TRANSLATOR AND EDITOR:
Rabbi David Strauss

MANAGING EDITOR:
Baruch Goldberg

EDITOR:
Dr. Edward L. Tepper

ASSOCIATE EDITOR:
Dr. Jeffrey M. Green

COPY EDITOR:
Alec Israel

BOOK DESIGNER:
Ben Gasner

GRAPHIC ARTIST:
Michael Etkin

TECHNICAL STAFF:
Muriel Stein
Rona Katz

Random House Staff

PRODUCTION MANAGER:
Richard Elman

ART DIRECTOR:
Bernard Klein

THE TALMUD

THE STEINSALTZ EDITION

VOLUME XII

TRACTATE KETUBOT

PART VI

Volume XII
Tractate Ketubot
Part VI

Random House
New York

THE TALMUD

תלמוד בבלי

THE STEINSALTZ EDITION

Commentary by Rabbi Adin Steinsaltz (Even Yisrael)

 Published in the United States by Random House, Inc., New York, and simultaneously in Canada by Random House of Canada Limited, Toronto.

This is an English translation of a work originally published in Hebrew by The Israel Institute for Talmudic Publications, Jerusalem, Israel.

Library of Congress Cataloging-in-Publication Data
(Revised for volume XII)
The Talmud
English, Hebrew, Aramaic.
Includes bibliograpical references.
Contents: v. 1. Tractate Bava metzia-
v. 12. Tractate Ketubot, pt. 6.
Accompanied by a reference guide.
I. Title.
BM499.5.E4 1989 89-842911
ISBN 0-394-57665-9 (guide)
ISBN 0-394-57666-7 (v. 1)
ISBN 0-679-42962-X (v. 12)

Random House website address: http://www.randomhouse.com/

Printed in the United States of America on acid-free paper

2 4 6 8 9 7 5 3

First Edition

This volume is dedicated in loving memory

of

parents: Serafina and Harry Falk

wife: Anne Falk

beloved son: Michael David Falk

dear son-in-law: Jules Bier

Publication of this volume made possible by Mr. Isidore Falk

The Steinsaltz Talmud in English

The English edition of the Steinsaltz Talmud is a translation and adaptation of the Hebrew edition. It includes most of the additions and improvements that characterize the Hebrew version, but it has been adapted and expanded especially for the English reader. This edition has been designed to meet the needs of advanced students capable of studying from standard Talmud editions, as well as of beginners, who know little or no Hebrew and have had no prior training in studying the Talmud.

The overall structure of the page is similar to that of the traditional pages in the standard printed editions. The text is placed in the center of the page, and alongside it are the main auxiliary commentaries. At the bottom of the page and in the margins are additions and supplements.

The original Hebrew-Aramaic text, which is framed in the center of each page, is exactly the same as that in the traditional Talmud (although material that was removed by non-Jewish censors has been restored on the basis of manuscripts and old printed editions). The main innovation is that this Hebrew-Aramaic text has been completely vocalized and punctuated, and all the terms usually abbreviated have been fully spelled out. In order to retain the connection with the page numbers of the standard editions, these are indicated at the head of every page.

We have placed a *Literal Translation* on the right-hand side of the page, and its punctuation has been introduced into the Talmud text, further helping the student to orientate himself. The *Literal Translation* is intended to help the student to learn the meaning of specific Hebrew and Aramaic words. By comparing the original text with this translation, the reader develops an understanding of the Talmudic text and can follow the words and sentences in the original. Occasionally, however, it has not been possible to present an exact literal translation of the original text, because it is so different in structure from English. Therefore we have added certain auxiliary words, which are indicated in square brackets. In other cases it would make no sense to offer a literal translation of a Talmudic idiom, so we have provided a close English equivalent of the original meaning, while a note, marked "lit.," explaining the literal meaning of the words, appears in parentheses. Our purpose in presenting this literal translation was to give the student an appreciation of the terse and enigmatic nature of the Talmud itself, before the arguments are opened up by interpretation.

Nevertheless, no one can study the Talmud without the assistance of commentaries. The main aid to understanding the Talmud provided by this edition is the *Translation and Commentary,* appearing on the left side of the page. This is Rabbi Adin Steinsaltz's highly regarded Hebrew interpretation of the Talmud, translated into English, adapted and expanded.

This commentary is not merely an explanation of difficult passages. It is an integrated exposition of the entire text. It includes a full translation of the Talmud text, combined with explanatory remarks. Where the translation in the commentary reflects the literal translation, it has been set off in bold type. It has also been given the same reference numbers that are found both in the original text and in the literal translation. Moreover, each section of the commentary begins with a few words of the Hebrew-Aramaic text. These reference numbers and paragraph headings allow the reader to move from one part of the page to another with ease.

There are some slight variations between the literal translation and the words in bold face appearing in the *Translation and Commentary.* These variations are meant to enhance understanding, for a juxtaposition of the literal translation and the sometimes freer translation in the commentary will give the reader a firmer grasp of the meaning.

The expanded *Translation and Commentary* in the left-hand column is intended to provide a conceptual understanding of the arguments of the Talmud, their form, content, context, and significance. The commentary also brings out the logic of the questions asked by the Sages and the assumptions they made.

Rashi's traditional commentary has been included in the right-hand column, under the *Literal Translation.* We have left this commentary in the traditional "Rashi script," but all quotations of the Talmud text appear in standard square type, the abbreviated expressions have all been printed in full, and Rashi's commentary is fully punctuated.

Since the *Translation and Commentary* cannot remain cogent and still encompass all the complex issues that arise in the Talmudic discussion, we have included a number of other features, which are also found in Rabbi Steinsaltz's Hebrew edition.

At the bottom of the page, under the *Translation and Commentary,* is the *Notes* section, containing additional material on issues raised in the text. These notes deepen understanding of the Talmud in various ways. Some provide a deeper and more profound analysis of the issues discussed in the text, with regard to individual points and to the development of the entire discussion. Others explain Halakhic concepts and the terms of Talmudic discourse.

The *Notes* contain brief summaries of the opinions of many of the major commentators on the Talmud, from the period after the completion of the Talmud to the present. Frequently the *Notes* offer interpretations different from that presented in the commentary, illustrating the richness and depth of Rabbinic thought.

The *Halakhah* section appears below the *Notes.* This provides references to the authoritative legal decisions reached over the centuries by the Rabbis in their discussions of the matters dealt with in the Talmud. It explains what reasons led to these Halakhic decisions and the close connection between the Halakhah today and the Talmud and its various interpreters. It should be noted that the summary of the Halakhah presented here is not meant to serve as a reference source for actual religious practice but to introduce the reader to Halakhic conclusions drawn from the Talmudic text.

English commentary and expanded translation of the text, making it readable and comprehensible

Hebrew/Aramaic text of the Talmud, fully vocalized, and punctuated

Literal translation of the Talmud text into English

Marginal notes provide essential background information

Hebrew commentary of Rashi, the classic explanation that accompanies all editions of the Talmud

Numbers link the three main sections of the page and allow readers to refer rapidly from one to the other

Notes highlight points of interest in the text and expand the discussion by quoting other classical commentaries

REALIA

קַלְתָּהּ **Her basket.** The source of this word is the Greek κάλαθος, kalathos, and it means a basket with a narrow base.

Illustration from a Greek drawing depicting such a basket of fruit.

CONCEPTS

פֵּאָה ***Pe'ah.*** **One of the presents left for the poor** (מַתְּנוֹת עֲנִיִּים). The Torah forbids harvesting "the corners of your field," so that the produce left standing may be harvested and kept by the poor (Leviticus 19:9).

The Torah did not specify a minimum amount of produce to be left as *pe'ah*. But the Sages stipulated that it must be at least one-sixtieth of the crop.

Pe'ah is set aside only from crops that ripen at one time and are harvested at one time. The poor are allowed to use their own initiative to reap the *pe'ah* left in the fields. But the owner of an orchard must see to it that each of the poor gets a fixed share of the *pe'ah* from places that are difficult to reach. The poor come to collect *pe'ah* three times a day. The laws of *pe'ah* are discussed in detail in tractate *Pe'ah*.

TRANSLATION AND COMMENTARY

[1]**and her husband threw her a bill of divorce into her lap or into her basket**, which she was carrying on her head, [2]would you say **here, too,** that **she would not be divorced**? Surely we know that the law is that she *is* divorced in such a case, as the Mishnah (*Gittin* 77a) states explicitly!

אֲמַר לֵיהּ [3]Rav Ashi **said** in reply **to** Ravina: The woman's **basket is** considered to be **at rest, and it is she who walks beneath it.** Thus the basket is considered to be a "stationary courtyard," and the woman acquires whatever is thrown into it.

MISHNAH הָיָה רוֹכֵב [4]If a **person was riding on an animal and he saw an ownerless object** lying on the ground, **and he said to another person** standing nearby, **"Give that object to me,"** [5]if **the other person took** the ownerless object **and said, "I have acquired it for myself,"** [6]he has **acquired it** by lifting it up, even though he was not the first to see it, and the rider has no claim to it. [7]But **if, after he gave** the object **to** the rider, the person who picked it up **said, "I acquired** the object **first,"** [8]**he** in fact **said nothing**. His words are of no effect, and the rider may keep it. Since the person walking showed no intention of acquiring the object when he originally picked it up, he is not now believed when he claims that he acquired it first. Indeed, even if we maintain that when a person picks up an ownerless object on behalf of someone else, the latter does *not* acquire it automatically, here, by *giving* the object to the rider, he makes a gift of it to the rider.

GEMARA תְּנַן הָתָם [9]**We have learned elsewhere** in a Mishnah in tractate *Pe'ah* (4:9): **"Someone who gathered *pe'ah*** — produce which by Torah law [Leviticus 23:22] is left unharvested in the corner of a field by the owner of the field, to be gleaned by the poor — **and said, 'Behold, this *pe'ah*** which I have gleaned **is** intended **for so-and-so the poor man,'** [10]**Rabbi Eliezer says:** The person who gathered the *pe'ah* **has acquired it**

בִּרְשׁוּת הָרַבִּים [1]וְזָרַק לָהּ גֵּט לְתוֹךְ חֵיקָהּ אוֹ לְתוֹךְ קַלְתָּהּ — [2]הָכָא נַמִי דְּלָא מִגָּרְשָׁה? [3]אֲמַר לֵיהּ: קַלְתָּהּ מֵינָח נַיְיחָא, וְאִיהִי דְּקָא מְסַגְּיָא מִתּוּתָהּ.

משנה [4]הָיָה רוֹכֵב עַל גַּבֵּי בְהֵמָה וְרָאָה אֶת הַמְּצִיאָה, וְאָמַר לַחֲבֵירוֹ "תְּנָה לִי", [5]נְטָלָהּ וְאָמַר, "אֲנִי זָכִיתִי בָּהּ", [6]זָכָה בָּהּ. [7]אִם, מִשֶּׁנְּתָנָהּ לוֹ, אָמַר, "אֲנִי זָכִיתִי בָּהּ תְּחִלָּה", [8]לֹא אָמַר כְּלוּם.

גמרא [9]תְּנַן הָתָם: "מִי שֶׁלִּיקֵּט אֶת הַפֵּאָה וְאָמַר, 'הֲרֵי זוֹ לִפְלוֹנִי עָנִי', [10]רַבִּי אֱלִיעֶזֶר

LITERAL TRANSLATION

in a public thoroughfare [1]and [her husband] threw her a bill of divorce into her lap or into her basket, [2]here, too, would she not be divorced?

[3]He said to him: Her basket is at rest, and it is she who walks beneath it.

MISHNAH [4][If a person] was riding on an animal and he saw a found object, and he said to another person, "Give it to me," [5][and the other person] took it and said, "I have acquired it," [6]he has acquired it. [7]If, after he gave it to him, he said, "I acquired it first," [8]he said nothing.

GEMARA [9]We have learned there: "Someone who gathered *pe'ah* and said, 'Behold this is for so-and-so the poor man,' [10]Rabbi Eliezer says:

RASHI

קלתה — סל שעל ראשה, שנותנת בה כלי מלאכתה וטווי שלה. הכי נמי דלא הוי גיטא — והאנן תנן במסכת גיטין (עז,א): זרק לה גיטה לתוך חיקה או לתוך קלתה — הרי זו מגורשת!

משנה לא אמר כלום — דאפילו אמרינן המגביה מציאה לחבירו לא קנה חבירו, כיון דיהבה ליה — קנייה ממה נפשך. אי קנייה קמא דלא מתכוין להקנות לחבירו — הא יהבה ניהליה במתנה. ואי לא קנייה קמא משום דלא היה מתכוין לקנות — הויא ליה הפקר עד דמטא לידיה דהאי, וקנייה האי במאי דעקרה מידיה דקמא לשם קנייה.

גמרא מי שליקט את הפאה — אדם בעלמא שאינו בעל שדה. דאי בבעל שדה — לא אמר רבי אליעזר זכה. דליכא למימר "מגו דזכי לנפשיה", דאפילו הוא עני מוזהר הוא שלא ללקט פאה משדה שלו, כדאמר בשחיטת חולין (קלא,ב): "לא תלקט לעני" — להזהיר עני על שלו.

NOTES

מִי שֶׁלִּיקֵּט אֶת הַפֵּאָה **If a person gathered *pe'ah*.** According to *Rashi*, the Mishnah must be referring to someone other than the owner of the field. By Torah law the owner of a field is required to separate part of his field as *pe'ah*, even if he himself is poor, and he may not take the *pe'ah* for himself. Therefore the "since" (מגו) argument

HALAKHAH

קַלְתָּהּ **A woman's basket.** "If a man throws a bill of divorce into a container that his wife is holding, she thereby acquires the bill of divorce and the divorce takes effect." (*Shulḥan Arukh, Even HaEzer* 139:10.)

הַמְלַקֵּט פֵּאָה עֲבוּר אַחֵר **A person who gathered *pe'ah* for someone else.** "If a poor person, who is himself entitled to collect *pe'ah*, gathered *pe'ah* for another poor person, and said, 'This *pe'ah* is for X, the poor person,' he acquires the *pe'ah* on behalf of that other poor person. But if the person who collected the *peah* was wealthy, he does not acquire the *pe'ah* on behalf of the poor person. He must give it instead to the first poor person who appears in the field," following the opinion of the Sages, as explained by Rabbi Yehoshua ben Levi. (*Rambam, Sefer Zeraim, Hilkhot Mattenot Aniyyim* 2:19.)

On the outer margin of the page, factual information clarifying the meaning of the Talmudic discussion is presented. Entries under the heading *Language* explain unusual terms, often borrowed from Greek, Latin, or Persian. *Sages* gives brief biographies of the major figures whose opinions are presented in the Talmud. *Terminology* explains the terms used in the Talmudic discussion. *Concepts* gives information about fundamental Halakhic principles. *Background* provides historical, geographical, and other information needed to understand the text. *Realia* explains the artifacts mentioned in the text. These notes are sometimes accompanied by illustrations.

The best way of studying the Talmud is the way in which the Talmud itself evolved - a combination of frontal teaching and continuous interaction between teacher and pupil, and between pupils themselves.

This edition is meant for a broad spectrum of users, from those who have considerable prior background and who know how to study the Talmud from any standard edition to those who have never studied the Talmud and do not even know Hebrew.

The division of the page into various sections is designed to enable students of every kind to derive the greatest possible benefit from it.

For those who know how to study the Talmud, the book is intended to be a written Gemara lesson, so that, either alone, with partners, or in groups, they can have the sense of studying with a teacher who explains the difficult passages and deepens their understanding both of the development of the dialectic and also of the various approaches that have been taken by the Rabbis over the centuries in interpreting the material. A student of this kind can start with the Hebrew-Aramaic text, examine Rashi's commentary, and pass on from there to the expanded commentary. Afterwards the student can turn to the Notes section. Study of the *Halakhah* section will clarify the conclusions reached in the course of establishing the Halakhah, and the other items in the margins will be helpful whenever the need arises to clarify a concept or a word or to understand the background of the discussion.

For those who do not possess sufficient knowledge to be able to use a standard edition of the Talmud, but who know how to read Hebrew, a different method is proposed. Such students can begin by reading the Hebrew-Aramaic text and comparing it immediately to the *Literal Translation*. They can then move over to the *Translation and Commentary*, which refers both to the original text and to the *Literal Translation*. Such students would also do well to read through the *Notes* and choose those that explain matters at greater length. They will benefit, too, from the terms explained in the side margins.

The beginner who does not know Hebrew well enough to grapple with the original can start with the *Translation and Commentary*. The inclusion of a translation within the commentary permits the student to ignore the *Literal Translation*, since the commentary includes both the Talmudic text and an interpretation of it. The beginner can also benefit from the *Notes*, and it is important for him to go over the marginal notes on the concepts to improve his awareness of the juridical background and the methods of study characteristic of this text.

Apart from its use as study material, this book can also be useful to those well versed in the Talmud, as a source of additional knowledge in various areas, both for understanding the historical and archeological background and also for an explanation of words and concepts. The general reader, too, who might not plan to study the book from beginning to end, can find a great deal of interesting material in it regarding both the spiritual world of Judaism, practical Jewish law, and the life and customs of the Jewish people during the thousand years (500 B.C.E.–500 C.E.) of the Talmudic period.

Contents

THE TALMUD
THE STEINSALTZ EDITION

VOLUME XII

TRACTATE KETUBOT

PART VI

Introduction to Chapter Nine

הַכּוֹתֵב לְאִשְׁתּוֹ

Since a marriage agreement between a man and a woman depends, with respect to finances, upon their wishes, a husband might make certain concessions to his wife regarding the obligations normally incumbent upon her in consequence of marriage. In this chapter two such concessions are examined in detail. The first concession discussed is the possibility that a husband might partially or fully waive the right to enjoy his wife's income. The second concession discussed is the possibility that he might waive his right to require her to take an oath when she collects her marriage settlement.

Regarding the concession of a husband's rights to his wife's usufruct property, the main discussion is related to the precise formulation of this concession and with determining its limits — how far does the wording of the concession extend?

The discussion of exempting the wife from taking an oath includes several issues. One case discussed is that of a wife who wishes to collect part of her marriage settlement and admits that she has already received a portion of it. Here she must take an oath, for there are grounds for suspicion that she might have received the entire sum in one way or another. Further, when a widow seeks to collect her settlement after her husband's death, she must swear to his heirs that the claim is well-founded and that she has received no payment. This is because the Sages decreed that the property of orphans may not be taken without an oath.

Another issue raised is the obligation to take an oath incumbent upon a wife who managed some or all of her husband's property. Here her obligation to take an oath is similar to that of any partner or employee who might be sued by the owner of the property and who must clear himself of suspicion of theft and the like. Further, the question is raised whether a wife must take an oath regarding the way she had administered her household. This chapter discusses both obligations and also the ways in which a husband may exempt his wife of the requirement to take an oath.

A wife's obligation to take an oath when she receives her marriage settlement is the basis of two further problems. What is the status of the wife's claim with respect to other claims against her husband's property? The other question concerns the nature of the document that a wife uses to collect her settlement. Does she collect on the basis of her ketubah deed, or has she other ways of collecting? And what is the law if she posessed two ketubah deeds?

הַכּוֹתֵב

[1]לְאִשְׁתּוֹ: ״דִּין וּדְבָרִים אֵין לִי בִּנְכָסַיִךְ״, [2]הֲרֵי זֶה אוֹכֵל פֵּירוֹת בְּחַיֶּיהָ, [3]וְאִם מֵתָה, יוֹרְשָׁהּ. [4]אִם כֵּן, לָמָּה כָּתַב לָהּ: [5]״דִּין וּדְבָרִים אֵין לִי בִּנְכָסַיִךְ״? [6]שֶׁאִם מָכְרָה וְנָתְנָה, קַיָּים.

LITERAL TRANSLATION

MISHNAH [1][If] someone wrote to his wife: "I have no claim (lit., 'litigation or dispute') on your property," [2]he enjoys [its] fruits during her lifetime, [3]and if she dies, he inherits her. [4]If so, why did he write her: [5]"I have no claim on your property"? [6]So that if she sold [it] or gave [it] away, it is valid.

RASHI

משנה הכותב אם כן למה כתב לה כו׳ — בגמרא מפרש טעמא.

TRANSLATION AND COMMENTARY

MISHNAH הַכּוֹתֵב לְאִשְׁתּוֹ [1]The property that a woman brings to her marriage from her father's home and is not recorded in her ketubah deed, and the property that she inherits or receives as a gift after marriage, is known as *nikhsei milog*, or "usufruct property." This property remains in her formal possession even after marriage. However, her husband is entitled to make use of this property and keeps all income deriving from it provided that he leaves the principal intact. If his wife predeceases him, he inherits the property along with the rest of her estate. Our Mishnah discusses the laws that apply to a husband who waived his rights to his wife's usufruct property. **If someone wrote his wife** the following stipulation: **"I will have no claim on your** usufruct **property,"** [2]**he** may still **enjoy its fruits during** the woman's **lifetime,** [3]**and if she dies** before him, **he inherits** the property from **her.** We assume that he meant only to waive his right to the property itself, but not his right to the property's usufruct. [4]**If so,** asks the Mishnah, **why did he write her:** [5]**"I will have no claim to your** usufruct **property,"** if his stipulation does not alter the existing situation? The Mishnah explains: [6]He wrote the stipulation to indicate **that if she sold** the property **or gave it away** as a gift, this transaction will be **valid.**

NOTES

דִּין וּדְבָרִים **Claim.** *Melekhet Shlomo* explains the redundant term דִּין וּדְבָרִים as follows: Not only does the husband waive his legal claim to his wife's property, but he also promises not to enter into a verbal dispute with his wife regarding this forfeiture.

אֵין לִי בִּנְכָסַיִךְ **I have no claim on your property.** As will be explained in the Gemara, the formulation "I have no claim on your property" expresses the husband's renunciation of his future rights to his wife's property. *Rashbam* (*Bava Batra* 43a) and others note that we find in Mishnaic Hebrew that the term "I do not have (אֵין לִי)" is used in the sense of "I will not have (לֹא יְהֵא לִי)."

שֶׁאִם מָכְרָה וְנָתְנָה, קַיָּים **So that if she sold it or gave it away, it is valid.** As the Gemara explains, in the case in our Mishnah, the husband stipulated with his wife at the time of their betrothal that he would have no claim to her property after their marriage. The Rishonim ask: The Mishnah implies that it is only because the husband waived his claim to his wife's property, that she may sell it or give it away. But this is difficult, for we learned earlier in the tractate (*Ketubot* 78a) that Rabban Gamliel taught that if a married woman sold or gave away property that she had received during her betrothal and brought into marriage, the transaction is valid, even if the husband did not waive his rights to the property. *Tosafot* (*Ketubot* 78b) explain that our Mishnah follows the view of the Sages who queried to Rabban Gamliel's view and asked: "if the man has rights over the woman, should he not obtain rights over her property and prevent her from selling or giving it away?" Our Mishnah teaches according to these Sages that if the husband had waived his rights to the property, her transaction is then valid. *Ramban,* in *Milḥamot,* takes a different approach and argues that our Mishnah teaches that the husband's waiver of his rights to his wife's property is required with respect to property that the woman acquired after she was already married. For if the woman sold or gave away such property and the husband had not renounced his rights during their betrothal, the transaction would not be valid. *Ramban* notes that the Jerusalem Talmud seems to discuss such a case, but concludes that the husband's waiver of his rights to his wife's property is not valid with respect to property that she acquires after marriage. He suggests that the Jerusalem Talmud is dealing with the case where he makes his renouncement only after marriage, but if he waived his rights to her property while she was still only betrothed to him, the waiver is indeed valid for property she acquires after marriage. *Rashba* and others argue that the Jerusalem Talmud should be understood according to its plain sense, when he renounced during the betrothal period. As for the difficulty raised here,

HALAKHAH

דִּין וּדְבָרִים אֵין לִי בִּנְכָסַיִךְ **I have no claim on your property.** "If someone wrote his wife (in the proper manner and at the proper time, as explained below): 'I will have no claim on your usufruct property,' and the woman sold the property or gave it away as a gift, the transaction is valid. But if she did not sell the property or give it away, the husband may enjoy the usufruct, and if she dies before him, he inherits the property from her," following the Mishnah. (*Rambam, Sefer Nashim, Hilkhot Ishut* 23:2; *Shulḥan Arukh, Even HaEzer* 92:1.)

SAGES

רַבִּי יְהוּדָה **Rabbi Yehudah (bar Il'ai).** See *Ketubot,* Part II, p. 30.

רַבָּן שִׁמְעוֹן בֶּן גַּמְלִיאֵל **Rabban Shimon ben Gamliel.** See *Ketubot,* Part I, pp. 120-1.

TRANSLATION AND COMMENTARY

כָּתַב לָהּ [1]If the husband **wrote** his wife: "I will **have no claim on your** usufruct **property, or on its fruits,"** [2]**he does not enjoy the fruits** of his wife's property **during her lifetime.** [3]**But if she dies** before him, **he inherits** the property from **her.** [4]**Rabbi Yehudah says:** Even if the husband waived his right to the usufruct of his wife's property, he may **still enjoy the fruits of the fruits** of that property, [5]**unless he wrote her** explicitly: "I will **have no claim on your property,** [6]**or on its fruits, or on the fruits of its fruits forever."** In this case, the husband purchased land with the income from his wife's property. That land belongs to his wife, but the husband is entitled to enjoy its usufruct unless he stated explicitly that he waives his right not only to the original usufruct, but also to the usufruct of the usufruct forever.

כָּתַב לָהּ [7]If the husband **wrote** his wife: "I will **have no claim on your** usufruct **property,** [8]**or on its fruits, or on the fruits of its fruits,** [9]neither **during your lifetime nor after your death,"** [10]**he does not enjoy the fruits** of the property **during** his wife's **lifetime.** [11]**And if she dies** before him, **he does not inherit** the property from **her.** [12]**Rabban Shimon ben Gamliel says: If she dies** before him, **he** does in fact **inherit** the property from **her,** [13]**because his stipulation is against** (i.e., contrary

[1]כָּתַב לָהּ: ״דִּין וּדְבָרִים אֵין לִי
בִּנְכָסַיִךְ וּבְפֵירוֹתֵיהֶן״, [2]הֲרֵי זֶה
אֵינוֹ אוֹכֵל פֵּירוֹת בְּחַיֶּיהָ. [3]וְאִם
מֵתָה, יוֹרְשָׁהּ. [4]רַבִּי יְהוּדָה
אוֹמֵר: לְעוֹלָם אוֹכֵל פֵּירֵי
פֵּירוֹת, [5]עַד שֶׁיִּכְתּוֹב לָהּ: ״דִּין
וּדְבָרִים אֵין לִי בִּנְכָסַיִךְ,
[6]וּבְפֵירוֹתֵיהֶן, וּבְפֵירֵי פֵּירוֹתֵיהֶן
עַד עוֹלָם״.
[7]כָּתַב לָהּ: ״דִּין וּדְבָרִים אֵין לִי
בִּנְכָסַיִךְ, [8]וּבְפֵירוֹתֵיהֶן, וּבְפֵירֵי
פֵּירוֹתֵיהֶן, [9]בְּחַיַּיִךְ וּבְמוֹתֵךְ״,
[10]אֵינוֹ אוֹכֵל פֵּירוֹת בְּחַיֶּיהָ,
[11]וְאִם מֵתָה, אֵינוֹ יוֹרְשָׁהּ. [12]רַבָּן
שִׁמְעוֹן בֶּן גַּמְלִיאֵל אוֹמֵר: אִם
מֵתָה, יִירָשֶׁנָּה, [13]מִפְּנֵי שֶׁמַּתְנֶה
עַל מַה שֶּׁכָּתוּב בַּתּוֹרָה,

LITERAL TRANSLATION

[1][If] he wrote her: "I have no claim on your property or on its fruits," [2]he does not enjoy [its] fruits during her lifetime. [3]But if she dies, he inherits her. [4]Rabbi Yehudah says: He still [may] enjoy the fruits of [its] fruits, [5]unless he writes her: "I have no claim on your property, [6]or on its fruits, or on the fruits of its fruit [and so on] forever."

[7][If] he wrote her: "I have no claim on your property, [8]or on its fruits, or on the fruits of its fruits, [9]during your lifetime or after your death," [10]he does not enjoy the fruits during her lifetime, [11]and if she dies, he does not inherit her. [12]Rabban Shimon ben Gamliel says: If she dies, he inherits her, [13]because he stipulated against what is written in the Torah,

RASHI

הכי גרסינן: רבי יהודה אומר לעולם הוא אוכל פירי פירות — וגמרא מפרש אלו הן פירי פירות. שמַתנה על מה שכתוב בתורה — דקסבר: ירושת הבעל דאורייתא. ובבבא בתרא (קיא,ב) נפקא לן מהאי קרא: "לשארו הקרוב אליו ממשפחתו וירש אותה"; האי "וירש אותה" יתירא הוא לדרשא שהאיש יורש את שארו, ו"שארו" זו אשתו. ואף על גב ד"שארו" דקרא לאו אשתו היא, דהא כתיב ביה "ונתתם את נחלתו לשארו", וליכא למימר שתירש האשה את בעלה, דהא "ממשפחתו" כתיב. מיהו גבי קרא יתירא ד"וירש אותה" דרשינן הכי: ונתתם את נחלתו לקרוב אליו ממשפחתו שארו וירש אותה — האיש יורש את אשתו.

NOTES

Rashba proposes another solution: If a married woman sold or gave away property which she had brought into the marriage, the transaction is indeed valid, even if the husband had not waived his rights to the property during their betrothal. But if the woman comes to ask about such a transaction before making it, she is told that she may not dispose of the property, following Bet Hillel (*Ketubot* 78a). Our Mishnah teaches that if the husband waived his rights to his wife's property while she was betrothed to him, she is told that she is free to sell the property or give it away as she pleases.

HALAKHAH

דִּין וּדְבָרִים אֵין לִי בִּנְכָסַיִךְ וּבְפֵירוֹתֵיהֶן **I have no claim on your property, nor on its fruit.** "If the husband wrote: 'I will have no claim on your usufruct property, nor on its usufruct,' he may not enjoy the usufruct during her lifetime. Rather the usufruct is sold, land is purchased with the proceeds, and the husband may enjoy its usufruct." (*Rambam, Sefer Nashim, Hilkhot Ishut* 23:3; *Shulḥan Arukh, Even HaEzer* 92:4.)

בִּנְכָסַיִךְ, וּבְפֵירוֹתֵיהֶן, וּבְפֵירֵי פֵּירוֹתֵיהֶן עַד עוֹלָם **On your property, nor on its fruit, nor on the fruit of its fruit.** "If the husband wrote his wife: 'I will have no claim on your usufruct property, nor on its usufruct, nor on the usufruct of its usufruct forever, neither during your lifetime, nor after your death,' he may not enjoy any usufruct during her lifetime. But if the woman predeceases her husband, he inherits the property," following the Gemara's ruling in accordance with the position of Rabban Shimon ben Gamliel below. (*Rambam, Sefer Nashim, Hilkhot Ishut* 23:7; *Shulḥan Arukh, Even HaEzer* 92:8.)

TRANSLATION AND COMMENTARY

to) **what is written in the Torah,** [1]**and whoever stipulates against what is written in the Torah, his stipulation is void.** According to Rabban Shimon ben Gamliel, the husband's right to succeed to his wife's estate is Biblical law, derived from the verse (Numbers 27:11): "Then you shall give his inheritance to his kinsman that is next to him from his family and he shall inherit it." "To his kinsman that is next to him" is interpreted to mean his wife. Since the husband is entitled to his wife's estate by Torah law, this right cannot be cancelled by an individual's stipulation.

GEMARA תָּנֵי רַבִּי חִיָּיא [2]We learned in our Mishnah that a husband can waive his rights to his wife's usufruct property by writing her a stipulation to that effect. **Rabbi Ḥiyya taught** a slightly different version of the Mishnah: **"If someone said to his wife,** etc." Even if the husband expressed his waiver verbally, without committing it to writing, the waiver is valid.

וְכִי כָּתַב לָהּ [3]The Gemara now raises an objection against the laws recorded in our Mishnah: **And if** the husband **wrote** his wife **such** a stipulation, and all the more so, if he only expressed his waiver verbally, [4]**what is done?** The wording of these stipulations cannot effect the transfer of property rights. [5]**For surely it was taught** in a Baraita: **"If** two parties jointly owned a certain property, and **one** of them **said** to the other, whether orally or in writing: [6]**'I will have no claim to this field,' or 'I will have no business with it,' or 'My hand will be removed from** the field,' [7]**he did not say anything.** Such formulations cannot effect a transfer of ownership from one partner to the other, so why should a similar formulation effect a waiver of a husband's rights to his wife's property?

[1]וְכָל הַמַּתְנֶה עַל מַה שֶּׁכָּתוּב בַּתּוֹרָה, תְּנָאוֹ בָּטֵל.

גמרא [2]תָּנֵי רַבִּי חִיָּיא: "הָאוֹמֵר לְאִשְׁתּוֹ".

[3]וְכִי כָּתַב לָהּ הָכִי, [4]מַאי הָוֵי? [5]וְהָתַנְיָא: "הָאוֹמֵר לַחֲבֵירוֹ: [6]'דִּין וּדְבָרִים אֵין לִי עַל שָׂדֶה זוֹ' וְ'אֵין לִי עֵסֶק בָּהּ', וְ'יָדִי מְסוּלֶּקֶת הֵימֶנָּה', [7]לֹא אָמַר כְּלוּם!"

LITERAL TRANSLATION

[1]and whoever stipulates against what is written in the Torah, his stipulation is void.

GEMARA [2]Rabbi Ḥiyya taught: "[If] someone said to his wife."

[3]And if he wrote her thus, [4]what is done? [5]But surely it was taught: "[If] someone said to his fellow: [6]'I have no claim to this field,' or 'I have no business with it,' or 'My hand is removed from it,' [7]he did not say anything."

RASHI

וכל המתנה כו' – אבל פירות תקנתא דרבנן היא, ומצי לאתנויי עלייהו.
גמרא תני: רבי חייא האומר לאשתו – ולא תני "כותב", דאשמועינן דבאמירה בעלמא נמי סליק נפשיה, בלא שום קנין וכתיבה. **וכי כתב לה מאי הוי** – וכל שכן אמירה. **האומר לחבירו** – כגון שדה של שותפין, ואמר האחד לחברו אחד מן הלשונות הללו, [בין בכתיבה בין באמירה]. **לא אמר כלום** – דאין כאן לשון מתנה.

BACKGROUND

כָּל הַמַּתְנֶה עַל מַה שֶּׁכָּתוּב בַּתּוֹרָה Whoever makes a stipulation against what is written in the Torah. This is a general problem in any legal system: What is the status of an agreement, part of which is against the law? In general it is assumed that the agreement itself is enforced, although the illegal clause has no effect. The Mishnah goes on to state that this principle applies not only with respect to various parts of an agreement, but also when a condition is attached to an agreement, according to which the entire agreement depends on the fulfillment of a certain condition. If it is illegal to fulfill the condition, we accept the agreement but invalidate the condition. However, if the agreement is formulated in such a way that it is clear that the entire contract depends on the satisfaction of an illegal condition, the entire agreement is void.

NOTES

תָּנֵי רַבִּי חִיָּיא: הָאוֹמֵר Rabbi Ḥiyya taught: If someone said. *Ra'ah* explains that the Gemara cites Rabbi Ḥiyya's reading of the Mishnah to lay the groundwork for the question that it is about to ask from the Baraita regarding jointly-owned property and the formulations which cannot effect a transfer of ownership from one partner to the other. For without Rabbi Ḥiyya, the Mishnah itself could have been understood as dealing with a husband who waived his rights to his wife's property in the best possible way, and he wrote a deed, which was accompanied by a formal act ratifying the deed (known as a *kinyan*). In such a case, the waiver is certainly valid, and the Baraita dealing with oral formulations would not present any difficulty. Hence, the Gemara cites Rabbi Ḥiyya's reading, "If someone said, etc.," which implies that a formal act ratifying the waiver was not performed, and the parallel reading of "If he wrote her," also in valued no *kinyan*. The Gemara then continues with its question from the Baraita, arguing that if the formulation "I will have no claim on this field" cannot effect a transfer of ownership from one partner to another, that same formulation should not be able to effect a waiver of the husband's rights to his wife's usufruct property (see also *Ritva, Ran,* and *Maharsha*).

אֵין לִי עֵסֶק בָּהּ I have no business with it. The formulations mentioned in the Baraita cannot effect a transfer of ownership, because, as *Tosafot* say, they are "inferior formulations," or as the Jerusalem Talmud explains, "a person cannot acquire with such a formulation." The Rishonim (*Tosafot* and others) ask: It was taught elsewhere (*Gittin* 43b) that if a master wrote his non-Jewish slave, "I will have no business with you," the slave's bondage is terminated, which implies that this wording is indeed a valid formulation for effecting a transaction. *Rabbenu Tam* distinguishes between a field and a slave. If a master said to his slave that he will have no business with him, the slave is released from bondage, because when the master

HALAKHAH

תָּנֵי רַבִּי חִיָּיא: הָאוֹמֵר Rabbi Ḥiyya taught: If someone said. "When the husband waives his rights to his wife's property, it makes no difference whether he waives them orally or commits his waiver to writing." (*Rambam, Sefer Nashim, Hilkhot Ishut* 23:2; *Shulḥan Arukh, Even HaEzer* 92:1.)

[1]אָמְרִי דְּבֵי רַבִּי יַנַּאי: [2]בְּכוֹתֵב לָהּ וְעוֹדָהּ אֲרוּסָה, כִּדְרַב כָּהֲנָא.
[3]דַּאֲמַר רַב כָּהֲנָא: [4]נַחֲלָה הַבָּאָה לְאָדָם מִמָּקוֹם אַחֵר, [5]אָדָם מַתְנֶה עָלֶיהָ שֶׁלֹּא יִירָשֶׁנָּה. [6]וְכִדְרָבָא, דְּאָמַר רָבָא: [7]הָאוֹמֵר: "אִי אֶפְשִׁי בְּתַקָּנַת חֲכָמִים כְּגוֹן זוֹ", שׁוֹמְעִין לוֹ.

LITERAL TRANSLATION

[1]They said in the academy of Rabbi Yannai: [2]When he wrote to her while she was still betrothed, in accordance with Rav Kahana. [3]For Rav Kahana said: [4][Regarding] an estate which comes to a person from another place, [5]a person may stipulate not to inherit it. [6]And in accordance with Rava, for Rava said: [7][If] someone said: "I do not want [benefit of] a Rabbinic enactment such as this," we listen to him.

TRANSLATION AND COMMENTARY

אָמְרִי [1]The scholars **in the academy of Rabbi Yannai said:** [2]In our Mishnah the husband **wrote** the stipulation **to her while she was still betrothed** to him. The husband does not acquire full rights to his wife's property at the betrothal but only after they are married. Therefore, the bridegroom may arrange with his betrothed that after they are married, he will not have any claim on her property. Renunciation before acquisition is valid. This is **in accordance with** the view of **Rav Kahana.**

דַּאֲמַר רַב כָּהֲנָא [3]**For Rav Kahana said:** One cannot waive one's share of the estate of a blood relative. [4]But **regarding an estate which** is to **come into his** possession **from another place,** such as from his wife, [5]**a person may stipulate not to inherit** the estate upon her death. [6]**And** this is also **in accordance with** the view of **Rava, for Rava said:** [7]**If someone said: "I do not want benefit of a Rabbinic enactment such as this," we listen to him.**

RASHI

בכותב לה ועודה ארוסה — ודאי מי שהקרקע שלו, ובא ליתנו לחבירו — צריך לשון מתנה. ומתניתין — בכותב לה עד שלא זכה בנכסים, ומתנה עמה שלא יזכה בהן לכשישאנה. ואין צריך לשון מתנה — שהרי אין לו עכשיו רשות בהן. **ממקום אחר** — שאינה ירושת אבותיו, אלא על ידי מעשיו תבא לו, כגון נחלת אשתו הבאה לו על ידי נשואין שלו. דהואיל ומשום תקנתא דידיה תקון רבנן, והוא בא למחול עליה — מוחל, וכדרב הונא. **בתקנת חכמים** — שתיקנו לטובתי, ואינה טובה לי. **כגון זו** — לקמן מפרש אהייא אתמר.

SAGES

רָבָא Rava. See *Ketubot,* Part I, p. 14.

NOTES

renounces his ownership, the slave automatically acquires himself. But regarding ones' half-ownership of a field, this formulation is too weak to transfer ownership because it does not imply that the field was given as a gift or even that the property was declared ownerless, and in any event a field cannot acquire itself.

בְּכוֹתֵב לָהּ וְעוֹדָהּ אֲרוּסָה When he wrote to her while she was still a betrothed woman. The Jerusalem Talmud also understands that the Mishnah is dealing with a husband who waived his rights to his wife's property during their betrothal. *Ran* adds that this waiver, whether oral or in writing, can only be made while the woman is betrothed. If the husband waived his rights to his future wife's property before betrothal (when there is no legal bond between them) the waiver is not valid as one cannot decline or transfer rights that are not yet in existence.

נַחֲלָה הַבָּאָה לְאָדָם מִמָּקוֹם אַחֵר An estate which comes to a person from an external source. *Rashi, Tosafot,* and others understand that during his betrothal period a man may renounce his right to inherit her estate because this right is only a Rabbinic enactment and a person may renounce a right conferred upon him by the Rabbis for his benefit. *Ramban* and his school argue that Rav Kahana does not mean to distinguish between a right to inherit under Torah law and that which is only by Rabbinic decree. For even if the husband's right to inherit his wife is Torah law, there would still be a difference between inheriting a blood relative and the husband's right to his wife's estate, which originates from an extrafamilial source. place, such as marriage. A person cannot renounce his share of a blood relative's estate, because he acquired that right the moment he was born. But a man only acquires the right to inherit his wife when they marry. Thus that right may be renounced before he marries.

וְכִדְרָבָא And in accordance with Rava. The Rishonim (see, for example, *Tosafot*) discuss at length why the Gemara had to cite Rava's statement after it had already presented Rav Kahana's ruling. *Rashba* (following *Ramban*'s understanding of the passage; see previous note) explains that without Rava we might have thought that Rav Kahana's ruling that a husband may renounce his right to his wife's estate, is only because this right is given to him by Torah law. However, the husband may not be able to an entitlement conferred upon him by Rabbinical enactment, such as the

HALAKHAH

בְּכוֹתֵב לָהּ וְעוֹדָהּ אֲרוּסָה If he wrote her while she was still only betrothed. "The husband's waiver of his rights to his wife's property by way of the formulation 'I will have no claim to your property' is only valid when the stipulation is made during their betrothal." (*Rambam, Sefer Nashim, Hilkhot Ishut* 23:2; *Shulḥan Arukh, Even HaEzer* 92:1.)

נַחֲלָה הַבָּאָה לְאָדָם מִמָּקוֹם אַחֵר An estate which comes to a person from another place. "If a man stipulated with his wife that he would not inherit her estate, he does not inherit it, but he may enjoy the usufruct during her lifetime. This only applies if the husband made the stipulation during the betrothal, or if he inserted it into the woman's ketubah deed at the time of marriage. But if he made the stipulation only after they were married, his stipulation is void, and he inherits her estate." (*Rambam, Sefer Nashim, Hilkhot Ishut* 23:6; *Shulḥan Arukh, Even HaEzer* 92:7; 69:7.)

TRANSLATION AND COMMENTARY

מַאי [1]The Gemara now clarifies Rava's statement: **What** was Rava referring to when he said that a person can renounce "a Rabbinic enactment **such as this**"? [2]The Gemara explains: Rava was referring to **what Rav Huna said in the name of Rav, for Rav Huna said in the name of Rav:** [3]**A woman can say to her husband: "I will not** exercise my Rabbinical right to **be maintained** by you, **and I will not** give you **any** proceeds of my **handiwork,** which I will use for my own support."

אִי הָכִי [4]The Gemara asks: **If** this is **so** that the Mishnah's ruling is based on the principle that a person can renounce a right which was conferred upon him for his benefit, then **even if she was** already **married** to him, he should be able to waive these rights, just as a married woman may surrender her right to maintenance and keep for herself the proceeds of her handiwork!

אָמַר אַבַּיֵּי [5]The Gemara now shows that property and maintenance rights are not analogous. **Abaye said:** Regarding **a married woman, her husband's rights** to her property **are like her rights** to that property. They are legal partners, and one partner cannot transfer his share of jointly-owned property to the other partner simply by renouncing his ownership. Thus the Mishnah can only be referring to a stipulation made before the husband became a joint-owner of his wife's property by marriage.

רָבָא אָמַר [6]**Rava** carries Abaye's argument a step further and **says: The husband's rights are** even **stronger than his wife's right** to her property. He, therefore, can certainly not waive of his rights with a formulation that expresses mere renunciation and not a clear declaration of his returning to her as a gift.

נָפְקָא מִינָּהּ [7]The Gemara now goes on to explain the practical difference between the views of Abaye and Rava. **There is a practical difference regarding a widow** whose husband died without children who **is** now **waiting for her brother-in-law** to take her in levirate marriage or release her from the levirate tie by performing *halitzah*. If the levir renounced his rights to his brother's widow's usufruct property before taking her as a wife, is the woman treated like a betrothed woman, in which case the renunciation formulation, "I will have no claim on your property," would indeed effect a waiver of his rights? Or is she treated like a married woman, in which case the renunciation would have no validity? Thus, according to Abaye who said that a husband's rights to his wife's property is equal to his wife's rights to that property, the levir's

[1]מַאי "כְּגוֹן זוֹ"? [2]כִּדְרַב הוּנָא אָמַר רַב. דְּאָמַר רַב הוּנָא אָמַר רַב: [3]יְכוֹלָה אִשָּׁה שֶׁתֹּאמַר לְבַעְלָהּ: "אֵינִי נִיזּוֹנֶת וְאֵינִי עוֹשָׂה".

[4]אִי הָכִי, אֲפִילּוּ נְשׂוּאָה נַמִּי!

[5]אָמַר אַבַּיֵּי: נְשׂוּאָה — יָדוֹ כְּיָדָהּ.

[6]רָבָא אָמַר: יָדוֹ עֲדִיפָא מִיָּדָהּ.

[7]נָפְקָא מִינָּהּ לְשׁוֹמֶרֶת יָבָם.

LITERAL TRANSLATION

[1]What is "such as this"? [2]Such as what Rav Huna said in the name of Rav. For Rav Huna said in the name of Rav: [3]A woman can say to her husband: "I will not be maintained and I will not do any handiwork."

[4]If so, even a married woman!

[5]Abaye said: [Regarding] a married woman — his rights (lit., "hand") are like her rights (lit., "hand").

[6]Rava said: His rights (lit., "hand") are stronger than her rights.

[7]There is a difference regarding a widow waiting for [levirate marriage to] her brother-in-law.

RASHI

מאי כגון זו — אהיכא אמרה רבא. כדרב הונא — אמזונות שתיקנו לאשה תחת מעשה ידיה. ואי אמרה: אי אפשי בתקנה זו שתיקנו חכמים לטובתי — שחשו לכל הנשים; זימנין דלא ספקי להו מזונות במעשה ידיהן, ותקנו להן מזונות ומעשה ידיהן לבעל, אני — איני צריכה לכך, מעוגנת אני ואי אפשי לעשות מלאכה, אמלא לי מזונות. או, יש לי אומנות יקרה יתר על כדי מזונותי. אי הכי — דטעמא משום דתקנתא דידיה הוא, ויכול למחול עליה, אמאי איצטריך דבי רבי ינאי לאוקמה בכותב לה ועודה ארוסה? אפילו נשואה נמי. ידו כידה — והרי הוא כשותף בהן. וכיון שנכסים שלו, צריך לשון מתנה, ואין מועיל בה לשון "דין ודברים". נפקא מינה לשומרת יבם — כלומר: לענין דין ודברים לא פליגי, דבין ידו כידה ובין ידו עדיפא מידה — אין מועיל בה לשון "דין ודברים" לסלקו. ופלוגתא דאביי ורבא — לענין שומרת יבם איצטריך. וביבמות אפליגו בה אביי ורבא בפרק "החולץ" (לט,א) גבי מתניתין דפרק דלעיל, בהאשה שומרת יבם שנפלו לה נכסים, דקתני: מתה מה יעשה בכתובתה כו׳, ואיפליגו בית שמאי ובית הלל. ואוקי אביי פלוגתייהו — בשנפלו לה כשהיא תחתיו דבעל, בחיי בעל הראשון. קסבר אביי: ידו כידה. לפיכך: כשמת ונפלה לפני יבם ומתה עד שלא נתיבמה — יורשיה ויורשי הבעל שניהם באים לירש, זה מכח אחותו וזה מכח אחיו. לבית שמאי — חלוקה עדיפא. ולבית הלל חזקה קמייתא עדיפא. לפיכך, נכסי מלוג בחזקת

NOTES

right to the usufruct of his wife's property, because the Rabbis might have augmented their enactment to give it more strength than by Torah law. Therefore, the Gemara cites the position of Rava, which teaches that even regarding Rabbinic enactments, a person can renounce a right conferred upon him for his own benefit.

נָפְקָא מִינָּהּ לְשׁוֹמֶרֶת יָבָם They differ regarding a widow waiting for her brother-in-law. Interpreting our Gemara in light of a similar discussion in *Yevamot* 39a, *Rashi* understands that the case where the views of Abaye and Rava lead to conflicting conclusions — the right to inherit a woman who died while she was waiting for her deceased

BACKGROUND

אֵינִי נִיזּוֹנֶת "I will not be maintained." Rav Huna maintains that when the Rabbis enacted the rights and duties of the husband and wife, the wife's right to maintenance was the primary enactment, passed into law for the woman's benefit so that she be guaranteed maintenance if she is unable to support herself with her own earnings. And in return for his duty to support his wife, the Rabbis enacted that the husband is entitled to the proceeds of her work, in order to avoid the enmity which might arise were a husband be required to support his wife, and not be entitled to the proceeds of her work. Since the woman's right to maintenance is primary, she can surrender that right and keep for herself the proceeds of her handiwork, should she decide that she can earn more than the amount of her maintenance. Our Mishnah teaches that just as a woman can renounce her right to maintenance, so can a man can renounce his right to enjoy the usufruct of his wife's property during her lifetime and inherit the property after her death. (Also see the discussion in tractate *Ketubot*, Part IV, pp. 256-57.)

שׁוֹמֶרֶת יָבָם A widow waiting for her brother-in-law. The legal position of a woman awaiting a levirate marriage is the subject of many discussions in the Talmud. On the one hand, no marriage connection exists, for the levir has not betrothed his brother's widow, so in that respect she is an unmarried woman. However, on the other hand, her connection with the levir (called "זיקה") prevents her from marrying anyone until the levir releases her through the ceremony of *halitzah*. Some authorities have argued that in this respect she is like a married woman, so that if she contracts marriage with a man other than the levir, that marriage does not take effect. Moreover, since the bond between a widow and her late husband's brother does not depend upon their personal choice, but rather is decreed by the Torah, it could be claimed that it is more powerful than an ordinary betrothal.

SAGES

אַבַּיֵי Abaye. See *Ketubot*, Part I, pp. 44-5.

רַב יוֹסֵף Rav Yosef. See *Ketubot*, Part I, p. 8.

רַב נַחְמָן Rav Naḥman. See *Ketubot*, Part IV, p. 169.

TRANSLATION AND COMMENTARY

right to his sister-in-law's property would be weaker than that of the woman. Therefore, the levir's renunciation of his rights should be effective. According to Rava who said that the husband's rights to his wife's property are even stronger than her rights, the levir's rights to his sister-in-law's property would be reduced (with respect to his brother) and be equivalent to the woman's rights. Thus the levir should not be able to renounce his rights to that property.

אִיבַּעְיָא לְהוּ [1]In discussion among the Sages, **it was asked:** [2]**What is the law if** the partner in the above Baraita not only renounced his rights to his half of the property, but **they reinforced** this renunciation **by making a valid act of acquisition,** known as a *kinyan*. A *kinyan* can be used not only to finalize a sale, but also to conclude and ratify other agreements, such as acceptance of responsibility with regard to a future action. Does the *kinyan* render a renunciation agreement valid? Do we say that the *kinyan* merely confirms what the partner had already said, namely that he will not raise a claim to the property? Then since the formulation expressing renunciation is not valid, confirming it with a *kinyan* adds nothing. Or do we say that the *kinyan* reinforces the renunciation declaration, so that it can effect a transfer of ownership of the property itself?

אָמַר רַב יוֹסֵף [3]**Rav Yosef said:** If a partner waived his rights to his half of jointly-owned property, using an ineffective renunciation formulation, [4]the act of **acquisition** which he performed **concerns** only the waiver of his **claim** to the property. The *kinyan,* therefore, cannot make the ineffective statement effective.

רַב נַחְמָן אָמַר [5]**Rav Naḥman** disagreed and **said:** In such a case, the act of **acquisition** which he performed **concerns** his ownership of **the land itself,** and so the *kinyan* does indeed effect a transfer of ownership.

[1]אִיבַּעְיָא לְהוּ: [2]קָנוּ מִיָּדוֹ, מַהוּ?
[3]אָמַר רַב יוֹסֵף: [4]מִדִּין וּדְבָרִים, קָנוּ מִיָּדוֹ.
[5]רַב נַחְמָן אָמַר: מִגּוּפָהּ שֶׁל קַרְקַע, קָנוּ מִיָּדוֹ.

LITERAL TRANSLATION

[1]It was asked of them: [2][If] they made an act of acquisition (lit., "acquired from his hand"), what [is the law]?

[3]Rav Yosef said: [4]Concerning his claim, it was acquired from his hand.

[5]Rav Naḥman said: Concerning the land itself, it was acquired from his hand.

RASHI

יורשי האב. ופליג רבא אדאביי, דאמר: אי דנפלו לה כשהיא תחתיו, דכולי עלמא — ידו של בעל עדיפא מידה, וכשמת עמד אחיו ליבמה במקומו והרי הוא כמותו, ואם מתה כשהיא שומרת יבם — אין ליורשיה בהן כלום, ומתניתין דבית שמאי — דנפלו לה כשהיא שומרת יבם. קנו מידו מהו — אברייתא דהאומר לחבירו "דין ודברים אין לי על שדה זו" קאי. אבל אמתניתין — לא מהניא קנין ליפות כחה. דהא במכירה בלא לשון מתנה סגי לאסתלוקי אפילו מגופה של קרקע, היכא דפריש, כדקתני סיפא. וטעמא דמתניתין דאמר "הרי זה אוכל פירות" לאו משום גריעותא דלשון "דין ודברים" הוא, אלא משום דלא פריש ממאי סליק נפשיה, ואמרינן ידה על התחתונה, כדמפרש לקמן, ואינה יכולה לומר: מן הכל נסתלקת. הילכך, מה לי קנו מה לי לא קנו. אלא אברייתא קא בעי לה, דקתני: לא אמר כלום. וטעמא — משום גריעותא דלישנא הוא. מהו — מי אמרינן: לא הקנה בחליפין הללו כלום, ולא אמר עליה אלא לשון "דין ודברים". או דלמא אין חליפין באים אלא לדבר שיש בו ממש, שזה קונה את הסודר ומקנה לו חפץ המכר או המַתָּנָה ועל גופה של קרקע קנו מידו, ומתנה גמורה היא. מדין ודברים קנו מידו — מה שפירש על הקנין קנו מידו, והוא לשון דין ודברים, ואינו כלום.

NOTES

husband's brother to take her in levirate marriage. Our commentary follows *Meiri* (whose explanation was arrived at independently by *Pnei Yehoshua*), who understands that there is a practical difference between Abaye and Rava in the case of a brother who renounced his rights to the property of his brother's widow who was bound to him by the levirate tie but not yet married to him.

קָנוּ מִיָּדוֹ, מַהוּ If he made an act of acquisition, what is the law? Our commentary follows *Rashi* and others who understand that the Gemara's question relates to the Baraita cited earlier regarding the partner who waived his rights to half of the property, using a formulation that expresses renunciation. The Baraita ruled that the renunciation is not valid, and the Gemara now asks about a situation where the partner reinforced his renunciation with a valid act of acquisition. Other Rishonim have difficulties with *Rashi's* position (see *Tosafot* and *Tosafot Rid*). *Rav Tzemaḥ Gaon, Rav Naḥshon Gaon* and *Tosafot* argue that

HALAKHAH

מִגּוּפָהּ שֶׁל קַרְקַע With respect to the land itself. "If a woman stipulated with her husband that he would waive a certain pecuniary right that he has with regard to her, and the stipulation was made only after they were married, the stipulation must be reinforced with a valid mode of acquisition, and then the stipulation is binding. If a man stipulated with his wife during their betrothal that he would have no claim to her property, and he performed a valid mode of acquisition, he waived his rights to the property itself, so that he is no longer entitled to any of the usufruct, but he does inherit the property after her death," following Rav Naḥman, according to *Rav Hai Gaon*. Other authorities disagree. According to *Rosh*, in such a case, the husband does not even inherit from his wife." (*Rambam, Sefer Nashim, Hilkhot Ishut* 23:1; *Shulḥan Arukh, Even HaEzer* 92:3.)

TRANSLATION AND COMMENTARY

אָמַר אַבַּיֵי [1]**Abaye said: The view of Rav Yosef stands to reason** [83B] **when** the other partner came to take possession of the property which had been waived to him, the partner that waived ownership **protested.** [2]**But if** the waiving partner **stood by** and allowed some time to pass before protesting against his partner's taking possession, [3]we assume that **the act of acquisition** that the first partner **performed related to** his ownership of **the land itself** and that he cannot now retract that transaction.

אָמַר אַמֵימָר [4]The Gemara records a final ruling on the matter: **Amemar said: The law is** that **the act of acquisition** which the partner performed relates to his ownership **of the land itself.**

אָמַר לֵיהּ רַב [5]**Rav Ashi** said to Amemar: Does your ruling apply even **when** the waiving partner **protested** against the other partner immediately, **or** does it apply only **when** he **stood by** and allowed time to pass before objecting? [6]The Gemara then asks: **What difference does it make?** [7]And it replies: The issue is whether or not Amemar rules **in accordance with Rav Yosef** when the waiving partner raises an immediate objection.

אָמַר לֵיהּ [8]Amemar **said to** Rav Ashi: **I did not hear** what Rav Yosef said — [9]**that is to say, I do not agree** with his position.

אִם כֵּן [10]We learned in the Mishnah that if someone wrote to his wife: "I have no claim on your property," he retains his right to the property's usufruct and his right to inherit the property from her. The Mishnah asked: **"If so why did** the man **write her** 'I have no claim on your property'? And it answered that he relinquished his right to protest his wife's selling it or giving it away as a gift. [11]The Gemara now asks: If indeed there is validity to the husband's renunciation, **let** the woman **say to** her husband: **"From all things you removed yourself"** and you also surrendered the right to enjoy the usufruct and to inherit the property!

אָמַר אַבַּיֵי [12]**Abaye said:** We apply here a general rule that when in doubt regarding the correct interpretation of a deed, **the deed holder has the weaker hand** and the deed must be interpreted in the way

[1]אָמַר אַבַּיֵי: מִסְתַּבְּרָא מִילְּתָא דְּרַב יוֹסֵף [83B] בְּעוֹרֵר, אֲבָל [2]בְּעוֹמֵד, [3]מִגּוּפָהּ שֶׁל קַרְקַע, קָנוּ מִיָּדוֹ.

[4]אָמַר אַמֵימָר: הִלְכְתָא: מִגּוּפָהּ שֶׁל קַרְקַע קָנוּ מִיָּדוֹ.

[5]אָמַר לֵיהּ רַב אַשִׁי לְאַמֵימָר: בְּעוֹרֵר אוֹ בְּעוֹמֵד? [6]לְמַאי נָפְקָא מִינָּהּ? [7]לְכִדְרַב יוֹסֵף.

[8]אָמַר לֵיהּ: לָא שְׁמִיעַ לִי, [9]כְּלוֹמַר, לָא סְבִירָא לִי.

[10]"אִם כֵּן, לָמָּה כָּתַב לָהּ וכו׳". [11]וְתֵימָא לֵיהּ: "מִכָּל מִילֵּי סְלִיקַתְּ נַפְשָׁךְ"!

[12]אָמַר אַבַּיֵי: יַד בַּעַל הַשְּׁטָר עַל הַתַּחְתּוֹנָה.

LITERAL TRANSLATION

[1]Abaye said: The view of Rav Yosef stands to reason [83B] when he protested, [2]but when he stood [by, even] with respect to the land itself,[3] he acquired [it] from his hand.

[4]Amemar said: The law is: With respect to the land itself he acquired [it] from his hand.

[5]Rav Ashi said to Amemar: When he protested or when he stood [by]? [6]What difference does it make (lit., "what comes out of it")? [7]According to Rav Yosef.

[8][Amemar] said to him: I did not hear it, [9]that is to say, I do not agree.

[10]"If so, why did he write her, etc." [11]But let her say to him: "From all things you removed yourself"!

[12]Abaye said: The deed holder has the weaker (lit., "lower") hand.

RASHI

בעורר – כשבא חברו זה להחזיק בחלקו מיד עמד וערער על המתנה ואמר: לא נתתי לך את השדה ודין ודברים בעלמא אמרתי לך שלא אריב עמך. אבל בעומד – יום או יומים ואחר כך ערער – לא, דהשתא הוא דקא הדר ביה ולמדוהו לטעון כך. ותימא ליה מכל מילי סליקת נפשך – כיון דאוקמת דבלשון זה יכול להסתלק, למה אינו מסולק מן הכל. יד בעל השטר על התחתונה – כל המוציא שטר על המוחזק בדבר מה שמפורש בשטר יכול לתבוע עליו. ואם השטר סתום, מורידים אותו לפחות שבמשמעות השטר. וכאן הבעל בא בתקנת

BACKGROUND

לָא שְׁמִיעַ לִי וכו׳ I did not hear it etc. This expression indicates that the Sage who used it (in this case, Amemar) wished to speak respectfully. Therefore he did not say explicitly that he disagreed ("לָא סְבִירָא לִי"). Rather he spoke tactfully and said that he had not heard of the matter, though he actually had heard of it. He meant that he did not believe that the opinion was worthy of consideration, but he spoke as though it had been unknown to him.

NOTES

the Gemara's question relates to a man who renounced his rights to his wife's property after he was married to her. The Gemara had just explained that a man cannot renounce his rights to his wife's property by way of a stipulation after they are married, and it now asks whether the renunciation is valid if it was accompanied by a valid mode of acquisition. Rav Yosef maintains that the renunciation is still not valid, and Rav Naḥman argues that it is. *Rav Hai Gaon* understands that the Gemara's question relates to a man who stipulated with his wife during their betrothal that he has no claim to her property. The Mishnah taught that in such a case the husband retains his rights to the usufruct of his wife's property during her lifetime and to the property itself after her death. He only relinquished his right to reclaim the property if it was sold or given away by his wife. The Gemara now asks whether it makes any difference if the husband's stipulation was accompanied by a valid act of acquisition. Rav Yosef maintains that the *kinyan* adds nothing. Rav Naḥman argues that if the husband reinforced his waiver with a *kinyan,* he does indeed forfeit his right to the usufruct of his wife's property, and perhaps even the right to succeed to her estate (see *Rosh* and Halakhah).

BACKGROUND

בּוּצִינָא טַב מִקָּרָא A cucumber is better than a gourd. *Rashi* explains that בּוּצִינָא and קָרָא are two names for a similar kind of fruit. The former term is used when the fruit is small, and the latter, when it is full grown. However, *Tosafot* prove by citing other passages that the two terms refer to different kinds of fruit. A בּוּצִינָא grows on the ground like a kind of cucumber, whereas a קָרָא is a kind of pumpkin, and the former ripens well before the latter. The purport of the expression remains the same: a person prefers something small in the present rather than hope to receive something larger that might or might not be available in the future ("a bird in the hand is worth two in the bush").

TRANSLATION AND COMMENTARY

most advantageous to the person against whom the deed is presented, for the burden of proof always fall upon the party holding the deed. If the woman presents the document and argues that her husband surrendered all his rights, and the husband claims that he only renounced his right to object to its sale, but not to the usufruct or to inherit the property, we accept his argument. Because the wife wishes to deprive her husband of the rights he would normally enjoy, the burden of proof falls upon her.

וְאֵימָא [1]However, according to the rule that the deed holder is at a disadvantage, you should **say** that the husband meant only to waive his right to enjoy **the fruits** of his wife's property during her lifetime, but he had no intention of waiving his right to prevent its sale. This interpretation of the husband's renunciation is the one most advantageous to him, for he would rather surrender his right to enjoy the usufruct of his wife's property during his lifetime, than give up his right to object to her selling it. For if she sells the property, he will not inherit it upon her death.

אֲמַר אַבַּיֵי [2]**Abaye said:** There is a popular adage that says: **A cucumber** now **is better than a gourd** in the future. So it is reasonable to assume that if the husband is giving up something, he prefers to waive his right to object to the sale of his wife's property, a hypothetical eventuality, and to continue enjoying the usufruct, an immediate and regular benefit.

וְאֵימָא [3]The Gemara now asks: Why should we not **say** that when the husband surrendered his right to his wife's property he meant only to waive his right of **inheritance,** but he had no intention of giving up his right to object to its sale. For regarding inheritance, his wife may outlive him; but if his wife sells it, he cannot enjoy the usufruct, an immediate benefit.

אֲמַר אַבַּיֵי [4]**Abaye said: Death is common,** so a husband's right to inherit his wife's property is one that is often exercised. [5]But it **is not common** for a woman to **sell** property that she inherited. The husband's right to object to such a sale is one that is not often exercised. [6]**And when a person removes himself** from exercising a right, [7]we assume that he is renouncing **a right that is not commonly** exercised, and not **a right that is commonly** exercised.

[1]וְאֵימָא: מִפֵּירֵי!
[2]אֲמַר אַבַּיֵי: בּוּצִינָא טַב מִקָּרָא.
[3]וְאֵימָא, מִירוּשָּׁה!
[4]אֲמַר אַבַּיֵי: מִיתָה שְׁכִיחָא; [5]מְכִירָה לָא שְׁכִיחָא. [6]וְכִי מְסַלֵּיק אִינִישׁ נַפְשֵׁיהּ, [7]מִמִּילְּתָא דְּלָא שְׁכִיחָא. מִמִּילְּתָא דִּשְׁכִיחָא לָא מְסַלֵּיק אִינִישׁ נַפְשֵׁיהּ.

LITERAL TRANSLATION

[1]But say, from [its] fruits!
[2]Abaye said: A cucumber is better than a gourd.
[3]But say, from [the] inheritance!
[4]Abaye said: Death is common; [5]a sale is not common. [6]And when a person removes himself, [7][it is] from something that is not common. From something that is common a person does not remove himself.

RASHI

חכמים על נכסי אשתו בשלשה דברים: לאכול פירות, ולירש, ואם תמכור — מכרה בטל, וזו מוציאה עליו שטר שכתבת לי דין ודברים אין לי בנכסייך, ולשון סילוק הוא זה. והוא יכול לטעון: ודאי לשון סילוק הוא, אבל לא נסתלקתי אלא מפחות שבדברים, וזו היא המכירה, אבל כל זמן שלא תמכור אוכל פירות. **ואימא מפירי** — מסלק נפשיה, שלא יאכל פירות בחייה, והוא פחות שבכולן. אבל אם תמכור, שמפסיד אף גוף הקרקע שהיה ראוי לירש אם תמות בחייו, יהא מכרה בטל ויירשנה. **בוצינא טב מקרא** — בוצינא — דלעת קטנה, קרא — דלעת גדולה. והאומר לחבירו: קח לך דלעת קטנה בגינתי, או המתן עד שיגדילו וקח גדולה. טוב לו ליקח הקטנה מיד, כי לא ידע מה יולד יום. אף כאן חביבה עליו אכילת פירות שהוא תדיר ומיד, מביטול מכר שאינו מיד אלא לכשתמכור ושמא לא תמכור. **ואימא מירושה** — סליק נפשיה. והוא הפחות, שמא לא תמות בחייו, אבל ממכירה לא סליק נפשיה שמא תמכור ויפסיד אכילת פירות שהוא עכשיו. **מכירה לא שכיחא** — שאין אשה רוצה למכור נכסי בית אביה.

NOTES

וְאֵימָא: מִפֵּירֵי But say, from its fruits. According to *Rashi,* the Gemara is suggesting that if the husband stipulated that he would have no claim on his wife's property, he meant to waive his right to enjoy the property's usufruct during her lifetime. However, if she sold the property and then died, he would still be able to reclaim the property from the buyer. The Rishonim point out that it follows from this that if a husband did not waive any of his rights to his wife's property, he would indeed be able to reclaim property which his wife had sold to another person. But this is difficult, for it is recorded that a husband can reclaim property that his wife sells by virtue of an enactment passed in the city of Usha. And the Gemara elsewhere (*Ketubot* 78b) implies that the Ushan enactment is not included in the Mishnah. *Ra'avad* answers that the Ushan enactment was actually passed before Rabbi Yehudah HaNasi compiled the Mishnah, and so its provision is included in Mishnaic law. The Gemara, in *Ketubot* 78b, means only that the enactment is not stated explicitly in the Mishnah.

מִיתָה שְׁכִיחָא Death is common. According to *Rashi* and *Tosafot,* the Gemara is arguing that the husband's right to inherit his wife's property is a right that is often exercised, because a wife often dies before her husband, as a result

[1]רַב אַשִׁי אֲמַר: ״בִּנְכָסַיִיךְ״, וְלֹא בְּפֵירוֹתֵיהֶן. [2]״בִּנְכָסַיִיךְ״, וְלֹא לְאַחַר מִיתָה.

[3]״רַבִּי יְהוּדָה אוֹמֵר: לְעוֹלָם הוּא אוֹכֵל פֵּירֵי פֵירוֹת״. [4]תָּנוּ רַבָּנַן: ״אֵלּוּ הֵן ׳פֵּירוֹת׳, וְאֵלּוּ הֵן ׳פֵּירֵי פֵירוֹת׳: [5]הִכְנִיסָה לוֹ קַרְקַע, וְעָשְׂתָה פֵּירוֹת, הֲרֵי הֵן פֵּירוֹת. [6]מָכַר פֵּירוֹת וְלָקַח מֵהֶן קַרְקַע, וְעָשְׂתָה פֵּירוֹת, [7]הֲרֵי הֵן פֵּירֵי פֵירוֹת״.

LITERAL TRANSLATION

[1]Rav Ashi said: "On your property," but not on its fruits. [2]"On your property," but not after [your] death.

[3]"Rabbi Yehudah says: He still [may] enjoy the fruits of [its] fruits." [4]Our Rabbis taught: "These are 'fruits' and these are 'fruits of fruits': [5][If] she brought [in] land to him, and it yielded produce, these are fruits. [6][If] he sold [this] produce and bought with it land, and it yielded produce, [7]these are fruits of [its] fruits."

RASHI

רב אשי אמר – אין לך אלא דקדוק הלשון. בנכסייך – אמר לה, אבל לא בפירותיהן, ובעודן שלה קאמר לה, דהא ״בנכסייך״ קאמר, ולא לאחר מיתה שבטל שמה מעליהן.

TRANSLATION AND COMMENTARY

רַב אַשִׁי [1]To explain why the husband's renunciation does not refer to all his rights, Rav Ashi sets aside the principle that the deed-holder is at a disadvantage and returns to the wording of the husband's renunciation. **Rav Ashi said,** the words, **"on your property,"** imply that the husband meant to waive his right to the property itself, **but not** his right to enjoy **its fuits.** [2]Moreover, the words, **"on your property,"** imply that he meant to waive his rights to his wife's property while it was still her's — i.e., during her lifetime — **but** he did **not** intend to surrender his right to inherit the property **after** her **death.**

רַבִּי יְהוּדָה [3]We learned in the Mishnah: If someone wrote to his wife: "I will have no claim on your property or its fruits," he does not enjoy its fruits during her lifetime. But if she predeceases him, he inherits the property from her. And **"Rabbi Yehudah says: He still** may **enjoy the fruits of its fruits,** unless he writes her explicitly: 'I will have no claim on your property, or on its fruits, or on the fruits of its fruits, forever.'" [4]**Our Rabbis taught** a Baraita that clarifies Rabbi Yehudah's position and defines the benefits that are known as **fruits** and those that are known as **fruits of fruits.** [5]For example, **if** a woman **brought land** into her marriage, **and** the land yielded produce, **these are** regarded as **fruits.** [6]**If he** then **sold this produce and bought land with** the proceeds, **and** that land later **yielded produce,** [7]**these are** regarded as **fruits of its fruits."**

NOTES

of complications arising from childbirth. *Meiri* challenges this statistical assumption, arguing that husbands usually die before their wives, either because they are more likely to enter into life-threatening situations, such as road travel or war, or because a man usually marries a younger woman. *Meiri* and *Ritva* therefore explain that the Gemara is arguing that it is more common for a woman to die before her husband than to sell the property which she brought into her marriage.

בִּנְכָסַיִיךְ, וְלֹא בְּפֵירוֹתֵיהֶן "On your property," but not on its fruit. According to *Ritva* and others, Rav Ashi agrees with Abaye that the Mishnah's ruling is based on the principle that in a case of doubt regarding the correct interpretation of a deed, the deed-holder is at a disadvantage. But they disagree about how we apply this principle. Abaye argues that we interpret the husband's formula of renunciation in such a way that he surrenders as little as possible. And Rav Ashi argues that we interpret the husband's formula of renunciation in the narrowest possible way. But according to *Tosafot* and others, Rav Ashi disagrees with Abaye about whether the principle that the deed-holder is at a disadvantage may be applied to the case in our Mishnah. Some explain that according to Rav Ashi this principle applies only when the deed-holder comes to collect a claim on the basis of the ambiguous deed. We then interpret the deed in the way most advantageous to the person against whom the claim is presented, for the burden of proof always falls upon the party putting forward the claim. But in our Mishnah, the husband wishes to collect the usufruct of his wife's property or inherit her against the deed of renunciation which she holds. It therefore lies on him to prove that he did not renounce those rights. Rav Ashi therefore explains that the wording of the husband's renunciation implies that he meant only to waive his right to object to the sale of his wife's property, but not his rights to enjoy the usufruct or inherit the property.

Rashba asks: If the words "on your property" imply that the husband meant to waive his right to his wife's property itself, but not his right to the property's usufruct, why then do we not say that someone who sells property to another person means to sell only the property itself, but not the usufruct? He answers that since, in general, property and its usufruct belong to the same person, we assume that when the property is sold, the usufruct is sold along with it. But regarding his wife's property, a husband may be entitled to the usufruct but have no rights to its principle or he may be entitled to inherit her estate, but have no right to the usufruct during her lifetime. Thus, we cannot assume that when the husband renounces his rights to his wife's property, he renounces all his rights, and so we interpret his renunciation in the narrowest way possible. *Ritva* argues that in the usual case of sale, when the transfer of ownership is clearly formulated, we do not interpret the wording narrowly and explain "property" to exclude usufruct. But here the husband uses an ambiguous formulation that expresses renunciation, and so we interpret each word as precisely as possible.

TRANSLATION AND COMMENTARY

אִיבַּעֲיָא לְהוּ [1]The following problem arose in discussion among the Sages and **it was asked: According to Rabbi Yehudah, is** the expression **"the fruits of its fruits" determinant,** so that even if the husband only waived his claim to the "fruits of the fruits" without mentioning "forever," he may not enjoy the usufruct of the usufruct of his wife's property, or the usufruct of that usufruct, as if he had written "forever"? [2]**Or is perhaps** the expression **"forever" determinant?** So that if the husband waived his claim to the "fruits" of his wife's property "forever," he may not enjoy not only the fruits, but also this usufruct and the usufruct of this secondary usufruct. [3]**Or perhaps** use of **both** expressions **is determinant?** So that if he wrote only the one of them, he would not have waived his claim to the usufruct of his wife's usufruct ad infinitum.

אִם תִּמְצֵי לוֹמַר [4]The Gemara challenges the suggestion that the expression "fruits of its fruits" is determinant. **If you wish to say that** the expression **"the fruits of its fruits" is determinant,** [5]**why then** was it necessary for the Mishnah to mention **"forever"?**

הָא קָא מַשְׁמַע לָן [6]The Gemara answers: The expression "forever" is explanatory, and **teaches us** that **if** the husband **just wrote** that he waives his claim to **"the fruits of its fruits"** [7]**he is considered as if he had written** that he waives his claim to all of the property's usufruct **"forever."**

וְאִם תִּמְצֵי לוֹמַר [8]The Gemara now questions its second suggestion: **And if you wish to say that** the expression **"forever" is determinant,** [9]**why then was it** necessary for the Mishnah to mention **"fruits of its fruits"?**

הָא קָא מַשְׁמַע לָן [10]The Gemara answers: The Mishnah wished **to teach us** that **even if** the husband **wrote her** that he would have no claim to his wife's property, or to its fruits, [11]or to **"the fruits of its fruits" — if he** also **wrote** the word **"forever,"** he did waive the usufruct of the usufruct of the usufruct of the property ad infinitum, but **if** he did **not** include that expression, he did **not.**

וְאִם תִּמְצֵי לוֹמַר [12]The Gemara now asks about its third option: **And if you wish to say that both** expressions **are determinant,** [13]**why then do both of them** need to be included in the husband's waiver?

[1]אִיבַּעֲיָא לְהוּ: לְרַבִּי יְהוּדָה, ״פֵּירֵי פֵּירוֹת״ דַּוְקָא, [2]אוֹ דִּלְמָא ״עַד עוֹלָם״ דַּוְקָא, [3]אוֹ דִּלְמָא תַּרְוַיְיהוּ דַּוְקָא?

[4]אִם תִּמְצֵי לוֹמַר ״פֵּירֵי פֵּירוֹת״ דַּוְקָא, [5]״עַד עוֹלָם״ לָמָּה לִי? [6]הָא קָא מַשְׁמַע לָן: כֵּיוָן דִּכְתַב לָהּ ״פֵּירֵי פֵּירוֹת״, [7]כְּמַאן דִּכְתַב לָהּ ״עַד עוֹלָם״ דָּמֵי.

[8]וְאִם תִּמְצֵי לוֹמַר ״עַד עוֹלָם״ דַּוְקָא, [9]״פֵּירֵי פֵּירוֹת״ לָמָּה לִי? [10]הָא קָא מַשְׁמַע לָן: אַף עַל גַּב דִּכְתַב לָהּ ״פֵּירֵי פֵּירוֹת״, [11]אִי כְּתַב לָהּ ״עַד עוֹלָם״, אִין; אִי לָא, לָא.

[12]וְאִם תִּמְצֵי לוֹמַר תַּרְוַיְיהוּ דַּוְקָא, [13]תַּרְתֵּי לָמָּה לִי?

LITERAL TRANSLATION

[1]It was asked of them: According to Rabbi Yehudah, is "fruits of its fruits" determinant (lit., "precise"), [2]or perhaps "forever" is determinant, [3]or perhaps [use of] both of them is determinant?

[4]If you wish to say [that] "fruits of its fruits" is determinant, [5]why [then] do I need "forever"?

[6]It [can] teach us: If he [just] wrote her "fruits of its fruits," [7]he is [considered as] one who wrote her "forever."

[8]And if you wish to say [that] "forever" is determinant, [9]why [then] do I need "fruits of its fruits"?

[10]It teaches us: Even if he wrote her "fruits of its fruits," [11]if he wrote her "forever," yes; if not, no.

[12]And if you wish to say [that] both of them are determinant, [13]why [then] do I need both of them?

RASHI

איבעיא להו לרבי יהודה — דתנא תרתי: ״ובפירי פירותיהן״ ״עד עולם״. **פירי פירות דוקא** — בהאי לישנא לחוד סגי לאסתלוקי מפירי פירות ומפירי דפירי פירות, ולא בעי ״עד עולם״. ואי כתב ״בפירותיהן עד עולם״ ולא כתב ״בפירי פירות״ — לא אסתלק מפירי פירות. **או דלמא עד עולם דוקא** — וב״עד עולם״ תליא מילתא, ו״בפירי פירות״ לא בעי למיכתב. ואי כתב ״מפירי פירות״, ולא כתב ״עד עולם״ — לא איסתלק מפירי דפירי פירות, או דלמא תרווייהו דוקא. **עד עולם למה לי** — למיתני מתניתין הואיל ולא צריך למיכתביה. **הא קא משמע לן כו׳** — והכי קאמר: עד שיכתוב ״ובפירי פירותיהן״ היינו ״עד עולם״. **פירי פירות למה לי** — למיתני מתניתין ליתני ״בפירותיהן עד עולם״ הואיל וביה תליא, והוא לשון פירות ופירי פירות. **הא קא משמע לן כו׳** — אין ודאי לא בעי למכתב, מיהו אי לא תני הוה אמינא דאי כתב ״פירי פירות״ הוה ככותב ״עד עולם״, להכי תני, למימר דאפילו כתב ״פירי פירות״ בעינן ״עד עולם״. **תרתי למה לי** — למיכתב בשטר.

NOTES

אוֹ דִּלְמָא תַּרְוַיְיהוּ דַּוְקָא Or perhaps use of both of them is determinant. *Maharam Shiff* notes that there is also a fourth possibility that use of either expression is determinant, for whether he wrote only "the fruits of its fruits," or he wrote only "fruits forever," either way the husband waives his right to the usufruct of his wife's property forever. He adds that *Tosafot* in fact understand the first possibility suggested by the Gemara in this manner, that

[1]צְרִיכָא. דְּאִי כָּתַב לָהּ ״פֵּירֵי פֵּירוֹת״, [2]וְלֹא כָּתַב לָהּ ״עַד עוֹלָם״, הֲוָה אָמִינָא פֵּירֵי פֵּירוֹת הוּא דְּלָא אָכֵיל, [3]אֲבָל פֵּירָא דְּפֵירֵי פֵּירוֹת אָכֵיל. [4]לְהָכִי, אִיצְטְרִיךְ ״עַד עוֹלָם״. [5]וְאִי כָּתַב לָהּ ״עַד עוֹלָם״, וְלֹא כָּתַב לָהּ ״פֵּירֵי פֵּירוֹת״, [6]הֲוָה אָמִינָא ״לְעוֹלָם״ אַפֵּירוֹת קָאֵי. [7]לְהָכִי, אִיצְטְרִיךְ ״פֵּירֵי פֵּירוֹת״.

[8]אִיבַּעֲיָא לְהוּ: [9]כָּתַב לָהּ: ״דִּין וּדְבָרִים אֵין לִי בִּנְכָסַיִךְ, וּבְפֵירֵי פֵּירוֹת״, [10]מַהוּ שֶׁיֹּאכַל פֵּירוֹת? [11]מִפֵּירֵי פֵּירוֹת סָלֵיק נַפְשֵׁיהּ, [12]מִפֵּירֵי לָא סָלֵיק נַפְשֵׁיהּ, [13]אוֹ דִּלְמָא מִכָּל מִילֵּי סָלֵיק נַפְשֵׁיהּ?

LITERAL TRANSLATION

[1]It is necessary. For if he wrote her "fruits of its fruits," [2]but did not write her "forever," I would have said [that] he does not enjoy the fruit of its fruit, [3]but fruits of the fruit of its fruit he does enjoy. [4]Therefore, it was necessary [to write] "forever." [5]And if he wrote her "forever," but did not write her "the fruits of its fruits," [6]I would have said [that] "forever" refers to the fruits [themselves]. [7]Therefore, it was necessary [to write] "fruits of its fruits."

[8]It was asked of them: [9][If] he wrote her: "I have no claim on your property, or on the fruits of its fruits," [10]what about his enjoying the fruits? [11]From the fruits of its fruits he removed himself, [12][but] from the fruits, he did not remove himself, [13]or perhaps from all things he removed himself?

TRANSLATION AND COMMENTARY

צְרִיכָא [1]The Gemara explains: **It is necessary** for the husband to write both expressions. **For if he** only **wrote** that he would have no claim on his wife's property, its usufruct, or on **"the fruits of its fruits,"** [2]**but did not** also **write her "forever," I would have said that he may not enjoy the fruits of its fruits** of his wife's property, for that usufruct he waived explicitly, [3]**but the fruits of the fruits of its fruits he may** indeed **enjoy.** [4]**Therefore, it is necessary** for the husband **to write** in his waiver the expression **"forever."** [5]**And if** he only **wrote** that he would have no claim on his wife's property or its usufruct **"forever," and he did not** also **write her "the fruits of its fruits,"** [6]**I would have said that in fact** the word "forever" **refers to the fruits** and nothing more. The husband may have meant to waive his claim to the usufruct of his wife's property this year, and forevermore, but not to waive the usufruct of the usufruct of his wife's property. [7]**Therefore, it was necessary** for the husband to **write** the expression **"the fruits of its fruits."**

אִיבַּעֲיָא לְהוּ [8]The Gemara now raises another question: In discussion among the Sages, **it was asked:** [9]**If someone wrote** his wife: **"I will have no claim on your property, or on the fruits of its fruits"** but he did not mention explicitly that he waives his right to the property's usufruct, [10]**what is** the law **regarding** the husband's **enjoying the fruit?** The Gemara now clarifies the two sides of the question: [11]Do we say that it was only **from** that which the husband specifically mentioned in his waiver, namely, **the fruit of its fruit,** did **he remove himself,** [12]**but from the usufruct** itself, which he did not mention, **he did not remove himself?** [13]**Or perhaps** we say that it was **from all things** — both the usufruct of the usufruct and the usufruct itself — that the husband **removed himself!**

RASHI

לעולם אפירות קאי — לא אוכל הפירות לעולם, לא בשנה זו ולא בשנים הבאות, אבל פירי פירות אוכל.

NOTES

writing "the fruits of its fruits" suffices by itself, and so too "forever." The Aharonim discuss this possibility at greater length.

לְעוֹלָם אַפֵּירוֹת קָאֵי **In fact it refers to the fruits alone.** Our commentary follows *Rashi,* who explains that had the husband not added the words "forever," he might have been understood as waiving his claim to the usufruct of his wife's property for only a single year. With "forever," he has waived his claim year after year. *Tosafot* argue that there is no reason to assume that the husband would distinguish between the first and subsequent years, if he did not add "forever." But *Ramat Shmuel* suggests that the husband may have been willing to waive his right to the usufruct of his wife's property for the first year because of his strong affection for her during the first year of marriage. *Tosafot* explain the Gemara differently: If the husband wrote that he would not have any claim to his wife's property, or to its usufruct "forever," but he did not also mention "the usufruct of its usufruct," we might have thought that the word "forever" teaches that the husband meant to waive his claim to the usufruct of his wife's property both during her lifetime and after her death. But he may never have meant to waive the usufruct of the usufruct of his wife's property. Therefore, it was necessary for the husband to include "the fruit of its fruit" in his deed in order to waive them.

פֵּירֵי פֵּירוֹת עַד עוֹלָם **The fruit of its fruit forever.** *Rabbenu Zerahyah HaLevi* asks: If the husband wrote that he waives his right to the usufruct of his wife's property, as well as his right to the usufruct of its usufruct forever, why not say that he meant only to waive his right to the usufruct and the usufruct of its usufruct forever, but not his right to the usufruct of the usufruct of the usufruct? He answers: If the husband waived only the usufruct of his wife's property, but not the usufruct of its usufruct, it can be argued that he added "forever" to show that he meant to waive his

TRANSLATION AND COMMENTARY

פְּשִׁיטָא [1]The Gemara answers: **It is obvious that** in such a case it was **from all things** that the husband **removed himself.** [2]**For if you say that** the husband **removed himself** only **from the fruits of the fruits** of his wife's property, **but from the fruits** themselves **he did not remove himself,** there is a difficulty. [3]**If he ate all the** property's **fruits, from where do fruits of the fruits come?**

וְלִיטַעֲמִיךְ [4]The Gemara introduces a counterargument: **According to this opinion,** how can we explain **that which we have learned in the Mishnah:** [5]**"Rabbi Yehudah says:** The husband still may **enjoy the fruits of its fruits** of his wife's property unless he writes explicitly: 'I will have no claim on your property, or on its fruits, or on the fruits of its fruits forever' "? Here too you should ask: [6]**Since she ate the fruits, from where do the fruits of its fruits come?** [7]**Rather,** you must **explain** that Rabbi Yehudah is dealing with a case where the wife consumed only a part of the usufruct, and what **she left over** was invested by her husband. [8]**Here too** in the case where the husband only removes himself from the usufruct of the usufruct, we deal with what **he left over** from the usufruct of his wife's property. The problem posed by the Gemara as to whether or not in such a case the husband also removed himself from the usufruct of his wife's property remains unresolved.

רַבָּן [9]We learned in our Mishnah: **"Rabban Shimon ben Gamliel says:** Even if the husband stipulated that he would have no claim on his wife's property after her death, **if she dies he inherits her,** because he stipulated against what is written in the Torah, and whoever stipulates against what is written in the Torah, his stipulation is void." [10]**Rav said: The law is in accordance with** the view of **Rabban Shimon ben Gamliel, but not for his reason.**

[1]פְּשִׁיטָא דְּמִכָּל מִילֵּי סָלֵיק נַפְשֵׁיהּ, [2]דְּאִי אָמְרַתְּ: מִפֵּירֵי פֵּירוֹת סָלֵיק נַפְשֵׁיהּ, מִפֵּירֵי לָא סָלֵיק נַפְשֵׁיהּ, [3]כֵּיוָן דְּאָכְלִינְהוּ לְפֵירוֹת, פֵּירֵי פֵּירוֹת מֵהֵיכָא? [4]וְלִיטַעֲמִיךְ, הָא דִּתְנַן: [5]"רַבִּי יְהוּדָה אוֹמֵר: לְעוֹלָם הוּא אוֹכֵל פֵּירֵי פֵּירוֹת, כו׳". [6]כֵּיוָן דְּאָכְלִינְהוּ לְפֵירֵי, פֵּירֵי פֵּירוֹת מֵהֵיכָא? [7]אֶלָּא, בִּדְשָׁיְירָא. [8]הָכָא נַמִי, בִּדְשָׁיֵיר.

[9]"רַבָּן שִׁמְעוֹן בֶּן גַּמְלִיאֵל אוֹמֵר כו׳". [10]אָמַר רַב: הֲלָכָה כְּרַבָּן שִׁמְעוֹן בֶּן גַּמְלִיאֵל, וְלָא מִטַּעֲמֵיהּ?

LITERAL TRANSLATION

[1]It is obvious that from all things he removed himself, [2]for if you say that from the fruits of its fruits he removed himself, [but] from the fruits he did not remove himself, [3]since he ate [all] the fruits, from where [do] fruits of the fruits [come]?

[4]But according to your opinion, that which we have learned [in the Mishnah]: [5]"Rabbi Yehudah says: He still may enjoy the fruits of its fruits, etc." [6]Since she ate the fruits, from where [do] fruits of its fruits [come]? [7]Rather, [explain] that she left [some] over. [8]Here too, when he left [some] over.

[9]"Rabban Shimon ben Gamliel says, etc." [10]Rav said: The law is in accordance with Rabban Shimon ben Gamliel, but not for his reason.

RASHI

הכי גרסינן – וליטעמיך דקתני רבי יהודה אומר כו׳ כיון דאכלתינהו לפירות, ולא גרסינן דאכלינהו. **אלא בדשיירא גרסינן הכא נמי בדשייר** – אם לא אכלן, ומכרן ולקח בהו קרקע ועשתה פירות, סילק נפשו מהן ולא מן הראשונים.

NOTES

right not only to the usufruct of property that was already in existence, but even usufruct that was not yet in existence. But if the husband waived not only the usufruct, but also the usufruct of the usufruct, the words "forever" can only be understood as teaching that he meant to waive his right to when the usufruct of the usufruct of the usufruct forever, for usufruct of usufruct is always not yet in existence. *Ramban* rejects this answer because the husband wrote his renunciation before marriage, the usufruct was not yet his. Then even renunciation of the usufruct forever should mean he renounced them all. The *Ramban* explains than when the husband mentioned not only the usufruct, but also the usufruct of the usufruct, and then he added the words "forever," those extra words surely teach that he meant to waive the usufruct of its usufruct, and its usufruct, and its usufruct forever, for there is no other way to formulate such a waiver.

אֶלָּא, בִּדְשָׁיְירָא **Rather, explain that she left some over.** *Rambam* maintains that if the husband waives his rights to enjoy the usufruct of his wife's property, he can compel her to sell the usufruct and buy land with the proceeds, so that he can enjoy the usufruct of the usufruct. The Rishonim note that this position is not supported by the simple understanding of our Gemara which implies that she may

HALAKHAH

רַבָּן שִׁמְעוֹן בֶּן גַּמְלִיאֵל אוֹמֵר **Rabban Shimon ben Gamliel says.** "If a man stipulated with his wife after he married her that he would not inherit her estate after her death, his stipulation is void. Even though the husband's right to his wife's inheritance is only by Rabbinic decree, the Rabbis reinforced their rulings in the same way as the laws of the

TRANSLATION AND COMMENTARY

מַאי הֲלָכָה [1]The Gemara asks: **What is the meaning of** Rav's statement that **the law is in accordance with** the view of **Rabban Shimon ben Gamliel, but not for the reason** that he offered? [2]If you **say that the law is in accordance with** the view of **Rabban Shimon ben Gamliel, who said that if** a woman **dies,** [3]her husband **inherits her,** even if he stipulated that he would have no claim on the property after her death, **but not for his reason.** [4]**For Rabban Shimon ben Gamliel maintains** that if **someone who stipulates against what is written in the Torah, his stipulation is void.** [5]**Rav,** however, agrees with the Tanna Rabbi Yehudah who **maintains** that concerning monetary matters, **a stipulation** contrary to Torah law **is valid.** Now, although Rav disagrees with Rabban Shimon ben Gamliel about the validity of a stipulation contrary to Torah law, he agrees that a widower inherits his late wife's property. [6]This is because Rav **maintains** that **the husband's** right to **inherit** his wife **is** not Torah law but a **Rabbinic decree.** And according to him, the verse cited above (Numbers 27:11), "the kinsman that is next to him....And he shall inherit it," refers not to a man's wife, but to the estate of someone related to him by blood. For that very reason, the husband cannot make a stipulation waiving his right to inherit his wife, [7]for **the Sages reinforced their enactment** and were **even more** stringent about them **than** they were about **the commands of the Torah.**

[84A] וְסָבַר רַב [8]The Gemara raises an objection against this interpretation of Rav's ruling: **But does Rav** really **maintain that** if someone makes a stipulation concerning monetary matters that is contrary to what is written in the Torah, **his stipulation is valid?** [9]**But surely it was stated** elsewhere that Rav maintained the contrary opinion. For it was stated: [10]If **someone says to his fellow:** "I am selling you this merchandise **on condition that you** waive **any claim of fraud against me,"** [11]**Rav said:** The sale is in effect, but the condition

[1]מַאי הֲלָכָה כְּרַבָּן שִׁמְעוֹן בֶּן גַּמְלִיאֵל, וְלָא מִטַּעֲמֵיהּ? [2]אִילֵימָא הֲלָכָה כְּרַבָּן שִׁמְעוֹן בֶּן גַּמְלִיאֵל — דְּאָמַר: אִם מֵתָה, [3]יִירָשֶׁנָּה, וְלָאו מִטַּעֲמֵיהּ — [4]דְּאִילּוּ רַבָּן שִׁמְעוֹן בֶּן גַּמְלִיאֵל סָבַר: מַתְנֶה עַל מַה שֶּׁכָּתוּב בַּתּוֹרָה, תְּנָאוֹ בָּטֵל. [5]וְרַב סָבַר: תְּנָאוֹ קַיָּים, [6]וְקָסָבַר: יְרוּשַּׁת הַבַּעַל דְּרַבָּנַן, [7]וַחֲכָמִים עָשׂוּ חִיזּוּק לְדִבְרֵיהֶם יוֹתֵר מִשֶּׁל תּוֹרָה.

[84A] [8]וְסָבַר רַב תְּנָאוֹ קַיָּים? [9]וְהָא אִיתְּמַר: [10]הָאוֹמֵר לַחֲבֵירוֹ: ״עַל מְנָת שֶׁאֵין לְךָ עָלַי אוֹנָאָה״, [11]רַב אָמַר: יֵשׁ לוֹ

LITERAL TRANSLATION

[1]What is [the meaning of] the law is in accordance with Rabban Shimon ben Gamliel, but not for his reason? [2]If you say [that] the law is in accordance with Rabban Shimon ben Gamliel — who said [that] if she dies, [3]he inherits her — but not for his reason — [4]for Rabban Shimon ben Gamliel maintains: Someone who stipulates against what is written in the Torah, his stipulation is void. [5]And Rav maintains: His condition is valid, [6]but he [also] maintains: The husband's inheritance is by Rabbinic decree, [7]and the Sages made a reinforcement for their enactments (lit., "words") greater than for those of the Torah.

[84A] [8]But does Rav maintain that his stipulation is valid? [9]But surely it was stated: [10]Someone who says to his fellow: "On condition that you do not have [a claim of] fraud against me," [11]Rav said: He has

RASHI

ורב סבר תנאו קיים — כרבי יהודה דאמר גבי מקדש את האשה: על מנת שאין ליך עלי שאר כסות ועונה — בדבר שבממון תנאו קיים. והכא אמאי יירשנה, דקסבר רב: ירושת הבעל דרבנן, וחכמים עשו חיזוק לדבריהם יותר משל תורה, להיות תנאו בטל. **על מנת שאין לך עלי דין אונאה** — אמכור לך חפץ זה.

NOTES

choose whether to consume all the usufruct of her property or to leave some of it over and invest it in land. They propose that *Rambam* must rely on the position of the Tosefta and Jerusalem Talmud (*Ketubot* 52a). *Rosh* argues that there is a passage in the Babylonian Talmud (*Bava Batra* 51a) that refutes *Rambam*'s view, and that our Gemara should be understood as implying that only if the wife decides to leave some of the usufruct over is that usufruct reinvested in land.

HALAKHAH

Torah and said that a condition that is contrary to the law is void," following Rav and the Gemara's conclusion about his position. (*Rambam, Sefer Nashim, Hilkhot Ishut* 12:9; *Sefer Mishpatim, Hilkhot Naḥalot* 1:8; *Tur, Even HaEzer* 69.)

עַל מְנָת שֶׁאֵין לְךָ עָלַי אוֹנָאָה **On condition that you do not have a claim of fraud against me.** "In a transaction where one party said to the other: 'On condition that you do not have a claim of fraud against me,' the defrauded party can

BACKGROUND

תְּנָאוֹ קַיָּים **A condition is valid.** If someone said to a woman: "Behold, you are betrothed to me on condition that you have no claims against me for food, clothing or conjugal relations," Rabbi Meir says that she is betrothed, but the condition is void, because it runs counter to the Torah law requiring a husband to provide his wife with food and clothing and to have sexual relations with her. But Rabbi Yehudah says that concerning monetary matters, such as the husband's obligation to provide his wife with food and clothing, a condition that runs counter to Torah law but has nevertheless been accepted is valid. Were the husband entitled to his wife's estate by Torah law, his stipulation waiving his right to the estate would therefore be valid.

וַחֲכָמִים עָשׂוּ חִיזּוּק לְדִבְרֵיהֶם יוֹתֵר מִשֶּׁל תּוֹרָה **The Sages made a reinforcement for their enactmants greater than for those of the Torah.** The laws of the Torah themselves are immutable, determining what a person must do what punishments he incurs by violating them. These are all determined and defined and cannot change with changing times and conditions. Rabbinical ordinances, however, are instituted for defined purposes, and the Sages who institute them also state the importance to be related to each ordinance. The Sages generally preferred that Rabbinical ordinances be less severe than Torah law. Hence, for example, when there is doubt regarding a Rabbinical ordinance, one tends toward leniency. However, in some instances, because of the importance of the matter, the Sages sought to strengthen their rulings, and when they instituted an ordinance, they also legislated the necessary severity. In this instance, Rav maintains that the Sages ordained that a husband should inherit his late wife's property, and that they gave this ordinance absolute authority, so that he could not waive his right to that inheritance.

BACKGROUND

אֵין לוֹ עָלָיו אוֹנָאָה He does not have a claim of fraud against him. The Torah states (Leviticus 25:14): "And if you sell anything to your neighbor or buy anything from the hand of your neighbor, do not defraud one another." From here the Sages derived that it is not permitted to sell an article for more than its market value, or to buy an article for less than its market value. There are three degrees of fraud, depending on the discrepancy between the market value of the article and the price actually paid: (1) fraud that need not be returned; (2) fraud that must be returned, but does not invalidate the sale; and (3) fraud that invalidates the sale. Hence, if someone stipulates that he is selling merchandise on condition that the buyer will waive any claim of fraud against him, he has made a condition contrary to Torah law. And Rav rules that in such a case, the condition is void. Thus, we see that according to Rav, a condition that runs counter to what is written in the Torah is void, even in cases concerning monetary matters.

TRANSLATION AND COMMENTARY

is invalid and the buyer retains his right to lodge **a claim of fraud against** the seller. [1]**And Shmuel said:** The buyer **does not** retain the right to lodge **a claim of fraud against** the seller, since he accepted the seller's condition.

אֶלָּא [2]**Rather,** Rav's position must be understood as follows: **The law is in accordance with** the view of **Rabban Shimon ben Gamliel who said** [3]**that if someone stipulates against what is written in the Torah, his stipulation is void — but not for his reason.** [4]**For Rabban Shimon ben Gamliel maintains** that if a husband stipulated that he would have no claim on his wife's property after she dies, and **she dies** before him, **he still inherits her,** because the husband's right to inherit his wife's estate is Biblical law, and the stipulation that he made to cancel that right is void. [5]**And Rav maintains** that **if** this woman **dies,** her husband **does not inherit her.** Because Rav maintains that the husband's right to his wife's inheritance is only by Rabbinic decree and he also maintains that the Rabbis' enactments are not as strong as Torah laws, his stipulation against the Rabbinic decree has force.

הַאי מְטַעֲמֵיהּ [6]The Gemara rejects this interpretation of Rav's position: According to **this** interpretation, Rav **is in accordance with** the **reason** Rabban Shimon ben Gamliel offered for his ruling, [7]**but** he does **not** rule **in accordance with his law!**

אֶלָּא [8]The Gemara suggests now a third way to understand Rav's position: **Rather, the law is in accordance with** the view of **Rabban Shimon ben Gamliel who said** [9]that **if** the husband stipulated that he would have no claim on his wife's property after her death, and **she dies** before him, **he** still **inherits her. But not for his reason,** [10]**for Rabban Shimon ben Gamliel maintains** that the husband is entitled to inherit from his wife by Torah law, and **regarding a Torah law a stipulation** that is contrary to what is written in the Torah is **void.** [11]**But regarding a Rabbinic decree,** such as the husband's right to the usufruct of his wife's property, **a condition** that runs counter to Torah law **is** indeed **valid.** [12]**And Rav** disagrees and **maintains** that **even regarding a Rabbinic decree a stipulation** that is contrary to their law **is** also **void.**

עָלָיו אוֹנָאָה. [1]וּשְׁמוּאֵל אָמַר: אֵין לוֹ עָלָיו אוֹנָאָה!
[2]אֶלָּא, הֲלָכָה כְּרַבָּן שִׁמְעוֹן בֶּן גַּמְלִיאֵל — דְּאָמַר: [3]הַמַּתְנֶה עַל מַה שֶּׁכָּתוּב בַּתּוֹרָה, תְּנָאוֹ בָּטֵל. וְלָאו מִטַּעֲמֵיהּ — [4]דְּאִילּוּ רַבָּן שִׁמְעוֹן בֶּן גַּמְלִיאֵל סָבַר: מֵתָה, יִירָשֶׁנָּה. [5]וְרַב סָבַר: מֵתָה, לֹא יִירָשֶׁנָּה.
[6]הַאי מִטַּעֲמֵיהּ, [7]וְלָא כְּהִילְכָתֵיהּ הוּא!
[8]אֶלָּא, הֲלָכָה כְּרַבָּן שִׁמְעוֹן בֶּן גַּמְלִיאֵל — דְּאָמַר: [9]אִם מֵתָה, יִירָשֶׁנָּה. וְלָאו מִטַּעֲמֵיהּ — [10]דְּאִילּוּ רַבָּן שִׁמְעוֹן בֶּן גַּמְלִיאֵל סָבַר: בִּדְאוֹרַיְיתָא תְּנָאוֹ בָּטֵל. [11]הָא בִּדְרַבָּנַן תְּנָאוֹ קַיָּים. [12]וְרַב סָבַר: אֲפִילּוּ בִּדְרַבָּנַן תְּנָאוֹ בָּטֵל.

LITERAL TRANSLATION

[a claim of] fraud against him. [1]And Shmuel said: He does not have [a claim of] fraud against him.

[2]Rather, the law is in accordance with Rabban Shimon ben Gamliel who said: [3]Someone who stipulates against what is written in the Torah, his stipulation is void — but not for his reason. [4]For Rabban Shimon ben Gamliel maintains: [If] she dies, he inherits her. [5]And Rav maintains: [If] she dies, he does not inherit her.

[6][But] this is in accordance with his reason, [7]but not in accordance with his law!

[8]Rather, the law is in accordance with Rabban Shimon ben Gamliel who said: [9]If she dies, he inherits her — but not for his reason. [10]For Rabban Shimon ben Gamliel maintains: Regarding a Torah law his stipulation is void. [11]But regarding a Rabbinic decree his stipulation is valid. [12]And Rav maintains: Even regarding a Rabbinic decree his stipulation is void.

RASHI

יש לו עליו — דמתנה על של תורה הוא: "אל תונו" (ויקרא כה). **ורב סבר אם מתה לא יירשנה** — דקסבר: ירושת הבעל דרבנן, ולא עשו חיזוק לדבריהן כשל תורה. **הא בדרבנן** — כגון זה, שהתנה שלא יאכל פירות. **ורב סבר** — אפילו תנאי הפירות נמי בטל, דחכמים עשו חיזוק לדבריהם כשל תורה, וכל שכן הירושה שהיא של תורה.

NOTES

אֲפִילּוּ בִּדְרַבָּנַן תְּנָאוֹ בָּטֵל Even regarding a Rabbinic decree his stipulation is void. *Rashi* understands that the Gemara here assumes that according to Rav any stipulation that runs counter to a Rabbinic decree is void, even a condition by which the husband waives his right to the usufruct of his wife's property. *Tosafot* object because according to

HALAKHAH

still pursue a claim of fraud, and can certainly do so if there was a stipulation that this transaction should not involve the laws of fraud," following Rav. (*Rambam, Sefer Kinyan, Hilkhot Mekhirah* 13:3; *Shulḥan Arukh, Ḥoshen Mishpat* 227:21.)

TRANSLATION AND COMMENTARY

הַאי כְּטַעֲמֵיהּ [1]The Gemara rejects also this interpretation of Rav's statement: According to **this** interpretation of Rav's statement Rav agrees with Rabban Shimon ben Gamliel about the **reason** offered for his ruling, that a stipulation that is contrary to Torah law is void, **and** he rules **in accordance with his law** that if the husband stipulated that he would have no claim on his wife's property after her death, he still inherits her. [2]But **Rav is only supplementing** what Rabban Shimon ben Gamliel said by adding that even a stipulation that is contrary to a Rabbinic decree is void!

אֶלָּא [3]**Rather,** Rav's position must be understood as follows: **The law is in accordance with** the view of **Rabban Shimon ben Gamliel who said** that **if** the husband waived claim to his wife's property after her death, and **she dies** before him, **he** still **inherits** from **her.** [4]**But** this is **not for** the **reason he** gives, [5]**for Rabban Shimon ben Gamliel maintains** that **the husband's** right to inherit from his wife **is by Torah law, and whoever stipulates against what is written in the Torah, his stipulation is void.** [6]**And Rav maintains** that **the husband's** right to his wife's **inheritance is** only **by Rabbinic decree.** [7]But the husband's stipulation is nevertheless void, for **the Sages reinforced their** own **enactments in the same way as the laws of the Torah,** voiding even stipulations against their own laws.

וְרַב סָבַר [8]The Gemara raises an objection against this interpretation of Rav's ruling as well: **But does Rav** really **maintain that the husband's** right to his wife's **inheritance is** only **by Rabbinic decree?**

[1]הַאי כְּטַעֲמֵיהּ וּכְהִילְכָתֵיהּ הוּא, [2]וְרַב מוֹסִיף הוּא!

[3]אֶלָּא, הֲלָכָה כְּרַבָּן שִׁמְעוֹן בֶּן גַּמְלִיאֵל, דְּאָמַר: אִם מֵתָה, יִירָשֶׁנָּה — [4]וְלָאו מִטַּעֲמֵיהּ. [5]דְּאִילּוּ רַבָּן שִׁמְעוֹן בֶּן גַּמְלִיאֵל סָבַר: יְרוּשַּׁת הַבַּעַל דְּאוֹרַיְיתָא, וְכָל הַמַּתְנֶה עַל מַה שֶּׁכָּתוּב בַּתּוֹרָה, [6]תְּנָאוֹ בָּטֵל. וְרַב סָבַר: יְרוּשַּׁת הַבַּעַל דְּרַבָּנַן, [7]וַחֲכָמִים עָשׂוּ חִיזּוּק לְדִבְרֵיהֶם כְּשֶׁל תּוֹרָה.

[8]וְרַב סָבַר יְרוּשַּׁת הַבַּעַל דְּרַבָּנַן?

LITERAL TRANSLATION

[1][But] this is in accordance with his reason and in accordance with his law, [2]and Rav is supplementing [it]!

[3]Rather, the law is in accordance with Rabban Shimon ben Gamliel who said: If she dies, he inherits her — [4]but not for his reason. [5]For Rabban Shimon ben Gamliel maintains: The husband's inheritance is by Torah law, and whoever stipulates against what is written in the Torah, his stipulation is void. [6]And Rav maintains: The husband's inheritance is by Rabbinic decree, [7]and the Sages made a reinforcement for their enactments (lit., "words") as [strong as] those of the Torah.

[8]But does Rav maintain that the husband's inheritance is by Rabbinic decree?

RASHI

האי כטעמיה וכהילכתיה הוא — סבירא ליה לרב כטעמיה דרבן שמעון — דמתנה על של תורה תנאו בטל, וכהילכתיה — דאם מתה יירשנה.

NOTES

Rashi Rav does not agree with any of the Tannaim of the Mishnah, since all of them accept that the husband can waive his right to the usufruct of his wife's property. *Tosafot* explain that even Rav would agree that such a stipulation is valid, because most women do not bring landed property into their marriage, and the Rabbis saw no need to reinforce an enactment that is enjoyed by a minority of husbands and to invalidate a stipulation made to waive it (see *Ketubot* 56b). *Rashba* explains that the Rabbis voided a husband's stipulation not to inherit his wife, because the Rabbinic enactment to inherit her is similar to Torah laws of inheritance. But they did not void his stipulation to waive his enjoying the usufruct of his wife's property, because that entitlement has no parallel in Torah law.

הֲלָכָה כְּרַבָּן שִׁמְעוֹן בֶּן גַּמְלִיאֵל The law is in accordance with Rabban Shimon ben Gamliel. The Geonim and later the Rishonim disagree about the final law. *Rabbenu Ḥananel, Rambam,* and others rule in accordance with Rabban Shimon ben Gamliel, either because the law always follows his positions as recorded in the Mishnah, or because Rav ruled in accordance with his view. But *Rif* and many other Rishonim rule in accordance with the anonymous Tanna of the Mishnah against Rabban Shimon ben Gamliel. They do so because the rule that the law always follows Rabban Shimon ben Gamliel's opinions is not absolute (see *Meiri*), and more importantly because the law is also in accordance with the view that in monetary matters, even a stipulation that runs counter to Torah law is valid. *Ramban, Ra'ah* and others discuss the matter at length, justifying *Rif's* ruling and reconciling that ruling with the Jerusalem Talmud. *Rabbenu Tam* (in *Sefer HaYashar*) rules in accordance with Rabban Shimon ben Gamliel, but for a different reason. *Rabbenu Tam* explains that since the husband inherits his wife by Torah law, he is like any other heir. Therefore as a son cannot stipulate that he will not inherit his father, so too a husband cannot stipulate that he will not inherit his wife.

וְרַב סָבַר יְרוּשַּׁת הַבַּעַל דְּרַבָּנַן But does Rav maintain that the husband's inheritance is by Rabbinic decree. The Jerusalem Talmud has a similar discussion of Rav's statement that the law is in accordance with the view of Rabban Shimon ben Gamliel, but not for his reason. The Jerusalem Talmud explains that Rav agrees that the husband inherits from his wife by Torah law, but he also maintains that regarding monetary matters a stipulation is valid even when it runs counter to Torah law. Thus, the husband's

TRANSLATION AND COMMENTARY

[1]**But surely we have learned** in the Mishnah (*Bekhorot* 52b): "The Torah states (Leviticus 25:25-28): 'If your brother becomes poor and sells of his possession...that which he sold shall remain in the hand of the buyer until the year of the Jubilee; and in the Jubilee it shall go out, and he shall return to possession.' From here we learn that if a person acquired land through a purchase or gift, he or his heirs must return that land to its original owner or his heirs during the Jubilee year. According to the first Tanna of the Mishnah, property that a husband inherits from his wife is not returned to the wife's relatives during the Jubilee year, as would be family property that she sold before marriage, for he is entitled to his wife's estate by Torah law. Rabbi Elazar says: The property must be returned to the wife's relatives during the Jubilee year, as in all land acquired through purchase or received as a gift, for the husband's right to the estate is only by Rabbinic decree. [2]**Rabbi Yoḥanan ben Beroka says: If someone inherits his wife's** estate, **he must return the property to the members of her family** during the Jubilee year, **and he deducts** a certain sum **from the payment** due for the return of their property." [3]**And** elsewhere **we discussed this statement** of Rabbi Yoḥanan ben Beroka, and asked: **What does he maintain?** The Gemara now clarifies this question: [4]**If** Rabbi Yoḥanan ben Beroka **maintains that the husband's** right to his wife's **inheritance is by Torah law, why must he return the property** to the members of his wife's family? Surely, he agrees that land that was passed down by subsequent inheritance need not be returned during the Jubilee year! [5]**And if** he maintains that the husband's right to his wife's inheritance is only **by Rabbinic decree, what is the function of** this **payment?** If the members of the woman's family are entitled to the family property, why must they pay the husband for its return? No compensation need be offered for land returned to its original owner during the Jubilee year! [6]**And Rav said** in answer to this question: **In fact,** Rabbi Yoḥanan ben Beroka **maintains that the husband's** right to his wife's **inheritance is by Torah law.** Ordinarily, the husband would not be required to return the property that he inherited from his wife to the members of her family, [7]**but here** we are dealing with a case **in which his wife left him** her **family's graveyard.** [8]**Because** his retaining

[1]וְהָתְנַן: [2]"רַבִּי יוֹחָנָן בֶּן בְּרוֹקָא אוֹמֵר: הַיּוֹרֵשׁ אֶת אִשְׁתּוֹ, יַחֲזִיר לִבְנֵי מִשְׁפָּחָה וִינַכֶּה לָהֶן מִן הַדָּמִים". [3]וַהֲוֵינַן בָּהּ: מַאי קָסָבַר? [4]אִי קָסָבַר: יְרוּשַּׁת הַבַּעַל דְּאוֹרַיְיתָא, אַמַּאי יַחֲזִיר? [5]וְאִי דְּרַבָּנַן, דָּמִים מַאי עֲבִידְתַּיְיהוּ? [6]וַאֲמַר רַב: לְעוֹלָם, קָסָבַר: יְרוּשַּׁת הַבַּעַל דְּאוֹרַיְיתָא, [7]וּכְגוֹן שֶׁהוֹרִישַׁתּוּ אִשְׁתּוֹ בֵּית הַקְּבָרוֹת. [8]מִשּׁוּם

LITERAL TRANSLATION

[1]But surely we have learned: [2]"Rabbi Yoḥanan ben Beroka says: [If] someone inherits his wife, he must return [the property] to the members of the family, and he deducts for them from the payment." [3]And we discussed it: What does he maintain? [4]If he maintains [that] the husband's inheritance is by Torah law, why must he return [the property]? [5]And if by Rabbinic decree, payment, what is its function (lit., "its work")? [6]And Rav said: In fact, he maintains [that] the husband's inheritance is by Torah law, [7]but here his wife left him a [family] graveyard. [8]Because

RASHI

יחזיר לבני משפחה – ביובל. **וינכה להם מן הדמים** – קא סלקא דעתך: יחזירם להם בדמים קלים. **אמאי יחזיר** – ירושה אינה חוזרת ביובל כדאמרי׳ בבכורות (נב,ב).

SAGES

רַבִּי יוֹחָנָן בֶּן בְּרוֹקָה Rabbi Yoḥanan ben Beroka. A Tanna of the third and fourth generations. See *Ketubot,* Part II, pp. 5-6.

TERMINOLOGY

וַהֲוֵינַן בָּהּ We discussed it. This expression means that we discussed the following topic elsewhere in another context.

NOTES

stipulation to waive his right to inherit from his wife should be valid. However, Rav invalidates the stipulation for a different reason. At the time it was formulated the husband had not yet acquired the estate, he therefore cannot make any stipulations about it. This passage in the Jerusalem Talmud is brought as support for *Rabbenu Ḥananel*'s ruling that the law is in accordance with the view of Rabban Shimon ben Gamliel. *Ramban* rejects this proof, arguing that the Jerusalem Talmud is dealing with a case where the husband made the stipulation after he was already married. Since he had already acquired the right to succeed to her estate, that right cannot be waived by way of a stipulation. But if he stipulated during the period of their betrothal (as our Gemara understands the case), he does not inherit his wife upon her death, as a person can renounce a right that he has not yet acquired.

יַחֲזִיר לִבְנֵי מִשְׁפָּחָה He must return the property to the members of the family. *Rashi* and *Tosafot* understand that when Rabbi Yoḥanan ben Beroka says that the husband must return the property of his wife's estate to the members of her family, he is talking about the Jubilee year. Some Rishonim even had a reading that stated this explicitly. Others, however, argue that since the Gemara concludes that we are dealing with a family graveyard, and that the property is returned in order not to shame the family, it stands to reason that the property is returned even before the Jubilee year, a principle that would follow from the Baraita regarding a person who sells his grave. *Tosafot* prove that the Mishnah must be talking about the Jubilee year. They explain that the husband is not required to return his wife's family's burial plot before then, because the family will only be shamed if the graveyard remains in an outsider's hands even after the Jubilee year, when all other properties return to their original owners. And that time it becomes clear to all that members of the family are buried on property belonging to an outsider. *Rashba* explains

TRANSLATION AND COMMENTARY

this traditional graveyard would **disgrace the family** of the wife, **the Rabbis said** that the husband should **take money** from the members of his wife's family **and return the graveyard** to them. [1]**And what** did Rabbi Yoḥanan ben Beroka mean when he said that "the husband **deducts for them** a certain sum **from the payment?** [2]He meant that the husband must deduct **the value of his wife's grave** if she is buried there, for it is the husband's duty to bear the costs of his wife's burial. [3]This is in keeping with what **was taught** in a Baraita: **"If someone sold** his family's graveyard which was to serve as **his** own **grave, or the path** leading **to his grave,** [4]**or the site** at which the funeral escort was **to halt** for lamentation or consolation upon returning from his burial, **or the site** at which **his eulogy** was to be delivered, when the seller dies, [5]**the** other **members of his family may come and bury him** in the family graveyard and conduct the funeral service there in the ordinary manner even **against the purchaser's will.** This is so, [6]**because** burying him elsewhere would **disgrace the family.** Thus, we see that Rav maintains that the husband's right to his wife's inheritance is by Torah law, against our last interpretation of Rav's ruling!

רַב לְטַעֲמֵיהּ [7]The Gemara answers: Rav's comment regarding the Mishnah in *Bekhorot* does not prove anything about Rav's own opinion about whether the husband's right to inherit his wife's estate is by Torah law, for **Rav said what he said according to the reasoning of Rabbi Yoḥanan ben Beroka.** Rav just explained Rabbi Yoḥanan ben Beroka's opinion. [8]**But** Rav himself **may not agree with him** on the matter. Thus, we may explain Rav's ruling on the Mishnah as was suggested above, that Rav maintains that the law is in accordance with the view of Rabban Shimon ben Gamliel, but not for his reason, for according to Rabban Shimon ben Gamliel, the husband inherits his wife by Torah law, whereas according to Rav, he inherits her only by Rabbinic decree.

MISHNAH מִי שֶׁמֵּת [9]**If someone died, and left a wife** who comes now to claim her ketubah, **and a creditor** who comes now to claim the debt owed him, **and heirs** who come now to claim the entire estate,

LITERAL TRANSLATION

of the disgrace (lit., "blemish") to the family, the Rabbis said: Take money and return [the graveyard]. [1]And what [is the meaning of] "he deducts for them from the payment"? [2]The value of his wife's grave. [3]As it was taught: "[If] someone sold his grave, or the path to his grave, [4][or the site for] his halting, or the site for his eulogy — [5]the members of the family may come and bury him [there] against [the purchaser's] will, [6]because of the disgrace (lit., 'blemish') to the family."

[7]Rav said [that] according to the reasoning of Rabbi Yoḥanan ben Beroka. [8]But he does not agree with him.

MISHNAH [9][If] someone died, and left a wife, and a creditor, and heirs,

פְּגַם מִשְׁפָּחָה אֲמוּר רַבָּנַן לִישְׁקוֹל דְּמֵי וְלִיהֲדַר, [1]וּמַאי ״יְנַכֶּה לָהֶן מִן הַדָּמִים״? [2]דְּמֵי קֶבֶר אִשְׁתּוֹ, [3]כִּדְתַנְיָא: הַמּוֹכֵר קִבְרוֹ וְדֶרֶךְ קִבְרוֹ, [4]מַעֲמָדוֹ וּמְקוֹם הֶסְפֵּידוֹ — [5]בָּאִין בְּנֵי מִשְׁפָּחָה וְקוֹבְרִין אוֹתוֹ בְּעַל כָּרְחוֹ, [6]מִשּׁוּם פְּגַם מִשְׁפָּחָה!

[7]רַב לְטַעֲמֵיהּ דְּרַבִּי יוֹחָנָן בֶּן בְּרוֹקָא קָאָמַר. [8]וְלֵיהּ לָא סְבִירָא לֵיהּ.

מִשְׁנָה [9]מִי שֶׁמֵּת, וְהִנִּיחַ אִשָּׁה וּבַעַל חוֹב וְיוֹרְשִׁין,

RASHI

משום פגם משפחה — גנאי הוא להם שיהיו אחרים נקברים עמהם, והם יקברו בקבורת אחרים. **דמי קבר אשתו** — שחייב הוא בקבורתה. **כדתניא** — לוקח בית הקברות מחזירו על כרחו. **וקוברים אותו בעל כרחו** — של לוקח. **אלא** — לא גרסינן.

BACKGROUND

פְּגַם מִשְׁפָּחָה **Disgrace to the family.** Wealthy families in the Mishnaic and Talmudic periods acquired burial plots for their private use. Such family plots, some containing splendid mausoleums, have been found in several places in Eretz Israel. These families were mortified when such a burial plot, which was so closely connected with them as a heritage, passed permanently out of their possession.

NOTES

that the husband who received his wife's family's graveyard by way of inheritance is not required to return the property until the Jubilee year, because he did nothing wrong. But someone who bought someone else's grave must return the property immediately, for such a purchase is inappropriate.

פְּגַם מִשְׁפָּחָה **Disgrace to the family.** *Rivan* and *Meiri* explain that it is a disgrace to the family if outsiders are buried in a graveyard that had been previously reserved for members of the family. *Rashi* adds that it is also a disgrace for members of a family to be buried in a graveyard belonging to somebody else.

HALAKHAH

הַמּוֹכֵר קִבְרוֹ **If someone sold his grave.** "If someone sold the plot of land in his family's graveyard which was to serve as his own grave, or the path leading to his grave, or the site at which the funeral escort was to halt or the site at which his eulogy was to be delivered, the other members of his family may bury him in the family graveyard against the purchaser's will, and then return the purchase money to him," following the Baraita. (*Rambam, Sefer Kinyan, Hilkhot Mekhirah* 24:17; *Shulḥan Arukh, Ḥoshen Mishpat* 217:7.)

¹וְהָיָה לוֹ פִּקָּדוֹן אוֹ מִלְוֶה בְּיַד אֲחֵרִים, ²רַבִּי טַרְפוֹן אוֹמֵר: יִנָּתְנוּ לַכּוֹשֵׁל שֶׁבָּהֶן. ³רַבִּי עֲקִיבָא אוֹמֵר: אֵין מְרַחֲמִין בַּדִּין, ⁴אֶלָּא יִנָּתְנוּ לַיּוֹרְשִׁין, ⁵שֶׁכּוּלָּן צְרִיכִין שְׁבוּעָה ⁶וְאֵין הַיּוֹרְשִׁין צְרִיכִין שְׁבוּעָה.

⁷הִנִּיחַ פֵּירוֹת תְּלוּשִׁין מִן הַקַּרְקַע, ⁸כָּל הַקּוֹדֵם בָּהֶן זָכָה בָּהֶן.

⁹זָכְתָה אִשָּׁה יוֹתֵר מִכְּתוּבָּתָהּ, וּבַעַל חוֹב יוֹתֵר עַל חוֹבוֹ, ¹⁰הַמּוֹתָר — רַבִּי טַרְפוֹן אוֹמֵר: יִנָּתְנוּ לַכּוֹשֵׁל שֶׁבָּהֶן. ¹¹רַבִּי עֲקִיבָא אוֹמֵר: אֵין מְרַחֲמִין בַּדִּין, ¹²אֶלָּא יִנָּתְנוּ לַיּוֹרְשִׁין, ¹³שֶׁכּוּלָּם צְרִיכִין שְׁבוּעָה, ¹⁴וְאֵין הַיּוֹרְשִׁין צְרִיכִין שְׁבוּעָה.

LITERAL TRANSLATION

¹and he had a deposit or a loan in someone else's hand, ²Rabbi Tarfon says: They must be given to the weakest among them. ³Rabbi Akiva says: We do not show compassion in law. ⁴Rather, they must be given to the heirs, ⁵for all of them require an oath, ⁶but the heirs do not require an oath.

⁷[If] he left produce that was detached from the ground, ⁸whichever [of these claimants] seizes it first, acquires it (lit., "them").

⁹[If] the woman acquired more than [the value of] her ketubah, or the creditor [acquired] more than [the value of] his debt — ¹⁰[with regard to] the excess, Rabbi Tarfon says: It must be given to the weakest among them. ¹¹Rabbi Akiva says: We do not show compassion in law. ¹²Rather, it must be given to the heirs, ¹³for all of them require an oath, ¹⁴but the heirs do not require an oath.

TRANSLATION AND COMMENTARY

¹**and** the deceased **had a deposit or a loan in someone else's hand** — that is, during his lifetime he deposited an article in someone else's safekeeping or extended a loan to another person, and the deposit or loan was still in that other person's possession. If the widow, the creditor, and the heirs all claim the deposit or loan, the Tannaim disagree about who is entitled to collect from it. ²**Rabbi Tarfon says:** The deposit or loan **must be given to the weakest** party **among** the three contesting for the property. ³**Rabbi Akiva says: We do not show compassion in** deciding **law.** ⁴But **rather** the dictates of the law must be strictly executed, and the deposit or loan must be given to the party with the strongest claim. Therefore, they **must be given to the heirs.** ⁵**For** whoever wishes to recover a debt (or ketubah) from the debtor's heirs **must** first **take an oath** that the debt is still outstanding. ⁶**But heirs** are **not required** to take such **an oath** in order to receive their inheritance.

הִנִּיחַ פֵּירוֹת ⁷If the deceased **left produce that was** already **detached from the ground** (and therefore is considered movable property), but the produce was not yet in anyone's possession, ⁸**whichever of those claimants seizes it first** — whether the widow, the creditor or the heirs — **acquires it.**

זָכְתָה אִשָּׁה ⁹**If the woman** seized detached produce and **acquired more than the value of her ketubah, or the creditor** seized such produce and **acquired more than the value of his debt,** the excess must be returned. ¹⁰**Regarding the excess, Rabbi Tarfon says: It must be given to the weakest** party **among them.** ¹¹**Rabbi Akiva** disagrees and **says: We do not show compassion in law.** ¹²**Rather,** the excess **must be given to the heirs,** ¹³**for whoever** wishes to recover a debt from the debtor's heirs **must** first **take an oath** that the debt is still outstanding. Without an oath, his claim is not recognized. ¹⁴**But the heirs are not required to take an oath** in order to receive their inheritance.

RASHI

משנה ינתנו לכושל שבהן — בגמרא מפרש מאי ניהו. ואף על גב דלא משתעבדי מטלטלי דיתמי לא לבעל חוב ולא לכתובה, הכא — דלאו ברשותייהו מנחי — סבירא לרבי טרפון דמוציאין מיד הלוה, או מיד מי שהפקדון אצלו, ונותנין לבעל חוב ולכתובה — שנתחייב בהן המת מחיים. ינתנו ליורשים — ולא מהניא תפיסה. שכולן צריכין שבועה — דתנן בפירקין: הבא ליפרע מנכסי יתומים — לא יפרע אלא בשבועה. וכל זמן שלא נשבעו — אין להם רשות בהם ואין אנו יודעין אם יש להם עליו כלום הלכך, משמת המת — זכו בהן היורשין וברשותן הן. כל הקודם בהן זכה — קדמו יורשין — זכו, ואין מוציאין מידם, דמטלטלי דיתמי לא משתעבדי לבעל חוב ולכתובה. קדם אחד מהן — האשה או המלוה — זכה הוא. דרבי טרפון אית ליה: תפיסה דלאחר מיתה מהניא. זכתה אשה יתר על כתובתה — אם קדמה ותפסה, ויש יותר מן הכתובה, או קדם בעל חוב ותפס, ויש בהן יותר על חובו. המותר ינתנו לכושל שבהן — זה בעל השטר, שידו על התחתונה. ואם יבואו ליד היתומים — שוב לא יוציא מהם לא אשה ולא בעל חוב.

BACKGROUND

אֵין מְרַחֲמִין בַּדִּין **We do not show compassion in law.** Rabbi Akiba maintains that whenever a Halakhic legal principle is involved, judgment must not deviate from the truth, as it is written in the Torah, "nor shall you show deference to a poor man in his dispute" (Exodus 23:3). In his opinion, there is room for mercy and charity, but not in a Halakhic decision, and in judging a case, one must follow the Halakhah alone.

SAGES

רַבִּי עֲקִיבָא **Rabbi Akiva.** The greatest of the Tannaim. See *Ketubot*, Part II, p. 206.

רַבִּי טַרְפוֹן **Rabbi Tarfon.** He was a priest who served in the Temple at the end of the Second Temple period. However, his main period of activity came later, to a large extent in association with Rabbi Eliezer and Rabbi Yehoshua. Rabbi Tarfon was wealthy and extremely generous. He seems to have been one of the first Sages to acknowledge the greatness of Rabbi Akiva. Although he was initially superior to the latter in wisdom and was probably older, he came to consider himself Rabbi Akiva's disciple. Rabbi Tarfon also trained a number of disciples, and we know that Rabbi Yehudah bar Il'ai was one of his students. His grandson was a Sage during the time of Rabbi Yehudah HaNasi.

NOTES

שֶׁכּוּלָּם צְרִיכִין שְׁבוּעָה **For all of them require an oath.** Some Rishonim argue that according to this reasoning, when the widow or the creditor are not required to take an oath, such as where the husband willingly exempted them from this obligation, the heirs are not given any preference, but rather the money or movable property that was deposited or loaned is given to the weakest party. The Jerusalem Talmud rejects this argument and claims that Rabbi Akiva's position is really based on a more fundamental principle, namely, that "this is by Torah law and this is

TERMINOLOGY

לָמָּה לִי לְמִיתְנֵי...לָמָּה לִי לְמִיתְנֵי **Why does he have to teach X, and why does he have to teach Y?** When the Gemara, in analyzing a Mishnah, finds an unnecessary repetition of seemingly identical cases, it often asks: "Why does the author of the Mishnah need to teach case X, and why does he then need to teach case Y? Surely one of the cases is superfluous!" The Gemara answers, using the expression צְרִיכָא, showing that the various cases are in fact necessary, and going on to explain why.

גמרא [1]לָמָּה לִי לְמִיתְנֵי מִלְוֶה, לָמָּה לִי לְמִיתְנֵי פִּקָּדוֹן? [2]צְרִיכָא, [3]דְּאִי תָּנָא מִלְוֶה, [4]בְּהָא קָאָמַר רַבִּי טַרְפוֹן, [5]מִשּׁוּם דְּמִלְוֶה לְהוֹצָאָה נִיתְּנָה, [6]אֲבָל פִּקָּדוֹן דְּאִיתֵיהּ בְּעֵינֵיהּ, [7]אֵימָא מוֹדֵי לֵיהּ לְרַבִּי עֲקִיבָא. [8]וְאִי תָּנָא הָא, [9]בְּהָא קָאָמַר רַבִּי עֲקִיבָא? [10]אֲבָל בְּהַךְ, אֵימָא מוֹדֵי לְרַבִּי טַרְפוֹן. [11]צְרִיכָא. [12]מַאי "לַכּוֹשֵׁל"? [13]רַבִּי יוֹסֵי בְּרַבִּי חֲנִינָא אוֹמֵר: לַכּוֹשֵׁל שֶׁבִּרְאָיָה,

LITERAL TRANSLATION

GEMARA [1]Why do I have to teach "a loan," [and] why do I have to teach "a deposit"? [2][Both] are necessary. [3]For if he had taught "a loan," [4][I would have said that only] in this [case] Rabbi Tarfon said, [5]because a loan is given for spending. [6]But [regarding] a deposit, which remains extant [7]I would say [that] he agrees with Rabbi Akiva. [8]And if he had taught the other, [9]["a deposit," I would have said that only] in that [case] Rabbi Akiva said? [10]But in this [case], I would say [that] he agrees with Rabbi Tarfon. [11][Therefore both] are necessary.

[12]What [is meant by] "to the weakest"? [13]Rabbi Yose the son of Rabbi Ḥanina says: To the weakest in proof.

TRANSLATION AND COMMENTARY

GEMARA לָמָּה לִי [1]**Why does** the Mishnah **have to teach** both the case of **"a loan" and** the case of **"a deposit"?** Surely it would have been sufficient to mention only one of them!

צְרִיכָא [2]The Gemara answers: The examples were well chosen, and **both are necessary.** [3]**For if** the Mishnah **had** only **taught** the case of "a loan," I **would have said that** [4]it is only **in this case** that **Rabbi Tarfon said** that the money goes to the weakest party, [5]**because a loan is given** to the borrower **for spending.** Until the loan is repaid, any money in the borrower's hand belongs to the borrower and cannot be regarded as being in the hands of his heirs. Rabbi Tarfon therefore maintains that the debts of the deceased can be collected from that money, because it has not yet become a part of the estate. [6]**But regarding** the case of **a deposit, which remains extant** in the hand of the bailee, [7]**I might have said that** Rabbi Tarfon **agrees with Rabbi Akiva** that the deposit must be given to the heirs, for it is considered to have been transferred to them at the moment of death, and the debts of the deceased cannot be collected from inherited movable property already acquired by the heirs. Therefore, it was necessary to teach the case of "a deposit" in the Mishnah, to show that Rabbi Tarfon's ruling applies also to deposits. [8]**And if** the Mishnah **had** only **taught** the case of **"a deposit,"** [9]**I would have said that** only **in that case** does **Rabbi Akiva say** that the property must be given to the heirs. [10]**But in the** case of a loan, **I might have said that** Rabbi Akiva **agrees with Rabbi Tarfon** that the loan must be given to the weakest party, for a loan is given to the borrower for spending and the money he holds cannot be considered as belonging to the heirs. Therefore, the Mishnah had to teach the case of a loan, to show that Rabbi Akiva's ruling applies also to loans. [11]**Therefore it was necessary** for the Mishnah to mention **both** a loan and a deposit, in order to establish that Rabbi Tarfon and Rabbi Akiva disagree about the law in both cases.

מַאי "לַכּוֹשֵׁל" [12]The Gemara now clarifies the position of Rabbi Tarfon: **What** did he mean by the words **"to the weakest** party"? [13]**Rabbi Yose the son of Rabbi Ḥanina says:** He meant that the property must be given **to the** party who is **weakest in proof,** i.e., the party whose document testifying to a lien on the debtor's property has the most recent date. Since the lien is created automatically at the time the obligation comes

RASHI

גמרא להוצאה ניתנה — ואינה קיימת בעין, דמחסרא גוביינא. ומשום הכי אמר רבי טרפון דלא מנחי ברשותא דיתמי. אבל פקדון דאיתיה בעיניה אימא כו׳ — דכל היכא דאיתיה — ברשותא דיתמי איתיה. לכושל שבראיה — למי ששטרו מאוחר, שלא יוכל לטרוף לקוחות הקודמים לו.

NOTES

not by Torah law." The money or movable property must be given to the heirs, because their right of succession is Torah law, whereas the widow and the creditor are only entitled to the property on account of a contractual agreement (see also *Ran*).

לַכּוֹשֵׁל בִּרְאָיָה **To the weakest in proof.** Our commentary follows *Rashi* and many other Rishonim who understand that the party weakest in proof is the one whose deed establishing a lien on his debtor's property is dated the latest, be it the creditor or the widow. *Rif, Rambam,* and *Rivan* explain that the party weakest in proof is the creditor. *Rif* explains that this is so because a creditor cannot collect his debt without first proving that he is owed money, whereas the widow can collect her ketubah even without presenting her ketubah deed. The Jerusalem Talmud cites Rabbi Yose bar Ḥanina's position that the weakest party is he who is weakest in proof, and gives the example of two creditors, one of whom gave the loan in the presence of witnesses and the other gave it in exchange for a deed of indebtedness. The creditor who lent money in the presence

SAGES

רַבִּי בִּנְיָמִין Rabbi Binyamin. He belonged to the sixth generation of Tannaim and was a student of Rabbi Akiva's. He is found in discussion with several of Rabbi Akiva's other students, though few of his teachings are recorded in the two Talmuds.

TRANSLATION AND COMMENTARY

into existence, the claimant holding the later deed is in the weakest position. For the claimant with the earliest deed could well have liens on a greater number of properties, as some of them may have been sold between the dates on the two deeds. [1]**Rabbi Yoḥanan** disagrees and **says:** "To the weakest party" means that it must be given **to pay the woman's ketubah.** The woman is considered the weaker party, for unlike a creditor a wife does not usually involve herself in her late husband's affairs and therefore would not uncover landed property from which she can collect her ketubah. She requires special assistance which the Rabbis gave her, [2]**in order to enhance her favor,** and make it easier for women to consent to offers of marriage.

כְּתַנָּאֵי [3]The Gemara notes that the dispute between the Amoraim, Rabbi Yose the son of Rabbi Ḥanina and Rabbi Yoḥanan, **is like** the dispute of the **Tannaim** about the same matter, as it was taught in a Baraita: **"Rabbi Binyamin says:** [4]The deposit or loan must be given **to the** party who is **weakest in proof, and this is** the **proper** action. [5]**Rabbi Elazar says:** The deposit or loan must be given **to the woman** as payment of her **ketubah, so that** men will find **favor** in women's eyes, and they will consent to enter into marriage."

הִנִּיחַ פֵּירוֹת [6]We learned in the Mishnah: **"If** someone died, and he **left produce that was** already **detached** from the ground, whichever claimant — the wife, the creditor, or the heirs — seizes it first, acquires it. If the woman acquired more produce than the value of her ketubah, or the creditor acquired more produce than the value of his debt, Rabbi Tarfon says: The excess must be given to the weakest party among them. And Rabbi Akiva says: The excess must be given to the heirs." The Gemara questions Rabbi Akiva's position: [7]**Why does Rabbi Akiva** mention only **"the excess"?** [8]According to his position, **all of the** produce **should belong to the heirs** from the time of death, and their seizure by a creditor or widow should not be recognized. Why then does Rabbi Akiva relate only to the excess?

אִין הָכִי נַמִי [9]The Gemara answers: **Yes, this is indeed so,** that according to Rabbi Akiva, whatever produce the creditor or the widow seizes must be given back to the heirs. [10]**But since Rabbi Tarfon spoke about the excess** and ruled that it must be given to the weakest party, [11]Rabbi Akiva **also taught** that **the excess** must be given to the heirs, even though the same law applies to the rest of the produce as well.

[1]רַבִּי יוֹחָנָן אָמַר: לִכְתוּבַּת אִשָּׁה, [2]מִשּׁוּם חִינָּא.
[3]כְּתַנָּאֵי, רַבִּי בִּנְיָמִין אוֹמֵר: [4]לַכּוֹשֵׁל שֶׁבָּרְאָיָה, וְהוּא כָּשֵׁר; [5]רַבִּי אֶלְעָזָר אוֹמֵר: לִכְתוּבַּת אִשָּׁה, מִשּׁוּם חִינָּא.
[6]״הִנִּיחַ פֵּירוֹת הַתְּלוּשִׁין״. [7]וְרַבִּי עֲקִיבָא, מַאי אִירְיָא מוֹתָר? [8]כּוּלְּהוּ נַמִי דְּיוֹרְשִׁין הָווּ!
[9]אִין הָכִי נַמִי, [10]וְאַיְּידֵי דְּאָמַר רַבִּי טַרְפוֹן ״מוֹתָר״, [11]תָּנָא אִיהוּ נַמִי ״מוֹתָר״.

LITERAL TRANSLATION

[1]Rabbi Yoḥanan says: To [pay] the woman's ketubah, [2]in order to [enhance her] favor.

[3]Like the Tannaim. "Rabbi Binyamin says: [4]To the weakest in proof, and this is proper. [5]Rabbi Elazar says: To [pay] the woman's ketubah, in order to [enhance her] favor."

[6]"[If] he left produce that was detached." [7]And Rabbi Akiva, why [did he] discuss "the excess"? [8]All of it also belongs to the heirs!

[9]Yes, this is indeed so, [10]but since Rabbi Tarfon spoke [about] "the excess," [11]he also taught "the excess."

RASHI

לכתובת אשה – היא קרויה ״כושל״, שאין דרכה לחזור אחר נכסי המת ולבקש היכן יש לו קרקע. **משום חינא** – שימצאו האנשים חן בעיני הנשים, ויהיו נשאות להן, שלא תדאגנה להפסיד כתובתן. **והוא כשר** – והדבר כשר והגון לעשות כן. **כולהו נמי דיורשין הוו** – כיון דטעמא דרבי עקיבא משום דלא נשבעו הוא, כי תפסי נמי אמאי זכו? הרי זכו בהן יורשים משעת מיתה, ונכסי דיתמי קא תפסי. **ואיידי דאמר רבי טרפון מותר** – אהדר ליה איהו נמי במאי דאיירו ביה. ולעולם בכולהו נמי אית ליה – דאפילו תפס – מפקינן ליה מיניה.

NOTES

of witnesses and cannot now collect his debt without those witnesses is the weakest in proof, as the creditor with the deed needs only his note. *Ra'ah* and *Ritva* cite the Jerusalem Talmud as saying also that if both creditors held deeds, the party whose deed establishes the most recent lien is considered to be the weakest in proof, like *Rashi.* The Jerusalem Talmud also cites the view of Rabbi Yoḥanan that the weakest party is the party who is physically the weakest, and as the Gemara concludes, is also the poorest.

מִשּׁוּם חִינָּא **In order to seek her favor.** Our commentary follows *Rashi,* who explains that the Rabbis allowed the woman to collect her ketubah, so that men will find favor in men's eyes, and as a result women will consent to their offers of marriage. According to *Rabbenu Ḥananel* (cited by *Tosafot*), the Rabbis allowed the woman to collect her ketubah, so that she should find favor in the eyes of men, and quickly find another husband.

[84B] [1]וְרַבִּי עֲקִיבָא, [2]תְּפִיסָה לָא מְהַנְיָא כְּלָל?
[3]אָמַר רָבָא אָמַר רַב נַחְמָן: וְהוּא שֶׁתָּפַס מֵחַיִּים.
[4]וּלְרַבִּי טַרְפוֹן, [5]דְּמַנְחֵי הֵיכָא?
[6]רַב וּשְׁמוּאֵל דְּאָמְרִי תַּרְוַיְיהוּ: וְהוּא שֶׁצְּבוּרִין וּמוּנָּחִין בִּרְשׁוּת הָרַבִּים, [7]אֲבָל בְּסִימְטָא, לָא.
[8]וְרַבִּי יוֹחָנָן וְרֵישׁ לָקִישׁ דְּאָמְרִי תַּרְוַיְיהוּ: אֲפִילּוּ בְּסִימְטָא.

LITERAL TRANSLATION

[84B] [1]And [according to] Rabbi Akiva, [2]does seizure not help at all?

[3]Rava said in the name of Rabbi Naḥman: [It does] when he seized during the [debtor's] lifetime.

[4]And according to Rabbi Tarfon, [5]where was [the produce] lying?

[6]Rav and Shmuel both said: And [he said] it when it was piled and lying in the public domain, [7]but in a side street, no. [8]And Rabbi Yoḥanan and Resh Lakish both said: Even in a side street.

TRANSLATION AND COMMENTARY

[84B] וְרַבִּי עֲקִיבָא [1]The Gemara now tries to clarify Rabbi Akiva's position: It was just concluded that, according to Rabbi Akiva, if a person died, and his creditor or widow seized movable property belonging to his estate, the property must be returned to the heirs, for it is in their possession from the time of death. Now, **according to Rabbi Akiva,** [2]**does** the creditor's **seizure** of the debtor's assets **have** no legal effect **at all?**

אָמַר רָבָא [3]The Gemara answers: **Rava said in the name of Rabbi Naḥman:** Even Rabbi Akiva agrees that the creditor's seizure has a legal effect, provided **that he seized** the movable property **during the debtor's lifetime.** During a debtor's lifetime, the creditor is not required to take an oath in order to collect the money that is owed him. Thus, the creditor acquires the property which he seizes from his debtor as payment of the debt. However, after the debtor dies, the seizure of his assets has no legal effect, for at the moment of his death, his assets are acquired by the debtor's heirs.

וּלְרַבִּי טַרְפוֹן [4]The Gemara tries now to clarify Rabbi Tarfon's position: **According to Rabbi Tarfon** who said that if a person died, leaving produce that was already detached from the ground, whichever of the claimants seizes the produce first acquires it, [5]**where was the produce lying** at the time of death so that it was not immediately acquired by the heirs?

רַב וּשְׁמוּאֵל [6]The Gemara records an Amoraic dispute about Rabbi Tarfon's opinion: **Rav and Shmuel both said:** The Mishnah refers to produce that **was piled and lying in the public domain,** where acts of acquisition cannot take effect. When the produce is lying in such a place the Rabbis do not consider the produce acquired by the heirs. [7]**But** if the produce was lying **in a side street** adjoining the public domain to which people withdraw in order to conduct their business, an area in which forms of acquisition can indeed take effect, the heirs immediately acquire the produce at the time of death, and so Rabbi Tarfon would agree that seizure from a side street has **no** effect. [8]But **Rabbi Yoḥanan and Resh Lakish both** disagree and **say:** According to Rabbi Tarfon, if any of the parties seized the produce while it was **even in a side street,** he acquires it.

RASHI

ורבי עקיבא תפיסה לא מהניא כלל – לשון שאלה הוא זה. אמר רב נחמן – מהניא היכא דתפס מחיים של מת. והכי גמר לה רב נחמן מרביה. דמנחי היכא – הנך פירות דקאמר רבי טרפון, דבשעת מיתה לא זכו בהן יורשין, אלא יזכה בהן הקודם. בסימטא – קרן זוית הסמוכה לרשות הרבים, ובני אדם העושין סחורה זה עם זה בשוק ורוצים לדבר דבריהם בנחת וישוב הדעת, מסתלקין לשם. אבל בסימטא לא – אמר רבי טרפון כל הקודם זכה. דכיון דמקום הראוי לקנין הוא כדאמרינן בעלמא (בבא בתרא פד,ב) דמשיכה קניא התם, אפילו למאן דאמר ברשות הרבים לא קניא – אין זה מקום הפקר, וזכו בהן יורשין משעת מיתה, והמחזיק בו שם – כמחזיק בו בביתם.

SAGES

רַב **Rav.** A Babylonian Amora of the first generation. See *Ketubot,* Part I, pp. 42-3.

שְׁמוּאֵל **Shmuel.** A Babylonian Amora of the first generation. See *Ketubot,* Part I, pp. 8-9.

LANGUAGE

סִימְטָא **Alley.** From the Latin *semita,* "footpath, small alley."

NOTES

וְרַבִּי עֲקִיבָא תְּפִיסָה לָא מְהַנְיָא כְּלָל **And according to Rabbi Akiva, does seizure not help at all.** The Rishonim offer several slightly different explanations of this question. Our commentary follows *Rashi,* who understands it as a question of clarification: According to Rabbi Akiva, is it only after the debtor's death that the creditor's seizure of his movable property has no legal effect, or is the creditor's seizure ineffective even when executed during the debtor's lifetime? *Tosafot* understand that the Gemara is raising a difficulty: Does Rabbi Akiva really maintain that the creditor's seizure of the debtor's movable goods is ineffective? But surely the Mishnah elsewhere (*Ketubot* 80b) implies otherwise, and it would be preferable to say that the Mishnah can be reconciled with the view of Rabbi Akiva.

שֶׁצְּבוּרִין וּמוּנָּחִין בִּרְשׁוּת הָרַבִּים **When it was piled and lying in the public domain.** The Jerusalem Talmud records a slightly different version of the disagreement: Rav and

HALAKHAH

וְהוּא שֶׁתָּפַס מֵחַיִּים **And that is where he seized during the debtor's lifetime.** "It is a mitzvah for the heirs of the deceased to pay his debts from the movable property which he left them, but they cannot be compelled to do so. The creditor can, however, recover his debt by seizing movable property during the debtor's lifetime. However, by Geonic

[1] דּוּן דַּיָּינֵי כְּרַבִּי טַרְפוֹן, [2] וְאַהְדְרֵיהּ רֵישׁ לָקִישׁ לְעוּבְדָא מִינַּיְיהוּ. [3] אֲמַר לֵיהּ רַבִּי יוֹחָנָן: עָשִׂיתָ כְּשֶׁל תּוֹרָה.
[4] לֵימָא בְּהָא קָמִיפַּלְגִי: [5] דְּמָר סָבַר: טָעָה בִּדְבַר מִשְׁנָה, חוֹזֵר. [6] וּמָר סָבַר: טָעָה בִּדְבַר מִשְׁנָה אֵינוֹ חוֹזֵר!

LITERAL TRANSLATION

[1] Judges ruled in accordance with Rabbi Tarfon, [2] and Resh Lakish overturned their ruling. [3] Rabbi Yoḥanan said to him: You treat (lit., "do") [it] like a Torah law!

[4] Shall we say that they disagree about this: [5] That the one Sage maintains: [If a judge] erred about a matter in the Mishnah, [the ruling] is overturned. [6] And the other Sage maintains: [If a judge] erred about a matter in the Mishnah, [the ruling] is not overturned.

TRANSLATION AND COMMENTARY

דּוּן דַּיָּינֵי [1] The Gemara now presents a series of illustrative cases: It once happened that a person died, and a creditor seized movable property of the estate before it entered into the physical possession of its heirs. When the matter came before the **judges**, they **ruled in accordance with** the view of **Rabbi Tarfon** that the seizure is valid. [2] When **Resh Lakish** was informed of the judges' decision, he **overturned their ruling** and awarded the property to the heirs, arguing that the law is in accordance with Rabbi Akiva. [3] **Rabbi Yoḥanan said to** Resh Lakish: By overturning the judges' ruling according to Rabbi Tarfon, you have demonstrated that **you treat** Rabbi Akiva's position as if **it** were **a Torah law**. But surely this is not the case, and so the judges' ruling should not have been overturned.

לֵימָא [4] The Gemara now seeks an explanation for the dispute between Resh Lakish and Rabbi Yoḥanan: **Shall we say that** Resh Lakish and Rabbi Yoḥanan **disagree about** the following issue? [5] **The one Sage** — Resh Lakish — **maintains** that **if a judge erred** in his decision regarding **a matter** ruled upon **in the Mishnah**, or about a clear and undisputed ruling in the Talmud, **the ruling is overturned.** [6] **And the other Sage** — Rabbi Yoḥanan — **maintains** that even **if a judge erred** in his decision regarding **a matter** ruled upon **in the Mishnah, the ruling is not overturned.**

RASHI

ואהדריה לעובדא — סבר לה כרבי עקיבא, דלא מהניא תפיסה. **עשית** — דברי רבי עקיבא כאילו הן הלכה למשה מסיני, שחזרת מעשה בית דין. דיי לנו לקיים הלכה כמותו לכתחילה, אבל משנעשה ונגמר הדין — אין לנו לחזור. **בדבר משנה** — דקיימא לן: הלכה כרבי עקיבא היכא דיחידאה פליג עליה. ואף על גב דלאו במשנה ממש תנינא לה, אלא שמעתא דאמוראי הוא, אמרינן בסנהדרין (לג,א) דחוזר: דאמרינן התם: אפילו טעה בדרב ושמואל? אמר ליה: אין.

NOTES

Resh Lakish maintain that, according to Rabbi Tarfon, the seizure of the debtor's movable property is effective if at the time of the debtor's death the property was resting even in a side street adjoining the public domain. But if it was in the house of the deceased, the heirs acquire the property along with the house at the time of death, so that its seizure by the wife or the creditor has no legal effect. Rabbi Yoḥanan disagrees and says that the seizure of the movable property is effective even if the property was in the house of the deceased at the time of his death, for a person's premises can only acquire movable property for him if the person intends to acquire the property thereby, and here the heirs had no such intention, for they mistakenly ought that the property was already theirs.

טָעָה בִּדְבַר מִשְׁנָה חוֹזֵר If someone erred about a matter in the Mishnah. According to the Jerusalem Talmud, Rabbi Yoḥanan and Resh Lakish do indeed disagree about an erroneous judgment regarding a matter ruled upon in the Mishnah. Both agree that if the judge ruled in error about an explicit Torah law, the ruling is overturned. They both also agree that if a court's mistaken decision resulted from an error in discretion, the ruling stands. They disagree about an error regarding a clear and undisputed ruling in the Mishnah or Talmud, following a discussion of its various aspects. Rabbi Yoḥanan likens such an error to an error in discretion, and so the ruling stands. Resh Lakish compares such an error to an error in explicit Torah law, in which case it is overturned.

HALAKHAH

enactment a creditor can collect from heirs even when they inherit movable property. Thus the creditor's seizure of his debtor's movable property is effective, even if he seized the property after the debtor's death. If the creditor has no witnesses to the debt, in which case he would not be able to collect from the heirs had he not seized movable property from them, once he has seized the property, he may take an oath and collect his debt from what he seized." (*Rambam, Sefer Mishpatim, Hilkhot Malveh VeLoveh* 11:8; *Shulḥan Arukh, Ḥoshen Misphat* 107:5.)

טָעָה בִּדְבַר מִשְׁנָה חוֹזֵר If someone erred about a matter in the Mishnah. "If a judge issued an erroneous ruling in a civil case about a matter that is clear and undisputed, against an explicit Mishnah or Gemara, the ruling is overturned, and a correct decision is issued." (*Rambam, Sefer Shofetim, Hilkhot Sanhedrin* 6:1; *Shulḥan Arukh, Ḥoshen Mishpat* 25:1.)

BACKGROUND

טָעָה בִּדְבַר מִשְׁנָה Erred about a matter in the Mishnah. Although the Jewish court system did not include a procedure for appeal, nevertheless legal decisions were reviewed by other Sages. Sometimes Sages with higher personal or legal authority would rebuke a lower court for committing an error in judgment.
In the case of a clear error, when it is possible to correct the decision, it is reversed. The kind of error for which a decision was reversed was one of basic fact — either the facts of the case, or the facts of the Halakhah, such as when a judge misquotes or otherwise mistakes the Mishnah.
The expression, "a matter in the Mishnah" was used during Talmudic times when the Mishnah was the only binding book of law. Later it was used to refer to an error about a matter that was clear in the Talmud or about a clear conclusion in a binding Halakhic code. These, too, are sufficient to reverse an earlier legal decision.

SAGES

רַבִּי יוֹחָנָן Rabbi Yoḥanan bar Nappaḥa. See *Ketubot*, Part II, pp. 15-16.

TRANSLATION AND COMMENTARY

לָא [1]However, this suggestion is not conclusive, and the Gemara says: **No,** both Resh Lakish and Rabbi Yoḥanan might **agree that if** a judge **erred** in his decision regarding **a matter** ruled upon **in the Mishnah, the ruling is** indeed **overturned.** [2]**And here** Resh Lakish and Rabbi Yoḥanan **disagree about** whether the judges in the case at hand issued an erroneous judgment: **The one Sage** — Rabbi Yoḥanan — **maintains** that when there is a dispute between Rabbi Akiva and another Sage, **the law is in accordance with Rabbi Akiva against his fellow** Sage, **but not against his master,** and Rabbi Tarfon was Rabbi Akiva's teacher, not his colleague. Hence the judges were correct in their ruling. [3]**And the other Sage** — Resh Lakish — **maintains** that when there is a dispute between Rabbi Akiva and another Sage, **the law is in accordance with Rabbi Akiva, even against his master.**

וְאִיבָּעֵית אֵימָא [4]The Gemara makes also another suggestion: **If you wish,** you can **say that all** — both Resh Lakish and Rabbi Yoḥanan — **agree that** when there is a dispute between Rabbi Akiva and another Sage, **the law is in accordance with Rabbi Akiva against his fellow** Sage, **but not against his master.** [5]**And here** Resh Lakish and Rabbi Yoḥanan **disagree about** the connection between Rabbi Akiva and Rabbi Tarfon: [6]**The one Sage** — Rabbi Yoḥanan — **maintains** that **Rabbi Tarfon was** Rabbi Akiva's **master,** and that the law does follow the view of Rabbi Tarfon. Consequently the judges were correct in their ruling. [7]**And the other Sage** — Resh Lakish — **maintains** that Rabbi Tarfon **was** Rabbi Akiva's **fellow** Sage. Thus, the law should follow the view of Rabbi Akiva, against Rabbi Tarfon, and so the judges delivered an erroneous judgment.

וְאִיבָּעֵית אֵימָא [8]Finally, it is suggested, **if you wish,** you can **say that** both **agree that** Rabbi Tarfon **was** indeed Rabbi Akiva's **fellow** Sage. [9]**And here** Resh Lakish and Rabbi Yoḥanan **disagree about** the tradition regarding the authority of Rabbi Akiva's rulings: **The one Sage** — Resh Lakish — **maintains** that **it was stated** specifically that **the law** is in accordance with Rabbi Akiva's position. Thus, the judges that ruled in accordance with the view of Rabbi Tarfon were in error. [10]**And the other Sage** — Rabbi Yoḥanan — **maintains** that when it was stated that the law follows the view of Rabbi Akiva, **it was** only **stated** that **we are inclined** to rule in accordance with the position of Rabbi Akiva. Therefore, if someone asks for a ruling on the matter, we issue a decision following the view of Rabbi Akiva. But if a judgment was issued in accordance with the view of Rabbi Tarfon, after the fact, it cannot be overturned.

קְרִיבֵיהּ דְּרַבִּי יוֹחָנָן [11]It was related that the **relatives of Rabbi Yoḥanan** were owed money and when the debtor died, they **seized a cow** which was to have passed down **to his orphaned** children as part of their inheritance. The seizure took place while the animal was standing in **a side street** before the heirs actually took possession of it. [12]The relatives **came before Rabbi Yoḥanan** for a ruling on the validity of their seizure,

[1]לָא, דְּכוּלֵּי עָלְמָא טָעָה בִּדְבַר מִשְׁנָה, חוֹזֵר. [2]וְהָכָא בְּהָא קָמִיפַּלְגִי: מָר סָבַר: הֲלָכָה כְּרַבִּי עֲקִיבָא מֵחֲבֵירוֹ וְלֹא מֵרַבּוֹ. [3]וּמָר סָבַר: הֲלָכָה אֲפִילּוּ מֵרַבּוֹ.

[4]וְאִיבָּעֵית אֵימָא: דְּכוּלֵּי עָלְמָא הֲלָכָה כְּרַבִּי עֲקִיבָא מֵחֲבֵירוֹ וְלֹא מֵרַבּוֹ. [5]וְהָכָא בְּהָא קָמִיפַּלְגִי: [6]מָר סָבַר: רַבִּי טַרְפוֹן רַבּוֹ הֲוָה. [7]וּמָר סָבַר: חֲבֵירוֹ הֲוָה.

[8]וְאִיבָּעֵית אֵימָא: דְּכוּלֵּי עָלְמָא חֲבֵירוֹ הֲוָה. [9]וְהָכָא בְּהָא קָמִיפַּלְגִי: מָר סָבַר: ״הֲלָכָה״ אִיתְּמַר. [10]וּמָר סָבַר: ״מַטִּין״ אִיתְּמַר.

[11]קְרִיבֵיהּ דְּרַבִּי יוֹחָנָן תָּפוּס פָּרָה דְּיַתְמֵי מִסִּימְטָא. [12]אֲתוֹ

LITERAL TRANSLATION

[1]No, all agree [that if a judge] erred about a matter in the Mishnah, [the ruling] is overturned. [2]And here they disagree about this: The one Sage maintains: The law is in accordance with Rabbi Akiva against his fellow, but not against his master. [3]And the other Sage maintains: The law [is in accordance with Rabbi Akiva] even against his master.

[4]And if you wish, say that all agree [that] the law is in accordance with Rabbi Akiva against his fellow, but not against his master. [5]And here they disagree about this: [6]The one Sage maintains: Rabbi Tarfon was his master. [7]And the other Sage maintains: He was his fellow.

[8]And if you wish, say that all agree [that] he was his fellow. [9]And here they disagree about this: The one Sage maintains: "The law" was stated. [10]And the other Sage maintains: "We are inclined" was stated.

[11]Relatives of Rabbi Yoḥanan seized the cow of orphans from a side street. [12]They came

RASHI

הלכה אתמר — הלכה כרבי עקיבא מחבירו. מטין אתמר — מטין ההוראה לכתחילה אחר רבי עקיבא ומיהו, אי עביד כאידך — לא מהדרינן עובדא. קריביה דרבי יוחנן — קרוביו.

SAGES

רֵישׁ לָקִישׁ **Resh Lakish.** See *Ketubot,* Part II, p. 12.

BACKGROUND

הֲלָכָה כְּרַבִּי עֲקִיבָא מֵחֲבֵירוֹ **The law is in accordance with Rabbi Akiva against his fellow.** This is one of the principles posited by Halakhic authorities. Many such principles are found in the Talmud, some of which are collected in tractate *Eruvin* (46a-47b). These principles guide the Sages of the Talmud and of following generations. Many of them are personal, such as that the Halakhah follows the House of Hillel against that of Shammai, that it follows Rabbi Yosef against Rabbi Yehudah, etc. There are also broader principles such as, "the Halakhah follows the anonymous Mishnah," or "the Halakhah follows a certain Rabbi as opposed to his colleague," no matter which Sage disagrees with him. There are also more restricted principles such as, "The Halakhah follows Rav against Shmuel regarding prohibitions, and it follows Shmuel against Rav in monetary matters." Sometimes the principles are formulated categorically, but they also may be formulated merely as a tendency, a certain opinion, such as a statement that "they were accustomed" to adopt a certain opinion. In the present case, we have discussion both of the wording of the principle and also of its precise meaning.

NOTES

אֲתוֹ לְקַמֵּיהּ דְּרַבִּי יוֹחָנָן **They came before Rabbi Yoḥanan.** *Tosafot* ask: It was stated above that even according to Rabbi

CONCEPTS

מִיגּוֹ From the midst of, since. An important legal argument, used to support the claim of one of the parties in a dispute. If one of the litigants could have made a claim more advantageous to his cause than he actually did, we assume he was telling the truth. The *miggo* argument may be expressed in the following way: "Since he could have made a better claim (for had he wanted to lie, he would presumably have put forward a claim more advantageous to himself), we assume that he must be telling the truth." For he could say: מַה לִּי לְשַׁקֵּר — "'What reason do I have to lie?'" There are, however, certain limitations governing the application of this principle; for example, אֵין מִיגּוֹ בִּמְקוֹם עֵדִים — "There is no *miggo* where there are witnesses." In other words, *miggo* is not effective where witnesses contradict the litigant's claim. The principle of *miggo* is the subject of profound legal analysis in the Talmud and its commentaries.

TRANSLATION AND COMMENTARY

and he **said to them:** "You **have lawfully seized** the cow, in accordance with the view of Rabbi Tarfon." [1] Rabbi Yoḥanan's relatives then **came before Rabbi Shimon ben Lakish** hoping that he would confirm Rabbi Yoḥanan's ruling, but he **said to them: "Go, return** the cow to your creditor's heirs," for the law is that the creditor's seizure of his deceased debtor's property has no legal validity." [2] The disappointed relatives then **came** back to **Rabbi Yoḥanan** to complain about Resh Lakish's judgment, but **he said to them: "What shall I do?** [3] Resh Lakish, who is **my equal** in stature and erudition, **disagrees with me,** and so I cannot overturn his decision."

הַהוּא בַּקָּרָא [4] It was further related that **a certain herdsman** was tending the animals that were inherited by **orphans.** A creditor of the deceased **seized an ox from** the herdsman as payment of the debt. [5] **The creditor said:** "It was already **during the debtor's lifetime** that **I seized** the ox, so the seizure is valid." [6] **And the herdsman said:** "It was only **after** the debtor's **death** that **he seized** it. [7] The creditor and the herdsman **came before Rav Naḥman, who said to** the herdsman: **"Do you have witnesses that** the creditor **seized** the ox from you?" [8] The herdsman **replied to** Rav Naḥman: **"No."** [9] Rav Naḥman then **said to** the herdsman: **"Since**

לְקַמֵּיהּ דְּרַבִּי יוֹחָנָן, אֲמַר לְהוּ: שַׁפִּיר תְּפַסְתּוּהָ. [1] אָתוּ לְקַמֵּיהּ דְּרַבִּי שִׁמְעוֹן בֶּן לָקִישׁ, אֲמַר לְהוּ: "זִילוּ אַהֲדוּר". [2] אָתוּ לְקַמֵּיהּ דְּרַבִּי יוֹחָנָן, אֲמַר לְהוּ: [3] "מָה אֶעֱשֶׂה, שֶׁכְּנֶגְדִּי חָלוּק עָלַי".
[4] הַהוּא בַּקָּרָא דְּיָתְמֵי דְּתָפְסֵי תּוֹרָא מִינֵּיהּ. [5] בַּעַל חוֹב אֲמַר: "מֵחַיִּים תְּפֵיסְנָא לֵיהּ". [6] וּבַקָּרָא אֲמַר: "לְאַחַר מִיתָה תְּפַסֵיהּ". [7] אָתוּ לְקַמֵּיהּ דְּרַב נַחְמָן, אֲמַר לֵיהּ: "אִית לָךְ סָהֲדֵי דְּתַפְסֵיהּ"? [8] אֲמַר לֵיהּ: "לָאו". [9] אֲמַר לֵיהּ: "מִגּוֹ דְּיָכוֹל

LITERAL TRANSLATION

before Rabbi Yoḥanan, [who] said to them: "You have seized it lawfully (lit., 'well')." [1] They came before Rabbi Shimon ben Lakish, [who] said to them: "Go, return [it]." [2] They came before Rabbi Yoḥanan, [who] said to them: "What shall I do? [3] My equal (lit., 'he that is opposite me') disagrees with me."
[4] [There was] a certain herdsman of orphans from whom [creditors] seized an ox. [5] The creditor said: "During the [debtor's] lifetime I seized it." [6] And the herdsman said: "After [his] death he seized it." [7] They came before Rav Naḥman, [who] said to [him]: "Do you have witnesses that he seized it?" [8] He said to him: "No." [9] He said to him: "Since he can

RASHI

זילו אהדור — דסבירא ליה כרבי עקיבא, דתפיסה דלאחר מיתה לאו כלום היא. שכנגדי — שקול כמותי. בקרא דיתמי — שומר בהמותיהם. דתפוס תורא מיניה — בעל חוב של מת תפסו בבית השומר.

NOTES

Yoḥanan we are inclined to rule in accordance with the position of Rabbi Akiva. How then could Rabbi Yoḥanan have said to his relatives that they seized the cow lawfully, against the ruling of Rabbi Akiva? *Tosafot* suggest that since the relatives had already seized the animal, it is considered as after the fact, and so Rabbi Yoḥanan said that their seizure is valid, even though they followed the view of Rabbi Tarfon. *Ritva* adds that in this case the relatives had already eaten the animal, a case that is surely after the fact (and we must explain that Resh Lakish's telling the relatives to return it refers to monetary compensation.)

אִית לָךְ סָהֲדֵי דְּתַפְסֵיהּ Do you have witnesses that he seized it. *Tosafot* and *Rivan* reject the reading: "...that he seized it after [the debtor's] death?" For if the herdsman has witnesses that the creditor seized the ox from him, even if they cannot testify that he seized the ox only after the debtor's death, the creditor's seizure of the animal is still not valid, for he can no longer claim in court that he had bought the animal. *Rabbenu Crescas Vidal* accepts the reading, arguing that even if the herdsman has witnesses that he seized the ox, if they cannot testify that the creditor did so after the debtor's death, the seizure is valid, for the creditor would still be believed via a slightly modified *miggo* argument: If he was a lier he could have claimed in court that he had returned the seized animal to the debtor, unbeknownst to the herdsman, and later purchased it.

Rabbenu Ḥananel and others write that if the creditor's claim that he had seized the animal during the debtor's lifetime is accepted, the herder has to pay the heirs for the animal, for the herdsman is a paid bailee who is liable for negligence. Therefore, the herdsman cannot serve as a witness that the creditor seized the animal only after the debtor's death, for he is an interested party and is disqualified from testifying. The Aḥaronim discuss why the herdsman cannot exempt himself from paying for the ox with the argument that he was acting in accordance with the rule of "Rabbi Natan's lien," which states that if one man [A] claims a certain sum from his neighbor [B] and this neighbor [B] claims that same sum from another neighbor [C] we collect from the one [C], and give it to the other [A].

HALAKHAH

מִגּוֹ דְּיָכוֹל לְמֵימַר Since he can say. "If a creditor claims that he seized property from his debtor during his lifetime, and the debtor's heirs claim that the creditor seized the property only after the debtor's death, the burden of proof falls upon the heirs," following Rav Naḥman. (*Rambam, Sefer Mishpatim, Hilkhot Malveh VeLoveh* 11:8.)

TRANSLATION AND COMMENTARY

the creditor **could have said:** [1]**'I bought** the ox from you, and so **it is** rightfully **in my possession,'** and his claim would have been accepted, for there are no witnesses who could have contradicted him. [2]**He can also say:** 'I **seized** the ox **during the debtor's lifetime."** Thus his claim is accepted. In certain situations a litigant's plea is accepted by the court, even when there is no evidence to support it. One such situation is a claim that is supported by the argument of *miggo* ("since"). If a litigant puts forward a certain plea, but could have lied and put forward a plea more advantageous to his interests, he is assumed to be telling the truth. In our case, the creditor claimed that he had seized the ox from the herdsman while the debtor was still alive. Had he wished to lie, he could have claimed that he bought the ox from the debtor or his heir. Since the creditor could have advanced a stronger claim, he is believed.

וְהָאָמַר רֵישׁ לָקִישׁ [3]The Gemara now questions Rav Naḥman's ruling: **But surely Resh Lakish said: Regarding livestock,** physical possession **does not** create **a presumption of ownership.** Livestock, strays from one field to the next. Thus, the fact that an animal is in the physical possession of a particular person does not necessarily mean that he is its rightful owner. Had the purchaser claimed without any additional proof, that he had bought the ox, he would not have been allowed to keep it. Thus the creditor's plea that he had seized the ox during his debtor's lifetime is not relatively strong claim that must be accepted as true.

שָׁאנֵי תּוֹרָא [4]The Gemara answers: **An ox is different** from other livestock, **for it is** generally **entrusted to** the care of **a herdsman,** and does not wander about freely. Thus, the rule that physical possession implies rightful ownership also applies to an ox.

דְּבֵי נְשִׂיאָה [5]Similarly, **members of the House of the Nasi** in Eretz Israel were once owed money. When the debtor died, the creditors **seized a** non-Jewish **maidservant** who had belonged to the deceased and now was to have passed **to his heirs.** In this case, too, the seizure took place while the maidservant was standing **in a side street** before the heirs actually took possession of her. When the two sides came for a ruling on the validity of the seizure, [6]**Rabbi Abbahu, Rabbi Ḥanina bar Pappi and Rabbi Yitzḥak Nappaḥa sat** as judges, **and Rabbi Abba sat next to them.** [7]Rabbi Abbahu **said to** the creditors: "**Your seizing** of the maidservant was **lawful,"** according to the view of Rabbi Tarfon. [8]**Rabbi Abba said to** the judges: **"Because** the creditors **are** members **of the House of the Nasi you** show **them favor?** [9]**But surely** we know about the similar case that was brought before **judges.** [10]They also **ruled in accordance with** the view of **Rabbi Tarfon and** when **Resh Lakish** heard the judgment, he **overturned their ruling.** Thus the maidservant should be returned to the heirs.

לְמֵימַר: [1]׳לָקוּחַ הוּא בְּיָדִי׳ — [2]יָכוֹל נַמִי לְמֵימַר: ׳מֵחַיִּים תְּפֵיסְנָא לֵיהּ׳״. [3]וְהָאָמַר רֵישׁ לָקִישׁ: הַגּוֹדְרוֹת אֵין לָהֶן חֲזָקָה! [4]שָׁאנֵי תּוֹרָא, דִּמְסִירָה לְרוֹעֶה. [5]דְּבֵי נְשִׂיאָה תְּפוּס אַמְתָא דְּיַתְמֵי מִסִּימְטָא. [6]יָתֵיב רַבִּי אַבָּהוּ וְרַבִּי חֲנִינָא בַּר פַּפִּי וְרַבִּי יִצְחָק נַפָּחָא, וְיָתֵיב רַבִּי אַבָּא גַּבַּיְיהוּ. [7]אֲמַר לְהוּ: ״שַׁפִּיר תְּפַסִיתוּהָ״. [8]אֲמַר לְהוּ רַבִּי אַבָּא: ״מִשּׁוּם דְּבֵי נְשִׂיאָה נִינְהוּ מַחְנְפִיתוּ לְהוּ? [9]וְהָא דּוּן דַּיָּינֵי כְּרַבִּי טַרְפוֹן, [10]וְאַהַדְרִיהּ רֵישׁ לָקִישׁ עוּבְדָא מִינַּיְיהוּ״!

LITERAL TRANSLATION

say: [1]'[Through] purchase it is in my hand' — [2]he can also say: 'During the [debtor's] lifetime I seized it.' "

[3]But surely Resh Lakish said: Regarding livestock there is no presumption of ownership.

[4]An ox is different, for it is entrusted to a herdsman.

[5][Members] of the house of the Nasi seized the maidservant of orphans from a side street. [6]Rabbi Abbahu and Rabbi Ḥanina bar Pappi and Rabbi Yitzḥak Nappaḥa sat, and Rabbi Abba sat next to them. [7]He said to them: "You have seized her lawfully (lit., 'well')." [8]Rabbi Abba said to them: "Because they are of the house of the Nasi you favor them? [9]But surely judges ruled in accordance with Rabbi Tarfon, [10]and Resh Lakish overturned their ruling!"

RASHI

הגודרות — בהמה דקה על שם ״גדרות לאן״ (במדבר לב). **אין להן חזקה** — אין המחזיק בהם יכול לומר ״לקוחין הן בידי״ — שמא מאלאן והכניסן בביתו, לפי שדרכן להלך בשדות.

SAGES

רַבִּי אַבָּהוּ **Rabbi Abbahu.** See *Ketubot,* Part II, p. 20.

רַבִּי אַבָּא **Rabbi Abba.** See *Ketubot,* Part II, p. 112.

רַבִּי יִצְחָק נַפָּחָא **Rabbi Yitzḥak Nappaḥa.** A prominent Palestinian Amora of the second and third generations. He was a disciple of Rabbi Yoḥanan and often presents teachings in the latters name. He also spent part of his life in Babylonia, where he was an important source of information about the teachings and customs of Eretz Israel.

רַב פַּפָּא **Rav Pappa.** See *Ketubot,* Part IV, p. 18.

NOTES

מִגּוֹ דְּיָכוֹל לְמֵימַר **Since he can say.** *Rosh* explains that were it not for the argument of *miggo,* the creditor's claim that he had seized the animal during the debtor's lifetime would not be accepted. Such a claim is regarded as a very

HALAKHAH

הַגּוֹדְרוֹת אֵין לָהֶן חֲזָקָה **Regarding livestock there is no presumption of ownership.** "Even though a person is generally believed when he claims that he is the rightful owner of the movable property found in his possesion, he

SAGES

רַב הוּנָא בְּרֵיהּ דְּרַב יְהוֹשֻׁעַ **Rav Huna the son of Rabbi Yehoshua.** A fifth-generation Babylonian Amora. See *Ketubot*, Part II, p. 80.

TRANSLATION AND COMMENTARY

יֵימָר בַּר חָשׁוּ [1]It was further related that **Yemar the son of Ḥashu was owed money by a certain man.** [2]The debtor **died, and left a boat** as part of his estate. Before the debtor's heirs took possession of the boat, [3]Yemar the son of Ḥashu **said to his agent:** "Go out and **seize** the boat **for me** as payment of the debt." [4]The agent **went and seized** the boat on behalf of the creditor. [5]**Rav Pappa and Rav Huna the son of Rav Yehoshua met the agent** after he seized it, **and said to him:** [6]**"You seized** movable property belonging to a debtor **on behalf** of one **creditor where** the debtor also **owes others.** [7]**And** about such a situation, **Rabbi Yoḥanan said: If someone seizes** movable property belonging to a debtor **on behalf** of one **of** his **creditors in a situation where** the debtor also **owes** money to **other** creditors, [85A] **he did not acquire**

[1]יֵימָר בַּר חָשׁוּ הֲוָה מַסֵּיק בֵּיהּ זוּזֵי בְּהַהוּא גַּבְרָא. [2]שְׁכֵיב וְשָׁבֵיק אַרְבָּא. [3]אֲמַר לֵיהּ לִשְׁלוּחֵיהּ: "זִיל תָּפְסָהּ נִיהֲלֵיהּ". [4]אֲזַל תְּפָסָהּ. [5]פָּגְעוּ בֵּיהּ רַב פַּפָּא וְרַב הוּנָא בְּרֵיהּ דְּרַב יְהוֹשֻׁעַ, אֲמַרוּ לֵיהּ: [6]"אַתְּ תּוֹפֵס לְבַעַל חוֹב בְּמָקוֹם שֶׁחָב לַאֲחֵרִים". [7]וְאָמַר רַבִּי יוֹחָנָן: הַתּוֹפֵס לְבַעַל חוֹב בְּמָקוֹם שֶׁחָב לַאֲחֵרִים, [85A] לֹא קָנָה".

LITERAL TRANSLATION

[1]Yemar the son of Ḥashu was owed money by a certain man. [2]He died, and left a boat. [3][Yemar] said to his agent: "Go seize it for me." [4]He went [and] seized it. [5]Rav Pappa and Rav Huna the son of Rav Yehoshua met [the agent, and] said to him: [6]"You seized on behalf of a creditor in a situation where [the debtor] owes others. [7]And Rabbi Yoḥanan said: [If] someone seizes on behalf of a creditor in a situation where [the debtor] owes others, [85A] he did not acquire."

RASHI

חשו — שם האיש. שכיב — הלוה. ארבא = ספינה. אמר ליה — יימר לשלוחיה: זיל תפסה. התופס לבעל חוב — שליח התופס מטלטלין של לוה לצורך בעל חוב. במקום שחב לאחרים — שמפסיד בעלי חובין אחרים בתפיסתו. לא קנה — דלאו כל כמיניה לחוב זה כדי לזכות את זה.

NOTES

weak plea, because the creditor himself admits that he had seized the animal from the oxherd and that it had entered into his possession without its owner's consent.

הַתּוֹפֵס לְבַעַל חוֹב **If someone seized on behalf of a creditor.** *Tosafot* conclude from the incident recorded in our Gemara that it makes no difference who seized the movable property on behalf of the creditor. If a debtor had several creditors, and someone seized movable property from him on behalf of one of his creditors, the seizure is not valid, even if the person who seized the property had been appointed to do so as an agent of the creditor. Elsewhere (*Bava Metzia* 10a), *Rashi* writes that the seizure is invalid only when an unauthorized person seized the property. But if the creditor appointed an agent to seize it for him, the seizure is valid, even when there are other creditors. *Shittah Mekubbetzet* distinguishes between an ordinary agent and an agent appointed in the presence of witnesses and whose authority is equal to that of the creditor himself. *Rabbenu Ḥananel* argues that an agent may not seize property on behalf of a single creditor, but a legal guardian, and perhaps even someone who was authorized with power of attorney, may indeed seize property on behalf of his ward or principal, even if the debtor also owes money to other people.

HALAKHAH

is not believed with respect to livestock, for the animal might have wandered into his possession of its own accord, or he might have seized it while it was wandering about in the public domain. If a person claims that he is the rightful owner of an animal which is now in somebody else's possession, and he has witnesses who can testify that the animal had once belonged to him, he can take an oath of the kind instituted in the post-Mishnaic period (*shevu'at hesset*) and reclaim his property. If he does not have such witnesses, the one in possession of the animal must take an oath, after which the animal remains in his possession. *Rema* adds that according to some authorities (*Tur* in the name of *Rashbam* and *Tosafot*), a person is believed about his claim that he is the rightful owner of a certain animal, if that animal was in his possession for three years. In a place where it is customary to entrust animals to a herdsman, so that they do not wander about on their own, animals are treated like any other movable property, so that a person is believed when he claims ownership of an animal found in his possession," following our Gemara. (*Rambam, Sefer Mishpatim, Hilkhot To'en VeNit'an* 10:1; *Shulḥan Arukh, Ḥoshen Mishpat* 135:1.)

הַתּוֹפֵס לְבַעַל חוֹב בְּמָקוֹם שֶׁחָב לַאֲחֵרִים **If someone seizes on behalf of a creditor in a situation where he owes others.** "If a person owed money to two or more creditors, but he did not have enough property to cover all of his debts, and someone seized movable property belonging to the debtor on behalf of one of the creditors, he did not acquire the property on his behalf. This law applies even if the person who seized the property had been appointed by the creditor as his agent, and even if he had been given power of attorney. But if the property was seized by the creditor's guardian, the guardian acquired the property on behalf of his ward." (*Rambam, Sefer Mishpatim, Hilkhot Malveh VeLoveh* 20:2; *Shulḥan Arukh, Ḥoshen Mishpat* 105:1.)

לֹא קָנָה **He did not acquire.** Elsewhere (*Bava Metzia* 10a), the Amoraim disagree about a person who found an object and picked it up with the intention that it should be acquired by somebody else. Rav Naḥman and Rav Ḥisda

TRANSLATION AND COMMENTARY

the property on the creditor's behalf, for he does not have the authority to acquire it." [1]After disqualifying the agent's seizure, Rav Pappa and Rav Huna the son of Rav Yehoshua both tried to **seize** the boat for **themselves,** for they too were creditors of the deceased. Each of the two Sages tried to seize the boat exclusively for himself. [2]**Rav Pappa rowed the oars,** [3]and **Rav Huna the son of Rav Yehoshua pulled it with a rope.** [4]**The one Sage said: "I acquired it** with a valid act of acquisition." [5]**And the other Sage said: "I acquired it** with a valid act of acquisition." [6]**Rav Pinehas the son of Ammi met them** [7]**and said to them:** "But surely **Rav and Shmuel both said:** Even according to Rabbi Tarfon, who said that whichever party seizes the deceased debtor's property first acquires it, [8]**that is only when** the property **was piled and lying in the public domain** at the time of the debtor's death." Rav Pinehas the son of Ammi assumed that the debtor's boat was moored along a river bank, which has the status of a side street. Thus, neither of them acquired the boat." [9]**They said** to Rav Pinehas the son of Ammi: **"We too seized** the boat while it was moving along **the current** in the middle **of the river,** which, with respect to acquisition, is equivalent to a public domain." [10]Rav Pappa and Rav Huna the son of Rav Yehoshua **came before Rava** for a ruling, and **he** rebuked them, **saying to them:** [11]"You two old gentlemen with your white beards are nothing but **white geese who strip people of their cloaks.** [12]Surely **Rav Nahman said:** Rabbi Akiva agrees that the creditor's seizure of the debtor's movable property is effective **only when he seizes** it **during the debtor's lifetime.** But you two Rabbis tried to seize the debtor's boat after he died. Since the law follows Rabbi Akiva, the seizure is not valid."

[1]תְּפָסוּהָ אִינְהוּ. [2]רַב פַּפָּא מִימְלַח מַלּוּחֵי; [3]רַב הוּנָא בְּרֵיהּ דְּרַב יְהוֹשֻׁעַ מַמְתַּח לָהּ בְּאַשְׁלָא. [4]מָר אֲמַר: "אֲנָא קָנֵינָא לָהּ לְכוּלָּהּ". [5]וּמָר אֲמַר: "אֲנָא קָנֵינָא לָהּ לְכוּלָּהּ". [6]פָּגַע בְּהוּ רַב פִּנְחָס בַּר אַמִי, [7]אֲמַר לְהוּ: רַב וּשְׁמוּאֵל דְּאָמְרִי תַּרְוַיְיהוּ: [8]וְהוּא שֶׁצְּבוּרִין וּמוּנָּחִין בִּרְשׁוּת הָרַבִּים! [9]אֲמַרוּ לֵיהּ: "אֲנַן נַמִי מֵחֲרִיפוּתָא דְּנַהֲרָא תָּפֵיסְנָא". [10]אֲתוּ לְקַמֵּיהּ דְּרָבָא, אֲמַר לְהוּ: [11]"קָאקֵי חִיוָּרֵי מְשַׁלְּחֵי גְּלִימֵי דְּאֱינָשֵׁי! [12]הָכִי אֲמַר רַב נַחְמָן: וְהוּא שֶׁתְּפָסָהּ מֵחַיִּים".

LITERAL TRANSLATION

[1]They [then] seized it themselves. [2]Rav Pappa rowed the oars; [3]Rav Huna the son of Rav Yehoshua pulled it with a rope. [4]One master said: "I acquired it all." [5]And the other master said: "I acquired it all." [6]Rav Pinehas the son of Ammi met them, [7][and] said to them: Rav and Shmuel both said: [8]And it is [only] when it was piled and lying in the public domain. [9]They said to him: "We too seized [it] from the current of the river." [10]They came before Rava, [who] said to them: [11]"White geese who strip people of [their] cloaks! [12]Thus said Rav Nahman: And it is [only] when he seized during the [debtor's] lifetime."

RASHI

תפסוה אינהו – שאף הם נושים בו מעות. **ממלח מלוחי** – מנהיגה בעוגין שלה שקורין *ריימ"ש בלעז. ממלח שקורין **וירני"ר בלעז. לשון "ויראו המלחים" (יונה א). **אנא קנינא כולה** – הנהגתי בריאה משל חבירי. **מחריפותא דנהרא** – לא מצאנוה על שפת הנהר, שהיא כסימטא, אלא מזה תפסנוה שהיה מוליכה באמצע הנהר, שכל הספינות הולכות שם, והוי כרשות הרבים. **קאקי** = אווזים. **חיורי** – על שזקנים היו. **משלחי גלימי דאינשי** = מפשיטין טליתות האנשים.

LANGUAGE (RASHI)

ריימ"ש* From the Old French *reims,* "oars."

וורירני"ר** From the Old French *werner,* "sail" (a boat).

LANGUAGE

קָאקֵי Geese. *Rashi* explains קָאקֵי as "geese." *Arukh,* however, observes that in Targum Yonatan (and apparently in certain Talmudic passages) this word translates the Hebrew קָאַת ("pelican"; others explain this as some kind of night bird of prey), a non-kosher bird (Leviticus 11:18).

SAGES

רַב פִּנְחָס בְּרֵיהּ דְּרַב אַמִי Rav Pinheas the son of Rav Ammi. He belonged to the fifth generation of Amoraim in Babylonia. He was a colleague of Rav Pappa and of Rav Huna, the son of Rav Yehoshua. The Sages of the following generation, such as Rav Yemar and even Rav Ashi heard his expositions and consulted him when in doubt. Only a few teachings in his name are found in the Talmud, but in several places.

רַב נַחְמָן Rav Nahman (bar Ya'akov). The famous Babylonian Amora of the third and fourth generations. See *Ketubot,* Part IV, p. 169

NOTES

קָאקֵי חִיוָּרֵי White geese. Our commentary follows *Rashi* and others, who understand the words קאקי חיורי as "white geese." Rava called Rav Pappa and Rav Huna white geese because they were advanced in years and their hair had turned white. It has been suggested that Rava's rebuke be understood as follows: Are old people like you still running after money? (*Hever ben Hayyim.*)

HALAKHAH

maintain that the other person does not acquire the found object, because the person who picked it up is similar to a person who seized a debtor's property on behalf of one of the debtor's several creditors, and the law is that in such a case he did not acquire the property on the creditor's behalf. Rabbi Yohanan disagrees and says that the other person does in fact acquire the found object. The Rishonim point out a difficulty: Here it is Rabbi Yohanan himself who says that if a person seized property on behalf of a creditor, he does not acquire the property on his behalf if the debtor also owes money to other people. Thus, he should agree that if a person picked up a found object on behalf of another person, that other person does not acquire the object! *Tosafot* and others resolve the difficulty by distinguishing between a found object and property seized in satisfaction of a debt. Property that a person can acquire for himself he can also acquire on behalf of someone else. Since a lost object is ownerless, the finder can acquire it for himself. Therefore he can also acquire it on behalf of another person. But the debtor's property is liened to his creditors. A person who does not possess a lien on the property cannot acquire it for himself, and so he can also not acquire it on behalf of one of the creditors, even if that creditor had appointed him as his agent to act on his behalf.

[1]אֲבִימִי בְּרֵיהּ דְּרַבִּי אַבָּהוּ הֲווּ מַסְּקֵי בֵּיהּ זוּזֵי בֵּי חוֹזָאֵי. [2]שַׁדְּרִינְהוּ בְּיַד חָמָא בְּרֵיהּ דְּרַבָּה בַּר אַבָּהוּ. [3]אֲזַל פָּרְעִינְהוּ. [4]אֲמַר לְהוּ: ״הֲבוּ לִי שְׁטָרָא״! [5]אֲמַרוּ לֵיהּ: ״סִיטְרָאֵי נִינְהוּ״. [6]אֲתָא לְקַמֵּיהּ דְּרַבִּי אַבָּהוּ, [7]אֲתָא לְקַמֵּיהּ: ״אִית לָךְ סָהֲדֵי דִּפְרַעְתִּינְהוּ״? [8]אֲמַר לֵיהּ: ״לָא״. [9]אֲמַר לֵיהּ: ״מִיגּוֹ דִיכוֹלִין לוֹמַר: ׳לֹא הָיוּ דְּבָרִים מֵעוֹלָם׳, [10]יְכוֹלִין נַמִי לְמֵימַר: ׳סִיטְרָאֵי נִינְהוּ׳״.

LITERAL TRANSLATION

[1]Avimi the son of Rabbi Abbahu owed money to [people from] Bei Hozai. [2]He sent it by way of Ḥama the son of Rabbah the son of Abbahu. [3]He went [and] repaid [the loan, [4]and] said to them: "Give me the promissory note!" [5]They said to him: "This is [money owed us] from other claims (lit., 'these are on the sides')." [6]He came before Rabbi Abbahu, [7][who] said to him: "Do you have witnesses that you paid them?" [8]He said to him: "No." [9]He said to him: "Since they can say: 'There was never such a thing,' [10]they can also say: 'This is [money owed us] from other claims (lit., "these are sides").'"

TRANSLATION AND COMMENTARY

אֲבִימִי [1]The Gemara now relates that **Avimi the son of Rabbi Abbahu** once **owed money to people from Bei Hozai,** a distant district. [2]Avimi **sent** the money **by way of Ḥama the son of Rabbah the son of Abbahu.** [3]Ḥama **went** to Bei Hozai **and repaid the loan** to Avimi's creditors. [4]**He** then **said to them: "Give me the promissory note** so that you cannot try to collect the same debt again." [5]The creditors **said to him: "The money** which we received from you settles a debt which Avimi **owed us aside** from the loan recorded in the promissory note. Avimi received two loans from us, one which was established orally, and another which was committed to writing. The oral loan is now paid back, but the written loan is still outstanding." [6]Ḥama **came before Rabbi Abbahu** for a ruling. [7]After hearing the details of the case, Rabbi Abbahu **said to** Ḥama: **"Do you have witnesses** who can testify **that you paid** Avimi's creditors any money?" [8]Ḥama **said to him: "No."** [9]Rabbi Abbahu **said to** Ḥama: "The creditors' claim is accepted, for it is supported by the argument of *miggo.* Here the creditors **could have** made a stronger argument and **said: 'There was never such a thing,** for he never paid us,' and their claim would have been accepted. [10]Thus **they can** advance the weaker argument and **also say: 'The money** which we received from you settles a debt which Avimi **owed us aside** from the loan recorded in the promissory note,' and their claim is accepted."

RASHI

מסקי ביה = נושים בו. **בי חוזאי** — אנשי אותה מדינה. **סיטראי** — מלד אחר היינו נושים בו, מלוה על פה, ומחמת אותה מלוה נחזיק בהם.

NOTES

סִיטְרָאֵי נִינְהוּ This is money owed us from other claims. A number of Rishonim (*Ran, Nimmukei Yosef,* and *Rabbenu Crescas Vidal*) conclude from our passage that when a debtor owes several separate debts to his creditor, and he paid back some of the money the creditor may determine which of the debts was repaid. *Rosh* appears to disagree and say that it is the debtor who ordinarily decides which of his debts he repays, but in the case discussed here the creditor's *miggo* gives him the power to assign the payment (see *Kovetz Shiurim*).

מִיגּוֹ דִיכוֹלִין לוֹמַר Since they can say. *Rosh* adds that without the *miggo*, the creditor would not have been believed, because it stands to reason that the debtor meant to pay back the loan for which there was a promissory note, rather than the loan which had been established orally (see previous note).

The Rishonim ask: This case should be treated like the case of the metal bar that was decided by Rabbi Abba. A single witness testified against a litigant who was unable to take the required oath to contradict his testimony. The litigant was ordered to pay (see *Bava Batra* 34a). Similarly, Ḥama who acted as Avimi's agent to repay his loan should be able to serve as a single witness that the creditor had received payment, obligating the creditor to take an oath to contradict that witness. But since the creditor admitted that he received the money and just claims that he received it as payment for a different debt, we should invoke the rule, set down by Rabbi Abba, that whoever is liable for an

HALAKHAH

יְכוֹלִין נַמִי לְמֵימַר: ׳סִיטְרָאֵי נִינְהוּ׳ They can also say: This is money owed us from other claims. "If a creditor presents his debtor with a certified bill of indebtedness, and the debtor claims that he already repaid his debt; the creditor then responds that he did indeed receive money from the debtor, but that payment was made for a different debt that had been established orally, and the debt recorded in the bill of indebtedness is still outstanding. The creditor is believed, provided the debtor had not paid him in the presence of witnesses. The creditor can collect the sum recorded in the bill (even without taking an oath, if the bill includes a provision exempting him from an oath)," following Rabbi Abbahu. The debtor can later sue the creditor for the money which he claims was collected from him unjustly, and the creditor must then take a *hesset* oath." (*Rambam, Sefer Mishpatim, Hilkhot Malveh VeLoveh* 14:9; *Shulḥan Arukh, Ḥoshen Mishpat* 58:1.)

SAGES

אֲבִימִי בְּרֵיהּ דְּרַבִּי אַבָּהוּ Avimi the son of Rabbi Abbahu. He was an Amora of Eretz Israel in the fourth generation. Avimi was the son of the famous Sage, Rabbi Abbahu, one of the greatest Sages of his generation in Torah and in prominence. Rabbi Avimi, the son of Rabbi Abbahu might have had a special position in the Great Yeshivah, and he was accustomed to citing sources from ancient Baraitot. His father, Rabbi Abbahu, expressed pride in this son for observing the commandment of honoring one's father according to the Halakhah. From the story told here, it appears that Avimi was a wealthy merchant who dealt in international trade on a large scale. Another source implies that he had five sons who were all ordained Sages.

חָמָא בְּרֵיהּ דְּרַב נַחְמָן Ḥama the son of Rav Naḥman. A Babylonian Amora of the third generation, Rav Ḥama was the son of the well-known Amora, Rabbah bar Ahuva. Rav Ḥama lived in Eretz Israel for some time. He may have gone there for purposes of commerce.

BACKGROUND

בֵּי חוֹזָאֵי Bei Hozai. Now called Huzistan, it was one of the larger provinces of the Persian kingdom, extending from the Elamite mountains to the Persian Gulf. This district was an important agricultural and commercial center, but it was very far from the main Jewish settlements in Babylonia. Since the journey there was arduous, and transportation in that direction was hard to come by, it could take a whole year to get to Bei Hozai and back, and such trips were therefore very expensive.

TRANSLATION AND COMMENTARY

לְעִנְיַן [1]The incident involving Avimi and Ḥama leads the Gemara to the following question: **What is the law regarding the agent's** obligation to offer **compensation** to the party whose debt he repaid for failing to recover the promissory note?

אֲמַר רַב אַשִׁי [2]**Rav Ashi said: We consider** the precise wording of the instructions given to the agent: [3]**If** the principal **said to** the agent: **"Take** back **the promissory note** from my creditor **and give** him **the money,"** the agent must **pay** the principal for the damage which he caused him, if he failed to follow the instructions. [4]But if the principal said to the agent: **"Give** my creditor **the money** that is due him, **and take** back **the promissory note,"** without explicitly instructing him to recover the note first, [5]the agent **is not required to pay** damages.

וְלָא הִיא [6]The Gemara notes: **But** the law **is not so.** [7]**For in any case** the agent **must pay** for the principal's loss if he failed to recover the note. [8]**For** the principal **can say to him: "I sent you for my benefit** i.e., to repay the documented loan, **and not to do me harm."** The fundamental law governing agents is that the agent must act in a manner most beneficial to the person he represents.

הַהִיא [9]It was further related that **there was a certain woman to whom** a man **entrusted a bag** holding **promissory notes.** [10]The man died, and **his heirs came and demanded** the bag of notes **from her.**

[1]לְעִנְיַן שַׁלּוּמֵי שָׁלִיחַ, מַאי?
[2]אֲמַר רַב אַשִׁי: חָזֵינַן. [3]אִי אֲמַר לֵיהּ: שְׁקוֹל שְׁטָרָא וְהַב זוּזֵי, מְשַׁלֵּם. [4]"הַב זוּזֵי וּשְׁקוֹל שְׁטָרָא", [5]לָא מְשַׁלֵּם.
[6]וְלָא הִיא. [7]בֵּין כָּךְ וּבֵין כָּךְ מְשַׁלֵּם, [8]דְּאָמַר לֵיהּ: "לְתַקּוּנֵי שַׁדַּרְתִּיךְ וְלָא לְעַוּוֹתֵי".
[9]הַהִיא אִיתְּתָא דַּהֲווּ מִיפַּקְדִי גַּבָּהּ מְלוֹגָא דִּשְׁטָרֵי. [10]אֲתוּ יוֹרְשִׁים, קָא תָּבְעֵי לֵיהּ מִינָּהּ.

LITERAL TRANSLATION

[1]Regarding compensation from the agent, what [is the law]?

[2]Rav Ashi said: We see: [3]If he said to him: "Take the promissory note and give the money," he pays. [4]"Give the money and take the promissory note," [5]he does not pay.

[6]But this is not so. [7][For] whether [he said] this or that he pays, [8]for he says to him: "I sent you to benefit [me], and not to do [me] harm."

[9][There was] a certain woman to whom was entrusted a bag of promissory notes. [10]The heirs came, [and] demanded it from her.

RASHI

לענין שלומי שליח – למשלם. מאי – מי הוה פושע, שהחזיר המעות עד שלא קבל מהם השטר? לתקוני שדרתיך – והיה לך לדקדק בתקנתי. דהוו מפקדי גבה – מאבי יתומים. מלוגא דשטרי – תיק מלא שטרות.

LANGUAGE

מְלוֹגָא Bag. This word is apparently derived from the Greek μολγός *molgos,* "leather bag."

NOTES

oath, but cannot take it. must pay! They answer that Ḥama was disqualified to serve as a witness because he was an interested party. Were the creditor's claim accepted, Ḥama would be obligated to compensate Avimi for his loss. *Ritva* adds that Ḥama would be regarded as an interested party even if he were not liable to offer monetary compensation, for he would be obligated to take a *hesset* oath that he fulfilled his mandate. Others write that since the creditor was only liable for an oath by Rabbinic enactment, it would not have been necessary for him to contradict the witness and swear that he had not received any money, but rather it would have sufficed for him to take an oath that the money he received was payment for a different debt.

לְתַקּוּנֵי שַׁדַּרְתִּיךְ I sent you to benefit me. According to a responsum of *Rabbi Naḥshon Gaon* (cited by *Rid*), whenever an agent could have acted to benefit his principal, but instead he caused his principal a financial loss, the agent is liable to pay. However, most of the Rishonim disagree and say that the agent is only liable if the debtor specifically mentioned the promissory note. But if the principal did not mention the note, or if he did not tell the agent to repay the loan in the presence of witnesses, the agent is not liable for the loss caused by his failure to secure the promissory note or repay the loan in front of witnesses (*Rabbenu Ḥananel, Rabbi Shimshon of Sens,* and others).

הַהִיא אִיתְּתָא There was a certain woman. *Meiri* explains that the Gemara's anecdote relates to a widow whose husband had deposited his promissory notes with her, and then when the man's heirs came and demanded them from her, she claimed that she had seized them during her husband's lifetime, so that she would be able to collect her ketubah with them. But *Meiri* says that the same law would apply in the case of an ordinary woman too.

HALAKHAH

לְתַקּוּנֵי שַׁדַּרְתִּיךְ I sent you to benefit me. "If the debtor's agent repaid the debt without witnesses, and the creditor later claimed that he received the payment for another debt that had been established orally, and not for the debt recorded in the bill of indebtedness which the debtor now wants returned to him, the agent is liable for any damage suffered by the debtor, whether the debtor had instructed him to take back the bill and hand over the money, or he had told him to repay the debt and then reclaim the bill," following the Gemara's conclusion. (*Rambam, Sefer Kinyan, Hilkhot Sheluḥin* 1:6; *Shulḥan Arukh, Ḥoshen Mishpat* 58:1.)

PEOPLE

בַּת רַב חִסְדָּא The daughter of Rav Ḥisda. One of Rav Ḥisda's daughters, was first married to Rami bar Ḥama and then, after his death, she married his friend Rava. The Talmud relates that this daughter of Rav Ḥisda uttered a kind of prophecy in her childhood, that she would marry both Rami bar Ḥama and Rava. Indeed, she waited more than ten years after the death of her first husband, until Rava's wife died.

The Talmud also indicates that there was a deep bond of respect and love between Rava and this wife of his. Rava was strongly attached to her and regarded her highly both for her knowledge of the Halakhah and also for the honesty of her heart. He also transmits teachings he heard from her. Perhaps Rav Mesharshiya, the son of Rava, was born to the daughter of Rav Ḥisda.

TRANSLATION AND COMMENTARY

[1] The woman **said to them: "During the lifetime** of the deceased **I had already seized** those promissory notes, to repay a debt he owed me." [2] The woman **came before Rav Naḥman** for a ruling on the matter; he **said to her:** [3] **"Do you have witnesses** that can testify **that** the owner of those notes **demanded** them back from you **during his lifetime, and you refused to return them to him** because of his debt?" [4] The woman **said to** Rav Naḥman: **"No."** [5] Rav Naḥman said: **"If so, this is** considered a case of **seizure** of debtor's property **after his death.** [6] **And** since the law is in accordance with the view of Rabbi Akiva that the creditor's **seizure** of the debtor's property **after his death has no** legal **validity,** the promissory notes must be returned to the heirs."

הַהִיא [7] The Gemara presents another illustrative anecdote: **A certain woman was required by the court** headed by **Rava to take an oath** in order to confirm her denial of a claim against her.

אָמְרָה לֵיהּ [8] Rava's wife, who was **Rav Ḥisda's daughter, said to him: "I** myself **know that** this woman **is suspected of lying under oath,"** and therefore she is not qualified to take an oath. [9] Accepting his wife's allegation, **Rava shifted the oath** from the woman **to the plaintiff** who claimed that she owed him money, which is the normal procedure in such cases. [10] On

[1] אֲמַרָה לְהוּ: ״מֵחַיִּים תָּפֵיסְנָא לְהוּ״. [2] אֲתַאי לְקַמֵּיהּ דְּרַב נַחְמָן, אֲמַר לָהּ: [3] ״אִית לֵיךְ סָהֲדֵי דִּתְבָעוּהּ מִינֵיךְ מֵחַיִּים, וְלָא יְהָבִית נִיהֲלֵיהּ״? [4] אֲמַרָה לֵיהּ: ״לָא״. [5] ״אִם כֵּן, הָוֵי תְּפִיסָה דִּלְאַחַר מִיתָה, [6] וּתְפִיסָה דִּלְאַחַר מִיתָה לֹא כְּלוּם הִיא״. [7] הַהִיא אִיתְּתָא דְּאִיחַיְּיבָא שְׁבוּעָה בֵּי דִינָא דְּרָבָא. [8] אֲמַרָה לֵיהּ בַּת רַב חִסְדָּא: ״יָדַעְנָא בָּהּ דַּחֲשׁוּדָה אַשְּׁבוּעָה״. [9] אַפְּכָהּ רָבָא לִשְׁבוּעָה אַשֶּׁכְּנֶגְדָּהּ. [10] זִימְנִין

LITERAL TRANSLATION

[1] She said to them: "During [his] lifetime I seized them." [2] She came before Rav Naḥman, [who] said to her: [3] "Do you have witnesses that he demanded it from you during [his] lifetime, and you did not give it to him?" [4] She said to him: "No." [5] "If so, it is seizure after [the debtor's] death, [6] and seizure after [the debtor's] death is nothing."

[7] [There was] a certain woman who was required [to take] an oath by the court of Rava.

[8] The daughter of Rav Ḥisda said to him: "I know that she is under suspicion regarding oaths." [9] Rava shifted the oath to the opposing party. [10] Once,

RASHI

מחיים תפיסנא להו – בחוב שהיה חייב לי החזקתי בהם. **הוי תפיסה דלאחר מיתה** – שכל זמן שהיה חי – היו פקדון בידך, והרי הן כמונחין ברשותיה. וכי אמרינן תפיסה מחיים – כגון שראהו קרוב למות, ותפס מטלטלין לשם חובו, ולא היו פקדון בידו. **דאיחייבא שבועה** – שהיה אדם תובעה ממון והיא כופרת. **בת רב חסדא** – אשתו של רבא. **לשבועה אשכנגדה** – התובע אותה ישבע ויטול כדתנן (שבועות מד,ג): ואלו נשבעין ונוטלין: שכנגדו חשוד על השבועה. **זימנין** – פעם אחרת.

NOTES

אִית לֵיךְ סָהֲדֵי דִּתְבָעוּהּ מִינֵיךְ מֵחַיִּים Do you have witnesses that he demanded it from you during his lifetime. The Rishonim ask: Why does the woman need witnesses to testify that the man who had deposited the promissory notes demanded them back from her, and that she refused? Let her be believed because of a *miggo* argument: Since she could have claimed that she originally bought the promissory notes from the deceased, she should be believed when she claims to have seized them during his lifetime! *Rabbenu Ḥananel, Rid,* and others answer that witnesses saw that she had originally received the promissory notes as a deposit, so that she could not have claimed that she had originally purchased them. *Tosafot* (see also *Rabbi Shimshon of Sens*) argue that since she had already claimed that she had seized notes deposited with her during her debtor's lifetime, she could not later have claimed that she had originally bought them. *Rif, Rabbenu Tam,* and others explain that the woman could not have claimed that she had purchased the promissory notes, because the transfer of promissory notes requires a deed of sale, and she could not have produced such a deed.

The Rishonim also deal at length with the question of whether the woman could have claimed that her debtor had given her the promissory notes as security for the debt which he owed her, so that she could retain them until the debt is repaid (see *Ramban, Ra'ah, Ritva,* and others).

דַּחֲשׁוּדָה אַשְּׁבוּעָה That you are under suspicion regarding oaths. Some of the Geonim explain that Rava Ḥisda's daughter claimed to know that the woman habitually swore falsely and in vain. Others explain that she knew that she regularly utters God's name in vain.

אַפְּכָהּ רָבָא לִשְׁבוּעָה Rava shifted the oath. Our commentary follows *Rashi,* who understands that the woman was obligated to take an oath required by Torah law to exempt

HALAKHAH

אִית לֵיךְ סָהֲדֵי דִּתְבָעוּהּ מִינֵיךְ מֵחַיִּים Do you have witnesses that he demanded it from you during his lifetime. "If someone received promissory notes as a deposit, and the depositor died, and the bailee claims that he had seized the notes during the depositor's lifetime as security for a debt which the depositor owed him — if he has witnesses

TRANSLATION AND COMMENTARY

another occasion, **when Rav Pappa and Rav Adda the son of Matena sat before** Rava, [1]**a certain note of indebtedness was brought before him,** so that he might rule on its validity. [2]**Rav Pappa said to** Rava: **"I** myself **know that this note was** already **been repaid."** [3]Rava **said to him: "Is there** perhaps **another person with you, Sir,** who can confirm your allegation?" [4]Rav Pappa **said to** [5]Rava: **"No."** Rava **said to** Rav Pappa: **"Even though you, Sir,** say so, testimony of only one **witness has** no legal **validity** here without the required second witness." [6]Hearing this exchange, **Rav Adda the son of Matena said to** Rava: **"But should not Rav Pappa be believed as** was **the daughter of Rav Ḥisda?** If you took her word alone, why not take Rav Pappa's word? [7]Rava replied, "As for my wife, **the daughter of Rav Ḥisda — I am** absolutely **certain** that she always tells the truth. [8]But as for **Master** — Rav Pappa — **I am not** absolutely **certain about him."**

אֲמַר רַב פַּפָּא [9]The Gemara seeks to draw a conclusion from the explanation which Rava gave for his ruling: **Rav Pappa said: Now that Master** — Rava — **has said:** [10]If a judge can say, **"I am** absolutely **certain about** a particular person that he always tells the truth," that declaration **has legal validity.** [11]Thus if **someone like my son Abba Mar about** whose honesty **I am** absolutely **certain** says that a certain bill of indebtedness has already been repaid, [12]**I may tear up the bill based on his words.**

הֲווּ יָתְבִי קַמֵּיהּ רַב פַּפָּא וְרַב אַדָּא בַּר מַתְּנָא, [1]אַיְיתוּ הַהוּא שְׁטָרָא גַּבֵּיהּ. [2]אֲמַר לֵיהּ רַב פַּפָּא: ״יָדַעְנָא בֵּיהּ דִּשְׁטָרָא פְּרִיעָא הוּא״. [3]אֲמַר לֵיהּ: ״אִיכָּא אִינִישׁ אַחֲרִינָא בַּהֲדֵיהּ דְּמָר״? [4]אֲמַר לֵיהּ: ״לָא״. [5]אֲמַר לֵיהּ: ״אַף עַל גַּב דְּאִיכָּא מָר, עֵד אֶחָד לָאו כְּלוּם הוּא״. [6]אֲמַר לֵיהּ רַב אַדָּא בַּר מַתְּנָא: ״וְלָא יְהֵא רַב פַּפָּא כְּבַת רַב חִסְדָּא״? [7]בַּת רַב חִסְדָּא — קִים לִי בְּגַוָּהּ. [8]מָר — לָא קִים לִי בְּגַוֵּיהּ״.

[9]אֲמַר רַב פַּפָּא: הָשְׁתָּא דַּאֲמַר מָר: [10]״קִים לִי בְּגַוֵּיהּ״ מִילְּתָא הִיא — [11]כְּגוֹן אַבָּא מָר בְּרִי דְּקִים לִי בְּגַוֵּיהּ, [12]קָרַעְנָא שְׁטָרָא אַפּוּמֵּיהּ.

LITERAL TRANSLATION

[when] Rav Pappa and Rav Adda the son of Matena sat before [Rava], [1]they brought a certain note [of indebtedness] before him. [2]Rav Pappa said to him: "I know that this note has been repaid." [3]He said to him: "Is there another person with you, Sir?" [4]He said to him: "No." [5]He said to him: "Even though there is you, Sir, one witness is nothing." [6]Rav Adda the son of Matena said to him: "But should not Rav Pappa be [believed] like the daughter of Rav Ḥisda?" [7]"The daughter of Rav Ḥisda — I am certain about her. [8]Master — I am not certain about him."

[9]Rav Pappa said: Now that Master said: [10]"I am certain about him" is something — [11][then regarding someone] like Abba Mar my son about whom I am certain, [12]I may tear up a bill [of indebtedness] based on his words (lit., "mouth").

RASHI

כבת רב חסדא — שהאמנת לחשוד את האשה על השבועה. דקים לי בגוה — דלא משקרא.

SAGES

רַב אַדָּא בַּר מַתְּנָא Rav Adda bar Matena. A Babylonian Amora of the fourth and fifth generations. See *Ketubot*, Part II, p. 250.

BACKGROUND

וְלָא יְהֵא רַב פַּפָּא וכו׳ But should not Rav Pappa, etc. Surprise is expressed here not only because Rav Ḥisda's daughter was a woman and not eligible to testify in court, but also because Rav Pappa was an important Sage even while he was Rava's student, so it would be proper to rely on his word.

As we see here, Rav Pappa accepted Rava's explanation without being insulted, because he understood that the matter depended not on his formal status as a Sage and the like, but rather on a judge's inner belief in a person's veracity. Although that person's testimony might not be valid judicially, with respect to understanding the matter, it is entirely convincing.

NOTES

herself from payment; Rava shifted the oath to the plaintiff, allowing him to swear and collect the sum that he was claiming. *Ritva* argues that Rava would certainly not have allowed the plaintiff to collect from the woman on the basis of his wife's allegation that the litigant was suspected of lying under oath. This parallels the Gemara's later argument that Rav Pappa would certainly not have torn up an apparently valid bill of indebtedness based on the testimony of a single witness who says that it was already repaid. Rather, *Ritva* explains that the woman was obligated to take an oath instituted by Rabbinic law in order to collect money owed her, and Rava shifted the oath to the other party, allowing him to swear and exempt himself from payment.

קִים לִי בְּגַוֵּיהּ I am certain about her. *Rav Sherira Gaon* and *Rav Hai Gaon* explain that when Rava said that he was certain about his wife's telling the truth, he did not merely mean that never knew her to lie, but rather that he is aware that she often suffered great pain and even financial loss, in order to avoid saying anything that could in any way be understood as being false.

HALAKHAH

that the depositor had demanded the notes back and he refused to return them to him, his seizure is valid, but if he does not have such witnesses, the seizure is not valid," following Rav Naḥman. (*Rambam, Sefer Mishpatim, Hilkhot Malveh VeLoveh* 11:8; *Shulḥan Arukh, Ḥoshen Mishpat* 64:1.)

״קִים לִי בְּגַוֵּיהּ״ מִילְּתָא הִיא "I am certain about him" is something. "A judge must adjudicate civil cases in accordance with his own perception of the truth, even in the absence of clear evidence. How so? If a certain party was obligated to take an oath, and the judge heard from someone in whom he had absolute trust (even a single witness, and even a woman) that that person was suspected of lying under oath, the judge is permitted to shift the oath to the other litigant. Similarly, if a judge heard from a person in whom he had absolute truth that a bill of indebtedness that was brought before him had already been repaid, he is permitted to impose an oath on the billholder before allowing him to collect the debt. This

[1] קָרַעֲנָא סָלְקָא דַּעְתָּךְ?
[2] אֶלָּא, מָרַעֲנָא שְׁטָרָא אַפּוּמֵּיהּ.
[3] הַהִיא אִיתְּתָא דְּאִיחַיְּיבָא שְׁבוּעָה בֵּי דִינָא דְּרַב בֵּיבָי בַּר אַבַּיֵּי. [4] אֲמַר לְהוּ הַהוּא בַּעַל דִּין: [5] ״תֵּיתֵי וְתִישְׁתַּבַּע בְּמָתָא;
[6] אֶפְשָׁר דְּמִיכְסְפָא וּמוֹדְיָא״.

LITERAL TRANSLATION

[1] Does it come to your mind [that he said] I may tear up?!

[2] Rather, [he said] I may impair a bill [of indebtedness] based on his words.

[3] [There was] a certain woman who was required [to take] an oath by the court of Rav Bevai the son of Abaye. [4] The [other] litigant said to them: [5] "Let her come and swear in town; [6] perhaps she will be embarrassed and confess."

TRANSLATION AND COMMENTARY

קָרַעֲנָא [1] The Gemara says in astonishment: **Do you think** that **I may tear up** the bill on the basis of the testimony of a single witness? Surely two witnesses are required for such drastic action!

אֶלָּא [2] The Gemara answers: **Rather,** Rav Pappa meant to **say** as follows: "**I may impair** the power of **the bill on the basis of what** an absolutely reliable person **says,**" and refrain from collecting the debt until the creditor proves that the debt in the bill had not been repaid.

הַהִיא [3] The Gemara further relates that **a certain woman was required by the court** headed by **Rav Bevai the son of Abaye to take an oath** to confirm her denial of a claim against her. [4] **The other litigant said to** the judges: "Do not administer the oath to the woman in your court. [5] But rather **let her come and swear in town** in the presence of her townspeople. [6] **Perhaps** she will see someone before whom **she is**

RASHI

קרענא סלקא דעתך – וכי אחד נאמן להוציא שטר חתום מיד המחזיק בו? אפוקי ממונא הוא, ותרי בעינן. מרענא – ולא אזדקק לגבות באותו שטר, ומקרע נמי לא קרענא ליה.

SAGES

רַב בֵּיבָי בַּר אַבַּיֵי **Rav Bevai bar Abaye.** A Babylonian Amora of the fifth generation, Rav Bevai was the son of Abaye, Rava's colleague. His teachers were Rav Yosef and his own father. His contemporaries were Rav Pappi and Rav Huna the son of Rav Yehoshua. His Halakhic teachings and Aggadic sayings are found in many places in the Talmud.

NOTES

מָרַעֲנָא שְׁטָרָא **I may impair a bill of indebtedness.** *Rashi* explains that impairing the bill of indebtedness means that the billholder cannot collect his debt until he brings additional proof that he had not been repaid. According to *Rivan,* the billholder cannot collect the debt even with an oath. But most Rishonim follow *Rabbenu Ḥananel* and *Rif,* who say that the billholder can collect the debt recorded in an impaired bill of indebtedness if he swears that the debt is still outstanding. *Tosafot* ask: The billholder would have to take an oath in order to collect the debt, even if the bill were not impaired, for we learned in the Mishnah below (87a) that if one witness testifies that a certain bill had been repaid, the billholder still cannot collect without first taking an oath to confirm his claim. What then is accomplished by Rav Pappa's certainty about his son's integrity which allows him to impair an otherwise valid bill of indebtedness? *Tosafot* and others answer that a judge can rely on a witness whom he is certain to be telling the truth, even if the witness is related to one of the parties involved in the case or otherwise disqualified from testifying. *Rabbenu Ḥananel* says that if the judge is absolutely certain about the honesty of a witness, he can impose an oath upon the billholder even if the bill of indebtedness explicitly exempts him from having to take an oath in order to collect his debt.

וְתִישְׁתַּבַּע בְּמָתָא **Let her swear in the town.** There are a number of different readings of this line. According to one reading, the plaintiff said to the judges: תִּישְׁתַּבַּע בְּמָאתִין – Let the woman swear in *our* town. As *Rivan* explains, the plaintiff asked that the woman take her oath in the town in which both of them lived, thinking that there might be someone who knows the truth and before whom she might be embarrassed to swear falsely. Some (*Meiri* and others) read: תִּישְׁתַּבַּע בְּמָתָא – Let the woman swear in *the* town. Let the woman take her oath in town with many people, where there might be somebody she knows well and before whom she is embarrassed to lie. According to a third reading, the plaintiff said בְּמָתַאי – in *my* town. The Rishonim discuss whether or not the creditor can compel the debtor to come to his town in order to take an oath which had been imposed upon him by a distant court. While the plaintiff is able to compel the defendant to stand trial outside his place of residence in a more reputable court, opinions differ as to whether he can compel him to take his oath in another place (see *Ramban, Ra'ah,* and *Ritva*).

HALAKHAH

is the law, following the rulings of Rava and Rav Pappa. But since the quality of the judges has declined in later generations, it was agreed that the courts may not issue rulings based on anything but clear evidence. Even today, if a judge suspects deception, he should not issue a ruling based on the evidence brought before him, but rather he should cross-examine the litigants until the truth emerges, or he should effect a compromise or disqualify himself from the case." (*Rambam, Sefer Shofetim, Hilkhot Sanhedrin* 24:1-2; *Shulḥan Arukh, Ḥoshen Mishpat* 15:5.)

תֵּיתֵי וְתִישְׁתַּבַּע בְּמָתָא **Let her come and swear in the town.** "The plaintiff can demand that the defendant take his oath where their business had been conducted and there are people who know about the matter, or where there are many people before whom the defendant might be embarrassed to take a false oath. The plaintiff cannot insist that the defendant go to that other place immediately, but rather he must wait until the defendant arrives there. The defendant must then take his oath, and he cannot say that he will only swear in his own city. (*Shulḥan Arukh, Ḥoshen Mishpat* 87:23, *Rema.*)

¹אֲמַרָה לְהוּ: ״כְּתְבוּ לִי זַכְוָותָא דְּכִי מִשְׁתַּבַּעֲנָא, יָהֲבֵי לִי״. ²אֲמַר לְהוּ רַב בֵּיבָי בַּר אַבַּיֵי: ״כְּתְבוּ לָהּ״. ³אֲמַר רַב פַּפִּי: ״מִשּׁוּם דַּאֲתִיתוּ מִמּוּלָאֵי, ⁴אָמְרִיתוּ מִילֵּי מוּלַיְתָא״? ⁵הָא אֲמַר רָבָא: הַאי אַשַּׁרְתָּא דְּדַיָּינֵי דְּמִיכַּתְבָא מִקַּמֵּי דְּנַחֲווּ סָהֲדֵי אַחֲתִימוֹת יְדַיְיהוּ — פְּסוּלָה. ⁶אַלְמָא, מֶיחֱזֵי כְּשִׁיקְרָא. ⁷הָכִי נַמִי מֶיחֱזֵי כְּשִׁיקְרָא.

⁸וְלֵיתָא, מִדְּרַב נַחְמָן. ⁹דְּאָמַר רַב נַחְמָן: אוֹמֵר הָיָה רַבִּי מֵאִיר: ¹⁰אֲפִילּוּ מְצָאוֹ בָּאַשְׁפָּה, וַחֲתָמוֹ, וּנְתָנוֹ לָהּ, כָּשֵׁר.

LITERAL TRANSLATION

[1]She said to them: "Write for me a favorable verdict so that when I swear, they will give [it] to me." [2]Rav Bevai the son of Abaye said to them: "Write her." [3]Rav Pappi said: "Because you come from short-lived people, [4]you speak short-lived words?" [5]Surely Rava said: A certification of judges that was written [on a note] before the witnesses gave evidence about their signatures (lit., "of their hands"), is invalid. [6]Evidently, [it] looks like a falsehood. [7]Here too it looks like a falsehood.

[8]But [this] is not so, because of Rav Naḥman. [9]For Rav Naḥman said: Rabbi Meir used to say: [10]Even if [the husband] found [a bill of divorce] in a heap of refuse, and [had] it signed, and gave it to her, it is valid.

TRANSLATION AND COMMENTARY

embarrassed to lie, **and** she may **confess** that her denial was false." [1]The woman **said to** the judges: "Please **write** your **favorable verdict in a document,** testifying that if I should appear before that court and take an oath I shall be released from paying the alleged debt. Draw up the document now, **so that when I take the oath, they will give me** the money without delay." [2]**Rav Bevai the son of Abaye said to them: "Write** the affidavit **for** the woman." [3]**Rav Pappi said** to Rav Bevai: **"Because you** are descendant **from short-lived people** (Abaye's family traced their lineage to the house of Eli, all of whose descendants were destined to be short-lived; see I Samuel 2:31), [4]**you speak short-lived words.** Your opinion must be rejected. [5]For **surely Rava said: A certification of judges** validating the authenticity of the witnesses' signatures **that was written** on the **note before the witnesses gave evidence about their signatures, is invalid.** This is because the standard language of the judges' document of certification implies that the testimony had already been heard. But if the testimony had not yet taken place at the time of the writing but eventually did occur, [6]the validation certificate is nevertheless invalid because it **appears** as a **false statement.** [7]**Here too** the document which the woman requested should be invalid, for **it looks like a falsehood.**

וְלֵיתָא [8]**But,** the Gemara concludes: Rava's ruling **is not** the law, as we know from what **Rav Naḥman** said. [9]**For Rav Naḥman said: Rabbi Meir said:** A bill of divorce must be written according to law, signed by witnesses, and delivered by the husband to the wife. It must include the names of the man and woman who are the parties to the divorce, but at the time of its drafting, the document need not be intended for that particular couple. [10]Therefore, **even if the husband found an** unsigned **bill of divorce** lying discarded **in a heap of refuse,** if witnesses then **signed** the document, **and** the husband **gave it to** his wife, the bill of divorce **is valid,** provided that the husband and wife have the same names as the man and woman on

RASHI

כתבו לי זכוותא — שבאתי לדין, ונפטרתי הימנו בשבועתי. **ממולאי** — בית עלי, שהן כרותי ימים. ולי נראה: ממולאי גבנונים, בעלי מומין, שאינן חיין כשאר בני אדם, לשון "שקל מוליא ושדי בגלא" (בבא בתרא נד,א). **אשרתא** — לשון חוזק כמו "יישר כחך" (יבמות סב,א). **אשרתא דשטרי** — קיום השטר, שכותבין דיינין: במותב תלתא הוינא ואתא פלוני ופלוני ואסהידו אחתימות ידייהו ואשרנוהו וקיימנוהו. **דניחוו** — שיעידו זה כתב ידי. **הכי נמי מיחזי בשיקרא** — לכתוב "נשבעה פלונית" ועדיין לא נשבעה.

LANGUAGE

דַּאֲתִיתוּ מִמּוּלָאֵי Because you come from short-lived people. The commentaries differ about the meaning of this expression, which appears in several places in the Talmud. Some explain this as "cut off, decreased," i.e., "people of decreased longevity"; thus, the Gemara alludes to the fact that Rav Bevai was a descendant of the house of Eli, who were condemned to die young (see I Samuel 2:33). Others, following *Bereshit Rabbah,* take ממלא as the name of a place where Eli's descendants lived. A third explanation is given by *Arukh,* who interprets מוּלָאֵי as "great, distinguished"; thus, Rav Pappi meant: "Since you are descended from distinguished scholars (Rabbah and Abaye), you say great things."

NOTES

כְּתְבוּ לִי זַכְוָותָא Write me a favorable verdict. *Rashi* explains that the woman asked that a document be drawn up stating that she had appeared before the court and taken an oath which exempted her from payment. It stands to reason that this document was to be deposited in the hands of a third party and given to her after she takes her oath. *Ritva* adds that such a document may be drawn up, but it may not be signed before she takes her oath, for in that case the document would not only look like a falsehood, it would be an actual falsehood.

מִמּוּלָאֵי From short-lived people. Several explanations have been offered for this expression, which appears in a number of places. *Rashi* explains the word מולאי as denoting a physical weakness. Abaye's family traced their lineage to the house of Eli, whose descendants were destined to be short-lived. Thus, Rav Pappi said the following: Because you are one of the descendants of Eli, all of whom are weak and short-lived, you put forward a weak argument.

Following *Bereshit Rabbah* (59:1), *Rashbam* (*Bava Batra* 137b) interprets the word מוּלָאֵי as meaning "residents of Mamla," a place inhabited by the descendants of the house of Eli. *Arukh* cites another explanation, according to which the word means "elevated." According to this explanation Rav Pappi said: Because you are descended from great people, you make excessive demands.

[1]וַאֲפִילּוּ רַבָּנַן לָא פְּלִיגִי עֲלֵיהּ דְּרַבִּי מֵאִיר אֶלָּא בְּגִיטֵּי נָשִׁים, דְּבָעֵינַן כְּתִיבָה לִשְׁמָהּ. [2]אֲבָל בִּשְׁאָר שְׁטָרוֹת, מוֹדוּ לֵיהּ. [3]דְּאָמַר רַב אַסִּי אָמַר רַבִּי יוֹחָנָן: שְׁטָר שֶׁלָּוָה בּוֹ וּפְרָעוֹ — [4]אֵינוֹ חוֹזֵר וְלֹוֶה בּוֹ, [5]שֶׁכְּבָר נִמְחַל שִׁיעְבּוּדוֹ. [6]טַעְמָא דְּנִמְחַל שִׁיעְבּוּדוֹ. [7]אֲבָל לְמֶיחֱזֵי [85B] כְּשִׁיקְרָא, [8]לָא חָיְישִׁינַן.

LITERAL TRANSLATION

[1]And even the Sages disagree with Rabbi Meir only about women's bills of divorce, [2]because we require that it be written [specifically] for her. But about other bills, they agree with him. [3]For Rav Assi said in the name of Rabbi Yoḥanan: A bill of indebtedness that has been [used to] borrow [money] which he repaid — [4]he may not borrow with it again, [5]for the lien was already cancelled. [6]The reason is that its lien was cancelled. [7]But that it looks [85B] like a falsehood, [8]we are not concerned.

TRANSLATION AND COMMENTARY

behalf of whom the document had originally been written. This is the position of Rabbi Meir. But the Sages disagree and say that the bill of divorce is not valid. [1]**And** Rav Naḥman added: **Even the Sages only disagree with Rabbi Meir about a bill of divorce, because** they maintain that there is a **requirement that** a woman's bill of divorce **be written specifically for her.** [2]**But about other bills,** which have no such requirement, the Rabbis **agree with** Rabbi Meir that the note can be drafted in advance. Support for this position may be brought from what [3]**Rav Assi said in the name of Rabbi Yoḥanan:** If **someone borrowed** money with a certain **bill of indebtedness** and then **repaid** the debt, [4]**he may not borrow again** with that bill of indebtedness — even if he borrows the same sum from the same lender on the same date as the first loan — [5]**for the lien** established by the bill of indebtedness **was already cancelled** when the first loan was repaid. Now, as Rabbi Yoḥanan stated, [6]**the reason** that the bill of indebtedness cannot be used again is **that the lien** which it established **was already cancelled.** [7]**But that** the bill of indebtedness **looks** [85B] **like a falsehood** because it had been drafted originally for a different loan, [8]**we are not concerned.** This is against the opinion of Rava who invalidates a document that looks like a falsehood.

RASHI

ופרעו — בו ביום. אינו חוזר ולוה בו — אפילו בו ביום. ואף על גב דלאו מוקדם הוא, שהרי ביום הלואה נכתב. שכבר נמחל שעבודו — משפרעו בטל השטר, ונמצאת מלוה השניה מלוה על פה, ואינו גובה מן הלקוחות. כשיקרא — שלא נכתב על מלוה זו. לא חיישינן — אם לא שיש בדבר ביטול שטר גמור.

NOTES

אֵינוֹ חוֹזֵר וְלֹוֶה בּוֹ **He may not borrow with it again.** *Rashi* writes that a promissory note which has already been repaid may not be used again, even if the original loan was repaid on the very day that it had been extended, so that the second loan can be contracted on the day recorded in the bill. The promissory note can certainly not be used again at some later date, for then the bill would be predated, enabling the creditor to collect his debt from property which his debtor had sold before he took the loan. *Ritva* adds that we might also be dealing with a promissory note that mentions only the month and year in which the loan was extended, but not the day of the month. In such a case the creditor's lien on the debtor's property begins only on the last day of the month recorded in the bill, and there is no need to limit the discussion to the unlikely case where the two loans were made on the same day.

לְמֶיחֱזֵי כְּשִׁיקְרָא, לָא חָיְישִׁינַן **That it looks like a falsehood, we are not concerned.** *Ritva* notes that we say that there is no concern only when there is the mere appearance of falsehood. But the court can certainly not give its approval

HALAKHAH

בְּגִיטֵּי נָשִׁים, דְּבָעֵינַן כְּתִיבָה לִשְׁמָהּ. **About women's bills of divorce, because we require that it be written specifically for her.** "A bill of divorce must be written and signed for the man and the woman whose marriage it terminates. If the bill of divorce was not specifically written for that man and woman, it is not valid. How so? If someone found a bill of divorce that had been written by a scribe who was practicing his art, or a bill of divorce that had been written for a different couple, and his name and his wife's name, and the name of his town and her town, match the personal and place names recorded in the bill of divorce, and he took the document and gave it to his wife in order to effect a divorce, the divorce is not valid." (*Rambam, Sefer Nashim, Hilkhot Gerushin* 3:4; *Shulḥan Arukh, Even HaEzer* 131:1.)

בִּשְׁאָר שְׁטָרוֹת, מוֹדוּ לֵיהּ **About other bills, they agree with him.** "A scribe may prepare promissory notes in advance, and he may even include the names of the lender and the borrower, and the sum of the loan, but he should leave the space designated for the date blank, so that the note not be predated." (*Shulḥan Arukh, Ḥoshen Mishpat* 48:1.)

נִמְחַל שִׁיעְבּוּדוֹ **Its lien was cancelled.** "A promissory note that was drawn up for one loan and then repaid may not be used for another loan — even if the second loan took place on the same day as the first, so that the note is not predated — for the lien established by the note was already cancelled," following Rabbi Yoḥanan. (*Rambam, Sefer Mishpatim, Hilkhot Malveh VeLoveh* 14:7; *Shulḥan Arukh, Ḥoshen Mishpat* 48:1.)

TRANSLATION AND COMMENTARY

הַהוּא גַּבְרָא [1]The Gemara now discusses a number of cases in which a litigant claims property found in the possession of someone who died. **A certain man deposited seven pearls that were tied up in a sheet in the house of Rabbi Meyasha the grandson of Rabbi Yehoshua ben Levi.** [2]**Rabbi Meyasha died** suddenly, **without having left** any **instructions** as to the disposition of the pearls. The person who had deposited the pearls claimed them, but Rabbi Meyasha's heirs argued that perhaps the pearls belonged to their father. [3]The depositor and the heirs **came before Rabbi Ammi,** who **said to them:** "I have two reasons for awarding the pearls to the claimant: [4]**First, because I know that Rabbi Meyasha the grandson of Rabbi Yehoshua ben Levi was not** a **wealthy** man, so the pearls were probably not his. [5]**And moreover, the depositor offered an identifying sign** for he asked for his seven pearls in a sheet." [6]The Gemara adds: **And**

[1]הַהוּא גַּבְרָא דְּאַפְקֵיד שַׁב מַרְגָּנִיתָא דְּצַיְירֵי בִּסְדִינָא בֵּי רַבִּי מְיָאשָׁא בַּר בְּרֵיהּ דְּרַבִּי יְהוֹשֻׁעַ בֶּן לֵוִי. [2]שְׁכֵיב רַבִּי מְיָאשָׁא וְלָא פְּקֵיד. [3]אֲתוֹ לְקַמֵּיהּ דְּרַבִּי אַמִי, אֲמַר לֵיהּ: [4]"חֲדָא, דְּיָדַעְנָא בֵּיהּ בְּרַבִּי מְיָאשָׁא בַּר בְּרֵיהּ דְּרַבִּי יְהוֹשֻׁעַ בֶּן לֵוִי דְּלָא אֲמִיד. [5]וְעוֹד, הָא קָא יָהֵיב סִימָנָא". [6]וְלָא אֲמָרַן

LITERAL TRANSLATION

[1][There was] a certain man who deposited seven pearls that were tied up in a sheet in the house of Rabbi Meyasha the son of the son of Rabbi Yehoshua ben Levi. [2]Rabbi Meyasha died and did not leave instructions. [3][The disputants] came before Rabbi Ammi, [who] said to them: [4]"First, since I know that Rabbi Meyasha the son of the son of Rabbi Yehoshua ben Levi was not wealthy. [5]And moreover, [the depositor] offered an identifying sign." [6]And we only say

RASHI

שב מרגניתא דצייריבסדינא — שבע מרגליות צרורות בסדין אחד הפקיד ביד רבי מיאשא. **ולא פקיד** — לא צוה לאנשי ביתו, שחטפתו מיתה. **אתו לקמיה דרבי אמי** — לתבוע את היורשין, והיורשין אומרים: שמא של אבינו היו. **דלא אמיד** — אינו עשיר. **סימנא** — דאמר: בסדין הם צרורות, והם שבע.

SAGES

רַבִּי מְיָאשָׁא בַּר בְּרֵיהּ דְּרַבִּי יְהוֹשֻׁעַ Rabbi Meyasha the grandson of Rabbi Yehoshua ben Levi. He was an Amora of the fourth generation in Eretz Israel. According to the Talmud, Rabbi Yehoshua ben Levi's son died during his father's lifetime. Rabbi Yehoshua ben Levi, who was one of the greatest scholars of his generation, raised his grandson, Rabbi Meyasha, and he was very involved in his upbringing from the time he was a little boy. Because he was raised by his grandfather, he is always called by his name. We also find that he transmits Torah teachings in his grandfather's name. He appears to have lived in Tiberias, where he was among the most important scholars. We find teachings by him in both Talmuds, as well as many Aggadic Midrashim.

NOTES

to an outright lie. Thus, the court could draft a document stating that the woman had taken an oath even before she actually did so, but it could not sign it until after the oath was taken. *Talmidei Rabbenu Yonah* argue that the principle that we are not concerned about the appearance of falsehood applied only when the apparent falsehood will ultimately turn out to be true, such as in our case, where the woman will indeed take the oath. But the court can certainly not give its approval to a document that is not true, and will always look spurious, even if the documented falsehood has no Halakhic ramifications.

הַהוּא גַּבְרָא דְּאַפְקֵיד There was a certain man who deposited. The Rishonim raised numerous questions about the arguments that Rabbi Ammi put forward to justify his rulings that the pearls found in Rabbi Meyasha's possession should be awarded to the party claiming to be their owner. First, even if Rabbi Meyasha was not known to be wealthy, he might have wished to conceal his wealth; perhaps he found the pearls or received them as a gift. Second, even if the claimant offered an identifying sign, such a sign does not usually suffice to remove property from the party holding it. Furthermore, were Rabbi Meyasha alive, he would have been believed to say that the pearls were his. Thus, the court should have presented this claim on behalf of his heirs, following the rule that any claim that could have been presented by the deceased is put forward by the court on behalf of his heirs. *Tosafot* argue that the court will only claim on behalf of the heirs if these claims are likely and reasonable. The arguments put forward by Rabbi Ammi, that Rabbi Meyasha was not known to be wealthy and that the claimant offered an identifying sign, were intended to demonstrate that it was unlikely that Rabbi Meyasha had owned the pearls. Most of the Rishonim (*Ramban*, explaining the position of *Rif, Ra'ah* in the name of *Rabbenu Zeraḥyah HaLevi,* and others) understand that witnesses saw that pearls had been deposited in Rabbi Meyasha's hands, so Rabbi Meyasha could not have claimed that they belonged to him. However, those witnesses could not identify the pearls or their owner. In such a case, the argument that Rabbi Meyasha was not known to be wealthy and the claimant's offering of an identifying sign are sufficient reasons to award the pearls to him.

הָא קָא יָהֵיב סִימָנָא He offered an identifying sign. *Rashi* explains that the claimant identified the pearls, saying that they were tied up in a sheet and that they were seven in number. *Tosafot* points out that elsewhere (*Yevamot* 115b), such an identifying sign is not considered proof of ownership and another sign must have been given.

The Rishonim and Aḥaronim discuss the circumstances under which an identifying sign can suffice to remove property from the party in whose possession that property is found. *Ahavat Zion* suggests that once it was established that the pearls did not belong to Rabbi Meyasha, they were treated as lost property, which the heirs were obligated to return on the basis of an identifying sign.

HALAKHAH

הַהוּא גַּבְרָא דְּאַפְקֵיד There was a certain man who deposited. "If someone claimed that he had deposited an object with a person who subsequently died, and he offers a manifest identifying sign for the object, and the judge knows that the deceased had not been a wealthy person who is likely to have owned such an object, the judge

SAGES

חָסָא Ḥasa. Very little is known about this scholar (he may be identical with the Rav Ḥasa mentioned in several other passages in the Talmud). In *Yevamot* (121b), the Gemara relates that he drowned in a pond, and since he died suddenly, it is only understandable why he died intestate.

רַב סָפְרָא Rav Safra. A Babylonian Amora of the third and fourth generations. See *Ketubot,* Part II, p. 112.

רַב דִּימִי Rav Dimi. A Babylonian Amora of the third and fourth generations. See *Ketubot,* Part II, pp. 243-44.

LANGUAGE

מְטַכְּסָא Silk. From the Greek μέταξα *metaxa,* meaning "raw silk."

LANGUAGE (RASHI)

צינד״ל* (read: צינדי״ר). From the Old French *cender,* a type of silk.

TRANSLATION AND COMMENTARY

we only say that we rely on such an identifying sign [1]**because** the claimant had **not** been **accustomed to** goi n **and out of** the house of the deceased. [2]**But** were the claimant **accustomed to go in and out of there,** [3]we would **say that** perhaps **another person deposited** the pearls, **and** the claimant **saw the deposit** in his house, enabling him to describe it.

הַהוּא גַּבְרָא [4]It was similarly related that **a certain man deposited a silver goblet in the house of Ḥasa.** [5]**Ḥasa died** suddenly **without having left instructions** as to the disposition of the goblet. [6]Hasa's heirs and the man who claimed ownership **came before Rav Naḥman** who **said to them:** [7]"The goblet must be returned to the depositor. **Firstly, I know that Hasa was not** a **wealthy** man. [8]**And moreover,** the claimant **offered an identifying sign."** [9]The Gemara adds: **And we only say** that we rely on such an identifying sign **because** the claimant **was not accustomed to go in and out of** the house of the deceased. [10]**But were** the claimant **accustomed to go in and out of there,** [11]we would **say that** perhaps **another person deposited the** goblet, **and the** claimant **saw the deposit** in his house, enabling him to provide an identifying mark.

הַהוּא דְּאַפְקֵיד [12]In a third instance, **a certain man deposited silk in the house of Rav Dimi the brother of Rav Safra.** [13]**Rav Dimi died** suddenly, **without having left instructions.** [14]**The depositor** and the heirs **came before Rabbi Abba,** who **said to them:** the silk must be returned to the depositor. [15]**First I know that Rav Dimi was not** a **wealthy** man, and he would not have owned such expensive fabric. [16]**And moreover,** the depositor **offered an identifying sign."** [17]The Gemara adds: **And we only say** that we rely on such an identifying sign **because** the claimant **was not accustomed to go in and out of** the house of the deceased. [18]**But were** the claimant **accustomed to go in and out of there,** [19]we would **say that** perhaps **another person deposited** the article, **and** this claimant **saw** it when he was in the house, enabling him to provide an identifying mark.

[1]אֶלָּא דְּלָא רָגִיל דְּעָיֵיל וְנָפֵיק לְהָתָם. [2]אֲבָל רָגִיל דְּעָיֵיל וְנָפֵיק לְהָתָם — [3]אֵימָא אִינִישׁ אַחֲרִינָא אַפְקֵיד וְאִיהוּ מִיחְזָא חֲזָא.

[4]הַהוּא גַּבְרָא דְּאַפְקֵיד כָּסָא דְּכַסְפָּא בֵּי חָסָא. [5]שְׁכֵיב חָסָא, וְלָא פְּקֵיד. [6]אֲתוֹ לְקַמֵּיהּ דְּרַב נַחְמָן אֲמַר לְהוּ: [7]"יָדַעְנָא בֵּיהּ בְּחָסָא דְּלָא אֲמִיד. [8]וְעוֹד, הָא קָא יָהֵיב סִימָנָא". [9]וְלָא אֲמָרַן אֶלָּא דְּלָא רָגִיל דְּעָיֵיל וְנָפֵיק לְהָתָם. [10]אֲבָל רָגִיל דְּעָיֵיל וְנָפֵיק לְהָתָם — [11]אֵימַר אִינִישׁ אַחֲרִינָא אַפְקֵיד וְאִיהוּ מִיחְזָא חֲזָא.

[12]הַהוּא דְּאַפְקֵיד מְטַכְּסָא בֵּי רַב דִּימִי אֲחוּהּ דְּרַב סָפְרָא. [13]שְׁכֵיב רַב דִּימִי, וְלָא פְּקֵיד. [14]אֲתָא לְקַמֵּיהּ דְּרַבִּי אַבָּא אֲמַר לֵיהּ: [15]"חֲדָא, דְּיָדַעְנָא בֵּיהּ בְּרַב דִּימִי דְּלָא אֲמִיד. [16]וְעוֹד, הָא קָא יָהֵיב סִימָנָא". [17]וְלָא אֲמָרַן אֶלָּא דְּלָא רָגִיל דְּעָיֵיל וְנָפֵיק לְהָתָם. [18]אֲבָל רָגִיל דְּעָיֵיל וְנָפֵיק לְהָתָם — [19]אֵימָא אִינִישׁ אַחֲרִינָא אַפְקֵיד, וְאִיהוּ מִיחְזָא חֲזָא.

LITERAL TRANSLATION

[1][this] because [the depositor] was not accustomed to go in and out of there. [2]But if he was accustomed to go in and out of there — [3]say that another person deposited [them] and he saw [the deposit].

[4][There was] a certain man who deposited a silver goblet in the house of Ḥasa. [5]Ḥasa died, and did not leave instructions. [6][The disputants] came before Rav Naḥman [who] said to them: [7]"I know that Ḥasa was not wealthy. [8]And moreover, [the depositor] offered an identifying sign." [9]And we only say [this] because [the depositor] was not accustomed to go in and out of there. [10]But if he was accustomed to go in and out of there — [11]say that another person deposited [it] and he saw [the deposit].

[12][There was] a certain man who deposited silk in the house of Rav Dimi the brother of Rav Safra. [13]Rav Dimi died, and did not leave instructions. [14][The depositor] came before Rabbi Abba [who] said to them: [15]"First, I know that Rav Dimi was not wealthy. [16]And furthermore, [the depositor] offered an identifying sign." [17]And we only say [this] because [the depositor] was not accustomed to go in and out of there. [18]But if he was accustomed to go in and out of there — [19]say another person deposited [it], and he saw [the deposit].

RASHI

שכיב חסא ולא פקיד — שטבע בנהר, כדאמר ביבמות בפרק בתרא (קכא,ב). **מטכסא** = לבוש משי *צינד״ל בלעז.

HALAKHAH

should take the object from the heirs and award it to the claimant, provided that the claimant was not accustomed to go in and out of the house of the deceased," following the rulings recorded in our Gemara. (*Rambam, Sefer Mishpatim, Hilkhot She'elah* 6:4; *Sefer Shofetim, Hilkhot Sanhedrin* 24:2; *Shulḥan Arukh, Ḥoshen Mishpat* 15:5.)

[1]הַהוּא דְּאָמַר לְהוּ: ״נְכָסַיי לְטוּבִיָּה״. [2]שְׁכֵיב, אֲתָא טוּבִיָּה. [3]אָמַר רַבִּי יוֹחָנָן: ״הֲרֵי בָּא טוּבִיָּה״.

[4]אֲמַר ״טוּבִיָּה״, [5]וַאֲתָא רַב טוּבִיָּה — [6]״לְטוּבִיָּה״ אֲמַר, [7]״לְרַב טוּבִיָּה״ לָא אֲמַר. [8]וְאִי אִינִישׁ דְּגִיס בֵּיהּ, [9]הָא גִּיס בֵּיהּ.

[10]אָתוּ שְׁנֵי טוּבִיָּה, [11]שָׁכֵן וְתַלְמִיד חָכָם, [12]תַּלְמִיד חָכָם קוֹדֵם; [13]קָרוֹב וְתַלְמִיד חָכָם, [14]תַּלְמִיד חָכָם קוֹדֵם.

[15]אִיבַּעֲיָא לְהוּ: [16]שָׁכֵן וְקָרוֹב, מַאי?

LITERAL TRANSLATION

[1][There was] a certain man who said to them: "My property to Toviyah." [2]He died, [and] Toviyah came. [3]Rabbi Yoḥanan said: "Indeed Toviyah has come."

[4][If the deceased] said "Toviyah," [5]and Rav Toviyah came — [6]he said "to Toviyah," [7]he did not say "to Rav Toviyah." [8]And if [Rav Toviyah] was a person with whom he had been familiar, [9]he was familiar with him.

[10][If] two Toviyahs came, [11][one] a neighbor and [the other] a Torah scholar, [12]the Torah scholar takes precedence; [13]a relative and a Torah scholar, [14]the Torah scholar takes precedence.

[15]It was asked of them: [16][If] a neighbor and a relative [came], what [is the law]?

TRANSLATION AND COMMENTARY

הַהוּא [1]In a similar vein, **a** dying **man said to** those who surrounded him as he lay on his deathbed: "Upon my death **my property** is to be given **to Toviyah."** [2]The man **died,** and shortly thereafter a man named **Toviyah came** to claim the property. [3]Asked about the matter, **Rabbi Yoḥanan said:** The deceased said give it to Toviyah, and now a man named **Toviyah came** to collect. Since there is only a single claimant, we give it to him.

אֲמַר טוּבִיָּה [4]The Gemara adds: **If** the dying man **said:** "Upon my death my property is to be given to **Toviyah,"** [5]**and** when he died a man named **Rav Toviyah came** to collect the property, the property is not given to him, [6]for the deceased had **said** that his property should be given **to "Toviyah,"** [7]and **he did not say to "Rav Toviyah,"** and so we assume that he had another person in mind. [8]But **if** this Rav Toviyah who came to collect the property **was a person with whom** the deceased **had been familiar,** the property must be given to him, [9]for we assume that since he **had been familiar with him,** the deceased called him by his casual name.

אָתוּ [10]The Gemara continues: If the dying man said: "Upon my death my property is to be given to Toviyah," and when he died, **two** people named **Toviyah came** to collect the property, the following regulations apply: [11]If one of the claimants is **a neighbor** of the deceased but not a Torah scholar, **and** the other is **a Torah scholar** but not a neighbor, [12]**the Torah scholar is given precedence.** [13]And even if one of the claimants is **a relative** of the deceased but not a Torah scholar, **and** the other is **a Torah scholar** but not a relative, [14]**the Torah scholar is given precedence.**

אִיבַּעֲיָא לְהוּ [15]In a discussion among the Sages, **it was asked:** If two people named Toviyah came to collect the property, [16]one of the claimants being **a neighbor** of the deceased **and** the other, his **relative, what is the law?**

RASHI

ההוא דאמר להו — בצוואת מיתה: נכסי לטוביה, ולא פירש לאיזה טוביה. דגיס ביה — רגיל אצלו, ומגו דגייסי אהדדי — קורא לו בשמו כאילו לא נסמך. תלמיד חכם קודם — דמסתמא אדם מצדיק מעשיו לזכות בשעת מיתה, דאמר מר (ברכות לד,ב): כל הנביאים לא נתנבאו אלא למהנה תלמידי חכמים מנכסיו.

NOTES

תַּלְמִיד חָכָם קוֹדֵם **The Torah scholar takes precedence.** *Rashi* explains that the Torah scholar is not given precedence, because he has preferential rights, but rather because we assume that the dying person wished to perform a good deed with his money, so he instructed that his property be given to a Torah scholar.

שָׁכֵן וְקָרוֹב **A neighbor and a relative.** *Rosh* and *Talmidei Rabbenu Yonah* note that when the Gemara speaks of a neighbor, it does not refer to someone living in the physical proximity of the deceased, but rather someone with whom he had an established business relationship. The verse cited by the Gemara, which speaks of a "close neighbor," supports this understanding, for one is not necessarily close with one's nearest physical neighbors.

HALAKHAH

נְכָסַיי לְטוּבִיָּה **My property to Toviyah.** "If a dying man left instructions that his property be given to Toviyah, and he died, and a person named Toviyah came to claim the property, the claimant is given the property, even if there are other Toviyahs whom the deceased might have had in mind. If the claimant was known as Rav Toviyah, he is not given the property, unless the deceased had been so familiar with him that he would have called him Toviyah. If two people named Toviyah came to collect the property, and one of them was a Torah scholar, the Torah scholar is given precedence to receive the property. If neither was a Torah scholar, but one was a relative or a neighbor, he

TRANSLATION AND COMMENTARY

תָּא שְׁמַע [1]The Gemara answers: **Come and hear** a solution to this problem from the verse which states (Proverbs 27:10): **"A neighbor near by is better than a brother far away."** We assume that the deceased had his neighbor in mind.

שְׁנֵיהֶם [2]The Gemara concludes this discussion with the following ruling: If two people came to collect the property, and **both** claimants **are relatives** of the deceased **or both are neighbors or both are** Torah scholars, [3]**the judges** use **their discretion** in deciding which of the two claimants should receive the property.

אֲמַר לֵיהּ [4]The Gemara now considers a new topic of discussion: **Rava said to the son of Rav Hiyya the son of Avin:** [5]**Come, I will tell you a fine** point of the law **that your father said:** [6]**Shmuel said: If a creditor sold a promissory note to his fellow, and** the creditor **then waived** the debtor's repayment of the debt, the debt **was waived.** This is because when a creditor assigns a debt to another person, he does not transfer the obligations of the debtor to him, but merely empowers him to collect the debt on his behalf and keep the proceeds. Thus, even if the creditor "sells" the debt, the debtor's obligation is to him and not to the buyer. Therefore he retains the right to cancel the debtor's obligation. [7]Not only the creditor himself, but **even his**

LITERAL TRANSLATION

[1]Come [and] hear: "A neighbor near is better than a brother far away."

[2][If] both of them are relatives or both of them are neighbors or both of them are scholars, [3]the discretion of the judges.

[4]Rava said to the son of Rav Hiyya the son of Avin: [5]Come, I will tell you a fine thing that your father used to say: [6]That which Shmuel said: [If] someone sold a promissory note to his fellow and then he waived it, it is waived, [7]and even an heir

תָּא שְׁמַע: "טוֹב שָׁכֵן קָרוֹב מֵאָח רָחוֹק". [2]שְׁנֵיהֶם קְרוֹבִים וּשְׁנֵיהֶם שְׁכֵנִים וּשְׁנֵיהֶם חֲכָמִים, [3]שׁוּדָא דְּדַיָּינֵי. [4]אֲמַר לֵיהּ רָבָא לִבְרֵיהּ דְּרַב חִיָּיא בַּר אָבִין: [5]תָּא, אֵימָא לָךְ מִילְּתָא מַעֲלְיְּיתָא דַּהֲוָה אָמַר אֲבוּךְ: [6]הָא דַּאֲמַר שְׁמוּאֵל: הַמּוֹכֵר שְׁטַר חוֹב לַחֲבֵירוֹ וְחָזַר וּמְחָלוֹ, מָחוּל, [7]וַאֲפִילוּ יוֹרֵשׁ

RASHI

שׁוּדָא דְּדַיָּינֵי = הַטָּלַת הַדַּיָּינִים. לְפִי מַה שֶּׁיִּרְאוּ דַּיָּינִים שֶׁהָיָה דַּרְכּוֹ שֶׁל מֵת לְקָרֵב אֶת זֶה יוֹתֵר מִזֶּה, אוֹ מִי שֶׁבִּשְׁנֵיהֶן טוֹב וְנוֹהֵג בְּדֶרֶךְ יְשָׁרָה, שָׁם לוֹמַר בּוֹ נָתְכַּוֵּין הַמֵּת לִזְכּוֹת. שׁוּדָא — כְּמוֹ "שָׂדִי בְּיַמָּא" (שמות טו) דִמְתַרְגְּמִינַן "יְרָה בִיס" הֵטִיל בְּיַם. וְחָזַר וּמְחָלוֹ — הַמּוֹכֵר, שֶׁהוּא מַלְוֶה, מְחָלוֹ לַלֹּוֶה. מָחוּל — דְּאָמַר לֵיהּ לוֹ לַלּוֹקֵחַ: לָאו בַּעַל דְּבָרִים דִּידִי אַתְּ. וַאֲפִילוּ יוֹרֵשׁ — שֶׁל מַלְוֶה מוֹחֵל.

NOTES

שׁוּדָא דְּדַיָּינֵי **The discretion of the judges.** *Rashi* explains that this expression means that the judges should assess to the best of their abilities to whom the deceased would have been more likely to bestow his property, based on the character of each of the claimants, and their relationship with the deceased. *Rivan, Rid,* and apparently *Rambam* as well, accept this explanation. But many Rishonim follow *Rabbenu Tam* who understands that "discretion" here means an arbitrary assignment of the property. Support for this position is brought from some readings of the Jerusalem Talmud, according to which שודא is a contracted form of the word שוחדא, bribe. Thus the assignment is made arbitrarily and not on the basis of logical assessment.

הַמּוֹכֵר שְׁטַר חוֹב לַחֲבֵירוֹ וְחָזַר וּמְחָלוֹ **If someone sold a promissory note to his fellow and then he waived it.**

Various explanations have been offered to justify the validity of the release granted by the original creditor after selling the bill of indebtedness. Most Rishonim (including *Rambam, Rashba, Ran,* and *Meiri*) follow *Rabbenu Tam* who says that the release is valid because it is only by Rabbinic enactment that a bill of indebtedness can be sold. By Torah law, a debt, being intangible cannot be transferred to a third party. When a creditor sells a promissory note, he does not really sell the debt, but rather he empowers the purchaser to collect the debt in his stead. Since the debt remains a personal obligation of the debtor to the creditor, the creditor retains the right to release the debtor from that obligation. (See *Tosafot* who cite this explanation and raise objections against it.) The Rishonim cite another explanation in the name of *Rabbenu Tam,* according to which every

HALAKHAH

is given precedence over the other claimant. If one of the two was a relative, and the other was a neighbor (a friend who had business dealings with the deceased; *Rema* in the name of *Tur*), the property is given to the neighbor. If both claimants were Torah scholars, or relatives, or neighbors, the judges should use their discretion in deciding which of the two the deceased had in mind," following the Gemara. (*Rambam, Sefer Kinyan, Hilkhot Zekhiyah* 11:2-3; *Shulḥan Arukh, Ḥoshen Mishpat* 253:29.)

הַמּוֹכֵר שְׁטַר חוֹב לַחֲבֵירוֹ וְחָזַר וּמְחָלוֹ **If someone sold a promissory note to his fellow and then he waived it.** "If

a creditor sold a promissory note to another person, and later released the debtor from his obligation to repay the debt, the release is valid. The creditor can release the debtor from his obligation, even if he had stipulated with the buyer that he would not be able to do so. Not only the creditor himself, but even his heir can release the debtor from his obligation to repay the debt, following Shmuel. A person cannot release a debt to himself, in order to cause a loss to the buyer. How so? If someone lent money to his son sold the debt to another person, and then died, the son who inherits the right to release his father's debtors cannot

TRANSLATION AND COMMENTARY

heir can waive the debt. Now, regarding Shmuel's ruling, Rav Ḥiyya the son of Avin said: Shmuel's ruling is limited to the sale of a promissory note to a third party. [1]But even **Shmuel agrees** that if **a woman** entering marriage **brought her husband a promissory note** drawn to her favor, [2]**and then she waived** the debtor's obligation to repay, **the release is not valid,** [3]**for** after a woman is married, her husband's **rights** to her property **are like her rights** to that property. Therefore, she can no longer release the debtor from his obligation.

קְרִיבָתֵיהּ דְּרַב נַחְמָן [4]It was reported that **a relative of Rav Naḥman sold her ketubah** to another person **at a discounted price** while she was still married. A person who buys a ketubah from a married woman is not willing to pay her the full amount recorded in the ketubah, for he will only collect that amount if the woman is divorced or widowed. If the woman predeceases her husband, the buyer will not receive anything. [5]As it turned out, the woman **was divorced,** entitling him to collect the ketubah settlement, but **she died** shortly thereafter, and her right to receive the settlement passed to her daughter. [6]The purchaser of the ketubah then **came and demanded it from her daughter.** [7]**Rav Naḥman said to** those around him: **Is there nobody** here

מוֹחֵל. [1]מוֹדֶה שְׁמוּאֵל בְּמַכְנֶסֶת שְׁטַר חוֹב לְבַעְלָהּ, [2]וְחָזְרָה וּמְחַלְתּוֹ, שֶׁאֵינוֹ מָחוּל, [3]מִפְּנֵי שֶׁיָּדוֹ כְּיָדָהּ.

[4]קְרִיבָתֵיהּ דְּרַב נַחְמָן זְבִינְתָּהּ לִכְתוּבָּתָהּ בְּטוֹבַת הֲנָאָה. [5]אִיגַּרְשָׁה, וּשְׁכִיבָה. [6]אָתוּ קָא תַּבְעֵי לָהּ לִבְרַתָּהּ. [7]אֲמַר לְהוּ רַב נַחְמָן: לֵיכָּא דְּלִיסְבָּא לָהּ

LITERAL TRANSLATION

can waive it. [1]Shmuel agrees [regarding] a woman who brought in a promissory note to her husband, [2]and then she waived it, [3]that it is not waived, for his rights (lit., "hand") are like her rights.

[4]A relative of Rav Naḥman sold her ketubah at a discount (lit., "a benefit of pleasure"). [5]She was divorced, and she died. [6][The purchaser] came [and] demanded it from her daughter. [7]Rav Naḥman said to them: Is there nobody to give her

RASHI

זבינתה לכתובתה — מכרה שעבוד כתובתה לאחרים, בעודה תחת בעלה.

בטובת הנאה — דבר מועט שאינו אלא כחיזוק טובה, שקורין *גרי״ד מפיק רצון ולפי שהלוקח מטיל מעותיו בספק — שמא תמות היא בחיי בעלה — מפחד, ואינו לוקחה אלא בדמים מועטים. הכי גרסינן: **אתו תבעי לה לברתה** — אתו לקוחות וקא תבעי לה לברתה, הבאה לגבות כתובת אמה מאביה, ולירש הכתובה מכח אמה. ואלו באין ליטול אותה הימנה, לומר: אמך מכרה לנו.

LANGUAGE (RASHI)

גרי״ד* From the Old French *gred,* meaning "favor."

NOTES

creditor has two claims on his debtor: the right to collect from his person, and the right to collect from his property. When a creditor sells a promissory note, he sells only the lien on the debtor's property, but the debtor's personal obligation cannot be transferred. Thus, the creditor can always release the debtor from his personal obligation, upon which the lien on his property is also cancelled. *Rav Tzemaḥ Gaon* and *Rabbenu Ḥananel* suggest that the creditor's release is only valid when he says that he examined his records and found that the debtor does not owe him the entire sum in the promissory note or thinks that he may have paid it. (See *Rif, Ramban,* and *Rid,* who raise objections against this position.)

מִפְּנֵי שֶׁיָּדוֹ כְּיָדָהּ **For his rights are like her rights.** Even though Rava himself stated above (83a) that a husband's rights are even stronger than his wife's rights, that was said with respect to his rights to property that she brought into the marriage. But here Rava means to say that once a woman is married, his hand is like her hand and his mouth is like her mouth, so that her release of her debtor from his obligation is not valid unless it is done together with her husband, just as his release of her debtor would not be valid unless she participates in that release. (*Maharshal,* following *Rif*).

תַּבְעֵי לָהּ לִבְרַתָּהּ **They demanded it from her daughter.** The Rishonim ask: Why did the party who bought the ketubah come and demand the settlement from the deceased woman's daughter? He should have gone to her

HALAKHAH

release himself from payment and argue that he should not be liable for the loss which he caused the buyer. Rather he must repay the debt in full to the buyer. There are those who disagree and say that a person can release a debt even to himself." Regarding the creditor's liability for the loss that he causes the buyer due to his releasing the debtor from his obligation to repay the debt, see below. (*Rambam, Sefer Kinyan, Hilkhot Mekhirah* 6:12; *Shulḥan Arukh, Ḥoshen Mishpat* 66:23.)

בְּמַכְנֶסֶת שְׁטַר חוֹב לְבַעְלָהּ, וְחָזְרָה וּמְחַלְתּוֹ **A woman who brought in promissory note to her husband, and then she waived it.** "If a woman was a creditor before marriage — whether the debt was established orally or it had been committed to writing — or if she lent out money after marriage, she cannot release her debtor from his obligation, for the woman does not have proprietary rights independent of her husband, even in her *milog* property." (*Rambam, Sefer Kinyan, Hilkhot Mekhirah* 6:13; *Shulḥan Arukh, Ḥoshen Mishpat* 66:28.)

קְרִיבָתֵיהּ דְּרַב נַחְמָן **A relative of Rav Naḥman.** "If a woman sold her ketubah while she was married, and then her husband died, and then she died, the heirs can waive their right to their mother's ketubah and thus cancel the sale, even if the husband had no other heirs and it turns out that the heirs released the ketubah obligation to themselves." (*Shulḥan Arukh, Even HaEzer* 105:6.)

TRANSLATION AND COMMENTARY

to advise the daughter [86A] **to go and release** her father from his obligation to pay **her mother's ketubah** settlement? Since a ketubah is a bill of indebtedness, if a man's wife sells her ketubah, she can release her husband from his obligation and deprive the buyer of his right to collect the sum recorded in the ketubah. As Shmuel said, not only the creditor himself, but even his heir can release the debtor from his obligation. In our case, it would be to the daughter's advantage to release her father from paying her mother's ketubah settlement, for that would prevent the money from passing to the buyer. Even though she too would be deprived of her mother's ketubah settlement temporarily, upon her father's death, she will **inherit** it from him. [1]The daughter **heard** what Rav Naḥman **said** and immediately **went and released** her father from his obligation to pay **it.** After considering what he had done, [2]**Rav Naḥman said: We have acted as lawyers.**

מֵעִיקָּרָא [3]The Gemara asks: **At first** when Rav Naḥman suggested counseling his relative **what** position **did he maintain, and in the end** when he regretted for having offered such advice, **what** position **did he maintain?**

מֵעִיקָּרָא סָבַר [4]The Gemara explains: **At first,** Rav Naḥman **maintained:** The verse states (Isaiah 58:7): **"And do not hide yourself from your own flesh,"** which teaches that one must come to the assistance of one's relatives.

עֵצָה [86A] תֵּיזִיל וְתֵיחֲלָה לִכְתוּבָּתָהּ דְּאִמָּהּ לְגַבֵּי אֲבוּהּ, וְתֵירְתָהּ מִינֵּיהּ? [1]שָׁמְעָה, אָזְלָה, אַחֵילְתָהּ. [2]אָמַר רַב נַחְמָן: עָשִׂינוּ עַצְמֵינוּ כְּעוֹרְכֵי הַדַּיָּינִין.

[3]מֵעִיקָּרָא מַאי סְבַר, וּלְבַסּוֹף מַאי סְבַר?

[4]מֵעִיקָּרָא סְבַר: "וּמִבְּשָׂרְךָ לֹא

LITERAL TRANSLATION

advice [86A] to go and waive her mother's ketubah [settlement] in favor of (lit., "towards") her father, and inherit it from him? [1]She heard, went, [and] waived [it]. [2]Rav Naḥman said: We have acted (lit., "made ourselves") as lawyers.

[3]At first what did he maintain, and at the end what did he maintain?

[4]At first he maintained: "And do not hide yourself from your own flesh."

RASHI

תיזיל ותיחלה כו׳ — דאמרינן: אפילו יורש מוחל, ואמה של זו מכרה להן שטר חוב שהיה לה על בעלה. **עשינו עצמינו** — כקרוב של בעל דין, או אוהבו, הבא אצל דיינין ועורכו בראיות אחר זכות אוהבו או קרובו. כך למדתי עצה לזו להפסיד שכנגדה. **מעיקרא** — כשאמר כן. **לבסוף** — כשנתחרט.

BACKGROUND

כְּעוֹרְכֵי הַדַּיָּינִין As lawyers. Rav Naḥman's words refer to a Mishnah that states: "Do not make yourself like the lawyers" (*Avot* 1:5). It should be recalled that in Jewish courts, as opposed to Greek and Roman courts, there were no attorneys. Moreover, the court always wanted to hear the basic claims of the litigants, without the intervention of legal counsel to give them another form. Attorneys were regarded as miscarriers of justice, because they instructed litigants about what claims to present rather than simply present matters as they saw them. Much of the Jewish conception of justice is based on the assumption that people who come to court are not aware of the legal consequences arising from their claims (as in the argument based on *"miggo,"* the advantageous claim a litigant might have raised, had he been willing to lie). Moreover, when legal counsel is given to one party, it necessarily causes some injustice to the other one.

TERMINOLOGY

מֵעִיקָּרָא מַאי סְבַר וּלְבַסּוֹף מַאי סְבַר? At first what did he maintain, and at the end what did he maintain? In cases where a scholar changes his mind, the Talmud may ask what the Rabbi's reasoning was initially, and why he later changed his opinion. As in this case Rav Naḥman obviously wanted to advice her relative, and then regretted it.

NOTES

husband who was liable for the obligation! *Rashi* explains that the buyer knew that the daughter was planning to collect her mother's settlement from her father. He went to the daughter either to collect it if it had already been received, and if not, to inform the daughter that he had purchased the ketubah. *Ritva* suggests that the daughter was her mother's ketubah deed, and the buyer went to demand that she deliver it to him so that he can go and collect from the husband. *Rabbenu Zeraḥyah Halevi* explains that the husband also died, and all of his property was inherited by the daughter, so the buyer had to go to her to collect. According to this understanding, when the Gemara states that the daughter should "go and waive her mother's ketubah to her father," it means that she should concede the ketubah settlement to her father's estate.

תֵּיזִיל וְתֵיחֲלָה To go and waive. All the Rishonim ask: What does the daughter gain by releasing her father from his obligation to pay her mother's ketubah settlement? As we will learn below, according to those that say a person is liable for indirect damage that he causes — a position maintained by Rav Naḥman himself — the creditor who releases his debtor from repayment must compensate a third party to whom he may have sold the promissory note. Thus, if the daughter takes Rav Naḥman's advice, she will have to compensate the purchaser for his loss! *Ri* (cited by *Tosafot*) and others answer that the daughter will only have to pay the discounted price that purchaser actually paid for the ketubah, the daughter gaining the difference between the full value of the ketubah and the price that the purchaser had paid for it. *Tosafot* and others suggest that in this case the daughter was a minor who was old enough to release her father from his obligation to pay her mother's ketubah settlement, but not old enough to be liable for the damage which she causes, directly or indirectly. Alternatively, the daughter was a married woman, from whom damages cannot be collected while she is married (*Ramban, Ra'ah*). *Rid* suggests that the daughter had no assets of her own from which the purchaser could have collected damages, and she had arranged with her father that he would give her her mother's ketubah settlement as a gift on the condition that it not be subject to collection (in which case, the money she holds would revert ot the father if the purchaser would attempt to collect it) or that the father would give it to her little by little so that she would never accumulate a sum large enough for the purchaser to collect. *Ra'avad* answers that a person who waives a debt that had already been sold to another person is only liable for indirect damages if he waived it in order to damage the purchaser. But here the daughter waives the ketubah settlement for her own benefit, so that she will inherit it from her father. *Ramban* cites others who argue that only the creditor himself is liable for the indirect damage caused by then waiving the debt, but the creditor's heirs are not liable for their waving it. *Ramban* rejects these last two positions, suggesting instead that perhaps Rav Naḥman made his suggestion only in order to convince the purchaser to reach a compromise with the daughter.

וּמִבְּשָׂרְךָ לֹא תִתְעַלָּם And do not hide yourself from your own flesh. *Ritva* writes that the daughter must have been a poor woman, and when Rav Naḥman advised her to

TRANSLATION AND COMMENTARY

[1]**And in the end,** Rav Naḥman **maintained:** Despite the importance of helping one's relatives, **an important person** like himself **is different,** and a Rabbinic authority must avoid even the appearance of impropriety.

גּוּפָא [2]Having made reference to the position of Shmuel, the Gemara now **returns to** it in greater detail: **Shmuel said: If** a creditor **sold a promissory note to his fellow, and** the creditor **then waived** the debtor's repayment of the debt, **the debt was waived.** Not only the creditor himself, [3]but **even** his **heir can waive** the debtor's obligation. Consequently, the third party who purchases the promissory note finds himself in a very vulnerable position. But there is a way for the buyer to overcome the difficulty, [4]as **Rav Huna the son of Rav Yehoshua said: If** the purchaser of the debt **is clever** and wishes to protect himself, [5]**he should jingle** some money **before the debtor, and** thereby convince him to **write a** new promissory **note** that is drawn up **in his name.** He now no longer needs the old note to collect his debt and has protected his rights.

אֲמַר אֲמֵימָר [6]Elsewhere (*Bava Kamma* 100a), the Sages disagree about whether or not a person is liable for indirect damage. This dispute has ramifications regarding the case of the creditor who sold a promissory note and subsequently released the debtor from his obligation to repay the debt. **Amemar said: The authority who maintains that a person is liable for indirect damage** [7]**would make** the creditor **pay** to the party who purchased the bill of indebtedness from him **the full value of the bill.** For when the creditor released the debtor from his obligation, he prevented the purchaser from recovering the debt. Even though the creditor

תִתְעַלָּם״. [1]וּלְבַסּוֹף סְבַר: אָדָם חָשׁוּב שָׁאנֵי.

[2]גּוּפָא: אֲמַר שְׁמוּאֵל: הַמּוֹכֵר שְׁטָר חוֹב לַחֲבֵירוֹ וְחָזַר וּמְחָלוֹ, מָחוּל, [3]וַאֲפִילּוּ יוֹרֵשׁ מוֹחֵל.

[4]אֲמַר רַב הוּנָא בְּרֵיהּ דְּרַב יְהוֹשֻׁעַ: וְאִי פִּקֵּחַ הוּא, [5]מְקַרְקֵשׁ לֵיהּ זוּזֵי, וְכָתַב לֵיהּ שְׁטָרָא בִּשְׁמֵיהּ.

[6]אֲמַר אֲמֵימָר: מַאן דְּדָאֵין דִּינָא דְּגַרְמֵי [7]מַגְבֵּי בֵּיהּ דְּמֵי שְׁטָרָא

LITERAL TRANSLATION

[1]And at the end he maintained: An important person is different.

[2]Returning to the above (lit., "the thing itself"): Shmuel said: [If] someone sold a promissory note to his fellow and then he waived it, it is waived, [3]and even an heir can waive it. [4]Rav Huna the son of Rav Yehoshua said: And if [the purchaser] is clever, [5]he should jingle coins [before the debtor], and he will write for [the purchaser] a note in his name.

[6]Amemar said: The one who maintains (lit., "judges") that there is liability for indirect damage [7]makes him pay the full value.

RASHI

אדם חשוב שאני — לפי שלמדין הימנו, ויש שיעשו אף שלא לקרובים. **ואי פקח הוא** — הלוקח. **מקרקש ליה זוזי** — ללוה, ושוכרו בהן לכתוב לו שטר חוב בשמו, קודם שיעשו קנוניא בין שניהם. **מאן דדאין דינא דגרמי** — המחייב את הגורם הפסד לחבירו. **מגבי ביה** — בהאי שטרא, מן המוחלו. **דמי שטרא**

LANGUAGE

מְקַרְקֵשׁ **Jingle.** This word, which is apparently onomatopoetic, means "making noise by shaking something."

SAGES

אֲמֵימָר **Amemar.** A Babylonian Amora of the fifth and sixth generations. See *Ketubot*, Part II, pp. 111-12.

NOTES

release her father from his obligation to pay out her mother's ketubah settlement, he must have told her that she must return to the buyer whatever he had paid for the ketubah. Otherwise he should not have advised the woman to cause the buyer a loss, even if she was his relative.

אָדָם חָשׁוּב שָׁאנֵי **An important person is different.** A respected scholar like Rav Naḥman should have been especially careful to avoid even the appearance of impropriety, so as not to lead people to think that he permitted his relative to cause the purchaser a loss and thereby result in a profanation of God's name (see previous note). Furthermore, others might ignore the special circumstances of the case, and infer from Rav Naḥman's actions that it is permissible to advise someone involved in a litigation, even if he is not a close relative (*Talmidei Rabbenu Yonah*).

מְקַרְקֵשׁ לֵיהּ זוּזֵי **He should jingle coins.** *Ritva* explains that the buyer should have the debtor write him a note promising to pay him the debt recorded in the original promissory note. Such a note establishes a new lien on the debtor's property from the day that it was drawn up, a lien that can no longer be cancelled by the creditor's waiver. However, the original creditor can still waive first the promissory note and its lien, preventing the purchaser from collecting from property sold between the dates on the two notes.

מַגְבֵּי בֵּיהּ דְּמֵי שְׁטָרָא מַעַלְיָא **Makes him to collect the full value of the bill.** According to some Geonim and Rishonim (see *Ri*, cited by *Tosafot*), the creditor is only liable for the

HALAKHAH

מְקַרְקֵשׁ לֵיהּ זוּזֵי **He should jingle coins.** "If a person bought a promissory note, and wishes to protect himself from a loss, he should persuade the debtor to either draw up a new note in his favor or to accept payment of the debt to the purchaser, which obligation he assumes by means of a valid mode of acquisition or in front of witnesses. Then the seller of the note will no longer be able to forgive the purchaser's right to collect." (*Shulḥan Arukh, Ḥoshen Mishpat* 66:23.)

מַגְבֵּי בֵּיהּ דְּמֵי שְׁטָרָא מַעַלְיָא **He collects with it the full value of the bill.** "A person is liable for the indirect damage he causes, following Rabbi Meir. Therefore, if a

SAGES

רַפְרָם Rafram. A Babylonian Amora of the six and seventh generations. See *Ketubot*, Part III, p. 127.

רַב אַשִׁי Rav Ashi. A sixth-generation Babylonian Amora. See *Ketubot*, Part I, p. 14.

BACKGROUND

כִּי כְּשׁוּרָא לְצַלְמֵי Like a beam for woodcarvers. This expression means, like a beam used to sculpt a form, which must be without flaws. It is used to express something done perfectly, without omitting anything.

TRANSLATION AND COMMENTARY

did not cause the other person any direct damage the loss which he indirectly caused him to suffer falls under the category of indirect damage for which a person is liable. [1]**The authority who does not maintain that a person is liable for indirect damage** [2]**would only make** the creditor pay him **the value of the paper** on which **the promissory note was written,** for that is the extent of the direct damage that he caused. [3]**There was an incident** in which a person caused a billholder indirect damage by making it impossible for him to recover his debt. The case was brought before Rav Ashi for a ruling, **and** through the force of his arguments **Rafram coerced Rav Ashi** into accepting the position that a person is liable for indirect damage which he causes. [4]Rav Ashi then **made** the defendant **pay** full compensation, exacting money from him with precision **similar to** the way a person selects **a beam** that is to be used **for** decorative **woodcarvings.**

מַעַלְיָא. [1]מַאן דְּלָא דָּאֵין דִּינָא דְּגַרְמֵי [2]מַגְבֵּי בֵּיהּ דְּמֵי נְיָירָא בְּעָלְמָא. [3]הֲוָה עוּבְדָא וְכַפְיֵיהּ רַפְרָם לְרַב אַשִׁי, [4]וְאַגְבֵּי בֵּיהּ כִּי כְּשׁוּרָא לְצַלְמֵי.

LITERAL TRANSLATION

[1]The one who does not maintain (lit., "judges") that there is liability for indirect damage [2]makes him pay only the value of the paper. [3]There was an incident, and Rafram coerced Rav Ashi, [4]and he made him pay like a beam for woodcarvers.

RASHI

מעליא – כל החוב שבתוכו. **ומאן דלא דאין כו׳** – פלוגתייהו בבבא קמא, בפרק בתרא (קטז,ב) ורבי מאיר אית ליה דינא דגרמי, כדתניא (שם, קב): נתייאש הימנה ולא גדרה – הרי זה קידש, וחייב באחריותו גבי כלאים. וקיימא לאן כוותיה. **מגבי ביה דמי ניירא בעלמא** – כלומר, אומר שלא מכר לו אלא הנייר, והרי הוא בידך. **כפייה רפרם לרב אשי** – שבא הדין לפני רב אשי, וסיבבו והקיפו בראיות ואגבי מדינא דגרמי. **כי בשורא לצלמי** – כלומר: גיבוי גמור, כל ההפסד. דקדק בו כאשר ידקדק הלוקח קורה לצור בה צורות, שלוקח ישרה וחלקה.

NOTES

amount which the purchaser actually paid for the promissory note, for that is the extent of the damage that he caused him. But *Rav Hai Gaon, Rabbenu Ḥananel, Rashi, Ramban* and many other Rishonim maintain that the creditor is liable for the full amount recorded in the promissory note. Some of these Rishonim note that the creditor is only liable for the full amount if the purchaser could actually have collected that sum from the debtor. Thus, in determining the creditor's liability, we must take into consideration the expenses that the purchaser would have incurred in collecting the debt (such as having to sell the debtor's field) as well whether the debtor had sufficient assets from which the debt could have been collected (*Ramban, Ra'ah, Ritva*).

דְּמֵי נְיָירָא בְּעָלְמָא Only the value of the paper. *Rashi* and others understand that according to the opinion that a person is not liable for indirect damage, the creditor who sells a promissory note and then waives the debt pays the purchaser nothing. The Gemara that says here that he pays the value of the paper on which the promissory note is written is merely borrowing a phrase used in a different case, in which a person burned someone else's promissory note and is in fact liable for the value of the paper (*Bava Kamma* 98a). In our case, the expression simply means that the bill remains in the purchaser's hands and that is all he gets. *Ramban* and others explain that according to those that do not collect indirect damages, the creditor must indeed pay the purchaser the value of the paper, for that is the value of the loss which he caused him. Before the creditor waived his debt the promissory note was like a pledge held by the purchaser "ensuring" his right to collect. But when the creditor waived the debt, the purchaser became obligated to return the promissory note to the debtor. Thus, the creditor caused the purchaser a direct loss, just as if he had burned the bill of indebtedness with his own hands.

כְּשׁוּרָא לְצַלְמֵי A beam for woodcarvers. *Rashi* explains that Rav Ashi acted in the same precise manner as a person who selects a perfectly straight and smooth beam for wood carvings. Rav Ashi scrupulously made the defendant pay full compensation for the damage that he caused. Similarly, *Rivan* explains that Rav Ashi collected full compensation without the slightest deviation, as straight as a beam used by woodcarvers. The Geonim explain that the wooden beam mentioned here was used for a lintel, which is usually decorated with carvings.

Ritva understands that the Gemara means that Rav Ashi collected compensation from land of the highest quality, as he would collect compensation from any other tortfeasor. *Ra'avad* explains that just as in the case of a carved beam, a person pays not only for the beam, but for the carvings as well, so too here Rav Ashi collected compensation for the full sum that was recorded in the bill of indebtedness, not merely what the purchaser had paid for it.

According to all these explanations — which were followed in our commentary — a case was brought before Rav Ashi for adjudication and he hesitated about issuing a decision until Rafram coerced him to collect compensation for indirect damage. An entirely different explanation of this passage has also been suggested: Rav Ashi himself caused damage to certain engravings on a beam, and Rafram ordered him to pay for the damage (*Arukh* of *Rash ben Gama*).

HALAKHAH

creditor sold a promissory note drawn to his favor and then the creditor waived the debt to the debtor, the waiver is valid, but the creditor is obligated to compensate the buyer for the damage by paying him the entire sum recorded in the bill from land of the best quality," following Amemar and Rafram. (*Rambam, Sefer Nezikin, Hilkhot Ḥovel U'Mazzik* 7:10; *Shulḥan Arukh, Ḥoshen Mishpat* 386:1.)

TRANSLATION AND COMMENTARY

אֲמַר אַמֵימָר [1]**Amemar said in the name of Rav Ḥama:** If **someone** with an outstanding debt divorced his wife and **is** now obligated to pay both **the woman's ketubah settlement and** a loan to his **creditor,** [2]**and** the debtor **has land and money,** [3]**we** tell him to settle his obligation to **the creditor with money, and** his obligation to **the woman with land.** [4]The creditor receives the money **in accordance** with what is due **him.** He lent out money and is repaid with money. The woman receives the land **in accordance with what** is due **her.** Since the husband in return for her agreement to marry him, obligated himself to pay his wife's ketubah settlement, and she relied on the lien on his land to insure payment of the ketubah, she gets the land.

וְאִי לָא [5]The Gemara now discusses a special case where the creditor and the woman come with identical liens on the debtors property, the promissory note and ketubah having the same date. **And if** in such a case, the man has no money and **only one parcel of land,** which **is sufficient** to settle **only one** of these obligations, [6]the land is **given to the creditor,** and **it is not given to the woman.** [7]**What is the reason?** The Rabbis enacted that the creditor should be given preferential treatment so that a lender not bolt his door to a potential borrower and refuse to extend him a loan. However, the Rabbis were not concerned that giving preferential treatment to the husband's creditor would deter women from marriage, [8]for **more than a man desires to marry, a woman desires to be married.**

[1]אֲמַר אַמֵימָר מִשְּׁמֵיהּ דְּרַב חָמָא: הַאי מַאן דְּאִיכָּא עֲלֵיהּ כְּתוּבַּת אִשָּׁה וּבַעַל חוֹב, [2]וְאִית לֵיהּ אַרְעָא וְאִית לֵיהּ זוּזֵי — [3]לְבַעַל חוֹב מְסַלְּקִינַן לֵיהּ בְּזוּזֵי, לְאִשָּׁה מְסַלְּקִינַן לָהּ בְּאַרְעָא. [4]הַאי כִּי דִּינֵיהּ וְהַאי כִּי דִּינֵיהּ. [5]וְאִי לָא אִיכָּא אֶלָּא חַד אַרְעָא וְלָא חַזְיָא אֶלָּא לְחַד — [6]לְבַעַל חוֹב יָהֲבִינַן לֵיהּ, לְאִשָּׁה לָא יָהֲבִינַן לָהּ. [7]מַאי טַעְמָא? [8]יוֹתֵר מִמַּה שֶּׁהָאִישׁ רוֹצֶה לִישָּׂא, אִשָּׁה רוֹצָה לְהִנָּשֵׂא.

LITERAL TRANSLATION

[1]Amemar said in the name of Rav Ḥama: Someone upon whom [rests the claims of] a woman's ketubah and a creditor, [2]and he has land, and he has money — the creditor, [3]we dismiss him with money, [and] the woman, we dismiss her with land. [4]This in accordance with his law, and this in accordance with [her] law.

[5]And if there is only one [parcel of] land, and it is sufficient for only one — [6]to the creditor we give it, to the woman we do not give it. [7]What is the reason? [8]More than a man desires to marry, a woman desires to be married.

RASHI

האי כי דיניה – זה הלוה מעות, וזו סמכה על שיעבוד הקרקע, והיא לא נתנה כלום. ואם בשביל נכסי צאן ברזל הנישומין בכתובה – הוא זכה בהן מיד, וזו צירפתן עם הכתובה על שיעבוד הקרקע. ולא חזיא אלא לחד – אין בה אלא כדי לאחד מהן. לבעל חוב יהבינן – שלא תנעול דלת. יותר משהאיש רוצה כו' – ולא חיישינן לומר משום חינא. ודוקא שהשטרות נכתבו ביום אחד, אבל אם קדמה זמן הכתובה – היא גובה.

SAGES

רַב חָמָא **Rav Ḥama.** A fifth-generation Babylonian Amora, Rav Ḥama came from Neharde'a and was apparently a student of Rava, although he may also have studied with Rava's teachers. After the death of Rav Naḥman bar Yitzḥak, Rav Ḥama served as the head of the Pumbedita Yeshivah for more than twenty years. Rav Ḥama was apparently a "scholar in residence" in the House of the Exilarch, which followed his Halakhic rulings. He also seems to have maintained contact with King Shapur of Persia. Thus, it was only natural that people who did business on his behalf benefited from his patronage.

BACKGROUND

יוֹתֵר מִמַּה שֶּׁהָאִישׁ רוֹצֶה וכו׳ **More than a man desires etc.** In comparing the status of the lender and that of the wife, one must remember that the lender in question extends a loan without interest, and without receiving any other profit. The lender is thus doing the borrower a great favor, and he must be encouraged by being reassured that he will not lose his property by extending the loan. Otherwise he and other potential lenders will not help needy people. Conversely, there was an assumption that women were more interested in marriage than men, for psychological, economic, and other reasons. Therefore, even if it should happen that, in some instance, a woman might not receive her settlement, this will not deter other women from marriage.

NOTES

וְלָא חַזְיָא אֶלָּא לְחַד **And it is fit for only one.** Like *Rashi,* most Rishonim explain that in this case the man had no money, and only one parcel of land, which did not suffice to settle both obligations, his wife's ketubah settlement and his debt. *Ritva* suggests an entirely different explanation: The man had one parcel of land whose value would have sufficed for both obligations, but the property was not fit to be divided between them, for when a small field is reparcelled its total value drops. Thus the question arose as which of the two would receive the land and then compensate the other with money.

לְבַעַל חוֹב יָהֲבִינַן **To the creditor we give it.** According to *Rashi* and *Rabbenu Ḥananel,* Amemar had to decide a case in which the man became indebted to his wife and his creditor on the same day, so that neither enjoys a preferential right of lien. The law follows the position of Shmuel (see *Ketubot* 94a) that if someone sold the same field to two different people, and two bills of sale for that field were issued on the same day, we do not say that the two buyers should divide the field, but rather that the judges use their discretion to deciding which party should be given title to the property. Amemar establishes that our

HALAKHAH

כְּתוּבַּת אִשָּׁה וּבַעַל חוֹב **A woman's ketubah and a creditor.** "If someone divorced his wife and is now obligated to pay the woman her ketubah settlement, and he had also borrowed money and is now obligated to repay his creditor, and he has land and money which together suffice to cover both obligations, he repays the creditor with the money, and he pays the ketubah settlement with the land. If the man only has land, and that land does not suffice to cover both obligations, and neither the woman nor the creditor enjoys a preferential right of lien, the land is given to the creditor, and if anything is left over, it is given to the woman. The same law applies if the man died and left a widow and a creditor and land to which neither party enjoys a preferential right of lien." (*Rambam, Sefer Nashim, Hilkhot Ishut* 17:4-5; *Shulḥan Arukh, Even HaEzer* 102:3-4.)

¹אֲמַר לֵיהּ רַב פַּפָּא לְרַב חָמָא: וַדַּאי דְּאָמְרִיתוּ מִשְּׁמֵיהּ דְּרָבָא: ²הַאי מַאן דְּמַסְּקֵי בֵּיהּ זוּזֵי וְאִית לֵיהּ אַרְעָא, ³וַאֲתָא בַּעַל חוֹב וְקָא תָּבַע מִינֵּיהּ, ⁴וַאֲמַר לֵיהּ: ״זִיל שְׁקוֹל מֵאַרְעָא״, ⁵אָמְרִינַן לֵיהּ: ״זִיל זַבֵּין אַתְּ וְאַיְיתֵי הַב לֵיהּ״? ⁶אֲמַר לֵיהּ: ״לָא״. ⁷״אֵימָא לִי גּוּפָא דְּעוּבְדָא הֵיכִי הֲוָה״. ⁸אֲמַר לֵיהּ: ״תּוֹלֶה מְעוֹתָיו בְּגוֹי הֲוָה, ⁹הוּא עָשָׂה

LITERAL TRANSLATION

[1]Rav Pappa said to Rav Ḥama: Is it right that you said [this] in the name of Rava: [2][If] someone owes money, [3]and he has land, [4]and the creditor came and demanded [payment] from him, and he said to him: "Go take from the land," [5]we say to him: "Go sell [it] yourself and bring [the money and] give [it to] him." [6]He said to him: "No." [7]"Tell me how the incident itself occurred?" [8]He said to him: "He attributed his money to a non-Jew. [9]He acted

TRANSLATION AND COMMENTARY

אֲמַר לֵיהּ [1]**Rav Pappa said to Rav Ḥama: Is it correct that you said** the following **in the name of Rava:** [2]**If someone owes money, and he has land** [3]**and the creditor came and demanded** repayment **from him,** [4]**and** the debtor **said to** the creditor: **"Go take** what I owe you **from the land,"** [5]**we say to** the debtor: "Your creditor is not required to exert himself and liquidate the assets which he receives from you. **Go** and **sell** your land, **and bring** your creditor the money **and give it to him."** Rav Pappa questioned this transmitted ruling of Rava because it is standard practice that when a debtor pays with land, the land itself goes to the creditor who deals with it as he sees fit (see *Gittin* 48b). [6]Rav Ḥama **said to** Rav Pappa: **"No,** I did not report such a position in the name of Rava." [7]Rav Pappa now asked: **"Tell me what incident occurred** that led people to think that you reported such a ruling." [8]Rav Ḥama **said to** Rav Pappa: In the case I was referring to, the debtor had money with which he could have repaid the creditor, but **he** had **claimed** that the **money belonged to a non-Jew,** and so the creditor could not recover his debt from that money. [9]The debtor **acted improperly,** and

BACKGROUND

תּוֹלֶה מְעוֹתָיו בְּנָכְרִי He attributed his money to a non-Jew. Although in principle there was no severe discrimination against the Jews in Babylonia, nevertheless, in fact, when a Jew wished to sue a non-Jew in a gentile court, the proceedings were not always honest. Sometimes those courts were unable to force violent men to obey their orders. Moreover, the laws and precedents were considerably different in gentile courts, so that a certain case might be decided differently in a gentile court. Therefore, it was frowned upon for a Jew to involve a fellow Jew in a suit with a gentile before a gentile court.

RASHI

ודאי דאמריתו כו' — לשון שאלה הוא: אמת הוא ששמעתי שאתם אומרים דבר זה של תימה, דמטרחינן ליה ללוה למכרה? והלא המלוה עיקר סמך שלו על הקרקע! **תולה מעותיו בעובד כוכבים הוה** — מעות היה לו לפרוע, ואומר של גוי הם.

NOTES

case of indebtedness has the same law, and the judges use their discretion and award the land to the creditor for the reason stated here. But most Rishonim follow *Rif,* who understands that Shmuel's ruling of a judge using discretions is limited to the case of two bills of sale for a certain property However, if bills of indebtedness were issued against the same debtor on the same day, and the debtor's property does not suffice to cover both debts, all agree that the two creditors divide the debtor's property. Hence in Amemar's case whenever the wife's and creditor's liens fall on the same property and it is not enough for both, the property should be divided between the two. However, if one of the parties went ahead and seized it, the seizure is valid because of his lien. Therefore, Amemar ruled that the property should be given to the creditor to encourage the granting of loans, as stated in the Gemara.

תּוֹלֶה מְעוֹתָיו בְּגוֹי He attributed his money to a non-Jew. Most commentators explain that the debtor claimed that the money that he had in his possession did not belong to him, but rather to a non-Jew, and so the creditor could not recover his debt from that money (see *Sefer HaYashar*). In such a case, the debtor may not repay his debt with land, but rather he must sell his land, and repay his debt with cash. *Rav Hai Gaon* writes that the Gemara might also be dealing with a case in which the debtor claimed that his land belonged to a non-Jew or even that a non-Jew had a claim on his property. Therefore the creditor did not want his debt to be repaid with the land, lest the non-Jew come to him. In such a case, the debtor is obligated to sell the property himself and repay his debt with cash.

עָשׂוּ בּוֹ שֶׁלֹּא כַּהוֹגֶן They acted toward him improperly. Rav Ḥama means to say that if we would have accepted the debtor's claim that the money which he had in his possession did not belong to him, Rava's court acted

HALAKHAH

מַאן דְּמַסְּקֵי בֵּיהּ זוּזֵי If someone owes money. "If a debtor has money, he cannot repay his creditor with land or movable goods. If he does not have money, he is not required to sell his land or movable goods, but can use them to repay his loan (his creditor having the choice between receiving land or movable goods). If the debtor claims that he does not have money or that the money he has belongs to someone else, he is not required to confirm his claim with an oath, but rather an imprecation is placed on anyone who knows that the debtor has money (and doesn't come forward). The same law applies if the debtor claims that the money in his possession belongs to a non-Jew. Some authorities maintain that if the debtor was known to be a wealthy man, we do not accept such a claim, and require the debtor to repay his loan with cash. If the debtor claimed that he does not have money to repay a certain debt, and was found to be lying, he is no longer believed to push off payment of that debt and the court forces him to liquidate his assets and repay his debt with the proceeds. *Rema* (in the name of *Tur*) writes that if the court thinks that the debtor is lying and concealing money, it can compel him to liquidate his assets and repay his debt with cash," following Rav Ḥama. (*Rambam, Sefer Mishpatim, Hilkhot Malveh VeLoveh* 11:7; *Shulḥan Arukh, Ḥoshen Mishpat* 101:1-2, 7.)

TRANSLATION AND COMMENTARY

therefore the court of Rava **acted improperly toward him,** forcing him to sell the land himself and repay his debt. That case was exceptional.

אֲמַר לֵיהּ [1]**Rav Kahana said to Rav Pappa:** [2]**According to you who said:** The debtor's duty to **repay his creditor is a religious duty** and not a legal obligation, the following question arises: [3]**If** the debtor **said: "It is not convenient for me to perform my religious duty," what is the law?**

אֲמַר לֵיהּ [4]Rav Pappa **said to** Rav Kahana: The debtor is flogged until he agrees to fulfill his obligation, for **we have learned** in a Baraita: "The maximum number of lashes that can be administered for a single transgression is thirty-nine. [5]**In what instances does this** limited punishment apply? [6]When there has been a violation of a **negative injunction.** [7]**But** where a person fails to carry out a **positive command — for example, where** a person was told: [8]**'Build a sukkah,' and he refuses to build it,** or he was told: **'Take a lulav,' and he refuses to take it."** [86B] [9]In such a case the lashes are administered to coerce the offender to fulfill his duty, and **he is flogged until his soul departs."** Since a debtor's duty to repay his creditor is also a positive command, the debtor who refuses to do so is flogged until he agrees to fulfill his obligation.

שֶׁלֹּא כַּהוֹגֶן, לְפִיכָךְ עָשׂוּ בּוֹ שֶׁלֹּא כַּהוֹגֶן.
[1]אֲמַר לֵיהּ רַב כָּהֲנָא לְרַב פַּפָּא: [2]לְדִידָךְ דְּאָמְרַתְּ: פְּרִיעַת בַּעַל חוֹב מִצְוָה, [3]אֲמַר: "לָא נִיחָא לִי דְּאִיעֲבֵיד מִצְוָה", מַאי?
[4]אֲמַר לֵיהּ: תָּנֵינָא: [5]בַּמֶּה דְּבָרִים אֲמוּרִים? [6]בְּמִצְוֹת לֹא תַעֲשֶׂה, [7]אֲבָל בְּמִצְוֹת עֲשֵׂה, כְּגוֹן שֶׁאוֹמְרִין לוֹ: [8]"עֲשֵׂה סוּכָּה" וְאֵינוֹ עוֹשֶׂה, "לוּלָב", וְאֵינוֹ עוֹשֶׂה [86B] [9]מַכִּין אוֹתוֹ עַד שֶׁתֵּצֵא נַפְשׁוֹ".

LITERAL TRANSLATION

improperly. Therefore, they acted improperly toward him."

[1]Rav Kahana said to Rav Pappa: According to you who said: [2]Repaying a creditor is a religious duty (lit., "a commandment"), [3][if] he said: "It is not convenient for me to perform my religious duty," what [is the law]?

[4]He said to him: We have learned: [5]"In what [instances] are these things said? [6]Regarding negative injunctions, [7]but regarding positive commands — for example, where they said to him: [8]'Build a sukkah,' and he does not build [it], '[Take] a lulav,' and he does not take (lit., 'do') [it], [86B] [9]they flog him until his soul departs."

RASHI

לדידך דאמרת כו' — במסכת ערכין בפרק "שום היתומין" (כג,א). **פריעת בעל חוב מצוה** — מלוה עליו לפרוע חובו ולאמת דבריו, דכתיב "הין צדק" שיהא "הן" שלך צדק ו"לאו" שלך צדק (בבא מציעא מט,א). **במה דברים אמורים** — דלוקה ארבעים. **מכין אותו** — קודם שעבר על העשה, ויש בידו לקיים.

NOTES

improperly when it required the debtor to liquidate his assets and repay his debt with cash. But, in fact, the court rejected the debtor's claim that the money found in his possession was not his, he therefore was required to pay cash. The court then acted in accordance with law and by requiring the debtor to sell the field if he wished to use that for payment (*Rabbenu Tam*).

פְּרִיעַת בַּעַל חוֹב מִצְוָה Repaying the creditor is a religious duty. Elsewhere (*Bava Batra* 174a), the Amoraim disagree about the nature of the debtor's obligation to repay his creditor. Rav Huna the son of Rav Yehoshua maintains that by Torah law the debtor is obligated to repay his debts, and the creditor enjoys a lien over the debtor's property that ensures that he will be repaid. But Rav Pappa maintains that the debtor's duty to repay his creditor is only a mitzvah, a religious duty, and not a legal obligation. Hence, the lien which the creditor exercises over the debtor's property would be only by Rabbinic enactment. *Ramban* writes that even according to the opinion that the debtor's duty is only a religious obligation, the court can nevertheless collect the debt from his property, for surely before we physically coerce the debtor with corporal punishment (see Gemara below), we forcibly seize his property.

Rashi notes the religious duty to repay a debt is derived from the verse (Leviticus 19:36): "You shall have a just hin (a liquid measure)." According to its plain meaning, the verse teaches that a person must use just weights and measures. But the Rabbis read the word "hin" as though it were "hen" — "yes", and said that the verse also wants to teach that your "yes" should be just, and your "no" should be just. A person should never break his word (see *Bava Metzia* 49a). Thus, a person who undertook to repay a loan has a religious obligation to keep his word and pay back his debt. But many Rishonim understand that this verse teaches only that a person should not say one thing and intend something else. Thus, a person is forbidden to take out a loan intending not to repay it. But if at the time that he borrowed the money he had full intention to pay it back, he does not violate the Rabbinic exegesis on this verse if he later defaults on the loan. Rather, the religious obligation to repay a loan is derived from the debtor's having to return a given pledge to the creditor, as it is said (Deuteronomy 24:11): "And the man to whom you have lend shall bring out the pledge to you" (see *Ramban, Ra'ah* and *Rashba*).

SAGES

רָמִי בַּר חָמָא Rami bar Ḥama. A Babylonian Amora of the fourth generation. See *Ketubot,* Part II, p. 57.

BACKGROUND

צִידֵּי רְשׁוּת הָרַבִּים Sides of a public domain. The edge of the public domain is a place where people generally do not walk, but it is near the public domain, and occasionally, when the public domain is crowded, people also walk on its edge. The Sages disagreed about the Halakhic status of the edge of the public domain both regarding carrying on Shabbat and also regarding the laws of acquisition.

TRANSLATION AND COMMENTARY

בָּעָא מִינֵּיהּ [1]The Gemara now raises an entirely different matter, which it will try to resolve in light of the view of Rav and Shmuel recorded earlier in our Gemara (84b): **Rami bar Ḥama asked Rav Ḥisda:** If a man said to his wife: [2]**"This is your bill of divorce, but you shall not be divorced with it until after thirty days** have passed," [3]**and** the woman took the document and **placed it at the side of a public domain** — an open area adjacent to a public domain which is available to the public but is not ordinarily used — and the bill of divorce was still lying there after thirty days, [4]**what is the law?** Is the woman's divorce valid or not?

אֲמַר לֵיהּ [5]**Rav Ḥisda said to** Rami bar Ḥama: The woman **is not divorced, because of** what **Rav and Shmuel** said. [6]**For Rav and Shmuel both said:** Rabbi Tarfon stated in our Mishnah that if a person died and left produce that had already been detached from the ground to which several parties have a legal claim, the claimant who seizes it first acquires it. [7]Rabbi Tarfon was referring to movable property that **was piled and lying in the public domain,** where an act of acquisition

[1]בָּעָא מִינֵּיהּ רָמִי בַּר חָמָא מֵרַב חִסְדָּא: [2]"הֲרֵי זֶה גִּיטֵּיךְ וְלֹא תִתְגָּרְשִׁי בּוֹ אֶלָּא לְאַחַר שְׁלֹשִׁים יוֹם", [3]וְהָלְכָה וְהִנִּיחַתּוֹ בְּצִידֵּי רְשׁוּת הָרַבִּים, [4]מַהוּ? [5]אֲמַר לֵיהּ: אֵינָהּ מְגוֹרֶשֶׁת, מִדְּרַב וּשְׁמוּאֵל. [6]דְּרַב וּשְׁמוּאֵל דְּאָמְרִי תַּרְוַיְיהוּ: [7]וְהוּא שֶׁצְּבוּרִין וּמוּנָּחִין בִּרְשׁוּת

LITERAL TRANSLATION

[1]Rami bar Ḥama asked Rav Ḥisda: [2]"This is your bill of divorce, but you shall not be divorced with it until after thirty days," [3]and she went and placed it at the sides of a public domain, [4]what [is the law]?

[5]He said to him: She is not divorced, because [the opinion of] Rav and Shmuel. [6]For Rav and Shmuel both said: [7]And [he said] it when it was piled and lying in the public domain.

RASHI

והלכה והניחתו כו׳ – ועודנו שם לאחר שלשים. **והוא שצבורין** – גבי מתניתין, דקתני: הקודם זכה. אלמא רשות הרבים לא קני ליה לבעלים מידי, אלא אלא כן מגביהו. הילכך, לאחר שלשים לאו ברשותה הוא דליהוי גירושין חיילי.

NOTES

הֲרֵי זֶה גִּיטֵּיךְ This is your bill of divorce. This passage is discussed at length by the Rishonim (with the exception of *Rif* who skipped it altogether, apparently because he maintains that the law does not follow the positions recorded here). What precisely did the husband say to his wife? If he simply said: "This is your bill of divorce, but you shall not be divorced with it until after thirty days have passed," then the divorce should not be valid, even if the woman placed it in her own courtyard. A bill of divorce must be handed directly to the woman, and here when the divorce became valid, the woman took possession of it on her own. *Tosafot, Ra'avad,* and others therefore argue that in this case the husband said: "This is your bill of divorce *from now,* but you shall not be divorced with it until after thirty days have passed." Hence, this case is comparable to the case of the cow discussed by Rav Naḥman, for as the Gemara explains elsewhere *(Ketubot* 82a), we must explain that the owner of the cow said to the buyer: "Go now and draw my cow into your possession, and acquire it retroactively *from now* after thirty days have passed." But *Ramban* and his disciples object to the *Tosafot*'s explanation because the Gemara concludes elsewhere (*Kiddushin* 59b) that if the husband said to his wife that she should be divorced from now and after thirty days, the validity of her divorce is in doubt. That is because it is not clear whether his saying "after thirty days" was a condition implying retroactive validity of the divorce or whether he had changed his mind and wants the bill of divorce to go into effect only after thirty days. *Ramban* argues that in this case the husband did not add the words *from now* but merely specified that the divorce would go into effect only after thirty days have passed. However, since the husband himself handed her the bill of divorce, she is not considered as having taken it by herself even if it only became valid at the end of the thirty day period, after she had placed it at the side of a public domain. However, the bill of divorce is not valid if it is not in her possession at the end of the thirty day period, and the question here is whether the bill of divorce resting at the side of the public domain is considered for this purpose as being in her possession.

צִידֵּי רְשׁוּת הָרַבִּים The side of a public domain. The Rishonim (*Tosafot* and others) point out that elsewhere (*Ketubot* 31b) the Gemara concludes that the law is in accordance with the opinion that the sides of a public domain are like a public domain, both with respect to the laws of Shabbat and with respect to the laws of acquisition. *Ritva* explains that here the Gemara is not asking whether an act of acquisition, such as *meshikhah,* can take effect in the area adjacent to a public domain. Rather it is asking whether or not something that was placed in an area adjacent to a public domain can be regarded as in the possession of the party who had acquired it.

מִדְּרַב וּשְׁמוּאֵל Because of Rav and Shmuel. The Rishonim ask: Rav and Shmuel spoke about produce that was piled

HALAKHAH

וְהִנִּיחַתּוֹ בְּצִידֵּי רְשׁוּת הָרַבִּים And she placed it at the side of the public domain. "If a man gave his wife a bill of divorce, but told her that she would not be divorced until after thirty days had passed, and the woman went and put it down in an area adjacent to the public domain, and the bill of divorce was lost or stolen after the thirty-day period

TRANSLATION AND COMMENTARY

cannot take effect. The produce cannot then be transferred automatically to the heirs, and the claimant taking it from there acquires it. [1]**And,** added Rav Ḥisda, with respect to this ruling, **the** open area running along **the side of a public domain** should be considered **like a public domain itself.** Similarly, if a bill of divorce that is lying in a public domain or beside it on the date when it becomes valid, it is not considered to be in the woman's possession and therefore the divorce does not take effect.

אַדְּרַבָּה [2]Rami bar Ḥama rejected Rav Ḥisda's argument: **On the contrary,** it stands to reason that the woman should indeed **be divorced, because of** what **Rav Naḥman** said: [3]**For Rav Naḥman said in the name of Rabbah the son of Avuha:** [4]**If someone said to another person:** "Go and **pull this cow** of mine as an act of acquisition (*meshikhah*), **but it shall not be acquired by you until after thirty days** have passed," and the other person pulled the cow into his possession, **he** does in fact **acquire** the cow after thirty days have passed, [5]**even if** at the end of that period when the cow was no longer in the buyer's physical possession, but rather **it was standing in a meadow** that did not belong to him or anyone else. Rav Naḥman therefore taught that a transaction to take place at a future date is valid, even if the object is not then in the buyer's physical possession, a law that should apply to the bill of divorce placed at the side of a public domain. Now, continued Rami bar Ḥama, [6]**is not the meadow** discussed by Rav Naḥman **the same as** the open area along **the side of a public domain** in Rami bar Ḥama's question dealing with the bill of divorce?

לָא [7]Rav Ḥisda rebutted Rami bar Ḥama's position: **No, a meadow has a status of its own** — it is a place where acts of acquisition can take place and possession of the cow standing there can be automatically transferred to the purchaser. **And** the area on **the side of a public domain has a status of its own** — acts of acquisition cannot be made there and the bill of divorce lying there is not automatically transferred to the woman. Therefore there is no proof from Rav Naḥman that the woman is divorced.

אִיכָּא דְּאָמְרִי [8]The Gemara now records a different version of the dispute between Rav Ḥisda and Rami bar Ḥama. **There are some** authorities **who say** that Rami bar Ḥama asked Rav Ḥisda: What is the law if a man said to his wife: "This is your bill of divorce, but you shall not be divorced with it until after thirty days have passed," and the woman took the document and placed it at the side of the public domain, and

הָרַבִּים. [1]וְצִידֵּי רְשׁוּת הָרַבִּים כִּרְשׁוּת הָרַבִּים דָּמוּ.
[2]אַדְּרַבָּה, מְגוֹרֶשֶׁת מִדְּרַב נַחְמָן. [3]דְּאָמַר רַב נַחְמָן אָמַר רַבָּה בַּר אֲבוּהּ: [4]הָאוֹמֵר לַחֲבֵירוֹ: "מְשׁוֹךְ פָּרָה זוֹ, וְלֹא תְּהֵא קְנוּיָה לְךָ עַד לְאַחַר שְׁלֹשִׁים יוֹם" — קָנָה, [5]וַאֲפִילּוּ עוֹמֶדֶת בְּאֲגַם. [6]מַאי לָאו הַיְינוּ אֲגַם וְהַיְינוּ צִידֵּי רְשׁוּת הָרַבִּים? [7]לָא, אֲגַם לְחוּד וְצִידֵּי רְשׁוּת הָרַבִּים לְחוּד.
[8]אִיכָּא דְּאָמְרִי: אָמַר לֵיהּ:

LITERAL TRANSLATION

[1]And the sides of a public domain are considered as the public domain.

[2]On the contrary, she is divorced because [the opinion of] Rav Naḥman. [3]For Rav Naḥman said in the name of Rabbah the son of Avuha: [4][If] someone said to his fellow: "Pull this cow, but it shall not be acquired by you until after thirty days," he acquired [it], [5]even if it is was standing in a meadow. [6]Is not a meadow the same as the sides of a public domain?

[7]No, a meadow [has a definition] by itself and the sides of a public domain by itself.

[8]There are [some] who say: He said to him:

RASHI

צידי רשות הרבים – סמוך לכתלים, שאין דרך בני אדם לעבור שם ולהתחכך בכותלים.

SAGES

רַבָּה בַּר אֲבוּהּ Rabbah bar Avuha. A Babylonian Amora of the second generation. See *Ketubot,* Part III, p. 154.

BACKGROUND

אֲגַם Meadow. Here the word means meadow, as it does in most Talmudic passages (and some Biblical verses, such as Jeremiah 51:32). In modern Hebrew, though אֲגַם means "pond, lake"; this term apparently refers to pasture land near sources of water (such as swamps) which does not belong to anyone and anyone may make us of it. Hence it was debated whether a meadow is a kind of public domain, because of its public use, or whether, because it is not heavily frequented, it might have a unique Halakhic status.

NOTES

and resting in a public domain (see above, 82a), but they said nothing about the area adjacent to a public domain. How then can Rav Ḥisda have inferred anything from what Rav and Shmuel said about the area adjacent to a public domain? They answer that since Rav and Shmuel discussed the public domain as distinct from a side street, it stands to reason that the area adjacent to a public domain is considered by them to be equivalent to the public domain itself (see *Rosh* and others).

HALAKHAH

had already passed, the divorce is valid, for the bill of divorce was laying where the woman had set it down when it became valid and that place is not considered a public domain," following the conclusion of the second version of the Talmudic passage. (*Rambam, Sefer Nashim, Hilkhot Gerushin* 9:3; *Shulḥan Arukh, Even HaEzer* 146:2.)

¹מְגוֹרֶשֶׁת, מִדְּרַב נַחְמָן. ²וְצִידֵּי רְשׁוּת הָרַבִּים כַּאֲגַם דָּמֵי.
³אַדְּרַבָּה, אֵינָהּ מְגוֹרֶשֶׁת מִדְּרַב וּשְׁמוּאֵל. ⁴מַאי לָאו הַיְינוּ רְשׁוּת הָרַבִּים וְהַיְינוּ צִידֵּי רְשׁוּת הָרַבִּים?
⁵לָא, רְשׁוּת הָרַבִּים לְחוּד, ⁶וְצִידֵּי רְשׁוּת הָרַבִּים לְחוּד.
מִשְׁנָה ⁷הַמּוֹשִׁיב אֶת אִשְׁתּוֹ חֶנְוָונִית, אוֹ שֶׁמִּינָּהּ אַפּוֹטְרוֹפְּיָא — הֲרֵי זֶה מַשְׁבִּיעָהּ כָּל זְמַן שֶׁיִּרְצֶה. ⁸רַבִּי אֱלִיעֶזֶר אוֹמֵר: אֲפִילּוּ עַל פִּילְכָּהּ וְעַל עִיסָּתָהּ.

LITERAL TRANSLATION

[1]She is divorced, because of Rav Naḥman. [2]And the sides of the public domain are considered as a meadow.

[3]On the contrary, she is not divorced, because of Rav and Shmuel. [4]Is not that the public domain the same as the side of the public domain?

[5]No, the public domain [has a] separate [status], [6]and the sides of a public domain [have a] separate [status].

MISHNAH [7][If] someone sets his wife up as a shopkeeper, or appointed her as an administrator, he may impose an oath upon her whenever he wishes. [8]Rabbi Eliezer says: Even regarding her spindle and her dough.

TRANSLATION AND COMMENTARY

it was still lying there after thirty days? Rav Ḥisda **said to him:** [1]The woman **is divorced, because of** what **Rav Naḥman** said in the name of Rabbah the son of Avuha: If someone said to another person: "Go and pull this cow of mine into your possession, but it shall not be acquired by you until after thirty days have passed," and that other person pulled the cow, he acquires the cow after thirty days have passed, even if the cow was then standing in a meadow. [2]**And,** added Rav Ḥisda, the open area **beside a public domain is considered as a meadow.**

אַדְּרַבָּה [3]Rami bar Ḥama rejected Rav Ḥisda's argument: **On the contrary,** it stands to reason that the woman **is not divorced, because of** what **Rav and Shmuel** said. For Rav and Shmuel said that when Rabbi Tarfon stated that the party who seizes produce belonging to the deceased acquires it, he was referring to property that was piled in the public domain. Now, argued Rami bar Ḥama, [4]**is not the public domain the same as** the open area **beside the public domain?** Therefore, the bill of divorce which is still lying beside the public domain after thirty days should not be considered to be in the woman's possession at the time that the divorce is to take effect, and so the divorce should not be valid.

לָא [5]Rav Ḥisda rebutted Rami bar Ḥama's argument: **No,** an analogy cannot be made between a public domain and an open area beside a public domain, for **a public domain has its own status,** [6]**and** the area on **the side of a public domain has its own status.**

MISHNAH הַמּוֹשִׁיב [7]The Rabbis enacted that in certain cases an oath can be imposed upon a defendant even if the plaintiff cannot claim with certainty that the defendant owes him money (see *Shevuot* 45a). For example, if someone suspects that his partner or tenant-farmer stole money from him, or did not keep a careful account of the money that the one owed the other, he can demand that an oath be administered to the partner or tenant-farmer, even if he cannot claim with certainty that he owes him money. Our Mishnah teaches that the same oath can be imposed on a married woman by her husband. Thus, **if someone set his wife up as a shopkeeper** to sell merchandise in his store, **or appointed her as an administrator** to manage his business, **he may impose an oath upon her whenever he wishes** if he suspects she is cheating him. [8]**Rabbi Eliezer says:** The husband may impose an oath upon his wife not only with respect to her handling of his business affairs, but **even regarding her spindle and dough,** if he suspects she is mismanaging the household accounts.

RASHI

משנה חנונית – למכור יינו ופירותיו בחנות. משביעה – שלא עיכבה בידה כלום. אפוטרופיא – להכניס ולהוציא פירותיו, ולשכור פועלים, ולישא וליתן.

LANGUAGE

אַפּוֹטְרוֹפְּיָא Administrator. This is the Aramaic feminine form for the Greek word, *apotropos*. It refers to a woman who has received a power of attorney to deal with matters and to act as she sees fit for the benefit of another, whether it be her husband or someone else.

BACKGROUND

פִּילְכָּהּ Her spindle. This does not refer to the spindle itself but to the yarn that the wife spins with it. Her husband suspects that she has been concealing some of the wool or flax or the thread that she produces.

NOTES

מַשְׁבִּיעָהּ כָּל זְמַן שֶׁיִּרְצֶה He may demand of her an oath whenever he wishes. *Shittah Mekubbetzet* writes that the husband may make his wife swear that she conducted his business honestly whenever and as often as he wishes. The Rabbis were concerned that because the woman labors on behalf of her husband, she might feel justified in withholding some of the profit from his business for herself.

However some Geonim ruled that the law does not

HALAKHAH

הַמּוֹשִׁיב אֶת אִשְׁתּוֹ חֶנְוָונִית If someone sets his wife up as a shopkeeper. "If a man set his wife up as a shopkeeper or appointed her as an administrator to oversee his property, he may make her swear that she conducted his business honestly, even if he only suspects something and cannot claim that he knows for sure that she cheated him.

TRANSLATION AND COMMENTARY

GEMARA **אִיבַּעְיָא לְהוּ** [1]There is a general rule that when a defendant is obliged to take an oath in order to free himself of a liability and the plaintiff has other claims against him, the plaintiff can force him to extend the oath to include a denial of these other claims, which of themselves would not require the defendant to take an oath. The extension of an oath is called *gilgul shevuah*. Now, in a discussion of our Mishnah by the Sages, **it was asked:** When **Rabbi Eliezer** said that the husband may impose an oath upon his wife even regarding her spindle and dough, **did he** mean that he may impose such an oath upon her **by attaching** an oath to an oath which she is already taking regarding her handling of his business. [2]**Or did he** mean that the husband may **directly** impose an oath upon his wife regarding specifically her management of household affairs?

תָּא שְׁמַע [3]The Gemara suggests an answer: **Come and hear** what was taught in the following Baraita: "The Sages **said to Rabbi Eliezer:** [4]'**A person cannot dwell in a basket** together **with a serpent** that could bite him at any moment.' Similarly, a woman would not be able to live with her husband, if he could at any moment impose an oath upon her regarding her handling of the day-to-day household affairs." [5]**Granted if you say** that Rabbi Eliezer meant that a husband may impose a direct oath regarding his wife's handling of domestic affairs, we **well** understand the Sages' argument. [6]**But if you say** that Rabbi Eliezer meant that the husband may only impose an oath upon his wife regarding household matters **by means of *gilgul shevuah*,** [7]then **what difference does it make to her?** If she must take an oath about her husband's business, then why should she care if she is obligated to include in her oath a denial of any mismanagement of her household?

דְּאָמְרָה לֵיהּ [8]The Gemara rejects: The Sages' argument that a wife would be in an intolerable position if her husband could force her to swear about her management of the household. **For the woman can** still **say to** her husband: **"Since you are so exacting with me** and also require of me now to include in my oath that I did not take for myself any of the wool which I spun for you or any of the dough which I kneaded for you, [9]**I am not able to live with you."**

גמרא [1]אִיבַּעְיָא לְהוּ: רַבִּי אֱלִיעֶזֶר עַל יְדֵי גִלְגּוּל קָאָמַר, [2]אוֹ לְכַתְּחִלָּה קָאָמַר? [3]תָּא שְׁמַע: ״אָמְרוּ לוֹ לְרַבִּי אֱלִיעֶזֶר: [4]׳אֵין אָדָם דָּר עִם נָחָשׁ בִּכְפִיפָה׳״. [5]אִי אָמְרַתְּ בִּשְׁלָמָא לְכַתְּחִלָּה, שַׁפִּיר. [6]אֶלָּא אִי אָמְרַתְּ עַל יְדֵי גִלְגּוּל, [7]מַאי נָפְקָא לָהּ מִינָּהּ? [8]דְּאָמְרָה לֵיהּ: ״כֵּיוָן דְּקָדֵייקַתְּ בַּתְרַאי כּוּלֵּי הַאי, [9]לָא מָצֵינָא דְּאָדוּר בַּהֲדָךְ״.

LITERAL TRANSLATION

GEMARA [1]It was asked of them: Did Rabbi Eliezer mean by attaching (lit., "rolling [on to an oath"]), [2]or did he mean directly?

[3]Come [and] hear: "They said to Rabbi Eliezer: [4]'A person cannot dwell in a basket with a serpent.'" [5]Granted if you meant directly, it is well. [6]But if you meant the attaching (lit., "rolling" [one oath into another]), [7]what difference is it to her?

[8]Because she [can] say to him: "Since you are so exacting with me, [9]I am not able to live with you."

RASHI

גמרא **על ידי גלגול קאמר** — דשמעיה לתנא קמא דאמר: משביעה על האפטרופסות, ולא על פילכה ועיסתה, ואפילו על ידי גלגול שבועת אפטרופסות. דכיון דשבועת אפטרופסות דרבנן, [דהא לא קטען ליה תובע טענת ברי, אלא: ״רצוני שתשבע לי״ — לא מגלגלין על ידה] שבועה אחריתי. ואתא רבי אליעזר למימר: היכא דהושיבה חנונית, מיגו דמישתבעה אאפטרופסות — משתבעה נמי על ידי גלגול על פילכה ועיסתה, דמגלגלין מדרבנן. **או לכתחלה קאמר** — דאפילו לא מינה אפוטרופיא משביעה על פלכה, שהרי אפוטרופסת היא. **בכפיפה** — בתוך קופה אחת. **שפיר** — דאמרה ליה: ״הואיל ומשבעת לי על פילכי — איני יכול לסבול קפדנותך״. **מאי נפקא לה מינה** — הרי נתחייבת לו שבועה, ומה יקשה לה גלגול זה אם לא עיכבה כלום? **הואיל וקא דייקת בתראי** — אינך אוהב ומאמין אותי, ולא מצינא לאידור בהדך.

CONCEPTS

גִּלְגּוּל שְׁבוּעָה The attaching [lit., "rolling"] of an oath; the adding of one oath to another. When a defendant is obliged to take an oath in order to free himself of a liability, the plaintiff can require him to extend the oath to include a denial of other claims by the plaintiff, which of themselves would not require the defendant to take an oath. This extension of the oath is called *gilgul shevuah*, "the adding of one oath to another."

BACKGROUND

אֵין אָדָם דָּר עִם נָחָשׁ בִּכְפִיפָה A person cannot dwell in a basket with a serpent. That is, one does not require a person to live in a condition of constant suspicion, like someone confined in a narrow space with a venomous serpent. For a person cannot live in constant apprehension and dread.

NOTES

follow this Mishnah, but rather the view of Rabbi Shimon recorded in the Mishnah below (87b) that an oath can only be imposed upon a wife when she claims her ketubah settlement. But *Rif* and most other codifiers ruled in accordance with our Mishnah (see Halakhah).

עַל יְדֵי גִלְגּוּל By means of an extended oath. The Jerusalem Talmud (cited by *Tosafot*) argues that Rabbi Eliezar's position seems reasonable, and asks for an

HALAKHAH

But if she is only involved in domestic matters, he cannot impose an oath upon her based on an uncertain claim, following the anonymous first Tanna of the Mishnah. Even if the husband set his wife up as a shopkeeper or appointed her as an administrator, he cannot impose an oath upon her until she comes to collect her ketubah settlement. According to a second opinion, he may impose an oath upon her whenever he chooses." (*Rambam, Sefer Kinyan, Hilkhot Sheluḥin VeShutafim* 9:1,4; *Shulḥan Arukh, Even HaEzer* 97:1-2; *Ḥoshen Mishpat* 93:1.)

תָּא שְׁמַע: ״הֲרֵי שֶׁלֹּא פָּטַר אֶת אִשְׁתּוֹ מִן הַנֶּדֶר וּמִן הַשְּׁבוּעָה, וְהוֹשִׁיבָהּ חֶנְוָנִית אוֹ שֶׁמִּינָּהּ אַפּוֹטְרוֹפְּיָא — הֲרֵי זֶה מַשְׁבִּיעָהּ כָּל זְמַן שֶׁיִּרְצֶה. לֹא הוֹשִׁיבָהּ חֶנְוָנִית, וְלֹא מִינָּהּ אַפּוֹטְרוֹפְּיָא — אֵינוֹ יָכוֹל לְהַשְׁבִּיעָהּ. רַבִּי אֱלִיעֶזֶר אוֹמֵר: אַף עַל פִּי שֶׁלֹּא הוֹשִׁיבָהּ חֶנְוָנִית, וְלֹא מִינָּהּ אַפּוֹטְרוֹפְּיָא — הֲרֵי זֶה מַשְׁבִּיעָהּ כָּל זְמַן שֶׁיִּרְצֶה, שֶׁאֵין לְךָ אִשָּׁה שֶׁלֹּא נַעֲשֵׂית אַפּוֹטְרוֹפְּיָא שָׁעָה אַחַת בְּחַיֵּי בַּעְלָהּ עַל פִּילְכָּהּ וְעַל עִיסָּתָהּ. אָמְרוּ לוֹ: אֵין אָדָם דָּר עִם נָחָשׁ בִּכְפִיפָה״. שְׁמַע מִינָּהּ: לְכַתְּחִלָּה. שְׁמַע מִינָּהּ.

מִשְׁנָה כָּתַב לָהּ: ״נֶדֶר

LITERAL TRANSLATION

[1]Come [and] hear: "[If] a man did not exempt his wife from a vow and from an oath, [2]and he set her up as a shopkeeper, or appointed her as an administrator, he may impose an oath upon her whenever he wishes. [3][If] he did not set her up as a shopkeeper, or appoint her as an administrator, [4]he may not impose an oath upon her. [5]Rabbi Eliezer says: Even if he did not set her up as a shopkeeper, or appoint her as an administrator, [6]he may impose an oath upon her whenever he wishes, [7]for there is no woman who is not appointed an administrator one hour during her husband's lifetime regarding her spindle and her dough. [8]They said to him: A person cannot dwell in a basket with a serpent." [9]Conclude from this: A direct [oath]. [10]Conclude from it.

MISHNAH [11][If] he wrote her:

RASHI

הרי שלא פטר — שלא כתב לה: ״נדר ושבועה אין לי עליך״. נדר — שנודרת לו: ״יאסרו עלי כל פירות שבעולם אם עיכבתי משלך כלום״, כדאמר במסכת גיטין (לד,ב): נמנעו מלהשביעה, התקין רבן גמליאל הזקן שתהא נודרת ליתומים כל מה שירצו וגובה כתובתה.

TRANSLATION AND COMMENTARY

תָּא שְׁמַע [1]Rabbi Eliezer's position is still unclear, so the Gemara offers another approach: **Come and hear** what was taught in the following Baraita: **"If** the husband **did not** explicitly **exempt his wife from** ever having to take **a vow or an oath** to counter claims which he might bring against her, [2]**and he set her up as a shopkeeper** to sell merchandise in his store, **or appointed her as an administrator** to oversee his property and manage his business, **he may impose an oath upon her whenever he wishes** and make her swear that she is not withholding money that is due him. [3]**If he did not set her up as a shopkeeper, or appoint her as an administrator** over his affairs, [4]**he may not impose an oath upon her.** [5]**Rabbi Eliezer says: Even if** the husband **did not set** his wife **up as a shopkeeper, or appoint her as an administrator,** [6]**he may impose an oath upon her whenever he wishes.** [7]**for there is no woman who is not appointed** as **an administrator** of her husband's affairs at least **one hour during her husband's lifetime regarding** the wool which she spins on **her spindle and the dough** which she kneads. [8]And the Sages **said to** Rabbi Eliezer: **A person cannot dwell in a basket** together **with a serpent."** Now, since the Baraita says that Rabbi Eliezer maintains that the husband can impose an oath upon his wife regarding her spindle and dough, even though he had never set her up as a shopkeeper or appointed her as an administrator, [9]it may be **concluded** from here that according to Rabbi Eliezer the husband may impose such an oath **directly,** and not just by means of *gilgul shevuah.* The Gemara accepts this argument and says: [10]Indeed, it is correct to **conclude** this **from** the Baraita quoted.

MISHNAH כָּתַב לָהּ [11]We learned in the previous Mishnah that if a man set his wife up as a shopkeeper in his store, or appointed her as an administrator over his affairs, he may impose an oath upon her whenever he wishes. And we learned earlier in the chapter (84a) that if a widow wishes to collect her ketubah

NOTES

explanation of the anonymous first Tanna's view. It suggests that according to the anonymous first Tanna, the husband cannot impose even an extended oath upon his wife regarding possible mismanagement of household activities, because allowing the husband to impose such an oath would undermine domestic peace and tranquility. Similarly the Jerusalem Talmud rules that a wife who broke a household dish is not liable for the damages, not as a paid bailee, nor even as an unpaid bailee, for holding the wife accountable for breaking domestic utensils would destroy domestic harmony.

כָּתַב לָהּ **If he wrote her.** *Ritva* and *Nimmukei Yosef* note that the Mishnah's ruling is not limited to a written exemption from her ever having to take an oath or a vow, for the same law applies in the case where he exempted her orally.

HALAKHAH

כָּתַב לָהּ: נֶדֶר וּשְׁבוּעָה **If he wrote her: I will have no claim of a vow or an oath.** "If the husband exempted his wife from taking an oath, she may collect her ketubah settlement without an oath. The scope of the exemption

TRANSLATION AND COMMENTARY

settlement from her late husband's heirs, she must first take an oath that she had not received it during her husband's lifetime. It also appears that in some cases (see the Mishnah, *Gittin* 34b), a wife is forced to take a conditional vow in place of an oath to confirm her claim. For example: "I will never benefit from such-and-such, if I have been paid my ketubah settlement." If a man **wrote** his wife: **"I will have no claim of a vow or an oath against you,"** [1]**he may not** later **impose an oath** or a vow **upon her,** whether he set her up as a shopkeeper or appointed her as an administrator, or with respect to her ketubah settlement. [2]**But he may impose an oath upon her heirs or her lawful successors** to collect her ketubah settlement. For example, the man divorced his wife, and she died before receiving her ketubah settlement and her heirs come to the husband to collect the settlement, he can require them to swear that they have no knowledge that their mother received payment. Similarly, if the woman sold her ketubah to another person while she was still married, and then she was divorced, and she died before she received her settlement, the husband may require the buyer of her ketubah to swear that he has no knowledge that the settlement was paid, and only then must he pay him. The heirs and the buyer must take such an oath, for the husband only exempted his wife from having to take an oath, but he did not exempt his wife's heirs or the buyers.

וּשְׁבוּעָה אֵין לִי עָלַיִךְ", [1]אֵין יָכוֹל לְהַשְׁבִּיעָהּ. [2]אֲבָל מַשְׁבִּיעַ הוּא אֶת יוֹרְשֶׁיהָ וְאֶת הַבָּאִים בִּרְשׁוּתָהּ.

LITERAL TRANSLATION

"I will have no [claim of] a vow or an oath against you," [1]he may not impose an oath upon her. [2]But he may impose an oath upon her heirs and her lawful successors (lit., "those who come in her stead").

RASHI

משנה אינו יכול להשביעה – בגמרא מפרש מהי שבועה פטרה. **אבל משביע הוא את יורשיה** – אם גירשה ומתה, ויורשיה תובעין הימנו כתובתה – נשבעים שבועת יורשין המפורשת במסכת שבועות (מה,א): שבועה שלא פקדתנו בשעת מיתה, ולא אמרה לנו קודם לכן, ולא מצאנו בין שטרותיה ששטר כתובתה פרוע. **ואת הבאים ברשותה** – אם מכרה כתובתה לאחרים, ונתגרשה ומתה, והלקוחות תובעין אותו – נשבעין אף הן שבועת היורשין.

NOTES

נֶדֶר וּשְׁבוּעָה A vow or an oath. *Tosafot* ask: Why did the Mishnah include the husband's mentioning "a vow" when he exempted his wife from having to swear to him? Surely we learned elsewhere (*Gittin* 35a) that only in the case of a widow did the Rabbis enact that she must take a vow in place of an oath, but when a divorcee is required to swear, she must take an oath. And the formulation, "*I* will have no claim of a vow or an oath against *you*," implies that the husband is referring to a possible future divorce! *Ramban* answers that while the Rabbis enacted that a widow may take only a vow and not an oath, a defendant can always impose a vow upon a claimant instead of the oath which he would otherwise have been obligated to take. Thus, if the husband did not explicitly exempt his wife from a vow, he can always argue that he only exempted her from an oath.

אֲבָל מַשְׁבִּיעַ הוּא אֶת יוֹרְשֶׁיהָ But he may impose an oath upon her heirs. *Rashi* explains that the Mishnah refers here to the oath that the husband can impose upon his divorced wife's heirs when they have the right to collect her ketubah settlement that was due her (see *Shevuot* 45a). The heirs can only collect their mother's settlement after swearing that she did not tell them during her lifetime or on her deathbed that she had already received payment, and that they did not find among her papers a document stating that it had been paid. Regarding someone who comes in the woman's stead to collect her ketubah, *Rashi* writes that we are dealing with a case when the woman sold her ketubah while she was still married, and then she was divorced, and then she died before the settlement was collected. The buyer who now seeks to collect the settlement from her former husband must take the same oath that would have been imposed upon her heirs: that to his knowledge the settlement had not been paid. *Rosh* notes that this law applies only if the woman died, but if she were still alive the buyer cannot collect with an oath, but rather she herself must take the oath, for the husband only exempted her from an oath if she comes to collect the settlement for herself. And this is possible because the husband only exempted her from an oath if she comes to collect the settlement for herself. *Ritva* argues that if the husband exempted his wife from an oath, the buyer can indeed collect the woman's ketubah settlement after taking the heir's oath, even if the woman is still alive. But if the husband did not exempt his wife from an oath, all agree that the buyer cannot collect her ketubah settlement unless the woman herself takes an oath that she has not received it.

HALAKHAH

depends on the way it was formulated. If the husband wrote that his wife would be exempted from taking an oath to him, he cannot impose an oath upon her, but he can impose an oath upon her heirs, or upon those who come in her stead, such as someone who purchased her ketubah from her," following the Mishnah (*Rambam, Sefer Nashim, Hilkhot Ishut* 16:19; *Sefer Mishpatim, Hilkhot Malveh VeLoveh* 15:7; *Shulḥan Arukh, Even HaEzer* 98:1; *Ḥoshen Mishpat* 71:1, 17.)

[1]״נֶדֶר וּשְׁבוּעָה אֵין לִי עָלַיִךְ, וְעַל יוֹרְשַׁיִךְ, וְעַל הַבָּאִים בִּרְשׁוּתֵךְ״ — [2]אֵינוֹ יָכוֹל לְהַשְׁבִּיעָהּ — לֹא הִיא וְלֹא יוֹרְשֶׁיהָ, [3]וְלֹא אֶת הַבָּאִים בִּרְשׁוּתָהּ. [4]אֲבָל יוֹרְשָׁיו מַשְׁבִּיעִין אוֹתָהּ, וְאֶת יוֹרְשֶׁיהָ, וְאֶת הַבָּאִים בִּרְשׁוּתָהּ.

[5]״נֶדֶר וּשְׁבוּעָה אֵין לִי וְלֹא לְיוֹרְשַׁי וְלֹא לַבָּאִים בִּרְשׁוּתִי עָלַיִךְ, וְעַל יוֹרְשַׁיִךְ, וְעַל הַבָּאִים בִּרְשׁוּתֵיךְ״ — [6]אֵינוֹ יָכוֹל לְהַשְׁבִּיעָהּ, [7]לֹא הוּא, וְלֹא יוֹרְשָׁיו, וְלֹא הַבָּאִים בִּרְשׁוּתוֹ. לֹא אוֹתָהּ, וְלֹא יוֹרְשֶׁיהָ, וְלֹא הַבָּאִים בִּרְשׁוּתָהּ.

[8]הָלְכָה מִקֶּבֶר בַּעְלָהּ לְבֵית

LITERAL TRANSLATION

[1]"[I will have no claim of] a vow or an oath against you, or your heirs, or your lawful successors" [2]he may not impose an oath — not upon her, nor her heirs, [3]nor her lawful successors. [4]But his heirs may impose an oath upon her, and her heirs, and her lawful successors.

[5]"Neither I nor my heirs nor my lawful successors will have [a claim of] a vow or an oath against you, or your heirs, or your lawful successors," [6]he may not impose an oath upon her — [7]not him, nor his heirs, nor his lawful successors, not upon her, nor her heirs, nor her lawful successors.

[8][If] she went from her husband's grave to her father's house,

TRANSLATION AND COMMENTARY

נֶדֶר וּשְׁבוּעָה [1]If the husband wrote his wife: **"I will have no claim of a vow or an oath against you, or your heirs, or your lawful successors** to collect your ketubah settlement," [2]**he may not** later **impose an oath** upon anyone — **not upon** the woman **herself, nor** upon **her heirs** if she was widowed and then died before receiving her ketubah, [3]**nor** upon **her lawful successors,** for he stated explicitly that he was exempting all of these parties from having to take an oath. [4]**But** if the husband died, **his heirs may impose an oath upon** his widow, **upon** her **heirs,** if she dies before collecting the settlement, **or upon her lawful successors.**

נֶדֶר וּשְׁבוּעָה [5]If the husband wrote his wife: **"Neither I nor my heirs nor my lawful successors** — if I sell my property and you come to collect your ketubah settlement from the buyer — **will have a claim of a vow or an oath against you, or your heirs, or your lawful successors,"** [6]**he may not impose an oath upon her** — [7]**not him, nor his heirs, nor his lawful successors, not upon her, nor** upon **her heirs, nor** upon **her lawful successors** to collect her ketubah settlement, for he exempted all of these parties from having to take any sort of oath whether to him, or to his heirs, or to those who come in his place.

הָלְכָה מִקֶּבֶר בַּעְלָהּ [8]If the husband exempted his wife from having to take an oath or a vow to him or to his heirs, and he died, and after he was buried, the woman **went** directly **from her husband's grave to her**

RASHI

אבל יורשיו משביעין אותה — אם נתאלמנה, והיא או יורשיה נפרעין מן היתומים — צריכים שבועה, שהרי לא פטרן אלא ממנו, אם תגבה כתובתה בחייו. **לבאין ברשותי** — אם אמכור נכסי, ואת באה ליפרע מלקוחות. **הלכה מקבר בעלה כו׳** — זו שפטרה בעלה מן השבועה. והכי תני בהדיא בתוספתא — דאהך שפטרה קאי. **לבית אביה** — שלא נתעסקה שוב בנכסים.

NOTES

אֲבָל יוֹרְשָׁיו מַשְׁבִּיעִין אוֹתָהּ **But his heirs may impose an oath upon her.** Following the Gemara in *Shevuot* 48a, the Rishonim note that the Mishnah must be dealing here with a woman who was first divorced and then died during her husband's lifetime, and later the husband died. Her heirs must first take the heir's oath, before collecting her settlement. But if the husband died before her, the woman's heirs cannot collect anything, for she herself would have had to take an oath before collecting her ketubah settlement from his heirs, and there is a rule that a person cannot pass an oath down to his heirs.

הַבָּאִים בִּרְשׁוּתִי **Those who come in my stead.** *Rabbenu Ḥananel* writes that if the husband exempted his wife from taking an oath to those who come in his stead, the exemption is valid only with respect to her collecting her ketubah settlement from someone who bought liened property from the husband after he granted her the exemption. But the woman is still obligated to take an oath if she wishes to collect her ketubah settlement from someone who purchased property from her husband before he granted the exemption.

הָלְכָה מִקֶּבֶר בַּעְלָהּ **If she went from her husband's grave.** Our commentary follows *Rashi* and most Rishonim, who understand that the Mishnah here is dealing with a

HALAKHAH

עָלַיִךְ וְעַל יוֹרְשַׁיִךְ **Against you or your heirs.** "If the husband wrote that the woman, her heirs, and those who come in her place would be exempt from taking an oath to him, he cannot impose an oath upon any of them, but an oath can be imposed upon them by the husband's heirs or those who come in his stead, such as someone who purchased property from him," following the Mishnah. (*Rambam, Sefer Nashim, Hilkhot Ishut* 16:20; *Shulḥan Arukh, Even HaEzer* 98:3; *Ḥoshen Mishpat* 71:17.)

אֵין לִי וְלֹא לְיוֹרְשַׁי **Neither I nor my heirs.** "If the husband wrote that the woman, her heirs, and those who come in her place would all be exempt from having to take an oath to him, his heirs, or those who come in his place, neither he, nor his heirs, nor those who come in his place can impose an oath upon her, her heirs, or those who come in her place," following the Mishnah. (*Shulḥan Arukh, Even HaEzer* 98:4.)

הָלְכָה מִקֶּבֶר בַּעְלָהּ **If she went from her husband's grave.** "If a woman had been exempt from having to take an oath

TRANSLATION AND COMMENTARY

father's house, and had nothing further to do with her late husband's property, [1]**or she returned to her father-in-law's house,** [2]**but had not been made an administrator** over her late husband's estate, [3]**the heirs may not impose an oath upon her** when she comes to collect her ketubah settlement, nor may they impose an oath upon her regarding her managing of her husband's property during his lifetime. [4]**And if** the woman **had been made an administrator** over her late husband's estate after his burial, **the heirs may impose an oath upon her regarding** her handling of the property from that time **on,** for the exemption from an oath which had been extended to her by her husband is no longer valid. [5]**But they may not impose an oath upon her regarding** her managing of the property **in the past** during her husband's lifetime.

GEMARA שְׁבוּעָה [6]The Gemara asks: **What** exactly **is the effect** of exempting a woman from taking **an oath** to her husband or his heirs? From which oath is the woman exempt?

אָמַר רַב יְהוּדָה [7]**Rav Yehudah said in the name of Rav:** [87A] In this case the husband intends to forgo his right to exact an oath from his wife, whom he had appointed as [8]**an administrator** over his property

אָבִיהָ, [1]אוֹ שֶׁחָזְרָה לְבֵית חָמִיהָ, [2]וְלֹא נַעֲשֵׂית אַפּוֹטְרוֹפְּיָא — [3]אֵין הַיּוֹרְשִׁין מַשְׁבִּיעִין אוֹתָהּ. [4]וְאִם נַעֲשֵׂית אַפּוֹטְרוֹפְּיָא — הַיּוֹרְשִׁין מַשְׁבִּיעִין אוֹתָהּ עַל הֶעָתִיד לָבֹא, [5]וְאֵין מַשְׁבִּיעִין אוֹתָהּ עַל מַה שֶּׁעָבַר.

גמרא [6]שְׁבוּעָה, מַאי עֲבִידְתָּהּ?

[7]אָמַר רַב יְהוּדָה אָמַר רַב: [87A] [8]עַל אַפּוֹטְרוֹפְּיָא שֶׁנַּעֲשֵׂית בְּחַיֵּי בַּעְלָהּ.

LITERAL TRANSLATION

[1]or she returned to her father-in-law's house, [2]and she had not been made an administrator, [3]the heirs may not impose an oath upon her. [4]And if she had been made an administrator, the heirs may impose an oath upon her regarding that which will come in the future, [5]but they may not impose an oath upon her regarding that which has passed.

GEMARA [6]An oath, what is its purpose (lit., "its work")?

[7]Rav Yehudah said in the name of Rav: [87A] [8][It is] for [a woman] who had been made an administrator during her husband's lifetime.

RASHI

על העתיד לבא – על עסק שלאחר מיתה, שלא עיכבה בידה כלום. דהשתא נכסים דיתמי נינהו, ולא מהניא בהו פטור דידיה. על שעבר – על עסק שבחיי בעלה.

גמרא שבועה מאי עבידתה – איזו שבועה סתם שאשה חייבת לבעלה או ליורשיו, דקתני: דכי לא פטרה – משביעה, וכי פטרה – אין משביעה. על אפוטרופיא – פוטרה בכתיבה זאת משבועת אפוטרופוס אם יושיבנה חנונית. אבל אם פגמה כתובתה, דתנן במתניתין: הפוגמת כתובתה לא תפרע אלא בשבועה – לא

NOTES

husband who exempted his wife from having to take an oath or a vow to him or to his heirs. The Mishnah teaches that the heirs cannot impose an oath upon his widow if she had nothing further to do with her late husband's property after his funeral. If, however, she was made an administrator over his estate after his burial, the heirs may impose an oath upon her regarding her handling of the property from that time on, for the exemption from an oath which had been extended to her by her husband is no longer valid. A certain difficulty arises from this explanation, for we already learned in the first part of the Mishnah that if the husband exempted his wife from having to take an oath or a vow to him or to his heirs, the heirs cannot impose an oath upon her about her handling of their father's property during his lifetime. *Rabbenu Shmuel of Narbonne* and others answer that this clause of the Mishnah teaches that if the husband exempted his wife from taking an oath about her handling of his property, the heirs cannot impose an oath upon her relating to that matter even by attaching that oath to another oath which she is otherwise obligated to take. (Whether or not an oath can be imposed upon a person who had been exempted by that individual from having to swear about the matter is the subject of a dispute among the Rishonim.)

Rav Hai Gaon, Rif and others understand that the Mishnah is dealing here with a husband who did not exempt his wife from taking an oath. It teaches nevertheless that the heirs cannot impose an oath upon his widow about her handling of their father's property during his lifetime, despite the ability of the father to have done so. *Rav Hai Gaon* explains that since the husband could have made her swear but did not do so, we infer that he waived his right to any claim against her, and the heirs cannot make her take an oath to them. *Ramban* and others discuss these opinions at length in light of the related passages in the Tosefta and Jerusalem Talmud.

HALAKHAH

about her handling of her husband's property, and she was not appointed as an administrator over his estate after his burial, her husband's heirs cannot impose an oath upon her about her handling of their father's property during his lifetime, even by extending another oath that she is otherwise obligated to take. According to some authorities, the heirs cannot impose such an oath upon her, even if her husband had not exempted her from having to swear. But if the woman was appointed as an administrator over her husband's estate after his burial, her husband's heirs can impose an oath upon her regarding her handling of the property from the time of the burial." (*Rambam, Sefer Kinyan, Hilkhot Sheluḥin VeShutafin* 9:4; *Shulḥan Arukh, Even HaEzer* 98:4.)

SAGES

רַב מָרְדְּכַי Rav Mordekhai. A Babylonian Amora of the sixth generation, Rav Mordekhai was a pupil of Avimi of Hagrunya, in whose name he transmitted many legal rulings to Rav Ashi. Rav Mordekhai appears several times in the Talmud in the company of Rav Ashi and his colleagues, Amemar and Mar Zutra.

TRANSLATION AND COMMENTARY

during his **lifetime.** (See the previous Mishnah, 86b.)

רַב נַחְמָן [1]**Rav Naḥman said in the name of Rabbah bar Avuha:** When the husband exempts his wife from an oath, he intends to exempt her even from the oath which he can impose upon her if **she impairs her ketubah** and admits that she had already received partial payment of the settlement, and all the more so she is exempt from the oath which her husband can impose upon her if he had appointed her as an administrator over his property.

אֲזַל רַב מָרְדְּכַי [2]**Rav Mordekhai went and repeated before Rav Ashi this discussion** of the dispute between Rav Yehudah and Rav Naḥman, and posed the following question: [3]**Granted according to the** Amora **who said** that if the husband writes that he will have no claim of an oath against his wife, she is exempt even from the oath which he can impose upon her if **she impairs her ketubah,** we understand why he might write her such an exemption. [4]**For the** woman **thinks** to herself: **Perhaps I will need money** some day, **and** then **take** a **partial payment** of **my ketubah** settlement. [5]**So she says to** him: **"Write me that you will not impose an oath upon me** when I come to collect the rest of my ketubah or have other dealings with you." And since she is already asking her husband to exempt her from an oath should she detract from her ketubah, she also asks him to grant her a general exemption from having to take any oath. [6]**But according to the** Amora **who said** that if the husband writes that he will have no claim of an oath against his wife, she is only exempt from the oath which he could have imposed upon her if **she had been appointed an administrator** over her husband's property **during his lifetime,** there is a difficulty. [7]How **did** the woman **know that** her husband **would** one day appoint **her an administrator,** [8]**so that she would have said to him: "Write me that you will not impose an oath upon me** regarding my management of your property"?

אֲמַר לֵיהּ [9]Rav Ashi **said to** Rav Mordekhai: Your tradition regarding Rav Yehudah's statement in the

[1]רַב נַחְמָן אָמַר רַבָּה בַּר אֲבוּהּ: עַל הַפּוֹגֶמֶת כְּתוּבָּתָהּ.

[2]אֲזַל רַב מָרְדְּכַי אֲמָרָהּ לִשְׁמַעֲתָא קַמֵּיהּ דְּרַב אַשִׁי: [3]בִּשְׁלָמָא לְמַאן דְּאָמַר: עַל הַפּוֹגֶמֶת כְּתוּבָּתָהּ, [4]דְּמַסְקָא אַדַּעְתָּהּ: "דִּלְמָא מִצְטָרְכֵי לִי זוּזֵי וְשָׁקֵילְנָא מִכְּתוּבַּתַאי", [5]וְאָמְרָה לֵיהּ: "כְּתוֹב לִי דְּלָא מַשְׁבַּעַתְּ לִי". [6]אֶלָּא לְמַאן דְּאָמַר: עַל אַפּוֹטְרוֹפְּיָא שֶׁנַּעֲשֵׂית בְּחַיֵּי בַּעְלָהּ — [7]אִיהִי מִי הֲוָת יָדְעָה דְּמוֹתִיב לָהּ אַפּוֹטְרוֹפְּיָא, [8]דְּאָמְרָה לֵיהּ: "כְּתוֹב לִי דְּלָא מַשְׁבַּעַתְּ לִי"? [9]אֲמַר לֵיהּ: אַתּוּן אַהָא

LITERAL TRANSLATION

[1]Rav Naḥman said in the name of Rabbah bar Avuha: [It is] for [a woman] who had impaired [the value of] her ketubah.

[2]Rav Mordekhai went [and] said the tradition before Rav Ashi: [3]Granted according to the one who said: For having impaired her ketubah, [4]because she thinks: "Perhaps I will need money and I will take [partial payment] settlement, of my ketubah," [5]and she said to him: "Write for me that you will impose no oath upon me." [6]But according to the one who said: For having been made an administrator during her husband's lifetime — [7]did she know that he would make her an administrator, [8]that she would have said to him: "Write for me that you will impose no oath upon me"?

[9]Rav Ashi said to him: You

RASHI

נפטרה מאותה שבועה על ידי תנאי זה.

דכי פטר לה משבועה דקא רמי הוא עלה, אבל שבועה דהיא גרמה לנפשה — לא פטר לה. על הפוגמת — וכל שכן משבועת אפוטרופיא, דמכל שבועה פטרה. אמרה לשמעתא — הך אתקפתא: בשלמא למאן דאמר כו׳ אותביה קמיה דרב אשי. כתוב לי דלא משבעת לי — ומיגו דרמיא אנפשה — תבעה ליה פטור כל שבועות.

NOTES

עַל הַפּוֹגֶמֶת כְּתוּבָּתָהּ **Who had impaired her ketubah.** Most Rishonim agree with *Ra'avad* who says that even according to the opinion that the husband exempted his wife from the oath which she would have to take if she impaired her ketubah, he did not exempt her from the oath which she would have to take against a single witness testifying that she already received her the entire settlement, for when the husband exempted his wife from an oath, he meant to say that she would be trusted more than himself, but not more than a single witness who testifies against her. According to *Rosh,* the husband's exemption also covers the oath that would be administered to his wife because of the testimony of a single witness.

אִיהִי מִי הֲוָת יָדְעָה **Did she know.** The Rishonim ask: Why not say that the Mishnah is dealing with a husband who exempted his wife from an oath when he appointed her as an administrator? *Rashba* answers that the Gemara assumes that our Mishnah, like the other Mishnayot in the chapter, refers to agreements made at the time of betrothal or during marriage. *Rivash* answers that the Amoraim do not argue about how to understand the Mishnah, but about the law, and if the husband exempted his wife from an oath when he appointed her as an administrator, all would agree that he exempted her from having to swear about her handling of his property, and nothing else.

LITERAL TRANSLATION

taught it about that; [1]we taught it about this: [2]"[If] she went from her husband's grave to her father's house, [3]or she returned to her father-in-law's house, and she had not been made an administrator, [4]the heirs may not impose an oath upon her. [5]And if she had been made an administrator, the heirs may impose an oath upon her regarding that which will come in the future, [6]but they may not impose an oath upon her regarding that which had passed." [7]That which had passed, what is it its purpose (lit., "its work")?

[8]Rav Yehudah said in the name of Rav: [It is] for [a woman] who had been made an administrator during her husband's lifetime. [9]But [for the time] between death and burial, they may impose an oath upon her. [10]And Rav Matena said: Even [for the time] between death

מַתְנִיתוּ לָהּ; [1]אֲנַן אַהָא מַתְנִינַן לָהּ: [2]"הָלְכָה מִקֶּבֶר בַּעְלָהּ לְבֵית אָבִיהָ, [3]אוֹ שֶׁחָזְרָה לְבֵית חָמִיהָ, וְלֹא נַעֲשֵׂית אַפּוֹטְרוֹפְּיָא, [4]אֵין הַיּוֹרְשִׁין מַשְׁבִּיעִין אוֹתָהּ. [5]וְאִם נַעֲשֵׂית אַפּוֹטְרוֹפְּיָא, יוֹרְשִׁין מַשְׁבִּיעִין אוֹתָהּ עַל הֶעָתִיד לָבֹא, [6]וְאֵין מַשְׁבִּיעִין אוֹתָהּ עַל שֶׁעָבַר". [7]שֶׁעָבַר, מַאי עֲבִידְתֵּיהּ?

[8]אֲמַר רַב יְהוּדָה אָמַר רַב: עַל אַפּוֹטְרוֹפְּיָא שֶׁנַּעֲשֵׂית בְּחַיֵּי הַבַּעַל. [9]אֲבָל בֵּין מִיתָה לִקְבוּרָה, מַשְׁבְּעִינַן לָהּ. [10]וְרַב מַתָּנָא אֲמַר: אֲפִילּוּ בֵּין מִיתָה

TRANSLATION AND COMMENTARY

name of Rav differs from ours. **You taught** that Rav Yehudah's statement was made **with respect to** the first clause of the Mishnah which deals with the husband who did not specify from which oath he meant to exempt his wife, and your understanding of Rav Yehudah's statement leads you to your difficulty, namely that no one would have anticipated that she would be appointed to administrate his property. [1]But **we taught** that Rav Yehudah's statement in the name of Rav was made **with respect to** a later clause in the Mishnah, that says: [2]**"If** the husband exempted his wife from having to take an oath or a vow to him or to his heirs, and he died, and after he was buried, the woman **went** directly **from her husband's grave to her father's house,** and had nothing further to do with her late husband's property, [3]**or she returned to her father-in-law's house, but had not been made an administrator** over her late husband's estate, [4]**the heirs may not impose an oath upon her.** [5]And if the woman **was made an administrator** over her late husband's estate after his burial, **the heirs may impose an oath upon her regarding the future.** [6]**But they may not impose an oath upon her regarding** the **past."** [7]And it was asked: Regarding **the past, what purpose** does the Mishnah have in mentioning it? This clause deals with the period following the husband's death.

אֲמַר רַב יְהוּדָה [8]In answer to this question **Rav Yehudah said in the name of Rav:** They may not impose an oath upon her **regarding her having been made an administrator** over her husband's property **during his lifetime,** for the husband had exempted her from having to take such an oath. [9]**But regarding** her managing of her husband's property **between** the time of his **death and** the time of his **burial, they may** indeed **impose an oath upon her,** for at that time the property already belongs to her husband's heirs, and so the exemption from an oath which she had received from her husband no longer applies. [10]**And Rav Matena** disagreed and **said: Even regarding** the woman's managing of her husband's property **between** the time of his **death and** the time of his **burial they may not impose an**

RASHI

אתון אהא מתניתו — להא דרב יהודה, ארישא דמתניתין דלא פריש בה בהי שבועה איירי, ואפלוגתיה דרב נחמן, וסבריתו דרב יהודה אדרב נחמן פליג, וקשיא לכו. **אנן** — אסיפא דמתניתין מתנינן לה, דמיירי בשבועת אפוטרופין בהדיא דקתני: ואם נעשית אפוטרופיא. ודרב נחמן לאו אפלוגתא דרב יהודה אתמר, אלא אפירושא דרישא אתמר. ורב מתנא פליג אדרב יהודה בסיפא בהי אפוטרופוס קאמר לשעבר, אבל בפוגמת — כולהו מודו דפטרה, דשבועה הבאה לה על ידי נכסיו היא. **שעבר מאי עבידתיה** — כלומר, עד מתי קרוי לשעבר, דלא אמרינן נכסי דיתמי נינהו, ואין תנאי שלו מועיל בהן. **אבל בין מיתה לקבורה** — כבר רמו נכסי קמי יתמי, ואין תנאי שלו מועיל בהן, שלא על ידי נכסיו באה לה.

NOTES

שֶׁעָבַר, מַאי עֲבִידְתֵּיהּ **That which had passed, what is its purpose.** *Rashi* and others understand that this expression is used here in an unusual sense: What is the precise meaning of the words "that which passed"? Regarding what past things may the heirs not impose an oath upon the widow? *Talmidei Rabbenu Yonah* explain this expression in its more usual sense: What place is there for an oath? Since she went straight from her husband's grave to her father's house, surely the heirs cannot make her swear that she did not take of the property after her husband's death, for she did not have any dealings with that property at that time. Similarly the heirs cannot make her swear about her handling of her husband's property during his lifetime, for he exempted her from taking such an oath. Why then did the Mishnah have to say that the heirs may not impose an oath upon the woman regarding that which passed?

TRANSLATION AND COMMENTARY

oath upon her. [1]**For the** Sages of **Neharde'a say:** When the court acts on behalf of an orphan and decides to sell some of his property, it must publicize the sale in order to get the best price. But when the property is sold to raise money **for** payment of **the poll tax, or** to provide **maintenance** for a widow and her daughters, **or** to cover **burial** expenses, [2]it **may be sold** even **without a public announcement,** because of the urgency of the need. According to this understanding of Rav Yehudah's statement, Rav Mordekhai's difficulty falls away, for Rav Yehudah might very well agree with Rav Naḥman that if the husband writes his wife that he will have no claim of an oath against his wife, he means to exempt her even from the oath which he could otherwise have imposed upon her if she impaired her ketubah.

אָמַר רַבָּה [3]**Rabbah said in the name of Rabbi Ḥiyya:** If a husband exempted his wife from taking an oath, using the formulation: [4]**"Without a vow and without an oath," he may not** later **impose an oath upon her,** [5]**but his heirs may** indeed **impose an oath upon her,** for the husband, not his heirs exempted her from taking an oath. But if he formulated the exemption as follows: [6]**"Free regarding a vow, free regarding an oath," neither he nor his heirs may impose an oath upon her,** [7]for with that formulation **he** meant **to say to her: "You are** in all cases **free from** having to **take an oath."**

לִקְבוּרָה — לָא מַשְׁבַּעִינַן לָהּ.
[1]דְּאָמְרִי נְהַרְדְּעֵי: לְכַרְגָּא, וְלִמְזוֹנֵי, וְלִקְבוּרָה, [2]מְזַבְּנִינַן בְּלָא אַכְרַזְתָּא.
[3]אָמַר רַבָּה אָמַר רַב חִיָּיא: [4]"דְּלָא נֶדֶר וּדְלָא שְׁבוּעָה", הוּא אֵינוֹ יָכוֹל לְהַשְׁבִּיעָהּ, [5]אֲבָל יוֹרְשִׁין מַשְׁבִּיעִין אוֹתָהּ. [6]"נָקִי נֶדֶר נָקִי שְׁבוּעָה", בֵּין הוּא וּבֵין יוֹרְשִׁין אֵין מַשְׁבִּיעִין אוֹתָהּ. [7]הָכִי קָאָמַר לָהּ: "מְנַקִּית מִשְּׁבוּעֲתָא".

LITERAL TRANSLATION

and burial they may not impose an oath upon her. [1]For the Neharde'ans say: For the poll tax, and for maintenance, and for burial, [2]we sell [land] without [public] announcement.

[3]Rabbah said in the name of Rabbi Ḥiyya: [4]"Without a vow and without of an oath," he may not impose an oath upon her, [5]but the heirs may impose an oath upon her. [6]"Free of a vow, free of an oath," neither he nor the heirs may impose an oath upon her. [7]Thus he said to her: "You are free from [taking] an oath."

RASHI

לכרגא — לפרוע למלך כסף גולגלתא דיתמי. ולמזוני — מזון האשה והבנות והיתומים. ולקבורה — לקבורת המת או היתומים. מזבנינן — נכסי דיתמי בלא אכרזתא. שאין שהות ומתון לדבר. והכי נמי לא משבעינן על אותה מכירה, דאי אפשר שלא תזלזל ותפסידתן, ונמצאת שבועת שקר. דלא נדר דלא שבועה — אם כתב לה לשון זה. נקי נדר — מנקית משבועתא, מדין שבועה.

BACKGROUND

דְּאָמְרִי נְהַרְדְּעֵי **The Neharde'ans say.** Although this expression is a general one and refers to the Sages of the city of Neharde'a, nevertheless the Sages in the Talmud (*Sanhedrin* 17b) apply it to a particular Sage, Rav Hama, who was one of the most important Rabbis of that city. Occasionally this expression is used because the opinion expressed is not only Rav Ḥama's personal view but reflects the approach taken by all the Sages of Neharde'a.

LANGUAGE

כַּרְגָּא **Poll tax.** This word apparently stems from the ancient Persian *charak*, a poll tax paid by all residents.

NOTES

אֲפִילּוּ בֵּין מִיתָה לִקְבוּרָה — לָא מַשְׁבַּעִינַן לָהּ **Even for the time between death and burial they may not impose an oath upon her.** Our commentary follows *Rashi,* who explains that the widow cannot be obligated to take an oath that she managed her husband's property in the best possible manner, for she may have been force to sell some of it at a discount to raise money for his funeral. *Tosafot* understand that during this period the woman cannot even be obligated to take an oath that she kept none of her husband's property for herself, lest (as the Jerusalem Talmud explains) she head straight back to her father's house and refrain from handling her husband's burial (see *Rid* who cites both explanations.)

לְכַרְגָּא, וְלִמְזוֹנֵי **For the poll tax, and for maintenance.** *Rashi* explains that the court can sell some of the orphans' property without a public announcement in order to raise money for their poll tax or to provide for their maintenance. *Tosafot* object because this construction implies that a public announcement would be necessary if the property was being sold to raise money to cover other needs of the orphan, a conclusion that is contradicted elsewhere in the Talmud. *Ritva* suggests that according to *Rashi* the poll tax and maintenance mentioned here are merely examples, and the court can indeed sell orphans' property without public announcement for any of their other needs. *Tosafot* explain that the Neharde'an Sages meant here to permit selling some of the orphan's property without a public announcement in order to pay the widow's poll tax, an obligation that falls upon her husband and his heirs.

HALAKHAH

בֵּין מִיתָה לִקְבוּרָה — לָא מַשְׁבַּעִינַן לָהּ **Between death and burial they may not impose an oath upon her.** "An oath cannot be imposed upon a widow regarding the property belonging to her husband that she sold between the time of his death and the time of his burial in order to cover his funeral expenses. Such an oath cannot be imposed upon her even by way of attaching it to an oath that she is otherwise obligated to take," following Rav Matena. (*Rambam, Sefer Kinyan, Hilkhot Sheluḥin* 9:4; *Shulḥan Arukh, Even HaEzer* 98:5.)

לְכַרְגָּא, וְלִמְזוֹנֵי, וְלִקְבוּרָה **For the poll tax, and for maintenance, and for burial.** "The court may sell an orphan's property even without a prior public announcement, when the sale is necessary in order to raise money for the payment of a poll tax, or to provide maintenance for a widow and her daughters, or to cover burial expenses," following the Neharde'an Sages. (*Rambam, Sefer Mishpatim, Hilkhot Malveh VeLoveh* 12:11; *Shulḥan Arukh, Even HaEzer* 104:3.)

TRANSLATION AND COMMENTARY

וְרַב יוֹסֵף [1]A very different tradition relating ot the second half of Rabbi Ḥiyya's position was taught by **Rav Yosef** who **said in the name of Rabbi Ḥiyya:** If the husband formulated his exemption as follows: **"Without a vow and without an oath,"** [2]**he may not** later **impose an oath upon** his wife, **but his heirs may** indeed **impose an oath upon her,** for the husband, not his heirs, exempted her from her obligation from taking an oath. But if the husband said: [3]**"Free from a vow, free from an oath," both he and the heirs may impose an oath upon her,** for he had no intention of exempting his wife from taking a vow. [4]Rather **he** meant to **say to her as follows: "Free** yourself from any suspicion by taking **an oath."**

שָׁלַח רַבִּי זַכַּאי [5]**Rabbi Zakkai sent** the following ruling **to Mar Ukva: Whether** the husband **wrote "without an oath," or** he wrote **"free of an oath," or** he wrote **"without a vow," or** he wrote **"free of a vow"** — [6]if he added the words **"regarding *my* property," he may not** later **impose an oath upon her,** [7]**but his heirs may** indeed **impose an oath upon her.** The phrase "regarding my property" implies that the wife's exemption from taking an oath would only apply during his lifetime while the property was still her husband's. After his death, however, the property would pass to his heirs, and the exemption no longer applies. But if he formulated his exemption, [8]saying **"regarding *this*** particular **property," neither he nor his heirs may impose an oath upon her.**

אָמַר רַב נַחְמָן [9]The Gemara now presents a different position on this matter: **Rav Naḥman said in the name of Shmuel who said in the name of Abba Shaul ben Imma Miryam:** [10]**Whether** the husband **wrote "without an oath," or** he wrote **"free of an oath,"** [11]**or** he wrote **"without a vow," or** he wrote **"free of a vow"** — [12]**whether he added** the words **"regarding *my* property," or** he added the words **"regarding *this* property,"** [13]by right **neither he nor his heirs may impose an oath upon her.** [14]**But what can I do?** [15]**The Sages said:** If **someone comes to collect** a debt **from the property of** his deceased debtor which had passed to his heirs, he **may not collect** anything without first taking **an oath** that he had not already been paid. No matter how the husband

[1]וְרַב יוֹסֵף אָמַר רַבִּי חִיָּיא: ״דְּלָא
נֶדֶר וּדְלָא שְׁבוּעָה״, [2]הוּא אֵינוֹ
יָכוֹל לְהַשְׁבִּיעָהּ, אֲבָל יוֹרְשִׁין
מַשְׁבִּיעִין אוֹתָהּ. [3]״נָקִי נֶדֶר, נָקִי
שְׁבוּעָה״, בֵּין הוּא וּבֵין יוֹרְשִׁין
מַשְׁבִּיעִין אוֹתָהּ. [4]הָכִי קָאָמַר
לָהּ: ״נַקִּי נַפְשָׁךְ בִּשְׁבוּעֲתָא״.
[5]שָׁלַח רַבִּי זַכַּאי לְמָר עוּקְבָא:
בֵּין ״דְּלָא שְׁבוּעָה״, בֵּין ״דְּנָקִי
שְׁבוּעָה״, בֵּין ״דְּלָא נֶדֶר״, וּבֵין
״דְּנָקִי נֶדֶר״ — [6]״בִּנְכָסַי״, הוּא
אֵינוֹ יָכוֹל לְהַשְׁבִּיעָהּ, [7]אֲבָל
יוֹרְשִׁין מַשְׁבִּיעִין אוֹתָהּ.
[8]״מִנִּכְסַיָּא אִילֵּין״ — בֵּין הוּא
וּבֵין יוֹרְשָׁיו אֵין מַשְׁבִּיעִין אוֹתָהּ.
[9]אָמַר רַב נַחְמָן אָמַר שְׁמוּאֵל
מִשּׁוּם אַבָּא שָׁאוּל בֶּן אִימָּא
מִרְיָם: [10]בֵּין ״דְּלָא שְׁבוּעָה״, בֵּין
״דְּנָקִי שְׁבוּעָה״, [11]בֵּין ״דְּלָא
נֶדֶר״ וּבֵין ״דְּנָקִי נֶדֶר״, [12]בֵּין
״מִנְּכָסַי״ וּבֵין ״מִנִּכְסַיָּא אִילֵּין״
— [13]בֵּין הוּא וּבֵין יוֹרְשָׁיו אֵין
מַשְׁבִּיעִין אוֹתָהּ. [14]אֲבָל מָה
אֶעֱשֶׂה? [15]שֶׁהֲרֵי אָמְרוּ חֲכָמִים:
הַבָּא לִיפָּרַע מִנִּכְסֵי יְתוֹמִים לֹא
יִפָּרַע אֶלָּא בִּשְׁבוּעָה.

LITERAL TRANSLATION

[1]And Rav Yosef said in the name of Rabbi Ḥiyya: "Without a vow and without an oath," [2]he may not impose an oath upon her, but the heirs may impose an oath upon her. [3]"Free [from a] vow, free [from an] oath," both he and the heirs may impose an oath upon her. [4]Thus he said to her: "Free yourself [by means of] an oath."

[5]Rabbi Zakkai sent to Mar Ukva: Whether [he wrote] "without an oath," or "free [from an] oath," or "without a vow," or "free [from a] vow" — [6]"regarding my property," he may not impose an oath upon her, [7]but the heirs may impose an oath upon her. [8]"Regarding this property," neither he nor his heirs may impose an oath upon her.

[9]Rav Naḥman said in the name of Shmuel who said in the name of Abba Shaul ben Imma Miryam: [10]Whether [he wrote] "without an oath," or "free [from an] oath," [11]or "without a vow," or "free [from a] vow," [12]whether [he added] "regarding my property," or "regarding this property," [13]neither he nor his heirs may impose an oath upon her. [14]But what can I do? [15]For the Sages said: Someone who comes to collect from the property of orphans may collect only with an oath.

SAGES

רַב יוֹסֵף **Rav Yosef.** A Babylonian Amora of the third generation. See *Ketubot,* Part II, p.102

רַב חִסְדָּא **Rav Hisda.** A Babylonian Amora of the second generation. See *Ketubot,* Part II, p.64.

מָר עוּקְבָא **Mar Ukva.** The Exilarch in Babylonia during the first generation of Amoraim. See *Ketubot,* Part V, p.34.

אַבָּא שָׁאוּל בֶּן אִמָּא מִרְיָם **Abba Shaul ben Imma Miryam.** We do not know who this scholar was or when he lived. The title "Abba" was apparently used as an honorific before "Rabbi" came into use.

Our scholar's mother's name was apparently mentioned to distinguish him from other Sages with the same first name and title, e.g., Abba Shaul without patronymic (in *Ketubot* 88b, two scholars by this name are mentioned!), or Abba Shaul ben Botnit. Other scholars, too, are occasionally identified by matronymics — apparently, because of their mothers' illustrious lineage (or because their mothers were distinguished for other reasons). Abba Shaul ben Miryam's mother's title, "Imma" ("mother"), is apparently an honorific for an important woman.

RASHI

נקי נפשך בשבועתא — אם יחשדוך, השבעי להם. אבל מה אעשה — דלעולם יורשין משביעין אותה אם מת הוא, והיא נפרעת מהם.

NOTES

הַבָּא לִיפָּרַע מִנִּכְסֵי יְתוֹמִים **Someone who comes to collect from the property of orphans.** The Geonim maintain that Rav Naḥman's ruling in accordance with the position of Abba Shaul ben Imma Miryam applies only when the

TRANSLATION AND COMMENTARY

had formulated the exemption for his wife, she must first take an oath before she can collect anything from his heirs.

וְאִיכָּא דְּאָמְרִי **¹There are some who say** that Abba Shaul ben Imma Miryam's position is known not only through an Amoraic tradition, but it is also recorded in **a Baraita** which taught: **²"Abba Shaul ben Imma Miryam said: Whether** the husband **wrote 'without an oath,'** or he wrote **'free regarding an oath,'** ³or he wrote **'without a vow,'** or he wrote **'free regarding a vow'** — **⁴whether he added** the words **'regarding my property,'** or he added the words **'regarding this property,'** ⁵by right **neither he nor his heirs may impose an oath upon her.** ⁶**But what can I do?** ⁷**The Sages said: If someone comes to collect a debt** from the property of his deceased debtor which had passed to his heirs, he **may collect** only by first taking **an oath** that he had not already **been paid."** ⁸And **Rav Naḥman said in the name of Shmuel: The law is in accordance with** the view of Abba Shaul **the son of Imma Miryam.**

MISHNAH הַפּוֹגֶמֶת כְּתוּבָּתָהּ ⁹**The following Mishnah discusses several cases of women who must first take an oath before collecting their ketubah settlement. If a woman impairs her ketubah** and admits that she had already received part of the sum recorded therein, but insists that part of the obligation is still outstanding, and her husband claims that she had already received her entire settlement, she **may not collect** the remainder **without** first taking **an oath** that she is still owed money.

LITERAL TRANSLATION

¹And there are [some] who say a Baraita: ²"Abba Shaul ben Imma Miryam said: Whether [he wrote] 'without an oath,' or **'free [from an] oath,' ³or 'without a vow,'** or **'free [from a] vow' — ⁴whether [he wrote] 'regarding my property,'** or **'regarding this property,' ⁵neither he nor his heirs may impose an oath upon her. ⁶But what can I do? ⁷For the Sages said: Someone who comes to collect from the property of orphans may collect only with an oath."** ⁸**Rav Naḥman said in the name of Shmuel: The law is in accordance with the son of Imma Miryam.**

MISHNAH ⁹**A woman who impairs her ketubah may not collect without an oath.**

וְאִיכָּא דְּאָמְרִי לָהּ מַתְנִיתָא: ²"אַבָּא שָׁאוּל בֶּן אִימָּא מִרְיָם אָמַר: בֵּין "דְּלָא שְׁבוּעָה", בֵּין "דְּנָקֵי שְׁבוּעָה", ³בֵּין "דְּלָא נֶדֶר", וּבֵין "נָקֵי נֶדֶר", ⁴בֵּין "מִנְּכָסַי", וּבֵין "מִנִּכְסַיָּא אִילֵּין" — ⁵בֵּין הוּא וּבֵין יוֹרְשָׁיו אֵין מַשְׁבִּיעִין אוֹתָהּ. ⁶אֲבָל מָה אֶעֱשֶׂה? ⁷שֶׁהֲרֵי אָמְרוּ חֲכָמִים: הַבָּא לִיפָּרַע מִנְּכְסֵי יְתוֹמִים לֹא יִפָּרַע אֶלָּא בִּשְׁבוּעָה". ⁸אָמַר רַב נַחְמָן אָמַר שְׁמוּאֵל: הֲלָכָה כְּבֶן אִימָּא מִרְיָם.

מִשְׁנָה ⁹הַפּוֹגֶמֶת כְּתוּבָּתָהּ — לֹא תִּפָּרַע אֶלָּא בִּשְׁבוּעָה.

RASHI

ואיכא דאמרי לה — להא דאבא שאול בן אימא מריס מתניתא, [ולא אמרו לה בלשון שמעתא דאמורא, כדאמרן דאמר שמואל משום אבא שאול, אלא מתניתא] היא, ואמר שמואל עלה הלכה כאבא שאול.

משנה הפוגמת כתובתה — כדמפרש ואזיל במתניתין גופה. לא תפרע — השאר. וגמרא מפרש טעמא.

NOTES

husband exempted his wife from an oath in general terms and at the time of betrothal, without specifying, as in the Mishnah, who the claimant will be. In this case, according to the Sages' enactment, she must still take an oath when collecting her ketubah settlement from his heirs. But if before he died, the husband left instructions that his widow be given her ketubah settlement without having to swear, she may indeed collect it without an oath, for the case is treated like that of a gift of a person on his deathbed. *Meiri* adds that even if the husband said clearly at the time of betrothal that he exempts her from taking an oath before him or his heirs, she must still take an oath to collect the ketubah settlement from the heirs, due to the Rabbinical enactment.

According to *Rif*, *Rambam*, and many other Rishonim, Abba Shaul's ruling only applies when the husband exempted his wife from an oath, using the expression "without an oath," "without a vow," or some other ambiguous formulation. But if the husband clearly exempted his wife from having to take an oath to him or to his heirs, even Abba Shaul agrees that she is not required to take an oath when she comes to collect her ketubah settlement from her husband's heirs. But many Rishonim (*Rabbenu Ḥananel, Rabbenu Tam*, the *Sages of Narbonne*, and others) disagree and say that a widow must always take an oath when she comes to collect her ketubah settlement from her husband's heirs, no matter how her husband formulated his exemption.

HALAKHAH

הֲלָכָה כְּבֶן אִימָּא מִרְיָם **The law is in accordance with the son of Imma Miryam.** "Even if the husband wrote "without an oath" or "without a vow," and even if he wrote "regarding this property," the husband's heirs may still impose an oath upon a widow when she comes to collect her ketubah settlement. She is only exempt from such an

oath if the husband explicitly exempted her from having to swear to his heirs." (*Rambam, Sefer Nashim, Hilkhot Ishut* 18:19; *Shulḥan Arukh, Even HaEzer* 98:6.)

הַפּוֹגֶמֶת כְּתוּבָּתָה **A woman who impairs her ketubah.** "If a woman comes to collect her ketubah settlement, and her husband claims that he already paid her the entire amount,

¹עֵד אֶחָד מְעִידָהּ שֶׁהִיא פְּרוּעָה — לֹא תִּפָּרַע אֶלָּא בִּשְׁבוּעָה. ²מִנִּכְסֵי יְתוֹמִים, ³וּמִנְּכָסִים מְשׁוּעְבָּדִים, ⁴וְשֶׁלֹּא בְּפָנָיו — לֹא תִּפָּרַע אֶלָּא בִּשְׁבוּעָה. ⁵״הַפּוֹגֶמֶת כְּתוּבָּתָהּ״, כֵּיצַד? ⁶הָיְתָה כְּתוּבָּתָהּ אֶלֶף זוּז, וְאָמַר לָהּ: ״הִתְקַבַּלְתְּ כְּתוּבָּתֵיךְ״, ⁷וְהִיא אוֹמֶרֶת: ״לֹא הִתְקַבַּלְתִּי אֶלָּא מָנֶה״ — ⁸לֹא תִּפָּרַע אֶלָּא בִּשְׁבוּעָה.

LITERAL TRANSLATION

¹[If] one witness testifies that it was paid, she may not collect without an oath. ²[If she comes to collect] from the property of orphans, ³or from mortgaged property, ⁴or in his absence, she may not collect without an oath. ⁵"A woman who impairs her ketubah," how so? ⁶[If] her ketubah was a thousand zuz, and he said to her: "You received your ketubah," ⁷and she says: "I received only a maneh," ⁸she may not collect without an oath.

RASHI

עד אחד מעידה כו׳ — בגמרא מפרש טעמא. **מנכסים משועבדים** — משום דאי הוה גבי מן הלוה גופיה, והוה טוען לוה: אשתבע לי דלא פרעתיך — אמרינן בשבועות דמשבעינן ליה, ואי לא טעין — לא טענינן ליה, הואיל ונקיט שטרא. אבל בשביל לקוחות — אנן טענינן: דלמא אי הוה גבית מן הלוה — הוה טעין לך: אישתבע לי דלא פרעתיך, ובעית אישתבועי. השתא אנן טענינן, ד״פתח פיך לאלם״ הוא. ומנכסי יתומים, ונפרעת שלא בפניו — כולהו משום האי טעמא.

TRANSLATION AND COMMENTARY

עֵד אֶחָד ¹If a woman comes to collect her ketubah settlement, and **one witness testifies** on behalf of her husband **that** it had already been **paid, she may not collect** anything **without** first taking **an oath** to confirm her claim.

מִנִּכְסֵי יְתוֹמִים ²If a widow **comes to collect** her ketubah settlement **from** her late husband's **property** that had passed to his heirs, she may not collect it without first taking an oath that she had not already received her payment. ³Similarly, if a woman wishes to collect the settlement **from property** that had been **mortgaged** to her ketubah, but was sold by her husband, she must first take an oath in order to collect the field (or its value) from the buyer. So too, if a woman was divorced and her husband went abroad before paying her ketubah settlement, ⁴and she asks the court to collect it from her husband's property **in his absence, she may not collect** anything **without** first taking **an oath** that she had not yet received payment.

הַפּוֹגֶמֶת כְּתוּבָּתָהּ ⁵The Mishnah now explains each of these cases in greater detail: **"A woman who impairs her ketubah,"** how so? ⁶**If** a woman's **ketubah was a thousand zuz,** and she came to collect the money after her divorce, **and** her ex-husband **said to her: "You** have already **received your ketubah** settlement," ⁷**and she said:** "To date **I received only a maneh** (one hundred zuz), the remainder being outstanding," ⁸**she may not collect** anything **without** first taking **an oath** that indeed she had not yet received the nine hundred zuz.

NOTES

מִנְּכָסִים מְשׁוּעְבָּדִים **From mortgaged property.** Almost all of the Rishonim conclude that even if the husband wrote a credence clause for his wife, exempting her from any oath which any one might otherwise force her to take, nevertheless, the woman cannot collect her ketubah settlement without an oath from property which her husband had sold to a third person. His willingness to believe his wife without an oath does not obligate the buyer to do the same. The buyer's standing is different from that of the heir, for the heir inherits the place of the deceased and assumes his rights and obligations, including the exemption from an oath that he may have granted his wife. *Rid* disagrees and also exempts the buyer from forcing her to take an oath, explaining that the husband's written exemption for his wife is in effect, a clause that also restricts the purchaser.

HALAKHAH

and she admits that she received part of the sum, she cannot collect the rest without first taking an oath that she is still owed the money," following the Mishnah. (*Rambam, Sefer Nashim, Hilkhot Ishut* 16:14; *Shulḥan Arukh, Even HaEzer* 96:7.)

עֵד אֶחָד מְעִידָהּ שֶׁהִיא פְּרוּעָה **One witness testifies that it was paid.** "If a woman comes to collect her ketubah settlement, and her husband claims that he already paid her the entire amount, and a single witness testifies that the woman received it either in part or in its entirety, she cannot collect it without first taking an oath that she is still owed the money," following the Mishnah. (*Rambam, Sefer Nashim, Hilkhot Ishut* 16:15; *Shulḥan Arukh, Even HaEzer* 96:8.)

מִנְּכָסִים מְשׁוּעְבָּדִים **From mortgaged property.** "A woman cannot collect her ketubah settlement from property which her husband had sold to another person without first taking an oath that she has not already received it," following the Mishnah. (*Rambam, Sefer Nashim, Hilkhot Ishut* 16:10; *Shulḥan Arukh, Even HaEzer* 96:9.)

מִנִּכְסֵי יְתוֹמִים **From the property of orphans.** "A widow cannot collect her ketubah settlement from her late husband's property which had passed to his heirs without first taking an oath that she had not already received it," following the Mishnah. (*Rambam, Sefer Nashim, Hilkhot Ishut* 16:19; *Shulḥan Arukh, Even HaEzer* 96:1.)

[1] "עֵד אֶחָד מְעִידָהּ שֶׁהִיא פְּרוּעָה", כֵּיצַד? [2] הָיְתָה כְּתוּבָּתָהּ אֶלֶף זוּז, וְאָמַר לָהּ: "הִתְקַבַּלְתְּ כְּתוּבָּתֵיךְ", [3] וְהִיא אוֹמֶרֶת: "לֹא הִתְקַבַּלְתִּי", [4] וְעֵד אֶחָד מְעִידָהּ שֶׁהִיא פְּרוּעָה — [5] לֹא תִּפָּרַע אֶלָּא בִּשְׁבוּעָה.

[6] "מִנְּכָסִים מְשׁוּעְבָּדִים", כֵּיצַד? [7] מָכַר נְכָסָיו לַאֲחֵרִים, וְהִיא נִפְרַעַת מִן הַלָּקוֹחוֹת — [8] לֹא תִּפָּרַע אֶלָּא בִּשְׁבוּעָה.

[9] "מִנִּכְסֵי יְתוֹמִים", כֵּיצַד? [10] מֵת, וְהִנִּיחַ נְכָסָיו לִיתוֹמִים, וְהִיא נִפְרַעַת מִן הַיְתוֹמִים — [11] לֹא תִּפָּרַע אֶלָּא בִּשְׁבוּעָה.

[12] "וְשֶׁלֹּא בְּפָנָיו", כֵּיצַד? [13] הָלַךְ לוֹ לִמְדִינַת הַיָּם, וְהִיא נִפְרַעַת שֶׁלֹּא בְּפָנָיו — [14] אֵינָהּ נִפְרַעַת אֶלָּא בִּשְׁבוּעָה.

[87B] [15] רַבִּי שִׁמְעוֹן אוֹמֵר: כָּל זְמַן שֶׁהִיא תּוֹבַעַת כְּתוּבָּתָהּ — הַיּוֹרְשִׁין מַשְׁבִּיעִין אוֹתָהּ. [16] וְאִם אֵינָהּ תּוֹבַעַת כְּתוּבָּתָהּ — אֵין הַיּוֹרְשִׁין מַשְׁבִּיעִין אוֹתָהּ.

LITERAL TRANSLATION

[1] "One witness testifying that it was paid," how so? [2] [If] her ketubah was a thousand zuz, and he said to her: "You received your ketubah," [3] and she says: "I did not receive [it]," [4] and one witness testified that it was paid, [5] she may not collect without an oath.

[6] "From mortgaged property," how so? [7] [If] he sold his property to others, and she collects from the buyer, [8] she may not collect without an oath.

[9] "From the property of orphans," how so? [10] If he died, and left property to [his] orphans, and she collects from the orphans, [11] she may not collect without an oath.

[12] "Or in his absence," how so? [13] [If] he went abroad, and she collects in his absence, [14] she may not collect without an oath.

[87B] [15] Rabbi Shimon says: Whenever she claims her ketubah, the heirs may impose an oath upon her. [16] And if she is not claiming her ketubah, the heirs may not impose an oath upon her.

TRANSLATION AND COMMENTARY

עֵד אֶחָד [1] **"One witness testifying that** the woman's' settlement **was** already **paid,"** **how so?** [2] **If it was a thousand zuz,** and she came to collect the money after having been divorced, **and** the ex-husband **said to her: "You** already **received** all the money for **your ketubah,"** [3] **and she said: "I did not** yet **receive** any part of **it,"** [4] **and one witness** came and **testified** in the husband's favor **that** it **had** indeed **been paid,** [5] **she may not collect** anything **without** first taking **an oath** to confirm her claim.

מִנְּכָסִים מְשׁוּעְבָּדִים [6] **"From mortgaged property,"** **how so?** [7] If the husband **sold property** that had been mortgaged under the lien established by her ketubah, and she was widowed or divorced, **and** the woman came to **collect** the field (or its value) **from the buyer** of the mortgaged property, [8] **she may not collect** anything from him **without** first taking **an oath** that she had not yet received her ketubah settlement.

מִנִּכְסֵי יְתוֹמִים [9] **"From the property of orphans,"** **how so?** [10] If the husband **died, and left property to** his heirs, **and** the widow came to **collect** her ketubah settlement **from** those **heirs,** [11] **she may not collect** anything **without** first taking **an oath** that she had not yet received her ketubah settlement.

וְשֶׁלֹּא בְּפָנָיו [12] **"Or in his absence,"** **how so?** [13] If the husband **went abroad** after divorcing his wife but without paying her ketubah settlement, **and she** comes now to **collect** it from her ex-husband's property **in his absence,** [14] **she may not collect** anything **without** first taking **an oath** that she had not yet received her ketubah settlement.

[87B] רַבִּי שִׁמְעוֹן אוֹמֵר [15] **Rabbi Shimon says: Whenever** a woman **claims her ketubah** settlement from her late husband's heirs, **the heirs may impose an oath upon her** that she has not yet received it. [16] **But if she is not claiming her ketubah** settlement from them, **the heirs may not impose an oath upon her.**

RASHI

רבי שמעון אומר כו׳ – בגמרא מפרש להיא קאי.

NOTES

וְשֶׁלֹּא בְּפָנָיו **Not in his presence.** Most of the Geonim maintain that the wife cannot collect her ketubah settlement from her husband's property in his absence without an oath even if he had written her a credence clause, relieving her of any oath that may be necessary. One possible explanation could be that we assume that he only waived the right to demand an oath when she collects from him personally, thinking that she would not have the

HALAKHAH

וְשֶׁלֹּא בְּפָנָיו **Not in his presence.** "If a woman comes to collect her ketubah settlement from her husband who divorced her and then went abroad, she may not collect from his property without first taking an oath that she did not already receive the settlement. If it is possible to go to the husband and return within thirty days, a messenger

TRANSLATION AND COMMENTARY

GEMARA סָבַר [1]**Rami bar Ḥama thought to say: This oath,** imposed upon a woman who impairs her ketubah, is **by Torah law.** [2]**For** the husband **claims** that he already paid his wife a settlement of **two hundred** zuz, **and** she **admits** that she received **from him a hundred** zuz. [3]Thus, the woman **admits to part of** her husband's **claim,** [4]**and by Torah law whoever admits to part of a claim** brought against him by a plaintiff **must swear** to support his claim if he is to be believed.

אָמַר רָבָא [5]**Rava said: There are two arguments** that can be raised **against this** position: [6]**First, all those who take an oath that** is mentioned in the Torah, [7]**take an oath** to exempt themselves **from payment.** The verse states (Exodus 22:10): "And the owner of it shall accept this [the oath], and he [the bailee] shall not pay," implying that a Torah oath falls upon the defendant, who would otherwise have been obligated to pay. But here the woman is the plaintiff, [8]for it is **she** who **swears and collects** what she claims is still owed her. Thus, her oath cannot be required by Torah law. [9]**And moreover,** by Torah law **an oath is not taken** when the defendant **denies** a claim that gives the plaintiff **a lien on** the defendant's **land.** Since all the husband's landed property is mortgaged to his wife's ketubah, a claim regarding it is considered a claim involving land, and there is a general rule that oaths are not imposed by the Torah in cases involving land.

גמרא [1]סָבַר רָמִי בַּר חָמָא לְמֵימַר: שְׁבוּעָה דְּאוֹרַיְיתָא, [2]דְּקָא טָעֵין מָאתַיִם, וְקָא מוֹדָה לֵיהּ בְּמָאָה, [3]הָוְיָא לֵיהּ הוֹדָאָה בְּמִקְצָת הַטַּעֲנָה, [4]וְכָל הַמּוֹדֶה בְּמִקְצָת הַטַּעֲנָה יִשָּׁבַע.

[5]אָמַר רָבָא: שְׁתֵּי תְּשׁוּבוֹת בַּדָּבָר: [6]חֲדָא, דְּכָל הַנִּשְׁבָּעִין שֶׁבַּתּוֹרָה, [7]נִשְׁבָּעִין וְלֹא מְשַׁלְּמִין. [8]וְהִיא נִשְׁבַּעַת וְנוֹטֶלֶת. [9]וְעוֹד, אֵין נִשְׁבָּעִין עַל כְּפִירַת שִׁעְבּוּד קַרְקָעוֹת!

LITERAL TRANSLATION

GEMARA [1]Rami bar Ḥama thought to say: [This oath regarding an impaired ketubah is] an oath by Torah law, [2]for he claims two hundred, and she admits to him a hundred, [3][which] is an admission to part of the claim, [4]and whoever admits to part of the claim must swear [by Torah law].

[5]Rava said: [There are] two arguments against this matter: [6]First, all those who swear by Torah [law], [7]swear and do not pay. [8]And she swears and collects. [9]And moreover, we do not swear [to confirm] the denial of a lien on land.

RASHI

גמרא שבועה דאורייתא — ונפקא מינה דלא מפכינן לה. **נשבעין ולא משלמין** — מי שתובעין אותו נשבע, שנאמר "ולקח בעליו ולא ישלם" מי שעליו לשלם הוא נשבע. כל שטרות שיעבוד קרקעות הן, ואין נשבעין על הקרקעות, כדאמרינן בשבועות (מב,ב) וב"הזהב" (בבא מציעא נז,ב).

NOTES

audacity to lie to his face and claim a settlement that she already had received. Alternatively, we might assume that since he had granted her credence when they were married he would have taken the precaution of demanding a receipt for the settlement when he paid her. In his absence, he obviously cannot produce it.

סָבַר רָמִי בַּר חָמָא **Rami bar Ḥama thought to say.** The Rishonim ask: How could Rami bar Ḥama have made such an elementary error and suggest that the oath imposed upon a woman who impairs her ketubah settlement is by Torah law? Surely the Mishnah states that a Torah oath is only taken by the defendant in order to support his denial of a claim brought against him (*Shavuot* 45a), but not regarding a claim involving land! They answer that Rami bar Ḥama never meant to say that the oath imposed upon a woman who impairs her ketubah settlement is by Torah law, but rather that when the Rabbis imposed their oath they did it in a manner similar to the Torah oath imposed upon a defendant who admits to part of the claim brought against him. However, Rava misunderstood his words and thought that he meant that the oath imposed upon the woman is by Torah law. The similarity between the oath administered to a woman who impairs her ketubah settlement and a Torah oath may be understood as follows: Since the woman is holding the ketubah deed, she is considered as if she were already in possession of the money that she can collect with it, and the husband who claims that the deed was already paid is in effect, coming

HALAKHAH

must be sent to inform him that his wife's ketubah settlement will be collected from his property. If he does not come, the woman can collect it from his property with an oath." (*Rambam, Sefer Nashim, Hilkhot Ishut* 16:15; *Shulḥan Arukh, Even HaEzer* 96:10.)

וְכָל הַמּוֹדֶה בְּמִקְצָת הַטַּעֲנָה יִשָּׁבַע **Whoever admits part of the claim must swear.** "If the defendant admitted part of a claim brought against him regarding movable goods, he must pay the amount admitted, and take a Torah oath regarding the rest." (*Rambam, Sefer Hafla'ah, Hilkhot Shevuot* 11:5; *Shulḥan Arukh, Ḥoshen Mishpat* 87:1.)

אֵין נִשְׁבָּעִין עַל כְּפִירַת שִׁעְבּוּד קַרְקָעוֹת **We do not swear to confirm the denial of a lien on land.** "The defendant is not liable for a Torah oath if he denied a claim regarding landed property, but the Rabbis enacted that he take a *hesset* oath." (*Rambam, Sefer Mishpatim, Hilkhot To'en VeNit'an* 5:1; *Shulḥan Arukh, Ḥoshen Mishpat* 95:1.)

TRANSLATION AND COMMENTARY

אֶלָּא [1]Rather, Rava said: The oath that may be imposed upon a woman who has received partial payment of her ketubah settlement is by Rabbinic decree. By Torah law the ketubah deed she puts forward is sufficient proof that her husband owes her the sum recorded therein. Her admission that part of the settlement had already been paid does not invalidate the evidence supplied by her ketubah deed that she is owed money. Why then did the Rabbis impose an oath in this case? [2]The party who pays back a debt is generally scrupulous about remembering the matter in case the claimant comes to ask for the money again. [3]But the party who is paid back a debt is not generally as scrupulous about remembering the details, as he was on the receiving end. In our case the husband claims with certainty that he already paid his wife her entire ketubah settlement, and she claims that she only received part of it. Thus, there is reason to think that the entire ketubah was indeed paid out, and she may have forgotten the details of the payment. [4]The Rabbis therefore cast an oath upon her so that she will be scrupulous in her dealings with the ketubah. For they assumed that she would not take the oath unless she were absolutely certain that she had not received the entire settlement.

[1]אֶלָּא, אֲמַר רָבָא: מִדְּרַבָּנַן. [2]דְּפָרַע דָּיֵיק. [3]דְּמִיפְּרַע לָא דָּיֵיק. [4]וּרְמוּ רַבָּנַן שְׁבוּעָה עֲלָהּ כִּי הֵיכִי דְּתֵידוּק.

[5]אִיבַּעֲיָא לְהוּ: פּוֹגֶמֶת כְּתוּבָּתָהּ בְּעֵדִים, מַהוּ? [6]אִם אִיתָא דִּפְרָעָהּ, [7]בְּעֵדִים הֲוָה פָּרַע לָהּ, [8]אוֹ דִּלְמָא אִיתְרַמּוּיֵי אִיתְרְמֵי לֵיהּ?

LITERAL TRANSLATION

[1]Rather, Rava said: [It is an oath] by Rabbinic decree. [2]The one who pays is scrupulous. [3]The one who collects is not scrupulous. [4]And the Rabbis cast an oath upon her so that she will be scrupulous.

[5]It was asked of them: [If] she impairs her ketubah before witnesses, what [is the law]? [6]If it is so that he paid her [the rest], [7]he would have paid her [again] before witnesses, [8]or perhaps [the first time] happened by chance?

RASHI

אלא אמר רבא מדרבנן — היא שבועה זו. מאי טעמא דפרע דייק כו'.
ואם תאמר: בלא פוגם נמי, הא קיימא לן בשבועות דאי אמר ליה: "אישתבע לי דלא פרעתיך" משבעינן ליה, והאי נמי — הא קא טעין ליה: "פרעתיך", ומה צורך בפגימה? וכן בעד אחד מעידה שפרועה — בלא עד נמי משבעינן לה! הא פרכינן ליה בשבועות: מה בין זה לפוגם שטרו? ומשנינן לה הכי: התם כי פגים ואמר ליה האי "פרעתיך" — משבעינן ליה ואפילו לא טען לו זה "השבע לי" — אבל כי לא פגים, אפילו אמר ליה "פרעתיך", אי לא אמר ליה בהדיא "אישתבע לי" — אמרינן ליה: זיל שלים, דהא נקיט שטרא. **פוגמת כתובתה בעדים** — התקבלתי מנה, ובפני עדים קיבלתיו. **מי אמרינן אי איתא דפרעה טפי בעדים הוה פרע** — דהא דק, וקא אייתי עדים לפרעון מנה קמא. **או דלמא** — לאו משום דדק הוא, אלא איתרמויי איתרמי דהוו עדים התם בההוא זימנא.

אִיבַּעֲיָא לְהוּ [5]In discussion among the Sages, it was asked: If a woman impaired her ketubah and claimed that she had already received a portion of it before witnesses, and her husband argued that he had already paid the entire amount, what is the law? Do we say that since the husband paid his wife some of her ketubah settlement before witnesses, he must be particularly careful about the way in which he pays his debts, [6]so that if it true that he later paid her the remainder, [7]surely he would also have paid her that sum before witnesses? Since the husband cannot bring witnesses, we should assume that the woman is still owed money, and so she should be able to collect the remainder of her settlement without an oath. [8]Or perhaps we say that it was just by chance that there were witnesses present at the first payment, and he might indeed have paid her the remainder of the ketubah settlement in the absence of witnesses, and so she must take an oath before she collects what she says is still due her.

NOTES

to collect money from her. When the woman impairs her ketubah settlement, she admits to part of her husband's claim, and, Rami bar Ḥama argues, she must take an oath similar to the Torah oath that is imposed when a defendant admits to part of the claim brought against him. (See *Ritva*, *Talmid HaRashba*, and Jerusalem Talmud, which states that the woman's oath is similar to a Torah oath, and that the woman is regarded as being in possession of her ketubah settlement.)

דְּמִיפְּרַע לָא דָּיֵיק The one who is paid is not precise. *Rabbenu Ḥananel* explains that the Rabbis imposed an oath upon the woman to make certain that she will be precise and not present a claim about which she is uncertain. The Rishonim ask: Why is the woman not believed on the basis of a *miggo* argument: Had she wished to lie, she could have denied receiving any of her ketubah settlement? Had she presented such a claim, she would have been believed without an oath. Hence she should also be believed when she claims that she received part of her ketubah settlement, but the rest is still outstanding! *Tosafot* answer that a *miggo*

HALAKHAH

פּוֹגֶמֶת כְּתוּבָּתָהּ בְּעֵדִים If she impairs her ketubah before witnesses. "When a divorcee seeks to collect her ketubah settlement, if her husband claims that he already paid her the entire amount, and she admits that she received part of the sum, then even if she brings witnesses that she received that amount, she cannot collect the rest of her

TRANSLATION AND COMMENTARY

תָּא שְׁמַע [1]The Gemara suggests that an answer to its question can be found in a Baraita: **Come and hear** what was taught: **"All who** take an oath by **Torah law** swear **and are** then exempt from **paying.** [2]**And these** listed below may by Rabbinic enactment take an oath to confirm their claims, **and** then **collect** what they demand: (1) [3]**A laborer** claiming his wages from an employer who says that he has already paid him; (2) [4]**The victim of a robbery.** This robbery was witnessed but without the witnesses being able to identify the object taken. If the victim names the article, and the intruder denies having taken it, the robbed person may take an oath and collect from the robber whatever he claims was stolen from him. (3) [5]**A person who was injured.** If a person was seen by witnesses entering his fellow's house whole and sound and exiting with an injury, and his fellow denies hunting him, the injured party may take an oath and collect compensation. (4) [6]**A person whose adversary was suspect about** lying under **oath.** If someone is liable for an oath in order to free himself from payment, but he is a suspected liar and therefore the oath cannot be administered to him, the oath is shifted to the plaintiff who may swear to

[1]תָּא שְׁמַע: ״כָּל הַנִּשְׁבָּעִין שֶׁבַּתּוֹרָה — נִשְׁבָּעִין וְלֹא מְשַׁלְּמִין: [2]וְאֵלּוּ נִשְׁבָּעִין וְנוֹטְלִין: [3]הַשָּׂכִיר, [4]וְהַנִּגְזָל, [5]וְהַנֶּחְבָּל, [6]וְשֶׁכְּנֶגְדּוֹ חָשׁוּד עַל

LITERAL TRANSLATION

[1]Come [and] hear: "All those who swear who are [mentioned] in the Torah swear and do not pay. [2]But these swear and take: [3]A laborer, [4]a victim of robbery, [5]and a person who was injured, [6]and a person whose adversary was suspect about oaths,

RASHI

ואלו נשבעין ונוטלין — שתקנו חכמים לישבע וליטול. וטעמייהו מפורש בשבועות בפרק ״כל הנשבעין״. **שכיר** — אמר לו: תן לי שכרי, והוא אומר: נתתי. **נגזל** — ראוהו שנכנס בביתו, אמר לו: תן לי כליי שנטלת, והוא אומר: לא נטלתי, והעדים ראו שילא והכלים תחת כנפי טליתו, ולא ידעו מה. **הנחבל** — ראוהו שנכנס לתוך ביתו וידו שלם, וילא חבול, אמר לו: חבלת בי, והוא אומר: לא חבלתי.

NOTES

argument cannot be invoked here, because we are not concerned that the woman is lying, but that she has not kept an accurate account. As *Talmid HaRashba* explains, a *miggo* argument is only valid when we suspect that the defendant might be lying. But here we are concerned only that the woman may not be sure about how much money she already received, and so the alternative plea is not relevant. *Ritva* answers that a *miggo* argument cannot be invoked if the alternative plea would have been more audacious than the actual plea, and here it would have taken more audacity for the woman to deny having received any part of her ketubah than to admit having received some of the money. Therefore a *miggo* argument is not accepted in the case of a person who admitted to part of a claim and asked to be exempt from an oath because had he wished to lie, he could have denied the entire claim. *Talmidei Rabbenu Yonah* argue that *miggo* is of no avail to allow the plaintiff to collect from the defendant. Furthermore, *miggo* is of no use to exempt a person from taking an oath.

HALAKHAH

ketubah settlement without first taking an oath that she is still owed the money." (*Rambam, Sefer Nashim, Hilkhot Ishut* 16:14; *Shulḥan Arukh, Even HaEzer* 96:7.)

כָּל הַנִּשְׁבָּעִין שֶׁבַּתּוֹרָה **All those who swear who are mentioned in the Torah.** "All the oaths imposed by Torah law are sworn by the defendant, and he takes them in order to deny a claim brought against him and exempt himself from payment. However in certain cases the Rabbis enacted that the plaintiff must take an oath so that he can collect the sum which he claims is owed him." (*Rambam, Sefer Mishpatim, Hilkhot To'en VeNit'an* 1:2; *Shulḥan Arukh, Ḥoshen Mishpat* 89:1.)

הַשָּׂכִיר **A laborer.** "If a laborer has witnesses that he worked for his employer, and he claims that he was not paid for his work, and his employer claims that he did pay him part or all of his wages, the laborer may take a Mishnaic oath and collect his wages." (*Rambam, Sefer Mishpatim, Hilkhot To'en VeNit'an* 1:2; *Shulḥan Arukh, Ḥoshen Mishpat* 89:2.)

הַנִּגְזָל **A victim of robbery.** "When someone was seen by witnesses entering empty-handed into somebody else's house, and they later saw him leaving the house with something concealed under his garment, if the homeowner claims that the intruder stole a certain article from him, and the intruder denies having taken it, the person who claims that he was robbed may take an oath and recover the stolen article from the intruder." (*Rambam, Sefer Nezikin, Hilkhot Gezelah* 4:1-2; *Shulḥan Arukh, Ḥoshen Mishpat* 90:1.)

הַנֶּחְבָּל **A person who was injured.** "When a person was seen by witnesses entering uninjured into another person's house, and they later saw him emerging from the house with an injury, if the injured party claims that the other person caused him the injury, and the accused denies the charge, the injured party may take an oath and collect compensation." (*Rambam, Sefer Nezikin, Hilkhot Ḥovel* 5:4; *Shulḥan Arukh, Ḥoshen Mishpat* 90:16).

שֶׁכְּנֶגְדּוֹ חָשׁוּד עַל הַשְּׁבוּעָה **A person whose adversary was suspect about oaths.** "If a person is liable for an oath, but he is a suspected liar — to whom an oath may not be administered — the oath is shifted to the plaintiff, who may swear and collect what he claims is owed him." (*Rambam, Sefer Mishpatim, Hilkhot Malveh VeLoveh* 16:5; *Shulḥan Arukh, Ḥoshen Mishpat* 92:7.)

הַשְּׁבוּעָה, [1]וְחֶנְוָנִי עַל פִּנְקָסוֹ, [2]וְהַפּוֹגֵם שְׁטָרוֹ שֶׁלֹּא בְּעֵדִים״. [3]שֶׁלֹּא בְּעֵדִים — אִין, [4]בְּעֵדִים — לָא! [5]״לָא מִיבָּעֲיָא״ קָאָמַר. [6]לָא מִיבָּעֲיָא ״בְּעֵדִים״, [7]דְּוַדַּאי צְרִיכָה שְׁבוּעָה. [8]אֲבָל שֶׁלֹּא בְּעֵדִים, [9]אֵימָא תֵּיהֱוֵי כְּמֵשִׁיב אֲבֵידָה, [10]וְתִשְׁקוֹל בְּלָא שְׁבוּעָה. [11]קָא מַשְׁמַע לָן.

LITERAL TRANSLATION

[1]and a shopkeeper regarding his account book, [2]and one who impairs his deed without witnesses." [3]Without witnesses — yes. [4]Before witnesses — no! [5]He is speaking [in the style of] "there is no need." [6]There is no need [to state] "before witnesses," [7]for she [then] certainly requires an oath. [8]But without witnesses, [9][one might] say [that] she would be like someone who returns a lost object, [10]and she should take without an oath. [11]It [therefore] tells us [otherwise].

TRANSLATION AND COMMENTARY

collect what he claims is owed him. (5) [1]**A shopkeeper regarding his account book.** In this case, a shopkeeper claims that he advanced goods or money to a third party at the request of a customer, and the transaction was duly recorded in this customer's name in his account book. If the third party denies having received anything from the shopkeeper, the shopkeeper may take an oath that he gave him and collect from the customer. [2]**And** (6) a creditor **who impairs the deed** he is holding by admitting that his debtor repaid part of his debt **without witnesses.** If the creditor claims that the debtor still owes him the rest of the sum, and the debtor argues that he paid his debt in full, the creditor may not collect the balance of the debt without first taking an oath that he is still owed the money." [3]The Gemara now suggests that an inference may be drawn from this Baraita: Since the creditor admits that his debtor paid back part his debt **without witnesses,** the creditor must **indeed** take an oath before collecting the remainder of the debt. [4]But it may be inferred from this that if the creditor says that the debtor repaid him **before witnesses,** he would **not** be required to take an oath before collecting the rest of the debt. Similarly, if a woman claimed that she had received part of her ketubah settlement from her husband before witnesses, she should be able to collect the remainder from him even without an oath.

לָא מִיבָּעֲיָא [5]However the Gemara immediately rejects this inference. The Baraita brought **was speaking in the style of "there is no need."** The Baraita intentionally chose to discuss a problematic case, regarding which one might have thought that a different ruling would apply, rather than the simpler case in which "there was no need" to state the law. [6]**There is no need to state** the law in the simpler case **when** the woman admits having received part of her ketubah settlement **before witnesses,** [7]**for** in that case **she certainly requires an oath** to collect the remainder. The payment was made in the presence of witnesses, so she could not have denied having received that part of the money. [8]**But** if she says that she received part of her ketubah settlement **without witnesses,** [9]**one might say that she would be** considered **like someone who restores a lost object** to its rightful owner. Since no one is there to testify that she already received a part of her ketubah settlement, if she were willing to lie, she could claim that she was still owed the entire amount. [10]Thus, **she should** be allowed to **collect** the rest of her ketubah settlement **without** having to take **an oath,** just as someone who returns a lost article is not required to swear that he did not keep some of it when the owner claims that he did not return all that was lost. [11]The Baraita **therefore tells us** that this is not so. And even if the woman admits having received a part of her ketubah settlement without witnesses, she cannot collect the rest of the settlement without first taking an oath that it was still owed to her.

RASHI

וחנוני על פנקסו — שכותב בו הקפותיו: כך צוני פלוני לתת לפועליו, ונתתי להם. והם אומרים: לא נטלנו. שניהם נשבעין ונוטלין הימנו. **דודאי צריכה שבועה** — על השאר. דהא דקא מודיא בהאי מנה — משום עדים הוא, ולאו השבת אבידה היא. **תיהוי כמשיב אבידה** — שהרי יש לה שטר שלם עליו, ואי בעיא, הויא אמרה: לא קבלתי כלום.

HALAKHAH

וְחֶנְוָנִי עַל פִּנְקָסוֹ **A shopkeeper regarding his account book.** "If a shopkeeper claims that he advanced money to laborers at their employer's request, and the laborers deny having received the money, the shopkeeper may take an oath and collect what he demands from the employer. So too can the laborers collect from the employer with an oath." (*Rambam, Sefer Mishpatim, Hilkhot To'en VeNit'an* 2:5; *Shulḥan Arukh, Ḥoshen Mishpat* 91:1.)

וְהַפּוֹגֵם שְׁטָרוֹ **One who impairs his deed.** "If the plaintiff presents a promissory note to the defendant for payment, and the defendant claims that he already paid him all that he owes him, and the plaintiff admits having received part of the debt, he has to take a Mishnaic oath that the balance is still due him." (*Rambam, Sefer Mishpatim, Hilkhot Malveh VeLoveh* 14:1; *Shulḥan Arukh, Ḥoshen Mishpat* 84:1.)

[1]אִיבַּעֲיָא לְהוּ: הַפּוֹגֶמֶת כְּתוּבָּתָהּ פָּחוֹת פָּחוֹת מִשָּׁוֶה פְּרוּטָה, מַהוּ? [2]מִי אָמְרִינַן: כֵּיוָן דְּקָא דָּיְיקָא כּוּלֵּי הַאי, קוּשְׁטָא קָא אָמְרָה, [3]אוֹ דִּלְמָא אִיעֲרוּמֵי קָא מַעַרְמָא?

[4]תֵּיקוּ.

[5]אִיבַּעֲיָא לְהוּ: פּוֹחֶתֶת כְּתוּבָּתָהּ, מַהוּ? [6]מִי אָמְרִינַן: הַיְינוּ פּוֹגֶמֶת, [7]אוֹ דִּלְמָא פּוֹגֶמֶת מוֹדְיָא בְּמִקְצָת, [8]הָא לָא קָא מוֹדְיָא בְּמִקְצָת?

[9]תָּא שְׁמַע: ״פּוֹחֶתֶת, תִּפָּרַע

LITERAL TRANSLATION

[1]It was asked of them: [If] she impairs her ketubah less than the value of a perutah, what [is the law]? [2]Do we say: Since she is so scrupulous, she speaks the truth, [3]or perhaps she is being deceitful?

[4]Let it stand.

[5]It was asked of them: [If] she reduces the [original] amount [written] in her ketubah, what [is the law]? [6]Do we say: This is [the same as] a woman who impairs her ketubah, [7]or perhaps, a woman who impairs [it] admits to [receiving] part, [8][but] this one does not admit to [receiving] part?

[9]Come [and] hear: "[If] she reduces the [original] amount [in her ketubah], she may

RASHI

פחות פחות משוה פרוטה – במנה שהיא מודה עליו שקיבלה, עושה עמו חשבון: כך נתת לי ביום פלוני, וכך ביום פלוני, ומצרפתן בחשבון אפילו פחות משוה פרוטה. **מהו** – צריכה שבועה על השאר, או לא? **פוחתת** – היתה כתובתה אלף זוז כתוב בשטר, והוא אומר: התקבלת כולה, והיא אומרת: לא התקבלתי כלום, אבל מודה אני שלא התנית עמי לכתובתי אלא מנה. **מודיא במקצת** – שנתקבלה קצת.

TRANSLATION AND COMMENTARY

אִיבַּעֲיָא לְהוּ [1]The Gemara now asks another question regarding a woman who admitted that a part of her ketubah settlement had been paid. In discussion among the Sages, **it was asked of them:** If a woman **impaired her ketubah** and admitted that she had already received some of what was due her, and she was so precise that she even **included various payments** that were **less than the value of a perutah** (an extremely small sum), and her husband argued that she had already received her entire ketubah settlement, **what is the law?** [2]**Do we say** that **since** the woman **is so precise** about the sums, surely **she** must be **speaking the truth,** and so she should collect the remainder without taking an oath? [3]**Or perhaps** do we say that she **is being deceitful?**

תֵּיקוּ [4]The Gemara offers no solution to this problem, and concludes: The problem raised here **remains** unresolved.

אִיבַּעֲיָא לְהוּ [5]The Gemara now discusses a slightly different problem: **The following problem arose** in discussion among the Sages: If a woman had a ketubah in which a certain sum was recorded as her settlement, and her husband claimed that she had already been paid that entire amount, and she denied having received any part of it, but **said that the amount originally** recorded **in her ketubah was** greater than the actual amount he agreed to pay and he still owes her the smaller sum, **what is the law?** [6]**Do we say** that the law in **this** case **is the same as** the law in the case of a woman **who impairs her ketubah,** for in both cases she admits that she is not entitled to the entire sum recorded in her ketubah deed? If so, she would have to take an oath before collecting what she claims is owed her. [7]**Or** do we say that when **a woman impairs** her ketubah, she **admits to** having received **a part** of it, [8]whereas in **this** case **she does not admit** to having received anything, but rather that from the outset the actual amount of her settlement was less than the amount recorded in the ketubah. If so, the woman may be able to collect what she claims is owed her without first taking an oath.

תָּא שְׁמַע [9]The Gemara argues that there is a Baraita which deals directly with this case: **Come and hear** what was taught in the following Baraita: "**If** a woman had a ketubah in which a certain sum was recorded as her settlement, and her husband claimed that she had already been paid the entire amount, and the woman denied having received any part of it, but **she said** that the **amount originally** recorded **in her ketubah**

NOTES

פּוֹחֶתֶת כְּתוּבָּתָהּ, מַהוּ If she reduces the original amount in her ketubah, what is the law. *Ritva* asks: Why should the law in the case of the woman who says that the true amount of her ketubah settlement was less than the sum recorded in her ketubah deed be the same as the law of a woman who impairs her ketubah? Since the former woman does not admit to having received any part of her settlement, there is no reason to say that she was imprecise in her records, and therefore there is no reason to make her swear! He answers that perhaps the Rabbis did not make this distinction, but rather once they imposed an oath on one woman whose ketubah settlement is

HALAKHAH

פּוֹחֶתֶת כְּתוּבָּתָהּ If she reduces the amount of her ketubah. "If a woman presents her husband with her ketubah deed of one thousand zuz, and the husband claims that he has already paid her the entire sum, and the woman denies having received any part of it, but claims that there was a secret trust between them that she would only ask for five hundred zuz, she collects the five hundred without an oath," following the Baraita and Rava the son of Rabbah. (*Rambam, Sefer Nashim, Hilkhot Ishut* 16:17; *Shulḥan Arukh, Even HaEzer* 96:14.)

TRANSLATION AND COMMENTARY

was greater than the actual amount he agreed to pay, **she may collect** the lesser amount which she says is owed her **without** taking **an oath. How so?** [1]**If** a woman's **ketubah** settlement **was a thousand zuz** according to what was written, [2]**and** her husband **said to her: 'You** already **received your** entire **ketubah** settlement,' [3]**and** she **says: 'I did not receive** anything, however its real value **is only a maneh** (a hundred zuz) and not a thousand zuz, [4]**she may collect** what she claims is actually owed her **without** taking **an oath."** Thus, the Baraita distinguishes between the case of a woman who admits that a portion of her settlement had already been paid and the case of a woman who admits that the settlement was less than the amount recorded in the deed.

בְּמַאי גָּבְיָא [5]The Gemara raises a question with respect to this last case: If the woman admits that the amount recorded in her ketubah is greater than the amount of the agreed settlement, then **with what does she collect** even that reduced amount? [6]You cannot say that she collects it **with the deed** that she holds, [7]for **that deed is a mere potsherd,** since she herself admits that the document is false!

אָמַר [8]**Rava the son of Rabbah said:** We are dealing here with a case **where** the woman **says:** "The ketubah deed which records the larger sum is a genuine document, properly drafted and signed. [9]But **there was** an agreement based on **trust between me and** my husband that — although he obligated himself to the full thousand zuz — I would never put forward a claim for the full amount recorded in the document. Therefore, the original question asked among the Sages must also be explained where he obligated himself to the full thousand zuz and she agreed never to claim the full amount. She may collect this amount without an oath — despite his denial of liability — based on the valid ketubah. However if she invalidates the ketubah by saying that her husband had only obligated himself to a hundred zuz, she has no valid deed to support her claim and she collects nothing provided that the husband swears to support his claim that he paid it all.

עֵד אֶחָד [10]The Gemara now examines the next clause of the Mishnah, which stated: **"If** a woman comes to collect her ketubah settlement, and **one witness testifies** on behalf of her husband **that it had** already **been paid,** she may not collect anything without first taking an oath to confirm her claim." [11]**Rami bar Ḥama thought to say** that the **oath** the Mishnah imposes upon the woman to refute the witness supporting her ex-husband is **by Torah law,** [12]**for the verse states** (Deuteronomy 19:15): **"One witness shall not rise up against a man for any iniquity, or for any sin."** This verse teaches that to punish someone — whether a corporal

שֶׁלֹּא בִּשְׁבוּעָה. כֵּיצַד? [1]הָיְתָה כְּתוּבָּתָהּ אֶלֶף זוּז, [2]וְאָמַר לָהּ: ׳הִתְקַבַּלְתְּ כְּתוּבָּתֵיךְ׳" [3]וְהִיא אוֹמֶרֶת: ׳לֹא הִתְקַבַּלְתִּי וְאֵינָהּ אֶלָּא מָנֶה׳ — [4]נִפְרַעַת שֶׁלֹּא בִּשְׁבוּעָה".

[5]בְּמַאי גָּבְיָא — [6]בְּהַאי שְׁטָרָא? [7]הַאי שְׁטָרָא חַסְפָּא בְּעָלְמָא הוּא!

[8]אָמַר רָבָא בְּרֵיהּ דְּרַבָּה: בְּאוֹמֶרֶת: [9]׳אֲמָנָה הָיְתָה לִי בֵּינִי לְבֵינוֹ׳".

[10]"עֵד אֶחָד מְעִידָהּ שֶׁהִיא פְּרוּעָה". [11]סְבַר רָמִי בַּר חָמָא לְמֵימַר: שְׁבוּעָה דְּאוֹרַיְיתָא, [12]דִּכְתִיב: "לֹא יָקוּם עֵד אֶחָד בְּאִישׁ לְכָל עָוֹן וּלְכָל חַטָּאת"

LITERAL TRANSLATION

collect without an oath. How so? [1][If] her ketubah was a thousand zuz, [2]and he said to her: 'You received your ketubah,' [3]and she says: 'I did not receive [it], but it is only a maneh,' [4]she may collect without an oath."

[5]With what does she collect — [6]with that deed? [7]That deed is a mere potsherd!

[8]Rava the son of Rabbah said: Where she says: [9]"There was a [secret] trust between me and him."

[10]"[If] one witness testifies that it was paid." [11]Rami bar Ḥama thought to say: [This is] an oath by Torah law, [12]for it is written: "One witness shall not rise up against a man for [determining] any iniquity, or for any sin" —

RASHI

במאי גביא — אפילו ההוא מנה? **בהאי שטרא** — הא חספא בעלמא הוא, שהיא אומרת: מזוייף הוא! **באומרת אמנה היתה ביני לבינו** — ששטר נכתב ונחתם כהוגן, ובפני העדים קבל עליו אלף זוז, אבל הוא האמין בי שלא אתבענו אלא מנה.

NOTES

similar to that of a defendant who admits to part of a claim, they imposed it on all such cases.

אֲמָנָה הָיְתָה לִי בֵּינִי לְבֵינוֹ **There was a secret trust between me and him.** *Ritva* explains that when the woman says that there was a verbal agreement based on trust between herself and her husband, she meant to say that her husband had indeed obligated himself to everything that is recorded in the ketubah deed, and so the lien established by the deed is still valid. But an agreement had been reached between them that she would not put forward a claim for the full amount recorded in the ketubah deed, an amount which he had exaggerated in order to enhance the honor of the two parties.

TRANSLATION AND COMMENTARY

punishment or a monetary fine — [1]a single witness **shall not rise up for determination of an iniquity or a sin.** For as a general rule, the testimony of two witnesses is required in order to impose a punishment (see Numbers 35:30). [2]**But** a single witness **can rise up** and offer his testimony so that another person will be required to take **an oath** to deny a claim that was supported by the witness. [3]**And the** Sage **said: Wherever two witnesses** will **obligate** a defendant **to pay** the plaintiff **money,** [4]**a single** witness will **obligate him to take an oath** to refute the witness and be believed that he owes nothing. Thus, it follows that if a single witness testified that a woman had already received her ketubah settlement by Torah law, she must swear that she had not yet received it, if she wishes to collect what she claims is still owed her.

[1]לְכָל עָוֹן וּלְכָל חַטָּאת הוּא דְּאֵינוֹ קָם, [2]אֲבָל קָם הוּא לִשְׁבוּעָה. [3]וְאָמַר מָר: כָּל מָקוֹם שֶׁהַשְּׁנַיִם מְחַיְּיבִין אוֹתוֹ מָמוֹן, [4]אֶחָד מְחַיְּיבוֹ שְׁבוּעָה. [5]אָמַר רָבָא: שְׁתֵּי תְּשׁוּבוֹת בַּדָּבָר: חֲדָא, דְּכָל הַנִּשְׁבָּעִין שֶׁבַּתּוֹרָה, [6]נִשְׁבָּעִין וְלֹא מְשַׁלְּמִין. [7]וְהִיא נִשְׁבַּעַת וְנוֹטֶלֶת. [8]וְעוֹד, אֵין נִשְׁבָּעִין עַל כְּפִירַת שִׁיעְבּוּד קַרְקָעוֹת! [9]אֶלָּא, אָמַר רָבָא: [10]מִדְּרַבָּנַן, כְּדֵי לְהָפִיס דַּעְתּוֹ שֶׁל בַּעַל.

LITERAL TRANSLATION

[1]for any iniquity or any sin he does not rise up. [2]But he rises up for [necessitating] an oath. [3]And the master said: Wherever two [witnesses] obligate him [to pay] money, [4]one [witness] obligates him [to take] an oath.

[5]Rava said: [There are] two arguments against this matter: First, that all those who swear by the Torah [law], [6]swear and do not pay. [7]And she swears and collects. [8]And moreover, we do not swear [to confirm the] denial of a lien on land.

[9]Rather, Rava said: [10][It is an oath] by Rabbinic decree, in order to appease the husband's mind.

RASHI

אחד מחייבו שבועה – על ממון, שאילו היו שנים היה משלם, עכשיו ישבע שהעד מכחש.

אָמַר רָבָא [5]**Rava said: There are two arguments** that can be raised **against this** position: **First, all those who take an oath** that is mentioned in the **Torah** [6]**take an oath** to exempt themselves from payment. But here the woman is the plaintiff, [7]for it is **she** who **swears** that she had not yet received her ketubah settlement, after which she **collects** what she claims is still owed her. Thus her oath cannot be required by Torah law. [8]**And moreover,** by Torah law **an oath is not taken** when the defendant **denies** a claim that gives the plaintiff has **a lien on** the defendant's **land.** An oath is administered only to rebut a claim regarding movable property. Since all the husband's land is mortgaged to his wife's settlement, a claim regarding it is considered a claim involving land. Thus, for this reason too, the oath that a woman must take here cannot be administered under Torah law.

אֶלָּא [9]**Rather, Rava said:** The **oath** imposed upon a woman to counter a single witness supporting her husband's claim that her ketubah settlement has been paid **is by Rabbinic decree.** By Torah law the woman could collect her ketubah settlement without an oath, for the validity of the ketubah she holds (which is signed by two witnesses) is not undermined by the testimony of a single witness that it had been paid. [10]But the Rabbis imposed an oath upon the woman **in order to appease her husband.** Since he is convinced that he has already paid the settlement, and even has a witness to confirm his claim, were the woman able to collect the settlement without even an oath, her husband would feel that he was being cheated.

NOTES

וְעוֹד, אֵין נִשְׁבָּעִין עַל כְּפִירַת שִׁיעְבּוּד קַרְקָעוֹת And furthermore, one does not swear to refute a denial of a lien on land. *Tosafot* raise the following question: The law that an oath is not imposed when the defendant denies a claim regarding land is derived from a verse dealing with the bailee's oath. Now, the verses dealing with the bailee's oath and those dealing with the oath taken by the defendant who admits part of the claim are mixed together, and so the law stated with respect to the one can be applied to the other. But how do we know that the oath imposed to rebut the claim of a single witness is also not administered when the claim involves land? *Ritva* answers that the verse found in the same passage (Exodus 22:10), "And the owner shall accept it, and he shall not pay," teaches that the laws derived from that passage apply to all cases where the defendant takes an oath and thereby exempts himself from having to pay.

HALAKHAH

אֲבָל קָם הוּא לִשְׁבוּעָה But he rises up for necessitating an oath. "Whenever the testimony of two witnesses would suffice to obligate a defendant to pay, the testimony of a single witness suffices to make him liable to take an oath to deny the claim brought against him." (*Rambam, Sefer Hafla'ah, Hilkhot Shevuot* 11:5; *Sefer Mishpatim, Hilkhot To'en VeNit'an* 1:1; *Sefer Shofetim, Hilkhot Edut* 5:1; *Shulhan Arukh, Hoshen Mishpat* 87:1.)

SAGES

רַב שֵׁישָׁא בְּרֵיהּ דְּרַב אִידִי **Rav Shesha the son of Rabbi Idi.** A Babylonian Amora of the fourth and fifth generations, Rav Shesha (or, as he is sometimes called, Rav Sheshet) was the son of the Sage, Rav Idi bar Avin, who belonged to the fifth generation of Babylonian Amoraim. Rav Shesha discusses Halakhic issues with Abaye and Rava and also with the greatest of their students.

LITERAL TRANSLATION

[1]Rav Pappa said: [88A] [2]If he is clever, he can bring her to an oath by Torah law. [3]He can give her her ketubah [again] in front of one witness, [4]and join the first witness to the last witness, [5]and consider the first [money] as a loan.

[6]Rav Shesha the son of Rav Idi strongly objected to this: [7]How can he join the first witness to the last witness?

[1]אֲמַר רַב פַּפָּא [88A] [2]אִי פִּיקֵּחַ הוּא, מַיְיתֵי לָהּ לִידֵי שְׁבוּעָה דְּאוֹרַיְיתָא. [3]יָהֵיב לָהּ כְּתוּבָּתָהּ בְּאַפֵּי חַד סָהֲדָא, [4]וְסָמֵיךְ סָהֲדָא קַמָּא אַסָּהֲדָא בַּתְרָא, [5]וּמוֹקִים לְהוּ לְהָנָךְ קַמָּאֵי בְּמִלְוֶה.

[6]מַתְקִיף לָהּ רַב שֵׁישָׁא בְּרֵיהּ דְּרַב אִידִי: [7]הֵיאָךְ סָמֵיךְ סָהֲדָא קַמָּא אַסָּהֲדָא בַּתְרָא?

TRANSLATION AND COMMENTARY

אֲמַר רַב פַּפָּא [1]Agreeing with Rava that the oath imposed upon a woman when a single witness testifies that her ketubah settlement has already been paid is only by Rabbinic decree, **Rav Pappa added:** [88A] [2]**If,** however, the woman's husband **is clever, he can bring** his wife **to** swear **an oath by Torah law.** How so? [3]**He can** pay **her her ketubah** settlement **again in front of another witness,** this time making sure to take back the ketubah deed, [4]**and** then **join the original witness with** this **second witness,** so that he now has two witnesses who can testify that his wife received her settlement. [5]**He can** then claim that the **money** that he had given her **the first** time was given to her **as a loan.** Since the husband has a witness who can support his claim that he had given his wife the money on that earlier occasion, he can impose an oath upon her by Torah law. The woman must either swear that she did not receive the money or pay her husband what he claims she owes him. The woman now becomes the defendant and is required to take an oath in order to deny a claim brought against her by her husband and supported by the testimony of a single witness. The oath does not relate to a claim for which the plaintiff, now the husband, has a lien on the defendant's property, for the loan was extended orally and a lien only comes into existence when a promissory note is written.

מַתְקִיף לָהּ [6]**Rav Shesha the son of Rav Idi strongly objected to this** suggestion: [7]**How can the husband join the original witness with the second witness?** The first witness did not see the woman receiving her ketubah settlement the second time, and the second witness did not see her being paid on the earlier occasion, and so the two witnesses are not testifying about the same event. If the woman denies having received any money on either occasion, there is only one witness who can contradict her claim with respect to the first payment, and only one witness who can contradict her about the second payment. In such a case, not only should the husband be unable to impose a Torah oath upon his wife, but she should be able to take another Rabbinic oath and collect her ketubah settlement a third time!

RASHI

אי פקח הוא — האי בעל. **לידי שבועה דאורייתא** — שהיא בשם או בכנוי, ואוחז ספר בידו, כדאמרינן בשבועות (לח,ב): וחמורה היא מאד. אבל שבועה דרבנן — קללה בעלמא, כעין שלנו. **יהיב לה כתובתה באפי חד סהדא** — פעם שניה. **וסמיך סהדא קמא אסהדא בתרא** — יביא את שניהם יחד לבית דין, שאם תכפור — יעידוה שניהם שנתקבלה כתובתה. **ומוקי להנך קמאי בהלואה** — יתבענה פרעון הראשון, ויאמר: מלוה הן אצלך, שהרי התקבלת כתובתיך שנית. וכשתכפור, ותאמר: לא קבלתי אלא הפעם הזאת. ועד אחד מעיד על הראשונה — איכא שבועה דאורייתא, נשבעת ולא משלמת. ואין כאן שיעבוד קרקעות, שלא מכח כתובה תובעה. **היכי סמיך כו'** — מה שראה זה לא ראה זה, ואם תכפור על שתיהן — אין כאן אלא עד אחד, ותשבע ותטול שלישית, ונמצא מפסיד.

NOTES

שְׁבוּעָה דְּאוֹרַיְיתָא **An oath by Torah law.** *Rashi* explains that a Torah oath is different from a Rabbinic oath in its gravity and in its administration. A Torah oath is taken by holding a Torah scroll in one's hand and swearing by God's name or by one of His substitute names. A Rabbinic oath is taken without holding a Torah scroll or mentioning God's name, and is similar to a declaration of a curse upon the party who is lying. Most Rishonim (see *Tosafot* and others), however, disagree and say that even a Rabbinic oath (at least a Mishnaic oath, namely, one that is recorded in the Mishnah, as opposed to a *hesset* oath which is only an Amoraic enactment) is taken by holding a Torah scroll in one's hand and swearing by God's name or by one of His substitute names. They explain that a Torah oath is distinguished from a Rabbinic oath in different ways: For example, even if the litigants agree, a Torah oath cannot be shifted to the plaintiff to enable him to swear and collect. Some note that this distinction is not relevant here in all cases. Because even a Rabbinic oath can only be shifted if it was to be taken by the defendant in order to exempt him from paying. But a Rabbinic oath which was to be taken by the plaintiff in order to allow him to collect cannot be shifted. Others (see *Ramban* and *Ra'ah*) propose that a Torah oath and a Rabbinic oath differ with respect to a person who is a suspected liar. If a suspected liar is obligated to take a Torah oath, the oath is shifted to the other party, who swear and collects. But if he is obligated to take a Rabbinic oath, the oath is not cancelled and shifted. Thus, in our Gemara's case, if the woman is only obligated to take a Rabbinic oath, and she is a suspected liar, she would collect her ketubah settlement even without an oath. But if she is obligated to take a Torah oath and she is suspect, the oath would be shifted to the husband. Another difference: If someone who refuses to take a Torah

[1]אֶלָּא, אֲמַר רַב שֵׁישָׁא בְּרֵיהּ דְּרַב אִידִי: [2]יָהֵיב לָהּ כְּתוּבָּתָהּ בְּאַפֵּי סָהֲדָא קַמָּא וְסָהֲדָא בַּתְרָא, [3]וּמוֹקִים לָהּ לְהָנָךְ קַמָּאֵי בְּהַלְוָאָה.

[4]מַתְקִיף לָהּ רַב אַשִׁי: [5]אַכַּתִּי יְכוֹלָה לְמֵימַר: "שְׁתֵּי כְּתוּבּוֹת הֲוַאי!"

[6]אֶלָּא, אֲמַר רַב אַשִׁי: הוּא דְּמוֹדַע לְהוּ.

LITERAL TRANSLATION

[1]Rather, Rav Shesha the son of Rav Idi said: [2]He can give her her ketubah in front of the first witness and the last witness, [3]and consider the first [money] as a loan.

[4]Rav Ashi strongly objected to this: [5][But] she can still say: "There were two ketubahs!"

[6]Rather, Rav Ashi said: When he informed them.

TRANSLATION AND COMMENTARY

אֶלָּא [1]**Rather, Rav Shesha the son of Rav Idi said:** If the husband wishes to bring his wife to swear an oath by Torah law, he can act as follows: [2]**He can pay her her ketubah** settlement again **in front of the original witness and a** second **witness,** so that he now has two witnesses who can testify that on that second occasion his wife received the money. [3]The husband **can** then claim that the **money** that he had given his wife **the first** time was given **as a loan.** Since he has a witness who can support his claim that he had given her the money on that earlier occasion, he can impose an oath upon her by Torah law. She must either swear that she did not receive the money or pay her husband what he claims she owes him.

מַתְקִיף לָהּ [4]**Rav Ashi strongly objected to this** strategy: Even if the husband pays his wife again in front of two witnesses, he should not be able to impose a Torah oath upon her regarding the money which he claims he gave her the first time. [5]For **she can still say** to him: "I held **two ketubah** deeds against you. When you paid me the first time, you paid out my first ketubah, and when you paid me the second time, you paid out my second ketubah. The first payment was not a loan." Indeed, the witness who attests to the first payment supports her claim, for he saw her receiving money as a payment of her ketubah, and not as a loan.

אֶלָּא [6]**Rather, Rav Ashi said:** If the husband wishes to make his wife take an oath by Torah law, **he must,** before he pays his wife's ketubah settlement again, **inform** the two witnesses and/or the judge that he had paid it once already. However, since she denies having received it and he has only one witness who can confirm his claim, he is paying it again before them so that he then can obligate his wife to take a Torah

RASHI

באפי סהדא קמא וסהדא בתרא — והוא הדין לשני עדים מן השוק. אבל עצה טובה היא, שיכיר העד הראשון ששתי פעמים פרע, ויכול להעיד על פרעון הכתובה עם חבירו, ועל הפרעון הראשון. **יכולה לומר שתי כתובות היו** — שתי שטרות היו לי עליך, בפרעון הראשון החזרתי לך אחת, ובשניה אחרת. והרי העד הראשון מעיד לסייעה, שראה שני הפרעונות לשם כתובה ולא לשם מלוה. **דמודע להו** — לסהדא קמא ובתרא לפני פרעון השני: דעו שכבר פרעתי לה כתובתה בפני אחד מכם, והיא כופרת. ואני רוצה לפורעה שנית לשם כתובה, שיהיו לי שני עדים בדבר, ואתבע את הראשונים, ויש לי עליהן עד אחד, ותתחייב שבועה דאורייתא. וכיון דשמעינהו, ולא מסייע לה האי עד קמא — תו לא מצית למימר שתי כתובות הוו, דמילתא דלא שכיחא הוא.

NOTES

oath and holds the property in dispute, the court removes it from his possession. But if he was only liable for a Rabbinic oath, the money is not removed from him if he does not swear. *Ra'avad* (in his notes to *Sefer HaMa'or*) proposes that the issue here raised by Rav Pappa is not the gravity of the oath that is to be taken. Rather Rav Pappa suggests a way by which the woman would be obligated to take two oaths: a Rabbinic oath in order to collect her ketubah settlement, and a Torah oath to exempt herself from the claim brought against her by her husband that is supported by a single witness.

יָהֵיב לָהּ כְּתוּבָּתָהּ בְּאַפֵּי סָהֲדָא קַמָּא וְסָהֲדָא בַּתְרָא **He can give her her ketubah settlement in front of the first witness and the last witness.** *Rashi* and others point out that if the husband wishes to bring his wife to swear an oath by Torah law, he does not have to pay her ketubah settlement again in front of the original witness and a second witness, for he can just as well pay it in front of two fresh witnesses. Rav Shesha only suggested that the husband should make his second payment in front of the original witness to spare him the trouble of looking for a third witness. *Rivash* explains that it is preferable for the original witness to be present when the second payment is made, so that the woman not be able to claim later that there had in fact been only one payment, and that the original witness and the second two witnesses are all testifying about the same payment.

שְׁתֵּי כְּתוּבּוֹת **Two ketubahs.** A woman could be entitled to two ketubahs for various different reasons: Her husband might have decided that he wanted to add to her ketubah settlement, and so he wrote her a second ketubah. Or else he might have divorced her, and then taken her back in marriage, and written her a second ketubah (even though he is not obligated by law to do so). Or else he might not have wanted to write a single ketubah for a very large sum, and so he divided that sum between two ketubah deeds (see *Rivan*).

דְּמוֹדַע לְהוּ **He informed them.** *Talmid HaRashba* explains that Rav Ashi means that the husband should inform the two witnesses in his wife's presence that he had already

TRANSLATION AND COMMENTARY

oath. In such a case, the woman cannot later claim that she received two payments for two ketubah deeds, for the witnesses are now aware of her denial of the first payment and she cannot now claim that that payment was for another ketubah.

מִנְּכָסִים מְשׁוּעְבָּדִים [1]We learned in our Mishnah: "If a woman comes to collect her ketubah settlement from property that had passed to her husband's heirs, or **from property** sold by her husband that had been **mortgaged** under the lien of her ketubah, she cannot collect from the buyer without first taking an oath that she had not yet received her ketubah settlement." [2]**We have learned elsewhere** in the Mishnah (*Shevuot* 45a): **"And similarly, a** creditor's heirs **may not collect** a debt that had been owed to their father **without** first taking **an oath** that to the best of their knowledge the debt had not yet been repaid."

מִמַּאן [3]The Gemara wishes to clarify this Mishnah: **From whom** can the creditor's heirs not collect without an oath? [4]**If you say** that the creditor's heirs come with the promissory note to collect the father's debt **from the debtor** himself, there is a difficulty. [5]**Surely their father** would have been able to **collect** from the debtor **without an oath,** for presentation of a promissory note, obviates the need for an oath. Why should the law applying to the creditor's heirs be more stringent than that applying to the creditor himself, [6]and require **them** to take **an oath?**

אֶלָּא [7]**Rather,** the Mishnah meant to **say as follows:** [8]**And similarly,** the creditor's heirs **may not collect from** the heirs of their father's debtor without first taking **an oath** that to the best of their knowledge the debt which had been owed to their father had not yet been repaid.

אָמַר רַב זְרִיקָא [9]**Rav Zerika said in the name of Rav Yehudah:** It follows from this understanding of the Mishnah that if the creditor's heirs take an oath, they may indeed collect the debt from the debtor's heirs. [10]But this ruling was **only taught when the heirs of the debtor said:** "Before he died, **Father said to us:** 'Indeed **I borrowed** money, **but** I already **repaid** the loan.'" The creditor's heirs must then take an oath that their father

[1]"מִנְּכָסִים מְשׁוּעְבָּדִים". [2]תְּנַן הָתָם: "וְכֵן, הַיְּתוֹמִים לֹא יִפָּרְעוּ אֶלָּא בִּשְׁבוּעָה." [3]מִמַּאן? [4]אִילֵימָא מִלֹּוֶה, [5]הָשְׁתָּא אֲבִיהֶן שָׁקֵיל בְּלָא שְׁבוּעָה, [6]וְאִינְהוּ בִּשְׁבוּעָה? [7]אֶלָּא, הָכִי קָאָמַר: [8]וְכֵן, הַיְּתוֹמִים מִן הַיְּתוֹמִים לֹא יִפָּרְעוּ אֶלָּא בִּשְׁבוּעָה. [9]אָמַר רַב זְרִיקָא אָמַר רַב יְהוּדָה: [10]לֹא שָׁנוּ אֶלָּא שֶׁאָמְרוּ יְתוֹמִים: "אָמַר לָנוּ אַבָּא 'לָוִיתִי

LITERAL TRANSLATION

[1]"From mortgaged property." [2]We have learned elsewhere: "And similarly, orphans may only collect with an oath."

[3]From whom? [4]If you say from a borrower — [5]now their father collects without an oath, [6]and they with an oath!

[7]Rather, thus he said: [8]And similarly, orphans from orphans may only collect with an oath.

[9]Rav Zerika said in the name of Rav Yehudah: [10]They only taught [this] when the orphans [of the debtor] said: "Father said to us: 'I borrowed

RASHI

תנן התם — בשבועות. אי נימא מלוה — שהלוה קיים, והיו מוציאין עליו שטר אביהן. לא שנו — דכי משתבעי שקלי. שאמרו יתומים — של לוה: לויתי ופרעתי — ישבעו אלו: שבועה שלא פקדנו, ולא אמר לנו אבא, ולא מצינו שובר בין שטרותיו שטר זה פרוע, ונוטלין.

NOTES

paid her her ketubah settlement and that he is paying out that obligation again because he has only one witness who can confirm that claim, and he wants to obligate his wife to take a Torah oath. If the woman remains silent, she cannot later claim that her husband had obligated himself to two ketubahs, but rather she must take a Torah oath that she does not owe him any money. But most Rishonim (see *Rashi* and *Ritva*) understand that it suffices if the husband explains to the witnesses why he is paying out his wife's ketubah, even if the woman is not present. In such a case, the woman's claim that her husband owed her two ketubahs is no longer supported by the witness who saw the first payment, as he saw no handing over of the ketubah deed and it is unusual for a woman to be entitled to two ketubah settlements. Our commentary follows *Rivan* who explains that the husband should inform the judge about what he plans to do. Before allowing her to take the second money, the judge will have the woman deny having received payment of her ketubah. In such a case, she cannot later claim that her husband had owed her two ketubah settlements, and that the money which was given to her on the earlier occasion was payment of one of them.

HALAKHAH

וְכֵן, הַיְּתוֹמִים **And similarly, orphans.** "All the laws that apply when the creditor's heirs come to collect their father's debt from the debtor apply also when they come to collect from the debtor's heirs, except that in the latter case, the creditor's heirs must also take an oath that they themselves did not collect from the debtor before he died." (*Rambam, Sefer Mishpatim, Hilkhot Malveh VeLoveh* 17:2; *Shulḥan Arukh, Ḥoshen Mishpat* 108:9.)

TRANSLATION AND COMMENTARY

did not inform them that the promissory note he was holding had been repaid, nor did they find among his papers any record of such a repayment. If the creditor's heirs take the oath, they may use the note to collect the debt from the debtor's heirs. [1]**But if** the debtor's heirs **said:** "Before his death, **Father said to us: 'I never borrowed** any money,'" [2]then the creditor's heirs **may not collect** anything from them **even with an oath.**

מַתְקִיף לַהּ [3]**Rava strongly objected to this** position: [4]**On the contrary,** there is a general rule that if a defendant **says, "I never borrowed** any money from the plaintiff," and his plea is contradicted by a promissory note or by witnesses who testify that he did borrow money from him, [5]he is considered **as if he said, "I** borrowed money from the plaintiff, but **did not repay** the loan." If he says he never took the loan, surely he never paid it back, and there is extant proof that there was a loan. By the same token, if the debtor's heirs said that their father told them that he had never borrowed any money from the creditor, and the creditor's heirs possess their father's promissory note, they should be able to collect the debt without having to take an oath.

אֶלָּא [6]The Gemara now suggests an alternative version of Rav Zerika's statement: **Rather, if** something **was said** in this context by Rav Zerika regarding the Mishnah in *Shevuot*, **it was said as follows:** [7]**Rav Zerika said in the name of Rav Yehudah:** It follows from this understanding that if the creditor's heirs take an oath, they may indeed collect the debt from the debtor's heirs. [8]But this ruling was **only taught when the heirs of the debtor said:** [9]"Before he died, **Father said to us:** 'Indeed, **I borrowed** money from the creditor, **but** I already **repaid** the loan.'" The creditor's heirs must then take an oath that their father did not inform them that the promissory note had been repaid, nor did they find among his papers any record of such a repayment. If the creditor's heirs take the oath, they may use the note to collect the debt from the debtor's heirs. [10]**But if** the debtor's heirs **said:** "Before his death, **Father said to us: 'I never borrowed** any money from the creditor,'" [11]the creditor's heirs **may collect** what they claim is owed them **without an oath.** [12]**For** if the defendant **says, "I never borrowed** any money from the plaintiff," and his plea is contradicted by a promissory note or by witnesses who testify that he did borrow money from him, [13]it is considered **as if he said, "I** borrowed money from the plaintiff, but **did not repay** the loan."

וּפָרַעְתִּי׳״. [1]אֲבָל אָמְרוּ: ״אָמַר לָנוּ אַבָּא: ׳לֹא לָוִיתִי׳״, [2]אַף בִּשְׁבוּעָה לֹא יִפָּרְעוּ.

[3]מַתְקִיף לַהּ רָבָא: [4]אַדְּרַבָּה, כָּל הָאוֹמֵר, ״לֹא לָוִיתִי״, [5]כְּאוֹמֵר, ״לֹא פָּרַעְתִּי״ דָּמֵי!

[6]אֶלָּא, אִי אִתְּמַר הָכִי אִתְּמַר: [7]אָמַר רַב זְרִיקָא אָמַר רַב יְהוּדָה: [8]לֹא שָׁנוּ אֶלָּא שֶׁאָמְרוּ יְתוֹמִים: [9]״אָמַר לָנוּ אַבָּא: ׳לָוִיתִי וּפָרַעְתִּי׳״. [10]אֲבָל אָמְרוּ: ״אָמַר לָנוּ אַבָּא: ׳לֹא לָוִיתִי׳״, [11]נִפְרָעִין שֶׁלֹּא בִּשְׁבוּעָה, [12]שֶׁכָּל הָאוֹמֵר, ״לֹא לָוִיתִי״, [13]כְּאוֹמֵר, ״לֹא פָּרַעְתִּי״ דָּמֵי.

LITERAL TRANSLATION

and repaid.'" [1]But [if] they said: "Father said to us: 'I did not borrow,'" [2]the [other orphans] may not collect even with an oath.

[3]Rava strongly objected to this: [4]On the contrary, whoever says, "I did not borrow," [5]is as if he said, "I did not repay"!

[6]Rather, if it was said, it was said as follows: [7]Rav Zerika said in the name of Rav Yehudah: [8]They only taught [this] when the orphans [of the debtor] said: [9]"Father said to us: 'I borrowed and repaid.'" [10]But [if] they said: "Father said to us: 'I did not borrow,'" [11]the [other orphans] may collect without an oath, [12]for whoever says, "I did not borrow," [13]is as if he said, "I did not repay."

RASHI

כאומר לא פרעתי דמי – דכיון דאמר לא לוה – מודה הוא שלא פרע, והרי שטר מוכיח עליו שלוה. **לא שנו** – דבעו שבועה.

NOTES

אַף בִּשְׁבוּעָה לֹא יִפָּרְעוּ They may not collect even with an oath. *Ritva* asks: Even if the debtor's heirs claim that their father had told that he had never borrowed any money from the creditor, how could the Gemara possibly have thought that the creditor's heirs cannot collect from the debtor's heirs even when they present a valid promissory note and take an oath? He answers that the Gemara might have thought that since the debtor spoke to his

HALAKHAH

אָמַר לָנוּ אַבָּא: ׳לֹא לָוִיתִי׳ Father said to us: I did not borrow. "If the creditor or his heirs come to collect a debt from the debtor's heirs with a promissory note and the debtor's heirs claim that their father told them that he had never assumed the debt recorded in that bill, the creditor or his heirs may collect the debt without taking an oath," following the Gemara's conclusion about Rav Yehudah's position. (*Rambam, Sefer Mishpatim, Hilkhot Malveh VeLoveh* 17:6; *Shulḥan Arukh, Ḥoshen Mishpat* 108:15.)

SAGES

רַב אַחָא שַׂר הַבִּירָה **Rav Aha Sar HaBirah.** See *Ketubot*, Part II, p.130.

LITERAL TRANSLATION

[1] "And she who collects in his absence may not collect without an oath." [2] Rav Aḥa Sar HaBirah said: An incident came before Rabbi Yitzḥak in Antioch, and he said: [3] They taught [this] only regarding a woman's ketubah, [4] in order to [seek her] favor. [5] But a creditor, no. [6] And Rava said in the name of Rav Naḥman: Even a creditor,[7] so that every so and so cannot take his fellow's money [as a loan] and go and settle abroad, [8] and you will [cause] bolting of the door before borrowers.

[1] "וְנִפְרַעַת שֶׁלֹּא בְּפָנָיו לֹא תִּפָּרַע אֶלָּא בִּשְׁבוּעָה". [2] אָמַר רַב אַחָא שַׂר הַבִּירָה: מַעֲשֶׂה בָּא לִפְנֵי רַבִּי יִצְחָק בְּאַנְטוֹכְיָא, וְאָמַר: [3] לֹא שָׁנוּ אֶלָּא לִכְתוּבַּת אִשָּׁה, [4] מִשּׁוּם חִינָּא. [5] אֲבָל בַּעַל חוֹב, לֹא. [6] וְרָבָא אָמַר רַב נַחְמָן: אֲפִילּוּ בַּעַל חוֹב, [7] שֶׁלֹּא יְהֵא כָּל אֶחָד וְאֶחָד נוֹטֵל מְעוֹתָיו שֶׁל חֲבֵרוֹ וְהוֹלֵךְ וְיוֹשֵׁב בִּמְדִינַת הַיָּם, [8] וְאַתָּה נוֹעֵל דֶּלֶת בִּפְנֵי לוֹוִין.

RASHI

שר הבירה — כך כינויו. לא שנו — שיורדין בית דין לנכסי אדם שלא בפניו.

TRANSLATION AND COMMENTARY

וְנִפְרַעַת [1] We learned in our Mishnah: "If a woman was divorced and her ex-husband went abroad before paying her ketubah settlement, and **she** asked the court to **collect** it from her husband's property **in his absence, she may not collect** anything **without** first taking **an oath** that she had not yet received it." [2] **Rav Aḥa Sar HaBirah said: An incident** similar to the case discussed in the Mishnah **came before Rabbi Yitzḥak in Antioch, and he said:** [3] The Mishnah's ruling that the court can collect a debt from a person's property in his absence applies **only to a woman's ketubah** settlement. [4] The Rabbis allowed her to collect in his absence **in order** that men will find **favor** in women's eyes, and they will more readily agree to marriage. [5] **But an** ordinary **creditor may not** collect from his debtor's property in his absence, even with an oath. [6] **And Rava said in the name of Rav Naḥman: Even an** ordinary **creditor** may recover his debt from the debtor's property in the debtor's absence provided that he takes an oath that the debt had not yet been paid. [7] This allowance was made **so that** a person **cannot take somebody else's money as a loan and go and settle abroad** without paying his debt. The Rabbis enacted this leniency in favor of the lender, [8] so that **the door** would **not be closed before borrowers.** Because extending a loan without interest is an act of charity. The Rabbis were concerned to allow lenders to collect debts in the borrowers' absence, so that they will not hesitate to grant loans.

NOTES

children on his deathbed, he is presumed to have spoken the truth. Thus, he is believed if he claimed that he never borrowed from the creditor. But he is not believed if he claimed that he borrowed money and paid it back, for he might have repaid a different creditor and confused the two.

אֲפִילּוּ בַּעַל חוֹב **Even a creditor.** Most of the Rishonim rule in accordance with the position of Rav Naḥman that even an ordinary creditor, and not just a divorcee with a ketubah, may recover his debt from an absent debtor's property, if he takes an oath that the debt has not yet been paid. But *Rabbenu Ḥananel* (see *Tosafot*) writes that it was not the customary practice to collect a debt from the debtor's property in his absence. The common practice is supported by the Jerusalem Talmud which asks in astonishment: Can a debt really be collected in the debtor's absence? The Jerusalem Talmud understands that our Mishnah is dealing with special circumstances, an interest bearing loan which the debtor had received from a non-Jew, and the Jew had undertaken to guarantee it. If the guarantor paid the non-Jew, he may collect from the debtor's property in his absence, for it is to the debtor's advantage not to pay any additional interest. But most of the Rishonim understand that the two Talmuds differ on the issue, and that we follow the Babylonian Talmud which rules in accordance with Rav Naḥman (see also *Arakhin* 22a).

Ritva writes that it follows according to Rav Naḥman's reasoning that the creditor can only collect from the debtor's property in his absence if the debtor left the place where he borrowed the money. But if the loan was extended in one place, and the creditor went to another

HALAKHAH

אֲפִילּוּ בַּעַל חוֹב **Even a creditor.** "If a creditor comes with a duly authenticated promissory note to collect a debt from his debtor's property in his absence, the court must send a messenger to the debtor to inform him of the proceedings, provided that the messenger can reach him and return within thirty days. The creditor covers the costs of the messenger, but may later recover his expenses from the debtor. If the messenger cannot reach the creditor and return within thirty days, the creditor may immediately take an oath that his debt has not yet been repaid and then collect the property, following Rava. If the debtor had written a credence clause in the note, stating explicitly that it would be valid even in the debtor's absence, the creditor can collect without an oath. *Rema* writes that according to some authorities (*Rivash*), the creditor can only collect from the debtor himself, but not from the debtor's heirs in their absence. Rather he must seek them out in their place of residence." (*Rambam, Sefer Mishpatim, Hilkhot Malveh VeLoveh* 13:1; *Shulḥan Arukh, Ḥoshen Mishpat* 106:1.)

[1]״רַבִּי שִׁמְעוֹן אוֹמֵר: כָּל זְמַן שֶׁתּוֹבַעַת כְּתוּבָּתָהּ וכו׳״. [2]רַבִּי שִׁמְעוֹן אַהַיָּיא?
[3]אָמַר רַבִּי יִרְמְיָה: אַהָא: [4]״וְנִפְרַעַת שֶׁלֹּא בְּפָנָיו לֹא תִּפָּרַע אֶלָּא בִּשְׁבוּעָה״ — [5]לָא שְׁנָא לִמְזוֹנֵי וְלָא שְׁנָא לִכְתוּבָּה. [6]וַאֲתָא רַבִּי שִׁמְעוֹן לְמֵימַר: כָּל זְמַן שֶׁתּוֹבַעַת כְּתוּבָּתָהּ, [7]יוֹרְשֶׁיהָ מַשְׁבִּיעִין אוֹתָהּ, [88B] [8]אֵינָהּ תּוֹבַעַת כְּתוּבָּתָהּ, אֵין יוֹרְשִׁין מַשְׁבִּיעִין אוֹתָהּ. [9]וְקָמִיפַּלְגִי בִּפְלוּגְתָּא דְּחָנָן וּבְנֵי כֹּהֲנִים גְּדוֹלִים, [10]דִּתְנַן: ״מִי שֶׁהָלַךְ לִמְדִינַת הַיָּם וְאִשְׁתּוֹ תּוֹבַעַת מְזוֹנוֹת, [11]חָנָן אוֹמֵר: תִּשָּׁבַע בַּסּוֹף, [12]וְלֹא תִּשָּׁבַע

LITERAL TRANSLATION

[1]"Rabbi Shimon says: Whenever she claims her ketubah, etc." [2]To which [clause] does Rabbi Shimon refer?

[3]Rabbi Yirmeyah said: To this one: [4]"And she who collects in his absence may not collect without an oath" — [5]no distinction is made between [collecting] maintenance and the ketubah (lit., "there is no difference . . . and there is no difference"). [6]And Rabbi Shimon came to say: Whenever she claims her ketubah, [7]the heirs (lit., "her heirs") may impose an oath upon her. [88B] [8][If] she is not claiming her ketubah, the heirs may not impose an oath upon her. [9]And they disagree about the [matter] in dispute between Ḥanan and the sons of the High Priests, [10]for we have learned: "[If] someone went abroad, and his wife claims maintenance, [11]Ḥanan said: She must swear at the end, [12]but need not swear

TRANSLATION AND COMMENTARY

רַבִּי שִׁמְעוֹן [1]We learned in the last clause of the Mishnah: **"Rabbi Shimon says: Whenever** a woman **claims her ketubah** settlement from her late husband's heirs, the heirs may impose an oath upon her that she has not yet received it. But if she is not claiming her ketubah settlement from them, the heirs may not impose an oath upon her." [2]**To which** clause of the Mishnah does **Rabbi Shimon**'s ruling relate?

אָמַר רַבִּי יִרְמְיָה [3]The Gemara will now offer a number of solutions to this question. **Rabbi Yirmeyah said:** Rabbi Shimon's ruling relates **to this** clause: "If a woman's ex-husband went abroad before paying her ketubah settlement, [4]and **she** asked the court to **collect** what is due her from her husband's property **in his absence, she may not collect without** first taking **an oath** that she had not yet received it." The Sages — the anonymous first Tanna of the Mishnah — [5]**made no distinction between** a woman who is still married and claims **maintenance** from an absentee husband's property **and the** case of a divorced woman who demands her **ketubah** settlement. In the former case, the wife must take an oath that her husband did not leave her with sufficient means of support, and in the latter case, the divorced woman must swear that she has not received her ketubah settlement. [6]**And Rabbi Shimon came** and **said: Whenever** a woman **claims her ketubah** settlement from her husband's heirs, [7]**his heirs may impose an oath upon her** that she has not yet received it. [88B] [8]**If she is not claiming her ketubah** settlement from **the heirs,** but only her maintenance, they **may not impose an oath upon her.** [9]**And** Rabbi Shimon and the Rabbis **disagree about the** same **matter that is disputed by Ḥanan and the sons of the High Priests.** [10]**For we have learned** elsewhere in the Mishnah (*Ketubot* 104b): **"If someone went abroad and his wife** comes before the court to **claim** the **maintenance** due her, the court may collect it from the husband's property in his absence. The Sages disagree about whether the wife must take an oath before collecting her maintenance. [11]**Ḥanan said:** The woman **must swear at the end** of her marriage (after receiving a bill of divorce or finding out that her husband died) when she comes to collect her ketubah settlement. At that time she must swear that her husband did not give her money or property from which to collect her ketubah. [12]**But** she **need not swear at the beginning** (while still married) when she comes to

RASHI

לא שנא למזוני — באה לבית דין, ותובעת מזונות מנכסי בעלה למכור קרקע ולזונה — נשבעת שלא הניח בידה מעות ליזון מהם. **ולא שנא לכתובה** — אם שלח לה גט. **אינה תובעת כתובתה אין היורשין משביעין אותה** — משום שבועת אפוטרופסת. דהויא לה אפוטרופוס שמינהו אבי יתומים, וסבירא ליה: לא ישבע כאבא שאול, דאמר: חילוף הדברים. וטעמייהו מפרש בגיטין בפרק ״הניזקין״ רבנן סברי: מינוהו בית דין לא ישבע — דאם כן מימנע ולא הוי אפוטרופוס, הואיל ואשדינן ליה. אבל מינהו אבי יתומים — לא מימנע, דאי לאו דהוה ליה הנאה מיניה בחייו — לא הוה מימני ליה. ואבא שאול סבר: מינהו אבי יתומים, אי ידע דמשבעי ליה — מימנע ולא הוי אפוטרופוס. אבל מינוהו בית דין, אף על גב דידע דמשבעי ליה — לא מימנע, דחשיבותא הוא לגביה דמהימן להו לבי דינא. תשבע סוף — כשתתאלמן או תתגרש

SAGES

רַבִּי שִׁמְעוֹן Rabbi Shimon. See *Ketubot*, Part I, pp.56-7.

רַבִּי יִרְמְיָה Rabbi Yirmeyah. An Amora of the third and fourth generations. See *Ketubot*, Part II, p. 231.

TERMINOLOGY

אַהַיָּיא To which case is he referring? Sometimes, when a concluding sentence in a Mishnah, a Baraita, or an Amoraic statement refers to or differs from an earlier statement in the same source, it is not clear to which of the previous statements it is referring. In such cases, the Talmud may ask: To which statement does this sentence refer?

NOTES

place to collect from the debtor's property there, he cannot collect from that property, unless he brings the debtor to court in the first place and receives a court order allowing him to seize the debtor's property wherever it may be found (see also Responsa of *Rivash*).

TRANSLATION AND COMMENTARY

collect her maintenance. [1]**The sons of the High Priests disagreed with** Ḥanan **and said:** The woman **must** even **swear at the beginning** that her husband did not leave her with money or property from which to support herself. [2]**And** she must also swear **at the end** when she comes to collect her ketubah settlement." [3]**Rabbi Shimon** agrees with **Ḥanan** who says that she need not swear to collect maintenance in his absence. [4]And **the Rabbis** agree with **the sons of the High Priests**, who rule that she must swear both to collect maintenance and to receive her ketubah.

מַתְקִיף לָהּ [5]**Rav Sheshet strongly objected to** Rabbi Yirmeyah's choice of the clause in the Mishnah with which Rabbi Shimon disagrees: **In the case** he chose **is it the heirs that impose an oath upon her?** When a man is abroad and his wife asks for a court order to collect her ketubah from his property, it is the court, not the heirs, that impose the oath? [6]Thus **Rabbi Shimon should have said that "the courts may impose an oath upon her!"** and he should not have mentioned "the heirs."

אֶלָּא [7]Rather, Rav Sheshet said: Rabbi Shimon's disagreement relates **to the clause** in the previous Mishnah (86b), which states: [8]**"If** a husband exempted his wife from taking an oath or a vow to him or to his heirs, and he died, and after he was buried his widow **went** directly **from her husband's grave to her father's house** and had nothing further to do with her late husband's property, [9]**or she returned to her father-in-law's house, but had not been made an administrator** over her late husband's estate, [10]**the heirs may not impose an oath upon her** when she comes to collect her ketubah settlement, nor may they impose an oath upon her regarding her managing of her husband's property during his lifetime. [11]**And if** a widow **had been made an administrator** over her late husband's estate after his burial, **the heirs may impose an oath upon her regarding** her handling of the property from that time **on,** for the exemption from an oath that had been extended to her by her husband is no longer valid. [12]**But they may not impose an oath upon her regarding** her managing of the property **in the past,** for the husband had exempted her from taking such an oath while he was alive." [13]**And**

בַּתְּחִלָּה. [1]נֶחְלְקוּ עָלָיו בְּנֵי כֹּהֲנִים גְּדוֹלִים וְאָמְרוּ: [2]תִּשָּׁבַע בַּתְּחִלָּה וּבַסּוֹף". [3]רַבִּי שִׁמְעוֹן כְּחָנָן; [4]רַבָּנַן כִּבְנֵי כֹּהֲנִים גְּדוֹלִים.

[5]מַתְקִיף לָהּ רַב שֵׁשֶׁת: הַאי, "יוֹרְשִׁין מַשְׁבִּיעִין אוֹתָהּ"? [6]"בֵּית דִּין מַשְׁבִּיעִין אוֹתָהּ" מִיבָּעֵי לֵיהּ!

[7]אֶלָּא, אֲמַר רַב שֵׁשֶׁת: אַהָא: [8]"הָלְכָה מִקֶּבֶר בַּעְלָהּ לְבֵית אָבִיהָ, [9]אוֹ שֶׁחָזְרָה לְבֵית חָמִיהָ, וְלֹא נַעֲשֵׂית אַפּוֹטְרוֹפְּיָא, [10]אֵין הַיּוֹרְשִׁים מַשְׁבִּיעִין אוֹתָהּ — [11]וְאִם נַעֲשֵׂית אַפּוֹטְרוֹפְּיָא — יוֹרְשִׁין מַשְׁבִּיעִין אוֹתָהּ עַל הֶעָתִיד לָבֹא, [12]וְאֵין מַשְׁבִּיעִין אוֹתָהּ עַל מַה שֶּׁעָבַר". [13]וַאֲתָא

LITERAL TRANSLATION

at the beginning. [1]The sons of the High Priests disagreed with him and said: She must swear at the beginning [2]and at the end." [3]Rabbi Shimon is like Ḥanan; [4]the Rabbis are like the sons of the High Priests.

[5]Rav Sheshet strongly objected to this: In this [clause], is it the heirs that impose an oath upon her? [6][Rabbi Shimon] should have [then said]: "The courts may impose an oath upon her!"

[7]Rather, Rav Sheshet said: [Rabbi Shimon refers] to this one: [8]"[If] she went from her husband's grave to her father's house, [9]or she returned to her father-in-law's house, and she had not been made an administrator, [10]the heirs may not impose an oath upon her. [11]And if she had been made an administrator, the heirs may impose an oath upon her regarding that which will come in the future, [12]but they may not impose an oath upon her regarding that which had passed." [13]And Rabbi Shimon came to say:

RASHI

ותתבע כתובה — תשבע שלא עיכבה בידה משל בעלה כלום. בתחילה — בפיסוק מזונות. האי יורשין וכו' — בתמיה, [כיון דא"נפרעת שלא בפניו" קאי, מאי לשון יורשין כאן]? הרי הוא קיים! הלכה מקבר בעלה כו' — אשה שכתב לה בעלה "נדר ושבועה אין לי ולא ליורשי עליך". העתיד לבא — על שנתעסקה אחר מיתה, דלאו מכח נכסי בעלה באה שבועה זו, אלא מכח נכסי יתומים. ונשבעת כדין אפוטרופוס, כדתנן בשבועות (מה,א): אלו נשבעין שלא בטענת ברי — השותפין והאריסין והאפוטרופין.

NOTES

הַאי "יוֹרְשִׁין מַשְׁבִּיעִין"? **Is it the heirs that impose an oath?** *Tosafot* ask: Why does the Gemara not answer that Rabbi Yirmeyah follows Shmuel, who says elsewhere (*Ketubot* 107a) that all agree that the court may not collect a wife's maintenance from her husband's property in his absence, and that Ḥanan and the sons of the High Priests only disagree when it is known that the husband died? Then it would be clear why Rabbi Shimon is talking about the heirs imposing an oath. *Rosh* answers: Rabbi Yirmeyah himself stated that Rabbi Shimon's ruling relates to the clause in

רַבִּי שִׁמְעוֹן לְמֵימַר: [1]כָּל זְמַן שֶׁתּוֹבַעַת כְּתוּבָּתָהּ — [2]יוֹרְשִׁין מַשְׁבִּיעִין אוֹתָהּ. [3]אֵינָהּ תּוֹבַעַת כְּתוּבָּתָהּ — אֵין הַיּוֹרְשִׁין מַשְׁבִּיעִין אוֹתָהּ. [4]וְקָמִיפַּלְגִי בִּפְלוּגְתָּא דְּאַבָּא שָׁאוּל וְרַבָּנַן, [5]דִּתְנַן: ״אַפּוֹטְרוֹפּוֹס שֶׁמִּינָּהוּ אֲבִי יְתוֹמִים — יִשָּׁבַע. [6]מִינּוּהוּ בֵּית דִּין — לֹא יִשָּׁבַע. [7]אַבָּא שָׁאוּל אוֹמֵר: חִילּוּף הַדְּבָרִים: [8]מִינּוּהוּ בֵּית דִּין — יִשָּׁבַע. [9]מִינָּהוּ אֲבִי יְתוֹמִים — לֹא יִשָּׁבַע״. [10]רַבִּי שִׁמְעוֹן כְּאַבָּא שָׁאוּל; [11]וְרַבָּנַן כְּרַבָּנַן.

LITERAL TRANSLATION

[1]Whenever she claims her ketubah, [2]the heirs may impose an oath upon her. [3][If] she does not demand her ketubah, the heirs may not impose an oath upon her. [4]And they disagree about the [matter] in dispute between Abba Shaul and the Rabbis, [5]for we have learned: "A guardian who was appointed by the father of the orphans must swear. [6][If] he was appointed by the court, he does not swear. [7]Abba Shaul said: The things are the reverse: [8][If] he was appointed by the court, he must swear. [9][If] he was appointed by the father of the orphans, he does not swear." [10]Rabbi Shimon is like Abba Shaul; [11]and the Rabbis are like the Rabbis.

TRANSLATION AND COMMENTARY

Rabbi Shimon came and said: [1]**Whenever** the widow **claims her ketubah** settlement from her husband's heirs, [2]**the heirs may impose an oath upon her** that she had not yet received any of it. [3]But **if she is not claiming her ketubah** settlement from them, **the heirs may not impose an oath upon her** regarding her managing of the property of her late husband's estate. [4]**And** Rabbi Shimon and the Rabbis **disagree about the matter in dispute between Abba Shaul and the Rabbis.** [5]**For we have learned** elsewhere in the Mishnah (*Gittin* 52a): "If a guardian (an administrator, especially of minors) was appointed to handle the affairs of a minor, his guardianship terminates when the ward reaches majority. At that time the guardian must relinquish all of the ward's property and the management of his affairs. If **the guardian had been appointed by the orphan's father** before he died, he **must** take an oath and **swear** that he has not misappropriated any of the ward's assets. [6]But **if he had been appointed by the court, he need not swear.** Court-appointed guardians do not receive any remuneration and there was concern that a person would not accept the court's request to serve as a guardian, were he required to take an oath when the guardianship is completed. However, a guardian who was appointed by the orphan's father usually accepts the position in return for some benefit he received, and there is little concern that his having to take an oath would prevent him from assuming the guardianship. [7]**Abba Shaul said: The** law **is** just **the reverse:** [8]If the guardian **was appointed by the court, he must** take an oath at the termination of his guardianship. [9]But **if he had been appointed by the orphan's father** before he died, **he need not take** such an oath. In Abba Shaul's opinion, a guardian appointed by the orphan's father usually accepts the position as a favor. The Rabbis did not impose an oath upon him, so as not to deter him from accepting the position. But a guardian who was appointed by the court benefits from the appointment, for he gains the reputation of being a trustworthy person. There is therefore no concern that he will refuse the position on account of the oath." [10]**Rabbi Shimon** agrees with **Abba Shaul** that when the guardian is appointed by the orphan's father, he need not swear that he is not holding any of his ward's assets. So too a widow need not swear about her handling of her husband's property even after her husband's burial. She is regarded by the Rabbis as a guardian appointed by a child's father. [11]**And the Rabbis** who disagree with Rabbi Shimon follow **the Rabbis** who disagree with Abba Shaul and say that if a guardian is appointed by the orphan's father, he must take an oath that he has not misappropriated any of

RASHI

ואתא רבי שמעון למימר – אם תובעת כתובתה – יורשין משביעין אותה שלא עיכבה משלהן לאחר מיתת אביהן כלום, כדין הבא ליפרע מנכסי יתומים. הכי גרסינן: רבי שמעון כאבא שאול, ורבנן דמתניתין כרבנן.

NOTES

the Mishnah that deals with a wife collecting maintenance from her husband's property in his absence. Thus, Rabbi Yirmeyah cannot be dealing with a case when it became known that the husband died, for then the woman would collect from her husband's heirs and not from his property in his absence.

HALAKHAH

אַפּוֹטְרוֹפּוֹס שֶׁמִּינָּהוּ אֲבִי יְתוֹמִים **A guardian who was appointed by the father of the orphans.** "A guardian who managed the property that a minor had inherited from his father must hand it over to the heirs on his reaching majority. The guardian does not have to give a detailed accounting of the expenditures and income involved in his guardianship. However, if he was appointed by a court, he must take an oath while holding a Torah scroll that he did not keep anything belonging to his ward. If a guardian was appointed by the ward's father, he is not required to take

[1]מַתְקִיף לָהּ אַבַּיֵי: הַאי ״כָּל זְמַן שֶׁתּוֹבַעַת כְּתוּבָּתָהּ״? [2]״אִם תּוֹבַעַת״ מִיבָּעֵי לֵיהּ!

[3]אֶלָּא, אֲמַר אַבַּיֵי: אַהָא: ״כָּתַב לָהּ: [4]׳נֶדֶר וּשְׁבוּעָה אֵין לִי עָלַיִךְ׳ — אֵינוֹ יָכוֹל לְהַשְׁבִּיעָהּ, כו׳. [5]׳נֶדֶר וּשְׁבוּעָה אֵין לִי וְלֹא לְיוֹרְשַׁי וְלֹא לַבָּאִים בִּרְשׁוּתִי עָלַיִךְ, וְעַל יוֹרְשַׁיִךְ, וְעַל הַבָּאִין בִּרְשׁוּתֵךְ׳ — [6]אֵין יָכוֹל לְהַשְׁבִּיעָהּ, לֹא הוּא, וְלֹא יוֹרְשָׁיו, וְלֹא הַבָּאִין בִּרְשׁוּתוֹ. לֹא הִיא, וְלֹא יוֹרְשֶׁיהָ, וְלֹא הַבָּאִין

LITERAL TRANSLATION

[1]Abaye strongly objected to this: Is this "Whenever she claims her ketubah"? [2]It should have said: "If she claims [her ketubah]"!

[3]Rather, Abaye said: [Rabbi Shimon refers] to this: "[If] he wrote her: '[4]I will have no [claim of] a vow or an oath against you,' he may not impose an oath upon her, etc. [5]'Neither I nor my heirs nor those who come with my authority will have [a claim of] a vow or an oath against you, or your heirs, or those who come with your authority,' [6]he may not impose an oath upon her — not him, nor his heirs, nor those who come with his authority, not upon her, nor her heirs, nor those who come

TRANSLATION AND COMMENTARY

his ward's assets. So too a widow must swear about her handling of her late husband's property after his burial, for she is treated as a guardian appointed by his ward's father.

מַתְקִיף לָהּ [1]**Abaye strongly objected to** Rav Sheshet's interpretation of the dispute between the Rabbis and Rabbi Shimon: If this is the correct understanding of Rabbi Shimon's position, **is** the phrase **"Whenever she claims her ketubah** settlement" appropriate? [2]Surely, Rabbi Shimon **should have said: "If she claims her ketubah** settlement." The Mishnah's formulation of his position, "Whenever she claims her ketubah," implies that Rabbi Shimon is more stringent than the Rabbis. They maintain that the widow is exempt from an oath even if she comes to collect her ketubah settlement. Rabbi Shimon disagrees and says that whenever she demands her ketubah settlement she must take an oath that she has not already received it. But according to Rav Sheshet, Rabbi Shimon is more lenient than the Rabbis, for the Rabbis maintain that the heirs may impose an oath upon the widow regarding her handling of her late husband's estate, and Rabbi Shimon maintains that they may only impose an oath upon her if she comes to collect her ketubah settlement. Thus, we would have expected Rabbi Shimon to formulate his position differently and say as follows: If she demands her ketubah, the heirs may impose an oath upon her!

אֶלָּא [3]**Rather, Abaye said:** Rabbi Shimon's ruling refers **to the** first clause in the previous Mishnah (86b) which states: [4]**"If** a man **wrote** for his wife: **'I will have no claim of a vow or an oath against you,' he may not** later **impose an oath** or a vow **upon her.** But he may impose an oath upon her heirs or those who come with her authority to collect her ketubah settlement. [5]If he wrote for his wife: **'Neither I nor my heirs nor those who come with my authority will have a claim of a vow or an oath against you, or your heirs, or those who come with your authority,'** [6]**he may not impose an oath upon her — not him, nor his heirs, nor those who come with his authority, not** upon **her, nor** upon **her heirs, nor** upon **those who come with her authority** to collect her ketubah settlement." According to the Rabbis, if the husband exempted his wife from having

RASHI

האי כל זמן שתובעת — בתמיה, הואיל ורבי שמעון לקולא מאי כל זמן? **אם תובעת מיבעי ליה** — אבל ״כל זמן״ משמע דשמעיה לתנא קמא דפטר לה משבועה אפילו תובעת כתובתה, ואמר ליה איהו: כל זמן שתובעת כתובתה — לא תפטרנה. **אלא אמר אביי** — ארישא פליג. דאמר: כתב לה נדר ושבועה כו׳ דפטורה מן השבועה אפילו כשנפרעת מן היתומים, ואתא רבי שמעון למימר: כל זמן שתובעת כתובתה מהן — משביעין אותה, כאבא שאול בן אימא מרים, דאמר לעיל: אבל מה אעשה שהרי אמרו הבא ליפרע מנכסי יתומין לא יפרע אלא בשבועה. ופליגי רבנן עליה דאבא שאול ורבי שמעון כאבא שאול. ורבנן דמתניתין כרבנן.

NOTES

!אִם תּוֹבַעַת״ מִיבָּעֵי לֵיהּ״ **It should have said: If she claims her ketubah settlement.** *Rabbenu Ḥananel* has a slightly different reading: "It should have said: If she does not claim her ketubah settlement." *Rosh* explains this second reading as follows: If Rabbi Shimon follows the position of Abba Shaul, he should have taught only the second half of his statement, for the first half of his statement implies that when the woman demands her ketubah settlement, the

HALAKHAH

an oath unless a clear claim was brought against him, following Abba Shaul. *Rema* writes that according to some authorities (*Mordekhai*), a guardian who was appointed by the ward's father and is exempt from an oath must give a full accounting of his expenditures with respect to his ward's property." (*Rambam, Sefer Mishpatim, Hilkhot Nahalot* 11:5; *Shulḥan Arukh, Ḥoshen Mishpat* 290:16.)

TRANSLATION AND COMMENTARY

to take an oath to his heirs, they may not impose an oath upon her even if she comes to collect her ketubah settlement from them. [1]**And Rabbi Shimon came and said: Whenever** the woman **claims her ketubah** settlement from them, **the heirs may** indeed **impose an oath upon her** and make her swear that she has not yet received it. [2]**And** Rabbi Shimon and the Rabbis **disagree about the matter in dispute between Abba Shaul ben Imma Miryam and the Rabbis** (see 87a). [3]**Rabbi Shimon** agrees with **Abba Shaul** ben Imma Miryam that no matter how the husband formulated the exemption that he had extended to his wife, she cannot collect her ketubah settlement from his heirs without first taking an oath that she had not yet received it. [4]**And the Rabbis** who disagree with Rabbi Shimon follow **the Rabbis** who disagree with Abba Shaul ben Imma Miryam and maintain that if the husband exempted his wife from taking a vow to him and his heirs, she can indeed collect her ketubah settlement from the heirs without first taking an oath.

מַתְקִיף לַהּ [5]**Rav Pappa strongly objected to** Abaye's explanation of the disagreement between Rabbi Shimon and the Rabbis: [6]**Granted** that this explanation accounts for the first half of Rabbi Shimon's ruling that **whenever** the widow **demands her ketubah** settlement, the heirs may impose an oath upon her, no matter how the husband's exemption had been formulated. [7]**But what** can be **said** about the second half of Rabbi Shimon's ruling that **if** the widow **does not demand her ketubah** settlement from the heirs, they may not impose an oath upon her? What is Rabbi Shimon adding here to what he had already said?

אֶלָּא [8]**Rather, Rav Pappa said:** From the first half of his ruling, it is clear that Rabbi Shimon disagrees with the Tanna of the previous Mishnah who taught that if the husband exempted his wife from taking an oath to him or to his heirs, the heirs may not impose an oath upon her when she comes to collect her ketubah settlement from them. However, in the second half of his ruling by negating the right of the heirs to make her swear when she is not coming to collect her ketubah settlement, [9]Rabbi Shimon is **coming** to oppose both the **view** of **Rabbi Eliezer and** the anonymous Tanna **who disagreed with** Rabbi Eliezer in the earlier Mishnah (86b). For the first Tanna there teaches that if someone sets up his wife as a shopkeeper to sell merchandise in his store, or appointed her as an administrator to oversee his property and manage his business, he may at any time impose an oath upon her that she is not withholding any money that is

בִּרְשׁוּתָהּ״. [1]וַאֲתָא רַבִּי שִׁמְעוֹן לְמֵימַר: כָּל זְמַן שֶׁתּוֹבַעַת כְּתוּבָּתָהּ — יוֹרְשִׁין מַשְׁבִּיעִין אוֹתָהּ. [2]וְקָמִיפַּלְגִי בִּפְלוּגְתָּא דְאַבָּא שָׁאוּל בֶּן אִימָּא מִרְיָם וְרַבָּנַן. [3]רַבִּי שִׁמְעוֹן כְּאַבָּא שָׁאוּל; [4]וְרַבָּנַן כְּרַבָּנַן.

[5]מַתְקִיף לָהּ רַב פַּפָּא: [6]הָתֵינַח: כָּל זְמַן שֶׁתּוֹבַעַת כְּתוּבָּתָהּ. [7]״אֵינָהּ תּוֹבַעַת כְּתוּבָּתָהּ״, מַאי אִיכָּא לְמֵימַר?

[8]אֶלָּא, אֲמַר רַב פַּפָּא: [9]לְאַפּוּקֵי מִדְּרַבִּי אֱלִיעֶזֶר וּמַחֲלוֹקְתוֹ.

LITERAL TRANSLATION

with her authority." [1]And Rabbi Shimon came to say: Whenever she claims her ketubah, the heirs may impose an oath upon her. [2]And they disagree about the [matter] in dispute between Abba Shaul ben Ima Miryam and the Rabbis. [3]Rabbi Shimon is like Abba Shaul; [4]and the Rabbis are like the Rabbis.

[5]Rav Pappa strongly objected to this: [6]Granted: Whenever she demands her ketubah. [7][But, "if] she is not claiming her ketubah". What is there to say?

[8]Rather, Rav Pappa said: [9][Rabbi Shimon comes] to exclude [the view] of Rabbi Eliezer and those who disagree with him.

RASHI

הא תינח כל זמן שתובעת — אתא לאפוקי מדרבנן. דאמרי: אף משבועת היתומים פטורה, ונפרעת בלא שבועה. ואתא רבי שמעון למימר: לא תפרע אלא בשבועה. **אינה תובעת כתובתה** — דמסקנא דמילתיה למאי תנייה, ולאפוקי ממאן? **אלא אמר רב פפא לאפוקי מדרבי אליעזר ומחלוקתו** — כלומר, לא תימא רבי שמעון א״כתב לה נדר ושבועה״ לחוד פליג, אלא אכולי מלתא דרבי אליעזר ובני מחלוקתו פליג, ארישא וסיפא. שמעינהו דקאמרי רבי אליעזר ורבנן: משביעה כל זמן שירצה שבועת אפוטרופיא היכא דלא פטרה מן הנדר ומן השבועה, ואפילו שלא בשעת תביעת כתובתה. ואם פטרה מן השבועה — אפילו יורשין אין משביעין אותה כשנפרעת מהם, כדקתני: נדר ושבועה אין לי ליורשי כו׳. ואתא רבי שמעון למימר: כל זמן שתובעת כתובתה יורשין משביעין אותה. ואפילו כתב לה ״נדר ושבועה אין ליורשי עליך״. כאבא שאול, אינה תובעת כתובתה — אין היורשין משביעין על אפוטרופיא שבחיי בעלה ואפילו לא פטרה מן השבועה, דלית ליה דרבי אליעזר ומחלוקתו דאמרי: משביעה כל זמן שירצה.

NOTES

heirs may impose an oath upon her even with respect to her handling of their father's property. But according to Abba Shaul, a guardian appointed by the orphans' father is never required to take such an oath, even by attachment.

אֶלָּא, אֲמַר רַב פַּפָּא **Rather Rav Pappa said.** Our commentary follows *Rashi* who understands that Rav Pappa adds to what Abaye had said. He accepts Abaye's interpretation of the first half of Rabbi Shimon's statement that Rabbi Shimon disagrees with the Tanna of the previous Mishnah, who taught that if a husband exempted his wife from taking an oath to him or to his heirs, the heirs may not impose an oath when she comes to collect her ketubah

LITERAL TRANSLATION

MISHNAH [1] [If] she presented a bill of divorce, [2] and there was no ketubah with it, [89A] she collects her ketubah [settlement].

משנה [1] הוֹצִיאָה גֵּט, [2] וְאֵין עִמּוֹ כְּתוּבָּה, [89A] גּוֹבָה כְּתוּבָּתָהּ.

RASHI

משנה הוציאה גט ואין עמו כתובה — קא סלקא דעתך באומרת ״אבד שטר כתובתי״. גובה כתובתה — ואינו יכול לטעון: פרעתיך והחזרת לי שטר כתובתיך וקרעתיו. משום דתנאי כתובה מעשה בית דין הוא, ומהכא נפקא לן בבבא מציעא: הטוען אחר מעשה בית דין — לא אמר כלום. מאי טעמא — כל מעשה בית דין כמאן דנקיט שטרא דמי.

TRANSLATION AND COMMENTARY

due him. Rabbi Eliezer goes further and says that the husband may also impose an oath upon his wife regarding her honest management of household affairs, even if he had not set her up as a shopkeeper or an administrator. In our Mishnah Rabbi Shimon disagrees with both of these positions. He teaches that if a woman does not demand her ketubah settlement from her husband's heirs, they may not impose an oath upon her regarding her handling of her husband's business or domestic affairs during his lifetime, even if he had not exempted her from taking such an oath. For Rabbi Shimon disagrees with the Tannaim of the earlier Mishnah and says that not even the husband himself can impose an oath upon his wife regarding her handling of his affairs.

MISHNAH הוֹצִיאָה גֵּט [1] If a woman **presented** her **bill of divorce** before the court and demanded payment of her ketubah settlement, [2] **but there was no ketubah** deed documenting his obligation, [89A] **she** may still **collect her ketubah** settlement.

NOTES

settlement. According to Rabbi Shimon, when the husband exempts his wife from swearing to the heirs, they may indeed impose an oath upon her. But, Rav Pappa adds in the second half of his statement, Rabbi Shimon intends to counter the position of Rabbi Eliezer and the Tanna disagreeing with Rabbi Eliezer in an earlier Mishnah. For according to Rabbi Shimon, if a widow does not demand her ketubah settlement from her husband's heirs, they cannot impose any type of oath upon her. *Ritva* notes that while this understanding of Rav Pappa is in itself reasonable, the term אֶלָּא ("rather") implies that Rav Pappa rejects the entire position of Abaye. There is, however, a reading that omits the word אֶלָּא.

Ra'avad agrees with *Rashi* about Rav Pappa's understanding of the first half of Rabbi Shimon's statement. As for the second half of that statement, *Ra'avad* suggests that according to Rav Pappa, Rabbi Shimon does not disagree with both Rabbi Eliezer and the anonymous first Tanna, but disagrees with Rabbi Eliezer in his dispute with the annonymous first Tanna. Therefore, when a widow does not demand her ketubah settlement, they may not impose an oath upon her regarding her handling of his domestic affairs. However, following the anonymous first Tanna, Rabbi Shimon agrees that they may still impose an oath regarding her handling of his business affairs.

Others understand that the word אֶלָּא is significant, and that Rav Pappa is offering an entirely new explanation. According to them, Rabbi Shimon means to say that when a widow demands her ketubah settlement from her late husband's heirs, the heirs may impose an oath upon her that she has not yet received it, and they may even make her take an oath on her handling of her husband's domestic affairs. This is in contrast to the anonymous first Tanna who disagrees with Rabbi Eliezer, and says that a wife can never be required to take an oath about her handling of her husband's domestic affairs. Rabbi Shimon then teaches that if a widow does not demand her ketubah settlement, her husband's heirs may not impose any oath upon. On this matter, he disagrees with both Rabbi Eliezer and the anonymous first Tanna, for those Tannaim agree that a wife can always be required to take an oath about her handling of her husband's business affairs (see *Sefer Zekhut* of *Ramban*).

These differences in the understanding of Rav Pappa are particularly significant according to those authorities, such as *Rabbenu Ḥananel, Rabbenu Tam,* and others who ruled that the Halakhah is in accordance with the position of Rabbi Shimon. These authorities took this stand because in all of the interpretations of Rabbi Shimon's position suggested by our Gemara, Rabbi Shimon follows the position that is accepted as the conclusive law. The Jerusalem Talmud also ruled explicitly according to Rabbi Shimon. But many Rishonim, including *Rif* and *Rambam,* ruled in accordance with the anonymous first Tanna of the Mishnah on 86b, against Rabbi Shimon.

גּוֹבָה כְּתוּבָּתָהּ **She collects her ketubah.** *Rashi* follows the Gemara in *Bava Metzia* 17a, which explains that this ruling is based on the principle formulated by Rabbi Yoḥanan: if a person claims that he already paid an obligation that falls upon him because of a Rabbinic enactment, his claim is not accepted. A husband's obligation to pay his wife her ketubah settlement does not stem from the ketubah deed

HALAKHAH

הוֹצִיאָה גֵּט וְאֵין עִמּוֹ כְּתוּבָּה **If she presented a bill of divorce, and there was no ketubah with it.** "If a woman presented her bill of divorce to the court and demanded payment of her ketubah settlement, but she does not have a ketubah deed, the following distinction applies: If the local custom is that women are not given ketubah deeds, she may collect the main portion of her ketubah settlement with her bill of divorce. But if the local custom is that women are given ketubah deeds, the woman may not collect anything without first producing her ketubah deed. However, the husband here is required to take a *hesset* oath to counter his wife's claim." (*Rambam, Sefer Nashim, Hilkhot Ishut* 16:28; *Shulḥan Arukh, Even HaEzer* 100:12.)

TRANSLATION AND COMMENTARY

כְּתוּבָּה [1]A woman **presented** her **ketubah** for collection, **but** did not have **the bill of divorce,** so her husband refused to pay her. [2]In court the woman **claimed: "I lost my bill of divorce** before collecting my ketubah settlement," [3]**and** her ex-husband **saying:** "She collected her ketubah settlement with her bill of divorce (as she claimed that her ketubah deed was lost), the bill of divorce was then torn up, and I was given a receipt to prevent her from collecting the ketubah settlement again; but **my receipt was** subsequently **lost**". [4]**And similarly,** if **a creditor presented a promissory note** to the court after the Sabbatical Year, **but he** claimed that the *prosbul* (a document authorizing the court to collect his debts after the Sabbatical Year), was lost — [5]the lender too **may not collect** the debt, for we are concerned that perhaps the lender did not arrange a *prosbul* and the debt was therefore cancelled by the Sabbatical Year.

[1]כְּתוּבָּה וְאֵין עִמָּהּ גֵּט, [2]הִיא אוֹמֶרֶת: "אָבַד גִּיטִּי", [3]וְהוּא אוֹמֵר: "אָבַד שׁוֹבְרִי"; [4]וְכֵן, בַּעַל חוֹב שֶׁהוֹצִיא שְׁטַר חוֹב, וְאֵין עִמּוֹ פְּרוֹזְבּוֹל, [5]הֲרֵי אֵלּוּ לֹא יִפָּרְעוּ.

LITERAL TRANSLATION

[1][if she presented] a ketubah, and there was no bill of divorce with it, [2][and] she says: "My bill of divorce was lost," [3]and he says: "My receipt was lost"; [4]and similarly, a creditor who presented a promissory note, [5]and there was no *prosbul* with it — they may not collect.

RASHI

אבד גטי — שלא הוצאתיו עליו לגבות כתובתי על ידו, כדתנן: גובה כתובתה. ולא קרעוהו בית דין, אלא אבד ממני. **והוא אומר אבד שוברי** — כבר הוצאתו בבית דין, ואמרת אבד שטר כתובתי, וגבו בית דין הכתובה על פי הגט, וקרעוהו. ולי נכתב שובר על הכתובה, שאם תוציאי עוד על יורשי שטר הכתובה, ותבואי לגבות מכח אלמנות לומר לא נתגרשתי ולא נפרעתי — יהיה השובר לעד, ואבד הימני. **וכן בעל חוב שהוציא שטר חוב** — אחר שביעית, ואין עמו פרוזבול. זה אומר: השמיטתו שביעית, וזה אומר: פרוזבול היה לי שלא תשמיטנו שביעית, ואבד. **הרי אלו לא יפרעו** — חיישינן שמא כבר גבתה בגט, וזה — השמיטתו שביעית.

LANGUAGE

פְּרוֹזְבּוֹל ***Prosbul.*** This word is clearly of Greek origin, although its precise etymology remains obscure. Some derive this προβολή from *probole*, "presentation of a case to the assembly," or "loan." Others derive it from the Greek προσβολή *prosbole*, "consummation of a sale" (other explanations have also been suggested).

CONCEPTS

פְּרוֹזְבּוֹל ***Prosbul.*** *Prosbul* is a legal document written during the Sabbatical Year, in which the creditor declares that he entrusts all debts due him to the court. Thus, the court, to which the laws of the Sabbatical Year do not apply, may collect these debts on the creditor's behalf after the Sabbatical Year is over. *Prosbul* was instituted by Hillel the Elder who was concerned that the wealthy would not lend to the poor, because they felt that the debts due them would be cancelled by the Sabbatical Year. Accordingly, Hillel instituted the *prosbul* to ensure that potential moneylenders would be able to collect the money due them after the Sabbatical Year.

NOTES

in the same way that a debtor's obligation to repay his creditor stems from the promissory note. Rather it is based on a Rabbinic enactment which entitles every woman to receive a ketubah settlement from her husband. Thus, as long as a woman has proof that she is entitled to collect her settlement, by producing her bill of divorce, for example, her husband cannot claim that he already paid the woman her settlement, even if she cannot produce her ketubah deed. We accept as law the position of Rabbi Meir who said that a man is obligated to write a ketubah deed for his wife. However, this ruling is meant to make the woman feel secure about her ketubah settlement and to prevent her sexual intercourse with her husband from being deemed an act of prostitution. The woman is not required to produce her ketubah deed in order to collect her ketubah settlement.

The Rishonim discuss whether or not the increment that a husband may add to his wife's ketubah settlement is considered part of the Rabbinic enactment regarding her ketubah. If the woman has witnesses that her husband obligated himself to an increment to her ketubah settlement, can she collect that increment without producing her ketubah deed, or is the increment like an ordinary obligation, which a debtor can claim had already been paid if his creditor cannot produce the promissory note?

הִיא אוֹמֶרֶת: אָבַד גִּיטִּי **She says: My bill of divorce was lost.** Our commentary follows *Rashi* and other Rishonim, who explain that the woman claims that she lost her bill of divorce before using it to collect her ketubah settlement (as the woman did in the first clause of the Mishnah), and so she is now entitled to her entire settlement. Her husband claims that she had already presented her bill of divorce, and collected her ketubah settlement. The woman's bill of divorce was then torn up, the husband was given a receipt for his payment, but, so he claims, the receipt was lost.

Ritva cites another explanation: The woman claims that she lost her bill of divorce, and the husband claims that she had already received her ketubah settlement on the basis of her bill of divorce, but that a receipt had been written on the bill of divorce itself, so that she would not be able to collect with it again. Thus, when she claimed that the bill of divorce was lost, the receipt was lost with it. *Rivan* suggests that the husband was not serious when he said that he lost the receipt. What he meant was that he does not believe his wife that she lost her bill of divorce, and that if she persists in her claim that she did not receive her settlement, he can counter that he had a receipt for his payment but it was lost.

וְאֵין עִמּוֹ פְּרוֹזְבּוֹל **And there was no *prosbul* with it.** The Torah stipulates that loans may not be collected by creditors after the seventh year of the seven-year cycle (see Deuteronomy 15:1-11). If, however, the loan contract had been given to the court for collection, the loan is not cancelled. When Hillel the Elder saw that many people were refusing to lend money in the years preceding the seventh year because they were afraid that they would not recover their money, he instituted a process — drawing up a document known as a *prosbul* — whereby the lender authorizes the court to collect his debts. When a *prozbul* is written by a creditor his debts are not cancelled by the Sabbatical Year.

The Rishonim note that elsewhere (*Gittin* 37b) the Tannaim disagree about whether a creditor is believed if he says that he had a *prosbul* but it was lost. Our Mishnah follows the view that the creditor is not believed regarding such a claim, but the law follows the view that the creditor is believed, for we assume that a person would not violate a prohibition if he had ample opportunity to write a *prosbul* and collect the rest in a permitted manner.

TRANSLATION AND COMMENTARY

רַבָּן שִׁמְעוֹן בֶּן גַּמְלִיאֵל [1]**Rabban Shimon ben Gamliel says:** In ordinary times a woman may not collect her ketubah settlement without a bill of divorce, and a borrower may not collect his debt after the Sabbatical Year without a *prosbul*. But [2]**from the time of danger and afterwards,** when Jewish observance was forbidden by the Roman authorities and people were afraid to preserve their bills of divorce and *prosbuls*, [3]**a woman** may **collect her ketubah** settlement even **without** presenting her **bill of divorce,** [4]**and a creditor** may **collect** his debt after the Sabbatical Year even **without** presenting **his** ***prosbul*,** for we assume that the documents were destroyed to avoid trouble with the authorities.

GEMARA שְׁמַע מִינָּהּ [5]The Gemara now suggests that a general conclusion may be drawn from our Mishnah. **Infer from** our Mishnah that when a creditor claims to have lost his promissory note and the debtor admits the debt, **we** tell the debtor to pay the debt and order the creditor to **write** him **a receipt.** [6]**If we do not** require her to **write a receipt, we should be concerned that** she is concealing her ketubah deed, and later **she will perhaps produce her ketubah** deed in another court, **and collect with it** a second time after the husband's death. Therefore, we should infer that in the related case where the creditor claims to have lost his promissory note he receives payment and writes a receipt. Elsewhere (*Bava Batra* 171b), the Tannaim and Amoraim disagree about this very case. According to one opinion, we require the debtor to pay and order the creditor to write a receipt, for the debtor admits the debt and it would be unfair to allow the creditor to remain unpaid. According to a second opinion, we permit the debtor to delay payment until the promissory note is returned to him. It would be unfair to order the debtor to accept a receipt, for if the receipt is ever lost, and the creditor produces his note, the debtor may be forced to pay it again. Our Mishnah supports the former opinion.

[1]רַבָּן שִׁמְעוֹן בֶּן גַּמְלִיאֵל אוֹמֵר: [2]מִן הַסַּכָּנָה וְאֵילָךְ, [3]אִשָּׁה גּוֹבָה כְּתוּבָּתָהּ שֶׁלֹּא בְּגֵט, [4]וּבַעַל חוֹב גּוֹבֶה שֶׁלֹּא בִּפְרוֹזְבּוֹל.

גמרא [5]שְׁמַע מִינָּהּ: כּוֹתְבִין שׁוֹבֵר. [6]דְּאִי אֵין כּוֹתְבִין שׁוֹבֵר, לֵיחוּשׁ דִּלְמָא מַפְּקָא לַהּ לִכְתוּבָּתָהּ וְגָבְיָא בַּהּ!

LITERAL TRANSLATION

[1]Rabban Shimon ben Gamliel says: [2]From [the time of] danger and afterwards, [3]a woman collects her ketubah [settlement] without a bill of divorce, [4]and a creditor collects without a *prosbul*.

GEMARA [5]Infer from this: We write a receipt. [6]For if we do not write a receipt, let us be concerned [that] perhaps she will present her ketubah, and collect with it!

RASHI

מן הסכנה – שגזרו גויים על המצות, והיו יראים לשמור גיטיהן, ומשקיבלתו שורפתו. וכן פרוזבוליהן. פרוזבול – במסכת גיטין מפרש, בפרק "השולח גט" (לד,ב): הלל התקין פרוזבול כדי שלא תשמט שביעית, שמוסר שטרותיו לבית דין שיגבו מן הלוה חובו כל זמן שיתבענו. דהשתא לא קרינן ביה "לא יגוש" – שאינו תובעו כלום, אלא הבית דין תובעו, שהפקירם היה הפקר והם יורדין לנכסיו.

גמרא שמע מינה – מדקתני: גובה כתובתה בהוצאת גט, ולא חיישׁ לאיערומי מערמא והדרא ומפקא כתובתה בבי דינא אחרינא, ותגבה לאחר מיתתו בתורת אלמנה, לומר: לא נתגרשתי ולא נפרעתי. דהא ודאי בתורת גרושה לא הדרא גביא, דהא קרעינן לגיטא. וכי הדרא מפקא לכתובתה בלא גט – תנן מתניתין: הרי אלו לא יפרעו. ומיהו, הוה לן למיחש (שלא) [שהיא] תמתין עד שימות. ותגבה בתורת אלמנה. ומדלא חייש, שמע מינה: כותבין שובר על כרחו של לוה, ואינו יכול להשמיט עצמו לומר: לא אפרע עד שתחזיר לי שטרי, שמא תחזור ותוציאנו. אלא אומרים לו: פרע, והוא יכתוב לך שובר. ופלוגתא היא בבבא בתרא (קעא,ב) וקיימא לן כמאן דאמר: אין כותבין, לפי שנמצא זה צריך לשמור שוברו מן העכברים. דלמא מפקא – לאחר מיתה. וגביא – בתורת אלמנה.

NOTES

כּוֹתְבִין שׁוֹבֵר **We write a receipt.** Elsewhere (*Bava Batra* 171b), the Tannaim disagree about whether a debtor may refuse to repay his debt until the promissory note which the creditor holds is returned to him, or whether the debtor is required to repay the debt and accept a receipt of payment.

According to *Rashi*, the law follows the position that a debtor is not obligated to accept a receipt, and so he is not required to repay a debt if his promissory note is not returned to him. *Tosafot* and other argue that the Gemara in *Bava Batra* implies that the law follows the position that the debtor can indeed be required to accept a receipt.

HALAKHAH

בַּעַל חוֹב גּוֹבֶה שֶׁלֹּא בִּפְרוֹזְבּוֹל **A creditor collects without a *prosbul*.** "Following the Sabbatical Year, a creditor is believed if he claims that he had a *prosbul* allowing him to collect his debts, but it was lost. Moreover, even if he himself did not put forward such a claim, the court asks him whether perhaps he had a *prosbul* and it was lost, and if he answers that indeed that was the case, he is believed, following Rabbi Yehudah (*Gittin* 37b). If he admits that he never had a *prosbul*, he forfeits his right to collect his debt. *Rema* adds (in the name of *Rashba*) that if the creditor left the courtroom without claiming that he once had a *prosbul*, but before the court announced its decision, he returned and put forward such a claim, he is believed. But he is not believed when he presents his claim after the court issued its ruling." (*Rambam, Sefer Zeraim, Hilkhot Shemittah* 9:24; *Shulḥan Arukh, Ḥoshen Mishpat* 67:33.)

TRANSLATION AND COMMENTARY

אָמַר רַב [1]**Rav said:** This inference from the Mishnah is unwarranted, for it **deals with a place where they do not write a ketubah** at all. In some places it was customary to dispense with writing a ketubah deed, for the basic obligations of the marriage contract are fixed by law. In such places the Sages had no fear that a woman might later produce a ketubah deed. Thus no receipt for payment was required.

וּשְׁמוּאֵל אָמַר [2]**And Shmuel said:** In our Mishnah we are dealing **even with a place where** it is the general custom to **write a ketubah.** There a woman can collect her ketubah settlement upon presentation of her bill of divorce, and her husband cannot withhold payment until she produces her ketubah deed.

וְלִשְׁמוּאֵל [3]The Gemara asks: **And according to Shmuel**'s understanding of the Mishnah, can we then conclude that when a creditor claims to have lost his promissory note and the debtor admits the debt, **we** require the debtor to pay the debt and order the creditor to **write** him **a receipt** for the money that he received?

אָמַר רַב עָנָן [4]The Gemara now clarifies the position of Shmuel. It is possible that, in general, we do not force payment and the writing of a receipt. For **Rav Anan said: I myself personally heard Mar Shmuel explain** his position as follows: [5]**In a place where** people **do not** ordinarily **write a ketubah** deed, our Mishnah refers to the exceptional case, [6]when the husband **said: "I wrote** my wife a ketubah deed." Thus, in order to avoid paying her ketubah settlement **he must prove** that he wrote a ketubah deed by producing witnesses to that effect. The Mishnah further limits itself to a case when he cannot bring such witnesses, and so the woman can collect her ketubah without producing a ketubah deed — for we assume that no such deed was ever written. [7]Conversely, **in a place where** people ordinarily **write** a ketubah deed, the Mishnah refers to a woman who **said:** "My husband **did not write** a ketubah deed **for me,"** an assertion that **she must prove.** The Mishnah further limits itself to a case when she brings witnesses to support her claim, and so she can collect her settlement without presenting a ketubah deed.

[1]אָמַר רַב: בְּמָקוֹם שֶׁאֵין כּוֹתְבִין כְּתוּבָּה עָסְקִינַן.
[2]וּשְׁמוּאֵל אָמַר: אַף בְּמָקוֹם שֶׁכּוֹתְבִין כְּתוּבָּה.
[3]וְלִשְׁמוּאֵל כּוֹתְבִין שׁוֹבֵר?
[4]אֲמַר רַב עָנָן: לְדִידִי מִיפַּרְשָׁא לִי מִינֵּיהּ דְּמָר שְׁמוּאֵל: [5]בְּמָקוֹם שֶׁאֵין כּוֹתְבִין, [6]וְאָמַר: ״כָּתַבְתִּי״ — עָלָיו לְהָבִיא רְאָיָה. [7]בְּמָקוֹם שֶׁכּוֹתְבִין, וְאָמְרָה: ״לֹא כָּתַב לִי״ — עָלֶיהָ לְהָבִיא רְאָיָה.

LITERAL TRANSLATION

[1]Rav said: We are dealing with a place where they do not write a ketubah.

[2]But Shmuel said: Even with a place where they write a ketubah.

[3]And according to Shmuel, do we write a receipt?

[4]Rav Anan said: [His intention] was explained to me personally by Mar Shmuel: [5]In a place where they do not write [a ketubah], [6]and he said: "I wrote," he must bring proof. [7]In a place where they write [a ketubah], and she said: "He did not write [one] for me," it is upon her to bring proof.

RASHI

במקום שאין כותבין כתובה — אלא סומכין על תנאי בית דין. **ולשמואל כותבין שובר** — בתמיה. **לדידי מיפרשא לי** — דלעולם אין כותבין שובר. והיינו טעמא דגובה כתובתה: דאי מקום שאין כותבין הוא, והוא אומר: כתבתי, וירא אני שמא תחזור ותוציאנה — עליו להביא ראיה. ואי מייתי ראיה — קתני מתניתין: גובה כתובתה. ואינו נאמן לומר: שניתי מנהג העיר. ואי מקום שכותבין הוא, והיא אמרה: לא כתב לי — עליה להביא ראיה. וכי קתני מתניתין: גובה כתובתה — שהביאה ראיה שלא כתב לה.

SAGES

רַב עָנָן **Rav Anan.** A Babylonian Amora of the second generation. See *Ketubot,* Part IV, p. 186.

NOTES

Hence the discussion in our Gemara is purely theoretical, for it seeks to reconcile our Mishnah with the view that the debtor is not obligated to accept a receipt. *Rid* and *Rivash* note that one can distinguish between a ketubah and other documented debts. In the case of an ordinary debt, the debtor might be required to repay and accept a receipt, and we are not concerned with his having to safeguard the receipt, following the Biblical aphorism "the borrower is the servant of the lender (Proverbs 22:7)." But in the case of a ketubah this aphorism does not apply. A husband might be allowed to delay payment of his wife's ketubah until she produces her ketubah deed.

רַב וּשְׁמוּאֵל **Rav and Shmuel.** *Ra'ah* summarizes the views of the various Amoraim as follows: Rav maintains that in a place where it is customary to write a ketubah deed for a woman, she cannot collect her ketubah settlement without producing the deed. Even if the woman has witnesses that her husband did not write her a ketubah deed, we assume that at some later date he did write a ketubah for her, in accordance with local custom. However,

HALAKHAH

בְּמָקוֹם שֶׁאֵין כּוֹתְבִין כְּתוּבָּה **A place where they do not write a ketubah.** "If a woman presented her bill of divorce to the court and demanded payment of her ketubah settlement, but she did not have a ketubah deed, the following distinction applies: If according to local custom women are not given ketubah deeds, the woman may

LITERAL TRANSLATION

[1] And even Rav retracted, for Rav said: [2] Whether in a place where they write or in a place where they do not write — [3] [with a] bill of divorce, she collects the main [settlement], [4] [with a] ketubah, she collects the increment. [5] And whoever wishes to object, let him come and object.

[6] We have learned: "[If she presented] a ketubah, and there was no bill of divorce with it, [7] [and] she says: 'My bill of divorce was lost,' [8] and he says: 'My receipt was lost,'

[1] וְאַף רַב הֲדַר בֵּיהּ, דַּאֲמַר רַב: [2] בֵּין בְּמָקוֹם שֶׁכּוֹתְבִין בֵּין בְּמָקוֹם שֶׁאֵין כּוֹתְבִין — [3] גֵּט, גּוֹבָה עִיקָּר. [4] כְּתוּבָּה, גּוֹבָה תּוֹסֶפֶת. [5] וְכָל הָרוֹצֶה לְהָשִׁיב, יָבֹא וְיָשִׁיב.

[6] תְּנַן: "כְּתוּבָּה, וְאֵין עִמָּהּ גֵּט, [7] הִיא אוֹמֶרֶת: 'אָבַד גִּיטִּי', [8] וְהוּא אוֹמֵר: 'אָבַד שׁוֹבְרִי',

RASHI

ואף רב — דאוקי מתניתין במקום שאין כותבין לחודיה. **הדר ביה** — ואוקי מתניתין בטעמא אחרינא, ואמר: בין במקום שכותבין ובין במקום שאין כותבין, כי מפקא גט בלא כתובה — גובה עיקר כתובתה, דהיינו מנה ומאתים. ו"גובה" דקתני מתניתין — עיקר קאמר, ולא תוספת. וכי מפקא כתובה בלא גט — גובה תוספת ולא עיקר, חיישינן שמא גבאתו על פי הגט. **וכל הרוצה להשיב יבא וישיב** — דאין לחוש מעתה לכלום.

TRANSLATION AND COMMENTARY

וְאַף רַב [1] The Gemara now argues that **even Rav** who said above that our Mishnah's ruling applies only where people do not ordinarily write a ketubah deed **retracted** this understanding, as **Rav** subsequently **said:** [2] **Whether in a place where** people ordinarily **write** a ketubah deed, **or in a place where they do not** ordinarily **write** such a deed, [3] if a woman presented her **bill of divorce** to the court, but was unable to produce her ketubah deed, **she** may **collect the main ketubah** settlement — the minimum amount that she is entitled to receive from her husband on the dissolution of their marriage: two hundred dinars in the case of a woman who was a virgin at the time of her marriage, or one hundred dinars in all other cases. For the main portion of a woman's ketubah is not an optional contractual obligation, but rather an obligation imposed upon the husband by Rabbinic enactment. But she cannot, without producing the deed, collect any amount that the husband may have added to the settlement. [4] And if the woman presented her **ketubah** to the court, but was unable to produce her bill of divorce, she cannot collect the main portion of her settlement, for she may already have collected it with her bill of divorce. However, **she can collect the increment** to her settlement, for she could not have collected it without her bill of divorce. [5] **And whoever wishes to** raise an **objection to this ruling, let him come and** raise an **objection.**

תְּנַן [6] But surely **we have learned** in the next clause of our Mishnah: "If a woman **presented** her **ketubah** deed to the court for collection, but did not have the **bill of divorce with it,** and the woman and her ex-husband disagree about what happened — [7] the woman **saying: "I lost my bill of divorce** before I had a chance to collect my ketubah settlement," [8] **and** her ex-husband **saying:** "My former wife already collected her ketubah settlement with her bill of divorce; her bill of divorce was torn up, and I was given a receipt, to prevent her from collecting it again, but that **receipt was lost"** — the woman may not collect her ketubah

NOTES

in a place where it is not the custom to write a ketubah deed, we rely on the Rabbinic enactment and allow her to collect her settlement with the bill of divorce alone. Shmuel disagrees and says that even where it is not customary to write a ketubah deed, if the husband can prove that he did provide his wife with such a deed, she cannot collect her ketubah settlement without producing that deed. And in a place where it is customary to write a ketubah deed, if the woman can prove that her husband did not write her such a deed, she can collect her ketubah with her bill of divorce. Rabbi Yoḥanan has a third opinion (see *Bava Metzia* 17a): Even where it is customary to write a ketubah deed, the husband must prove that he did indeed give his wife such a deed. If the husband is unable to provide such proof, the woman can collect her ketubah settlement by virtue of the Rabbinic enactment.

וְאַף רַב הֲדַר בֵּיהּ And even Rav retracted. *Ayelet Ahevim* explains that Rav retracted his first explanation, because the Mishnah's formulation, "[If she presented her] ketubah," implies that we are dealing with a place where it is

HALAKHAH

collect the main portion of her settlement with her bill of divorce. But in a place where women are customarily given ketubah deeds, the woman may not collect anything without first producing her ketubah deed. If the husband claims he has already paid the settlement, he is required to take a *hesset* oath to confirm his claim," following Shmuel and Rav Anan (*Gra*). Opinions differ about a place where women are not customarily given ketubah deeds, and witnesses came forth to testify that a particular woman was indeed given a ketubah deed. According to some authorities, the woman may not collect her settlement without first producing her ketubah deed. And according to others, she may collect the settlement with her bill of divorce (if she claims to have lost the ketubah). (*Rambam, Sefer Nashim, Hilkhot Ishut* 16:28; *Shulḥan Arukh, Even HaEzer* 100:9,12.)

LITERAL TRANSLATION

[1]and similarly a creditor who presented a promissory note, and there was no *prosbul* with it — [2]they may not collect." [3]Granted according to Shmuel, he interprets it in a place where they do not write [a ketubah], [4]and he said: "I wrote," [5]and we say to him: Bring proof. [6]And if he does not bring proof, we say to him: Go, pay it. [7]But according to Rav, [8]granted that she does not collect the main [settlement], [9][but] let her at least collect the increment!

[10]Rav Yosef said: With what are we dealing here? Where there are no witnesses to the divorce. [11][And] since he can say:

[1]וְכֵן בַּעַל חוֹב שֶׁהוֹצִיא שְׁטַר חוֹב וְאֵין עִמּוֹ פְּרוֹזְבּוֹל — [2]הֲרֵי אֵלּוּ לֹא יִפָּרְעוּ״. [3]בִּשְׁלָמָא לִשְׁמוּאֵל, מוֹקֵי לָהּ בְּמָקוֹם שֶׁאֵין כּוֹתְבִין, [4]וְאָמַר: ״כָּתַבְתִּי״, [5]דְּאָמְרִינַן לֵיהּ: אַיְיתֵי רְאָיָה. [6]וְאִי לָא מַיְיתֵי רְאָיָה, אָמְרִינַן לֵיהּ: זִיל, פְּרָעֵיהּ. [7]אֶלָּא לְרַב, [8]נְהִי דְּעִיקָּר לָא גָּבְיָא, [9]תּוֹסֶפֶת מִיהָא תִּיגְבֵּי!

[10]אֲמַר רַב יוֹסֵף: הָכָא בְּמַאי עָסְקִינַן? כְּשֶׁאֵין שָׁם עֵדֵי גֵירוּשִׁין. [11]מִיגּוֹ דְּיָכוֹל לְמֵימַר:

RASHI

בשלמא לשמואל — דאמר: בין עיקר בין תוספת — נפרעין על פי הגט. **מוקי לה** — הא דקתני: לא יפרעו. **במקום שאין כותבין** — ומשום הכי מהימן במאי דאמר: פרעתי על פי הגט, דאמר: כשתבעתני על פי הגט אמרתי בבית דין: כתבתי לה כתובה, ויראה אני שלא תחזור ותוציאנה. ואמרו לי: הבא ראיה, ולא מצאתי ראיה. ואמרו לי: פרע, ובקשתי מהן שיכתבו לי שובר, הואיל ועל כרחי אני זקוק לפרוע — טוב לי שיהיה לי שובר, וכתבוהו לי, ואבד. **אלא לרב** — דאמר: אין נפרעין על פי הגט אלא עיקר, אמאי לא יפרעו, נהי דעיקר לא גביא כו׳.

TRANSLATION AND COMMENTARY

settlement, for we are concerned that perhaps she had indeed already received it. [1]**And similarly,** if **a creditor presented a promissory note** to the court after the Sabbatical Year, **but he did not have a** ***prosbul,*** [2]the lender **may not collect** the debt, for we are concerned that perhaps a *prosbul* was not written." [3]**Granted according to Shmuel** we can understand why the woman presenting her ketubah without a bill of divorce may not collect her settlement. For he can **explain** that this clause of the Mishnah is dealing with **a place where** people **do not** ordinarily **write a ketubah** deed. And when his wife came to court to collect her settlement with her bill of divorce alone, [4]the ex-husband **claimed I wrote** her a ketubah deed, and should not be required to pay until she produces it. When the husband puts forward such an argument, [5]**we say to him: Bring proof** that you wrote a ketubah deed against the prevailing custom. [6]**If he cannot bring** such **proof**, **we say to him: Go, pay** your wife her ketubah based on the bill of divorce, and accept a receipt, so that she will not be able to collect her ketubah again with the deed. If the wife then comes with the ketubah without the bill of divorce and the husband says that he paid the settlement based on the bill of divorce (which was torn by the court) and was given a receipt that was lost, the husband's claim is accepted because it is customary in this place to collect with the bill of divorce. [7]**But according to Rav** who said that when a woman presents her bill of divorce before the court, but not her ketubah deed, she can collect only the basic portion of her ketubah, but not the increment, we do not understand the Mishnah's ruling that a woman cannot collect her settlement with only the ketubah deed. [8]**Granted that she cannot collect the main** portion of her **ketubah** settlement, for the husband can claim that he already paid it when she presented her bill of divorce. [9]**But let her at least collect the increment** specified in her ketubah, which could not have been collected with her bill of divorce!

אֲמַר רַב יוֹסֵף [10]**Rav Yosef said:** There is no difficulty, for we can explain according to Rav that **we are dealing here with** a woman who has **no witnesses** to testify **to her divorce.** [11]**And since** the husband **can** deny

NOTES

customary to write a ketubah. Others explain that since the Mishnah did not state explicitly that its ruling was limited to a specific case, it stands to reason that it applies to all places.

HALAKHAH

כְּשֶׁאֵין שָׁם עֵדֵי גֵירוּשִׁין When there are no witnesses to the divorce. "If a woman presented her ketubah deed to the court and demanded payment of her settlement, but she does not have a bill of divorce, and the husband admits that he divorced his wife, but claims that he already paid her both the main portion of her settlement and also the increment, and she wrote him a receipt for the money, but the receipt was lost — he is believed about the increment, for he could have claimed that he had never divorced his wife, and thus he would be exempt from paying her the increment to her ketubah. The husband can require his wife to take an oath holding a Torah scroll regarding the principal, after which he must pay her that sum, and he himself is required to take a *hesset* oath regarding the increment." (*Rambam, Sefer Nashim, Hilkhot Ishut* 16:27; *Shulḥan Arukh, Even HaEzer* 100:11.)

"לֹא גֵּירַשְׁתִּיהָ", [89B] [1]יָכוֹל לְמֵימַר: "גֵּירַשְׁתִּיהָ וְנָתַתִּי לָהּ כְּתוּבָּתָהּ".

[2]הָא מְדְקָתָנֵי סֵיפָא: [3]"רַבָּן שִׁמְעוֹן בֶּן גַּמְלִיאֵל אוֹמֵר: מִן הַסַּכָּנָה וְאֵילָךְ, [4]אִשָּׁה גּוֹבָה כְּתוּבָּתָהּ שֶׁלֹּא בְּגֵט, [5]וּבַעַל חוֹב שֶׁלֹּא בִּפְרוֹזְבּוֹל" — [6]בִּדְאִיכָּא עֵדֵי גֵירוּשִׁין עָסְקִינַן, [7]דְּאִי לֵיכָּא עֵדֵי גֵירוּשִׁין, בְּמַאי גָּבְיָא?

[8]אֶלָּא, כּוּלָּהּ רַבָּן שִׁמְעוֹן בֶּן גַּמְלִיאֵל הִיא; [9]וְחַסּוּרֵי מִיחַסְּרָא,

LITERAL TRANSLATION

"I did not divorce her," [89B] [1]he can say: "I divorced her and gave her her ketubah settlement." [2]Surely since the last clause states: [3]"Rabban Shimon ben Gamliel says: From [the time of] danger and afterward, [4]a woman collects her ketubah settlement without a bill of divorce, [5]and a creditor without a *prosbul*" — [6]we must be dealing with when there are witnesses to the divorce, [7]for if there are no witnesses to the divorce, with what does she collect? [8]Rather, the entire [Mishnah] follows Rabban Shimon ben Gamliel; [9]but it is lacking,

TRANSLATION AND COMMENTARY

his obligation altogether and **say: "I did not divorce** my wife, and so I do not have to pay out her her ketubah settlement," and his claim would have been accepted, [89B] [1]**he can** also **say:** "Indeed **I divorced her, but I** already **paid her her ketubah** settlement — the main portion as well as the increment." Since the husband's claim is supported by the legal inference called *miggo* (lit., "since"; see above 84b), we accept it.

הָא מְדְקָתָנֵי סֵיפָא [2]The Gemara now questions the suggestion that the Mishnah deals with a woman who could not find witnesses to her divorce: **Surely since the last clause** of the Mishnah **states:** [3]**"Rabban Shimon ben Gamliel says: From the time of danger and afterwards,** when Jewish observance was forbidden by the Roman authorities and people were afraid to preserve their bills of divorce and *prosbuls*, [4]**a woman** may **collect her ketubah** settlement even **without** presenting her **bill of divorce,** [5]**and a creditor** may collect his debt after the Sabbatical Year even **without** presenting his ***prosbul*."** [6]It follows that **we must be dealing** here in the Mishnah **with a case when there are witnesses** who can testify **to the divorce,** [7]**for if there are no witnesses to the divorce,** how can the woman **collect** her ketubah settlement? Thus, the Mishnah must be referring to when she has witnesses, and the objection raised above against the position of Rav has not been countered.

אֶלָּא [8]The Gemara answers: **Rather,** according to Rav an entirely different understanding of the Mishnah must be adopted: **The entire Mishnah** can be interpreted as reflecting the view of **Rabban Shimon ben Gamliel,** as the Gemara now explains: [9]The text of the Mishnah **is lacking** — several sentences are missing from it.

NOTES

לֹא גֵּירַשְׁתִּיהָ **I did not divorce her.** The Rishonim ask: How can the husband have denied his obligation altogether by saying that he never divorced his wife? Surely, it was taught elsewhere (*Ketubot* 22b) that a woman who says that she was divorced by her husband is believed! *Tosafot* answer that we believe her only when she is testifying to her marital status. However, if she comes to court and demands payment of her ketubah settlement because she was divorced, she is not believed, for we are concerned that she may be making this claim only to collect the money. *Rabbenu Shimshon of Sens* suggests that in this instance it was known that the husband and wife had been fighting. In such a case, the woman is not believed when she claims without proof that she was divorced, if that claim is denied by her husband. *Ra'avad* answers that in this case the woman claims that she has just been divorced, and her claim is not accepted, for it is not likely that she would have lost her bill of divorce so quickly. *Ritva* argues that a woman who claims that she was divorced is believed with respect to collecting the basic ketubah settlement, but not with respect to the increment.

יָכוֹל לְמֵימַר: גֵּירַשְׁתִּיהָ **He can say: I divorced her.** The Rishonim challenge the validity of this *miggo* argument: How can we believe the husband's claim that he divorced his wife and paid the ketubah settlement because he could have said that he never divorced her? Had he said that, he would have been obligated to provide her with maintenance and put himself in a less advantageous position. *Tosafot* answer: Even if the husband had claimed that he never divorced his wife, he would not have been required to provide her with maintenance, for this is similar to a case where the plaintiff demands wheat, and the defendant admits owing barley. There the defendant is exempt from any obligation, for that to which he admitted was not demanded of him. Here too the husband would have been exempt from maintenance, for his wife demanded her ketubah settlement, and he admitted to maintenance. *Rosh* argues that since the woman claims that she was divorced, she is considered as if she had explicitly admitted that her husband does not owe her any maintenance. *Ritva* answers that the husband is believed when he says that he paid his wife her ketubah settlement, because he could have claimed that he had never divorced his wife and that when they were married his wife had specifically exempted him from maintenance.

כּוּלָּהּ רַבָּן שִׁמְעוֹן בֶּן גַּמְלִיאֵל **Rather the entire [Mishnah] follows Rabban Shimon ben Gamliel.** *Rivan* and *Ritva* omit the word "rather," for the explanation proposed here does

HALAKHAH

מִן הַסַּכָּנָה וְאֵילָךְ **From the time of danger and afterwards.** "In a place where it is dangerous for a woman to preserve her bill of divorce, she is believed when she says that she was divorced, and she may collect her entire ketubah on

TRANSLATION AND COMMENTARY

[1]**It should be taught as follows:** "If a woman presented her ketubah to the court for collection, but she did not have a bill of divorce, and she claims that she never received her settlement, whereas her husband argues that he already paid it to her, but he lost the receipt, she **may not collect** her settlement, for we are concerned that perhaps she had indeed already received it." The Gemara now cites the crucial section that had been omitted from the Mishnah: [2]**In what case do we say this?** [3]When **there are no witnesses** who can testify **about the divorce.** Here the husband is believed with the legal principle of *miggo*: he could have claimed that he had never divorced the woman and does not yet owe her her ketubah. [4]**But when there are witnesses to the divorce,** in which case the husband cannot present such an argument, the woman **may collect the increment** to her settlement with her ketubah deed, for (according to Rav) she could not have collected the increment with her bill of divorce alone. [5]As for **the basic** sum of the **ketubah, if she can present her bill of divorce, she may collect it,** [6]**but if she cannot present her bill of divorce, she may not collect** it, for she might have presented her bill of divorce in a different court and collected the basic portion of her ketubah settlement. All of this applies in ordinary times. [7]But **from the time of danger and afterwards** when Jewish observance was forbidden by the Roman authorities and women were afraid to preserve their bills of divorce, [8]**even if** a woman **cannot present her bill of divorce, she may collect** the basic portion of her ketubah." [9]And the Mishnah concludes: **"For Rabban Shimon ben Gamliel says: From the time of danger and afterwards, a woman may collect her ketubah** even **without** presenting **her bill of divorce,** [10]**and a creditor** may collect his debt after the Sabbatical Year even **without** presenting **his *prosbul*,** for we assume that these documents were destroyed so as not to get into trouble with the authorities."

אָמְרִי לֵיהּ [11]**Rav Kahana and Rav Assi said to Rav: According to you who said** that in normal times only [12]**if a woman presents her bill of divorce, can she collect the basic** portion of her **ketubah** settlement, there

[1]וְהָכִי קָתָנֵי: הֲרֵי אֵלּוּ לֹא יִפָּרְעוּ. [2]בַּמֶּה דְּבָרִים אֲמוּרִים? [3]כְּשֶׁאֵין שָׁם עֵדֵי גֵירוּשִׁין. [4]אֲבָל יֵשׁ שָׁם עֵדֵי גֵירוּשִׁין, גָּבְיָא תּוֹסֶפֶת. [5]וְעִיקָּר? אִי מַפְּקָא גִּיטָּא, גָּבְיָא, [6]וְאִי לָא מַפְּקָא גִּיטָּא, לָא גָּבְיָא. [7]וּמִן הַסַּכָּנָה וְאֵילָךְ, [8]אַף עַל גַּב דְּלָא מַפְּקָא גִּיטָּא, גָּבְיָא, [9]שֶׁרַבָּן שִׁמְעוֹן בֶּן גַּמְלִיאֵל אוֹמֵר: מִסַּכָּנָה וְאֵילָךְ, אִשָּׁה גּוֹבָה כְּתוּבָּתָהּ שֶׁלֹּא בְּגֵט, [10]וּבַעַל חוֹב שֶׁלֹּא בִּפְרוֹזְבּוּל. [11]אָמְרִי לֵיהּ רַב כָּהֲנָא וְרַב אַסִּי לְרַב: לְדִידָךְ דְּאָמְרַתְּ: [12]גֵּט,

LITERAL TRANSLATION

[1]and it teaches as follows: Now these do not collect. [2]About what are these things said? [3]Where there are no witnesses to the divorce. [4]But where there are witnesses to the divorce, she may collect the increment. [5]And the basic [settlement]? If she presents a bill of divorce, she may collect [it], [6]but if she does not present a bill of divorce, she may not collect. [7]And from [the time of] danger and afterward, [8]even if she did not present a bill of divorce, [9]she may collect, for Rabban Shimon ben Gamliel says: From [the time of] danger and afterward, a woman collects her ketubah settlement without a bill of divorce, [10]and a creditor [collects] without a *prosbul*.

[11]Rav Kahana and Rav Assi said to Rav: According to you who said: [12][If she presents] a bill of divorce,

RASHI

ואי לא לא גביא – חיישינן שמא כבר גבתה על פי הגט.

NOTES

not contradict the previous explanation, but rather it completes it. *Ra'ah* notes that once the Gemara says that the text of the Mishnah is defective and that several missing sentences must be inserted, there is no longer any need to say that the entire Mishnah must be interpreted as reflecting only the view of Rabban Shimon ben Gamliel. The Gemara argues that the entire Mishnah follows Rabban Shimon ben Gamliel, because it assumes that there is no Tanna who would disagree with his distinction between before and after the time of danger (see also *Ritva*). Or else, the Gemara prefers to explain that the entire Mishnah follows the position of Rabban Shimon ben Gamliel, because the Mishnah does not cite the position of an anonymous first Tanna with whom Rabban Shimon ben Gamliel supposedly disagrees.

לְדִידָךְ דְּאָמְרַתְּ **According to you who said.** *Tosafot* and others ask: Why do Rav Kahana and Rav Assi raise their question only according to Rav? That same question — how does a woman who was widowed from marriage collect her ketubah settlement — can also be asked according to Shmuel with respect to a place where it is customary not to write a ketubah deed. For in such a place, Shmuel

HALAKHAH

the basis of that claim, even without bringing witnesses to testify to her divorce. *Rambam* writes that if the husband claims that he did not divorce his wife, he must pay her the main ketubah settlement, but he is not required to pay her the increment to her ketubah unless she can prove that he divorced her." (*Tur, Even HaEzer* 100.)

TRANSLATION AND COMMENTARY

is a difficulty. [1]For **how would a woman who was widowed from marriage collect** her settlement? [2]Surely, she does so **with witnesses to her husband's death.** [3]**But** if a woman can collect the basic portion of her ketubah settlement with her bill of divorce alone **we should be concerned that perhaps** the widow's husband had **divorced her** before he died **and she will** first collect her ketubah from his heirs with witnesses to his death, and then appear before another court, [4]**produce her bill of divorce, and collect** her ketubah **with it** again!

בְּיוֹשֶׁבֶת [5]Rav answered: A widow can only collect her ketubah settlement if she can prove that **she was living with her husband** until the time of his death, so there is no concern that she will subsequently produce a bill of divorce.

וְדִלְמָא [6]The Gemara asks: **But perhaps** the husband **divorced** his wife immediately before **his death** without it becoming a matter of public knowledge.

אִיהוּ הוּא [7]The Gemara answers: We are not concerned about such a possibility, for in such a case, if the woman manages to collect two ketubah settlements, **it is** the husband **who caused himself** and his heirs **the loss.**

אַלְמָנָה [8]The Gemara now asks a similar question: According to Rav who said that a woman can only collect the basic portion of her ketubah settlement if she presents her bill of divorce, there is a difficulty. For how **does a woman who was widowed from betrothal collect** her ketubah settlement? [9]Surely, she collects it **with witnesses to her bridegroom's death,** for she cannot adduce any other proof that she is entitled to it. [10]**But** if a woman can collect the basic portion of her ketubah settlement with her bill of divorce alone, **we should be concerned that perhaps** the widow's bridegroom had **divorced her** before he died, **and she will** collect her ketubah settlement from the heirs with witnesses to his death, and then go to another court, [11]**produce her bill of divorce, and collect** it again! Here it cannot be argued that the widow can only collect her ketubah settlement if she proves that she had been living together with her husband, for a betrothed woman does not live with her husband!

אֶלָּא [12]The Gemara answers: **Rather,** if she cannot prove that she was not divorced, a widow can collect her ketubah settlement from her husband's heirs if she writes a receipt for the money. For **when it is**

גּוֹבָה עִיקָּר. [1]אַלְמָנָה מִן הַנִּשּׂוּאִין, בְּמַאי גָּבְיָא? [2]בְּעֵדֵי מִיתָה. [3]וְלֵיחוּשׁ דִּלְמָא גֵּירְשָׁהּ, [4]וּמַפְּקָא לְגִיטָּא וְגָבְיָא בֵּיהּ! [5]בְּיוֹשֶׁבֶת תַּחַת בַּעְלָהּ. [6]וְדִלְמָא סָמוּךְ לְמִיתָה גֵּירְשָׁהּ! [7]אִיהוּ הוּא דְּאַפְסִיד אַנַּפְשֵׁיהּ. [8]אַלְמָנָה מִן הָאֵירוּסִין, בְּמַאי גָּבְיָא? [9]בְּעֵדֵי מִיתָה. [10]וְלֵיחוּשׁ דִּלְמָא גֵּירְשָׁהּ, [11]וּמַפְּקָא גִּיטָּא וְגָבְיָא! [12]אֶלָּא, בְּמָקוֹם דְּלָא אֶפְשָׁר,

LITERAL TRANSLATION

she collects the basic [ketubah settlement]. [1][But] a widow from marriage, with what does she collect? [2]With witnesses to [the husband's] death. [3]But let us be concerned that perhaps he had divorced her, [4]and she will present her bill of divorce and collect with it! [5]When she was living with her husband. [6]But perhaps soon before [his] death he divorced her! [7][Then,] it is he who caused himself the loss. [8]But a widow from betrothal, with what does she collect? [9]With witnesses to [the bridegroom's] death. [10]But let us be concerned that perhaps he had divorced her, [11]and she will present her bill of divorce and collect with it! [12]Except in a place where it is not possible

RASHI

אלמנה במאי גביא — כתובה שלה. על כרחך בעדי מיתה, שמת בעלה ומחזרת שטר כתובה ליורשים, וקורעין אותו. **ניחוש שמא גירשה** — והדרא ומפקא גיטא בבי דינא אחרינא, ותגבה עיקר. **ביושבת תחת בעלה** — אין אלמנה גובה כתובתה, אלא אם כן מכירין אותה שבשעת מיתתו היתה יושבת תחתיו. **אלמנה מן האירוסין** — שלא ישבה תחתיו מעולם. **אלא במקום דלא אפשר כו׳** — אלא לא תימא ביושבת תחת בעלה, דאפילו הלך למדינת הים נמי, ושמעו בו שמת — גובה כתובתה, ולא חיישינן לדלמא גירשה והדרא מפקא לגיטה. דאמרינן להו: תכתוב לכם שובר. דבמקום שאין לומר הערמה, ואי אפשר לה לגבות אם באת לחוש לכל אלה, כגון זו, וכגון נשרפה כתובתה בעדים — לא נמנענה מלהגבות כתובתה, ותכתוב שובר.

NOTES

agrees that a woman can collect her settlement even without producing a ketubah deed. *Ra'ah* answers that Rav Kahanah and Rav Assi were Rav's disciples, and so they directed their question to their master. Moreover, the difficulty is greater according to Rav, for according to Rav, the question arises even where it is customary to write a woman a ketubah deed.

אַלְמָנָה מִן הָאֵירוּסִין **A widow from betrothal.** According to some Rishonim, it is obvious to the Gemara that a betrothed woman is entitled to a ketubah by Rabbinic enactment, even if her husband did not write one for her, and that Mar Kashisha is only looking for Tannaitic support for this entitlement (see *Rash, Ramban, Ra'ah* and others). But *Rambam* and *Ra'avad* rule that a betrothed woman is not entitled to a ketubah settlement if her husband did not obligate himself by writing a ketubah for her.

כָּתְבִינַן שׁוֹבֵר. [1]דְּאִי לָא תֵּימָא הָכִי, עֵדֵי מִיתָה גּוּפַיְיהוּ, [2]נֵיחוּשׁ דִּלְמָא מַפְּקָא עֵדֵי מִיתָה בְּהַאי בֵּי דִינָא וְגָבְיָא, [3]וַהֲדַר מַפְּקָא בְּבֵי דִינָא אַחֲרִינָא, וְגָבְיָא! [4]אֶלָּא, וַדַּאי, בְּמָקוֹם דְּלָא אֶפְשָׁר, [5]כָּתְבִינַן שׁוֹבֵר.

[6]אֲמַר לֵיהּ מָר קַשִּׁישָׁא בְּרֵיהּ דְּרַב חִסְדָּא לְרַב אַשִׁי: אַלְמָנָה מִן הָאֵירוּסִין מְנָלַן דְּאִית לָהּ כְּתוּבָּה? [7]אִילֵימָא, מֵהָא: [8]״נִתְאַרְמְלָה אוֹ נִתְגָּרְשָׁה, בֵּין מִן הָאֵירוּסִין בֵּין מִן הַנִּשּׂוּאִין, גּוֹבָה אֶת הַכֹּל״ — [9]דִּלְמָא דְּכָתַב לָהּ! [10]וְכִי תֵּימָא: אִי כָּתַב לָהּ, מַאי לְמֵימְרָא? [11]לְאַפּוּקֵי מִדְּרַבִּי אֶלְעָזָר בֶּן עֲזַרְיָה, דְּאָמַר: [12]״שֶׁלֹּא כָּתַב לָהּ אֶלָּא עַל מְנָת שֶׁהוּא כּוֹנְסָהּ״.

LITERAL TRANSLATION

[otherwise], we write a receipt. [1]For if you do not say so, [regarding] witnesses to [the husband's] death themselves, [2]let us be concerned that perhaps she will present witnesses to [his] death in this court and collect, [3]and then present [the witnesses] in a different court, and collect! [4]Rather, certainly, where it is not possible [otherwise], [5]we write a receipt.

[6]Mar Kashisha the son of Rav Ḥisda said to Rav Ashi: A widow from betrothal, from where do we [know] that she has a ketubah settlement? [7]If you say, from here: [8]"[If] she was widowed or divorced, whether from betrothal or from marriage, she collects the whole [ketubah settlement]" — [9]perhaps when he wrote her [a ketubah]! [10]And if you say: If he wrote her [a ketubah], what [does the Tanna mean] to say? [11]To exclude Rabbi Elazar ben Azaryah, who said: [12]"For he only wrote [the increment] for her on condition that he marry her."

TRANSLATION AND COMMENTARY

impossible to be certain that a creditor will not collect his debt again, **we** do indeed allow him to collect and **write** the debtor **a receipt.** [1]**For if you do not say** that in certain situations we do indeed require the creditor to write the debtor a receipt, it may be asked how a widow can ever collect her ketubah settlement on the basis of the **witnesses** testifying **to her husband's death,** even if she had been living with her husband when he died. [2]**We should** always **be concerned that perhaps** the woman **will present witnesses to** her husband's **death in one court, and collect** her ketubah settlement on the basis of their testimony, [3]**and then** she will present **the witnesses in a different court, and collect** it again. [4]**Rather,** it must **certainly** be concluded that **when it is impossible** to be certain in any other way that a creditor will not be able to collect his debt twice, [5]**we** allow him to collect if he **writes** the debtor **a receipt.**

אֲמַר לֵיהּ [6]**Mar Kashisha the son of Rav Ḥisda said to Rav Ashi:** A woman who was **widowed from betrothal, from where do we know that she is entitled** by law **to** receive **a** basic **ketubah** settlement, even if her bridegroom did not write one for her? Perhaps, the Rabbinic enactment entitling a woman to a ketubah settlement was only for a married woman. [7]**If you say** that we know a betrothed woman is entitled to a settlement by virtue of the law **from** the Mishnah (*Ketubot* 54b), which states: [8]**"If a woman was widowed or divorced, whether from betrothal or from marriage, she collects the whole** amount of her **ketubah,** I will respond that this Mishnah proves nothing, [9]for **perhaps** it refers to a case **when** the husband **wrote** his betrothed wife **a ketubah** deed. [10]**You might respond** to this: If it indeed refers to a case **when** the husband **wrote** a ketubah deed, **what does the Tanna mean to** teach us? In such a case the husband surely undertook to pay her her ketubah! [11]I can then answer that the anonymous first Tanna of that Mishnah came **to** negate the position of **Rabbi Elazar ben Azaryah, who said** immediately afterward in the Mishnah: "If the woman was widowed or divorced from marriage, she collects the entire amount of her ketubah, the basic portion and the increment. But if she was widowed or divorced from betrothal, she collects only the basic settlement, but not the increment, [12]**for** the husband **only wrote the increment** of the ketubah **for her on** the **condition that he marry her,** and here she was widowed or divorced before then." Thus, the anonymous first Tanna of the Mishnah had to teach us that a widow from betrothal, who had a ketubah, collects both the basic portion and the increment.

RASHI

עדי מיתה גופייהו — במקום שאין כותבין כתובה, ואין היורשין יכולין לומר לה: החזירי לנו שטר כתובתך, ניחוש כו׳. **מר קשישא ומר ינוקא** — שני בניס היו לרב חסדא, ושם שניהם שוין, אלא שהגדול קורין לו מר קשישא, ולצעיר קורין לו מר ינוקא. **אלמנה מן האירוסין** — דאית לה כתובה בתנאי בית דין, אם לא כתב לה. **מנלן** — דקאמר לעיל: עדי מיתה גופייהו ליחוש דלמא מפקא והדרא ומפקא. על כרחך חדא מינייהו גביא בלא שטרא, שהרי בפרעון ראשון החזירה השטר אם כתב לה, וקא חייש להדרא ומפקא. אלמא: יש לה כתובה בתנאי בית דין בלא שום כתובה, מנלן? **את הכל** — עיקר ותוספת. **לא כתב לה** — התוספת אלא על מנת לכונסה, ואם מת באירוסין — אין לה אלא עיקר כתובה.

SAGES

רַבִּי אֶלְעָזָר בֶּן עֲזַרְיָה **Rabbi Eliezer ben Azaryah.** See *Ketubot*, Part II, pp. 205-6.

[1]דַּיְקָא נַמִי, דְּקָתָנֵי: [2]״גּוֹבָה אֶת הַכֹּל״. [3]אִי אָמְרַתְּ, בִּשְׁלָמָא, דִּכְתַב לָהּ, [4]מִשּׁוּם הָכִי גּוֹבָה אֶת הַכֹּל. [5]אֶלָּא אִי אָמְרַתְּ דְּלָא כְּתַב לָהּ, [6]מַאי ״גּוֹבָה אֶת הַכֹּל״? [7]מָנֶה מָאתַיִם הוּא דְּאִית לָהּ!

[8]וְאֶלָּא, מִדְּתָנֵי רַב חִיָּיא בַּר אָבִין: [9]״אִשְׁתּוֹ אֲרוּסָה, לֹא אוֹנֵן וְלֹא מִיטַּמֵּא לָהּ. [10]וְכֵן, הִיא לֹא אוֹנֶנֶת וְלֹא מִיטַּמְּאָה לוֹ. [11]מֵתָה, אֵינוֹ יוֹרְשָׁהּ. [12]מֵת הוּא, גּוֹבָה כְּתוּבָּתָהּ״.

LITERAL TRANSLATION

[1]It is also precise, for it teaches: "[2]She collects the whole [ketubah settlement]." [3]If you say, granted, when he wrote her [a ketubah], [4]therefore she collects it all. [5]But if you say that he did not write [one for] her, [6]what [is the meaning of] "she collects the whole [ketubah settlement]"? [7]The maneh or two hundred [dinars] is [always] what she has!

[8]Rather, [we know about a betrothed woman's ketubah] from what Rav Ḥiyya bar Avin taught: [9]"[For] his betrothed bride, he does not mourn or defile himself for her. [10]And similarly, she does not mourn or defile herself for him. [11][If] she dies, he does not inherit from her. [12][If] he dies, she collects her ketubah settlement."

TRANSLATION AND COMMENTARY

דַּיְקָא נַמִי [1]Moreover: The wording of the anonymous first Tanna's position **is also precise,** and thus supports this argument, **for** the Tanna **teaches:** "If she was widowed or divorced, whether from betrothal or from marriage, [2]**she collects the whole** amount of her **ketubah.**" [3]**Granted if you say that** the Mishnah refers to a case when the husband **wrote** his wife a ketubah deed, [4]**therefore** we understand why the Tanna said that the betrothed woman **collects the whole** amount of her ketubah, i.e., the basic portion and its increment. [5]**But if you say that** the Mishnah refers to a case when the husband **did not write** his wife a ketubah deed, and she now seeks to collect her settlement by virtue of the law, [6]**what** did the Tanna mean when he said that the woman **collects the whole** amount of her ketubah? [7]**A maneh** in the case of a virgin **or two hundred dinars** in the case of a non-virgin **is always what she** is entitled to receive, for she can only collect an increment if was been recorded in her ketubah deed!

וְאֶלָּא [8]**Rather,** evince proof that a woman widowed from betrothal receives a ketubah settlement by virtue of law **from** the Baraita that **was taught by Rav Ḥiyya bar Avin:** [9]"If **a betrothed woman** died, her husband is not subject to the laws of acute **mourning** (*aninut*), which forbid him from partaking of sacrifices, **and** if the husband was a priest, **he** may not **defile himself** by coming into contact with **her** corpse. A priest is forbidden to contract ritual impurity through proximity with a corpse, except for his closest relatives, which include his wife but not his betrothed. [10]**And similarly,** if a man died, his betrothed bride is not subject to the laws of acute **mourning,** nor is she required to **defile herself for him,** if others are available to arrange his funeral. [11]**If** a betrothed woman **died,** her husband **does not inherit from her,** for a man does not inherit from his wife until she is married. [12]But **if** the groom **died,** his betrothed bride **collects her ketubah** settlement." Thus, the Baraita states explicitly that a widow from betrothal is entitled to a ketubah.

RASHI

אלא אי אמרת בשלא כתב לה — ובתנאי בית דין הוא דגביא, לאלמנה מנה ומאתים לבתולה הוא דאית לה שהרי אין כאן תוספת. **לא אונן** — ליאסר בקדשים. **ולא מיטמא לה** — אם כהן הוא, ד״שארו״ כתיב. **ולא מטמאה לו** — אינה חייבת להתעסק בו וליטמא בו, בין כהנת בין ישראלית. אף על פי שמצוה ליטמא למתים האמורים בפרשה, כדכתיב (ויקרא כא): ״לה יטמא״ — זו אינה חייבת. ולאו משום כהנת נקט לה, שלא הוזהרו כהנות מליטמא למתים. **אינו יורשה** — דגבי ירושת הבעל ״שארו״ כתיב ״לשארו הקרוב אליו ממשפחתו וירש אותה״ — מכאן שהבעל יורש את אשתו.

NOTES

לֹא אוֹנֵן **He does not mourn.** During the period of acute mourning, between the time of the death of a close relative and the time of his burial, the mourner is forbidden to eat second-tithe, first-fruit offerings, and sacrificial food. If the mourner is a priest, he may also not take part in the Temple service. The Baraita teaches that if a betrothed woman died, her husband is not subject to these laws, nor is a woman governed by these laws upon the death of her betrothed husband.

וְלֹא מִיטַּמְּאָה **And he does not defile himself.** The Baraita that teaches that a man does not defile himself upon the death of his betrothed bride is referring to a priest, who is ordinarily forbidden to defile himself by coming into contact with a corpse, but is permitted to defile himself by coming into contact with the corpse of a close relative. The Baraita teaches that while the priest may defile himself for his married spouse, he may not defile himself for his betrothed bride. But the daughter of a priest is not forbidden to contract ritual impurity through proximity with a corpse. Thus, when the Baraita teaches that a woman does not defile herself for her betrothed husband, it is not referring specifically to the daughter of a priest, but rather to any

TRANSLATION AND COMMENTARY

דִּלְמָא [1]The Gemara rejects this proof as well: **Perhaps** the Baraita is referring to a husband who **voluntarily wrote** his wife a **ketubah** deed. [2]But **you** might **say** to this: **If** in fact the Baraita does refer to a husband who **voluntarily wrote** a ketubah deed for his betrothed wife, **what does the** Tanna of the Baraita **mean to** teach us? In such a case the husband surely undertook to pay his wife her ketubah when their marriage ends. But this argument can be rebutted as follows: [3]Since the Tanna desired **to teach: "If** a betrothed woman **died,** her husband **does not inherit** her." The Tanna also adds the law of a voluntary ketubah to teach us that despite the bridegroom's obligating himself to pay his betrothed a ketubah settlement, he nevertheless does not inherit her. The Gemara's original question — from where do we know that a widow from betrothal is entitled to receive a ketubah settlement — remains unanswered.

[1]דִּלְמָא, דְּכָתַב לַהּ! [2]וְכִי תֵּימָא: אִי כָּתַב לַהּ, מַאי לְמֵימְרָא? [3]״מֵתָה אֵינוֹ יוֹרְשָׁהּ״ אִיצְטְרִיכָא לֵיהּ.

[4]אֲמַר לֵיהּ רַב נַחְמָן לְרַב הוּנָא: לְרַב דְּאָמַר: ״גֵּט גּוֹבָה עִיקָּר״, [5]לֵיחוּשׁ דִּלְמָא מַפְּקָא גִּיטָּא בְּהַאי בֵּי דִינָא וְגָבְיָא, [6]וְהַדְרָא מַפְּקָא בְּבֵי דִינָא אַחֲרִינָא וְגָבְיָא! [7]וְכִי תֵּימָא: דְּקָרְעִינַן לֵיהּ, [8]אָמְרָה: בָּעֵינָא לְאִנְּסוּבֵי בֵּיהּ.

LITERAL TRANSLATION

[1]Perhaps, he [voluntarily] wrote [a ketubah] for her! [2]And if you say: If he [voluntarily] wrote her, what [does the Baraita mean] to say? [3]It was necessary for it [to state]: "[If] she dies, he does not inherit from her."

[4]Rav Naḥman said to Rav Huna: According to Rav who said: "[If she presents] a bill of divorce, she collects the basic [ketubah settlement]," [5]let us be concerned that perhaps she will present a bill of divorce in this court and collect, [6]and then present [it] in a different court and collect! [7]And if you say: We tear it, [8]she will say: I wish to be married with it!

RASHI

מתה אינו יורשה איצטריכא ליה – משום ״מתה אינו יורשה״ איצטריך ליה למיתני: מת הוא גובה כתובתה, לאשמעינן, דבדכתב לה כתובה עסקינן. ואף על גב דאיקרבו לאחתוני כולי האי – אינו יורשה.

בעינא לאינסובי ביה – שיהיה בידי לראיה שנתגרשתי, שלא יאמרו עלי: אשת איש היא.

BACKGROUND

דְּקָרְעִינַן לֵיהּ **We tear it.** The tearing of a bill of divorce, which has become standard practice over the years regarding every bill of divorce that is properly written and delivered, was performed after the bill of divorce was delivered to a wife. The bill of divorce is then folded and its ends are cut on an angle, so that it will be cut both horizontally and vertically. This manner of tearing is known as the tearing of the court, and it does not invalidate the bill of divorce as evidence that the divorced woman may remarry.

אֲמַר לֵיהּ [4]**Rav Naḥman said to Rav Huna: According to Rav who said** that **if a woman presents a bill of divorce,** but not her ketubah deed, **she** can **collect the basic ketubah** settlement, but not the increment, a difficulty arises: [5]**We should be concerned that perhaps she will present her bill of divorce in** one **court, and collect** her settlement in accordance with Rav's position, [6]**and then** later **she will present** her bill of divorce **in a different court, and collect** again. [7]**And if you say** that in order to prevent a woman from collecting twice, **we tear** up the bill of divorce when she receives payment, this is not a satisfactory solution, [8]for the woman **can** object and **say:** I do not want my bill of divorce destroyed, for **I wish to be married** and need **it** for proof that I am eligible.

NOTES

Jewish woman. Even though a person is ordinarily obligated to defile himself and arrange for the burial of a close relative, a betrothed woman is not required to defile himself upon the death of her bridegroom (*Rashi*). Alternatively, one can explain that the Baraita teaches that during the period of the Festivals, when a person is obligated to be in a state of ritual purity, a betrothed woman is forbidden to defile herself for her bridegroom (*Rivan*).

דְּקָרְעִינַן לֵיהּ **We tear it.** The Rishonim ask: A woman does not necessarily have to come court to collect her ketubah settlement. If a man pays his wife without dragging the matter to court, what protection does he have that his wife will not later produce her bill of divorce in court, and collect her ketubah again? *Ra'ah* answers that if the husband pays his wife her ketubah settlement outside of court, he has no protection other than requesting a receipt. But if a husband pays his wife her ketubah in court, there is no concern, for the bill of divorce is torn up, and a certification of divorce is then written on the back of the torn document (see also *Rosh*).

Ritva notes that the Gemara implies that when a woman comes to collect her ketubah settlement with a bill of divorce, the bill of divorce must be torn up, and it does not suffice to write a receipt for the husband in the bill itself. This is so because whatever is inserted into the bill of divorce might later be erased, and the woman could come to collect her ketubah again. *Ritva* concludes from this that a bill of divorce or any other deed is legally valid even if it contains erasures (see also *Maharam Shiff*).

בָּעֵינָא לְאִנְּסוּבֵי **I wish to be married.** The Rishonim ask: Why should the woman need her bill of divorce in order to remarry? Surely a woman who claims that she was divorced from her husband is believed! *Rivan* answers that a woman who claims that she was divorced is only believed if she made that claim in her ex-husband's presence. It would appear from *Rashi* that even though a woman without a divorce deed is believed if she claims that she is divorced, she can still object to having her bill of divorce torn up, for she can argue that she needs it to silence possible rumors that she is still a married woman.

TRANSLATION AND COMMENTARY

דְּקָרְעִינַן לֵיהּ [1]**Rav Huna replied:** Indeed, **we** can **tear** it up to prevent her claiming two ketubah settlements, but to allay her objection, the court will certify the bill of divorce, and **write on the back of** the torn document: [2]**We tore this bill of divorce, not because it is an invalid bill of divorce,** [3]**but rather so that** the woman **not** be able to **collect** her ketubah **with it a second time.** She now has proof of divorce if she wishes to remarry.

MISHNAH שְׁנֵי גִיטִּין [4]If a woman presents **two bills of divorce and two ketubah** deeds, meaning that a man married a woman, divorced her, remarried her, and later divorced her again, and each time he married her, he gave her a ketubah, [5]**she may collect two ketubah settlements,** one for each marriage. [6]But if she produces **two ketubah** deeds **and** only **one bill of divorce,** meaning that her husband wrote her two ketubah deeds during the course of a single marriage, and then divorced her, [7]or if she produces **one ketubah** deed **and two bills of divorce,** meaning that her husband divorced her, remarried her without writing her a second ketubah deed, and then divorced her a second time, [8]**or** if she produces **one ketubah** deed **and one bill of divorce and** two of witnesses who testify to **her husband's death,** meaning that her husband married her, granted her a divorce, remarried her without writing her a second ketubah, and then he died — [9]in each of these cases the woman **may collect only one ketubah** settlement. [10]Because if a man **divorces his wife, and remarries her** before she collected her ketubah settlement, we assume — if he did not write her a new ketubah — [11]that **he remarries her on the basis of** what was written in **her first ketubah.**

[1]דְּקָרְעִינַן לֵיהּ, וְכָתְבִינַן אַגַּבֵּיהּ: [2]גִּיטָּא דְּנַן קְרַעֲנוּהִי, לָאו מִשּׁוּם דְּגִיטָּא פָּסוּל הוּא, [3]אֶלָּא דְּלָא תֶּיהֱדַר וְתִיגְבֵּי בֵּיהּ זִמְנָא אַחֲרִינָא.

משנה [4]שְׁנֵי גִיטִּין וּשְׁתֵּי כְתוּבּוֹת — [5]גּוֹבָה שְׁתֵּי כְתוּבּוֹת. [6]שְׁתֵּי כְתוּבּוֹת וְגֵט אֶחָד, [7]אוֹ כְּתוּבָּה וּשְׁנֵי גִטִּין, [8]אוֹ כְּתוּבָּה וְגֵט וּמִיתָה — [9]אֵינָהּ גּוֹבָה אֶלָּא כְּתוּבָּה אַחַת, [10]שֶׁהַמְגָרֵשׁ אֶת אִשְׁתּוֹ וְהֶחֱזִירָהּ, [11]עַל מְנָת כְּתוּבָּה הָרִאשׁוֹנָה מַחֲזִירָהּ.

LITERAL TRANSLATION

[1][Rav Huna replied:] We tear it, and write on back of it: [2]We tore this bill of divorce, not because it is an invalid bill of divorce, [3]but rather so that she not collect with it another time.

MISHNAH [4][If she presents] two bills of divorce and two ketubahs — [5]she collects two ketubah settlements. [6]Two ketubahs and one bill of divorce, [7]or a ketubah and two bills of divorce, [8]or a ketubah and a bill of divorce and [proof of her husband's] death, [9]she may collect only one ketubah settlement, [10]for a man who divorces his wife and remarries her, [11]remarries her on the basis of the first ketubah.

RASHI

משנה שני גיטין ושתי כתובות — זמן ראשונה קודם לזמן גט ראשון, וזמן כתובה שניה קודם לגט שני. גובה שתי כתובות — שהרי גירשה והחזירה, וכתב לה כתובה שניה. אבל קדמו שתי הכתובות לגט הראשון — לא. שהרי כשהחזירה לא כתב לה כתובה, ותנן בסיפא: שתי כתובות וגט — אינה גובה אלא אחת [למדנו שהכותב לאשתו שתי כתובות — אינה גובה אלא אחת. ואי משום דאיגרשא והדרה — הא תנן: כתובה ושני גיטין — אין לה אלא אחת] שעל מנת כתובה הראשונה החזירה. שתי כתובות וגט — שקדמו שתיהן לגט. ובגמרא מפרש למאי כתב להו. כתובה ושני גיטין — כתובה בנשואין הראשונים, וגירשה והחזירה ולא כתב לה כתובה, וחזר וגירשה.

HALAKHAH

שְׁנֵי גִיטִּין וּשְׁתֵּי כְתוּבּוֹת **Two bills of divorce and one ketubah.** "If a woman produces two bills of divorce and two ketubah deeds, and the earlier ketubah predates the first bill of divorce, and the later ketubah predates the second bill of divorce, she may collect both ketubot," following the Mishnah. (*Rambam, Sefer Nashim, Hilkhot Ishut* 16:29; *Shulḥan Arukh, Even HaEzer* 100:13.)

שְׁתֵּי כְתוּבּוֹת וְגֵט אֶחָד **Two ketubahs and one bill of divorce.** "If a woman produces two ketubah deeds and one bill of divorce, she may collect only one ketubah. With which ketubah does she collect? If both ketubah deeds were written for the same sum, the second one cancels the first, so that she may only seize property that had been sold to a third party after the second ketubah had been drawn up. If the second ketubah deed was written for a larger sum than the first, but it did not state explicitly that the husband was adding to his wife's first ketubah, the woman may collect the first ketubah settlement from property that had been sold after the first ketubah had been drawn up, or she may collect the second ketubah settlement from property that had been sold after the second ketubah had been drawn up. If the second ketubah deed stated explicitly that the husband was adding to his wife's ketubah, the woman may collect the sum recorded in the first ketubah from property that had been sold after the first ketubah was written, and the additional sum, from property that had been sold after the second ketubah was written, following Rav Pappa. These laws apply only when the ketubah deeds were both written either during the woman's betrothal or her marriage. But if the first was written during her betrothal and the other during her marriage, she may only collect the second ketubah." (*Rambam, Sefer Nashim, Hilkhot Ishut* 16:29; *Shulḥan Arukh, Even HaEzer* 100:14.)

כְּתוּבָּה וּשְׁנֵי גִטִּין **A ketubah and two bills of divorce.** "If a woman produces two bills of divorce and only one ketubah deed, she may collect only one ketubah, for it is assumed that someone who divorces his wife and then remarries her, remarries her on the basis of what was written in her first ketubah." (*Rambam, Sefer Nashim, Hilkhot Ishut* 16:30; *Shulḥan Arukh, Even HaEzer* 100:15.)

TRANSLATION AND COMMENTARY

GEMARA אִי בָּעֲיָא [1] Our Mishnah teaches that when a woman produces two ketubah deeds, dated before her bill of divorce, she may collect only one of them. But it does not specify which of the two she may collect. The Gemara asks: Is this to say that **if** the woman **prefers, she may collect** the first ketubah, [2] **and if she** prefers otherwise, **she may collect the** other one. [3] **Shall we say that** the Mishnah **is a refutation of what Rav Nahman said in the name of Shmuel.** [4] **For Rav Nahman said in the name of Shmuel:** [5] **If two contracts** of sale or gift **were issued** for the same transaction involving land, **one** dated **later than the other,** [6] **the second** contract **cancels the first.** This ruling is of significance when the contract includes a clause that guarantees the transaction by pledging the seller's immovable property as security for the sale or gift. Under this guarantee, if the seller's creditors seize the land on the basis of a lien they hold on it, the purchaser may recover its value from the seller's other property that was mortgaged by the guarantee. Rav Nahman teaches that if two bills of sale were issued for the same transaction, the second cancels the first. Thus if the purchaser collects under the guarantee, he can collect only from property that the seller possessed at the time of the second contract and not from property that he had at the time of the first contract but subsequently sold. Now, our Mishnah seems to refute the position of Rav Nahman, for it implies that if a woman has two ketubahs and prefers to collect under the liens of the earlier one, she may do so.

לָאו אִתְּמַר עֲלָהּ [7] The Gemara argues that there is no contradiction between the Mishnah and Rav Nahman's ruling: **Was not** the following clarification **stated** with respect to **this ruling of Rav Nahman:** [8] **Rav Pappa said: Rav Nahman agrees that if** something was added to the second contract — for example, the first contract spoke of a field and the second contract mentioned the field as well as an **added date-palm** — then the second contract does not cancel the first one completely? [9] We assume that the original owner **wrote** the second **contract for the addition** that was contained in it. Rav Nahman's ruling that the second contract cancels the first one therefore applies only when nothing was added to the second contract. [10] **Here too** the Mishnah refers to a husband who **added** something **for** his wife in **the** second **ketubah,** obligating himself to pay her more. Thus this it is not in conflict with Rav Nahman's ruling as explained by Rav Pappa.

גמרא [1] אִי בָּעֲיָא, בְּהַאי גָּבְיָא, [2] אִי בָּעֲיָא בְּהַאי גָּבְיָא. [3] לֵימָא, תֶּיהֱוֵי תְּיוּבְתָּא דְּרַב נַחְמָן אָמַר שְׁמוּאֵל, [4] דְּאָמַר רַב נַחְמָן אָמַר שְׁמוּאֵל: [5] שְׁנֵי שְׁטָרוֹת הַיּוֹצְאִין בָּזֶה אַחַר זֶה, [6] בִּיטֵּל שֵׁנִי אֶת הָרִאשׁוֹן! [7] לָאו אִתְּמַר עֲלָהּ: [8] אָמַר רַב פַּפָּא: וּמוֹדֶה רַב נַחְמָן, דְּאִי אוֹסֵיף בֵּיהּ דִּיקְלָא, [9] לְתוֹסֶפֶת כְּתָבֵיהּ? [10] הָכָא נַמִי, בְּדְאוֹסֵיף לָהּ.

LITERAL TRANSLATION

GEMARA [1] [Apparently] if she wishes, she may collect with this one, [2] [and] if she wishes she may collect with that one. [3] Shall we say that this is a refutation of [what] Rav Nahman [said] in the name of Shmuel, [4] for Rav Nahman said in the name of Shmuel: [5] [If] two contracts were issued one after the other, [6] the second cancels the first.

[7] Was it not stated about this [ruling]: [8] Rav Pappa said: And Rav Nahman agrees that if he added a date-palm, [9] he wrote [it] for the addition? [10] Here too, when he added [to the ketubah] for her.

RASHI

גמרא אי בעיא בהאי גביא — בתמיה. וא"שתי כתובות וגט" קאי, דקתני: אין לה אלא כתובה אחת. ולא קתני: אין לה אלא כתובה אחרונה. אלמא: אי ניחא לה למיטרף לקוחות מזמן ראשון — טרפה. **בזה אחר זה** — זמנו של זה קודם לזה, ושניהם על הלואה אחת או על מכר אחד. **ביטל שני את הראשון** — ואינו טורף אלא מזמן שני. דכיון דכתב לשטרא בתרא — אחליה לשיעבוד קמא. **דאי אוסיף ביה דקלא** — בשטר שני. **לתוספת כתביה** — ולא אחליה לשיעבוד לבטל זמן שטר ראשון. ותרוייהו מיהא לא גביא, מדלא כתב לה: צביתי ואוסיפית לה הך אקמייתא. אלא שטר כתובה יתירא כתב לה, ולא הזכיר בה את הראשונה. הכי קאמר: אם תתרצי למחול שיעבוד של ראשונה — גבי כתובה זו המרובה, ואם לאו — גבי הראשונה המועטת. הלכך, הי מינייהו דבעיא, גביא. והכי פרשינן בפירקין קמאי. וכי אמר רב נחמן: ביטל שני את הראשון — בדלא אוסיף ביה מידי. דאי לאו לבטולי קמא אתא — למאי כתביה?

NOTES

שְׁנֵי שְׁטָרוֹת **Two contracts.** According to *Rashi,* Rav Nahman's ruling about two contracts, that the later-dated contract cancels the earlier one, applies not only to contracts of sale and gift, but to loan contracts as well. But most Rishonim (*Rif, Ramban, Rosh,* and others) disagree and say that Rav Nahman's ruling applies only to contracts of sale or gift, or to ketubahs, for if a creditor holds two loan contracts from the same debtor, the second does not cancel the first, but rather he collects them both, because we assume that the two loan contracts were drawn up for two separate loans. (See *Ramban,* who reconciles a passage from the Jerusalem Talmud relating to this issue with the position of Rif; and also *Meiri,* who cites a different reading of the Jerusalem Talmud passage.)

TRANSLATION AND COMMENTARY

תָּנוּ רַבָּנַן [1]We learned in our Mishnah that if a woman presents one ketubah deed and one bill of divorce and a set of witnesses who testify to her husband's death, she may collect only one settlement. The Gemara now records a Baraita that clarifies the scope of this ruling: **Our Rabbis taught: "If** a woman **presented a bill of divorce and a ketubah** deed **and** a set of witnesses who testify to **her husband's death,** [90A] the following distinction applies: [2]**If** the date on **the bill of divorce** is earlier than the date on **the ketubah** deed, showing that her husband divorced her and then wrote her a new ketubah when he married her again, [3]she **may collect two ketubah** — one with her bill of divorce from her first marriage, and another with the ketubah deed and proof of her husband's death. [4]But **if** the date on **the ketubah** deed is earlier than the date on in **the bill of divorce,** showing that her husband divorced and remarried her without paying the old ketubah settlement or writing her a new one, [5]**she may** then **collect only one ketubah** settlement. Why, though is she not entitled to a separate ketubah for each marriage? [6]That is because if **someone divorces his wife, and** then **remarries her** before paying the settlement, and he does not write a new ketubah deed, [7]we assume that **he remarries her on the basis of** what he wrote for her in **the first ketubah."**

MISHNAH קָטָן [8]If **a minor was married off by his father,** and he then reached legal majority, (his thirteenth birthday) his wife's **ketubah,** which had been written while he was still a minor **remains valid.** [9]**For** it was **on the basis of** this **ketubah** that **he kept her** as his wife after reaching majority. [10]Similarly, if **a man converted** to Judaism and **his wife converted** along **with him,** [11]the woman's **ketubah** which had been written while the two were not yet Jewish, **remains valid.** [12]**For** it was **on the basis of** this **ketubah** that **he kept her** as his wife after their conversion.

LITERAL TRANSLATION

[1]Our Rabbis taught: "[If] she presented a bill of divorce and a ketubah and [proof of her husband's] death, [90A] [2]if the bill of divorce precedes the ketubah, [3]she may collect two ketubah. [4][If] the ketubah precedes the bill of divorce, [5]she may collect only one ketubah, [6]for a man who divorces his wife and remarries her, [7]remarries her on the basis of the first ketubah."

MISHNAH [8]A minor whose father married him off — her ketubah remains valid, [9]for on the basis of that [ketubah] he kept her [when he came of age]. [10]A convert whose wife converted with him — [11]her ketubah remains valid, [12]for on the basis of that [ketubah] he kept her.

[1]תָּנוּ רַבָּנַן: ״הוֹצִיאָה גֵּט וּכְתוּבָּה וּמִיתָה, [90A] [2]אִם גֵּט קוֹדֵם לַכְּתוּבָּה — [3]גּוֹבָה שְׁתֵּי כְתוּבּוֹת. [4]כְּתוּבָּה קוֹדֶמֶת לַגֵּט — [5]אֵינָהּ גּוֹבָה אֶלָּא כְּתוּבָּה אַחַת, [6]שֶׁהַמְגָרֵשׁ אֶת אִשְׁתּוֹ וְהֶחֱזִירָהּ, [7]עַל מְנָת כְּתוּבָּה הָרִאשׁוֹנָה הֶחֱזִירָהּ.

מִשְׁנָה [8]קָטָן שֶׁהִשִּׂיאוֹ אָבִיו — כְּתוּבָּתָהּ קַיֶּימֶת, [9]שֶׁעַל מְנָת כֵּן קִיְּימָהּ. [10]גֵּר שֶׁנִּתְגַּיְּירָה אִשְׁתּוֹ עִמּוֹ — [11]כְּתוּבָּתָהּ קַיֶּימֶת, [12]שֶׁעַל מְנָת כֵּן קִיְּימָהּ.

RASHI

ומיתה — ועדי מיתה. ובאה לגבות שתי כתובות, אחת בתורת גרושין, ואחת בתורת אלמנות. אם גט קודם לכתובה — הרי כתב לה כתובה שנית כשהחזירה.

משנה כתובתה קיימת — שכתב לה כשהוא קטן. ולגבי גר — כתובה שכתב לה בהיותו גוי.

NOTES

גֵּר שֶׁנִּתְגַּיְּירָה אִשְׁתּוֹ עִמּוֹ **A convert whose wife converted with him.** *Rid* offers a novel interpretation of our Mishnah, according to which the Mishnah refers to a non-Jew who had married a Jewish woman, written her a ketubah, and later converted to Judaism. Only in such a case does the woman's ketubah of two hundred dinars remain valid, for here the ketubah deed was drawn up for a woman who was fit to have a ketubah. But if two gentiles were married, and both of them later converted to Judaism, the woman is only entitled to a ketubah of a hundred dinars, for a ketubah written for a gentile woman has no legal validity whatsoever. *Rivash* rejects this interpretation, for both linguistic and legal reasons. As for the law regarding a non-Jewish couple who converted, *Rambam* agrees that the woman is only entitled to a ketubah of a hundred dinars, for even if the man married her after she had converted, she would only be entitled to a ketubah of that sum.

HALAKHAH

גֵּט וּכְתוּבָּה וּמִיתָה **A bill of divorce and a ketubah and her proof of husband's death.** "If a widow produces a bill of divorce and a ketubah deed that was dated later than the bill of divorce, she may collect the basic portion of a ketubah with her bill of divorce, and whatever sum is recorded in the ketubah deed with that deed. If the ketubah deed was dated earlier than the bill of divorce, she may collect only one ketubah, for it is assumed that the husband remarried his wife on the basis of her first ketubah," following the Baraita. (*Rambam, Sefer Nashim, Hilkhot Ishut* 16:30; *Shulḥan Arukh, Even HaEzer* 100:16.)

קָטָן שֶׁהִשִּׂיאוֹ אָבִיו **A minor whose father married him off.** "If a boy at least nine years old was married off by his father, his wife is not entitled to a ketubah settlement. If the two engaged in sexual intercourse after the boy reached majority, the woman is entitled to the basic settlement (two

TRANSLATION AND COMMENTARY

GEMARA אָמַר רַב הוּנָא [1]The Mishnah teaches that a ketubah written by a minor or a non-Jew is valid after the minor reaches majority or the non-Jew converts to Judaism. **Rav Huna said: This only** applies with respect **to the maneh** (written for a non-virgin), **or two hundred dinars** (written for a virgin), the basic ketubah settlement to which a woman is entitled by virtue of law. A woman may collect this amount because her entitlement stems from a Rabbinic enactment. [2]**But the increment** which the husband added to the wife's ketubah **may not** be collected if the ketubah deed was written while the husband was a minor or a non-Jew, because a ketubah deed written by a minor or a non-Jew is invalid. [3]**And Rav Yehudah** disagreed with Rav Huna and **said: She** may **even** collect **the increment** which the minor or the non-Jew added to the ketubah, once the husband reaches his majority or is converted.

מֵיתִיבֵי [4]**An objection was raised** against the position of Rav Yehudah from a Baraita that stated: **"If** a man wrote his wife a ketubah while he was still a minor or a non-Jew, and then when he reached majority or converted to Judaism he **added** a certain amount to his wife's original ketubah, and later the woman was divorced or widowed, **she may take what** her husband **added** to her ketubah after he reached majority or converted." [5]Apparently, that amount that he **added** after he reached majority or converted, **may be** collected. [6]But the amount **not** added to the ketubah after he reached majority or converted, which was included in the original ketubah deed, may **not** be collected. But Rav Yehudah said the original increment may be collected.

LITERAL TRANSLATION

GEMARA [1]Rav Huna said: They only taught [this regarding] the maneh [and] two hundred [dinars]. [2]But the increment she does not have. [3]And Rav Yehudah said: She even has the increment.

[4]They raised an objection [to Rav Yehudah]: "[If] they added [something] (lit., 'renewed it'), she takes what they added." [5][What] they added — yes. [6][What] they did not add — no!

גמרא [1]אָמַר רַב הוּנָא: לֹא שָׁנוּ אֶלָּא מָנֶה מָאתַיִם. [2]אֲבָל תּוֹסֶפֶת אֵין לָהּ. [3]וְרַב יְהוּדָה אָמַר: אֲפִילוּ תּוֹסֶפֶת יֵשׁ לָהּ. [4]מֵיתִיבֵי: "חִידְּשׁוֹ, נוֹטֶלֶת מַה שֶּׁחִידְּשׁוֹ". [5]חִידְּשׁוֹ — אִין. [6]לֹא חִידְּשׁוֹ — לָא!

RASHI

גמרא אלא מנה מאתים — שהן תנאי בית דין. דאילו בשטר לא גביא, דתקספא בעלמא הוא. חידשו — קטן משהגדיל, וגר משנתגייר אם הוסיפו כלום על כתובה ראשונה. מה שחידשו — וקא סלקא דעתין: מה שחידשו על מנה מאתים.

NOTES

אֲפִילוּ תּוֹסֶפֶת יֵשׁ לָהּ **She even has the increment.** A similar question is discussed in the Jerusalem Talmud, which asks whether in the cases discussed in our Mishnah, the woman is only entitled to the basic portion of her ketubah settlement, or also to the ketubah conditions, the additional rights to which a woman is entitled by virtue of her ketubah. *Meiri* discusses whether the woman's right to recover her dowry upon the dissolution of her marriage is treated like the main portion of her ketubah or like the increment.

לֹא שָׁנוּ אֶלָּא מָנֶה **They only taught this regarding the maneh.** *Tosafot* ask: If the woman is only entitled to a maneh or two hundred dinars, then what does the Mishnah mean when it says: "For on the basis of that ketubah he kept her"? For even if the husband had never written a ketubah for the woman, she would still be entitled to a maneh or two hundred dinars, for that is the amount to which every woman is entitled by law! *Tosafot* answer that

the Mishnah teaches that if the woman was a virgin when she first married, she is still entitled to a settlement of two hundred dinars, even though she was no longer a virgin when her husband reached majority or converted, for it was on the basis of her original ketubah that he kept her as his wife. *Ritva* and *Rosh* answer in the name of *Rabbenu Tam* that without the Mishnah we might have thought that if a husband wrote a ketubah for his wife when he was a minor or a non-Jew, his wife would be less entitled to a ketubah than if he never wrote her a ketubah. For if no ketubah was written, the woman relies on the Rabbinic enactment, but if the husband wrote his wife a ketubah when he was a minor or a non-Jew, she relies on a ketubah deed which is void. Thus, the Mishnah teaches that the woman is entitled to a settlement, for it was on the basis of the woman's original ketubah that the husband kept her as his wife. *Ritva* adds that without the Mishnah we might have thought that the woman is not entitled to a settlement, for

HALAKHAH

hundred dinars if she was a virgin, and a hundred dinars if not). But she is not entitled to the increment to her ketubah that her husband had written while he was still a minor, following the Mishnah and Rav Huna. Her collection of the basic settlement does not derive from her written ketubah deed, but rather from the Rabbinic enactment entitling every woman to a settlement. She therefore

cannot collect from property that had been sold to a third party by the husband while he was still only a minor. These laws also apply to a man who converted to Judaism together with his wife, except that according to *Rambam* such a woman is only entitled to a ketubah settlement of a hundred dinars." (*Rambam, Sefer Nashim, Hilkhot Ishut* 11:7; *Shulḥan Arukh, Even HaEzer* 67:11.)

TRANSLATION AND COMMENTARY

אֵימָא [1]The Gemara rebuts this objection: **Say** that the Baraita means as follows: She may collect not only the entire original ketubah settlement, but she may **even** take **what** her husband later **added** to her ketubah after he reached majority or converted.

וְהָא לָא [2]The Gemara does not accept this: **But surely** the Baraita **did not** state the law this way, but rather as follows: [3]**"If** the husband **added** a certain amount to his wife's original ketubah after he reached majority or converted, **she may** collect **what** her husband **added**. [4]But **if he did not then add** to his wife's ketubah, she only collects the main settlement. If she was **a virgin** at the time of her marriage, she **collects two hundred** dinars, **and** [5]if she was **a widow,** she collects **a maneh."** Thus, the Baraita states explicitly that the wife is not entitled to the increment of the ketubah written when the husband was a minor or non-Jew, [6]and this is **a** conclusive **refutation of** the position of **Rav Yehudah!**

רַב יְהוּדָה [7]The Gemara now explains Rav Yehudah's mistake: **Rav Yehudah was misled by** the wording of **our Mishnah.** [8]**He thought** that when the Mishnah stated that the **ketubah** that had been written while the husband was still a minor or a non-Jew **remains valid,** [9]it **was referring to the** woman's **entire** ketubah. [10]**But this is not so,** [11]for the Mishnah **refers** only **to the basic** portion of the woman's **ketubah** to which the woman is entitled by virtue of the law, not to the increment which the husband may add as he wishes.

[1]אֵימָא: אַף מַה שֶׁחִידְּשׁוּ.
[2]וְהָא לָא תָּנֵי הָכִי: [3]"חִידְּשׁוּ, נוֹטֶלֶת מַה שֶׁחִידְּשׁוּ. [4]לֹא חִידְּשׁוּ, [5]בְּתוּלָה גּוֹבָה מָאתַיִם, וְאַלְמָנָה מָנֶה". [6]תְּיוּבְתָּא דְּרַב יְהוּדָה!
[7]רַב יְהוּדָה מַתְנִיתִין אַטְעִיתֵיהּ. [8]הוּא סָבַר: "כְּתוּבָּתָהּ קַיֶּימֶת [9]אַכּוּלָּהּ מִילְּתָא קָאֵי. [10]וְלָא הִיא — [11]אַעִיקַּר כְּתוּבָּה קָאֵי.

הדרן עלך הכותב לאשתו

LITERAL TRANSLATION

[1]Say: Even what they added.

[2]But surely it did not say that, [3][but rather]: "[If] they added [something], she takes what they added. [4][If] they did not add, [5]a virgin collects two hundred, and a widow a maneh." [6]A refutation of Rav Yehudah!

[7]Rav Yehudah was misled by our Mishnah. [8]He thought: "Her ketubah remains valid" [9]refers to the entire thing. [10]But this is not so — [11]it refers to the basic ketubah.

RASHI

אף מה שחידשו — על תוספת כתובה. אכולה מילתא — על כל הכתוב בשטר כתובה.

הדרן עלך הכותב לאשתו

NOTES

when the husband reached majority or converted, he did not perform a second marriage ceremony, and in such a case the Rabbis may not have enacted a ketubah. The Mishnah teaches she is, in fact, entitled to a settlement because we say that it was on the basis of the woman's original ketubah that the husband kept her as his wife. *Hafla'ah* offers a similar answer: Since sexual intercourse effects betrothal, but not marriage, we might have thought that when the husband engages in sexual intercourse with his wife after he reaches majority or converts, she is considered betrothed, not married, and so according to those who maintain that a betrothed woman is not entitled to a settlement, this woman would also not be entitled to a ketubah.

Rambam disagrees with *Tosafot* and maintains that if a non-Jew wrote his non-Jewish wife a ketubah, and then later the two converted to Judaism, the woman is only entitled to a settlement of a maneh, even if she was a virgin when she first married. What then does the Mishnah mean when it says that it was on the basis of the woman's original ketubah that her husband kept her as his wife? *Tosafot Yom Tov* explains that the Mishnah teaches that the husband must pay out his wife's ketubah in the currency circulating where the couple were married originally, and not in the currency circulating where they lived after they converted. Following the Jerusalem Talmud, *Melekhet Shlomo* suggests that the Mishnah teaches that the woman is only entitled to her ketubah settlement if the couple engaged in sexual intercourse after their conversion. But if they did not engage in sexual intercourse, the woman is not entitled to a ketubah settlement.

בְּתוּלָה גּוֹבָה מָאתַיִם **A virgin collects two hundred.** *Tosafot* maintain that in the case under discussion, the woman cannot collect her settlement from property that her husband had sold to a third party, for the ketubah deed written before he reached majority or converted is not a valid legal document, and does not create a lien on his property. She can, therefore, only collect from free property in her husband's possession at the time of the dissolution of their marriage. According to *Meiri,* this woman's ketubah indeed creates a lien and she can therefore collect it from property that the husband sold. He raises the question whether the woman exercises a lien over her husband's property from the time of their original marriage, or only from the time that he kept her as his wife after reaching majority or having converted. He concludes that she only exercises a lien from that later time.

Conclusion to Chapter Nine

Regarding a husband's right to his wife's usufruct property, it is agreed that he has the right to waive his rights to the fruit of this property (by a written deed or an oral statement), if he does so before the marriage. However, he cannot waive his right to inherit his wife's property if she predeceases him.

Regarding the obligation to take an oath, it was decided that in the interest of domestic tranquility, a husband may not ordinarily require his wife to take an oath regarding her administration of the household. However, he or his heirs may require her to take an oath if she has become a storekeeper or a custodian of his property. If a wife is in possession of her marriage contract, ordinarily she may collect her settlement without taking an oath. However, if she has received an advance payment of part of the settlement ("impaired" it), or if she admits that the sum written in the marriage contract is greater than the amount upon which they initially agreed ("decreased" it), she must take an oath, and in any event she is required to take an oath to collect from her husband's heirs.

Most of the aforementioned oaths are subject to exemption. If a husband has stated in writing that he exempts his wife from the obligation of taking an oath, she is exempt from that obligation, depending upon the exact conditions that he stipulated with her (exemption only regarding his claim from her, for him and his heirs, for her and her heirs, and so on).

When others advance claims against an estate, and the moveable property is insufficient to pay all the claims, the heirs have priority, unless one of the creditors preempted them and seized the property while his debtor was still living.

Although the marriage contract is the principal proof needed to collect the settlement, nevertheless, when no marriage document is extant, a divorced wife or widow collects the major portion of the marriage settlement if she possesses a bill of divorce or can produce witnesses that her husband is dead. If a wife possesses two marriage contracts from her husband, if other documents and testimony establish that her husband had given her both marriage contracts to supplement one another, she collects both settlements. Otherwise she collects only one.

Introduction to Chapter Ten

מִי שֶׁהָיָה נָשׂוּי

This chapter deals at length with a problem that was begun in the previous chapter: When a man dies, leaving several wives, how do they (and their heirs) divide the property among them to pay the obligation of their marriage settlement?

Evidently if the property was sufficient to pay all their claims, no problem is incurred. However, several questions arise when the amounts of the marriage settlements exceed the amount of the estate. This issue comprises three essential problems. First, which wife has priority in collecting the marriage settlement, and how is this priority determined in practice? The second problem: How is the property divided when the amounts of the marriage settlements are not equal, and one wife has a larger claim than her fellow? In such a situation (as in the division of assets among partners with unequal shares) there are several possibilities: that each claimant shall receive an equal share; that the claimants shall receive shares proportional to their claims; or that one of the claimants shall receive priority.

The third problem arises regarding a *ketubat benin dikhrin* ("a marriage contract of male children"). One of the conditions of a marriage contract is that the sons of each wife shall be entitled to inherit their mother's marriage settlement after her death, in addition to their portion of the total inheritance. Since marriage settlements are not always equal, and sometimes one wife may have few sons, there is reason to examine how one may reconcile the claims of the various sons regarding these inheritances.

All of these problems become more complex when one of the wives waives her portion only for one person. This gives rise to a system of claims in which the various claimants have relative priority which obligates a practical solution.

These problems and judgments associated with them are the main subject of this chapter.

מִי

[1]שֶׁהָיָה נָשׂוּי שְׁתֵּי נָשִׁים וּמֵת — [2]הָרִאשׁוֹנָה קוֹדֶמֶת לַשְּׁנִיָּה, [3]וְיוֹרְשֵׁי הָרִאשׁוֹנָה קוֹדְמִין לְיוֹרְשֵׁי שְׁנִיָּה.

[4]נָשָׂא אֶת הָרִאשׁוֹנָה, וּמֵתָה, [5]נָשָׂא שְׁנִיָּה, וּמֵת הוּא — [6]שְׁנִיָּה וְיוֹרְשֶׁיהָ קוֹדְמִין לְיוֹרְשֵׁי הָרִאשׁוֹנָה.

LITERAL TRANSLATION

MISHNAH [1][If] someone was married to two women and he died, [2]the first takes precedence over the second, [3]and the heirs of the first take precedence over the heirs of the second.

[4][If] he married the first, and she died, [5][and] he married the second, and he died, [6]the second or her heirs take precedence over the heirs of the first.

RASHI

משנה מי שהיה נשוי. יורשי הראשונה – אם מתו נשיו אחריו, עד שלא הספיקו לגבות. נשא ראשונה ומתה – בחייו. נשא שניה ומת הוא, ויורשי הראשונה באין ותובעין כתובת בנין דכרין, כמו ששנינו (כתובות נג,ב): בנין דכרין דיהוון ליכי מינאי כו׳, או רוצים לחלוק ירושת אביהם. שניה ויורשיה קודמין – שהיא בעלת חוב. אבל ראשונים באין לירש את אביהן, דהא ״אינון ירתון״ תנן, לפיכך פורעין את החוב תחילה, והשאר ירושה.

TRANSLATION AND COMMENTARY

MISHNAH מִי שֶׁהָיָה נָשׂוּי [1]If a man **was married to two women,** and the ketubah deed of one wife was dated earlier than that of the other, **and** the husband **died** and then each of the two widows sought to collect their ketubah settlement from the property of his estate, but the estate was insufficient to cover both obligations, [2]**the** man's **first** wife **takes precedence over** his **second** wife. This is because the first wife's lien on her husband's property was established before that of his second wife. The first wife is entitled to collect whatever she can from her late husband's estate, and the second wife collects only from what remains. Similarly, if both wives died before they could collect their settlements, and their heirs then came to collect them from the husband's heirs, [3]**the heirs of the** man's **first wife take precedence over the heirs of** his **second wife.**

נָשָׂא אֶת הָרִאשׁוֹנָה [4]**If someone was married to a woman, and she died** during his lifetime, so that he inherited her entire estate and her sons became entitled to collect her ketubah settlement upon his death by virtue of the enactment of *ketubat benin dikhrin*, [5]**and** then the husband **took a second wife, but** subsequently **he died,** [6]**the second wife** or **her heirs** who come to collect her ketubah settlement **take precedence over the first wife's heirs** who come to collect the settlement by virtue of the enactment of *ketubat*

NOTES

מִי שֶׁהָיָה נָשׂוּי **If someone was married.** *Melekhet Shelomo* explains that the previous chapter concluded with the laws applying to one woman with two ketubot, and so this chapter opens with the laws applying to two women with two ketubahs. Moreover, the fourth chapter of this tractate outlined the husband's various obligations to his wife. The subsequent chapters dealt at greater length with some of the ketubah conditions, such as the wife's right to maintenance, and this chapter continues with a discussion of the ketubah condition known as *ketubat benin dikhrin*.

כְּתוּבַּת בְּנִין דִּכְרִין ***Ketubat benin dikhrin.*** If a woman predeceases her husband, he inherits her entire estate, including the dowry she brought into the marriage. But the Rabbis enacted that when the husband dies, the ketubah settlement he did not have to pay and the dowry he inherited from his wife pass to the male children of that marriage, and only then is the rest of the man's estate divided among all his heirs. While this provision was usually written explicitly into the ketubah deed, the ketubah settlement and the dowry pass down to her sons even if the document did not contain this clause (see *Ketubot* 52b). This ketubah condition, known as the *ketubat benin dikhrin* ("ketubah of male children"), was instituted by the Rabbis in order to ensure that the dowry provided by the bride's father would remain in the hands of his descendants. This assurance encourages a father to give his daughter a larger dowry and thus improve her chances of finding a suitable husband.

הָרִאשׁוֹנָה קוֹדֶמֶת לַשְּׁנִיָּה **The first one takes precedence over the second one.** The Tosefta and the Jerusalem

HALAKHAH

מִי שֶׁהָיָה נָשׂוּי שְׁתֵּי נָשִׁים **If someone was married to two women.** "If a man was married to two women and he died, an later his two widows also died, the following distinction applies: If the women had taken the widow's oath before they died (swearing that they had not collected their ketubahs), the women's sons inherit their mother's ketubahs by Torah law (and not by virtue of the enactment of *ketubat benin dikhrin*). The heirs of the man's first wife take precedence over the heirs of his second wife. If the women had not taken the widow's oath before they died, the women's sons do not inherit their mother's ketubahs (for a widow cannot collect her ketubah without first taking the oath), and so the women's ketubahs are divided up evenly between all the sons, just like the rest of the man's estate," following the Mishnah and the Gemara's conclusion in *Shevuot* 45a. (*Rambam, Sefer Nashim, Hilkhot Ishut* 19:8; *Shulḥan Arukh, Even HaEzer* 111:11).

נָשָׂא אֶת הָרִאשׁוֹנָה וּמֵת **If he married the first one, and died.** "If a man was married to two women, and one of his two wives died during his lifetime, and his second wife

TRANSLATION AND COMMENTARY

benin dikhrin. Because the *ketubat benin dikhrin* has the characteristics of an inheritance, the sons may only collect it after all other obligations of the estate have been satisfied.

GEMARA מִדְּקָתָנֵי [1]The Gemara suggests using the Mishnah to derive a related law: **Since** the Mishnah **teaches:** "If the husband's estate does not suffice to cover both obligations, the claim of his **first** wife **takes precedence over** that of his **second** wife," [2]**and it does not teach** more simply: **"The** man's **first wife has** a ketubah settlement, **but** his **second** wife **does not have** one" — [3]**this proves by implication that if the second wife proceeded and seized** property belonging to her late husband's estate, and thereby prevented the first wife from recovering her settlement, [4]**we do not take** the seized property **from her** and give it to the husband's first wife. The Gemara attempts to generalize this conclusion: [5]**Infer from this** that if a debtor's property does not suffice to satisfy all of his creditors, and **a later creditor,** one whose lien upon the debtor's property was established after that of another creditor, **proceeded and collected** his debt from the debtor's property, [6]**whatever** the later creditor succeeded in **collecting he collected** legally. We do not take the property from him and give it to the earlier creditor, who had the preferential rights to the property.

גמרא [1]מִדְּקָתָנֵי: ״הָרִאשׁוֹנָה קוֹדֶמֶת לַשְּׁנִיָּה״, [2]וְלָא קָתָנֵי: ״הָרִאשׁוֹנָה יֵשׁ לָהּ, וְהַשְּׁנִיָּה אֵין לָהּ״ — [3]מִכְּלָל דְּאִי קָדְמָה שְׁנִיָּה וְתָפְסָה, [4]לָא מַפְּקִינַן מִינָּהּ. [5]שְׁמַע מִינָּהּ: בַּעַל חוֹב מְאוּחָר שֶׁקָּדַם וְגָבָה, [6]מַה שֶּׁגָּבָה גָּבָה!

LITERAL TRANSLATION

GEMARA [1]Since it teaches: "The first takes precedence over the second," [2]and it does not teach: "The first has and the second does not have" — [3][this proves] by implication that if the second proceeded and seized, [4]we do not take it away from her. [5]Infer from this: A later creditor who proceeded and collected, [6]what he collected he collected.

RASHI

גמרא מדקתני — לישנא דקודמת ולא קתני כו׳ — ועל כרחך כשאין שם אלא כדי כתובה אחת קאמר. דאי לא — מאי נפקא מינה דקודמת? שמע מינה — קודמת לכתחילה. אבל אם קדמה שניה ותפסה — לא מפקינן מינה.

NOTES

Talmud state that it is only with respect to collecting her ketubah settlement that a man's first wife takes precedence over his second wife. But neither woman has a preferential right with respect to collecting maintenance from her late husband's estate.

בַּעַל חוֹב מְאוּחָר שֶׁקָּדַם וְגָבָה **A later creditor who went ahead and collected.** The validity of a later creditor's taking of his debtor's property in the face of an earlier creditor's prior lien is the subject of a Tannaitic dispute, below, 94a. *Ramban* explains that this dispute depends upon a second dispute - namely, whether the creditor's lien on his debtor's property is Torah law or a Rabbinic enactment. Those who maintain that the later creditor's collection stands also maintain that the lien on a debtor's property is a Rabbinic enactment and not Torah law. The Rabbis enacted this lien so that the creditor may collect from that property even after it was sold to a third party. The lien was intended to overcome a person's reluctance to extend loans, for a borrower might sell all of his property and make it impossible to recover the loan (see also *Tosafot*). Thus, the Rabbis enacted that a creditor may recover his debtor's property from the buyer, but they did not enact that he can recover it from a later creditor who proceeded to take the property before him. They had no concern that a person would refrain from granting a loan on account of such a possibility. (Others suggest that a creditor can recover his debt from his debtor's property that was sold to a third party, because the buyer did something improper when purchasing property over which the creditor had a lien, an argument that does not apply in the case of a plurality of creditors; see *Meiri*). But according to those who say that a later creditor's taking of his debtor's property is not valid, and that the earlier creditor may recover the property from him, a creditor's lien over his debtor's property is by Torah law. Alternatively, they may also maintain that the lien is only by Rabbinic enactment, but once the lien was enacted, the Rabbis do not distinguish between a buyer and a later creditor, and the lien of the prior creditor remains even when the property is delivered to the other creditor.

HALAKHAH

died only after his death, and he had sons from both marriages, the following distinction applies: If the second wife had taken the widow's oath before she died, her sons inherit her ketubah by Torah law, and then the sons of the first wife inherit their mother's ketubah by virtue of the enactment of *ketubat benin dikhrin,* and whatever is left is then divided evenly between all the sons. If the second wife died before taking the widow's oath, the sons of the first wife inherit their mother's ketubah by virtue of the enactment of *ketubat benin dikhrin*, and whatever is left is then divided evenly between all the sons," following the Mishnah, and the Gemara in *Shevuot*. (*Rambam, Sefer Nashim, Hilkhot Ishut* 19:7; *Shulḥan Arukh, Even HaEzer* 111:8).

TRANSLATION AND COMMENTARY

לְעוֹלָם [1]The Gemara rejects this conclusion: **In fact, I can** tell **you** that in the case of a plurality of creditors, [2]**whatever** property a later creditor **collected was not** legally **collected,** and the earlier creditor may recover it from him. [3]**And what** does the Mishnah mean when it states: "The man's first wife **takes precedence** over his second wife"? [4]**It means** that the first wife has an **absolute** right to the property that cancels out the second's wife's right of recovery. Moreover, the term "takes precedence" can indeed be used to mean an all-embracing right. [5]**For we have learned** elsewhere **in the Mishnah** regarding the rights of inheritance (*Bava Batra* 116a): **"A son takes precedence over a daughter."** The son has an absolute right to his father's estate, so that even if the daughter seized the property, it must be returned to the son.

אִיכָּא דְּאָמְרִי [6]There are **some who** report a different version of this passage, in which the Gemara uses the Mishnah to derive an exactly opposite conclusion: [7]**Since** the Mishnah teaches the general expression "takes precedence over" but **does not teach** explicitly: [8]**"If the second** wife **proceeded and seized** property belonging to her late husband's estate, and thus prevented the first wife from recovering her ketubah settlement, **we do not take** the seized property **from her** and give it to the husband's first wife" — [9]**this proves by implication that if the** man's **second wife proceeded and seized** property belonging to her late husband's estate, [10]**we** do in fact **take** the seized property **away from her** and give it to the husband's first wife. [11]Thus, we may **infer from this** that if a debtor's property does not suffice to satisfy all of his creditors, and **a later creditor proceeded and collected** his debt from the debtor's property, [12]**whatever** the later creditor **collected was not collected** legally, and the earlier creditor with the prior lien may recover the property from him.

לְעוֹלָם [13]The Gemara rejects this conclusion: **In fact, I can** tell **you** that in the case of a plurality of creditors, [14]**whatever** the later creditor succeeded in **collecting was collected** legally. The Mishnah did not state this explicitly because the first half of the Mishnah was formulated under the stylistic influence of the second half. [15]**Since** the Tanna wanted to **teach** in the second clause: "If a man's first wife died, and then he remarried and later he himself died, [16]**the** man's **second** wife **or her heirs** who come to collect the later ketubah settlement **take precedence over the first wife's heirs** who come to collect the settlement by virtue of the enactment of *ketubat benin dikhrin.* In this later case, the Tanna could not have stated that if the first wife's heirs seized property, we do not take it away from them, for seizure by the first wife's heirs is surely invalid. Any property they take would be mortgaged to the second wife's ketubah settlement. *Ketubat benin dikhrin* has the status of an inheritance and does not have its own property lien. Thus for reasons of parallelism [90B] the Tanna **also taught** the first clause in the same style: [17]"If a man died leaving two widows, his **first** wife **takes precedence over** his **second** wife in recovering her ketubah."

[1]לְעוֹלָם, אֵימָא לָךְ: [2]מַה שֶׁגָּבָה, לֹא גָּבָה. [3]וּמַאי "קוֹדֶמֶת"? [4]לְגַמְרֵי קָתָנֵי. [5]כְּדִתְנַן: "בֵּן קוֹדֵם לְבַת".
[6]אִיכָּא דְּאָמְרִי: [7]מִדְּלָא קָתָנֵי: [8]"אִם קָדְמָה שְׁנִיָּה וְתָפְסָה, אֵין מוֹצִיאִין מִיָּדָהּ" — [9]מִכְּלָל דְּאִי קָדְמָה שְׁנִיָּה וְתָפְסָה, [10]מַפְּקִינַן מִינָּהּ. [11]שְׁמַע מִינָּהּ: בַּעַל חוֹב מְאוּחָר שֶׁקָּדַם וְגָבָה, [12]מַה שֶׁגָּבָה, לֹא גָּבָה!
[13]לְעוֹלָם אֵימָא לָךְ: [14]מַה שֶׁגָּבָה, גָּבָה. [15]אַיְּידֵי דְּתָנָא: [16]"שְׁנִיָּה וְיוֹרְשֶׁיהָ קוֹדְמִין לְיוֹרְשֵׁי הָרִאשׁוֹנָה", [90B] תָּנָא נַמִי: [17]"הָרִאשׁוֹנָה קוֹדֶמֶת לַשְּׁנִיָּה".

LITERAL TRANSLATION

[1]In fact, I can say to you: [2]What he collected, he did not collect. [3]And what is [meant by] "she takes precedence"? [4]It means [lit., "states"] absolutely. [5]As we have learned [in the Mishnah]: "A son takes precedence over a daughter."

[6]There are [some] who say: [7]Since it does not teach: [8]"If the second proceeded and seized, we do not take it away from her" — [9][this proves] by implication that if the second proceeded and seized, [10]we remove it from her. [11]Infer from this: A later creditor who proceeded and collected, [12]what he collected he did not collect [legally].

[13]In fact, I can say to you: [14]What he collected, he collected [legally]. [15][But] since he taught: [16]"The second or her heirs take precedence over the heirs of the first," [90B] he also taught: [17]"The first takes precedence over the second."

RASHI

לגמרי — שאין לשניה כלום. כדתנן: בן קודם לבת — ועל כרחך — קודם לגמרי הוא. איידי — דבעי למיתני סיפא: שניה ויורשיה, לישנא ד"קודמין", ולא שייך למיתני בה: אם קדמו ותפסו אין מוציאין מידם — דהא ודאי מוציאין אם תפסו והחזיקו בקרקע, דהא נכסי אישתעבוד לשטר דבעל חוב. תנא נמי — רישא, לישנא דלכתחילה "קודמת", ולא תנא: אם קדמה ותפסה אין מוציאין.

LITERAL TRANSLATION

[1]"If he married the first." [2]Infer from this three [things]. [3][In the first instance,] infer from this: [If] one [wife died] during his lifetime and one after his death, the [first wife's sons] have the ketubah of male children, [4]and we are not concerned about quarreling.

[5]From where [do we know this]? [6]Since it states: "The second and her heirs take precedence over the heirs of the first." [7]They take precedence, [8]but if there is, the [first wife's heirs] take.

[1]״נָשָׂא אֶת הָרִאשׁוֹנָה״. [2]שְׁמַע מִינָּהּ תְּלָת. [3]שְׁמַע מִינָּהּ: אַחַת בְּחַיָּיו וְאַחַת בְּמוֹתוֹ, יֵשׁ לָהֶן כְּתוּבַּת בְּנִין דִּכְרִין, [4]וְלָא חָיְישִׁינַן לְאִינְצוּיֵי.

[5]מִמַּאי? [6]מִדְּקָתָנֵי: ״שְׁנִיָּה וְיוֹרְשֶׁיהָ קוֹדְמִים לְיוֹרְשֵׁי רִאשׁוֹנָה״. [7]מִיקְדָּם הוּא דְּקָדְמִי, [8]הָא אִיכָּא שָׁקְלִי.

TRANSLATION AND COMMENTARY

נָשָׂא [1]We learned in the Mishnah: **"If someone was married to a woman,** and she died during his lifetime, and he remarried and then died, the claim of the second wife or her heirs to her ketubah settlement takes precedence over that of the first wife's heirs, who collect the settlement by virtue of the enactment of *ketubat benin dikhrin.*" [2]The Gemara notes: The following **three** conclusions may **be inferred from the** Mishnah's ruling: [3]In the first instance, **infer from this** Mishnah that if a man was married to two women, **one** of whom died **during his lifetime, and** the second died only **after his death,** the sons of the first wife inherit their mother's ketubah settlement from their father by virtue of the enactment of ***ketubat benin dikhrin,*** [4]**and we are not concerned** that allowing them to take their mother's ketubah will give rise to **quarreling** between the brothers. Since the sons of the first wife collect their *ketubat benin dikhrin* as an inheritance before the entire estate is appraised and divided up, we might be concerned that the second wife's sons will object that their half-brothers are inheriting an unfairly large portion of their father's estate. Our Mishnah implies that *ketubat benin dikhrin* was applied even if one of the man's wives outlived him, and not only when both wives predeceased him, in which case, both groups of half-brothers collect an inheritance of *ketubat benin dikhrin.*

מִמַּאי [5]The Gemara now asks: **From where** in the Mishnah **do we know this?** [6]**From** what the Mishnah **states: "The second** wife **or her heirs** who come to collect the ketubah settlement which is due her as a widow **take precedence over the first wife's heirs** who claim the *ketubat benin dikhrin.*" [7]Since the Mishnah teaches that the second wife's heirs **take precedence** over the first wife's heirs, it must refer to an estate insufficient to cover both ketubah settlements, and so it rules that the second wife's heirs collect first. [8]**But** this implies that **if** the estate **is** sufficiently large to cover both settlements, the first wife's heirs do indeed **take** the *ketubat benin dikhrin.*

RASHI

שמע מינה אחת בחייו ואחת במותו יש להן — לראשונים כתובת בנין דכרין. ולא אמרינן: כי תקון בנין דכרין — היכא דמתו שתיהן בחייו, וכתובת האחת מרובה משל חברתה — אלו נוטלין כתובת אמן ואלו נוטלין כתובת אמן, והשאר חולקין בשוה. דהשתא אתו תרוייהו בתורת בנין דכרין, שהוא ירושת האב, ולא אתי לאינצויי. אבל אחת בחייו ואחת במותו, דיורשי שניה באין על כתובת אמן בתורת ירושת חוב אמן, ולא מאביהם באה להם, ובני ראשונה באין ליטול חלק יתר מכח ירושת האב, דהא ״ירתון״ תנן — לא שקלי, דלמא אתו לאינצויי, ולומר: לא תטלו בירושת אבינו יותר ממנו — הא לא אמרינן.

NOTES

אַחַת בְּחַיָּיו וְאַחַת בְּמוֹתוֹ **One wife died during his lifetime and one after his death.** According to *Rav Hai Gaon, Rav Sherira Gaon, Rabbenu Ḥananel* and others, only if one of the wives died during her husband's lifetime and the second one died after his death that the first wife's sons inherit their mother's ketubah by virtue of the enactment of *ketubat benin dikhrin.* But if the second wife is still alive and claims her ketubah settlement, the sons of the first wife do not inherit their mother's ketubah settlement. We are concerned that giving it to them will give rise to a quarrel with the second wife if there is not enough money to pay both. Other Geonim (and so too *Ramban* and others) disagree and say that the first wife's sons do inherit their mother's ketubah settlement even if the second wife is still alive. They support their position from the Mishnah that teaches: "The second one or her heirs take precedence over

HALAKHAH

אַחַת בְּחַיָּיו וְאַחַת בְּמוֹתוֹ **One during his lifetime and one after his death.** "If a man was married to two women, and one of his wives died during his lifetime, and his second wife died after his death, the sons of both women inherit their mothers' ketubah settlements, and we are not concerned that they will quarrel. The sons of the first wife inherit their mother's ketubah settlement by virtue of the enactment of *ketubat benin dikhrin,* even if after it is collected, a dinar surplus will not remain to be divided evenly among all the brothers, for the second wife's ketubah settlement is considered such a surplus." (*Rambam, Sefer Nashim, Hilkhot Ishut* 19:7; *Shulḥan Arukh, Even HaEzer* 111:8.)

LITERAL TRANSLATION

[1] And [in the second instance,] infer from this: The [second wife's] ketubah is considered as a surplus for the other [ketubah].

[2] From where [do we know this]? [3] Since it does not state: "If there is there a surplus of a dinar."

[4] And [in the third instance] infer from this: [5] The ketubah of male children may not be seized from mortgaged property. [6] For if it enters your mind that it may be seized from

[1] וּשְׁמַע מִינָּהּ: כְּתוּבָּה נַעֲשֵׂית מוֹתָר לַחֲבֶרְתָּהּ.

[2] מִמַּאי? [3] מִדְּלָא קָתָנֵי: "אִם יֵשׁ שָׁם מוֹתָר דִּינָר".

[4] וּשְׁמַע מִינָּהּ: [5] כְּתוּבַּת בְּנִין דִּכְרִין לָא טָרְפָה מִמְּשַׁעְבְּדֵי.

[6] דְּאִי סָלְקָא דַּעְתִּין טָרְפָה

TRANSLATION AND COMMENTARY

וּשְׁמַע מִינָּהּ [1] The Gemara now explains the second inference: **Infer from this** Mishnah that **the ketubah** settlement collected by the second wife or her heirs **is considered a surplus** of the estate that allows **the other** ketubah settlement to be paid out as a *ketubat benin dikhrin*. We learned in the Mishnah below (91a) that sons only inherit their mother's ketubah settlement if the father left an estate large enough so that, after the ketubah settlement is paid, at least a dinar is left to be divided evenly among all the brothers as an inheritance. As the Gemara explains above (52b), this surplus is necessary to prevent the Biblical laws of inheritance from being totally uprooted by the Rabbinic enactment of *ketubat benin dikhrin*. Our Mishnah implies that the surplus dinar is not necessary if one of the wives outlived her husband, and she or her heirs came to collect her ketubah settlement from his estate. For in that case the ketubah settlement is collected as a debt owed by the husband that his heirs must pay out of their inheritance. The Biblical laws of inheritance are thus fulfilled with the payment of the second wife's ketubah settlement, and the first wife's sons can collect their mother's ketubah settlement as a *ketubat benin dikhrin*.

מִמַּאי [2] The Gemara now asks: **From where** in the Mishnah **do we know this?** [3] The Gemara explains: **Since** the Mishnah **does not state** explicitly that the first wife's heirs only inherit their mother's ketubah settlement **if a surplus of** at least **a dinar** will remain after the second wife's ketubah settlement is collected, it follows that they inherit her ketubah settlement, even if nothing at all will be left to be shared with the sons of the second wife.

וּשְׁמַע מִינָּהּ [4] The third inference that may be drawn from the Mishnah is as follows: **Infer from this** Mishnah that unlike a widow or divorcee who collects her ketubah settlement from pledged property, [5] the enactment regarding ***ketubat benin dikhrin*** does not allow the sons **to seize** the **property that was** originally **pledged** as security for their mother's ketubah and was later sold to a third party. As explained earlier in the tractate (52b), if a woman predeceases her husband, the Rabbis enacted that upon their father's death, her sons receive her ketubah settlement as an inheritance, and heirs are only entitled to property that was in the testator's possession at the time of his death. The Gemara now explains the basis of this inference: [6] **For if you think that** the enactment of *ketubat benin dikhrin* **allows** the sons **to seize property pledged** as payment of their mother's ketubah, as is maintained by the scholars of Mata Meḥasya (see above, 55a) — why should the second wife's heirs take precedence over the first wife's heirs?

RASHI

כתובה נעשית מותר לחברתה — דאף על גב דלא תקון כתובת בנין דכרין אלא אם כן יש מותר על שתי הכתובות דינר, דלא מיעקרא נחלה דאורייתא, כדתנן בפרקין — ופרשינן טעמא בפרק "נערה שנתפתתה" (כתובות נב,ב) — הני מילי כי מתו שתיהן בחייו, דתרווייהו אתו בתורת בנין דכרין. אבל אחת בחייו ואחת במותו, שהשניה נגבית בתורת חוב — אין לך ירושה גדולה מזו, ולא מיעקרא נחלה דאורייתא. שכשמת נפלו נכסים לפני יורשין, וכשילא שטר חוב על אביהן — אלו ואלו עושין מלוה לפרוע חובת אביהן, והיא היא ירושתן. לפיכך כתובה זו נעשית כמותר לירושה, וגובין בני הראשונה כתובת בנין דכרין. [לא טרפי ממשעבדי — דלא תימא "יתבון" תנן, ובעל חוב הוו, ושעבודם קודם, ויטרפו מבני השניה שהן בעלי חובות מאוחרין. אלא יורשין הן, ו"ירתון" תנן, ולא גבו ממשעבדי].

NOTES

the heirs of the first one," which implies that when the second wife claims her ketubah settlement she takes precedence over the first wife's heirs, but if the estate is sufficiently large the latter do inherit their mother's ketubah settlement.

HALAKHAH

כְּתוּבַּת בְּנִין דִּכְרִין לָא טָרְפָה מִמְּשַׁעְבְּדֵי **The ketubah of male children does not seize from mortgaged property.** "A son who inherits his mother's ketubah settlement by virtue of the enactment of *ketubat benin dikhrin* may not seize property that was pledged as security for the woman's ketubah and later sold to a third party. Rather he may only take his mother's ketubah from the free property of his father's estate." (*Rambam, Sefer Nashim, Hilkhot Ishut* 19:9; *Shulḥan Arukh, Even HaEzer* 111:13.)

TRANSLATION AND COMMENTARY

[1] **Let the first wife's sons come and seize** their mother's ketubah settlement **from the** property that **the second wife's sons** collected as payment of their mother's ketubah, for the former wife's ketubah has a prior lien?

מַתְקִיף לָהּ [2] **Rav Ashi strongly objected** to these first two inferences: **From where do we derive these conclusions?** [3] **Perhaps in fact I can say to you** that if a man was married to two women, **one of whom died during his lifetime, and the** second died only **after his death,** [4] **the first wife's sons do not** inherit their mother's ketubah settlement as a *ketubat benin dikhrin*. [5] **What then is the meaning of** the Mishnah's ruling: "The second wife or her heirs **take precedence** over the first wife's heirs" — a ruling that was understood above as implying that in this case the first wife's heirs can inherit their mother's ketubah settlement. [6] **I can say to you** that the Mishnah **stated** this **with regard to inheritance,** and it meant to teach: The second wife or her heirs take precedence and have priority in collecting the ketubah settlement, after which the first wife's heirs take their share of what is left in the estate. [7] **And if you** argue that if the Mishnah is dealing with the inheritance of the father's estate, **why** then **do I refer** to his first wife's sons as **"the first wife's heirs"?** We are dealing with their inheriting from their father not their mother! But this is not really difficult, for I can say that this phrase was formulated to preserve stylistic parallelism. [8] **Since** the Tanna wanted to **teach** that **"the second wife or her heirs"** take precedence in collecting her ketubah settlement, [9] the Tanna **also** referred to the first woman's sons as **"the first wife's heirs."**

וּדְקָאָמְרַתְּ [10] Rav Ashi now rejects the Gemara's second conclusion: **And regarding what you said** that the Mishnah implies that **the ketubah** settlement collected by the second wife or her heirs **is considered a surplus** of the estate that allows heirs to collect their *ketubat benin dikhrin* first, this too is not necessarily true. [11] **For**

LITERAL TRANSLATION

mortgaged property, [1] let the sons of the first [wife] come and seize from the sons of the second.
[2] Rav Ashi strongly objected: From where? [3] Perhaps in fact I can say to you: [If] one [wife died] during his lifetime and one after his death, [4] the [first wife's sons] do not have the ketubah of male children. [5] And what is [the meaning of] "they take precedence"? [6] This is stated with regard to inheritance. [7] And if you say: Why do I need "the heirs of the first"? [8] Since he taught: "The second and her heirs," [9] he also taught: "The heirs of the first."
[10] And regarding what you said: "The [second wife's] ketubah is considered as a surplus for the other [ketubah]," [11] I may still

מִמְּשַׁעְבְּדֵי, [1]לֵיתוּ בְּנֵי רִאשׁוֹנָה וְלִטְרְפִינְהוּ לִבְנֵי שְׁנִיָּה. [2]מַתְקִיף לָהּ רַב אַשִׁי: מִמַּאי? [3]דִּלְמָא לְעוֹלָם אֵימָא לָךְ: אַחַת בְּחַיָּיו וְאַחַת בְּמוֹתוֹ, [4]אֵין לָהֶן כְּתוּבַּת בְּנִין דִּכְרִין. [5]וּמַאי "קוֹדְמִין"? [6]לְנַחֲלָה קָתָנֵי! [7]וְכִי תֵּימָא: "יוֹרְשֵׁי הָרִאשׁוֹנָה" לָמָּה לִי? [8]אַיְּידֵי דְּתָנָא: "שְׁנִיָּה וְיוֹרְשֶׁיהָ", [9]תָּנָא נַמִי: "לְיוֹרְשֵׁי הָרִאשׁוֹנָה". [10]וּדְקָאָמְרַתְּ: "כְּתוּבָּה נַעֲשֵׂית מוֹתָר לַחֲבֶרְתָּהּ", [11]דִּלְמָא

RASHI

וּמַאי קוֹדְמִין — דְּמַשְׁמַע: הָא אִי אִיכָּא מִידֵי לְמִשְׁקַל בַּתְרַייהוּ — שְׁקָלוּ. קוֹדְמִין לְנַחֲלָה — לֹא שֶׁיִּטְּלוּ הָרִאשׁוֹנִים אַחֲרֵיהֶם כְּתוּבַּת אֵמָן, אֶלָּא שֶׁיִּטְּלוּ אַחֲרֵיהֶם חֵלֶק בְּמוֹתָר, כְּדֶרֶךְ חוֹלְקֵי יְרוּשָׁה. יוֹרְשֵׁי הָרִאשׁוֹנָה לְמָה לִי — דִּקְרוֹ לְהוּ "יוֹרְשֵׁי רִאשׁוֹנָה", הֲלֹא לֹא מִכְּחָה וְלֹא מִתַּקַּנְתָּהּ הֵן בָּאִין לִירַשׁ, וְאַמַּאי קָתָנֵי לְיוֹרְשֵׁי הָרִאשׁוֹנָה? הָכִי גָּרְסִינַן: אַיְּידֵי דְּתָנָא שְׁנִיָּה וְיוֹרְשֶׁיהָ תָּנָא נַמִי לְיוֹרְשֵׁי הָרִאשׁוֹנָה — אַיְּידֵי דְּקָרֵי לְהוּ לִבְנֵי שְׁנִיָּה יוֹרְשֵׁי הָאֵם, דְּאִינְהוּ מִינָּהּ קָא יָרְתֵי. קְרֵינְהוּ לִבְנֵי רִאשׁוֹנָה נַמִי עַל שֵׁם יוֹרְשֶׁיהָ. וְלֹאו מִשּׁוּם דְּמִידַּהּ קָא יָרְתֵי, אֶלָּא שְׁמָא בְעָלְמָא, כְּלוֹמַר לִבְנֵי הָרִאשׁוֹנָה.

NOTES

וְלִטְרְפִינְהוּ לִבְנֵי שְׁנִיָּה **Let them seize from the sons of the second one.** *Ramban* derives a more general principle from our passage: Whenever a person is not entitled to recover payment of a debt from assets that the debtor sold to a third party (such as a undocumented loan), neither can he recover it from mortgaged assets in the possession of the debtor. Thus, if a person borrowed from two different lenders, one of whom had a promissory note that created a lien over the debtor's property, and the other had only an undocumented loan, the creditor with the oral obligation can only collect his money after the creditor with the promissory note has been paid. *Ramban* questions the authenticity of a responsum attributed to *Rav Hai Gaon,* according to which the creditor with an earlier oral

obligation enjoys a preferential right to recover the money owed him over the creditor with the promissory note written later. *Rav Hai Gaon* argues that a creditor with an oral obligation does not collect his debt from purchased land because the existence of an oral obligation is not widely known, and it was necessary to protect the purchaser who had no way of knowing about the lien. But the creditor with the oral obligation does enjoy the preferential right of recovering his debt from property held by the debtor, because by Torah law the creditor enjoys a lien over the debtor's property even if his debt was established orally. (See also *Ra'ah* who agrees with *Ramban,* and *Rashba* who agrees with *Rav Hai Gaon.*)

TRANSLATION AND COMMENTARY

I **may still** reply **to you** [1]that **the ketubah** settlement collected by the second wife or her heirs **is not considered a surplus** of the estate that would allow **the other** ketubah to be paid out. [2]**But, here** the Mishnah refers to an estate in which, after the first wife's heirs collect her ketubah, **a surplus of** at least **a dinar will** still **remain.** This was not stated explicitly, because the Mishnah is not dealing here with that issue.

וְאַחַת בְּחַיָּיו [3]The Gemara now notes the institution of *ketubat benin dikhrin* when a man was married to two women, **one** of whom died **during his lifetime, and the second** died **after his death, is the subject of a Tannaitic dispute:** [4]**For it was taught** in a Baraita: **"If** a man's two wives **died, one during his lifetime, and the second** only **after his death,** the Tannaim disagree about whether the sons of the woman who died during her husband's lifetime collect a *ketubat benin dikhrin.* [5]**Ben Nannas says: The sons of the** wife who died **first can say to the sons of the** wife who died afterward: [6]**You** come to collect your mother's ketubah settlement as **the sons of a creditor,** for upon our father's death your mother became a creditor of his estate and you have now inherited that obligation. [7]**Take your mother's ketubah** settlement, **and leave,** for we are entitled to the rest of our father's estate by virtue of the enactment of *ketubat benin dikhrin.* [8]**Rabbi Akiva says:** This is not so, for when the husband died during his second wife's lifetime, the right to **inherit** their mother's ketubah settlement **jumped away from the first wife's sons,** [9]**and landed before the second wife's sons,** so that they all have an

לְעוֹלָם אֵימָא לָךְ: [1]אֵין כְּתוּבָּה נַעֲשֵׂית מוֹתָר לַחֲבֶרְתָּהּ. [2]וְהָכָא הוּא דְּאִיכָּא מוֹתָר דִּינָר.

[3]וְאַחַת בְּחַיָּיו וְאַחַת בְּמוֹתוֹ תַּנָּאֵי הִיא. [4]דְּתַנְיָא: "מֵתוּ, אַחַת בְּחַיָּיו, וְאַחַת בְּמוֹתוֹ, [5]בֶּן נַנָּס אוֹמֵר: יְכוֹלִין בְּנֵי הָרִאשׁוֹנָה לוֹמַר לִבְנֵי הַשְּׁנִיָּה: [6]בְּנֵי בַּעֲלַת חוֹב אַתֶּם. [7]טְלוּ כְּתוּבַּת אִמְּכֶם, וּצְאוּ. [8]רַבִּי עֲקִיבָא אוֹמֵר: כְּבָר קָפְצָה נַחֲלָה מִלִּפְנֵי בְּנֵי הָרִאשׁוֹנָה, [9]וְנָפְלָה לִפְנֵי בְּנֵי הַשְּׁנִיָּה".

LITERAL TRANSLATION

say to you: [1]The ketubah is not considered as a surplus for the other. [2]But here is when there is a surplus of a dinar.

[3]And [if] one [wife died] during his lifetime and one after his death is [the subject of] a Tannaitic dispute. [4]For it was taught: "If they died, one during his lifetime, and one after his death, [5]Ben Nannas says: The sons of the first can say to the sons of the second: [6]You are the sons of a creditor. [7]Take your mother's ketubah, and leave. [8]Rabbi Akiva says: The inheritance already jumped away from the sons of the first [wife], [9]and landed before the sons of the second."

RASHI

והכא בדאיכא מותר דינר — קאמר. אי האי "קודמין ליורשי הראשונה" קודמין לכתובת בנין דכרין הוא — איכא לאוקומה בדאיכא מותר דינר. ואף על גב דלא תני "אם יש שם מותר דינר" — הא קתני לה לקמן: היה שם מותר דינר כו'. ותרתי זימני לא איצטריך למיתני. **תנאי היא** — אי שקלי בני ראשונה כתובת בנין דכרין אי לא. **אתם בני בעלת חוב אתם טלו כתובת אמכם וצאו** — על כרחך בדליכא מותר דינר קמיירי, מדקתני "וצאו". ואי דאיכא נחלה יותר על שתי כתובות — מאי "וצאו" דקא אמרי להו? נהי נמי דשקלי בני ראשונה כתובת בנין דכרין — שארא מיהא פלגי. אלא בדליכא, והכי קאמרי להו: אתם בני בעלת חוב אתם, וכתובת אמכם — הואיל וחוב היא, ואינכם באין בתורת בנין דכרין — לא בעינן מותר דינר. דאין לך נחלה דאורייתא יפה מזו שאנו ואתם פורעים חובת אבינו. הלכך, טלו אותה וצאו, ואנו נטול השאר בכתובת בנין דכרין. **רבי עקיבא אומר כבר קפצה נחלה כו'** — משעה שמת הבעל בחייה של שניה קפצה נחלת בנין דכרין מלפני בני הראשונה. **ונפלה** — להיות נחלה, כשאר ירושה, אף לבני השניה. ואפילו הוי הכא מותר דינר — לא הוו שקלי בני הראשונה כתובת בנין דכרין, דבאחת בחייו ואחת במותו לא איתקן.

NOTES

מוֹתָר דִּינָר **A surplus of a dinar.** According to some authorities, the ketubah settlement collected by the second wife or her heirs is only considered as a surplus of the estate, if the estate is large enough to cover both ketubot. But if the sum of the two ketubot is greater than the estate, the law of *ketubat benin dikhrin* does not apply. However, most Rishonim maintain that as long as the estate is larger than the second wife's ketubah settlement, its payment fulfills the Biblical laws of inheritance, and whatever is left may be collected by the first wife's heirs as a *ketubat benin dikhrin* (see *Rosh* and *Ritva*).

וְאַחַת בְּחַיָּיו וְאַחַת בְּמוֹתוֹ תַּנָּאֵי הִיא **And if one wife died during his lifetime and one after his death is the subject of a Tannaitic dispute.** *Shittah Mekubbetzet* asks: Why does the Gemara state here categorically that this matter is the subject of a Tannaitic dispute? It should have asked tentatively: Shall we say that this Tannaitic dispute (לֵימָא כְּתַנָּאֵי)? This is precisely what it asks after citing the Baraita: Do they not disagree about this? *Shittah Mekubbetzet* answers: The Gemara means to say: The law regarding the case of a man who was married to two women, one of whom died during his lifetime, and the second died after his death, is indeed the subject of a Tannaitic dispute. However after citing the Baraita, the Gemara begins to clarify the precise point of this disagreement: Do they disagree about whether the first wife's sons are entitled at all to their mother's ketubah settlement, or do they disagree about whether or not the ketubah settlement collected by the second wife or her heirs is considered as a surplus of the estate, or about some other issue?

[1]מַאי לָאו בְּהָא קָא מִיפַּלְגִי? [2]דְּמָר סָבַר: אַחַת בְּחַיָּיו וְאַחַת בְּמוֹתוֹ, [3]יֵשׁ לָהֶן כְּתוּבַּת בְּנִין דִּכְרִין, [4]וּמָר סָבַר: אַחַת בְּחַיָּיו וְאַחַת בְּמוֹתוֹ, [5]אֵין לָהֶן כְּתוּבַּת בְּנִין דִּכְרִין.

[6]אֲמַר רַבָּה: אַשְׁכַּחְתִּינְהוּ לְרַבָּנַן דְּבֵי רַב דְּיָתְבֵי וְקָאָמְרִי: [7]דְּכוּלֵּי עָלְמָא, אַחַת בְּחַיָּיו וְאַחַת בְּמוֹתוֹ, [8]יֵשׁ לָהֶן כְּתוּבַּת בְּנִין דִּכְרִין. [9]וְהָכָא בִּכְתוּבָּה נַעֲשֵׂית מוֹתָר לַחֲבֶרְתָּהּ, [10]וְהוּא הַדִּין לְבַעַל חוֹב קָמִיפַּלְגִי. [11]מָר סָבַר: כְּתוּבָּה נַעֲשֵׂית מוֹתָר לַחֲבֶרְתָּהּ, [12]וְהוּא הַדִּין לְבַעַל חוֹב. [13]וּמָר סָבַר: אֵין כְּתוּבָּה נַעֲשֵׂית מוֹתָר לַחֲבֶרְתָּהּ, [14]וְהוּא הַדִּין

LITERAL TRANSLATION

[1]Do they not disagree about this? [2]One Sage maintains: [If] one [wife died] during his lifetime and one after his death, [3]the [first wife's sons] have the ketubah of male children, [4]and the other Sage maintains: [If] one [wife died] during his lifetime and one after his death, [5]they do not have the ketubah of male children?

[6]Rabbah said: I found the Rabbis of the academy sitting and saying: [7]All agree that [if] one [wife died] during his lifetime and one after his death, [8]the [first wife's sons] have the ketubah of male children. [9]And here they disagree about [whether] the [second wife's] ketubah is considered a surplus for the other [ketubah], [10]and likewise [about a debt owed to] a creditor. [11]One Sage maintains: The [second wife's] ketubah is considered as a surplus for the other [ketubah], [12]and likewise [the debt owed to] a creditor. [13]And the other Sage maintains: The [second wife's] ketubah is not considered a surplus for the other [ketubah], [14]and likewise [a debt owed]

TRANSLATION AND COMMENTARY

equal claim of inheritance." [1]**Do not** these Tannaim **disagree about this very issue?** [2]**One Sage** — Ben Nanas — **maintains** that if **one** of his wives died **during his lifetime, and the** second died only **after his death,** [3]the **sons** of the **first wife inherit** their mother's **ketubah** settlement through the enactment of ***ketubat benin dikhrin.*** Ben Nannas says that the first wife's sons can send the second wife's sons away after the latter have received their mother's ketubah settlement, because, in this case, nothing will be left of their father's estate once the first wife's sons have taken their mother's ketubah settlement. Nevertheless they do inherit that settlement, because the Biblical laws of inheritance were fulfilled when the second wife's heirs received their mother's ketubah. [4]**The other Sage** — Rabbi Akiva — **maintains if one** of his **wives died during his lifetime, and the** second died only **after his death,** [5]the sons of the first woman **do not** inherit their mother's ketubah settlement through the enactment of ***ketubat benin dikhrin.*** Thus, after payment of the second wife's settlement, the rest of the father's estate is divided equally among all the sons.

אֲמַר רַבָּה [6]**Rabbah said: I found the Rabbis of the academy sitting and saying:** [7]**All agree** — both Ben Nannas and Rabbi Akiva — **that** if **one wife died during his lifetime, and** the second died only **after his death,** [8]the **first wife's sons do** in fact inherit their mother's ketubah settlement as a ***ketubat benin dikhrin.*** Therefore, this is not the issue under dispute in the Baraita. [9]**Here** the Tannaim **disagree about whether** or not **the ketubah** collected by the second wife or her heirs **is considered a surplus** of the estate that allows **the other ketubah** to be paid out to the first wife's sons as a *ketubat benin dikhrin.* [10]They also disagree about whether or not **a debt** collected by **a creditor** of the deceased can be considered as a surplus that allows the distribution of *ketubat benin dikhrin.* [11]**One Sage** — Ben Nanas — **maintains** that **the ketubah** settlement collected by the second wife or her heirs **is considered a surplus** of the estate that allows **the other** wife's ketubah to be paid out to his first wife's heirs as a *ketubat benin dikhrin.* [12]**And likewise** the payment of **a debt owed to a creditor** of the deceased — if it amounts to at least one dinar — also fulfills the requirement of a surplus allowing the distribution of the rest of the estate as *ketubat benin dikhrin,* if both wives died before the husband. [13]**The other Sage** — Rabbi Akiva — **maintains** that **the ketubah** settlement collected by the second wife or her heirs **is not considered a surplus** of the estate that allows **the other** wife's ketubah settlement to be paid out as a *ketubat benin dikhrin.* [14]**And likewise** the payment of **a debt owed to a creditor** of the deceased does not allow his sons to collect their mother's ketubah settlement as a *ketubat benin dikhrin.* Thus, the second wife's sons collect the ketubah settlement which was due to their mother, and then the rest of the father's estate is divided equally between the sons of the first wife and the sons of the second wife. The first wife's sons do not inherit their mother's ketubah, because in this case, a surplus of a dinar

RASHI

דכולי עלמא יש להן — וטעמא דרבי עקיבא הכא משום דליכא מותר דינר הוא, וקסבר: אין כתובה נעשית מותר לחברתה, ואפילו השניה חוב. והוא הדין לבעל חוב היכא דמתו שתיהן בחייו, דתרוייהו אתו בתורת בנין דכרין ויש שם מותר דינר, והוא משועבד לבעל חוב — לא הוי מותר.

לְבַעַל חוֹב. [1]וְאָמִינָא לְהוּ אֲנָא: בְּבַעַל חוֹב, [2]כּוּלֵּי עָלְמָא לָא פְּלִיגִי דְּהָוֵי מוֹתָר. [3]כִּי פְּלִיגִי, בִּכְתוּבָּה.

[4]מַתְקִיף לָהּ רַב יוֹסֵף: [5]אִי הָכִי, ״רַבִּי עֲקִיבָא אוֹמֵר: [6]כְּבָר קָפְצָה נַחֲלָה״? [7]״אִם יֵשׁ מוֹתָר דִּינָר״ מִיבָּעֵי לֵיהּ!

LITERAL TRANSLATION

to a creditor. [1]And I said to them: Regarding [a debt owed to] a creditor, [2]nobody disagrees that it is considered a surplus. [3]When they disagree, [it is] regarding a ketubah.

[4]Rav Yosef strongly objected to this: [5]If so, "Rabbi Akiva says: [6]The inheritance already jumped away"? [7]He should have [said]: "If there is a surplus of a dinar."

TRANSLATION AND COMMENTARY

would not remain after they take the ketubah settlement, and the ketubah settlement collected by the second wife's sons is not considered a surplus of the estate. [1]**And I,** Rabbah, **said to** those Rabbis: I disagree with what you said **regarding** the payment of **a debt owed to a creditor** of the deceased, [2]for in my opinion **all agree** — both Ben Nannas and Rabbi Akiva — **that it is considered a surplus** of the estate which allows all the sons to collect their mothers' ketubah settlements by virtue of the enactment of *ketubat benin dikhrin.* That debt falls equally upon all the brothers, and so it must be collected from the assets which all of the brothers inherited from their father. [3]But I do agree with you that Ben Nannas and Rabbi Akiva **disagree about the ketubah** settlement collected by the second wife's sons. Ben Nannas maintains that it is like any other debt, and is considered a surplus, allowing the first wife's sons to receive their mother's ketubah settlement first as a *ketubat benin dikhrin.* Rabbi Akiva disagrees and maintains that the ketubah obligation is unlike a debt to an outsider, for it does not fall equally upon all the brothers. The second wife's sons do not share in paying out that debt; on the contrary, they collect it. Thus, the Biblical laws of inheritance are not fulfilled by paying the second wife's ketubah settlement. Hence the first wife's sons cannot collect their mother's ketubah settlement as a *ketubat benin dikhrin* unless a dinar is left in the estate after both settlements are paid.

מַתְקִיף לָהּ [4]**Rav Yosef strongly objected to** Rabbah's interpretation of the dispute between Ben Nannas and Rabbi Akiva: [5]**If** it is **so** that these Tannaim disagree about whether the ketubah settlement collected by the second wife's sons is considered a surplus, then why does the Baraita states: **"Rabbi Akiva says** that when the father died before his second wife, [6]the right to **inherit** their mother's ketubah settlement **jumped away from the first wife's sons and landed** before **the second wife's sons,** so that they have an equal claim to the property?" This implies that if the second wife dies after her husband, his first wife's sons can never inherit their mother's ketubah settlement. [7]Rabbi Akiva **should have said: "If a surplus of** at least **a dinar** will remain after the first wife's sons collect her ketubah settlement, they may indeed take it. But if such a surplus will not remain, the first wife's ketubah settlement is divided equally among all the brothers."

RASHI

בבעל חוב כולי עלמא לא פליגי דהוי מותר – הואיל והשטר יוצא על כולם – נמצאו כולם פורעין, והיא נחלה שלהן, שעשו בהן מצות פריעת חוב אביהם. **כי פליגי בכתובה** – באחת בחייו ואחת במותו, שהשניה חוב היא, פליגי; בן ננס סבר: הרי זו כשאר חוב, והוי מותר. ורבי עקיבא סבר: לאו כשאר חוב דמי, כיון דאינהו גופייהו קא שקלי. והלכך, הנך בני שניה מקבלין ולא פורעין. נמצא שאין כאן נחלה דאורייתא, ולא איתקן ירושת בנין דכרין דרבנן למיעקר נחלה דאורייתא. **אי הכי** – דהא לחודא הוא דפליג רבי עקיבא – משום דליכא מותר, ואי הוה מותר – לא פליג, מאי "כבר קפצה נחלה" דמשמע: אין כאן תורת בנין דכרין כלל, הכי אבעי ליה למימר: אם יש שם מותר נוטלין ואם לאו אין נוטלין.

NOTES

בְּבַעַל חוֹב, כּוּלֵּי עָלְמָא לָא פְּלִיגִי דְּהָוֵי מוֹתָר **Regarding a debt owed to a creditor, nobody disagrees that it is considered a surplus.** This explanation of the Tannaitic dispute is supported by Rabbi Akiva's response to Ben Nanas' argument in the Baraita: "The sons of the first one can say to the sons of the second one: You are the sons of a creditor." Since Rabbi Akiva makes no mention of the creditor, he presumably agrees that the payment of a debt owed to an ordinary creditor is considered as a surplus of the husband's estate, and that he only disagrees about whether payment of the second wife's ketubah is treated as the payment of an ordinary debt (*Shittah Mekubbetzet*).

As for the distinction between the second wife's ketubah settlement and an ordinary debt, our commentary follows *Rashi* and others who explain that the second wife's settlement is unlike any other debt, for the second wife's

HALAKHAH

בְּבַעַל חוֹב, כּוּלֵּי עָלְמָא לָא פְּלִיגִי **Regarding a debt owed to a creditor, nobody disagrees.** "A debt owed to a creditor is regarded as a surplus of the husband's estate which allows his sons to collect their mother's ketubah settlement by virtue of the enactment of *ketubat benin dikhrin.*" (*Rambam, Sefer Nashim, Hilkhot Ishut* 19:6; *Shulḥan Arukh, Even HaEzer* 111:6.)

[1]אֶלָּא אֲמַר רַב יוֹסֵף: בְּאַחַת בְּחַיָּיו וְאַחַת בְּמוֹתוֹ קָא מִיפַּלְגִי. [2]וְהָנֵי תַּנָּאֵי כִּי הָנֵי תַּנָּאֵי. [3]דְּתַנְיָא: ״נָשָׂא אֶת הָרִאשׁוֹנָה וּמֵתָה, נָשָׂא אֶת הַשְּׁנִיָּה וּמֵת הוּא, [4]בָּאִין בָּנֶיהָ שֶׁל זוֹ לְאַחַר מִיתָה, וְנוֹטְלִין כְּתוּבַּת אִמָּן. [5]רַבִּי שִׁמְעוֹן אוֹמֵר: אִם יֵשׁ מוֹתָר דִּינָר, אֵלּוּ נוֹטְלִין כְּתוּבַּת אִמָּן, [6]וְאֵלּוּ נוֹטְלִין כְּתוּבַּת אִמָּן. [7]וְאִם לָאו, חוֹלְקִין בְּשָׁוֶה״. [8]מַאי לָאו בְּהָא קָא מִיפַּלְגִי, [9]דְּמָר סָבַר: אַחַת בְּחַיָּיו וְאַחַת בְּמוֹתוֹ, [10]יֵשׁ לָהֶן כְּתוּבַּת בְּנִין דִּכְרִין, [11]וּמָר סָבַר: אַחַת בְּחַיָּיו וְאַחַת בְּמוֹתוֹ, [12]אֵין לָהֶם כְּתוּבַּת בְּנִין דִּכְרִין!

LITERAL TRANSLATION

[1]Rather, Rav Yosef said: They disagree about [if] one [wife died] during his lifetime and one after his death. [2]And these Tannaim are like those Tannaim. [3]For it was taught: "[If] he married the first and she died, [and] he married the second one and he died, [4]the sons of this one come after [her] death, and take their mother's ketubah. [5]Rabbi Shimon says: If there is a surplus of a dinar, these take their mother's ketubah, [6]and these take their mother's ketubah. [7]But if not, they divide equally." [8]Do they not disagree about this, [9]that one Sage maintains: [If] one [wife died] during his lifetime and one after his death, [10]the [first wife's sons] have the ketubah of male children, [11]and the other Sage maintains: [If] one [wife died] during his lifetime and one after his death, [12]they do not have the ketubah of male children.

TRANSLATION AND COMMENTARY

אֶלָּא [1]**Rather, Rav Yosef said:** Ben Nanas and Rabbi Akiva **disagree about** whether the law regarding *ketubat benin dikhrin* applies if a man was married to two women, **one** of whom died **during his lifetime and the second** died only **after his death,** as had been suggested above. [2]**And these Tannaim** disagree about the very same issue which was in dispute between **the following Tannaim,** [3]**for it was taught** in another Baraita: **"If someone was married to a woman, and she died** during his lifetime, **and** then the husband **took a second wife, and** later **he died,** and subsequently the second wife died as well, [4]**the woman's sons come after her death and take their mother's ketubah** settlement (it will be explained below whether this refers to the sons of the first or second wife). [5]**Rabbi Shimon says: If** the father left an estate large enough so that **a surplus of** at least **a dinar** will remain after the first wife's sons take their mother's ketubah settlement, the second wife's sons **take their mother's ketubah** settlement, [6]**and** the first wife's sons **take their mother's ketubah** settlement as *ketubat benin dikhrin.* [7]**But if** a surplus of at least a dinar will **not** remain after the sons of both wives collect their respective settlements, the second wife's sons take her settlement, and the rest of the father's estate is **divided equally** between all the sons." Now, Rav Yosef assumes that when the anonymous first Tanna of the Baraita said that the woman's sons come after her death and take their mother's ketubah settlement, he was referring to the sons of the second wife who collect the settlement due to her mother as a widow. But the first wife's sons do not inherit their mother's ketubah settlement. Rav Yosef therefore suggests that the Baraita should be understood as follows: [8]**Do not** the anonymous first Tanna and Rabbi Shimon **disagree about this** very issue? [9]**One Sage** — Rabbi Shimon — **maintains** that if a man was married to two women, **one** of whom died **during his lifetime, and the** second died only **after his death,** [10]the sons of the **woman** who died **first inherit** their mother's ketubah settlement from their father by virtue of the enactment of ***ketubat benin dikhrin.*** But this enactment only applies when a surplus of at least a dinar will remain after both settlements are paid, because the settlement collected by the second wife's sons is not considered a surplus. [11]**And the other Sage** — the anonymous first Tanna of the Baraita — **maintains** that if **one** of a man's two wives died **during his lifetime, and the second** died only **after his death,** [12]the first wife's sons **do not inherit** their mother's ketubah settlement as ***ketubat benin dikhrin.*** Therefore, the second wife's

RASHI

אלא אמר רב יוסף כו' — כדפרישית ברישא, דאפילו הוה בה מותר אתא רבי עקיבא למימר: דהואיל ואחת במותו ליכא כתובת בנין דכרין לבני ראשונה, וכל שכן כי ליכא. **באים בניה של זו** — קא סלקא דעתך אבני שניה קאי, והכי קאמר: באים בני השניה, שהיא בעלת חוב, ונוטלין כתובת אמם. אבל לבני ראשונה — אין כאן כתובה, דקסבר: אחת בחייו ואחת במותו אין להם. **חולקין בשוה** — את המותר על כתובת החוב.

NOTES

sons do not have a share in paying that debt, but are in fact, its collectors. And the Biblical laws of inheritance are only fulfilled when the payment of a debt falls equally upon all the heirs. *Ritva* cites another explanation: Since the heirs of the deceased are commanded to pay his debts, the Biblical laws of inheritance are viewed as having been fulfilled when those debts are paid. But paying the widow her ketubah settlement, while obligatory, is not included in that commandment, and so the Biblical laws of inheritance are not viewed as having been fulfilled when that obligation is paid.

[1]לָא, דְּכוּלֵּי עָלְמָא אַחַת בְּחַיָּיו וְאַחַת בְּמוֹתוֹ, [2]יֵשׁ לָהֶן כְּתוּבַּת בְּנִין דִּכְרִין [91A] [3]וְהָכָא בְּדִינָר מְקַרְקְעֵי קָמִיפַּלְגִי. [4]מָר סָבַר: מְקַרְקְעֵי — אִין; [5]מִטַּלְטְלֵי — לָא. [6]וּמָר סָבַר: אֲפִילּוּ מִטַּלְטְלֵי.

[7]וּמִי מָצֵית אָמְרַתְּ הָכִי? [8]וְהָתְנַן, רַבִּי שִׁמְעוֹן אוֹמֵר: ״אֲפִילּוּ יֵשׁ שָׁם נְכָסִים שֶׁאֵין לָהֶם אַחֲרָיוּת אֵינָן כְּלוּם, [9]עַד שֶׁיְּהֵא שָׁם נְכָסִים שֶׁיֵּשׁ לָהֶן אַחֲרָיוּת יָתֵר עַל שְׁתֵּי כְתוּבּוֹת דִּינָר״!

[10]אֶלָּא, הָכָא בְּדִינָר מְשַׁעְבְּדֵי קָמִיפַּלְגִי. [11]מָר סָבַר: מִבְּנֵי חוֹרִין — אִין; [12]מִמְּשַׁעְבְּדֵי — לָא. [13]וּמָר סָבַר: אֲפִילּוּ מִמְּשַׁעְבְּדֵי.

LITERAL TRANSLATION

[1]No, for all agree that [if] one [wife died] during his lifetime and one after his death, [2]they have the ketubah of male children. [91A] [3]And here they disagree about a [surplus of a] dinar of land. [4]One Sage maintains: Land — yes; [5]movable goods — no. [6]And the other Sage maintains: Even movable goods.

[7]But can you say this? [8]But surely we have learned: "Rabbi Shimon says: Even if there is movable property (lit., "property without responsibility") it is nothing, [9]until there is there landed property (lit., "property with responsibility"), a dinar in excess of the two ketubahs."

[10]Rather, here they disagree about a [surplus of a] dinar of mortgaged property. [11]The one Sage maintains: Of free [landed] property — yes; [12]of mortgaged property — no. [13]And the other Sage maintains: Even from mortgaged property.

TRANSLATION AND COMMENTARY

sons collect their mother's ketubah settlement, which is due to her as a widow, and the rest of the father's estate is divided equally among all the sons.

לָא [1]The Gemara rejects this explanation of the Baraita: These Tannaim do **not** necessarily argue about this issue, **for** I can tell you that both Tannaim of the Baraita **agree that** if **one** of a man's two wives died **during his lifetime, and the second** died only **after his death,** [2]the first wife's sons **do** in fact **inherit** their mother's ketubah settlement as ***ketubat benin dikhrin.*** [91A] [3]**And here** the Tannaim **disagree about** whether the enactment of *ketubat benin dikhrin* applies only when **the dinar surplus** which will remain to be divided among all the brothers is **land.** [4]**One Sage** — the anonymous first Tanna of the Baraita — **maintains** that the remaining dinar must be of **land,** if the enactment is to apply; [5]if only **movable goods** are left, the enactment does **not** apply. [6]**And the other Sage** — Rabbi Shimon — **maintains** that the enactment applies **even** when only **movable goods** will remain.

וּמִי מָצֵית [7]The Gemara raises an objection: **But can you** really **say** that **this** is the view of Rabbi Shimon? [8]**Surely we have learned** in the next Mishnah: **"Rabbi Shimon says: Even if** the father's estate includes **movable property, it is not** regarded as **anything** with respect to the requirement that a dinar surplus remain after all the sons have taken their mothers' ketubah settlements, for the enactment of *ketubat benin dikhrin* does not apply unless [9]**there is a dinar** of **landed property in excess of the two ketubah** settlements."

אֶלָּא [10]**Rather, here** in the Baraita the Tannaim **disagree about** whether the enactment of *ketubat benin dikhrin* applies when **the dinar** surplus is **property that was mortgaged** to the father's creditor. [11]**One Sage** — the anonymous first Tanna of the Baraita — **maintains** that if a dinar of **landed property free** of any lien will remain after both ketubah settlements are collected, the enactment of *ketubat benin dikhrin* **indeed** applies. [12]But if the **property** in excess of the settlements **was mortgaged** to the father's creditor, the enactment does **not** apply. [13]**And the other Sage** — Rabbi Shimon — **maintains** that the enactment applies **even** when only **mortgaged property** will remain. The Baraita refers to a case in which only land that is mortgaged to creditors would remain after the sons of both wives take their mothers' settlements. Thus, the anonymous first Tanna says that first wife's sons do not inherit their mother's settlement. And Rabbi Shimon disagrees and says that if a surplus of at least a dinar will remain, even if it only consists of mortgaged property, the first wife's sons do inherit their mother's ketubah settlement as *ketubat benin dikhrin.*

BACKGROUND

נְכָסִים שֶׁיֵּשׁ לָהֶם אַחֲרָיוּת Lit., property with responsibility, i.e., morgagable property, real estate, immovable property, land; usually real estate, which can be mortgaged to guarantee a loan, and from which debts may ultimately be paid. Written contracts normally establish a lien on all of a persons landed property (the Geonim subsequently decreed that debts may be collected from movable property as well). Special modes of acquisition must be used to purchase land, although one who purchases can, at the same time, acquire movable property together with the land. One who purchases land can acquire separate lots located in different areas, or even in different countries, simultaneously. A *prosbul* — a special document of release, permitting loans to be collected after the Sabbatical Year — may only be written if the debtor owns land. However, since all Jews are Halakhically assumed to own at least 4 cubits by 4 cubits of land in Eretz Israel, this land may be used either for the establishing of liens or for writing a *prosbul.*

RASHI

בדינר מקרקעי קמיפלגי — אי בעינן הוא מותר, שיהא שם שתי כתובות ודינר מקרקעות. והכא בדליכא מותר דינר אלא מטלטלי, משום הכי אמר תנא קמא דאין בני ראשונה נוטלין, ואתא רבי שמעון למימר: הואיל ויש מותר דינר כל דהו — שקלי. ומר סבר אפילו ממשעבדי — רבי שמעון סבר: חוב הוי מותר.

NOTES

בְּדִינָר מְשַׁעְבְּדֵי **About a dinar of mortgaged property.** Our commentary follows *Rashi* and most Rishonim who understand that in the case under discussion, the portion of the husband's estate remaining after the distribution of the ketubah settlements is mortgaged to a debt owed to an outside creditor. *Talmid HaRashba* (cited by *Shittah Mekubbetzet*) suggests that in the case under discussion, the property is mortgaged to the heirs in such a manner that

¹אִי הָכִי, ״רַבִּי שִׁמְעוֹן אוֹמֵר: אִם יֵשׁ שָׁם מוֹתָר דִּינָר״? ²״כֵּיוָן שֶׁיֵּשׁ שָׁם מוֹתָר דִּינָר״ מִיבָּעֵי לֵיהּ!
³אֶלָּא בְּפָחוֹת מִדִּינָר קָמִיפַּלְגִי. ⁴מָר סָבַר: דִּינָר — אִין; ⁵פָּחוֹת מִדִּינָר — לָא. ⁶וּמָר סָבַר: אֲפִילּוּ פָּחוֹת מִדִּינָר.
⁷וְהָא רַבִּי שִׁמְעוֹן דִּינָר קָאָמַר!

LITERAL TRANSLATION

[1] If so, "Rabbi Shimon says: If there is a surplus of a dinar"? [2] He should have [said]: "Since there is a surplus of a dinar."

[3] Rather, they disagree about [a surplus of] less than a dinar. [4] The one Sage maintains: A dinar — yes; [5] less than a dinar — no. [6] And the other Sage maintains: Even less than a dinar.

[7] But surely Rabbi Shimon said a dinar!

TRANSLATION AND COMMENTARY

אִי הָכִי [1] However, according to this explanation of the Tannaitic dispute, the Baraita's formulation is difficult: **If** it is **so** that these Tannaim disagree about whether mortgaged property is considered a surplus, then why does the Baraita state: **"Rabbi Shimon says: If** the father left an estate large enough so that **a surplus of** at least **a dinar** will remain after the first wife's sons take their mother's ketubah settlement, the second wife's sons take their mother's settlement, then the first wife's sons take theirs"? Since a dinar's worth of mortgaged landed property remains in excess of the settlements, and Rabbi Shimon comes to say that this too is considered a surplus, [2] the Baraita **should have stated: "Since there is a surplus of a dinar** (even though the property is mortgaged) it is considered a surplus, and the first wife's sons may inherit their mother's ketubah settlement as a *ketubat benin dikhrin*"!

אֶלָּא [3] **Rather,** explain that the Tannaim **disagree about** whether the enactment of *ketubat benin dikhrin* applies when the **surplus** that remains to be divided among all the brothers is **less than a dinar.** [4] **One Sage** — the anonymous first Tanna of the Baraita — **maintains** that if a surplus of at least **a dinar** will remain after the sons of both wives take their mothers' settlements, the enactment of *ketubat benin dikhrin* **indeed** applies. [5] But if the surplus will be **less than a dinar,** the enactment does **not** apply. [6] **And the other Sage** — Rabbi Shimon — **maintains** that the enactment applies **even** when **less than a dinar** will remain after the settlements are taken. And in the case discussed by our Baraita less than a dinar surplus remains. Thus the anonymous first Tanna says that the second wife's sons collect their mother's ketubah settlement, but not the first wife's sons. And Rabbi Shimon says the other sons do inherit their mother's ketubah settlement.

וְהָא רַבִּי שִׁמְעוֹן [7] The Gemara raises an objection: **But surely Rabbi Shimon stated** explicitly in the Baraita that a surplus of at least **a dinar** must remain for a *ketubat benin dikhrin* to be collected!

RASHI

הכי גרסינן: אי הכי רבי שמעון אומר אם יש מותר דינר — ואברייתא קאי, הואיל ודאיכא מותר מוקמת לה אלא שמשועבד, ורבי שמעון לקולא קאמר — הכי איבעי ליה למימר: הואיל ויש שם מותר דינר אלו נוטלין כו'. ובי תימא איפוך — פירושא דפרשינן בפלוגתייהו איפוך, ואימא: "באין בניה של זו" דקאמר תנא קמא — אבני ראשונה קאי, וקאמר דשקלי כתובת בנין דכרין. ואתא רבי שמעון למימר: אם יש שם מותר דינר — כולם נוטלין. ואם לאו, אלא פחות מדינר יש — חולקים בשוה. והא תנא קמא דמתניתין — דקאמר רבי שמעון עלייהו: אפילו יש שם נכסים שאין להם אחריות אינם כלום. דינר קאמר — דקתני: היה שם יתר דינר כו', ותנא קמא דמתניתין הוא תנא קמא דברייתא.

NOTES

they have no rights to the principal but are entitled to enjoy the usufruct. For example, they might have inherited property that was originally mortgaged to their father by a Suran mortgage. The question then arises whether that property is considered part of the estate through which the Biblical laws of inheritance can be fulfilled, thereby allowing the first wife's heirs to inherit her ketubah settlement. *Rashash* suggests that in the case under discussion, the portion of the husband's estate exceeding the value of the ketubah settlements is property that had been mortgaged to the husband but not yet collected. The Tannaim then disagree about the issue that is in dispute elsewhere (*Bava Batra* 124a), whether such property is considered to be in the heirs' actual possession or only potentially due them.

בְּפָחוֹת מִדִּינָר **About less than a dinar.** *Penei Yehoshua* asks: How could the Gemara possibly have suggested that Rabbi Shimon maintains that the enactment of *ketubat benin dikhrin* applies when the surplus to be divided is less than a dinar, when in both the Mishnah and the Baraita Rabbi Shimon speaks explicitly about a surplus of a dinar? He answers that the Gemara thought that Rabbi Shimon meant primarily to disagree with the anonymous first Tanna of the Mishnah who says that the enactment of *ketubat benin dikhrin* applies even when the surplus consists of movable goods, for according to Rabbi Shimon the enactment applies only when it consists of land. And here even property less than a dinar suffices, for land does not have a clearly set price (as we see from the rule that land is not subject to the laws of *ona'ah*). Rabbi Shimon only spoke of a dinar because the anonymous first Tanna of the Mishnah who allows even movable goods, requires a dinar (see also *Ayelet Ahevim*).

TRANSLATION AND COMMENTARY

וְכִי תֵּימָא [1]The Gemara suggests an answer to this objection, but quickly rejects it: **You might say** that the Tannaim of the Baraita do indeed disagree about whether the enactment of *ketubat benin dikhrin* applies when the surplus that remains to be divided among all the brothers is less than a dinar, but the viewpoints attributed to each of the Tannaim should be **reversed:** The anonymous first Tanna of the Baraita maintains that the enactment applies even if the surplus is less than a dinar, and Rabbi Shimon requires a surplus of at least a dinar. But this revised explanation of the Tannaitic dispute is also difficult, [2]for **the** anonymous **first Tanna of the** next **Mishnah**, with whom Rabbi Shimon also disagrees, **stated** that the enactment of *ketubat benin dikhrin* applies only when there is a surplus of at least **a dinar!** Rabbi Shimon disagrees with both the first Tanna of that Mishnah and the first Tanna of our Baraita. Consequently, the Tannaim of our Baraita cannot be arguing about a surplus of less than a dinar!

אֶלָּא [3]**Rather,** you must **explain** the Tannaitic dispute in one of **the first two ways** suggested above, that the Tannaim disagree either about whether the enactment of *ketubat benin dikhrin* applies when the dinar surplus consists of movable goods or about whether it applies to land that was mortgaged to the late father's creditor. [4]But to counter the objections raised above, the viewpoints attributed to each of the Tannaim should be **reversed.** The first Tanna says that the first wife's sons receive their mother's ketubah settlement by virtue of the enactment of *ketubat benin dikhrin,* even if the surplus consists of movable goods or mortgaged property. Rabbi Shimon disagrees and says that only if there will be a surplus of at least a dinar of landed property which is free of any lien, do the first wife's sons inherit their mother's ketubah settlement. Otherwise the Rabbinic enactment does not apply.

אֲמַר מָר זוּטְרָא [5]The Gemara now concludes this discussion with a practical ruling: **Mar Zutra said in the name of Rav Pappa:** [6]**The law is** that if a man was married to two women, **one** of whom died **during his lifetime, and the second** died only **after his death,** [7]the sons of the first wife **inherit** their mother's ketubah settlement by virtue of the enactment of ***ketubat benin dikhrin.*** [8]**And** the law is that **the ketubah** settlement collected by the second wife or her heirs **is considered as a surplus** of the estate that allows **the other** settlement to be paid to the first wife's heirs as a *ketubat benin dikhrin.*

[1]וְכִי תֵּימָא: אֵיפּוּךְ — [2]תַּנָּא קַמָּא דְּמַתְנִיתִין נַמִי דִּינָר קָאָמַר!

[3]אֶלָּא, כִּי הָנָךְ תְּרֵי לִישָּׁנֵי קַמָּאֵי, [4]וְאֵיפּוּךְ.

[5]אֲמַר מָר זוּטְרָא מִשְּׁמֵיהּ דְּרַב פַּפָּא: [6]הִלְכְתָא: אַחַת בְּחַיָּיו וְאַחַת בְּמוֹתוֹ, [7]יֵשׁ לָהֶן כְּתוּבַּת בְּנִין דִּכְרִין, [8]וּכְתוּבָּה נַעֲשֵׂית מוֹתָר לַחֲבֶרְתָּהּ.

LITERAL TRANSLATION

[1]And if you should say: Reverse [the opinions] — [2]the first Tanna of the Mishnah also said a dinar! [3]Rather, [explain it] like those first two versions, [4]and reverse [the opinions].

[5]Mar Zutra said in the name of Rav Pappa: [6]The law is: [If] one [wife died] during his lifetime and one after his death, [7]they have the ketubah of male children, [8]and the [second wife's] ketubah is considered a surplus for the other.

RASHI

אלא כי הני תרי לישני קמאי — בדינר מקרקע או בדינר משעבדי. **ואיפוך** — תרילותא והכי קאמר תנא קמא: באין בניה של ראשונה גם הם, ונוטלין כתובת אמן משום תנאי בנין דכרין. ואף על גב דליכא אלא מותר דינר מטלטלי או משעבדי. ואתא רבי שמעון למימר: אם יש מותר דינר מקרקעי ובני חרי — אלו נוטלין כו׳. והשתא דרבי שמעון לחומרא, ולא שייך לאותובי: הואיל ויש שם מבעי ליה!

SAGES

מָר זוּטְרָא Mar Zutra. See *Ketubot,* Part III, p. 85.

NOTES

אֵיפּוּךְ Reverse it. Our commentary follows *Rashi,* who explains that when the Gemara proposes that the viewpoints attributed to each of the Tannaim should be reversed, it means to suggest that an entirely new interpretation of the Baraita be adopted, according to which the anonymous first Tanna teaches that the sons of the first wife may collect their mother's ketubah settlement, even if the remaining surplus is less than a dinar, and Rabbi Shimon disagrees and says that a surplus of at least a dinar is required. But according to *Tosafot* and most Rishonim, the Baraita itself reads: "The sons of the second one come after her death, and take their mother's ketubah settlement." Thus, when the Gemara suggests that the viewpoints attributed to each of the Tannaim be reversed, it means that the Baraita refers to a case in which there is no surplus whatsoever: According to the anonymous first Tanna, if there is no surplus whatsoever, the sons of the second wife collect their mother's ketubah settlement, but the sons of the first wife do not collect their mother's ketubah. But if there is a surplus, even if it is less than a dinar, the sons of the first wife collect their mother's ketubah settlement by virtue of the enactment of *ketubat benin dikhrin.* Rabbi Shimon disagrees and says that the enactment only applies if there will be a surplus of at least a dinar.

¹בִּשְׁלָמָא אִי אַשְׁמְעִינַן: אַחַת בְּחַיָּיו וְאַחַת בְּמוֹתוֹ, ²יֵשׁ לָהֶן כְּתוּבַּת בְּנִין דִּיכְרִין, ³וְלָא אַשְׁמְעִינַן: כְּתוּבָּה נַעֲשֵׂית מוֹתָר לַחֲבֶרְתָּהּ, ⁴הֲוָה אָמִינָא: אִי אִיכָּא מוֹתָר דִּינָר, אִין, ⁵אִי לָא, לָא. ⁶אֶלָּא לִישְׁמְעִינַן כְּתוּבָּה נַעֲשֵׂית מוֹתָר לַחֲבֶרְתָּהּ, ⁷וַאֲנָא יָדַעְנָא מִשּׁוּם דְּאַחַת בְּחַיָּיו וְאַחַת בְּמוֹתוֹ, ⁸יֵשׁ לָהֶן כְּתוּבַּת בְּנִין דִּכְרִין!

⁹אִי אַשְׁמְעִינַן הָכִי, ¹⁰הֲוָה אָמִינָא כְּגוֹן שֶׁנָּשָׂא שָׁלֹשׁ נָשִׁים וּמֵתוּ שְׁתַּיִם בְּחַיָּיו וְאַחַת בְּמוֹתוֹ, ¹¹וְהַךְ דְּמָיְית לְאַחַר מִיתָה יוֹלֶדֶת נְקֵבָה הִיא, ¹²וְלָאו בַּת יְרוּשָּׁה הִיא. ¹³אֲבָל אַחַת בְּחַיָּיו וְאַחַת בְּמוֹתוֹ, וְהָא דִּלְאַחַר מִיתָה

LITERAL TRANSLATION

¹Granted had [Rav Pappa only] taught us: [If] one [wife died] during his lifetime and one after his death, ²they have the ketubah of male children, ³but he did not teach us: The [second wife's] ketubah is considered a surplus for the other, ⁴I might have said [that] if there a surplus of a dinar, yes, ⁵[and] if not, no. ⁶But let him teach us [only that] the [second wife's] ketubah is considered a surplus for the other, ⁷and I would know [that this is] because [if] one [wife died] during his lifetime and one after his death, ⁸they have the ketubah of male children.

⁹Had he taught us [just] that, ¹⁰I might have said [that Rav Pappa ruled] as when he married three women, and two died during his lifetime and one after his death, ¹¹and she who died after his death had given birth to a girl, ¹²and she is not fit to inherit.

¹³But [if] one [wife died] during his lifetime and one after his death, and the one [who died] after his death had given

TRANSLATION AND COMMENTARY

בִּשְׁלָמָא ¹The Gemara now asks why Rav Pappa had to rule on both matters. **Granted** that **had** Rav Pappa only **taught us** that if **one** of a man's two wives died **during his lifetime, and the second** died **after his death,** ²the first wife's sons **inherit** their mother's ketubah settlement by virtue of the enactment of ***ketubat benin dikhrin,*** ³but he did not teach us that **the ketubah** settlement collected by the second wife or her heirs **is considered a surplus** of the estate that allows **the other** ketubah settlement to be paid, ⁴**I might have** mistakenly **concluded that** only **if there is a surplus of** at least **a dinar** in excess of the two settlements, do the first wife's sons **indeed** inherit their mother's settlement. ⁵**But if** there is **no** such surplus, they do **not** inherit it, for the ketubah collected by the second wife or her heirs is not considered a surplus. ⁶**But** Rav Pappa **could have taught us** only **that the ketubah** settlement collected by the **second wife** or her heirs **is considered a surplus** of the estate that allows **the other** settlement to be paid, ⁷**and I would** have **known** by myself **that** if **one** of a man's two wives died **during his lifetime, and the second** died only **after his death,** ⁸the first wife's sons **inherit** her ketubah settlement as a *ketubat benin dikhrin.* Otherwise, regarding what is the second wife's ketubah settlement considered a surplus?!

אִי אַשְׁמְעִינַן ⁹The Gemara now explains why both rulings were in fact necessary: **Had** Rav Pappa only **taught us that** the ketubah settlement collected by one wife or her heirs is considered as a surplus of the estate, ¹⁰**I might have** mistakenly **concluded** that this ruling is relevant only **if** a man **married three woman, two of whom** died **during his lifetime and the third** died **after his death,** ¹¹**and** the woman **who died after** her husband **had** only **a daughter,** ¹²**who does not have the right of inheritance** in the presence of sons. Rav Pappa teaches that the ketubah settlement collected by the third wife's daughter as a debt owed to her mother is considered a surplus of the estate which allow the sons of the other two wives to inherit their mother's ketubah settlements as *ketubot benin dikhrin.* There is no concern that allowing the sons to inherit their mothers' ketubah settlements will lead to a quarrel between those sons and the third wife's daughter, for in any case the daughter would not have inherited any of her father's estate.

אֲבָל ¹³**But** if **one** of a man's two wives died **during his lifetime and the second one** died **after his death, and the** woman **who died after** her husband **had a son** who has same right of inheritance as his half-brothers,

RASHI

ואנא ידענא כו׳ — דאי בשתיהן בחייו, דתרוייהו בתורת בנין דכרין אתו — לא מצי למימר כתובה נעשית מותר לחברתה — דהא לאו פריעת חוב הוא. ואי הכא לא בעינן מותר — היכא איתקן? דלאו בת ירושה — וליכא למיחש לאינצויי, דהא לית לה בנכסים כח אלא כתובת אמה. ובני שתים הראשונות שהם זכרים, ובאים לירש — יש בהם שכתובת אמן גדולה משל חברתה, ואומרים: טלו כתובת אמכם כבנין דכרין, ואנו נטול כתובת אמנו. ואי משום דליכא מותר דינר — הרי פרענו בין שנינו הכתובה השלישית, והיא נעשית מותר לשתים שבחייו. ומריבה אין כאן, דאלו ואלו בתורת בנין דכרין נוטלין הכתובות. וזו שנטלה משום חוב — אין לה לריב, שהרי אינה יורשת, שתוכל לומר: אתם יורשים הכתובות יתר על החלוקה.

TRANSLATION AND COMMENTARY

[1]I might have **said** that *ketubat benin dikhrin* was not enacted, for **we should be concerned** that applying the law there might give rise to **quarreling** between the brothers. For in such a case, the second wife's son collects her ketubah settlement as her heir. Thus, he might object to his half-brothers inheriting their mother's ketubah settlement from their father's estate as a *ketubat benin dikhrin*, and thereby reducing the residue of their father's estate. [2]**Therefore,** Rav Pappa came to **teach us** that we are not concerned about the possibility of such quarreling, and that the enactment of *ketubat benin dikhrin* applies even when the man had a son by the wife who outlived him.

MISHNAH מִי שֶׁהָיָה נָשׂוּי [3]The next Mishnah continues its discussion of the regulations governing the enactment of *ketubat benin dikhrin,* some of which have already been mentioned. Suppose the following situation arises: **Someone was married to two women, and they** both **died** during his lifetime, so that he inherited both of their estates, **and afterward he** too **died,** so that his estate fell to his sons for inheritance. [4]Now **the sons** of the wife whose ketubah was larger **demand their mother's ketubah** settlement and that their half-brothers receive the *ketubat benin dikhrin.* [5]**But** the father's entire estate **is only** large enough to cover **the two ketubot.** In such a case the enactment of *ketubat benin dikhrin* does not apply, [6]and the sons **divide** their father's estate **equally** in accordance with Torah law. But **if** the father left an estate large enough so that after the two ketubot are [7]collected, **a surplus of** at least **a dinar** will remain to be divided, the sons of one wife **take their mother's ketubah** settlement, [8]**and** the sons of the second wife **take their mother's ketubah** settlement, and whatever is left is then divided equally among all the brothers. As the Gemara explained above (52b), a surplus of at least one dinar must remain to be divided evenly among all of the brothers, so that the Biblical laws of inheritance are not totally uprooted by the Rabbinic enactment of *ketubat benin dikhrin.*

יוֹלֶדֶת זָכָר הִיא — [1]אֵימָא לֵיחוּשׁ לְאִינְצוּיֵי. [2]קָא מַשְׁמַע לָן.

מִשְׁנָה [3]מִי שֶׁהָיָה נָשׂוּי שְׁתֵּי נָשִׁים וּמֵתוּ, וְאַחַר כָּךְ מֵת הוּא, [4]וִיתוֹמִים מְבַקְּשִׁין כְּתוּבַּת אִמָּן, [5]וְאֵין שָׁם אֶלָּא שְׁתֵּי כְתוּבּוֹת, [6]חוֹלְקִין בְּשָׁוֶה. [7]הָיָה שָׁם מוֹתָר דִּינָר, אֵלּוּ נוֹטְלִים כְּתוּבַּת אִמָּן, [8]וְאֵלּוּ נוֹטְלִים כְּתוּבַּת אִמָּן.

LITERAL TRANSLATION

birth to a boy — [1]say that we should be concerned about quarreling. [2][Therefore] it teaches us.

MISHNAH [3][If] someone was married to two women, and they died, and afterward he died, [4]and the orphans demand their mother's ketubah, [5]but there is [enough for] only (lit., "there is not there but") two ketubot, [6]they divide equally. [7][If] there was (lit., "there was there") a surplus of a dinar, they take their mother's ketubah, [8]and they take their mother's ketubah.

RASHI

ליחוש לאנצויי — שיכול לומר בנה של זו: בעלת חוב אתה, למה תירשו את אבא יותר ממני? שאתה בא ליטול כתובת אמך יתר על החלוקה, אם נטלתי אני כתובת אמי — לא מאבי ירשתי אלא מאמי.

משנה ויתומים מבקשים כתובת אמן — שכתובת אמם מרובה משל חברתה, ואומרים בניה: כתובת בנין דכרין נטול, וכן אתם, והשאר נחלוק. **חולקין בשוה** — כשאר כל ירושה, לפי הגולגולת.

NOTES

וִיתוֹמִים מְבַקְּשִׁין כְּתוּבַּת אִמָּן **The orphans demand their mother's ketubah.** *Rashi* and most of the other Rishonim (following the Baraita cited in the Gemara) explain that in the case under discussion, one wife had a larger ketubah than the other. This is why her sons demand that the two settlements be distributed, and only afterwards should the remainder of the estate be divided, as this would give them a larger portion of their father's estate. *Rivan* suggests that the Mishnah might also be dealing with a case in which the two ketubahs were for the same amount, but one woman had fewer sons than the other and those sons demanded that their mother's ketubah settlement be divided among them, and the other woman's ketubah settlement be divided among her sons, and only then should the rest of their father's estate be evenly divided between all the brothers. In that way they will receive a larger portion of their father's estate.

מוֹתָר דִּינָר **A surplus of a dinar.** *Tosafot Yom Tov* points out that we find elsewhere (as in *Ketubot* 95b) that the Mishnah can speak of a dinar, but the same law applies to even less than a dinar. Here, however, the Mishnah is precise (see *Bet Yosef*), as is obvious above from the Tannaitic disagreement about a surplus of less than a dinar. Thus the enactment of *ketubat benin dikhrin* applies only if

HALAKHAH

אֵין שָׁם אֶלָּא שְׁתֵּי כְתוּבּוֹת **There are only two ketubot.** "If a man was married to two women, and they both died during his lifetime, and then he died, and his estate was only large enough to cover both women's ketubah settlements, but no surplus would remain after they were distributed, the enactment of *ketubat benin dikhrin* does not apply, and so all the brother's divide their father's estate equally between them." (*Rambam, Sefer Nashim, Hilkhot Ishut* 19:3; *Shulhan Arukh, Even HaEzer* 111:2.)

TRANSLATION AND COMMENTARY

אִם אָמְרוּ יְתוֹמִים [1]If the father's estate was only large enough to cover the two settlements, but **the** sons inheriting the larger one **said: "We will overvalue our father's property by a dinar more** than its actual market value" — [2]reasoning **that they would** then **be able to take their mother's ketubah** settlement, because a dinar surplus with which to fulfill the Biblical laws of inheritance would remain after both settlements are distributed — **we do not listen to them** to overvalue the estate. [3]**But rather the property** of the estate **is appraised by the court.**

הָיוּ שָׁם [4]A person's estate includes property that was actually in his possession at the time of his death, as well as property that was due but not yet in his possession, such as property or money that he was to inherit, or money due from debtors or distant bailees. Regarding the requirement that a surplus of a dinar must remain after the two settlements are distributed, **property that was potentially due** to the father **is not considered as if it were** in his possession.

רַבִּי שִׁמְעוֹן אוֹמֵר [5]**Rabbi Shimon says: Even if** the father's estate includes **movable property, it is not** considered **anything** with respect to the requirement that a dinar surplus must remain after the two ketubah settlements are distributed, for the enactment of *ketubat benin dikhrin* does not apply unless [6]**there is land** worth **a dinar in excess of the two ketubot.**

[1]אִם אָמְרוּ יְתוֹמִים: ״אֲנַחְנוּ מַעֲלִים עַל נִכְסֵי אָבִינוּ יָפֶה דִּינָר״, [2]כְּדֵי שֶׁיִּטְּלוּ כְּתוּבַּת אִמָּן — אֵין שׁוֹמְעִין לָהֶן, [3]אֶלָּא שָׁמִין אֶת הַנְּכָסִים בְּבֵית דִּין.

[4]הָיוּ שָׁם נְכָסִים בְּרָאוּי, אֵינָן כְּבַמּוּחְזָק.

[5]רַבִּי שִׁמְעוֹן אוֹמֵר: אֲפִילּוּ יֵשׁ שָׁם נְכָסִים שֶׁאֵין לָהֶם אַחֲרָיוּת, אֵינָן כְּלוּם, [6]עַד שֶׁיִּהְיוּ שָׁם נְכָסִים שֶׁיֵּשׁ לָהֶן אַחֲרָיוּת, יוֹתֵר עַל שְׁתֵּי הַכְּתוּבּוֹת דִּינָר.

LITERAL TRANSLATION

[1]If the orphans said: "We will overvalue our father's property by a dinar," [2]so that they may take their mother's ketubah, we do not listen to them, [3]but we appraise the property in court.

[4][If] there was property that was potentially due [to the deceased], it is not considered as held [by him].

[5]Rabbi Shimon says: Even if there is movable property (lit., "property without responsibility"), it is nothing, [6]until there is there landed property (lit., "property with responsibility"), a dinar in excess of the two ketubot.

RASHI

אם אמרו יתומים — בני הכתובה הגדולה. **הרי אנו מעלין על נכסי אבינו** — מעלין דמיהן לקבלם עלינו ביוקר כדי דינר יותר על שווין, כדי שיהיה שם מותר דינר, ויטלו כתובת אמם. **היו שם נכסים בראוי** — שראויה ליפול להם ירושה מאבי אביהם אחר מות אביהם, ולכשתפול — יהיה שם מותר דינר בשתי הירושות. **אינן כבמוחזק** — אינן נחשבין עכשיו להיות כאילו הן מוחזקין בהן כבר, ויש כאן מותר דינר.

NOTES

a surplus of at least a dinar will remain after the two ketubah settlements are collected. *Gilyon HaShas* explains that a dinar was required, because the surplus is needed in order to fulfill the Biblical laws of inheritance, and those laws are only fulfilled if each of the heirs receives at least a perutah's worth of the estate. Since there is no knowing how many children will inherit, the Rabbis set the surplus at a dinar.

שָׁמִין אֶת הַנְּכָסִים בְּבֵית דִּין We appraise the property in a court. *Ritva* writes that the Mishnah emphasizes that the property must be assessed by the court in order to teach that even if the property might be sold later at the inflated price proposed by the sons of the woman with the larger ketubah, the value of the property is set in accordance with its market price at the time of the father's death. Moreover, even if another person came to court with the sons and offered the higher price, the property must still be assessed by the court.

רַבִּי שִׁמְעוֹן אוֹמֵר Rabbi Shimon says. In the Jerusalem Talmud, the Amoraim disagree about this Tannaitic dispute.

HALAKHAH

אֲנַחְנוּ מַעֲלִים עַל נִכְסֵי אָבִינוּ We will overvalue our father's property. "If the sons of the deceased said that they would accept their father's property at a dinar more than its actual market value, so that they would be able to take their mother's ketubah settlement, we do not listen to them. Rather the court assesses how much the estate was worth at the time of the father's death, and if it did not exceed the value of the two ketubah settlements by at least a dinar, the enactment of *ketubat benin dikhrin* does not apply." (*Rambam, Sefer Nashim, Hilkhot Ishut* 19:5; *Shulhan Arukh, Even HaEzer* 111:5.)

הָיוּ נְכָסִים בְּרָאוּי If property was due. "The enactment of *ketubat benin dikhrin* does not apply if after the two ketubah settlements are distributed a dinar surplus will not remain from assets that were in the father's possession at the time of his death, even if a dinar surplus will remain if one considers property that was due him at that time," following the Mishnah. (*Shulhan Arukh, Even HaEzer* 111:3.)

נְכָסִים שֶׁיֵּשׁ לָהֶן אַחֲרָיוּת Property with responsibility. "According to some authorities, the enactment of *ketubat benin dikhrin* only applies if the estate of the deceased includes land worth as much as his two wives' ketubahs,

TRANSLATION AND COMMENTARY

GEMARA תָּנוּ רַבָּנַן [1]**Our Rabbis** taught a related Baraita: "If **one** wife had a ketubah of **a thousand** dinars, **and a second** had a ketubah of **five hundred** dinars, and they died before their husband, and then the husband died, the following regulations apply: [2]**If a surplus** of at least **a dinar will remain** after the two ketubah settlements are distributed, [3]the sons of the first wife **take their mother's ketubah** settlement, **and** the sons of the second wife **take their mother's ketubah,** and whatever remains is divided evenly among all the brothers. [4]**And if** a dinar surplus will **not** remain after the two settlements are distributed, the enactment of *ketubat benin dikhrin* does not apply, and so the entire estate **is divided equally** among all of the brothers."

פְּשִׁיטָא [5]The Gemara now lays the groundwork for an inquiry, indicating first which issue has an obvious answer, and then setting out that issue which must still be resolved: **It is obvious that if** the father's estate **was sufficient** at the time of his death, **but** by the time the sons came to collect their mothers' ketubah settlements, the value of the estate had **depreciated** and there was no longer a dinar surplus, the sons may still take their mothers' settlements, [6]for **they already acquired them** at the time of their father's death as *ketubat benin dikhrin.* [7]But what is the law if the father's estate **was insufficient** at the time of his death, **but** when they came to collect, the estate had **appreciated** and was sufficient to cover both settlements with a dinar surplus? Which valuation do we use, the one at the time of death, or the one at the time of the distribution of the estate?

LITERAL TRANSLATION

GEMARA [1]Our Rabbis taught: "To this [wife] a thousand [dinars], and to this one five hundred, [2]if there is there a surplus of a dinar, [3]these [sons] take their mother's ketubah, and these take their mother's ketubah. [4]And if not, they divide equally."

[5]It is obvious [that if the properties were] sufficient and [they] depreciated, [6]the heirs already acquired them. [7][If] they were worth little and [they] appreciated, what [is the law]?

גמרא [1]תָּנוּ רַבָּנַן: "לָזוֹ אֶלֶף, וְלָזוֹ חֲמֵשׁ מֵאוֹת, [2]אִם יֵשׁ שָׁם מוֹתָר דִּינָר, [3]אֵלּוּ נוֹטְלִין כְּתוּבַּת אִמָּן, וְאֵלּוּ נוֹטְלִין כְּתוּבַּת אִמָּן. [4]וְאִם לָאו, יַחְלְקוּ בְּשָׁוֶה.

[5]פְּשִׁיטָא, מְרוּבִּין וְנִתְמַעֲטוּ, [6]כְּבָר זָכוּ בָּהֶן יוֹרְשִׁין. [7]מוּעָטִין וְנִתְרַבּוּ, מַאי?

RASHI

גמרא **מרובים** — בשעת מיתה. ואילו שמאום באותה שעה — היה שם מותר דינר. **ונתמעטו** — שהוזלו קודם ששמאו בבית דין. **כבר זכו בהם** — יורשי כתובה הגדולה, לזכות בכתובת אמם משעת מיתה, שהיה שם מותר דינר.

NOTES

According to Rabbi Mana, the Tannaim disagree about whether the husband's estate must include land worth as much as the two ketubahs, but all agree that the surplus of a dinar can be in movable goods. According to Rabbi Yose the son of Rabbi Bon, all agree that the *ketubat benin dikhrin* only applies if the husband's estate includes land worth as much as the two ketubahs, but the Tannaim disagree about whether the dinar surplus must be land or whether movable goods suffice.

Rambam in his Commentary to the Mishnah rules in accordance with Rabbi Shimon, but he apparently changed his mind in his Mishneh Torah, where he speaks about the dinar surplus without mentioning that it must be in land. (*Rambam's* rulings might perhaps be understood in light of the Amoraic dispute recorded in the Jerusalem Talmud.)

לָזוֹ אֶלֶף **To this one a thousand.** *Rivan* explains that this Baraita explains why the sons might prefer to have the two ketubah settlements distributed to the respective women's sons, and only afterward divide the rest of the father's estate equally among them.

פְּשִׁיטָא, מְרוּבִּין וְנִתְמַעֲטוּ **It is obvious they were sufficient and they depreciated.** The Rishonim ask: Why is the law if the husband's estate depreciated more obvious than if the estate appreciated? *Ra'ah, Ritva* and others explain that it was obvious to the Gemara that if the husband's estate decreased in value so that there no longer remains a dinar surplus, the sons do collect their mothers' ketubah settlements. Because the Rabbis enacted *ketubat benin dikhrin* as an inheritance, it stands to reason that we consider the value of the estate at the time of the husband's death. But the Gemara was in doubt about how to rule if the husband's estate increased in value: Do we say that here too we look at the estate's value at the time of the husband's death, when there was no dinar surplus, or do we allow them to collect now that there is a dinar surplus, and the Biblical laws of inheritance will not be totally

HALAKHAH

but not if the estate includes only movable goods. The dinar surplus which must remain after the two ketubah settlements are distributed may, however, consist of movable goods," against Rabbi Shimon. Some authorities maintain that today *ketubat benin dikhrin* may be collected even from movable goods. (*Shulhan Arukh, Even HaEzer* 111:14.)

מְרוּבִּין וְנִתְמַעֲטוּ **If they were sufficient and became insufficient.** "The court assesses the estate of the deceased at the time of his death, and if it did not exceed the value

TRANSLATION AND COMMENTARY

תָּא שְׁמַע [1]An answer is implied in the following anecdote: **Come and hear** the following incident: **The properties of the house of the son of Tzartzur were insufficient** at the time of his death to cover the ketubah settlements of his two wives and leave a surplus of at least a dinar. **But** by the time the sons came to collect, the **value** of the estate had **appreciated,** so that a surplus dinar would remain. [2]The sons **came before Rav Amram** to ask him whether each set of sons should collect their mother's ketubah settlement as *ketubat benin dikhrin*, or whether the enactment does not apply and the sons must divide the estate equally among themselves. Rav Amram turned to the sons of the wife with the smaller ketubah, [3]and **said to them: "Go** out **and appease** your half-brothers from your inheritance. They thought they would inherit their mother's ketubah settlement in addition to their share of your father's estate, but the entire estate will be divided evenly among all the brothers." [4]The sons of the woman with the smaller ketubah **did not listen** to Rav Amram, [5]so **he said to them: "If you do not appease** your brothers, **I will wound you with a thorn that does not cause blood to flow,"** meaning that he would place them under a ban." [6]Rav Amram then **sent them before Rav Naḥman** so that he might adjudicate the matter. After hearing the case, [7]Rav Naḥman **said to them: Just as** we did when the father's estate **was sufficient** at the time of death to cover both ketubah settlements and still leave a surplus of at least a dinar, but later before the sons actually came to collect their mother's ketubahs, the estate **depreciated** and became insufficient to cover the two ketubahs with a dinar surplus, [91B] [8]each set of **heirs acquired their** mother's ketubah settlement, for we follow the valuation taken at the time of death — [9]**so too,** when the estate **was** originally **insufficient** to cover both settlements and leave a dinar surplus, but the estate later appreciated in value **and became sufficient,** [10]all the **heirs acquire** an equal share of their father's estate. Here too we accept the valuation at the time of death: At that time there would not have been a dinar surplus, and so the enactment of *ketubat benin dikhrin* does not apply.

LITERAL TRANSLATION

[1]Come [and] hear: The properties of the house of the son of Tzartzur were worth little and they increased [in value], [2]and they came before Rav Amram. [3]He said to them: "Go and appease them." [4]They did not listen to him. [5]He said to them: "If you do not appease them, I will wound you with a thorn that does not cause blood to flow." [6]He sent them before Rav Naḥman, [7]who said to them: Just as [if] the [properties] were sufficient, and [they] depreciated, [91B] [8]the heirs acquired them, [9]so too [where] they were insufficient, [10]and [their value] appreciated, the heirs acquired them.

[1]תָּא שְׁמַע: דְּנִיכְסֵי דְּבֵי בַּר צַרְצוּר מוּעָטִין וְנִתְרַבּוּ הָווּ, [2]וַאֲתוּ לְקַמֵּיהּ דְּרַב עַמְרָם. [3]אֲמַר לְהוּ: ״זִילוּ פַּיְיסִינְהוּ״. [4]לָא אַשְׁגַּחוּ. [5]אֲמַר לְהוּ: ״אִי לָא מְפַיְּיסִיתוּ לְהוּ, מָחֵינָא לְכוּ בְּסִילְוָא דְּלָא מַבַּע דָּמָא״. [6]שַׁדְּרִינְהוּ לְקַמֵּיהּ דְּרַב נַחְמָן, [7]אֲמַר לָהֶן: כְּשֵׁם שֶׁמְּרוּבִּין, וְנִתְמַעֲטוּ, [91B] [8]זָכוּ בָּהֶן יוֹרְשִׁין, [9]כָּךְ מוּעָטִין, וְנִתְרַבּוּ, [10]זָכוּ בָּהֶן יוֹרְשִׁין.

RASHI

זילו פייסינהו — ליורשי כתובה הגדולה. **סילוא דלא מבע דמא** — קוץ שאינו מוציא דם בנוקבו בבשר. כלומר, שמתא ונדוי. **סילוא דלא מבע דמא** — קוץ שאינו מוציא דם בנוקבו בבשר. כלומר, שמתא ונדוי. **זכו בהן** — יורשי כתובה הקטנה לחלוק הכל בשוה, הואיל ובשעת מיתה לא הוה בהו מותר.

LANGUAGE

סִילְוָא Thorn. The meaning of this word is similar to the Arabic شلاه (*sulaa*), meaning the spike of a palm. These are the small leaves in the frond of palms that harden over time and form sharp spikes, which make painful wounds.

It appears that in Mishnaic Hebrew this is the word סול and might be connected to the Biblical Hebrew סלון (Ezekiel 2:6, 28:24), which also means a sharp thorn.

NOTES

uprooted? *Meiri* explains the Gemara's doubt about the second case as follows: If the husband's estate appreciated, do we say that it is considered as if there had already been a dinar surplus at the time of his death, or do we say that this surplus is like property that was due to the husband, which, as the Mishnah taught, is not considered as being in his possession? (See also *Talmid HaRashba*.)

וְנִתְמַעֲטוּ And they depreciated. Most of the Rishonim understand that the Gemara is discussing an estate that depreciated, so that it no longer sufficed to cover the two ketubah settlements and leave the dinar surplus. *Rivan* suggests that it might have become known that some of the assets of the estate had not actually belonged to the husband. But most authorities (*Ramban, Ra'ah,* and others) reject this explanation, arguing that in this case the estate did not depreciate. Rather the initial appraisal of the estate was in error.

כָּךְ מוּעָטִין, וְנִתְרַבּוּ So too if they were insufficient, and their value appreciated. Our commentary follows *Rashi, Rabbenu Ḥananel, Rambam,* and most Rishonim. In their

HALAKHAH

of his wives' two settlements by at least a dinar, the enactment of *ketubat benin dikhrin* does not apply. An appraisal is made of the estate at the time of the man's death, even if the value of the property increased or decreased later," following Rav Naḥman. *Rema* writes that this only applies if the estate decreased in value after the man's death, but if it is discovered that some of the assets did not belong to the deceased, the estate is reassessed (following *Ran,* and others). (*Rambam, Sefer Nashim, Hilkhot Ishut* 19:5; *Shulḥan Arukh, Even HaEzer* 111:5.)

TRANSLATION AND COMMENTARY

סימן [1]The Gemara now presents a series of related cases introduced by **mnemonic: A thousand, one hundred, mitzvah, ketubah, Ya'akov, obligated himself** with a loan, **his fields, opponent, protests.**

הַהוּא גַּבְרָא [2]The first case involves **a certain man who owed a thousand zuz.** [3]This man **had two mansions, one** of which **he sold for five hundred zuz, and the second** of which he sold to the same purchaser **for** another **five hundred zuz.** When the debtor failed to repay his debt, the creditor took steps to recover the debt from the debtor's property. A debt established by a deed provides the creditor with a lien on all of the debtor's property, allowing him to exact payment of the debt from that property even if it had subsequently been sold to a third party — provided that the debtor has no other free property to cover the debt. [4]Thus, **the creditor came** to the purchaser of the mortgaged property **and seized one of** the mansions from him as partial satisfaction of the debt. [5]When the creditor was about **to seize the other** mansion to cover the remainder, [6]the purchaser of the mansions **took a thousand zuz, went to** the creditor, [7]**and said to him: "If** the mansion you have already taken **is worth a thousand zuz to you, very well.** Keep it as payment for the entire debt, and I will keep the other mansion for myself. [8]**If** you are **not** willing to accept one mansion in lieu of a thousand zuz, **take the thousand zuz** in cash, return the first mansion **and be off!"** The purchaser of mortgaged property has the right to pay the debt in cash and keep the property (see *Bava Metzia* 15b). Here the purchaser wants to retain both mansions by paying back the entire debt. No matter what financial arrangement the buyer reaches with the creditor, the original borrower must still pay the buyer back.

[1]סִימָן: אֶלֶף, וּמֵאָה, מִצְוָה, בִּכְתוּבָּה, יַעֲקֹב, זָקַף, שְׂדוֹתָיו, בִּדְבָרִים, עֲסִיקִין.
[2]הַהוּא גַּבְרָא דַּהֲווּ מַסְּקִי בֵּיהּ אַלְפָּא זוּזֵי. [3]הֲווּ לֵיהּ תְּרֵי אַפַּדְנֵי. זַבְּינְהוּ חֲדָא בַּחֲמֵשׁ מְאָה וַחֲדָא בַּחֲמֵשׁ מְאָה. [4]אֲתָא בַּעַל חוֹב טְרַפָא לַחֲדָא מִינַּיְיהוּ. [5]הֲדַר קָטָרֵיף לְאִידָךְ. [6]שְׁקַל אַלְפָּא זוּזֵי וְקָא אָזֵיל לְגַבֵּיהּ, [7]אֲמַר לֵיהּ: "אִי שָׁוְיָא לָךְ אַלְפָּא זוּזֵי, לְחַיֵּי, [8]וְאִי לָא, שְׁקִיל אַלְפָּא זוּזֵי וְאִיסְתַּלֵּק"!

LITERAL TRANSLATION

[1]Mnemonic: A thousand, one hundred, mitzvah, ketubah, Ya'akov, obligated himself [with a loan], his fields, opponent, protests.

[2]A certain man owed a thousand zuz. [3]He had two mansions. He sold one for five hundred [zuz] and the other for five hundred [zuz]. [4]The creditor came and seized one of them. [5]Then he came back [and wanted] to seize the other. [6][The purchaser] took a thousand zuz and went to him, [7][and] said to him: "If it is worth a thousand zuz to you, very well. [8]But if not, take the thousand zuz, and be off!"

RASHI

מסקי ביה — נושים בו. שקל — לוקח, אלפא זוזי. אי שויא לך — הסיא חדא, לקבלה בחוב שלך ותניח לי את זו. ואיסתלק — מתרוייהו.

NOTES

view, we consider the estate to have been transferred to the heirs at the time of the husband's death, whether it increases or decreases in value. Since, at the time of the husband's death, the estate did not then cover the two ketubah settlements with a dinar surplus, the enactment of *ketubat benin dikhrin* does not apply. Thus all the heirs acquire an equal share of their father's estate. *Tosafot* also cite the opposite interpretation in the name of *Ri*; who maintains that each set of sons acquire their respective mothers' ketubah settlements, regardless of whether the estate rose or fell in value. According to this explanation, the phrase "the heirs acquired them" has the same meaning in both cases. (See also *Rivan*.)

טְרַפָא לַחֲדָא **He seized one.** *Ritva* points out in the case discussed by the Gemara, the creditor did not actually seize one of the mansions from the purchaser. For in such a case the purchaser cannot demand that the creditor return the property to him in exchange for money. Rather, in the case under discussion, the creditor came with a *tirpa*, the court document authorizing him to seize property from the purchaser, and he wished to seize first one mansion and then the other. Our commentary follows *Meiri*, who explains the Gemara in its more literal sense, that the property was actually seized. However, by overvaluing its worth, the purchaser is able to recover the mansion from the creditor. Since the debt was not yet fully restored, the purchaser caused the creditor no damage.

HALAKHAH

הַהוּא גַּבְרָא דַּהֲווּ מַסְּקִי **A certain man owed.** "If someone bought two fields, each one for a maneh, and the seller owed his creditor two hundred dinars, and the creditor seized one of the fields purchased by the buyer as partial satisfaction of the debt owed him, and the creditor then came to seize the second field for that part of his debt which was still outstanding, the buyer can tell the creditor to accept the first field as full payment for the debt owed him, or else accept two hundred dinars in cash. If the creditor accepted the first field as full payment for the debt owed him, the buyer can only recover one maneh from the seller (the debtor), following Rav Avira. *Rema* notes that this ruling only applies if one person bought the two fields. But if the two fields were purchased by two different

SAGES

רָבִינָא Ravina. A Babylonian Amora of the fifth and sixth generations. See *Ketubot,* Part II, p. 18.

TRANSLATION AND COMMENTARY

סָבַר [1]**Rami bar Ḥama thought to say** that **this** case **is** similar to that of **our Mishnah,** where we learned: [2]"**If** the father's estate was only large enough to cover the two ketubah settlements, but **the sons** inheriting the larger ketubah **said:** '[3]**We will overvalue our father's property at a dinar more** than its actual market value.' As explained earlier, if a surplus of one dinar is not left after the ketubah settlements are paid, the sons all inherit an equal share of the estate. By retroactively overvaluing the estate by one dinar, the sons whose mother's ketubah settlement was larger manage to gain a larger share of their father's estate. This legal fiction is not permitted. Similarly, we should not allow the purchaser to overvalue property that has already come into the creditor's possession, enabling him to pay the whole debt and retrieve the seized property.

אֲמַר לֵיהּ [4]**Rava said to** Rami bar Hama: But **are** the two cases really **the same?** [5]**There, the sons** of the woman with the smaller ketubah would **suffer a loss** if the father's estate were assessed at more than its value, for they would then receive their mother's settlement rather than an equal share in their father's estate. [6]But **here, would** the creditor **suffer a loss** if the property purchased from the debtor were assessed at more than its value? [7]Surely the creditor **gave** the debtor **a thousand** zuz when he extended him a loan, **and** now **he takes a thousand** zuz from the purchaser in payment of the debt! In any event, the borrower must still compensate the purchaser for his loss.

וְטִירְפָּא [8]The Gemara asks: If the creditor decided to accept the one mansion as full payment of the thousand zuz debt, **for what sum should** the court **write** the purchaser **a *tirpa*,** the document permitting a purchaser allowing to recover the value of the seized property from the debtor? Should the *tirpa* given to this purchaser state that the creditor seized property valued at a thousand zuz, for the creditor accepted the property as full payment of the thousand-zuz debt? Or should it state that the creditor seized property valued at five hundred zuz, for that is the amount that the purchaser actually paid for the property? [9]**Ravina said:** The *tirpa* should be written **for a thousand** zuz. [10]**Rav Avira said:** It should be written **for five hundred** zuz.

[1]סָבַר רָמִי בַּר חָמָא לְמֵימַר: הַיְינוּ מַתְנִיתִין: [2]״אִם אָמְרוּ יְתוֹמִים: [3]׳הֲרֵי אָנוּ מַעֲלִין עַל נִכְסֵי אָבִינוּ יָפֶה דִּינָר׳״.

[4]אֲמַר לֵיהּ רָבָא: מִי דָּמֵי? [5]הָתָם, אִית לְהוּ פְּסֵידָא לְיָתְמֵי; [6]הָכָא מִי אִית לֵיהּ פְּסֵידָא? [7]אַלְפָּא יָהֵיב, וְאַלְפָּא שָׁקֵיל.

[8]וְטִירְפָּא בְּכַמָּה כָּתְבִינַן? [9]רָבִינָא אֲמַר: בְּאַלְפָּא. [10]רַב עֲוִירָא אֲמַר: בַּחֲמֵשׁ מְאָה.

LITERAL TRANSLATION

[1]Rami bar Ḥama thought to say: This is our Mishnah: "[2]If the orphans said: '[3]We will overvalue our father's property by a dinar.'"

[4]Rava said to him: Are they the same? [5]There, [some of] the orphans have a loss; [6]here, does [the creditor] have a loss? [7]He gave a thousand, and he takes a thousand.

[8]And for how much do we write the *tirpa*? [9]Ravina said: For a thousand. [10]Rav Avira said: For five hundred.

RASHI

היינו מתניתין – ממתניתין מלינן למיגמר האי דינא, דלא מצי טעין ליה האי לוקח הכי, שהיה מעלה על דמיה. **אית להו פסידא** – לבני כתובה הקטנה בהעלותן של אלו. **וטירפא בכמה כתבינן** – הרי לוקח זה מכרה לנושה באלף זוז לפלותו מחובו, וחוזר לבית דין לכתוב לו שטר טירפא על זה שמכרה לו באחריות. והרי טרפוה ממנו בדמי אלף זוז שהיה מחויב, בכמה כתבינן ליה טירפא? באלפא כשיעור החוב, או בחמש מאה, שהרי כך קנאה ממנו?

NOTES

וְטִירְפָּא בְּכַמָּה כָּתְבִינַן And for how much do we write the *tirpa*. The Rishonim ask: If the creditor seized property from the purchaser, it means that his debtor did not have any free land from which his debt could have been satisfied. What then can the purchaser do with his *tirpa*? It cannot be argued that the debtor may indeed have had other free assets, but he had designated the mansions as a hypothec, specifying that the creditor may exact payment only from the mansions and no other landed property, free property. For in such a case the purchaser could surely not have requested that the creditor allow him to keep the property in exchange for money. Rather, in the case under discussion, at the time of the sale, the debtor subjected the sale to a lien not only on the property already in his possession, but also on property that he might purchase in the future. Therefore, the purchaser needs the *tirpa* document to seize any property that the debtor may buy in the future (*Ramban, Ritva,* and others).

HALAKHAH

buyers, one buyer cannot say to the creditor that he must accept the field which he had seized from the other buyer as full payment for the debt owed him, or else accept payment for the entire debt in cash, for the creditor can argue that the one buyer has no standing regarding the field which he had seized from the other." (*Rambam, Sefer Mishpatim, Hilkhot Malveh VeLoveh* 18:9; *Shulḥan Arukh, Ḥoshen Mishpat* 114:3.)

TRANSLATION AND COMMENTARY

וְהִלְכְתָא [1]**The law is** that in such a case the *tirpa* is written **for five hundred** zuz. The debtor still owes the original creditor five hundred zuz. If he also had to pay a thousand zuz to the buyer, he would be severely disadvantaged.

הַהוּא גַּבְרָא [2]The Gemara continues with an almost identical story: **A certain man owed a hundred zuz.** [3]This man **had two small parcels of land,** [4]**one** of which **he sold for fifty zuz, and the second** of which he sold to the same purchaser **for** another **fifty zuz.** When the debtor failed to repay his debt, and the creditor took steps to recover the debt from the debtor's property over which he exercised a lien. [5]**The creditor came** to the purchaser of the mortgaged property **and seized one of** the parcels of land in partial satisfaction of the debt. [6]When the creditor was about **to seize the other** parcel of land to cover the remainder, [7]the purchaser **took a hundred zuz, went to** the creditor, [8]**and said to him: "If** the parcel of land you have taken **is worth a hundred zuz to you, very well.** Keep it as payment for the entire debt, and I will keep the second parcel of land for myself. [9]**If** you are **not** willing to accept the one parcel of land in lieu of a hundred zuz, **take the hundred zuz** in cash that I am ready to offer you, return the first parcel of land, **and be off!"**

סָבַר רַב יוֹסֵף [10]**Rav Yosef thought to say** that **this** case **is** similar to that of **our Mishnah,** where we learned: [11]**"If** the father's estate was only large enough to cover the two ketubah settlements, but **the sons** inheriting the larger one **said:** 'We will overvalue our father's property at a dinar more than its actual market value.' Just as in the Mishnah we do not allow the sons to overvalue their father's estate to collect the larger settlement, here too we should not allow the purchaser to overvalue the property in the possession of the creditor, which would allow him to retrieve the seized parcel of land.

אֲמַר לֵיהּ [12]**Abaye said to** Rav Yosef: But **are** the two cases really **the same?** [13]**There, the sons** of the woman with the smaller settlement would **suffer a loss** if the father's estate were assessed at more than its value, for they would then receive their mother's ketubah rather than a share of their father's estate equal to that of their half-brothers. [14]But **here, what loss would** the creditor **suffer?**

מְאָה יָהֵיב [15]Surely the creditor **gave** the debtor **a hundred** zuz when he extended him a loan, **and** now **he takes a hundred** zuz from the purchaser as payment of the debt!

[1]וְהִלְכְתָא: בְּחָמֵשׁ מְאָה.
[2]הַהוּא גַּבְרָא דַּהֲווּ מַסְּקֵי בֵּיהּ מְאָה זוּזֵי. [3]הֲווּ לֵיהּ תְּרֵי קְטִינֵי דְאַרְעָא. [4]חַד זַבִּינְהוּ בְּחַמְשִׁין, וְחַד בְּחַמְשִׁין. [5]אֲתָא בַּעַל חוֹב טָרְפָא לְחַד מִינַּיְיהוּ. [6]הֲדַר אֲתָא וְקָטָרֵיף לְאִידָךְ. [7]שְׁקַל מְאָה זוּזֵי וְקָאָזֵיל לְגַבֵּיהּ, [8]וַאֲמַר לֵיהּ: "אִי שָׁוְיָא לָךְ מְאָה זוּזֵי, לְחַיֵּי. [9]וְאִי לָא, שְׁקוֹל מְאָה זוּזֵי, וְאִיסְתַּלֵּק"!
[10]סָבַר רַב יוֹסֵף לְמֵימַר: הַיְינוּ מַתְנִיתִין: [11]"אִם אָמְרוּ יְתוֹמִים כו׳".
[12]אֲמַר לֵיהּ אַבַּיֵי: מִי דָּמֵי? [13]הָתָם, אִית לְהוּ פְּסֵידָא לְיָתְמֵי; [14]הָכָא, מַאי פְּסֵידָא אִית לֵיהּ? [15]מְאָה יָהֵיב, מְאָה שָׁקֵיל.

LITERAL TRANSLATION

[1]And the law is: For five hundred.

[2]A certain man owed a hundred zuz. [3]He had two small parcels of land. [4]One he sold for fifty [zuz], and the other for fifty [zuz]. [5]The creditor came and seized one of them. [6]He came back [and wanted] to seize the other. [7][The purchaser] took a hundred zuz and went to him, [8]and said to him: "If it is worth a hundred zuz to you, very well. [9]But if not, take the hundred zuz, and be off!"

[10]Rav Yosef thought to say: This is our Mishnah: [11]"If the orphans said, etc."

[12]Abaye said to him: Are they the same? [13]There, [some of] the orphans have a loss; [14]here, what loss does [the creditor] have?

[15]He gave a hundred, [and] he takes a hundred.

RASHI

קטיני דארעא – שדות קטנות.

NOTES

וְהִלְכְתָא: בְּחָמֵשׁ מְאָה **And the law is: For five hundred.** Most Rishonim understand that the creditor decided to accept the one mansion as full payment of the thousand zuz debt. (See *Rivan* and *Ramban*, who explain that the debtor was apparently in desperate need of money, and so he sold the property to the buyer at half of its true value. Or alternatively, the creditor wanted to keep the mansion, even if this meant waiving the remainder of his loan.) The question now arises whether the buyer should be given a *tirpa* for five hundred zuz, for the amount that he had actually paid for the property, or should he be given a *tirpa* for a thousand zuz, the price that the creditor accepted for keeping the property (see *Rid*)?

תְּרֵי קְטִינֵי דְאַרְעָא **Two small parcels of land.** Most of the Rishonim understand that the debtor sold the two mansions or the two small parcels of land to the same purchaser. But if he sold them to two different people, the second purchaser cannot remove the creditor from both properties

TRANSLATION AND COMMENTARY

וְטִירְפָּא [1]As in the first case, the Gemara asks: If the creditor decided to accept the one small parcel of land as full payment of the hundred zuz debt, **for** what sum **does** the court **write** the purchaser **a** ***tirpa,*** the document enabling the purchaser to recover the value of the seized property from the creditor? Should the *tirpa* state that the creditor seized property in the value of a hundred zuz? Or should it state that the creditor seized property in the value of fifty zuz? [2]**Ravina said:** The ***tirpa*** should be written **for a hundred** zuz. [3]**Rav Avira said:** It should be written **for fifty** zuz.

וְהִלְכְתָא [4]The Gemara sums up with a practical ruling: **The law is** that in such a case the ***tirpa*** is written **for fifty** zuz.

הַהוּא גַּבְרָא [5]In a somewhat similar case, **a certain man owed a hundred zuz.** [6]The debtor **died, and left** his heirs **a small parcel of land that was worth** only **fifty zuz.** Since the debts of the deceased are recoverable from the land in his estate, [7]**the creditor came to seize** that small parcel of land as partial satisfaction of the debt. [8]**The** debtor's **heirs** wanted to keep the land, and so they **went** to the creditor **and** paid **him fifty zuz,** the value of the land, for the heirs have the right to pay in cash rather than surrender the property over which the creditor exercises a lien. But the creditor later claimed that the heirs had given him the fifty zuz as payment of their father's remaining debt. [9]So **he** came **again to seize** the small parcel of land. [10]The heirs **came before Abaye** to obtain a ruling on the matter, [11]and he **said to them: It is a meritorious deed for the sons** of the deceased **to repay their father's debts** from the assets which they inherited from him, even from moveable property. [12]Therefore, **with that first** payment of **money** we assume that **you** wished to **perform the meritorious deed** of repaying your father's debt. And since you repaid only part of it, the lien which your father's creditor exercises is still in effect. [13]Thus **when he** comes **now to seize** that small parcel of land again, **he** comes **by right to seize** that property. The Gemara adds the following

[1]וְטִירְפָּא בְּכַמָּה כָּתְבִינַן? [2]רָבִינָא אֲמַר: בְּמֵאָה. [3]רַב עֲוִירָא אֲמַר: בְּחַמְשִׁין. [4]וְהִלְכְתָא: בְּחַמְשִׁין. [5]הַהוּא גַּבְרָא דְּהָווּ מַסְּקֵי בֵּיהּ מֵאָה זוּזֵי. [6]שְׁכִיב, שְׁבַק קְטִינָא דְּאַרְעָא דַּהֲוָה שָׁוְיָא חַמְשִׁין זוּזֵי. [7]אֲתָא בַּעַל חוֹב וְקָטָרֵיף לֵיהּ. [8]אֲזוּל יָתְמֵי יְהַבוּ לֵיהּ חַמְשִׁין זוּזֵי. [9]הֲדַר קָטָרֵיף לָהּ. [10]אֲתוּ לְקַמֵּיהּ דְּאַבַּיֵי, [11]אֲמַר לְהֶן: מִצְוָה עַל הַיְּתוֹמִים לִפְרוֹעַ חוֹב אֲבִיהֶן. [12]הָנֵי קַמָּאֵי מִצְוָה עֲבַדִיתוּ. [13]הָשְׁתָּא כִּי טָרֵיף, בְּדִין קָטָרֵיף.

LITERAL TRANSLATION

[1]And for how much do we write the *tirpa*? [2]Ravina said: For a hundred. [3]Rav Avira said: For fifty. [4]And the law is: For fifty.

[5]A certain man owed a hundred zuz. [6]He died, [and] left a small parcel of land that was worth fifty zuz. [7]The creditor came and seized it. [8]The orphans went [and] gave him fifty zuz. [9]He seized it again. [10]They came before Abaye, [11][who] said to them: It is a meritorious deed for the orphans to repay their father's debt. [12][With] that first [money] you performed a meritorious deed. [13]Now when he seizes, he seizes by right.

RASHI

מצוה על היתומים לפרוע חוב אביהן – משום כבוד אביהן. אלא שאין לבית דין לכופן על כך, דלאו מצות עשה מפורשת היא כסוכה וכלולב, אלא מצוה בעלמא, דרבנן. **בדין קא טריף** – שנכסי הלוה נשתעבדו לו.

NOTES

by paying him off. However, *Meiri* suggests that the same law applies if the debtor sold the two properties to two different buyers. According to him, the second story reads: "To one he sold for fifty [zuz], and to the other for fifty [zuz]." This also resolves the difficulty raised by *Shittah Mekubbetzet* — what does the case of the two parcels of land add to the case of the two mansions? According to *Meiri,* in the first story case, the debtor sold the two properties to a single buyer, whereas in the second case, he sold the two properties to two different people.

הָנֵי קַמָּאֵי מִצְוָה עֲבַדִיתוּ **With the first money you performed a meritorious deed.** According to *Rashi,* it is meritorious deed for the sons of the deceased to pay their father's debts as a show of respect to their late father. But this is only a moral duty, not a formal Rabbinic obligation, and the courts cannot compel them to pay the debts against their will. *Rabbenu Ḥananel* disagrees and says that just as a debtor is commanded to pay his debts, and the courts can compel him to do so, so too his heirs are commanded to repay his debts, and the courts can compel

HALAKHAH

שְׁבַק קְטִינָא דְּאַרְעָא **He left a small parcel of land.** "If the deceased owed his creditor two hundred dinars, but he left land that was worth only a hundred dinars,and when the creditor came to seize that property from his debtor's heirs as partial satisfaction of the debt, they gave him a hundred dinars' worth of the movable goods that their father had left them, the creditor can still seize the land as satisfaction of the rest of the debt, following Abaye. But if the heirs stated explicitly that they were paying the creditor for the field which he wished to seize from them, the creditor cannot seize the land for the rest of his debt," following the Gemara's conclusion (see *Sma, Shakh*). (*Rambam, Sefer Mishpatim, Hilkhot Malveh VeLoveh* 18:10; *Shulḥan Arukh, Ḥoshen Mishpat* 107:6.)

[1]וְלָא אֲמָרָן: דְּלָא אֲמַרוּ לֵיהּ: [2]הָנֵי חַמְשִׁין זוּזֵי דְּמֵי דְּאַרְעָא קְטִינָא. [3]אֲבָל אֲמַרוּ לֵיהּ: הָנֵי חַמְשִׁין זוּזֵי דְּמֵי אַרְעָא קְטִינָא, [4]סַלּוּקֵי סַלְקוּהּ.

[5]הַהוּא גַּבְרָא דְּזַבְּנָהּ לִכְתוּבָּתָהּ דְּאִימֵּיהּ בְּטוֹבַת הֲנָאָה, [6]וַאֲמַר לֵיהּ: אִי אָתְיָא אֵם וּמְעַרְעֲרָא,

LITERAL TRANSLATION

[1]And we only said this when [the orphans] did not say to him: [2]These fifty zuz are payment for the small parcel of land. [3]But if they said to him: These fifty zuz are payment for the small parcel of land, [4]they removed him.

[5]A certain man sold his mother's ketubah settlement for a small benefit (lit., "benefit of pleasure"), [6]and said to him: If Mother comes and protests [the sale],

RASHI

דלא אמרו ליה – כשפרעו את הראשונים. דמי קטינא – כשאר מכר, ולא כפריעת החוב. דזבנה לכתובתה דאימיה – שהיתה נשואה לאחר, ומכר כתובתה בחיי בעלה. בטובת הנאה – בדבר מועט, מפני שהוא ספק: שמא תמות וירשנה בעלה, או אפילו ימות בעלה בחייה – שמא ימות הבן בחייה, ולא תבא הזכות לידו, ואין ללוקח בה כלום, דלא היה זה שלומו. אמר ליה אי אתיא אימא וקא מערערא

TRANSLATION AND COMMENTARY

qualification to this ruling: [1]**We only say** that the payment made by the heirs does not cancel the lien on the inherited landed property **if** the heirs **did not say to** the creditor: [2]**These fifty zuz** that we are giving you **shall be** considered as **payment for the small parcel of land** that you came to seize from us. [3]**But if** the heirs **said to** the creditor when they paid him the money: **These fifty zuz shall be** considered as **payment for the small parcel of land** which you came to seize, [4]the lien is cancelled and the debtor **is sent away** without having any further claim to the property, though he is still owed fifty zuz.

הַהוּא גַּבְרָא [5]In a related case, **a certain man sold** the rights to **his mother's ketubah** settlement **for a benefit** of money. The woman had remarried, and her son sold the settlement that she would receive from her second husband if he predeceased her, and which the son would later inherit from her if she died before her second husband. He could only sell the settlement for a small sum, because of the speculative nature of this sale. Moreover, the son was acting here on his own initiative, and his mother still retained the right to sell her ketubah settlement to another buyer. When he sold him the ketubah settlement, [6]the son **said to** the buyer: **If** my **mother comes and protests** against the sale of her ketubah and sells it to

NOTES

them to do so. Legal authorities note that this commandment only applies if the sons inherited assets from their father, even if only movable goods. But if they did not inherit anything from their father, they are not required pay his debts from their own money.

דְּמֵי דְּאַרְעָא קְטִינָא Payment for the small parcel of land. *Rashi* explains that if the heirs said to the creditor: "These fifty zuz shall be considered as payment for the land," we see the fifty zuz as purchase money for the land, and not as a repayment of their father's debt. The Rishonim infer from this that if a later creditor of their father came to seize the property from the heirs, he cannot do so, for the heir already bought the property from the earlier creditor and it is no longer part of the estate (see also Jerusalem Talmud, *Ketubot* 10:6). So too if an earlier creditor seized the property from the heirs. They can recover his purchase money from the later creditor from whom he bought it (see *Ramban, Ritva,* and others).

זַבְּנָהּ לִכְתוּבָּתָהּ דְּאִימֵּיהּ He sold his mother's ketubah settlement. The Rishonim offer different explanations of this case. According to *Rashi,* the son sold the rights to the settlement that his mother would receive from her second husband if he predeceased her, and which the son would later inherit from her if she dies before her husband. He could not sell the settlement for the full amount stated in the ketubah deed, because of the speculative nature of this sale. The Rishonim point out a difficulty with this explanation: A person cannot sell something that has not yet come into existence, or has not yet come into his possession. Thus, how could someone sell his mother's ketubah settlement before he had any control over it? The seller certainly must return the purchase money to the buyer. *Rabbenu Tam* (cited by *Tosafot*) concludes from this that when the Gemara states elsewhere (*Bava Metzia* 16a) that if a person sold "what he will inherit from his father," the sale is not valid, because the seller did not specify the specific property that he was to inherit. But if he sold "this field which he will inherit from his father," the sale is indeed valid. Here too, the son's sale of his mother's ketubah settlement before it actually came into his possession is a valid sale (see also *Rid*). *Rashi* also offers a second explanation, according to which we are dealing here with a case in which the son sold property that had been designated by his father for the payment of his mother's

HALAKHAH

דְּזַבְּנָהּ לִכְתוּבָּתָהּ דְּאִימֵּיהּ בְּטוֹבַת הֲנָאָה He sold his mother's ketubah settlement for a benefit. "If someone sold his mother's ketubah settlement during his father's lifetime, so that if his father dies first, and then his mother, and he then inherits her ketubah settlement, the buyer will be entitled to collect it. If the son stipulated with the buyer that if his mother protests against the sale of her ketubah settlement, he will not restore the purchase money to him, and the mother died without having protested against the sale, the son cannot protest against the sale in place of his mother, for he surely accepted responsibility for his own protest," following Rava. (*Shulḥan Arukh, Even HaEzer* 105:7.)

BACKGROUND

רְאוּבֵן וְשִׁמְעוֹן Reuven and Shimon. The Sages used the names of Jacobs sons as standard names, like John Doe, instead of using more general expressions like "a man," "another man," etc. In these cases the names stand for anyone and have no particular significance except convenience. But in some cases these names, as well as those of the Patriarchs and Matriarchs, are used to indicate people who are related to each other. For example, three brothers might be called Reuven, Shimon, and Levi, and the father might be called Jacob, etc.

[1]לָא מְפַצֵּינָא לָךְ. [2]שְׁכִיבָא אִימֵּיהּ וְלָא אִיעַרְעֲרָא, [3]וַאֲתָא אִיהוּ וְקָא מְעַרְעֵר. [4]סָבַר רָמִי בַּר חָמָא לְמֵימַר: אִיהוּ בִּמְקוֹם אִימֵּיהּ קָאֵי. [5]אֲמַר לֵיהּ רָבָא: נְהִי דְּאַחֲרָיוּת דִּידָהּ לָא קַבֵּיל עֲלֵיהּ, [6]אַחֲרָיוּת דִּידֵיהּ מִי לָא קַבֵּיל?

[7]אֲמַר רָמִי בַּר חָמָא: רְאוּבֵן שֶׁמָּכַר שָׂדֶה לְשִׁמְעוֹן שֶׁלֹּא בְּאַחֲרָיוּת, [8]וַאֲתָא שִׁמְעוֹן וּמְכָרָהּ לִרְאוּבֵן בְּאַחֲרָיוּת [92A] [9]וַאֲתָא בַּעַל חוֹב דִּרְאוּבֵן

LITERAL TRANSLATION

[1]I will not compensate you. [2]His mother died and did not protest, [3]but [the son] came and protested. [4]Rami bar Ḥama thought to say: He stands in his mother's place. [5]Rava said to him: Granted that he did not accept responsibility upon himself for her [protest], [6][but] did he not accept responsibility for his own [protest]?

[7]Rami bar Ḥama said: [If] Reuven sold a field to Shimon without a guarantee, [8]and Shimon came and sold it [back] to Reuven with a guarantee, [92A] [9]and Reuven's creditor

TRANSLATION AND COMMENTARY

someone else, [1]**I will not restore the** purchase **money to you,** for I do not accept any responsibility regarding this sale. [2]As it turned out, after his mother's second husband died, **she,** too, **died without having protested** against the sale, [3]**but the son** himself then **came and protested** against it. He claimed that since he stands in his mother's stead, he now has the right to protest against the sale and keep his mother's ketubah settlement for himself. He further argued that he is not required to restore the purchase money to the buyer, for he sold him the ketubah without accepting any responsibility regarding the sale. [4]**Rami bar Ḥama thought to say** that the son **stands in his mother's place,** and so he may cancel the sale without having to pay compensation. [5]**Rava said to him: Granted that** the son **did not accept responsibility upon himself for his mother's protest,** [6]**but** is it reasonable to say that he **did he not** even **accept responsibility for his own protest?** His mother's possible protest was not under his control, but his own actions are.

אֲמַר [7]In a related matter: **Rami bar Ḥama said: If Reuven sold a field to Shimon without a guarantee,** with no obligation to restore the purchase money if a creditor seized the property, nor did he mortgage other property to the buyer as security for the sale — [8]**and** then **Shimon came and sold it back to Reuven with a guarantee** for the sale, agreeing to restore the purchase money if the property were seized, and mortgaging his other property as security, [92A] [9]**and** then **Reuven's creditor came and**

RASHI

לא מפצינא לך — והמעות לא אחזיר לך, דשלא באחריות אני מוכר לך. **אתא איהו וקא מערער** — לומר: אני תחת אמי עומד, ואטלנו. ואף המעות לא אחזיר — דשלא באחריות סבירת וקבילת. **אחריות דנפשיה** — אם יצא הוא ויערער — דין הוא שיחזיר לו מעותיו. ונהי נמי דחוזר במכירת הקרקע, דאין אדם מקנה דבר שלא זכה בו, כדתניא (בבא מציעא טז,א): מה שאירש מאבא מכור לך — לא אמר כלום. והא לא דמיא לגוזל שדה ומכרה, וחזר ולקחה מבעלים הראשונים, דקיימא לן בה (בבא מציעא טו,ב): מה מכר ראשון לשני — כל זכות שתבא לידו. דהתם — לקחה דוקא, דטרח אבתרה וזבנה, כי היכי דליקום בהימנותיה עם לוקח. אבל נפלה זו בירושה — אמרינן התם: ירושה ממילא הוה, ולא טרח למיקם בהימנותיה, וחוזר במכירתו ומחזיר המעות. לשון אחר: דזבנה לכתובתה דאימיה בטובת הנאה — שדה שייחד אביו לאמו לכתובתה, ומת, ונפלו נכסים לפני זה. וכל זמן שלא עמדה בדין, אם מכרה זה — המכר קיים, ואינו יכול לחזור, שהרי יורש הוא, וכל הנכסים לפניו — אלא שחייב לתת כתובה לאמו כשתתבענו. ועל שדה זו שעבודה מוטל, והיא יכולה לטורפה מיד הלוקח. ומשום דאמר ליה האי: אי אתיא אמי ומערערא — לא מפצינא לך ותפסיד מעותיך, לא מכרה אלא בדבר מועט. **שלא באחריות** — כל מי שיטרפנה מידך, אפילו בדין — לא אחזיר לך המעות. **ומכרה לראובן** — בעלים הראשונים. **באחריות** — שכל מי שיטרפנה בדין יפצנה לו. **ואתא בעל חוב דראובן** — שהיה שטרו קודם למכירה ראשונה שמכרה ראובן לשמעון. ואילו בא ומצאה ביד שמעון — הכי נמי הוה טריף לה.

NOTES

ketubah. The father died, and that property along with the rest of the father's estate passed into the son's hands as his inheritance. Thus, the son could sell the property, but since it was mortgaged to his mother's ketubah settlement, she could still seize the property from the purchaser. Since the son did not want to accept responsibility for the sale, he could only sell the property for a small amount of money, and not its true value (see also *Ra'avad, Ra'ah, Ritva,* and *Meiri*). *Rav Hai Gaon* proposes a different explanation: The woman was dying, and her son sold her ketubah settlement in order to cover her funeral expenses. We learned elsewhere (*Bava Metzia* 16a) that in such a case, the sale is valid. But the son stipulated with the buyer that if his mother recovered, and she objected to the sale, he would not return the purchase money to him. The mother did recover and did not object to the sale, but she later died. The son then objected to the sale. Thus, the question arose as to whether the son was obligated to compensate the buyer for the money that he had paid for the ketubah settlement.

אַחֲרָיוּת דִּידֵיהּ מִי לָא קַבֵּיל But did he not accept responsibility for his own protest. Some commentators have inferred from this passage that even if a person stated explicitly that he was selling property without accepting any responsibility for the sale, he is nevertheless responsible for any loss that he himself may later cause the buyer. But the

TRANSLATION AND COMMENTARY

seized the field **from him** — the creditor's lien on the property predating Reuven's sale of the property to Shimon — [1]**the law is that Shimon must go and reimburse** Reuven, for he sold him the field with a guarantee, but Reuven is not required to give Shimon anything, for he sold him the field without any guarantee.

אָמַר לֵיהּ רָבָא [2]**Rava said to** Rami bar Ḥama: **Granted that** Shimon **accepted upon himself the responsibility** of restoring the purchase money to Reuven if the field is seized by a creditor as payment **for a debt** incurred by Shimon himself, or by **others,** who may have owned the field before it first entered Reuven's possession, and their creditors had a lien on it. [3]**But did** Shimon **accept upon himself the responsibility** of restoring the purchase money to Reuven in the event that the field is seized by a creditor as payment **for a debt** incurred by Reuven **himself?** Thus, Shimon is not required to compensate Reuven if the field which he sold him is confiscated by Reuven's own creditor.

וּמוֹדֶה רָבָא [4]The Gemara now notes that **Rava agrees** with Rami bar Ḥama **that if Reuven inherited a field from** his father **Ya'akov, and** then **sold it to Shimon without a guarantee** protecting him from seizure by creditors, [5]**and** then **Shimon came and sold** the field back **to Reuven with a guarantee** against seizure, [6]**and** then **Ya'akov's creditor came and seized** the field **from** Reuven, [7]**the law is that Shimon must go and restore**

וְקָטָרֵיף לֵיהּ מִינֵּיהּ, [1]דִּינָא הוּא דְּאָזֵיל שִׁמְעוֹן וּמְפַצֵּי לֵיהּ.
[2]אֲמַר לֵיהּ רָבָא: נְהִי דְּאַחֲרָיוּת דְּעָלְמָא קַבֵּיל עֲלֵיהּ, [3]אַחֲרָיוּת דְּנַפְשֵׁיהּ מִי קַבֵּיל עֲלֵיהּ?
[4]וּמוֹדֶה רָבָא, בִּרְאוּבֵן שֶׁיָּרַשׁ שָׂדֶה מִיַּעֲקֹב וּמְכָרָהּ לְשִׁמְעוֹן שֶׁלֹּא בְּאַחֲרָיוּת, [5]וַאֲתָא שִׁמְעוֹן וּמְכָרָהּ לִרְאוּבֵן בְּאַחֲרָיוּת, [6]וַאֲתָא בַּעַל חוֹב דְּיַעֲקֹב וְקָטָרֵיף לֵיהּ מִינֵּיהּ, [7]דִּינָא הוּא,

LITERAL TRANSLATION

came and seized it from him, [1]the law is that Shimon must go and compensate him.

[2]Rava said to him: Granted that he accepted upon himself responsibility for [debts of] others, [3][but] did he accept upon himself responsibility for [Reuven's] own [debts]?

[4]But Rava agrees [that if] Reuven inherited a field from Ya'akov, and sold it to Shimon without a guarantee, [5]and Shimon came and sold it [back] to Reuven with guarantee, [6]and Ya'akov's creditor came and seized it from him, [7]the law is

RASHI

דינא הוא דאזיל שמעון ומפצי ליה — כשם שאילו מכרה שמעון זה לאיש אחר באחריות, ובא בעל חוב דראובן וטורפה — היה שמעון מפלהו, ועל ראובן לא יוכל לחזור — שהרי שלא באחריות לקחה הימנו. כך כשמכרה לראובן עצמו — יפלה לו. **נהי דאחריות דעלמא** — כל העוררים עליה שלא מחמת ראובן, קיבל עליה שמעון. **אחריות דנפשיה** — ערעור הבא לו מחמת עצמו.

LANGUAGE

מְפַצֵּי Compensate. The meaning of the word פצה here is, "to rescue," as in the verse from Psalms 144,10: "Who delivers David, His servant, from the evil sword." Here, too, he saves his friend from the challenge. However, the meaning of the verb changed over time, to denote compensation for damage that has caused.

NOTES

Rishonim rejected this position, arguing that in this case the seller did accept responsibility for the sale (whether explicitly or implicitly). He merely excluded from this responsibility any loss to the buyer that might arise on account of his mother's protest (*Ritva, Rabbenu Crescas*).

אַחֲרָיוּת דְּנַפְשֵׁיהּ מִי קַבֵּיל עֲלֵיהּ **But did he accept responsibility upon himself for his own debts?** According to this reading (that of *Rashi* and the standard editions of the Talmud), Rava speaks of Shimon: Granted that Shimon accepted the responsibility of restoring the purchase money to Reuven if the field is seized by a creditor for a debt incurred by Shimon himself, or others, who held a lien on the property when it was still in the hands of the owner who originally sold it to Reuven. But did Shimon accept responsibility to restore the purchase money to Reuven if the field is seized by a creditor for a debt incurred by Reuven himself? *Rav Hai Gaon, Rif,* and others had a different reading: "Granted that he did not accept upon himself responsibility for [debts of] others, [but] did he not accept upon himself responsibility for his own [debts]?" According to this reading, Rava refers to Reuven: Even though Reuven did not accept responsibility for restoring the purchase money to Shimon if the property is seized for a debt incurred by somebody else, surely he accepted the responsibility of restoring the purchase money to Shimon if the property is seized for a debt which he himself incurred!

HALAKHAH

נְהִי דְּאַחֲרָיוּת **Granted that he accepted responsibility.** "If Reuven sold a field to Shimon without accepting responsibility for the sale, and then Shimon sold it back to Reuven with responsibility for the sale, and then Reuven's creditor seized the field from him, Reuven cannot recover the purchase price from Shimon. Even though Reuven did not accept responsibility for the sale, he nevertheless accepted upon himself responsibility regarding himself," following Rava. (*Rambam, Sefer Kinyan, Hilkhot Mekhirah* 19:10; *Shulḥan Arukh, Ḥoshen Mishpat* 226:2.)

וּמוֹדֶה רָבָא, בִּרְאוּבֵן שֶׁיָּרַשׁ שָׂדֶה **And Rava agrees that if Reuven inherited a field.** "If Reuven inherited a field from his father and sold it to Shimon without accepting responsibility for the sale, and then Shimon sold it back to him with responsibility for the sale, and then the creditor of Reuven's father came and seized the field from him, Reuven can recover the purchase price from Shimon, for, even according to Rava, Reuven had never accepted responsibility for seizure of the field by his father's creditors." (*Rambam, Sefer Kinyan, Hilkhot Mekhirah* 19:10; *Shulḥan Arukh, Ḥoshen Mishpat* 226:2.)

דְּאָזֵיל שִׁמְעוֹן וּמְפַצֵּי לֵיהּ מִינֵּיהּ. [1]מַאי טַעְמָא? [2]בַּעַל חוֹב דְּיַעֲקֹב כְּבַעַל חוֹב דְּעָלְמָא דָּמֵי.
[3]אֲמַר רָמִי בַּר חָמָא: רְאוּבֵן שֶׁמָּכַר שָׂדֶה לְשִׁמְעוֹן בְּאַחֲרָיוּת, וְזָקַף עָלָיו בְּמִלְוֶה, [4]וּמֵת רְאוּבֵן, וַאֲתָא בַּעַל חוֹב דִּרְאוּבֵן וְקָטָרֵיף לָהּ מִשִּׁמְעוֹן, [5]וּפַיְּיסֵיהּ בְּזוּזֵי — [6]דִּינָא הוּא דְּאָמְרִי לֵיהּ בְּנֵי רְאוּבֵן: אֲנַן מִטַּלְטְלֵי שְׁבַק אֲבוּן גַּבָּךְ, [7]וּמִטַּלְטְלֵי דְּיָתְמֵי לְבַעַל חוֹב לָא מִשְׁתַּעְבְּדִי.

LITERAL TRANSLATION

that Shimon must go reimburse to him for it. [1]What is the reason? [2]Ya'akov's creditor is considered like any other creditor.

[3]Rami bar Ḥama said: [If] Reuven sold a field to Shimon with a guarantee, and made [the payment] for him into a loan, [4]and Reuven died, and Reuven's creditor came to seize it from Shimon, [5]and he pacified him with money — [6]the law is that Reuven's sons can say to him: [Regarding] us, our father left movable goods with you, [7]and the movable goods of orphans are not mortgaged to the creditor.

TRANSLATION AND COMMENTARY

the purchase **money to** Reuven. [1]**What is the reason** that Rava agrees with Rami bar Ḥama in such a case? [2]Shimon must restore the purchase money to Reuven because **Ya'akov's creditor is considered like any other creditor** who may have had a lien on the property before it came into Reuven's possession.

אָמַר [3]The Gemara continues: **Rami bar Ḥama said: If Reuven sold a field to Shimon with a guarantee** against seizure, but Shimon did not have enough money to pay for his purchase, **and** so Reuven **converted** the purchase money **into a loan,** accepting a promissory note from Shimon. [4]**And Reuven** later **died, and** then **Reuven's creditor came to seize** the field **from Shimon** — the creditor's lien on the property predating Shimon's purchase of it — [5]**and** Shimon **settled with** the creditor by giving him the **money** that he had owed Reuven for the field. Reuven's heirs then demanded that Shimon repay the loan that he had received from their father, and Shimon countered that he had already paid that money to Reuven's creditor. [6]**The law is** as follows: **Reuven's heirs can say to** Shimon: The money that **our father left** with **you** as a loan is considered **movable property,** [7]**and the movable property** that **the sons** inherit from their father **is not mortgaged to the** father's **creditor.** Even though our father accepted responsibility for the sale, you cannot recover the purchase money from the money that you owed him. Being movable, that money is not mortgaged to cover your loss of the field. Thus, you must still repay the loan which you received from our father, and it is no concern of ours that you will end up paying twice to keep the field.

RASHI

כבעל חוב דעלמא דמי — המעורר עליה שלא מחמת ראובן, אלא מחמת מי שמכר לו לראובן תחלה. וכשם שאם לקחה ראובן מלוי ומכרה לשמעון, שאינו אחיו, שלא באחריות, וחזר שמעון ומכרה לראובן באחריות, ובא בעל חוב דלוי, הקודם לשטר מכירה ראשונה, וטורפה מראובן — צריך שמעון לפצותו, שהרי באחריות מכרה, והוא לקחה שלא באחריות. אף כשירשה ראובן מיעקב ומכרה, ובא בעל חוב דיעקב — יפצנו שמעון, ולא אמרינן דראובן כרעיה דאבוה הוא ואחריות דראובן לא קיבל עליה שמעון. **וזקפן עליו במלוה** — שלא נתן לו שמעון דמי השדה, אלא כתב לו שטר חוב עליהם. **ופייסיה בזוזי** — במעות דמי השדה שהיה חייב ליתמי, פייס את הנושה, בשביל ראובן, שבאחריות מכרה לו. **מטלטלי שביק אבון גבך** — והיה בעל חוב של אבינו מסולק ממנו, שאין לנו קרקע. והמעות לא היה לך ליתן, דמטלטלי דיתמי לא משתעבדי לבעל חוב. ועתה גם אתה אין לך לחזור עלינו על האחריות, לפי שאין לנו קרקע מאבינו.

NOTES

וְזָקַף עָלָיו בְּמִלְוֶה **And he made the payment for him into a loan.** According to some Rishonim, the phrase "he made the payment for him into a loan" (וְזָקַף עָלָיו בְּמִלְוֶה) is not to be meant literally, for the same law applies even if Reuven did not convert the purchase money into an official loan by accepting a promissory note from Shimon. The Gemara means only that Shimon did not yet pay Reuven for the field and still owes him the purchase money. Others, however, argue that the phrase is to be meant literally, for if Reuven did not convert the purchase money into a loan, and Shimon later paid Reuven's other debt, Reuven's heirs cannot require Shimon to repay the loan. For if the purchase money had not been officially converted into a loan, we assume that Shimon was allowed to retain the money as a pledge for the guarantee he received with his purchase of the property (see *Tosafot, Ra'ah,* and others).

HALAKHAH

שֶׁמָּכַר שָׂדֶה לְשִׁמְעוֹן בְּאַחֲרָיוּת וְזָקַף עָלָיו בְּמִלְוֶה **If he sold a field with responsibility, and made the payment into a loan.** "If Reuven sold a field to Shimon accepting responsibility for the sale, and Reuven converted the purchase money owed him by Shimon into a loan, and Reuven died, and his debtor came to seize the field from Shimon, and Shimon paid the creditor the money that Reuven had owed him, Reuven's heirs can still demand that Shimon repay the loan which he had received from their father," following Rami bar Ḥama. (*Rambam, Sefer Mishpatim, Hilkhot Malveh VeLoveh* 11:10; *Tur, Ḥoshen Mishpat* 101.)

[1]אֲמַר רָבָא: אִי פִּקֵּחַ אִידָךְ, מַגְבֵּי לְהוּ נִיהֲלַיְיהוּ אַרְעָא, [2]וַהֲדַר גָּבֵי לָהּ מִינַּיְיהוּ, [3]כְּרַב נַחְמָן. [4]דְּאָמַר רַב נַחְמָן אָמַר רַבָּה בַּר אֲבוּהּ: יְתוֹמִים שֶׁגָּבוּ קַרְקַע בְּחוֹבַת אֲבִיהֶן, [5]בַּעַל חוֹב חוֹזֵר וְגוֹבֶה אוֹתָהּ מֵהֶן. [6]אָמַר רַבָּה: רְאוּבֵן שֶׁמָּכַר כָּל שְׂדוֹתָיו לְשִׁמְעוֹן, [7]וְחָזַר שִׁמְעוֹן וּמָכַר שָׂדֶה אַחַת לְלֵוִי, [8]וַאֲתָא בַּעַל חוֹב דִּרְאוּבֵן — [9]רָצָה, מִזֶּה גּוֹבֶה, [10]רָצָה, מִזֶּה גּוֹבֶה.

LITERAL TRANSLATION

[1]Rava said: If the other one is clever, he will pay [the orphans] with land, [2]and then collect it [back] from them, [3]like Rav Naḥman. [4]For Rav Naḥman said in the name of Rabbah bar Avuha: [If] orphans collected land [as payment] for a debt owed to their father, [5]the [father's] creditor can come and collect it from them. [6]Rabbah said: [If] Reuven sold all his fields to Shimon, [7]and Shimon then sold one field to Levi, [8]and Reuven's creditor came — [9][if] he wishes, he may collect from this one, [10][if] he wishes, he may collect from that one.

TRANSLATION AND COMMENTARY

אֲמַר רָבָא [1]**Rava said: If** Shimon **is clever,** when Reuven's heirs come to collect the money from him **he will pay them with** the field in question or an equivalent plot of **land.** [2]He can **then collect it** back **from them,** due to the guarantee that Reuven had given him against seizure of the property. [3]This is **in accordance with** the opinion of **Rav Naḥman.** [4]**For Rav Naḥman said in the name of Rabbah bar Avuha:** If a man was owed money, and died, and his **heirs collected land as payment for the debt owed their father,** [5]**the father's** own **creditor can** then **come and collect** that land **from** the heirs, just as if they had inherited the land as part of their father's estate.

אָמַר רַבָּה [6]The Gemara continues with a related matter: **Rabbah said: If Reuven sold all of his fields to Shimon,** [7]**and then Shimon sold one** of those **fields to Levi,** [8]**and** then **Reuven's creditor came** to recover money that was owed him from property that had been sold to Shimon and Levi and mortgaged to the creditor as security for the loan, the creditor may decide from whom to seize the property. [9]**If he prefers, he may collect from this one,** [10]**if he prefers, he may collect from that one,** for he exercises a lien over all of Reuven's former property.

RASHI

מגבי להו ארעא — כשתבעוהו היתומים יפרע להן קרקע בדמי המעות. **והדר גבי מנייהו** בשביל אחריות אביהם. ולא מצו למימר: לא ירשנו קרקע זה מאבינו אלא לקחנוהו במעות, דאמר להו: על ידי שעבוד חוב אביכם באה לכם, והרי היא לכם כירושת קרקע שלקח אביכם בחייו. **בעל חוב** — של אביהם. **חוזר וגובה אותה מהם** — כאילו נפלה להם ממש בירושה. **כל שדותיו** — בשטר אחד. דבשני שטרות אין גובין מלוי, אלא אם כן לקח משמעון אותה שלקח מראובן באחרונה, דמצי אמר ליה: הניח לך שמעון מקום לגבות הימנו כשלקח את זו, ואין זו בשעבודך, דאין נפרעין מנכסים משועבדים במקום שיש בני חורין. **רצה מזה גובה רצה מזה גובה** — וכדמסיים ואזיל: דזבן לוי משמעון בינונית, דשעבוד בעל חוב עליה, ולא שבק בינונית משל ראובן אלל שמעון.

NOTES

מַגְבֵּי לְהוּ נִיהֲלַיְיהוּ אַרְעָא **He will pay them with land.** Many Rishonim ask: How can Shimon pay Reuven's heirs with land, when we learned earlier in the tractate (*Ketubot* 86a) that a debtor can not pay his debt with land if he has money? Some suggest therefore that Shimon did not have any money with which to pay Reuven's heirs. But then the wording of Rava's statement — "If the other one is clever" — is difficult. *Meiri* suggests that he might mean: If Shimon is clever, and he has no money, he will not sell land and pay his debt with money, but rather he will pay with land and then collect it back from Reuven's heirs.

Most Rishonim, however, understand that Shimon had money, and they explain the matter in different ways: *Rivan* explains that if Shimon is clever, he could say that he has no free money to pay the debt, for we only say that a debtor must sell his land and pay his debt with the proceeds if the debtor acted inappropriately, for example by claiming that the money in his possession belonged to a non-Jew (see *Ketubot* 86a). *Tosafot* suggest that a debtor is forbidden to pay his debt with land only if it makes no difference to him how he pays. But if paying with money would cause him a loss, as in this case, the debtor can indeed repay his debt with land, even if he has money. *Ra'avad* argues that a debtor is required to repay his debt with money only if he himself had received money from his creditor. But here the debtor received land, so he can also pay his debt with land. *Ritva* proposes that by right Shimon cannot pay his debt with land. But if he is clever he will persuade Reuven's heirs to accept land, and then collect it back from him, for not everybody is familiar with Rav Naḥman's ruling.

רָצָה מִזֶּה גּוֹבֶה **If he wishes, he collects from this one.** According to *Rashi,* Shimon bought all of Reuven's fields at once. But if Shimon bought Reuven's fields at various

HALAKHAH

אִי פִּקֵּחַ אִידָךְ **If the other one is clever.** "If Shimon is clever, then when Reuven's heirs come to collect the money which Shimon had owed their father, he will pay them with the land that he had purchased from Reuven, and then seize it back from them as repayment of the money he had given to Reuven's creditor," following Rabbah bar Avuha. (*Rambam, Sefer Mishpatim, Hilkhot Malveh VeLoveh* 11:10; *Tur, Ḥoshen Mishpat* 101.)

יְתוֹמִים שֶׁגָּבוּ קַרְקַע **If orphans collected land.** "If heirs collected land as payment of a debt owed their father, their father's creditor can come and collect that land from them as payment of a debt," following Rabbah bar Avuha. (*Rambam, Sefer Mishpatim, Hilkhot Malveh VeLoveh* 11:9; *Shulḥan Arukh, Ḥoshen Mishpat* 107:1.)

רָצָה מִזֶּה גּוֹבֶה **If he wishes, he collects from this one.** "If Reuven sold all his fields to Shimon in a single transaction,

¹וְלָא אֲמָרָן אֶלָּא דְּזַבְנָהּ בֵּינוֹנִית. ²אֲבָל זַבְנָהּ עִידִית וְזִבּוּרִית, ³מָצֵי אֲמַר לֵיהּ: ⁴לְהָכִי, טָרְחִי וּזְבִינִי אַרְעָא דְּלָא חַזְיָא לָךְ. ⁵וּבֵינוֹנִית נַמִי, ⁶לָא אֲמָרָן אֶלָּא דְּלָא שְׁבַק בֵּינוֹנִית דִּכְוָותָהּ [92B] ⁷אֲבָל שְׁבַק בֵּינוֹנִית דִּכְוָותָהּ, ⁸מָצֵי אֲמַר לֵיהּ: "הִנַּחְתִּי לְךָ מָקוֹם לִגְבּוֹת הֵימֶנּוּ".

LITERAL TRANSLATION

¹And we said [this] only if he sold land of medium quality. ²But if he sold land of the highest or the lowest quality, ³[Levi] can say to [the creditor]: ⁴Therefore, I made the effort and bought land that is not fit for you. ⁵And also [regarding] land of medium quality, ⁶we said [this] only if he did not leave land of intermediate quality like it. [92B] ⁷But if he left land of medium quality like it, ⁸[Levi] can say to him: "I left you a place from which to collect".

TRANSLATION AND COMMENTARY

¹However, **we only said** that the creditor may collect from Levi's purchased property **if** Shimon **sold him land of medium quality.** ²**But if** Shimon **sold** Levi **land of the highest quality or** land of **the lowest quality,** the creditor cannot collect from Levi, ³for Levi **can say to him:** "I wished to avoid having my land confiscated by a creditor. ⁴**Therefore I made the effort and bought land to which you are not entitled.**" All of a debtor's landed property is subject to a lien, that is exercised by claimants when the debtor cannot meet his obligations. If the land consists of fields of different quality, the following rules apply: Compensation for damage may be extracted from land of the highest quality; a wife's ketubah settlement may be collected even from land of the poorest quality; and all other obligations may be recovered only from land of medium quality. If Levi bought from Shimon land of the highest or of the lowest quality, he can refuse to pay Reuven's creditor, arguing that he should collect his debt from land of medium quality that is in Shimon's possession. ⁵Moreover, **even** if Levi bought **land of medium quality** from Shimon ⁶**we only say** that the creditor may collect his debt from Levi **if** Levi bought all of the medium quality land that Shimon had purchased earlier from Reuven, and thus **he did not leave** any equivalent **land of medium quality** in Shimon's hands. [92B] ⁷**But if** Levi **left** in Shimon's hands **land of medium quality similar to** the land he bought from him, the creditor cannot collect from Levi, ⁸for **Levi can say to him:** "**I left you property** with Shimon **from which to collect.**"

RASHI

הלכך, רצה לגבות משמעון עידית — גובה, דאמר ליה: אתה לקחת כל השדות ונכנסת תחת ראובן להשתעבד לחובי, וכל זמן שאמצא משל ראובן אצלך כלום — לא אטריח את לוי, שהניח לי מקום לגבות. רצה — מלוי גובה, כגון אם לא ימצא אצל שמעון משל ראובן אלא זיבורית — גובה בינונית מלוי. דאמר ליה: לקחת את שעבודי בינונית שדיני מוטל עליה. ואף על גב דאילו לקחה לוי לבינונית זו מראובן, והניח אצלו זיבורית — לא היה יכול בעל חוב דראובן לחזור על לוי, כדתנן: אין נפרעין מנכסים משועבדים במקום שיש בני חורין, ואפילו הן זיבורית. התם הוא — דראובן בעל חובו הוא, ואמור רבנן: מפני תקון העולם, כל זמן שיש אצל בעל חובו כדי חובו — לא יטרוף לקוחות. אבל כאן — שמעון לאו בעל חובו הוא, ואף עליו מכח טירפא הוא בא.

NOTES

times, Reuven's creditor can only recover the money owed him from the field that Shimon purchased last, for that field remained as free property in Reuven's possession after all the other fields had been sold, and a creditor may not recover his money by taking land from a purchaser if the debtor still owns land. *Tosafot* disagree, but most of the Geonim and Rishonim accept *Rashi*'s position.

Most Rishonim understand that the creditor may even collect land of the poorest quality from Shimon. Although the Rabbis enacted that a creditor can demand collection from property of medium quality, if he wishes he can also collect from land of the poorest quality. But he cannot collect from land of the highest quality, for a creditor cannot collect from this property even from the debtor himself. According to *Rashi*, however, the creditor can collect even land of the highest quality from Shimon (see *Ritva* who rejects this position and refers to it as a great mistake). *Rav Hai Gaon* agrees with *Rashi*, and explains that since Shimon bought all of the property that Reuven had mortgaged to his creditor, preventing the creditor from collecting his debt from Reuven, Shimon acted improperly and is considered as if he had stolen from the creditor. Therefore, the creditor can collect even from property of the highest quality from Shimon, as is due him from someone who did him damage.

אֲבָל שְׁבַק בֵּינוֹנִית דִּכְוָותָהּ **But if he left land of medium quality like it.** Some of the Rishonim note that Levi must leave land with Shimon of exactly the same quality as the

HALAKHAH

and then Shimon sold one of those fields to Levi, Reuven's creditor can recover the money which Reuven owes him from either Shimon or Levi. The creditor can only collect from Levi, if Levi had purchased land of medium quality from Shimon. But if he had purchased land of the highest quality or land of the lowest quality, he cannot collect from Levi, but only from Shimon. Even if Levi had purchased land of medium quality from Shimon, Reuven's creditor can only recover his debt from him, if Levi did not leave in Shimon's hands land of medium quality like the land he had bought from him," following Rabbah. (*Rambam, Sefer Mishpatim, Hilkhot Malveh VeLoveh* 19:3; *Shulhan Arukh, Hoshen Mishpat* 119:1.)

CONCEPTS

עִידִּית **Land of the highest quality.** Landed property may be of three qualities: עִידִּית — the highest; בֵּינוֹנִית — the medium; זִיבּוּרִית — the lowest. If the law requires a person to make a payment of money, and he does not have it, his land may be confiscated as payment. In such circumstances the following rules apply: Compensation for damage must be paid at least from the medium quality; and a persons obligations to his wife resulting from their marriage contract — the ketubah — must be made from land of the highest quality.

TRANSLATION AND COMMENTARY

אֲמַר אַבַּיֵי [1] In another ruling concerning property that was sold with a guarantee: **Abaye said: If Reuven sold a field to Shimon with a guarantee** for the sale, [2] **and** then **Reuven's creditor came** to Shimon **to seize** the field **from him,** [3] **the law is that Reuven can take** the creditor to court, if he has claims that would prevent the creditor from collecting,

LITERAL TRANSLATION

[1] Abaye said: [If] Reuven sold a field to Shimon with a guarantee, [2] and Reuven's creditor came and seized it from him, [3] the law is that Reuven can go

[1] אֲמַר אַבַּיֵי: רְאוּבֵן שֶׁמָּכַר שָׂדֶה לְשִׁמְעוֹן בְּאַחֲרָיוּת, [2] וַאֲתָא בַּעַל חוֹב דִּרְאוּבֵן וְקָטְרֵיף לָהּ מִינֵּיהּ, [3] דִּינָא הוּא דְּאָזֵיל רְאוּבֵן

RASHI

דינא הוא דאזיל ראובן ומפצי ליה – אם יש לו עליו שום גלגול דברים, לחשוב חוב כנגד חוב, או: אישתבע לי דלא פרעתיך. לאו בעל דברים דידי את – איני טורף ממך כלום.

NOTES

land that he bought. If the land that he left with Shimon is even slightly better than the land that he bought, he cannot send the creditor to Shimon, for Shimon's land is of high quality compared to Levi's land, and a creditor cannot collect from high quality land when medium quality land is available (*Talmidei Rabbenu Yonah*).

Tosafot and others point out that the Gemara is not to be understood literally when it said that if Levi left land of medium quality in Shimon's possession, he can say to Reuven's creditor: "I left property with Shimon from which you can collect your debt," for that argument can only be put forward by a buyer who bought property directly from the debtor, but not from a derivative purchaser who bought from the first buyer. Rather, the Gemara must be interpreted more broadly, and it means to say that Levi can refuse the creditor with the following argument: Had the two properties of medium quality remained with Shimon, he could have decided from which of the two to give you. So, too, I can decide that you should collect your debt from the property of medium quality in Shimon's possession, for Shimon sold it to me along with all the attendant rights and privileges. According to this explanation the land held by Reuven can be of any medium quality and need not be of the exact same grade as that held by Levi.

דִּינָא הוּא דְּאָזֵיל רְאוּבֵן **The law is that Reuven can go.** *Netziv* (in his novellae to *Bava Kamma*) writes that Reuven is required by law to go to court and put forward any claims that will help Shimon retain possession of the property that Reuven's creditor wishes to seize. This obligation stems from the guarantee that Reuven accepted at the time of the sale. *Netziv's* position is supported by the Gemara's formulation: "The law is," which implies that we are dealing here with a legal obligation. But the *Netziv* apparently did not see *Ritva's* comment to our passage, in which he notes that Reuven is not obligated to go to court on Shimon's behalf, for he can argue that the obligations stemming from his guarantee have force once the property is actually seized. Rather, Abaye means to teach that Reuven may, if he wishes, take the creditor to court for his own benefit, and the creditor cannot dismiss him with the argument that he has no legal standing.

דְּאָזֵיל רְאוּבֵן **That Reuven can go.** Reuven can go to court to force his creditor to accept money rather than seize the land he has sold to Shimon. Of course he may also deny that the alleged creditor has a valid claim at all. The Rishonim all ask: What difference does it make whether Reuven or Shimon goes to court? They offer numerous answers to this question: *Rashi* explains that if Reuven claims that he already repaid the debt, or that the creditor's loan is offset by a claim that Reuven has against him, the creditor cannot collect from Shimon's property without first taking an oath that Reuven still owes him the money. *Tosafot* object that a creditor can never collect from mortgaged property that was sold to a third party without first taking such an oath. *Penei Yehoshua* counters that it nevertheless makes a difference who presents the claim, for if Reuven himself comes to court and challenges the creditor, the creditor might back down and admit that the debt has been repaid. *Rivan* suggests that only Reuven can argue that the debt was not yet due, and so the creditor is not yet entitled to recover the loan from mortgaged property. *Tosafot* propose that only Reuven can argue that the promissory note held by the creditor, which is required for seizure, is forged. But this is difficult, for even if Reuven does not present such an argument, the court does not allow a creditor to collect from mortgaged property without first authenticating the signatures on the promissory note. *Tosafot* and *Ramban* (in *Bava Kamma*) suggest that if Shimon has already presented his pleas before the court, he cannot return and add an additional plea, but Reuven may make his pleas after Shimon has completed his case. Others propose that if Shimon granted the creditor credence, waiving his right to demand an oath, or if he agreed to accept the testimony of the creditor's father (a witness that is otherwise disqualified under Torah law), Reuven can still impose an oath upon the creditor, or reject this witness. Alternatively, if the creditor is liable for to Reuven to take an oath regarding some other matter, Reuven can also impose an oath upon him regarding this debt by means of an extended oath (see above 86b) *Ramban* suggests that the property may have depreciated between the time that Reuven had sold it to Shimon and the time that the creditor came to seize it. Thus Reuven prefers to repay the debt with money so that he will not be obligated to compensate Shimon according to the higher purchase price. *Rosh* suggests that Reuven can insist that the case be heard in a court of higher authority that sits in a place to which Shimon is unable to travel. *Ittur* (and *Ramban* and his disciples) argues that Reuven designated the property as an hypothec, collateral specifically dedicated for the loan, in which case Shimon, as a purchaser, cannot give the creditor money, but Reuven retains the right to do so. Alternatively, the property may have been designated as an hypothec, and Shimon had made certain improvements to it, the debt being equivalent to the value of the property before the improvements. In such a case Shimon cannot insist that he keep a small parcel of the land to cover the improvements he made, but the creditor is entitled to take the entire property, and pay Shimon for the improvements. Reuven, however, can demand to keep a small parcel of the land representing the value of the improvements. *Rosh* (in the name of *Rivam;* and so too *Ramban, Nimmukei Yosef,*

TRANSLATION AND COMMENTARY

[1]and thereby **rescue** the field for Shimon. [2]Here the creditor **cannot say to** Reuven: [3]"I have not come to confiscate your property, therefore **you are not my adversary** in this case." Presumably the creditor wants the particular property he seeks to seize, but he cannot refuse Reuven's offer in this manner, [4]for Reuven **can say to him:** "I sold the property to Shimon with a guarantee. [5]Thus, **whatever you collect from** Shimon in satisfaction of the debt that you claim I owe you **will come back to me** to restore to him. You must therefore answer the claims that I bring against you." [6]**And there are some** authorities **who say** that Reuven can go to court with the creditor **even** if he sold the field to Shimon **without a guarantee.** Even though Shimon will have no monetary claim against Reuven if his property is confiscated, the creditor still cannot argue that Reuven has no legal standing in the case, [7]for **Reuven can say to him: "I do not want Shimon to have** any **resentment against me** because I sold him a field that was later confiscated by my creditor."

[1]וּמְפַצֵּי לֵיהּ, [2]וְלָא מָצֵי אָמַר לֵיהּ: [3]"לָאו בַּעַל דְּבָרִים דִּידִי אַתְּ", [4]מִשּׁוּם דְּאָמַר לֵיהּ: [5]"דְּמַפְּקַתְּ מִינֵּיהּ עָלַי הָדַר". [6]וְאִיכָּא דְּאָמְרִי: אֲפִילּוּ שֶׁלֹּא בְּאַחֲרָיוּת נַמִי, [7]דְּאָמַר לֵיהּ: "לָא נִיחָא לִי דְּתֶהֱוֵי לֵיהּ לְשִׁמְעוֹן תַּרְעוֹמֶת עָלַי".
[8]אָמַר אַבַּיֵי: רְאוּבֵן שֶׁמָּכַר שָׂדֶה לְשִׁמְעוֹן שֶׁלֹּא בְּאַחֲרָיוּת, [9]וְיָצְאוּ עָלָיו [93A] עֲסִיקִין, [10]עַד שֶׁלֹּא הֶחֱזִיק בָּהּ, יָכוֹל לַחֲזוֹר בּוֹ, [11]מִשֶּׁהֶחֱזִיק בָּהּ, אֵינוֹ יָכוֹל

LITERAL TRANSLATION

[1]and compensate him, [2]and [the creditor] cannot say to him: [3]"You are not my adversary," [4]for [Reuven] can say to him: [5]"What you collect from him comes back to me." [6]And there are [those] who say: Even without a guarantee too, [7]for he can say to him: "It is not agreable to me for Shimon to have resentment against me."

[8]Abaye said: [If] Reuven sold a field to Shimon without a guarantee, [9]and protests went out about it, [93A] [10]as long as he did not take possession, he can retract, [11][but] once he took possession, he may not retract,

RASHI

דמפקת מיניה עלי הדר – מה שאתה מוציא ממנו, יחזור עלי. **ואיכא דאמרי אפילו שלא באחריות נמי** – מכרה ראובן לשמעון, לא מצי אמר ליה בעל חוב לראובן: לאו בעל דברים דידי את. **עסיקין** = עוררין. **עד שלא החזיק בה יכול לחזור בו** – אם לא נתן מעות. **אין יכול לחזור בו** – שהקרקע נקנה בחזקה כי אמר ליה "חזק וקני". ויש שמחזיקין מיד ונותנין מעות לאחר זמן, ומשהחזיק בה נתחייב המעות.

אָמַר אַבַּיֵי [8]**Abaye said: Suppose Reuven sold a field to Shimon without guaranteeing** the sale, [9]**and protests** about Reuven's title to the field **were** then **raised** by someone claiming to be its true owner. If Shimon wishes to cancel the transaction to avoid possible loss of the property, the following rules apply: [93A] [10]**As long as** Shimon **did not** yet **take possession** by performing *ḥazakah* — an act which demonstrates ownership, such as fencing the property, or opening a gateway — **he can withdraw.** For even if he reached an agreement to purchase the field, it is not his until he performs an act of acquisition. [11]**But once** Shimon **performs** *ḥazakah*, **he can no longer withdraw** from the transaction and must pay Reuven the stipulated purchase price. Shimon cannot now argue that he was deceived when making the purchase,

NOTES

and others) argues that even if there is no practical difference between the claims that could be presented by Shimon or by Reuven, Reuven might be a more clever or experienced litigant who is better able to present his claims in court.

לָאו בַּעַל דְּבָרִים דִּידִי אַתְּ **You are not my opponent.** The Rishonim discuss the relevance of our passage to the issue of a person being represented in court by a proxy. It would seem from here that a person cannot be represented by someone else, otherwise Reuven would not have to resort to the argument, "Whatever you collect from him comes back to me." Rather he could simply come to court as Shimon's advocate. Note that this argument is only valid according to some of the approaches cited in the previous note, for there are pleas mentioned above that Reuven can present only as an interested party, with independent legal standing (see *Shittah Mekubbetzet*).

עַד שֶׁלֹּא הֶחֱזִיק בָּהּ **As long as he did not take possession.** The Rishonim disagree about this case. According to *Rashi*, the buyer did not yet pay the seller for the property, and

HALAKHAH

דְּאָזֵיל רְאוּבֵן וּמְפַצֵּי לֵיהּ **The law is that Reuven can go and compensate him.** "Even if Reuven sold a field to Shimon without accepting responsibility for the sale, if Reuven's creditor came to Shimon to seize the field from him, Reuven can enter into litigation with the creditor, who cannot argue that Reuven has no legal standing in the case," following the opinion in the Gemara introduced by the phrase "there are those who say." (*Rambam, Sefer Kinyan, Hilkhot Mekhirah* 19:9; *Shulḥan Arukh, Ḥoshen Mishpat* 226:1.)

עַד שֶׁלֹּא הֶחֱזִיק בָּהּ **As long as he did not perform *hazakah*.** "If Reuven sold a field to Shimon, who then performed one

לַחֲזוֹר בּוֹ, [1]מִשּׁוּם דְּאָמַר לֵיהּ: ״חַיְיתָא דְּקִיטְרֵי סָבְרַתְּ וְקַבֵּילַתְּ״.

[2]וּמֵאֵימַת מַחֲזִיק בָּהּ? [3]מִכִּי דָּיֵישׁ אַמִּצְרֵי.

[4]אִיכָּא דְּאָמְרִי: אֲפִילּוּ בְּאַחֲרָיוּת נַמִי, [5]דְּאָמַר לֵיהּ: ״אַחֲוֵי טִירְפָּךְ וַאֲשַׁלֵּם לָךְ״.

TRANSLATION AND COMMENTARY

[1]for Reuven **can say to him: "You** knowingly **agreed to buy a sack of knots,** an inferior piece of merchandise without examining what it contained. I sold you the field without accepting responsibility for the sale, and so you should have realized that there might be some problem regarding my title to the property."

וּמֵאֵימַת [2]The Gemara asks: **When** does the buyer **take possession** of the field? [3]**When he walks along its borders,** to determine what must be done to maintain it.

אִיכָּא דְּאָמְרִי [4]The Gemara continues: Regarding the possibility of cancelling the transaction, **there are those** authorities **who say** that **even** if Reuven sold the field to Shimon **with a guarantee** for the sale, once Shimon has performed *ḥazakah* on the field, he cannot withdraw from the transaction on account of protests to Reuven's title. [5]**For** Reuven **can say to him: "Show me the *tirpa*,** the court document allowing the protester to seize the field which you purchased from me, **and I will refund** the purchase money. Until then, the transaction stands, for the protester may not be able to prove his case."

LITERAL TRANSLATION

[1]for [Reuven] can say to him: "A bag of knots you agreed [to buy] and received."

[2]And from when has he taken possession? [3]When he treads along the borders.

[4]There are [those] who say: Even with a guarantee as well, [5]for [the seller] can say to him: "Show me your *tirpa* and I will pay you."

RASHI

חייתא = שק קטן. **דקיטרי** — מלא קשרים. **סברת וקבילת** — בדמי שתיכות כסף. כלומר, נתרצית לאבד מעותיך מספק. **אפילו באחריות נמי** — מכרה לו, אינו יכול לחזור בו מחמת עסיקין. ולא אמרינן: סוף סוף עליה הדר, ואטרוחי דייני למה לן. **דאמר ליה אחוי טירפך** — שטר טירפא מבית דין, שכתבו לך שיצאה השדה מידך בדין, ותחזור עלי לטרוף. **ואשלם לך** — וכל זמן שלא יצתה מידך — לא אשלם, שהרבה עוררין שאין זוכין בדין.

BACKGROUND

חַיְיתָא דְּקִיטְרֵי A sack of knots. Here *Rashi* explains the phrase חַיְיתָא דְּקִיטְרֵי as "a sack full of knots." *Rivan* and *Rashi* in *Bava Kamma* understand the phrase as "a tied sack full of air," an empty sack. *Nemmukei Yosef* (in *Bava Kamma*) explains it as "a tied sack of unknown contents."

NOTES

he, therefore, did not yet acquire it. Abaye teaches us that until the buyer takes possession with a valid act of acquisition — such as a *ḥazakah* — he may withdraw from the transaction without moral stigma. According to *Rabbenu Tam,* the buyer did indeed pay for the property, but the transaction took place where payment does not finalize a transaction involving land. Rather a bill of sale or some other valid act of acquisition is required. Abaye teaches that until act of acquistion has been performed, the buyer may withdraw from the transaction, and he is not liable to the Rabbinic curse that applies to someone who reneges on a purchase after payment has been made. But according to most Rishonim (*Rivam,* cited by *Tosafot, Ramban, Ra'ah, Ritva,* and others) a valid act of acquisition had been performed in this case, and protests against the seller's title were then raised. The Gemara is discussing an additional act of *ḥazakah* that the purchaser may perform to indicate that he agrees to the purchase without reservation and waives his right to claim that it was made under false premises (see below, Note, s.v., ומאימת מחזיק).

וּמֵאֵימַת מַחֲזִיק בָּהּ? And when does he take possession with an act of *ḥazakah*. *Tosafot* and others ask: Why does the Gemara ask here about taking possession with a *ḥazakah,* when the laws of acquisition by way of *ḥazakah* are recorded in detail in *Bava Batra*? *Tosafot* answer that since the buyer has paid for the property, a lesser type of *ḥazakah* suffices. But most Rishonim follow *Rivam* (cited by *Tosafot*) that the Gemara is not asking here about the standard mode of acquisition known as *ḥazakah,* since the buyer has already acquired the property through some other valid mode of acquisition. Here an additional act of *ḥazakah* is necessary to demonstrate his agreement to acquire the property despite the challange to the seller's title. Until the buyer performs that *ḥazakah,* he can nullify the transaction, claiming that it was made under false premises. Thus, the Gemara must clarify what type of *ḥazakah* is referred to here.

מִכִּי דָּיֵישׁ אַמִּצְרֵי When he treads along the borders. The Rishonim disagree about the meaning of this phrase. *Tosafot* explain that the *ḥazakah* discussed here is performed when the buyer walks along the borders of his field to determine what he must do in order to maintain the property. *Rivan* and *Ritva* explain that this means that the buyer raises and reinforces the boundary ridge demarcating the field. *Rif* and *Rambam* understand that in the case under discussion the buyer bought a field adjacent to one that he already owned. *Ḥazakah* is performed when he removes the boundary ridge separating the two fields in order to combine them into a single field.

HALAKHAH

of the various modes of acquisition, but before he used the property, protests about Reuven's title to the field were voiced, Shimon can still retract from the transaction, and Reuven must return the purchase money to him. But if Shimon has used the property, even if he only removed the border and levelled it with the rest of the field, he can no longer withdraw from the transaction," following the opinion in the Gemara introduced by the words "There are those who say" that this ruling applies even if Reuven sold the field to Shimon with responsibility. According to *Rosh* and others, this ruling only applies if Shimon has not yet paid for the field (*Sma*). (*Rambam, Sefer Kinyan, Hilkhot Mekhirah* 19:2; *Shulḥan Arukh, Ḥoshen Mishpat* 226:5.)

TRANSLATION AND COMMENTARY

MISHNAH מִי שֶׁהָיָה נָשׂוּי [1]**If a man was married to three women, and he died,** and the three widows come now to collect their ketubah settlements, and all three ketubah deeds were signed on the same day, so that none of them has a preferential right, but the three ketubot were not equal in value — [2]**one** wife having **a ketubah of a maneh** (one hundred dinars), **the second** having **a ketubah of two hundred** dinars, **and the third** having **a ketubah of three hundred** dinars — [3]and the husband's estate amounts to **only a maneh**, the three wives **divide the estate equally,** each woman taking property worth a third of a maneh (thirty-three and a third dinars), for each of them has a ketubah of at least a hundred dinars, and thus each of them has an equal claim to the hundred dinars of the estate.

הָיוּ שָׁם מָאתַיִם [4]If the husband's estate amounts to **two hundred dinars, the woman who has the ketubah of a maneh takes** property worth **fifty** dinars, [5]**and the woman who has the ketubah of two hundred** dinars **and the woman who has the ketubah of three hundred** dinars divide equally what is left of the estate, [6]**each taking** property to the value of **three gold dinars,** which is equivalent to seventy-five silver dinars.

משנה [1]מִי שֶׁהָיָה נָשׂוּי שָׁלֹשׁ נָשִׁים וּמֵת, [2]כְּתוּבָּתָהּ שֶׁל זוֹ מָנֶה, וְשֶׁל זוֹ מָאתַיִם, וְשֶׁל זוֹ שְׁלֹשׁ מֵאוֹת, [3]וְאֵין שָׁם אֶלָּא מָנֶה — חוֹלְקִין בְּשָׁוֶה. [4]הָיוּ שָׁם מָאתַיִם — שֶׁל מָנֶה נוֹטֶלֶת חֲמִשִּׁים, [5]שֶׁל מָאתַיִם וְשֶׁל שְׁלֹשׁ מֵאוֹת, [6]שְׁלֹשָׁה שְׁלֹשָׁה שֶׁל זָהָב.

LITERAL TRANSLATION

MISHNAH [1][If] a man was married to three women and died, [and] the ketubah of this one is a maneh, [2]and of this one two hundred, and of this one three hundred, [3]and there is only a maneh, they divide [it] equally.

[4][If] there were two hundred, [she who has a ketubah] of a maneh takes fifty, [5]and [she who has a ketubah] of two hundred and [she who has a ketubah] of three hundred, [6][each takes] three (lit., "three three") gold [dinars].

RASHI

משנה של זו מנה ושל זו מאתים כו' — ושלשתן נחתמו ביום אחד. דאי בתלתא יומי — הקודמת בשטר קודמת בגיבוי. **חולקות בשוה** — שהרי כח שלשתן שוה בשעבוד מנה, דבכולהו איכא מנה. **היו שם מאתים** — אין לבעלת מנה שעבוד אלא במנה ראשון, אבל במנה שני — אין שעבוד לשטרה של מנה. **נוטלת חמשים** — בגמרא פריך עלה. **שלש של זהב** — שלשה דינרי זהב, וכל דינר זהב עשרים וחמשה דינרי כסף, כדאמר ב"הזהב" (בבא מציעא מה,ב). ושל מאתים כחה שוה במאתים לבעלת שלש מאות, שהרי מאתים משועבדים לשטרה.

NOTES

הָיוּ שָׁם מָאתַיִם **If there are two hundred.** The underlying principle of the Mishnah is that if a man is married to several women, each with a ketubah of a different sum, they each have liens of different strength on the husband's property. If the husband dies without leaving enough assets to pay all the settlements, each widow collects from the property of her husband's estate in accordance with the strength of her lien. But, as the Gemara explains, the calculations recorded in the Mishnah cannot all be reconciled with this principle, and some of the cases there must be restricted to special situations, such as if the widows come to an agreement among themselves (Shmuel's approach) or if different portions of the husband's estate came into their possession on separate occasions (the approach of Rav Ya'akov of Nehar Pekod). *Rav Sa'adyah Gaon,* however, suggests a novel interpretation of the Mishnah that does not require special situations. It is built on the principle that if the husband's estate amounts to less than the largest of his wives' ketubahs, the portion that is equal to or less than the value of each widow's ketubah, is shared evenly by them all. But from the portion of the estate that exceeds the sum of her ketubah, she takes her proportionate share. If the husband's estate is equal to or larger than the largest of his wives' ketubot, the entire estate is divided proportionately between the women. Thus, if the husband left assets of a maneh — a sum that does not exceed any of the ketubot — the three widows divide the property evenly among themselves. If he left an estate of two hundred dinars — a sum which exceeds the ketubah of a maneh — the first hundred dinars is divided evenly among the three widows, but as for the second hundred dinars, the woman with the ketubah of a maneh takes her proportionate share, a sixth, and the other two women share what is left. Thus the widow with a ketubah of a maneh receives fifty dinars (thirty-three and a third from the first hundred dinars and sixteen and two-thirds from

HALAKHAH

מִי שֶׁהָיָה נָשׂוּי שָׁלֹשׁ נָשִׁים **If someone was married to three women.** "If a man was married to four women — one having a ketubah of one hundred dinars, the second having a ketubah of two hundred dinars, the third having a ketubah of three hundred dinars, and the fourth having a ketubah of four hundred dinars — and all four ketubot were signed on the same day, and the man died, but his estate does not suffice to cover all four obligations, the estate is divided up among his widows as follows: If when the estate is divided up evenly among all the widows, the one with the smallest ketubah will receive the entire amount or less, the estate is divided evenly among them. If the estate is larger than that, the assets are divided evenly among all the widows until the one with the smallest ketubah receives all that is due her. What is left is then divided evenly among the other three widows until the one with the second smallest ketubah receives all that is due her, and so on. The same law applies if there are multiple

TRANSLATION AND COMMENTARY

הָיוּ שָׁם [1]If the husband's estate amounts to **three hundred dinars, the woman who has the ketubah of a maneh takes** property worth **fifty** dinars, [2]**the woman who has the ketubah of two hundred** dinars **takes** property worth **a maneh** (one hundred dinars), **and the woman who has the ketubah of three hundred** dinars **takes** property worth **six gold dinars,** which is equal to a hundred and fifty silver dinars.

וְכֵן שְׁלֹשָׁה [3]**And similarly** where **three** people **formed a partnership** to purchase merchandise, with each person investing a different sum, **and** the total value of their investments **decreased or increased,** if the partners now wish to dissolve the partnership **they divide** the assets **in the same manner** as they invested.

GEMARA שֶׁל מָנֶה [4]We learned in the Mishnah that if one wife has a ketubah of a hundred dinars, the second a ketubah of two hundred dinars, and the third a ketubah of three hundred dinars, and the husband's estate amounts to only two hundred dinars, the woman with the ketubah of one hundred dinars (maneh) takes fifty dinars. The Gemara asks: Does the woman **who has a ketubah of a maneh** really **take** property worth **fifty dinars?** Her claim to the first hundred dinars of the estate is shared equally with the two other wives, [5]so **she** should only take property worth **thirty-three and a third** dinars, a third of the first hundred dinars of the estate!

[1]הָיוּ שָׁם שְׁלֹשׁ מֵאוֹת, שֶׁל מָנֶה נוֹטֶלֶת חֲמִשִּׁים, [2]וְשֶׁל מָאתַיִם מָנֶה, וְשֶׁל שְׁלֹשׁ מֵאוֹת שִׁשָּׁה שֶׁל זָהָב.
[3]וְכֵן שְׁלֹשָׁה שֶׁהִטִּילוּ לַכִּיס, פִּיחֲתוּ אוֹ הוֹתִירוּ כָּךְ הֵן חוֹלְקִין.

גמרא [4]שֶׁל מָנֶה נוֹטֶלֶת חֲמִשִּׁים? [5]תְּלָתִין וּתְלָתָא וְתִילְתָּא הוּא דְּאִית לָהּ!

LITERAL TRANSLATION

[1][If] there were there three hundred, [she who has a ketubah] of a maneh takes fifty, [2]and [she who has a ketubah] of two hundred [takes] a maneh, and [she who has a ketubah] of three hundred [takes] six gold [dinars].

[3]And similarly three who formed a partnership (lit., "cast into a purse"), [and the investments] decreased or increased, they divide in this manner.

GEMARA [4][She who has a ketubah] of a maneh takes fifty? [5]She has thirty-three and a third!

RASHI

היו שם שלש מאות — מנה ראשון משועבד לכולן, והשני לבעלת מאתים ולבעלת שלש מאות, והשלישי לבעלת שלש מאות לבדה. **של מנה נוטלת חמשים** — בגמרא פריך עלה. **ושל מאתים מנה** — בגמרא מפרש לה. **ששה של זהב** — הם מאה וחמשים זוז. **שהטילו לכיס** — מעות לקנות סחורה לשכר. **כך הן חולקין** — כל אחד ואחד נוטל בשכר והפסד לפי מעותיו.

גמרא תלתין ותלתא ותילתא הוא דאית לה — דהיינו שליש של מנה, שהרי אין לה חלק במנה שני.

NOTES

the second hundred dinars), and the other two women receive seventy-five dinars each (thirty-three and a third dinars plus forty-one and two-thirds dinars). If the husband left an estate of three hundred dinars — a sum that is equal to the largest of the ketubot — the property is divided proportionately among the widows. The one with a ketubah of a maneh receives fifty dinars, the one with a ketubah of two hundred dinars receives a maneh, and the one with a ketubah of three hundred dinars receives a hundred-and-fifty dinars.

וְכֵן שְׁלֹשָׁה שֶׁהִטִּילוּ לַכִּיס **And similarly three who formed a partnership.** The Rishonim agree that when each of several partners invested a different sum and the value of their investment decreased or increased, and they now wish to divide up the assets, each partner receives his share in proportion to his initial investment. Thus, the term "And similarly" poses a certain difficulty, for then the law applying to the partners is not the same as that applying to three wives with ketubot of different amounts. *Rabbenu Ḥananel* explains that the term "And similarly" refers to the particular law applying to the three wives, when the husband's estate amounts to three hundred dinars, in which case (but for a different reason) each of the women receives a sum in proportion to the size of her ketubah.

תְּלָתִין וּתְלָתָא **Thirty-three.** Most of the Rishonim follow *Rashi, Rif,* and others who say that the underlying principle of our Mishnah is that each widow exercises a lien on the estate that is equal to the amount of her ketubah. Thus, when the husband left assets worth only a maneh, each of his widow exercises a lien over all his property, and it is divided equally among them. If the husband left property worth two hundred dinars, all three widows exercise a lien over the first hundred dinars of property, but the one with a ketubah of a maneh has no claim to the second hundred dinars of property. Thus she should receive only thirty-three and a third dinars (her share of the first hundred dinars), and the second maneh should be divided evenly between the other two widows, giving them each eighty-three and a third dinars). If the husband left property worth three hundred dinars, the widow with the ketubah of a maneh

HALAKHAH

creditors, none of whom enjoys a preferential right of recovering his debt, and the debtor's property does not suffice to cover all his obligations." The law follows Rabbi Yehudah HaNasi, against Rabbi Natan, in accordance with the understanding of *Rif.* (*Rambam, Sefer Nashim, Hilkhot Ishut* 17:8; *Shulḥan Arukh, Even HaEzer* 96:18; *Rambam, Sefer Mishpatim, Hilkhot Malveh* 20:4; *Shulḥan Arukh, Ḥoshen Mishpat* 104:10.)

[1]אָמַר שְׁמוּאֵל: בִּכוֹתֶבֶת בַּעֲלַת מָאתַיִם לְבַעֲלַת מָנֶה: [2]״דִּין וּדְבָרִים אֵין לִי עִמָּךְ בְּמָנֶה״: [3]אִי הָכִי, אֵימָא סֵיפָא: [4]״שֶׁל מָאתַיִם וְשֶׁל שְׁלֹשׁ מֵאוֹת שָׁלֹשׁ שָׁלֹשׁ שֶׁל זָהָב״, [5]תֵּימָא לָהּ: ״הָא סָלְקַתְּ נַפְשָׁךְ מִינָּהּ״! [6]מִשּׁוּם דְּאָמְרָה לָהּ: [7]״מִדִּין וּדְבָרִים הוּא דְּסַלִּיקִי נַפְשַׁאי״. [8]״הָיוּ שָׁם שְׁלֹשׁ מֵאוֹת וכו׳״.

LITERAL TRANSLATION

[1]Shmuel said: When the one with [a ketubah of] two hundred writes to the one with [a ketubah of] a maneh: [2]"I have no claim (lit., "litigation or dispute") against you regarding a maneh."

[3]If so, say the next (lit., "last") clause: [4]"[She who has a ketubah] of two hundred and [she who has a ketubah] of three hundred, [each takes] three gold [dinars]." [5]She may say to her: "Surely you relinquished (lit., 'removed yourself from') it!"

[6]Because she can say to her: [7]"It is from litigation that I removed myself."

[8]"[If] there were three hundred, etc."

TRANSLATION AND COMMENTARY

אָמַר שְׁמוּאֵל [1]**Shmuel said:** The Mishnah is dealing with a case **when the woman with the ketubah of two hundred** dinars **wrote to the woman with the ketubah of a maneh:** [2]"When you collect your settlement, **I will not sue you for the maneh** of our husband's property on which you exercise a lien, as I do not want you to lose part of your ketubah settlement on my account." Thus, the widows with the ketubot of a maneh and of three hundred dinars divide the first hundred dinars worth of property between themselves, as the arrangement leaves the widow with the ketubah of a maneh property worth fifty dinars.

אִי הָכִי [3]The Gemara asks: **If** indeed the Mishnah is dealing with **such** a case, there is a difficulty, for you must **consider** what was taught in **its next clause:** "If the husband's estate amounts to only two hundred dinars...[4]the woman with the ketubah **of two hundred** dinars **and** the woman with the ketubah **of three hundred** dinars divide what is left of the estate equally between themselves, **each taking three gold dinars,** which is equivalent to seventy-five silver dinars." Now if the woman with the ketubah of two hundred dinars waived her rights to the first hundred dinars of her husband's estate, why should she receive seventy-five dinars? [5]**Let the woman** with the ketubah of three hundred dinars **say to her: "Surely you removed yourself from** all claims regarding the first hundred dinars!"

מִשּׁוּם [6]The Gemara answers: The woman with the ketubah of two hundred dinars takes property worth seventy-five dinars, **because she can say to** the woman with the ketubah of three hundred dinars: "I never waived my right to our late husband's estate. [7]I just **agreed not to raise a claim** against the woman with the ketubah of a maneh, enabling her to collect fifty dinars by virtue of her lien on the first hundred dinars of the estate. But I never agreed not to raise a claim against you. Since we have an equal claim to the remaining hundred and fifty dinars, we should divide that sum equally between ourselves."

הָיוּ שָׁם [8]We learned in the next clause of the Mishnah: **"If** the husband's estate amounts to **three hundred** dinars, the widow with the ketubah of a maneh takes fifty dinars, the one with the ketubah of two hundred dinars takes a maneh, and the one with the ketubah of three hundred dinars takes six gold dinars, which

RASHI

דין ודברים אין לי עמך במנה — כשתבואי לדין לא אריב עמך במנה המשועבד לך, ולא יתמעט חלקך בשבילי. הלכך, היא ובעלת שלש מאות חולקות אותו. **תימא לה** — בעלת שלש מאות לבעלת מאתים: הא סליקת נפשיך ממנה, ואין לך לחלק אלא במנה שני. **מדין ודברים סליקת נפשאי** — לא נתתי חלקי במתנה, ומה שגבתה — לא בשליחותי גבתה, שתאמר לי: נטלה זו חלקך. אני סילקתי עצמי מלריב עמה ולמעט חלקה במנה, וגבר ידה לגבות חצי המנה בשעבוד שטרה. עכשיו אני באה לחלוק עמך בנותר, שלא סילקתי עצמי מלריב עמך, ושעבודי ושעבודך שוים.

NOTES

should receive thirty-three and a third dinars, the widow with the two-hundred-dinar ketubah should receive a third of the first maneh and half of the second maneh, giving her eighty-three and a third dinars, and the third widow should receive a third of the first maneh, half of the second maneh, and all of the third maneh, giving her a total of one hundred and eighty-three and a third dinars. But our Mishnah is dealing with a special case, as is explained in the Gemara by Shmuel and Rav Ya'akov of Nehar Pekod.

בִּכוֹתֶבֶת בַּעֲלַת מָאתַיִם **Where the one with a ketubah of two hundred writes.** *Ritva* notes that according to this explanation, the widow with the three-hundred-dinar ketubah must consent to the arrangement between the other two, because they cannot bilaterally reach an agreement that will cause a loss to the third widow. *Meiri* writes that the woman with the three-hundred-dinar ketubah was present when the other two reached their agreement, and she remained silent, tacitly agreeing to waive a portion of her share.

TRANSLATION AND COMMENTARY

is equivalent to a hundred and fifty silver dinars." Again the Gemara asks: [1]Does the woman **who has the ketubah of two hundred** dinars really **take** property worth **a maneh?** We have established that our Mishnah refers to a case in which the widow with the two-hundred-dinar ketubah wrote the widow with the ketubah of a maneh that she would not raise a claim against her regarding the first hundred dinars of their late husband's estate. Now the woman with the two-hundred-dinar ketubah has no claim whatsoever on the third hundred dinars of the property, because she has a claim only on the second hundred dinars and fifty dinars of the first hundred dinars. [2]Therefore, **she should** only be entitled to property **seventy-five** dinars, as her claim is shared equally with the woman who has a ketubah of three hundred dinars!

אָמַר שְׁמוּאֵל [3]**Shmuel said:** Here **the woman with the ketubah of three hundred** dinars **wrote to the woman with the ketubah of a maneh:** "When you collect your ketubah, [4]**I will not raise a claim against you regarding the maneh** of our husband's property on which you exercise a lien." The widow with the two-hundred-dinar ketubah did not relinquish any of her rights. Thus, the widow with the ketubah of a maneh and the one with the two-hundred-dinar ketubah divide the first hundred dinars worth of property, and the one with the two-hundred-dinar ketubah and the one with the three-hundred-dinar ketubah divide the second hundred dinars of property. The third hundred dinars belongs exclusively to the woman with the three-hundred-dinar ketubah. Hence, the widow with the ketubah of a maneh receives property worth fifty dinars, the one with the two-hundred-dinar ketubah receives property worth a maneh, and the one with the three-hundred-dinar ketubah receives property worth a hundred and fifty dinars.

רַב יַעֲקֹב [5]The Gemara now presents an entirely different explanation of our Mishnah: **Rav Ya'akov from Nehar Pekod said in the name of Ravina:** [6]**The earlier clause** of the Mishnah, regarding an estate of two hundred dinars (which is actually the second case of the Mishnah) — **deals with** women who **seized** a portion of their late husband's estate **on two** separate **occasions,** [7]**and** similarly **the later clause**, regarding an estate of three hundred dinars — **deals with** women who **seized** property **on two** separate **occasions.** How so? [8]**The first clause** of the Mishnah **deals with seizures on two** separate **occasions:** [9]**When** assets worth **seventy-five** dinars **fell** into their hands **on one occasion,** [10]**and** assets worth **a hundred and twenty-five** dinars **fell** into their hands **on a second occasion.** When they took possession of the seventy-five dinars of property, each of the widows had an equal claim to the property, so it was divided equally. Later, when the hundred and twenty-five dinars of property came into their possession, the widow with the ketubah of a maneh has an

[1]שֶׁל מָאתַיִם מָנֶה? [2]שִׁבְעִים וַחֲמִשָּׁה הוּא דְּאִית לָהּ!
[3]אָמַר שְׁמוּאֵל: בְּכוֹתֶבֶת בַּעֲלַת שְׁלֹשׁ מֵאוֹת לְבַעֲלַת מָאתַיִם וּלְבַעֲלַת מָנֶה: [4]"דִּין וּדְבָרִים אֵין לִי עִמָּכֶם בְּמָנֶה".
[5]"רַב יַעֲקֹב מִנְּהַר פְּקוֹד מִשְּׁמֵיהּ דְּרָבִינָא אֲמַר: [6]רֵישָׁא בִּשְׁתֵּי תְפִיסוֹת, [7]וְסֵיפָא בִּשְׁתֵּי תְפִיסוֹת. [8]רֵישָׁא בִּשְׁתֵּי תְפִיסוֹת, [9]דְּנָפְלוּ שִׁבְעִין וַחֲמִשָּׁה בְּחַד זִימְנָא, [10]וּמֵאָה וְעֶשְׂרִים וַחֲמִשָּׁה בְּחַד זִימְנָא.

LITERAL TRANSLATION

[1][She who has a ketubah] of two hundred [takes] a maneh? [2][But] she has only seventy-five.

[3]Shmuel said: When the one with [the ketubah of] three hundred writes to the one with [the ketubah of] two hundred and to the one with [the ketubah of] a maneh: [4]"I have no claim (lit., 'litigation or dispute') against you for a maneh."

[5]Rav Ya'akov from Nehar Pekod said in the name of Ravina: [6]The earlier (lit., "first") clause [deals] with two seizures, [7]and the later (lit., "last") clause [deals] with two seizures. [8]The earlier clause [deals] with two seizures, [9]when seventy-five fell [into their hands] at one time, [10]and a hundred and twenty-five [fell into their hands] at another time.

RASHI

שבעים וחמשה הוא דאית לה — דהא כיון דאוקימנא בכותבת בעלת מאתים כו' — אין לה לחלוק מעתה אלא במאה וחמשים, אבל במנה שלישי — אין לה כלום. אמר שמואל — סיפא בכותבת בעלת שלש מאות כו', ובעלת מאתים לא כתבה כלום. הלכך, מנה ראשון חולקות בעלת מאתים ובעלת מנה, ומנה שני חולקות בעלת מאתים ובעלת שלש מאות. ומנה שלישי כולה לבעלת שלש מאות. רבינא אמר — לא תוקמה בכותבת, אלא בשתי תפיסות, שתפסו מטלטלין לכתובתן ולא נמצאו להן מאתים בפעם אחת, אלא בשתי פעמים.

NOTES

בִּשְׁתֵּי תְפִיסוֹת **With two seizures.** The term *tefisah*, "seizure," ordinarily refers to movable goods. But this leads to a certain difficulty, for a widow cannot collect her ketubah settlement from the movable assets of her late husband's estate. According to *Rashi*, the women here seized movable property during their husband's lifetime, in which case they may indeed retain it for their ketubah settlements. *Ritva* suggests that the husband had explicitly

TRANSLATION AND COMMENTARY

outstanding claim on seventy-five dinars of it, as do the other two widows. Since all three widows have an equal claim to seventy-five dinars of this new property, each one first receives another twenty-five dinars, giving each one a total of fifty dinars. The remaining fifty dinars of the estate are then divided between the women with the two-hundred-dinar and three-hundred-dinar ketubot. Thus each of the two widows end up with seventy-five dinars worth of property. [1]Similarly, **the later clause** of the Mishnah **deals with seizures** of the late husband's estate **on two** separate **occasions:** [2]Assets worth **seventy-five** dinars **fell** into their hands **on one occasion,** [3]**and** assets worth **two hundred and twenty-five fell** into their hands **on a second occasion.** When they took possession of the seventy-five dinars of property, if each of them had an equal claim to the property, so it was divided equally. When another two hundred and twenty-five dinars of property came into their possession, the widow with the ketubah of a maneh is left with a claim for another seventy-five dinars, the woman with the two-hundred-dinar ketubah, with a claim for another hundred and seventy-five dinars, and the woman with the three-hundred-dinar ketubah, a claim for another two hundred seventy-five dinars. Since all three of them have an equal claim to at least another seventy-five dinars of this property, each of them first receives another twenty-five dinars, leaving one hundred and fifty dinars, yet to be apportioned. Regarding this remaining property, the woman with a ketubah of two hundred dinars and the woman with a ketubah of three hundred dinars have an equal claim to yet another hundred dinars, so this is divided equally between them, giving them another fifty dinars of property each. Fifty dinars of property remains, to which only the widow with the three-hundred-dinar ketubah is entitled. Thus, the widow with the ketubah of a maneh receives fifty dinars (first twenty-five dinars, then another twenty-five dinars), the widow with the ketubah of two hundred dinars receives a hundred dinars (first twenty-five dinars, then another seventy-five dinars), and the widow with the ketubah of three hundred dinars receives a hundred and fifty dinars (first twenty-five dinars, then a hundred and twenty-five dinars.)

תַּנְיָא [4]**It was taught** in a Baraita that the Mishnah's ruling is subject to a Tannaitic dispute: "The Mishnah's ruling that when a man's estate does not suffice to cover all of his wives' ketubahs, each of them collects according to the extent of their liens as determined by the size of their ketubahs **is the Mishnah** taught **by Rabbi Natan.**[5] But **Rabbi** Yehudah HaNaSi **says: I do not agree with the position of Rabbi Natan regarding this** matter, for until her settlement is paid in full, a woman exercises a lien over all of her husband's property.

[1]סֵיפָא בִּשְׁתֵּי תְפִיסוֹת, [2]דִּנְפַלוּ שִׁבְעִים וַחֲמִשָּׁה בְּחַד זִימְנָא, [3]וּמָאתַיִם וְעֶשְׂרִים וַחֲמִשָּׁה בְּחַד זִימְנָא.

[4]תַּנְיָא: ״זוֹ מִשְׁנַת רַבִּי נָתָן: [5]רַבִּי אוֹמֵר: אֵין אֲנִי רוֹאֶה דְּבָרָיו שֶׁל רַבִּי נָתָן בְּאֵלּוּ,

LITERAL TRANSLATION

[1]The later clause [deals] with two seizures, [2]where seventy-five fell [into their hands] at one time, [3]and two hundred and twenty-five [fell into their hands] at another time.

[4]It was taught: "This is the Mishnah of Rabbi Natan: [5]Rabbi says: I do not accept (lit., "see") the words of Rabbi Natan in these [matters],

RASHI

דנפלו להן שבעים וחמשה בחד זימנא — ובאו לדון עליהם. אמרינן להו: חולקות בשוה, שהרי שעבוד שלשתן על מנה. **ומאה ועשרים וחמשה בחד זימנא** — בעלת מנה כבר גבתה עשרים וחמשה, ובאת לריב על שבעים וחמשה. הלכך, שבעים וחמשה משועבדים לכולנה וחולקין אותן, הרי ביד כל אחת חמשים. והמותר אין לבעלת מנה חלק בו, היינו דקאמר: של מאתים ושל שלש מאות — שלשה שלשה של זהב. **סיפא בשתי תפיסות כו׳ ומאתים ועשרים וחמשה בחד זימנא** — שבעים וחמשה מינייהו — יד כולן שוין בו. ובעלת מאתים שלא גבתה בתפיסה ראשונה אלא עשרים וחמשה, באה לריב על שניה על מאה שבעים וחמשה, ופלגי שבעים וחמשה בין שלשתן, ונמצא ביד כל אחת חמשים. ומאה בין בעלת מאתים ובעלת שלש מאות, וחצי מאה שנשאר כולה לבעלת שלש מאות. נמצאת של מנה נוטלת חמשים, ושל מאתים מנה, ושל שלש מאות מאה חמישים, שהן ששה דינרי זהב. **אין אני רואה דבריו של רבי נתן באלו** — שאין זה דומה לשלשה שהטילו לכיס. דהתם שבח מעות שהשביחו מעותיהן שקלי, הלכך כל אחד יטול לפי מעותיו. אבל הכא, טעמא משום שיעבודא הוא, וכל נכסיו אחראין לכתובתה. הלכך, שלש המנים משועבדין לבעלת מנה כשאר חברותיה, עד שתגבה כל כתובתה, לפיכך חולקות בשוה.

NOTES

mortgaged his movable property to his wives' ketubahs, so they had the right to seize it. Alternatively, the women may have collected land from a third person who had bought it from the husband, for this too is called *tefisah*. *Meiri* explains that the women seized money belonging to their husband that had been kept overseas and arrived in two separate installments.

זוֹ מִשְׁנַת רַבִּי נָתָן **This is the Mishnah of Rabbi Natan.** *Rivan* and *Rabbenu Yonatan* explain that the Baraita means to say that the Mishnah follows the viewpoint of Rabbi Natan, who says elsewhere (*Bava Metzia* 117b) that if a building of two stories collapsed, and the owners of the upper and lower stories do not desire to rebuild the structure, but rather to sell the property, the owner of the

TRANSLATION AND COMMENTARY

Hence when a man's estate is insufficient, [1]his widows **divide** the property **equally** among themselves, regardless of the relative size of their ketubot."

וְכֵן שְׁלֹשָׁה [2]We learned in the last clause of our Mishnah: **"And similarly,** when **three** people **formed a partnership** to purchase merchandise together, each investing a different amount, if the value of their investment decreased or increased, and the partners wish now to dissolve the partnership, they divide up the assets in **the manner** in which they invested, each partner receiving his proportional share." [3]**Shmuel said: If two** people **formed a partnership, this one** investing **a maneh** (one hundred dinars) **and that one** investing **two hundred** dinars, [93B] they **divide the profits** equally **down the middle,** each partner taking an equal share of the profits.

אָמַר רַבָּה [4]**Rabbah said: Shmuel's position stand to reason when** the partners **bought an ox for plowing and** that ox still **stands ready for plowing** — that is, ready for business operations. Here an ox is merely an example for investment in equipment that will be used to make a profit. The profits earned from the ox's

[1]אֶלָּא חוֹלְקוֹת בְּשָׁוֶה״. [2]״וְכֵן שְׁלֹשָׁה שֶׁהִטִּילוּ״. [3]אָמַר שְׁמוּאֵל: שְׁנַיִם שֶׁהִטִּילוּ לַכִּיס, זֶה מָנֶה וְזֶה מָאתַיִם — [93B] הַשָּׂכָר לָאֶמְצַע. [4]אָמַר רַבָּה: מִסְתַּבְּרָא מִילְּתֵיהּ דִּשְׁמוּאֵל בְּשׁוֹר לַחֲרִישָׁה וְעוֹמֵד

LITERAL TRANSLATION

[1]but rather they divide equally."

[2]"And similarly three who formed a partnership (lit., 'cast into a purse')." [3]Shmuel said: [If] two formed a partnership, this one a maneh, and that one two hundred, [93B] the profit is [divided equally] in the middle. [4]Rabbah said: The words of Shmuel stand to reason regarding an ox for plowing that stands [ready]

RASHI

השכר לאמצע – חולקין בשוה. **שור לחרישה** – שלקחו בהן שור לחרוש וחורשין בו, ואין חלקו של זה מועיל בלא חלקו של זה כלום – הלכך חולקין בשוה, אבל שור לחרישה, והשביח בבשר, ושחטוהו.

NOTES

lower story takes two-thirds of the proceeds, and the owner of the upper story takes one-third. Here too, Rabbi Natan says that each of the women collects property from their late husband's estate in proportion to the value of her ketubah.

אֶלָּא חוֹלְקוֹת בְּשָׁוֶה **But rather they divide equally.** Our commentary follows *Rashi,* who understands that, according to Rabbi Yehudah HaNasi, in all the cases of our Mishnah the three widows divide up their husband's estate evenly. Thus, when the estate was three hundred dinars, each woman receives a hundred dinars. According to this, Rabbi Yehudah HaNasi only disagrees with Rabbi Natan about the second and third cases of the Mishnah. *Rabbenu Ḥananel* (cited by *Tosafot*) rejects this position, arguing that it would be unjust for all the women to receive an equal share of their husband's estate. Rather, Rabbi Yehudah HaNasi means that each widow takes an equal share of her husband's property for each maneh that is due her as her ketubah settlement, leaving them with portions proportional to the value of their ketubot. According to this approach, Rabbi Yehudah HaNasi only disagrees with Rabbi Natan about the first and second cases of the Mishnah. *Rif* discusses this passage at great length, and even adds a detailed explanation in Arabic. According to *Rif* (and following him, *Rambam*), Rabbi Yehudah HaNasi maintains that the husband's property is divided evenly among all three women until the widow with the smallest ketubah receives all that is due her. The remainder is then divided evenly between the other two widows, until the widow with the next smallest ketubah receives all that is due her. The remainder is then taken by the widow with the largest ketubah. According to this, Rabbi Yehudah HaNasi disagrees with Rabbi Natan regarding the last two cases of the Mishnah. In both instances he would award a third of the estate to each of the widows, as the one with the smallest ketubah must receive all that is due her before allowing the others to take a larger share of the estate.

הַשָּׂכָר לָאֶמְצַע **The profit is divided down the middle.** Our commentary follows *Rashi* and others, who explain Shmuel's position in accordance with the rationale put forward in the Jerusalem Talmud. When an ox stands ready for plowing it can be argued that the profits earned from its work should be divided equally between the partners, because neither partner's share of the animal could have produced any profit without the share belonging to the other. The Jerusalem Talmud applies this rationale to the purchase of an expensive jewel by two partners, neither of whom could have purchased it on his own. Each partner is entitled to an equal share of the profit, regardless of the size of his initial investment, because neither of the investors could have made a profit without the other. When the ox stands ready for slaughter — the case in dispute between Rabbah and Rav Hamnuna — the law is more problematic. In the parallel case discussed in the Jerusalem Talmud, the two partners have purchased merchandise that could have been purchased in a smaller quantity by either one. The Jerusalem Talmud suggests that even in such a case profits earned from that partnership should be divided evenly between the two partners, because the partner who made the larger initial investment might not necessarily have made the same percentage of profit on his investment without the help of his partner, or if his partner had competed with him by lowering his prices. The Jerusalem Talmud records a disagreement about whether a partnership — in the absence of any explicit stipulations — is assumed to have been made with the understanding that the profits would be divided equally between the partners, regardless of initial investment, or whether a partnership is assumed to have been made with the understanding that the profits would be divided among the partners in proportion to the initial investment.

לַחֲרִישָׁה. [1] אֲבָל בְּשׁוֹר לַחֲרִישָׁה וְעוֹמֵד לִטְבִיחָה, [2] זֶה נוֹטֵל לְפִי מָעוֹתָיו וְזֶה נוֹטֵל לְפִי מָעוֹתָיו.
[3] וְרַב הַמְנוּנָא אָמַר: אֲפִילּוּ שׁוֹר לַחֲרִישָׁה וְעוֹמֵד לִטְבִיחָה, [4] הַשָּׂכָר לָאֶמְצַע.
[5] מֵיתִיבֵי. ״שְׁנַיִם שֶׁהֵטִילוּ לַכִּיס, זֶה מָנֶה וְזֶה מָאתַיִם, הַשָּׂכָר לָאֶמְצַע״. [6] מַאי לָאו בְּשׁוֹר לַחֲרִישָׁה וְעוֹמֵד לִטְבִיחָה, [7] וּתְיוּבְתָּא דְרַבָּה!

LITERAL TRANSLATION

for plowing. [1] But regarding an ox for plowing that stands [ready] for slaughter, [2] this one takes according to his money, and that one takes according to his money.

[3] And Rav Hamnuna said: Even [regarding] an ox for plowing, that stands [ready] for slaughter, [4] the profit is [divided equally] in the middle.

[5] They raised an objection: "Two who formed a partnership, this one [investing] a maneh, and that one [investing] two hundred, the profit is in the middle." [6] Is it not regarding an ox for plowing, that stands [ready] for slaughter [7] and it is a refutation of Rabbah!

TRANSLATION AND COMMENTARY

plowing are here divided equally between the two partners. The relative size of each partner's initial investment is irrelevant, because neither partner's share of the animal could not have produced any profits without the share belonging to the other. [1] **But if** the partners **bought an ox for plowing, and** that ox now **stands ready for slaughter,** that is, ready for dissolving the partnership and dividing the profits gained from selling the meat, [2] **this one takes** his share **in proportion to the** sum of **money** that he invested in the partnership, **and** similarly **the other one takes** his share **in proportion to the** sum of **money** that he invested. Here the money is divided in proportion to the initial investment, for each partner's share of the animal produces profits independently of the other partner's share.

וְרַב הַמְנוּנָא [3] **Rav Hamnuna** disagreed with Rabbah and **said: Even if** partners **bought an ox for plowing, and** that ox now **stands ready for slaughter,** [4] the partners split **the profit** earned from the sale of the meat equally **down the middle,** each partner receiving an equal share of the profits.

מֵיתִיבֵי [5] **An objection was raised** against Rabbah's position from a Baraita that stated: "If **two** people **formed a partnership, this one investing a maneh, and that one investing two hundred** dinars, they **divide the profit equally down the middle.**" This Baraita is difficult according to Rabbah; because it does not specify the case dealt with. [6] **Does** it **not** apply even **to an ox bought for plowing** that **stands ready for slaughter,** and the two partners wish to dissolve the partnership? [7] If so, the Baraita **is a refutation of Rabbah,** who claims that in such a case they divide the profits in proportion to their initial investments.

RASHI

זה נוטל לפי מעותיו כו׳ — שהרי מתחלק לאבריו. והא דנקט ראשית מקחן לחרישה — רבותא אשמועינן, דאף על גב דמעיקרא אדעתא דלמיפלג בשוה נחות לשותפות, השתא דשבח בבשר ושחטוהו, והוא מתחלק לאבריו — יטול איש לפי מעותיו.

NOTES

שׁוֹר לַחֲרִישָׁה וְעוֹמֵד לִטְבִיחָה **An ox for plowing and it stands ready for slaughter.** *Rivan* offers a second interpretation of this passage, according to which each of the partners purchased an ox with his own money, and they then joined together in order to use the animals as a team for plowing. Later when the animals became fattened the partners decided to sell them for slaughter.

אֲפִילּוּ שׁוֹר לַחֲרִישָׁה **Even an ox for plowing.** The Rishonim disagree about the position of Rav Hamnuna. Some understand that he formulated his position — "even an ox for plowing and it stands ready for slaughter" — following the terminology of Rabbah, but his ruling that the two partners divide the profits equally applies even if the ox was originally purchased for slaughter. But others argue that Rav Hamnuna was discriminative, and that only if the ox was initially purchased for plowing does he maintain that the two partners divide the profits evenly between them, for in such a case they intended to set up a partnership in which each would have an equal claim to the profits. But if the ox was purchased for slaughter from the outset, we assume that they intended to form a partnership in which each partner would take profits in proportion to his initial investment. In fact, all agree that when partners make an explicit agreement regarding how to divide up the profits, their agreement is binding.

There is a secondary disagreement according to those Rishonim who maintain that Rav Hamnuna does not distinguish between an animal that was purchased from the outset for plowing or for slaughter. According to *Rabbenu Ḥananel, Rif* and *Rambam*, Rav Hamnuna's ruling that the

HALAKHAH

שְׁנַיִם שֶׁהֵטִילוּ לַכִּיס **Two who formed a partnership.** "If several people formed a partnership, each one contributing a different sum, and the partnership enjoyed a profit or suffered a loss, the profit or loss is divided evenly among the partners, and not in proportion to each partner's initial investment. Had they bought an ox for slaughter, each partner would have taken a share of its meat in proportion to his initial investment when it was slaughtered. But if the ox was sold, the profit or loss is divided evenly between the partners," following Shmuel and Rav Hamnuna. (*Rambam, Sefer Mishpatim, Hilkhot Sheluḥim VeShutafim* 4:3; *Shulḥan Arukh, Ḥoshen Mishpat* 176:5.)

TRANSLATION AND COMMENTARY

לָא [1]The Gemara rebuts this objection: **No,** the Baraita is dealing with **an ox for plowing** that **stands ready for plowing.** In that case all agree that each of the partners receives an equal share of the profits.

אֲבָל שׁוֹר [2]The Gemara questions this understanding of the Baraita: **But what** then **is the law regarding an ox for plowing,** that **stands ready for slaughter,** and the partners wish to dissolve the partnership? Can you say, as Rabbah maintains, [3]that in such a case **one** partner **takes** his share **in proportion to the** sum of **money** that he had initially invested **and** similarly **the other** partner **takes** his share **in proportion to the money** that he had invested? If indeed these two cases are governed by different regulations, then the Baraita should not have gone on to teach a completely new case. [4]**Instead of teaching in its next clause: "If one** person **bought** a strong ox **with** two hundred dinars of **his own money, and the other** person **bought** a weaker ox **with** a hundred dinars of **his own money, and they then joined together** as partners, [5]**one** partner **takes** his share of the profits earned from the animals' plowing **in proportion to the** amount of **money** that he had initially invested, **and the other** partner **takes** his share **in proportion to the** sum of **money** that he had invested," the Baraita — if it were in agreement with Rabbah — should have continued discussing the case described in its first clause, in which the two pooled their money to buy a single animal. [6]It **should have taught the** following **distinction: When does this** ruling **apply** that the partners split their earnings equally? [7]When the partners **bought an ox for plowing and it** still **stands ready for plowing,** and they now divide the profits earned from the animal's work. [8]**But if** the partners **bought an ox for plowing, and** the ox now **stands ready for slaughter,** and for dissolving the partnership, [9]**this one takes** his share in the sale of the animal's meat **in proportion to the** amount of **money** that he had initially invested, **and the other one takes** his share **in proportion to the** amount of **money** that he had invested!

הָכִי נַמִי [10]The Gemara answers: **This indeed** is what the Tanna **said,** for the Baraita should be understood as if it had taught as follows: [11]**When does this** ruling **apply** that the partners divide the earnings equally between themselves? [12]**When** partners **bought an ox for plowing and it** still **stands ready for plowing,** and they

[1]לָא, בְּשׁוֹר לַחֲרִישָׁה וְעוֹמֵד לַחֲרִישָׁה.
[2]אֲבָל שׁוֹר לַחֲרִישָׁה וְעוֹמֵד לִטְבִיחָה, [3]מַאי — זֶה נוֹטֵל לְפִי מְעוֹתָיו, וְזֶה נוֹטֵל לְפִי מְעוֹתָיו? [4]אַדְּתָנֵי סֵיפָא: "לָקַח זֶה בְּשֶׁלּוֹ, וְזֶה בְּשֶׁלּוֹ, וְנִתְעָרְבוּ [5]— זֶה נוֹטֵל לְפִי מְעוֹתָיו, וְזֶה נוֹטֵל לְפִי מְעוֹתָיו" — [6]לִיפְלוֹג וְלִיתְנֵי בְּדִידֵיהּ: בַּמֶּה דְּבָרִים אֲמוּרִים? [7]בְּשׁוֹר לַחֲרִישָׁה וְעוֹמֵד לַחֲרִישָׁה. [8]אֲבָל בְּשׁוֹר לַחֲרִישָׁה וְעוֹמֵד לִטְבִיחָה, [9]זֶה נוֹטֵל לְפִי מְעוֹתָיו, וְזֶה נוֹטֵל לְפִי מְעוֹתָיו!
[10]הָכִי נַמִי קָאָמַר: [11]בַּמֶּה דְּבָרִים אֲמוּרִים? [12]בְּשׁוֹר לַחֲרִישָׁה וְעוֹמֵד לַחֲרִישָׁה.

LITERAL TRANSLATION

[1]No, regarding an ox for plowing, that stands [ready] for plowing.

[2]But regarding an ox for plowing, that stands [ready] for slaughter, [3]what [is the law] — this one takes according to his money, and that one takes according to his money? [4]Instead of the teaching in the last clause: "[If] this one bought with his own [money], and that one bought with his own [money], and they [then] joined together, [5]this one takes according to his money, and that one takes according to his money" — [6]let it distinguish and teach about itself: In what [case] are these things said? [7]Regarding an ox for plowing that stands [ready] for plowing. [8]But regarding an ox for plowing and it stands [ready] for slaughter, [9]this one takes according to his money, and that one takes according to his money!

[10]This is indeed [what] he said: [11]In what [case] are these things said? [12]Regarding an ox for plowing that stands [ready] for plowing.

RASHI

לקח זה בשלו – שוורים בריאים במאתים. וזה בשלו – שוורים כחושים במנה. זה נוטל לפי מעותיו – דשור כחוש אין עבודתו דומה לשל בריא. ליפלוג בדידיה – אף כשהטילו לכיס מעות, ולקחו בהמה אחת, יחלוקו. ולימא, זה נוטל לפי מעותיו וזה נוטל לפי מעותיו כו׳.

NOTES

profits are divided evenly only applies when the animal was sold before it was slaughtered. But if it was sold after it was slaughtered (or generally, if the partners enter into a partnership regarding merchandise that can be divided up for sale), the profits are divided in proportion to each partner's initial investment. *Rosh, Ra'ah* and *Ritva* disagree and say that Rav Hamnuna rules in all cases that the profits are divided evenly.

TRANSLATION AND COMMENTARY

divide the profits earned from the animal's work. [1]**But** if the partners had bought **an ox for plowing, and** the ox now **stands ready for slaughter,** and they divide the profits earned from the sale of the animal's meat, [2]**it is considered as if one had bought** a strong ox **with his own** greater sum of **money, and the other had bought** a weaker ox **with his own** smaller sum of **money, and** only then **did they join together** as partners. [3]So **one** partner **takes** his share of the profits **in proportion to the** amount of **money** that he had initially invested, **and the other** partner **takes** his share of the profits **in proportion to the** amount of **money** that he had invested.

תְּנַן [4]The Gemara now raises an objection to Shmuel's ruling from what **we have learned** in our Mishnah: **"And similarly** if **three** people **invested in a partnership** to purchase merchandise, each one investing a different sum, **and** the total value of their investments **decreased or increased,** when the partners dissolve the partnership, **they divide** up the assets **in the same manner,** each partner receiving a proportional share of his initial investment." The Gemara asks regarding the language of the Mishnah: [5]**Is it not** that the expression **"they decreased" means** that the partnership's assets **decreased in real value,** [6]**and** the expression **"they increased" means** that the partnership's assets **increased in real value?** The increase or decrease is profit or loss. Thus, the Mishnah's ruling contradicts Shmuel, who said that the profits of a partnership are divided equally among the partners, regardless of how much each of them initially invested!

אָמַר רַב נַחְמָן [7]**Rav Naḥman said in the name of Rabbah bar Avuha:** There is really **no** difficulty,

[1]אֲבָל בְּשׁוֹר לַחֲרִישָׁה וְעוֹמֵד לִטְבִיחָה, [2]נַעֲשָׂה כְּמִי שֶׁלָּקַח זֶה בְּשֶׁלּוֹ, וְזֶה בְּשֶׁלּוֹ, וְנִתְעָרְבוּ, [3]זֶה נוֹטֵל לְפִי מְעוֹתָיו, וְזֶה נוֹטֵל לְפִי מְעוֹתָיו.

[4]תְּנַן: "וְכֵן שְׁלֹשָׁה שֶׁהִטִּילוּ לַכִּיס, פָּחֲתוּ אוֹ הוֹתִירוּ, כָּךְ הֵן חוֹלְקִין". [5]מַאי לָאו "פָּחֲתוּ" פָּחֲתוּ מַמָּשׁ, [6]"הוֹתִירוּ" הוֹתִירוּ מַמָּשׁ!

[7]אָמַר רַב נַחְמָן אָמַר רַבָּה בַּר

LITERAL TRANSLATION

[1]But regarding an ox for plowing that stands [ready] for slaughter, [2]it becomes as if this one bought with his own [money], and that one bought with his own [money], and they [then] joined together, [3][therefore] this one takes according to his money, and that one takes according to his money.

[4]We have learned: "And similarly three who formed a partnership, [and the investments] decreased or increased, they divide in this manner." [5]Is it not that "they decreased" [means] they actually decreased [in value] [6][and] "they increased" [means] they actually increased [in value].

[7]Rav Naḥman said in the name of Rabbah bar

RASHI

פחתו פחתו ממש כו׳ – וקתני: כך הן חולקין לפי המעות, ומיובתא דשמואל.

NOTES

תְּנַן: וְכֵן שְׁלֹשָׁה שֶׁהִטִּילוּ לַכִּיס **We have learned: And similarly three who invested.** *Rashi* writes that the Gemara cites our Mishnah as an objection to Shmuel. Some understood that according to *Rashi,* there are three different opinions regarding the division of profits among partners who invested different amounts: That of Shmuel, Rabbah, and Rav Hamnuna. Thus *Rashi* maintains that according to Shmuel, the partners always divide the profits evenly. Our Mishnah is only difficult according to Shmuel but not according to Rabbah or Rav Hamnuna. According to Rabbah, the Mishnah can be understood as dealing with a case like an ox that was purchased for plowing and now stands ready for slaughter. According to Rav Hamnuna, it is equivalent to an ox that was purchased for slaughter and now stands ready for slaughter. But *Ritva* and others (see *Tosafot*) understand that Rabbah and Rav Hamnuna disagree about Shmuel's position, and that the Gemara's objection based on the Mishnah follows Rav Hamnuna's understanding of Shmuel. These Rishonim maintain that according to Rav Hamnuna, the partners always divide the profits evenly.

פָּחֲתוּ אוֹ הוֹתִירוּ **"They increased" means new coins.** The Jerusalem Talmud resolves this difficulty in the same manner. Some authorities note that this law applies whenever the value of the money increased, as when it was revalued by government decree.

HALAKHAH

פָּחֲתוּ אוֹ הוֹתִירוּ **They decreased or increased.** "The ruling that the partners divide the profit or loss evenly between them, and not in proportion to each partner's initial investment, only applies if the partners invested the joint funds and realized a profit or loss. But if the funds were not invested, but appreciated or depreciated because of fluctuations in the value of currency, the profit or loss is divided between the partners in proportion to each partner's initial investment. *Rema* notes that all the more so do the partners divide the profit or loss in proportion to their initial investments, if they each contributed merchandise to the partnership, and that merchandise is intact." (*Rambam, Sefer Mishpatim, Hilkhot Sheluḥim VeShutafim* 4:3; *Shulḥan Arukh, Ḥoshen Mishpat* 176:5.)

אֲבוּהּ: לָא, [1]"הוֹתִירוּ" זוּזֵי חֲדַתֵי, [2]"פָּחֲתוּ" אַסְתֵּירָא דְּצוּנִיתָא.

מִשְׁנָה [3]מִי שֶׁהָיָה נָשׂוּי אַרְבַּע נָשִׁים וּמֵת, [4]הָרִאשׁוֹנָה קוֹדֶמֶת לַשְּׁנִיָּה, [5]וּשְׁנִיָּה לַשְּׁלִישִׁית, וּשְׁלִישִׁית לָרְבִיעִית. [6]וְרִאשׁוֹנָה נִשְׁבַּעַת לַשְּׁנִיָּה,

LITERAL TRANSLATION

Avuha: No, [1]"they increased" [relates to] new coins, [2][and] "they decreased" [relates to] a coin [useful only] for a callus.

MISHNAH [3][If] someone was married to four women and [he] died, [4]the first one takes precedence over the second, [5]and the second over the third, and the third over the fourth.

[6]And the first takes an oath to the second,

TRANSLATION AND COMMENTARY

[1]for when the Mishnah says that the partnership's assets **"increased,"** it refers to getting rid of old coins and taking in **new ones,** although the nominal value of their initial capital had not changed. New coins, circulate more easily than old ones. Thus the partnership's assets increased somewhat in value. In this situation, the Mishnah rules that when the partnership is dissolved, each partner receives his share of the coins in accordance with his initial investment. However, when Shmuel said that the profits earned through a partnership are divided equally between the partners, he was referring to a real increase in the nominal value of the business' assets. [2]When the Mishnah says that the partnership's assets **"decreased,"** it means that the coins held by the partnership were removed from circulation because they were disqualified by the authorities, so that now the **coins** could only be **used** as a remedy **for calluses.** It was customary for a person with a callus on his foot to bind a coin that had been removed from circulation to the afflicted area in order to prevent chafing. These coins — which were part of the partnership capital before they were disqualified — are worth less than coins that circulate as currency. Thus the partnership's assets suffered a loss in value. The Mishnah rules that when the partnership is dissolved, each partner receives his share of these disqualified coins in accordance with his initial investment. If, however, the business actually lost money, the partners divide the loss equally between them, in agreement with Shmuel.

MISHNAH מִי שֶׁהָיָה [3]If someone married four women, and their four ketubah deeds were drawn up on different dates, **and** the husband **died,** and the estate was insufficient to cover all of the obligations, [4]**the** man's **first wife takes precedence over** his **second** wife in recovering her ketubah, [5]his **second** wife takes precedence **over the third, and** his **third** wife takes precedence **over the fourth.**

וְרִאשׁוֹנָה נִשְׁבַּעַת [6]If the man's second wife is concerned that her husband's estate will not suffice to cover her ketubah, she may demand that **the first** wife **take an oath to her** that she did not receive her settlement

RASHI

זוזי חדתי — שמטילין זוזים ישנים, ונתנו ונשאו בהם עד שנעשו חדשים, ויוצאין הם בהוצאה. הלכך, חולקים לפי המעות, דכל חד מאי דיהיב שקיל. אבל אם הותירו יותר על החשבון — השכר לאמצע. **איסתרי דצוניתא** — שנפסלה המטבע, ואין יוצאת בהוצאה, ומי שיש לו מכה בפיסת רגלו מתחת, קושר מהם שם. דמעליא ליה חלודה דידהו, וצורתא דידהו כדאמרינן במסכת שבת (סה,א): יוצאין בסלע שעל הצינית, ומפרש: מאי צינית — בת ארעא. דכיון דישנו בעין — נוטל כל אחד כחשבון שהטיל. אבל אם פחתו מאה או חמשים זוז — זה מפסיד מחצה, וזה מחצה, שהשכר וההפסד לאמצע.

משנה הראשונה נשבעת לשניה — אם שניה טוענת: הואיל ואת באת ליטול תחלה — השבעי לי שלא גבית משל בעלי כלום, דלמא לא משתייר לי נכסים כשיעור כתובתי. ואף שלישית תאמר כן לשניה, ורביעית לשלישית. אבל הרביעית — נפרעת שלא בשבועה. וכגון שהיתומים גדולים. וקסבר האי תנא: כי אמרו רבנן הבא ליפרע מנכסי יתומים לא יפרע אלא בשבועה — ביתומים קטנים אמרו, ולא בגדולים.

BACKGROUND

אַסְתֵּירָא דְּצוּנִיתָא **A coin for a callus.** It appears that צִנִּית is an infected swelling or blistering of the foot. Perhaps contact with the metal also helped cure the injury. Today as well certain metallic powders are used to cure wounds.

However, the Jerusalem Talmud defines צִנִּית as gout, a very painful disease that mainly affects toe joints.

NOTES

אַרְבַּע נָשִׁים **Four wives.** *Tosafot* and others ask: Why does the Mishnah deal with a case where a man married four women, when the same laws apply when a man married only three women? *Talmid HaRashba* explains that the Mishnah implies the advice that a man should not marry more than four women (advice that the Gemara offers explicitly in *Yevamot* 44a). *Rivan* suggests that since the previous Mishnah dealt with a man who married three women, our Mishnah deals with a man who had four wives. *Meiri* argues that the Mishnayot are arranged in order: The chapter opens with a case where a man had two wives, it then proceeds to discuss the case of three wives, and here, four wives.

הָרִאשׁוֹנָה קוֹדֶמֶת לַשְּׁנִיָּה **The first takes precedence over the second.** *Talmid HaRashba* explains that the first wife takes precedence over the second, even if the husband's

HALAKHAH

הָרִאשׁוֹנָה קוֹדֶמֶת לַשְּׁנִיָּה **The first one takes precedence over the second.** "If a man married four women, and their four ketubah deeds were drawn up on different dates, and the man died, whichever woman was married first takes precedence over the next wife in recovering her ketubah. The first wife must take an oath to the second wife that

[1] וּשְׁנִיָּה לַשְּׁלִישִׁית, וּשְׁלִישִׁית לָרְבִיעִית, [2] וְהָרְבִיעִית נִפְרַעַת שֶׁלֹּא בִּשְׁבוּעָה.

[3] בֶּן נַנָּס אוֹמֵר: וְכִי מִפְּנֵי שֶׁהִיא אַחֲרוֹנָה נִשְׂכֶּרֶת? [4] אַף הִיא לֹא תִּפָּרַע אֶלָּא בִּשְׁבוּעָה.

[5] הָיוּ יוֹצְאוֹת כּוּלָּן בְּיוֹם אֶחָד, [6] כָּל הַקּוֹדֶמֶת לַחֲבֶרְתָּהּ, אֲפִילּוּ שָׁעָה אַחַת, זָכְתָה. [7] וְכָךְ הָיוּ כּוֹתְבִין בִּירוּשָׁלַיִם שָׁעוֹת.

[8] הָיוּ כּוּלָּן יוֹצְאוֹת בְּשָׁעָה אַחַת, [9] וְאֵין שָׁם אֶלָּא מָנֶה, חוֹלְקוֹת בְּשָׁוֶה.

גמרא [10] בְּמַאי קָמִיפַּלְגִי?

LITERAL TRANSLATION

[1] and the second to the third, and the third to the fourth, [2] and the fourth receives payment without an oath.

[3] Ben Nannas says: And should she profit because she is last? [4] She too is not paid without an oath.

[5] [If] all [the ketubot] were issued (lit., "went out") on the same day, [6] each [woman whose ketubah] comes before the other, even [by] one hour, acquires [it]. [7] And thus they would write in Jerusalem the hour.

[8] If all were issued at the same hour, [9] and there is only a maneh, they divide equally.

GEMARA [10] About what do they disagree?

RASHI

אף היא לא תפרע כו׳ — ובגמרא מפרש פלוגתייהו במאי. **היו כולן יוצאות ביום אחד** — כלומר יוצאות לפנינו ומלמדות שכולן נכתבו ביום אחד. **כל הקודמת לחברתה שעה אחת** — בכתובתה. **זכתה** — אם השעות מפורשות בתוכן. כגון, באחת כתוב: ביום פלוני בשעה שלישית, ובשניה בשעה רביעית, וכן בכולן.

TRANSLATION AND COMMENTARY

during her husband's lifetime, and only after taking the oath may she collect what is due her. And similarly, [1] **the** man's **second** wife must take an oath **to his third** wife, and **his third** wife must take an oath **to his fourth** wife, each woman swearing to the woman with the subsequent lien that she has not collected her settlement. [2] **But the** man's **fourth** wife **receives payment** even **without** taking **an oath** to the others that she had not already received her ketubah.

בֶּן נַנָּס [3] **Ben Nannas** disagrees with the first Tanna of the Mishnah and **says:** Why **should the** fourth **woman profit** and be free of an oath just **because she is the last** to receive payment? [4] **She too does not receive payment without** first taking **an oath** that she has not collected her settlement.

הָיוּ יוֹצְאוֹת כּוּלָּן [5] Until now the Mishnah has assumed that the respective ketubah deeds were drawn up on different days. But **if all the ketubah deeds were issued on the same day,** the hour at which the deed was written determines the priority of the liens. [6] **The woman with** the **ketubah** deed that was written **before** that of **the other, even** if the difference between the two is only **an hour, acquires** her ketubah settlement before the other. [7] **And thus** it was customary **in Jerusalem to write** into the ketubah deed **the hour** at which it was written, so that there be no question about whose lien was established first.

הָיוּ כּוּלָּן [8] The Mishnah concludes: **If** a man was married to several women, and **all** of their ketubah deeds **were issued** on the same day and **at the same hour,** so that nobody has a preferential right of recovering her ketubah, and the husband died, [9] **and** his estate **amounts to only a maneh,** the widows **divide** the estate **equally.**

GEMARA בְּמַאי קָמִיפַּלְגִי [10] The Gemara asks: **About what do** the anonymous first Tanna of the Mishnah and Ben Nannas **disagree?**

NOTES

estate suffices to cover all his obligations. If it later turns out that the property which the first wife collected did not belong to her husband, she can seize the property that the second wife collected.

וְכָךְ הָיוּ כּוֹתְבִין בִּירוּשָׁלַיִם **And thus they would write in Jerusalem.** *Talmidei Rabbenu Yonah* write that where it is not customary to record the time in the ketubah, we assume that the parties did not wish the lien to be established until the end of the day. Hence, if a man's several wives all had ketubah deeds that were issued on the same day, each of them has an equal lien on her husband's property, even if there are witnesses that one ketubah deed was drawn up before the other.

בְּמַאי קָמִיפַּלְגִי **About what do they disagree.** Our commentary follows *Rivan* who understands this phrase in its usual sense, as an inquiry into the theoretical basis for

HALAKHAH

she has not received her ketubah settlement, the second wife must take such an oath to the third wife, the third wife must take such an oath to the fourth wife, and the fourth wife must take such an oath to the heirs," following Ben Nannas. (*Rambam, Sefer Nashim, Hilkhot Ishut* 17:1; *Shulhan Arukh, Even HaEzer* 96:16.)

הָיוּ יוֹצְאוֹת כּוּלָּן בְּיוֹם אֶחָד **If all went out on the same day.** "If a man was married to several women, and all their ketubah deeds were issued on the same day (or at the same hour where such information is recorded in the ketubah deed), each woman takes an equal share of her late husband's property, for nobody enjoys a preferential

TRANSLATION AND COMMENTARY

אָמַר שְׁמוּאֵל [1]**Shmuel said:** [94A] [2]Ben Nannas's objection arises **when one of** the fields collected by the first three wives **was found to be a field that did not** actually **belong to** the husband. Concerned that the field that she had received would be taken away by its rightful owner, the wife holding that field wished to impose an oath upon her husband's fourth wife that she had not already collected her ketubah settlement. If she refuses to swear, she cannot collect the property, which will then remain as security for the concerned woman. [3]The Tannaim of our Mishnah **argue about** whether the fourth wife must take such an oath to collect her settlement. The theoretical issue underlying their dispute is the matter of **a later creditor**, whose lien upon the debtor's property was established after that of another creditor. If the later creditor **went ahead and collected** his debt from the debtor's property, thereby forestalling an earlier creditor from utilizing his preferential right of recovery, [4]**the** anonymous **first Tanna** of the Mishnah **maintains** that **what he collected was not collected legally,** so the earlier creditor may take it from him. Thus, it is immaterial whether the fourth wife takes an oath. In any event, if the other wife's field is confiscated by its rightful owner, she can recover her settlement from that of the fourth wife, who is like a later creditor who seized property to which the third wife had an earlier lien. [5]**And Ben Nannas maintains** that if a later creditor and seized property to which another creditor had an earlier lien, **what** the later creditor **collected was collected legally.** In his view, the wife with the "stolen" field, will not be able to retrieve anything from the fourth wife if it is confiscated. Hence she can demand that the fourth wife swear that she has not already collected her settlement, and only then may the fourth wife take what is due her.

(אָמַר) רַב נַחְמָן [6]**Rav Naḥman said in the name of Rabbah bar Avuha:** [7]In fact, **all** the Tannaim — both the anonymous first Tanna of the Mishnah and Ben Nannas — **agree that** if a later creditor seized property to which another creditor had an earlier lien, **what he collected was not collected legally.** All therefore also agree that if the third wife's field is confiscated by its rightful owner, she can seize the field that the fourth wife received as her ketubah settlement. Why, then, does Ben Nannas maintains that the fourth wife must take an oath before receiving property for her ketubah settlement. The anonymous first Tanna of the

[1]אָמַר שְׁמוּאֵל [94A] [2]כְּגוֹן שֶׁנִּמְצֵאת אַחַת מֵהֶן שָׂדֶה שֶׁאֵינָהּ שֶׁלּוֹ, [3]וּבְבַעַל חוֹב מְאוּחָר שֶׁקָּדַם וְגָבָה קָמִיפַּלְגִי. [4]תָּנָא קַמָּא סָבַר: מַה שֶׁגָּבָה לֹא גָּבָה. [5]וּבֶן נַנָּס סָבַר: מַה שֶּׁגָּבָה, גָּבָה.

[6](אָמַר) רַב נַחְמָן אָמַר רַבָּה בַּר אֲבוּהּ: [7]דְּכוּלֵּי עָלְמָא מַה שֶּׁגָּבָה לֹא גָּבָה. וְהָכָא

LITERAL TRANSLATION

[1]Shmuel said: [94A] [2]As when one of [the fields] was found to be a field that is not his, and they argue [3]about a later creditor who went first and collected. [4]The first Tanna maintains: What he collected he did not collect [legally]. [5]And Ben Nannas maintains: What he collected, he collected [legally].

[6]Rav Naḥman said in the name of Rabbah bar Avuha: [7]All agree [that] what he collected he did not collect [legally]. And here

RASHI

כגון שנמצאת אחת — מן השלש שדות שגבו שלש נשים ראשונות. **שדה שאינה שלו** — שנודע שגזלה, וסוף שיבואו בעלים ויטלוה ממנה. וכשבאה רביעית לגבות כתובתה משדה רביעית — באה זו ועומדת לאמר: למחר יבא הנגזל ויטול שדהו מידי, ונמצאתי קרחת. רצוני שתשבעי שלא גבית כתובתיך בחיי הבעל. **ובבעל חוב מאוחר שקדם וגבה קמיפלגי תנא קמא סבר מה שגבה לא גבה** — הלכך למה תשבע? אם יבא הנגזל ויטרוף מזו — תחזור היא על הרביעית, ותטול ממנה מה שגבתה, דהויא לה רביעית בעל חוב מאוחר. **ובן ננס סבר מה שגבה גבה** — ואין השלישית חוזרת עליה, לפיכך יכולה להשביעה. **דכולי עלמא מה שגבה לא גבה** — ושבועה דבן ננס טעמא מאי — דקסבר: חיישינן שמא תכסיף הרביעית הזאת את השדה שהיא גובה. דכי חזיא דלא משבעינן לה ידעא דהדרא שלישית עילוה כשיטלו מה שבידה, ולא חיישא הך רביעית לאשבוחי לארעא, אלא שמטה ואכלה. ותנא קמא לא חייש ל"שמא תכסיף".

SAGES

בֶּן נַנָּס **Ben Nannas.** His full name is Rabbi Shimon ben Nannas, one of the Sages of the Mishnah. It appears that he was a colleague of Rabbi Akiva (though younger than him) and of Rabbi Yishmael. The Talmud quotes his rulings on a number of occasions, and his opponent in Halakhic discussions is frequently Rabbi Akiva.

The Talmud makes no mention of his personal history or family background. The only reference we find to Ben Nannas's personality is the superlative praise accorded him by Rabbi Yishmael (*Bava Batra* 125b): "A person who desires to gain wisdom should occupy himself with civil law…and a person who desires to occupy himself with civil law should study under Shimon ben Nannas."

NOTES

a dispute between the Tannaim. *Ritva* argues that the Gemara here raises a question about Ben Nannas's opinion: Why does Ben Nannas require the fourth wife to take an oath? The viewpoint of the anonymous first Tanna of the Mishnah stands to reason, for the other three wives have already received their ketubah settlements and will not suffer a loss even if the fourth woman had received her settlement before her husband died!

HALAKHAH

right of recovering her ketubah settlement." (*Rambam, Sefer Nashim, Hilkhot Ishut* 17:3; *Shulḥan Arukh, Even HaEzer* 96:17.)

מַה שֶּׁגָּבָה גָּבָה **What he collected he did not collect.** "In the case of a plurality of creditors, the one whose lien had been established has priority in recovering his debt, whether from the debtor himself or from a buyer who purchased landed property from him. If a later creditor collected his debt from the debtor's property on which another creditor had an earlier lien, the property is removed from him." (*Rambam, Sefer Mishpatim, Hilkhot Malveh* 20:1; *Shulḥan Arukh, Ḥoshen Mishpat* 104:1.)

TRANSLATION AND COMMENTARY

Mishnah and Ben Nannas [1]**disagree about whether** or not **we are concerned that** the fourth wife **will perhaps** misuse the collected property and **allow** it **to deteriorate.** [2]**One Sage** — Ben Nannas — **maintains** that **we are concerned that** if the fourth wife collects the property without first taking an oath, she will understand that the property is not firmly in her possession and **will allow it to deteriorate,** and the other wife will recover a damaged field. [3]**And the other Sage** — the anonymous first Tanna of the Mishnah — **maintains** that **we are not concerned that** the fourth wife **will allow** the property which she collects **to deteriorate** and therefore there is no reason to impose an oath upon her.

אַבַּיֵי אָמַר [4]The Gemara now suggests a third way to understand the Tannaitic dispute: **Abaye said:** The Mishnah deals with an oath that can be required by the husband's heirs from all the wives. According to Abaye, the anonymous first Tanna of the Baraita and Ben Nannas **disagree about the** Baraita **taught by Abaye the Elder,** [5]**for Abaye the Elder taught** a Baraita that clarifies the ruling that a creditor may not recover his debt from the debtor's orphaned heirs without first taking an oath that the debt is still outstanding. The Baraita states: **"The orphans about which** the Rabbis **spoke** include even **adult** heirs, [6]**and it is not necessary to say** that **minors** are also included." Surely a creditor cannot recover a debt from his debtor's orphaned children without first taking an oath, for minors are not competent to dispute the claims brought against their deceased father. The Baraita teaches that without an oath a creditor cannot even recover a debt from his debtor's adult heirs, because they may not have been familiar enough with their father's business dealings to know if he had paid his debt. Now, our Mishnah refers to widows who seek to collect their ketubah

[1]בְּחָיְישִׁינַן שֶׁמָּא תַּכְסִיף קָמִיפַּלְגִי. [2]מָר סָבַר: חָיְישִׁינַן שֶׁמָּא תַּכְסִיף. [3]וּמָר סָבַר: לָא חָיְישִׁינַן שֶׁמָּא תַּכְסִיף.
[4]אַבַּיֵי אָמַר: דְּאַבַּיֵי קַשִּׁישָׁא אִיכָּא בֵּינַיְיהוּ, [5]דְּתָנֵי אַבַּיֵי קַשִּׁישָׁא: "יְתוֹמִים שֶׁאָמְרוּ, גְּדוֹלִים, [6]וְאֵין צָרִיךְ לוֹמַר

LITERAL TRANSLATION

[1]they disagree about [whether] we are concerned that perhaps she will allow [it] to deteriorate. [2]One Sage maintains: We are concerned that perhaps she will allow it to deteriorate. [3]And the other Sage maintains: We are not concerned that she will allow it to deteriorate.

[4]Abaye said: That [teaching] of Abaye the Elder is [the difference] between them, [5]for Abaye the Elder taught: "The orphans about which they spoke are adults, [6]and it is not necessary to say [that] minors [are included]."

RASHI

דאביי קשישא איכא בינייהו — והיתומים באים להשביעה. ולא בנמלאת שדה שאינה שלו מיירי. **יתומים שאמרו** — הבא ליפרע מהם לא יפרע אלא בשבועה — **אף** בגדולים אמרו.

NOTES

בְּחָיְישִׁינַן שֶׁמָּא תַּכְסִיף About whether we are concerned that perhaps she will allow it to deteriorate. Our commentary follows *Rashi* who understands that Ben Nannas is concerned that if the fourth wife is allowed to collect her ketubah settlement without an oath, she will fear that the property might not remain in her possession forever, and will not take proper care of it. We therefore impose an oath upon her so that she will have the same apparent status as the other wives and watch over her property as carefully as other wives watch over theirs. *Ramban* questions whether we impose an oath here only to deceive the fourth wife. *Ramban* himself explains that the other wives can argue that they do not want the fourth wife to take the property, for she may already have collected her ketubah settlement, and they might have to collect the property from her later. Meanwhile, she might allow the property to deteriorate. But if the fourth wife takes an oath that she has not yet received her ketubah settlement, the other women cannot keep her from taking possession of the property until one of the other wives advances a claim on it (see also *Ra'ah,* and others).

Rav Sherira Gaon suggests an entirely different interpretation, according to which the term שֶׁמָּא תַּכְסִיף means: "Perhaps she will be embarrassed." Ben Nannas maintains that the fourth wife must also take an oath, for we are concerned that if an oath is imposed only on the first three, they might suffer embarrassment because they were not trusted, while the fourth wife was given her property without an oath.

דְּאַבַּיֵי קַשִּׁישָׁא אִיכָּא בֵּינַיְיהוּ That of Abaye the Elder is between them. There are practical differences between the various explanations offered for the dispute between Ben Nannas and the anonymous first Tanna of the Mishnah. According to the first two explanations, the law is in accordance with the anonymous first Tanna, whereas according to the third explanation, the law is in accordance with Ben Nannas, for his position is supported by the Baraita taught by Abaye the Elder. The law, in fact, follows

HALAKHAH

יְתוֹמִים שֶׁאָמְרוּ גְּדוֹלִים The orphans about which they spoke. "A creditor cannot collect from his debtor's heirs without first taking an oath, even if those heirs are adults," following Abaye the Elder, and the conclusion of the Gemara in *Gittin* 50b. (*Rambam, Sefer Mishpatim, Hilkhot Malveh* 14:1; *Shulḥan Arukh, Ḥoshen Mishpat* 108:17.)

קְטַנִּים". [1]תַּנָּא קַמָּא לֵית לֵיהּ דְּאַבָּיֵי קַשִּׁישָׁא, [2]וּבֶן נַנָּס אִית לֵיהּ דְּאַבָּיֵי קַשִּׁישָׁא.

[3]אָמַר רַב הוּנָא: הָנֵי תְּרֵי אַחֵי וּתְרֵי שׁוּתָּפֵי דְּאִית לְהוּ דִּינָא בַּהֲדֵי חַד, [4]וַאֲזַל חַד מִינַּיְיהוּ בַּהֲדֵיהּ לְדִינָא [5]לָא מָצֵי אִידָךְ לְמֵימַר לֵיהּ: "אַתְּ לָאו בַּעַל דְּבָרִים דִּידִי אַתְּ", [6]אֶלָּא שְׁלִיחוּתֵיהּ עֲבַד.

[7]אִקְלַע רַב נַחְמָן לְסוּרָא, שַׁיְילוּהִי: [8]כִּי הַאי גַּוְונָא,

LITERAL TRANSLATION

[1]The first Tanna does not agree with Abaye the Elder, [2]and Ben Nannas agrees with Abaye the Elder. [3]Rav Huna said: [If there were] two brothers or two partners who have a lawsuit against an individual, [4]and one of- them went with him for litigation [5]the other one cannot say [to this individual]: "You are not my opponent," [6]but [the first one] performed his agency.

[7]Rav Naḥman happened to come to Sura, [where] they asked him: [8]In such a situation,

RASHI

תרי אחי ותרי שותפי – או תרי שותפי. **ואזל חד מינייהו בהדיה לדינא** – בדבר השותפות, ויצא השותף חייב. **לא מצי** – שותף חבירו, למימר לבעל הדין. **אנת לאו בעל דברים דידי את** – בדין זה שנתחייב חברי – אני אדין עמך בחלקי.

TRANSLATION AND COMMENTARY

settlements from their husband's adult heirs. [1]**The** anonymous **first Tanna** of the Mishnah **does not agree with** the Baraita taught by **Abaye the Elder,** so he rules that the fourth wife may collect her ketubah settlement without first taking an oath that she has not already collected it. [2]**And Ben Nannas agrees with** the Baraita taught by **Abaye the Elder** and rules that she must take an oath, just like the others.

אָמַר רַב הוּנָא [3]**Rav Huna said:** Suppose **two brothers** inherited their father's estate but had not yet divided it, **or two partners** in business have **a lawsuit against someone.** [4]**If one of the** brothers or partners **went** to court by himself to deal with **the litigation,** and lost, [5]**the other** brother or partner **cannot** deny his half of the liability and **say** to **the individual** who won the lawsuit: **"You were not my opponent** in any litigation. The lawsuit that you won related only to my bother's portion of the estate, or my partner's portion of the business." [6]**But rather** we say that the brother or partner who responded to the lawsuit and lost **was acting as an agent** of the other, and the liability falls equally on both of them.

אִקְלַע [7]**Rav Naḥman happened to come to Sura, where he was asked:** [8]In a case **like this,** when one of

NOTES

Ben Nannas. The fourth wife must take an oath before collecting her settlement from the estate. *Rambam* and *Bertinoro* explain the Mishnah in the manner suggested by Shmuel and not as did Abaye. It would appear that they preferred the simple reading of the Mishnah, which implies that the women take oaths to each other, and not to the heirs.

תְּרֵי אַחֵי וּתְרֵי שׁוּתָּפֵי **Two brothers or two partners.** It has been suggested Rav Huna had to mention both the case of the two brothers and that of the two partners. For had he mentioned only the former case, we might have thought that it is only there where the two brothers automatically inherited property from the same estate that we consider the brother who responded to the lawsuit to be acting as agent for the other, but where two people joined together voluntarily as partners, perhaps the law is different. And had Rav Huna mentioned only the two partners, we might have thought that it is only in the case where partners join together of their own volition do we say that the partner who responded to the lawsuit was acting as the agent of the other partner, but in the case of the two brothers, perhaps the law is different (*Ḥever ben Ḥayyim*).

לָא מָצֵי אִידָךְ לְמֵימַר **The other one cannot say.** Our commentary follows *Rashi* and most Rishonim who understand that Rav Huna means that the other brother or partner cannot say to the plaintiff: You must bring my half of your claim in a separate suit. According to this explanation the phrase, "You are not my opponent," is not to be taken literally, for the brother or partner does not claim that the plaintiff has no standing in the case, but rather that the decision in his brother's or his partner's suit should not apply to him. *Ritva* explains that this phrase falls under the category of phrases that have different meanings in different passages. *Ran* cites an entirely different explanation in the name of *Rambam:* Rav Huna maintains that the plaintiff cannot say to the brother or partner who comes to court that he by himself is not his opponent in this case and that his brother or partner must also appear, so that he not be required to bring a second suit against him at some later point. Rather, the one brother or partner may appear in court on behalf of the other as his agent.

HALAKHAH

תְּרֵי אַחֵי וּתְרֵי שׁוּתָּפֵי **Two brothers or two partners.** "One of several brothers who had not yet divided their father's estate or one of several partners may present a claim against another person on behalf of all the brothers or partners without formal authorization from the others," following Rav Huna. (*Rambam, Sefer Kinyan, Hilkhot Sheluḥin VeShutafim* 3:3; *Shulḥan Arukh, Ḥoshen Mishpat* 122:9.)

TRANSLATION AND COMMENTARY

two partners entered into litigation with a third party, and lost, [1]**what is the law?** [2]Rav Naḥman **said to them:** Your answer **is** found in **our Mishnah,** which teaches: [3]**"The** man's **first** wife **takes an oath to his second** wife that she has not already received her ketubah settlement during her husband's lifetime, and only then may she collect what is due her. [4]Similarly, **the** man's **second** wife must take an oath **to his third** wife, and **his third** wife must take an oath **to his fourth** wife." [5]**But** the Mishnah **does not state** that the man's **first** wife **must** also **take an oath to his third** or fourth wife, even though they might also be legitimately concerned that their husband's estate will not suffice to pay their ketubot after the first wife receives her ketubah settlement. [6]**What is the reason** that the third or fourth wife cannot demand an oath of the first wife? [7]**Is it not that** the second, third, and fourth wives are seen as having a joint claim against the first wife, and when the second wife demanded an oath of the first wife, **she was** also **acting as** the other wives' **agent,** and the one oath suffices for all of them? So too in the case of two partners, one partner was acting as the other partner's agent in the common lawsuit.

מִי דָּמֵי [8]The Gemara rejects the analogy: But **is** the case of our Mishnah really **similar** to the case about which Rav Naḥman was asked to issue a ruling? [9]**There,** in the case of the Mishnah, the third and fourth wives cannot impose an oath upon the first wife after she swore to the second wife, because **an oath** taken **to one** person is exactly the same as **an oath** taken **to a hundred** people. [10]But **here,** in the case of the partners, the second partner **can say:** [11]**"Had I been there, I would have pleaded more effectively** and won the case. Thus, my partner should not be regarded as having acted as my agent."

וְלָא אֲמָרַן [12]The Gemara notes: **And we only say** that the third party must also sue the second partner opponent must also sue the second partner **if** the second partner **was not in town** at the time of the first lawsuit. In that case it can be argued that the partner who responded to the lawsuit was acting on his own. [13]**But if** the second partner **was in town** at the time, **he should have come** to court and participated in the litigation. If he failed to do so, it must be because he agreed to have his partner to act as his agent.

[1]מַאי? [2]אֲמַר לְהוּ: מַתְנִיתִין הִיא: [3]"הָרִאשׁוֹנָה נִשְׁבַּעַת לַשְּׁנִיָּה, [4]וּשְׁנִיָּה לַשְּׁלִישִׁית, וּשְׁלִישִׁית לָרְבִיעִית". [5]וְאִילּוּ רִאשׁוֹנָה לַשְּׁלִישִׁית לָא קָתָנֵי. [6]מַאי טַעְמָא? [7]לָאו מִשּׁוּם דִּשְׁלִיחוּתָהּ עָבְדָה?
[8]מִי דָּמֵי? [9]הָתָם שְׁבוּעָה לְאֶחָד וּשְׁבוּעָה לְמֵאָה. [10]הָכָא, אָמַר: [11]"אִילּוּ אֲנָא הֲוַאי, טָעֵינְנָא טְפֵי".
[12]וְלָא אֲמָרַן אֶלָּא דְּלָא אִיתֵיהּ בְּמָתָא, [13]אֲבָל אִיתֵיהּ בְּמָתָא, אִיבָּעֵי לֵיהּ לְמֵיתֵי.

LITERAL TRANSLATION

[1]what [is the law]? [2]He said to them: It is our Mishnah: [3]"The first takes an oath to the second, [4]and the second to the third, and the third to the fourth." [5]But it does not state: The first to the third. [6]What is the reason? [7]Is it not that [the second] performed her agency?
[8]Is it similar? [9]There, an oath to one is [like] an oath to a hundred. [10]Here, [the other one] says: [11]"Had I been [there], I would have pleaded better."
[12]And we only say this when he was not in town, [13]but if he was in town, he should have come.

RASHI

ואילו ראשונה לשלישית לא קתני – דתשבע לפי שנשבעה. ולא אמרן – שיחזיר וידון. אלא דלא הוה – האי שותף במתא, כשבא חבירו לדין.

HALAKHAH

שְׁבוּעָה לְאֶחָד וּשְׁבוּעָה לְמֵאָה **An oath to one, and an oath to a hundred.** "If two partners had a claim against someone, and one of the partners presented the claim against him, and the defendant took an oath to free himself of liability, the other partner cannot demand that the defendant take another oath, for an oath taken to one person is the same as an oath taken to a hundred people." (*Shulḥan Arukh, Ḥoshen Mishpat* 176:24.)

וְלָא אֲמָרַן אֶלָּא דְּלָא אִיתֵיהּ בְּמָתָא **And we only say this where he was not in town.** "One of several partners may present a claim on behalf of all the partners without formal authorization from the others. If he loses the case, another partner cannot say, that had he been there, he would have presented other arguments and won, for the partner who lost can ask him why did he not come to court and present his arguments. Thus, if the other partner was out of town at the time, he can bring another claim. Consequently, the partner's legal adversary can refuse to go to court with the one partner regarding a claim presented on behalf of all the partners without formal authorization from the others. *Rema* writes that the former ruling only applies if the partners were the plaintiffs. But if they were the defendants, and one partner responded to the suit on behalf of all the partners without receiving formal authorization from them, the other partners can argue that they are not bound by the decision that was delivered against them (*Ravyah*)." (*Rambam, Sefer Kinyan, Hilkhot Sheluḥim VeShutafim* 3:3; *Shulḥan Arukh, Ḥoshen Mishpat* 122:9, 176:25-26.)

TRANSLATION AND COMMENTARY

אִתְּמַר [1]**It was stated** that the Amoraim disagree about the following matter: If someone sold the same field to two different people, and **two bills** of sale for that field **were issued on the same day,** [2]**Rav says:** The two buyers **divide** the field, for there is no way to decide whose claim is stronger. [3]**Shmuel** disagrees and **says: The judges** may **use their discretion** in deciding which of the two buyers should be given title of the property.

לֵימָא רַב [4]The Gemara now proposes that this Amoraic disagreement is based on a Tannaitic dispute regarding an entirely different matter: **Shall we say that Rav said** that the two buyers divide the field because he **agrees with Rabbi Meir,** [36]**who said** that **the witnesses who sign** the bill of divorce **effect the divorce,** [94B] **and** that **Shmuel, who said** that the judges may use their discretion, **agrees with Rabbi Elazar,** [1]**who said** that **the witnesses to the delivery** of the bill of divorce **effect the divorce?** A woman's bill of divorce should be signed by two witnesses and delivered to her in the presence of two witnesses. However, the Tannaim

LITERAL TRANSLATION

[1]It was stated: [Regarding] two deeds that were issued on the same day, [2]Rav said: They divide. [3]And Shmuel said: The judges [use their] discretion. [4]Shall we say that Rav says as Rabbi Meir, [36]who said: The signing witnesses effect the divorce, [94B] and Shmuel said like Rabbi Elazar, [1]who said: The witnesses of delivery effect the divorce?

[1]אִתְּמַר: שְׁנֵי שְׁטָרוֹת הַיּוֹצְאִים בְּיוֹם אֶחָד, רַב אָמַר: חוֹלְקִין. [2]וּשְׁמוּאֵל אָמַר: שׁוּדָא דְּדַיָּינֵי. [3]לֵימָא רַב דְּאָמַר כְּרַבִּי מֵאִיר, [4]דְּאָמַר: עֵדֵי חֲתִימָה כָּרְתִי, [94B] וּשְׁמוּאֵל דְּאָמַר כְּרַבִּי אֶלְעָזָר, [5]דְּאָמַר: עֵדֵי מְסִירָה כָּרְתִי?

RASHI

שני שטרות – מכר שדה אחת לשני בני אדם ביום אחד. **שודא דדייני** – לפי ראות עיני הדיינין יטילו הזכות והחובה. **שודא** – לשון השלכה. כמו "ירה בים" דמתרגם "שדי בימא" (שמות טו). **כרבי מאיר דאמר** – לענין גט, עדי חתימה עיקר כריתות, וכן לענין השטרות. ואלו שניהם נחתמו ביום אחד ובמקום שאין כותבין שעות – גלו דעתייהו דאין מקפידין על הקודם לחבירו, ואפילו זה שחרית וזה במנחה – אין זה גובה יותר מזה. הלכך, מאי שודא דדייני איכא למימר? אין אדם יכול ליפות כחו של זה משל זה! **ושמואל דאמר כרבי אלעזר דאמר** – אף על פי שאין עליו עדים אלא שנתנו בפני עדים גובה מנכסים משועבדים

BACKGROUND

שׁוּדָא דְּדַיָּינֵי **The discretion of the judges.** Just as the Rishonim disagreed about the Halakhic meaning of this concept, they also disagreed about the meaning of the words. In *Rashi's* opinion, שׁוּדָא is derived from the root שדא,, meaning "to throw." However, according to *Tosefot,* שׁוּדָא is an abbreviated form of שׁוּחֲדָא, meaning "bribery." The gutteral letter ח would have fallen out as in many words in the Babylonian Talmud, under the influence of the local language. Thus the expression would mean something that was done without justification, as though the judges had received some bribe. Major support for this interpretation comes from the parallel passage in the Jerusalem Talmud (*Ketubot* 10:5), which states in the name of Shmuel, שׁוּחֲדָא דְּדַיָּינֵי.

NOTES

שְׁנֵי שְׁטָרוֹת **Two deeds.** The Jerusalem Talmud which cites Shmuel's position that in certain cases the judges may use their discretion in deciding the law, distinguishes between the case where two deeds of sale were issued to two different people for the same property, and the case where a single deed was issued for one of two properties, but it is not clear to which of them the deed relates.

Rashi, Rif, and many other Rishonim understand that Rav and Shmuel only disagree about a case where two bills of sale or gift were issued for the same field on the same day. But where a debtor issued two bills of indebtedness to two different creditors on the same day, and the debtor's property does not suffice to cover both obligations, even Shmuel agrees that the two creditors divide the debtor's property evenly. *Rabbenu Ḥananel* disagrees and says that Rav and Shmuel disagree about all deeds, even bills of indebtedness (see *Rif, Ramban, Ra'ah,* and *Tosafot,* who discuss the issue at length).

עֵדֵי חֲתִימָה כָּרְתִי **The witnesses to the signing separate.** The dispute between Rabbi Meir and Rabbi Elazar refers primarily to a woman's bill of divorce. According to Rabbi Meir, the witnesses' signatures on the bill of divorce turn the document into an instrument that can effect a divorce. While it is certainly necessary for the bill of divorce to be delivered to the woman, the divorce is valid even if there are no witnesses present at the time of delivery. According to Rabbi Elazar, witnesses must be present when the bill of divorce is delivered, and it is only by Rabbinic decree that witnesses must sign the bill of divorce. The Rishonim discuss at length the relationship between the viewpoint of Rabbi Meir that it is the witnesses who sign the bill of divorce who effect the divorce, and Rav's position that where two deeds of sale for the same property were issued on the same day to two different people, the buyers divide the field equally (see *Tosafot*). *Ra'ah* and others explain that according to Rabbi Meir, after the buyer receives the bill of sale, he acquires what is sold to him from the time that the witnesses signed the bill, even if the bill was written many days before delivery. Thus, if two bills of sale were signed on the same day, they take effect at the same time, no matter when they were delivered, and so the two buyers divide the property evenly between themselves.

וּשְׁמוּאֵל דְּאָמַר כְּרַבִּי אֶלְעָזָר **And Shmuel said like Rabbi Elazar.** *Ritva* explains the Gemara as follows: Rabbi Meir

HALAKHAH

שְׁנֵי שְׁטָרוֹת הַיּוֹצְאִים בְּיוֹם אֶחָד **Two deeds which go out on one day.** "If two bills of sale or gift were issued on the same day for the same property, the judges may use their discretion and decide to whom the property should be given," following Shmuel, whose position is accepted as law in civil matters. (*Rambam, Sefer Kinyan, Hilkhot Zekhiyah U'Matanah* 5:6; *Shulḥan Arukh, Ḥoshen Mishpat* 240:3.)

עֵדֵי מְסִירָה כָּרְתִי **The witnesses of delivery effect the divorce.** "If two deeds of sale were issued for the same property on the same date, the claimant who has witnesses that the bill of sale was delivered to him first acquires the property," following Shmuel, whose position is accepted as law in civil matters. (*Rambam, Sefer Kinyan, Hilkhot Zekhiyah* 5:7; *Shulḥan Arukh, Ḥoshen Mishpat* 240:4.)

עֵדֵי מְסִירָה **The witnesses of delivery.** "A bill of divorce

TRANSLATION AND COMMENTARY

disagree about which pair of witnesses is absolutely essential to validate the divorce. According to Rabbi Meir, the witnesses' signatures on the bill of divorce turn the document effective, even if no witnesses are present at the time of delivery. Rabbi Elazar disagrees and says that by Torah law witnesses need not sign the bill of divorce, but they must be present at its delivery. The Gemara suggests that the disagreement between Rav and Shmuel about promissory notes parallels the dispute between Rabbi Meir and Rabbi Elazar about bills of divorce. Just as Rabbi Meir says that the validity of a bill of divorce depends on the witnesses who sign it, so too Rav says that a bill of sale derives its validity from the witnesses who sign it. Since both bills of sale for the field were issued on the same day, both buyers have equal claim to the property. Therefore it is divided. Further, just as Rabbi Elazar says that the validity of a bill of divorce depends on the witnesses present at its delivery, so too Shmuel says that a bill of sale derives its validity from the witnesses present when it is handed to the buyer. Thus, even if both bills of sale have the same date, it is unlikely that they were handed over to the two buyers at the same time. The buyer who received the bill of sale first acquired the property. However, since we do not know which of them was first, the judges are given the discretion to decide which of buyers should be given possession of the property, based on whom they think the seller would have wanted to sell the property, for it is preferable that the judges give it to the most probable claimant, than for the property to be divided between the buyers.

לָא [1]The Gemara rejects this argument: **No, all** of the Amoraim — both Rav and Shmuel — might **agree with Rabbi Elazar** who said that the witnesses of delivery validate a bill of divorce or bill of sale, [2]**but here they disagree about the following** issue: [3]**Rav maintains:** In cases of doubt, **it is preferable to divide** the property so that the person who is in fact entitled to it will definitely receive at least part of what is due to him. [4]**And Shmuel maintains:** In such cases **it is better for the judges** to use their **discretion** and decide to which

LITERAL TRANSLATION

[1]No, for all agree with Rabbi Elazar, [2]and here they disagree about this: [3]Rav maintains: Dividing is preferable. [4]And Shmuel maintains: The discretion of the judges is preferable.

[1]לָא, דְּכוּלֵּי עָלְמָא כְּרַבִּי אֶלְעָזָר, [2]וְהָכָא בְּהָא קָמִיפַּלְגִי: [3]רַב סָבַר: חֲלוּקָה עֲדִיפָא. [4]וּשְׁמוּאֵל סָבַר: שׁוּדָא דְּדַיָּינֵי עֲדִיפָא.

RASHI

שאין העדים חותמין על הגט אלא מפני תיקון העולם, שמא ימותו עדי מסירה או ילכו למדינת הים. אלמא עדי מסירה עיקר. והכא יש לומר, שמא האחד היה חביב עליו יותר וקדם ומסרו לו ואת השני הטעה, וכי לא ידעינן נימא שודא דדייני לפי מה שהם רואים מי מהם היה רגיל אצלו יותר, דשודא עדיפא מחלוקה. דכולי עלמא כר׳ אלעזר — דקיימא לן כוותיה בגטין, ואיכא למימר שודא ואיכא למימר חלוקה, ובהא פליגי.

NOTES

and Rabbi Elazar disagree about two issues. First, according to Rabbi Meir, a divorce can only be effected by the witnesses who sign the bill of divorce, and not by the witnesses to the bill's delivery, whereas according to Rabbi Elazar, the witnesses to the bill's delivery can also effect the divorce. And second, Rabbi Meir maintains that the witnesses who sign a bill of sale effect the transfer of ownership, even if the bill did not reach the hands of the buyer until much later, whereas Rabbi Elazar maintains that witnesses who sign a bill of sale only effect the transfer of ownership when the bill reaches the hands of the buyer. Thus, according to Rabbi Eliezer, a bill that was not delivered on the day that it was signed is invalid, for it is a predated bill of sale. Now, there are four possibilities regarding two bills of sale that were signed on the same day. They may have been delivered (1) simultaneously on the day they were signed, or (2) one after the other on the day they were signed, or (3) they may have been delivered simultaneously on some other day, or (4) one after the other on some other day. According to Rabbi Meir, in three of those cases (possibilities 1, 3, and 4), buyers acquire the property, so it should be divided between them. Only in one case (possibility 2) is the property acquired by the buyer who receives his bill of sale first. So in that case, if it is not know who received the bill of sale first, property should be awarded according to the judge's discretion. As with the three possible situations, Rabbi Meir would divide the property between the two buyers in this situation as well, for there is a greater chance that justice will be done. But according to Rabbi Elazar there are only two possibilities: both bills of sale were delivered simultaneously on the day they were signed, or they were delivered one after the other on that day. If they were delivered on some later day, they are invalid. Since it is most likely that the two bills of sale were delivered one after the other, only one of the buyers actually acquired the property. Thus, Rabbi Elazar would rule that it is preferable to award it in accordance with the judges' discretion.

HALAKHAH

must be signed by two witnesses and delivered to the woman in the presence of two witnesses. If a bill of divorce was signed by two witnesses, but there were no witnesses present at the time of delivery, or if a bill of divorce was delivered in the presence of two witnesses, but not signed by witnesses, it is valid. According to some authorities, if it is known that no witnesses were present at the time of delivery, the bill of divorce is invalid, even if it was signed by witnesses. But a bill of divorce that is signed by witnesses is assumed to have been delivered in the presence of two witnesses." (*Rambam, Sefer Nashim, Hilkhot Gerushin* 1:15; *Shulḥan Arukh, Even HaEzer* 133:1.)

TRANSLATION AND COMMENTARY

of the two the property was most probably sold, then the rightful owner could well receive his property, whereas if the property is divided, the rightful owner will surely lose half of what belongs to him.

וּמִי מָצֵית [1]The Gemara objects: **But can you** really **say that Rav agrees with Rabbi Elazar** regarding a bill of sale? [2]**But surely Rav Yehudah said in the name of Rav: The law is in accordance with** the position of **Rabbi Elazar regarding bills of divorce** [3]**And** Rav Yehudah added: **When I reported this** ruling **before Shmuel, he said:** The law is in accordance with the position of Rabbi Elazar **even regarding bills of sale.** Now, since Rav Yehudah reports that Shmuel added to Rav's ruling and said that the law follows Rabbi Elazar even regarding bills of sale, [4]**this proves by implication that Rav** himself **maintains that regarding bills of sale,** he does **not** agree with the position of Rabbi Elazar!

אֶלָּא [5]**Rather,** argues the Gemara, **it is clear** that we must say, as suggested above, that the Amoraic disagreement parallels the earlier Tannaitic dispute, **Rav agrees with Rabbi Meir,** [6]**and Shmuel agrees with Rabbi Elazar.**

מֵיתִיבֵי [7]**An objection was raised** against Shmuel's position from a Baraita that deals specifically with the case about which he and Rav argue: "If someone sold the same field to two different people, and **two bills** of sale for that field **were issued on the same day,** the two buyers **divide** the field between themselves." [8]This Baraita seems to be **a** conclusive **refutation of** the position **of Shmuel,** who argues that the judges should use their discretion.

אָמַר לָךְ שְׁמוּאֵל [9]But **Shmuel can say to you: Whose** position **does this** Baraita follow? [10]**It** follows the position of **Rabbi Meir,** who said that the signatures of witnesses on a bill of divorce, and by extension, a bill of sale effect the divorce or purchase. [11]**But I said** what I said **in accordance with** the position of **Rabbi Elazar,** who ruled that the witnesses to the delivery of the bill effect the divorce or sale. Therefore, the property is acquired by the party who received his bill of sale first. If we do not know which of the buyers was first, the judges are given the discretion to decide which of the two should be given possession of the property.

אִי רַבִּי מֵאִיר [12]The Gemara now questions the attribution of the Baraita to Rabbi Meir: **If the Baraita** follows the position of **Rabbi Meir,** there is a difficulty, for **consider** what is stated in **the next clause** of that Baraita: [13]**"If** the seller **wrote** a bill of sale for a certain property **to one** buyer, but did not deliver it to him before **he wrote and delivered** a second bill of sale for that same property **to another** buyer, **the party to whom he delivered** the bill of sale first **acquired** the property." [14]**Now, if the Baraita** follows the position of **Rabbi Meir, why did** the party to whom the seller delivered the bill of sale first **acquire** the property? [15]**But surely** Rabbi Meir **said** that the **witnesses who sign** the bill of divorce **effect the divorce,** and, by extension

[1]וּמִי מָצֵית מוֹקְמַתְּ לֵיהּ לְרַב כְּרַבִּי אֶלְעָזָר? [2]וְהָאָמַר רַב יְהוּדָה אָמַר רַב: הֲלָכָה כְּרַבִּי אֶלְעָזָר בְּגִיטִּין. [3]כִּי אֲמַרִיתָהּ קַמֵּיהּ דִּשְׁמוּאֵל, אֲמַר: אַף בִּשְׁטָרוֹת. [4]מִכְּלָל דְּרַב סָבַר: בִּשְׁטָרוֹת, לָא!

[5]אֶלָּא מְחַוַּורְתָּא, רַב כְּרַבִּי מֵאִיר, [6]וּשְׁמוּאֵל כְּרַבִּי אֶלְעָזָר.

[7]מֵיתִיבֵי: "שְׁנֵי שְׁטָרוֹת הַיּוֹצְאִים בְּיוֹם אֶחָד — חוֹלְקִין". [8]תְּיוּבְתָּא דִּשְׁמוּאֵל!

[9]אָמַר לָךְ שְׁמוּאֵל: הָא מַנִּי? [10]רַבִּי מֵאִיר הִיא, [11]וַאֲנָא דַּאֲמַרִי כְּרַבִּי אֶלְעָזָר.

[12]אִי רַבִּי מֵאִיר, אֵימָא סֵיפָא: [13]"כָּתַב לְאֶחָד וּמָסַר לְאַחֵר, זֶה שֶׁמָּסַר לוֹ קָנָה. [14]וְאִי רַבִּי מֵאִיר, אַמַּאי קָנָה? [15]הָאָמַר: עֵדֵי חֲתִימָה כָּרְתִי!

LITERAL TRANSLATION

[1]But can you establish Rav as [the opinion of] Rabbi Elazar? [2]But surely Rav Yehudah said in the name of Rav: The law is in accordance with Rabbi Elazar regarding bills of divorce. [3][And] when I said this before Shmuel, he said: Also regarding bills [of sale]. [4][This proves] by implication that Rav maintains [that] regarding bills [of sale], no!

[5]Rather, it is clear [that] Rav [said] as Rabbi Meir, [6]and Shmuel [said] as Rabbi Elazar.

[7]They objected: "Two deeds that were issued (lit., 'go out') the same day — they divide." [8]A refutation of Shmuel!

[9]Shmuel can say to you: Whose is this? [10]It is Rabbi Meir. [11]And I said as Rabbi Elazar.

[12]If it is Rabbi Meir, say the last clause: [13]"[If] he wrote to one, and [then wrote and] delivered to another, the one to whom he delivered acquired [it]." [14]And if it is Rabbi Meir, why did he acquire [it]? [15]But surely he said: The signing witnesses effect the divorce!

RASHI

חולקין — אלמא חלוקה עדיפא. **רבי מאיר היא** — וליכא למימר שודא בחתימתו. **כתב לאחד** — השטר, ולא מסר לו עד שכתב שטר שני לאחר עליה ומסר לו. **ואי רבי מאיר כו׳** — אלא לאו רבי אלעזר, ואיכא למימר שודא ואיכא למימר חלוקה, וקתני "חולקין" — אלמא חלוקה עדיפא.

[1]תַּנָּאֵי הִיא, דְּתַנְיָא: [2]״וַחֲכָמִים אוֹמְרִים: יַחֲלוֹקוּ. [3]וְכָאן אָמְרוּ: מַה שֶׁיִּרְצֶה הַשָּׁלִישׁ יַעֲשֶׂה״. [4]אִמֵּיהּ דְּרָמִי בַּר חָמָא כְּתַבְתִּינְהוּ לְנִכְסָהּ לְרָמִי בַּר חָמָא בְּצַפְרָא. [5]לְאוֹרְתָא

LITERAL TRANSLATION

[1]It is [a dispute between] the Tannaim, for it was taught: [2]"And the Sages say: They divide. [3]And here they said: Whatever the trustee wishes he may do." [4]The mother of Rami bar Ḥama wrote over her property to Rami bar Ḥama in the morning. [5]That evening

RASHI

תנאי היא – איכא למ״ד שודא עדיף ואיכא למ״ד חלוקה עדיפא. וחכמים אומרים כו׳ – בשלהי פרק קמא דגטין: ״הולך מנה לפלוני״. והלך וביקשו ולא מצאו, שמת – יחזרו למשלח. מת המשלח – יחזרו ליורשים כו׳ עד וחכמים אומרים: יחלוקו יורשי משלח ויורשי מי שנשתלחו לו. וכאן אמרו: מה שירצה שליש יעשה, דהיינו שליח יעשה, אלמא שודא עדיפא. אמיה דרמי בר חמא כו׳ – ולא נודע למי מסרה תחלה שטר מתנה.

TRANSLATION AND COMMENTARY

the signature on a bill of sale effect the purchase. Therefore, you must say that the Baraita follows the position of Rabbi Elazar, who says that a bill of sale derives its validity from the witnesses who are present when it is handed to the buyer. In its first clause the Baraita teaches that when we do not know who received his bill of sale first, it is preferable to divide the property than to allow the judges to use their discretion. Thus, the Baraita appears indeed to be a conclusive refutation of Shmuel's position!

תַּנָּאֵי הִיא [1]This issue — whether in cases of doubt as to which of two parties is entitled to certain property it is preferable to divide the property or to allow the judges to use their discretion — **is** the subject of **a Tannaitic dispute, for it was taught** in a Baraita: "If someone sent money by way of an agent, but when the agent arrived he found that the intended recipient had died, he should return the money to his principal. If, meanwhile the principal also died, there is a disagreement among the Tannaim. Rabbi Natan and Rabbi Ya'akov say: The money should be returned to the principal's heirs. Some say: The money should be given to the heirs of the intended recipient. [2]**The Sages say:** The heirs of the principal and the heirs of the intended recipient should **divide** the money between them. [3]**And here** in Babylonia the Rabbis **said: Whatever the agent wishes** to do with the money, **he may do.** He may use his discretion to decide whether the money should be given to the heirs of the principal, or to those of the intended recipient." Thus, we see that the Tannaim disagree about whether it is preferable to divide disputed money between the two claimants, or it is preferable to award the money to one of parties in accordance with the discretion of the agent who is now holding the money or, as in our case, in accordance with the discretion of the judges before whom the case was brought for adjudication.

אִמֵּיהּ דְּרָמִי בַּר חָמָא [4]It was related that **one morning the mother of Rami bar Ḥama wrote** a deed of gift assigning all of **her property to Rami bar Ḥama,** [5]and **that evening she wrote** a second deed of gift assigning

SAGES

רָמִי בַּר חָמָא וְאָחִיו Rami bar Ḥama and his brother. Both of these brothers were Sages in their own right, and both were sons-in-law of Rav Ḥisda. It appears that Rami bar Ḥama was the eldest and also the greatest Torah scholar. He was famous for his sharp intellect, because of which some said of him that he occasionally was negligent regarding details because of the acuity of his mind. He frequented the greatest scholars of the earlier generation and was a student and colleague of theirs, mainly his father-in-law, Rav Ḥisda, Rav Naḥman, and Rav Sheshet (who greatly valued this student of his and often spoke in his praise). His disagreements with Rava are documented at length, and after Rami bar Ḥama's death, Rava married his widow, the daughter of Rav Ḥisda. The teachings of Mar (sometimes he is also called Rav) Ukva bar Ḥama are also cited frequently in the Talmud.

NOTES

וַחֲכָמִים אוֹמְרִים: יַחֲלוֹקוּ And the Sages say: They divide. As the Gemara explains elsewhere (*Gittin* 14b), the Tannaim disagree about an agent who was ordered to bring money to a certain person, and the intended recipient died before he was given the money, and the principal died before the agent returned the money to him. Two issues are in dispute: (1) When someone instructs his agent to "bring money to a certain person," does he mean the agent to acquire it on the recipients behalf? If that is so, the intended recipient acquires the money as soon as the agent receives it, and it is inherited by his heirs as soon as the intended recipient dies. Alternatively, the principal may simply that the money should be physically given to the other person? In this case, if the intended recipient dies before getting the money, it must be returned to the principal or to the principal's heirs. (2) After a person dies, are we commanded to fulfill the wishes that he expressed before his death? If so, the money should be given to the intended recipient's heirs, even if the intended recipient did not acquire the money before he died. But if there is no such commandment, then the money should be returned to the principal's heirs. If there is a doubt about either of these two issues, the money should be divided between the two sets of heirs.

מַה שֶׁיִּרְצֶה הַשָּׁלִישׁ יַעֲשֶׂה Whatever the third person wishes he may do. *Ritva* brings support from here to *Rabbenu Tam* and others who understand that when the judges are given discretion, their award can be arbitrary, without any assessment of intention, for the Gemara compares Shmuel's position that the judges should use their discretion in awarding the property disputed by the two buyers with the ruling of the Babylonian Rabbis that the agent may do with the money as he sees fit. *Rivan,* follows *Rashi's* position that when the judges are given discretion, they must award the money to the party to whom they think the seller or donor would have wanted to receive the money. He explains that here, too, the agent may not decide arbitrarily who should be given the money. Rather he must assess the nature of principal's gift. If it was so generous that it would seem that he would have wanted it to reach the intended recipient's heirs, the money is given to those heirs, but if not, the money is returned to the heirs of the principal.

אִמֵּיהּ דְּרָמִי בַּר חָמָא The mother of Rami bar Ḥama. The Rishonim discuss the relationship between the story related here about Rami bar Ḥama and Mar Ukva bar Ḥama and a similar story related about these two brothers in *Bava Batra* 151a. *Tosafot* and most Rishonim argue that despite

TRANSLATION AND COMMENTARY

all of **her property to Mar Ukva bar Ḥama,** Rami bar Ḥama's brother, and it was not known who received the deed of gift first. [1]**Rami bar Ḥama came before Rav Sheshet** for a ruling on the case, and Rav Sheshet **established him** as **owner of the property.** [2]His brother **Mar Ukva** bar Ḥama then **came before Rav Naḥman,** and Rav Naḥman **established him as owner of the property.** [3]**Rav Sheshet came before Rav Naḥman, and said to him: "What is the reason that Master acted in this manner,** awarding the property to Mar Ukva?" [4]Rav Naḥman **said to** Rav Sheshet in reply: **"And what is the reason that Master acted in that manner,** awarding the property to Rami bar Ḥama?" [5]Rav Sheshet **said to him:** "I awarded the property to Rami bar Ḥama, **because** the writing of his deed of gift **preceded** the writing of his brother's deed of gift." [6]Rav Naḥman **said to** Rav Sheshet: **"Do we live in Jerusalem where they write** in the bill **the hour** that the bill was written? Where we live, the time of the transaction is not recorded in the deed of gift. Hence we assume that the parties do not wish the transaction to take effect until the end of the day. Since the two parties hold deeds of gift having the same date, neither party has better title to the property." [7]Rav Sheshet asked Rav Naḥman once again: **"What then is the reason that Master acted in this manner,** awarding the property to Mar Ukva, rather than having the two brothers divide it?" [8]Rav Naḥman **said to him:** "Following Shmuel, I utilized **the discretion** that is given **to judges** in such cases. It seemed to me that Mar Ukva was his mother's favorite." [9]Rav Sheshet **said to** Rav Naḥman: "If so, then **I too** should be regarded as having utilized **the discretion** that is given **to judges** in such cases. My ruling, which was issued first, should be regarded as final." [10]Rav Naḥman **said to** Rav Sheshet in reply: "Two arguments may be raised against your argument. **First, I am an** official **judge,**

כְּתַבְתִּינְהוּ לְמָר עוּקְבָא בַּר חָמָא. [1]אֲתָא רָמִי בַּר חָמָא לְקַמֵּיהּ דְּרַב שֵׁשֶׁת, אוֹקְמֵיהּ בְּנִכְסָא. [2]אֲתָא מָר עוּקְבָא לְקַמֵּיהּ דְּרַב נַחְמָן, אוֹקְמֵיהּ בְּנִכְסָא. [3]אֲתָא רַב שֵׁשֶׁת לְקַמֵּיהּ דְּרַב נַחְמָן, אֲמַר לֵיהּ: מַאי טַעְמָא עֲבַד מָר הָכִי? [4]אֲמַר לֵיהּ: "וּמַאי טַעְמָא עֲבַד מָר הָכִי"? [5]אֲמַר לֵיהּ: "דְּקָדֵים". [6]אֲמַר לֵיהּ: "אַטּוּ בִּירוּשָׁלַיִם יָתְבִינַן, דְּכָתְבִינַן שָׁעוֹת"? [7]"אֶלָּא מָר מַאי טַעְמָא עֲבַד הָכִי"? [8]אֲמַר לֵיהּ: "שׁוּדָא דְּדַיָּינֵי". [9]אֲמַר לֵיהּ: "אֲנָא נַמִי שׁוּדָא דְּדַיָּינֵי"! [10]אֲמַר לֵיהּ: "חֲדָא, דַּאֲנָא דַּיָּינָא וּמָר

LITERAL TRANSLATION

she wrote over her property to Mar Ukva bar Ḥama. [1]Rami bar Ḥama came before Rav Sheshet, [who] established him [as owner] of the property. [2]Mar Ukva came before Rav Naḥman [who] established him [as owner] of the property. [3]Rav Sheshet came before Rav Naḥman, [and] said to him: "What is the reason that Master acted thus?" [4]He said to him: "And what is the reason that Master acted thus?" [5]He said to him: "Because it preceded." [6]He said to him: "Do we sit in Jerusalem where they write the hours?" [7][Rav Sheshet queried:] "Rather what is the reason that Master acted thus?" [8]He said to him: "The judges [use their] discretion." [9]He said to him: "I too say the judges [use their] discretion." [10][Rav Naḥman] said to him: "Firstly, I am a judge and Master

RASHI

אטו בירושלים יתבינן כו׳ – וכיון דלא הקפידו בני מקום לכתוב שעות, גילו מנהגם שאין הולכים אחר הקודם לבו ביום, ושניהם שוים. **אלא מר מאי טעמא עבד הכי** – ולא אמר יחלוקו. **שודא דדייני** – כרבי אלעזר דאמר: עדי מסירה כרתי. ולי נראה שזה היה חביב לה יותר וקדמה ומסרה לו תחלה. **אמר ליה אנא נמי** – תיהוי דידי שודא דדייני, וכיון שפסקתי אני הדין, שוב אין לך כח להוציא מידו, שהרי יצא מבית דין זכאי בשודא דדייני. **אנא דיינא** – על פי ראש גלותא והישיבה. **אנא דיינא** – על פי ראש גלותא והישיבה.

NOTES

the obvious similarities between the two stories, they relate to two different incidents, Here we are dealing with a gift made by their mother when she was still healthy, and which was effected through a deed of gift without any additional act of acquisition. However, in *Bava Batra* the gift was made while she was on her deathbed. *Rif* cites the view of one of the Geonim that the two stories relate to the same incident, and that the version recorded here is a corrupted form of the version recorded in Bava Batra.

דַּאֲנָא דַּיָּינָא I am a judge. The Rishonim ask how Rav

HALAKHAH

אַטּוּ בִּירוּשָׁלַיִם יָתְבִינַן Do we sit in Jerusalem. "If two bills of sale were issued on the same day for the same property, and it was the local practice to include the hour of sale in the bill of sale, whichever buyer seizes the property first acquires it. If it was not the local practice to include the hour of sale in the bill of sale, the judges are given the discretion to decide to whom the property should be given." (*Rambam, Sefer Kinyan, Hilkhot Zekhiyah* 5:6; *Shulḥan Arukh, Ḥoshen Mishpat* 240:3.)

חֲדָא, דַּאֲנָא דַּיָּינָא First, I am the judge. "According to some authorities, when hearing cases dealing with property of doubtful title, only an authorized judge has discretion to award it." (*Shulḥan Arukh, Ḥoshen Mishpat* 240:3, *Rema.*)

לָאו דַּיָּינָא. [1]וְעוֹד, מֵעִיקָּרָא לָאו בְּתוֹרַת הָכִי אָתֵית לָהּ״. [2]הָנְהוּ תְּרֵי שְׁטָרֵי דַּאֲתוּ לְקַמֵּיהּ דְּרַב יוֹסֵף. [3]חַד הֲוָה כָּתוּב ״בְּחַמְשָׁא בְּנִיסָן״. [4]וְחַד הֲוָה כָּתוּב בֵּיהּ ״בְּנִיסָן״ סְתָמָא. [5]אוֹקְמֵיהּ רַב יוֹסֵף לְהַהוּא דְּחַמְשָׁא בְּנִיסָן בַּנְּכָסִים. [6]אֲמַר לֵיהּ אִידָךְ: ״וַאֲנָא אַפְסִיד״? [7]אֲמַר לֵיהּ: ״אַתְּ, יָדְךָ עַל הַתַּחְתּוֹנָה, אֵימָא בַּר עֶשְׂרִים וְתִשְׁעָה בְּנִיסָן אַתְּ״! [8]אֲמַר לֵיהּ: ״וְנִכְתּוֹב לִי מָר [95A] טִירְפָּא מֵאִיָּיר וְאֵילָךְ״!

LITERAL TRANSLATION

is not a judge. [1]And furthermore, at the beginning it was not because of this [reason] that you came to that [decision]."

[2]There were two [guaranteed] bills [of sale] that came before Rav Yosef. [3]In one was written "the fifth of Nisan." [4]And in one was written "in Nisan," without specifying. [5]Rav Yosef established the one [whose bill read] "the fifth of Nisan" [as owner] of the property. [6]The other one said to him: "And should I suffer a loss?" [7]He said to him: "You are at a disadvantage (lit., 'your hand is lower'), [as he can] say that your [bill] was of the twenty-ninth of Nisan!" [8]He said to him: "Let the Master write me [95A] a *tirpa* [authorizing seizure] from Iyyar on wards!"

TRANSLATION AND COMMENTARY

authorized by the Exilarch and the head of the academy to issue rulings, while **Master is not an** authorized **judge.** [1]**And furthermore, it was not at first because of this,** the discretion given to judges, **that you came to the decision** to award the property to Rami bar Ḥama. Rather you thought that he was entitled to the property because his deed of gift was written first."

הָנְהוּ תְּרֵי שְׁטָרֵי [2]It was further related that a certain person sold the same property with a guarantee to two different people, and the **two guaranteed bills of sale were brought to Rav Yosef** to decide who had legal title to the property. [3]**One** of the bills **was dated "the fifth of** the month of **Nisan,"** [4]**and the other was dated "in** the month of **Nisan,"** the day of the month **not being specified.** [5]**Rav Yosef established the one whose bill** was dated **"the fifth of Nisan" as** the legal **owner of the property.** [6]Unhappy with that ruling, **the other** buyer **said to** Rav Yosef: "Why **should I suffer a loss?** Perhaps my bill of sale was written first!" [7]Rav Yosef **said to him**: "Since your bill does not record the day of Nisan on which it was written, **you are at a disadvantage,** for the other buyer can **say that it** was written on the **twenty-ninth of Nisan,** after his purchase on the fifth of Nisan." [8]The unfortunate buyer **said to** Rav Yosef: "Then **let Master write me** [95A] **a *tirpa* authorizing** me **to seize** property purchased from the seller **from** the first of **Iyyar onward** (the day after the twenty-ninth of Nisan). Such property was surely mortgaged by the guarantee in my bill of sale!"

RASHI

לאו בתורת הכי אתית לה — לא אמרת טעם שלך משום שודא דדייני אלא משום דקדים בחתימה כרבי מאיר, ובזו טעית, דהא לאו בירושלים יתבינן. הנהו תרי שטרי — של מכר שיצאו על שדה אחת. טירפא — לטרוף לקוחות מראש חדש אייר, שהרי מכרה לו באחריות.

NOTES

Naḥman could have said to Rav Sheshet that he is a judge and Rav Sheshet is not, when it is clear that Rav Sheshet was one of the greatest Torah scholars of his generation. *Rashi, Rid,* and others explain that Rav Naḥman was an official judge, authorized by the Exilarch to serve in that capacity, whereas Rav Sheshet never received such authorization, even though he was a great scholar. *Ra'ah* argues that Rav Sheshet was indeed an authorized judge, but since Rav Naḥman was a greater expert on civil law than he was, he should not have offered his opinion on a matter that fell under Rav Naḥman's jurisdiction (see also *Rabbenu Ḥananel*).

Rabbenu Ḥananel reports that he had a tradition that the law allowing a judge to use his discretion in deciding a case applies only to cases involving land. *Tosafot* disagree and say that judicial discretion may be used even in cases involving money or movable goods.

הָנְהוּ תְּרֵי שְׁטָרֵי **There were two bills.** Our commentary follows *Rashi* and others who explain that we are dealing here with two guaranteed bills of sale that were written for the same property. *Ra'ah* suggests that this is the case of a debtor who wrote two promissory notes for two different creditors, and the two creditors come to sieze the same free property remaining in the debtor's possession. *Ritva* notes that both explanations are correct, and that there is no practical difference between them. *Ra'ah* cites another explanation in the name of *Rabbi Shlomo of Montpelier*, according to which the bill dated the fifth of Nisan was a bill of indebtedness, and the bill dated in Nisan was a guaranteed bill of sale.

אֵימָא בַּר עֶשְׂרִים וְתִשְׁעָה בְּנִיסָן אַתְּ **Say that you are one of the twenty-ninth of Nisan.** *Talmidei Rabbenu Yonah* explain that the buyer holding the bill dated in the month of Nisan is at the disadvantage, because the rights accorded to him by the document in his hand are not clear, whereas the rights accorded the other buyer by the document which he holds are clear. Alternatively, the failure of his deed of sale to specify the day on which the transaction took place suggests that it took place at the end of the month, and it was for that very reason that he did not want the date to be included.

TRANSLATION AND COMMENTARY

[1]Rav Yosef **said to** the buyer: "Those **purchasers can** turn you away by **claiming:** [2]**'Your bill of sale was** written **on the first of Nisan,** and you are the legal owner of property that was taken by the other buyer. Therefore you have no claim on land that I subsequently obtained from the seller! You must recover the property from him. The Gemara now asks: Since the purchaser with the guaranteed bill of sale without a clear date is dismissed both by the other buyer and by the holder of land mortgaged to his guarantee, [3]**what** can he do **to remedy** his situation? Since at least one of the holders of the guaranteed bill of sale has the right to collect from the sold mortgaged properties, [4]**let** the **two** original **purchasers write a power of attorney to each other.** The unfortunate buyer can then claim the mortgaged field because if its owner rejects him by saying that he is the real purchaser of the property, he removes the power of attorney and demands the field for the second purchaser. The holder of the mortgaged property now has no way to escape him.

[1]אֲמַר לֵיהּ: יָכְלֵי לְמֵימַר לָךְ: [2]אַתְּ בַּר חַד בְּנִיסָן אַתְּ! [3]מַאי תַּקַּנְתֵּיהּ? [4]נִכְתְּבוּ הַרְשָׁאָה לַהֲדָדֵי.

משנה [5]מִי שֶׁהָיָה נָשׂוּי שְׁתֵּי נָשִׁים, וּמָכַר אֶת שָׂדֵהוּ, [6]וְכָתְבָה רִאשׁוֹנָה לַלּוֹקֵחַ: [7]"דִּין וּדְבָרִים אֵין לִי עִמְּךָ", [8]הַשְּׁנִיָּה מוֹצִיאָה מֵהַלּוֹקֵחַ, [9]וְרִאשׁוֹנָה

LITERAL TRANSLATION

[1]He said to him: "The [purchasers] can say to you: [2]'Your [bill of sale] was of the first of Nisan!'" [3]What is his remedy? [4]Let them write a power of attorney to one another.

MISHNAH [5][If] someone was married to two women, and he sold his field, [6]and the first one wrote to the buyer: [7]"I have no claim (lit., 'claim or dispute') against you," [8]the second one can remove [it] from the buyer, [9]and the first

RASHI

יכלי למימר – לקוחות. **את בר חד בניסן את** – ושטרך קודם, ושלא כדין נטלה ממך. **מאי תקנתיה** – דהאי.

נכתבו הרשאה להדדי – יבקש מאת חברו בר חמשה בניסן, וימסור לו שטרו, ויכתוב לו הרשאה עליו לטרוף לקוחות. ואם יאמרו לו: בר חד בניסן את, אומר להם: אני בא לטרוף בשביל מעות של חמשה בניסן, שהרי לשנינו מכרה באחריות, ואני בא בהרשאה עליכם מכחו. ואם יאמרו לו: הוא קדם, ואת בר כ"ט בניסן היית, אומר להם: אני בא מחמת עצמי.

משנה ומכר את שדהו – המשועבד לכתובות. **הראשונה** – שנשאת תחלה. **השניה מוציאה** – כשימות בעלה.

In order to understand this passage the three buyers have to be labelled. Buyer number one is the person whose deed to a field was dated the fifth of Nisan. Buyer number two is the one whose deed to the same field was dated simply "Nisan," and whose claim to the field was rejected. Buyer number three purchased a different field from the original seller after the end of Nisan. By rights, buyer number two should be able to seize that field, since his purchase was guaranteed. As we have seen, buyer number three argued that buyer number two has a claim not against him but against buyer number one. However, if buyers number one and two exchange powers of attorney, buyer number three cannot reject their claim in that way. By telling buyer number two to recover the field from buyer number one, buyer number three is acknowledging that buyer number one has a claim against him. Buyer number two can then produce the power of attorney given to him by buyer number one and lodge the claim against buyer number three in behalf of buyer number one.

MISHNAH מִי שֶׁהָיָה נָשׂוּי [5]If a man had two wives, and the ketubah deed of one was dated earlier than that of the other, **and** the husband **sold his field** over which both them exercized a lien, but which was not sufficient for both ketubah settlements, [6]**and the** man's **first** wife, who had the preferential lien, **wrote to the buyer** of the property: [7]**"I will have no claim against you** regarding this field," thereby renouncing her right to seize that field from him as payment of her ketubah settlement, and the husband later died, [8]**the** man's **second** wife **can take** the field **away from the buyer,** for she never waived her right to collect her ketubah settlement from that property. [9]**And** then **the** man's **first** wife can remove the field **from the second**

HALAKHAH

מִי שֶׁהָיָה נָשׂוּי שְׁתֵּי נָשִׁים If a man was married to two women. "If a man was married to two women, and he sold a field over which both women exercised a lien for their ketubah settlements, and before the buyer purchased the field from the husband, he obtained a waiver from the first wife of her right to seize the field from him as payment of her ketubah settlement, and he reinforced that waiver with an act of acquisition, and the husband died or divorced his two wives, and there were no other assets from which the women could collect their ketubah settlements, the second wife can seize the field from the buyer. Then the first wife can seize the field from the second wife, and then the buyer can seize the field from the first wife. The cycle repeats itself over and over until the three parties reach a compromise." (*Rambam, Sefer Nashim, Hilkhot Ishut* 17:12; *Shulḥan Arukh, Even HaEzer* 100:4.)

LANGUAGE

חֲלִילָה **In turn.** The meaning of this word here refers to the image of a dance, something done in a circle, something that turns. חוֹזֵר חֲלִילָה means "to repeat over and over again, circularly."

TRANSLATION AND COMMENTARY

wife, for she has the preferential right of recovery and did not waive her right to collect from the second wife. [1]**And** then **the buyer** can remove the field **from the first** wife, for she had waived her right to dispute with him over that field, [2]**and the cycle repeats itself** over and over again — the second wife seizes from the buyer, the first wife seizes from the second wife, and the buyer seizes from the first wife — [3]**until the three** parties **make a compromise among themselves** and come to an agreement about how to divide the field.

וְכֵן, בַּעַל חוֹב [4]**A similar** situation exists in the case of **a creditor.** [5]And **a similar** situation also exists in the case of **a woman who is** her husband's **creditor.**

מִן הַשְּׁנִיָּה, [1]וְהַלּוֹקֵחַ מִן הָרִאשׁוֹנָה, [2]וְחוֹזְרוֹת חֲלִילָה, [3]עַד שֶׁיַּעֲשׂוּ פְּשָׁרָה בֵּינֵיהֶם. [4]וְכֵן, בַּעַל חוֹב. [5]וְכֵן, אִשָּׁה בַּעֲלַת חוֹב.

גמרא [6]וְכִי כָּתְבָה לֵיהּ, מַאי הָוֵי? [7]וְהָתַנְיָא: "הָאוֹמֵר לַחֲבֵירוֹ: [8]'דִּין וּדְבָרִים אֵין לִי עַל שָׂדֶה זוֹ'; וְ'אֵין לִי עֵסֶק בָּהּ'; וְ'יָדַי מְסוּלֶּקֶת הֵימֶנָּה', [9]לֹא אָמַר כְּלוּם"! [10]הָכָא בְּמַאי עָסְקִינַן? [11]בְּשֶׁקָּנוּ מִיָּדָהּ.

LITERAL TRANSLATION

one from the second one, [1]and the buyer from the first one, [2]and they go around in turn [3]until they make a compromise among themselves.

[4]And similarly, a creditor. [5]And similarly, a woman who is a creditor.

GEMARA [6]And when she writes him, what is done? [7]But surely it was taught: "[If] someone said to his fellow: [8]'I have no claim to this field'; or 'I have no business with it'; or 'My hand is removed from it,' [9]he did not say anything"! [10]With what are we dealing here? [11]When they made an act of acquisition (lit., "acquired it from her hand").

RASHI

וכן בעל חוב וכן אשה בעלת חוב – מפרש בגמרא.

גמרא בשקנו מידה – ואמרינן ב"הכותב לאשתו" דהיכא דקנו מידו, מגופה של קרקע קנו מידו.

GEMARA וְכִי כָּתְבָה לֵיהּ [6]The Gemara raises an objection against our Mishnah: If the wife **writes** the buyer that she will have no claim regarding the field which he had purchased from her husband, **what has she accomplished?** [7]**Surely it was taught** in a Baraita: **"If** two parties jointly owned a certain property, and **one** of them **said** to the other: [8]**'I will have no claim to this field,'** or **'I will have no business with it,'** or **'My hand will be removed from** the field,' [9]**he did not say anything.** He did not effect a transfer of ownership of his half of the field to his partner, for he did not use a formulation that implies a gift." If the formulation "I will have no claim to this field" cannot transfer ownership rights to a partner, why should a similar formulation be able to effect a waiver of the woman's right to collect from property mortgaged to her ketubah?

הָכָא בְּמַאי עָסְקִינַן [10]The Gemara answers: **We are dealing** in the Mishnah **with** a case **when** in addition to the woman's verbal waiving of her rights, [11]the buyer also **performed a** valid **act of acquisition** to render the woman's renunciation legally binding. This procedure, called a *kinyan,* can be used not only to finalize a sales transaction, but also to conclude and ratify actions that are not sales, such as the waiving of rights, discussed in our Mishnah.

NOTES

וְרִאשׁוֹנָה מִן הַשְּׁנִיָּה **And the first from the second.** *Ra'avad* asks: Why does the Gemara use this Mishnah to prove that if a later creditor collected his debt from the debtor's property, thereby forestalling an earlier creditor from utilizing his preferential right of recovery, whatever the later creditor succeeded in obtaining was not collected legally, and so the earlier creditor may take it away from him (see above, 94a)? Our Mishnah states explicitly that the man's first wife can take the property on which she had a preferential lien from the second wife. *Ra'avad* answers that there is no proof from our Mishnah, for it might be dealing with a field that the husband had designated as a hypotheque, a dedicated mortgage for the first woman's ketubah settlement. *Ramban* questions the validity of this answer, and offers a different solution: In our Mishnah, the second wife has not taken the field away from the buyer, but rather both wives come to court with a claim on the property.

וְחוֹזְרוֹת חֲלִילָה **And they move about in a circle.** *Ritva* (in the name of *Rabbi Shimshon of Sens*) writes that the Mishnah does not mean that the parties actually seize the property from each other over and over again, for the court would not recover the property for one party if it will be immediately seized again by another. Rather, the Mishnah means that since the disputants are involved in a never-ending cycle, the various parties should compromise.

וְכִי קָנוּ מִיָּדָהּ **And when they made an act of acquisition.** *Shittah Mekubbetzet* discusses why the Gemara prefers to explain the Mishnah with the example of a woman who made a weak statement transferring her rights and strengthened it with an act of acquisition. The Gemara could have interpreted the Mishnah broadly and explained that its use of the woman's statement: "I will have no claim against you" is not to be taken literally. He merely indicates that she transferred her rights, and the written waiver she actually employed was composed in a legally binding

TRANSLATION AND COMMENTARY

וְכִי קָנוּ מִיָּדָהּ [1]The Gemara now raises another objection: But even **if** the buyer reinforced the wife's waiver by **performing a valid act of acquisition, what has he accomplished?** [2]**Let** the woman later **say** to the buyer: "When I waived my right to collect from that field, **I did** so only **to please my husband.** I saw that he wanted to sell his field and did not want to quarrel with him." [3]**Have we not learned** elsewhere in the Mishnah (*Gittin* 55b): **"If someone bought property from a man,** and that property was set aside to guarantee the seller's wifes ketubah, **and then he bought from his wife** her rights to the property, **the purchase is invalid."** [4]**Conclude,** therefore **that** the **woman can say:** "When I sold my rights to my husband's property, [5]**I did so** only **to please my husband,** but I did not really intend to sell those rights." Here too in our Mishnah why should the first wife not be able to claim that she really did not mean to waive her rights to recover her ketubah from the sold property?

אָמַר רַב זֵירָא [6]**Rav Zera said in the name of Rav Ḥisda: There is** really **no difficulty,** for the Tannaim disagree about this very matter. [7]**Our Mishnah** here in *Ketubot* is in accordance with the view of **Rabbi Meir** who maintains that a woman cannot free herself from an agreement by claiming that she acted only to please

LITERAL TRANSLATION

[1]When they made an act of acquisition, what is done? [2]Let her say: "I did it to please my husband"! [3]Have we not learned: "[If] someone bought [property] from a man, and then he bought [it] from [his] wife, the sale is invalid." [4]Consequently, [conclude that] she can say: [5]"I did it to please my husband."

[6]Rav Zera said in the name of Rav Ḥisda: There is no difficulty. [7]This is [according to] Rabbi Meir;

[1]וְכִי קָנוּ מִיָּדָהּ, מַאי הָוֵי? [2]תֵּימָא: "נַחַת רוּחַ עָשִׂיתִי לְבַעְלִי"! [3]מִי לָא תְּנַן: "לָקַח מִן הָאִישׁ וְחָזַר וְלָקַח מִן הָאִשָּׁה, מִקָּחוֹ בָּטֵל. [4]אַלְמָא, יְכוֹלָה הִיא שֶׁתֹּאמַר: [5]"נַחַת רוּחַ עָשִׂיתִי לְבַעְלִי"!

[6]אָמַר רַב זֵירָא אָמַר רַב חִסְדָּא: לָא קַשְׁיָא. [7]הָא רַבִּי מֵאִיר;

RASHI

מקחו בטל – משמע לגמרי ואפילו בחיי הבעל. ובבבא בתרא מוקמינן לה באחת מאותן שלש שדות: או ייחדה לה לכתובתה או כתב לה בתוך הכתובה או שהכניסה לו שום משלה.

NOTES

manner. In either case, the Gemara's question, "Let her say: 'I did it to please my husband,' would apply." *Shittah Mekubbetzet* answers that had the Gemara interpreted the Mishnah's text more broadly, it could have been argued that is the buyer purchased the woman's rights first, and only later did he buy the property itself from the husband. In such a situation, we clearly do not believe her claim that she sold her rights to please her husband. The Gemara understood the Mishnah's text literally in order to eliminate that suggestion. Thus the question remains as to why the woman cannot argue that she only waived her right to recover her ketubah settlement from the field sold by her husband in order to please him.

לָקַח מִן הָאִישׁ **If someone bought something from a man.** *Ritva* asks: Elsewhere (*Bava Batra* 49b), the Gemara explains that in the Mishnah in *Gittin* the husband sold property that had been especially designated for his wife's ketubah. Either this was property that the husband had set aside as a hypotheque for his wife's ketubah, or property that his wife brought into the marriage as part of her dowry. Although all of the husband's property is technically mortgaged to his wife's ketubah, she relies on collecting her settlement from the property which had been especially designated for that purpose. Hence she can claim that she sold the rights to that property only in order to please her husband. However, regarding the remainder of the husband's property perhaps his wife cannot put forward this claim! *Ritva* answers that the woman can always argue that she sold her rights in the property only to please her husband. The difference between property which had been especially designated for her ketubah and the rest of her husband's property is that regarding the former the sale is automatically invalid, whereas regarding the rest of the husband's property, the sale is valid until the woman objects to the sale. Other Rishonim disagree with *Ritva* and maintain that even in the case of property especially designated for the wife's ketubah, the sale is valid until she claims that she agreed to the sale only to please her husband.

וְחָזַר וְלָקַח מִן הָאִשָּׁה **And then he bought it from his wife.** *Rivan* notes that the term "bought" implies that the buyer paid the woman something for her agreement to waive her rights to her husband's property.

נַחַת רוּחַ עָשִׂיתִי לְבַעְלִי **I did it to please my husband.** If a person discloses in advance that a transaction he is about to conclude is being done against his will, it is void. Such

HALAKHAH

לָקַח מִן הָאִישׁ **If someone bought property from a man.** "If a husband sold or gave away property over which his wife exercised a lien for her ketubah settlement, and the wife stated in writing that she would not bring a claim against the buyer regarding that property, and she even reinforced that waiver with an act of acquisition, she can still collect her ketubah settlement from that property. For she can claim that she only agreed to the sale in order to please her husband." (*Rambam, Sefer Nashim, Hilkhot Ishut* 17:11; *Sefer Kinyan, Hilkhot Mekhirah* 30:3; *Shulḥan Arukh, Even HaEzer* 90:17.)

[1] הָא רַבִּי יְהוּדָה, [2] דְּתַנְיָא: "כָּתַב לָרִאשׁוֹן, וְלֹא חָתְמָה לוֹ, לַשֵּׁנִי וְחָתְמָה לוֹ, אִיבְּדָה כְּתוּבָּתָהּ; [3] דִּבְרֵי רַבִּי מֵאִיר. [4] רַבִּי יְהוּדָה אוֹמֵר: יְכוֹלָה הִיא שֶׁתֹּאמַר: [5] 'נַחַת רוּחַ עָשִׂיתִי לְבַעְלִי; [6] אַתֶּם, מַה לָּכֶם עָלַי?'". [7] וְרַבִּי סָתַם לָהּ הָכָא כְּרַבִּי מֵאִיר, [8] וְסָתַם לָהּ הָתָם כְּרַבִּי יְהוּדָה? [9] אֲמַר רַב פַּפָּא: [10] בִּגְרוּשָׁה, וְדִבְרֵי הַכֹּל.

LITERAL TRANSLATION

[1] that is [according to] Rabbi Yehudah, [2] as it was taught: "[If] he wrote [a bill of sale] for the first one, and [his wife] did not sign for him, for the second one, and she did sign for him, she lost her ketubah; [3] [these are] the words of Rabbi Meir. [4] Rabbi Yehudah says: She can say: [5] 'I did it to please my husband; [6] [so] why are you [disputing] with me?'"

[7] And [would] Rabbi teach here anonymously according to Rabbi Meir, [8] and teach there anonymously according to Rabbi Yehudah?

[9] Rav Pappa said: [Our Mishnah deals with] a divorcee, [10] and according to everyone.

RASHI

כתב לראשון – שטר מכר על שדה אחת. ולא חתמה לו – לא הודית באותו מכר, וכתב שטר אחר ללוקח שני על שדה אחרת, וחתמה לו. אבדה כתובתה – אם אין שם בני חורין, שהרי הראשון אומר: הנחתי ליך מקום לגבות הימנו. יכולה היא שתאמר כו' – מן השני תגבה. ורבי – דסתמינהו למשניות, הכא בכתובות סתם לן כרבי מאיר, ובמסכת גיטין סתם לן מקחו בטל כרבי יהודה. אמר רב פפא – מתניתין כשהיתה גרושה ואחר כך כתבה לו ללוקח כן.

TRANSLATION AND COMMENTARY

her husband, [1] and the Mishnah in *Gittin* follows the view of **Rabbi Yehudah,** who maintains that a woman can indeed present such an argument. [2] **For it was taught** in a Baraita: **"If a man wrote a bill** of sale **for one** field, **and** his wife **did not sign** the document **for him** to approve the sale, and then he wrote a bill of sale **for a second** field, **and** this time his wife **signed** and approved the document **for him**, the woman **lost her** rights to collect **her ketubah** settlement from either field. She cannot collect from the second field, because she renounced her rights to it when she approved to its sale. She also cannot collect even from the first field, because its buyer can argue that when he purchased it, he left the husband with the second property from which the woman could collect her ketubah settlement. Therefore, he should not have to suffer a loss if she later waived her rights to that other property. [3] **This is the position of Rabbi Meir.** [4] **Rabbi Yehudah** disagrees and **says:** The woman did not lose her rights to collect her ketubah settlement, for **she can say** to the second buyer: 'When I agreed to my husband's sale of the property, [5] **I did** so only **to please my husband,** but I did not really mean to sell my rights to the field. [6] **Why** then **are you disputing with me?'"**

וְרַבִּי [7] The Gemara asks: Granted that this explanation reconciles the contradiction between the Mishnah in *Ketubot* and the Mishnah in *Gittin*. But is it reasonable that **Rabbi** Yehudah HaNasi **taught** the Mishnah **here** in *Ketubot* **anonymously according to** the opinion of **Rabbi Meir,** [8] **and he taught** the Mishnah **there** in *Gittin* **anonymously according to** the opinion of **Rabbi Yehudah?**

אֲמַר רַב פַּפָּא [9] **Rav Pappa said** that the difficulty posed by the Mishnah in *Gittin* can be resolved as follows: The Mishnah in *Gittin* is dealing with a field that was sold while the woman was married. It follows the opinion of Rabbi Yehudah and rules that the wife can say that she was only trying to please her husband, and therefore her sale of her rights is invalid. [10] By contrast, the Mishnah here in *Ketubot* is dealing with a woman who was already **a divorcee** when she waived her right to the field that was purchased from her ex-husband. In such a case **all agree** — even Rabbi Yehudah — that her waiver is binding, for a divorcee cannot argue that any of her actions were prompted by a desire to please her husband.

NOTES

a declaration must ordinarily be made in the presence of witnesses. *Rabbenu Yehonatan* notes that in our case such a notification is not necessary, for even if the wife did not make such a declaration, we assume that she agreed to the sale of her husband's property only in order to please him and did not declare this before witnesses because she was afraid that the matter would become known to him and he would become angry and accuse her of preparing herself for divorce or widowhood.

כָּתַב לָרִאשׁוֹן, וְלֹא חָתְמָה לוֹ **If he wrote a bill for the first one, and she did not sign for him.** The Rishonim ask: Why should the first buyer ask the wife to sign the bill of sale? If she comes later to claim her ketubah settlement from that property, he can argue that when he purchased it, he left land with the husband from which she could collect! *Ra'ah* and others answer that the first buyer would like her to approve his purchase, because property that he left behind might turn out to be stolen, or else it might be seized by some other creditor, and the woman would then be able to collect her ketubah settlement from the property that he had bought.

לַשֵּׁנִי וְחָתְמָה לוֹ **For the second one, and she signed for him.** The rationale of Rabbi Meir's position is clear: The first time that the woman refused to give her consent to the sale of property, she demonstrated that she was willing to oppose his will. Consequently she cannot argue later that

TRANSLATION AND COMMENTARY

רַב אַשִׁי אֲמַר [1]**Rav Ashi said:** In fact, you can say that both Mishnayot deal with women who surrendered their rights while they were married, and **both are according to** the view of **Rabbi Meir.** [2]**Rabbi Meir only says** that a woman cannot argue that she acted to please her husband **in** the case of the Baraita, when the husband sold his property to **two** different **buyers,** and his wife refused to sign for one sale but agreed to the second sale. In such a case, the woman forfeit her right to collect her ketubah settlement from any of the sold property, [3]**for** the buyers **can say to her: "If indeed you acted** only **to please your husband, you should have done** the same **with respect to the first** sale." If she refused to agree to the first sale, that showed that she was willing to displease her husband, and she is, therefore, not believed when she claims that she acted only to please him in the second sale. [4]**But** in the case of the Mishnah in *Gittin,* the husband sold property to only **one buyer.** [5]**Even Rabbi Meir agrees** that the sale is not valid, for the woman can argue that she acted only to please her husband and did not intend to give up her rights to the property. [6]**However, in our Mishnah** the husband **wrote someone else** a bill of sale on his property prior to the sale mentioned in the Mishnah, and his wife refused to sign it. He then sold the property to someone else, at which time she consented. In such a case the woman cannot argue that her consent to the second transaction was only given in order to please her husband.

תְּנַן הָתָם [7]**We have learned elsewhere** in the Mishnah (*Gittin* 48b): "An injured party, a creditor, or a divorced woman **cannot be paid** what is due them **from property that had been mortgaged** to the debt but is now in the hands of a buyer, **if free** landed **property** still **remains** for collection in the hands of the tortfeasor, the debtor or the husband. The injured party cannot collect from purchased property, [8]**even if** the free property available to them **is property of the poorest quality,** although ordinarily he would have been entitled to collect from land of higher quality."

[1]רַב אַשִׁי אֲמַר: כּוּלָּהּ רַבִּי מֵאִיר הִיא, [2]וְעַד כָּאן לָא קָאָמַר רַבִּי מֵאִיר הָתָם אֶלָּא בִּשְׁנֵי לָקוֹחוֹת, [3]דְּאָמְרִי לָהּ: "אִי אִיתָא דְּנַחַת רוּחַ עָבְדַתְּ, לְקַמָּא אִיבָּעֵי לָךְ לְמֵיעֱבַד". [4]אֲבָל בְּלוֹקֵחַ אֶחָד, [5]אֲפִילּוּ רַבִּי מֵאִיר מוֹדֶה. [6]וּמַתְנִיתִין דִּכְתַב לֵיהּ לְאַחֵר.

[7]תְּנַן הָתָם: "אֵין נִפְרָעִין מִנְּכָסִים מְשׁוּעְבָּדִים בְּמָקוֹם שֶׁיֵּשׁ נְכָסִים בְּנֵי חוֹרִין, [8]וַאֲפִילּוּ הֵן זִיבּוּרִית".

LITERAL TRANSLATION

[1]Rav Ashi said: Both are (lit., "all of it is") [according to] Rabbi Meir, [2]and Rabbi Meir only said [his opinion] there in [the case of] two buyers, [3]for they can say to her: "If indeed you did it to please [your husband], you should have [also] done it for the first one." [4]But with one buyer, [5]even Rabbi Meir agrees. [6]And our Mishnah [was learnt] when he wrote [a bill of sale] to someone else.

[7]We have learned elsewhere: "They are not paid from mortgaged property in a place where there is free property, [8]even if it is property of the poorest quality."

RASHI

רב אשי אמר — אפילו יושבת תחתיו, ותרוייהו סתמי כרבי מאיר, ומתניתין דגיטין דלקח מן האיש וחזר ולקח מן האשה להכי מקחו בטל, דעד כאן לא קאמר רבי מאיר בברייתא: איבדה כתובתה, אלא בשני לקוחות, והא חזינן דבראשון לא עשתה נחת רוח לבעלה, הלכך לא מצית למימר כי חתמה לשני: נחת רוח עשיתי לבעלי. **ומתניתין** — דהכא דאשמעינן מינה חתימתה קיימת. **בדכתב** — הבעל לאחר קודם לזה, ולא חתמה לו, ולזה חתמה.

NOTES

when she agreed to the second sale, she did so only in order to please him. As for Rabbi Yehudah's position *Rivan* explains that the woman can argue that since she refused her husband once already, she was afraid to do so again. However, she never really meant to waive her rights to that portion of her husband's property.

HALAKHAH

אֶלָּא בִּשְׁנֵי לָקוֹחוֹת **There in the case of two buyers.** "If a husband sold property over which his wife exercised a lien for her ketubah settlement, and he asked her to waive her rights to the property, but she refused to do so, and then the husband sold the same property or some other property to a second buyer, and this time when he asked her to waive her rights to the property, she agreed and reinforced the waiver with an act of acquisition, she cannot later collect her ketubah settlement from that property. After she refused her husband the first time, she cannot claim that she agreed to the second sale only in order to please him," following Rabbi Meir and Rav Ashi. (*Rambam, Sefer Nashim, Hilkhot Ishut* 19:2; *Shulhan Arukh, Even HaEzer* 90:17.)

אֵין נִפְרָעִין מִנְּכָסִים מְשׁוּעְבָּדִים **They are not paid from mortgaged property.** "A creditor cannot collect the money owed him from property that had been mortgaged to the debt but is now in the hands of a buyer, if free property remains in the hands of his debtor. This is true even if the free property is of the poorest quality, and the mortgaged property is of intermediate or of the highest quality," following the Mishnah in *Gittin.* (*Rambam, Sefer Mishpatim, Hilkhot Malveh* 19:2; *Shulḥan Arukh, Ḥoshen Mishpat* 111:8.)

[1]אִיבַּעְיָא לְהוּ: אִישְׁתַּדּוּף בְּנֵי חָרֵי, [2]מַהוּ דְּלִיטְרוֹף מִמְּשַׁעְבְּדֵי?

[3]תָּא שְׁמַע: ״כָּתַב לָרִאשׁוֹן, וְלֹא חָתְמָה לוֹ, [4]לַשֵּׁנִי וְחָתְמָה לוֹ, [5]אִיבְּדָה כְּתוּבָּתָהּ; [6]דִּבְרֵי רַבִּי מֵאִיר״. [7]וְאִי סָלְקָא דַּעְתָּךְ אִישְׁתַּדּוּף בְּנֵי חָרֵי, [8]טָרֵיף מִמְּשַׁעְבְּדֵי, [9]נְהִי דְּאִיבְּדָה כְּתוּבָּתָהּ מִשֵּׁנִי, [10]מֵרִאשׁוֹן מִיהָא תִּיגְבֵּי!

[11]אָמַר רַב נַחְמָן בַּר יִצְחָק: מַאי ״אִיבְּדָה״? [12]אִיבְּדָה מִשֵּׁנִי.

[13]אָמַר רָבָא: שְׁתֵּי תְּשׁוּבוֹת בַּדָּבָר: [14]חֲדָא, דְּ״אִיבְּדָה״ לְגַמְרֵי מַשְׁמַע. [15]וְעוֹד, תַּנְיָא:

LITERAL TRANSLATION

[1]It was asked of them: [If] the free property was struck [by hot winds], [2]what about seizing mortgaged property?

[3]Come [and] hear: "[If] he wrote [a bill of sale] for the first one, and she did not sign for him, [4]for the second one and she did sign for him, [5]she lost her ketubah; [6][these are] the words of Rabbi Meir." [7]And if it should enter your mind that [if] the free property was struck [by hot winds], [8]he seizes from mortgaged property, [9]granted that she lost [collecting] her ketubah from the second one, [10][but] she should at least collect from the first one!

[11]Rav Naḥman bar Yitzḥak said: What is [the meaning of] "she lost"? [12]She lost [collecting] from the second one.

[13]Rava said: [There are] two answers against this matter: [14]First, "she lost" implies entirely. [15]And furthermore, it was taught:

TRANSLATION AND COMMENTARY

אִיבַּעְיָא לְהוּ [1]The following **question was raised** among the Sages who were studying this Mishnah: **If,** after part of the debtor's property was purchased by a buyer, **the free property** that remained in the debtor's hands **was struck by hot winds,** or otherwise damaged, and its value dropped so that it was no longer sufficient to cover his debt, [2]**may** the creditor then **seize mortgaged property** that was sold?

תָּא שְׁמַע [3]The Gemara suggests that an answer to this question may be found in the Baraita which had been cited earlier: **Come and hear**: "If a man **wrote a bill** of sale **for one** field, **and** his wife **did not sign** the document **for him,** showing her disapproval of the sale, [4]and then he wrote a bill of sale **for a second** field, **and** this time his wife **signed** and approved the sale **for him,** [5]the woman **lost her** rights to collect **her ketubah** settlement from either of the fields. [6]**These are the words of Rabbi Meir."** [7]**Now if it should enter your mind that if the free property** remaining in a debtor's possession **was struck by hot winds** and ruined, [8]the creditor **may seize** what is owed him **from mortgaged property** that had been sold, you are contradicted by the Baraita. [9]**Granted that** the woman **lost** her right to collect **her ketubah** settlement **from the second** field, as she explicitly renounced her rights to that property. [10]**But she should at least** be able to **collect** her ketubah settlement **from the first** field. It was explained above that the woman cannot collect her ketubah from the first field, because the buyer can argue that when he had purchased the field from the husband, he had left him with other property from which she could collect her ketubah, and so he should not have to suffer a loss if the woman later waived her rights to that other property. But if when the free property remaining in the debtor's hands is damaged by winds and ruined, the creditor can collect his debt from mortgaged property that had been sold to a buyer, even though the buyer can argue that when he had purchased the field, he had left the debtor with other property from which the creditor could collect his debt, the woman who renounced her rights to collect her ketubah from the second field should be able to collect her ketubah from the first field, even though the buyer can argue that when he had purchased the field, he had left the husband with other property from which the woman could collect her ketubah!

אָמַר רַב נַחְמָן [11]**Rav Naḥman bar Yitzḥak said:** Nothing can be proven from this Baraita, for it can be argued that **what** the Baraita meant when it stated: "The woman **lost** her right to collect her ketubah," [12]was that **she lost** her right to collect her ketubah **from the second** field, to which she explicitly renounced her rights. But she may indeed be able to collect her ketubah from the first field. Similarly, a creditor can collect his debt from property which the debtor had sold to a third party, if the free property which the buyer had left behind was ruined.

אָמַר רָבָא [13]**Rav said: Two arguments** may be raised **against this suggestion:** [14]**First,** the expression **"she lost** her ketubah" **implies** that she lost it **entirely,** and she cannot collect from either of the fields. [15]**And furthermore,** a parallel case in which a creditor cannot collect from either field **was taught** explicitly in another

RASHI

אישתדוף בני חרי – לאחר שלקחו הלקוחות. אישתדוף = נתקלקלו. מראשון מיהא תגבי – שהרי נתקלקל זכותה במקום שהניח לה לגבות, והוה ליה כאישתדוף. ועוד תניא – דמראשון לא תגבה.

TRANSLATION AND COMMENTARY

Baraita: [1]"If a person **borrowed** money **from someone and** later divided and **sold his** mortgaged **property to two** different people, **and the creditor** wrote nothing to the first buyer, but he **wrote to the second buyer:** [2]'**I will have no claim against you** regarding the property that you purchased from my debtor,' not only does the creditor waive his claim against the second buyer, [3]but **he** also **has no claim against the first** buyer. [4]This is **because** the first buyer **can say** to the creditor: 'When I purchased property from the debtor, **I left** him with free **property from which you could collect** your debt, and I should not have to suffer a loss if you waived your right to collect your debt from that other property.'" Notwithstanding, neither the Baraita dealing with the woman who waived her right to collect her ketubah settlement from her husband's sold property, nor the Baraita dealing with the creditor who waived his right to collect his debt from his debtor's sold property teaches us a thing about the case involving free property that was ruined. [5]For **there** the woman or the creditor **caused themselves damage with their own hands** by waiving their right to collect from the property. Their acts cannot impair the rights of the first purchaser of the field, who left free property with the creditor from which they could collect.

[1] ״לָוָה מִן הָאֶחָד וּמָכַר נְכָסָיו לִשְׁנַיִם, וְכָתַב בַּעַל חוֹב לְלוֹקֵחַ שֵׁנִי: [2] ׳דִּין וּדְבָרִים אֵין לִי עִמְּךָ׳, [3] אֵין לוֹ עַל לוֹקֵחַ רִאשׁוֹן כְּלוּם, [4] מִפְּנֵי שֶׁיָּכוֹל לוֹמַר: ׳הִנַּחְתִּי לְךָ מָקוֹם לִגְבּוֹת הֵימֶנּוּ׳״. [5] הָתָם, אִיהוּ דְּאַפְסִיד נַפְשֵׁיהּ בְּיָדַיִם.

LITERAL TRANSLATION

[1]"[If] he borrowed from one and sold his property to two, and the creditor wrote to the second buyer: [2]'I have no claim (lit., "claim or dispute") against you,' [3]he has no [claim] against the first one, [4]because he can say: 'I left you a place from which to collect.'" [5]There, he caused himself damage with his own hands.

RASHI

הכי גרסינן: התם איהו דאפסיד אנפשיה — וכולה רבא קאמר לה, לא תימא מאי איבדה כתובתה משני, דאף מראשון איבדה אפילו הכי לא נפשוט מינה אישתדוף בני חרי לא טריף ממשעבדי, דהתם היא דאבדה כתובתה.

והא דקתני: אין לו על לוקח ראשון כלום חד טעמא הוא, האי דלא הדר גבי מהראשון משום דאפסיד נפשיה בידים שכתב לשני: דין ודברים אין לי עמך, ולא דמי לאישתדוף.

NOTES

אִיהוּ דְּאַפְסִיד נַפְשֵׁיהּ **There he caused himself damage.** Our commentary follows *Rashi* who explains that this line is a continuation of Rava's statement. Rava first demonstrates that the Baraita must mean that the woman lost her ketubah settlement entirely, and that she cannot collect from either of the fields. He then concludes that the Baraita dealing with the woman who waived her right to collect her ketubah settlement from the property that her husband sold to the second buyer, and the Baraita dealing with the creditor who waived his right to collect his debt from the property that his debtor had sold to a second buyer prove nothing about the case when the free property remaining in the debtor's hands was ruined by the winds. For in the cases discussed in the Baraitot, the wife and the creditor damaged themselves with their own hands. *Tosafot* argue that according to *Rashi's* explanation, the Gemara should read: *Rather* (אֶלָּא) there he caused himself damage with his own hands. (*Ittur* cites a reading which includes the word אֶלָּא.) *Tosafot* explain that this line is the Gemara's argument against Rava: In the Baraita dealing with the creditor, he caused himself damage, and therefore he cannot even collect from the first buyer. But the woman who waived her right to collect her ketubah settlement from the property that was sold to the second buyer, is not

HALAKHAH

לָוָה מִן הָאֶחָד וּמָכַר נְכָסָיו לִשְׁנַיִם **If he borrowed from one and sold his property to two.** "If a debtor sold two fields to two different people, and his creditor exercised a lien upon that property, and the creditor wrote to the second buyer that he would not bring a claim against it, and he reinforced his waiver with an act of acquisition, the creditor cannot recover his debt from the property purchased by the first buyer. The first buyer can argue that when he purchased the property from the debtor, he left him with free property from which the creditor could collect, and it was the creditor who caused himself a loss when he waived his right to collect from the property purchased by the second buyer. Similarly, if a husband sold two fields to two different people and his wife exercised a lien over these fields and waived her right to collect her ketubah settlement from the property purchased by the second buyer, she cannot even collect from the first buyer. But if she waived her right to collect from the property purchased by the first buyer, she can still collect from the second buyer. If the husband sold property to one buyer, but his wife did not agree to the sale, and then he sold the same property or some other property to a second buyer, and this time his wife agreed to the sale, she cannot collect her ketubah settlement from the second buyer." According to some authorities (*Tosafot*), the woman can still collect from the first buyer. According to others (*Rashi, Rambam,* and others), she cannot collect her ketubah from the first buyer. (*Rambam, Sefer Mishpatim, Hilkhot Malveh* 19:8; *Shulḥan Arukh, Ḥoshen Mishpat* 118:1; *Even HaEzer* 100:3.)

LANGUAGE

פַּרְדֵּיסָא Orchard. This word is found in the Bible, in the Song of Songs and Ecclesiastes, and its source is a Persian term meaning "garden." It was borrowed with more or less closely related meanings by many languages, as in English, "paradise."
From Talmudic and Midrashic sources, it appears that the "pardes" is a grove of various kinds of fruit trees, and some claim that its main function was decorative.

[1] אֲמַר לֵיהּ רַב יֵימָר לְרַב אַשִׁי: [95B] [2] וְהָא מַעֲשִׂים בְּכָל יוֹם! [3] דְּהַהוּא גַּבְרָא דְּמִישְׁכֵּן לֵיהּ פַּרְדֵּיסָא לְחַבְרֵיהּ לְעֶשֶׂר שְׁנִין, [4] וְקַשׁ לְחָמֵשׁ שְׁנִין, וַאֲתָא לְקַמַּיְיהוּ דְּרַבָּנַן, [5] וְכָתְבוּ לֵיהּ טִירְפָּא!

[6] הָתָם נַמִי אִינְהוּ הוּא דְּאַפְסִידוּ אַנַּפְשַׁיְיהוּ. [7] כֵּיוָן דַּהֲווּ יָדְעִי דְּפַרְדֵּיסָא עֲבִיד דְּקִישׁ, [8] לָא אִיבָּעֵי לְהוּ לְמִיזְבַּן.

[9] וְהִלְכְתָא: אִישְׁתַּדּוּף בְּנֵי חָרֵי, [10] טָרְפָא מִמְּשַׁעְבְּדֵי.

LITERAL TRANSLATION

[1] Rav Yemar said to Rav Ashi: [95B] [2] But surely there are [legal] acts every day! [3] For [there was] a certain man who mortgaged an orchard to his fellow for ten years, [4] but it aged after five years, and he came before the Rabbis, [5] and they wrote him a *tirpa*!

[6] There too they caused themselves damage. [7] Since they knew that the orchard was liable to age, [8] they should not have bought [a mortgaged field].

[9] And the law is: [If] the [remaining] free property was struck [by hot winds], [10] he seizes from mortgaged property.

RASHI

והא מעשים בכל יום – דדיינין דינין דכיון דאשתדוף בני חרי טריף ממשעבדי. **פרדיסא** = כרם. **לעשר שנים** – שיאכלנה עשר שנים ותחזור לבעלים בלא מעות, דכתב ליה: "במשלם שניא אילין תיפוק ארעא דין בלא כסף". **וקש** = הזקין. **איהו אפסיד אנפשיה** – לוקח שלקח שדה מיד זה שמשכן כרם זה באחריות לאוכלו עשר שנים. **עביד דקיש** – והדר מלוה על הלקוחות.

TRANSLATION AND COMMENTARY

אֲמַר לֵיהּ [1] **Rav Yemar said to Rav Ashi:** [95B] [2] Is there any question about a creditor's seizing the debtor's mortgaged property from its purchaser, if the free property still in the debtor's hands was struck by hot winds and ruined? **But surely it is a common** that the courts rule, in such cases, that the creditor to seize mortgaged property from its purchasers! [3] **For example, a certain man mortgaged his orchard to another person for** a period of **ten years,** entitling the lender to enjoy the fruit of the mortgaged land, over that period in payment of his loan. [4] **But after five years** the trees **aged** and no longer produced salable fruit. The creditor **came before the Rabbis** demanding that the rest of his loan be repaid, [5] **and they wrote him a** *tirpa*, conferring upon him the right to seize other property that had been bought by a third party. This ruling shows that if a creditor can no longer collect his debt from unsold property, he can collect his debt from property that had been purchased by others.

הָתָם נַמִי [6] The Gemara answers: This incident proves nothing about the case where the property that was struck by hot winds and ruined, for **in the case** of the orchard **too,** it was the purchaser who **caused himself damage.** [7] **Since he knew that the orchard** held by the creditor **was liable to age** and stop producing salable fruit, and the creditor would then recover his debt from other property belonging to the debtor, [8] the buyer **should never have bought** any property from the debtor. But if the buyer purchased property from the debtor, and the debtor's free property was later battered by the winds and ruined, perhaps the creditor cannot collect from the property in the buyer's possession. The buyer can argue that when he bought the property, he left property in the debtor's possession from which the creditor could collect his debt, and he had no reason to anticipate that the remaining field would be ruined by the winds.

וְהִלְכְתָא [9] The Gemara concludes this discussion with a practical ruling: **The law is** that **if the free property** remaining in the debtor's possession **was struck by hot winds** and ruined, [10] the creditor may **seize the property that had been mortgaged** to the debt and later sold to another person.

NOTES

regarded as having caused herself the damage. A wife cannot collect her ketubah settlement during her husband's lifetime unless she is divorced, and if she remains married and predeceases him, she will never collect it. We therefore allow her to collect her ketubah settlement from the first buyer. This disagreement in understanding the Gemara also has practical ramifications as well (see Halakhah).

HALAKHAH

אִישְׁתַּדּוּף בְּנֵי חָרֵי If the free property was struck. "If the debtor's free property is ruined, the creditor may collect what is due him from property that had been mortgaged to the debt and later sold to someone else," following the Gemara's conclusion. This ruling only applies if the debtor's free property was ruined. But if it was stolen, the creditor cannot collect from mortgaged property, because circumstances might change and the land may eventually be retrieved from the bandits and become available for collection (*Rashba*). *Rema* adds that if the debtor left the Jewish faith (and no longer subjects himself to the Jewish court system), so that it will be impossible to collect a debt from him, the creditor can indeed collect from mortgaged property (*Rosh*). (*Rambam, Sefer Mishpatim, Hilkhot Malveh* 19:2; *Shulḥan Arukh, Ḥoshen Mishpat* 111:12-13.)

TRANSLATION AND COMMENTARY

אָמַר אַבַּיֵי [1] **Abaye said:** If a man said to an unmarried woman: **"My property** shall belong **to you** for the rest of your life, **but after you** die, what remains in your estate shall not go to your heirs, but rather **to so-and-so,"** [2] **and** then the woman **married, her husband is** regarded as if **he had bought** that property. [3] Therefore, **where there is a husband, the person** to whom that other man had promised his property **after** the woman dies **has no claim** to it even after the woman's death. Because when a person receives a gift of property even for a limited period (such as the woman in Abaye's teaching) he has total possession including the right of sale. Therefore, the stipulation made by the bestower of the gift does not apply to property the recipient had sold before her death.

[1] אָמַר אַבַּיֵי: "נְכָסַי לֵיךְ, וְאַחֲרַיִךְ לִפְלוֹנִי", [2] וְעָמְדָה וְנִיסֵּת, בַּעַל לוֹקֵחַ הָוֵי, [3] וְאֵין לְ"אַחֲרַיִךְ" בִּמְקוֹם בַּעַל כְּלוּם. [4] כְּמַאן? [5] כִּי הַאי תַּנָּא, דְּתַנְיָא: [6] "'נְכָסַי לֵיךְ, וְאַחֲרֶיךָ לִפְלוֹנִי', [7] יָרַד הָרִאשׁוֹן וּמָכַר, הַשֵּׁנִי מוֹצִיא מִיַּד הַלָּקוֹחוֹת; [8] דִּבְרֵי רַבִּי. [9] רַבָּן שִׁמְעוֹן בֶּן גַּמְלִיאֵל אוֹמֵר: אֵין לַשֵּׁנִי אֶלָּא מַה שֶׁשִּׁיֵּיר רִאשׁוֹן".

LITERAL TRANSLATION

[1] Abaye said: "My property to you, and after you to so-and-so," [2] and she stood up and married, the husband is a buyer, [3] and "[so-and-so] after you" where there is a husband has nothing.

[4] According to whom [is this statement]? [5] [It is] according to the following Tanna, who taught: [6] "'My property to you, and after you to so-and-so,' [7] [if] the first one went down and sold [it], the second one removes [it] from the hand of the buyer; [8] [these are] the words of Rabbi. [9] Rabban Shimon ben Gamliel says: The second one only has what the first one left [behind]."

RASHI

נכסי ליך – אמר לפנויה נכסי ליך ואחריך לפלוני. כי האי תנא – כרבי שמעון דאמר: מכירתו מכירה.

כְּמַאן [4] The Gemara asks: **In accordance with whose** opinion did Abaye issue this ruling? [5] The Gemara answers: **In accordance with the following Tanna**, Rabban Shimon ben Gamliel, who **taught** in a Baraita: [6] "If someone said to another person: **'My property** shall belong **to you** for the rest of your life, **but after you** die it shall belong **to so-and-so,'** [7] and **the first** recipient **went and sold** the property to a third party, **the second one** who was supposed to receive the property **may take it away from the buyer.** [8] **This is the position of Rabbi** Yehudah HaNasi, who maintains that the property was only given to the first recipient to use, but he was not permitted to sell it. [9] **Rabban Shimon ben Gamliel** disagrees and **says: The second one is only entitled to what the first one left** after him when he died. But he is not entitled to property sold by the first recipient during his lifetime." Rabban Shimon ben Gamliel's ruling supports that of Abaye: If a woman who received a gift of property marries, her husband is considered a purchaser, and the designated second recipient loses his claim to the property.

NOTES

וְאֵין לְ"אַחֲרַיִךְ" בִּמְקוֹם בַּעַל כְּלוּם **And "so-and-so after you" where there is a husband has nothing.** *Meiri* (in the name of *Sefer Hashlamah*) writes that even if the husband died before his wife, the person who was to receive the property after her death loses his claim to the property, for she is regarded as if she had sold the property to someone and then bought it back from him.

HALAKHAH

נְכָסַי לֵיךְ, וְאַחֲרַיִךְ לִפְלוֹנִי **My property to you, and after you to so-and-so.** "If a dying person said to an unmarried woman: 'My property shall belong to you for the rest of your life, but after your death, it shall belong to so-and-so, and the woman married, her husband is regarded as a buyer. Therefore, the other person to whom the property had been promised cannot take the property away from the husband after the woman's death, following Abaye's first ruling. But if the dying person gave the woman the property under those conditions while she was married, and the woman died, the other person to whom the property had been promised can remove the property from the husband," following Abaye's second ruling. Therefore, if the woman sold the property while she was married, and then she died, the property remains with the buyer. (*Rambam, Sefer Kinyan, Hilkhot Zekhiyah U'Matanah* 12:12; *Shulḥan Arukh, Ḥoshen Mishpat* 248:8.)

אֵין לַשֵּׁנִי אֶלָּא מַה שֶּׁשִּׁיֵּיר רִאשׁוֹן **The second one only has what the first one left behind.** "If a dying person said to another person: 'My property shall belong to you for the rest of your life, but after your death, it shall belong to so-and-so, the recipient of the property is forbidden to sell or give away the property and may only enjoy the usufruct during his lifetime. After his death the property passes to the other person to whom it was promised. If the recipient nevertheless sold the property or gave it away, the second person to whom it was promised is only entitled to whatever the first one leaves behind when he dies," following Rabban Shimon ben Gamliel. (*Rambam, Sefer Kinyan, Hilkhot Zekhiyah U'Matanah* 12:3, 8-9; *Shulḥan Arukh, Ḥoshen Mishpat* 248:1, 3.)

וּמִי אֲמַר אַבַּיֵי הָכִי? [2]וְהָאָמַר אַבַּיֵי: אֵיזֶהוּ רָשָׁע עָרוּם? [3]זֶה הַמַּשִּׂיא עֵצָה לִמְכּוֹר בִּנְכָסִים כְּרַבָּן שִׁמְעוֹן בֶּן גַּמְלִיאֵל!
[4]מִי קָאָמַר "תִּינָּשֵׂא"? [5]"נִשֵּׂאת" קָאָמַר.
[6]וְאָמַר אַבַּיֵי: "נְכָסַי לֵיךְ, וְאַחֲרַיִךְ לִפְלוֹנִי", [7]וּמָכְרָה וּמֵתָה — הַבַּעַל מוֹצִיא מִיַּד הַלָּקוֹחוֹת, [8]וְ"אַחֲרַיִךְ" מִיַּד בַּעַל, [9]וְלוֹקֵחַ מִיַּד "אַחֲרַיִךְ". [10]וּמוֹקְמִינַן לְכוּלְּהוּ בִּידָא דְּלוֹקֵחַ.

LITERAL TRANSLATION

[1]But did Abaye say this? [2]But surely Abaye said: Who is a cunning scoundrel? [3]He who gives advice to sell property according to [the ruling of] Rabban Shimon ben Gamliel!

[4]Did [Abaye] say: "She should marry"? [5]He said: "She married."

[6]And Abaye said: "My property to you, and after you to so-and-so," [7]and she sold [it] and died, the husband removes it from the buyers' hand, [8]and "[so-and-so] after you" from the husband, [9]and the buyer from "[so-and-so] after you." [10]And we establish [the ownership of] all of the [property] in the hand of the buyer.

TRANSLATION AND COMMENTARY

וּמִי אֲמַר [1]The Gemara asks: **But did Abaye** really **say** that once the woman marries the person who was to receive the property after the woman's death loses his claim to the property? [2]**But surely Abaye** himself **said: Who is** considered to be **a cunning scoundrel?** [3]**He who advises** others **to sell property in accordance with** the position of **Rabban Shimon ben Gamliel**, thus depriving the second party from receiving the property that was intended for him. If Abaye was so displeased by the position of Rabbi Shimon ben Gamliel, why would he have ruled in accordance with it?

מִי קָאָמַר [4]The Gemara answers: There is really no difficulty with Abaye's two statements. **Did Abaye** ever **say** in this case that the woman who received the property **should marry** somebody, thereby depriving the second designated recipient from ever receiving that property? [5]No, **he** only **said** that if **she married,** the other person to whom the property had been promised no longer has a claim to it.

וְאָמַר אַבַּיֵי [6]The Gemara continues with a related statement of Abaye. **Abaye said:** If a man said to a woman: "**My property** shall belong **to you** for the rest of your life, **but after you** die, it shall not go to your heirs, but rather **to so-and-so,"** [7]**and she sold** the property **and died, her husband may take** the property **away from the buyer,** for he is regarded as having obtained primary rights to this property as part of his wife's usufruct property (see *Ketubot* 78b), which he inherits from her if she dies and which, under the enactment of Usha, he may seize from anyone to whom his wife may have sold it. [8]The second designated recipient who was supposed to receive the property **after the woman's** death may then remove the property **from the husband,** for according to the donor's instructions it was he who was to receive the property after her death. [9]**And the one who bought** the property from the woman may then come and **take it away from** the second designated recipient, following the position of Rabban Shimon ben Gamliel, that if the first recipient sold the property during his lifetime, the sale is valid. [10]**And** in the end **we leave all of** the property **in the hand of the buyer.**

RASHI

ואמר אביי נכסי ליך כו׳ — לקמן מוקמי לה אשמעתא בתרייתא באומר לנשואה. הבעל מוציא מיד הלוקח — אם בא לדון עמו יכול הוא לזכות בדין שהוא לוקח ראשון. ואחריך — יכול להוציא מיד הבעל. דכי אמר אביי: "אין לאחריך במקום הבעל כלום" — שנתן לה כשהיא פנויה וניסת, אבל באומר לנשואה הכי קאמר לה: "אחריך" — ליקני, בעל לא ליקני. ולוקח מיד אחריך — כרבי שמעון דאמר דמכירת הראשון מכירה. ומוקמינן לה בידא דלוקח — אין בית דין נזקקין [בפעם הזאת אם בא להוציאן מיד הלוקח, שאין הפעם הזאת דומה לראשונה מתחלה שנכנס להם לוקח זה מכח מכירת האשה ומיד האשה יכול הבעל לטעון: "אני לקחתי ראשון". אבל בזו שהוציאן מיד אחריך שאין הבעל זוכה אלא בדין אין בית דין נזקקין] לבעל, כדקאמר טעמיה לקמיה.

NOTES

מִי קָאָמַר תִּינָּשֵׂא **Does it say: "She should marry."** *Ritva* asks: The Gemara's resolution of the apparent contradiction between Abaye's two statements is obvious. What then did the Gemara think when it asked its question? He suggests that the Gemara first thought that the word וְנִיסַּת, "and she was married," can be understood as implying that she should get married and thereby deprive the second recipient from receiving the property after her

HALAKHAH

אֵיזֶהוּ רָשָׁע עָרוּם **Who is a cunning scoundrel?** "Someone who advises a person to sell property that he had received as a gift under the condition that it should remain in his possession during his lifetime and pass to someone else after his death, is considered a wicked scoundrel," following Abaye. (*Rambam, Sefer Kinyan, Hilkhot Zekhiyah U'Matanah* 12:3,8-9; *Shulḥan Arukh, Ḥoshen Mishpat* 248:1, 3.)

TRANSLATION AND COMMENTARY

מַאי שְׁנָא [1]The Gemara asks: **Why is** the law in this case **different from that which we have learned** in our Mishnah: "If a man was married to two women, and he sold a field, and if the man's first wife, who had a preferential right of recovering her ketubah settlement from that property waived her rights to the field to the buyer, and then the husband died, his second wife can seize the field from the buyer. The first wife can then take the field away from the second wife, and then the buyer can take it away from the first wife, [2]**and the cycle repeats itself until the three** parties **reach a compromise among themselves."** Thus, we see that in a case of revolving claims, the court does not impose a solution. Rather it waits for the parties to reach agreement. Why then in the similar case discussed by Abaye does the property stop changing hands when it comes back into the buyer's possession?

[1]מַאי שְׁנָא מֵהָא דִּתְנַן: [2]״וְחוֹזְרוֹת חָלִילָה, עַד שֶׁיַּעֲשׂוּ פְּשָׁרָה בֵּינֵיהֶן״? [3]הָתָם אִית לְהוּ פְּסֵידָא לְכוּלְּהוּ. [4]הָכָא לוֹקֵחַ הוּא דְּאִית לֵיהּ פְּסֵידָא. [5]אֲזַל רַפְרָם אֲמַר לִשְׁמַעְתָּא קַמֵּיהּ דְּרַב אַשִׁי. [6]מִי אֲמַר אַבַּיֵי הָכִי? [7]וְהָאָמַר אַבַּיֵי: [8]״נְכָסַי לִיךְ, וְאַחֲרַיִךְ לִפְלוֹנִי״, [9]עָמְדָה וְנִיסֵּת, [10]בַּעַל לוֹקֵחַ הָוֵי, וְאֵין לְ״אַחֲרַיִךְ״ בִּמְקוֹם בַּעַל כְּלוּם! [11]אֲמַר לֵיהּ: הָתָם דַּאֲמַר לָהּ כְּשֶׁהִיא פְּנוּיָה. [12]הָכָא דַּאֲמַר לָהּ כְּשֶׁהִיא נְשׂוּאָה. [13]מַאי קָאָמַר לָהּ? [14]״אַחֲרַיִךְ״ — לִיקְנֵי, [15]בַּעַל — לָא לִיקְנֵי.

LITERAL TRANSLATION

[1]How is this different from what we have learned: [2]"And they go around in turn until they make a compromise among themselves"?

[3]There there is a loss to all of them. [4]Here it is [only] the buyer who has a loss.

[5]Rafram went [and] said this discussion before Rav Ashi. [6]But did Abaye say this? [7]Surely Abaye said: [8]"My property to you, and after to you to so-and-so," [9][and] she stood up married, [10]the husband is a buyer, and "[so-and-so] after you" where there is a husband has nothing.

[11]Rav Ashi said to him: There [her benefactor] said [it] to her when she was unmarried. [12]Here he said to her when she was married. [13][And] what did he say to her? [14]"After you," [so-and-so] should acquire [it]; [15][but your] husband should not acquire [it].

הָתָם [3]The Gemara answers: In the case of the Mishnah, **there is a loss to each** of the parties — the first wife, the second wife, and the buyer. They all have valid claims to it. Therefore, the court waits until the parties come to an agreement on their own. [4]But **here** in the case discussed by Abaye **it is** only **the buyer who would suffer a loss** if the property is taken away from him, for he paid for it. Since the others received it as a gift, the property stops changing hands once it reverts to the buyer.

אֲזַל רַפְרָם [5]The Gemara continues: **Rafram went and reported this** latter **discussion of** Abaye's law **before Rav Ashi,** and then asked him: [6]**Did Abaye** really **say this?** [7]**But surely** this ruling is contradicted by another ruling issued by Abaye, for **Abaye said** as reported above: If a man said to a woman: [8]**"My property** shall belong **to you** for the rest of your life, **but after you** die, what remains in your estate shall not go to your heirs, but rather **to so-and-so,"** [9]**and** then the woman **rose and married, her husband is** regarded as if **he had bought** that property. [10]Therefore, **where there is a husband, the person** to whom that other man had promised his property **after** the woman dies **has no claim** to the property. How could Abaye have ruled that the property goes to the buyer, when elsewhere he ruled that the property goes to the husband?

אֲמַר לֵיהּ [11]Rav Ashi **said to** Rafram: **There** — in his first law — Abaye ruled that the property goes to the husband because **her benefactor** had **spoken to** her **when she was** still **unmarried.** In such a case the benefactor's instructions do not prevent the husband from obtaining possession of the property. [12]But **here,** Abaye ruled that the property goes to the buyer, because her benefactor had **spoken to** her after **she was married.** [13]**What** then **did** the benefactor mean when **he said to her:** "My property shall belong to you for the rest of your life, but after you die, it shall not go to your heirs, but rather to so-and-so"? [14]He meant: The person to whom I have promised the property **after your** death **should** indeed **acquire** the property; [15]but **your husband should not acquire** it. Here the specifically states that the woman's husband shall not gain

NOTES

death. For we find in the first Mishnah of our tractate and elsewhere that the word is used in that sense. Therefore, the Gemara had to clarify that here Abaye meant that if she received such a gift, and then married, the other person to whom the property had been promised no longer has a claim to it. But Abaye did not imply that the woman should act in that manner.

דַּאֲמַר לָהּ כְּשֶׁהִיא נְשׂוּאָה He said to her when she was married. Some Rishonim prove from our passage that when someone gives a married woman property as a gift, we assume that he wishes the property to remain in her possession, even though the husband will enjoy the right of usufruct, and we do not say that whatever the woman acquires is automatically acquired by her husband (see *Tosafot, Kiddushin* 24a). Others rebut this proof, arguing that this is a particular instance, in which the donor stated

TRANSLATION AND COMMENTARY

possession of his property. Therefore the property goes to the buyer, for while it is in the wife's possession, she is entitled to sell it and her husband cannot object to the sale. (In fact, the husband nevertheless retains the right to enjoy the usufruct of the land, a right that the woman cannot transfer to the buyer.)

וְכֵן בַּעַל חוֹב [1] We learned in the Mishnah: "**A similar** situation exists in the case of **a creditor.** And a similar situation also exists in the case of a woman who is her husband's creditor." [2] **A Tanna taught** a Baraita that clarifies these two rulings: "**A similar** situation exists in the case of **a creditor,** when the debtor sold to **two** different **buyers** two fields over which the creditor exercised a lien — the two fields together equalling the debt. If the creditor wrote a waiver to the second buyer, stating: "I will have no claim against you regarding the field that you bought," thereby renouncing his right to collect his debt from that propertys, the creditor can still seize the first buyer's field as partial payment of the debt, and then the first buyer can seize the second buyer's field, provided that the first buyer had purchased his field with responsibility. The second buyer can then seize the field that the creditor has seized from the first buyer, for the creditor had waived to him his right to recover his debt from his field (which, in effect, he did when he seized the guaranteed field of the first buyer). The cycle then repeats itself over and over until the three parties reach an agreement about how to divide up the property. [3] A **similar** situation also exists in the case of **a woman who is** her husband's **creditor,** i.e., a woman whose husband owes her her ketubah, **and** he sold to **two** different **buyers** two fields which had been mortgaged to his wife's ketubah, their combined value equal in value to her ketubah, and if she wrote a waiver to the second buyer, stating: "I will have no claim against you regarding the field that you bought from my husband," thus renouncing her right to collect her ketubah from that property, the woman can still seize the first buyer's field as partial payment of her ketubah, and the first buyer can seize the second buyer's field, provided that the first buyer had purchased his field with responsibility, and then the second buyer can seize the field which the woman had seized from the first buyer, for the woman had waived to him her right to recover her ketubah from his field, and the cycle repeats itself over and over until the three parties reach an agreement about how to divide up the property.

LITERAL TRANSLATION

[1] "And similarly, a creditor." [2] [A Tanna] taught: [3] "And similarly, a creditor and two buyers, and similarly, a woman who was a creditor and two buyers.

[1] "וְכֵן בַּעַל חוֹב". [2] תָּנָא: "וְכֵן, בַּעַל חוֹב וּשְׁנֵי לָקוֹחוֹת, [3] וְכֵן אִשָּׁה בַּעֲלַת חוֹב וּשְׁנֵי לָקוֹחוֹת.

הדרן עלך מי שהיה נשוי

RASHI

וכן בעל חוב ושני לקוחות — ראובן נושה בשמעון מנה, ולו שתי שדות ומכרן לשנים, זו בחמשים וזו בחמשים. וכתב בעל חוב ללוקח שני: דין ודברים אין לי עמך — בעל חוב נוטל מיד הראשון. וכאן אין לומר: הנחתי מקום שתגבה הימנו, שהרי חובו כנגד שתיהן. ולוקח ראשון מוציא מיד השני, ובעל חוב חוזר ומוציא אף זו מן הראשון, ולוקח שני מבעל חוב וחוזרין חלילה עד שיעשו פשרה. **וכן אשה בעלת חוב** — שהיה לה חוב כתובתה על בעלה, ומכר שתי שדותיו לשנים ואין בשניהם אלא כדי כתובתה. וכתבה לשני: דין ודברים אין לי עמך — האשה מוציאה מיד לוקח ראשון, והוא מן השני. והאשה מן הראשון, והשני מן האשה, ולוקח ראשון מיד השני, וחוזרין חלילה.

הדרן עלך מי שהיה נשוי

NOTES

explicitly that he is giving the woman a gift on condition that it will not pass into her husband's possession.

וְכֵן בַּעַל חוֹב And similarly, a creditor. Our commentary follows *Rashi* and most Rishonim, who understand that the Baraita is dealing here with a debtor who sold two fields to two buyers, the combined value of the two fields equalling the debt. *Rambam* understands that the debtor sold a single field equal in value to the debt to one buyer, and that buyer sold the property to a second buyer (see also *Hafla'ah*).

וְכֵן אִשָּׁה And similarly, a woman. The Rishonim ask: The various different cases discussed by the Mishnah are all based on the same principle. Why then was it necessary for the Mishnah to include all three cases — that of the man with the two wives, that of the creditor and the two buyers, and that of the woman and the two buyers? *Rivan* answers that indeed it was not necessary for the Mishnah to include all three cases, for there is no reason to distinguish between the cases. *Tosafot* and *Maharshal* demonstrate that had the Mishnah not mentioned all three cases, it would have been possible to argue that the law would be different in the various cases.

HALAKHAH

וְכֵן, בַּעַל חוֹב וּשְׁנֵי לָקוֹחוֹת And similarly, a creditor and two buyers. "If a debtor sold to two different buyers two fields over which his creditor exercised a lien, and the creditor promised the second buyer in writing that he would not bring a claim against him regarding the property that he had bought, and he reinforced this waiver with an act of acquisition, the creditor can still seize the first buyer's field. Then the first buyer can seize the second buyer's field, and then the second buyer can seize the field that the creditor had seized from the first buyer. The cycle repeats itself until the three parties reach an agreement. This ruling applies if the debt equalled the value of the two fields," following the Gemara. Further, if the debt was for a maneh, and the debtor sold to two different people two fields, each of which was worth a maneh, and if the creditor waived his right to collect his debt from the second buyer, and it turned out that the field purchased by the first buyer did not belong to the debtor, or that it had been designated as a hypotheque in favor of a prior creditor, the same law applies. (See *Rambam, Sefer Mishpatim, Hilkhot Malveh* 19:5; *Shulḥan Arukh, Ḥoshen Mishpat* 118:2-4.)

Conclusion to Chapter Ten

Regarding the priority of women in collecting their ketubah settlements (as well as other creditors in collecting various debts, and all holders of promissory notes), a wife whose ketubah was written earlier has priority over wives whose ketubot were writtten later. The date of a deed is defined by the day, month, and year when it was written, and all deeds written on the same day are regarded as having been written simultaneously, unless they were written in a place where people are scrupulous about recording the hour of writing as well. Priority in collecting a ketubah settlement exists only when all of the claimants are alive (or, regarding inheritance, when all of them have died), but the claim of a ketubah settlement as a debt has priority over the claim of a ketubah settlement as an inheritance.

Regarding the division of property among unequal ketubah claims (when none has priority) there were many disagreements. In the opinion of most legal authorities, the wife with the smallest claim has preference, and she receives a relatively larger part of her total claim, and the wife with the largest claim for a ketubah settlement does not receive more, except from the residue of the property. By contrast, in most other matters this approach is not taken in dividing property among unequal partners. Regarding the law of *ketubat benin dikhrin* (the ketubah of male children) the general rule was adopted that this law was not applied unless a dinar remained in the estate after deduction of all the ketubah settlements. And if the estate was not that large, the law of inheritance was not completely suspended, since it was from the Torah, but the heirs divided the property equally. Moreover, the law of *ketubat benin dikhrin* was restricted to property already in hand and not property that is expected to be received, and the residue of a dinar is not taken into account unless it is real estate.

If one of the wives completely waives her claim to a creditor, a situation arises in which there are reciprocal claims which cannot be resolved (חוֹזְרוֹת חֲלִילָה) except through compromise.

Introduction to Chapter Eleven

אַלְמָנָה נִיזּוֹנֶת

This chapter mainly deals with the way in which a widow collects what is due her from her late husband's estate.

The widow has two principal monetary claims to her husband's property: the right to be supported (for a widow from marriage), and the right to her ketubah settlement. The widow is entitled to support so long as she has not claimed the ketubah settlement. After she has collected it, her husbands heirs have no other financial obligation to his widow.

The main problem in collecting the kebubah settlement and support is the collection itself. When the heirs are adults, they collect for the widow, but when they are minors, the widow must collect the money herself, and it must be examined how and under what conditions she may sell property to collect what is due her. By the way, another subject was raised: what happens when the property is sold for less than its value? Under what circumstances is the sale rescinded and when is it confirmed, and who has the responsibility when such a mistake has been made?

Another problem raised in this chapter concerns wives who have some Halakhic flaw in their marriages. When do such wives receive ketubah settlements and additional perquisits, and when do they receive nothing?

These problems and other questions that derive from them are the main subjects of this chapter.

TRANSLATION AND COMMENTARY

MISHNAH We learned earlier in the tractate (*Ketubot* 43a) that a widow is entitled to maintenance from her late husband's estate by virtue of the provisions of her ketubah. She does not inherit from her husband when he dies, but she is entitled to be maintained from his property and to continue living in his house throughout her widowhood, until she receives her ketubah settlement. Our Mishnah discusses this right and the ensuing obligations: [1] After a man dies, his **widow is maintained from the property** of his estate which passes to his **orphaned** children or other **heirs** as their inheritance, [2] and therefore **her handiwork** and earnings **belong to them.** It was taught elsewhere (*Ketubot* 47b) that the Sages ruled that a husband is liable for his wife's maintenance, in exchange for which he is entitled to her handiwork and earnings. Similarly, our Mishnah teaches that his heirs are entitled to his widow's earnings while she is maintained from the estate which they inherited. When the widow dies, her late husband's heirs (unless they are also her heirs) **are not responsible for** the costs of her burial and related expenses. [3] Rather, **her heirs, the heirs of her ketubah** settlement, **are obligated** to bear the costs of **her burial**. Elsewhere (*Ketubot* 47b), we learned that the Sages enacted that a husband must bear the costs of his wife's burial, in exchange for which he is entitled to the dowry recorded in her ketubah, which he inherits upon her death. But the husband's heirs do not inherit his widow's ketubah settlement when she dies, for it passes to her own heirs. Since they collect her ketubah settlement, they must pay for her burial.

LITERAL TRANSLATION

MISHNAH [1] A widow is maintained from the property of the orphans. [2] Her handiwork is theirs, and they are not responsible for her burial. [3] Her heirs the heirs of her ketubah are responsible for her burial.

אַלְמָנָה

[1] נִיזּוֹנֶת מִנִּכְסֵי יְתוֹמִים. [2] מַעֲשֵׂה יָדֶיהָ שֶׁלָּהֶן, וְאֵין חַיָּיבִין בִּקְבוּרָתָהּ. [3] יוֹרְשֶׁיהָ יוֹרְשֵׁי כְתוּבָּתָהּ — חַיָּיבִין בִּקְבוּרָתָהּ.

RASHI

משנה אלמנה ניזונת. אין חייבין בקבורתה — אם מתה, שהרי יורשיה גובין כתובתה מיורשי הבעל, ועליהן לקוברה, שהרי בעלה תחת כתובתה חייב בקבורתה, עכשיו שאינו יורשה, היא תקבור עצמה.

NOTES

יוֹרְשֶׁיהָ יוֹרְשֵׁי כְתוּבָּתָהּ Her heirs the heirs of her ketubah. It was explained earlier in the tractate (81a) that this formulation, "her heirs the heirs of her ketubah," which at first glance appears to be redundant, teaches that if a woman has more than one set of heirs, the obligation to cover the costs of her burial falls on the heirs who succeed to her ketubah. Such a situation can arise if a woman's husband died without children, and she was waiting for her husband's brother to take her in levirate marriage or perform *ḥalitzah*, in which case part of her estate goes to her husband's heirs and part of her estate goes to her father's heirs.

Rambam concludes from the formulation of our Mishnah, "her heirs the heirs of her ketubah," that the obligation to cover the costs of a widow's burial only falls upon her heirs if they actually inherit her ketubah settlement. But if for some reason they do not succeed to it, and it remains in the hands of her husband's heirs, the obligation to bury the woman falls upon the husband's heirs. This could occur if she died before she had the opportunity to take an oath that she had not received her ketubah settlement from her husband during his lifetime. Others conclude from this that if there was no ketubah settlement to inherit (for example, if the husband died without leaving any assets), neither the husband's heirs nor his widow's heirs are obligated to bury her. Rather she is buried from the community's charity fund. *Ra'avad* and others (see Halakhah) point to difficulties in *Rambam's* position, and they argue that the obligation to cover the woman's burial costs falls upon those who are fit to inherit her ketubah settlement, even if for some reason they do not actually inherit it (see also *Talmid HaRashba* in *Shittah Mekubbetzet*).

HALAKHAH

אַלְמָנָה נִיזּוֹנֶת A widow is maintained. "A widow is entitled to maintenance from the property of her husband's estate that passed to his heirs for the duration of her widowhood, even if that right was not stipulated in the her ketubah deed, for it is a right due her under the ketubah conditions," following the Gemara's conclusion in *Ketubot* 52b and 54a. (*Rambam, Sefer Nashim, Hilkhot Ishut* 18:1; *Shulḥan Arukh, Even HaEzer* 93:3.)

מַעֲשֵׂה יָדֶיהָ שֶׁלָּהֶן Her handiwork is theirs. "Since a man's heirs are required to maintain his widow, her handiwork and earnings belong to them. The heirs cannot tell the widow to maintain herself out of her own earnings, but she may waive her maintenance and keep her earnings for herself." (*Rambam, Sefer Nashim, Hilkhot Ishut* 18:6; *Shulḥan Arukh, Even HaEzer* 95:1.)

אֵין חַיָּיבִין בִּקְבוּרָתָהּ They are not responsible for her burial. "A man's heirs are not responsible for the costs of his widow's burial, but rather those who inherit her ketubah settlement are obligated to cover those expenses. According to *Rambam*, if she died before she had the opportunity to take an oath that she had not received her ketubah settlement during her husband's lifetime, his heirs are liable for the costs of her burial. But his position was not accepted by other Rishonim." (*Ra'avad, Tur, Tosafot.*) (*Rambam, Sefer Nashim, Hilkhot Ishut* 18:6; *Shulḥan Arukh, Even HaEzer* 89:4; 94:7.)

TRANSLATION AND COMMENTARY

GEMARA [1]**The following problem arose** in discussion among the Sages: We learned earlier in the tractate (*Ketubot* 43a) that opinions differ about whether or not a husband's heirs may compel his widow to receive her ketubah settlement, and thus forfeit her right to be maintained by them. According to the custom of the people of Jerusalem and the Galilee, the choice lies entirely in the widow's hands. But according to the custom of the people of Judea, the choice is placed in the hands of the heirs. This alternative practice was formally stipulated in the ketubah deed in Judea. Now, the precise formulation of our Mishnah is in question, and so it is not clear whether the Mishnah follows the custom of Jerusalem and the Galilee, or that of Judea. [2]**Did we learn** in the Mishnah: "A man's widow **is maintained** (נִיזוֹנֶת) from the property that passes to his heirs, and her handiwork belongs to them," as the Mishnah appears in the standard editions? [3]**Or did we learn** in the Mishnah: "A man's widow **who is maintained** (הַנִּיזוֹנֶת) from the property that passes to his heirs — her handiwork belongs to them." The Gemara now explains the significance of the difference between these two formulations. [4]**Did we learn** in the Mishnah: "A man's widow **is maintained** from the heirs' property," which implies that she is always entitled to maintenance, unless she demands her ketubah settlement? [5]If so, the Mishnah was formulated **in accordance with** the custom of **the people of** Jerusalem and **the Galilee,** according to which a husband's heirs **cannot deprive** his widow of her maintenance against her wishes. [6]**Or perhaps we learned** in the Mishnah: "A widow **who is maintained** from the heirs' property," which implies that a man's widow is not always entitled to maintenance. [7]In that case the Mishnah was formulated **in accordance with** the custom of **the people of Judea,** according to which the provision of maintenance is dependent on the heirs, [8]**and if they want,** they can compel her to receive her ketubah settlement, and then **they do not** have to **give her** maintenance.

[96A] תָּא שְׁמַע [9]The Gemara suggests an answer to its question: **Come and hear** what **Rabbi Zera said in the name of Shmuel:** [10]**What a widow finds belongs to her.** The Gemara now considers this ruling in light of the two possible interpretations of our Mishnah: [11]**Granted if you say** that **we learned** in the Mishnah: "A man's widow **who is maintained** from his heir's property." This implies that widow are not always maintained from the heir's property. In this light we **well** understand Shmuel's ruling, which could refer to a widow who is not to maintenance from her late husband's heirs. Therefore she is entitled to keep what she finds. [12]**But if you say** that **we learned** in the Mishnah: "A man's widow **is maintained** from the property which passed to his heirs," this implies that a widow is always entitled to maintenance unless she demands her ketubah settlement. So why would she be entitled to what she finds?

גמרא [1]אִיבַּעְיָא לְהוּ: [2]״נִיזוֹנֶת״ תְּנַן, [3]אוֹ ״הַנִּיזוֹנֶת״ תְּנַן? [4]״נִיזוֹנֶת״ תְּנַן, [5]וּכְאַנְשֵׁי גָלִיל, וְלָא סַגִּי דְּלָא יָהֲבֵי לָהּ? [6]אוֹ דִּלְמָא ״הַנִּיזוֹנֶת״ תְּנַן, [7]כְּאַנְשֵׁי יְהוּדָה, [8]וְאִי בָּעוּ, לָא יָהֲבֵי לָהּ?

[96A] [9]תָּא שְׁמַע: אָמַר רַבִּי זֵירָא אֲמַר שְׁמוּאֵל: [10]מְצִיאַת אַלְמָנָה לְעַצְמָהּ. [11]אִי אָמְרַתְּ בִּשְׁלָמָא ״הַנִּיזוֹנֶת״ תְּנַן, שַׁפִּיר. [12]אֶלָּא אִי אָמְרַתְּ ״נִיזוֹנֶת״ תְּנַן,

LITERAL TRANSLATION

GEMARA [1]It was asked of them: [2]Did we learn: "Is maintained," [3]or did we learn: "Who is maintained?" [4]Did we learn: "Is maintained," [5]and like the people of the Galilee, and it is impossible that they not give [it] to her? [6]Or perhaps we learned: "Who is maintained," [7]and like the people of Judea, [8]and if they want, they do not give [it] to her.

[96A] [9]Come [and] hear: Rabbi Zera said in the name of Shmuel: [10]What a widow finds belongs to her. [11]Granted if you say we learned, "Who is maintained," it is well. [12]But if you say we learned, "Is maintained,"

RASHI

גמרא אנשי גליל היו כותבין: את תהא יתבת בביתי. ומיתזנא מנכסי כל ימי מיגר ארמלותיך בביתי. באנשי יהודה — היו כותבין: עד שירצו היורשין ליתן ליך כתובתיך. לפיכך אם רצו היורשין — נותנין לה כתובתה ופוטרין אותה. הניזונת תנן — והכי קתני: אלמנה הניזונת מנכסי יתומים — מעשה ידיה שלהם, כל זמן שהם רוצים לזונה. אי אמרת בשלמא הניזונת תנן — וסתם לן תנא כאנשי יהודה. שפיר — איכא לאוקמי להא דשמואל — בשאינה ניזונת. אלא אי אמרת ניזונת תנן — וסתם לן כאנשי גליל, וליכא אלמנה שאינה ניזונת — אמאי מציאתה לעצמה?

NOTES

אִי אָמְרַתְּ ״נִיזוֹנֶת״ תְּנַן If you say: We learned: "Is maintained." Our commentary follows *Rashi,* who understands that the Gemara asked about the precise wording of the Mishnah in order to establish whether the Mishnah was formulated in accordance with the custom of the people of Jerusalem and Galilee or in accordance with the custom

TRANSLATION AND COMMENTARY

[1] **Let the heirs** who are obligated to maintain her **be** treated just **like the husband.** [2] **Just as** when a wife is maintained by her **husband, what she finds belongs to him** (as we learned earlier in the tractate, 65b), [3] **so too here** where she is maintained from property that passed to her husband's heirs, **what she finds should belong to those heirs!**

לְעוֹלָם אֵימָא לָךְ [4] The Gemara rejects this argument: **In fact, I can say to you** that **we learned** in the Mishnah: "A man's widow **is maintained** from the property which passed to his heirs," and nevertheless, Shmuel's ruling that a widow is entitled to what she finds is perfectly understandable. [5] **What is the reason that the Rabbis said** that **what a woman** finds while she is married **belong to her husband?** [6] **So that there be no** feelings of **enmity** between them. [7] But **here** in the case of the heirs, **let there be enmity.**

אָמַר רַבִּי יוֹסֵי בַּר חֲנִינָא [8] **Rabbi Yose bar Hanina said: All** the **that a woman** is obligated to **perform for her husband,** such as cooking, baking, and laundry, as is explained earlier in the tractate (59b), [9] **a widow** is obligated to **perform for his heirs,** [10] **except pouring** wine into his **cup, making** his **bed, and washing his face, his hands, and his feet,** because these three tasks are acts of intimacy, which a woman must perform only for her husband.

[1] נֶיהֱווּ כְּבַעַל. [2] מָה בַּעַל מְצִיאַת אִשָּׁה לְבַעְלָהּ, [3] הָכָא נַמִּי מְצִיאַת אִשָּׁה לַיּוֹרְשִׁים!
[4] לְעוֹלָם אֵימָא לָךְ: "נִיזּוֹנֶת" תְּנַן. [5] טַעְמָא מַאי אֲמוּר רַבָּנַן מְצִיאַת אִשָּׁה לְבַעְלָהּ? [6] דְּלָא תֵּיהֱוֵי לָהּ אֵיבָה. [7] הָנֵי תֵּיהֱוֵי לְהוּ אֵיבָה.
[8] אָמַר רַבִּי יוֹסֵי בַּר חֲנִינָא: כָּל מְלָאכוֹת שֶׁהָאִשָּׁה עוֹשָׂה לְבַעְלָהּ, [9] אַלְמָנָה עוֹשָׂה לַיּוֹרְשִׁים, [10] חוּץ מִמְּזִיגַת הַכּוֹס, וְהַצָּעַת הַמִּטָּה, וְהַרְחָצַת פָּנָיו יָדָיו וְרַגְלָיו.

LITERAL TRANSLATION

[1] let [the heirs] be like the husband. [2] Just as [with] a husband — what a woman finds belongs to her husband, [3] so too here — what a woman finds [should belong] to the heirs!

[4] In fact I can say to you [that] we learned, "Is maintained." [5] What is the reason that the Rabbis said that what a woman finds belong to her husband? [6] So there will be no enmity. [7] Here, let there be enmity.

[8] Rabbi Yose bar Hanina said: All service that a woman performs for her husband, [9] a widow performs for the heirs, [10] except pouring the cup, and arranging the bed, and washing his face, his hands, and his feet.

RASHI

ניהוו – יורשים כבעל? תיהוי להו איבה – דעל כרחם זנים אותה. אבל מעשה ידיה שתקנו לבעלה תחת מזונות – הוי ליורשים. כל מלאכות – השנויות בפרק "אף על פי" (כתובות נט,ב): טוחנת ואופה כו׳. חוץ ממזיגת הכוס כו׳ – שהן מלאכות המקרבות חיבה והרגל דבר, כדאמרינן נמי בהא מסכתא (ד,ב) שאין נדה עושה אותן לבעלה.

NOTES

of the people of Judea. *Tosafot* and others (see *Ritva*) raise various objections to this explanation of our passage. They suggest that the Gemara was first examining the law regarding the widow's handiwork only according to the custom of the people of Judea. According to that custom, if the Mishnah reads, "a man's widow is maintained," the to the widow's handiwork even while they are maintaining her. But if the Mishnah reads: "A man's widow who is maintained," then it teaches that even according to the custom of the people of Judea, a widow's handiwork belongs to her husband's heirs while they provide her with maintenance. The Gemara tries to resolve this problem concerning the custom of Judea from Shmuel's statement that what a widow finds belongs to her. Granted if you say that the Mishnah reads: "A man's widow who is maintained," following the custom of Judea, it can be argued that Shmuel ruled according to that custom (even though he himself rules elsewhere in accordance with the custom of Jerusalem and Galilee). He teaches here that even though the heirs are entitled to the widow's handiwork, they are not entitled to what she finds. Those who interpret the Gemara in this manner argue: If you say that the Mishnah reads: "A man's widow is maintained," following the custom of Jerusalem and Galilee, whereas according to the custom of the people of Judea, the widow's handiwork belongs to her, how can we understand Shmuel's statement? It would have been unnecessary to say that according to the custom of Judea, what a widow finds belongs to her, for according to that custom she is even entitled to her handiwork. And according to the custom of the people of Jerusalem and Galilee, where the heirs cannot deprive the widow of her maintenance, they should be treated just like the husband, and so they should indeed be entitled to what she woman's finds. The Gemara ultimately rejects this argument, and says that the Mishnah does in fact read: "A man's widow is maintained," and Shmuel's ruling was issued in accordance with the custom of the people of Jerusalem and Galilee, for a distinction can be made between a widow's handiwork and her finds.

חוּץ מִמְּזִיגַת הַכּוֹס Except for pouring the cup. *Rashi* explains that a widow is not required to perform these tasks for her husband's heirs, for they are acts of intimacy that a woman should only perform for her husband. *Rivan* writes that she is exempt from performing these tasks for her husband's heirs, for it would be degrading for her to perform these tasks for anyone but her husband.

[1]אָמַר רַבִּי יְהוֹשֻׁעַ בֶּן לֵוִי: [2]כָּל מְלָאכוֹת שֶׁהָעֶבֶד עוֹשֶׂה לְרַבּוֹ, [3]תַּלְמִיד עוֹשֶׂה לְרַבּוֹ, חוּץ מֵהַתָּרַת (לוֹ) מִנְעָל.
[4]אֲמַר רָבָא: לָא אֲמָרָן אֶלָּא בְּמָקוֹם שֶׁאֵין מַכִּירִין אוֹתוֹ, [5]אֲבָל בְּמָקוֹם שֶׁמַּכִּירִין אוֹתוֹ, לֵית לָן בָּהּ.
[6]אֲמַר רַב אַשִׁי: וּבְמָקוֹם שֶׁאֵין מַכִּירִין אוֹתוֹ נַמִי, [7]לָא אֲמָרָן אֶלָּא דְּלָא מַנַּח תְּפִלִּין. [8]אֲבָל מַנַּח תְּפִלִּין, [9]לֵית לָן בָּהּ.
[10]אָמַר רַבִּי חִיָּיא בַּר אַבָּא אָמַר רַבִּי יוֹחָנָן: [11]כָּל הַמּוֹנֵעַ תַּלְמִידוֹ מִלְּשַׁמְּשׁוֹ — כְּאִילּוּ מוֹנֵעַ מִמֶּנּוּ חֶסֶד, [12]שֶׁנֶּאֱמַר: ״לַמָּס מֵרֵעֵהוּ חָסֶד״.
[13]רַב נַחְמָן בַּר יִצְחָק אוֹמֵר: אַף פּוֹרֵק מִמֶּנּוּ יִרְאַת שָׁמַיִם,

LITERAL TRANSLATION

[1]Rabbi Yehoshua ben Levi said: [2]All service that a slave performs for his master, [3]a disciple performs for his master, except untying his shoe.
[4]Rava said: We only said [this] in a place where they do not recognize [the disciple], [5]but in a place where they recognize him, there is no [concern].
[6]Rav Ashi said: And in a place where they do not recognize him, [7]we also only said [this] if he has not put on tefillin. [8]But if he has put on tefillin, [9]there is no [concern].
[10]Rabbi Ḥiyya bar Abba said in the name of Rabbi Yoḥanan: [11]Whoever prevents his disciple from serving him [is considered] as if he is preventing him from [performing] acts of lovingkindness, [12]as it is stated: "Who avoids from his friend, lovingkindness."
[13]Rav Naḥman bar Yitzḥak said: He even removes from him the fear of Heaven,

TRANSLATION AND COMMENTARY

אָמַר רַבִּי יְהוֹשֻׁעַ בֶּן לֵוִי [1]The subject of service brings to mind the tasks that a disciple must perform for his teacher: **Rabbi Yehoshua ben Levi said:** [2]**All the tasks that a** non-Jewish **slave** is obliged to **perform for his master,** [3]**a disciple** is obliged to **perform for his teacher, except untying his shoes,** for the performance of such a menial task might lead observers to mistakenly conclude that the disciple is, in fact, a non-Jewish slave.

אֲמַר רָבָא [4]The Gemara now restricts Rabbi Yehoshua ben Levi's ruling: **Rava said: This** ruling that the disciple is not obliged to untie his master's shoes **only applies in a place where** people **do not recognize the disciple**, and so they are liable to mistake him for the master's slave. [5]**But in a place where** people **recognize him** as a disciple, is he indeed obliged to untie his master's shoes, for **there is no concern** that people will mistakenly conclude that he is the master's slave.

אֲמַר רַב אַשִׁי [6]Further restricting Rabbi Yehoshua ben Levi's ruling, **Rav Ashi said: Even in a place where** people **do not recognize** the disciple, [7]**this** ruling **only applies** when the disciple **is not** seen in public **wearing** his **tefillin**, for a man wearing tefillin would not be mistaken for a slave. [8]**But if he is** seen **wearing tefillin**, the disciple is indeed obliged to untie his master's shoes, [9]for **there is no concern** that people will think that he is a slave, because slaves never wear tefillin.

אָמַר רַבִּי חִיָּיא בַּר אַבָּא[24] **Rabbi Ḥiyya bar Abba said in the name of Rabbi Yoḥanan:** [10]**Whoever** waives his honor and **prevents his disciple from serving him** in the manner that disciples are obliged to serve their masters **is considered as if he were preventing him from performing acts of lovingkindness,** [11]**as the verse states** (Job 6:14): **"who avoids lovingkindness that is due from his friend** (לַמָּס מֵרֵעֵהוּ חָסֶד)." This difficult verse is usually translated, "To him that is afflicted, lovingkindness is due from his friend," but here it is understood by Rabbi Yohanan as follows: He who removes himself (לַמָּס) from his friend (מֵרֵעֵהוּ), such as a master who prevents his disciple from serving him, prevents his disciple from fulfilling his obligation of performing acts of lovingkindness (חֶסֶד).

רַב נַחְמָן בַּר יִצְחָק [12]**Rav Naḥman bar Yitzḥak said:** When a master prevents his disciple from serving him, not only does he prevent the disciple from fulfilling his obligation to perform acts of lovingkindness, but **he**

BACKGROUND

הַתָּרַת נַעַל וּתְפִלִּין **Untying someone else's shoe and tefillin.** In many sources in the Bible and Talmud shoes appear to be regarded as particularly contemptible. For that reason one does not enter a holy place wearing shoes (see Exodus 3:5 and elsewhere). Hitting someone with a shoe or throwing one's shoe at someone is regarded as a very grave insult (see Psalms 60:10). Therefore, it is thought that only a slave would remove someone else's shoes.

By contrast, putting on tefillin, aside from its being a positive commandment which a slave is not required to perform, has a special aspect of honor, which is how the Sages understood the verse, "wrap yourself in your glory" (Ezekiel 24:17) as relating to tefillin.

RASHI

חוץ מהתרת מנעל – שהרואה אומר: עבד כנעני הוא. מנח תפילין לית לן בה – שאין דרך עבדים להניח תפילין. למס מרעהו חסד – המּמיס עצמו מרעהו – ממיס ממנו חסדים. ואית דמפקא לה מדכתיב לעיל מיניה "ותושיה נדחה ממני" וסמיך ליה "למס מרעהו חסד".

NOTES

כָּל הַמּוֹנֵעַ תַּלְמִידוֹ מִלְּשַׁמְּשׁוֹ **Whoever prevents his disciple from serving him.** *Rivan* suggests that Rabbi Yoḥanan understands that the word לַמָּס is used here in the sense of "remove, slip away," as in (Deuteronomy 20:8): "Lest his brothers heart slip away (ימס) like his heart."

Regarding a master's obligation to allow his disciple to serve him, it has been explained that inasmuch as a disciple must fear his master much in the same way as he fears Heaven, the disciple must also serve his master in every way, just as he must serve Heaven (*Iyyun Ya'akov*). Moreover, a disciple who attends to his master's must remain close to his master at all times. Therefore he always

TRANSLATION AND COMMENTARY

even removes from him his fear of Heaven, [1]**as the** very same **verse continues** (Job 6:14): **"He foresakes the fear of the Almighty."**

אָמַר רַבִּי אֶלְעָזָר [2]Returning to the matter of a widow, **Rabbi Elazar said:** Even though the Gemara concluded elsewhere that a widow may only collect her maintenance from her late husband's land, and not from his movable goods (*Ketubot* 69b), if **a widow seized movable goods** from her late husband's estate **for her maintenance,** [3]**the seizure is valid.**

תַּנְיָא נַמִי הָכִי [4]The Gemara notes that **the same ruling was also taught** in a Baraita that stated: "If **a widow seized movable goods** from her late husband's estate **for her maintenance,** [5]**her seizure is valid,** and the movable goods are not taken away from her.

וְכֵן [6]**And similarly, when Rav Dimi came** to Babylonia from Eretz Israel, **he said:** [7]**It** once **happened that the daughter-in-law of Rabbi Shabbetai** was widowed, and she **seized a** leather **pouch full of coins** from her late husband's estate for her maintenance, [8]**and the Sages did not have the power to take** the money away **from her.**

[1]שֶׁנֶּאֱמַר: "וְיִרְאַת שַׁדַּי יַעֲזוֹב". [2]אָמַר רַבִּי אֶלְעָזָר: אַלְמָנָה שֶׁתָּפְסָה מִטַּלְטְלִין בִּמְזוֹנוֹתֶיהָ — [3]מַה שֶּׁתָּפְסָה תָּפְסָה. [4]תַּנְיָא נַמִי הָכִי: "אַלְמָנָה שֶׁתָּפְסָה מִטַּלְטְלִין בִּמְזוֹנוֹתֶיהָ — [5]מַה שֶּׁתָּפְסָה תָּפְסָה". [6]וְכֵן, כִּי אֲתָא רַב דִּימִי אָמַר: [7]מַעֲשֶׂה בְּכַלָּתוֹ שֶׁל רַבִּי שַׁבְּתַי שֶׁתָּפְסָה דִּסְקַיָּא מְלֵאָה מָעוֹת, [8]וְלֹא הָיָה כֹּחַ בְּיַד חֲכָמִים לְהוֹצִיא מִיָּדָהּ.

LITERAL TRANSLATION

[1]as it is stated: "He foresakes the fear of the Almighty."

[2]Rabbi Elazar said: A widow who seized movable goods for her maintenance — [3]what she seized she seized.

[4]It has also been taught thus: "A widow who seized movable goods for her maintenance — [5]what she seized she seized."

[6]And similarly, when Rav Dimi came he said: [7]It happened that the daughter-in-law of Rabbi Shabbetai seized a pouch full of coins, [8]and the Sages did not have the power to remove it from her.

RASHI

מה שתפסה תפסה — ולא מפקינן מינה. ואף על גב דפסקינן הלכתא בפרק "מציאת האשה" (כתובות סט,ב): ממקרקעי ולא ממטלטלי, הואיל ותפסה — תפסה. דסקיא = שק של עור, שקורין *טשינ"א.

LANGUAGE

דִּסְקַיָּא Pouch. This derives from the Greek δισάκκιον, *disakkion*, meaning "a double sack, one that was placed on the back of an animal."

LANGUAGE (RASHI)

טשינ"א* In manuscripts: בישצ"א. From the Old French *besace*, meaning "a double sack placed on the back of an animal."

NOTES

has the opportunity to learn from him, both theoretical knowledge and practical conduct. Thus, a master who prevents his disciple from serving him deprives him of the lovingkindess of the Torah, and even causes him to cast off his fear of Heaven (*Ir Binyamin*; see also second explanation of *Rashi*).

אַלְמָנָה שֶׁתָּפְסָה מִטַּלְטְלִין A widow who seized movable goods. The Rishonim disagree about how to understand this passage. According to *Halakhot Gedolot, Rabbenu Ḥananel,* and others, our Gemara is dealing with a widow who seized her husband's movable goods during his lifetime. What she had seized during her husband's lifetime for maintenance may be kept, but what she had seized during his lifetime for her ketubah settlement is taken away from her. But if the widow seized her husband's movable goods after his death, her seizure is void even if she seized them for her maintenance. *Rif, Rivan,* and many other Rishonim disagree, and say that our Gemara is dealing with a case where the widow seized movable goods from her husband's estate after his death. Regarding this situation, Ravina ruled that the movable goods seized for her ketubah settlement are taken away from her, but the movable goods seized for maintenance may be kept. But if she seized the movable goods during her husband's lifetime, the seizure is valid even if the goods were seized for her ketubah settlement.

The Rishonim explain why the widow's seizure of her late husband's movable goods is valid for maintenance. Since the Rabbis did not allow a widow to collect maintenance from land that had been sold by her husband to a third party, they decreed that her seizure of movable goods for maintenance is valid. However, a widow may collect her ketubah from land that had been sold to a third party. Therefore her seizure of her husband's movable goods for this purpose is not valid (*Rivan* and others). Similarly, *Rabbi Crescas Vidal* writes that since the heirs can take loans, thereby mortgaging the land that they had inherited from the late husband, the widow can be deprived of her maintenance. The Rabbis, therefore, validated her seizure of movable goods. Furthermore, since maintenance is a matter of central importance to a widow, the Rabbis strengthened her position.

תָּפְסָה דִּסְקַיָּא מְלֵאָה מָעוֹת She seized a pouch full of coins. The Jerusalem Talmud records a dispute between the Amoraim as to whether a woman who seized some of her husband's movable goods for her maintenance is required to show the court how much property she seized. According to some authorities, she is not required to do so, however, when she comes to collect her ketubah settlement, she must take an oath that she did not receive more than what was her due. *Riva* (cited by *Talmidei Rabbenu Yonah*) writes that if the widow seized movable goods that exceeded the value of her ketubah settlement, the excess is taken away so that the heirs will not suffer a loss.

לֹא הָיָה כֹּחַ בְּיַד חֲכָמִים לְהוֹצִיא מִיָּדָהּ The Sages did not have the power to take it away from her. *Rivan* explains that since a widow's right to maintenance from the husband's movable property was disputed (see above, 51a), the Sages were unable to prove conclusively that she must surrender the pouch full of coins that she had seized for her maintenance.

TRANSLATION AND COMMENTARY

אֲמַר רָבִינָא [1]The Gemara now restricts Rabbi Elazars ruling: **Ravina said: This** ruling validating a widows seizure of her late husband's movable goods **was only said** if the woman seized the movable goods **for** her **maintenance,** [2]**but** if she seized them **for her ketubah** settlement, the seizure is not valid, and **we take** them **away** from her.

מַתְקִיף לָהּ [3]**Mar bar Rav Ashi strongly objected to this** distinction taught by Ravina: **Why should** the law **be different** regarding a who woman seized movable goods for her **ketubah** settlement? [4]Is it **because** in principle it should only be collected **from** her late husband's **land, and not from movable goods?** [5]But surely in principle a woman should **also** collect her **maintenance only from** the **land** of her husband's estate, **and not from the movable goods!** [6]**Rather,** say that just as when a woman seizes movable goods **for** her **maintenance, the seizure is valid** after the fact, [7]**so too** when she seizes movable goods **for her ketubah** settlement, the seizure is also valid.

אֲמַר לֵיהּ [8]In support for Ravina's position, **Rav Yitzḥak bar Naftali said to Ravina:** [9]**We said in the name of Rava in accordance with your** ruling.

[1]אֲמַר רָבִינָא: וְלָא אֲמָרַן אֶלָּא לִמְזוֹנֵי, [2]אֲבָל לִכְתוּבָּה, מַפְּקִינַן מִינָּהּ.

[3]מַתְקִיף לָהּ מָר בַּר רַב אָשֵׁי: מַאי שְׁנָא לִכְתוּבָּה? [4]דְּמִמְּקַרְקְעֵי וְלָא מִמִּטַּלְטְלֵי? [5]מְזוֹנוֹת נַמִי מִמְּקַרְקְעֵי וְלָא מִמִּטַּלְטְלֵי! [6]אֶלָּא, לִמְזוֹנֵי מַאי דְּתָפְסָה תָּפְסָה, [7]הָכִי נַמִי לִכְתוּבָּה.

[8]אֲמַר לֵיהּ רַב יִצְחָק בַּר נַפְתָּלִי לְרָבִינָא: [9]הָכִי אָמְרִינַן מִשְּׁמֵיהּ דְּרָבָא כְּוָותָיךְ.

[10]אָמַר רַבִּי יוֹחָנָן מִשְּׁמֵיהּ דְּרַבִּי יוֹסֵי בֶּן זִימְרָא: [11]אַלְמָנָה שֶׁשָּׁהֲתָה שְׁתַּיִם וְשָׁלֹשׁ שָׁנִים וְלֹא תָּבְעָה מְזוֹנוֹת, [12]אִיבְּדָה מְזוֹנוֹת.

[13]הַשְׁתָּא שְׁתַּיִם אִיבְּדָה, [14]שָׁלֹשׁ מִיבַּעְיָא?

[15]לָא קַשְׁיָא. [16]כָּאן — בַּעֲנִיָּה; [17]כָּאן — בַּעֲשִׁירָה.

LITERAL TRANSLATION

[1]Ravina said: And we only said [this] regarding maintenance, [2]but for her ketubah, we take it [away].

[3]Mar bar Rav Ashi strongly objected to this: Why is a ketubah different? [4]Because it is [collected] from land and not from movable goods? [5]Maintenance too is [collected] from land and not from movable goods! [6]Rather, [say]: For maintenance, what she seized she seized, [7]so too for [her] ketubah.

[8]Rav Yitzḥak bar Naftali said to Ravina: [9]We say in the name of Rava in accordance with your [ruling].

[10]Rabbi Yoḥanan said in the name of Rabbi Yose ben Zimra: [11][If] a widow waited two or three years and did not demand maintenance, [12]she forfeited her maintenance.

[13]Now [if for] two she forfeited, [14]is it necessary [to mention] three?

[15]There is no difficulty. [16]Here — with [regard to] a poor woman; [17]here — with [regard to] a wealthy woman.

RASHI

עשירה — היכולת בידה להמתין. הלכך, אי נמי לא תבעה — לאו מחילה היא עד שלש שנים. אבל ענייה, מדלא תבעתן — מחלתן.

אָמַר רַבִּי יוֹחָנָן [10]Since the Mishnah mentions a widow's right of maintenance from the husband's estates, the Gemara now discusses various aspects of this right and how a widow may lose her it. **Rabbi Yoḥanan said in the name of Rabbi Yose ben Zimra:** [11]**If a widow waited for two or three years** after her husband died **without demanding maintenance** from his heirs, [12]**she forfeited her maintenance.**

הַשְׁתָּא שְׁתַּיִם אִיבְּדָה [13]The Gemara asks: Why does Rabbi Yoḥanan speak about a woman who waited "two or three years" before demanding her ketubah. **If** a woman who waited **for two** years before demanding her maintenance **forfeited** her right to be maintained by her husband's heirs, [14]**was it necessary to mention** that she forfeited her right to maintenance if she waited **three** years before demanding maintenance?

לָא קַשְׁיָא [15]The Gemara answers: **There is** really **no difficulty** in this formulation. [16]**Here,** in the first instance, Rabbi Yoḥanan refers to **a poor woman** for whom two years is a long time. [17]But **there,** in the later instance, Rabbi Yoḥanan refers to **a wealthy woman** who can support herself for two years from her own resources. We do not assume that a rich woman waived her right to be maintained from her husband's property unless she waited at least three years without demanding it from the heirs.

NOTES

אַלְמָנָה שֶׁשָּׁהֲתָה **If a widow waited.** The Jerusalem Talmud records a very different version of this ruling, according to which a widow forfeits her maintenance if she allowed two or three months to pass without demanding her maintenance. It has been noted that since a widow's maintenance is paid monthly, it stands to reason that the law should be formulated in terms of months, and not years. *Ramban* writes that while a widow does not forfeit her right to maintenance unless she allows two or three years to pass without presenting a claim, a married woman who does not demand her maintenance forfeits her maintenance immediately.

TRANSLATION AND COMMENTARY

אִי נַמִי [1]The Gemara now offers a second answer: **Alternatively,** the formulation can be explained as follows: When Rabbi Yoḥanan says that a widow forfeited her right to be maintained from her husband's property after two years, he is dealing **with a brazen woman** who is not embarrassed to come to court to demand her rights. But where he says that she does not forfeit her maintenance unless she went three years without it, [2]he is dealing **with a modest woman** who is more hesitant about bringing her claims before a court. In her case we give her three years to demand what is due her.

אֲמַר רָבָא [3]The Gemara adds a limitation to Rabbi Yoḥanan's ruling: **Rava said: This** ruling, that after a certain time a widow forfeits her right to maintenance, **only applies** to the maintenance that was due her **in the past.** [4]**But she** still **retains** her right to maintenance in **the future,** once she presents her claim.

בָּעֵי רַבִּי יוֹחָנָן [5]**Rabbi Yoḥanan asked: If the** husband's **heirs say: "We** already **gave** his widow her maintenance," [6]**and the** woman **says: "I did not receive** anything from them," **upon which party does the burden of proof fall?**

[96B] נִכְסֵי בְּחֶזְקַת [7]The Gemara now explains the two sides of the question: Do we say that **the** late husband's **property stands** now **in the** presumptive **possession of his heirs,** for they inherited it upon his death, [8]**and** so the obligation **falls upon the widow to bring proof** that she is entitled to her maintenance, for she is trying to remove property from the heirs' presumptive possession? [9]**Or** do we **perhaps** say that **the** late husband's **property stands** now **in the** presumptive **possession of the widow,** for it is mortgaged to her maintenance, which is one of the conditions of her ketubah, [10]**and** so the obligation **falls upon the heirs to adduce proof** that she has received what is due her, for it is they who are trying to remove the property from her presumptive possession?

[1]אִי נַמִי: כָּאן — בִּפְרוּצָה; [2]כָּאן — בִּצְנוּעָה. [3]אֲמַר רָבָא: לָא אֲמָרָן אֶלָּא לְמַפְרֵעַ, [4]אֲבָל לְהַבָּא, יֵשׁ לָהּ. [5]בָּעֵי רַבִּי יוֹחָנָן: יְתוֹמִים אוֹמְרִים: ״נָתַנְנוּ״, [6]וְהִיא אוֹמֶרֶת: ״לֹא נָטַלְתִּי״, עַל מִי לְהָבִיא רְאָיָה? [96B] [7]נִכְסֵי בְּחֶזְקַת יַתְמֵי קַיְימֵי, [8]וְעַל אַלְמָנָה לְהָבִיא רְאָיָה? [9]אוֹ דִּלְמָא נִכְסֵי בְּחֶזְקַת אַלְמָנָה קַיְימֵי, [10]וְעַל הַיְּתוֹמִים לְהָבִיא רְאָיָה?

LITERAL TRANSLATION

[1]Or else: Here — with [regard to] a brazen woman; [2]here — with [regard to] a modest woman.

[3]Rava said: We only said [this] for past [maintenance], [4]but for the future, she has.

[5]Rabbi Yoḥanan asked: [If] the orphans say: "We gave," [6]and she says: "I did not take," upon whom [falls the obligation] to bring proof?

[96B] [7]Does the property stand in the possession of the orphans, [8]and it [falls] upon the widow to bring proof? [9]Or perhaps the property stands in the possession of the widow, [10]and it [falls] upon the orphans to bring proof?

RASHI

עשירה — היכולת בידה להמתין. הלכך, אי נמי לא תבעה — לאו מחילה היא עד שלש שנים. אבל ענייה, מדלא תבעתן — מחלתן. **צנועה** — בושה לבא לבית דין, הלכך בשתי שנים לאו מחילה היא. **אלא למפרע** — אותן שתי שנים שעברו אבדה. **נתננו** — דמי מזונות לשנה הבאה. **נכסי** — הבעל. **בחזקת יתמי** — והיא המוציאה מהם, ועליה להביא עדים שהודו יתומים בפניהם שלא קבלה. וכל זמן שלא תביא עדים — לא תגבה. **בחזקת אלמנה קיימי** — שהרי נשתעבדו בתנאי בית דין.

NOTES

יְתוֹמִים אוֹמְרִים: ״נָתַנְנוּ״ If the orphans say: "We gave." *Rashi* writes that Rabbi Yoḥanan asked about heirs who claim that they already gave the widow the maintenance she would require in the future. *Tosafot* argue that the heir's claim that they gave the widow the maintenance that was due to her in the past. But if they claim that they had paid her in advance for the future, the burden of proof surely falls on them and not on the widow (see also Jerusalem Talmud).

וְעַל אַלְמָנָה לְהָבִיא רְאָיָה And it falls upon the widow to adduce proof. Some of the Geonim (*Netivot* and others) explain the Gemara in an entirely different matter, according to which the disagreement between the heirs and the widow is not about whether or not the woman has received her maintenance, but rather about whether or not she has received payment of her ketubah settlement.

עַל הַיְּתוֹמִים לְהָבִיא רְאָיָה It falls upon the orphans to adduce proof. The Rishonim all agree that even if the

HALAKHAH

עַל מִי לְהָבִיא רְאָיָה Upon whom falls the obligation to bring proof. "If a widow demands her maintenance from her husband's heirs, and they claim that they have paid it, and she denies having received anything from them, the following distinction applies: If the woman has not yet remarrieds, it is the heir's obligation to prove that she had indeed received her maintenance. If they fail to do so, she may take a *hesset* oath and collect her maintenance from them. If she has remarried, it is her obligation to prove that she has not yet received her maintenance. If she fails to do so, the heirs must take a *hesset* oath that they already paid it," following Levi. (*Rambam, Sefer Nashim, Hilkhot Ishut* 18:27; *Shulḥan Arukh, Even HaEzer* 93:15.)

TRANSLATION AND COMMENTARY

תָּא שְׁמַע [1] The Gemara proposes a solution to Rabbi Yoḥanan's question: **Come and hear** a Baraita that **Levi taught:** "If the husband's heirs claim that they have given his widow her maintenance, and she denies having received anything from them, the following distinction applies: [2] **As long as the widow has not** yet **remarried,** the obligation **falls upon** her husband's **heirs to adduce proof** that she had indeed received her maintenance. Thus, we can conclude from this first clause of the Baraita that her late husband's property is considered to be in her possession. [3] But **if** the woman **remarried,** and she now seeks to collect what had been due her as a widow, the obligation **falls upon her to bring proof** that she never received her maintenance. Once she remarries, her late husband's property is no longer in her presumptive possession."

אָמַר רַב שִׁימִי בַּר אַשִׁי [4] **Rav Shimi bar Ashi said:** The issue raised by Rabbi Yoḥanan is actually the subject of **a Tannaitic dispute,** for we learned in a Baraita: [5] "When a widow **sells** some of her late husband's property in order to satisfy a claim that she has against the estate, **she** should **write** in the witnessed bill of sale that is given to the purchaser: [6] '**This** property **I sold for my maintenance,'** or '**This** property **I sold for my ketubah** settlement.' [7] **This is the position of Rabbi Yehudah.** [8] **Rabbi Yose** disagrees and **says: She** should **sell** her husband's property, **and write** the purchaser a bill of sale **without specifying** why the property was sold, [9] **and thus her position will be stronger.** For she can decide later whether the proceeds of the sale should count towards payment of her ketubah settlement, or as payment of her maintenance." The Gemara now explains how this Tannaitic dispute is related to Rabbi Yoḥanan's query:

LITERAL TRANSLATION

[1] **Come [and] hear,** for Levi taught: [2] "A widow, as long as she has not married — it [falls] upon the orphans to bring proof. [3] [If] she married — it [falls] upon her to bring proof."

[4] Rav Shimi bar Ashi said: [This is] a Tannaitic dispute: [5] "She sells [property] and writes: [6] 'These I sold for maintenance, and these I sold for the ketubah.' [7] These are the words of Rabbi Yehudah. [8] Rabbi Yose says: She sells [the property] and writes without specifying, [9] and thus her position is stronger."

תָּא שְׁמַע, דְּתָנֵי לֵוִי: "אַלְמָנָה כָּל זְמַן שֶׁלֹּא נִיסֵת — עַל הַיְּתוֹמִים לְהָבִיא רְאָיָה, [3] נִיסֵת — עָלֶיהָ לְהָבִיא רְאָיָה". [4] אָמַר רַב שִׁימִי בַּר אַשִׁי: כְּתַנָּאֵי: [5] "מוֹכֶרֶת וְכוֹתֶבֶת: [6] 'אֵלּוּ לִמְזוֹנוֹת מָכַרְתִּי, וְאֵלּוּ לִכְתוּבָּה מָכַרְתִּי'. [7] דִּבְרֵי רַבִּי יְהוּדָה. [8] רַבִּי יוֹסֵי אוֹמֵר: מוֹכֶרֶת וְכוֹתֶבֶת סְתָם, [9] וְכֵן כֹּחָהּ יָפֶה".

RASHI

נשאת — וְהִיא בָּאָה לִתְבּוֹעַ מְזוֹנוֹת שֶׁל שְׁנֵי שֶׁעָבְרוּ. **עָלֶיהָ לְהָבִיא רְאָיָה** — דְּמַשְׁנִיסֵת אֵין הַנְּכָסִים בְּחֶזְקָתָהּ. **וְכוֹתֶבֶת אֵלּוּ לִמְזוֹנוֹת** — בַּשְּׁטָרוֹת הַמְּכִירָה שֶׁהִיא כּוֹתֶבֶת לַלָּקוֹחוֹת, כּוֹתֶבֶת אֶת הַמְּכוֹר לִמְזוֹנוֹת. וּכְשֶׁהִיא מוֹכֶרֶת לְגַבֵּי כְּתוּבָּה תְּפָרֵשׁ בְּתוֹךְ הַשְּׁטָר: לִכְתוּבָּה מָכַרְתִּי. **וְכָךְ כֹּחָהּ יָפֶה** — כִּדְבָעֵינַן לְפָרוֹשֵׁי.

NOTES

heirs are unable to prove that they had paid the widow her maintenance, she can only collect it after she takes an oath. According to most Rishonim, she must take a *hesset* oath (a post-Mishnaic oath which differs from a Torah or a Mishnaic oath in both its administration and its severity). Since the late husbands property is regarded as standing in the presumptive possession of the widow, she is regarded as if she were holding a pledge. Thus she is seen as taking an oath in order to free herself from payment, and she is only required to take a *hesset* oath. But according to some Rishonim (see *Ritva* and *Rashba*), *Rambam* requires the woman to take a Mishnaic oath that is similar in severity to a Torah oath, for according to *Rambam*, even a person who holds a pledge against another person is regarded as if he were collecting payment from him, and so he is liable for a Mishnaic oath.

וְכֵן כֹּחָהּ יָפֶה **And thus her position is stronger.** *Rashi*

explains that the widows position is stronger if she does not specify in the bill of sale the purpose for which she sold her husbands property. Even if she sold her husband's property for her ketubah settlement, she can later claim that she had sold it for her maintenance and then collect her ketubah settlement from property which had been sold to a third party. *Tosafot* argue that while this reasoning is correct, it would appear that the Gemara does not consider this explanation until later, when it cites the statement of Abaye the Elder. Here the Gemara understands that the widow's position is stronger if she does not specify in the bill of sale the purpose for which she sold her husband's property, because if the heirs later claim that she had waived her right to her maintenance, she can claim that she had sold her husband's property for that purpose. According to the Jerusalem Talmud, the womans position is stronger if she does not specify why

HALAKHAH

מוֹכֶרֶת וְכוֹתֶבֶת: אֵלּוּ לִמְזוֹנוֹת מָכַרְתִּי **She sells and writes: These I sold for maintenance?** "It is advisable for the widow that when she sells of her late husband's property for her ketubah settlement, she should write in the bill of sale that the property is being sold for that purpose, so that

people will not call her a gluttonous woman, thinking that she sold all the property for her maintenance. If she is not concerned that people will call her a gluttonous woman, it advantageous to her not to write that the property was sold for her ketubah settlement." (*Tur, Even HaEzer* 103.)

[1]מַאי לָאו בְּהָא קָמִיפַּלְגִי: [2]לְרַבִּי יְהוּדָה דַּאֲמַר: בָּעֵי לְפָרוּשֵׁי — [3]סָבַר: נִכְסֵי בְּחֶזְקַת יַתְמֵי קַיְימֵי, [4]וְעַל הָאַלְמָנָה לְהָבִיא רְאָיָה. [5]וְרַבִּי יוֹסֵי סָבַר. לָא בָּעֵי לְפָרוּשֵׁי, נִכְסֵי בְּחֶזְקַת אַלְמָנָה קַיְימֵי, [6]וְעַל הַיְּתוֹמִים לְהָבִיא רְאָיָה.

[7]מִמַּאי? [8]דִּלְמָא דְּכוּלֵּי עָלְמָא נִכְסֵי בְּחֶזְקַת אַלְמָנָה קַיְימֵי, [9]וְעַל הַיְּתוֹמִים לְהָבִיא רְאָיָה. [10]וְרַבִּי יְהוּדָה עֵצָה טוֹבָה קָא מַשְׁמַע לָן, [11]דְּלָא לִיקְרוּ לָהּ רַעַבְתָנוּתָא. [12]דְּאִי לָא תֵּימָא הָכִי, הָא דְּבָעֵי רַבִּי יוֹחָנָן,

LITERAL TRANSLATION

[1]Is it not that they disagree about this: [2]According to Rabbi Yehudah who says: She must specify — [3]he maintains: The property stands in the possession of the orphans, [4]and it [falls] upon the widow to bring proof. [5]And Rabbi Yose maintains: She need not specify. [As] the property stands in the possession of the widow, [6]and it [falls] on the orphans to bring proof.

[7]From what [is this inferred]? [8]Perhaps all agree that the property stands in the possession of the of the widow, [9]and it [falls] upon the orphans to bring proof. [10]And Rabbi Yehudah is giving us good advice, [11]so that [people] should not call her a glutton. [12]For if you do not say that, let Rabbi Yohanan resolve what

RASHI

מאי לאו בהא פליגי דרבי יהודה דאמר הפירוש יפה לה סבר נכסי בחזקת יתמי קיימי — ואי לא פירשה מה לכתובה ומה למזונות, סוף כשתבא לתבוע, יאמרו לה: מה שמכרת — לכתובה מכרת, וקבלת כתובתך. ואם תאמר להם: אם כן, תנו לי מזונות שאכלתי — הם יאמרו: נתננו ליך מטלטלין תמיד במזונותיך, והם נאמנים. **ורבי יוסי סבר נכסי בחזקת אלמנה קיימי** — והיא תחזיק בהם לצורך מזונותיה וכתובתה, ועליהם להביא ראיה. לפיכך הסתם יפה לה, מפני לקוחות שלקחו שדות מבעלה. שאם יכלו כל נכסי היתומים — תחשוב כל מה שמכרה למזונות, ועל הלקוחות שלקחו מבעלה תחזור על כתובתה. שאם תפרש ״לכתובה מכרתי״ — לא תוכל שוב לנתקן למזונות, ועל הלקוחות לא תחזור על מזונותיה, דתנן (גיטין מח,ב): אין מוציאין למזון האשה והבנות מנכסים משועבדים. **דלא ליקרו לה רעבתנותא** — הרואה שמוכרת כל קרקעות אלו, סבור שמוכרתן למזונות, מוציא עליה שם רעבתנותא, ושוב אין אדם נושאה.

TRANSLATION AND COMMENTARY

[1]**Is it not** true **that these** Tannaim **disagree about this** very issue: [2]**Rabbi Yehudah who says** that the woman **must specify** in the bill of sale why the husband's property was being sold, [3]**maintains** that **the** husband's **property stands in the** presumptive **possession** of his **heirs,** [4]**and** so the obligation **falls upon** his **widow to adduce proof** that she is still owed maintenance or her ketubah settlement. According to Rabbi Yehudah, the woman should specify why she sold her husband's property, because if she fails to do so, she might suffer. When she seeks to collect her ketubah settlement from the heirs, they can argue that the property that she sold was in payment for it. If she counters that she sold the property for her maintenance, the heirs can claim that they had already paid it, and they would be believed. [5]**And Rabbi Yose maintains** that the woman **need not specify** in the bill of sale why the property was being sold, because he is of the opinion that **the** husband's **property stands in the** presumptive **possession of the widow,** [6]**and** so the obligation **falls upon the heirs to adduce proof** that she had already received what is due her, either the ketubah settlement or the maintenance.

מִמַּאי [7]The Gemara now rejects this argument: **From what** do you **infer** that these Tannaim disagree about this matter? [8]**Perhaps** they **all** — both Rabbi Yehudah and Rabbi Yose — **agree that the** late husband's **property stands in the** presumptive **possession of his widow,** [9]**and** so the obligation **falls upon his heirs to adduce proof** that she has received all that was due her. [10]**And** when **Rabbi Yehudah** said that the widow should specify in the bill of sale the purpose for which the property was sold, he was merely **offering** the widow the **sound advice.** She should write in the bill of sale which property she is selling for maintenance and which she is selling for her ketubah settlement, [11]**so that** people will **not call her a gluttonous woman,** thinking that she sold all of the property for maintenance. Rabbi Yehudah suggests that by protecting her reputation, she also increases her chances for remarriage. We can support this understanding of Rabbi Yehudah, [12]**for if you do not say this,** there is a certain difficulty regarding **Rabbi Yohanan's** original query as to who must bring proof regarding payment of the widow's maintenance. Why should this question have bothered him at all?

NOTES

she sold the property, because if a creditor claims that he had extended a loan not recorded in writing to the woman's husband after he had married her, she can claim that she had sold the property for her ketubah settlement, and her lien precedes the creditors loan. If a creditor comes with a promissory note given by her husband before his marriage, she can claim that she sold her husband's property for her maintenance, in which case the creditor cannot recover from her what she had already spent (see *Ramban* and others who discuss the Jerusalem Talmud passage).

דְּלָא לִיקְרוּ לָהּ רַעַבְתָנוּתָא **So that they not call her a greedy woman.** *Ḥatam Sofer* asks: would the Rabbis have advised the widow to specify that she had sold her

SAGES

אַבַּיֵי קַשִּׁישָׁא Abaye the Elder. This Amora, very few of whose teachings are presented in the Talmud, apparently belonged to the second generation of Amoraim in Babylonia. The epithet קַשִּׁישָׁא, "the Elder," was given to him to distinguish him from the better known Abaye, Rava's colleague, who was much younger than he and belonged to the fourth generation of Amoraim.

TRANSLATION AND COMMENTARY

[1] **He should have simply resolved** his problem **from a Mishnah** in our chapter (97b) that states: [2] "A widow **may sell** some of her late husband's property **for her maintenance** on her own **without** the supervision of **a court, and she** should **write** in the bill of sale that is given to the purchaser: [3] 'I **sold this** property **for my maintenance.**'" Rabbi Yoḥanan should have inferred from this anonymous Mishnah, which follows the ruling of Rabbi Yehudah and is apparently accepted without reservation, that the late husband's property stands now in the presumptive possession of his heirs. Hence the widow must prove that she is still entitled to maintenance. Since Rabbi Yoḥanan did not resolve his query from the Mishnah, [4] it must follow that an answer **cannot be inferred from the Mishnah,** [5] **for** the Mishnah might have meant only to **offer** the widow the **sound advice.** [6] **Here** in the Baraita we should **also** say that Rabbi Yehudah agrees with Rabbi Yose that the property is in the presumptive possession of the widow, but that Rabbi Yehudah meant to **offer** the widow **advice** about how to sell some of her husband's property and at the same time protect her good name.

אִי נַמִי [7] The Gemara now suggests a diametrically opposite way to understand the Baraita: **Alternatively**, you can say that **all** the Tannaim — both Rabbi Yehudah and Rabbi Yose — **agree that the** late husband's **property stands in the** presumptive **possession of the heirs**, so that if they claim that they already paid her maintenance, the widow must prove that she did not yet receive it. [8] **And the reason** why **Rabbi Yose** said that the widow should not specify in the bill of sale the purpose of selling the property, [9] should be explained as taught by **Abaye the Elder.** [10] **For Abaye the Elder said: To what** can the position of **Rabbi Yose be compared?** [11] **To** the law that applies when **a person on his deathbed said: "Give two hundred zuz to so-and-so my creditor."** Here the dying man's instructions are ambiguous, for he might have meant that the creditor should be repaid the two hundred zuz that was owed him, or else that he should be given a two-hundred zuz gift. In such a case, the creditor may decide: [12] **If he wishes, he may take** the two hundred zuz as repayment **for his debt,**

[1] תִּפְשׁוֹט לֵיהּ מִמַּתְנִיתִין: [2] ״מוֹכֶרֶת לִמְזוֹנוֹת שֶׁלֹּא בְּבֵית דִּין, וְכוֹתֶבֶת: [3] ׳אֵלּוּ לִמְזוֹנוֹת מָכַרְתִּי׳״! [4] אֶלָּא, מִמַּתְנִיתִין לֵיכָּא לְמִשְׁמַע מִינָּהּ, [5] דְּעֵצָה טוֹבָה קָא מַשְׁמַע לָן. [6] הָכָא נַמִי עֵצָה טוֹבָה קָא מַשְׁמַע לָן.

[7] אִי נַמִי: דְּכוּלֵּי עָלְמָא — נִכְסֵי בְּחֶזְקַת יַתְמֵי קַיְימֵי, [8] וְהַיְינוּ טַעְמָא דְּרַבִּי יוֹסֵי — [9] כִּדְאַבַּיֵי קַשִּׁישָׁא. [10] דְּאָמַר אַבַּיֵי קַשִּׁישָׁא: מָשָׁל דְּרַבִּי יוֹסֵי לְמָה הַדָּבָר דּוֹמֶה? [11] לְשְׁכִיב מְרַע שֶׁאָמַר: ״תְּנוּ מָאתַיִם זוּז לִפְלוֹנִי בַּעַל חוֹבִי״. [12] רָצָה, בְּחוֹבוֹ נוֹטְלָן,

LITERAL TRANSLATION

[1] he asked from our Mishnah: [2] "She may sell [property] for [her] maintenance without a court, and she writes: [3] 'I sold these for my maintenance.'" [4] Rather, from our Mishnah it cannot be inferred, [5] for [we can say that] it is giving us good advice. [6] Here also — he is giving us good advice.

[7] Or also: All agree that the property stands in the possession of the orphans, [8] and this is the reason of Rabbi Yose — [9] as [taught by] Abaye the Elder. [10] For Abaye the Elder said: To what can [this teaching of] Rabbi Yose be compared? [11] To a person on his deathbed who said: "Give two hundred zuz to so-and-so my creditor." [12] [If] he wishes, he may take them for his debt,

RASHI

דאי לא תימא הכי — דטעמא דרבי יהודה לאו משום נכסי בחזקת יתמי הוא. הא דבעי רבי יוחנן — על מי להביא ראיה; נהי דמתניתא דפלוגתא דרבי יהודה ורבי יוסי לא שמיע ליה, מתניתין מיהא שמיע ליה, שהמשנה נשנית תמיד בבית המדרש. **תפשוט ליה ממתניתין —** דעל אלמנה להביא ראיה, דמתניתין נמי מלרכה לה לפרושי, כרבי יהודה. **דעצה טובה קא משמע לן —** דלא ליקרו לה רעבתנותא. **אי נמי דכולי עלמא —** היכא דאמרו יתומים "נתננו" — על אלמנה להביא ראיה, ואפילו הכי לרבי יוסי הסתם יפה לה לטריפת לקוחות שבחיי בעלה לכתובה, כמו שפירשתי, וכדתני אביי קשישא.

NOTES

husbands property for her ketubah settlement, so that people would not call her a greedy women, when doing so weakens her position, so that she might suffer a financial loss? He answers that Rabbi Yehudah maintains that if the widow later claims that she sold her husbands property for her maintenance, when in fact she sold it for her ketubah settlement, she is guilty of fraud. It would be wrong to advise anyone in a manner that might lead to fraud.

תְּנוּ מָאתַיִם זוּז Give two-hundred zuz. The Rishonim (see *Tosafot* and others) discuss at length the relationship between our passage and a similar passage in *Bava Batra* which deals with a person lying on his deathbed who said: "Give so-and-so my creditor as he is fit to receive." They distinguish between various different possible formulations:

HALAKHAH

לִשְׁכִיב מְרַע שֶׁאָמַר: ״תְּנוּ״ A person on his deathbed who said: "Give." "If a person on his deathbed said: 'Give two hundred zuz to so-and-so my creditor as he is fit to receive,' the creditor is given two hundred zuz in addition

TRANSLATION AND COMMENTARY

he may take the money **as a gift.** [97A] [1]But **if he takes the two hundred zuz as a gift, is this not his most advantageous option?**

כֵּיצַד מוֹכֶרֶת [2]The Gemara asks: **How does** the widow **sell** her late husband's **property** for her **maintenance**? [3]The Amoraim disagree: **Rabbi Daniel bar Rav Ketina said in the name of Rav Huna:** [4]**Once every twelve months,** the widow may **sell** some of her late husband's property. [5]**The buyer** does not give her one payment, but rather he should **give her** a twelfth of the purchase money **once every thirty days** for **support.**

[1]רָצָה, בְּמַתָּנָה נוֹטְלָן. [97A] [2]אִם בְּמַתָּנָה נוֹטְלָן, לֹא כָּךְ יָפֶה כֹּחוֹ?

[3]כֵּיצַד מוֹכֶרֶת? [4]אָמַר רַבִּי דָּנִיֵּאל בַּר רַב קְטִינָא אָמַר רַב הוּנָא: [5]מוֹכֶרֶת אַחַת לִשְׁנֵים עָשָׂר חֹדֶשׁ, [6]וְלוֹקֵחַ מְפַרְנֵס אַחַת לִשְׁלֹשִׁים יוֹם.

LITERAL TRANSLATION

[1][and if] he wishes, he may take them as a gift. [97A] [2]If he takes them as a gift, is this not his strongest position?

[3]How does she sell [property for maintenance]? [4]Rabbi Daniel bar Rav Ketina said in the name of Rav Huna: [5]She sells once every twelve months, [6]and the buyer provides [her] support once every thirty days.

RASHI

אם נטלן במתנה לא כך כחו יפה — שיוכל לטרוף לקוחות על החוב, ולא יוכל לטרוף על המתנה. **אף זו** — על המזונות לא תוכל לטרוף לקוחות, ועל הכתובה תטרוף אותם. ואם מפני היתומים שלא יאמרו: הכל לכתובה מכרת, ונתקבלת כתובתיך — יכולה היא להעמיד עדים שיראו את הנמכר למזונות. ואם תצטרך לכך — יבאו ויעידו. ואת הנמכר לכתובה — לא תודיע, מפני הלקוחות. **מוכרת לשנים עשר חודש** — כדי מזונות של שנה תמכור יחד. **והלוקח** — לא ימסור לה כל המעות, אלא דמי מזונות של חדש בחדש. שאם תינשא — יחזור מה שבידו ליורשים.

NOTES

Whether the dying man said, "Give to so-and-so," or he said: "Give to so-and-so my creditor," or he said, "Give to so-and-so my creditor as he is fit to receive."

רָצָה, בְּמַתָּנָה נוֹטְלָן If he wishes, he may take them for his debt. According to most Rishonim, if a dying person instructed that two hundred zuz be given to his creditor, the creditor is entitled to collect both his debt and a gift of two hundred zuz. Abaye the Elder teaches that the creditor may decide whether to take the two hundred zuz as repayment of his debt or as a gift. No matter how he chooses, he may still collect the other obligation, if there is property from which it can be collected. But some Rishonim understand that the creditor is given the option to choose between taking the two hundred zuz as repayment of his debt, or waiving his debt and taking the two hundred zuz as a gift (*Ra'avad;* see also *Ritva*).

אַחַת לִשְׁנֵים עָשָׂר חֹדֶשׁ Once every twelve months. The Gemara does not explain the rationale underlying the periods of time mentioned in our passage. But it would appear that the different positions are based on practices in different locales regarding the sale of land. The Jerusalem Talmud records only the first opinion that the widow may sell her late husband's property to the amount of her maintenance for the coming year.

אַחַת לִשְׁלֹשִׁים יוֹם Once every thirty days. The Jerusalem Talmud explains that the widow is given enough money to support herself for a month, so as not to cause the heirs a loss, for she might remarry or demand her ketubah settlement, after which she is not entitled to maintenance from the property of her late husband's estate. Even though the widow is only given enough money to support herself for the next month, the Rabbis permitted her to sell property to the amount of her maintenance for an entire year, so as not to require her to sell property every month. *Rivan* adds that they allowed her to sell property that will cover her maintenance for an entire year, because it might be difficult to find a buyer who is willing to purchase a smaller parcel of land. Selling land in small parcels can also damage the heirs, as the price per unit will generally be lower than when it is sold in larger segments.

HALAKHAH

to the sum which the dying person had owed him. If the dying person said: 'Give two hundred zuz to so-and-so as repayment of my debt,' the creditor is given whatever sum the dying person had owed him. And if the dying person did not say 'as he is fit to receive,' nor did he say 'as repayment of my debt,' the creditor is given the option of deciding whether to take the two hundred zuz as repayment of his debt or as a gift," following our Gemara and the Gemara in *Bava Batra* 138b. Some authorities (*Tur*) disagree and say that if the dying person said: "Give two hundred zuz to so-and-so my creditor," without adding anything else, the creditor receives that sum as a gift. *Rema* accepts the first opinion. (*Rambam, Sefer Kinyan, Hilkhot Zekhiyah U'Matanah* 11:19; *Shulḥan Arukh, Ḥoshen Mishpat* 253:8.)

כֵּיצַד מוֹכֶרֶת How does she sell. "A widow may sell some of her late husband's property in order to cover her maintenance for the next six months. The buyer should not give her the money all at once, but rather make a payment once every thirty days. After six months, the widow may sell more of her late husband's property in order to cover her maintenance for the next half year," following Amemar. *Rema* notes that this law only applies to the sale of land. But today when a widow may collect maintenance from the chattel in her husband's estate husband, she may only sell one object at a time to cover her support. If the widow is unable to find a buyer who is willing to purchase land in the quantity that will cover her maintenance for only the next six months, she may sell a larger parcel of land if the court deems this necessary (*Ritva* in the name of *Ramah*). (*Rambam, Sefer Nashim, Hilkhot Ishut* 18:21; *Shulḥan Arukh, Even HaEzer* 93:30-31.)

TRANSLATION AND COMMENTARY

[1] **And Rav Yehudah said: Once every six months**, the widow may **sell** some of her late husband's property maintenance for the coming half year, [2] and **the buyer** should **give her** one-sixth of the money **once every thirty days the support.**

תַּנְיָא כְּוָותֵיהּ [3] The Gemara now demonstrates that this issue was a subject of dispute among the Tannaim: An anonymous Baraita **was taught in accordance with** the position of **Rav Huna,** stating: [4] "Once **every twelve months,** the widow may **sell** some of her late husband's property, **and the buyer** should **give her** one-twelfth of the purchase money once **every thirty days,** for **support.**" [5] And another anonymous Baraita **was taught in accordance with** the position of **Rav Yehudah,** stating: [6] "Once **every six months,** the widow may **sell** property, [7] **and the buyer** should **give her** one-sixth of the money **once every thirty days,** so that she can **support herself."**

אֲמַר אַמֵימָר [8] The Gemara concludes this discussion with a practical ruling on the matter: **Amemar said:** [9] **The law is** in accordance with the view of Rav Yehudah that once **every six months,** the widow may **sell, and,** [10] **the buyer** should **give her** one-sixth of the money once **every thirty days** so that she can **support herself.**

אֲמַר לֵיהּ [11] **Rav Ashi said to Amemar: What** do you think **about** the position **of Rav Huna?**

אֲמַר לֵיהּ [12] Amemar **said to** Rav Ashi: **I did not hear** what Rav Huna said, [13] **that is to say, I do not agree with** his view.

בָּעוּ מִינֵּיהּ [14] **Rav Sheshet was asked** the following question: **If** a widow **sold** part of her late husband's property **for maintenance,** [15] **can she** later **seize** the sold property from the buyer for payment **of her ketubah** settlement? All the husband's property is mortgaged to his wife's ketubah, so that if his estate is insufficient to cover that obligation, the widow may collect it from land that the husband or his heirs may have transferred to others. Rav Sheshet was asked whether a widow can recover her ketubah settlement from her husband's property that she herself had sold for maintenance. The Gemara explains:

[1] וְרַב יְהוּדָה אָמַר: מוֹכֶרֶת לְשִׁשָּׁה חֳדָשִׁים, [2] וְלוֹקֵחַ מְפַרְנֵס אַחַת לִשְׁלֹשִׁים יוֹם.

[3] תַּנְיָא כְּוָותֵיהּ דְּרַב הוּנָא: [4] "מוֹכֶרֶת לִשְׁנֵים עָשָׂר חֹדֶשׁ, וְלוֹקֵחַ מְפַרְנֵס אַחַת לִשְׁלֹשִׁים יוֹם". [5] תַּנְיָא כְּוָותֵיהּ דְּרַבִּי יְהוּדָה: [6] "מוֹכֶרֶת לְשִׁשָּׁה חֳדָשִׁים, [7] וְלוֹקֵחַ מְפַרְנֵס אַחַת לִשְׁלֹשִׁים יוֹם".

[8] אֲמַר אַמֵימָר: [9] הִלְכְתָא: מוֹכֶרֶת לְשִׁשָּׁה חֳדָשִׁים, [10] וְלוֹקֵחַ מְפַרְנֵס אַחַת לִשְׁלֹשִׁים יוֹם.

[11] אֲמַר לֵיהּ רַב אַשִׁי לְאַמֵימָר: דְּרַב הוּנָא מַאי? [12] אֲמַר לֵיהּ: לָא שְׁמִיעַ לִי, [13] כְּלוֹמַר, לָא סְבִירָא לִי.

[14] בָּעוּ מִינֵּיהּ מֵרַב שֵׁשֶׁת: מוֹכֶרֶת לִמְזוֹנוֹת, [15] מַהוּ שֶׁתַּחֲזוֹר וְתִטְרוֹף לִכְתוּבָּה?

LITERAL TRANSLATION

[1] And Rav Yehudah said: She sells every six months, [2] and the buyer provides [her] support once every thirty days.

[3] It was taught in accordance with Rav Huna: [4] "She sells every twelve months, and the buyer provides [her] support once every thirty days." [5] It was taught in accordance with Rav Yehudah: [6] "She sells every six months, [7] and the buyer provides [her] support once every thirty days."

[8] Amemar said: [9] The law is: She sells every six months, [10] and the buyer provides support [once] every thirty days.

[11] Rav Ashi said to Amemar: What about [the teaching of] Rav Huna?

[12] He said to him: I did not hear it, [13] that is, I do not agree with it.

[14] They asked Rav Sheshet: [If] she sells [property] for maintenance, [15] what about [her] going back and seizing [the sold property] for her ketubah?

RASHI

מהו שתחזור ותטרוף – אותם הקרקעות עצמן.

NOTES

לְשִׁשָּׁה חֳדָשִׁים Every six months. *Ramah* writes that if the widow is unable to find a buyer who is willing to purchase a parcel of land that covers just six months of maintenance, the court may use its discretion and allow her to sell a larger parcel of land, the proceeds of which will provide for a longer period of maintenance. According to some of the Geonim, the six-month limit only applies the first time that she sells property for her maintenance. The Rabbis allowed her to sell her husband's property without the court's supervision so that she would not have to go to court immediately following her husband's death. Therefore they enacted that she may sell property to cover her maintenance for the first six months of her widowhood. Subsequently when she wishes to sell her husband's property under court supervision, the court may authorize her to sell enough to cover a longer period of maintenance.

מַהוּ שֶׁתַּחֲזוֹר וְתִטְרוֹף What about her going back and seizing? According to *Rosh,* the same question can be asked about a woman who sold her husband's property for her ketubah settlement, but did not collect the entire amount from the sale, and she seizes it back from the buyer for the remainder (see also *Ran*). The Aḥaronim consider this issue, comparing and differentiating between property sold by the woman for maintenance and property sold for her ketubah settlement (see *Maharam Shiff, Ketzot HaḤoshen*).

TRANSLATION AND COMMENTARY

[1]Those who posed the question were in doubt about the law formulated by **Rav Yosef,** [2]**for Rav Yosef said:** If someone sold land, and the seller's creditors came and seized the property for payment of a debt owed them by the seller, the purchaser is entitled to obtain his purchase money from the seller's other property, for the seller's other property is mortgaged to him as a guarantee against seizure. [3]Now, **if a widow sold** part of her late husband's **property** for maintenance or her ketubah settlement, **the guarantee** for the transaction **falls upon the heirs.** If one of the husband's prior creditors seizes the property, it is the heirs' responsibility to compensate the purchaser for his loss, for it was their obligation to pay the widow her maintenance and her ketubah settlement. [4]**And** similarly **if the court sold** part of the husband's property for his widow's maintenance or her ketubah settlement, **the guarantee** to compensate the purchaser against seizure a **falls upon the heirs.** In light of this ruling, the question was put before Rav Sheshet: [5]**What is the law** in our case, when the widow herself sold of her late husband's property for maintenance? [6]Do we say that **since the guarantee** for sale of the property **falls upon the heirs,** the woman may indeed **seize** for payment of her ketubah settlement the property that she herself had sold for her maintenance, just like any creditor with a prior lien on his debtor's property? [7]**Or perhaps** we say that the heirs **can say to** the widow: [8]**Granted that you did not accept upon yourself guarantee regarding other** creditors who may come to seize the property. [9]**But surely did you not** at least **accept a guarantee regarding you yourself?**

אֲמַר לֵיהּ [10]Rav Sheshet **answered them: You have** already **learned** a Baraita that answers your question: [11]"A widow may **keep selling** her late husband's **property** for maintenance **until** what **is left** with the heirs

[1]קָמִיבָּעֲיָא לְהוּ בִּדְרַב יוֹסֵף, [2]דְּאָמַר רַב יוֹסֵף: [3]אַרְמַלְתָּא דְּזַבֵּין אַחֲרָיוּת אַיַּתְמֵי. [4]וּבֵי דִינָא דְּזַבֵּין אַחֲרָיוּת אַיַּתְמֵי. [5]מַאי? [6]כֵּיוָן דְּאַחֲרָיוּת אַיַּתְמֵי, טָרְפָא? [7]אוֹ דִלְמָא מָצֵי אָמְרִי לַהּ: [8]נְהִי דְּאַחֲרָיוּת דְּעָלְמָא לָא קַבִּילַתְּ עִילָּוָךְ. [9]אַחֲרָיוּת דְּנַפְשָׁךְ מִי לָא קַבּוּלֵי קַבִּילַתְּ? [10]אֲמַר לֵיהּ: תְּנֵיתוּהָ: [11]"מוֹכֶרֶת וְהוֹלֶכֶת עַד כְּדֵי כְּתוּבָּתָהּ,

LITERAL TRANSLATION

[1]They were in doubt about [the ruling] of Rav Yosef, [2]for Rav Yosef said: [3][If] the widow sold [property], the guarantee is upon the orphans. [4]And [if] the court sold, the guarantee is upon the orphans. [5]What [is the law]? [6]Since the guarantee is upon the orphans, she may seize? [7]Or perhaps, they can say to her: [8]Granted that you did not accept upon yourself a regarding others. [9][But] surely did you not accept upon yourself a guarantee regarding you yourself? [10]He said to them: You have learned it: [11]"She continues to sell [property] until [there is left] the value of her ketubah,

RASHI

ארמלתא דזבין – שדה יתומים, למזונות או לכתובה, וקבלה עליה אחריות. אחריות איתמי – אחריות הלקוחות חוזר על היתומים, שהרי עליהן היה החוב. טרפא – והם יחזרו על היתומים. מוכרת והולכת – למזונות. עד – שלא יותר קרקע ליורשים, אלא שיעור כתובתה.

NOTES

אַחֲרָיוּת דְּנַפְשָׁךְ מִי לָא קַבּוּלֵי קַבִּילַתְּ But did you not accept upon yourself a guarantee regarding you yourself. *Tosafot* and others discuss the difference between this case and Rava's ruling earlier in the tractate (92a), according to which we do indeed say that even when a person does not guarantee the sale of land regarding the seizure of others, he must accept responsibility for his own seizure. Some suggest that in that case, the seller specified that the land was being sold without a guarantee, whereas here the sale includes a guarantee. However, it does not fall upon the widow who sold the property, but rather upon the heirs. *Ra'ah* infers from our passage that the seller always guarantees against seizure, so that he cannot later reverse his sale on grounds that were known to him at the time of the transaction. *Ra'ah* and his disciples discuss the issue of whether a guardian who sells property belonging to his ward is treated as a principal, so that he too accepts upon himself responsibility for his own seizure.

עַד כְּדֵי כְּתוּבָּתָהּ Until the value of her ketubah. *Rif* understands that this Baraita teaches that a widow may

HALAKHAH

אַחֲרָיוּת אַיַּתְמֵי The guarantee is upon the orphans. "If a widow sold of her late husband's property, with or without supervision of the court, the guarantee against seizure of the property falls upon her late husband's heirs," following the Gemara. (*Rambam, Sefer Nashim, Hilkhot Ishut* 17:13; *Shulḥan Arukh, Even HaEzer* 93:29.)

מוֹכֶרֶת וְהוֹלֶכֶת עַד כְּדֵי כְּתוּבָּתָהּ She continues to sell until there is left the value of her ketubah. "A widow may continue to sell of her late husband's property for her maintenance until all that is left in the hands of his heirs is property to the value of her ketubah settlement, and then she collects the rest as the settlement, following *Rashi* and others. According to *Rif,* if the usufruct of the late husband's estate does not suffice to cover his widow's maintenance, the widow may only collect maintenance from the assets of the estate up to the value of her ketubah

BACKGROUND

זַבִּין וְלָא אִיצְטְרִיכוּ לֵיהּ If someone sold property, and subsequently did not need the money. It is unclear why this issue is discussed in our Gemara, and several suggestions have been proposed to explain its inclusion. There is a certain similarity between this issue and the issue of a widow selling her late husband's property for her maintenance, for it might happen subsequently to the sale of property for six months of maintenance that she no longer is entitled to maintenance (for example, if she remarries). *Ayelet Ahevim* suggests that we can be dealing here with a widow who planned to remarry and therefore sold of her late husband's property in order to collect the ketubah settlement, and then her wedding plans were cancelled. The Jerusalem Talmud records a similar incident, when the husband's heirs wished to exempt themselves from paying his widow's maintenance, so they deceived her and told her that someone wished to marry her. The woman sold some of her husband's property for her ketubah settlement, but the transaction was voided when it became clear that the sale of the property and the woman's waiver of her right to maintenance had been made in error.

TRANSLATION AND COMMENTARY

is equivalent to **the value of her ketubah** settlement, [1]**and she** then **relies on collecting her ketubah** settlement **from the** property **that is left** in their possession." [2]**Infer from this** Baraita as follows: [3]**If the** widow **left** property with the heirs from which to collect her ketubah settlement, she may **indeed** collect it from that property. [4]But **if she did not leave** any property for her ketubah settlement, but she sold it all for her maintenance, she may **not** then seize the property that she had sold for maintenance in payment for her ketubah settlement. For were this the Baraita's intent, it should have taught that the widow may keep selling her late husband's property for her maintenance until nothing is left.

וְדִלְמָא עֵצָה טוֹבָה [5]The Gemara raises another possibility: **Perhaps** the widow may indeed collect her ketubah settlement from property which she herself had sold for her maintenance, but the Baraita meant **to teach us** some **good advice.** [6]The Baraita advises the widow **not** to put herself in a position where she will have to seize the property back to pay her ketubah settlement, thereby sullying her reputation and causing herself to **be called a swindler.** However, by right she may indeed collect her ketubah settlement from the buyer.

אִם כֵּן [7]But **if** this is **so,** the Baraita **should have taught** as follows: The widow may continue **to** sell property until there is enough left for her ketubah settlement, and she **collects her ketubah** settlement **from what is left** with the heirs. [8]**What is the meaning** of the expression: **"She relies on** collecting"? [9]**Conclude from this** that the Baraita was formulated precisely. [10]It teaches that **if** the widow **left** property with the heirs from which to collect her ketubah settlement, she may **indeed** do so. [11]But **if she did not leave** any property for her ketubah settlement, she may **not** later seize property that she had sold earlier for her maintenance.

אִיבַּעֲיָא לְהוּ [12]**The following question arose** in discussion among the Sages: **If someone sold** land in order to raise money for a specific purpose, **and subsequently** he **did not need the money** for that purpose,

[1]וְסָמֵךְ לָהּ שֶׁתִּגְבֶּה כְּתוּבָּתָהּ מִן הַשְּׁאָר. [2]שְׁמַע מִינָּהּ: [3]שִׁיְּירָא — אִין; [4]לָא שִׁיְּירָא — לָא. [5]וְדִלְמָא עֵצָה טוֹבָה קָא מַשְׁמַע לָן, [6]דְּלָא לִיקְרוּ לָהּ הַדְרִינָתָא! [7]אִם כֵּן, לִיתְנֵי ״גּוֹבָה כְּתוּבָּתָהּ מִן הַשְּׁאָר״. [8]מַאי ״סָמֵךְ לָהּ״? [9]שְׁמַע מִינָּהּ: [10]שִׁיְּירָא — אִין; [11]לָא שִׁיְּירָא — לָא. [12]אִיבַּעֲיָא לְהוּ: זַבִּין וְלָא אִיצְטְרִיכוּ לֵיהּ זוּזֵי,

LITERAL TRANSLATION

[1]and she relies on collecting her ketubah from what is left." [2]Conclude from here: [3][If] she left over — yes; [4][if] she did not leave over — no.

[5]But perhaps it teaches us good advice, [6]so that they will not call her a swindler!

[7]If so, let it teach: She collects her ketubah from what is left. [8]What is [meant by] "She relies on"? [9]Conclude from this: [10][If] she left over — yes; [11][if] she did not leave over — no.

[12]It was asked of them: [If] someone sold [property], and [subsequently] did not need the money,

RASHI

וסמך לה — ואותו השאר יהא סמך לה לגבות משם כתובתה. **זבין ולא איצטריכו ליה זוזי** — מכר שדהו, ואנו יודעים שהיה חפץ לקנות שדה פלוני, או פרגמטיא פלונית באותן מעות. **ולא איצטריכו ליה זוזי** — שחזרו בהן המוכרים.

NOTES

continue to sell her late husband's property for her maintenance until the sum that she has collected equals the value of her ketubah settlement, but no more. It has been suggested that *Rif* maintains that since the widow's right to maintenance stems from a ketubah condition, it stands to reason that the sum total of the maintenance which she collects cannot exceed the value of her ketubah settlement. Others explain (see *Rabbenu Ḥananel* and others) that as long as the widow has not sold property for her maintenance in excess of the value of her ketubah settlement, then even if she sold property worth more than her monthly maintenance, the heirs can deduct this excess and recover what is owed them when she collects her ketubah settlement. But if she already collected maintenance for a sum that exceeds her ketubah settlement, the heirs have no way of recovering what is owed them. The Rishonim note that *Rif* appears to have retracted his position in his later years (see Halakhah).

וְלָא אִיצְטְרִיכוּ לֵיהּ זוּזֵי And did not need the money. According to *Rashi* and others (see *Rivan* and *Ra'ah*), in this case it is known that the seller sold his property in order to raise money for a specific purpose. But *Rav Hai Gaon*

HALAKHAH

settlement, but no more. But this opinion is rejected by most Rishonim (*Rambam, Rosh,* and others, and according to *Ra'avad,* even *Rif* himself retracted from this position)." (*Rambam, Sefer Nashim, Hilkhot Ishut* 18:21; *Shulḥan Arukh, Even HaEzer* 93:13.)

שִׁיְּירָא — אִין If she left over — yes. If a widow sold some of her late husband's property for maintenance, the guarantee for the transaction falls upon her late husband's heirs, but she may still not collect her ketubah settlement from property thats she herself had sold earlier for her maintenance." (*Shulḥan Arukh, Even HaEzer* 93:29.)

זַבִּין וְלָא אִיצְטְרִיכוּ לֵיהּ זוּזֵי If someone sold, and did not need the money. "If someone sold property and stated at the time of the sale that he was selling the property in order to use the proceeds for a specific purpose, this is considered a condition to the sale, so that if he did not

TRANSLATION AND COMMENTARY

[1]can the seller **withdraw from the sale,** [2]**or can he not withdraw from the sale?** Since the seller no longer needs the money for the specific purpose for which he had sold his property, do we say that the sale is considered as having been made in error? Or do we say that his intentions regarding what to do with the money of the sale are irrelevant to the validity of the transaction?

תָּא שְׁמַע [3]The Gemara proposes a solution: **Come and hear** the following story: **There was a certain man who sold land to Rav Pappa,** [4]**because he needed** to raise **money to buy oxen.** [5]But **in the end** the seller **did not need the money** for that purpose. He wished to cancel the sale, [6]**and Rav Pappa returned his land to him.**

רַב פַּפָּא [7]The Gemara rejects this example as general proof: **Rav Pappa was acting beyond** the strict **requirements of the law.** He returned the land out of a sense of moral duty.

תָּא שְׁמַע [8]The Gemara now offers another example: **Come and hear** the following story: **There once was a drought in Neharde'a** that caused the price of wheat to soar, [9]**and everybody sold their mansions** in order to buy food. [10]**In the end, wheat arrived** in the city, and its price dropped. [11]**Rav Naḥman said to** the Neharde'an townspeople: **The law is that the mansions** must be **returned to their** former **owners.**

הָתָם [12]However, this example also offers no general proof, because **there, in the case of the Neharde'a drought, the sales were also in error** at the very time they were made, [13]**for it turned out,** unknown to the townsfolk, **that the ship was standing anchored in the bend [of the river],** a short distance from Neharde'a. This was a standard case of a sale made on the basis of incomplete knowledge. It therefore has no bearing on a case when the situation changes after the sale, which was the basis of the question under discussion, and it could well be that in such a case Rav Naḥman would uphold the sale.

[1]הָדְרִי זְבִינֵי, [2]אוֹ לָא הָדְרִי זְבִינֵי?

[3]תָּא שְׁמַע: דְּהַהוּא גַּבְרָא דְּזַבֵּין אַרְעָא לְרַב פַּפָּא, [4]דְּאִצְטְרִיכוּ לֵיהּ זוּזֵי לְמִיזְבַּן תּוֹרֵי. [5]לְסוֹף, לָא אִיצְטְרִיכוּ לֵיהּ, [6]וְאַהַדְרֵיהּ נִיהֲלֵיהּ רַב פַּפָּא לְאַרְעֵיהּ.

[7]רַב פַּפָּא לִפְנִים מִשּׁוּרַת הַדִּין הוּא דַּעֲבַד.

[8]תָּא שְׁמַע: דְּהַהוּא בַּצּוֹרְתָא דַּהֲוָה בִּנְהַרְדְּעָא, [9]זַבְּנִינְהוּ כּוּלֵּי עָלְמָא לְאַפַּדְנַיְיהוּ. [10]לְסוֹף, אָתוּ חִיטֵּי. [11]אֲמַר לְהוּ רַב נַחְמָן: דִּינָא הוּא, דְּהָדְרִי אַפַּדְנֵי לְמָרַיְיהוּ.

[12]הָתָם, נַמִי זְבִינֵי בְּטָעוּת הָווּ, [13]דְּאִיגְלַאי מִילְּתָא דְּאַרְבָּא בְּעִקּוּלֵי הֲוָה קַיְימָא.

LITERAL TRANSLATION

[1]can the sale be voided, [2]or can the sale not be voided?

[3]Come [and] hear: That [there was] a certain man who sold land to Rav Pappa, [4]because he needed money to buy oxen. [5]In the end, he did not need [the money], [6]and Rav Pappa returned his land to him.

[7]Rav Pappa was acting beyond the requirements of the law (lit., "inside the line of justice").

[8]Come [and] hear: That [there was] a certain drought in Neharde'a, [9][and] everybody sold their mansions. [10]In the end, wheat arrived. [11]Rav Naḥman said to them: The law is that the mansions must be returned to their owners.

[12]There, also the sales were in error, [13]for it turned out that the boat was standing in the bend [of the river].

RASHI

בצורתא – יוקר הבא בשערים פתאום.

זבנינהו לאפדנייהו – לקנות חטין.

דארבי בעקולי הוו קיימי – שעל ידי שגדל הנהר הוארכו הספינות ללכת עקלקלות. ואילו ידעו המוכרים כן – לא היו מוכרים בתיהם, ומשעת מכירה הוה ליה טעות. אבל היכא דמכירה לאו בטעות הואי, כגון חזרו בהן מוכרי החיטין לאחר שמכרו אלו בתיהם, או שבאו חיטין ממקום אחר, שעדיין לא נעקרו ממקומם – לא הדרי.

BACKGROUND

בַּצּוֹרְתָא בִּנְהַרְדְּעָא A drought is Neharde'a. Although the city of Neharde'a was located where the Malka River flows into the Euphrates, it was still on the edge of the Syrian desert. Although its fields were well irrigated by canals from the rivers, a year without rain and a consequent fall in the water level could mean that only some of the fields were irrigated, causing a drought.

NOTES

and other Geonim, *Tosafot* and most Rishonim argue that even if the seller's intentions are known to us, his mental reservations fall under the category of "matter of intent" (דְּבָרִים שֶׁבַּלֵּב), which have no legal effect. Rather, here the seller stated explicitly to the purchaser at the time of sale that he was selling his property for a designated purpose. *Tosafot* discuss when such a statement of intent is sufficient and when a formal condition is required. According to *Rabbenu Ḥananel,* such a statement made at the time of the transaction can nullify the sale of land, but not the sale

HALAKHAH

need the money for the stated purpose, he may return the purchase money and recover his property," following the Gemara's conclusion. "But if he sold the property without any such specification, even if he had in mind to use the proceeds for a specific purpose, and even if it appears that indeed he sold the property for that purpose, the seller is bound by the transaction," following the conclusion of the Gemara in *Kiddushin. Rema* writes that this law only applies to the sale of land, but if a person sold movable goods, the sale is binding unless the seller attached an explicit condition to the sale (*Tur* in the name of *Rashi* and *Rabbenu Ḥananel*). He also adds that if the seller's intentions were clearly apparent, he may cancel the transaction even if he did not mention his intentions at the time of the sale (*Tosafot* and *Rosh*). According to some authorities, a mental reservation is valid in the case of a gift (*Hagahot Alfasi*). (*Rambam, Sefer Kinyan, Hilkhot Mekhirah* 11:8-9; *Shulḥan Arukh, Ḥoshen Mishpat* 207:3-4.)

אי הָכִי, הַיְינוּ דַּאֲמַר לֵיהּ רָמִי בַּר שְׁמוּאֵל לְרַב נַחְמָן: [2] אִם כֵּן, נִמְצֵאת מַכְשִׁילָן לֶעָתִיד לָבֹא! [3] אֲמַר לֵיהּ: אַטּוּ כָּל יוֹמָא בַּצּוֹרְתָא שְׁכִיחָא? [4] אֲמַר לֵיהּ: אִין, בַּצּוֹרְתָא בִּנְהַרְדְּעָא מַשְׁכַּח שְׁכִיחָא.

[5] וְהִלְכְתָא: זַבֵּין, וְלָא אִיצְטְרִיכוּ לֵיהּ זוּזֵי, [6] הָדְרִי זְבִינֵי.

מִשְׁנָה [7] אַלְמָנָה בֵּין מִן הָאֵירוּסִין בֵּין מִן הַנִּשּׂוּאִין, מוֹכֶרֶת שֶׁלֹּא בְּבֵית דִּין.

TRANSLATION AND COMMENTARY

אִי הָכִי [1] **If** it is **so** that in this case the ship was anchored in the river's band near Neharde'a, this would explain the discussion of **what Rami bar Shmuel said to Rav Naḥman** and Rav Naḥman's reply. [2] As Rami bar Shmuel asked: **If** it is **so** that the law requires returning the mansions, **it turns out that you will cause them to stumble in the future!** The people of Neharde'a will think that as a general rule, sales of property can be voided if some time in the future the reason for his selling the property is no longer relevant.

אֲמַר לֵיהּ [3] Rav Naḥman **replied to** Rami bar Shmuel: **Is it every day that a drought occurs?** [4] Rami bar Shmuel **said to** Rav Naḥman: **Yes, a drought in Neharde'a is frequent,** and ships are also likely to be held up. However, if Rav Naḥman's ruling was based on the broader principle that whenever a person sells property, and the reason for the sale becomes irrelevant, the sale is void, the discussion between Rami bar Shmuel and Rav Naḥman about the frequency of droughts in Neharde'a would be irrelevant to Rav Naḥman's decision.

וְהִלְכְתָא [5] **And the law is: If someone sold** indeed property for a specific purpose, and subsequently it turned out **that he did not need the money,** [6] **the sale is void.**

MISHNAH אַלְמָנָה [7] **A widow may sell** her late husband's property for her maintenance, or her ketubah settlement even **without** the supervision of **a court — whether** she was widowed during the period of her **betrothal,** so that she is only entitled to her ketubah settlement, but not to maintenance, from her husband's estate, **or** she was widowed after her **marriage,** so that she is also entitled to maintenance.

LITERAL TRANSLATION

[1] If so, this is what Rami bar Shmuel said to Rav Naḥman: [2] If so, it turns out that you will cause to stumble in the future!

[3] He said to him: Is it every day that a drought occurs (lit., "is found")? [4] He said to him: Yes, a drought in Neharde'a is frequent.

[5] And the law is: [If] someone sold [property], and [subsequently] did not need the money, [6] the sale is void.

MISHNAH [7] A widow, whether from betrothal or from marriage, may sell [property] without a court.

RASHI

אי הכי היינו ודאי דאמר ליה כו׳ נמצאת מכשילן — דאי בעי לזבוני קרקע לא ימצאו קונים. **ואמר ליה אין בצורתא בנהרדעא משכח שכיח** — וחיישינן לדלמא אתו ארבי דקיימי בעקולי, והדרי זביניהו. שמע מינה: טעמא משום מקח טעות הוי. דאי בדאתו חטין ממקום קרוב, או שבאו לאלו לבדם, דטעמא משום זבין ולא אילטריכו ליה זוזי הוה — מידי דלא שכיח הוא, וליכא מכשול.

משנה בין מן הארוסין — שאין לה מזונות, ומוכרת לכתובה. **בין מן הנשואין** — שהיא מוכרת למזונות — מוכרת שלא בבית דין.

NOTES

of movable goods. *Ra'ah* adds that the seller can only cancel the transaction if he obtains money from another source, or if he acquires what he wanted in another manner, but the transaction is not voided if he changed his mind and decided that he does not want to purchase what he had originally intended to buy.

מִן הַנִּשּׂוּאִין — מוֹכֶרֶת שֶׁלֹּא בְּבֵית דִּין **From marriage — she may sell without a court.** Our commentary follows *Rashi* and most Rishonim, who explain that according to the anonymous first Tanna of the Mishnah, both a widow from betrothal, who can sell her husband's property only for her ketubah settlement, and a widow from marriage, who can also sell her husband's property for her maintenance, may sell the property without the court's supervision. Rabbi Shimon disagrees and says that a widow from marriage may sell her late husband's property without the court's supervision for maintenance, as this is an urgent matter. But a widow from betrothal who sells her husband's property only for her ketubah settlement, or a widow from marriage who comes to collect her ketubah settlement, may only sell property under court supervision, because this matter is not as urgent, and, in addition, is only a one time sale. *Ritva* argues that if this explanation were true, the Mishnah should not have explained the

HALAKHAH

אַלְמָנָה בֵּין מִן הָאֵירוּסִין בֵּין מִן הַנִּשּׂוּאִין **A widow, whether from betrothal or from marriage.** "A widow, whether she was widowed during the period of her betrothal or after her marriage, may sell some of her late husband's property for her ketubah settlement even without the court's supervision, provided that she sells it under the supervision of three people who are experts at assessing the value of the property," following the anonymous Tanna of our Mishnah and the Gemara's conclusion in *Bava Metzia.* If she sold the property by herself without any supervision, but at the correct price, the sale is valid (*Rambam).* Some authorities (*Ramban*) disagree, and say that the sale is void. (*Rambam, Sefer Nashim, Hilkhot Ishut* 17:13; *Shulḥan Arukh, Even HaEzer* 103:1.)

TRANSLATION AND COMMENTARY

רַבִּי שִׁמְעוֹן אוֹמֵר [1]**Rabbi Shimon** disagrees and **says:** If she was widowed **from marriage,** and she wishes to sell her late husband's property for her maintenance, [2]**she may sell** the property even **without** the supervision of **a court,** for the money is needed for immediate needs, and she cannot wait until the court has a chance to consider her situation. [3]But if she was widowed **from betrothal,** and she wishes to sell her late husband's property for her ketubah settlement, **she may only sell** the property under the supervision of **a court,** [4]**for** a widow from betrothal **is not entitled to maintenance,** [5]**and a woman who is not entitled to maintenance may only** sell her late husband's property under the supervision of **a court.**

GEMARA בִּשְׁלָמָא [6]The Gemara examines the position of the anonymous first Tanna of the Mishnah: **Granted** that **a widow from marriage** may sell her late husband's property without the supervision of a court, [7]**because** she may sell the property **for her maintenance** without delay. [97B] [8]**But why** may **a widow from betrothal** sell her late husband's property without the supervision of a court, like anybody else who seeks to collect a debt from his debtor's property?

אֲמַר עוּלָּא [9]**Ulla said:** The Rabbis permitted a widow from betrothal to sell the property without the supervision of a court **in order to enhance her favor** in the eyes of a potential suitor. They wanted to make it easier for her to collect her ketubah settlement so that she will quickly find another husband.

רַבִּי יוֹחָנָן אָמַר [10]**Rabbi Yoḥanan said:** The Rabbis allowed a widow from betrothal to sell the property outside court, [11]**because a man does not want his wife to suffer** the **humiliation associated with** the public examination of her affairs **in a court** of law.

[1]רַבִּי שִׁמְעוֹן אוֹמֵר: מִן הַנִּשּׂוּאִין — [2]מוֹכֶרֶת שֶׁלֹּא בְּבֵית דִּין. [3]מִן הָאֵירוּסִין — לֹא תִּמְכּוֹר אֶלָּא בְּבֵית דִּין, [4]מִפְּנֵי שֶׁאֵין לָהּ מְזוֹנוֹת, [5]וְכָל שֶׁאֵין לָהּ מְזוֹנוֹת לֹא תִּמְכּוֹר אֶלָּא בְּבֵית דִּין.

גמרא [6]בִּשְׁלָמָא מִן הַנִּשּׂוּאִין, [7]מִשּׁוּם מְזוֹנֵי. [97B] [8]אֶלָּא מִן הָאֵירוּסִין מַאי טַעְמָא? [9]אֲמַר עוּלָּא: מִשּׁוּם חִינָּא.

[10]רַבִּי יוֹחָנָן אָמַר: [11]לְפִי שֶׁאֵין אָדָם רוֹצֶה שֶׁתִּתְבַּזֶּה אִשְׁתּוֹ בְּבֵית דִּין.

LITERAL TRANSLATION

[1]Rabbi Shimon says: From marriage — [2]she may sell without a court. [3]From betrothal — she may only sell in court, [4]for she does not have maintenance, [5]and any [woman] who does not have maintenance may only sell in court.

GEMARA [6]Granted [a widow] from marriage, [7]because of maintenance. [97B] [8]But [a widow] from betrothal, what is the reason?

[9]Ulla said: In order to [enhance her] favor.

[10]Rabbi Yoḥanan said: [11]Because a man does not want his wife to be humiliated in court.

RASHI

רבי שמעון אומר מן הנשואין — שהיא מוכרת למזונות. מוכרת שלא בבית דין — שאי אפשר לה להיות יושבת ומתענה עד שיזדקקו לה בית דין. אבל מן האירוסין, שאין מכירתה אלא לכתובה — לא תמכור אלא בבית דין.

גמרא אלא מן האירוסין מאי טעמא — לא אטרחוה רבנן [לבא] לבית דין, ככל שאר מוציאי שטר חוב? משום חינא — שיהו בעליהן לחן בעיניהן, ולא ימנעו הנשים מלינשא לאנשים.

NOTES

disagreement between the first Tanna and Rabbi Shimon in terms of a widow from marriage and a widow from betrothal. In fact, when either of them sell property for their ketubah settlement, both the first Tanna and Rabbi Shimon agree that she must sell under court supervision. The Mishnah should then have set up the disagreement between them as centering on whether the widow is selling property for maintenance or selling it for her ketubah settlement. Hence the Mishnah should be explained as dealing with the sale of property for the ketubah settlement alone. According to the anonymous first Tanna of the Mishnah, both a widow from betrothal, who does not forfeit maintenance when she sells her husband's property for her ketubah settlement, and a widow from marriage, who does forfeit her maintenance when she sells her husband's property, may sell their husband's property for her ketubah settlement without the court's supervision. Rabbi Shimon disagrees and says that a widow from marriage may sell her husband's property for her ketubah settlement without the court's supervision, for she will then forfeit her maintenance, and the heirs will benefit. But a widow from betrothal, who gets no maintenance, may only sell her husband's property with the court's supervision.

משום חִינָּא **In order to enhance her favor.** Most commentators explain this expression following the opinion of *Rabbenu Ḥananel*, meaning that one grants certain rights to women so that they will find favor with men, who will wish to marry them. However, *Rashi* explains "in order to enhance her favor" as meaning that men will appear gracious to women, so that they will wish to remarry. For if they encounter difficulties after the dissolution of their first marriage, they will not want to do so. However, not only is *Rashi*'s interpretation difficult to reconcile with the text here (see *Ritva* and others), it also contradicts another passage of the Gemara (see above, 86a), which states that women wish to be married more than men wish to marry them (see also *Meiri*, who discusses this and reconciles the opinions so as even to include *Rashi*'s approach).

LITERAL TRANSLATION

[1]What is [the difference] between them? [2]There is [a difference] between them of a divorced woman. [3]According to the one who says: In order to [enhance her] favor [4]a divorcee also needs favor. [5]According to the one who says: Because a man does not want his wife be humiliated in court [6]he does not care about [his] divorcee.

[7]We have learned: "But a divorcee may only sell in court." [8]Granted according to the one who says: Because a man does not want his wife to be humiliated in the court [9]he does not care about [his] divorcee. [10]But according to the one who says: In order to [enhance her] favor, [11]a divorcee also needs favor! [12]Whose is this? [13]It is Rabbi Shimon.

[1]מַאי בֵּינַיְיהוּ? [2]אִיכָּא בֵּינַיְיהוּ גְּרוּשָׁה. [3]לְמַאן דְּאָמַר: מִשּׁוּם חִינָּא, [4]גְּרוּשָׁה נַמִי בָּעֲיָא חֵן. [5]לְמַאן דְּאָמַר: לְפִי שֶׁאֵין אָדָם רוֹצֶה שֶׁתִּתְבַּזֶּה אִשְׁתּוֹ בְּבֵית דִּין, [6]גְּרוּשָׁה לָא אִיכְפַּת לֵיהּ. [7]תְּנַן: "וּגְרוּשָׁה לֹא תִּמְכּוֹר אֶלָּא בְּבֵית דִּין". [8]בִּשְׁלָמָא לְמַאן דְּאָמַר: לְפִי שֶׁאֵין אָדָם רוֹצֶה שֶׁתִּתְבַּזֶּה אִשְׁתּוֹ בְּבֵית דִּין, [9]גְּרוּשָׁה לָא אִיכְפַּת לֵיהּ. [10]אֶלָּא לְמַאן דְּאָמַר מִשּׁוּם חִינָּא, [11]גְּרוּשָׁה נַמִי בָּעֲיָא חֵן! [12]הָא מַנִּי? [13]רַבִּי שִׁמְעוֹן הִיא.

RASHI

גרושה נמי בעיא חן – תקנתא דמשום חינא. שהרי תקנת חכמים היא, ולא מאהבת האיש. הלכך מה לי אהובה מה לי שנואה? רבי שמעון היא – דלית ליה חינא. דגבי אלמנה מן האירוסין נמי, משום דלכתובה קא מזבנה, אמר: לא תמכור אלא בבית דין.

TRANSLATION AND COMMENTARY

מַאי בֵּינַיְיהוּ [1]The Gemara asks: **What is** the practical **difference between** the reasons given by Ulla and Rabbi Yoḥanan? [2]The Gemara answers: **There is** a **difference between them** regarding **a divorcee.** [3]**According to** Ulla **who said** that a widow may sell her late husband's property outside court, **in order to enhance her favor** in the eyes of suitors, the same law should also apply to a divorcee, [4]for **a divorcee also requires favor** to find another husband. [5]But **according** to Rabbi Yoḥanan **who said** that a widow is permitted to sell the property out of court, **because a man does not want his wife to suffer humiliation in court,** this law would be limited to the case of a widow who was presumably on good terms with her husband at the time of his death. [6]But a former husband **does not care** if **his divorcee** is humiliated.

תְּנַן [7]The Gemara now tries to adduce support for Rabbi Yoḥanan from the next anonymous Mishnah where **we have learned: "But a divorcee may only sell** her former husband's property for her ketubah settlement under the supervision of **a court."** [8]**Granted** that **according to** Rabbi Yoḥanan **who said** that a widow may sell her husband's property out of court because **a man does not want his wife to be humiliated in court,** we understand the next Mishnah's ruling about the divorcee, [9]for a man **does not care** if **his divorcee** is humiliated. [10]**But according to** Ulla **who said** that the Rabbis permitted a widow to sell property for her ketubah settlement out of court **in order to enhance her favor,** we find it difficult to understand the next Mishnah. The same law should apply to a divorcee, [11]because **a divorcee also needs favor** if she is find another husband!

הָא מַנִּי [12]The Gemara rejects this argument: **In accordance with whose** viewpoint was the next Mishnah taught? [13]That Mishnah follows the position of **Rabbi Shimon** of our Mishnah, who rules that a woman entitled to a ketubah settlement, but not to maintenance may only sell her husband's property under the court supervision. Thus, a divorcee who wishes to sell property for her ketubah settlement may only do so in court, for she is not entitled to maintenance. Thus there is no contradiction between this later Mishnah and Ulla's position, because he and Rabbi Yoḥanan are responding to the anonymous first Tanna of our Mishnah, who rules that even a widow from betrothal who receives no maintenance may sell out of court.

NOTES

גְּרוּשָׁה לָא אִיכְפַּת לֵיהּ **He does not care about a divorcee.** This is the approach taken by our Talmud. However the Jerusalem Talmud explains at length that a man does not even wish to see his divorced wife humiliated, and to some extent he is commanded to make sure she is not humiliated because of the law, "do not turn away from your flesh." Some commentators hold that the ruling here refers to a woman divorced from betrothal, with whom the husband had not yet had any intimate contact. It can also be said that while he may not wish to see her humiliated, he nevertheless would not fear the slight humiliation of appearing in court.

HALAKHAH

גְּרוּשָׁה לֹא תִּמְכּוֹר אֶלָּא בְּבֵית דִּין **A divorcee may only sell in court.** "Even though a widow may sell her late husband's property out of court, a divorcee may not sell her husband's property without such supervision, following Rabbi Yoḥanan. So too a widow who has remarried may not sell her first husband's property without the court's supervision." *Ḥelkat Meḥokek* explains that a man is not concerned about the humiliation suffered by his widow

[1]אִי רַבִּי שִׁמְעוֹן, הָא תָּנָא לֵיהּ רֵישָׁא: [2]״מִן הָאֵירוּסִין — [3]לֹא תִּמְכּוֹר כו׳״!

[4]מַהוּ דְּתֵימָא: אַלְמָנָה מִן הָאֵירוּסִין הוּא, [5]דְּלָא נָפֵישׁ חֵן דִּידָהּ. [6]אֲבָל גְּרוּשָׁה דְּנָפֵישׁ חֵן דִּידָהּ, [7]אֵימָא תִּיבָּעֵי חֵן.

[8]הָא נַמִי תָּנֵינָא: [9]״כָּל שֶׁאֵין לָהּ מְזוֹנוֹת״. [10]לְאַתּוּיֵי מַאי? [11]לָאו לְאַתּוּיֵי גְּרוּשָׁה!

[12]לָא! לְאַתּוּיֵי מְגוֹרֶשֶׁת וְאֵינָהּ מְגוֹרֶשֶׁת [13]כִּדְרַבִּי זֵירָא.

TRANSLATION AND COMMENTARY

אִי רַבִּי שִׁמְעוֹן [1]The Gemara questions this attribution: However, **if** the next Mishnah follows the position of **Rabbi Shimon,** there is a certain difficulty, for **surely** Rabbi Shimon already **taught** this position **in the** second **clause** of his ruling as given in our Mishnah: [2]"If a woman was widowed **from betrothal,** and she wishes to sell her late husband's property for her ketubah settlement, [3]**she may only sell** in court, for such a woman does not receive maintenance." Now, it follows from this that a divorcee, too, should not be permitted to sell her husband's property for her ketubah settlement except in court, for she is not entitled to maintenance from her husband's property. Why then should it have been necessary for this to be stated explicitly in the next Mishnah?

מַהוּ דְּתֵימָא [4]The Gemara answers: Had the law applying to a divorcee not been stated explicitly in the next Mishnah, it might have been possible to distinguish between a widow from betrothal and a divorcee. For **you might have** mistakenly **said** that according to Rabbi Shimon only **a widow from betrothal** must sell her late husband's property in court, [5]for **her need for** enhanced **favor is not** so **great,** since she is still a virgin and would not have difficulty finding another husband. [6]**But** regarding **a divorcee** who is no longer a virgin and **whose need for favor is** therefore very **great,** [7]**you might have** said that even Rabbi Shimon agrees **that** she **needs** help to enhance her **favor** in the eyes of potential suitors. Thus, it was necessary for the next Mishnah to state explicitly that a even a divorcee may only sell the property in court.

הָא נַמִי תָּנֵינָא [8]The Gemara continues this line of questioning: But **this** explicit statement in the next Mishnah regarding a divorcee **was** also **taught** by implication in our Mishnah, which concludes with the following general rule: [9]**"Any woman who is not entitled to maintenance may only sell** her husband's property under the supervision of a court." [10]**What new information** does this line of the Mishnah **add?** [11]**Does it not include** the law applying to **a divorcee?** Thus, we return to our earlier difficulty: Why was it necessary for this law of a divorcee to have been stated explicitly in the next Mishnah?

לָא [12]**No,** the general rule recorded at the end of the first Mishnah **adds** the law applying to **a** betrothed **woman who is divorced but not divorced,** a betrothed woman the validity of whose divorce is in doubt. For example, if a man threw a bill of divorce to his wife who was standing in the public domain, and it is not clear whether the bill landed on the ground closer to her (in which case she is divorced) or closer to him (in which case she is not divorced), the validity of the woman's divorce is in doubt, and she cannot remarry until her husband gives her a second bill of divorce. [13]The Mishnah **follows** the position of **Rabbi Zera,**

LITERAL TRANSLATION

[1]If it is Rabbi Shimon, surely he taught it in the first clause: [2]"From betrothal — [3]she may only sell, etc."

[4]You might have [mistakenly] said: A widow from betrothal — [5]whose [need for] favor is not great. [6]But a divorcee whose [need for] favor is great, [7]say that she needs [enhanced] favor.

[8]This too was taught: [9]"Any [woman] who does not have maintenance." [10]To include (lit., "bring") what [new information]? [11]Is it not to include a divorcee!

[12]No! To include a woman who is divorced and not divorced [13][and] like Rabbi Zera.

RASHI

דלא נפיש חן דידה — שלא היתה לה חיבת ביאה ולא ירע בעיני הנשים אם הוטרחה זו. **אימא תבעי חן** — ואפילו לרבי שמעון. **הא נמי תנינא** — בסיפא דמילתיה דרבי שמעון. **לאו לאתויי גרושה** — מן הנשואין. דאי מן האירוסין — הא אשמעינן אלמנה, וכל שכן גרושה. **מגורשת ואינה מגורשת** — ומן האירוסין. ולא לאשמעינן דלא תמכור לכתובתה אלא בבית דין — דהא מאלמנה שמעינן לה. אלא אגב אורחיה אשמעינן דמגורשת ואינה מגורשת, כגון זרק לה גיטה; ספק קרוב לה ספק קרוב לו ברשות הרבים — אין לה מזונות מן היתומים אם מת. **כדרבי זירא** — דאמר: בעלה חייב במזונותיה בחייו. [ואשמעינן מתניתין דדוקא בחייו], משום דמעוכבת בשבילו להנשא. אבל לאחר מיתה — לא, דדלמא גרושין הוו, ואין לה מזונות, דמספיקא לא מפקינן ממונא. **יורשיה** יורשי כתובתה — גרסינן, ולא גרסינן ויורשי.

HALAKHAH

after she remarries. But *Be'er HaGolah* and *Gra* explain that this ruling follows Ulla, according to *Rabbenu Ḥananel*; see also *Ḥelkat Meḥokek* who cites *Rashba* who rules in accordance with Ulla. (*Rambam, Sefer Nashim, Hilkhot Ishut* 17:13; *Shulḥan Arukh, Even HaEzer* 103:3.)

מְגוֹרֶשֶׁת וְאֵינָהּ מְגוֹרֶשֶׁת A woman who is divorced and not divorced. "A woman the validity of whose divorce is in doubt is entitled to maintenance from her husband during

TRANSLATION AND COMMENTARY

[1]**for Rabbi Zera said: Wherever** the Sages **said** that a betrothed woman **is divorced but not divorced,** [2]the Rabbis legislated that her **husband is responsible for her maintenance** until he grants her a valid divorce or dies, as he is the cause of her inability to remarry. Regarding the woman in this situation, the Mishnah teaches, that once her husband dies and she is no longer entitled to maintenance, she may not sell his property out of court. Moreover, this teaching implies that while the husband is alive and she is entitled to maintenance, she may sell his property out of court. The Mishnah thus teaches that a betrothed woman whose divorce is of doubtful validity may can sell her husband's property out of court, although her right to maintenance stems from a special Rabbinic enactment.

תָּא שְׁמַע [3]The Gemara offers another proof for the position of Rabbi Yoḥanan: **Come and hear** what was taught in a Baraita: [4]**"Just as** a widow **may sell** her husband's property for her ketubah settlement **without** the supervision of **a court,** [5]**so** too **her heirs, the heirs of her ketubah, may sell** her husband's property for her ketubah settlement **without** the supervision of **a court."** [6]**Granted** that **according to** Rabbi Yoḥanan **who said** that the Rabbis permitted a widow to sell her husband's property out of court [7]**because a man does not want his wife to be humiliated in court,** we understand this Baraita's ruling. [8]**Just as he does not want** his wife **to be humiliated** in court, [9]so **too he does not want her heirs to be humiliated.** [10]**But according to** Ulla **who said** that the Rabbis permitted a widow to sell her husband's property out of court **to enhance her favor,** we do not understand the Baraita, [11]for **how does favor** play a role **regarding her heirs?**

תַּרְגְּמָהּ עוּלָּא [12]**Ulla** can **explain** that Baraita as follows: The Baraita is dealing with a case such as when the widow's **daughter or sister inherited her** ketubah, for they too are in need of favor to marry.

MISHNAH מָכְרָה כְּתוּבָּתָהּ [13]**If** a widow **sold** the main part of **her ketubah** settlement, the hundred or two hundred dinars to which every woman is entitled, and she now wishes to collect the additional amounts that her husband had added on his own, **or** if she sold only **a portion of** her basic ketubah settlement, and she now wishes to collect the rest, [14]**or if she pledged** the entire main part of **her ketubah** settlement

[1]דְּאָמַר רַבִּי זֵירָא: כָּל מָקוֹם שֶׁאָמְרוּ ״מְגוֹרֶשֶׁת וְאֵינָהּ מְגוֹרֶשֶׁת״, [2]בַּעַל חַיָּיב בִּמְזוֹנוֹתֶיהָ.

[3]תָּא שְׁמַע: [4]״כְּשֵׁם שֶׁמּוֹכֶרֶת שֶׁלֹּא בְּבֵית דִּין, [5]כָּךְ יוֹרְשֶׁיהָ יוֹרְשֵׁי כְתוּבָּתָהּ, מוֹכְרִים שֶׁלֹּא בְּבֵית דִּין״. [6]בִּשְׁלָמָא לְמַאן דְּאָמַר: [7]לְפִי שֶׁאֵין אָדָם רוֹצֶה שֶׁתִּתְבַּזֶּה אִשְׁתּוֹ בְּבֵית דִּין, [8]כִּי הֵיכִי דְּאִיהִי לָא נִיחָא לֵיהּ דְּתִתְבַּזֵּי, [9]יוֹרְשֶׁיהָ נַמִי לָא נִיחָא לֵיהּ דְּלִיבַזּוּ. [10]אֶלָּא לְמַאן דְּאָמַר: מִשּׁוּם חִינָּא, [11]יוֹרְשֶׁיהָ מַאי חֵן אִיכָּא?

[12]תַּרְגְּמָהּ עוּלָּא: כְּגוֹן שֶׁיְּרַשְׁתָּהּ בִּתָּהּ אוֹ אֲחוֹתָהּ.

משנה [13]מָכְרָה כְּתוּבָּתָהּ אוֹ מִקְצָתָהּ, [14]מִשְׁכְּנָה כְּתוּבָּתָהּ

LITERAL TRANSLATION

[1]For Rabbi Zera said: Wherever they said "She is divorced and not divorced," [2]the husband is responsible for her maintenance.

[3]Come [and] hear: [4]"Just as [a widow] sells without a court, [5]so do her heirs, the heirs of her ketubah, sell without a court." [6]Granted according to the one who says: [7]Because a man does not want his wife to be humiliated in court [8]just as he is not pleased when she is humiliated, [9]he is also not pleased when her heirs are humiliated. [10]But according to the one who said: In order to [enhance her] favor — [11]what favor is there with regard to her heirs?

[12]Ulla explained it: As when her daughter or her sister inherited her.

MISHNAH [13][If] she sold her ketubah or a portion of it, [14][or if] she pledged her ketubah

RASHI

מאי חן איכא – הרי הנטרחים לבית דין אנשים הן. שירשתה בתה או אחותה – דמשום דידה בעינן תקנתא, שלא תמשך מלהנשא.

משנה לא תמכור את השאר כו׳ – רבי שמעון קאמר לה. דאמר: אין מוכרת שלא בב״ד אלא למזונות. וזו, מכיון שגבתה מקצתה לא תמכור את השאר כו׳ – רבי שמעון קאמר לה דאמר אין מוכרת שלא בבית דין אלא למזונות וזו מכיון שגבתה מקצתה – אין לה מזונות. והכי מוקי לה בגמרא כרבי שמעון.

HALAKHAH

his lifetime until he grants her a valid divorce. But after his death, his heirs are not liable for her maintenance, for she cannot claim with certainty that she is entitled to such maintenance," following Rabbi Zera and the Gemara's conclusion. (*Rambam, Sefer Nashim, Hilkhot Ishut* 18:25; *Shulḥan Arukh, Even HaEzer* 93:2.)

מָכְרָה מִקְצָת כְּתוּבָּתָהּ If she sold a portion of her ketubah. "A widow who sold, pledged, or gave away as a gift a portion of her ketubah settlement, may sell some of her late husband's property for the rest of it out of court, provided that she sells it under the supervision of three people who are experts at assessing the value of the property. She may repeatedly sell some of her husband's property for her ketubah settlement, each sale providing

[1]אוֹ מִקְצָתָהּ, [2]נָתְנָה כְּתוּבָּתָהּ לְאַחֵר אוֹ מִקְצָתָהּ. [3]לֹא תִּמְכּוֹר אֶת הַשְּׁאָר אֶלָּא בְּבֵית דִּין. [4]וַחֲכָמִים אוֹמְרִים: מוֹכֶרֶת הִיא אֲפִילּוּ אַרְבָּעָה וַחֲמִשָּׁה פְּעָמִים. [5]וּמוֹכֶרֶת לִמְזוֹנוֹת שֶׁלֹּא בְּבֵית דִּין [6]וְכוֹתֶבֶת: ״לִמְזוֹנוֹת מָכַרְתִּי״. [7]וּגְרוּשָׁה לֹא תִּמְכּוֹר אֶלָּא בְּבֵית דִּין.

גמרא [8]מַתְנִיתִין מַנִּי? [9]רַבִּי שִׁמְעוֹן הִיא, [10]דְּתַנְיָא: ״מָכְרָה כְּתוּבָּתָהּ, [11]מִשְׁכְּנָה כְּתוּבָּתָהּ, [12]עָשְׂתָה כְּתוּבָּתָהּ אַפּוֹתֵיקִי לְאַחֵר, [13]אֵין לָהּ מְזוֹנוֹת. [14]דִּבְרֵי רַבִּי מֵאִיר. [15]רַבִּי שִׁמְעוֹן אוֹמֵר: אַף עַל פִּי שֶׁלֹּא מָכְרָה וְלֹא מִשְׁכְּנָה כְּתוּבָּתָהּ אֶלָּא מֶחֱצִיתָהּ, [16]אִבְּדָה מְזוֹנוֹתֶיהָ.

LITERAL TRANSLATION

[1]or a portion of it, [2][or if] she gave her ketubah or a portion of it to another person, she may not sell the remainder [of her ketubah], except in court. [3]But the Sages say: [4]She may sell [property], even four or five times. [5]And she may sell [property] for [her] maintenance without a court [6]and writes: "I sold [these] for my maintenance." [7]But a divorcee may only sell in court.

GEMARA [8]Whose is our Mishnah? [9]It is Rabbi Shimon, [10]for it was taught: "[If] she sold her ketubah, [11][or if] she pledged her ketubah, [12][or if] she made her ketubah a pledge to another person, [13]she does not have maintenance. [14][These are] the words of Rabbi Meir. [15]Rabbi Shimon says: Even if she sold or only pledged only half of her ketubah, [16]she has lost her maintenance."

TRANSLATION AND COMMENTARY

[1]**or a portion of it** as security for a debt that she owed, [2]**or if she gave** the entire main part of **her ketubah** settlement **or a portion of it** as a gift **to another person,** [3]she **may sell** her husband's property to collect **the remainder,** the additional amounts or whatever is left of the main part of the ketubah settlement, but only under the supervision of **a court.** [4]**But the Sages** disagree and **say:** The widow **may repeatedly sell** her husband's property out of court, **even in four or five installments.** [5]**And** until she collects her entire ketubah settlement, **she may** also **sell** her husband's property **for her maintenance** on her own **without** the supervision of **a court.** [6]When a widow sells her husband's property for her maintenance, **she** should **write** in the bill of sale: **"I sold this** property **for my maintenance."** [7]**But a divorcee,** who is not entitled to maintenance, **may only sell** her husband's property for her ketubah settlement under the supervision of **a court.**

GEMARA מַתְנִיתִין מַנִּי [8]The Gemara asks: **Which Tanna's** view does the first part of **our Mishnah** follow? [9]And it answers: It reflects the opinion of **Rabbi Shimon,** [10]**for it was taught** in a Baraita: **"If a** widow **sold her** entire **ketubah** settlement, [11]**or if she pledged her** entire **ketubah** settlement as security for a debt, [12]**or if she made her** entire **ketubah** a specific pledge **for a debt** that she owed to **another person,** [13]**she is not entitled to maintenance** from her husband's property. But if she sold, pledged, or made only a portion of her ketubah settlement a specific pledge, she is still entitled to maintenance from her husband's property. [14]**This is the position of Rabbi Meir.** [15]**Rabbi Shimon** disagrees and **says: Even if** the widow **sold or pledged only half of her ketubah** settlement, [16]**she** already **forfeited her** right to **maintenance** from her husband's property. Therefore when she seeks to collect the rest of her ketubah settlement, she must sell the property under the supervision of a court."

RASHI

וחכמים אומרים מוכרת היא – לכתובתה, אפילו לפרקים. ואף על פי כן – מוכרת בינתיים למזונות שלא בבית דין. **וכותבת** – בשטר המכירה. **למזונות מכרתי** – משום עלה טובה, כדאמר לעיל. **וגרושה לא תמכור** – לכתובתה. **אלא בבית דין** – למאן דאמר טעמא משום אינו רוצה שתתבזה כו׳ – הא לא איכפת ליה, ודברי הכל היא. ולמאן דאוקי טעמא משום חינא הא – רבי שמעון היא.

גמרא מתניתין מני – תנא קמא דמתניתין. **מכרה כתובתה** – כולה, אין לה מזונות דברי רבי מאיר. אבל מכרה מקצתה – יש לה מזונות.

NOTES

נָתְנָה כְּתוּבָּתָהּ לְאַחֵר **She gave her ketubah settlement to another.** *Ran* and others wrote that it makes no difference to whom she gave the ketubah settlement. Even if she gave it as a gift to the orphans, legally she is seen has having given it away. The Jerusalem Talmud says that if she gave the ketubah settlement to the orphans by ceding it to them, she does receive maintenance, for one does not do her the injustice of denying her that right.

HALAKHAH

only a portion of it," following the opinion of the Sages, as explained in the Gemara. (*Rambam, Sefer Nashim, Hilkhot Ishut* 17:18; *Shulḥan Arukh, Even HaEzer* 103:1.)

מוֹכֶרֶת לִמְזוֹנוֹת שֶׁלֹּא בְּבֵית דִּין **She may sell for her maintenance without a court.** "A widow may sell her late husband's property for her maintenance out of court, and without a public announcement of the sale, provided that she sells the property under the supervision of three people who are experts at assessing the value of the property." (*Rambam, Sefer Nashim, Hilkhot Ishut* 18:20; *Shulḥan Arukh, Even HaEzer* 93:25.)

[1]לְמֵימְרָא, דְּרַבִּי שִׁמְעוֹן סָבַר דְּלָא אָמְרִינַן: [2]מִקְצָת כֶּסֶף כְּכָל כֶּסֶף, [3]וְרַבָּנַן סָבְרִי אָמְרִינַן: [4]מִקְצָת כֶּסֶף כְּכָל כֶּסֶף? [5]הָא אִיפְּכָא שָׁמְעִינַן לְהוּ, [6]דְּתַנְיָא: "'וְהוּא אִשָּׁה בִּבְתוּלֶיהָ' — [7]פְּרָט לְבוֹגֶרֶת שֶׁכָּלוּ בְּתוּלֶיהָ. [8]דִּבְרֵי רַבִּי מֵאִיר. [9]רַבִּי אֶלְעָזָר וְרַבִּי שִׁמְעוֹן מַכְשִׁירִין בְּבוֹגֶרֶת". [10]הָתָם בִּקְרָאֵי פְּלִיגִי. [11]רַבִּי מֵאִיר סָבַר: "בְּתוּלָה" — [12]אֲפִילּוּ מִקְצָת בְּתוּלִים. [13]"בְּתוּלֶיהָ" — [14]עַד דְּאִיכָּא כּוּלְּהוּ בְּתוּלִים. [15]"בִּבְתוּלֶיהָ" — [16]בִּכְדַרְכָּהּ אִין;

LITERAL TRANSLATION

[1]Is this to say that Rabbi Shimon maintains that we do not say: [2][Her being owed] part of the money is like [being owed] all of the money, [3]and the Sages maintain [that] we do say: [4][Her being owed] part of the money is like [her being owed] all of the money? [5]But surely we heard them [taking] the opposite [position], [6]for it was taught: "'And he [shall take] a wife in her virginity' — [7]to the exclusion of an adult woman whose virginity is diminished. [8][These are] the words of Rabbi Meir. [9]Rabbi Elazar and Rabbi Shimon allow an adult woman." [10]There they disagree about [expounding] the verses. [11]Rabbi Meir maintains: "A virgin" [means retaining] [12]even part of her virginity. [13]"Her virginity" [means] [14]until [she retains] all of her virginity. [15]"In her virginity" [means] [16]through vaginal (lit., "natural" intercourse) yes;

TRANSLATION AND COMMENTARY

לְמֵימְרָא [1]The Gemara now analyzes the positions of Rabbi Shimon and the Sages of our Mishnah in greater detail: **Is this to say that Rabbi Shimon maintains that we do not say** that a widow who is still entitled to [2]**part of** her ketubah settlement **money is** considered **as** if she were still entitled to **all of** her ketubah settlement **money?** This position implies that a widow who sold or pledged all of her ketubah settlement is no longer entitled to maintenance. [3]**And,** in contrast, does it mean that **the Rabbis** of the Mishnah **maintain that we do** indeed **say** that a widow who is still entitled to [4]**part of** her ketubah settlement **money is** considered **as** if she were still entitled to **all of** her ketubah settlement **money,** and therefore she is entitled to maintenance even if she has already sold or pledged a part of it? [5]**But** this interpretation of their dispute is difficult, for **surely we heard** from another Tannaitic source that Rabbi Shimon and his disputants **take opposite** stands, [6]**for it was taught** in a Baraita dealing with an entirely different subject: "It is written regarding the High Priest, (Leviticus 21:13): **'And he shall take a wife in her virginity.'** [7]This verse **excludes an adult** woman and means that the High Priest may not marry a girl who has already reached the age of twelve-and-a-half, at which point she considered a full adult. After that time her **virginity is diminished,** her hymen having undergone some physical degeneration during puberty. [8]**This is the position of Rabbi Meir.** [9]**Rabbi Elazar and Rabbi Shimon allow** the High Priest to marry **an adult woman."** Rabbi Shimon seems to be of the opinion that since an adult woman still retains part of her virginity she is considered a full virgin, which contradicts what he appears to maintain in our Mishnah, that a woman who still retains rights to part of her ketubah settlement does not retain rights to all of her ketubah settlement!

הָתָם [10]The Gemara answers: You may not compare these two issues, since **there** in the Baraita the Tannaim **disagree about** how to expound **the** Biblical **verse.** [11]**Rabbi Meir maintains** that had the verse stated: "He shall take a wife who is **a virgin** (בְּתוּלָה)," we would say that the High Priest may marry a woman [12]**even** if she has only **part of her virginity,** having reached full adulthood at the age of twelve-and-a-half, so that her virginity is diminished. [13]However, the verse speaks of **"her virginity** (בְּתוּלֶיהָ)," teaching that the High Priest may only take as his a wife a woman who still has [14]**all of her virginity,** a girl who has not yet reached the age of twelve-and-a-half. [15]And the extra letter *bet* ("in") in the expression **"in her virginity"** teaches that if the girl had engaged in sexual intercourse [16]**in the natural manner** (vaginal intercourse), she

RASHI

לא אמרינן מקצת כסף — מוהר הבתולות, שיש לה עדיין עליהם — הרי הוא ככולו, ויתן לה מזונות. פרט לבוגרת — ולא אמרינן מקצת בתולים ככל הבתולים. בתוליה — אי הוה כתיב "והוא אשה בתולה יקח". בבתוליה — במקום בתולים הקפיד הכתוב, אבל נבעלה שלא כדרכה, והיא נערה — כשרה לכהן גדול.

HALAKHAH

פְּרָט לְבוֹגֶרֶת **To the exclusion of a grown woman.** "The High Priest is bound by a positive commandment to marry a virgin who is a *na'arah* (a girl between the ages of twelve and twelve-and-a-half). But if she has reached full maturity at the age of twelve-and-a-half, she is forbidden to him," following Rabbi Meir, whose viewpoint is accepted as law in *Yevamot* 60a. (*Rambam, Sefer Kedushah, Hilkhot Issurei Bi'ah* 17:13.)

[1]שֶׁלֹּא כְּדַרְכָּהּ לָא. [2]רַבִּי אֶלְעָזָר וְרַבִּי שִׁמְעוֹן סָבְרִי: [3]״בְּתוּלָה״ — שְׁלֵמָה מַשְׁמַע. [4]״בְּתוּלֶיהָ״ — אֲפִילּוּ מִקְצָת בְּתוּלִים. [98A] [5]״בִּבְתוּלֶיהָ״ — שֶׁיְּהוּ כָּל בְּתוּלֶיהָ קַיָּימִין, [6]בֵּין בִּכְדַרְכָּהּ בֵּין שֶׁלֹּא כְּדַרְכָּהּ.

[7]הַהִיא אִיתְּתָא דְּתָפְסָה כָּסָא דְּכַסְפָּא בִּכְתוּבָּתָהּ, [8]קָתָבְעָה מְזוֹנֵי. [9]אֲתַאי לְקַמֵּיהּ דְּרָבָא, [10]אֲמַר לְהוּ לְיָתְמֵי: ״זִילוּ, הֲבוּ לָהּ מְזוֹנוֹת. [11]לֵית דְּחָשׁ לְהָא דְּרַבִּי שִׁמְעוֹן, [12]דְּאָמַר: לָא אָמְרִינַן: מִקְצָת כֶּסֶף כְּכָל כֶּסֶף״.

[13]שְׁלַח לֵיהּ רַבָּה בְּרֵיהּ דְּרָבָא לְרַב יוֹסֵף: מוֹכֶרֶת שֶׁלֹּא בְּבֵית דִּין, [14]צְרִיכָה שְׁבוּעָה, אוֹ אֵין צְרִיכָה שְׁבוּעָה?

LITERAL TRANSLATION

[1]through anal (lit., "unnatural" intercourse) no. [2]Rabbi Elazar and Rabbi Shimon maintain: [3]"A virgin" implies [retaining] full virginity. [4]"Her virginity" implies [retaining] even part of her virginity. [98A] [5]"In her virginity" [means] that all of her virginity exists, [6]whether [impaired] by vaginal (lit., "natural") [intercourse] or anal (lit., "unnatural") [intercourse].

[7][There was] a certain woman who seized a silver goblet for [a portion of] her ketubah, [8][and] she demanded her maintenance. [9]She came before Rava, [10][who] said to the orphans: "Go, give her maintenance. [11]There is nobody who is concerned about the [ruling] of Rabbi Shimon, [12]who said: We do not say: Part of the money is like all of the money."

[13]Rabbah the son of Rava sent to Rav Yosef: [If] she sells without a court, [14]does she require an oath, or does she not require an oath?

TRANSLATION AND COMMENTARY

is **indeed** unfit to marry the High Priest. [1]But if she had engaged in sexual intercourse **in an unnatural manner** (anal intercourse), she is **not** disqualified from marrying the High Priest. [2]**Rabbi Elazar and Rabbi Shimon** understand this verse differently. They **maintain** that had the verse stated: [3]"He shall take a wife who is **a virgin** (בְּתוּלָה)," this would have **implied** that the High Priest may only marry a woman who has **full virginity,** who has not yet reached the age of twelve-and-a-half, so that her hymen is still fully intact. [4]Therefore, the verse speaks of **"her virginity** (בְּתוּלֶיהָ)" teaching that the High Priest may marry a woman **even** if she has only **part of her virginity,** having reached full adulthood at the age of twelve-and-a-half, so her virginity is diminished. [98A] [5]And the expression **"in her virginity** (בִּבְתוּלֶיהָ)" teaches that the High Priest may only marry a woman if **all of her virginity exists** and she had not engaged in any type of sexual intercourse, [6]**whether vaginal or anal.** In any event, that Tannaitic disagreement about how to interpret Scripture has no bearing on the dispute in our Mishnah about part of a sum being regarded as full payment.

הַהִיא אִיתְּתָא [7]It was related that a widow **seized a silver goblet** that had belonged to her husband as partial payment **of her ketubah** settlement, [8]**and she** continued to **demand her maintenance** from his heirs, since she had not yet collected the entire amount. Her husband's heirs countered that she was no longer entitled to her maintenance, for she had already received a portion of her ketubah settlement. [9]The woman **came before Rava** for a ruling, and after hearing the case, [10]he **said to the heirs: "Go and give her the maintenance** that is due her, [11]for **nobody is concerned about the ruling of Rabbi Shimon,** [12]**who said** that **we do not say** that a widow who is still **owed part of** her ketubah **money is** considered **as** if she were still **owed all of** her ketubah **money."**

שְׁלַח לֵיהּ [13]**Rabbah the son of Rava sent Rav Yosef** the following question: **If** a widow **sells** her late husband's property on her own **without** the supervision of **a court,** [14]**is she required** to take **an** oath that she did not take more than what was due her, **or is she not required** to take such **an oath?**

RASHI

בתוליה קיימין – לענין בעילה, שלא נבעלה אפילו שלא כדרכה. **דתפסה כסא דכספא** – ולא היה בו שיעור כתובתה. **צריכה שבועה** – שלא גבתה יותר.

NOTES

לֵית דְּחָשׁ There is nobody who is concerned. *Ritva* explains that it was necessary for Rava to say this because, as was stated earlier, the anonymous Tanna of the Mishnah reflects the view of Rabbi Shimon, and so there was reason to say that the law should follow his position. Rava teaches that, notwithstanding, nobody accepts the viewpoint of Rabbi Shimon as law.

צְרִיכָה שְׁבוּעָה She requires an oath. The Rishonim disagree about the nature of this oath. Our commentary follows *Rashi,* who understands that the Gemara is asking

HALAKHAH

בֵּין בִּכְדַרְכָּהּ Whether in the natural manner. "A woman who engaged in sexual intercourse, whether in a natural (vaginal) manner or in an unnatural (anal) manner, is no longer regarded as a virgin, and therefore forbidden to the High Priest," following Rav in *Yevamot* 83b. (*Rambam, Sefer Kedushah, Hilkhot Issurei Bi'ah* 17:14.)

[1]וְתִבָּעֵי לָךְ הַכְרָזָה! [2]אֲמַר לֵיהּ: הַכְרָזָה לָא קָמִיבָּעֲיָא לִי, [3]דְּאָמַר רַבִּי זֵירָא אָמַר רַב נַחְמָן: [4]אַלְמָנָה שֶׁשָּׁמָה לְעַצְמָהּ לֹא עָשְׂתָה וְלֹא כְלוּם. [5]הֵיכִי דָּמֵי? [6]אִי דְּאַכְרוּז, [7]אַמַּאי לֹא עָשְׂתָה וְלֹא כְלוּם? [8]אֶלָּא לָאו דְּלָא אַכְרוּז, [9]וּלְעַצְמָהּ הוּא דְּלֹא עָשְׂתָה וְלֹא כְלוּם. [10]הָא לְאַחֵר מַה שֶּׁעָשְׂתָה עָשְׂתָה.

TRANSLATION AND COMMENTARY

וְתִבָּעֵי לָךְ הַכְרָזָה [1]Rav Yosef sent back the following reply: Why do you ask about an oath? **You should ask about an announcement** of sale! If a widow wishes to sell her husband's property on her own without the supervision of a court, it is necessary for there to be a public announcement of the sale in order to achieve the highest bid for the sale?

אֲמַר לֵיהּ [2]Rabbah **said to** Rav Yosef: I did not ask that question, because **I am not in doubt about an announcement** of sale, [3]**for Rabbi Zera said in the name of Rav Naḥman:** [4]If a **widow appraised** her husband's **property by herself,** and took it as payment of her ketubah settlement in accordance with her own evaluation, **she did nothing.** Her actions are not binding, and her husband's heirs can take back the property and pay her her ketubah settlement with money. Now, it may be asked: [5]**How do we** visualize the ruling of Rav Naḥman? [6]**If she** publicly **announced** the sale, and took the property at the price offered by the highest bidder, [7]**why did she do nothing?** She should be treated like any buyer, who would acquire the property with the highest bid. [8]**Rather, she did not** publicly **announce** the sale. [9]**And** Rav Naḥman ruled that if the widow took the property **for herself** for her ketubah settlement in accordance with her own appraisal of the property, **she did nothing.** [10]**But** it follows from this that if she sold it **to someone else, what she did, she did,** and the sale is valid, even without a public announcement. For that reason, Rabbah did not ask Rav Yosef about a public announcement.

LITERAL TRANSLATION

[1]And you should ask about an announcement [of sale]!

[2][Rava] said to him: I am not in doubt about an announcement [of sale], [3]for Rabbi Zera said in the name of Rav Naḥman: [4]A widow who appraised [the property] by herself did not do anything. [5]How so (lit., "What is it like")? [6]If she announced [the sale], [7]why did she not do anything? [8]Rather [say] it is if she did not announce, [9]and [if she took it] for herself she did not do anything. [10]But [if she sold it] to someone else, what she did, she did.

RASHI

ששמה לעצמה — לקחה שדה היתומים לעצמה בשומת כתובתה. **לא עשתה ולא כלום** — ואם רצו היתומים להגבותה מעות לאחר זמן — חוזרין ונוטלין אותה.

NOTES

whether the widow is required to take an oath that she did not take more than what was her due. *Tosafot* suggest that the Gemara is asking whether she must take an oath that she did not sell her late husband's property at a reduced price. The Rishonim ask: Since the widow is not permitted to sell her husband's property entirely on her own — for it must be assessed by three expert appraisers — why should there be any concern that she took more than her due or that she sold the property at less than its market value? *Ramban* answers that when a woman sells her husband's property without the court's supervision, three expert appraisers must assess the value of the property, but then the woman may sell it on her own. Thus, she might have found a buyer who purchased the property at more than its assessed value, giving her more than her due. There is no such concern when the woman sells her husband's property under the court's supervision. *Ramban* suggests that the Gemara is asking about an oath that the widow did not receive payment of her ketubah settlement during her husband's lifetime. Must she take that oath before she sells her husband's property, or can she sell it and then take the oath (see also *Rid*)?

וְתִבָּעֵי לָךְ הַכְרָזָה And you should ask about an announcement of sale. Some Rishonim explain Rav Yosef's question as follows: Since a public announcement of sale is required, it would have to be made before the woman takes her oath. Rabbah should first have asked about whether it is necessary for the widow to announce the

HALAKHAH

אַלְמָנָה שֶׁשָּׁמָה לְעַצְמָהּ A widow who appraised property by herself. "If a widow assessed her late husband's property on her own, and then took it for herself as payment of her ketubah settlement, her action is not valid, even if she publicly announced the sale," following the Gemara's conclusion. If three laymen assessed the property, her action is valid (*Rambam,* according to *Maggid Mishneh*). According to some authorities (*Tur,* following *Rabbenu Ḥananel*), her action is not valid unless the property was assessed by three authorized judges. (*Rambam, Sefer Nashim, Hilkhot Ishut* 17:14; *Shulḥan Arukh, Even HaEzer* 93:27-28; 103:5.)

הָא לְאַחֵר מַה שֶּׁעָשְׂתָה עָשְׂתָה But for someone else, what she did, she did. "If a widow sold some of her late husband's property on her own at the property's market price, the transaction is valid, and she must take the widow's oath," following the Gemara's conclusion. This ruling applies to movable goods, but if the widow sold landed property, the transaction is not valid unless the property was assessed by others, even three laymen (*Rashba*). According to some authorities (*Rosh*), a court must collect her ketubah settlement for her. *Rema* writes that according to some authorities (*Halakhot Gedolot, Ri Tov Elem*) even in the case of movable goods, the transaction

[1]לְעוֹלָם דְּאַכְרוּז, [2]וּדְאָמְרִי לָהּ: מַאן שָׁם לֵיךְ? [3]כִּי הַאי דְּהַהוּא גַּבְרָא דְּאַפְקִידוּ גַּבֵּיהּ כִּיסְתָא דְּיָתְמֵי. [4]אֲזַל שָׁמָהּ לְנַפְשֵׁיהּ בְּאַרְבַּע מְאָה זוּזֵי. [5]אִיַּיקַּר קָם בְּשִׁית מְאָה. [6]אֲתָא לְקַמֵּיהּ דְּרַבִּי אַמִי. [7]אֲמַר לֵיהּ: מַאן שָׁם לָךְ?

[8]וְהִלְכְתָא: צְרִיכָה שְׁבוּעָה [9]וְאֵינָהּ צְרִיכָה הַכְרָזָה.

משנה [10]אַלְמָנָה שֶׁהָיְתָה כְּתוּבָּתָהּ מָאתַיִם, וּמָכְרָה

LITERAL TRANSLATION

[1]In fact, [it is] when she announced [the sale], [2]and where they said to her: Who appraised [it] for you? [3]Like that man with whom were deposited corals [belonging] to orphans. [4]He went and appraised them for himself at four hundred zuz. [5]They appreciated in value to six hundred [zuz]. [6]He came before Rav Ammi, [7][who] said to him: Who appraised [it] for you?

[8]And the law is: She requires an oath, [9]and she does not require an announcement.

MISHNAH [10]A widow whose ketubah was two hundred [dinars] — [if] she sold [property]

RASHI

מאן שם ליך – ממי קבלת מכירה זו? לא מבית דין ולא מיתומין, לפיכך לא יצא הקרקע מרשות היתומין. אבל היכא דשמת לאחריני – נפק מרשות היורשין, שהרי נתנו לה חכמים רשות למכור. **כיסתא** = מספוא. לשון אחר: "כסיתא" גרס = עצי אלמוגים, שקורין קורא"ל.

TRANSLATION AND COMMENTARY

לְעוֹלָם דְּאַכְרוּז [1]The Gemara rejects this argument: **In fact,** Rav Naḥman could be dealing here with a widow who publicly **announced** the sale of her husband's property and offered it to the highest bidder, but in the end she took it as payment in accordance with her own highest bid. [2]In such a case **we say to her: Who appraised** the property **for you?** [3]This is **similar to** the incident involving **a man with whom were deposited corals belonging to orphans.** [4]The man had the corals **appraised by himself** before a layman's court **at four hundred zuz** and then bought them. [5]In the end, the corals **appreciated in value** so that they were now worth **six hundred zuz.** [6]The man **came before Rav Ammi** to ask him who is entitled to the profit, [7]and Rav Ammi **said to him: Who appraised** the corals **for you?** Since you appraised them by yourself, they remain in the orphans' possession, and the profit is theirs.

וְהִלְכְתָא [8]The Gemara concludes this discussion with a practical ruling: **And the law is:** A widow who sold her late husband's property on her own without the supervision of a court **is required** to take **an oath** that she did not take more than what was her due. [9]**But she is not required to announce** the sale and offer the property to the highest bidder.

MISHNAH אַלְמָנָה [10]If **a widow had a ketubah of two hundred dinars, and she sold** property belonging to

NOTES

sale. *Ra'ah* and *Ritva* add that the law regarding the oath is dependent upon the law regarding the announcement, because if the widow announced the sale of her husband's property, she should no longer be required to take an oath, since we know how much she received for the property.

מַאן שָׁם לֵיךְ? **Who appraised it for you?** The Rishonim disagree about how to understand this phrase. According to *Rashi* and *Tosafot,* this phrase should not be understood in its literal sense, but rather as follows: Who authorized you to take the property for yourself? For as *Rashi* understands the Gemara, the widow did not receive the property from the court, or from her husband's heirs (see also *Sefer Mikkaḥ U'Mimkar*). *Eshel Avraham* explains that although the widow is regarded in some respects as an agent of the court for the purpose of selling her late husband's property, she is authorized only to sell it, but not to take it.

The Geonim and *Rivan* understand the phrase according to its literal sense: Who appraised the property for you? Perhaps the property was worth more than the amount at which you appraised it, or perhaps the three appraisers who assessed the property were not precise in their appraisal, because they knew that you were planning to take the property.

הַהוּא גַּבְרָא דְּאַפְקִידוּ גַּבֵּיהּ **That man with whom were deposited.** The Rishonim note: Even when a deposit is liable to be ruined or to diminish in value, the bailee may not sell it without first receiving permission from the court, and even then he may not buy the property himself! How then could the bailee himself have bought the corals that had been entrusted to him? *Rabbi Crescas Vidal* suggests that the corals were entrusted to the bailee for the purpose of selling them on behalf of the orphans.

HALAKHAH

is only valid if the widow took her oath before selling the property. (*Rambam, Sefer Nashim, Hilkhot Ishut* 17:14; *Shulḥan Arukh, Even HaEzer* 96:5.)

אֵינָהּ צְרִיכָה הַכְרָזָה **She does not require an announcement.** "If a widow sells some of her late husband's property for her ketubah settlement without the court's supervision, she is not required to announce the sale, but the property must be assessed by three expert appraisers," following the Gemara's conclusion. (*Rambam, Sefer Nashim, Hilkhot Ishut* 17:13; *Shulḥan Arukh, Even HaEzer* 103:1.)

מָכְרָה שָׁוֶה מָנֶה בְּמָאתַיִם **If she sold a maneh's worth of property for two hundred.** "If a woman had a ketubah of two hundred dinars, and she sold property belonging to her husband's estate that was worth only a maneh for two

[1] שָׁוֶה מָנֶה בְּמָאתַיִם אוֹ שָׁוֶה מָאתַיִם בְּמָנֶה — נִתְקַבְּלָה כְּתוּבָּתָהּ.

[2] הָיְתָה כְּתוּבָּתָהּ מָנֶה, וּמָכְרָה שָׁוֶה מָנֶה וְדִינָר בְּמָנֶה — מִכְרָהּ בָּטֵל. [3] אֲפִילּוּ הִיא אוֹמֶרֶת: "אַחֲזִיר דִּינָר לַיּוֹרְשִׁין", מִכְרָהּ בָּטֵל.

[4] רַבִּי שִׁמְעוֹן בֶּן גַּמְלִיאֵל אוֹמֵר: לְעוֹלָם מִכְרָהּ קַיָּים, [5] עַד שֶׁתְּהֵא שָׁם כְּדֵי שֶׁתְּשַׁיֵּיר [6] בְּשָׂדֶה בַּת תִּשְׁעָה קַבִּין, [7] וּבְגִנָּה בַּת חֲצִי קַב, [8] וּכְדִבְרֵי רַבִּי עֲקִיבָא בֵּית רוֹבַע.

[9] הָיְתָה כְּתוּבָּתָהּ אַרְבַּע מֵאוֹת זוּז, וּמָכְרָה לָזֶה בְּמָנֶה

LITERAL TRANSLATION

worth a maneh for two hundred [dinars], or [property] worth two hundred [dinars] for a maneh, [1] she has received her ketubah.

[2] [If] her ketubah was a maneh, and she sold [property worth] a maneh and a dinar for a maneh, the sale is invalid. [3] Even if she said: "I will return a dinar to the heirs," the sale is invalid.

[4] Rabban Shimon ben Gamliel says: In fact, the sale is valid, [5] unless there is [an undervaluation] leaving [6] [an area] of nine *kavs* in a field, [7] or [an area] of half a *kav* in a garden, [8] and according to Rabbi Akiva, [an area] of a quarter of a *kav*.

[9] [If] her ketubah was four hundred zuz, and she sold [property] for a maneh to one person,

TRANSLATION AND COMMENTARY

her husband's estate that was **worth** only **a maneh** (one hundred dinars) **for two hundred** dinars, **or** she sold property that was **worth two hundred** dinars **for** only **a maneh**, [1] **she** is regarded as having **received her** entire **ketubah** settlement, and she cannot present her husband's heirs with any further claim.

הָיְתָה כְּתוּבָּתָהּ מָנֶה [2] If the widow **had a ketubah of a maneh, and she sold** property belonging to her husband's estate that was **worth a maneh and a dinar for a maneh, the sale is invalid,** for the woman only has a right to sell property up to the value of her ketubah, and she sold property that was worth a dinar more than her entitlement. [3] **Even if** the woman **said: "I will return the** extra **dinar to the heirs," the sale is invalid.**

רַבִּי שִׁמְעוֹן בֶּן גַּמְלִיאֵל [4] **Rabban Shimon ben Gamliel** disagrees and **says: In fact, the sale is valid,** [5] **unless** the undervaluation of the property **was so large that** were it not for the error, **there would be left** in the hands of the heirs a plot which would by itself be fit to be tilled. [6] **In** the case of **a** grain **field,** this is **an area** that is fit for the sowing **of nine** *kavs* of seed (3750 square cubits), the minimum size of a grain field that is fit to be tilled, [7] **or in** the case of **a** vegetable **garden,** an area that is fit for the sowing **of half a** *kav* of seed (208 1/3 square cubits), the minimum size of a vegetable garden that is fit to be tilled, [8] **and according to Rabbi Akiva, an area** that is fit for the sowing **of a quarter** *kav* of seed (104 1/6 square cubits).

הָיְתָה כְּתוּבָּתָהּ [9] If the widow **had a ketubah of four hundred zuz, and she sold** property belonging to her husband's estate to four different people, **to one** she sold property worth a maneh **for a maneh,**

BACKGROUND

שָׂדֶה בַּת תִּשְׁעָה קַבִּין **An area of nine** ***kavs.*** Land measurement in the Talmud was based on an estimate of the area of a field which could be sown with a certain quantity of wheat. One *bat se'ah,* the area that could be sown with a *se'ah* of seeds, equalled 2,500 square cubits. Consequently, depending on varying estimates of the cubit, the area of *bat tish'a kabin,* the area that could be sown with nine *kabin* of seeds, was 950-1400 square meters, and the area of *bat ḥatzi kav,* the area that could be sown with half a *kav,* was 50-60 square meters, and *beit rova,* a quarter *kav,* was half of that.

RASHI

משנה שוה מאתים במנה נתקבלה כתובתה — דאמרינן לה: את אפסדת.

מכרה בטל — שאותו דינר אין לה רשות למכור, נמצא שכל המכר טעות, שהרי בבת אחת היה. **לעולם מכרה קיים** — והיא תחזיר את הדינר ליורשין, דמה הפסידתן. **עד שיהא** — באונאה, כדי שאילו לא היתה האונאה היה משתייר בשדה בת תשעה קבין, או האונאה עצמה תשעה קבין. והוא הדין אם נשאר ליתומים שם לבד האונאה תשעה קבין. דכיון דיש ליתומים קרקע שם כשיעור שדה — יאמרו לה: אין רצוננו למכור קרקע הראוי לנו. אבל אם אין האונאה ראויה להצטרף לכדי שדה — לא הפסידתן כלום. **ובגנה בת חצי קב** — שזה שיעור גנה. **וכדברי רבי עקיבא** — ששמענו ממנו במקום אחר: בבית רובע הוא שיעור גנה.

NOTES

שָׁוֶה מָנֶה בְּמָאתַיִם **Property worth a maneh for two hundred dinars.** The Jerusalem Talmud asks: If the widow sold property worth a maneh for two hundred dinars, why should she be regarded as having received her entire ketubah? Surely, the buyer can cancel the purchase on the grounds that he had overpaid for the property, and so the purchase had been made in error. The Jerusalem Talmud answers that the property appreciated in value after the

HALAKHAH

hundred dinars, or she sold property that was worth two hundred dinars for only a maneh, she is regarded as having received her entire ketubah settlement." (*Rambam, Sefer Nashim, Hilkhot Ishut* 17:15; *Shulḥan Arukh, Even HaEzer* 103:6.)

מָכְרָה שָׁוֶה מָנֶה וְדִינָר בְּמָנֶה **If she sold a maneh and a dinar's worth of property for a maneh.** "If a woman had a ketubah of a maneh, and she sold property belonging to her husband's estate that was worth a maneh and a dinar for a maneh, the sale is invalid, even if the woman is willing to return the extra dinar to the heirs," following the anonymous first Tanna of the Mishnah. (*Rambam, Sefer Nashim, Hilkhot Ishut* 17:15; *Shulḥan Arukh, Even HaEzer* 103:7.)

הָיְתָה כְּתוּבָּתָהּ אַרְבַּע מֵאוֹת זוּז **If her ketubah was four hundred zuz.** "If a woman had a ketubah of four hundred dinars, and she sold property belonging to her husband's estate to four different people, selling property to the first

TRANSLATION AND COMMENTARY

to another person she sold property worth a maneh **for a maneh,** and so on, [1]**and to the last** she sold property worth **a maneh and a dinar for a maneh — the sale** made to the **last** buyer **is invalid** (following the anonymous first Tanna of the Mishnah), [2]**but the sales** made to **all the rest of them are valid,** for each sale is a separate transaction.

GEMARA מַאי שְׁנָא [3]The Gemara raises a question about the Mishnah's first ruling: **What is the difference** between the first two cases in the Mishnah that caused the Tanna to take seemingly opposite stands in forming his ruling? If a widow sold **property worth two hundred** dinars **for a maneh** the Mishnah teaches that the heirs can **say to** her: "You have no further claim to your ketubah settlement, for you already took from the estate what was due you, and [4]**you caused** yourself **a loss** by selling the property below value." [5]Why then, if the widow sold **property worth a maneh for two hundred** dinars, [6]**should** she not **be able to say** to the heirs: "I am entitled to another hundred dinars, for I took property worth only a maneh and it was I who **caused the profit,** and so that extra money should belong to me, and not count as payment of by ketubah."

אָמַר [7]**Rav Naḥman said in the name of Rabbah bar Avuha:** [98B] [8]**Here** in our Mishnah **Rabbi Yehudah HaNasi taught** us the principle: If someone sent an agent to purchase merchandise on his behalf, and the agent purchased the merchandise for less than what his principal was ready to spend, [9]**all** of the profit goes **to** the principal, **the owner of the money.** The agent cannot argue that his business acumen was responsible for the gain, so he should receive the profit. This matter is the subject of a Tannaitic dispute, [10]**as it was taught** in a Baraita: If someone sent an agent to purchase merchandise on his behalf at a certain price, and the seller **gave** the agent **one more piece of merchandise** than the price would have ordinarily warranted, [11]**all** of the profit goes **to the agent;** [12]**this is the position of Rabbi Yehudah.**

וְלָזֶה בְּמָנֶה, [1]וְלָאַחֲרוֹן יָפֶה מָנֶה וְדִינָר בְּמָנֶה, [2]שֶׁל אַחֲרוֹן — בָּטֵל, [3]וְשֶׁל כּוּלָּן — מִכְרָן קַיָּים.

גמרא [4]מַאי שְׁנָא שָׁוֶה מָאתַיִם בְּמָנֶה? דְּאָמְרִי לָהּ: [5]"אַתְּ אַפְסַדְתְּ". [6]שָׁוֶה מָנֶה בְּמָאתַיִם נַמִי, [7]תֵּימָא: "אֲנָא אַרְוַוחְנָא"!

[8]אֲמַר רַב נַחְמָן אֲמַר רַבָּה בַּר אֲבוּהּ: [98B] [9]כָּאן שָׁנָה רַבִּי: [10]הַכֹּל לְבַעַל הַמָּעוֹת. [11]כִּדְתַנְיָא: "הוֹסִיפוּ לוֹ אַחַת יְתֵירָה, [12]הַכֹּל לַשָּׁלִיחַ. [13]דִּבְרֵי

LITERAL TRANSLATION

and [property] for a maneh to another [and so on] [1]and to the last person a maneh and a dinar for a maneh — [2]the last one's [sale] is invalid, [3]but the sale of all [the rest] of them is valid.

GEMARA [4]Why is [the sale of] two hundred [dinars'] worth [of property] for a maneh different, that they say to her: [5]"You caused the loss." [6]A maneh's worth [of property] for two hundred also, [7]let her say: "I caused the profit"!

[8]Rav Naḥman said in the name of Rabbah bar Avuha: [98B] [9]Here Rabbi taught: [10]All [profits belong] to the owner of the money. [11]As it was taught: "[If] they added for [the agent] one extra [bit of merchandise], [12]it is all for the agent. [13][These are] the words

RASHI

כאן שנה רבי — במשנתינו למדנו רבי. **הכל לבעל המעות** — השולח שלוחו לשוק לסחורה ולקח בזול — הכל לבעל המעות, ולא מצי למימר אנא ארווחי. **כדתניא** — דאיכא פלוגתא דתנאי בהא מילתא, ומסקנא שמעינן דבדבר שאין לו קצבה אית ליה לרבי יוסי: הכל לבעל המעות. וסתם לן רבי במתניתין דהלכה — כרבי יוסי. **דמתניתין נמי** — דבר שאין לו קצבה הוא, דכל קרקע נמכר באומד, זה בפחות וזה ביוקר. **הוסיפו לו אחת יתירה** — בתוספתא דמסכת דמאי היא.

NOTES

sale and is now worth two hundred dinars. The buyer then has no reason to retract from his purchase. Resh Lakish argues that the sale is binding, and the buyer cannot retract, because the laws of *ona'ah* (overpaying) do not apply to the sale of land.

שֶׁל אַחֲרוֹן — בָּטֵל The last one's sale is invalid. Note that only if the widow sold property worth a maneh and a dinar for a maneh to the last buyer is the sale invalid. For at that point she only had the right to sell property worth a maneh, and when she sold property worth a maneh and a dinar, she was selling property belonging to the heirs. But if the widow sold property worth a maneh and a dinar for a maneh to one of the first three buyers, the sale is valid, and she is regarded as having received payment towards her ketubah of a maneh and a dinar. (This would be legally identical to the sale of property worth two hundred dinars for a maneh, regarding which we said earlier in the Mishnah that the sale is valid, and the woman is regarded as having received two hundred dinars of her ketubah.) (*Rivan, Meiri.*)

HALAKHAH

buyer worth a maneh for a maneh, and so to the second, and so to the third, but to the fourth buyer she sold property worth a maneh and a dinar for a maneh, the first three sales are valid, but the fourth sale is invalid," following the Mishnah. (*Rambam, Sefer Nashim, Hilkhot Ishut* 17:16; *Shulḥan Arukh, Even HaEzer* 103:8.)

TRANSLATION AND COMMENTARY

[1] **Rabbi Yose** disagrees and **says:** The principal and the agent **divide** the profit between them."

וְהָתַנְיָא [2] The Gemara asks: **But surely** the position of Rabbi Yose **was taught** otherwise in a different Baraita: **"Rabbi Yose says:** [3] **All** of the profit goes **to** the principal, **the owner of the money."**

אֲמַר רָמִי בַּר חָמָא [4] **Rami bar Ḥama says: There is** really **no difficulty.** [5] **Here,** in the first Baraita, we are dealing **with something that has a fixed price.** If the seller added extra merchandise to the sale, we assume that the extra merchandise was also valued at that fixed price, but was given as a gift. Because it is not clear whether the seller meant the gift to go to the principal or to his agent, they divide it between them. But **there,** in the second Baraita, we are dealing **with something that does not have a fixed price,** and is sold for its approximate value. Here too in our Mishnah, when the widow sells her husband's land for her ketubah settlement, and the purchaser bought a maneh worth of land for two hundred dinars, he did not intend to give the extra maneh as a gift to the widow. Rather he was buying the property at an inflated price and the extra money belongs to the principal, the heirs, who can designate it to pay the remaining hundred dinars of the widow's ketubah settlement.

רַבִּי יְהוּדָה. [1] רַבִּי יוֹסֵי אוֹמֵר: חוֹלְקִין״.
[2] וְהָתַנְיָא: ״רַבִּי יוֹסֵי אוֹמֵר: [3] הַכֹּל לְבַעַל הַמָּעוֹת״.
[4] אֲמַר רָמִי בַּר חָמָא: לָא קַשְׁיָא.
[5] כָּאן בְּדָבָר שֶׁיֵּשׁ לוֹ קִצְבָּה, כָּאן בְּדָבָר שֶׁאֵין לוֹ קִצְבָּה.

LITERAL TRANSLATION

of Rabbi Yehudah. [1] Rabbi Yose says: They divide." [2] But surely it was taught: "Rabbi Yose says: [3] All [profits belong] to the owner of the money." [4] Rami bar Ḥama says: There is no difficulty. [5] Here [it refers] to something that has a fixed price, here to something that has no fixed price.

RASHI

שיש לו קצבה — כגון קטנית הנמכר בחנות במדה, מלא כלי בפרוטה. אם הוסיפו אחת יתירה — חולקין, דמתנה הואי; יש לומר לשליח נתנה, ויש לומר לבעל מעות נתנה. דבר שאין לו קצבה — כגון טלית וחלוק וירק הנמכרים באומד, פעמים מוותר למכור בזול ופעמים בלמלוס — הכל לבעל מעות, שאין כאן מתנה אלא מכר.

NOTES

חוֹלְקִין **They divide.** The Rishonim disagree about why, according to Rabbi Yose, the principal and agent divide the extra merchandise. Our commentary follows *Rashi, Rivan, Ramban,* and others, who explain that since we assume that the seller intended to give the extra merchandise as a gift, and we do not know whether he gave it to the principal or to the agent, the extra merchandise is divided between the two parties. But according to the Geonim and *Rif* , even if we assume that the seller gave the extra merchandise to the agent, he must still divide the profit, because had the principal not sent the agent to purchase merchandise, he would not have received the gift. The two are therefore regarded as partners regarding the extra merchandise. There are various practical differences between the two explanations. If the seller stated explicitly that he was giving the extra merchandise as a gift to the agent, or if the seller gave the agent extra merchandise because of a pricing error on his part (assuming that the error does not nullify the transaction), or if the agent misled the seller and said that he was purchasing it for himself — according to *Rashi,* the entire profit goes to the agent, for the seller surely did not wish the extra merchandise to be given as a gift to the principal. But according to the Geonim and *Rif,* the agent must divide the extra merchandise with his principal, for he would not have made any profit had he not been acting as his agent. The Aḥaronim note that the Jerusalem Talmud (*Demai* 6:8) supports *Rif.*

Taz raises a question according to *Rashi's* explanation: If a doubt exists as to whom the seller wished to give the extra merchandise, the agent should not have to share it with his principal, for the extra merchandise is now in the agent's possession, and a person is assumed to have rightful title to any property in his possession! *Taz* answers that since there are grounds to say that all of the extra merchandise should go to the principal, there is no presumption that the agent has rightful title to that merchandise, even when in his possession. The argument put forward in *Taz*'s question might explain the position of Rabbi Yehudah that all of the profit goes to the agent.

דָּבָר שֶׁיֵּשׁ לוֹ קִצְבָּה **Something that has a fixed price.** According to *Rav Hai Gaon,* "something that has a fixed price" refers to movable goods, and "something that does not have a fixed price" refers to land, for as we learned elsewhere, the laws of *ona'ah* (overcharging) do not apply to land, because it does not have a fixed price. Our commentary follows *Rashi, Rif,* and most Rishonim, who explain that the phrase "something that has a fixed price," refers to merchandise that is sold at a set price per unit,

HALAKHAH

דָּבָר שֶׁיֵּשׁ לוֹ קִצְבָּה **Something that has a fixed price.** "If someone sent an agent to purchase merchandise that has a fixed price per unit, and the seller added extra merchandise to the sale, the extra merchandise is divided between the principal and the agent. If he sent the agent to purchase merchandise that does not have a set price per unit, all of the extra merchandise added to the sale by the seller belongs to the agent," following Rav Pappa. *Rema* (following *Ramban* and *Ran*) writes that if the seller stated explicitly that he was giving the extra merchandise to the agent, then all the extra merchandise belongs to the agent, even if the merchandise has a set price (see also *Sma, Shakh,* and *Taz,* who disagree with *Rema*'s ruling). (*Rambam, Sefer Kinyan, Hilkhot Sheluḥin* 1:4; *Shulḥan Arukh, Ḥoshen Mishpat* 183:6.)

TRANSLATION AND COMMENTARY

אָמַר רַב פַּפָּא [1]**Rav Pappa said: The law is:** [2]**When** the merchandise is **something that has a fixed** market **price,** the principal and the agent **divide** the profit between them, [3]and if it is **something that does not have a set** market **price, all** the profit goes **to** the principal, **the owner of the money.**

מַאי קָא מַשְׁמַע לָן [4]The Gemara asks: **What does** Rav Pappa **teach us?** Surely this is what Rami bar Ḥama just taught us!

שִׁינּוּיָא [5]The Gemara answers: Rav Pappa teaches us that **the answer proposed** by Rami bar Ḥama to the Gemara's question **is a** satisfactory **answer,** and so it may serve as the basis for a practical Halakhic decision.

אִיבַּעְיָא לְהוּ [6]**The following question arose** in discussion among the Sages: **If one said to his agent:** [7]**"Sell for me a** ***letekh*** of my land (a *letekh* being an area equivalent to half a *kor*)," [8]**and the** agent **went and sold for him an** entire ***kor*** of his land, **what is the law?** The sale of the second *letekh,* which was sold without the owner's authorization, is certainly not valid. But what about the first *letekh*? The Gemara explains the two sides of the question: Do we say that the agent is regarded as having only [9]**added to what** his principal **had instructed,** [10]**but the sale of a** ***letekh*** of land, which was done in accordance with his mandate, **was nevertheless valid?** [11]**Or** do we say **perhaps** that since the agent exceeded his authority, he is regarded as having **violated** his **instructions?** [12]Thus, **even** the sale of **the** ***letekh*** of land **would not be valid.**

אָמַר רַב יַעֲקֹב [13]**Rav Ya'akov from Nehar Pekod said in the name of Ravina:** [14]**Come and hear** a resolution to this problem from a Mishnah dealing with the subject of *me'ilah,* the misappropriation of consecrated property (*Me'ilah* 6:1): [15]**"If someone said to his agent: 'Give** one **piece** of meat **to** each of **my guests,'** [16]**and** the agent **said** to the guests: 'Each of you should **take two** pieces of meat,' [17]**and** the guests **took three** pieces of meat each, and it turned out that the meat that they had eaten was consecrated property, **all of them are guilty of** ***me'ilah.*** The host is guilty, because he instructed the agent to give the guests the first piece; the agent is guilty, because he told the guests to take a second piece; and the guests are guilty, because they took a third piece on their own." The Gemara now explains how this Mishnah resolves the

LITERAL TRANSLATION

[1]Rav Pappa said: The law is: [2][When] something has a fixed price, they divide. [3][When] something does not have a fixed price, all [profits belong] to the owner of the money.

[4]What does [Rav Pappa] teach us?

[5][That] the answer that we answered is an answer.

[6]It was asked of them: [If] one said to [his agent]: [7]"Sell for me a *letekh,*" [8]and he went and sold for him a *kor,* what [is the law]? [9]He [merely] added to [the owner's] instructions, [10]and the *letekh* was at all events acquired. [11]Or perhaps, he violated [the owner's] instructions, [12]and even the *letekh* was not acquired.

[13]Rav Ya'akov from Nehar Pekod said in the name of Ravina: [14]Come [and] hear: [15]"If the host said to his agent: 'Give a piece to the guests,' [16]and he said: 'Take two,' [17]and they took three — all of them are guilty of *me'ilah.*"

[1]אֲמַר רַב פַּפָּא: הִלְכְתָא: [2]דָּבָר שֶׁיֵּשׁ לוֹ קִצְבָּה, חוֹלְקִין. [3]דָּבָר שֶׁאֵין לוֹ קִצְבָּה, הַכֹּל לְבַעַל הַמָּעוֹת.

[4]מַאי קָא מַשְׁמַע לָן?

[5]שִׁינּוּיָא דְּשַׁנֵּינַן שִׁינּוּיָא הוּא.

[6]אִיבַּעְיָא לְהוּ: אֲמַר לֵיהּ: [7]"זַבֵּין לִי לִיתְכָא", [8]וַאֲזַל וְזַבֵּין לֵיהּ כּוֹרָא, מַאי? [9]מוֹסִיף עַל דְּבָרָיו הוּא, [10]וְלִיתְכָא מִיהָא קָנֵי. [11]אוֹ דִלְמָא, מַעֲבִיר עַל דְּבָרָיו הוּא, [12]וְלִיתְכָא נַמִי לָא קָנֵי?

[13]אֲמַר רַב יַעֲקֹב מִנְּהַר פְּקוֹד מִשְּׁמֵיהּ דְּרָבִינָא: [14]תָּא שְׁמַע: [15]"אָמַר בַּעַל הַבַּיִת לִשְׁלוּחוֹ: 'תֵּן לָהֶן חֲתִיכָה לָאוֹרְחִין', [16]וְהוּא אוֹמֵר: 'טְלוּ שְׁתַּיִם', [17]וְהֵן נָטְלוּ שָׁלֹשׁ — כּוּלָּן מָעֲלוּ".

RASHI

אמר ליה זבין לי ליתכא — אמר לשלוחו: מכור משדותי בית חצי כור. **וליתכא מיהא קני** — לוקח, ואם בא בעל הבית לחזור — אינו חוזר. **תן להם חתיכה** — חתיכה מבשר שיש לי בכלי. **והוא אמר להם טלו שתים** — שתים כל אחד מכם. **והם נטלו שלש** — ולבסוף נמצא בשר של הקדש. **כולן מעלו** — בעל הבית מעל — שהאחת היתה מדעתו, והשליח מעל בשניה, והאורחין בשלישית.

NOTES

so that if the seller gave the agent more merchandise than the purchase price would have warranted, the extra merchandise is presumed to have been a gift, whereas "something that does not have a fixed price" refers to merchandise that is sold after the parties bargain, so that no presumption can be made that any of the merchandise was intended as a gift.

HALAKHAH

תֵּן לָהֶן חֲתִיכָה לָאוֹרְחִין Give a piece to the guests. "If someone said to his agent: 'Give a piece of meat to each of my guests,' and the agent told them each to take two pieces, and the meat they had taken proved to be consecrated property, the sender is guilty of *me'ilah,* but the agent is exempt, for he is regarded as having violated his

CONCEPTS

מְעִילָה ***Me'ilah.*** The laws regarding the unintentional, unlawful use of consecrated property, are written in abbreviated form in Scripture (Leviticus 5:14-16), and expanded upon greatly in tractate *Me'ilah.* Anyone who benefits from consecrated property or damages it though use is guilty of *me'ilah.* The intentional, unlawful use of consecrated property, a different offence, is a severe sin punishable by death at the hand of Heaven, according to some authorities, and by lashes, according to others. One who commits *me'ilah* even under duress, must repay the Temple for the loss he caused or the benefit he gained, plus a fine of one-fifth of the value of the loss or of the benefit he gained. He must also bring a special sacrifice, a guilt-offering for trespass. *Me'ilah* is a special case regarding which the rule that "there is no agency for crime" does not apply. If someone commits a crime at the behest of someone else, only the person who actually committed the deed is liable for punishment. In the case of *me'ilah,* however, if an agent was sent by someone else to make use of property which turned out to be consecrated, the sender is the one who transgressed. However, the sender is only liable if the agent fulfilled his agency as instructed. If the agent deviated from his instructions, it is he, and not his sender, who is guilty of *me'ilah.*

[1]אִי אָמְרַתְּ בִּשְׁלָמָא מוֹסִיף עַל דְּבָרָיו הָוֵי, [2]מִשּׁוּם הָכִי בַּעַל הַבַּיִת מָעַל. [3]אֶלָּא אִי אָמְרַתְּ מַעֲבִיר עַל דְּבָרָיו הָוֵי, [4]בַּעַל הַבַּיִת אַמַּאי מָעַל? [5]וְהָתְנַן: ״הַשָּׁלִיחַ שֶׁעָשָׂה שְׁלִיחוּתוֹ, בַּעַל הַבַּיִת מָעַל. [6]לֹא עָשָׂה שְׁלִיחוּתוֹ, שָׁלִיחַ מָעַל״. [7]הָכָא בְּמַאי עָסְקִינַן? דַּאֲמַר לְהוּ: [8]״טְלוּ אַחַת מִדַּעְתּוֹ שֶׁל בַּעַל הַבַּיִת וְאַחַת מִדַּעְתִּי״, [9]וּשְׁקַלוּ אִינְהוּ תְּלָת.

LITERAL TRANSLATION

[1]Granted if you say [that] he added to his instructions, [2]this is why the host is guilty of *me'ilah.* [3]But if you say [that] he violated his instructions, [4]why is the host guilty of *me'ilah?* [5]Surely we have learned: "[If] the agent performed his agency, the host is guilty of *me'ilah.* [6]If he did not perform his agency, the agent is guilty of *me'ilah.*"

[7]What are we dealing with here? When he said to them: [8]"Take one with the consent of the host, and one with my consent," [9]and they took three.

RASHI

אחת מדעת בעל הבית — והרי עשה בה שליחותו.

TRANSLATION AND COMMENTARY

problem that was raised above. [1]**Granted if you say** that an agent who exceeded his authority is regarded as merely having **added to what** his principal **had told** him to do, [2]we understand **why** the Mishnah rules that **the host is guilty of *me'ilah,*** for regarding the first piece of meat, the agent is viewed as having performed his agency. The law of agency, in the case of *me'ilah*, differs from agencies to commit other transgressions such as theft or murder in which we rule that there is no agency to commit a transgression. The agent who commits a crime is acting on his own and bears all moral and legal responsibility for his deed. However, regarding *me'ilah,* the sender is himself guilty of the transgression if his agent misappropriated consecrated property as he instructed. [3]**But if you say** that an agent who exceeded his authority is regarded as having **negated his** principal's **instructions** and was acting on his own, [4]**why is the sender guilty of *me'ilah?*** [5]**Surely we learned** in that very same Mishnah: **"If the host** unintentionally gave an agent instructions about giving consecrated property to guests, and **the agent performed his agency** exactly as instructed, **the host is guilty of *me'ilah.*** [6]But **if** the agent **did not perform his agency** and deviated from his sender's instructions such as giving a piece of liver to the guests rather than a piece of ordinary meat, it is **the agent,** and not his sender, who **is guilty of *me'ilah.*"**

הָכָא בְּמַאי עָסְקִינַן [7]The Gemara rejects this argument: **There** in the Mishnah in *Me'ilah* the agent **said to** each of the guests: [8]**"Take one** piece of meat **with the consent of** your **host, and** take **one** piece **with my consent,"** [9]**and** the guests **took three** pieces of meat. In such a case, we surely say that agent fulfilled the host's agency regarding the first piece of meat, and that he clearly added to his agency and acted on his own authority when he told the guests to take the second piece. Therefore, the sender is liable for *me'ilah.* But if an agent exceeded his authority without stating explicitly that he was acting on his own for this additional act, we are still in doubt whether the agent was acting for the principal with respect to his original charge or he had violated his instructions.

NOTES

בַּעַל הַבַּיִת אַמַּאי מָעַל **Why is the host guilty of *me'ilah.*** *Ritva* and others ask (see also *Tosafot*): Why does the Gemara only ask about the sender? The same question could have been asked with regard to the agent. If an agent who exceeded his authority is regarded as having violated his commission, why is the agent guilty of *me'ilah?* Surely, the agent told the guest to take two, and the guest, acting on his own, took three! He answers that the Gemara could indeed have asked about the agent as well, but it would then have given an answer similar to that given for the sender.

The Jerusalem Talmud points out a contradiction between the law applying to *me'ilah* of consecrated things and the law applying to *terumah.* Regarding *terumah*, if an agent sets aside a larger percentage of the produce as *terumah* than he had been instructed to put away, none of the produce he separated is considered as *terumah.* Why then is the sender guilty of *me'ilah* if his agent added to his instructions and gave the guest more than what he had been instructed? It answers that regarding *terumah*, the grain set aside in accordance with the sender's instructions and that set aside by the agent on his own were mixed together, and so his separation of the *terumah* is entirely void. But regarding our case of *me'ilah,* we are dealing with separate pieces of meat. The piece that had been given to the guest on the principal's authority can be seen as having been given in accordance with his instructions, so he is liable for *me'ilah.*

וְאַחַת מִדַּעְתִּי **And one with my consent.** *Rambam* rules that if the principal told the agent to give one piece to the guest, and the agent told the guest to take two pieces, the principal is liable for *me'ilah,* but not the agent. An

HALAKHAH

agency. If the agent told each of the guests to take two pieces on his own initiative, both the sender and his agent are guilty of *me'ilah.* If in such a case each of the guests took three pieces, all three are guilty of *me'ilah* — the sender, his agent, and the guests" (see *Kesef Mishneh* who explains the Gemara according to *Rambam*). (*Rambam, Sefer Avodah, Hilkhot Me'ilah* 7:1.)

TRANSLATION AND COMMENTARY

תָּא שְׁמַע [1]The Gemara tries now to resolve this question from our Mishnah: **Come and hear** what we have learned: "If a widow **had a ketubah of a maneh, and she sold** property belonging to her husband's estate that was **worth a maneh and a dinar for a maneh, the sale is invalid.** Even if the woman said: 'I will return the extra dinar to the heirs,' the sale is invalid." The Gemara wishes to understand what is the case under discussion: [2]**Is** the Mishnah **not** dealing with a widow who **sold** property belonging to her husband's estate that was **worth a maneh and a dinar for a maneh and a dinar?** In other words, the woman sold her husband's property for its full market value, incurring no loss. [3]**But what** does the Mishnah mean when it says that the woman sold the property **"for a maneh,"** a formulation that appears to implies that she sold the property for less than its full value? This can be explained to mean that the woman sold property belonging to her husband's estate worth a maneh and a dinar [4]**for the maneh that was due her** for her ketubah settlement. [5]**But what** does the Mishnah then mean when it says that the sale is invalid **"even"** if the woman says that she will return the extra dinar to the heirs? Surely the widow would have to return the extra dinar to the heirs, for the woman is only entitled to a ketubah of a maneh! The Mishnah can be explained to mean that the sale is invalid [6]**even if** the widow says: **"I will return the dinar to the heirs with a dinar of land,** meaning that she will buy back a dinar's worth of land and return it to the heirs, and they will not suffer any loss. [7]Now, the Mishnah **teaches** that in such a case **the** entire **sale is invalid,** even the sale of a maneh's worth of property. Since the widow is regarded as the heirs' agent, it follows from this that whenever an agent exceeds his authority, we view him as having violated his principal's instructions completely. Therefore, whatever he did is null and void.

אָמַר [8]**Rav Huna the son of Rav Natan said: No,** in the case discussed in the Mishnah, the widow **reduced the price** and sold the property below its market value. She sold property worth a maneh and a dinar for only a maneh, making the sale is invalid, because she caused the heirs the loss of a dinar.

[99A] הָא מִדְּסֵיפָא בִּדְאוֹזִיל [9]The Gemara raises an objection: **But surely since the last clause** of the Mishnah **deals with** a widow who **reduced the price** of property belonging to her husband's estate and sold it below its actual market value, [10]**the earlier clause** of the Mishnah **must be dealing with** a widow who **did not reduce the price** of the property, but rather sold it at its full market value, since the Mishnah does not teach the same law twice. [11]**For the last clause** of the Mishnah **states:** "If the widow **had a ketubah of four hundred zuz,**

LITERAL TRANSLATION

[1]Come [and] hear: "[If] her ketubah was a maneh, and she sold [property] worth a maneh and a dinar for a maneh, her sale is invalid." [2]Is this not when she sold [property] worth a maneh and a dinar for a maneh and a dinar? [3]And what is [meant by] "for a maneh"? [4]For her maneh. [5]And what is [meant by] "Even[...]"? [6]Even if she says: "I will return the dinar to the heirs as a dinar of land." [7]And it teaches: Her sale is invalid.

[8]Rav Huna the son of Rav Natan said: No! When she lowered the price.

[99A] [9]But surely since the last clause [deals] with when she reduced the price, [10]the first clause [must be dealing] with when she did not reduce the price, [11]for the last clause states: "[If] her ketubah was

[1]תָּא שְׁמַע: ״הָיְתָה כְּתוּבָּתָהּ מָנֶה, וּמָכְרָה שָׁוֶה מָנֶה וְדִינָר בְּמָנֶה, מִכְרָהּ בָּטֵל״. [2]מַאי לָאו דְּזַבֵּין שָׁוֶה מָנֶה וְדִינָר בְּמָנֶה וְדִינָר? [3]וּמַאי ״בְּמָנֶה״? [4]מָנֶה שֶׁלָּהּ. [5]וּמַאי ״אֲפִילּוּ״? [6]אֲפִילּוּ הִיא אוֹמֶרֶת: ״אַחֲזִיר אֶת הַדִּינָר לַיּוֹרְשִׁים בְּדִינָר מְקַרְקְעֵי״. [7]וְקָתָנֵי: מִכְרָהּ בָּטֵל! [8]אֲמַר רַב הוּנָא בְּרֵיהּ דְּרַב נָתָן: לָא! בִּדְאוֹזִיל.

[99A] [9]הָא מִדְּסֵיפָא בִּדְאוֹזִיל, [10]הָוֵי רֵישָׁא בִּדְלָא אוֹזִיל, [11]דְּקָתָנֵי סֵיפָא: ״הָיְתָה כְּתוּבָּתָהּ

RASHI

מאי לאו דזבין שוה מנה ודינר במנה ודינר — שלא היה במנה ודינר שום טעות. **ומאי במנה** — דקתני. **במנה שלה** — כלומר, בשביל מנה שהיה לה להתקבל מכרה שוה מנה ודינר ובשויו. **ומאי אפילו היא אומרת** — פשיטא דעל כרחך של יתומים הוא. **דינר מקרקעי** — אחזיר, ואקנה מן הלוקח שוה הדינר, ואחזירנו להם. **בדאוזיל** — ומשום הכי מכרה בטל, דטעתה שמכרה שוה מנה ודינר במנה. **הא מדסיפא כו׳** — דתרתי בדאוזיל? למה לי לאשמועינן?

NOTES

objection was raised against this ruling while the principal should indeed be liable for *me'ilah,* because the agent is regarded as having performed his agency regarding the first piece, the agent should also be liable for *me'ilah,* because of what he added regarding the second piece! *Ri Korkos* (cited by *Kesef Mishneh*) answers that the principal is understood as having instructed the agent to give the guest at least one piece of meat. Thus the agent is not regarded as having added to his principal's instructions when he told the guest to take two pieces. He too should not be liable for *me'ilah,* unless he explicitly told the guests to take the second piece on his own initiative (see also *Hatam Sofer*).

אַרְבַּע מֵאוֹת זוּז, [1]מָכְרָה לָזֶה בְּמָנֶה וְלָזֶה בְּמָנֶה, וְלָאַחֲרוֹן יָפֶה מָנֶה וְדִינָר בְּמָנֶה, [2]שֶׁל אַחֲרוֹן — מִכְרָהּ בָּטֵל, [3]וְשֶׁל כּוּלָּן מִכְרָן קַיָּים״!

[4]לָא, רֵישָׁא וְסֵיפָא בְּדְאוֹזִיל. [5]וְסֵיפָא הָא קָא מַשְׁמַע לָן: [6]טַעְמָא דְּאוֹזִיל בְּדִיָתְמֵי. [7]אֲבָל בְּדִידָהּ, מִכְרָהּ קַיָּים.

[8]הָא מִדְּרֵישָׁא שָׁמְעַתְּ מִינָּהּ: [9]״הָיְתָה כְּתוּבָּתָהּ מָאתַיִם — וּמָכְרָה שָׁוֶה מָנֶה בְּמָאתַיִם, [10]אוֹ שָׁוֶה מָאתַיִם בְּמָנֶה, נִתְקַבְּלָה כְּתוּבָּתָהּ״!

[11]מַהוּ דְּתֵימָא, הָתָם הוּא דְּאִיסְתַּלְּקָא לָהּ מֵהַאי בֵּיתָא לְגַמְרֵי. [12]אֲבָל הָכָא נִיגְזוֹר מָנֶה

LITERAL TRANSLATION

four hundred zuz, [1]and she sold [property] for a maneh to one [person], and for a maneh to another, and to the last person a maneh and a dinar for a maneh — [2]the last one's [sale] is invalid, [3]but the sale of all [the rest] of them is valid."

[4]No, the first clause and the last clause [deal] with when she reduced the price. [5]And the last clause teaches us this: [6]The reason [the sale is invalid] is that she reduced the price of the [property] of the orphans. [7]But [if she reduced the price] on her [own account], the sale is valid.

[8]But surely you can infer this from the first clause: [9]"[A widow] whose ketubah was two hundred [dinars] [if] she sold [property] worth a maneh for two hundred [dinars], [10]or [property] worth two hundred [dinars] for a maneh, she has received her ketubah."

[11]Lest you say [the sale is valid] there, when she removed herself entirely from that household. [12]But here we should pass a regulation [invalidating] the first maneh

TRANSLATION AND COMMENTARY

[1]**and she sold** property belonging to her husband's estate to four different people — **to one** she sold property worth a maneh **for a maneh, to another** person she sold property worth a maneh **for a maneh,** to the third person she sold property worth a maneh for a maneh, [2]**and to the last one** she sold property worth **a maneh and a dinar for a maneh, the sale** made to the **last** buyer **is invalid,** [3]**but the sales** made to **all the rest of them are valid."**

לָא [4]The Gemara answers: **No,** both **the earlier clause** of the Mishnah **and the later clause** of the Mishnah **deal with** a widow who **sold** property belonging to her husband's estate **at a reduced price** below its true market value. [5]**And** as for the objection that in that case the later clause is redundant, it can be argued that **the later clause teaches us the following:** [6]**The reason why the sale is invalid is that she sold** property **at a reduced price on the heirs' account.** The widow sold property for her ketubah to four different people, but it was only to the last buyer that she sold property below its market value. Since after the last sale, she would have had no further claim against her husband's estate, his heirs would suffer a loss by her reducing the price. Therefore, that last sale is invalid. [7]**But if** the widow **sells** property **at a reduced price on her** own **account, the sale is valid.** That is, when she sells property at a reduced price to one of the first three buyers, while she still has an additional claim against her husband's estate, the sale is valid, because she must bear the loss and deduct it from what the heirs still owe her for the ketubah.

הָא מִדְּרֵישָׁא [8]The Gemara objects: **But surely this** law **can be inferred from the first clause** of the Mishnah which states: [9]"If **a widow had a ketubah of two hundred dinars, and she sold** property belonging to her husband's estate that was **worth** only **a maneh** (one hundred dinars) **for two hundred** dinars, [10]**or** she sold property that was **worth two hundred** dinars **for** only **a maneh, she** is regarded as having **received her** entire **ketubah,** and she cannot present her husband's heirs with any further claim." The Mishnah states explicitly that if a woman sells her husband's property at a reduced price, even at half of its true market value, the sale is valid, and it is she who bears the loss! Why then should the Mishnah repeat this law in the last clause?

מַהוּ דְּתֵימָא [11]The Gemara answers: It was nevertheless necessary for the Mishnah to teach us this regulation again, for had we only had the first clause of the Mishnah, **you might have said** that **the sale** at a reduced price **is valid** only **when** the widow **removed herself entirely from** her husband's **house.** Since she has collected her entire ketubah and has no further claims against her husband's estate, there is no reason for the Rabbis to invalidate the sale. [12]**But here** the widow still has a claim against the estate for the rest of her ketubah, so you might have said that **we should rule** that if the widow sold **the first maneh** below

RASHI

דאוזיל בדיתמי — שלא היה לה עוד עליהם כלום, שהרי באחרון טעתה. **אבל בדידה** — כגון שטעתה אצל אחד מן הראשונים, שהיה הטעות עליה, שהרי יש לה עוד לגבות ולמכור מהן — מכרה קיים, דאין אונאה בקרקעות. וכל שכן שאין כאן שתות שיעור אונאה. **נתקבלה כתובתה** — ולא אמרינן: מכרה בטל. **התם הוא דאיסתלקא לה** — במכירה ראשונה מהאי ביתא לגמרי, וליכא למיגזר מידי. אבל הכא, דבמכירה ראשונה לא איסתלקא לה — אימא: אם טעתה במנה ראשון נמי יהא מכרה בטל.

NOTES

נִיגְזוֹר מָנֶה רִאשׁוֹן **Let us pass a regulation invalidating the first maneh.** *Ritva* asks: Perhaps, when a widow sold her

רִאשׁוֹן אַטּוּ מָנֶה אַחֲרוֹן. [1]קָא מַשְׁמַע לָן.
[2]וְאִיכָּא דְּאָמְרִי: הָא לָא תִּיבָּעֵי לָךְ הֵיכָא דַּאֲמַר לֵיהּ: [3]״זִיל זַבֵּין לִי לִיתְכָא״, וְזַבֵּין לֵיהּ כּוֹרָא, [4]דְּוַדַּאי מוֹסִיף עַל דְּבָרָיו הָוֵי. [5]כִּי תִּיבָּעֵי לָךְ דַּאֲמַר לֵיהּ: ״זִיל, זַבֵּין לִי כּוֹרָא״, [6]וְאָזֵיל וְזַבֵּין לֵיהּ לִיתְכָא. [7]מַאי? [8]מִי אָמְרִינַן: אֲמַר לֵיהּ: ״דְּטָבָא לָךְ עֲבַדִי לָךְ, [9]דְּאִי לָא מִצְטָרְכֵי לָךְ זוּזֵי, לָא מָצֵית הָדְרַתְּ בֵּיהּ״. [10]אוֹ דִּלְמָא

TRANSLATION AND COMMENTARY

its market price that the sale is invalid because she also sold **the last maneh** below its market price. [1]Therefore, the last clause of the Mishnah comes to **inform us that this is not so.**

וְאִיכָּא דְּאָמְרִי [2]The Gemara now suggests that the previous discussion of an agent who sold a *kor* instead of *letekh* should have taken an entirely different course: **There are some who say: You should not have asked about** someone who **said to his agent:** [3]**"Go, sell for me a** ***letekh*** of my land," **and** the agent **sold an** entire ***kor*** of his land **for him.** [4]**Since** in such a case we **certainly** say that the agent is regarded as having **added to what** his principal **had told** him to do, and the sale of the first ***letekh*** of land is valid. [5]Rather, what **you should have asked about** is **when** someone **said to his** agent: **"Go, sell for me a** ***kor*** of my land," [6]**and** the agent **sold** only **a** ***letekh*** of land **for him.** [7]**What is the law** in such a case? [8]**Do we say** that the agent **can say to his** principal: **"I acted for you in your best interests.** [9]**For** had I sold the entire ***kor,*** and then later **it** would have **turned** out that **you did not need** all **the money, you would not have** been able to **retract from** the transaction. If we accept this argument, the sale is valid. [10]**Or** do we **perhaps** say that the principal **can say to his** agent: "Your good intentions notwithstanding, I still would have preferred to sell the entire *kor* of

LITERAL TRANSLATION

on account of the last maneh. [1]He informs us [that this is not so].

[2]And there are [some] who say: You should not ask about [the case] where [someone] said to [his agent]: [3]"Go, sell for me a *letekh,*" and he sold for him a *kor,* [4]for [there] he certainly added to [the owner's] instructions. [5]You should ask about [the case] when [someone] said to [his agent]: "Go, sell for me a *kor,*" [6]and he went and sold for him a *letekh.* [7]What [is the law]? [8]Do we say: He can say to him: "I acted for you in your best interests, [9]for if [it turns out that] you do not need the money, you cannot retract from it." [10]Or perhaps

RASHI

אטו מנה אחרון – דלא ניתי למימר: מכרה קיים, קא משמע לן, דאפילו הכי – דוקא דטעתה במנה אחרון, אבל במנה ראשון – מכרה קיים. **דאי לא מצטרכי לך זוזי** – ותתחרט במכירתך, לא היית יכול לחזור אס מכרתיה.

NOTES

husband's property below its market price, the sale is invalid even when it was for the first maneh of her ketubah settlement. However, the Mishnah ruled that the sales made to the first three buyers are valid because in these instances she sold the parcels for the proper price! He answers that if this were so, the Mishnah should have taught the case when the woman sold land for the first maneh below its market price, and we would have understood that if the sale is invalid when we could have retrieved the loss from the remainder of her ketubah, all the more so would the sale be invalid when she sold the last maneh below its market value and the loss would fall on the heirs.

דְּטָבָא לָךְ עֲבַדִי לָךְ I acted in your best interests. *Ra'ah, Ritva,* and others explain that the Gemara does not discuss a principal who gave the agent clear instructions, and the agent decided on his own to act differently for the principal's own good. In such a case the agent is certainly regarded as having negated his principal's instructions, and the sale is not valid. The Gemara, however, is asking about an agent who could have understood from his principal's instructions that he was permitted to sell up to a *kor* of land, and so he sold only a *letekh,* thinking that he was doing him a favor, for a person generally prefers not to sell his property unless it is absolutely necessary (*Rivan*). Thus, the agent might be regarded as having performed his agency and merely modified it by selling only a *letekh.* Most of the Rishonim rule that even in such a case the agent is regarded as having negated his principal's instructions, and

HALAKHAH

דַּאֲמַר לֵיהּ: ״זִיל זַבֵּין לִי לִיתְכָא״ If he said to him: Buy me a *letekh.* "If someone said to his agent: 'Sell for me a *bet se'ah* of my land,' and the agent sold two *bet se'ahs,* the agent is regarded as having added to what his principal had told him to do, and only the sale of a single *bet se'ah* is valid. However, the buyer may retract from the sale, arguing that he only wanted to purchase a field that is two *bet se'ahs* in area." (*Rambam, Sefer Kinyan, Hilkhot Sheluḥin* 1:4; *Shulḥan Arukh, Ḥoshen Mishpat* 182:8.)

דַּאֲמַר לֵיהּ: ״זִיל, זַבֵּין לִי כּוֹרָא״ If he said to him: Buy me a *kor.* "If someone said to his agent: 'Sell for me two *bet se'ahs* of my land,' and the agent sold only one *bet se'ah,* the agent is regarded as having negated his principals instructions, and the sale is null and void." (According to *Rif,* this is the conclusion that may be inferred from our Gemara. *Maggid Mishneh* adds that since the Gemara does not resolve this issue, this case is regarded as doubtful, and when a matter is doubtful we do not remove land from the known owner's possession.) (*Rambam, Sefer Kinyan, Hilkhot Sheluḥin* 1:4; *Shulḥan Arukh, Ḥoshen Mishpat* 182:9.)

אֲמַר לֵיהּ: [1]״לָא נִיחָא לִי דְּלִיפְּשׁוּ שְׁטָרֵי עִילָּוַאי״?
[2]אֲמַר רַבִּי חֲנִינָא מִסּוּרָא: תָּא שְׁמַע: [3]״נָתַן לוֹ דִּינָר שֶׁל זָהָב וְאָמַר לוֹ: [4]׳הָבֵא לִי חָלוּק׳, [5]וְהָלַךְ וְהֵבִיא לוֹ בְּשָׁלֹשׁ חָלוּק וּבְשָׁלֹשׁ טַלִּית, [6]שְׁנֵיהֶם מָעֲלוּ״.
[7]אִי אָמְרַתְּ בִּשְׁלָמָא שָׁלִיחַ כִּי הַאי גַּוְונָא עוֹשֶׂה שְׁלִיחוּתוֹ, [8]וּמוֹסִיף עַל דְּבָרָיו [9]הָוֵי, מִשּׁוּם הָכִי בַּעַל הַבַּיִת מָעַל. [10]אֶלָּא אִי אָמְרַתְּ מַעֲבִיר עַל דְּבָרָיו הָוֵי, [11]אַמַּאי מָעַל?

LITERAL TRANSLATION

[the owner] can say to [the agent]: [1]"It is not agreeable to me to have many [people holding] deeds [of sale] against me."

[2]Rabbi Ḥanina of Sura said: Come [and] hear: [3]"[If] he gave [his agent] a golden dinar, and said to him: [4]'Bring me a shirt,' [5]and he went and brought him a shirt for three [selas] and a cloak for three [selas], [6]both of them are guilty of *me'ilah*." [7]Granted if you say [that] an agent like this performed his agency, [8]but he [merely] added to his instructions — [9]therefore the principal (lit., "householder") is guilty of *me'ilah*. [10]But if you say [that] he violated his instructions, [11]why is [the principal] guilty of *me'ilah*?

TRANSLATION AND COMMENTARY

of land in one sale, [1]for **I do not want many people** to be **holding deeds of sale against me?"** (This is disadvantageous, because they can summon the seller to court if their properties are seized by his creditors.) If we accept this position, then the sale is invalid.

אֲמַר רַבִּי חֲנִינָא [2]**Rabbi Ḥanina of Sura said: Come and hear** a resolution to this problem from a Mishnah dealing with the subject of misappropriation (*Me'ilah* 21a): [3]**"If** someone **gave his** agent **a golden dinar** (equivalent to twenty-five silver dinars, or six selas), **and said to him:** [4]**'Bring me a shirt** with this money,' [5]**and** the agent **brought him a shirt** that he purchased **for three selas** (half of the money) **and a cloak** purchased **for three selas** (the other half of the money), and the golden dinar turned out to be consecrated property, [6]**both** the sender and the agent **are guilty of *me'ilah*."** As when someone told his agent to sell for him a *kor* of land, and he sold only a *letekh*, here, too, the sender told his agent to spend one golden dinar on a shirt, and he spent only three selas on it. [7]**Granted** there is no problem **if you say that an agent** who acted **in this manner** is regarded as having **performed his agency** when he bought a shirt for only three selas [8]**and he merely added to** his principal's **instructions** when he also bought the cloak. [9]We can **then** readily understand why the Mishnah rules that **the principal is** also **guilty of *me'ilah*.** [10]**But if you say that** an agent who acted in this manner is regarded as having **negated** his principal's **instructions,** and nothing that he did is considered as fulfillment of his agency, [11]**why then is the principal guilty of *me'ilah?*** Surely we learned in the Mishnah cited earlier that if the agent deviated from his sender's instructions, it is only the agent, and not the sender, who is guilty of *me'ilah*! His act has definite legal consequences. Hence if an agent was instructed to sell a *kor* of land, but he sold only a *letekh* of land, since he did not radically alter his commission, he is considered as having acted in the principal's behalf, and the sale is valid.

RASHI

דינר של זהב — שוה עשרים וחמשה דינרין כסף, כדאמרינן ב״הזהב״ (בבא מציעא מד,ב) והם ששה סלעים. והביא לו בשלש סלעים חלוק — דהוי דומיא ״דזבין לי כורא״ וזבין ליתכא, שהרי צוהו למכור כל הדינר בחלוק. אמאי מעל — אף על גב דליכא למימר הכא טעמא דאפושי שטרי, מיהו, אי בעלמא מעביר על דבריו הוי — על כרחין לא עשה שליחותו.

NOTES

the sale is not valid (see *Rif* and *Ramban*). However, others, including *Rav Hai Gaon*, ruled that if someone sells less than what he was instructed by his principal, the sale is valid.

דְּלִיפְּשׁוּ שְׁטָרֵי עִילָּוַאי That I have many deeds against me. The Rishonim offer various explanations of why the principal does not want to have many people holding his deeds of sale. *Ri* says that a person prefers to sell his property to a single buyer, rather than several different buyers, because he wishes to avoid having court cases with several different parties should disagreements arise in the future. *Rabbenu Tam* argues that a person prefers to sell his property to a single buyer, because he wishes to avoid the expenses and efforts of writing out individual deeds of sale to different buyers. There is a practical difference between these two explanations when the principal's property was sold with two deeds of sale to a single buyer. *Meiri* suggests that a person does not want to jeopardize his credit rating by becoming known as someone in constant need of selling property, a situation made more acute by having many purchasers.

דִּינָר שֶׁל זָהָב A golden dinar. Following the Gemara in *Bava Metzia* 44b, *Rashi* explains that a golden dinar is equal to twenty-five silver dinars, or six selas, and so the Mishnah

HALAKHAH

נָתַן לוֹ דִּינָר שֶׁל זָהָב If he gave him a golden dinar. "If someone gave his agent two perutahs of consecrated money and told him to buy a citron with the money, and the agent spent one perutah on a citron, and he purchased a pomegranate with the second perutah, the agent is guilty of *me'ilah*, and the principal is free of liability. But if the

[1]הָכָא בְּמַאי עָסְקִינַן דְּאַיְיתֵי לֵיהּ שָׁוֶה שֵׁשׁ בְּשָׁלֹשׁ.
[2]אִי הָכִי, שָׁלִיחַ אַמַּאי מָעַל?
[3]אַטַּלִּית.
[4]אִי הָכִי, אֵימָא סֵיפָא: [5]"רַבִּי יְהוּדָה אוֹמֵר: אַף בָּזֶה בַּעַל הַבַּיִת לֹא מָעַל, [6]מִפְּנֵי שֶׁיָּכוֹל לוֹמַר: 'חָלוּק גָּדוֹל הָיִיתִי מְבַקֵּשׁ וְאַתָּה הֵבֵאתָ לִי חָלוּק קָטָן וְרַע'".
[7]מַאי "רַע"? [8]רַע בְּדָמִים, [9]דְּאָמַר לֵיהּ: אִי אַיְיתִית לִי בְּשִׁית, [10]כָּל שֶׁכֵּן דַּהֲוָה שָׁוֶה תַּרְתֵּי סְרֵי.

LITERAL TRANSLATION

[1]Here we are dealing with when he brought him [a shirt] worth six for three.
[2]If so, why is the agent guilty of *me'ilah*?
[3]For the cloak.
[4]If so, say the last clause: [5]"Rabbi Yehudah says: Even in this [case] the principal is not guilty of misappropriation, [6]because he can say: 'I wanted a large shirt, and you brought me a shirt that is small and bad.'"
[7]What is [meant by] "bad"? [8]Bad with respect to the money, [9]for [the principal] can say to [his agent]: Had you brought me [a shirt] for six [selas], [10]it surely (lit., "all the more so") would have been worth twelve [selas].

RASHI

שוה שש — דהוה ליה עשה שליחותו, דחלוק בת שש אמר ליה. אטלית — שהסלעים האחרונים מדעתו הוציאם, ולא מדעת בעל הבית. רע בדמים — שקנאו בדמים מועטים, והוא נוחו לקנותו בשש. ואם תאמר: מאי אכפת ליה. דאמר ליה: אי אייתית לי בשית כל שכן — דמרווחנא טפי, דהוי שוה תרתי סרי סלעים גדולים. שהלוקח הרבה ביחד מוזלי גביה טפי.

TRANSLATION AND COMMENTARY

הָכָא בְּמַאי עָסְקִינַן [1]The Gemara rejects this argument: **There** in the Mishnah in *Me'ilah* **we are dealing with an** agent who **brought a shirt worth six** selas that he purchased **for** only **three** selas. In such a case, we surely say that the agent performed his agency, for the sender received precisely what he asked for, and so he is guilty of *me'ilah*. But if an agent deviated from his instructions and sold only a *letekh* of his principal's land instead of a *kor*, perhaps we do not see the agent as having performed his agency, and so the sale is not valid.

אִי הָכִי [2]The Gemara asks: But **if** we are dealing with a case where the agent brought his sender a shirt worth six selas, **why is the agent guilty of** ***me'ilah?*** Surely the agent performed his agency, and as we learned in the Mishnah cited earlier, if an agent performed his agency, it is his sender, and not the agent, who is guilty of *me'ilah*!

אַטַּלִּית [3]The Gemara answers: He is guilty **because of the cloak** that he bought with the three selas of consecrated money that were left over. When he made that purchase, he was no longer acting under his mandate.

אִי הָכִי [4]The Gemara raises another objection: But **if** it is **so** that the Mishnah refers to an agent who brought his principal a shirt worth six selas, there is a difficulty. If you **read the next clause** of that Mishnah, you will realize that this interpretation is incorrect. [5]For we learned there: **"Rabbi Yehudah** disagrees with the anonymous first Tanna and **says: Even in this case the sender is not guilty of** ***me'ilah,*** [6]**because he can say** to his agent: **I wanted a large shirt, and you brought me a shirt that is small and bad."** Now, if indeed the agent brought his sender a shirt worth six selas as he had requested, how can the sender argue that it is small and bad?

מַאי "רַע"? [7]The Gemara answers: **What is** meant here by the sender's complaining of the shirt's being **"bad"?** [8]**Bad with respect to the money,** meaning that it was a "bad" purchase. [9]The principal **can say to** the agent: "If the seller was so pressed for money that you were able to buy a shirt worth six selas for only three selas, then **had you brought me a shirt for six** selas as I had instructed, [10]**it surely have been worth twelve selas."**

NOTES

in *Me'ilah* is dealing with an agent who spent half of the golden dinar — three selas — on a shirt, and the other half of the golden dinar — the remaining three selas — on a cloak. *Rivan* notes that this is not precise, for a golden dinar is equal to six selas and a silver dinar (a sela is equal to four silver dinars). Thus, when the Mishnah said that the agent bought a shirt and a cloak for three selas apiece, it must have meant that he spent three selas and half a silver dinar on each. *Tosafot* write that a golden dinar is actually equal to twenty-four silver dinars. As for the Gemara in *Bava Metzia* which states that a golden dinar is equal to twenty-five silver dinars, that includes the commission of a silver dinar that must be paid to the moneychanger for changing silver dinars into a golden dinar.

HALAKHAH

citron that the agent purchased for a perutah was actually worth two perutahs, both the agent and the principal are guilty of *me'ilah*," following the Sages, in accordance with the Gemara's understanding of their position. (*Rambam, Sefer Avodah, Hilkhot Me'ilah* 7:4.)

TRANSLATION AND COMMENTARY

דַּיְקָא נַמִי [1]Moreover, this last interpretation **is indeed precise, for** a related Baraita **teaches: "Rabbi Yehudah agrees about** the law applying to someone who gave his agent one gold dinar and asked him to buy **legumes** with that money, and the agent spent three selas on legumes and three selas on some other item, and the golden dinar proved to be consecrated property. [2]In such a case **both of them** — the principal and the agent — **are guilty of** *me'ilah,* [99B] [3]**for** legumes are sold at a fixed price, regardless of the quantity being purchased. A certain measure of **legumes are** sold **for a sela, and** a proportionately smaller measure of **legumes are** sold **for a perutah.** In such a case, both the sender and the agent are guilty of *me'ilah*: the sender because he asked the agent to purchase the legumes, and the agent because he was acting on his own when he purchased the other item." [4]**Infer from this** that the Mishnah is dealing with an agent who bought a shirt worth six selas for three selas, and that Rabbi Yehudah maintains that the sender is not guilty of *me'ilah*, because he can argue that, had the agent spent six selas on the shirt as he had been instructed, he could have bought a much better shirt. Thus, we understand why he agrees about the agent who bought legumes: The sender is guilty of *me'ilah*, because the agent would not have received larger discount had he spent all of the money on the legumes as instructed.

הֵיכִי דָמֵי [5]The Gemara now clarifies the case discussed in this Baraita: **How do you envision** the case of the Baraita? [6]**If you say** that it refers to **a place where** legumes **are sold by** approximate **appraisal,** [7]then **when** the buyer **pays** the seller **a sela,** the seller does in fact **lower the price for him more,** so even legumes do not have a fixed price!

אֲמַר רַב פַּפָּא [8]**Rav Pappa said:** The Baraita refers to **a place where** the sellers **measure** out the legumes **with utensils,** and the seller **says to** the buyer: It makes no difference to me how much you buy. [9]**Each utensil**ful sells **for a perutah.**

[1]דַּיְקָא נַמִי, דְּקָתָנֵי: "מוֹדֶה רַבִּי יְהוּדָה בְּקִטְנִית, [2]שֶׁשְּׁנֵיהֶם מָעֲלוּ. [99B] [3]שֶׁהַקִּטְנִית בְּסֶלַע וְקִטְנִית בִּפְרוּטָה. [4]שְׁמַע מִינָּהּ. [5]הֵיכִי דָּמֵי? [6]אִילֵימָא בְּאַתְרָא דִּמְזַבְּנֵי בְּשׁוּמָא, [7]הֵיכָא דְּיָהֵיב לֵיהּ סֶלַע מוֹזְלֵי גַּבֵּיהּ טְפֵי! [8]אֲמַר רַב פַּפָּא: בְּאַתְרָא דְּכָיְילֵי בְּכַנֵּי, [9]דְּאָמַר לֵיהּ כַּנָּא כַּנָּא בִּפְרוּטָה.

LITERAL TRANSLATION

[1]It is also precise, for it teaches: "Rabbi Yehudah agrees about legumes, [2]that both of them are guilty of *me'ilah,* [99B] [3]for legumes are for a sela, and legumes are for a perutah." [4]Infer from this.

[5]What is it like? [6]If you say in a place where they sell with an appraisal, [7]where he gives him a sela, he lowers the price for him more!

[8]Rav Pappa said: In a place where they measure with utensils, [9]for he says to him: Each utensil for a perutah.

RASHI

דיקא נמי — ד"רע" דקאמר רבי יהודה רע בדמים קאמר, ובדאייתי ליה שוה שש, וטעמא כדאמרן מדקתני מודה בקטנית. דהתם לא מצי למימר: כל שכן דאי מייתית בדינר זהב היה שוה יותר מכפלים, דהוו מוזלי גבך טפי. שהקטנית בסלע — היא קטנית בפרוטה, לפי חשבון פרוטות בסלע. דמשום דזבין טפי לא מוזלי גביה, כדמסיים ואזיל: באתרא דמזבני בכני. כנא כנא בפרוטה — אם אתה חפץ יותר — שלא עוד וקח. ואם רישא חלוק רע ממש קאמר, שאינה שוה אלא שלש. ודכוותה גבי קטנית — דאמר ליה: הבא לי בסלע פולין, והביא לו בחצי סלע כשוה חצי סלע, ובחצי סלע אחר הביא לו מין אחר — אמאי מעל בעל הבית? לימא ליה: לשוה סלע הייתי צריך פולין! בשומא — באומד.

NOTES

שֶׁהַקִּטְנִית בְּסֶלַע **For legumes are for a sela.** *Rashi* explains as follows how this Baraita proves that the Mishnah in *Me'ilah* is dealing with an agent who bought his sender a shirt worth six selas for three selas: If the Mishnah is dealing with an agent who bought his sender a shirt worth three selas for three selas, then why should Rabbi Yehudah distinguish between the case of the shirt and the case of the legumes? In both cases, the principal sent his agent to purchase something for a particular amount of money, and in both cases the agent purchased only half of what he was supposed to buy and spent the rest of the money on something that the principal did not want! Rather, the Mishnah must be dealing with an agent who bought a shirt worth six selas for three selas, and Rabbi Yehudah argues that the principal is not guilty of *me'ilah,* because he can argue that the agent acted wrongly. Had he spent all six selas on a shirt, he would have received an even greater discount. In the parallel case with the legumes, Rabbi Yehudah agrees that the principal is guilty of *me'ilah,* because the price of legumes is fixed, and the principal cannot put forward a similar argument. *Ra'ah* notes: Even if the Mishnah is dealing with an agent who bought a shirt worth three selas for three selas, Rabbi Yehudah can distinguish between a shirt and legumes. In the case of the legumes, the agent can argue that the principal can sell the other item which he had purchased for him and purchase legumes with the proceeds. He would then have exactly what he wanted (an argument which cannot be made about a shirt). Thus, the agent should be regarded as having fulfilled his agency, and so the principal should indeed be guilty of *me'ilah*! *Ritva* answers that the principal can answer that he does not want to start buying and selling.

TRANSLATION AND COMMENTARY

תָּא שְׁמַע [1]The Gemara now tries to resolve this problem from our Mishnah: **Come and hear** what we have learned in our Mishnah: "If the widow **had a ketubah of four hundred zuz,** [2]**and she sold** property belonging to her husband's estate to four different people — **to one** she sold property worth a maneh **for a maneh, and to another** person she sold property worth a maneh **for a maneh,** and to a third person she sold property worth a maneh for a maneh, [3]**and to the last one** she sold property worth **a maneh and a dinar for a maneh** — [4]**the sale** made to the **last** buyer **is invalid, and the sales** made to **all the rest of them are valid."** Technically, the widow was authorized to sell property belonging to her husband's estate as his heirs' agent, and from the outset her mandate was to sell property worth four hundred zuz, the value of her ketubah. But she sold property worth only a maneh — once, twice, and then a third time. The Mishnah rules that all of those sales are valid, because each time the property was sold for the correct price. We do not say that the sales are null and void, because the widow strayed from her mandate when she sold property worth only a maneh, instead of property worth four hundred zuz. It should follow from this that if a person instructed his agent to sell a *kor* of land, and the agent sold only a *letekh*, the sale is valid.

כְּדַאֲמַר [5]The Gemara rejects this argument: The problem raised above cannot be resolved from our Mishnah. **Rav Shesha the son of Rav Idi said** that an estate was made up of **small parcels of land,** does not have to be sold all at once. [6]**Here** our Mishnah refers to an estate made up of several **small parcels of land** rather than a single unit for sale. Thus the widow was permitted to make separate sales. But if a person instructed his agent to sell a *kor* of land that was fit to be sold as a single unit, and the agent went ahead and sold only a *letekh* of the property, the sale might indeed be invalid, because the agent departed from the instructions which he received from his principal.

פְּשִׁיטָא [7]The Gemara continues with a new problem: **It is obvious** that **if someone said** to his agent: "Sell my property **to one** person, **and not to two** people," and the agent sold the property to two people, the agent departed from his instructions, and so the transactions are null and void, [8]for **surely** the sender **said**

[1]תָּא שְׁמַע: ״הָיְתָה כְּתוּבָּתָהּ אַרְבַּע מֵאוֹת זוּז, [2]מָכְרָה לָזֶה בְּמָנֶה וְלָזֶה בְּמָנֶה, [3]וְלָאַחֲרוֹן יָפֶה מָנֶה וְדִינָר בְּמָנֶה — [4]שֶׁל אַחֲרוֹן בָּטֵל, וְשֶׁל כּוּלָּן מִכְרָן קַיָּים!

[5]כְּדַאֲמַר רַב שֵׁישָׁא בְּרֵיהּ דְּרַב אִידִי: בִּקְטִינֵי. [6]הָכָא נַמִי בִּקְטִינֵי.

[7]פְּשִׁיטָא, אֲמַר: ״לְאֶחָד וְלֹא לִשְׁנַיִם״, [8]הָאֲמַר לֵיהּ: ״לְאֶחָד

LITERAL TRANSLATION

[1]Come [and] hear: "[If] her ketubah was four hundred zuz, [2]and she sold for a maneh to one, and for a maneh to another, [3]and to the last one a maneh and a dinar's worth for a maneh — [4]the last one's [sale] is invalid, and the sale of all [the rest] of them is valid."

[5]As Rav Shesha the son of Rav Idi said: With small parcels [of land]. [6]Here too with small parcels [of land].

[7]It is obvious [that if] he said: "To one, and not to two," [8]surely he said to him: "To one,

RASHI

של כולן מכרן קיים — והא הכא, דלזבוני בארבע מאה שדרוה, ומכרה לראשון במנה — דהיינו ״זבין לי כורא״ וזבין ליה ליתכא. **בקטיני** — לא היו שדות הללו יחד, ואין ראוין לאדם אחד. דמעיקרא אדעתא דהכי נעשית שליח. **פשיטא אמר** — לשלוחו: מכור לי בית כור משדותי ולאחד ולא לשנים. **האמר לאחד ולא לשנים** — ואפילו אם תמצא לומר זבין לי כורא וזבין ליה ליתכא מכרו קיים — הכא בטל, דגלי דעתיה דקפיד באפוסי שטרי.

NOTES

הָיְתָה כְּתוּבָּתָהּ If her ketubah. *Ra'ah* notes that it might be argued that our Mishnah does not resolve our problem, for the woman does not really sell the property belonging to her husband's estate as his heirs' agent. Rather she is a creditor who exercises a lien over her husband's estate and sells his property on her own behalf. He explains that the Gemara argues that if we were to accept the principal's claim that he does not want there to be many deeds of sale against him, then the widow should not be permitted to sell her husband's property to four different buyers without the heirs' consent. The heirs might prefer to pay the woman her ketubah settlement in cash rather than have her sell the property to four different buyers and thus multiply the number of deeds of sale against them. Similarly, *Ritva* argues that even if the widow is not regarded as the heirs' agent, if we were to accept the validity of the principal's claim that he does not want there to be many deeds of sale against him, then the widow should not be permitted to act to the heirs' detriment and sell her husband's property to four different buyers, if it is at all possible for her to sell the property to a single buyer.

פְּשִׁיטָא, אֲמַר: ״לְאֶחָד וְלֹא לִשְׁנַיִם״ It is obvious that if he said: To one, and not to two. The Rishonim discuss the relationship between the problem posed here regarding a

HALAKHAH

לְאֶחָד וְלֹא לִשְׁנַיִם To one, and not to two. "If someone said to his agent: 'Sell my field to one person,' and the agent sold the field to two people, the agent is regarded as having departed from his instructions, and so the sale

TRANSLATION AND COMMENTARY

to his agent: "Sell my property **to one** person, **and not to two** people." [1]But **what is the law if someone said to** his agent: "Sell my property **to one** person," [2]**without specifying** explicitly that he does not want him to sell it to two people?"

רַב הוּנָא אָמַר [3]Rav Huna **said:** The sender told his agent to sell his property **to one** person, **and** by this he meant that the property was to be sold to one person only, [4]and **not to two** people.

רַב חִסְדָּא [5]Rav Ḥisda and **Rabbah bar Rav Huna both said:** The sender may have told his agent to sell his property **to one** person, [6]but he meant that the property could be sold **even to two** people. [7]He may have said that his property should be sold **to one** person, but he meant that it could be sold **even to a hundred** people.

אִיקְלַע [8]It was related that **Rav Naḥman happened to come to Sura,** [9]and **Rav Ḥisda and Rabbah bar Rav Huna went in** to see **him.** [10]**The** two Sages **said to** the visiting scholar: Regarding a case **like this,** when someone told his agent to sell his property to one person, and the agent sold the property to two people, [11]**what is the law?**

אֲמַר לְהוּ [12]Rav Naḥman **said to** Rav Ḥisda and Rabbah bar Rav Huna: The sender may have told his agent to sell his property **to one** person, [13]but the agent is regarded as having performed his agency **even** if he sold the property **to two** people. [14]The sender may have ordered his agent to sell his property **to one** person, but the agent is regarded as having performed his agency **even** if he sold the property **to a hundred** people.

וְלֹא לִשְׁנַיִם״. [1]אֲמַר לֵיהּ: ״לְאֶחָד״, [2]סְתָמָא, מַאי?
[3]רַב הוּנָא אֲמַר: לְאֶחָד, [4]וְלֹא לִשְׁנַיִם.
[5]רַב חִסְדָּא וְרַבָּה בַּר רַב הוּנָא דְּאָמְרִי תַּרְוַיְיהוּ: לְאֶחָד, [6]וַאֲפִילּוּ לִשְׁנַיִם. [7]לְאֶחָד, וַאֲפִילּוּ לְמֵאָה.
[8]אִיקְלַע רַב נַחְמָן לְסוּרָא. [9]עוּל לְגַבֵּיהּ רַב חִסְדָּא וְרַבָּה בַּר רַב הוּנָא. [10]אָמְרוּ לֵיהּ: כִּי הַאי, גַּוְונָא [11]מַאי?
[12]אֲמַר לְהוּ: לְאֶחָד, [13]וַאֲפִילּוּ לִשְׁנַיִם. [14]לְאֶחָד, וַאֲפִילּוּ לְמֵאָה.

LITERAL TRANSLATION

and not to two." [1][If] he said to him: "To one," [2]without specifying, what [is the law]?

[3]Rav Huna said: To one, [4]and not to two.

[5]Rav Ḥisda and Rabbah bar Rav Huna both said: To one, [6]and even to two. [7]To one, and even to a hundred.

[8]Rav Naḥman happened to come to Sura. [9]Rav Ḥisda and Rabbah bar Rav Huna went in to him. [10]They said to him: Like this, [11]what [is the law]?

[12]He said to them: To one, [13]and even to two. [14]To one, and even to a hundred.

RASHI

אמר ״לאחד״ סתמא — ולא פירש ״ולא לשנים״ מי הוי גלוי דעתא או לא? לאחד ואפילו לשנים — דלאו אורחייהו דאינשי דקפדי. והאי נמי לא קפיד. אלא אורחא לאישתעויי הכי. ואי הוה קפיד הוה מפרש ליה: ולא לשנים.

NOTES

principal who told his agent to sell his property to one person, and the agent sold it to two people, and the problem posed above regarding a principal who told his agent to sell a *kor* of his property, and the agent sold only a *letekh.* This issue is particularly problematic according to *Rif,* who rules that when the agent sold only a *letekh* of his principal's property instead of a *kor,* the agent is regarded as having departed from his principal's instructions. The principal can argue that he does not want there to be many deeds of sale outstanding against him. However, regarding the problem raised here, he rules in accordance with Rav Ḥisda that if the principal did not specify that the agent must sell the property only to a single buyer, the sale is valid even if the agent sold the property to a hundred different buyers. This seems to indicate that the principal cannot argue that he does not want there to be many deeds of sale against him. *Ramban* and others distinguish between the two problems and explain that here we are dealing with an agent who sold the property to various buyers with a single deed of sale, and the issue is whether or not the principal can object and argue that he does not want to have to deal with more than one party should any disagreements arise (see also *Tosafot* and *Ra'ah*).

Rav Hai Gaon rules on the earlier question that if the agent sold only a *letekh* of his principal's property instead of a *kor,* the sale is valid, for the agent is regarded as having performed his agency and added to it. He understands that the Gemara's discussion about the principal who told his agent to sell his property to one person, and the agent sold it to two people is actually a resolution of the earlier question, for it implies that the sale of less than what the agent was instructed to sell does not invalidate the sale.

HALAKHAH

is void," following the simple understanding of the Gemara, and the reading of *Rabbenu Ḥananel* and *Rif* (*Kesef Mishneh*). *Rema* writes that according to some authorities (*Tur,* following the reading of *Rashi*), this ruling only applies if the agent sold the property with two bills of sale. (*Rambam, Sefer Kinyan, Hilkhot Sheluḥin* 1:4; *Shulḥan Arukh, Ḥoshen Mishpat* 182:10.)

לְאֶחָד סְתָמָא, מַאי To one, without specifying, what is the law. "If someone said to his agent: 'Sell my field,' without adding any specifications, then even if he sold the property to a hundred different buyers, the sale is valid, following the reading of *Rabbenu Ḥananel* and *Rif,* and the position of Rav Ḥisda and Rav Naḥman. This ruling only applies if the property was sold with one bill of sale (following *Ri* in

[1]אָמְרוּ לֵיהּ: אַף עַל גַּב דְּטָעָה שָׁלִיחַ?
[2]אֲמַר לְהוּ: דְּטָעָה שָׁלִיחַ, לָא קָאָמִינָא.
[3]אָמְרוּ לֵיהּ: וְהָאָמַר מָר: [4]אֵין אוֹנָאָה לְקַרְקָעוֹת!
[5]הָנֵי מִילֵּי הֵיכָא דְּטָעָה בַּעַל הַבַּיִת. [6]אֲבָל טָעָה שָׁלִיחַ, [7]אֲמַר לֵיהּ: "לְתַקּוּנֵי שְׁדַרְתִּיךְ וְלֹא לְעַוּוּתֵי".
[8]וּמְנָא תֵּימְרָא דְּשָׁאנֵי בֵּין שָׁלִיחַ לְבַעַל הַבַּיִת? [9]דִּתְנַן: "הָאוֹמֵר לִשְׁלוּחוֹ: 'צֵא וּתְרוֹם',

LITERAL TRANSLATION

[1]They said to him: Even though the agent erred? [2]He said to them: Where the agent erred, I did not say.

[3]They said to him: But surely master said: [4]There is no *ona'ah* regarding land.

[5]These words [apply] where the master of the house erred. [6]But [if] the agent erred, [7]he can say to him: "I sent you to benefit [me], and not to harm [me]."

[8]And from where do you say that there is a difference between the agent and the master of the house? [9]As we have learned: "[If] someone says to his agent: 'Go out and separate *terumah*,'

RASHI

ואף על גב דטעה שליח – ומכר בזול, נימא נמי דמקחו קייס? **והאמר מר אין אונאה לקרקעות** – גרסינן. ומשנה היא בפרק "הזהב".

TRANSLATION AND COMMENTARY

אָמְרוּ לֵיהּ [1]Rav Ḥisda and Rabbah bar Rav Huna **said to** Rav Naḥman: Do we say that **the agent** is regarded as having performed his agency **even if he erred** and sold the property below its market price?

אֲמַר לְהוּ [2]Rav Naḥman **said to them:** If **the agent erred, I did not say** that he is regarded as having performed his agency. Rather the sale is null and void.

אָמְרוּ לֵיהּ [3]Rav Ḥisda and Rabbah bar Rav Huna **said to** Rav Naḥman: **But surely master said:** [4]**The laws of overcharging and underpaying do not apply to land.** The Torah states (Leviticus 25:14): "And if you sell anything to your neighbor or buy anything from the hand of your neighbor, do not defraud one another." From here the Sages derived that it is not permitted to overcharge or underpay. However, since the verse speaks of "your neighbor's hand," it is understood as referring to ordinary movable goods that can be transferred from hand-to-hand, but not to land. Because the laws of unfair profit do not apply to real estate, the sale of the sender's property should be valid, even if the agent undercharged!

הָנֵי מִילֵּי [5]Rav Naḥman answered: **That ruling** only **applies if the principal** himself **erred.** [6]**But if the agent erred** and sold his principal's property below its market value, the sale is null and void, [7]for the sender **can say to** his agent: **"I sent you for my benefit, and not for my detriment."**

וּמְנָא תֵּימְרָא [8]The Gemara explains: **And from where do you know that there is a difference between** an error committed by a person's **agent and** an error committed by **the person** himself? [9]This is derived from a Mishnah in which **we have learned** (*Terumot* 4:4): **"If someone said to his agent: 'Go out and separate *terumah*** (a certain portion of a person's produce which he must set aside and give to a priest) from my

NOTES

וְהָאָמַר מָר **But surely master said.** The standard editions of the Gemara follow *Rashi's* reading: "But surely Master said." *Rashi* explains that Rav Ḥisda and Rabbah bar Rav Huna raised an objection from a Mishnah in *Bava Metzia* 56a. *Rabbenu Tam* in his *Sefer HaYashar* strongly objects to *Rashi*'s emendation of the text. Most Rishonim reject *Rashi*'s reading (for if it were correct, the Gemara should read: וְהָתְנַן, "But surely we learned in a Mishnah"). Those Rishonim maintain that the Gemara should read: "But surely it was Master who said: There is no excess profit for land, basing the question on Rav Naḥman's own ruling. *Ritva* explains that the question was raised on the basis of Rav Naḥman's own ruling, because according to some Amoraim, the Mishnah's ruling that land is not subject to the laws of excess profit only applies when the overcharge is one-sixth or less, but if the overcharge is more than one-sixth, even land is subject to cancellation of the sale. According to Rav Naḥman, however, the laws of excess profit do not apply to land at all.

HALAKHAH

Tosafot), or if the property was sold with more than one bill of sale, but the agent saw to it that all the bills of sale were drawn up and signed by witnesses (*Rabbenu Tam*). (*Rambam, Sefer Kinyan, Hilkhot Sheluḥin,* 1:4; *Shulḥan Arukh, Ḥoshen Mishpat* 182:11.)

טָעָה שָׁלִיחַ **Where the agent erred.** "If an agent erred and overpaid even the smallest amount for property which he purchased for his principal whether he bought land or movable goods, the transaction is void, for the principal can say to his agent: 'I sent you for my benefit, and not for my detriment,' following the Gemara. (*Rambam, Sefer Kinyan, Hilkhot Sheluḥin* 1:2; *Shulḥan Arukh, Ḥoshen Mishpat* 182:2-3.)

אֵין אוֹנָאָה לְקַרְקָעוֹת **There is no *ona'ah* regarding land.** "Landed property is not subject to the laws of *ona'ah*. Even if property worth a thousand dinars was sold for a dinar, or if property worth a dinar was sold for a thousand dinars, the transaction is valid, following the simple understanding of our Gemara. *Rema* adds that some authorities maintain that the transaction is invalid if the buyer paid more than

TRANSLATION AND COMMENTARY

produce,' but he did not tell him how much *terumah* to separate, [1]the agent should **separate *terumah*** from the produce **in accordance with** his understanding of **the intention of the owner** of the produce. The Torah does not specify the amount of *terumah* that must be set aside; a person may fulfill his obligation by giving even a single kernel of grain from an entire crop. But the Sages established a measure: one-fortieth for a generous gift, one-fiftieth for an average gift, and one-sixtieth for a miserly gift. If an agent was sent to separate *terumah*, without being told how much to set aside, but he knows that his sender is generous, average, or miserly, he should separate terumah from the produce accordingly. [2]If the agent **does not know the intention of the** produce's **owner, he should separate *terumah* according to the average gift, one-fiftieth** of the crop. [3]**If** the agent who does not know his sender's intention **subtracted ten,** by separating one-fortieth instead of one-fiftieth, **or** he **added ten,** by separating one-sixtieth instead of one-fortieth, **the *terumah*** which he separated **is *terumah*."** This Mishnah determines the margin of error within an agent's actions on behalf of his principal are valid. [4]**However,** this criterion does not apply to the owner of produce. **Regarding the owner** of the produce himself, **it was taught** in a Baraita: [5]**"If someone separated *terumah*, and he obtained** a portion much larger than necessary, **even one-twentieth** of the crop, **the *terumah*** which he separated **is** nevertheless ***terumah*."**

תָּא שְׁמַע [6]The Gemara again proposes that the problem of the agent's responsibility can be resolved from our Mishnah: **Come and hear** what we have learned in our Mishnah: "If a widow **had a ketubah of four hundred zuz,** [7]**and she sold** property belonging to her husband's estate to four different people — **to one** she sold property worth a maneh **for a maneh, and to another** person she sold property worth a maneh **for a maneh,** and to a third person she sold property worth a maneh for a maneh, [8]**and to the last one** she sold

[1]תּוֹרֵם כְּדַעַת בַּעַל הַבַּיִת. [2]וְאִם אֵינוֹ יוֹדֵעַ דַּעְתּוֹ שֶׁל בַּעַל הַבַּיִת, תּוֹרֵם בְּבֵינוֹנִית, אֶחָד מֵחֲמִשִּׁים. [3]פִּיחֵת עֲשָׂרָה, אוֹ הוֹסִיף עֲשָׂרָה, תְּרוּמָתוֹ תְּרוּמָה״. [4]וְאִילּוּ גַּבֵּי בַּעַל הַבַּיִת, תַּנְיָא: [5]״תָּרַם וְעָלָה בְּיָדוֹ אֲפִילּוּ אֶחָד מֵעֶשְׂרִים, תְּרוּמָתוֹ תְּרוּמָה״.

[6]תָּא שְׁמַע: ״הָיְתָה כְּתוּבָּתָהּ אַרְבַּע מֵאוֹת זוּז, [7]מָכְרָה לָזֶה בְּמָנֶה וְלָזֶה בְּמָנֶה, [8]וְלָאַחֲרוֹן

LITERAL TRANSLATION

[1]he separates *terumah* according to the intention of the master of the house. [2]And if he does not know the intention of the master of the house, he separates *terumah* according to the average [gift], one-fiftieth. [3][If] he subtracted ten, or added ten, his *terumah* is *terumah*." [4]But regarding the master of the house, it was taught: [5]"[If] he separated terumah, and he obtained even one-twentieth, his *terumah* is *terumah*."

[6]Come [and] hear: "[If] her ketubah was four hundred zuz, [7]and she sold for a maneh to one, and for a maneh to another, [8]and to the last one

RASHI

תורם כדעת בעל הבית — כפי מה שהוא מכיר בו; אם עין יפה — אחד מארבעים, ואם עין רעה — אחד מששים. **פיחת עשרה** — שתרם אחד מארבעים. **תרומתו תרומה** — דאמר ליה: בהכי אמדתיך. **הוסיף עשרה** — אחד מששים. **ואילו גבי בעל הבית תניא כו'** — והכא תניא: פיחת עשרה — תרומתו תרומה, אבל טפי — לא. **תא שמע היתה כתובתה כו'** — ואי אפושי שטרי קפידא היא, נהי נמי דיתומין לא גלו דעתייהו — אנן מיהא דיד יתומין בעינן למיהוי, אית לן למימר: מכרן בטל.

NOTES

מָכְרָה לָזֶה בְּמָנֶה **She sold one maneh to one.** Our Mishnah deals with a woman who sold the property of her husband's estate to four different people. Rav Shesha limits the Mishnah's ruling to the sale of four separate parcels of land. The Jerusalem Talmud discusses the sale of the property to the four different buyers with a single deed.

HALAKHAH

twice the value of the land (*Tur*, in the name of *Rabbenu Ḥananel* and *Rosh*, and as it follows from other passages). (*Rambam, Sefer Kinyan, Hilkhot Mekhirah* 13:8; *Shulḥan Arukh, Ḥoshen Mishpat* 227:29.)

תּוֹרֵם כְּדַעַת בַּעַל הַבַּיִת **He separates *terumah* according to the intention of the master of the house.** "If someone told his agent to separate *terumah* from his produce, but did not tell him how much to separate, he should separate *terumah* in accordance with his understanding of the intention of his principal. If the agent knows that his principal is miserly, he should set aside as *terumah* one-sixtieth of the produce. If he knows him to be generous, he should set aside as *terumah* one-fortieth of the produce. If he does not know, he should separate *terumah* according to the average gift, one fiftieth of the produce," following the Mishnah. (*Rambam, Sefer Zeraim, Hilkhot Terumot* 4:7.)

תָּרַם וְעָלָה בְּיָדוֹ **If he separated *terumah*, and he obtained.** "If someone separated *terumah* from his produce and obtained a portion much larger than necessary, even one-twentieth of the crop, the *terumah* which he separated is *terumah*." (*Rambam, Sefer Zeraim, Hilkhot Terumot* 3:6.)

TRANSLATION AND COMMENTARY

property worth **a maneh and a dinar for a maneh** — [1]**the sale** made to the **last** buyer **is invalid, and the sales** made to **all the rest of them are valid."** Now, the widow was acting as the agent of her husband's heirs', and it stands to reason that her mandate was to sell the property to a single buyer, so as not to multiply the deeds of sale which stand against the heirs. Nevertheless, the Mishnah rules that if she sold the property to several buyers, each of the transactions is valid, provided that the property was sold for the correct price.

אָמַר [2]**Rav Shesha the son of Rav Idi said:** The problem raised by the Gemara, about an agent who sold land to more than one buyer cannot be resolved from our Mishnah, for it is dealing **with** an estate made up of **small parcels of land,** not a single unit for sale. Thus, the widow's original mandate allowed her to sell the property as separate units to different people. But if someone instructed his agent to sell his property to one person, and the land was fit to be sold as a single unit, and the agent sold the property to two or more people, the transactions are indeed invalid. We assume that the landowner was particular about the matter, and the agent departed from the instructions which he had received.

MISHNAH שׁוּם הַדַּיָּינִין [3]If a court of **judges appraised** the property of the deceased which passed to his heirs in order to sell it and pay his widow her ketubah settlement or his creditors the money which the deceased had owed them, and the court erred, [4]and **sold** the property **for a sixth less** than its actual market value, **or** it **sold** the property **for a sixth more** than its actual market value, [5]**the sale is invalid.**

רַבָּן שִׁמְעוֹן בֶּן גַּמְלִיאֵל [6]**Rabban Shimon ben Gamliel says: The** court's **sale** of the property **is valid,** even if the error was for more than a sixth, [7]**for if** it is **so** that an error of a sixth nullifies the transaction, **in what**

שָׁוֶה מָנֶה וְדִינָר בְּמָנֶה — [1]שֶׁל אַחֲרוֹן בָּטֵל, וְשֶׁל כּוּלָּן מִכְרָן קַיָּים!

[2]אָמַר רַב שֵׁישָׁא בְּרֵיהּ דְּרַב אִידִי: בִּקְטִינֵי.

משנה [3]שׁוּם הַדַּיָּינִין, [4]שֶׁפִּיחֲתוּ שְׁתוּת אוֹ הוֹסִיפוּ שְׁתוּת — [5]מִכְרָן בָּטֵל.

[6]רַבָּן שִׁמְעוֹן בֶּן גַּמְלִיאֵל אוֹמֵר: מִכְרָן קַיָּים, [7]אִם כֵּן, מַה כֹּחַ

LITERAL TRANSLATION

a maneh and a dinar's worth for a maneh — [1]the last one's [sale] is invalid, and the sale of all [the rest] of them is valid."

[2]Rav Shesha the son of Rav Idi said: With small parcels [of land].

MISHNAH [3]The appraisal of the judges, [4]when they subtracted a sixth or added a sixth — [5]their sale is invalid.

[6]Rabban Shimon ben Gamliel says: Their sale is valid, [7][for] if so, what is the power

NOTES

According to Resh Lakish, even in such a case, only the sale made to the last buyer is invalid. Rabbi Yoḥanan disagrees and says that since the sale made to the last buyer is invalid, all the sales made through that bill of sale are invalid as well.

שֶׁפִּיחֲתוּ שְׁתוּת אוֹ הוֹסִיפוּ שְׁתוּת **Where they subtracted a sixth or added a sixth.** *Rivan* notes that the words "subtracted" and "added" can both be understood in two ways. Either they subtracted in favor of the heirs or they subtracted in favor of the buyer, and similarly, they added in favor of the heirs or they added in favor of the buyer. There is, however, no practical difference between the two explanations.

מִכְרָן בָּטֵל **Their sale is invalid.** The Rishonim note: Granted that the sale it invalid if the court appraised the property for a sixth less than its actual market value, for their error caused a loss to the orphans. But why is the sale invalid if the court sold the property for a sixth more than its actual worth? Surely, the law is that land is not subject to the laws of excess profit! (There are, in fact, some Rishonim who interpreted our Mishnah as referring to movable goods because of this question; see *Meiri.*) *Ramban* explains that an ordinary buyer would not be able to invalidate the sale because he overpaid, for land is not subject to laws of excess profit. But here the widow or the creditor went to court to collect the money owed them, and they were obliged to take the property at the price set by the court through its appraisal. Such a sale is invalid if the property was appraised at more than its actual market price. *Ra'ah* suggests that the sale is invalid even if the property was purchased by another buyer, for the Rabbis did not distinguish between property sold for less than its market value and property sold for more than its market value. *Rid* proposes that since the court erred in its appraisal of the property, whatever they did is invalid.

HALAKHAH

שׁוּם הַדַּיָּינִין, שֶׁפִּיחֲתוּ שְׁתוּת **The appraisal of the judges, where they subtracted a sixth.** "If the court erred while selling property belonging to orphans (whether landed property or movable goods), and sold it for a sixth more or a sixth less than its actual market value, the sale is null and void. But if the court erred by less than a sixth, the sale is valid," following the anonymous first Tanna of the Mishnah. (*Rambam, Sefer Kinyan, Hilkhot Mekhirah* 13:10; *Shulḥan Arukh, Ḥoshen Mishpat* 109:3.)

TRANSLATION AND COMMENTARY

way is the court's authority stronger than that of a private individual? [1]**But if** the court sold the property after having **drawn up a letter of examination,** publicly announcing the sale of the property in order to attract the highest bidder, [2]then **even if a maneh's worth** of property **was sold for two hundred** zuz, [3]**or** if **two hundred** dinars' **worth** was sold **for a maneh, the sale is valid.**

GEMARA אִיבַּעְיָא לְהוּ [4]The following **problem arose** in discussion: If **an agent** erred and sold property belonging to the deceased for less than its actual value, **whom is he like?** Do we treat him like a widow, about whom we learned in the previous Mishnah that if she sold property belonging to her husband for even a dinar less than its actual value, the sale is invalid? Or do we treat him like a court, in which case the sale is valid as long as he did not err by more than a sixth of the property's actual value?

[100A] רָבָא [5]**Rava said in the name of Rav Naḥman: An agent** who erred and property belonging to the deceased sold for less than its actual value **is** treated **like a** court of **judges.**

רַב [6]**Rav Shmuel bar Bisna said in the name of Rav Naḥman:** He is treated **like a widow.**

רָבָא אָמַר [7]The Gemara now explains the rationale underlying the two opposing opinions: **Rava said in the name of Rav Naḥman: An agent is** treated **like a** court of **judges.** [8]**Just as judges sell** the property belonging to the deceased on behalf of someone else, such as a widow who wishes to collect her ketubah settlement, or a creditor who wishes to collect his debt, and **not for themselves, so too an agent sells** property on behalf of someone else and **not for himself.** Consequently the Sages reinforced the transactions executed by the court or an agent, and declared them valid as long as the court or the agent did not err by one-sixth of the property's value. [9]**A widow is excluded** from this regulation, because **she sells** the property belonging to her husband's estate **for herself.**

בֵּית דִּין יָפֶה? [1]אֲבָל אִם עָשׂוּ אִגֶּרֶת בִּקּוֹרֶת בֵּינֵיהֶן, [2]אֲפִילּוּ מָכְרוּ שָׁוֶה מָנֶה בְּמָאתַיִם [3]אוֹ שָׁוֶה מָאתַיִם בְּמָנֶה, מִכְרָן קַיָּים.

גמרא [4]אִיבַּעְיָא לְהוּ: שָׁלִיחַ כְּמַאן? [100A] [5]רָבָא אָמַר רַב נַחְמָן: שָׁלִיחַ כְּדַיָּינִין. [6]רַב שְׁמוּאֵל בַּר בִּיסְנָא אָמַר רַב נַחְמָן: כְּאַלְמָנָה. [7]רָבָא אָמַר רַב נַחְמָן שָׁלִיחַ כְּדַיָּינִין. [8]מַה דַּיָּינִין לָאו לְדִידְהוּ, אַף שָׁלִיחַ נַמִי לָאו לְדִידֵיהּ. [9]לְאַפּוּקֵי אַלְמָנָה דִּלְדִידָהּ.

LITERAL TRANSLATION

of the court? [1]But if they made a letter of examination between them, [2]even if they sold a maneh's worth for two hundred, [3]or two hundred's worth for a maneh, their sale is valid.

GEMARA [4]It was asked of them: The agent is like whom? [100A] [5]Rava said in the name of Rav Naḥman: An agent is like judges.

[6]Rav Shmuel bar Bisna said in the name of Rav Naḥman: Like a widow.

[7]Rava said in the name of Rav Naḥman: An agent is like judges. [8]Just as judges [sell] not for themselves, so too an agent also [sells] not for himself. [9]To the exclusion of a widow, [who sells] for herself.

RASHI

משנה אגרת בקורת – הכרזה. ולשון בקורת — שמבקרין אותה בני אדם על ידי הכרזה.

גמרא שליח כמאן — שליח דטעה, כמאן דיינין ליה? כאלמנה דיינין ליה, שבטעות כל דהו בטל, כדתנן: שוה מנה ודינר במנה — מכרה בטל. או כדיינין הוא — ועד דטעה בשתות. לאו לדידהו — לאו לצורך עצמן מוכרים.

NOTES

אִגֶּרֶת בִּקּוֹרֶת **A letter of examination.** The Jerusalem Talmud explains that *iggeret bikoret* means a public announcement of the sale of the property. *Rashi* understands the term in the same manner, adding that as a result of the announcement, which apparently was done by way of an *iggeret,* a scroll that was open to public view, as opposed to a private document, people would come and "visit" (*bikkur*) the property and examine what was being offered for sale. *Rambam* understands the term as "letter of examination." After the court would announce the sale of the property, it would draw up a document stating that the appraisal and announcement had been conducted after careful examination of the entire matter (see also *Tosafot Yom Tov*).

שָׁלִיחַ כְּמַאן **The agent is like whom.** According to *Rabbenu Tam* (whose position was accepted by most of the Rishonim), the Gemara's discussion here refers to an agent who was appointed by the court, but regarding an ordinary agent, even the slightest error invalidates his transactions. As the Gemara stated above, his principal can argue that he had sent him for his benefit, not for his detriment.

לְאַפּוּקֵי אַלְמָנָה דִּלְדִידָהּ **To the exclusion of a widow.** *Rivan* explains that since the agent sells the property on behalf

HALAKHAH

אִם עָשׂוּ אִגֶּרֶת בִּקּוֹרֶת **If they made a letter of examination.** "If the court publicly announced the sale of the orphans property, and carefully appraised its value, then even if it erred and sold property worth a maneh for two hundred dinars or property worth two hundred dinars for a maneh, the sale is valid," following the Mishnah. (*Rambam, Sefer Mishpatim, Hilkhot Malveh* 12:11; *Shulḥan Arukh, Ḥoshen Mishpat* 109:3; *Even HaEzer* 104:3.)

TRANSLATION AND COMMENTARY

רַב [1] **Rav Shmuel bar Bisna said in the name of Rav Naḥman.** The agent is treated **like a widow.** [2] **Just as a widow is** only **one** person, **so too an agent is** only **one** person. Hence the Sages ruled that if the widow or the agent sold property belonging to the deceased for anything less than its full market value, the transaction is null and void. [3] **A court** of judges **is excluded** from this regulation, **because** a court consists **of many** judges, and so the Sages declared its actions valid as long as it did not commit an error of one-sixth of the property's value.

וְהִלְכְתָא [4] The Gemara concludes this discussion with a practical ruling on the matter: **The law is** that **an agent is** treated **like a widow,** so that if he sold property belonging to the deceased for even a dinar less than its actual value, the sale is null and void.

וּמַאי שְׁנָא [5] The Gemara asks: **How is** this case **different from that which we have learned** in the Mishnah (Terumot 4:4): [6] **"If someone said to his agent: 'Go out and separate** terumah from my produce,' but he did not tell him how much terumah to separate, [7] the agent should **separate** terumah from the produce **in accordance with** his understanding of **the intention of the owner** of the produce. [8] **If** the agent **does not know the intention of the** produce's **owner,** [9] **he should separate** terumah **according to the average gift, one-fiftieth** of the crop. [10] **If** the agent who does not know his sender's intention **subtracted ten,** by separating one-fortieth instead of one-fiftieth, **or** he **added ten,** by separating one-sixtieth instead of one-fortieth, [11] **the** terumah **which he separated is** terumah." If an agent's sale is invalid if he sold property for even one dinar less than its market value, why do we not say that the terumah which he separated from his principal's produce is not terumah, if he separated one-fortieth or one-sixtieth of the crop?

LITERAL TRANSLATION

[1] Rav Shmuel bar Bisna said in the name of Rav Naḥman. [2] Like a widow: Just as a widow is one, so too an agent is one. [3] To the exclusion of a court which is many.

[4] And the law is: An agent is like a widow.

[5] And how is it different from what we have learned: [6] "[If] someone says to his agent: 'Go out and separate terumah,' [7] he separates terumah according to the intention of the master of the house. [8] And if he does not know the intention of the master of the house, [9] he separates terumah according to the average [gift], one-fiftieth. [10] [If] he subtracted ten, or added ten, [11] his terumah is terumah."

[1] רַב שְׁמוּאֵל בַּר בִּיסְנָא אֲמַר רַב נַחְמָן כְּאַלְמָנָה. [2] מַה אַלְמָנָה יְחִידָה, אַף שָׁלִיחַ יָחִיד. [3] לְאַפּוּקֵי בֵּית דִּין דְּרַבִּים נִינְהוּ. [4] וְהִלְכְתָא: שָׁלִיחַ כְּאַלְמָנָה. [5] וּמַאי שְׁנָא מֵהָא דִּתְנַן: [6] "הָאוֹמֵר לִשְׁלוּחוֹ 'צֵא וּתְרוֹם', [7] תּוֹרֵם כְּדַעַת בַּעַל הַבַּיִת. [8] וְאִם אֵינוֹ יוֹדֵעַ דַּעְתּוֹ שֶׁל בַּעַל הַבַּיִת, [9] תּוֹרֵם בְּבֵינוֹנִית אֶחָד מֵחֲמִשִּׁים. [10] פִּיחֵת עֲשָׂרָה אוֹ הוֹסִיף עֲשָׂרָה, [11] תְּרוּמָתוֹ תְּרוּמָה".

NOTES

of someone else, he has no personal interest in selling it below its market price. Thus, his transactions are valid as long as he did not err by one-sixth of the property's value. But the widow who sells the property on her own behalf has an interest in selling it below its market price, for she is interested in selling it as soon as possible to collect her ketubah settlement. Thus her transactions are not valid if she sold the property for even one dinar less than its actual price.

שָׁלִיחַ כְּאַלְמָנָה **An agent is like a widow.** Rav Hai Gaon concludes, apparently from this passage, that an agent is treated like a widow, in that he cannot sell any of the property on his own, but only under the supervision of three other people, even if they are not authorized judges. But most of the Rishonim did not accept this position.

פִּיחֵת עֲשָׂרָה **If he subtracted ten.** According to those Rishonim who maintain that the Gemara's discussion is limited to a court-appointed agent, this question can be

understood as follows: If an agent for terumah can make an error, and the terumah which he separated is still terumah, then all the more so if a court-appointed agent made an error, the transaction which he executed should still be valid (Ramban). Ritva explains that if we were to say that a minor error made by a court-appointed agent does not invalidate a transaction, then we could say that the Rabbis treated an agent for terumah like a court-appointed agent. But if even a minor error invalidates a transaction contracted by a court-appointed agent, then why is terumah of an agent who made an error still terumah? Rosh writes that the Mishnah regarding terumah teaches that if an agent made a reasonable error, his actions are still valid. If so, the transactions of a court-appointed agent should be valid even if he made an error, provided that the error is reasonable, that is, less than one-sixth.

HALAKHAH

שָׁלִיחַ כְּאַלְמָנָה **The agent is like a widow.** "If an agent erred and overpaid or undercharged even the slightest amount, the transaction is null and void," following the Gemara's conclusion. This law applies even if the agent was appointed by a court. Rema writes that some authori-

ties (Rivash) maintain that if a judge was appointed by government decree, and he sold property by way of an agent, that agent is treated like a court. (Rambam, Sefer Kinyan, Hilkhot Mekhirah 13:9; Hilkhot Sheluhin 1:2; Shulḥan Arukh, Even HaEzer 104:6; Ḥoshen Mishpat 109:6.)

TRANSLATION AND COMMENTARY

הָתָם [1]The Gemara asks: **There** in the Mishnah in *Terumot,* the agent's *terumah* is *terumah,* **because some people separate *terumah* in a miserly manner,** and set aside only one-sixtieth of the crop, [2]**and others separate *terumah* in a** most **generous manner,** and set aside one-fortieth of the crop, [3]the agent **can say to** his sender: **"I assessed you** as one who separates *terumah* in a miserly manner, or as someone who separates *terumah* in a generous manner." [4]**But here,** the agent sold the property of the deceased at a reduced price below its market value, which **was an error,** and the principal **can say to** his agent: [5]**"You should not have committed** such **an error."** The agent's error invalidates the transaction.

אָמַר [6]The Gemara continues: **Rav Huna bar Ḥanina said in the name of Rav Naḥman: The law is in accordance** with the position of **the Sages** in the Mishnah (the anonymous first Tanna) who said that if judges erred in their appraisal of property, and sold it for one-sixth less or more than its actual market value, the sale is invalid.

וְלֵית לֵיהּ [7]The Gemara asks: **Does Rav Naḥman not accept** the argument put forward by Rabban Shimon ben Gamliel, that the court's sale of the property must be valid, even if the error was for more than one-sixth, for if not so, **in what way is the court's authority stronger** than that of a private individual? [8]**But surely Rav Naḥman said in the name of Shmuel: If** a person died, and his **heirs came to divide their father's property** among themselves, [9]**the court appoints a custodian for** any heir that is still a minor, **and** each

[1]הָתָם, כֵּיוָן דְּאִיכָּא דְּתוֹרֵם בְּעַיִן רָעָה,[2]וְאִיכָּא דְּתוֹרֵם בְּעַיִן יָפָה, [3]אָמַר לֵיהּ: ״לְהָכִי אֲמַדְתִּיךְ״. [4]אֲבָל הָכָא, טָעוּתָא הוּא, אָמַר לֵיהּ: [5]״לָא אִיבָּעֵי לָךְ לְמִיטְעֵי״.

[6]אָמַר רַב הוּנָא בַּר חֲנִינָא אָמַר רַב נַחְמָן: הֲלָכָה כְּדִבְרֵי חֲכָמִים.

[7]וְלֵית לֵיהּ לְרַב נַחְמָן: מָה כֹּחַ בֵּית דִּין יָפֶה? [8]וְהָאָמַר רַב נַחְמָן אָמַר שְׁמוּאֵל: יְתוֹמִים שֶׁבָּאוּ לַחֲלוֹק בְּנִכְסֵי אֲבִיהֶן, [9]בֵּית דִּין מַעֲמִידִין לָהֶן אַפּוֹטְרוֹפּוֹס וּבוֹרְרִין לָהֶם חֵלֶק יָפֶה.

LITERAL TRANSLATION

[1]There, since there is one who separates *terumah* in a miserly manner (lit., "with a bad eye"), [2]and there is one who separates *terumah* generously (lit., "with a good eye"), [3]he can say to him: "Thus I assessed you." [4]But here, it is an error, he can say to him: [5]"You should not have erred."

[6]Rav Huna bar Ḥanina said in the name of Rav Naḥman: The law is as the words of the Sages.

[7]Does Rav Naḥman not maintain: What is the power of the court? [8]But surely Rav Naḥman said in the name of Shmuel: [If] orphans came to divide up their father's property, [9]the court appoints a custodian for them, and they select a good portion for them.

RASHI

בית דין מעמידין להן אפוטרופוס – לכל אחד ואחד מן הקטנים. ובוררין להם – כל אפוטרופוס לתינוק שלו.

NOTES

כֵּיוָן דְּאִיכָּא דְּתוֹרֵם **Since there is someone who separates *terumah*.** *Ḥatam Sofer* explains: Since the owner of the produce knows that there are three different levels of generosity, and he did not specify with his agent how much *terumah* he should separate from his produce, it follows of someone else, he has no personal interest in selling it below its market price. Thus, his transactions are valid as that he relied on the agent's assessment of how much *terumah* he would like to have separated. But regarding an agent who sold property for less than its market value, the owner certainly did not give his agent permission to make an error.

יְתוֹמִים שֶׁבָּאוּ לַחֲלוֹק **If the orphans came to distribute.** *Rambam* understands that in the case discussed by the Gemara, some of the heirs had reached adulthood, while others were still minors. It would appear that he understood the case in this manner, because if all the heirs were minors, there would be no reason to divide the property now. *Rabbenu Tam,* however, writes that in the case discussed by the Gemara, all of the heirs were still minors (and so too it would appear from *Rashi*).

מַעֲמִידִין לָהֶן אַפּוֹטְרוֹפּוֹס **The court appoints a guardian for them.** *Rashi, Rabbenu Ḥananel,* and others understand that the court appoints a separate guardian for any heir that is still a minor, and each guardian protects the interests of his own ward. According to *Rambam* and *Rosh,* the court appoints one guardian who looks out for all the heirs that are still minors.

Regarding the selection of portions for each of the minors, *Rabbenu Ḥananel* maintains that the property should be divided up by drawing lots. Others, however, maintain that each guardian selects a portion of the estate.

HALAKHAH

יְתוֹמִים שֶׁבָּאוּ לַחֲלוֹק **If the orphans came to divide.** "If the heirs of the deceased wished to divide their father's property, the court appoints a custodian for any heir that is still a minor, and each custodian selects a fair portion of the estate for his ward. When the minors later reach majority, they cannot object to the way in which their father's estate had been divided, for the division was executed under the supervision of the court. But if the court

TRANSLATION AND COMMENTARY

custodian **selects** for his ward **a good portion** of the estate. [1]**If** the minors later **reached majority,** and were dissatisfied with the portions that they had received, **they can protest** and demand that their father's assets be redistributed. [2]**And Rav Naḥman himself** disagreed with Shmuel and **said: If** the minors **reached majority, they cannot protest,** [3]**for if** they can do **so, in what way is the court's authority stronger** than that of a private individual? Thus, we see that Rav Naḥman himself utilizes the argument put forward by Rabban Shimon ben Gamliel!

לָא קַשְׁיָא [4]The Gemara answers: [5]**There is** really **no difficulty. There** in our Mishnah the court **erred** and sold the property for one-sixth more or less than its actual value. Regarding such a case, Rav Naḥman rules that the law is in accordance with the position of the Sages that the sale is invalid. [6]But **here** the court **did not err,** and each of the heirs received all that was due him. Regarding such a case, Rav Naḥman accepts the argument of Rabban Shimon ben Gamliel.

אִי דְּלָא טָעוּ [7]The Gemara asks: **If** the court **did not commit an error** when it divided up the property of the deceased, [8]then **about what can** the heirs possibly **object?**

בְּרוּחוֹת [9]The Gemara answers: The heir wishes to object **about the side** of his father's property which he had been given. He would have preferred to receive his share on a different side of his father's property. Regarding such a case, Rav Naḥman ruled that the heir cannot object to the division of his father's estate.

כִּי אֲתָא [10]It was related that **when Rav Dimi came** to Babylonia from Eretz Israel, **he said: It** once **happened that Rabbi** Yehudah HaNasi **acted in accordance with the Sages** of our Mishnah concerning a judicial error in the appraisal of property, which was sold for one-sixth less than or more than its actual market value. He ruled that the sale is invalid. [11]**Perata the son of Rabbi Elazar ben Perata** and **the grandson of Rabbi Perata the Great said to** Rabbi Yehudah HaNasi: The court's sale of the property must be valid, [12]otherwise **in what way is the court's authority stronger** than that of a private individual? [13]**Rabbi** Yehudah HaNasi accepted this argument and **retracted his ruling.**

רַב דִּימִי [14]The Gemara continues: **Rav Dimi taught** this incident in the way that it has just been reported. [15]**Rav Safra taught** a slightly different version of the story: **It** once **happened that Rabbi** Yehudah HaNasi **wished to act in accordance with the Sages** of our Mishnah, who ruled that if judges erred in their appraisal of property, and sold it for one-sixth less than or more than its actual market value, the sale is invalid. But before Rabbi Yehudah HaNasi issued the ruling, [16]**Perata the son of Rabbi Elazar ben Perata** and **the**

LITERAL TRANSLATION

[1][If] they reached majority, they can protest. [2]And Rav Naḥman himself said: [If] they reached majority, they cannot object, [3][for] if so, what is the power of the court?

[4]It is not difficult. [5]This, when they erred; [6]this, when they did not err.

[7]If they did not err, [8]about what can they object?

[9]About the sides.

[10]When Rav Dimi came, he said: It happened that Rabbi acted in accordance with the Sages. [11]Perata the son of Rabbi Elazar ben Perata the grandson of Rabbi Perata the Elder said before him: [12]If so, what is the power of the court? [13]And Rabbi retracted the ruling (lit., "incident").

[14]Rav Dimi taught thus. [15]Rav Safra taught thus: It happened that Rabbi wished to act in accordance with the Sages. [16]Perata the son

[1]הִגְדִּילוּ, יְכוֹלִין לִמְחוֹת. [2]וְרַב נַחְמָן דִּידֵיהּ אָמַר: הִגְדִּילוּ אֵין יְכוֹלִין לִמְחוֹת, [3]אִם כֵּן, מַה כֹּחַ בֵּית דִּין יָפֶה!

[4]לָא קַשְׁיָא. [5]הָא דְּטָעוּ; [6]הָא דְּלָא טָעוּ.

[7]אִי דְּלָא טָעוּ, [8]בְּמַאי יְכוֹלִין לִמְחוֹת?

[9]בְּרוּחוֹת.

[10]כִּי אֲתָא רַב דִּימִי, אָמַר: מַעֲשֶׂה וְעָשָׂה רַבִּי כְּדִבְרֵי חֲכָמִים. [11]אָמַר לְפָנָיו פְּרָטָא בְּנוֹ שֶׁל רַבִּי אֶלְעָזָר בֶּן פְּרָטָא בֶּן בְּנוֹ שֶׁל רַבִּי פְּרָטָא הַגָּדוֹל: [12]אִם כֵּן, מַה כֹּחַ בֵּית דִּין יָפֶה? [13]וְהֶחֱזִיר רַבִּי אֶת הַמַּעֲשֶׂה.

[14]רַב דִּימִי מַתְנֵי הָכִי. [15]רַב סָפְרָא מַתְנֵי הָכִי: מַעֲשֶׂה וּבִיקֵּשׁ רַבִּי לַעֲשׂוֹת כְּדִבְרֵי חֲכָמִים. [16]אָמַר לְפָנָיו פְּרָטָא בְּנוֹ

SAGES

רַבִּי פְּרָטָא Rabbi Perata. Rabbi Perata belonged to a family of Sages of which we can trace three generations: Rabbi Perata the Great who apparently lived at the time of the destruction of the Temple; his son Rabbi Elazar ben Perata who was one of the Sages of the Sanhedrin in Yavneh and lived for many years, until the persecutions at the time of the Emperor Hadrian (he was saved from execution by a miracle); and his son, Rabbi Perata, who lived at the time of Rabbi Yehudah HaNasi. There might also have been a second Elazar ben Perata, the son of the younger Rabbi Perata, who lived during the first and second generation of Amoraim in Eretz Israel.

RASHI

אי דלא טעו – למה ימחו. **ברוחות** – טוב לי ליטול חלקי במזרח, שיש לי אצלה שדה שנפלה לי מבית אבי אמי. **והחזיר רבי את המעשה** – דנראה בעיניו טעם הגון מה ששנינו במשנתנו: אם כן מה כח בית דין יפה.

HALAKHAH

erred in their assessment and awarded the minors one-sixth less than what was due them, they can object, and the estate must be redivided after the minors reach majority," following Rav Naḥman and the Gemara's conclusion. (*Rambam, Sefer Mishpatim, Hilkhot Naḥalot* 10:4; *Shulḥan Arukh, Ḥoshen Mishpat* 289:1.)

TRANSLATION AND COMMENTARY

grandson of Rabbi Perata the Greater said to him: [1]**If** it is **so** that the sale is invalid, then **in what way is the court's authority stronger** than that of a private individual? [2]**Rabbi** Yehudah HaNasi accepted this argument, and **did not issue this ruling.**

לֵימָא בְּהָא קָמִיפַּלְגִי [3]The Gemara now tries to explain the difference between the two versions of this story, which hinge on the expression, "he wished to." **Shall we say that** Rav Dimi and Rav Safra **disagree about the following** issue? [4]**One Sage,** Rav Dimi, **maintains** that **if** a judge **issued an erroneous ruling about** a clear **Mishnaic law,** [5]**the ruling is subject to revision.** Since Rav Dimi maintains that an erroneous ruling of this nature is subject to revision, he can say that Rabbi Yehudah Ḥanasi first ruled in accordance with the Sages and then retracted his ruling after his error was demonstrated to him. [6]**And the other Sage,** Rav Safra, **says:** If a judge issued an erroneous ruling about a clear Mishnaic law, the ruling **is** nevertheless final and **not subject to revision.** In his view, had Rabbi Yehudah HaNasi already issued his ruling, he could not have retracted it.

לָא [7]The Gemara rejects this argument: **No, all** might **agree,** both Rav Dimi and Rav Safra, **that if someone issued an erroneous ruling about** a clear **Mishnaic law,** [8]**the ruling is subject to revision.** The two Amoraim do not disagree about a point of law; they simply received two different versions of the story. [9]**One Sage,** Rav Dimi, **says that the incident occurred this** way, [10]**and the other Sage,** Rav Safra, **says that the incident occurred that** way.

אָמַר רַב יוֹסֵף [11]**Rav Yosef said: If a widow sold** some of her late husband's property for her maintenance or for her ketubah settlement, [12]**the responsibility** of restoring the buyer's purchase money, **falls upon the heirs,** should it turn out that the property did not belong to the husband, or that it had been mortgaged to a prior creditor, and it was seized from the buyer by its rightful owner or by the creditor. The buyer may recover his loss from the other property which the heirs inherited, for that property is mortgaged to him to protect him against such a possibility. [13]**And,** similarly, **if the court sold** some of the late husband's property for his widow's maintenance or her ketubah settlement, or for the maintenance of his daughters, **the responsibility** of restoring the buyer's purchase money **falls upon the heirs,** should the property be seized from him by the property's rightful owner or by a prior creditor.

שֶׁל רַבִּי אֶלְעָזָר בֶּן פְּרָטָא בֶּן בְּנוֹ שֶׁל רַבִּי פְּרָטָא הַגָּדוֹל: [1]אִם כֵּן, מַה כֹּחַ בֵּית דִּין יָפֶה? [2]לֹא עָשָׂה רַבִּי אֶת הַמַּעֲשֶׂה.

[3]לֵימָא בְּהָא קָמִיפַּלְגִי? [4]מָר סָבַר: טָעָה בִּדְבַר מִשְׁנָה, [5]חוֹזֵר, [6]וּמָר סָבַר: אֵינוֹ חוֹזֵר.

[7]לָא, דְּכוּלֵּי עָלְמָא טָעָה בִּדְבַר מִשְׁנָה, [8]חוֹזֵר. [9]וּמָר סָבַר: הָכִי הֲוָה מַעֲשֶׂה. [10]וּמָר סָבַר: הָכִי הֲוָה מַעֲשֶׂה.

[11]אָמַר רַב יוֹסֵף: אַרְמַלְתָּא דְּזַבִּינָה, [12]אַחֲרָיוּת אַיַּתְמֵי. [13]וּבֵית דִּין דְּזַבִּין, אַחֲרָיוּת אַיַּתְמֵי.

LITERAL TRANSLATION

of Rabbi Elazar ben Perata the grandson of Rabbi Perata the Elder said before him: [1]If so, what is the power of the court? [2]Rabbi did not issue the ruling.

[3]Shall we say that they disagree about this? [4]One Sage maintains: [If] someone erred about a Mishnaic law, [5][the ruling] is overturned. [6]And the other Sage says: [The ruling] is not overturned.

[7]No, all agree [that if] someone erred about a Mishnaic law, [8][the ruling] is overturned. [9]And the one Sage says: Thus was the incident. [10]And the other Sage says: Thus was the incident.

[11]Rav Yosef said: [If] a widow sold, [12]the responsibility [falls] upon the orphans. [13]And [if] the court sold, the responsibility [falls] upon the orphans.

RASHI

לימא בהא פליגי — רב דימי ורב ספרא. רב דימי סבר: דיין הטועה בדבר המשנה, שלא עשה כמשנה — חוזר, ולא אמרינן מה שעשה עשוי וישלם מביתו, אלא בטועה בשיקול הדעת, כמו שמפורש בסנהדרין. והאי נמי — דבר משנה הוא, שאף על פי שנחלקו חכמים על רבן שמעון — הרי נתן טעם לדבריו. ורב ספרא שאינו שונה עשה והחזיר, סבר: אם עשה — לא היה יכול לחזור. **אחריותא איתמי** — אם נמצאת השדה גזולה או משועבדת לאחר, וטרפה מן הלוקח בחובו — חוזר הלוקח על היתומים. שהאלמנה שליח של יתומים היתה. **וכן בי דינא דזבין** — שדה יתומים למזון האשה והבנות — אחריות איתמי.

NOTES

טָעָה בִּדְבַר מִשְׁנָה If someone erred about a Mishnaic law. *Rivan* explains that Rabbi Yehudah HaNasi's ruling in accordance with the Sages is considered to be an erroneous ruling about a clear Mishnaic law, because, as a rule, the law follows Rabban Shimon ben Gamliel whenever his position is recorded in the Mishnah. *Rashi,* however, writes

HALAKHAH

טָעָה בִּדְבַר מִשְׁנָה, חוֹזֵר If someone erred about a Mishnaic law. "If a judge issued an erroneous judgment in a civil case, committing an error regarding a clearly decided law in the Mishnah, Gemara, or later authorities, the judgment is subject to revision. *Rema* adds that some maintain (*Tur,* in the name of *Rosh*) that a Rabbinic authority may disagree

[1]פְּשִׁיטָא!
[2]אַלְמָנָה לָא אִיצְטְרִיכָא לֵיהּ.
[3]כִּי אִיצְטְרִיךְ לֵיהּ — בֵּי דִינָא.
[4]מַהוּ דְּתֵימָא: [100B] [5]כָּל דְּזַבֵּין מִבֵּי דִינָא, אַדַּעְתָּא לְמֵיפַּק לֵיהּ קָלָא הוּא דְּזַבֵּין. [6]קָא מַשְׁמַע לָן.
[7]״רַבָּן שִׁמְעוֹן בֶּן גַּמְלִיאֵל אוֹמֵר כו׳״. [8]וְעַד כַּמָּה?
[9]אֲמַר רַב הוּנָא בַּר יְהוּדָה אֲמַר רַב שֵׁשֶׁת: עַד פַּלְגָּא.
[10]תַּנְיָא נַמִי הָכִי: [11]״אָמַר רַבָּן שִׁמְעוֹן בֶּן גַּמְלִיאֵל: בֵּית דִּין שֶׁמָּכְרוּ שָׁוֶה מָאתַיִם בְּמָנֶה, [12]אוֹ שָׁוֶה מָנֶה בְּמָאתַיִם, מִכְרָן קַיָּים.

LITERAL TRANSLATION

[1]This is obvious!

[2][Regarding] a widow, it was not necessary. [3]When was it necessary — [regarding] the court. [4]Lest you say: [100B] [5]Whoever buys from the court, buys on the assumption that a voice had gone forth. [6]It teaches us.

[7]"Rabban Shimon ben Gamliel says, etc." [8]And how much?

[9]Rav Huna bar Yehudah said in the name of Rav Sheshet: Up to half.

[10]It was also taught thus: [11]"Rabban Shimon ben Gamliel said: [If] a court sold two hundred's worth [of property] for a maneh, [12]or a maneh's worth for two hundred, their sale is valid."

TRANSLATION AND COMMENTARY

פְּשִׁיטָא [1]The Gemara asks: **This** ruling **is obvious,** for surely the widow did not sell her own property, so responsibility for the sale cannot fall upon her! She sold her late husband's property, which now belongs to his heirs, so the responsibility should certainly fall upon those heirs!

אַלְמָנָה [2]The Gemara answers: **Regarding a widow** who sold some of her late husband's property, **it was not necessary** for Rav Yosef to teach us that the responsibility for the sale falls upon the heirs, for as was explained above, this is obvious. [3]Regarding **which** case **was it necessary** to say that the responsibility for the sale falls upon the heirs? Regarding a **court** that sold some of the husband's property. [4]**For you might have said** [100B] [5]that **whoever buys** property **from a court buys** the property **on the assumption that an announcement has been made** publicizing the sale, so that if anybody had grounds to contest it, surely he would have come forward and presented his claim. Hence it is unlikely that anybody will come and claim the property, and the buyer is regarded as having waived his right to compensation should the property later be seized from him. [6]Thus, Rav Yosef **teaches us** that even if the court sold the husband's property, responsibility for the sale falls upon the heirs.

רַבָּן [7]We learned in our Mishnah: **"Rabban Shimon ben Gamliel says:** If a court erred in its appraisal of property, and sold it for more or less than its actual value, the sale is valid." [8]The Gemara asks: **How large** may the error be for the sale to remain valid?

אֲמַר [9]**Rav Huna bar Yehudah said in the name of Rav Sheshet:** Even if the court sold the property **for** only **half** of its actual value, or for twice its actual value, the sale is valid.

תַּנְיָא נַמִי הָכִי [10]The Gemara notes that **the same thing was also taught** in a Baraita which stated: [11]**"Rabban Shimon ben Gamliel said: If a court sold two hundred's worth** of property **for** only **a maneh,** [12]**or** if it sold **a maneh's worth** of property **for two hundred** dinars, **the sale is valid."** Since the Baraita did not give an example of an even larger error, it follows that if the error was larger, the sale is not valid.

RASHI

כל דזבין מבי דינא אדעתא דנפיק ליה קלא זבין – לפי שהן מוכרים בהכרזה, ובטוח הלוקח שאילו היו עליה עסיקין – היו יוצאין ומערערין. הלכך שלא באחריות הוא לוקח, קא משמע לן.

NOTES

that the ruling is considered to be erroneous because Rabban Shimon ben Gamliel gave a persuasive explanation of his position. It would appear that *Rashi* did not accept *Rivan*'s explanation, because he thought that the rule that the law is in accordance with Rabban Shimon ben Gamliel might not yet have been formulated in Rabbi Yehudah HaNasi's day.

אַדַּעְתָּא לְמֵיפַּק לֵיהּ קָלָא **On the assumption that a voice had gone forth.** *Rashi* and most of the Rishonim explain that if someone buys property through a court, he is confident that nobody will come and seize it from him, for the sale was publicized and nobody had come to contest it. Thus, unless the buyer explicitly stipulated that he was buying the property on condition that the transaction is guaranteed, he is regarded as having purchased the property without such a guarantee (see also *Rid*). *Rivan* objects that we might have thought that someone who buys property through a court thinks that a court-supervised sale cannot be contested, and so he does not expect the transaction to be subject to an additional guarantee.

HALAKHAH

with earlier post-Talmudic authorities if he can demonstrate through persuasive arguments that the law is not in accordance with their position. But he should not treat lightly a stringency that was accepted by authorities whose works are widely accepted in the Jewish community, unless he has a tradition that the common practice does not follow that stringency." (*Piskei Mahari.*) (*Rambam, Sefer Shofetim, Hilkhot Sanhedrin* 6:1; *Shulhan Arukh, Hoshen Mishpat* 25:1.)

[1]אָמַר אַמֵימָר מִשְּׁמֵיהּ דְּרַב יוֹסֵף: בֵּית דִּין שֶׁמָּכְרוּ בְּלֹא הַכְרָזָה, [2]נַעֲשׂוּ כְּמִי שֶׁטָּעוּ בִּדְבַר מִשְׁנָה וְחוֹזְרִין נַעֲשׂוּ? [3]וַדַּאי טָעוּ. [4]דִּתְנַן: [5]״שׁוּם הַיְּתוֹמִין — שְׁלֹשִׁים יוֹם, [6]וְשׁוּם הַהֶקְדֵּשׁ — שִׁשִּׁים יוֹם. [7]וּמַכְרִיזִין בַּבֹּקֶר וּבָעֶרֶב. [8]אִי מֵהַהִיא הֲוָה אָמִינָא: הָנֵי מִילֵּי שָׁלִיחַ, [9]אֲבָל בֵּית דִּין לָא. [10]קָא מַשְׁמַע לָן. [11]אֵיתִיבֵיהּ רַב אַשִׁי לְאַמֵימָר: [12]״שׁוּם הַדַּיָּינִין שֶׁפִּחֲתוּ שְׁתוּת אוֹ הוֹתִירוּ שְׁתוּת — מִכְרָן בָּטֵל״. [13]הָא שָׁוֶה בְּשָׁוֶה, מִכְרָן קַיָּים, [14]מַאי לָאו דְּלָא אַכְרוּז?

LITERAL TRANSLATION

[1]Amemar said in the name of Rav Yosef: [If] a court sold without an announcement, [2]it is as if they erred in a Mishnaic law, and they retract. [3]It is as if they certainly erred, [4]for we have learned: [5]"The appraisal of the orphans — thirty days, [6]and the appraisal of consecrated property — sixty days. [7]And they announce morning and evening." [8]If from that, I might have said: Those words [apply to] an agent, [9]but the court — no. [10]It teaches us. [11]Rav Ashi objected to Amemar: [12]"The appraisal of the judges, when they subtracted one-sixth or added one-sixth — their sale is invalid." [13]But for what it is worth, their sale is valid. [14]Is it not when they did not announce?

TRANSLATION AND COMMENTARY

אָמַר אַמֵימָר [1]**Amemar said in the name of Rav Yosef: If a court sold** property **without** first publicly **announcing** the sale in order to attract the highest bidder, [2]**it is** considered **as if it** had **issued an erroneous ruling regarding a Mishnaic law, and** so the sale **is canceled.**

וַדַּאי טָעוּ [3]The Gemara questions the formulation of Amemar's statement: Why does Amemar say that in such a case, **it is** considered **as if** the court had issued an erroneous ruling regarding a Mishnaic law? The court **certainly erred** about a Mishnaic law when it sold the property without first publicly announcing the sale, [4]**for we have learned** in a Mishnah (*Arakhin* 6:1): "Property belonging to orphans and consecrated property must be appraised by three people with the necessary expertise before it may be sold. [5]**The appraisal of** property belonging to **orphans** must be followed by a public announcement of the sale for **thirty** consecutive **days** in order to attract the highest bidder. [6]**The appraisal of consecrated property** must be followed by a public announcement of the sale for **sixty** consecutive **days.** [7]**These announcements are made morning and evening** when workmen set out and return home." The Mishnah states explicitly that the sale of property belonging to orphans must be properly advertised. It follows that if the court sold such property without first publicizing the sale, they committed an error with respect to a Mishnaic law.

אִי מֵהַהִיא [8]The Gemara answers: **If** we only had **that** Mishnah, **I might have said** that **the** Mishnah's **regulation** just **applies to an agent** who wishes to sell property belonging to orphans. [9]**But if the court** wishes to sell property belonging to orphans, a public announcement might **not** be necessary. [10]Therefore, Amemar came to **teach us** that even a court is required to announce the sale, and if it failed to do so, it is considered as having made an error about a Mishnaic law.

אֵיתִיבֵיהּ [11]**Rav Ashi raised an objection against Amemar's** position from our Mishnah in which we have learned: [12]"If a court of **judges appraised** property incorrectly, and **sold** it **for one-sixth less** than its actual market value, **or** it **sold** the property **for one — sixth more** than its actual market value, **the sale is invalid."** [13]**But** it follows from the Mishnah that if the court did not appraise the property incorrectly, but rather it sold the property **for what it was worth, the sale is valid.** [14]Now, **is not** the Mishnah dealing with a case **when** the sale of the property **was not announced?**

RASHI

וחוזרין — ואין אומרין: מה שעשה עשוי וישלם מביתו, אלא הדרי דייני. **נעשו** — בתמיה, הא ודאי טעו בדבר השנוי במשנה! **שום ההקדש** — גזבר המוכר קרקע של הקדש. **ששים יום** — מוסיפים ימי הכרזה.

CONCEPTS

הַכְרָזָה **An announcement.** The procedures surrounding the public announcement of the court's intention to sell property are discussed in tractate *Arakhin*. The sale of orphan's property was advertised for thirty days prior to the sale, if the announcement was made daily, or for sixty days if it was made only on Mondays and Thursdays. In the latter case the announcements would only be made on eighteen days, but since they were made over a two-month period, we assume that anyone potentially interested in purchasing the property would hear about the sale. The public announcement of the sale followed an appraisal of the property's worth. The announcement was made in the morning, when workmen set out to work, so that they could inform their employers about the upcoming sale, and in the evening when workmen return home, so that they can get up early the next morning and examine the property.

HALAKHAH

בֵּית דִּין שֶׁמָּכְרוּ בְּלֹא הַכְרָזָה **If a court sold without an announcement.** "If a court sold property without first publicly announcing the sale, it is considered having issued an erroneous ruling regarding a Mishnaic law. So the sale is canceled, and the property is sold again with a public announcement. *Rema* adds that if the court sold property when there are few buyers, as during a plague or a war, some authorities say that the sale is valid, but others disagree and consider the property as having been sold without an announcement." (*Rambam, Sefer Mishpatim, Hilkhot Malveh* 12:10; *Shulḥan Arukh, Even HaEzer* 104:2; *Ḥoshen Mishpat* 109:3.)

שׁוּם הַיְתוֹמִין — שְׁלֹשִׁים יוֹם **The appraisal of the orphans — thirty days.** "If a court wishes to sell property belonging to orphans, the property must be appraised and then the sale must be announced for thirty consecutive days, or for sixty days every Monday and Thursday. The announcements must be made morning and evening when workmen set out for work and return home," following the Mishnah cited in our Gemara. (*Rambam, Sefer Mishpatim, Hilkhot Malveh* 12:8; *Shulḥan Arukh, Even HaEzer* 104:1; *Ḥoshen Mishpat* 109:1.)

שׁוּם הַהֶקְדֵּשׁ **The appraisal of consecrated property.** "Land that had been consecrated to the Temple treasury and that

TRANSLATION AND COMMENTARY

לָא, בִּדְאַכְרוּז [1]Amemar answered: **No,** the Mishnah is dealing with a case **when a** public **announcement** preceded the sale.

הָא מִדְּסֵיפָא [2]The Gemara asks: **But surely since the last clause** of the Mishnah deals with a case **when a** public **announcement** preceded the sale, [3]**the first clause** must be dealing with a case **when a** prior **announcement** had not been made, [4]**for the last clause states: "If** the court sold the property after having **drawn up a letter of examination,** publicly announcing the sale of the property in order to attract the highest bidder, then **even if a maneh's worth** of property **was sold for two hundred** zuz, [5]**or** if **two hundred** dinars' **worth** was sold **for a maneh, the sale is valid."**

אֶלָּא לְעוֹלָם [6]The Gemara answers: **Rather,** the first clause of the Mishnah is **in fact** dealing with a case **when a** public **announcement did not** precede the sale, **and** nevertheless the Mishnah's ruling does **not** pose any **difficulty** for Amemar, for he can argue as follows: [7]**Here,** Amemar says that if a court sold property without first publicly announcing the sale, the sale is canceled. He is talking about the sale of **assets** belonging to orphans, which **must be announced** in advance, as when the court sold land. [8]And **here,** the Mishnah implies that if the court sold property without first publicly announcing the sale, but at the proper price, the sale is valid. The Mishnah is talking about the sale of **assets** which **would not** ordinarily be **announced.** [9]The Gemara explains: **These are the assets** the sale of which **would not** ordinarily **be announced:** [10]Non-Jewish **slaves, movable goods, and promissory notes** held by the heirs for debts that had been owed to their father. [11]The Gemara explains: **What is the reason** that the sale of slaves would not be preceded by a public announcement?

[1]לָא, בִּדְאַכְרוּז. [2]הָא מִדְּסֵיפָא בִּדְאַכְרוּז, [3]הָוֵי רֵישָׁא בִּדְלָא אַכְרוּז, [4]דְּקָתָנֵי סֵיפָא: ״אִם עָשׂוּ אִגֶּרֶת בִּקּוֹרֶת, אֲפִילּוּ מָכְרוּ שָׁוֶה מָנֶה בְּמָאתַיִם, [5]אוֹ שָׁוֶה מָאתַיִם בְּמָנֶה — מִכְרָן קַיָּים״. [6]אֶלָּא לְעוֹלָם בִּדְלָא אַכְרוּז, וְלָא קַשְׁיָא. [7]כָּאן בִּדְבָרִים שֶׁמַּכְרִיזִין עֲלֵיהֶן; [8]כָּאן בִּדְבָרִים שֶׁאֵין מַכְרִיזִין עֲלֵיהֶן. [9]וְאֵלּוּ הֵן דְּבָרִים שֶׁאֵין מַכְרִיזִין עֲלֵיהֶן: [10]הָעֲבָדִים, וְהַמִּטַּלְטְלִין, וְהַשְּׁטָרוֹת. [11]עֲבָדִים טַעְמָא מַאי?

LITERAL TRANSLATION

[1]No, when they announced.

[2]But surely since the last clause is when they announced, [3]the first clause is when they did not announce, [4]for the last clause states: "If they made a letter of examination, even if they sold a maneh's worth for two hundred, [5]or two hundred's worth for a maneh, their sale is valid."

[6]Rather, in fact when they did not announce, and it is not difficult. [7]Here, with things that they announce; [8]here, with things that they do not announce. [9]And these are the things that they do not announce: [10]Slaves, and movable goods, and promissory notes. [11]Slaves — what is the reason?

RASHI

שמא יגנבו — כשנאספין לראותם כדי ללוקחם. [השטרות — שמוכרין שטר חוב של יתומים לאחרים].

NOTES

כָּאן בִּדְבָרִים שֶׁמַּכְרִיזִין Here with things that they announce. *Rav Hai Gaon* and *Rosh* maintain that if the court announced the sale of property which for one reason or another did not require announcement, either because it was of a kind that did not require announcement, or because it was sold at a time when an announcement was not necessary, or because the property was sold in a place where it was not the practice to announce such a sale, the sale is governed by the same laws that apply to the sale of property which requires an announcement. An error does not invalidate the sale unless the property was sold for less than half of its worth. According to *Rif* and *Rambam,* however, the sale of property which does not require announcement is canceled by an error of one-sixth, even if the court announced the sale.

הָעֲבָדִים Slaves. *Rosh* writes that even though the slaves whom heirs inherited from their father are not mortgaged to their father's debts, the court may decide to sell the slaves in order to repay the debts, rather than sell the land. *Tosafot* suggest that we are dealing here with a creditor who seized the slaves during the father's lifetime, in which case the creditor may indeed collect his debt from the slaves.

וּשְׁטָרוֹת And deeds. It may be asked: Rather than sell

HALAKHAH

is now offered for sale must first be appraised and then the sale must be announced publicly for sixty consecutive days," following the Mishnah cited in our Gemara. (*Rambam, Sefer Hafla'ah, Hilkhot Arakhin* 4:27.)

בִּדְבָרִים שֶׁאֵין מַכְרִיזִין עֲלֵיהֶן With things that they do not announce. "If the court sold property that does not require a public announcement, and it erred by one-sixth, the sale is canceled. If the error was less than one-sixth, the sale is valid." (*Rambam, Sefer Mishpatim, Hilkhot Malveh* 12:11; *Shulḥan Arukh, Even HaEzer* 104:4; *Ḥoshen Mishpat* 109:3.)

בִּדְבָרִים שֶׁאֵין מַכְרִיזִין עֲלֵיהֶן With things that they do not announce. "The following may be sold without a public announcement: Slaves, movable goods, and promissory notes," following our Gemara. (*Rambam, Sefer Mishpatim, Hilkhot Malveh* 12:11; *Shulḥan Arukh, Even HaEzer* 104:4; *Ḥoshen Mishpat* 109:3.)

LANGUAGE

כַּרְגָּא **Poll-tax.** This word apparently stems from the ancient Persian *charak*, meaning "land-tax."

LITERAL TRANSLATION

[1]Lest they hear and run away; [2]movable goods and promissory notes — [3]lest they be stolen.

[4]And if you wish, say: [5]Here, at a time that they announce; [6]here, at a time that they do not announce, [7]for the Neharde'ans say: For the poll tax, for maintenance, and for burial, [8]we sell without an announcement.

[9]And if you wish, say: Here, in a place where they announce; [10]here, in a place where they do not announce, [11]for Rav Naḥman said: Never did they make a letter of examination in Neharde'a. [12]They understood from this [that it was] because

[1]שֶׁמָּא יִשְׁמְעוּ וְיִבְרְחוּ; [2]מִטַּלְטְלִין וּשְׁטָרוֹת — [3]שֶׁמָּא יִגָּנְבוּ.

[4]וְאִיבָּעֵית אֵימָא: [5]כָּאן בְּשָׁעָה שֶׁמַּכְרִיזִין; [6]כָּאן בְּשָׁעָה שֶׁאֵין מַכְרִיזִין, [7]דְּאָמְרִי נְהַרְדְּעֵי: לְכַרְגָּא, לִמְזוֹנֵי, וְלִקְבוּרָה [8]מְזַבְּנִינַן בְּלָא אַכְרַזְתָּא.

[9]וְאִיבָּעֵית אֵימָא: כָּאן בְּמָקוֹם שֶׁמַּכְרִיזִין, [10]כָּאן בְּמָקוֹם שֶׁאֵין מַכְרִיזִין, [11]דַּאֲמַר רַב נַחְמָן: מֵעוֹלָם לֹא עָשׂוּ אִגֶּרֶת בִּקּוֹרֶת בִּנְהַרְדְּעָא. [12]סְבוּר מִינָּהּ, מִשּׁוּם

RASHI

בשעה שמכריזין — כדמפרש, שיש שעה שאין פנאי להמתין משך ימי הכרזה, כגון לכרגא ולמזוני ולקבורה.
לכרגא — לפרוע למלך כסף גולגולת היתומים.

TRANSLATION AND COMMENTARY

[1]**Lest** the slaves **hear** that they were about to be sold, **and run away.** [2]And what is the reason that the sale of **movable goods and promissory notes** would not be preceded by a public announcement? [3]**Lest they be stolen.**

וְאִיבָּעֵית אֵימָא [4]The Gemara offers another resolution of the difficulty: **And if you wish,** you can **say:** [5]**Here,** where Amemar says that if a court sold property without first publicly announcing the sale, the sale is canceled, he is talking about the sale of orphan's property **at at time when** it **must be announced.** [6]And **here,** where the Mishnah implies that if the court sold property without a prior announcement, but at the proper price, the sale is valid, it is talking about the sale of property **at a time when** it need **not be announced,** such as when the property must be sold immediately, and there is no time for announcements to be made. [7]**For the Neharde'an Sages said:** When orphans' property is sold in order to raise money **for** payment of **the poll-tax, or** to provide **maintenance** for a widow or the daughters of the deceased, **or to** cover **burial** expenses, [8]it **may be sold** even **without a public announcement**. These are pressing needs.

וְאִיבָּעֵית אֵימָא [9]The Gemara offers yet another resolution of the difficulty: **And if you wish,** you can **say: Here,** where Amemar says that if a court sold property without first announcing the sale, the sale is canceled, he is talking about the sale of property **in a place where** it was the common practice to **announce** such a sale. [10]And **here,** where the Mishnah implies that if the court sold property without a prior announcement, but at the proper price, the sale is valid, it is talking about the sale of property **in a place where** it was the common practice **not** to **announce** such a sale. [11]**For Rav Naḥman said: A letter of examination** announcing the sale of property belonging to orphans **was never drawn up in Neharde'a.** [12]At first **it was understood from** Rav Naḥman's statement that a letter of examination was never drawn up in Neharde'a, **because** the

NOTES

promissory notes held by orphans, why does the court not simply collect the debts recorded by those notes? We might be dealing with orphans who need the money right away, but the debts were not yet due. Or else, the court might fear that it will be unable to collect from the debtor, and so it is preferable to sell the notes. Even though it is likely that the promissory notes will have to be sold at a discount, the courts may sell them without a public announcement, as explained in the Gemara.

לְכַרְגָּא, לִמְזוֹנֵי **For the poll-tax, for maintenance.** *Ramban* notes that it was not necessary for the Neharde'an Sages to tell us that we do not delay burial for thirty days in order

HALAKHAH

בְּשָׁעָה שֶׁאֵין מַכְרִיזִין **At a time that they do not announce.** "If the court sold land when it was not necessary to announce the sale, and they erred by one-sixth, the sale is invalid, even if it was announced. If they erred by less than one-sixth, the sale is valid, even if the sale was not announced. *Rema* writes that some authorities (*Tur* in the name of *Rosh*) maintain that if the sale was announced, it is valid, even if the announcement was not necessary." (*Rambam, Sefer Mishpatim, Hilkhot Malveh* 12:11; *Shulḥan Arukh, Even HaEzer* 104:4; *Ḥoshen Mishpat* 109:3.)

לְכַרְגָּא, לִמְזוֹנֵי, וְלִקְבוּרָה **For the poll-tax, for maintenance, and for burial.** "When property is sold in order to raise money to cover funeral costs, the maintenance of his widow or orphaned daughters, or the poll-tax, it is not necessary to announce the sale, following the Neharde'ans. A similar law applies if money had been borrowed for one of these purposes, and land must now be sold to repay the loan (*Tur, Maggid Mishneh* in the name of *Tosafot*)." (*Rambam, Sefer Mishpatim, Hilkhot Malveh* 12:11; *Shulḥan Arukh, Even HaEzer* 104:4; *Ḥoshen Mishpat* 109:3.)

בְּמָקוֹם שֶׁאֵין מַכְרִיזִין **In a place where they do not announce.** "If the court sold land when it was not the

TRANSLATION AND COMMENTARY

Neharde'an Sages **were experts at appraisal,** and it was not necessary for them to announce the sale of orphans' property in order to establish the proper price. [1]But **Rav Yosef bar Manyume said: I myself heard from Rav Naḥman** that orphans' property would be sold in Neharde'a without prior public announcement, [2]**because** those who responded to the announcement and purchased the property **would be called** in a derogatory manner: **"People who eat property which had been announced** by the court for sale." It was thought ill of them for exploiting the orphans' plight.

אָמַר רַב יְהוּדָה [3]**Rav Yehudah said in the name of Shmuel:** [4]As for **movable goods that belong to orphans,** the property **is appraised, and** then **sold immediately,** to keep it from deteriorating and causing the heirs a loss.

רַב חִסְדָּא [5]**Rav Ḥisda said in the name of Avimi:** [6]Movable goods belonging to orphans **should be sold in the markets** on the market day, when it should bring the highest price.

וְלָא פְּלִיגִי [7]The Gemara notes: Rav Yehudah and Rav Ḥisda **do not disagree:** [8]Rav Ḥisda's ruling applies **when the market** day **is close** at hand, and so there is no concern that the property will become ruined before it is sold. [9]And Rav Yehudah's ruling applies **when the market** day **is far** off, and the goods must be sold immediately to keep them from being spoiled before they can be sold in the market.

דְּבְקִיאֵי בְּשׁוּמָא. [1]אֲמַר לֵיהּ רַב יוֹסֵף בַּר מַנְיוּמֵי: לְדִידִי מִיפַּרְשָׁא לִי מִינֵּיהּ דְּרַב נַחְמָן: [2]מִשּׁוּם דְּקָרוּ לְהוּ: ״בְּנֵי אָכְלֵי נִכְסֵי דְּאַכְרַזְתָּא״.

[3]אָמַר רַב יְהוּדָה אָמַר שְׁמוּאֵל: [4]מִטַּלְטְלִין שֶׁל יְתוֹמִים — שָׁמִין אוֹתָן וּמוֹכְרִין אוֹתָן לְאַלְתַּר.

[5]רַב חִסְדָּא אָמַר אֲבִימִי: [6]מוֹכְרִין אוֹתָן לַשְּׁוָוקִים.

[7]וְלָא פְּלִיגִי: [8]הָא דְּמִיקַּרַב שׁוּקָא; [9]הָא דְּמִרָחַק שׁוּקָא.

LITERAL TRANSLATION

they were experts at appraisal. [1]Rav Yosef bar Manyume said to him: It was explained to me personally by Rav Naḥman: [2]Because they call them: "People who eat property that had been announced."

[3]Rav Yehudah said in the name of Shmuel: [4]Movable goods belonging to orphans — they appraise them, and sell them immediately.

[5]Rav Ḥisda said in the name of Avimi: [6]They sell them to markets.

[7]And they do not disagree: [8]This, when the market is close; [9]this, when the market is far.

RASHI

משום דקרו להו כו׳ — גנאי וחרפה היא להם כשקונים נכסים שבית דין מוכרין. לפי שמחמת דוחק, שהנושה לוחץ את היתומים או את הלוה, לוקחים הלקוחות בזול. ומבזין אותן, וקורין להן: ״אוכלי שדות הכרזה״. לאלתר — סמוך למיתת אביהן, שלא ירקבו. דמקרב שוקא — יומא דשוקא.

NOTES

to enable the court to announce the sale of orphan's property. Rather, the Neharde'an Sages come to teach us that the court is not even required to announce the sale on the first day. *Tosafot* and others understand that we are dealing with a case where orphans borrowed money in order to pay the poll-tax, to maintain the widow, or to cover funeral expenses, and now orphans' property must be sold to repay the loan. The Neharde'an Sages teach that even though there is no pressing need to sell the property right away, the property may be sold immediately without a public announcement, for were we to delay the sale for thirty days so that the sale could be properly announced, people might refrain from lending out money in such situations.

מִשּׁוּם דְּקָרוּ לְהוּ Because they call them. *Rashi* and most Rishonim understand that this derogatory expression would be applied to those who bought property that had been announced for sale by the court, for they were suspected of taking advantage of the orphans' plight, buying up their property and paying them less than what it was worth. *Rivan* adds two more explanations: This expression would be applied to those creditors who would accept orphans' property as payment of their debts, according to the price that was established by way of the announcement. Or else, it would be applied to those who announced the sale, and accepted a fee for their services.

דְּמִיקַּרַב שׁוּקָא Where the market is close. Our commentary follows *Rashi, Rivan,* and others who explain the term "market" as "market day," such as, if the market day is close, the court waits until then to sell orphans' property, and if it is still far off, it sells the property right away. *Rambam* understands the term literally, that is, if the market itself is close by, the goods are taken there and sold, but if it is far away, and one is concerned that the goods might become damaged while on the road, it is preferable to sell the property right away.

HALAKHAH

common practice to announce such a sale, and they erred by one-sixth, the sale is not valid, even if it was announced. If they erred by less than one-sixth, the sale is valid, even if it was not announced. *Rema* writes that some authorities (*Tur* in the name of *Rosh*) maintain that if the sale was announced, it is valid, even if the announcement was not necessary." (*Rambam, Sefer Mishpatim, Hilkhot Malveh* 12:11;

מוֹכְרִין אוֹתָן לְאַלְתַּר They sell them immediately. "Movable goods belonging to orphans are appraised by the court and sold immediately, and if the market is nearby, the goods are brought there and sold," following the Gemara. (*Rambam, Sefer Mishpatim, Hilkhot Malveh* 12:11; *Shulḥan Arukh, Even HaEzer* 104:4; *Ḥoshen Mishpat* 109:3.)

TRANSLATION AND COMMENTARY

רַב כָּהֲנָא [1]It was related that **Rav Kahana** once **had in his possession beer belonging to Rav Mesharshiya bar Ḥilkiyah the orphan.** [2]Rav Kahana **put off** selling the beer **until the festival** approached. [3]Rav Kahana **explained: Even though** the beer **might become sour** if I wait until the festival, [4]it **will bring in money in cash** then, for the demand for beer is at its highest, and I will not have to sell anything on credit.

רָבִינָא הֲוָה [5]It was further related that **Ravina** once **had in his possession wine belonging to the orphan, Ravina the Younger, his sister's son.** [6]Ravina **also had** in his possession **wine** that belonged to **himself.** [7]**He was** planning to **bring** his own wine **to Sikhra** in order to sell it there. [8]**He came before Rav Ashi, and said to him: What is the law about bringing** Ravina Junior's wine to Sikhra along **with my** own wine? Must I be concerned that something will happen to the wine on the way, or not? [9]Rav Ashi **said to** Ravina: **Go,** and take your nephew's wine along with you, **for it is no better than yours.** Since you are willing to take your own wine all the way to Sikhra in order to sell it there, you must think that is the best place to sell the wine. Thus, you are allowed to do the same with your nephew's wine as well.

MISHNAH הַמְמָאֶנֶת [10]The Mishnah lists three types of women who are not entitled to certain payments which women are ordinarily entitled to receive from their husbands: (1) **The *mema'enet.*** Under Torah law, a minor girl can be married off by her father without her consent, and the marriage is binding. But a minor girl whose father has died cannot be married. Recognizing that orphan girls would benefit most from a child marriage, the Rabbis instituted that a minor orphan girl could be married off by her mother or brothers with her consent. However, this marriage would not be completely binding until the girl reached the age of majority. Until then she could annul the marriage retroactively by simply refusing to go on with it. A girl who annuls her marriage in this way is called a *mema'enet* (lit., "refuser"). (2) [11]**The second-degree relative.** Under Torah law, incestuous relationships between certain close relatives are prohibited (Leviticus 18:6-18). The Rabbis extended this law and prohibited relationships between other, more distant, relatives, called

[1]רַב כָּהֲנָא הֲוָה בִּידֵיהּ שִׁכְרָא דְּרַב מְשָׁרְשִׁיָּא בַּר חִילְקַאי יַתְמָא. [2]שָׁהְיֵיהּ עַד רִיגְלָא. [3]אֲמַר: אַף עַל גַּב דְּנָפַל בֵּיהּ אִיצַצְתָּא, [4]מַיְיתֵי זוּזָא חֲרִיפָא. [5]רָבִינָא הֲוָה בִּידֵיהּ חַמְרָא דְּרָבִינָא זוּטִי יַתְמָא בַּר אַחְתֵּיהּ. [6]הֲוָה לְדִידֵיהּ נַמִי חַמְרָא. [7]הֲוָה קָמַסֵּיק לֵיהּ לְסִיכְרָא. [8]אֲתָא לְקַמֵּיהּ דְּרַב אַשִׁי. אֲמַר לֵיהּ: מַהוּ לְאַמְטוּיֵי בַּהֲדַן? [9]אֲמַר לֵיהּ: זִיל, לָא עָדִיף מִדִּידָךְ.

משנה [10]הַמְמָאֶנֶת, [11]הַשְּׁנִיָּה,

LITERAL TRANSLATION

[1]Rav Kahana had in his hand beer belonging to Rav Mesharshiya bar Ḥilkiyah the orphan. [2]He put it off until the festival. [3]He said: Even though it might become sour, [4]it brings in money in cash.

[5]Ravina had in his hand wine belonging to the orphan, Ravina the Younger, his sister's son. [6]He himself also had wine. [7]He was bringing it to Sikhra. [8]He came before Rav Ashi. He said to him: What [is the law] about bringing it with his? [9]He said to him: Go, it is no better than yours.

MISHNAH [10]The *mema'enet,* [11]the second-degree relative,

RASHI

איצצא – טעם הקרוב להחמיץ, *איגרו"ס בלע"ז. **זוזא חריפא** – ממהר לצאת. לפי שהכל צריכין לכך, ומביאין מעות, ואין מקיפין להן באשראי. **לסיכרא** – שם מקום. **מהו לאמטויי** – שיש לחוש שלא תטבע הספינה.

משנה השניה – שניה לעריות, שהן מדברי סופרים, המפורש ביבמות בפרק שני (כא,א).

LANGUAGE

אִיצַצְתָּא Sour. According to *Rashi* this means to turn slightly acidic. Some scholars have sought the source of this word in Greek, and although there is a similar word, the Aramaic word is probably not derived from it. Even today certain inexpensive wines become acidic over time and are liable to turn completely to vinegar. *Rabbenu Gershom,* in the *Introduction to the Arukh,* explains אִיצַצְתָּא (or, in his version, אוצא) in the sense of a financial loss, explaining that when the wine is brought for sale, it brings a lower price, though there is some profit, for other things that can also be bought cheaply.

LANGUAGE (RASHI)

איגרו"ם* The correct reading should be איגרו"ר. From the Old French *ergror,* meaning "sourness, acidity."

SAGES

רָבִינָא זוּטִי Ravina the Younger. Ravina the Younger is the last Sage named Ravina. According to the epistle of *Rav Sherira Gaon,* this refers to Ravina the son of Rav Huna. He was a student of Rav Ashi and continued in the work of editing the Talmud. The Amoraic period ends with Ravina's death, and it was followed by the Saboraic period.

As explained here, Ravina's father died when he was a young boy, living him an orphan under the tutelage of his uncle, who was also named Ravina. That uncle had been a student of Rava and was a colleague of Rav Ashi.

NOTES

רַב מְשָׁרְשִׁיָּא בַּר חִילְקַאי יַתְמָא Rav Mesharshiya bar Ḥilkiyah the orphan. This incident occurred while Rav Mesharshiya was still a young orphan, before he became "Rav" Mesharshiya the Talmudic scholar (see *Rivan*).

רִיגְלָא The festival. Most Rishonim understand the term *rigla* as festival. Rav Kahana put off selling the beer until the festival approached, for many people would then be involved in their holiday shopping, prices would be high, and payment would be made in cash. *Rivan* proposes an alternate explanation, according to which the term *rigla* refers to the anniversary of the death of a great Torah scholar. On which day many of his disciples would gather together for Torah study, so that the day resembled a market day.

הַמְמָאֶנֶת The *mema'enet.* *Melekhet Shelomo* explains that since we have been dealing in this chapter with the

HALAKHAH

הַמְמָאֶנֶת אֵין לָהּ כְּתוּבָּה The *mema'enet* does not have a ketubah. "A *mema'enet* is not entitled to the main portion of her ketubah settlement, but she is entitled to the increment to it. If the husband went abroad, and the girl had borrowed money for her maintenance or ransom, and later she annulled the marriage by way of refusal, the husband is not required to return any money to her, even if he had enjoyed the usufruct of her property before she refused him," following the Mishnah. (*Rambam, Sefer Nashim, Hilkhot Ishut* 24:5; *Shulḥan Arukh, Even HaEzer* 116:5.)

הַשְּׁנִיָּה אֵין לָהּ כְּתוּבָּה The second-degree relative does not have a ketubah. "A woman who is a second-degree relative of her husband is not entitled to the main portion

¹וְהָאַיְלוֹנִית אֵין לָהֶן כְּתוּבָּה, ²וְלֹא פֵּירוֹת, ³וְלֹא מְזוֹנוֹת, ⁴וְלֹא בְּלָאוֹת. ⁵אִם מִתְּחִלָּה נְשָׂאָהּ לְשֵׁם אַיְלוֹנִית יֵשׁ לָהּ כְּתוּבָּה. ⁶אַלְמָנָה לְכֹהֵן גָּדוֹל, גְּרוּשָׁה

LITERAL TRANSLATION

[1]and the *aylonit* do not have a ketubah, [2]nor produce, [3]nor maintenance, [4]nor worn-out [clothing]. [5]If from the outset he married her as an *aylonit*, she has a ketubah.

[6]A widow to the High Priest, a divorcee

TRANSLATION AND COMMENTARY

"second-degree relatives," including, for example, the relationship between a man and his grandmother. An incestuous marriage between first-degree relatives, prohibited by Torah law, is not valid and does not require a bill of divorce to dissolve it. By contrast, an incestuous marriage between second-degree relatives is prohibited by Rabbinic decree, but is legally valid, and the husband is required by law to divorce his wife. (3) [1]**The *aylonit.*** A sexually underdeveloped woman who is incapable of bearing children, because she suffers from a physical defect that causes her to lack the normal signs of puberty, is called an *aylonit (*lit., "female ram"). A marriage with an *aylonit* is legal, but if the husband was not aware of her condition at the time of the marriage, the marriage is not valid, since it was entered into under false pretenses. As soon as the husband discovers his wife's condition, the marriage may be annulled without need for a bill of divorce. The Mishnah rules that these three types of woman **are not entitled to** the following four financial benefits that apply to other women: (1) **The ketubah** settlement— the basic sum of money that the Rabbis require a husband to pay when he divorces his wife. (2) [2]**The produce** that grew on the wife's property while she was married. (3) [3]**The maintenance** which a husband is ordinarily obligated to provide his wife while they are married. (4) [4]The **clothing which** the woman brought into her marriage as part of her dowry and **wore out** during her marriage. [5]**If** the husband was aware of his wife's condition **from the outset** and **he married her** knowing that she was **an *aylonit,*** she **is entitled to a ketubah** settlement, as well as the other payments mentioned above.

אַלְמָנָה [6]If **a widow** was married **to the High Priest,** or if **a divorcee or a *ḥalutzah*** (a woman whose

RASHI

אין להן כתובה — ממאנת — משום דמעלמה יוצאה, שניה — קנסא דרבנן הוא, כדאמרינן ביבמות בפרק "יש מותרות" (פה,ב): מפני שהיא מרגילתו לנושאה, שאינה מפסדת כלום בנשואין, שאינה נפסלת בהן, וולדה כשר. **איילונית** — משום דמקח טעות הוא. **ולא פירות** — דין פירות, והוא פירקונה שתקנו חכמים תחת פירות נכסי מלוג שהוא אוכל — אין לה, ואם נשבית — אינו חייב לפדותה. דתנאי כתובה ככתובה, וכיון דאין לה כתובה — אין לה תנאי כתובה [ואית דאמרי: כלומר, אף לא פירות; אם אכלן — אין משלם לה פירות נכסי מלוג שאכל. ואף על גב דקיימא לן בפרקין דלעיל כתובות (מז,ב) תקנו פירקונה תחת פירות נכסי מלוג שהוא אוכל, כדתנן: לא כתב לה "אם תשתבאי אפרקינך" — חייב לפדותה. והאי לא קרינן בה "ואותבינך לי לאינתו" אפילו הכי לא ישלם פירות, דתנאי כתובה ככתובה; כי היכי דקנסוה רבנן דלא גביא נכסי צאן ברזל שהכניסה לו משלה בתורת כתובה — קנסוה נמי דלא תגבה מיניה פירות שאכל בתנאי כתובה של פירי, שהוא תנאי בית דין שאינו כתוב בשטר הכתובה, ואף דין פירות], וכן מזונות נמי — תנאי כתובה נינהו. ולקמן בפרק בתרא כתובות (קז,ב) אמרינן: כיצד אמרו "ממאנת אין לה מזונות"? אי אתה יכול לומר ביושבת תחתיו — שהרי בעלה חייב במזונותיה, אלא שאם הלך למדינת הים ולוותה ואכלה, ועמדה ומיאנה — אינו משלם. **ולא בלאות** — שחקי בגדים שהביאה לו בשומא, ולבשן הוא — אינו מחזירן לה בלאותה. **אלמנה לכהן גדול** — יש לה כתובה, מפני שהיא פסולה וולדה פסול על ידי נשואין — לפיכך אינה מרגילתו, אלא הוא מרגילה ומשדלה לינשא לו, לפיכך קנסו אותו ליתן כתובה.

NOTES

widow's right to maintenance after her husband's death, this Mishnah teaches that a second-degree relative is not entitled to maintenance even during her husband's lifetime. And since it teaches that the second-degree relative is not entitled to maintenance, it teaches that she is also not entitled to various other financial arrangements that apply to other women. And since it teaches the laws applying to a second-degree relative, it teaches that the same laws also apply to a *mema'enet* and an *aylonit.*

וְלֹא פֵּירוֹת Nor produce. The Rishonim disagree about what the Mishnah means when it says that these women are not entitled to produce. This certainly cannot be understood in its plain sense, for a woman is never entitled to the usufruct of her property, but rather it goes to her husband. *Rashi* and others explain that the Mishnah means that the Rabbinic enactment that was instituted in exchange for the husband's right to benefit from the usufruct of his wife's property — such as, the husband's obligation to ransom his wife should she fall into captivity — does not apply to these women. According to the Jerusalem Talmud (and so too according to the second explanation offered by *Rashi* and *Rambam*), the Mishnah means that if the husband of one of these women enjoyed the usufruct of his wife's property, he is not obligated to return any money to her.

אַלְמָנָה לְכֹהֵן גָּדוֹל A widow to a High Priest. At first glance, it is strange that a second-degree relative who is only

HALAKHAH

of her ketubah settlement or to her ketubah conditions, but she is entitled to the increment to the settlement. She is not entitled to maintenance, and the husband is not required to return the usufruct of her property which he enjoyed while they were married." (*Rambam, Sefer Nashim, Hilkhot Ishut* 24:2; *Shulḥan Arukh, Even HaEzer* 116:4.)

אַלְמָנָה לְכֹהֵן גָּדוֹל A widow to a High Priest. "If a man married a woman who was forbidden to him by Torah law

TRANSLATION AND COMMENTARY

husband died without children, and then underwent the *ḥalitzah* ceremony freeing her from the levirate tie) was married **to an ordinary priest,** [1]or if **a** ***mamzeret*** (a woman born from an incestuous or an adulterous relationship) **or a** ***netinah*** (a female descendant of the Gibeonites, a people who converted to Judaism during the days of Joshua, but were later forbidden to marry other Jews) was married **to an ordinary Jew,** [2]or if **a Jewish woman** was married **to a** ***natin*** (a male descendant of the Gibeonites) **or a** ***mamzer*** (a man born from an incestuous or an adulterous relationship) — in all these cases, even though the marriage is forbidden by Torah law, [3]the woman **is** nevertheless **entitled to a ketubah** settlement, as well as the other payments mentioned above.

GEMARA רַב תָּנֵי [4]**Rav taught** a Baraita which states: "If **a minor** girl was married off by her mother or her brothers, and her husband terminated the marriage while she was still a minor by giving her **a bill of divorce,** she **is not entitled to a ketubah** settlement, for by Torah law, the marriage is not binding. When the Rabbis enacted that a girl who was orphaned from her father could be married off by her mother or her brother, they did not enact that she would be entitled to a ketubah settlement. [5]**And all the more so, a** ***mema'enet*** is not entitled to a ketubah settlement, for her husband did not divorce her, but rather she left him."

שְׁמוּאֵל תָּנֵי [6]**Shmuel taught** a Baraita which disagrees: **"A** ***mema'enet*** **is not entitled to a ketubah** settlement, [7]**but** if a minor girl was married off by her mother or her brothers, and her husband terminated the marriage while she was still a minor by giving her **a bill of divorce,** she **is entitled to a ketubah** settlement, for she is treated like any other divorcee."

וַחֲלוּצָה לְכֹהֵן הֶדְיוֹט, [1]מַמְזֶרֶת וּנְתִינָה לְיִשְׂרָאֵל, [2]בַּת יִשְׂרָאֵל לְנָתִין וּלְמַמְזֵר — [3]יֵשׁ לָהֶם כְּתוּבָּה.

גמרא [4]רַב תָּנֵי: "קְטַנָּה יוֹצְאָה בְּגֵט אֵין לָהּ כְּתוּבָּה. [5]וְכָל שֶׁכֵּן מְמָאֶנֶת.

[6]שְׁמוּאֵל תָּנֵי: "מְמָאֶנֶת אֵין לָהּ כְּתוּבָּה, [7]אֲבָל יוֹצְאָה בְּגֵט יֵשׁ לָהּ כְּתוּבָּה".

LITERAL TRANSLATION

or *ḥalutzah* to an ordinary priest, [1]a *mamzeret* or a netinah to an ordinary Jew, [2]a daughter of Israel to a *natin* or a *mamzer* — [3]they have a ketubah.

GEMARA [4]Rav taught: "A minor who goes out with a bill of divorce does not have a ketubah. [5]And all the more so a *mema'enet*."

[6]Shmuel taught: "A *mema'enet* does not have a ketubah, [7]but [a minor] who goes out with a bill of divorce has a ketubah."

RASHI

גמרא רב תני קטנה היוצאה בגט אין לה כתובה — קסבר: אין נישואי קטנה אלא כמפותה, בעלמא.

NOTES

forbidden to her husband by a Rabbinic decree is not entitled to a ketubah settlement or the ketubah conditions, whereas a widow married to a High Priest who is forbidden to him by Torah law has all the rights of a married woman. Two explanations are offered (both in the Jerusalem Talmud and in the Babylonian Talmud, *Yevamot* 85b): First, it is not necessary to reinforce a Torah prohibition, but a Rabbinic enactment requires reinforcement, so that it not be treated lightly, and so the Rabbis said that a second-degree relative is not entitled to a ketubah settlement. And second, in the case of a second-degree relative, it is usually the woman who persuades the man to marry her, for a woman is more interested in marriage than a man, and their marriage which is only forbidden by Rabbinic decree does not disqualify her or her children from marrying into the priesthood. Thus, in order to discourage the woman from pursuing such a marriage, the Rabbis penalized her saying that she is not entitled to a ketubah settlement. But in the case of a widow married to a High Priest, it may be assumed that it was the High Priest who pursued the marriage and persuaded the widow to marry him, for their marriage disqualifies the woman and her children from marrying into the priesthood. Thus, there is no need to penalize the woman, but rather it is the husband who should be penalized and made to pay his wife a ketubah settlement.

רַב תָּנֵי: קְטַנָּה **Rav taught: A minor.** The Mishnah in the Jerusalem Talmud (and so too *Rif*) reads: "The orphan girl, the second-degree relative, and the *aylonit*," substituting "orphan girl" for "*mema'enet*." *Pnei Yehoshua* explains that the dispute between Rav and Shmuel is based on this ambiguous reading of the Mishnah. Rav understood that the Mishnah's ruling applies to any orphan girl who was married off by her mother or brothers, and not just a *mema'enet*, whereas Shmuel limited the Mishnah's ruling to a *mema'enet*.

HALAKHAH

(by a prohibition punishable by flogging, but not by execution or excision), and he knew that she was forbidden to him when he married her, the woman is entitled to her ketubah settlement," following the Mishnah. (*Rambam, Sefer Nashim, Hilkhot Ishut* 24:4; *Shulḥan Arukh, Even HaEzer* 116:1.)

יוֹצְאָה בְּגֵט יֵשׁ לָהּ כְּתוּבָּה **A woman who leaves with a bill of divorce has a ketubah.** "If a minor girl was married off by her mother or brothers and later divorced by her husband with a bill of divorce, she is entitled to her ketubah settlement, she is disqualified from marrying his relatives (and he is disqualified from marrying her relatives), she is disqualified from marrying into the priesthood, and she is required to wait three months before remarrying," following Shmuel. (*Rambam, Sefer Nashim, Hilkhot Gerushin* 11:16-17, 22; *Shulḥan Arukh, Even HaEzer* 155:10.)

[1]וְאַזְדָא שְׁמוּאֵל לְטַעֲמֵיהּ, דְּאָמַר שְׁמוּאֵל: [2]מְמָאֶנֶת אֵין לָהּ כְּתוּבָּה. [3]יוֹצְאָה בְּגֵט יֵשׁ לָהּ כְּתוּבָּה. [4]מְמָאֶנֶת — לֹא פְּסָלָהּ מִן הָאַחִין, [5]וְלֹא פְּסָלָהּ מִן הַכְּהוּנָּה. [6]יוֹצְאָה בְּגֵט — פְּסָלָהּ מִן הָאַחִין, [7]וּפְסָלָהּ מִן הַכְּהוּנָּה. [8]מְמָאֶנֶת אֵינָהּ צְרִיכָה לְהַמְתִּין שְׁלֹשָׁה חֳדָשִׁים. [101A] [9]יוֹצְאָה בְּגֵט צְרִיכָה לְהַמְתִּין שְׁלֹשָׁה חֳדָשִׁים.

[10]מַאי קָא מַשְׁמַע לָן? [11]תָּנֵינָא כּוּלְּהוּ: הַמְמָאֶנֶת בְּאִישׁ — [12]הוּא מוּתָּר בִּקְרוֹבוֹתֶיהָ, וְהִיא מוּתֶּרֶת בִּקְרוֹבָיו. [13]וְלֹא פְּסָלָהּ מִן הַכְּהוּנָּה. [14]נָתַן לָהּ גֵּט, הוּא אָסוּר בִּקְרוֹבוֹתֶיהָ, וְהִיא אֲסוּרָה בִּקְרוֹבָיו. [15]וּפְסָלָהּ מִן הַכְּהוּנָּה״.

LITERAL TRANSLATION

[1]And Shmuel follows his own opinion, for Shmuel said: [2]A *mema'enet* does not have a ketubah. [3][A minor] who goes out with a bill of divorce has a ketubah. [4]A *mema'enet* — he did not disqualify her from the brothers, [5]nor did he disqualify her from the priesthood. [6][A minor] who goes out with a bill of divorce — he disqualified her from the brothers, [7]and he disqualified her from the priesthood. [8]A *mema'enet* need not wait three months. [101A] [9][A minor] who goes out with a bill of divorce must wait three months.

[10]What does he teach us? [11]We learned all of them: "One who refuses a man — [12]he is permitted to her relatives, and she is permitted to his relatives. [13]And he did not disqualify her from the priesthood. [14][If] he gave her a bill of divorce, he is forbidden to her relatives, and she is forbidden to his relatives. [15]And he disqualified her from the priesthood."

TRANSLATION AND COMMENTARY

וְאַזְדָא שְׁמוּאֵל לְטַעֲמֵיהּ [1]The Gemara notes: **Shmuel follows his own opinion** stated elsewhere, **for Shmuel said:** The laws applying to a *mema'enet* differ in various ways from the laws applying to a minor girl who was married off by her mother or her brothers and later divorced by her husband while she was still a minor. [2]A ***mema'enet* is not entitled to a ketubah** settlement, but a minor girl who was married off by her mother or her brothers and later [3]**divorced with a bill of divorce is entitled to a ketubah** settlement. [4]In the case of **a *mema'enet*,** the marriage **did not disqualify her from** marrying one of her former husband's **brothers** or some other close relative. For when a girl refuses her husband, the marriage is nullified retroactively, and she is considered never to have been married at all. [5]**Nor did** the husband **disqualify** the girl **from** marrying into **the priesthood,** for she is not treated like a divorcee. But if a minor girl was married off by her mother or her brothers, [6]and later **divorced** her husband **with a bill of divorce,** the husband **disqualified her from** marrying one of **his brothers** or some other close relative, for he is considered as having been married to her. [7]The husband also **disqualified** the girl **from** marrying into **the priesthood,** for she is treated like a divorcee. [8]A ***mema'enet* need not wait three months** to remarry after refusing her husband, for her first marriage is nullified retroactively, and she is considered never to have been married at all. Therefore she is not governed by the Rabbinic legislation barring a woman from remarrying within three months of the termination of her previous marriage. [101A] [9]But a minor girl who was **divorced** by her husband **with a bill of divorce must wait three months** before she remarries, for she is treated like a divorcee.

מַאי קָא מַשְׁמַע לָן [10]The Gemara asks: **What does** Shmuel **teach us** with these various rulings? [11]**We** already **learned all of these** laws in the following Mishnah (*Yevamot* 108a): "If a minor girl was married off by her mother or her brothers, but she **refused** to remain married to **the man,** [12]**he is permitted to** marry **her relatives, and she is permitted to** marry **his relatives,** because after a girl refuses her husband, the marriage is completely annulled. [13]The husband also **did not disqualify** the girl **from** marrying into **the priesthood,** for annulment is not divorce. [14]But **if** the man **gave** the girl **a bill of divorce** while she was still a minor, **he is forbidden to** marry **her relatives, she is forbidden to** marry **his relatives,** [15]**and she is disqualified from** marrying into **the priesthood,** for she is treated like any other divorced woman."

RASHI

לא פסלה מן האחין — שמותרת לקרוביו כאנוסה וכמפותה, דתנן (יבמות צז,א): נושא אדם אנוסת אביו כו'. **ולא פסלה מן הכהונה** — משום גרושה. שאין אלו גירושין. אלא עקירת נשואים הראשונים, דאמרה: אי אפשי בקדושי אמי. **ממאנת אינה צריכה להמתין שלשה חדשים** — לאחר מיאונה. דעקרתינהו לנשואין, ואינה בכלל שאר תקנות שגזרו חכמים לכל שאר הנשואות, שצריכות להמתין אחר יציאתן מבעליהן שלשה חדשים. **יוצאה בגט צריכה להמתין** — ואף על גב דליכא לספוקי קטנה במעוברת — לא חילקו חכמים בתקנתן בנשואות.

HALAKHAH

מְמָאֶנֶת — לֹא פְּסָלָהּ A *mema'enet* — he did not disqualify her. "A *mema'enet* is not entitled to her ketubah settlement, nor is she disqualified from marrying one of her husband's brothers or other close relatives, nor is she disqualified from marrying into the priesthood, nor is she required to wait three months after refusing her husband before she remarries," following Shmuel. (*Rambam, Sefer Nashim, Hilkhot Gerushin* 11:16-17, 22; *Shulḥan Arukh, Even HaEzer* 155:10.)

TRANSLATION AND COMMENTARY

צְרִיכָה לְהַמְתִּין [1]The Gemara answers: **It was necessary for** Shmuel **to teach** us **that** a divorced minor girl **must wait three months** before remarrying, [2]**for we did not learn** this in the Mishnah. The Rabbis enacted that a woman who was divorced or widowed must wait three months before she remarries to preclude doubt about the paternity of any child who might subsequently be born. We might have thought that this regulation does not apply to a minor, for is unlikely to be pregnant. Shmuel teaches that we do not make this distinction, and a minor who was divorced must also wait three months before remarrying. Once he taught this law, he also mentioned the other differences between a *mema'enet* and a minor girl who was married off by her mother or her brothers and then divorced while still a minor.

לֵימָא כְּתַנָּאֵי [3]The Gemara suggests that the same dispute occurred between two earlier scholars: **Shall we say that this** disagreement between Rav and Shmuel **is** actually **the subject of a Tannaitic dispute?** [4]For we learned in a Baraita: **"Rabbi Eliezer says:** When **a minor** girl marries on her own without her father, her **act has no** legal **validity.** [5]Therefore, **her husband is not entitled to** the objects **that she finds, nor to the handiwork** that she produces. [6]He is **not authorized to nullify her vows, he does not inherit** from **her** when she dies, **and** if he is a priest, **he is not permitted to defile himself** by coming into contact **with her** corpse. [7]**The general rule is:** The girl **is not** considered **like an** ordinary **wife in any respect,** [8]**except that** if she wishes to terminate the marriage **she is required** to formally declare her **refusal** to remain with her husband. [9]**Rabbi Yehoshua** disagrees and **says:** When **a minor** girl marries on her own without her father, her **act has** legal **validity.** [10]Therefore, **her husband is entitled to** the objects **that she finds, as well as the handiwork** that she produces. [11]He is **authorized to nullify her vows, he inherits** from **her** when she dies, [12]**and** if he is a priest, **he must defile himself** by coming into contact **with her** corpse. [13]**The general rule is:** The girl **is** considered **like an** ordinary **wife in every respect, except that she may terminate her marriage by** formally declaring her **refusal** to remain with her husband, and a bill of divorce is not necessary." [14]**Shall we say that Rav agrees with Rabbi Eliezer** that a girl who marries without her father is not an ordinary wife, and so she is not entitled to a ketubah settlement, [15]**and Shmuel agrees with Rabbi Yehoshua** that such a girl is indeed an ordinary wife, and so she is also entitled to a ketubah settlement?

[1]צְרִיכָה לְהַמְתִּין שְׁלֹשָׁה חֳדָשִׁים אִיצְטְרִיכָא לֵיהּ, [2]דְּלָא תְּנַן. [3]לֵימָא כְּתַנָּאֵי: [4]״רַבִּי אֱלִיעֶזֶר אוֹמֵר: אֵין מַעֲשֵׂה קְטַנָּה כְּלוּם, [5]וְאֵין בַּעְלָהּ זַכַּאי בִּמְצִיאָתָהּ, וְלֹא בְּמַעֲשֵׂה יָדֶיהָ, [6]וְלֹא בַּהֲפָרַת נְדָרֶיהָ, וְאֵינוֹ יוֹרְשָׁהּ, וְאֵינוֹ מִיטַּמֵּא לָהּ. [7]כְּלָלוֹ שֶׁל דָּבָר: אֵינָהּ כְּאִשְׁתּוֹ לְכָל דָּבָר, [8]אֶלָּא שֶׁצְּרִיכָה מֵיאוּן. [9]רַבִּי יְהוֹשֻׁעַ אוֹמֵר: מַעֲשֵׂה קְטַנָּה כְּלוּם, [10]וּבַעְלָהּ זַכַּאי בִּמְצִיאָתָהּ, וּבְמַעֲשֵׂה יָדֶיהָ, [11]וּבַהֲפָרַת נְדָרֶיהָ, וְיוֹרְשָׁהּ [12]וּמִיטַּמֵּא לָהּ. [13]כְּלָלוֹ שֶׁל דָּבָר: הֲרֵי הִיא כְּאִשְׁתּוֹ לְכָל דָּבָר, אֶלָּא שֶׁיּוֹצְאָה בְּמֵיאוּן״. [14]לֵימָא רַב דְּאָמַר כְּרַבִּי אֱלִיעֶזֶר, [15]וּשְׁמוּאֵל דְּאָמַר כְּרַבִּי יְהוֹשֻׁעַ״?

LITERAL TRANSLATION

[1]It was necessary for him [to teach that] she must wait three months, [2]for we had not learned [it].

[3]Shall we say it is [the subject of] a Tannaitic dispute: [4]"Rabbi Eliezer says: A minor's act is nothing, [5]and her husband is not entitled to [what she] finds, nor her handiwork, [6]nor the nullification of her vows, and he does not inherit from her, nor does he defile himself for her. [7]The principle of the matter: She is not like his wife in any respect, [8]except that she requires refusal. [9]Rabbi Yehoshua says: A minor's act is something, [10]and her husband is entitled to [what she] finds, and her handiwork, [11]and the nullification of her vows, and he inherits from her, and he defiles himself for her. [12]The principle of the matter is: She is like his wife [13]in every respect, except that she leaves with refusal." [14]Shall we say that Rav said like Rabbi Eliezer, [15]and Shmuel said like Rabbi Yehoshua?

NOTES

בַּהֲפָרַת נְדָרֶיהָ כו׳ **And the nullification of her vows, etc.** The ruling of Rabbi Yehoshua, that the husband has certain financial rights regarding his minor wife are to be viewed as a Rabbinical ordinance, for the Sages have the authority to institute ordinances and remove property from its owners. However, a question arose regarding matters that were not financial in nature: The revocation of vows and the contraction of ritual impurity. In tractate *Niddah* it states that since the girl is a minor, her vows are not valid according to the Torah, and they only apply according to

HALAKHAH

אֵין מַעֲשֵׂה קְטַנָּה כְּלוּם **A minor's act is nothing.** "If a minor girl was married off by her mother or brothers, her husband is entitled to what she finds and handiwork, and if she dies, he inherits from her," following Rabbi Yehoshua against Rabbi Eliezer. (*Rambam, Sefer Nashim, Hilkhot Ishut* 22:4; *Shulḥan Arukh, Even HaEzer* 155:10.)

[1]אַלִּיבָּא דְּרַבִּי אֱלִיעֶזֶר, [2]כּוּלֵּי עָלְמָא לָא פְּלִיגִי. [3]כִּי פְּלִיגִי — אַלִּיבָּא דְּרַבִּי יְהוֹשֻׁעַ. [4]שְׁמוּאֵל כְּרַבִּי יְהוֹשֻׁעַ. [5]וְרַב: עַד כָּאן לָא קָאָמַר רַבִּי יְהוֹשֻׁעַ הָתָם אֶלָּא מִדִּידָהּ לְדִידֵיהּ. [6]אֲבָל מִדִּידֵיהּ לְדִידָהּ, לָא.

[7]״וְלֹא בְּלָאוֹת״. [8]אֲמַר לֵיהּ רַב הוּנָא בַּר חִיָּיא לְרַב כָּהֲנָא: אָמְרַתְּ לָן מִשְּׁמֵיהּ דִּשְׁמוּאֵל: [9]לֹא שָׁנוּ אֶלָּא נִכְסֵי מְלוֹג,

LITERAL TRANSLATION

[1]According to Rabbi Eliezer, [2]everyone (lit., "the whole world") does not disagree. [3]When do they disagree — according to Rabbi Yehoshua. [4]Shmuel [says] like Rabbi Yehoshua. [5]And Rav [says]: Until here Rabbi Yehoshua only stated [his opinion] there [regarding] from her to him. [6]But from him to her, no.

[7]"Nor worn-out clothing." [8]Rav Huna bar Ḥiyya said to Rav Kahana: You said to us in the name of Shmuel: [9]They only taught [this] regarding *milog* property,

TRANSLATION AND COMMENTARY

אַלִּיבָּא [1]The Gemara rejects this suggestion: Shmuel must indeed agree with Rabbi Yehoshua, but Rav does not necessarily agree with Rabbi Eliezer. The Gemara explains: **According to** the viewpoint of **Rabbi Eliezer** that a minor girl who marries without her father is not in any way like a married woman, [2]**everyone** — both Rav and Shmuel — **agrees** that the girl is not entitled to a ketubah settlement. [3]**They** only **disagree according to** the viewpoint of **Rabbi Yehoshua.** [4]**Shmuel agrees with Rabbi Yehoshua** that the minor girl is considered in every way like a married woman (except that she can terminate the marriage by declaring her refusal to remain with her husband), and so it follows that she is entitled to a ketubah settlement. [5]**And Rav says** that **Rabbi Yehoshua only stated his opinion** that the girl is considered like a married woman **with respect to** the obligations which fall **upon a woman toward her husband.** He receives what she finds and the handiwork which she produces, and he inherits from her. [6]**But with respect to** the obligations which fall **upon a man toward his wife,** such as a ketubah, and all the rights which stem from the ketubah conditions, the girl is **not** a married woman. The Rabbis enacted that an orphaned minor girl can contract marriage by herself or through her mother or brothers for her own benefit, for they feared that if she were not married, nobody would take care of her, or that she might be exploited. Since the Rabbis wanted the girl to find a husband, they imposed upon her all the obligations of an ordinary wife. They ruled that her husband is entitled to what she finds, her handiwork, and her estate. But they did not bestow upon her all the rights of a married woman, and so she is not entitled to a ketubah settlement.

״וְלֹא בְּלָאוֹת״ [7]We have learned in our Mishnah: "A *mema'enet*, a second-degree relative, and an *aylonit* are not entitled to the **clothing which** the woman brought into the marriage as part of her dowry and **wore out** during her marriage." [8]**Rav Huna bar Ḥiyya said to Rav Kahana: You said to us in the name of Shmuel:** [9]**This ruling only applies to** clothing which the woman brought into the marriage as ***milog* property,**

RASHI

אליבא דרבי אליעזר כולי עלמא לא פליגי — כלומר, הא דאמרת שמואל דאמר כרבי יהושע ולא כרבי אליעזר — שפיר קאמרת, דמודה שמואל לרבי אליעזר אין כתובה לשום קטנה. דהשתא ירושתה ומציאתה, דמדידה לדידיה, קאמר דלא מיתוקמא בה תקנתא דרבנן — כל שכן כתובתה, דמדידיה לדידה. שהרי כשתקנו חכמים נשואין ליתומה על ידי אמה ואחיה — להנאתה ולטובתה תקנו. כדאמרינן ביבמות בפרק "חרש שנשא את הפקחת" — כדי שלא יהו נוהגים בה הפקר, שאין קטנה יודעת לשמור עצמה מלהתפתות. **כי פליגי אליבא דרבי יהושע** — כלומר הא דאמרת דרב כרבי אליעזר ולא כרבי יהושע — ליתא, דרב — אפילו לרבי יהושע אמרה. **עד כאן לא קאמר רבי יהושע** — דמעשיה קיימין — אלא מדידה לדידיה, כגון ירושתה ומעשה ידיה ומציאתה שיהו לבעל, כי היכי דלא לימנעו מלישא אותה. וחכמים גזרו שתנשא, כדי שלא ינהגו בה הפקר. **אבל מדידיה לדידה** — כגון כתובה ותנאי כתובה. **צאן ברזל** — לאן שהוא קשה ומתקיים לה כברזל, לפי שקיבל עליו אחריות. **נכסי מלוג** — שהכניסה לו, ולא שמאום בכתובה, והקרן לאשה ופירות לבעל.

LANGUAGE

נִכְסֵי מְלוֹג *Milog* property. The Rishonim found it difficult to interpret this word. Some claimed that it was related to the root מְלוֹג meaning "to soak leather to remove the hair from it," for here, too, the husband "soaks" the profit from the property. Others claimed it was derived from the Greek λόγος, *logos*, a word, meaning that this was property that came to a man through speech and agreement. However, it appears that the word stood by itself, and it has been shown to have an ancient Akkadian root, meaning "property brought by a wife to her husband."

NOTES

Rabbinical law. Therefore the Sages could ordain that the husband has the right to revoke them. However, according to those who maintain מוּפְלָא סָמוּךְ לְאִישׁ — an expression meaning that a person close to majority has the faculty of discretion — a year before a child reaches majority, his or her vows are valid, if the child understands what a vow is. According to Rava's approach, any woman who vows does so with her husband's consent. In other words, her vows are conditional upon his authorization. If so, this also applies to a minor if she is a married woman in every respect. Regarding ritual impurity, *Tosafot* argue that since the husband inherits from her, her relatives are unwilling to arrange her funeral, so that he is commanded to do so, and even a priest must contract ritual impurity for a person whom he is commanded to bury.

HALAKHAH

בְּלָאוֹת מְמָאֶנֶת The worn-out clothing of a *mema'enet*. "A *mema'enet* may take back whatever remains of the property that she brought into the marriage, but the husband is not responsible for property which she brought into the marriage, whether *milog* property or *tzon barzel* property, that was lost or worn out during the marriage. According

LANGUAGE

נִכְסֵי צֹאן בַּרְזֶל ***Tzon barzel* property.** This colorful expression, similar to those found in Roman law, is used to describe the status of this type of property, which is like iron sheep for its owners: It never wears out because someone else (in this case, the husband) takes it upon himself to preserve its value. The image is appropriate for another reason as well, because the property brings no income to its owner, and only its constant value is retained.

TRANSLATION AND COMMENTARY

[1]**but regarding** clothing which she brought into the marriage as ***tzon barzel* property** the woman **has** the right to demand their return. A married woman's property is divided into two categories, *milog* property and *tzon barzel* property. The latter is the property that a woman brings into the marriage and entrusts to her husband's responsibility, and he undertakes to restore its equivalent to his wife upon the dissolution of their marriage. The husband may use the property as he sees fit, and any profit or loss accruing from this use is his. He bears full responsibility, however, for the property, and if he dies or divorces her, the value of the property as fixed in the ketubah must be restored. *Milog* property is property the principal of which remains in the wife's possession, while the usufruct belongs to the husband. He has no responsibility regarding the principal, both its gain and loss being only hers. Upon dissolution of the marriage, the property returns to the woman as it stands. *Milog* property includes all of the woman's property which is not *tzon barzel* property, whether it was brought by the woman at the time of the marriage, or acquired afterwards by way of inheritance or gift. Rav Kahana taught that the Mishnah's ruling regarding the women who are not entitled to their worn-out clothing applies only to *milog* property, but not to *tzon barzel* property.

הָוֵי בָּהּ [2]**Rav Pappa raised a question about** Rav Kahana's statement: **Regarding which** of the women mentioned in the Mishnah did Rav Kahana say what he said? [3]**If you say** that he was referrring **to a *mema'enet*,** there is a difficulty, [4]for **if** the worn-out clothing still **exists, she should** be entitled to **take both** the clothing that she brought into the marriage as *milog* property and the clothing that she brought in as *tzon barzel* property, for the marriage was dissolved, and there is no reason to penalize the girl. [5]**And if** the worn-out clothing in both categories **no longer exists,** since it was worn-out completely, **she should not** be entitled to **collect** the value of **either** of them. Her husband can argue that since he did not divorce the girl, but rather she declared her refusal to remain married, he should not be obligated to compensate her for the property which wore out during the period of their marriage.

אֶלָּא [6]**Rather,** Rav Kahana must have been referring to **an *aylonit*.** But this too is difficult, [7]for **if** the worn-out clothing still **exists,** the woman **should** be entitled to **take** clothing from **both** categories. Once the

[1]אֲבָל נִכְסֵי צֹאן בַּרְזֶל אִית לָהּ.
[2]הָוֵי בָּהּ רַב פַּפָּא: אַהַיָּיא?
[3]אִילֵימָא אַמְמָאֶנֶת — [4]אִי
דְּאִיתְנְהוּ, אִידִי וְאִידִי שָׁקְלָא.
[5]וְאִי דְּלֵיתְנֵהוּ, אִידִי וְאִידִי לָא
שָׁקְלָא!
[6]אֶלָּא, אַאַיְילוֹנִית. [7]אִי
דְּאִיתְנְהוּ, אִידִי וְאִידִי שָׁקְלָא.

LITERAL TRANSLATION

[1]but regarding *tzon barzel* property she has.
[2]Rav Pappa discussed it: Regarding which? [3]If you say regarding a *mema'enet* — [4]if they exist, this and that she takes. [5]And if it does not exist, this and that she does not take!
[6]Rather, regarding an *aylonit.* [7]If they exist, this and that she takes.

RASHI

נכסי צאן ברזל — הנישומין בכתובתה "ודא נדוניא דהנעלת ליה מבית אבוה". והוא מקבל עליו אחריות להחזירן לה כשתצא ממנו. **אבל** — בלאות, דנכסי צאן ברזל — אית לה. **אי דאיתנהו** — קיימין. **אידי ואידי אית לה** — שאין לנו לקונסה. **ואי דליתנהו** — קיימין. **אידי ואידי** — בין נכסי מלוג בין דצאן ברזל — לית לה. שיכול לומר: שלי הוצאתי, שהרי ברשות בית דין נשאתיה, וכשאוציאנה — אחזור מה שקבלתי עלי בכתובה. ובנכסי מלוג נמי אף על פי שלא ברשות הוציאם — מיהו יכול לומר: אין לי להחזירן עד שאגרשנה, שמא תמות בחיי ואירשנה. **אי דאיתנהו אידי ואידי שקלא** — שהרי הוא מוציאה מדעת.

NOTES

אִידִי וְאִידִי לָא שָׁקְלָא **This and that she does not take.** *Rashi* found it difficult to explain why she cannot take her usufruct property that was used by her husband, for after the marriage is annulled by her refusal, it is entirely without legal consequences, as if it had never taken place. (For that reason the *mema'enet* is viewed as a woman who had never been married at all with respect to prohibitions affecting once-married women.) If this is the case, why should her ex-husband receive her usufruct property? *Rashi* explains that he can argue, "I am not required to return it unless I divorce her, because she might die, and I will inherit from her." Other Rishonim expressed surprise at this statement, because she has left him completely. *Ritva* explains that *Rashi*'s explanation must be understood differently and revised as follows: The husband argues that since he married the girl according to a Rabbinical ordinance, he believed her to be his wife, and that he used her property with Rabbinical permission, and the Rabbis did not rule that he had to return it. *Ran* explains that the husband believed that Rav Naḥman's ruling was correct, and that his use of her property and the benefit he derived from it, even though that property was worn out because of his use, was usufruct, and everyone agrees that he does not have to return usufruct.

HALAKHAH

בְּלָאוֹת אַיְילוֹנִית **The worn-out clothing of an *aylonit*.** "If a woman was discovered to be an *aylonit* or forbidden to her husband because of a negative Torah commandment, and ... to *Shulḥan Arukh*, the husband must pay her for *tzon barzel* property that was lost." (*Rambam, Sefer Nashim, Hilkhot Ishut 24:9*; *Shulḥan Arukh, Even HaEzer* 155:10.)

[1]אִי דְּלֵיתְנְהוּ, אִיפְּכָא מִיבָּעֵי לֵיהּ: [2]נִכְסֵי מְלוֹג דְּבִרְשׁוּתָהּ קָיְימֵי, אִית לָהּ. [3]נִכְסֵי צֹאן בַּרְזֶל דְּלָאו בִּרְשׁוּתָהּ קָיְימֵי, לֵית לָהּ.

[4]אֶלָּא, אַשְׁנִיָּה. [5]וְקָנְסוּ רַבָּנַן לְדִידָהּ בְּדִידֵיהּ, [6]וּלְדִידֵיהּ בְּדִידָהּ.

[7]אָמַר רַב שִׁימִי בַּר אַשִׁי: שְׁמַע מִינָּהּ מִדְּרַב כָּהֲנָא: עַיְּילָא לֵיהּ גְּלִימָא, קַרְנָא הָוֵי, [8]וְלָא מְכַסֵּי לָהּ וְאָזֵיל עַד דְּבָלֵי.

LITERAL TRANSLATION

[1]If they do not exist, he should have [said] the opposite: [2][Regarding] *milog* property which stands in her possession, she has. [3][Regarding] *tzon barzel* property which does not stand in her possession, she does not have.

[4]Rather, regarding a second-degree [relative]. [5]And the Rabbis penalized to her from him, [6]and to him from her.

[7]Rav Shimi bar Ashi said: Infer from Rav Kahana: If she brought in to him a cloak, it is principle, [8]and he does not continue to wear it until it is worn-out.

TRANSLATION AND COMMENTARY

marriage was terminated, she should be entitled to take back whatever belongs to her. [1]And **if** the worn-out clothing **no longer exists,** because it was destroyed or worn-out completely, Rav Kahana **should have said** just **the opposite** if he thinks that there is reason to exempt the husband from the obligation to restore the value of her property, because he had no reason to suspect that she was an *aylonit*. [2]**Regarding** the clothing that the *aylonit* brought into the marriage as ***milog*** **property** and **which remained in her possession** throughout the marriage, **she should be entitled** to recover its value from her husband. [3]And **regarding** the clothing that the *aylonit* brought in as ***tzon barzel*** **property** and **which** therefore **did not remain in her possession** during the period of her marriage, **she should not be entitled** to recover the value of that property from her husband.

אֶלָּא [4]Thus Rav Kahana could not have been referring to either a *mema'enet* or an *aylonit*. **Rather** must have been referring to a woman who was forbidden to her husband because she was his **second-degree relative.** [5]**And the Rabbis** imposed penalties on both the woman and her husband in order to deter such forbidden marriages. They **penalized her** with respect to what she should be entitled to collect **from him,** her ketubah settlement, her maintenance, and compensation for the *milog* property which became worn-out. [6]**And** they penalized **him** with respect to what he should have been entitled to keep **from her,** her *tzon barzel* property which became worn-out.

אָמַר [7]**Rav Shimi bar Ashi said: Infer from** what **Rav Kahana** said: **If** a woman **brought a cloak for** her husband as part of her *milog* property, wearing the garment **is** considered consumption of **principle.** A husband is entitled to the usufruct of his wife's *milog* property, but he is not permitted to consume the principle. [8]Thus, he **may not cover himself with** the cloak and continue to wear it **until it is worn-out,** for in that way he consumes the principal.

RASHI

ואי דליתנהו – ומפני שלא היה לו להעלות בדעתו שמא תמצא אילונית אתה פוטרו, אם באת לחלוק בהן. **איפכא מבעי ליה נכסי מלוג דברשותה קיימי** – שלא היה לו לבלותן וללובשן. **אית לה** – אי סבירא לך עיילא ליה גלימא – קרנא הוי. **נכסי צאן ברזל** – שהוא קבל עליו אחריותן, ברשות הוליאן. **אשניה** – שהם נשואי עבירה. **וטעמא דידה** – משום קנסא, וכגון דליתנהו. **וקנסו רבנן כו׳** – כלומר, מדינא – איפכא מיבעי ליה, אלא חכמים הפכו את הדבר לעקור מהן תורת נשואין – קנסו אותה ממה שהיה ראוי לגבות משלו, ומאי ניהו – מנה מאתים, ומזונות, ובלאות דנכסי מלוג שהוליא שלא ברשות. **ולדידיה בדידה** – ואותו קנסו במה שהיה ראוי לו משלה – בלאות דנכסי לאן ברזל שהוליא ברשות. **שמע מינה מדרב כהנא** – דאמר: שניה אין לה בלאות דנכסי מלוג, וטעמא משום דקנסו רבנן לדידה בדידיה. הא אשה כשרה – גובה אותן ממנו, ואף על גב דלא איתנהו. **עיילא ליה גלימא** – בנכסי מלוג, שלא שמוה עליו בנדונייתה. **קרנא הוי** – וקיים לאשה לימכר וליקח בו קרקע, והוא אוכל פירות, ולא אמרינן: לבישתה הן הן פירותיה, ונכסי בה ויזיל.

HALAKHAH

her husband did not know this at the time of the marriage, he is not liable for *tzon barzel* property that was lost or stolen or worn out or ruined, but he must pay for *milog* property that was lost or stolen," following the Gemara. (*Rambam, Sefer Nashim, Hilkhot Ishut* 22:8; *Shulḥan Arukh, Even HaEzer* 116:1.)

בְּלָאוֹת שְׁנִיָּה The worn-out clothing of a second-degree relative. "If a woman was forbidden to her husband because she was his second-degree relative, she is not entitled to a ketubah settlement, but regarding her dowry she is treated like any other woman. Thus, her husband is liable for her *tzon barzel* property that was lost or stolen, but he is not responsible for her *milog* property." (*Rambam, Sefer Nashim, Hilkhot Ishut* 22:7-8; *Shulḥan Arukh, Even HaEzer* 116:4.)

עַיְּילָא לֵיהּ גְּלִימָא If she brought in to him a cloak. "If a woman brought a garment or utensil into her marriage as *milog* property, the husband may use it until it is entirely worn out, and if he divorces her, he is not obligated to compensate her for her worn-out *milog* property," following Rav Naḥman. (*Rambam, Sefer Nashim, Hilkhot Ishut* 22:34; *Shulḥan Arukh, Even HaEzer* 85:13.)

[1]וְהָאָמַר רַב נַחְמָן: פֵּירָא הָוֵי! [2]דְּרַב נַחְמָן פְּלִיגָא. [3]״אֵין לָהֶן כְּתוּבָּה״. [4]אָמַר שְׁמוּאֵל: לֹא שָׁנוּ אֶלָּא מָנֶה מָאתַיִם, [5]אֲבָל תּוֹסֶפֶת יֵשׁ לָהֶן. [6]תַּנְיָא נַמִּי הָכִי: ״נָשִׁים שֶׁאָמְרוּ חֲכָמִים: [7]׳אֵין לָהֶן כְּתוּבָּה׳, [8]כְּגוֹן הַמְמָאֶנֶת וַחֲבְרוֹתֶיהָ, [9]אֵין לָהֶן מָנֶה מָאתַיִם, [10]אֲבָל תּוֹסֶפֶת יֵשׁ לָהֶן. [11]נָשִׁים שֶׁאָמְרוּ חֲכָמִים: ׳יוֹצְאוֹת שֶׁלֹּא בִּכְתוּבָּה׳, [12]כְּגוֹן עוֹבֶרֶת עַל דָּת, וַחֲבְרוֹתֶיהָ, [13]אֵין לָהֶן תּוֹסֶפֶת, וְכָל שֶׁכֵּן מָנֶה מָאתַיִם.

LITERAL TRANSLATION

[1]But surely Rav Naḥman said: It is fruit! [2]Rav Naḥman disagrees.

[3]"They do not have a ketubah." [4]Shmuel said: They only taught [about] a maneh and two hundred, [5]but the increment they have.

[6]It was also taught thus: "The women about whom the Sages said: [7]'They do not have a ketubah,' [8]like a *mema'enet* and the others like her, [9]do not have a maneh or two hundred, [10]but they have the increment. [11]The women about whom the Sages said: 'They leave without a ketubah,' [12]like one who violates the law, and the others like her, [13]do not have the increment, and all the more so the maneh or two hundred.

TRANSLATION AND COMMENTARY

וְהָאָמַר רַב נַחְמָן [1]The Gemara raises a question: **But surely Rav Naḥman said** earlier in the tractate: If a woman brought a cloak for her husband as part of her *milog* property, wearing the garment **is** considered enjoyment of its **usufruct**. Thus, the husband may wear the cloak until it is completely worn-out, for the rags to which the cloak will become reduced can be preserved for the woman as her principal.

דְּרַב נַחְמָן [2]The Gemara answers: **Rav Naḥman disagrees** with Rav Kahana.

אֵין לָהֶן כְּתוּבָּה [3]We learned in the Mishnah: "A *mema'enet*, a second-degree relative, and an *aylonit* **are not entitled to their ketubah** settlement." [4]**Shmuel said: This ruling only applies to** the main portion of the settlement, the minimum amount that a woman is entitled by law to receive from her husband or his estate upon the dissolution of her marriage, **a maneh** in the case of a woman who is not a virgin, **and two hundred** zuz in the case of a virgin. [5]**But the increment** to the ketubah which the husband may add on his own even **these** women **are entitled to** receive.

תַּנְיָא נַמִּי הָכִי [6]The Gemara notes that **the same** thing **was also taught** in a Baraita: **"The women about whom the Sages said:** [7]**'They are not entitled to their ketubah** settlement,' [8]**like a *mema'enet* and the others** that are **like her,** a second-degree relative or an *aylonit,* [9]**are not entitled to** receive the main portion of the settlement, **the maneh or the two hundred** zuz to which every woman is entitled by law. [10]**But they are entitled to** receive **the increment** that the husband may add on his own to the minimum amount set by law. [11]And **the women about whom the Sages said: 'They may be divorced** from their husbands **without** receiving payment of **their ketubah** settlement, [12]**like** a woman **who violates the law** of Moses or Jewish custom (see *Ketubot* 72a), **and the others** that are **like her,** such as a woman who was found to be bound by vows or to have a serious physical defect (see *Ketubot* 72b), [13]**are not** even **entitled** to receive **the increment** to the ketubah which the husband may add voluntarily, **and all the more so** are they not entitled **to the maneh or**

RASHI

והאמר רב נחמן – ב״האשה״. **אבל תוספת יש לה** – דמתנה בעלמא יהיב לה בחיבת ביאה. [**נשים שאמרו בהן חכמים** – לשון ״אין להן כתובה״ – יש להן תוספת] נשים שאמרו חכמים ״לשון יוצאות שלא בכתובה״ – כל תורת גיבוי הפקיעו מהן. **עוברת על דת** – בפרק ״המדיר״ (כתובות עב,א). **וחברותיה** – נמצאו עליה נדרים או מומין, והמקללת יולדיו בפניו.

NOTES

הַמְמָאֶנֶת וַחֲבְרוֹתֶיהָ **The *mema'enet* and the others like her.** Many Rishonim wondered why the *aylonit* should have the right to the increment to her ketubah settlement, because taking her in marriage was clearly a transaction made in error. *Ramban* argues that since her husband married her, and he wishes to keep her while she is his, he can be seen as agreeing to give her the increment as a gift. *Ra'ah* and other Rishonim maintain that only the second-degree relative retains the increment to her ketubah settlement, because marriage to her was not a transaction made in error, like marriage to an *aylonit* or to a woman who proved to have a physical blemish.

HALAKHAH

תּוֹסֶפֶת יֵשׁ לָהֶן **The increment they have.** "If a man married a woman and did not know that she was an *aylonit* or a woman who was forbidden to him because of a negative commandment, or if he married a second-degree relative, or if he married a minor girl and she later refused him, none of these women is entitled to the main portion of the ketubah settlement, but she is entitled to the increment," following Shmuel. (*Rambam, Sefer Nashim, Hilkhot Ishut* 24:2,5; *Shulḥan Arukh, Even HaEzer* 116:1,5; 155:10.)

עוֹבֶרֶת עַל דָּת, וַחֲבְרוֹתֶיהָ **One who violates the law, and the others like her.** "If a man was obligated to divorce his wife because she was suspected of having committed adultery, or because she violated Torah law or Jewish custom, she is not entitled to a ketubah settlement, ketubah

[1]וְהַיּוֹצֵאת מִשּׁוּם שֵׁם רַע נוֹטֶלֶת מַה שֶּׁלְּפָנֶיהָ וְיוֹצְאָה.
[2]מְסַיֵּיעַ לֵיהּ לְרַב הוּנָא, דְּאָמַר רַב הוּנָא: [3]זִינְּתָה, לֹא הִפְסִידָה [101B] [4]בְּלָאוֹתֶיהָ קַיָּימִין.
[5]תָּנֵי תַּנָּא קַמֵּיהּ דְּרַב נַחְמָן: [6]"זִינְּתָה, הִפְסִידָה בְּלָאוֹתֶיהָ קַיָּימִין".
[7]אֲמַר לֵיהּ: אִם הִיא זִינְּתָה, כֵּלֶיהָ מִי זַנַּאי? [8]תְּנֵי: "לֹא הִפְסִידָה בְּלָאוֹתֶיהָ קַיָּימִין".
[9]אָמַר רַבָּה בַּר בַּר חָנָה אָמַר רַבִּי יוֹחָנָן: זוֹ דִּבְרֵי רַבִּי מְנַחֵם סְתִימְתָּאָה. [10]אֲבָל חֲכָמִים אוֹמְרִים: זִינְּתָה, לֹא הִפְסִידָה בְּלָאוֹתֶיהָ קַיָּימִין.
[11]"אִם מִתְּחִלָּה נְשָׂאָהּ כו׳".
[12]אָמַר רַב הוּנָא: אַיְלוֹנִית אִשָּׁה

LITERAL TRANSLATION

[1]And she who leaves because of a bad name takes what is before her and leaves."

[2]This supports Rav Huna, for Rav Huna said: [3][If] she committed adultery, she did not lose [101B] [4]her existing worn-out [clothing].

[5]A Tanna taught before Rav Naḥman: [6]"[If] she committed adultery, she lost her existing worn-out [clothing]."

[7]He said to him: If she committed adultery, did her garments commit adultery? [8]Teach: "She did not lose her existing worn-out [clothing]."

[9]Rabbah bar Bar Ḥanah said in the name of Rabbi Yoḥanan: These are the words of Rabbi Menahem reported anonymously. [10]But the Sages say: [If] she committed adultery, she did not lose her existing worn-out [clothing].

[11]"If from the outset he married her, etc." [12]Rav Huna said: An *aylonit* is a wife

TRANSLATION AND COMMENTARY

two hundred zuz to which every woman is entitled by law. [1]**And a woman who must be divorced** from her husband **because of the suspicion** that she committed adultery **takes what remains before her** of the property that she had brought into the marriage, **and leaves."**

מְסַיֵּיעַ לֵיהּ [2]The Gemara adds that **this** Baraita **supports Rav Huna, for Rav Huna said:** [3]Even **if** a woman **committed adultery, she did not lose** [101B] [4]**her** right to take the **worn-out clothing,** as well as the rest of the property which she brought into the marriage, **which** still **exists.**

תָּנֵי תַּנָּא [5]**A Tanna taught** an opposing Baraita **before Rav Naḥman:** [6]**"If** a woman **committed adultery, she lost her** right to take the **worn-out clothing,** as well as the rest of the property which she brought into the marriage, **which** still **exists."**

אֲמַר לֵיהּ [7]Rav Naḥman **said to** the Tanna: **If** indeed the woman **committed adultery, does** this mean that **her garments committed adultery?** Surely there is no reason to penalize the woman by depriving her of her clothing. [8]Rather, **teach** the Baraita as follows: "If a woman committed adultery, **she did not lose her** right to take the **worn-out clothing,** as well as the rest of the property which she brought into the marriage, **which** still **exists."**

אָמַר [9]**Rabbah bar Bar Ḥanah said in the name of Rabbi Yoḥanan: This** Baraita **follows the position of Rabbi Menahem,** whose opinion was **reported** here **anonymously.** [10]**But the Sages** disagree and **say:** Even **if** a woman **committed adultery, she did not lose her** right to take the **worn-out clothing,** as well as the rest of the property which she brought into the marriage, **which** still **exists.**

אִם מִתְּחִלָּה נְשָׂאָהּ [11]We have learned in our Mishnah: **"If** the husband was aware of his wife's condition **from the outset** and **he married her** knowing that she was an ***aylonit,*** she is entitled to a ketubah settlement as well as the other payments mentioned in the Mishnah." The Amoraim disagree about whether or not the Mishnah's distinction regarding an *aylonit* applies also to the women mentioned in the last clause of the Mishnah. [12]**Rav Huna said:** If someone was married to **an *aylonit,*** she **is** in some cases treated like

RASHI

והיוצאת משום שם רע — שזינתה. **מה שבפניה** — בנכסי מלוג קאמר. **בלאותיה קיימין** — בלאות שהן קיימין לא הפסידה. **זו דברי רבי מנחם** — הא סתמא דתני תנא קמיה דרב נחמן הפסידה רבי מנחם אמרה. **דסתימתאה הוא** — הרבה משמועותיו נשנו סתם במשנה ובברייתא. **אשה ואינה אשה** — פעמים היא כאשתו פעמים אינה כאשתו.

NOTES

כֵּלֶיהָ מִי זַנַּאי Did her garments commit adultery. *Rav Hai Gaon* applies this reasoning to the case of a married woman who converted to another religion. Such a woman is treated like a woman who committed adultery. Her heirs can claim the property which she had brought into her marriage, for they can argue that if indeed the woman left Judaism, does this mean that her property was guilty of the same transgression?

זוֹ דִּבְרֵי רַבִּי מְנַחֵם These are the words of Rabbi Menahem. *Ritva* explains that there is no disagreement between Rav Naḥman and Rabbi Yoḥanan. Rav Naḥman agrees with Rabbi Yoḥanan that Rabbi Menahem maintains that a

HALAKHAH

conditions, or the increment to her ketubah. She may take whatever is left of the property which she had brought into the marriage, but her husband is not obligated to compensate her for any property which was lost or worn out," following the Baraita. (*Rambam, Sefer Nashim, Hilkhot Ishut* 24:10; *Shulḥan Arukh, Even HaEzer* 115:5.)

TRANSLATION AND COMMENTARY

his **wife, and** in other cases she **is not** treated like his **wife.** [1]But if **a widow** was married **to the High Priest,** she **is in all cases** treated like his **wife.** How so? [2]If a man was married to **an** *aylonit,* she **is** in some cases treated like his **wife and** in other cases she **is not** treated like his **wife.** [3]If the husband **knew about** his wife's condition at the time that he married her, **she is entitled to** receive **her ketubah** settlement. [4]**If he did not know about** her condition at the time of their marriage, **she is not entitled to** receive **her ketubah** settlement. [5]But if **a widow** was married **to the High Priest,** she **is in all cases** treated like his **wife.** [6]Therefore, **whether he knew** at time that he married her that she was a widow, **or he did not know** then that she was a widow, the woman **is** always **entitled to her ketubah** settlement. [7]**Rav Yehudah** disagreed and **said: Both in the case** of an *aylonit* **and in the case** of a widow married to the High Priest, the woman **is** sometimes treated like **an** ordinary **wife, and** at other times **she is not** treated like **an** ordinary **wife.** How so? [8]**If** the husband **knew about** his wife's physical condition or personal status when he married her, **she is entitled to** receive **her ketubah** settlement. [9]And **if he did not know** these things about his wife at the time of their marriage, she **is not entitled to** receive **her ketubah** settlement.

מֵיתִיבֵי [10]**An objection was raised** against Rav Huna from a Baraita in which it was taught: [11]**"If** a man **married** his wife **on the presumption that she was** forbidden to him, for example, if the High Priest married a woman after she informed him that she was a widow, [12]**and it turned out that** the woman **was indeed** forbidden to him as he had thought, **she is entitled to** receive **her ketubah** settlement." [13]Now, it may be inferred from this Baraita that if a man married **without such a presumption,** and only later did he discover that she was in fact forbidden to him, she **is not entitled to her ketubah** settlement, against Rav Huna!

לָא תֵּימָא [14]The Gemara answers: **Do not infer** from the Baraita that if someone married a woman **without presuming** that she was forbidden to him, and only later he discovered that she was in fact forbidden to him, the woman **is not entitled to her ketubah** settlement. [15]**Rather, infer** from the Baraita as follows: **If** someone **married on the presumption that** his wife **was** not forbidden to him, as when a High Priest married a woman after she assured him that she had never been previously married, **and** then later **it turned out that she was** indeed forbidden to him, [16]**she is not entitled to her ketubah** settlement.

וְאֵינָהּ אִשָּׁה. [1]אַלְמָנָה אִשָּׁה גְּמוּרָה. [2]אַיְלוֹנִית אִשָּׁה וְאֵינָהּ אִשָּׁה. [3]הִכִּיר בָּהּ, יֵשׁ לָהּ כְּתוּבָּה; [4]לֹא הִכִּיר בָּהּ, אֵין לָהּ כְּתוּבָּה; [5]אַלְמָנָה אִשָּׁה גְּמוּרָה. [6]בֵּין הִכִּיר בָּהּ בֵּין לֹא הִכִּיר בָּהּ, יֵשׁ לָהּ כְּתוּבָּה. [7]וְרַב יְהוּדָה אוֹמֵר: אַחַת זוֹ וְאַחַת זוֹ אִשָּׁה וְאֵינָהּ אִשָּׁה. [8]הִכִּיר בָּהּ, יֵשׁ לָהּ כְּתוּבָּה; [9]לֹא הִכִּיר בָּהּ, אֵין לָהּ כְּתוּבָּה.

[10]מֵיתִיבֵי: [11]"כְּנָסָהּ בְּחֶזְקַת שֶׁהִיא כֵּן, [12]וְנִמְצֵאת שֶׁהִיא כֵּן, יֵשׁ לָהּ כְּתוּבָּה". [13]הָא סְתָמָא, אֵין לָהּ כְּתוּבָּה!

[14]לָא תֵּימָא: "הָא סְתָמָא", אֵין לָהּ כְּתוּבָּה. [15]אֶלָּא אֵימָא: כְּנָסָהּ בְּחֶזְקַת שֶׁאֵינָהּ כֵּן, וְנִמְצֵאת שֶׁהִיא כֵּן, [16]אֵין לָהּ

LITERAL TRANSLATION

and she is not a wife. [1]A widow [to the High Priest] is entirely a wife. [2]An *aylonit* is a wife and she is not a wife. [3][If] he knew about her, she has a ketubah; [4][if[he did not know about her, she does not have a ketubah. [5]A widow [to the High Priest] is entirely a wife. [6]Whether he knew about her or he did not know about her, she has a ketubah. [7]And Rav Yehudah says: Both in this [case] and in that [case] she is a wife and she is not a wife. [8][If] he knew about her, she has a ketubah; [9][if] he did not know about her, she does not have a ketubah."

[10]They raised an objection: [11]"[If] he married her on the presumption that she was so, [12]and it turned out that she was so, she has a ketubah." [13]But ordinarily, she does not have a ketubah!

[14]Do not say: "But ordinarily", she does not have a ketubah. [15]Rather, say: [If] he married her on the presumption that she was not so, and it turned out that she was so, [16]she does not have

RASHI

אלמנה – לכהן גדול. **בחזקת שהיא כן** – שהודיעתו שהיא אלמנה. **הא סתמא** – הוה ליה – לא הכיר בה. **אין לה** – תיובתא דרב הונא. **בחזקת שאינה כן** – שהטעתו, ואמרה לו: לא נתקדשתי לאדם מעולם.

NOTES

woman who committed adultery loses her right to take the worn-out clothing which still exists, and so the Baraita could have been understood without emendation. But Rav Naḥman altered the Baraita to make it follow the Halakhah, for the Baraita was taught anonymously, implying that it should be accepted as law. Rabbi Yoḥanan argues that it is preferable to establish the Baraita as following the position of Rabbi Menaḥem, rather than to emend it.

TRANSLATION AND COMMENTARY

[1]**But** if a man married a woman **without presuming** that she was forbidden to him, and only later discovered that she was in fact forbidden to him, **what is the law?** [2]**She is entitled to** her ketubah settlement.

אַדְתָּנֵי [3]The Gemara reformulates its objection against Rav Huna: If so, **rather than stating:** "If someone married a woman **on the presumption that she was** forbidden to him, [4]**and** the woman **indeed** turned out to be forbidden to him as he had thought, she **is entitled to** receive **her ketubah** settlement." [5]The Tanna **should have taught us** the law applying when someone married a woman **without presuming** that she was forbidden to him, and then later she proved to be forbidden to him. Even then she is entitled to her ketubah settlement, [6]**and** we would have been able to infer from this that **all the more so** is she entitled to it if her husband married her on the presumption that she was forbidden to him! [7]**And furthermore,** it was explicitly **taught** in another Baraita: **"If** a man **married** a woman **knowing** that she was forbidden to him, **and it turned out** that she was indeed forbidden to him **as he had known,** she **is entitled to** receive **her ketubah** settlement. [8]But **if he married her without knowing** that she was forbidden to him, and later she proved to be forbidden to him, **she is not entitled to** receive **her ketubah** settlement."

תְּיוּבְתָּא דְּרַב הוּנָא [9]The Gemara concludes: **This is** indeed **a** conclusive **refutation of** the position of **Rav Huna.**

רַב הוּנָא [10]The Gemara now explains that **Rav Huna was led into error by our Mishnah.** [11]**He thought** that **since** the Mishnah **distinguishes with respect to an** *aylonit* — that if the husband knew about her condition at the time of the marriage she is entitled to her ketubah settlement, but if he did not know about it at that time, she is not entitled to it — [12]**and it does not make that** same **distinction with respect to a widow** who was married to a High Priest, [13]**it follows that with respect to a widow, even** if the High Priest married her **without knowing** about her personal status, she **is entitled** to her ketubah settlement. [14]**But** in truth **it is not so,** [15]for **when** the Mishnah **taught** the law **regarding a widow,** [16]**it was assuming the distinction** that had already been **stated with respect to an** *aylonit.*

כְּתוּבָּה. [1]אֲבָל סְתָמָא, מַאי? [2]אִית לַהּ.
[3]אַדְתָּנֵי "בְּחֶזְקַת שֶׁהִיא כֵּן, [4]וְנִמְצֵאת שֶׁהִיא כֵּן, יֵשׁ לָהּ כְּתוּבָּה" — [5]לַשְׁמְעִינַן "סְתָמָא", [6]וְכׇל שֶׁכֵּן הָא! [7]וְעוֹד, תָּנֵי: "כְּנָסָהּ בְּיָדוּעַ, וְנִמְצֵאת בְּיָדוּעַ, יֵשׁ לָהּ כְּתוּבָּה. [8]כְּנָסָהּ סְתָם, אֵין לָהּ כְּתוּבָּה".
[9]תְּיוּבְתָּא דְּרַב הוּנָא!
[10]רַב הוּנָא מַתְנִיתִין אַטְעִיתֵיהּ. [11]הוּא סָבַר: מִדְּקָא מַפְלִיג בְּאַיְלוֹנִית, [12]וְלָא קָמַפְלִיג בְּאַלְמָנָה, [13]מִכְּלַל דְּאַלְמָנָה אֲפִילּוּ בִּסְתָמָא נַמִי אִית לַהּ. [14]וְלָא הִיא. [15]כִּי קָתָנֵי לָהּ לְאַלְמָנָה, [16]אַפְּלוּגְתָּא דְּאַיְלוֹנִית קָאֵי.

הדרן עלך אלמנה ניזונת

LITERAL TRANSLATION

a ketubah. [1]But ordinarily, what [is the law]? [2]She has.

[3]Rather than stating "on the presumption that she was so, [4]and it turned out that she was so, she has a ketubah" — [5]he should have taught us "ordinarily", [6]and all the more so that [case]! [7]And furthermore, he taught: "[If] he married her knowing, and it turned out as it was known, she has a ketubah. [8][If] he married her ordinarily, she does not have a ketubah."

[9]This is a refutation of Rav Huna.

[10]Rav Huna was misled by our Mishnah. [11]He thought: Since it distinguishes with respect to an *aylonit*, [12]and it does not distinguish with respect to a widow, [13]it follows that regarding a widow, even ordinarily she has. [14]But it is not so. [15]When it taught about a widow, [16]it was referring to the distinction [stated] with respect to an *aylonit.*

RASHI

אבל סתמא — שלא התנה עמה, ומיהו לא הכיר בה — יש לה. **כנסה בידוע** — שהיא אלמנה. **מדקא מפליג באיילונית** — דאם מתחלה נשאה לשם איילונית יש לה. **כי קתני לה לאלמנה** — וקאמר יש לה כתובה. **אפלוגתא דאיילונית קאי** — לאחר שחילק באיילונית, ופירש הכיר בה יש לה כתובה, שנאה לאלמנה אללה, וקאמר: אף אלמנה נמי, שהכיר בה ונשאה לשם אלמנה — יש לה כתובה.

הדרן עלך אלמנה ניזונת

Conclusion to Chapter Eleven

Support for a widow is collected from her late husband's estate, but the widow sells some of her husband's property every time to cover support for a year, and she receives payment from the buyer every thirty days. If a widow has not demanded support for a long time (two or three years), she loses her retroactive right to that support, but she is entitled to support from that time on. A widow may sell part of her husband's estate to collect her ketubah settlement, either all at once or in installments, and she need not sell in particular before an ordained court. Rather she may do that before three men who are expert appraisers of prices.

If a widow sells her husband's estate for less than its value, the sale is rescinded. This also applies to an emissary. But in the case of sale by a court, the sale is rescinded only if the error came to as much as a sixth of the total value (שְׁתוּת) and if they proclaimed the sale (אִיגֶּרֶת בִּקּוֹרֶת) it stands in any event.

In general, if an emissary departs from his employer's instruction, his action is voided, though in some cases he can be seen as adding things and not as completely voiding them.

Regarding women whose marriage is flawed, it was said that the שְׁנִיָּה (who is incestuous according to Rabbinical law), the אַיְילוֹנִית (a barren woman) whom the husband did not recognize as such, and the girl who was married as a minor and refuses to remain married upon reaching majority, receive neither the main ketubah settlement nor any additional perquisites. But those who are forbidden according to the Torah, if their marriage is valid retroactively, do receive a ketubah settlement. However a woman who is divorced from her husband because she has committed a transgression receives neither the main ketubah settlement nor any increment.

Introduction to Chapter Twelve

הַנּוֹשֵׂא אֶת הָאִשָּׁה

This chapter begins with a law that stands by itself, the case of a man who has promised to support the daughter of his wife from a previous marriage. It investigates the Halakhic meaning of such a promise and the relation between it and the other stipulations of the ketubah. However, the main concern of this chapter is a continuation from the previous chapter, regarding a widow's rights.

Two topics are discussed regarding this subject: One is the place and conditions of the widow's residence where she is entitled to live, and how she may use her dwelling; the second topic is the length of time in which she is entitled to demand the ketubah settlement from her late husband's heirs. Although there is no time limit regarding collection of a promissory note, in this instance, since the widow has benefitted from her late husband's property (by receiving support), there are grounds to say that she has waived her claim against his heirs.

This chapter investigates these issues and matters associated with them.

הַנּוֹשֵׂא

[1]אֶת הָאִשָּׁה, וּפָסְקָה עִמּוֹ כְּדֵי שֶׁיָּזוּן אֶת בִּתָּהּ חָמֵשׁ שָׁנִים, [2]חַיָּיב לְזוּנָהּ חָמֵשׁ שָׁנִים. [3]נִיסֵּת לְאַחֵר, וּפָסְקָה עִמּוֹ כְּדֵי שֶׁיָּזוּן אֶת בִּתָּהּ חָמֵשׁ שָׁנִים, [4]חַיָּיב לְזוּנָהּ חָמֵשׁ שָׁנִים. [5]לֹא יֹאמַר הָרִאשׁוֹן: ״לִכְשֶׁתָּבֹא אֶצְלִי, אֲזוּנָהּ״, [6]אֶלָּא מוֹלִיךְ לָהּ

LITERAL TRANSLATION

MISHNAH [1][If] someone married the woman, and she stipulated with him that he would maintain her daughter for five years, [2]he is obligated to maintain her for five years.

[3][If] she married somebody else, and she stipulated with him that he would maintain her daughter for five years, [4]he is obligated to maintain her for five years. [5]The first one may not say: "When she comes to me, I will maintain her," [6]but rather he must send her

RASHI

משנה הנושא את האשה, לזון את בתה – שהיה לה מאיש אחר. נשאת – האם, לאחר שגירשה הראשון, לכשתבא אצלי – כלומר, אם הייתי מקיים את אמה – הייתי זנה.

TRANSLATION AND COMMENTARY

MISHNAH הַנּוֹשֵׂא אֶת הָאִשָּׁה [1]The chapter opens with a the case of a husband who freely undertook upon himself to maintain his wife's daughter from a previous marriage: **If someone married a woman** who already had a daughter **and she stipulated with him that he would maintain her daughter for** a period of **five years,** [2]**he is obligated to maintain** the daughter **for five years** in accordance with the stipulation.

נִיסֵּת לְאַחֵר [3]If the woman was divorced from that husband before the five years had passed, and **she married somebody else, and** also **stipulated with him that he would maintain her daughter for** a period of **five years,** [4]**he** too **is obligated to maintain** the daughter **for five years,** even though the daughter is still collecting maintenance from the woman's previous husband. [5]In such a case, **the previous husband may not say: "If** my former wife's daughter **comes to my house, I will maintain her,"** [6]**but rather he must send** the daughter **her**

NOTES

הַנּוֹשֵׂא אֶת הָאִשָּׁה **If someone married the woman.** *Melekhet Shelomo* asks: Why does the Mishnah state: "If someone married *the* woman [הַנּוֹשֵׂא אֶת הָאִשָּׁה]," rather than: "If someone married *a* woman [הַנּוֹשֵׂא אִשָּׁה]"? He suggests that since the Mishnah is dealing with a husband who undertook to maintain his wife's daughter for five years, it must be referring to a woman of particular distinction, or else the husband would not have undertaken such an obligation. Hence, the expression *the* woman, indicates that she is a woman of distinction. This explanation, also sheds light on the last Mishnah of the previous chapter, which deals with a man who married a woman who was forbidden to him. It stands to reason there too that the woman must have stood out in some way, whether in her beauty or her wealth or the like, for otherwise he would not have taken her as his wife.

כְּדֵי שֶׁיָּזוּן אֶת בִּתָּהּ חָמֵשׁ שָׁנִים **That he would maintain her daughter for five years.** *Tosafot Yom Tov* explains why the Mishnah chose to discuss the case of a woman who stipulated with her husband that he must maintain her daughter from a previous marriage for a period of *five* years. A woman may not remarry as long as she is still nursing her infant, which in the Talmudic period generally continued until the child reached the age of two. This woman wishes to ensure that her daughter will be taken care of while she is regarded a young child whose parents are obligated to support her, i.e., until she reaches the age of seven. Therefore she stipulated with her husband that he must support her daughter for five years.

The Jerusalem Talmud explains that the husband must maintain his wife's daughter during the first five years of their marriage, whether food was particularly expensive during that period or it was cheap (see also Halakhah). It adds that if the husband did not maintain the daughter when food prices were high, and price of food subsequently dropped, he must repay the wife for her daughter's maintenance according to the higher prices if his failure to maintain her was his fault. But if it was his wife's fault, he only has to pay her the value of the daughter's maintenance according to the current, lower prices.

לִכְשֶׁתָּבֹא אֶצְלִי **When she comes to me.** *Rashi* explains this to mean that the previous husband may not say: "If my wife were still married to me, I would have continued to maintain the daughter." The Mishnah negates this

HALAKHAH

פָּסְקָה עִמּוֹ כְּדֵי שֶׁיָּזוּן אֶת בִּתָּהּ **If someone married a woman, and stipulated with him that he would maintain her daughter for five years.** "If someone married a woman, and she stipulated with him that he would maintain her daughter from a previous marriage for a period of five years, he is obligated to provide the daughter with food and drink for the first five years of the marriage, whether food was expensive during those years or it was cheap," following the Mishnah. (*Rambam, Sefer Nashim, Hilkhot Ishut* 23:17; *Shulḥan Arukh, Even HaEzer* 114:1.

נִיסֵּת לְאַחֵר, וּפָסְקָה עִמּוֹ **If she married somebody else, and stipulated with him.** "If a woman had stipulated with her husband that he would maintain her daughter for five years, and she was divorced from him, and then she married somebody else, and made the same stipulation with him, one of the two husbands is obligated to provide the woman's daughter with her actual maintenance, and the other is obligated to pay her the value of her maintenance," following the Mishnah. (*Rambam, Sefer Nashim, Hilkhot Ishut* 23:17; *Shulḥan Arukh, Even HaEzer* 114:8.)

מְזוֹנוֹתֶיהָ לְמָקוֹם שֶׁאִמָּהּ. [1]וְכֵן לֹא יֹאמְרוּ שְׁנֵיהֶם: ״הֲרֵי אָנוּ זָנִין אוֹתָהּ כְּאֶחָד״. [2]אֶלָּא, אֶחָד זָנָהּ, [3]וְאֶחָד נוֹתֵן לָהּ דְּמֵי מְזוֹנוֹת.

[4]נִיסֵּת, הַבַּעַל נוֹתֵן לָהּ מְזוֹנוֹת, [5]וְהֵן נוֹתְנִין לָהּ דְּמֵי מְזוֹנוֹת. [6]מֵתוּ, בְּנוֹתֵיהֶן נִיזּוֹנוֹת מִנְּכָסִים בְּנֵי חוֹרִין, [7]וְהִיא נִיזּוֹנֶת מִנְּכָסִים מְשׁוּעְבָּדִים, [8]מִפְּנֵי שֶׁהִיא כְּבַעֲלַת חוֹב.

LITERAL TRANSLATION

her maintenance to the place where her mother [lives]. [1]And so too the two of them may not say: "We will maintain her together." [2]But rather, one maintains her, [3]and one gives her money for maintenance.

[4][If] she married, the husband gives her maintenance, [5]and they give her money for maintenance.

[6][If] they died, their [own] daughters are maintained from free property, [7]and she is maintained from mortgaged property, [8]for she is like a creditor.

TRANSLATION AND COMMENTARY

maintenance to the place where her mother and she **are living.** [1]**And so too, the two husbands cannot say: "We will join together** and **maintain her** between the two of us." [2]**But rather, one** of them must **provide her with** her actual **maintenance** — food, shelter, clothing, etc. — [3]**and the other one** must **pay her the value of her maintenance.**

נִיסֵּת [4]**If** the daughter **married** while her mother's current and previous husbands were obligated to maintain her, **the** daughters own **husband** must **provide her with** her actual **maintenance** in accordance with his obligation to maintain his wife, [5]**and** her mother's two husbands must each **pay her the value of her maintenance** in accordance with the stipulations that her mother had made with them.

מֵתוּ [6]**If** the mother's two husbands **died, their** own **daughters may collect their maintenance from** the **free property** of their father's estates. By Torah law, if a man has sons, they, not his daughters inherit his estate. However, the Rabbis enacted that a man's minor daughters are entitled to maintenance from the estate of their deceased father until they are betrothed or reach majority (see *Ketubot* 52b). A daughter may only collect her maintenance from the free assets of her father's estate, which are still in the hands of her brothers who inherited the estate, and not from assets mortgaged or sold by her brothers. [7]**But** the daughter whom the mother had before her last two marriages, whom the deceased husbands had undertaken to maintain **may collect her maintenance** until the end of the stipulated maintenance period even **from the assets** of their estates **which** their heirs **had mortgaged** or sold to a third party, [8]**for she is like a creditor** who may collect a debt from mortgaged property.

RASHI

בנותיהן נזונות מנכסים בני חורין — ולא ממשועבדים. דתנן (גיטין מח,ב): אין מוציאין לאכילת פירות ולשבח קרקעות ולמזון האשה והבנות מנכסים משועבדים. **והיא נזונת** — אותה הבת. **שהיא כבעלת חוב** — שיש לה עליהן שטר מזונות.

NOTES

argument and insists that he must keep his undertaking to maintain his wife's daughter even following divorce. *Rashash* argues that the Mishnah can be understood more simply as follows: The husband cannot say that he will only maintain the daughter while she is living in his house, unlike the husbands heirs who may put forward such an argument regarding their father's widow. This latter view is adopted in our commentary.

וְאֶחָד נוֹתֵן לָהּ דְּמֵי מְזוֹנוֹת And one gives her money for maintenance. *Ritva* (following the Jerusalem Talmud) notes that whenever a person undertakes to provide another person with maintenance, that other person may opt to receive the value of his maintenance in cash, rather than the maintenance itself.

נִיסֵּת, הַבַּעַל נוֹתֵן לָהּ מְזוֹנוֹת If she married, the husband gives her maintenance. The Jerusalem Talmud notes that even while the daughter is being maintained by her step-father, she is entitled to keep her handiwork for herself. Furthermore, it teaches that if the daughter became ill, she is treated as if she were married, which means according to *Meiri* that if the daughter ate less because of illness, her mother's husband who undertook her maintenance is obligated to pay her in cash for the food that she did not eat.

שֶׁהִיא כְּבַעֲלַת חוֹב For she is like a creditor. The Rishonim note that the daughter is not like a creditor in all respects, for if she dies, her mother's husband is not obligated to pay the value of her maintenance to her heirs. While there are those who maintain otherwise, the Jerusalem Talmud concludes that the husband's obligation terminates with the daughter's death, for that obligation is personal, rather than financial, in nature.

HALAKHAH

נִיסֵּת, הַבַּעַל נוֹתֵן לָהּ מְזוֹנוֹת If she married, the husband gives her maintenance. "If the daughter married while her mother's current and previous husbands were obligated to maintain her, the daughters own husband must provide her with her actual maintenance, and her mother's two husbands must pay her the value of her maintenance," following the Mishnah. (*Rambam, Sefer Nashim, Hilkhot Ishut* 23:18; *Shulḥan Arukh, Even HaEzer* 114:10.)

[1] הַפִּקְחִים הָיוּ כּוֹתְבִים: [2] ״עַל מְנָת שֶׁאָזוּן אֶת בִּתֵּךְ חָמֵשׁ שָׁנִים כָּל זְמַן שֶׁאַתְּ עִמִּי״.

גמרא [3] אִתְּמַר: [4] הָאוֹמֵר לַחֲבֵירוֹ: ״חַיָּיב אֲנִי לְךָ מָנֶה״ — [5] רַבִּי יוֹחָנָן אָמַר: חַיָּיב. [6] וְרֵישׁ לָקִישׁ אָמַר: פָּטוּר. [7] הֵיכִי דָּמֵי? [8] אִי דַּאֲמַר לְהוּ: ״אַתֶּם עֵדַיי״, [9] מַאי טַעֲמָא דְּרֵישׁ לָקִישׁ דְּקָפָּטַר? [10] אִי דְּלָא אֲמַר לְהוּ: ״אַתֶּם עֵדַיי״, [11] מַאי טַעֲמָא דְּרַבִּי יוֹחָנָן דְּקָמְחַיֵּיב? [12] לְעוֹלָם דְּלָא קָאָמַר לְהוּ:

TRANSLATION AND COMMENTARY

הַפִּקְחִים [1] **Clever people** marrying a woman with a daughter from a previous marriage **would write** a condition stating: [2] "I will marry you **on condition that I will maintain your daughter for** a period of **five years,** but only **as long as you are with me** as my wife."

GEMARA אִתְּמַר [3] **It was stated** that the Amoraim disagreed about the following question: [4] **If someone said to another person: "I owe you a maneh"** — [5] **Rabbi Yoḥanan said:** He **is liable** for the maneh. [6] **And Resh Lakish said:** He **is free of liability.**

הֵיכִי דָּמֵי [7] The Gemara clarifies the issue in dispute: **How do you visualize the case?** [8] **If** the he **said** to two of the people who were present: **"You are my witnesses** that I admit owing this other person a maneh," [9] **what is the rationale of Resh Lakish who said** that he **is free of liability?** Surely an admission before witnesses is irrevocable. [10] And **if** the admittor **did not say** to those present: **"You are my witnesses,"** [11] **what is the rationale of Rabbi Yoḥanan who said** that the admittor **is liable?** Surely the admittor can later claim that he had not been serious when he admitted owing money to the other person!

לְעוֹלָם [12] The Gemara explains: **In fact,** the Amoraic dispute refers to someone who **did not say to** those

LITERAL TRANSLATION

[1] The clever ones would write: [2] "On condition that I will maintain your daughter for five years as long as you are with me."

GEMARA [3] It was stated: [4] [If] someone said to his fellow: "I owe you a maneh" — [5] Rabbi Yoḥanan said: He is liable. [6] And Resh Lakish said: He is free of liability.

[7] How is [the case] to be visualized (lit., "what is it like")? [8] If he said to them: "You are my witnesses," [9] what is the reason of Resh Lakish who said he is free of liability? [10] If he did not say to them: "You are my witnesses," [11] what is the reason of Rabbi Yoḥanan who said he is liable?

[12] In fact, when he did not say to them:

RASHI

כל זמן שאת עמי – ולא אם אמות, או תמותי או אגרשיך. **גמרא** אי דאמר להו – לשומעין. אתם עדיי – שאני מודה לו. מאי טעמא דריש לקיש דפטר – הא אנן תנן בסנהדרין (כט,ב): עד שיאמרו: בפנינו הודה לו, אלמא: הודה בפני עדים – חייב. אי לא אמר להו – לשומעין ״אתם עדיי״. מאי טעמא דרבי יוחנן – הא קיימא לן התם בסנהדרין: וצריך שיאמר אתם עדיי! הכי גרסינן: לעולם דלא אמר להו

NOTES

חַיָּיב אֲנִי לְךָ מָנֶה I owe you a maneh. There are two different explanations of the entire discussion: According to *Rashi, Tosafot,* and other Rishonim, the Gemara discusses here the liability of a person who admits owing money to someone else. The Gemara assumes that the admission of a debt before two competent witnesses is valid evidence of such liability, and that the admission of a debt without such witnesses is generally not binding, consequently, the Gemara must construct the case about which Rabbi Yoḥanan and Resh Lakish disagree, such as the admission by way of a written but unsigned document, or a document drawn up by someone else and delivered in the presence of two witnesses (see Note, below, s.v., אַלִּימָא מִילְּתָא דִּשְׁטָרָא). *Rif, Rabbenu Tam,* and many other Rishonim understand that Rabbi Yoḥanan and Resh Lakish do not argue about the admission of an already existing obligation, but rather about whether or not an admission is capable of creating a new obligation. *Ritva* and others discuss at length various different aspects of these issues, as well as the relationship between the laws governing an admission that confirms an existing obligation and the laws governing an admission which creates a new obligation. The Rishonim also discuss the relationship between the discussion here and the related discussion in the Jerusalem Talmud.

אִי דְּלָא אֲמַר לְהוּ: אַתֶּם עֵדַיי If he did not say to them: You are my witnesses. The Rishonim discuss the two

HALAKHAH

הַפִּקְחִים הָיוּ כּוֹתְבִים The clever ones would write. "If the husband wrote his wife that he would maintain her daughter as long as she remains married to him, and the woman died or he divorced her (and even if he later remarried her), he is no longer obligated to maintain the woman's daughter," following the Mishnah. (*Shulḥan Arukh, Even HaEzer* 114:11.)

חַיָּיב אֲנִי לְךָ מָנֶה I owe you a maneh. "If someone obligates himself for a sum of money to another person, he must pay him that sum, even if he did not actually owe him anything. How so? If someone said to two witnesses: 'Be my witnesses that I owe So-and-so money,' or if he wrote that other person a note stating: 'I owe you money,' or if he said to him before witnesses: 'I owe you money, and the debt is recorded in writing,' even if he did not say to the witnesses: 'Be my witnesses,' he must pay the other person the sum that he admitted owing him, even if both parties agree and the witnesses know that a previous debt had never really existed," following Rabbi Yoḥanan, against Resh Lakish. (*Rambam, Sefer Kinyan, Hilkhot Mekhirah* 11:15; *Shulḥan Arukh, Ḥoshen Mishpat* 40:1.)

TRANSLATION AND COMMENTARY

present: [1] **"You are my witnesses** that I admit owing this other person a maneh." [2] **And here we are dealing with an** unsigned **promissory note** written in his hand that said: **"I owe you a maneh."** [3] **Rabbi Yoḥanan said:** He **is liable** for the maneh, [4] for an admission by way of **an** unsigned **written document is as strong** and irrevocable **as when** the admittor **said to** two of the people who were present: [5] **"You are my witnesses** that I admit owing this other person money." [6] And **Resh Lakish said:** The admittor **is free of liability,** [7] for an admission by way of **an** unsigned **written document is not as strong** and irrevocable as an oral admission before designated witnesses.

תְּנַן [8] The Gemara now relates this dispute to our Mishnah, in which **we have learned: "If someone married a woman** who had a daughter **and she stipulated with him that he would maintain her daughter for** a period of **five years,** [9] **he is obligated to maintain** the daughter **for five years** in accordance with the stipulation. [10] **"Is not** the Mishnah referring to a case where the husbands obligation to maintain his step-daughter was recorded in an unsigned written document? For if the Mishnah refers to an obligation recorded in a signed deed, what does it teach us? Surely the husband is obligated to maintain his wifes daughter in accordance with the liability that he had undertaken! Thus, the Mishnah poses a difficulty for Resh Lakish who maintains that an admission of this sort does not establish liability!

[1] ״אַתֶּם עֵדַיי״, [2] וְהָכָא בְּמַאי עָסְקִינַן — דַּאֲמַר לֵיהּ: ״חַיָּיב אֲנִי לָךְ מָנֶה בִּשְׁטָר״, [3] רַבִּי יוֹחָנָן אָמַר: חַיָּיב, [4] אַלִּימָא מִילְּתָא דִּשְׁטָרָא, כְּמַאן דַּאֲמַר לְהוּ [5] ״אַתֶּם עֵדִים״ דָּמֵי; [6] רֵישׁ לָקִישׁ אָמַר: פָּטוּר, [7] לָא אַלִּימָא מִילְּתָא דִּשְׁטָרָא.

[8] תְּנַן: הַנּוֹשֵׂא אֶת הָאִשָּׁה, וּפָסְקָה עִמּוֹ לָזוּן אֶת בִּתָּהּ חָמֵשׁ שָׁנִים — [9] חַיָּיב לְזוּנָהּ חָמֵשׁ שָׁנִים; [10] מַאי לָאו כִּי הַאי גַּוְונָא?

LITERAL TRANSLATION

[1] "You are my witnesses." [2] But here what are we are dealing with? When he said to him in a promissory note: "I owe you a maneh." [3] Rabbi Yoḥanan said: He is liable. [4] The case of a promissory not is as strong as if he had said to them: [5] "You are my witnesses." [6] Resh Lakish said: He is free of liability. [7] The case of a promissory note is not as strong.

[8] We have learned: "[If] someone married a woman, and stipulated with her that he would maintain her daughter for five years, [9] he is obligated to maintain her for five years." [10] Is it not like this?

RASHI

אתם עדיי והכא במאי עסקינן בשטרא — שמסר לו שטר בפניהו, וכתוב בו: אני חייב לך מנה. ואף על פי שכתב ידו הוא, הואיל ולא חתם — פטור. והא דתנן (כתובות כא,א): הוציא עליו כתב ידו שהוא חייב לו — גובה מנכסים בני חורין — כגון שחתם בו "אני פלוני לויתי מנה מפלוני", כדמוכח בפרק "האשה שנתארמלה" (שם) דאמר אביי: לכתוב חתימת ידיה אחספא, אבל אמגילתא — לא. מאי טעמא — דלמא משכח ליה כו' ותנן: הוציא עליו כתב ידו כו.' אלמא בחתימת ידיה קמיירי. אבל הכא, הכי כתב ליה: חייב אני לך מנה, ולא חתם בו. **אלימא מלתא דשטרא** — הואיל ובפני עדים מסר לו. **מאי לאו כי האי גוונא** — [מה עדות יש לה לאחר זמן בדבר זה? לאו כי האי גוונא], שמוסר לה שטר בפני עדים, וכתוב בו: פלוני קבל עליו כך. ואין שם לא קנין ולא חתימה. דאי הוה שטר חתום בידה — מאי למימרא?

NOTES

pleas that one can put forward in order to revoke an admission that was not made in the presence of two witnesses. If the admission was made voluntarily, he can revoke it by arguing that he had made the admission for a special reason: — in order to make people think that he is in debt, and has little net capital. Or, if he made the admission in response to a demand put forward by an alleged creditor, he can argue that he had not been serious when he admitted owing him the money.

אַלִּימָא מִילְּתָא דִּשְׁטָרָא The case of a promissory note is as strong. *Rashi* and *Tosafot* understand that we deal here with someone who has admitted in a document that he owed money to another person. They disagree about the specifics of that document, whether it was written by the hand of the purported debtor but was not signed, or whether it was not drawn up in his own hand, but there are witnesses who saw that he gave the document to the purported creditor (see also *Sefer HaYashar*). *Rabbenu Ḥananel* understood the matter in an entirely different manner. He maintains that in this case someone made an oral admission that he owed another person money, that debt having been evidenced by a written deed of indebtedness. Here, he is bound by his admission, even if it was not made in the presence of two witnesses. Moreover, he cannot argue that he had not been serious about his admission, or that he had made it only in order to give the appearance of being in debt to others.

תְּנַן: הַנּוֹשֵׂא We have learned: If someone married. *Rashi,* following his position that the Gemara here is dealing with the evidential value of an admission by way of an unsigned document, argues that the Mishnah must be dealing with a similar case. The husband must have admitted in such a document that he owed his wife's daughter maintenance. For if the Mishnah were dealing with a signed document testifying to the obligation, it is obvious that the husband would be liable for the daughter's maintenance. *Rif* and others who understand that we are dealing here with the possibility of creating an obligation by way of an admission can explain the Gemara more simply. They argue that the Mishnah is dealing with a similar case, in which the husband wishes to create a new obligation to maintain his wife's daughter.

[102A] [1]לָא, בִּשְׁטָרֵי פְּסִיקְתָּא, [2]וְכִדְרַב גִּידֵּל. [3]דְּאָמַר רַב גִּידֵּל אָמַר רַב: [4]״כַּמָּה אַתָּה נוֹתֵן לִבְנְךָ״? ״כָּךְ וְכָךְ״, [5]״וְכַמָּה אַתָּה נוֹתֵן לְבִתְּךָ״? ״כָּךְ וְכָךְ״. [6]עָמְדוּ וְקִידְּשׁוּ, קָנוּ. [7]הֵן הֵן הַדְּבָרִים הַנִּקְנִין בַּאֲמִירָה. [8]תָּא שְׁמַע: [9]״כָּתַב לְכֹהֵן ״שֶׁאֲנִי חַיָּיב לְךָ חָמֵשׁ סְלָעִים״, [10]חַיָּיב לִיתֵּן לוֹ חָמֵשׁ סְלָעִים,

TRANSLATION AND COMMENTARY

[102A] לָא [1]**No,** in the case treated by the Mishnah, the husband's obligation to maintain his step-daughter was recorded in the **bill of agreement** which was drawn up when he and his wife agreed to marry. Before a marriage, a pre-nuptial agreement may be drawn up between the parties themselves or their respective parents, specifying the date and place of the proposed marriage, and the financial obligations of the parties, such as the dowry to be brought into the marriage by the bride. Such a document is signed by witnesses. The Mishnah teaches that the agreement is binding, even if it was not ratified by a formal act of acquisition, [2]for the law is **in accordance with** the position that was later formulated by **Rav Gidel.** [3]**For Rav Gidel said in the name of Rav:** If the father of the bride asked the father of the groom: [4]**"How much will you give your son** when he marries?" and the groom's father answered: "I will give him **such-and-such";** [5]and then the father of the groom asked the father of the bride: **"How much will you give your daughter** as her dowry?" and the bride's father answered: "I will give her **such-and-such";** [6]and the parties **stood up and** the groom **betrothed** the bride, all the obligations undertaken by the parents are **valid and binding,** even if a formal act of acquisition was not performed to ratify the agreement, [7]for such obligations **are matters that are effected by** mere **verbal agreement.** Since the case in the Mishnah involves a bill of agreement that was duly attested to by competent witnesses, it has no bearing on the matter in dispute between Resh Lakish and Rabbi Yoḥanan.

תָּא שְׁמַע [8]The Gemara now presents another difficulty entailed to the position of Resh Lakish: **Come and hear** what was taught in the following Mishnah (*Bekhorot* 51a): [9]**"If someone wrote to a priest** through whom he wished to redeem his first-born son: **I owe you five selas** — the sum designated by the Torah that is to be given to a priest for the redemption of a first-born son, [10]**he is obligated to give** that priest **five selas,**

LITERAL TRANSLATION

[102A] [1]No, with bills of agreement, [2]and in accordance with Rav Gidel. [3]For Rav Gidel said in the name of Rav: [4]"How much will you give your son?" "Such-and-such." [5]"And how much will you give your daughter?" "Such-and-such." [6][If] they stood up and betrothed, they acquired. [7]These are the matters that are acquired with speech.

[8]Come [and] here: [9]"[If] he wrote to a priest: That I owe you five selas, [10]he is obligated to give him five selas,

RASHI

לא בשטרי פסיקתא — החתן והכלה פוסקין תנאים שביניהם בשני עדים, והעדים חותמים עדות גמורה. ואם תאמר: אם כן מאי למימרא איצטריך. כגון דליכא קנין אלא דברים. ואשמעינן כדרב גידל, דלא בעי קנין.

NOTES

בִּשְׁטָרֵי פְּסִיקְתָּא **With bills of agreement.** The question was raised: If the Gemara establishes that our Mishnah follows the position of Rav Gidel that the obligations undertaken by the bride and groom are valid and binding even if effected by a verbal agreement, why was it necessary to say that the Mishnah is dealing with obligations that were recorded in a bill of agreement? Some commentators suggest that since the Gemara is assuming that the entire Mishnah is dealing with the same case, and one of its later clauses deals with the step-daughter's entitlement to collect maintenance from assets which had been mortgaged or sold to a third party, the Mishnah must be dealing with a written obligation, otherwise the daughter would only be entitled to collect her maintenance from free assets (*Maharam Shiff, Rabbi Akiva Eiger,* and *Ayelet Ahevim*).

חַיָּיב לִיתֵּן...וּבְנוֹ אֵינוֹ פָּדוּי **He is obligated to give...but his son is not redeemed.** As is the case with the rest of the Gemara's discussion, here too the Rishonim explain the Gemara's question and answer it in accordance with the two alternative approaches to understanding the case in

HALAKHAH

כַּמָּה אַתָּה נוֹתֵן לִבְנְךָ? **How much will you give your son?** "If a man and a woman promised to marry each other, and he said to her: 'How much will your bring in to the marriage as your dowry, and she said: 'Such-and-such, and she asked him: 'How much will you give me, and he said: 'Such-and-such; or if the fathers of the bride and groom undertook similar obligations, and the parties stood up and the groom betrothed the bride, all the obligations undertaken by the various parties are binding, even if the agreement was not ratified by a formal act of acquisition, for these are matters that are effected by mere verbal agreement," following Rav Gidel. (*Rambam, Sefer Kinyan, Hilkhot Zekhiyah* 6:17; *Shulḥan Arukh, Even HaEzer* 51:1.)

כָּתַב לְכֹהֵן **If he wrote to a priest.** "If someone wrote to a priest: 'I owe you five selas for the redemption of my son,' he is obligated to give the priest the five selas, but his first-born son is still not redeemed," following the Mishnah in *Bekhorot.* (*Rambam, Sefer Zeraim, Hilkhot Bikkurim* 11:7; *Shulḥan Arukh, Yoreh De'ah* 305:4.)

TRANSLATION AND COMMENTARY

but his first-born **son is not redeemed** by the unsigned promissory note. Therefore the father must give that priest or another one an additional five selas for the boy's redemption." This Mishnah is consistent with the ruling of the Rabbi Yoḥanan who maintains that an admission of this sort establishes liability. The father is obligated to give the priest five selas because he admitted to him in writing that he owed him that money, but his son is not redeemed. The son is only redeemed if his father gave the priest five selas because of the obligation imposed upon him by Torah law, and not because of an obligation which he himself established. But according to Resh Lakish who maintains that an admission of this sort does not establish liability, why is the father obligated to give the priest five selas?

שָׁאנֵי הָתָם [1]The Gemara answers: **There it is different.** The father must give the priest five selas, [2]**because he is obligated to him by Torah law** to do so, even if he did not admit in writing that he owes him money.

אִי הָכִי [3]The Gemara asks: **If** he had to pay anyway, **why did** the father feel it necessary to **write** an obligation to the priest?

כְּדֵי לְבָרֵר [4]The Gemara answers: He did so, **in order to select for himself a** particular **priest** to receive the money. Even though the father is obligated by Torah law to redeem his son, he is given the discretion to decide to which priest he will give the redemption money.

אִי הָכִי [5]The Gemara asks: **If so, why is his son not redeemed** when he gives the money to the priest?

כְּדְעוּלָּא [6]The Gemara answers: The matter should be understood **in accordance with** what **Ulla** said, [7]**for Ulla said: By Torah law,** the son **is** in fact **redeemed when** the father **gives** the five selas to the priest. [8]**What then is the reason that** the Sages **said** that the son is not redeemed? [9]The Sages issued **a decree** that the son is not redeemed, **lest** people **say:** A father may **redeem** his son **with a promissory note,** whereas the law is that only silver or its equivalent in moveable property can effect his redemption.

אֲמַר רָבָא [10]**Rava said:** The controversy between Rabbi Yoḥanan and Resh Lakish is **like** an earlier dispute between **the Tannaim** recorded in the following Baraita: [11]**"If** a third party gave his **guarantee after the**

LITERAL TRANSLATION

but his son is not redeemed."

[1]It is different there, [2]because he is obligated to him by Torah law.

[3]If so, why did he write?

[4]In order to select for himself a priest.

[5]If so, why is his son not redeemed?

[6]In accordance with Ulla, [7]for Ulla said: By Torah law, he is [indeed] redeemed when he gives. [8]But what is the reason that they said: His son is not redeemed? [9]A decree lest they say: They redeem with bills [of indebtedness].

[10]Rava said: [This is like [a dispute between] Tannaim: [11]"[If] the guarantee follows the signing of the bills,

וּבְנוֹ אֵינוֹ פָּדוּי!

[1]שָׁאנֵי הָתָם, [2]דִּמְשׁוּעְבַּד לֵיהּ מִדְּאוֹרַיְיתָא.

[3]אִי הָכִי, אַמַּאי כָּתַב?

[4]כְּדֵי לְבָרֵר לוֹ כֹּהֵן.

[5]אִי הָכִי, בְּנוֹ אַמַּאי אֵינוֹ פָּדוּי? [6]כְּדְעוּלָּא, [7]דְּאָמַר עוּלָּא: דְּבַר תּוֹרָה פָּדוּי לִכְשֶׁיִּתֵּן. [8]וּמַאי טַעֲמָא אָמְרוּ: בְּנוֹ אֵינוֹ פָּדוּי? [9]גְּזֵירָה שֶׁמָּא יֹאמְרוּ: פּוֹדִין בִּשְׁטָרוֹת.

[10]אֲמַר רָבָא, כְּתַנָּאֵי: [11]״עָרֵב הַיּוֹצֵא אַחַר חִיתּוּם שְׁטָרוֹת,

RASHI

לברר לו כהן – שלא יתננו לכהן אחר. אי הכי – דטעמא משום שיעבודא דאורייתא הוא, והוה ליה כמעיד עדים וחותמים – אמאי אין בנו פדוי? שמא יאמרו: פודין – את הבכור בשטרי חוב שיש לו על אחר, ומסרו לכהן בפדיונו. דאתי למימר: מה לי האי שטרא ומה לי האי שטרא? ואנן תנן במסכת בכורות: אין פודין לא בעבדים ולא בשטרות ולא בקרקעות. וילפינן לה התם מקראי בפרק ״יש בכור לנחלה״. לאחר חיתום שטרות – תחת חתימת העדים כתוב:

NOTES

which Rabbi Yoḥanan and Resh Lakish have their dispute. We are dealing with the evidential value of an admission recorded in an unsigned document, or with the possibility of creating an obligation by way of an admission. *Tosafot* and others discuss at length how this part of the discussion fits in with the two approaches, focusing in particular upon how it can be reconciled with *Rashi*s explanation.

שֶׁמָּא יֹאמְרוּ: פּוֹדִין בִּשְׁטָרוֹת **Lest they say: They redeem with bills.** Elsewhere (*Bekhorot* 41a), the Gemara derives in various ways (using the hermeneutical principles of כְּלָל וּפְרָט ("generalization and detail") and ריבּוּי וּמִיעוּט ("amplification and restriction") that a person cannot redeem his first-born son with something without intrinsic value. Thus, promissory notes are excluded, for they have no intrinsic value, but serve only as evidence of a debt.

HALAKHAH

עָרֵב הַיּוֹצֵא אַחַר חִיתּוּם שְׁטָרוֹת **If a guarantor follows the signing of the bills.** "If a guarantor undertook his obligation after the witnesses had signed a bill establishing the debt, and he wrote: 'I am the guarantor of this loan, and it is clear that this was written in his hand, or there are witnesses who confirm that it was his handwriting — some

TRANSLATION AND COMMENTARY

witnesses attached their **signatures to the bill** of indebtedness, [1]the creditor can only **collect** his debt **from the free property** that is found in the guarantor's possession, and not from property which he later sold to someone else. Although the guarantor agreed in writing to pay the debt if the borrower defaults, since he did so only after the principal obligation was created, the guarantee is treated like an oral, undocumented debt, which can only be collected from the debtor's free assets and not from property that was transferred by the debtor to a third party. [2] **An incident** such as this **was** once **brought before Rabbi Yishmael, and he said:** [3]The creditor can only **collect** his debt **from the free property** found in the guarantor's possession. [4]**Ben Nannas said to him:** If the guarantee was undertaken only after the principal obligation was created, the creditor **may not collect from the guarantors free property, nor from the property which he sold,** for the guarantee has no legal validity. [5]Rabbi Yishmael **said to** Ben Nannas: **Why** not? [6]Ben Nannas **said to** Rabbi Yishmael: **If someone was strangling somebody in the marketplace,** demanding that he repay the money that was owed him, [7]**and a third party happened upon them, and said to** the creditor: [8]**Leave him** alone **and I will give you** the money that he owes you — even though he obligated himself to repay the debtor's debt, **he is free** of all **liability,** [9]**for it was not because of** the creditors **trust** in the guarantor **that** he **had** originally **lent** the money **to** the debtor. A guarantee is only binding if it was undertaken before the creation of the principal obligation, for in that case the guarantor knows that the loan was given only because the lender trusted him, and we assume that he really intended to assume responsibility for the debt. Hence, if a guarantee is committed to writing after the witnesses signed the note establishing the principal obligation, it has no legal validity. [10]**Shall we say** that **Rabbi Yoḥanan,** who says that if someone wrote to another person: "I owe you a maneh," he is liable for the maneh, **agrees with Rabbi Yishmael,** who says that if the guarantor wrote the debtor: "I am your guarantor," he is responsible for the debt, [11]**and** that **Resh Lakish,** who said that a written admission to a debt, the admittor is free of liability, **agrees with Ben Nannas,** who says that accepting a guarantee after the fact is not binding?

LITERAL TRANSLATION

[1]he collects from free property. [2]An incident was brought before Rabbi Yishmael, and he said: [3]He collects from free property. [4]Ben Nannas said to him: He collects neither from free property nor from mortgaged property. [5][Rabbi Yishmael] said to him: Why? [6]He said to him: If someone was strangling his fellow in the market, [7]and his fellow found him and said to him: [8]Leave him and I will give you [the money], he is free of liability, [9]for it was not because of his trust that he lent to him." [10]Shall we say that Rabbi Yoḥanan said like Rabbi Yishmael, [11]and Resh Lakish said like Ben Nannas?

[1]גּוֹבֶה מִנְּכָסִים בְּנֵי חוֹרִין. [2]מַעֲשֶׂה בָּא לִפְנֵי רַבִּי יִשְׁמָעֵאל, וְאָמַר: [3]גּוֹבֶה מִנְּכָסִים בְּנֵי חוֹרִין. [4]אָמַר לוֹ בֶּן נַנָּס: אֵינוֹ גּוֹבֶה לֹא מִנְּכָסִים בְּנֵי חוֹרִין וְלֹא מִנְּכָסִים מְשׁוּעְבָּדִים. [5]אָמַר לוֹ: לָמָּה? [6]אָמַר לוֹ: הֲרֵי שֶׁהָיָה חוֹנֵק אֶת חֲבֵירוֹ בַּשּׁוּק, [7]וּמְצָאוֹ חֲבֵירוֹ וְאָמַר: לוֹ: [8]הַנַּח לוֹ, וַאֲנִי אֶתֵּן לְךָ — פָּטוּר, [9]שֶׁלֹּא עַל אֱמוּנָתוֹ הִלְוָהוּ״. [10]לֵימָא רַבִּי יוֹחָנָן דְּאָמַר כְּרַבִּי יִשְׁמָעֵאל, [11]וְרֵישׁ לָקִישׁ דְּאָמַר כְּבֶן נַנָּס!

RASHI

פלוני ערב, והוא מודה בדבר. גובה מנכסים בני חורין — המלוה מן הערב, ולא מנכסים משועבדים. כיון דלאחר חיתום השטר הוא, הויא לה כמלוה על פה.

NOTES

גּוֹבֶה מִנְּכָסִים בְּנֵי חוֹרִין **He collects from free property.** As a general rule, a creditor may collect his debt from landed assets that the debtor had sold to another person only if that debt is recorded in writing and signed by witnesses. Only then do we say that the debt has a *kol* (lit., "voice"), so that the purchaser is assumed to have known that the property which he bought was mortgaged to the creditor. But if the debt was established orally, there is no *kol,* and the creditor cannot collect the debt from property that is now in the hands of a purchaser. Similarly, if a guarantor undertook his obligation only after the witness had signed the promissory note establishing the debt, his obligation is regarded as a debt that had been established orally. Such a debt can be collected only from the debtor's free property, unlike a debt that was established in writing, and which can even be collected from a third party who bought property from the debtor.

HALAKHAH

authorities maintain that the guarantor is liable to repay the debt from his free assets, even if an act of acquisition was not performed, following Rabbi Yishmael. And other authorities maintain that the guarantor bears no liability, unless he obligated himself with an act of acquisition, following Ben Nannas. According to *Rambam,* even if the guarantor undertook his liability before the witnesses who signed the original bill of indebtedness, if he obligated himself only after the money had been given to the debtor, he bears no liability unless he undertook the obligation by way of an act of acquisition." (*Rambam, Sefer Mishpatim Hilkhot Malveh* 26:1; *Shulḥan Arukh, Ḥoshen Mishpat* 129:4.)

[1]אַלִּיבָּא דְּבֶן נַנָּס כּוּלֵּי עָלְמָא לָא פְּלִיגִי, [102B] [2]כִּי פְּלִיגִי אַלִּיבָּא דְּרַבִּי יִשְׁמָעֵאל. [3]רַבִּי יוֹחָנָן כְּרַבִּי יִשְׁמָעֵאל, [4]וְרֵישׁ לָקִישׁ: עַד כָּאן לָא קָאָמַר רַבִּי יִשְׁמָעֵאל הָתָם. [5]אֶלָּא דְּשַׁיָּיךְ לֵיהּ לְשִׁיעְבּוּדָא דְּאוֹרַיְיתָא. [6]אֲבָל הָכָא לָא שַׁיָּיךְ שִׁיעְבּוּדָא דְּאוֹרַיְיתָא.

[7]גּוּפָא, אָמַר רַב גִּידֵּל אָמַר רַב: [8]"כַּמָּה אַתָּה נוֹתֵן לִבְנְךָ"? "כָּךְ וְכָךְ". [9]"וְכַמָּה אַתָּה נוֹתֵן לְבִתְּךָ"? "כָּךְ וְכָךְ". [10]עָמְדוּ וְקִידְּשׁוּ, קָנוּ. [11]הֵן הֵן הַדְּבָרִים

TRANSLATION AND COMMENTARY

אַלִּיבָּא [1]The Gemara rejects this suggestion: **Regarding the** position of **Ben Nannas, all agree** — both Rabbi Yoḥanan and Resh Lakish — that if someone wrote to another person: "I owe you a maneh," he is free of all liability. [102B] [2]**They** only **disagree about** the position of [3]**Rabbi Yishmael. Rabbi Yoḥanan follows Rabbi Yishmael,** without distinguishing between the two issues. Just like Rabbi Yishmael said that it the guarantor wrote to the debtor: "I am your guarantor," he is responsible for his debt, so too Rabbi Yoḥanan said that if someone wrote to another person: "I owe you a maneh," he is liable to pay him that amount. [4]**And Resh Lakish** maintains that **Rabbi Yishmael only stated his opinion there** in the case of a guarantor because a guarantor [5]**is obligated** to repay the debtor's loan **under Torah law,** as the verses states (Genesis 43:9): "I will be surety for him." [6]**But here,** when someone merely said to another person: "I owe you a maneh," even Rabbi Yoḥanan agrees that he is not liable for the money, for accepting to pay a non-existent loan does not **carry an obligation under Torah law.**

גּוּפָא [7]Having referred to the position reported by Rav Gidel in the name of Rav, the Gemara now **returns to the subject** and analyzes it at greater length: **Rav Gidel said in the name of Rav:** If the father of the bride asked the father of the groom: [8]**"How much will you give your son** when he marries?" and the groom's father answered: "I will give him **such-and-such"**; [9]and then the father of the groom asked the father of the bride: **"How much will you give your daughter** as her dowry?" and the bride's father answered: "I will give her **such-and-such"**; [10]and the parties **stood up and** the groom **betrothed** the bride, all the obligations undertaken by the parents are **valid and binding,** even if a formal act of acquisition was not performed to ratify the agreement, [11]for such obligations **are matters that are effected by** mere **verbal**

LITERAL TRANSLATION

[1]Regarding [the position of] Ben Nannas there is no disagreement. [102B] [2]Where they disagree is with regard to the position of Rabbi Yishmael. [3]Rabbi Yoḥanan is like Rabbi Yishmael, [4]but Resh Lakish [can say to you]: Rabbi Yishmael stated [his opinion] only where there [5]is an obligation under the Torah law. [6]But here there is no obligation under Torah law.

[7]Returning to the statement quoted above (lit., "the thing itself"), Rav Gidel said in the name of Rav: [8]"How much will you give your son?" "Such-and-such." [9]And how much will you give your daughter?" "Such-and-such." [10][If] they stood up and betrothed, they acquired. [11]These are the things

RASHI

אליבא דבן ננס כולי עלמא לא פליגי — כלומר, בהא שפיר קאמרת דרבי יוחנן כרבי ישמעאל ולא כבן ננס, דמודה רבי יוחנן דלבן ננס פטור. דהשתא, ומה ערב דשיעבודא דאורייתא הוא, דכתיב "אנכי אערבנו" (בראשית מג) כי ליכא עדים — פטור, כל שכן כהאי גוונא. **כי פליגי כו'** — כלומר, הא דמוקמת ריש לקיש כבן ננס ולא כרבי ישמעאל, ליתא, דאמר לך ריש לקיש: אנא אפילו לרבי ישמעאל קא פליגנא אדרבי יוחנן. **ערב** — שיעבודא דאורייתא. **אבל הכא** — "פלוני חייב" — ליכא שיעבודא דאורייתא.

NOTES

כַּמָּה אַתָּה נוֹתֵן לִבְנְךָ **How much will you give your son.** The Jerusalem Talmud limits the marriage obligations that are effected by mere verbal agreement to those undertaken by the fathers of the bride and groom, and any obligations accepted by other relatives. Similarly it limits the regulation to a bride and a groom who are both marrying for the first time (see Halakhah). These limitations appear to be based on what is stated in our Gemara, that the parents agree to the conditions of the betrothal and obligate themselves to each other because of the benefit that they enjoy from entering each others' family — a benefit that is enjoyed primarily on the occasion of their childrens first marriage.

עָמְדוּ וְקִידְּשׁוּ **If they stood up and betrothed.** *Rashbam, Ra'ah* and others understand that this ruling is limited to an agreement about the conditions of the betrothal, immediately after which the groom "stood up" and betrothed his bride. But if he betrothed her at some later

HALAKHAH

הֵן הֵן הַדְּבָרִים הַנִּקְנִים בַּאֲמִירָה **These are the things that are acquired with speech.** "If the father of the groom promised a certain sum of money on behalf of his son, and the father of the bride promised a certain sum as his daughter's dowry (whether she was still a minor, or she had already reached adulthood; following the Gemara's conclusion), and the groom betrothed his bride, all the obligation's are binding, for they are matters that are effected by mere verbal agreement. This ruling only applies to obligations undertaken by the father of the bride, but not

הַנִּקְנִים בַּאֲמִירָה. [1]אֲמַר רָבָא: מִסְתַּבְּרָא מִילְּתָא דְּרַב בְּבִתּוֹ נַעֲרָה, [2]דְּקָא מָטֵי הֲנָאָה לִידֵיהּ. [3]אֲבָל בּוֹגֶרֶת, [4]דְּלָא מָטֵי הֲנָאָה לִידֵיהּ, לָא. [5]וְהָאֱלֹהִים! [6]אֲמַר רַב: אֲפִילּוּ בּוֹגֶרֶת. [7]דְּאִי לָא תֵּימָא הָכִי, אֲבִי הַבֵּן מַאי הֲנָאָה אָתָא לִידֵיהּ? [8]אֶלָּא, בְּהַהִיא הֲנָאָה דְּקָמִיחַתְּנֵי אַהֲדָדֵי, [9]גָּמְרֵי וּמַקְנֵי לַהֲדָדֵי.

[10]אֲמַר לֵיהּ רָבִינָא לְרַב אַשִׁי: דְּבָרִים הַלָּלוּ נִיתְּנוּ לִיכָּתֵב [11]אוֹ לֹא נִיתְּנוּ לִיכָּתֵב?

LITERAL TRANSLATION

that are acquired with speech. [1]Rava said: Rav's statement stands to reason with respect to his daughter who is a *na'arah*, [2]where benefit comes to his hand. [3]But [with respect to] a *bogeret*, [4]where benefit does not come to his hand, no. [5]But, by God! [6]Rav said: Even [with respect to] a *bogeret*. [7]For if you do not say this, what benefit comes to the hand of the father of the son? [8]Rather, with that benefit that they become an extended family (lit., "marry each other"), [9]they agree and obligate themselves to one another.

[10]Ravina said to Rav Ashi: Are these things given to be written [11]or are they not given to be written?

TRANSLATION AND COMMENTARY

agreement. [1]**Rava said: Rav's position stands to reason with respect to** a **daughter** who **is a** ***na'arah,*** a maturing girl between the age of twelve and twelve-and-a-half, whose father has the right to betrothe her and is entitled to keep the betrothal money for himself. [2]Since **he receives benefit** from his daughter's betrothal, we assume that he really meant to accept the various obligations to which he agreed. [3]**But with respect to** the case of **a** ***bogeret,*** a young girl who has reached legal majority at the age of twelve-and-a-half and whose father no longer has rights to her betrothal money, the obligations undertaken by the parents are not binding. [4]Since the father of the bride **does not receive** any **benefit** from his daughter's betrothal, there is no reason to assume that he meant to commit himself to the obligations that he had accepted. [5]Rava continues: **But, by God!** [6]**Rav said** what he said **even with respect to** the case of **a** ***bogeret.*** [7]**For if you do not say so, what benefit does the father of the groom derive** from his son's betrothal? A father's liability for the obligations which he had accepted cannot be dependent upon the financial benefit which he derives from his child's betrothal. The father of the groom does not enjoy any such benefit. Nevertheless, the obligations which he undertook are binding. Thus, the father of the bride should also be liable for the obligations which he had accepted, even if his daughter is a *bogeret,* and he enjoys no financial benefit from her betrothal. However, the couple's parents do not accept the obligations for their financial benefit. [8]**Rather,** it is **because of the benefit that** the parents enjoy **joining each other's family** [9]that **they agree** to the conditions of the betrothal **and obligate themselves to each other.**

אֲמַר לֵיהּ רָבִינָא [10]**Ravina said to Rav Ashi: May these matters** — the financial obligations undertaken verbally by the bride and groom or their parents as a condition to their betrothal — **be committed to writing** in a formal witnessed deed, so that the obligations can be collected from mortgaged property, [11]**or may they not be committed to writing** in such a deed, and so the obligations can only be collected from free assets?

RASHI

דקא מטי הנאה לידיה — כסף קדושיה לאביה. **אבי הבן** — אביו של חתן. **ניתנו ליכתב** — נתנו חכמים כתיבה לדבר, אם באו להחתים עדים בדברים הללו שהן בלא קנין. **לא ניתנו ליכתב** — דלא ליטרוף ממשעבדי. **וכיון דליכא קנין** — לא משתעבדי נכסי.

NOTES

occasion, the conditions are not binding unless they were ratified by an act of acquisition. *Ri* and others disagree and say that the term "stood up" has a more general meaning which does not necessarily denote immediacy, and so the betrothal conditions are binding even when the betrothal took place at some later date (see *Ritva*).

וְהָאֱלֹהִים **By God.** *Ritva* infers from here that a person is permitted to use such language, which includes an oath by God's name, with respect to something that he did not actually hear, provided that he is absolutely convinced of its logical necessity.

נִיתְּנוּ לִיכָּתֵב **They are given to be written.** The Rishonim understand Ravina's question and the ensuing discussion in various ways. Our commentary follows *Rashi* and others

HALAKHAH

those undertaken by her mother or brother, and it only applies to obligations undertaken at the time of the parties first marriage (following the Jerusalem Talmud). The parties can only obligate themselves with respect to property that was in their possession at the time, but not with respect to property that will only come into their possession at some time in the future." (*Rambam, Sefer Nashim, Hilkhot Ishut* 23:13; *Sefer Kinyan, Hilkhot Zekhiyah* 6:17; *Shulḥan Arukh, Even HaEzer* 51:1.)

לֹא נִיתְּנוּ לִיכָּתֵב **They are not given to be written.** "The financial obligations undertaken by the bride and groom, or their parents, as a condition to their betrothal may not be committed to writing. Thus, even if they were committed to writing, the parties cannot collect with the signed note

TRANSLATION AND COMMENTARY

אֲמַר לֵיהּ [1]Rav Ashi **said to** Ravina: These financial obligations which were undertaken verbally **may not be committed to writing** in a formal deed.

אֵיתִיבֵיהּ [2]Ravina **raised an objection** against Rav Ashi's position from our Mishnah in which we have learned: **"Clever people** marrying a woman with a daughter from a previous marriage **would write** a condition stating: [3]'I will marry you **on condition that I will maintain your daughter for** a period of **five years,** but only **as long as you are with me** as my wife.'" Thus, we see that the betrothal conditions may indeed be committed to writing!

מַאי כּוֹתְבִין [4]Rav Ashi answered: **What is the meaning of** the expression **"they would write"** as it is used here in our Mishnah? [5]The Mishnah means that the clever people **would state** verbally that they would maintain the daughter from a previous marriage only while they were still married.

וְקָרֵי לֵיהּ [6]Ravina asked: But **does** the Tanna ever **refer to a verbal statement** using the term **"writing"?**

אִין [7]Rav Ashi answered: **Yes** he does, for **we have** surely **learned** in the Mishnah (*Ketubot* 83b): [8]**"If someone wrote** for **his wife: 'I will have no claim to your property.'"** [9]**And Rabbi Ḥiyya taught** a slightly different version of the Mishnah, according to which it should read: **"If someone said** to his wife," ruling that the husband's waiver is valid, even if he only stated it verbally. Thus, we see that the Mishnah can use the term "writing" even in reference to a verbal statement.

[1]אֲמַר לֵיהּ: לֹא נִיתְּנוּ לִיכָּתֵב.
[2]אֵיתִיבֵיהּ: ״הַפִּקְחִין הָיוּ כּוֹתְבִין: [3]׳עַל מְנָת שֶׁאָזוּן אֶת בִּתֵּךְ חָמֵשׁ שָׁנִים כָּל זְמַן שֶׁאַתְּ עִמִּי׳״!
[4]מַאי ״כּוֹתְבִין״? [5]אוֹמְרִים.
[6]וְקָרֵי לֵיהּ לַאֲמִירָה ״כְּתִיבָה״?
[7]אִין, וְהָתְנַן: [8]״הַכּוֹתֵב לְאִשְׁתּוֹ: ׳דִּין וּדְבָרִים אֵין לִי בִּנְכָסַיִךְ׳״.
[9]וְתָנֵי רַבִּי חִיָּיא: ״הָאוֹמֵר לְאִשְׁתּוֹ״.

LITERAL TRANSLATION

[1]He said to him: They are not given to be written [as a formal document].

[2]He raised an objection: "The clever ones would write: [3]'On condition that I will maintain your daughter for five years as long as you are with me.'"

[4]What is [meant by] "they [would] write"? [5]They [would] say.

[6]Does [the Tanna] call speech "writing"?

[7]Yes, for surely we have learned: [8]"[If] someone writes his wife: 'I have no claim (lit., "litigation or dispute") to your property.'" [9]And Rabbi Ḥiyya taught: "[If] someone said to his wife."

NOTES

(see *Rivan* and *Rid)* who explain that Ravina asked whether the financial obligations undertaken verbally by the bride and groom or their parents as a condition to their betrothal may or may not be committed to writing in a formal deed. Since these verbal obligations with no act of acquisition can only be collected from free assets, do we allow them to be written in a document and signed by witnesses, enabling them now to be collected even from mortgages? *Rabbenu Tam* and *Rabbenu Ḥananel* understand the Gemara in a different manner: Must these obligations be committed to writing in a formal deed, for if they were not committed to writing they may not be collected even from free assets? Or is it unnecessary to record them in writing, for even without committing the obligations to writing, they may be collected even from mortgaged property? *Ra'avad* and *Rabbenu Zeraḥyah HaLevi* suggest that the Gemara means as follows: May the obligations be committed to writing by one of the parties without the consent of the other, for even when written down, verbal agreements may not be collected from mortgaged property? In that case, the writing adds nothing to the lien, but serves only as a reminder regarding the obligations. Or may the obligations not be committed to writing without the consent of the two parties, for writing them down strengthens the lien, for then the obligations can be collected even from mortgaged property?

הַפִּקְחִין הָיוּ כּוֹתְבִין **The clever ones would write.** The objection raised from our Mishnah is understood in different ways, depending on the various approaches to understanding the question raised by the Gemara. (See the previous note.) According to *Rashi,* the proof from our Mishnah is that the obligations undertaken by the parties may indeed be committed to writing. According to *Rabbenu Tam,* the Mishnah proves that the obligations must be committed to writing, for if not, why do clever people write down the conditions that they attach to the betrothal this would be unnecessary if they could collect on the basis of the verbal agreement alone. And *Ra'avad* explains that the Mishnah proves that committing the obligations to writing does not allow them to be collected from mortgaged property. Otherwise someone who commits himself in writing to maintain his wife's daughter for five years, provided they remain married, is not clever but is damaging himself, for when he does so he subjects his property to a lien on mortgaged assets in the daughter's favor.

HALAKHAH

from mortgaged property," following Rav Ashi. *Bet Shmuel* adds that this only applies if the document merely records the parties mutual verbal obligations. But if it was formulated in the manner of a promissory note, the parties may indeed collect from mortgaged property. (*Rambam, Sefer Nashim, Hilkhot Ishut* 23:13; *Sefer Kinyan, Hilkhot Zekhiyah* 6:17; *Shulḥan Arukh, Even HaEzer* 51:1.)

TRANSLATION AND COMMENTARY

תָּא שְׁמַע [1]The Gemara now cites a Baraita which seems to contradict Rav Ashi's position that the betrothal conditions may not be committed to writing: **Come and hear: "Bills of betrothal or marriage may not be written without the consent of** both parties, the groom and the bride." [2]**But** it follows from this Baraita that **with the consent** of both parties, bills of betrothal or marriage **may** indeed **be written. Is not** the Baraita referring to **bills of agreement** which record the promises made by each party regarding their respective financial obligations? Thus, we see that the betrothal conditions may indeed be committed to writing!

לָא [3]The Gemara rejects this proof: **No,** that Baraita is dealing with **actual bills of betrothal,** in which the groom writes to his wife: "Behold you are consecrated to me with this deed according to the laws of Moses and Israel." The Baraita teaches that such bills may not be written without the consent of both parties, [4]**as** it was later taught by **Rav Pappa and Rav Sherevya.** [5]**For it was stated** that the Amoraim disagreed about the following issue. **If** the groom specifically **wrote** a bill of betrothal for his bride, **but without her consent,** [6]**Rabbah and Ravina said: The betrothal is valid.** [7]**Rav Pappa and Rav Sherevya said: The betrothal is not valid.**

תָּא שְׁמַע [8]The Gemara now tries to disprove Rav Ashi's position from another section of our Mishnah: **Come and hear** what we have learned in our Mishnah: [9]"If the mother's two husbands **died, their** own **daughters may collect their maintenance from** the **free property** of their father's estates. [10]**But** the mother's daughter from her first marriage, whom her two later husbands had undertaken to maintain for a period of five years, **may collect her maintenance** until the end of that period even **from the assets** of their estates

[1]תָּא שְׁמַע: "אֵין כּוֹתְבִין שְׁטָרֵי אֵירוּסִין וְנִשּׂוּאִין אֶלָּא מִדַּעַת שְׁנֵיהֶם". [2]הָא מִדַּעַת שְׁנֵיהֶם כּוֹתְבִין, מַאי לָאו שְׁטָרֵי פְּסִיקְתָּא?

[3]לָא! שְׁטָרֵי אֵירוּסִין מַמָּשׁ, [4]כִּדְרַב פַּפָּא וְרַב שֵׁרֵבְיָא. [5]דְּאִיתְּמַר: כְּתָבוֹ לִשְׁמָהּ, וְשֶׁלֹּא מִדַּעְתָּהּ, [6]רַבָּה וְרָבִינָא אָמְרִי: מְקוּדֶּשֶׁת. [7]רַב פַּפָּא וְרַב שֵׁרֵבְיָא אָמְרִי: אֵינָהּ מְקוּדֶּשֶׁת.

[8]תָּא שְׁמַע: [9]"מֵתוּ, בְּנוֹתֵיהֶן נִיזּוֹנוֹת מִנְּכָסִים בְּנֵי חוֹרִין, [10]וְהִיא נִיזּוֹנֶת מִנְּכָסִים

LITERAL TRANSLATION

[1]Come [and] hear: "They may not write bills of betrothal or marriage without the consent of both of them." [2]But with the consent of both of them, they [may] write. Is it not [referring to] bills of agreement?

[3]No! It refers to actual bills of betrothal, [4]like Rav Pappa and Rav Sherevya. [5]For it was stated: [If] he wrote [a bill of betrothal] specifically for her (lit., "in her name"), but not with her consent, [6]Rabbah and Ravina said: She is betrothed. [7]Rav Pappa and Rav Sherevya said: She is not betrothed.

[8]Come [and] hear: [9]"[If] they died, their [own] daughters are maintained from free property, [10]and she [the stepdaughter] is maintained from mortgaged

RASHI

שטרי אירוסין ממש — שטר שמקדש בו את האשה "הרי את מקודשת לי" כותב בשטר ומוסר לה. ואשמעינן דצריך לכתוב על פיה, כדרב פפא ורב שרביא, דאמרי: כתבו שלא מדעתה — אינה מקודשת.

NOTES

לִשְׁמָהּ, וְשֶׁלֹּא מִדַּעְתָּהּ **To her name, but not with her knowledge.** The Gemara in *Kiddushin* (9b) explains that the Amoraim disagree about the Halakhic ramifications of the *gezerah shavah* (analogy) drawn between marriage and divorce. Rabbah and Ravina argue that just as a bill of divorce must be written specifically for the woman but not necessarily with her knowledge, so too a bill of betrothal must be written specifically for her, but not necessarily with her consent. Rav Pappa and Rav Sherevya argue that just as a bill of divorce must be written with the consent of the party who conveys title, i.e., the husband who conveys to his wife title over herself, allowing her to remarry; so too a bill of betrothal must be written with the consent of the party who conveys title, i.e., the bride, who conveys to the groom title over herself, forbidding herself to all other men.

בְּנוֹתֵיהֶן נִיזּוֹנוֹת **Their daughters are maintained.** *Tosafot* asks: Since this clause of the Mishnah precedes the clause dealing with the clever people who would protect themselves by carefully wording their obligations, why does the Gemara first raise an objection against Rav Ashi's position from the later clause, before raising its objection from this earlier clause? *Tosafot* answers that it is common for the

HALAKHAH

אֵין כּוֹתְבִין שְׁטָרֵי אֵירוּסִין **They may not write bills of betrothal.** "Bills of betrothal and marriage (as well as bills of agreement) may not be written without the consent of both parties, the groom and the bride." (*Rambam, Sefer Mishpatim, Hilkhot Malveh* 24:1; *Tur, Even HaEzer* 51.)

לִשְׁמָהּ, וְשֶׁלֹּא מִדַּעְתָּהּ **If he wrote it in her name, but not with her consent.** "A bill of betrothal must be written specifically for the bride whom the groom betrothes, and if it was not written specifically for her, the betrothal is not valid. A bill of betrothal must also be written with the woman's consent. If the bill was written without the woman's consent, the authorities disagree about the law. According to *Rambam,* the betrothal is not valid, following Rav Pappa and Rav Sherevya. According to *Shulḥan Arukh*

TRANSLATION AND COMMENTARY

which their heirs **had mortgaged** or sold to a third party, [1]**for she is like a creditor** who may collect his debt from mortgaged property." This proves that the financial obligations undertaken by the bride or groom may indeed be committed to writing, for a creditor may not collect his debt from mortgaged property unless the obligation was recorded in a promissory note.

הָכָא [2]The Gemara rebuts this argument: **Here** in the Mishnah **we are dealing with** the parties who **performed a** formal symbolic act of acquisition to ratify their obligations and any agreement ratified by an act of acquisition may be committed to writing.

אִי הָכִי [3]The Gemara objects: However, **if** this were **so** that the Mishnah is dealing with a case where the parties performed an act of acquisition to ratify the obligations undertaken by them, then **the** two husbands' own **daughters** should **also** be able to collect their maintenance from mortgaged property, for the obligations assumed toward them would also be included in the act of acquisition!

בְּשֶׁקָּנוּ לָזוֹ [4]The Gemara answers: No. The Mishnah is dealing with a case **where an act of acquisition was performed regarding this one,** the woman's daughter from her first husband, enabling the girl to collect her maintenance even from mortgaged property, [5]**but an act of acquisition was not performed regarding the others,** the daughters from her second and third husbands. Therefore they may only collect their maintenance from the free assets of their father's estates.

וּמַאי פָּסְקָא [6]The Gemara now asks: **But why this arbitrary decision?** Why should we assume that the act of acquisition was performed to protect the rights of the stepdaughter, but not the rights of his own daughter?

אִיהִי דַּהֲוַאי [7]The Gemara answers: Regarding the woman's daughter **who was born at the time that the act of acquisition** was performed, **the act of acquisition is effective,** and so the daughter can collect the maintenance due her from mortgaged property. [8]But regarding the woman's daughters from her second and third husbands **who were not born when the act of acquisition** was performed, **the act of acquisition is not effective,** and so those daughters can only collect their maintenance from the free assets of their father's estates. This follows the rule that an act of acquisition cannot create obligations regarding something that does not exist.

מְשׁוּעְבָּדִים, [1]מִפְּנֵי שֶׁהִיא כְּבַעֲלַת חוֹב״!

[2]הָכָא בְּמַאי עָסְקִינַן? בְּשֶׁקָּנוּ מִיָּדוֹ.

[3]אִי הָכִי, בָּנוֹת נַמִי!

[4]בְּשֶׁקָּנוּ לָזוֹ [5]וְלֹא קָנוּ לָזוֹ.

[6]וּמַאי פָּסְקָא?

[7]אִיהִי דַּהֲוַאי בִּשְׁעַת קִנְיָן — מְהַנֵּי לָהּ קִנְיָן. [8]בָּנוֹת דְּלָא הָווּ בִּשְׁעַת קִנְיָן — לָא מְהַנֵּי לְהוּ קִנְיָן.

LITERAL TRANSLATION

property, [1]for she is like a creditor!"

[2]With what are we dealing here? Where they acquired it from him.

[3]If so, [their own] daughters too!

[4]When they acquired for this one [5]and not for that one.

[6]But why [this arbitrary] decision?

[7][The daughter] who was there at the time of the acquisition — the act of acquisition is effective for her. [8]The daughters who were not there at the time of the acquisition — the acquisition is not effective for them.

RASHI

שהיא כבעלת חוב — ואי לא דנקיטא שטר מי טרפא ממשעבדי? **מאי פסקא** — בתמיה: וכי דבר פסוק הוא לחכמים שקונין לבת האשה ולא לבנות? ששנו סתם במשנה: בנותיהן ניזונות מבני חורין והיא ניזונת ממשועבדים.

NOTES

Gemara to arrange the discussion in such a way that allows for a variety of questions and answers. Had the Gemara referred to the earlier clause first and given the answer which it supplies, it could no longer have asked from the later clause, for that difficulty could have been resolved in the same way. *Ramat Shmuel* suggests that the Gemara first referred to the later clause maintaining "writing" explicitly, because the difficulty that it poses is more readily apparent. (See also *Hafla'ah* for another answer.)

HALAKHAH

(following *Rosh*), the validity of the betrothal is in doubt, for the matter was not resolved in the Gemara, nor conclusively decided about by the Rishonim (see also *Bet Shmuel*)." (*Rambam, Sefer Nashim, Hilkhot Ishut* 3:4; *Shulḥan Arukh, Even HaEzer* 32:1.)

בְּשֶׁקָּנוּ מִיָּדוֹ **Where they performed an act of acquisition.** "If a man obligated himself to provide his wife's daughter with maintenance, and he died, the daughter may collect her maintenance from mortgaged property, provided that the obligation was accompanied by the performance of an act of acquisition, or the husband had committed his obligation to writing. But otherwise she may not collect her maintenance from mortgaged property." (*Rambam, Sefer Nashim, Hilkhot Ishut* 23:18; *Shulḥan Arukh, Even HaEzer* 114:4.)

[1]מִי לָא עָסְקִינַן דַּהֲוַאי בִּשְׁעַת קִנְיָן, [2]וְהֵיכִי דָּמֵי? [3]כְּגוֹן דְּגֵרְשָׁהּ וְאַהַדְרָהּ!

[4]אֶלָּא, אִיהִי דְּלֵיתָא בִּתְנַאי בֵּית דִּין — [5]מְהַנֵּי לָהּ קִנְיָן. [6]בָּנוֹת דְּאִיתְנְהוּ בִּתְנַאי בֵּית דִּין — [7]לָא מְהַנֵּי לְהוּ קִנְיָן.

[8]מִגְרַע גָּרְעֵי?

[9]אֶלָּא, בְּנוֹתָיו הַיְינוּ טַעֲמָא: [10]כֵּיוָן דְּאִיתְנְהוּ בִּתְנַאי בֵּית דִּין, [11]אֵימַר צְרָרֵי אַתְפְּסִינְהוּ.

LITERAL TRANSLATION

[1]Are we not dealing [even with the situation] where they were [present] at the time of the acquisition, [2]and what is it like? [3]As when he divorced her and took her back!

[4]Rather, she [the stepdaughter] who is not [included] in the court[-mandated] stipulations — [5]the acquisition is effective for her. [6]The daughters who are [included] in the court [-mandated] stipulations — [7]the acquisition is not effective for her.

[8]Can they be worse?

[9]Rather, [regarding] his [own] daughters, this is the reason: [10]Since they are [included] in the court[-mandated] stipulations, [11]say that [we fear that] he gave them bundles [of money].

TRANSLATION AND COMMENTARY

מִי לָא עָסְקִינַן [1]The Gemara asks: **Can we not be dealing** in the Mishnah **with a** woman whose daughters from her second and third husbands **were** also **born at the time that the act of acquisition** was performed? [2]**And how can we visualize such a case?** [3]**If** each of the husbands had married the woman, fathered a daughter from her, **divorced her, and** later **he took her back** as his wife. Even in such a case the Mishnah would imply that the daughters of the second and third husbands can only collect their maintenance from the free assets of their father's estates. But the Mishnah is dealing with a case where an act of acquisition was performed to ratify the obligations undertaken by the husbands, why should those other daughters — present at the time of the act of acquisition — not be able to collect their maintenance from mortgaged property?

אֶלָּא [4]**Rather,** answers the Gemara, the matter must be understood as follows: The woman's daughter from her first marriage **is not included in the Rabbinic enactment** that entitles a woman's daughters to maintenance from her husband's estate. This enactment only applies to daughters from that husband. [5]Therefore **the act of acquisition is effective** for the daughter from an earlier union, who otherwise would not have been entitled to maintenance and as a result she can collect even from the estate's mortgaged property. [6]But regarding **the** woman's **daughters** from her second and third husbands **who are included in the Rabbinic enactment,** [7]**the act of acquisition is not effective,** and they can collect their maintenance only from the free property of their father's estate.

מִגְרַע גָּרְעֵי [8]The Gemara objects: Does it stand to reason that because the woman's daughters from her second and third husbands are entitled to maintenance from their fathers' estates by virtue of a Rabbinic enactment, their position **should be worse** than that of her daughter from her first marriage who is not entitled to maintenance by virtue of that enactment? To the contrary, their position should be even stronger!

אֶלָּא [9]**Rather,** suggests the Gemara, **this is the reason** that **the** second and third husbands' own **daughters** cannot collect their maintenance from mortgaged property: [10]**Since** those daughters **are included in the Rabbinic enactment,** which entitles a woman's daughters to maintenance from their father's estate, [11]we **say** that it is likely that those husbands concerned themselves with their daughters maintenance even before they died and **gave them bundles of money** for ensuring their maintenance. They cannot collect their maintenance from mortgaged property, for they might already have received all that is due them. But the woman's daughter from her first husband is not included in the Rabbinic enactment, and so we have no reason to think that her second or third husband might have given her anything before he died. Thus, that daughter can collect her maintenance even from mortgaged property.

RASHI

מי לא עסקינן כו׳ — וכי אי אפשר שיהו אף הבנות בשעת קנין? כגון דגרשה ואהדרה וכתב לה התנאים הללו. ואפילו הכי תנן סתמא: בנותיהן ניזונות מבני חורין ולא ממשועבדים. **בתנאי בית דין** — "בנן נוקבן דיהויין ליכי מינאי" כו׳. **מיגרע גרעי** — בתמיה. **צררי אתפסינהו** — לפני מותו מסר להם צרורות כספים למזונותיהן.

NOTES

צְרָרֵי אַתְפְּסִינְהוּ **He gave them bundles of money.** *Tosafot* and other Rishonim explain why one might think here that the father had given his minor daughter bundles of money before he died, whereas in other passages we find no such concern.

Ritva and others point out that there is a similar concern regarding a widow: Her husband might have left her money for her ketubah settlement before he died. Therefore only if the widow takes an oath that she did not receive anything from her husband, may she collect her ketubah settlement from mortgaged property. Here, however, because there is near certainty that a father will leave his daughter money for her maintenance, they did not allow her to collect her maintenance from mortgaged property even if she takes an oath that she received nothing from her father.

TRANSLATION AND COMMENTARY

לֹא יֹאמַר הָרִאשׁוֹן [1] We learned in the Mishnah: "If the woman was divorced from her second husband before the five years had passed, and she married somebody else, and also stipulated with him that he would maintain her daughter from her first marriage for a period of five years, he too is obligated to maintain the daughter for five years in accordance with his stipulation, even though the daughter is still collecting maintenance from the woman's previous husband. In such a case, **the previous husband cannot say:** If my former wife's daughter comes to my house, I will maintain her, but rather he must send the daughter her maintenance to the place where her mother and she are living, her new husband's home." [2] **Rav Ḥisda said:** The fact that the Mishnah states that the husband must send the daughter her maintenance "to the place where her mother is," [3] **teaches** that even a grown-up, unmarried **daughter** always goes to **live with her mother.**

מִמַּאי דִּבְגְדוֹלָה עָסְקִינַן [4] The Gemara questions this inference: **From where does** Rav Ḥisda **know that we are dealing with an adult** stepdaughter? [5] **Perhaps we are dealing with a** daughter who is still a **minor,** [6] **and** she goes and lives with her mother **because of a** certain **incident that occurred.** [7] **For it was taught** in a Baraita: **"If a man dies, and left a minor son to his mother,** [8] **and the father's heirs say: 'Let** the boy **grow up with us,** [9] **and the mother** objects and **says: Let my son grow up with me,** [10] **the child is left in the custody of his mother, and he is not left in the custody of** a relative **who is fit to inherit from him,** for we are concerned for the child's life, lest the relative try to kill him in order to succeed to his property. [11] Indeed, **it** once **happened that** an orphaned boy was left in the custody of relatives who were fit to inherit from him, and **they murdered him** for his money **on Pesaḥ eve."** Here too the Mishnah might be dealing a girl who inherited her father's estate because he died without sons. It teaches that she remains with her mother, and not with relatives who are fit to inherit from her, for we are concerned that those relatives might try to kill her and inherit her property.

[1] "לֹא יֹאמַר הָרִאשׁוֹן". [2] אָמַר רַב חִסְדָּא: [3] זֹאת אוֹמֶרֶת, בַּת אֵצֶל אִמָּהּ.

[4] מִמַּאי דִּבְגְדוֹלָה עָסְקִינַן? [5] דִּלְמָא בִּקְטַנָּה עָסְקִינַן, [6] וּמִשּׁוּם מַעֲשֶׂה שֶׁהָיָה! [7] דְּתַנְיָא: "מִי שֶׁמֵּת, וְהִנִּיחַ בֵּן קָטָן לְאִמּוֹ, [8] יוֹרְשֵׁי הָאָב אוֹמְרִים: 'יְהֵא גָּדֵל אֶצְלֵנוּ', [9] וְאִמּוֹ אוֹמֶרֶת: 'יְהֵא בְּנִי גָּדֵל אֶצְלִי', [10] מַנִּיחִין אוֹתוֹ אֵצֶל אִמּוֹ, וְאֵין מַנִּיחִין אוֹתוֹ אֵצֶל רָאוּי לְיוֹרְשׁוֹ. [11] מַעֲשֶׂה הָיָה וּשְׁחָטוּהוּ עֶרֶב הַפֶּסַח"!

LITERAL TRANSLATION

[1] "The first one cannot say." [2] Rav Ḥisda said: [3] This teaches [that] a daughter's [proper place] is with her mother.

[4] From where [do you know] that we are dealing [in the Mishnah] with an adult [stepdaughter]? [5] Perhaps we are dealing with a minor, and [she is with the mother] [6] because of the incident that occurred! [7] For it was taught: "[If] someone died, and left a minor son to his mother, [8] [and] the heirs of the father say: 'Let him grow up with us,' [9] and his mother says: 'Let my son grow up with me,' [10] we leave him with his mother, and we do not leave him with someone who is fit to inherit from him. [11] It happened that they slaughtered him on Pesaḥ eve."

RASHI

זאת אומרת הבת אצל האם — דקתני "למקום שאמה" ולא קתני "לבית אביה" — למדנו שכן הוא הדין, שתגדל הבת אצל אמה. **ובת הניזונת מן הנכסים** — זנין אותה בבית אמה, ואין כופין אותה לדור אצלם. **דלמא בקטנה עסקינן** — ומשום הכי לא קתני בת אצל אחין. **משום מעשה שהיה** — [ואיכא למיחש נמי שמא] יהרגוה בשביל לירש עישור נכסים שלה. אבל גדולה, דלא חיישינן לרציחה — אימא לך דתשב אצל האחין.

NOTES

וּשְׁחָטוּהוּ עֶרֶב הַפֶּסַח They slaughtered him on Pesaḥ eve. There are various different readings of this line in the Talmudic manuscripts and in the Rishonim: "on Pesaḥ eve," "on Rosh HaShanah eve," and "on the first evening." *Rabbi Ya'akov Emden* explains that according to the reading "on Pesaḥ eve," the Baraita wishes to emphasize that the

HALAKHAH

בַּת אֵצֶל אִמָּהּ A daughter is by her mother. "If a man divorces his wife, their daughter stays with her mother until she is married, even if the mother remarries. If the husband has enough money to give to charity, he may be compelled to provide his daughter's maintenance in her mother's house, and after his death, she may collect her maintenance from his estate in accordance with the ketubah conditions," following Rav Ḥisda. *Rema* adds that this ruling only applies if the court thinks that it is better for the daughter to be with her mother. But if the court thinks that it is better for the girl to be with her father, the mother cannot force the court to grant her custody over her daughter (following *Maharam Padua*). (*Rambam, Sefer Nashim, Hilkhot Ishut* 21:18; *Shulḥan Arukh, Even HaEzer* 82:7.)

TRANSLATION AND COMMENTARY

אִם כֵּן [1]The Gemara answers: **If** it is **so** that a distinction is made between a daughter who is still a minor and a daughter who has already reached adulthood, then the Mishnah **should have stated** that the husband must send the daughter her maintenance **in the place where she is** without specifying where that might be. If she is still a minor, she must live with her mother, and if she is already an adult, she may live with other relatives. [103A] [2]**What is** the meaning of the categorical statement that the husband must send the daughter her maintenance **"in the place where her mother is"**? [3]**Infer from this,** as Rav Ḥisda did, that **a daughter** always goes and **lives with her mother,** [4]there being **no distinction made between a** daughter who already reached **adulthood and** a daughter who is still **a minor.**

לֹא יֹאמְרוּ שְׁנֵיהֶם [5]We learned in the Mishnah: "If two men each obligated himself to maintain a woman's daughter, **the two may not say:** 'We will join together and maintain her between the two of us. Rather each one must fulfill his obligation separately, one providing the girl with actual maintenance, and the other paying her the value of her maintenance.'" [6]It was related that **there was a certain man who rented out his mill to someone else,** and the two agreed that instead of paying a rental fee, the renter would pay with his labor and grind the mill owner's grain, providing him with all the flour that he needs for his domestic needs. [7]**In the end,** The mill owner **became wealthy, and he bought** another **mill and a donkey** to turn the millstone, and he was no longer in need of the renter's services. [8]The mill owner approached the renter and **said to him: "Until now I would grind** my grain **with you** without being charged, and I accepted your services in lieu of a rental fee. [9]**Now** that I have bought a mill and a donkey, and no longer need you to grind my grain, I want you to start **paying me rent** in cash." [10]The renter **said to** the mill owner: "When I rented your mill, we agreed that in exchange **I would grind** your grain **for you.** Thus, you cannot come now and demand money from me, just because you no longer need my grinding." [11]When the matter was brought before **Ravina,**

[1]אִם כֵּן, לִיתְנֵי ״לְמָקוֹם שֶׁהִיא״ [103A] [2]מַאי ״לְמָקוֹם שֶׁאִמָּהּ״? [3]שָׁמְעַתְּ מִינָּהּ: בַּת אֵצֶל הָאֵם. [4]לָא שְׁנָא גְּדוֹלָה וְלָא שְׁנָא קְטַנָּה.

[5]״לֹא יֹאמְרוּ שְׁנֵיהֶם וכו׳״. [6]הַהוּא גַּבְרָא דְּאוֹגַר לֵיהּ רֵיחַיָּא לְחַבְרֵיהּ לִטְחִינָה, [7]לְסוֹף, אִיעַתַּר, זַבֵּין רֵיחַיָּא וְחַמְרָא. [8]אֲמַר לֵיהּ: ״עַד הָאִידָּנָא הֲוָה טָחֵינְנָא גַּבָּךְ. [9]הָשְׁתָּא הַב לִי אַגְרָא.״ [10]אֲמַר לֵיהּ: ״מִיטְחַן טָחֵינְנָא לָךְ״ [11]סָבַר רָבִינָא

LITERAL TRANSLATION

[1]If so, let it state: To the place where she is. [103A] [2]What is [meant by] "to the place of her mother?" [3]Infer from this: A daughter is with her mother. [4]No distinction is made between an adult and a minor.

[5]"The two of them may not say, etc." [6][There was] a certain man who rented out a mill to his fellow [in return] for grinding. [7]Ultimately, he became wealthy [and] bought [another] mill and a donkey. [8]He said to him: "Until now I would grind with you. [9]Now, give me rent." [10]He said to him: "I will [continue to] grind for you." [11]Ravina thought

RASHI

אם כן — דיש חילוק בין גדולה לקטנה. **ניתני** מוליך לה מזונות **למקום שהיא** — דמשמע לגדולה במקום שהיא, ולקטנה במקום שהיא. **מאי למקום שאמה** — דקתני מילתא פסיקתא, שמע מינה: כל בת אצל האם. **דאוגר ליה ריחיא לחבריה לטחינה** — לא התנה שוכר לתת מעות למשכיר, אלא שיטחון לו למזונות ביתו בשכרו. **לסוף איעתר** — משכיר. **זבין ריחיא וחמרא** — לטחון בה מזונות ביתו.

NOTES

relatives were so eager to kill the boy that they were not even concerned about becoming ritually impure, and therefore be unfit to bring the Paschal sacrifice. *Eshel Avraham* explains that according to the reading "on Rosh HaShanah eve," the Baraita stresses that the relatives were so eager to kill the boy that they were not even deterred by the Day of Judgment. It would appear that the text underwent internal censorship in order to avoid blood libels (see the marginal note in the *Vilna Shas*).

בַּת אֵצֶל הָאֵם **A daughter is with her mother.** According to some Rishonim (see *Rosh*), this ruling only applies to a widow. The daughter goes to live with her mother and not with her father's heirs, who are responsible for her maintenance, lest they do her harm in order to free themselves of their obligations. But if a woman was divorced from her husband, the daughter remains with her father, and does not go to live with her mother. *Ramah* (following the Geonim) disagrees and proves from our Gemara that a daughter always goes to live with her mother, whether the woman was widowed or divorced.

לָא שְׁנָא גְּדוֹלָה וְלָא שְׁנָא קְטַנָּה **No distinction is made between an adult and a minor.** A minor girl is placed in her mother's custody, both because of the danger of leaving her with her father's heirs, and because she is in need of

HALAKHAH

הַהוּא גַּבְרָא דְּאוֹגַר **There was a certain man who rented.** "If someone rented a mill in return for which he would grind a certain amount of the mill-owner's grain each month, and the mill-owner became wealthy, and no longer

לְמֵימַר: הַיְינוּ מַתְנִיתִין: [1]לֹא יֹאמְרוּ שְׁנֵיהֶם: ׳הֲרֵי אָנוּ זָנִין אוֹתָהּ כְּאֶחָד׳. [2]אֶלָּא אֶחָד זָנָהּ, וְאֶחָד נוֹתֵן לָהּ דְּמֵי מְזוֹנוֹת״. [3]אֲמַר לֵיהּ רַב עֲוִירָא: מִי דָּמֵי? [4]הָתָם חַד כְּרֵיסָא אִית לָהּ, תַּרְתֵּי כְּרֵיסָתָא לֵית לָהּ, [5]הָכָא מָצֵי אֲמַר לֵיהּ: טְחוֹן וְזַבֵּין, טְחוֹן וְאוֹתֵיב.

[6]וְלָא אֲמָרַן אֶלָּא דְּלֵית לֵיהּ טְחִינָא לְרֵיחַיָּא. [7]אֲבָל אִית לֵיהּ טְחִינָא לְרֵיחַיָּא, [8]כְּגוֹן זוֹ כּוֹפִין אוֹתוֹ עַל מִדַּת סְדוֹם.

LITERAL TRANSLATION

to say: This is our Mishnah: [1]"The two of them may not say: 'We will maintain her together.' [2]Rather, one maintains her, and one gives her money for maintenance."

[3]Rav Avira said to him: Are they similar? [4]There she has one stomach, two stomachs she does not have. [5]Here he can say: Grind and sell, grind and keep.

[6]And we only say [this] when he does not have [other] grinding for his mill. [7]But [if] he has [other] grinding for his mill, [8][in cases] like this we coerce him [to pay rent] on account of the morals of Sodom.

TRANSLATION AND COMMENTARY

he first **thought to say** that **this** case **is** similar to the case of **our Mishnah:** "If two men each obligated himself to maintain a woman's daughter, [1]**the two cannot say: 'We will** join **together** and **maintain her** between the two of us,' each providing half of the daughter's maintenance. [2]**But rather, one** of them must **provide her with** her actual **maintenance, and** the other **one** must **pay her the value of her maintenance."** We see from our Mishnah that, once the circumstances changed, one of the two husbands became obligated to pay the girl the value of her maintenance in cash, despite the previous agreement. So too then, now that the mill owner no longer needs the renter's grinding, he should be able to demand that the rental fee for his mill be paid in cash.

אֲמַר לֵיהּ [3]**Rav Avira said to** Ravina: **Are** these two cases really **similar?** [4]**There** in the case of the Mishnah, the daughter **has** only **one stomach,** and **not two.** It is not possible for both husbands to provide her with actual maintenance, so one of them pays her the value of her maintenance. [5]But **here** the tenant **can say** to the mill owner: **"Grind** grain with the new mill that you purchased, **and sell** it to others, and then **grind** the grain that you need for your domestic needs with me, **and keep** it for yourself." Since the mill owner can use the new mill, and still exercise his right to grind grain with his tenant without charge, he cannot insist that the tenant pay his rent in cash.

וְלָא אֲמָרַן [6]The Gemara notes: **This ruling** that the tenant cannot be obligated to pay the mill owner in cash **only applies** if he **has no grain to grind in his mill,** so he can argue that rather than sitting idle and paying his rent in cash, he wishes to pay his rent with his labor and grind the mill owner's grain in accordance with the original agreement. [7]**But if** the tenant **has grain to grind in his mill** for other people, and he can charge a fee for his services, and then pay his rent to the mill owner in cash, the mill owner can indeed insist on being paid with money. [8]In a case **like this,** we invoke the principle that **force may be used against a** person who follows **the morals of Sodom,** in other words, claiming a right, the waiver of which would cause him no harm, but would allow another person to benefit.

RASHI

אחד זנה ואחד נותן לה דמי מזונות — ולא אמרינן: שניהם יתנו לה מזונות, ואף על פי שלא פסק לה דמים מתחלה אלא מזונות — חייבוהו לתת דמיהם, כשיש לה מזונות ממקום אחר. הכא נמי, אף על פי שלא פסק אלא טחינה, עכשיו שאינו צריך — יתן דמים. **טחון וזבין** — באותה שלקחת. **טחון ואותיב** — למזונותיך באותה שאצלי. **ולא אמרן** — דלא יהיב דמי. **אלא דלית ליה טחינא לריחיא** — שאין שוכר מוצא לטחון בשכר כל שעה, לפיכך אומר לו: אני יושב בטל, אטחון לך ולא אתן דמים. **אבל** — כל זמן שמוצא לטחון, טוחן בשכר, ונותן לזה דמים. **מדת סדום** — זה נהנה וזה לא חסר, לא היו עושין טובה.

NOTES

her mother's care (for this reason a young boy is also placed in his mother's custody). A daughter who has already reached adulthood goes to live with her mother, because she is in need of her mother's instruction regarding matters of modesty, and also in order to avoid violating the transgression of secluding herself with a man (see *Rivan*).

HALAKHAH

needed to grind his grain with his renter, the following ruling applies: If the tenant has grain which he must grind for himself or others, he can be compelled to pay his rent in cash. But if he does not have any other grain to grind, the tenant can insist on paying his rent with his services by grinding the mill-owner's grain," following Rav Avira and the Gemara's conclusion. (*Rambam, Sefer Mishpatim, Hilkhot Sekhirut* 7:8; *Shulḥan Arukh, Ḥoshen Mishpat* 318.)

TRANSLATION AND COMMENTARY

MISHNAH אַלְמָנָה שֶׁאָמְרָה [1]**If a widow said** to her late husband's heirs: **"I do not want to move out of my husband's house,"** [2]**the heirs cannot say to her: "Go** and live in **your father's house, and we will maintain you** there." [3]**But rather they must maintain her** in her late husband's house as she desires, [4]**and they must provide her with a** suitable **dwelling in keeping with her social status,** for among the ketubah conditions guaranteed to every woman is the right to reside in her husband's house and be maintained there from the property of his estate for the duration of her widowhood.

אָמְרָה [5]If the widow **said** to the heirs: **"I do not want to move out of my father's house,"** and she asked them to send her maintenance there, [6]**the heirs can say to her: "If you** agree to **live with us** in your late husband's house, **we will provide you with** your **maintenance.** [7]**But if you do not** agree to **live with us** there, **we will not provide you with** your **maintenance."**

אִם הָיְתָה טוֹעֶנֶת [8]**If** the widow **claimed** that she wants to return to her father's house, rather than continue to live in her late husband's house, **because she is** still **a young girl and** the heirs, her husband's sons from another marriage, **are** still **young boys,** and it would be improper for them all to live under the same roof, [9]the heirs **must maintain her in her father's house.**

GEMARA תָּנוּ רַבָּנַן [10]**Our Rabbis taught** the following Baraita: "A widow who continues to live in her late husband's house is entitled to **use that residence in the** same **way that she had used it during her husband's lifetime.** [11]So too she may make use of her husband's **manservants and maidservants in the** same **way that**

משנה [1]אַלְמָנָה שֶׁאָמְרָה: "אִי אֶפְשִׁי לָזוּז מִבֵּית בַּעְלִי" — [2]אֵין הַיּוֹרְשִׁין יְכוֹלִין לוֹמַר לָהּ: "לְכִי לְבֵית אָבִיךְ, וְאָנוּ זָנִין אוֹתָךְ". [3]אֶלָּא זָנִין אוֹתָהּ, [4]וְנוֹתְנִין לָהּ מָדוֹר לְפִי כְבוֹדָהּ.

[5]אָמְרָה: "אִי אֶפְשִׁי לָזוּז מִבֵּית אַבָּא" — [6]יְכוֹלִין הַיּוֹרְשִׁין לוֹמַר לָהּ: "אִם אַתְּ אֶצְלֵנוּ, יֵשׁ לִיךְ מְזוֹנוֹת. [7]וְאִם אֵין אַתְּ אֶצְלֵנוּ, אֵין לִיךְ מְזוֹנוֹת". [8]אִם הָיְתָה טוֹעֶנֶת מִפְּנֵי שֶׁהִיא יַלְדָּה וְהֵן יְלָדִים, [9]זָנִין אוֹתָהּ, וְהִיא בְּבֵית אָבִיהָ.

גמרא [10]תָּנוּ רַבָּנַן: "מִשְׁתַּמֶּשֶׁת בַּמָּדוֹר כְּדֶרֶךְ שֶׁמִּשְׁתַּמֶּשֶׁת בְּחַיֵּי בַּעְלָהּ, [11]בַּעֲבָדִים וּשְׁפָחוֹת — כְּדֶרֶךְ

LITERAL TRANSLATION

MISHNAH [1][If] a widow said: "I do not want to move from my husband's house," [2]the heirs cannot say to her: "Go to your father's house, and we will maintain you." [3]But rather they must maintain her, [4]and they must give her a dwelling in keeping with her dignity.

[5][If] she said: "I do not want to move from my father's house," [6]the heirs can say to her: "If you are with us, you will have maintenance. [7]But if you are not with us, you will not have maintenance."

[8]If she claimed because she is a young girl and they are young boys, [9]they must maintain her while she is in her father's house.

GEMARA [10]Our Rabbis taught: "She uses the residence in the way that she used [it] during her husband's lifetime, [11][making use of] the manservants and the maidservants in the way

RASHI

משנה אי אפשי לזוז מבית בעלי — ללאת מבית בעלי.

NOTES

נוֹתְנִין לָהּ מָדוֹר לְפִי כְבוֹדָהּ **They must give her a dwelling in keeping with her dignity.** *Ritva* and *Rashba* infer from here that the widow does not share the entire house with her husband's heirs, but rather they assign a particular section of the house to her that is in keeping with her social status. *Rabbi Crescas Vidal* disagrees, arguing that the Baraita cited in the Gemara, according to which the widow is entitled to use her husband's residence in the same way that she had used it during his lifetime, implies that she is allowed to occupy the entire house.

מִפְּנֵי שֶׁהִיא יַלְדָּה **Because she is a young girl.** Most of the Rishonim explain that the widow here is not the mother of her husband's sons, for it is only in such a case that we are concerned about possible improprieties. *Talmidei*

HALAKHAH

אִי אֶפְשִׁי לָזוּז מִבֵּית אַבָּא **I do not want to move from my father's house.** "If the widow says that she does not want to leave her father's house, her husband's heirs can say to her that if she lives in their house, they will provide all of her maintenance, but if she chooses to remain in her father's house, they will only give her the sum that would have been added to their household expenses had she lived there with them," following the Mishnah and the Gemara's conclusion. If she claims that she does not want to remain with the heirs in her late husband's house, because she is young, and they are young, the heirs are obligated to provide her maintenance in her father's home. *Rema* adds that according to some authorities, this only applies if the woman was not the boys' mother. (*Rambam, Sefer Nashim, Hilkhot Ishut* 18:4; *Shulḥan Arukh, Even HaEzer* 94:6.)

מִשְׁתַּמֶּשֶׁת בַּמָּדוֹר **She uses the residence.** "Just as a widow is maintained from her late husband's property, so too she is given clothing, housewares, and a residence from his

שֶׁמִּשְׁתַּמֶּשֶׁת בְּחַיֵּי בַּעְלָהּ,
[1]בְּכָרִים וּכְסָתוֹת — כְּדֶרֶךְ שֶׁמִּשְׁתַּמֶּשֶׁת בְּחַיֵּי בַּעְלָהּ,
[2]בִּכְלֵי כֶסֶף וּבִכְלֵי זָהָב — כְּדֶרֶךְ שֶׁמִּשְׁתַּמֶּשֶׁת בְּחַיֵּי בַּעְלָהּ,
[3]שֶׁכָּךְ כָּתַב לָהּ: [4]׳וְאַתְּ תְּהֵא יָתְבַתְּ בְּבֵיתִי וּמִיתְזְנָא מִנְּכָסַי כָּל יְמֵי מִגַּר אַרְמְלוּתֵיךְ בְּבֵיתִי׳״.
[5]תָּנֵי רַב יוֹסֵף: ״׳בְּבֵיתִי׳ — וְלֹא בְּבִקְתִּי״
[6]אָמַר רַב נַחְמָן: יְתוֹמִים שֶׁמָּכְרוּ מְדוֹר אַלְמָנָה — לֹא עָשׂוּ וְלֹא כְלוּם.

LITERAL TRANSLATION

that she made use [of them] during her husband's lifetime, [1]the mattresses and pillows in the way that she made use [of them] during her husband's lifetime, [2]the silver utensils and the gold utensils in the way that she made use [of them] during her husband's lifetime, [3]for he writes her as follows: [4]'And you will live in my house and be maintained from my property all the days that you live in widowhood in my house.'"

[5]Rav Yosef taught: "'In my house' — but not in my hut."

[6]Rav Naḥman said: [If] the orphans sold the widow's residence, they did not do anything.

TRANSLATION AND COMMENTARY

she had made use of them during her husband's lifetime. [1]Similarly, she is entitled to use **the mattresses and pillows in the** same **way that she had used them during her husband's lifetime,** [2]and she is entitled to use **the silver and gold utensils in the** same **way that she had** made **use** of **them during her husband's lifetime.** In general, the widow is entitled to the same standard of living that she enjoyed during her husband's lifetime, [3]**for** her husband **had written** in her ketubah deed **as follows:** [4]'After I die, **you will live in my house and be maintained from my property all the days that you live in widowhood in my house.'"**

תָּנֵי רַב יוֹסֵף [5]**Rav Yosef taught** the following Baraita: "The husband writes for his wife: 'After I die, you will live **in my house,' but** he does not write: 'You will live **in my hut.'** The widow is entitled to continue living where she had lived with her husband, provided it was a proper house, and his heirs cannot send his widow back to her paternal home, even if they are willing to provide for her maintenance there. They must allocate a part of that house as a residence for their father's widow, according to her social status. But if the husband left behind only a hut, the heirs are not obligated to maintain his widow there. They are not required to crowd into the hut or move out of it altogether on her account. In such a case, they can send the widow back to her father's house, and send her maintenance there."

אָמַר רַב נַחְמָן [6]**Rav Naḥman said: If the** husband's **heirs sold his widow's residence, the sale is not valid,** for as long as the woman wishes to continue living in her husband's house, the property cannot be sold.

RASHI

גמרא ולא בבקתי — בית צר כעין צריף. כדאמרינן במסכת שבת (עז,ב) בקתא = בי עקתא. אם היה מדור שלו צר — לא קבל עליו להוציא את בניו ולהושיבה.

NOTES

Rabbenu Yonah suggest that the husband died without sons, and the woman does not want to share her husband's house with his brothers who inherited his estate.

בְּבֵיתִי — וְלֹא בְּבִקְתִּי In my house — but not in my hut. Our commentary follows *Rashi,* who explains that the heirs of the deceased husband are not required to share living quarters with the widow if all that the husband left was a hut. Instead, they can send her back to her father's home, and send her maintenance there. *Rivan* explains that the heirs cannot compel her to accept as her residence a hut which they offer to build her. (See also *Meiri.*)

HALAKHAH

property, or she continues to live in the house that she had lived in during his lifetime. *Rema* notes that if the widow lives with the heirs in her late husband's house, she is not given use of the whole house, but rather they set aside for her an apartment that befits her social status (following *Rashba* and *Ran*). According to some authorities (*Mordekhai*), the heirs can give her a fitting apartment in a different house. The widow is not permitted to rent out the apartment that she receives from her husband's heirs (*Rashba*). The widow may use the household utensils and servants as she had used them during her husband's lifetime (when her husband was away; Jerusalem Talmud)," following the Baraita. (*Rambam, Sefer Nashim, Hilkhot Ishut* 18:2; *Shulḥan Arukh, Even HaEzer* 94:1.)

בְּבֵיתִי — וְלֹא בְּבִקְתִּי In my house, but not in my hut. "If the late husband's house collapsed, or if he did not own a house, but rather he lived in a rented house, the heirs must provide his widow with a residence in keeping with her honor. If the husband's house was small, the heirs cannot be compelled to allow the widow to live there with them, but rather they may provide her with an alternative residence (*Be'er HaGolah*)." (*Rambam, Sefer Nashim, Hilkhot Ishut* 18:3; *Shulḥan Arukh, Even HaEzer* 94:5.)

יְתוֹמִים שֶׁמָּכְרוּ מְדוֹר אַלְמָנָה If the heirs sold the widow's residence. "If the husband's heirs went ahead and sold his widow's residence, the sale is not valid," following Rav Naḥman. (*Rambam, Sefer Nashim, Hilkhot Ishut* 18:3; *Shulḥan Arukh, Even HaEzer* 94:4.)

[1]וּמַאי שְׁנָא מִדְּרַבִּי אַסִּי אָמַר רַבִּי יוֹחָנָן? [2]דְּאָמַר רַבִּי אַסִּי אָמַר רַבִּי יוֹחָנָן: יְתוֹמִים שֶׁקָּדְמוּ וּמָכְרוּ בִּנְכָסִים מוּעָטִין, מַה שֶּׁמָּכְרוּ מָכְרוּ!
[3]הָתָם לָא מִשְׁתַּעְבְּדִי לָהּ מֵחַיִּים. [4]הָכָא מִשְׁתַּעְבְּדִי לָהּ מֵחַיִּים.
[5]אָמַר אַבַּיֵי: נְקִיטִינַן: מְדוֹר אַלְמָנָה שֶׁנָּפַל — [6]אֵין הַיּוֹרְשִׁין חַיָּיבִין לְבְנוֹתוֹ.
[7]תַּנְיָא נַמִי הָכִי: ״מְדוֹר אַלְמָנָה שֶׁנָּפַל — אֵין הַיּוֹרְשִׁין חַיָּיבִין לִבְנוֹתוֹ; [8]וְלֹא עוֹד, אֶלָּא

LITERAL TRANSLATION

[1]And how is this different from [what] Rabbi Assi said in the name of Rabbi Yoḥanan. [2]For Rabbi Assi said in the name of Rabbi Yoḥanan: [If] orphans went ahead and sold the small amount of [inherited] property, what they sold, they sold.
[3]There they were not mortgaged to her during [the father's] lifetime. [4]Here they were mortgaged to her during [his] lifetime.
[5]Abaye said: We maintain: A widow's residence that collapsed, [6]the heirs are not obligated to rebuild it.
[7]It was also taught thus: "A widow's residence that collapsed — the heirs are not obligated to rebuild it. [8]And not only [this], but

TRANSLATION AND COMMENTARY

וּמַאי שְׁנָא [1]The Gemara asks: **And how is this different from what Rabbi Assi said in the name of Rabbi Yoḥanan,** [2]**for Rabbi Assi said in the name of Rabbi Yoḥanan: If** a man's **heirs sold the small amount of property** which their father had left them, **whatever they sold is sold.** We learned elsewhere in the Mishnah (*Ketubot* 108b) that if someone died, leaving sons and daughters and only a small estate, which would not suffice to maintain both the sons and the daughters until the daughters reach adulthood, the daughters take precedence and are maintained from the estate, and the sons are sent out to beg for charity. Rav Assi teaches that if the father left only a small estate, and the sons improperly sold it all, the sale is nevertheless valid. Why then is the sale not valid, if the husband's heirs improperly sold his widow's residence?

הָתָם [3]The Gemara answers: **There,** in the case of the small estate, the property **was not mortgaged to the** daughters' **support during** the father's **lifetime,** for the daughters' right to maintenance only begins when their father died. [4]But **here,** regarding the widow's residence, the property **had been** already **mortgaged to** the woman's **support during** her husband's **lifetime,** as a husband is obligated to provide his wife with a home.

אָמַר אַבַּיֵי [5]**Abaye said: We maintain** as follows: If **a widow's residence collapsed** or became otherwise unfit for habitation, [6]her late husband's **heirs are not obligated to rebuild it** for her.

תַּנְיָא נַמִי הָכִי [7]**The same thing was also taught** in a Baraita: "If **a widow's residence collapsed** or became otherwise unfit for habitation, her late husband's **heirs are not obligated to rebuild it for her.** [8]**Moreover, even**

RASHI

בנכסים מועטין – שהבנות זוכות בהן, כדתנן (כתובות קח,ב): הבנות יזונו והבנים ישאלו על הפתחים. **וקדמו** – קודם שיבואו לבית דין, ומכרום.

NOTES

מִשְׁתַּעְבְּדִי לָהּ מֵחַיִּים They were mortgaged to her during his lifetime. *Eshel Avraham* prefers the reading found in certain manuscripts and cited by some Rishonim: "There she did not seize it during [his] lifetime. Here she seized it during [his] lifetime." If the husband's heirs sold his widow's residence, the sale is null and void, for she lived there during her husband's lifetime and cannot be evicted. But if a man's sons sold the small amount of property left them by their father, the sale is valid, because the daughters had not seized the property for their maintenance during their father's lifetime.

מְדוֹר אַלְמָנָה שֶׁנָּפַל A widow's residence which collapsed. According to most Rishonim, if a widow's residence collapsed, she loses her right to that residence, but the heirs are required to find her alternative quarters. But some disagree and argue that if the widow had been assigned a particular residence, and it collapsed, she loses her right to lodging from her husband's estate (see *Meiri*).

HALAKHAH

יְתוֹמִים שֶׁקָּדְמוּ וּמָכְרוּ בִּנְכָסִים מוּעָטִין If orphans first sold the small amount of property. "If the deceased left only a small estate that does not suffice to cover the costs of maintaining both the sons and the daughters until the daughters reach adulthood, and the sons improperly sold the property, the sale is nevertheless valid," following Rabbi Yoḥanan. (*Rambam, Sefer Nashim, Hilkhot Ishut* 19:19; *Shulḥan Arukh, Even HaEzer* 112:14.)

מְדוֹר אַלְמָנָה שֶׁנָּפַל A widow's residence that collapsed. "If the widow's residence collapsed, her late husband's heirs are not obligated to rebuild it for her. Even if the widow offered to rebuild the house at her own expense, the heirs are not required to permit her to do so. She may not even repair the house, but rather she must live there as is, or leave," following the Baraita. The law regarding the case of a widow who renovated her late husband's house was not decided, and so we follow the principle that we do not remove property from the party who enjoys presumptive possession (see *Bet Shmuel,* who cites a disagreement about who is regarded as enjoying presumptive possession). (*Rambam, Sefer Nashim, Hilkhot Ishut* 18:2; *Shulḥan Arukh, Even HaEzer* 94:2.)

אֲפִילּוּ הִיא אוֹמֶרֶת: ׳הַנִּיחוּנִי וְאֶבְנְנוּ מִשֶּׁלִּי׳, [1]אֵין שׁוֹמְעִין לָהּ.
[2]בָּעֵי אַבַּיֵי: שִׁיפְּצָהּ, מַאי?
[3]תֵּיקוּ.
[4]״אָמְרָה: ׳אִי אֶפְשִׁי׳״. [5]וְלֵיתְבוּ לָהּ כִּי יָתְבָה הָתָם!
[6]מְסַיַּיע לֵיהּ לְרַב הוּנָא, דְּאָמַר רַב הוּנָא: [7]בִּרְכַּת הַבַּיִת בְּרוּבָּהּ.
[8]וְלֵיתְבוּ לָהּ לְפִי בִּרְכַּת הַבַּיִת!
[9]הָכִי נַמִי.

LITERAL TRANSLATION

even if she says: 'Let me, and I will rebuild it from my own [resources],' [1]they do not [have to] listen to her."

[2]Abaye asked: [If] she fixed it, what [is the law]?

[3]Let [the question] stand [unresolved].

[4]"If she said: 'I do not want.'" [5]Let them give her [maintenance] as if she were living there!

[6]This supports Rav Huna, for Rav Huna said: [7]The blessing of a house is [in proportion to] the number of its residents (lit., "its many").

[8]So let them give her according to the blessing of the house!

[9]Indeed so.

TRANSLATION AND COMMENTARY

if the widow **says** to the heirs: **'Leave me, and I will rebuild** the house **at my own** expense, [1]the heirs **do not** have to **listen to her.'** Once the house collapses or becomes unsuitable for living, she loses her right to live there."

בָּעֵי אַבַּיֵי [2]**Abaye asked: If** the widow only **renovated** her late husband's house so it would stand longer, **what is the law?** Do we say that as long as the house stands the woman may not be evicted from it? Or do we say that the woman had no right to make any changes in the house, and so she may only live in the house for as long as it would have stood without the renovations?

תֵּיקוּ [3]Not having any apparent solution, the Gemara concludes: Let Abaye's question **stand unanswered.**

אָמְרָה [4]We learned in the Mishnah: **"If** the widow **said** to the heirs: **'I do not want** to move out of my father's house,' and she asked them to send her maintenance there, the heirs can say to her: 'We are ready to provide you with your maintenance if you live with us in your late husband's house, but if you insist on living in your father's house, we will not maintain you.'" [5]The Gemara proposes: **Let** the heirs **provide** the widow with **her** maintenance in her father's house **as if she were living there** with them in her late husband's home! What difference does it make to the heirs where the woman is living?

מְסַיַּיע לֵיהּ [6]The Gemara answers: **This supports** what **Rav Huna** said, **for Rav Huna said:** [7]**Blessing** is found **in a house in proportion to the number** of people living there. The heirs can argue that if the widow lives with them in her late husband's house, the cost of her maintenance does not add very much to their household expenses. But if she moves out of the house and returns to her paternal home, the cost of her maintenance is much greater.

וְלֵיתְבוּ לָהּ [8]The Gemara asks: Granted that if the widow returns to her father's home, the heirs should not be obligated to maintain her in a manner that would suffice to maintain a single person in an independent household. But **let them** at least **provide** the widow with **her** maintenance **in accordance with the blessing** that would be brought **to their house** were she still living there! Let them give her whatever would be added to their household expenses were she to decide to continue living in her late husband's home!

הָכִי נַמִי [9]The Gemara answers: **That indeed** is what the Mishnah means: If the widow says that she wishes to remain in her father's house, the heirs are not required to provide her with maintenance needed by a single person as an independent household, but they must give her whatever she would have costed them had she decided to continue living in their house.

RASHI

שיפצה – חזקה בדקיה. **מאי** – מי אמרינן: לא מפקינן לה כל ימים שיכול להתקיים, או דלמא אמרינן לה: לאו כל כמינך? **ברכת הבית ברובה** – בני אדם שעוזרין זה את זה משתכרין, ומזל דרבים עדיף. **וליתבו לה** – לפי מה שנתמעטה ברכת הבית ביציאתה!

NOTES

וְלֵיתְבוּ לָהּ לְפִי בִּרְכַּת הַבַּיִת **So let them give her according to the blessing of the house.** The Rishonim explain this in various different ways: *Rashi* explains that the abundance found in a house is proportionate to the size of the household, because the members of the household help each other, and that mutual help leads to greater profits, and also because a large group of people has better luck and fortune than a single individual. *Rivan* suggests that discounts are available when items are purchased in bulk, and so the heirs may deduct from the maintenance which they send to their father's widow that sum which they would have saved if the woman were living with them in their house. *Rabbenu Ḥananel* writes that the Gemara refers here to household costs, which do not increase with the size of the household, in keeping with what is stated elsewhere: The same candle which illuminates for a single

TRANSLATION AND COMMENTARY

אָמַר רַב הוּנָא [1]**Rav Huna said: The words of the Sages** are instructive not only regarding specific Halakhic issues, but also about matters relating to **blessing, wealth, and healing.** [2]Their teaching about **the blessing** bestowed upon a house is **what we have** just **said:** Rav Huna's principle that blessing is found in a home in proportion to the number of people living there. [3]The Sages also teach us about achieving **wealth, as we have learned** in the Mishnah (*Bava Batra* 84b): **"If someone sold produce to another person,** and the two parties agreed on a price, **and** the buyer **drew the produce into his possession,** then even if **he did not measure** out the produce, **he acquired** it, for drawing the produce into one's possession is a valid mode of acquisition. [4]But **if** the seller **measured** out the produce for the buyer, **but** the buyer **did not draw** the produce **into his possession, he did not acquire** it, for a valid mode of acquisition was not performed. [5]**If** the buyer **is clever,** and he wants to acquire the produce even before he draws it into his possession, so that the buyer will not be able to retract, **he should rent** from the seller **the place** where the produce is resting, for a person's premises — either his own or those rented by him — can acquire for him any movable property resting within." Thus, we see that the Mishnah offers us sound business advice. [6]The words of the Sages teach us also about ways of **healing, as we have learned** in the Mishnah (*Pesaḥim* 39b): [7]**"A person may not chew** grains of **wheat, and place them on his wound on Pesaḥ, for they become fermented** by way of his saliva, and are thus forbidden on Pesaḥ because of the prohibition against making leavened dough." In this Mishnah, the Sages also offer us medical advice.

[1]אָמַר רַב הוּנָא: לְשׁוֹן חֲכָמִים בְּרָכָה, לְשׁוֹן חֲכָמִים עוֹשֶׁר, לְשׁוֹן חֲכָמִים מַרְפֵּא. [2]בְּרָכָה, הָא דַּאֲמָרַן. [3]עוֹשֶׁר, דִּתְנַן: הַמּוֹכֵר פֵּירוֹת לַחֲבֵירוֹ, מָשַׁךְ וְלֹא מָדַד — קָנָה, [4]מָדַד וְלֹא מָשַׁךְ — לֹא קָנָה, [5]וְאִם הָיָה פִּקֵּחַ — שׂוֹכֵר אֶת מְקוֹמוֹ. [6]מַרְפֵּא, דִּתְנַן: [7]לֹא יִלְעוֹס אָדָם חִטִּין וְיַנִּיחַ עַל גַּבֵּי מַכָּתוֹ בְּפֶסַח, מִפְּנֵי שֶׁמַּחְמִיצוֹת.

LITERAL TRANSLATION

[1]Rav Huna said: [From] the words of the Sages — a blessing, [from] the words of the Sages — wealth, [from] the words of the Sages — healing. [2]A blessing — what we [just] said. [3]Wealth — for we have learned: "[If] someone sold produce to his fellow, [and] he drew [the produce into his possession], but did not measure [it], he acquired [it]. [4][If] he measured [it], but did not draw [it into his possession], he did not acquire [it]. [5]And if he is clever, he rents its place." [6]Healing — for we have learned: [7]"A person may not chew [grains of] wheat and place [them] on his wound on Pesaḥ, for they become fermented."

RASHI

לשון חכמים — יש ללמוד ממנה ברכה, ועושר, ורפואה. **אם היה פקח** — זה שלוקח פירות הרבה, ואין לו שהות למושכם, אלא נתן מעות. **שוכר את מקומו** — דהוי לה כי שכירו, ושכירו קונה לו. הרי אתה למד מכאן סחורה, שלא יוכל המוכר לחזור — הרי לך עושר למוד מלשון חכמים. **לא ילעוס כו'** — למדת שהחטים הלעוסין יפה למכה.

NOTES

person illuminates for a hundred people. If the widow wishes to be maintained by the heirs in her father's house, they are not obligated to pay for such things, for were the woman living with them in their house, they would not have to spend anything extra on her.

בִּשְׁעַת פְּטִירָתוֹ שֶׁל רַבִּי At the time of Rabbi's departure. *Rivan* and *Ra'avad* explain that the story about Rabbi Yehudah HaNasi's deathbed instructions is recorded here, because our Mishnah teaches that the widow must be given an apartment in keeping with her honor and social status, and Rabbi Yehudah HaNasi instructed his children to be careful about the honor which they must show his widow. The connection between the two is even stronger according to the version of Rabbi Yehudah HaNasi's testament found in the Jerusalem Talmud, for there it is reported that Rabbi Yehudah HaNasi instructed that his widow not be removed from his house after his death, in keeping with our Mishnah (*Rosh, Ritva*). The Jerusalem Talmud adds that it was necessary for Rabbi Yehudah HaNasi to say this, even though the matter is stated explicitly in the Mishnah. Otherwise we might have thought that the Nasi's house is designated for the Nasi's use, but it is not regarded as a private residence where his widow may continue to reside after his death.

HALAKHAH

אִם הָיָה פִּקֵּחַ שׂוֹכֵר אֶת מְקוֹמוֹ If he is clever, he rents its place. "If the seller measured out produce for the buyer, the buyer does not acquire the produce until he draws it into his possession. But if the buyer rented from the seller the place where the produce is resting, he acquires the produce even without drawing it into his possession, provided that he was standing there or the area was fenced in." (*Rambam, Sefer Kinyan, Hilkhot Mekhirah* 3:6-7; *Shulḥan Arukh, Ḥoshen Mishpat* 198:5.)

לֹא יִלְעוֹס אָדָם חִטִּין A person may not chew wheat. "A person may not chew wheat on Pesaḥ in order to place the grain on a wound, for the wheat kernels become fermented when they come into contact with his saliva." (*Rambam, Sefer Zemanim, Hilkhot Ḥametz U'Matzah* 5:19; *Shulḥan Arukh, Oraḥ Ḥayyim* 466:1.)

TRANSLATION AND COMMENTARY

תָּנוּ רַבָּנַן [1]The Gemara proceeds to a new discussion: **Our Rabbis taught** the following Baraita: **"At the time that Rabbi** Yehudah HaNasi **was dying, he said** to his attendants: [2]**'I need my sons,** for I have important things to tell them.' Rabbi Yehudah HaNasi's **sons** were summoned, and they **went in to** see **him.** [3]Rabbi Yehudah NaNasi **said to them:** 'After I die, **be careful about your mother's honor.** [4]**Let** my **candle** continue to **burn in its place** as it did during my lifetime. [5]**Let** my **table** continue to **be set in its place** as it was while I was alive. [6]**Let** my **bed** continue to **be made in its place** just as it was during my lifetime. [7]**Yosef of Haifa and Shimon of Efrat — they attended to me during my lifetime, and** so it is fitting that **they** continue to **attend to me after my death.'"**

הִזָּהֲרוּ [8]The Gemara now analyzes each line of Rabbi Yehudah HaNasi's testament: Rabbi Yehudah HaNasi instructed his sons: **"Be careful about your mother's honor."** [9]Surely Rabbi Yehudah HaNasi's sons were obligated to honor their mother **by Torah law, for the verse states** (Exodus 20:12): **"Honor your father and mother."**

אֵשֶׁת אָב הֲוַאי [10]The Gemara answers: The woman was not actually his sons' mother, but rather their stepmother, **the wife of their father,** who is not included in that commandment.

אֵשֶׁת אָב נַמִי [11]The Gemara asks: But surely the obligation to honor one's **father's wife is also by Torah life, as it was taught** in a Baraita: [12]"The verse states (Exodus 20:12): **'Honor your father and mother.'** Both the words 'your father' and the words 'your mother' are preceded by the word *et* (אֶת) — the particle of the objective case. Although that word is a normal feature of Biblical style, since it is not absolutely necessary, and since it may also mean *with,* it may be understood as an extending the meaning of the Biblical words. [13]Thus, the expression **'your father (אֶת אָבִיךָ)'** may be understood as alluding to the person

[1]תָּנוּ רַבָּנַן: בִּשְׁעַת פְּטִירָתוֹ שֶׁל רַבִּי, אָמַר: [2]לְבָנַי אֲנִי צָרִיךְ, נִכְנְסוּ בָּנָיו אֶצְלוֹ. [3]אָמַר לָהֶם: הִזָּהֲרוּ בִּכְבוֹד אִמְּכֶם; [4]נֵר יְהֵא דָּלוּק בִּמְקוֹמוֹ, [5]שׁוּלְחָן יְהֵא עָרוּךְ בִּמְקוֹמוֹ, [6]מִטָּה תְּהֵא מוּצַּעַת בִּמְקוֹמָהּ; [7]יוֹסֵף חֲפָנִי, שִׁמְעוֹן אֶפְרָתִי, הֵם שִׁמְּשׁוּנִי בְּחַיַּי וְהֵם יְשַׁמְּשׁוּנִי בְּמוֹתִי".

[8]הִזָּהֲרוּ בִּכְבוֹד אִמְּכֶם". [9]דְּאוֹרַיְיתָא הִיא, דִּכְתִיב: "כַּבֵּד אֶת אָבִיךָ וְאֶת אִמֶּךָ"!

[10]אֵשֶׁת אָב הֲוַאי.

[11]אֵשֶׁת אָב נַמִי דְּאוֹרַיְיתָא הִיא, דְּתַנְיָא: [12]"כַּבֵּד אֶת אָבִיךָ וְאֶת אִמֶּךָ", [13]"אֶת אָבִיךָ" — זוֹ

LITERAL TRANSLATION

[1]Our Rabbis taught: "At the time of Rabbi's passing, he said: [2]'I need my sons.' His sons went in to him, [3][and] he said to them: 'Be careful about your mother's honor. [4]Let [my] candle burn in its place. [5]Let [my] table be set in its place. [6]Let [my] bed be made in its place. [7]Yosef of Haifa [and] Shimon of Efrat — they attended to me during my lifetime, and they will attend to me after my death.'"

[8]"Be careful about your mother's honor." [9][But] this is by Torah law, for it is written: "Honor your father and mother"!

[10]She was the wife of [their] father.

[11]A father's wife is also by Torah law, as it was taught: [12]"'Honor your father and mother.' [13]'Your father' — this is

RASHI

נר יהא דלוק במקומו — אצל השולחן כמו בחיי, דכל ערב שבת היה בא לביתו משנפטר, כדלקמן. יוסף חפני — דמן חיפה. את אביך — כל אתין רבויין.

NOTES

כְּבוֹד אִמְּכֶם **Your mother's honor.** *Rabbi Ya'akov Emden* notes that even in Scripture a stepmother is referred to as a mother. For Jacob said to Joseph: "Shall I and your mother and your brothers come to bow down ourselves to you (Genesis 37:10)." Joseph's mother had already died, so Jacob must have been referring to Joseph's stepmother. *Iyyun Ya'akov* suggests that Rabbi Yehudah HaNasi might have referred to his sons' stepmother as their mother, because she had raised them (see also *Rashi* to Genesis 37:10).

אֵשֶׁת אָב **Your father's wife.** According to *Rambam,* a person is obligated to honor his father's wife and his mother's husband by Torah law, but the obligation to honor one's eldest brother is only by Rabbinic enactment. *Meiri* argues that even though our Gemara implies that these obligations are all by Torah law, they are in fact only by Rabbinic enactment. *Shittah Mekubbetzet* writes that the duty to honor one's eldest brother is an independent obligation, unconnected to the obligation to honor one's parents, and so it persists even after the parents' death.

HALAKHAH

אֶת אָבִיךָ — זוֹ אֵשֶׁת אָבִיךָ **Your father — this is your father's wife.** "A person is obligated to honor his father's wife during his lifetime, even if she is not his mother. And similarly, a person is obligated to honor his mother's husband during her lifetime, even though he is not his father. It is commendable to honor one's parent's spouse,

אֵשֶׁת אָבִיךָ, [1]"וְאֶת אִמֶּךָ" — זוֹ בַּעַל אִמְּךָ, [2]וי"ו יְתֵירָה — לְרַבּוֹת אֶת אָחִיךָ הַגָּדוֹל! [3]הָנֵי מִילֵּי מֵחַיִּים, [4]אֲבָל לְאַחַר מִיתָה — לָא.

[5]"נֵר יְהֵא דָּלוּק בִּמְקוֹמוֹ, שׁוּלְחָן יְהֵא עָרוּךְ בִּמְקוֹמוֹ, [6]מִטָּה תְּהֵא מוּצַּעַת בִּמְקוֹמָהּ". [7]מַאי טַעְמָא? [8]כָּל בֵּי שִׁמְשֵׁי הֲוָה אָתֵי לְבֵיתֵיהּ.

[9]הַהוּא בֵּי שִׁמְשָׁא אֲתַאי שִׁבַּבְתָּא קָא קַרְיָה אַבָּבָא, [10]אָמְרָה אַמְתֵיהּ: שְׁתִיקוּ, דְּרַבִּי יָתֵיב! [11]כֵּיוָן דִּשְׁמַע שׁוּב לָא אֲתָא, [12]שֶׁלֹּא לְהוֹצִיא לַעַז עַל צַדִּיקִים הָרִאשׁוֹנִים.

LITERAL TRANSLATION

your father's wife. [1]'And your mother' — this is your mother's husband. [2]The extra *vav* — [this is] to include your eldest brother."

[3]This applies (lit., "these words") during [his father's] lifetime. [4]But after death — no.

[5]"Let [my] candle burn it its place. [6]Let [my] table be set in its place. Let [my] bed be made in its place." [7]What is the reason? [8]Every Friday afternoon (lit., "at twilight") he would come to his house.

[9]One Friday afternoon a neighbor came, and knocked on the door. [10]His maidservant said: "Quiet, for Rabbi sits." [11]After he heard [this], he did not come again, [12]so as not to spread evil talk about earlier (lit., "the first") righteous men.

TRANSLATION AND COMMENTARY

who is 'with your father,' **your father's wife,** your stepmother. [1]And similarly, the expression **'and your mother** (וְאֶת אִמֶּךָ)' may be understood as alluding to the person who is 'with your mother,' [2]**your mother's husband,** your stepfather. And so too **the extra *vav,*** the particle which precedes the words 'your mother' and means *and,* may be understood as extending this obligation to include **one's eldest brother."** Thus, the question returns: Why did Rabbi Yehudah HaNasi have to instruct his sons to honor their stepmother, which they are obligated to do by Torah law?

הָנֵי מִילֵּי [3]The Gemara answers: The Torah obligation to honor one's stepmother **only applies during** the father's **lifetime.** [4]**But after** his **death,** the son is **no** longer obligated by Torah law to honor his stepmother. Thus, it was necessary for Rabbi Yehudah HaNasi to instruct his sons that they should continue honoring their stepmother even after his death.

נֵר יְהֵא דָּלוּק [5]The Gemara continues with its analysis of Rabbi Yehudah HaNasi's testament in which he instructed his sons: **"Let** my **candle** continue to **burn it its** regular **place,** and **let** my **table** continue to **be set in its** regular **place,** [6]and **let** my **bed** continue to **be made in its** regular **place."** [7]**What is the reason** that Rabbi Yehudah HaNasi instructed his sons to act in this way? This is because even after his death, [8]Rabbi Yehudah HaNasi **would visit at his house every Friday afternoon,** revealing himself to his family members, and so he asked to have his personal items — his candle, his table, and his couch — be arranged for him in the usual manner.

הַהוּא בֵּי שִׁמְשָׁא [9]The Gemara relates that **once on a Friday afternoon,** while Rabbi Yehudah HaNasi was making his weekly visit, **a neighbor** of his **came, and knocked on the door.** [10]**His maidservant** answered, and **said** to the neighbor: **"Quiet, for Rabbi** Yehudah HaNasi **is sitting** here with us." [11]**When** Rabbi Yehudah HaNasi **heard** that his maidservant had revealed that he made weekly visits, **he** decided **never to come** back **again,** [12]**so as not to spread derogatory talk about the righteous men** of **earlier** generations. He was concerned that people might begin to think less of those righteous men of earlier generations who did not return and reveal themselves to their families after they died.

RASHI

וי"ו יתירה — ד"ואת אמך". **הני מילי** — דחייב בכבוד אשת אביו בחיי אביו. **בי שמשי** — ערב שבת. ונראה בעיני: לפי שבין השמשות שלו שגור בפי כל, והכל חרדים אליו לגמור מלאכתן עד שלא תחשך, קרו ליה בי שמשי. **שלא להוציא לעז כו'** — לומר: לא צדיקים היו, שלא היה להן רשות לבא לביתם כמו רבי.

NOTES

כָּל בֵּי שִׁמְשֵׁי הֲוָה אָתֵי לְבֵיתֵיהּ **Every Friday afternoon he would come to his house.** Similar stories are related in various sources about several righteous figures, and their meaning remains unclear. *Maharsha* notes that it was fitting

The Aḥaronim discuss various aspects of this obligation, whether it applies only to a person's eldest brother, or to all of his older brothers, and whether it also applies to an older sister.

HALAKHAH

even after the parent's death," following the Baraita, and the story regarding Rabbi Yehudah HaNasi's testament. (*Rambam, Sefer Shofetim, Hilkhot Mamrim* 6:15; *Shulḥan Arukh, Yoreh De'ah* 240:21.)

לְרַבּוֹת אֶת אָחִיךָ הַגָּדוֹל **To include your older brother.** "A person is obligated to honor his older brother, whether the brother is from his father's side or his mother's side. *Rema* adds that this applies even if the younger brother is a greater Torah scholar than his older brother (following *Rosh* and *Smag*)." (*Rambam, Sefer Shofetim, Hilkhot Mamrim* 6:15; *Shulḥan Arukh, Yoreh De'ah* 240:22.)

SAGES

יוֹסֵף חֵפָנִי וְשִׁמְעוֹן אֶפְרָתִי Yosef of Haifa and Shimon of Efrat. We do not know very much about these attendants of Rabbi Yehudah HaNasi. Their surnames seem to based on the names of the places where they were born or lived. Yosef of Haifa might be identified with Rabbi Yose the Tall mentioned in *Midrash Shemot Rabbah*. It was said about him that wherever he arrived, Rabbi Yehudah HaNasi was sure to appear there shortly thereafter.

TRANSLATION AND COMMENTARY

יוֹסֵף חֵפָנִי [1]The Gemara continues: Rabbi Yehudah HaNasi concluded his testament with the following instructions: **"Yosef of Haifa and Shimon of Efrat — they attended to me during my lifetime, and** it is fitting that **they** continue to **attend to me after my death."** [2]People **thought** at first **that** Rabbi Yehudah HaNasi **was talking about** who would attend to him in **this world** and arrange his funeral and burial. [3]But **when they saw that their** two **biers went out before the bier** of Rabbi Yehudah HaNasi, [4]**they said: Infer from this that** Rabbi Yehudah HaNasi must have been **talking about** who would attend to him in **the world to come.** [5]**And** the reason **that** Rabbi Yehudah HaNasi had to **say** that Yosef of Haifa and Shimon of Efrat would attend to him in the world to come was so **that people should not say** that Rabbi Yehudah HaNasi's two attendants did not live to attend to his funeral [6]because **they** were **guilty of some** sinful act, [7]**and it was** only **Rabbi** Yehudah HaNasi's **merit that had protected them** from punishment up **until now.**

אָמַר לָהֶן [8]The Gemara now continues with the Baraita that reports what Rabbi Yehudah HaNasi said on his deathbed: "Rabbi Yehudah HaNasi **said** to his attendants: **'I need the Sages of Israel,** for I have important things to tell them as well.' [9]**The Sages of Israel** were summoned, and they **went in to see him.** [10]Rabbi Yehudah HaNasi **said to them: 'Do not eulogize me in the towns,** [103B] **and** quickly **reestablish the academy** for regular Torah study **thirty days after** my death. [11]**My son Shimon is wise.** [12]**My son Gamliel will be the** next **Nasi.** [13]**Ḥanina bar Ḥama will sit at the head** at the academy.'"

אַל תִּסְפְּדוּנִי בָּעֲיָירוֹת [14]The Gemara now analyzes each line of this portion of Rabbi Yehudah HaNasi's testament: Rabbi Yehudah HaNasi instructed the Sages: **"Do not eulogize me in the towns."** [15]**It was thought**

[1]״יוֹסֵף חֵפָנִי, שִׁמְעוֹן אֶפְרָתִי, הֵם שִׁמְּשׁוּנִי בְּחַיַּי וְהֵם יְשַׁמְּשׁוּנִי בְּמוֹתִי״. [2]סְבוּר מִינָּהּ, בְּהָדֵין עָלְמָא הוּא דְּקָאָמַר, [3]כֵּיוָן דְּחָזוּ דְּקָדֵים עַרְסַיְיהוּ לְעַרְסֵיהּ, [4]אָמְרִי: שְׁמַע מִינָּהּ לְהַהוּא עָלְמָא הוּא דְּקָאָמַר, [5]וְהַאי דַּאֲמַר הָכִי דְּלָא לֵימְרוּ: [6]מִילְּתָא הֲוַאי לְהוּ, [7]וְעַד הָאִידָּנָא נַמִי זְכוּתוֹ דְּרַבִּי הוּא דְּאַהֲנְיָא לְהוּ.

[8]״אָמַר לָהֶן: לְחַכְמֵי יִשְׂרָאֵל אֲנִי צָרִיךְ, [9]נִכְנְסוּ אֶצְלוֹ חַכְמֵי יִשְׂרָאֵל. [10]אָמַר לָהֶן: ׳אַל תִּסְפְּדוּנִי בָּעֲיָירוֹת, [103B] וְהוֹשִׁיבוּ יְשִׁיבָה לְאַחַר שְׁלֹשִׁים יוֹם. [11]שִׁמְעוֹן בְּנִי חָכָם. [12]גַּמְלִיאֵל בְּנִי נָשִׂיא. [13]חֲנִינָא בַּר חָמָא יֵשֵׁב בָּרֹאשׁ׳״.

[14]״אַל תִּסְפְּדוּנִי בָּעֲיָירוֹת״. [15]סְבוּר

LITERAL TRANSLATION

[1]"Yosef of Haifa [and] Shimon of Efrat — they attended to me during my lifetime, and they will attend to me after my death." [2]They thought from this that he was talking about this world. [3]When they saw that their biers went out before his bier, [4]they said: Infer from this that he was talking about that world. [5]And what he said [was] in order that [people] would not say [6][that] they had done some [sinful] act, [7]and until now it was also Rabbi's merit that protected them.

[8]"He said to them: 'I need the Sages of Israel.' [9]The Sages of Israel went in to him, [10][and] he said to them: 'Do not eulogize me in the towns, [103B] and set up the academy after thirty days. [11]Shimon my son is wise. [12]Gamliel my son will be the Nasi. [13]Ḥanina bar Ḥama will sit at its head.'"

[14]"Do not eulogize me in the towns." [15]They thought

RASHI

סבור מינה בהדין עלמא — שהיה מצוה שיתעסקו בקבורתו. **דקדים ערסייהו לערסיה** — הם נקברו תחלה. **והאי דאמר הכי** — שנזקק להודיע שימותו וישרתוהו. **דלא לימרו** — אינשי עלייהו, כשימותו: מילתא דאיסורא הוה בהו, שלא זכו להתעסק בו. ואיגלאי מילתא דהאי דלא שכיבו בשני דרבי — זכותיה דרבי אגנא עלייהו. **עיירות** — גדולות על הכפרים, וכרכין גדולים מהם. **והושיבו ישיבה** — לעסוק בתורה. **לאחר שלשים יום** — של פטירתי מיד, ולא תהיו עסוקין בהספד. **שמעון בני חכם** — הוא. ולקמן פריך: מאי קאמר? **חנינא בר חמא ישב בראש** — הישיבה.

NOTES

that Rabbi Yehudah HaNasi, who was otherwise known as "our holy Rabbi," should return on Friday afternoon in anticipation of the holy day of Sabbath. The *Zohar* writes in several places (*Bereshit* 7:1; *Vayera* 115:2; and elsewhere) that a righteous man has a spiritual image that corresponds to his physical body, and that the righteous man sometimes appears before other people in that form. *Pardes Rimonim* explains that Rabbi Yehudah HaNasi instructed that his light should be lit, meaning that the light of his Torah should continue to illuminate for others, and that his table should be arranged, meaning that his disciples should continue to study his Torah, and be maintained at his expense.

וְהוֹשִׁיבוּ יְשִׁיבָה And set up the academy after thirty days. Rabbi Yehudah HaNasi left these instructions because he knew that after his death, the troubles of the Jewish people would only multiply, and he was concerned that due to the combination of persecutions and excessive mourning, the public would neglect their Torah studies (*Pnei Yehoshua*).

מִינָּהּ, מִשּׁוּם טִרְחָא הוּא דְּקָאָמַר. [1]כֵּיוָן דַּחֲזוּ דְּקָסָפְדֵי בַּכְּרַכִּים, [2]וְקָאָתוּ כּוּלֵּי עָלְמָא, [3]אָמְרוּ: שְׁמַע מִינָּהּ מִשּׁוּם יְקָרָא הוּא דְּקָאָמַר.

[4]״הוֹשִׁיבוּ יְשִׁיבָה לְאַחַר שְׁלֹשִׁים יוֹם״. [5]דְּלָא עֲדִיפְנָא מִמֹּשֶׁה רַבֵּינוּ, [6]דִּכְתִיב: ״וַיִּבְכּוּ בְנֵי יִשְׂרָאֵל אֶת מֹשֶׁה בְּעַרְבוֹת מוֹאָב שְׁלֹשִׁים יוֹם״. [7]תְּלָתִין יוֹמִין סָפְדִין בִּימָמָא וְלֵילְיָא. [8]מִכָּאן וְאֵילָךְ סָפְדוּ בִּימָמָא וְגָרְסֵי בְּלֵילְיָא, אוֹ סָפְדוּ בְּלֵילְיָא וְגָרְסֵי בִּימָמָא, [9]עַד דְּסָפְדֵי תְּרֵיסַר יַרְחֵי שַׁתָּא.

LITERAL TRANSLATION

from this that he said it on account of the inconvenience [to the villagers]. [1]When they saw that they were eulogizing [him] in the big cities, [2]and everybody came, [3]they said: Infer from this that he said this on account of [his] honor.

[4]"Set up the academy after thirty days". [5]For I am no more privileged than Moses our Master, [6]as it is written: "And the children of Israel wept for Moses on the plains of Moab thirty days." [7]They eulogized by day and at night thirty days. [8]From then on they eulogized by day and studied at night, or they eulogized at night and studied by day, [9]until they eulogized for twelve months of the year.

RASHI

סבור מינה משום טורח – דבני כפרים דסמיכו לעיירות ואתו למספדיה. כיון דחזו דקא אספדוהו בכרכין, וקא אתו כולי עלמא מעיירות ומכפרים, אמרי: משום יקרא הוא דקאמר.

TRANSLATION AND COMMENTARY

at first **that** Rabbi Yehudah HaNasi had **said** that **because** he was concerned about **inconveniencing** the people living in outlying villages who would have to travel to the towns to hear the eulogies. [1]But **when** the Sages saw **that** Rabbi Yehudah HaNasi **was being eulogized in the big cities,** [2]**and that everybody** — including the villagers — **came** to participate in the ceremonies, [3]**they said: Infer from this that** Rabbi Yehudah HaNasi had **said** that he does not want to be eulogized in the towns, **because of the honor** due his office. The eulogies conducted in the big cities drew much larger audiences, in keeping with the honor that befits the Nasi of Israel.

הוֹשִׁיבוּ יְשִׁיבָה [4]The Gemara continues: Rabbi Yehudah HaNasi instructed the Sages: "Quickly **reestablish the academy** for regular Torah study **thirty days after** my death — [5]**for I am no more privileged than Moses our Master,** [6]about whom **the verse states** (Deuteronomy 34:8) **"And the children of Israel wept for Moses on the plains of Moab thirty days;** and the days of weeping and mourning for Moses were ended." [7]For **thirty days** the Sages **eulogized** Rabbi Yehudah HaNasi both **by day and at night.** [8]**From then on they eulogized** him **by day and studied** Torah **at night or** else **they eulogized** him **at night, and studied** Torah **by day,** [9]**until** a year had passed and **they** had **eulogized** him **for twelve months.**

NOTES

מִשּׁוּם טִרְחָא On account of inconvenience. *Rivan* writes that Rabbi Yehudah HaNasi asked that he not be eulogized in the towns, because there were so many towns that it would take a great effort to deliver a eulogy in every town through which his bier would pass. According to the Jerusalem Talmud, Rabbi Yehudah HaNasi asked that he not be eulogized in the towns because of the quarreling that might arise due to crowding in the small towns. *Meiri* explains that Rabbi Yehudah HaNasi was concerned that the city dwellers would be upset if the residents of the smaller towns do not come to the cities to participate in the eulogies held there. Others explain that the people would quarrel about the town in which the eulogy was to be held, and they would not go to the neighboring town if their own town was not chosen.

מִשּׁוּם יְקָרָא On account of his honor. *Maharsha* asks: But surely we learned elsewhere that Rabbi Yehudah HaNasi was extremely modest! Why then was he concerned about the honor that would be shown him after his death? He explains that Rabbi Yehudah HaNasi regarded the honor that would be shown him at his funeral as honor shown to the Torah, and while he was permitted to forgo personal honor, he was not permitted to waive the honor to the Torah. Similarly, *Bet Aharon* writes that Rabbi Yehudah HaNasi acted as he did so that the people would honor other Torah scholars, and a person is not permitted to act modestly when acting in that manner will harm others. Throughout the generations, various Rabbinic figures asked that no special honor be shown them after their deaths, but when they died their requests were not heeded.

תְּרֵיסַר יַרְחֵי שַׁתָּא Twelve months. A disciple is like a son. Just as a son must mourn the death of a parent for twelve months, so too a disciple must mourn the death of his teacher for a full year. And since Rabbi Yehudah HaNasi

HALAKHAH

תְּלָתִין יוֹמִין סָפְדִין Thirty days they eulogized. "One should not weep over the deceased for more than three days, nor eulogize him for more than a week. These rules apply to an ordinary person. But the time periods are extended for a Torah scholar in accordance with his honor. In any case, one should not weep over the death of a Torah scholar for more than thirty days, nor eulogize him for more than twelve months — the mourning period that had been observed for Moses and Rabbi Yehudah HaNasi." (*Rambam, Sefer Shofetim, Hilkhot Evel* 13:10; *Shulhan Arukh, Yoreh De'ah* 394:1-2.)

TRANSLATION AND COMMENTARY

הַהוּא יוֹמָא [1]It was related that **on the day of Rabbi** Yehudah HaNasi's **funeral a heavenly voice issued forth, stating:** [2]**"Everybody who attended Rabbi** Yehudah HaNasi's **funeral is destined for life in the world to come."** [3]It was further related that **there was a certain launderer who would come before Rabbi** Yehudah HaNasi **every day,** [4]**and** it so happened that on **the day of the funeral he did not come.** [5]**When** the launderer **heard that** Rabbi Yehudah HaNasi had died, he was overcome with grief, and **he went up to the roof,** jumped **and fell to the ground, and died.** [6]A second **heavenly voice issued forth, stating: "That launderer is also destined for life in the world to come."**

שִׁמְעוֹן [7]Rabbi Yehudah HaNasi's last testament continued: **"My son Shimon is wise.** My son Gamliel will be the next Nasi." [8]**What did he** mean when he **said** this?

הָכִי קָאָמַר [9]The Gemara explains: **He meant as follows: Even though my son Shimon is wiser** than his brother, [10]**my son Gamliel will be the** next **Nasi.**

אֲמַר לֵוִי [11]**Levi asked: Was it necessary** for Rabbi Yehudah HaNasi **to say** that his son Gamliel would take over as Nasi? Gamliel was the eldest, he was entitled to inherit the position?

אֲמַר [12]**Rabbi Shimon the son of Rabbi** Yehudah HaNasi mockingly **answered: It was** indeed **necessary for you and for your limping** question (an expression used to make fun of Levi, who happened to be crippled)!

מַאי קַשְׁיָא לֵיהּ [13]The Gemara asks: **What was** Rabbi Shimon's **difficulty** with Levi's question that he answered him so contemptuously? [14]**Surely the verse states** (II Chronicles 21:3): **"But he gave the kingdom**

[1]הַהוּא יוֹמָא דְּאַשְׁכַּבְתֵּיהּ דְּרַבִּי נָפְקָא בַּת קָלָא, וְאָמְרָה: [2]״כָּל דַּהֲוָה בְּאַשְׁכַּבְתֵּיהּ דְּרַבִּי מְזוּמָּן הוּא לְחַיֵּי הָעוֹלָם הַבָּא״. [3]הַהוּא כּוֹבֵס כָּל יוֹמָא הֲוָה אָתֵי קַמֵּיהּ, [4]הַהוּא יוֹמָא לָא אֲתָא, [5]כֵּיוָן דִּשְׁמַע הָכִי, סָלֵיק לְאִיגְּרָא וְנָפַל לְאַרְעָא וּמִית. [6]יָצְתָה בַּת קוֹל וְאָמְרָה: ״אַף הַהוּא כּוֹבֵס מְזוּמָּן הוּא לְחַיֵּי הָעוֹלָם הַבָּא.״

[7]״שִׁמְעוֹן בְּנִי חָכָם״. [8]מַאי קָאָמַר?

[9]הָכִי קָאָמַר: אַף עַל פִּי שֶׁשִּׁמְעוֹן בְּנִי חָכָם, [10]גַּמְלִיאֵל בְּנִי נָשִׂיא.

[11]אֲמַר לֵוִי: צְרִיכָא לְמֵימַר?

[12]אֲמַר רַבִּי שִׁמְעוֹן בַּר רַבִּי: צְרִיכָא לָךְ וּלְמִטְלַעְתָּךְ.

[13]מַאי קַשְׁיָא לֵיהּ? [14]הָא קְרָא קָאָמַר: ״וְאֶת הַמַּמְלָכָה נָתַן

LITERAL TRANSLATION

[1][On] the day of Rabbi's funeral a heavenly voice issued forth, and said: [2]"All who were at Rabbi's funeral are destined for life in the world to come." [3][There was] a certain launderer [who] every day would come before him, [4][and] that day he did not come. [5]When he heard that, he went up to the roof, and fell to the ground, and died. [6]A heavenly voice issued forth and said: "Even that launder is destined for life in the world to come."

[7]"Shimon my son is wise." [8]What is he saying?

[9]He says thus: Even though Shimon my son is wise, [10]Gamliel my son will be the Nasi.

[11]Levi said: Was it necessary to say [this]?

[12]Rabbi Shimon bar Rabbi said: It was necessary for you and for your limp.

[13]What was difficult for him? [14]Surely the verse states: "But he gave the kingdom

RASHI

יומא דאשכבתיה — יום פטירתו. **צריכא למימר** — דרבן גמליאל דבכור הוי נשיאה. **לך ולמטלעתך** — פִּסֵּחַ היה, כדאמרינן בעלמא (סוכה נג,א) לוי אחוי קידה ואטלע. **מאי קשיא ליה** — לרבי שמעון ברבי, דאמר: צריכא למימר, אמאי צריכא — הא קרא כתיב!

NOTES

was considered the teacher of all Israel, all the people mourned him for a year.

הַהוּא כּוֹבֵס **A certain launderer.** *Rabbi Ya'akov Emden* suggests that perhaps this is the same launderer who is reported elsewhere (*Nedarim* 41a) to have heard Rabbi Yehudah HaNasi's teachings, and later when Rabbi Yehudah HaNasi forgot something, he reminded him about what he had once learned from him.

סָלֵיק לְאִיגְּרָא **He went up to the roof.** This passage gives rise to a serious difficulty, for it is stated elsewhere that a person who commits suicide has no place in the world to come, and here it is reported that the launderer who committed suicide is destined for life in the world to come. *Rabbi Ya'akov Emden* suggests that the launderer's death did not fall under the category of suicide, for it was an act of madness which resulted from his great distress over Rabbi Yehudah HaNasi's passing. Others suggest that the prohibition against suicide does not apply to someone who kills himself for the sake of Heaven or to sanctify God's name (*Eshel Avraham*). This conclusion follows from various statements made by the Rabbis regarding King Saul and others. This position appears to have been accepted in practice by a number of Rabbis who committed suicide at the time of the Crusades.

צְרִיכָא לָךְ וּלְמִטְלַעְתָּךְ **It was necessary for you and your limp.** There are those who wondered why Rabbi Shimon the son of Rabbi Yehudah HaNasi spoke so contemptuously to Levi. Some try to soften the remark by pointing out that Levi acquired his lameness through his study of Torah, while he demonstrated to Rabbi Yehudah HaNasi how the

TRANSLATION AND COMMENTARY

to Yehoram, because he was the firstborn." Thus, we see that a firstborn is entitled to inherit his father's position, and it should not have been necessary for Rabbi Yehudah HaNasi to have left instructions on the matter!

הַהוּא [1]The Gemara answers: **That one,** Yehoram, **could fill the place of his father,** Jehoshafat, for there was nobody more fitting for the kingship. [2]**But Rabban Gamliel could not fill his father's place,** for his brother Shimon was indeed wiser. Hence it was necessary for Rabbi Yehudah HaNasi to say that Gamliel, and not Shimon, should be appointed as Nasi after him.

וְרַבִּי [3]The Gemara asks: **And what is the reason that** Rabbi Yehudah HaNasi **acted in that manner** appointing Rabban Gamliel as his successor, and not Rabbi Shimon?

נְהִי דְּאֵינוֹ מְמַלֵּא [4]The Gemara answers: **While** Rabban Gamliel **could not fill his father's place in** terms of **wisdom,** [5]**he did fill his father's place in** terms of **fear of sin** and piety, and so his appointment was appropriate.

חֲנִינָא בַּר חָמָא [6]Rabbi Yehudah HaNasi instructed the Sages: **"Ḥanina bar Ḥama will sit at the head** of the academy." [7]At first **Rabbi Ḥanina refused to accept** the appointment, [8]**because** he thought that the appointment should go to **Rabbi Afes** who **was two-and-a-half years older than him.** [9]But while **Rabbi Afes presided** over the academy, [10]**Rabbi Ḥanina sat outside,** for he was Rabbi Afes's superior in scholarship, and he thought it would be inappropriate for him to sit inside as if he were his disciple. [11]While he sat outside, **Levi went and sat next to** Rabbi Ḥanina and studied Torah with him. [12]After **Rabbi Afes died, Rabbi Ḥanina** accepted the appointment that he had now received from Rabbi Yehudah HaNasi and **sat at the head** of the academy. [13]**Levi** had **no one with whom to sit** and study Torah on his level of scholarship, **and so he went to Babylonia.** [14]Levi's arrival in Babylonia was a main

לִיהוֹרָם כִּי הוּא הַבְּכוֹר״. [1]הַהוּא מְמַלֵּא מָקוֹם אֲבוֹתָיו הֲוָה, [2]וְרַבָּן גַּמְלִיאֵל אֵינוֹ מְמַלֵּא מְקוֹם אֲבוֹתָיו הֲוָה. [3]וְרַבִּי, מַאי טַעְמָא עֲבַד הָכִי? [4]נְהִי דְּאֵינוֹ מְמַלֵּא מְקוֹם אֲבוֹתָיו בְּחָכְמָה, [5]בְּיִרְאַת חֵטְא מְמַלֵּא מְקוֹם אֲבוֹתָיו הֲוָה. [6]״חֲנִינָא בַּר חָמָא יֵשֵׁב בָּרֹאשׁ״. [7]לֹא קִיבֵּל רַבִּי חֲנִינָא, [8]שֶׁהָיָה רַבִּי אָפֵס גָּדוֹל מִמֶּנּוּ שְׁתֵּי שָׁנִים וּמֶחֱצָה. [9]יְתֵיב רַבִּי אָפֵס בְּרֵישָׁא, [10]וִיתֵיב רַבִּי חֲנִינָא אַבָּרָאי, [11]וַאֲתָא לֵוִי וִיתֵיב גַּבֵּיהּ. [12]נָח נַפְשֵׁיהּ דְּרַבִּי אָפֵס וִיתֵיב רַבִּי חֲנִינָא בְּרֵישָׁא, [13]וְלָא הֲוָה לֵיהּ לְלֵוִי אִינִישׁ לְמֵיתַב גַּבֵּיהּ וְקָאָתָא לְבָבֶל. [14]וְהַיְינוּ

LITERAL TRANSLATION

to Yehoram, because he was the firstborn." [1]That one could fill his father's place, [2]but Rabban Gamliel could not fill his father's place. [3]And Rabbi, what is the reason that he acted thus? [4]While he could not fill his father's place in wisdom, [5]he could fill his father's place in the fear of sin. [6]"Ḥanina bar Ḥama will sit at the head." [7]Rabbi Ḥanina did not accept [this] [8]because Rabbi Afes was older than him by two-and-a-half years. [9]Rabbi Afes sat at the head, [10]and Rabbi Hanina sat outside, [11]and Levi came and sat next to him. [12]Rabbi Afes died (lit., "his soul rested"), and Rabbi Ḥanina sat at the head, [13]and Levi had no one to sit next to, and he went (lit., "came") to Babylonia. [14]And this is what

RASHI

ההוא ממלא מקום אבותיו הוה — כלומר, אין באחיו חשוב ממנו. **אבל כאן** — הרי אחיו חכם ממנו. **יתיב רבי חנינא אבראי** — חוץ לבית המדרש, שלא היה נכפף לרבי אפס. **וקאתא** — לבבל.

LANGUAGE

רַבִּי אָפֵס **Rabbi Afes.** The name Afes appears to be a corruption of the Latin name, Appius.

SAGES

רַבִּי אָפֵס **Rabbi Afes.** Rabbi Afes served as Rabbi Yehudah HaNasi's scribe, and, as is mentioned here, he headed the academy for a certain period of time after Rabbi Yehudah HaNasi's death. The Talmud cites very few rulings or statements in his name. The younger members of Rabbi Yehudah HaNasi's generation were primarily involved in the final editing of the Mishnah and collection of the Baraitot, and their positions are usually recorded in an anonymous fashion under the heading: רַבּוֹתֵינוּ — "Our Rabbis said."

NOTES

High Priest would bow to the ground on Yom Kippur. Still it is difficult to understand why Rabbi Shimon should have mocked Levi's disability.

הַהוּא מְמַלֵּא מְקוֹם אֲבוֹתָיו הֲוָה That one could fill his father's place. *Maharsha* asks: Jehoshafat was a righteous king, but his son Yehoram was wicked. How then can the Gemara have said that Yehoram filled his father's place. *Maharsha* suggests that During Jehoshafat's lifetime, Yehoram was indeed a righteous man, and it was only after his death that Yehoram turned wicked. Others propose that although he was a wicked man, Yehoram was the best among the sons of Jehoshafat. The same can also be said about Rabbi Yehudah HaNasi that the son whom he chose as his successor was the best among his sons for this position, but not necessarily equal to Rabbi Yehudah HaNasi.

HALAKHAH

מְמַלֵּא מְקוֹם אֲבוֹתָיו He could fill his father's place. "A public appointment is regarded as an inheritance which is passed down from parent to child to grandchild. This only applies if the son fills his father's place in wisdom and the fear of God. If he fills his place in the fear of God, but not in wisdom, he is put into his father's position and is then taught," following our Gemara. (*Rambam, Sefer Avodah, Hilkhot Kelei HaMikdash* 14:20; *Sefer Shofetim, Hilkhot Melakhim* 1:7; *Shulḥan Arukh, Yoreh De'ah* 245:22, *Rema*.)

SAGES

רַבִּי חֲנִינָא בַּר חָמָא Rabbi Ḥanina bar Ḥama. A first-generation Amora of Eretz Israel. See *Ketubot,* Part II, pp. 153-4.

TRANSLATION AND COMMENTARY

event that **people related to Rav** as follows: [1]**"A great man has come to Neharde'a,** [2]**and he limps, and he has expounded** as follows: 'A woman **is permitted** to walk in the public domain on Shabbat with **a crown** on her head.' Crowns are worn only by women of high status, who do not remove their jewels in the public domain. Thus there is no concern that wearing such an ornament will lead to a violation of the Shabbat law." [3]Hearing about Levi's arrival in Babylonia, Rav **said: "Infer from this that Rabbi Afes** must have **died,** [4]**and Rabbi Ḥanina** now **sits at the head** of the academy, [5]**and Levi was** therefore left **with nobody to sit with** and study Torah, **and he came** to Babylonia."

וְאֵימָא [6]The Gemara questions this inference: How was Rav so sure that this was the course of the events? Why did he not **say that** it was **Rabbi Ḥanina** who **died,** [7]**and Rabbi Afes** continued to **preside** over the academy **as he had presided** until then, [8]**and** since **Levi no** longer **had anybody to sit with** and study Torah, **he** went to Babylonia?

אִיבָּעֵית אֵימָא [9]The Gemara answers: **If you wish,** you can **say** that if it would have been Rabbi Ḥanina who died, and Rabbi Afes was still presiding over the academy, **Levi would have subjected himself to Rabbi Afes** and entered the academy, for he had sat outside not because he regarded himself as Rabbi Afes' superior, but rather to show honor to Rabbi Ḥanina.

וְאִי בָּעֵית אֵימָא [10]The Gemara suggests an alternative answer: **And if you wish,** you can **say: Since Rabbi** Yehudah HaNasi had **said:** [11]**"Ḥanina bar Ḥama will sit at the head** of the academy," **it could not have been that he never presided,** [12]**for the verse states regarding righteous people** (Job 22:28): **"You shall decree a thing, and it shall be established for you,"** which teaches that a righteous person's decrees always come true.

וְהָא [13]The Gemara now asks why Rabbi Yehudah HaNasi's appointed Rabbi Ḥanina to head the academy: **But surely there was Rabbi Ḥiyya** who was the most appropriate candidate for the position!

נָח נַפְשֵׁיהּ [14]The Gemara answers: Rabbi Ḥiyya had by that time already **died.**

וְהָאָמַר רַבִּי חִיָּיא [15]The Gemara asks: **But surely Rabbi Ḥiyya said:** [16]**"I saw Rabbi** Yehudah HaNasi's **grave, and I shed tears over it."**

[1]דְּאָמְרִי לֵיהּ לְרַב: "גַּבְרָא רַבָּה אִקְלַע לִנְהַרְדְּעָא, [2]וּמְטַלַּע, וְדָרֵישׁ: 'כְּלִילָא שָׁרֵי'". [3]אָמַר: שְׁמַע מִינָּהּ נָח נַפְשֵׁיהּ דְּרַבִּי אָפֵס, [4]וִיתֵיב רַבִּי חֲנִינָא בְּרֵישָׁא, [5]וְלָא הֲוָה לֵיהּ לְלֵוִי אִינִישׁ לְמֵיתַב גַּבֵּיהּ, וְקָאָתָא.
[6]וְאֵימָא: רַבִּי חֲנִינָא נָח נַפְשֵׁיהּ, [7]וְרַבִּי אָפֵס כִּדְיָתֵיב יָתֵיב, [8]וְלָא הֲוָה לֵיהּ לְלֵוִי אִינִישׁ לְמֵיתַב גַּבֵּיהּ, וְקָאָתָא?
[9]אִיבָּעֵית אֵימָא: לֵוִי לְרַבִּי אָפֵס מֵיכַף הֲוָה כָּיֵיף לֵיהּ.
[10]וְאִי בָּעֵית אֵימָא: כֵּיוָן דְּאָמַר רַבִּי: [11]"חֲנִינָא בַּר חָמָא יֵשֵׁב בָּרֹאשׁ", לָא סַגִּי דְּלָא מָלֵיךְ, [12]דִּכְתִיב בְּהוּ בְּצַדִּיקִים: "וְתִגְזַר אֹמֶר וְיָקָם לָךְ".
[13]וְהָא הֲוָה רַבִּי חִיָּיא!
[14]נָח נַפְשֵׁיהּ.
[15]וְהָאָמַר רַבִּי חִיָּיא: [16]"אֲנִי רָאִיתִי קִבְרוֹ שֶׁל רַבִּי, וְהוֹרַדְתִּי עָלָיו דְּמָעוֹת"!

LITERAL TRANSLATION

they said to Rav: [1]"A great man came to Neharde'a, and he limps, [2]and he expounded: 'A crown is permitted.'" [3]He said: "[I] infer from this [that] Rabbi Afes died, [4]and Rabbi Ḥanina sat at the head, [5]and Levi had no one to sit next to, and he came."

[6]But say that Rabbi Ḥanina died, [7]and Rabbi Afes sat as he sat, [8]and Levi had no one to sit next to, and he came?

[9]If you wish, say: Levi would have subjected himself to Rabbi Afes.

[10]And if you wish, say: Since Rabbi said: [11]"Ḥanina bar Ḥama will sit at the head," it could not have been that he did not preside, [12]for it is written about righteous people: "You shall decree a thing, and it shall be established for you."

[13]But surely there was Rabbi Ḥiyya!

[14]He died.

[15]But surely Rabbi Ḥiyya said: [16]"I saw Rabbi's grave, and I shed tears over it."

RASHI

כלילא שרי — לצאת בה בשבת. מאי טעמא — מאן דרכה למיפק בכלילא — אשה חשובה, ואשה חשובה לא שלפא ומחויא, בפרק "במה אשה יוצאה" (שבת נט,ב). **מיכף הוה כייף ליה** — קודם שיגלה ממקומו, אבל לרבי חנינא לא כייף. **והא הוה רבי חייא** — ולמנייה רבי ראש ישיבה. **קברו של רבי** — ארונו של רבי, הורדתי עליו דמעות.

HALAKHAH

כְּלִילָא שָׁרֵי A crown is permitted. "A woman is permitted to walk in the public domain on Shabbat with a crown on her head, for only a wealthy woman goes out with such an ornament, and she would not remove her jewels in order to show them to others," following Levi. (*Rambam, Sefer Zemanim, Hilkhot Shabbat* 19:10; *Shulḥan Arukh, Oraḥ Ḥayyim* 303:5.)

LITERAL TRANSLATION

[1]Reverse [the parties].

[2]But surely Rabbi Ḥiyya said: The day that Rabbi died holiness ceased to exist!

[3]Reverse [it].

[4]But surely it was taught: "When Rabbi became ill, Rabbi Ḥiyya came in to him, and found him crying. [5]He said to him: 'Master, why are your crying?' [6]Surely it was taught: '[If] someone died laughing, it is a good sign for him. [If he died] crying, it is a bad sign for him. [7]With his face upward, it is a good sign for him. With his face downward, it is a bad sign for him. [8]With his face toward the people, it is a good sign for him. [With his face] toward the wall, it is a bad sign for him. [9]With a green face, it is a bad sign for him. [10]With a yellow or red face, it is a good sign for him. [11][If] he died on Friday, it is a good sign for him. On Saturday night, it is a bad sign for him. [12][If] he died on Yom Kippur eve, it is a bad sign for him. [13]On the night following Yom Kippur, it is a good sign for him. [14][If] he died from an intestinal disease, it is a good sign, [15]for the majority of righteous people die from an intestinal disease.'

[1]אִיפּוּךְ.

[2]וְהָאָמַר רַבִּי חִיָּיא: אוֹתוֹ הַיּוֹם שֶׁמֵּת רַבִּי בָּטְלָה קְדוּשָּׁה!

[3]אִיפּוּךְ.

[4]וְהָתַנְיָא: ״כְּשֶׁחָלָה רַבִּי, נִכְנַס רַבִּי חִיָּיא אֶצְלוֹ וּמְצָאוֹ שֶׁהוּא בּוֹכֶה. [5]אָמַר לוֹ: ׳רַבִּי, מִפְּנֵי מָה אַתָּה בּוֹכֶה׳? [6]וְהָתַנְיָא: ׳מֵת מִתּוֹךְ הַשְּׂחוֹק, סִימָן יָפֶה לוֹ. מִתּוֹךְ הַבְּכִי, סִימָן רַע לוֹ. [7]פָּנָיו לְמַעְלָה, סִימָן יָפֶה לוֹ. פָּנָיו לְמַטָּה, סִימָן רַע לוֹ. [8]פָּנָיו כְּלַפֵּי הָעָם, סִימָן יָפֶה לוֹ. כְּלַפֵּי הַכּוֹתֶל, סִימָן רַע לוֹ. [9]פָּנָיו יְרוּקִּין, סִימָן רַע לוֹ. [10]פָּנָיו צְהוּבִּין וַאֲדוּמִּים, סִימָן יָפֶה לוֹ. [11]מֵת בְּעֶרֶב שַׁבָּת, סִימָן יָפֶה לוֹ. בְּמוֹצָאֵי שַׁבָּת, סִימָן רַע לוֹ. [12]מֵת בְּעֶרֶב יוֹם הַכִּיפּוּרִים, סִימָן רַע לוֹ. [13]בְּמוֹצָאֵי יוֹם הַכִּיפּוּרִים, סִימָן יָפֶה לוֹ. [14]מֵת מֵחוּלִי מֵעַיִים, סִימָן יָפֶה לוֹ, [15]מִפְּנֵי שֶׁרוּבָּם שֶׁל צַדִּיקִים מִיתָתָן בְּחוֹלִי מֵעַיִים׳.

TRANSLATION AND COMMENTARY

אִיפּוּךְ [1]The Gemara answers: **Reverse** the names and report the matter as follows: Rabbi Yehudah HaNasi said: "I saw Rabbi Ḥiyya's grave, and I shed tears over it."

וְהָאָמַר רַבִּי חִיָּיא [2]The Gemara cites another statement of Rabbi Ḥiyya which implies that he outlived Rabbi Yehudah HaNasi: **But surely Rabbi Ḥiyya said: The day that Rabbi** Yehudah HaNasi **died holiness ceased to exist!**

אִיפּוּךְ [3]Again the Gemara answers: **Reverse** the names and say that Rabbi Yehudah HaNasi said that on the day that Rabbi Ḥiyya died, holiness ceased to exist.

וְהָתַנְיָא [4]**But surely it was taught** in a Baraita: **"When** Rabbi Yehudah HaNasi **became ill** and lay on his deathbed, **Rabbi Ḥiyya came in to** visit **him, and found him crying.** [5]Rabbi Ḥiyya **said to** Rabbi Yehudah HaNasi: **'Master, why are you crying?** [6]**Surely it was taught** as follows: **"If someone died laughing, it is a good sign for him,** but **if he died crying, it is a bad sign for him.** [7]If he died **facing upward, it is a good sign for him,** but if he died **facing downward, it is a bad sign for him.** [8]If he died **facing the people, it is a good sign for him,** but if he died **facing the wall, it is a bad sign for him.** [9]If he died **with a green face, it is a bad sign for him,** [10]but if he died **with a yellow or a red face, it is a good sign for him.** [11]If **he died on Friday, it is a good sign for him,** because he goes immediately to enjoy the Shabbat rest, but if he died **on Saturday night, it is a bad sign for him.** [12]If he died on **Yom Kippur eve, it is a bad sign,** for he died before his sins were pardoned, [13]but if he died **on the night following Yom Kippur, it is a good sign for him,** as he had achieved atonement. [14]If **he died from an intestinal disease, it is a good sign,** [15]**for most righteous people die from an intestinal disease.'**

RASHI

בערב שבת סימן יפה – שיכנס למנוחה מיד. **במוצאי יום הכפורים** – נמחלו עוונותיו וסימן יפה לו.

NOTES

בָּטְלָה קְדוּשָּׁה Holiness ceased to exist. *Rivan, Tosafot,* and others understand this as a figure of speech. Upon the death of Rabbi Yehudah Ḥanasi, who was otherwise known as *Rabbenu HaKadosh,* "our Master, the holy one," holiness ceased to exist. But *Ra'avad, Ran,* and many others explain this passage in accordance with what is stated in the Jerusalem Talmud that on the day that Rabbi Yehudah HaNasi died, the holiness of the priesthood was cancelled. Even priests were obligated to defile themselves and participate in his funeral, as if he were a corpse who has nobody to bury him.

סִימָן יָפֶה לוֹ It is a good sign for him. *Rivan* notes that he does not understand the meaning of each of these signs, with the exception of dying on Friday, which is a good sign, for the deceased immediately enters into the Sabbath rest, and dying on the night following Yom Kippur, which is another good sign, for his sins had just been pardoned.

מִיתָתָן בְּחוֹלִי מֵעַיִים They die from an intestinal disease. Dying from an intestinal disease inducing diarrhea is regarded as a good sign, for as the Jerusalem Talmud

SAGES

רַבִּי חִיָּיא **Rabbi Ḥiyya.** One of the last of the Tannaim. See *Ketubot,* Part II, pp. 199-200.

TRANSLATION AND COMMENTARY

[1]Rabbi Yehudah HaNasi **said to him: 'I am crying because of the Torah** that I will be unable to study **and the commandments** that I will be unable to observe after I die.' " Thus, we see that Rabbi Ḥiyya was still alive when Rabbi Yehudah HaNasi was on his deathbed!

אִיבָּעֵית אֵימָא [2]The Gemara answers: **If you wish,** you can **say** as was suggested above that the names should be **reversed,** and that it was Rabbi Yehudah HaNasi who visited Rabbi Ḥiyya while he was dying.

וְאִיבָּעֵית אֵימָא [3]The Gemara suggests an alternative answer: **And if you wish,** you can **say** that there is **in fact no** reason to **reverse** the names, and the traditions cited above according to which Rabbi Ḥiyya outlived Rabbi Yehudah HaNasi are correct. [4]**Rabbi Ḥiyya** was indeed the candidate of choice for the position of head of the academy, but he **was** particularly **involved in** the performance of righteous acts, [5]**and Rabbi** Yehudah HaNasi **thought** to himself: "If **I** appoint Rabbi Ḥiyya to preside over the academy, this will **prevent him** from performing those righteous deeds." [6]**And** Rabbi Ḥiyya's unusual piety is made clear in the following story: **When Rabbi Ḥanina and Rabbi Ḥiyya were** once **quarreling,** [7]Rabbi Ḥanina **said to** Rabbi Ḥiyya: **"Why you** take it upon yourself to **quarrel with me?** [8]For I am so well versed that **if God forbid the Torah were forgotten from Israel, I could restore** all the forgotten matters **by way of my argumentation."** [9]And **Rabbi Ḥiyya answered him:** "But **I act so that the Torah will not be forgotten from Israel.** [10]**For I bring flax** seeds, **and sow** them, and harvest the flax, **and weave nets** from the flax, **and hunt deer** with the nets, [11]**and feed the meat** of the deer **to orphans** who would otherwise go hungry. [12]**I make scrolls** of parchment **from the hides of the deer, and go to a city which has no teacher of young children,** [13]**and write the Five Books** of the Torah **for five** different **children, and teach the six orders of the Mishnah to six** different **children.** [14]**To each of** the children **I say: 'Teach** the book or **the order** that I taught you **to** each of **the other** children,' and in that way each child learns the Five Books of the Torah and the six orders of the Mishnah." [15]**And this is what Rabbi** Yehudah HaNasi was referring to when he **said: "How great are the**

[1]אֲמַר לֵיהּ: ׳אֲנָא אַתּוֹרָה וּמִצְוֹת קָא בָּכֵינָא׳״! [2]אִיבָּעֵית אֵימָא: אֵיפּוּךְ. [3]וְאִיבָּעֵית אֵימָא: לְעוֹלָם, לָא תֵּיפּוּךְ. [4]רַבִּי חִיָּיא עָסוּק בְּמִצְוֹת הֲוָה, [5]וְרַבִּי סָבַר: ״לָא אַפַּגְרֵיהּ״. [6]וְהַיְינוּ דְּכִי הָווּ מִינְצוּ רַבִּי חֲנִינָא וְרַבִּי חִיָּיא, [7]אֲמַר לֵיהּ רַבִּי חֲנִינָא לְרַבִּי חִיָּיא: ״בַּהֲדֵי דִּידִי מִינְצַתְּ? [8]דְּאִם חַס וְשָׁלוֹם נִשְׁתַּכְּחָה תּוֹרָה מִיִּשְׂרָאֵל, מַהֲדַרְנָא לֵיהּ מִפִּלְפּוּלִי״! [9]אֲמַר לֵיהּ רַבִּי חִיָּיא: ״אֲנָא עָבְדִי דְּלָא מִשְׁתַּכְּחָה תּוֹרָה מִיִּשְׂרָאֵל. [10]דְּאַיְיתִינָא כִּיתָּנָא וְשָׁדְיָינָא, וּמְגַדַּלְנָא נִישְׁבֵּי וְצָיְידְנָא טַבְיָא, [11]וּמַאֲכִילְנָא בִּישְׂרָא לְיָתְמֵי, [12]וַאֲרִיכְנָא מְגִילָּתָא מִמַּשְׁכֵי דְּטַבְיָא, וְסָלֵיקְנָא לְמָתָא דְּלֵית בָּהּ מַקְרֵי דַּרְדְּקֵי, [13]וְכָתֵיבְנָא חַמְשָׁא חוּמְשֵׁי לְחַמְשָׁא יָנוּקֵי, וּמַתְנֵינָא שִׁיתָּא סִידְרֵי לְשִׁיתָּא יָנוּקֵי. [14]לְכָל חַד וְחַד אָמְרִי לֵיהּ: אַתְנֵי סִידְרָךְ לְחַבְרָךְ״. [15]וְהַיְינוּ דְּאָמַר רַבִּי: ״כַּמָּה

LITERAL TRANSLATION

[1]He said to him: 'I am crying because of the Torah and the commandments.' "

[2]If you wish, say: Reverse [it].

[3]And if you wish, say: In fact, do not reverse [it].

[4]Rabbi Ḥiyya was busy with commandments, [5]and Rabbi thought: "I will not prevent him." [6]And this [was the case] when Rabbi Ḥanina and Rabbi Ḥiyya were quarreling, [7]Rabbi Ḥanina said to Rabbi Ḥiyya: "Why quarrel with me? [8]For if, God forbid, the Torah should be forgotten from Israel, I could restore it through my argumentation." [9]Rabbi Ḥiyya said to him: "I act so that the Torah shall not be forgotten from Israel. [10]For I bring flax, and sow, and weave nets, and hunt deer, [11]and feed the meat to orphans [12]and I make scrolls from the hides of the deer, and I go a city that has no teachers of young children, [13]and I write the Five Books [of the Bible] to five children, and I teach the six orders [of the Mishnah] to six children. [14]To each of them I say: 'Teach your order to your fellow.' " [15]And this is what Rabbi said: "How

RASHI

לא אפגריה — לא אבטלי ממצות. **שדיינא** = זרענא. **ומגדלנא נישבי** — מקלע אני מכמורת. ודומה לו: אין פורסין נשבין ליונים (בבא בתרא כג,א). **וציידנא טביי** — צביים. **ואריכנא מגילתא** — ומתקן אני קלפים. ארוכנא — לשון תיקון, כדאמר במסכת סוכה (מד,ב): ארוך או לא ארוך, כלומר מתוקן או אינו מתוקן. ובספר עזרא (סימן ד) נמי כתיב ״וערות מלכא לא ארוך לנא למחזא״.

NOTES

states, such a disease wipes the entire body clean. Others suggest that those who die from an intestinal disease remain alert until the final moments of their lives, and so they do not have to abandon their Torah studies until the very end.

TRANSLATION AND COMMENTARY

acks of Ḥiyya!" [1]When **Rabbi Shimon the son of Rabbi** Yehudah HaNasi, heard his father praise Rabbi Ḥiyya so highly, he **said to him:** "Are Rabbi Ḥiyya's acts **even greater than yours?"** [2]Rabbi Yehudah HaNasi **said to him: "Yes."** [3]**Rabbi Yishmael the son of Rabbi Yose** then **asked him:** "Are Rabbi Ḥiyya's acts **even greater than** those of my **father,** Rabbi Yose?" [4]Rabbi Yehudah HaNasi **said to him: "God forbid, let such a thing not be** said **in Israel,** for there is nobody whose deeds are greater than those of your fathers's."

אָמַר לָהֶן [5]Rabbi Yehudah HaNasi's deathbed instructions continued: "Rabbi Yehudah HaNasi **said to** his attendants: **'I need** to see **my younger son.'** [6]**Rabbi Shimon went in to** visit with **him.** [7]Rabbi Yehudah HaNasi **transmitted to him the principles of wisdom,** teaching him all of the fundamentals of the Torah. [8]Rabbi Yehudah HaNasi then **said to** his attendants: "Now **I need** to see **my older son.** [9]**Rabban Gamliel went in to** see his father. [10]Rabbi Yehudah HaNasi **transmitted him the principles of** handling the **presidency.** [11]Rabbi Yehudah HaNasi **said to him: 'My son, conduct your presidency with the exalted,** surrounding yourself with the nation's elite, [12]and **cast your fear upon the disciples,** treating them with a heavy hand.'"

אֵינִי [13]The Gemara asks: **Is it** really **so** that this is the best way for the Nasi to conduct his presidency? [14]**But surely the verse states** (Psalms 15:4): **"But he honors them that fear the Lord."** [15]**And a Sage said: This is** referring to **Jehoshafat the king of Judah.** [16]**When he saw a Torah scholar, he would** immediately

גְּדוֹלִים מַעֲשֵׂה חִיָּיא״! [1]אָמַר לוֹ רַבִּי שִׁמְעוֹן בְּרַבִּי: ״אֲפִילּוּ מִמְּךָ״? [2]אֲמַר לֵיהּ: ״אִין״. [3]אֲמַר לֵיהּ רַבִּי יִשְׁמָעֵאל בְּרַבִּי יוֹסֵי: ״אֲפִילּוּ מֵאַבָּא״? [4]אֲמַר לֵיהּ: ״חַס וְשָׁלוֹם, לֹא תְּהֵא כָּזֹאת בְּיִשְׂרָאֵל״.

[5]״אָמַר לָהֶן: ׳לִבְנִי קָטָן אֲנִי צָרִיךְ׳. [6]נִכְנַס רַבִּי שִׁמְעוֹן אֶצְלוֹ. [7]מָסַר לוֹ סִדְרֵי חָכְמָה. [8]אָמַר לָהֶן: לִבְנִי גָּדוֹל אֲנִי צָרִיךְ. [9]נִכְנַס רַבָּן גַּמְלִיאֵל אֶצְלוֹ. [10]וּמָסַר לוֹ סִדְרֵי נְשִׂיאוּת. [11]אָמַר לוֹ: ׳בְּנִי, נְהוֹג נְשִׂיאוּתְךָ בְּרָמִים, [12]זְרוֹק מָרָה בַּתַּלְמִידִים׳״.

[13]אִינִי? [14]וְהָא כְּתִיב: ״וְאֶת יִרְאֵי ה׳ יְכַבֵּד״. [15]וְאָמַר מָר: זֶה יְהוֹשָׁפָט מֶלֶךְ יְהוּדָה. [16]כְּשֶׁהָיָה רוֹאֶה תַּלְמִיד חָכָם,

LITERAL TRANSLATION

great are the acts of Ḥiyya!" [1]Rabbi Shimon the son of Rabbi, said to him: "Even [greater] than yours?" [2]He said to him: "Yes." [3]Rabbi Yishmael the son of Rabbi Yose, said to Rabbi: "Even [greater] than father's?" [4]He said to him: "God forbid, let there not be such a thing in Israel."

[5]"He said to them: 'I need my younger son.' [6]Rabbi Shimon went in to him. [7]He transmitted to him the orders of wisdom. [8]He said to them: 'I need my eldest son.' [9]Rabban Gamliel went in to him. [10]And he transmitted to him the orders of the presidency. [11]He said to him: 'My son, conduct your presidency [together] with the exalted, [12][and] cast fear upon the disciples.'"

[13]Is this so? [14]But surely it is written: "But he honors them that fear the Lord." [15]And the Sage said: This is Jehoshafat the king of Judah. [16]When he saw a Torah scholar,

RASHI

לא תהא כדבר הזה בישראל – כלומר, שלא אומר כדבר זה לעולם. **נהוג נשיאותך ברמים** – שתהא יושב בין הגדולים. **זרוק מרה** – אימה, שתהא אימתך עליהם.

NOTES

אֲפִילּוּ מִמְּךָ Even greater than yours? It is similarly reported in the Jerusalem Talmud that Rabbi Yehudah HaNasi would demonstrate his respect to Rabbi Ḥiyya by asking him to enter the room before him.

נְהוֹג נְשִׂיאוּתְךָ בְּרָמִים Conduct your presidency with the exalted. *Maharsha* proposes that Rabbi Yehudah HaNasi advised his son to act presidentially even with respect to the "exalted," those who were men of importance. *Arukh* cites the reading: "Conduct your presidency with money [בְּדָמִים, rather than בְּרָמִים]," which the Geonim understood as follows: Conduct your presidency as if it were something of great value, which no one would part with except for a large sum of money. Or alternatively: Even if you receive money from the people, do not belittle yourself before them.

HALAKHAH

זְרוֹק מָרָה בַּתַּלְמִידִים Cast fear upon the disciples. "Even though the Sages said that someone who is particular about his honor will not succeed as a teacher, that only applies when the students do not understand a particularly difficult matter. But if a master sees that his disciples are not attending to their studies, he must show them his anger, and put them to shame in order to sharpen them," following the instructions left by Rabbi Yehudah HaNasi for his son Rabban Gamliel. (*Rambam, Sefer Mada, Hilkhot Talmud Torah* 4:5; *Shulḥan Arukh, Yoreh De'ah* 246:11.)

הָיָה עוֹמֵד מִכִּסְאוֹ וּמְחַבְּקוֹ וּמְנַשְּׁקוֹ, וְקוֹרֵא לוֹ: [1]רַבִּי, רַבִּי, מָרִי, מָרִי!
[2]לָא קַשְׁיָא. הָא בְּצִינְעָא. [3]הָא בְּפַרְהֶסְיָא.
[4]תַּנְיָא: רַבִּי מוּטָּל בְּצִיפּוֹרִי, [5]וּמָקוֹם מוּכָן לוֹ בְּבֵית שְׁעָרִים.
[6]וְהָתַנְיָא: "צֶדֶק צֶדֶק תִּרְדֹּף" — [7]הַלֵּךְ אַחַר רַבִּי לְבֵית שְׁעָרִים!
[8]רַבִּי בְּבֵית שְׁעָרִים הֲוָה, [9]אֶלָּא כֵּיוָן דַּחֲלַשׁ, אַמְטִיוּהִי לְצִיפּוֹרִי, [104A] דִּמְדַלְיָא, [10]וּבְסִים אֲוִירָא.
[11]הַהוּא יוֹמָא דְּנָח נַפְשֵׁיהּ דְּרַבִּי, גָּזְרוּ רַבָּנַן תַּעֲנִיתָא. [12]וּבָעוּ רַחֲמֵי. [13]וְאָמְרִי: "כָּל מַאן דְּאָמַר 'נָח נַפְשֵׁיהּ דְּרַבִּי' יִדָּקֵר בַּחֶרֶב". [14]סְלִיקָא אַמְתֵיהּ דְּרַבִּי לְאִיגְּרָא, אָמְרָה: [15]"עֶלְיוֹנִים מְבַקְּשִׁין אֶת רַבִּי, וְהַתַּחְתּוֹנִים מְבַקְּשִׁין אֶת רַבִּי.

LITERAL TRANSLATION

he would rise from his throne, and hug him, and kiss him, and call him: [1]"My teacher, my teacher, my master, my master"!

[2]It is not difficult. This, in private. [3]This, in public.

[4]It was taught: "Rabbi was lying [ill] in Sepphoris, [5]and a place [for burial] was ready for him in Bet She'arim."

[6]But surely it was taught: "'Justice, justice shall you pursue'— [7]follow Rabbi to Bet She'arim."

[8]Rabbi was in Bet She'arim,[9] but when he became ill, they moved him to Sepphoris, [104A] because it is higher, [10]and its air is pleasant.

[11]The day that Rabbi died the Rabbis decreed a fast, [12]and they prayed for mercy. [13]And they said: "Whoever says [that] Rabbi died will be pierced with a sword." [14]Rabbi's maidservant went up to the roof, [and] said: [15]"The heavenly creatures desire Rabbi, and the earthly creatures desire Rabbi.

RASHI

בצינעא — מכבד כל אחד ואחד. בפרהסיא — מטיל עליהם אימה, להודיע נשיאותו. רבי מוטל — בחליו בצפורי, ומקום קברו מוכן לו בבית שערים. דמדליא — דאמרינן במסכת מגילה (דף ו): למה נקרא שמה צפורי — שיושבת בראש ההר, כציפור.

TRANSLATION AND COMMENTARY

rise up from his throne, hug and kiss him, and call out to **him:** [1]**"My teacher, my teacher, my master, my master!"**

לָא קַשְׁיָא [2]The Gemara answers: **There is no difficulty. This** act of Jehoshafat is the way that a king or Nasi should relate to Torah scholars **in private,** [3]and the advice of Rabbi Yehudah HaNasi is the way he should relate to them **in public.**

תַּנְיָא [4]The Gemara continues: **It was taught** in a Baraita: **"Rabbi** Yehudah HaNasi **was lying** on his deathbed **in Sepphoris,** [5]**and a** burial **place was** made **ready for him in Bet She'arim."**

וְהָתַנְיָא [6]The Gemara asks: **But surely it was taught** otherwise in another Baraita: "The verse which states (Deuteronomy 16:21): **'Justice, justice shall you pursue,'** teaches that a person should seek out justice by following a great Torah scholar to the academy where he teaches. [7]This means that one should follow **Rabbi** Yehudah HaNasi **to Bet She'arim."** Thus, we see that Rabbi Yehudah HaNasi's permanent residence was in Bet She'arim, and not in Sepphoris!

רַבִּי [8]The Gemara answers: **Rabbi** Yehudah HaNasi indeed **lived in Bet She'arim,** [9]**but when he became ill, he was moved to Sepphoris** for medical reasons, [104A] **for** Sepphoris **is** situated at a **higher** altitude than Bet She'arim, [10]**and its climate is** more **pleasant.**

הַהוּא יוֹמָא [11]It was related that **the day that Rabbi** Yehudah HaNasi **died the Rabbis had decreed** to be observed as **a fast,** [12]**and** everybody **prayed for** God's **mercy,** so that Rabbi Yehudah HaNasi's would recover from his illness. [13]**And they said: "Whoever proclaims that Rabbi** Yehudah HaNasi **died will be pierced with a sword."** [14]**Rabbi** Yehudah HaNasi's **maidservant went up to the roof** of the house **and said:** [15]**"The heavenly creatures desire Rabbi** Yehudah HaNasi up in Heaven, **and the earthly creatures desire** him on earth.

BACKGROUND

בֵּית שְׁעָרִים **Bet She'arim.** Bet She'arim was a small city in the northwestern corner of the Jezreel valley, situated on what is known today as the hill of al-Sheikh Burayk. It served as the seat of the Sanhedrin during the days of Rabbi Yehudah HaNasi. Even though Rabbi Yehudah HaNasi moved in his later years to Sepphoris on account of his failing health, he was buried in Bet She'arim. It was apparently for this reason that the catacombs of Bet She'arim became an especially important burial place. For several hundred years, leading families in Eretz Israel and outside of it would bring their dead to Bet She'arim to be buried there. Bet She'arim's burial grounds were excavated in recent years, and many of the epitaphs and sarcophagi have survived intact.

NOTES

הָא בְּצִינְעָא; הָא בְּפַרְהֶסְיָא **This, in private; this in public.** The king must be severe with the Sages, for there is a special rule that the fear of the king must be cast upon his people. Just as it is forbidden for others to treat his position lightly, so too he himself must do nothing to compromise his own honor.

כָּל מַאן דְּאָמַר נָח נַפְשֵׁיהּ דְּרַבִּי **Whoever says that Rabbi died.** *Rivan* explains that the Sages did not want to be informed of Rabbi Yehudah HaNasi's death, because they wanted to pray for him, and they would not be able to continue to do so once they knew he was dead.

עֶלְיוֹנִים מְבַקְּשִׁין אֶת רַבִּי **The heavenly creatures desire Rabbi.** *Maharsha* explains that man has a heavenly side — his soul, and an earthly side — his body. Heaven and earth

HALAKHAH

הָא בְּצִינְעָא. הָא בְּפַרְהֶסְיָא **This, in private. This, in public.** "The king is obligated to honor Torah scholars. When the Sages of Israel appear before him, he must stand up before them, and seat them at his side. But this only applies inside the king's castle and out of the public eye. But in public, he may not stand up and show respect to anyone, so that his fear be cast on the whole nation. (*Rambam, Sefer Shofetim, Hilkhot Melakhim* 2:5.)

[1]יְהִי רָצוֹן שֶׁיָּכוֹפוּ תַּחְתּוֹנִים אֶת הָעֶלְיוֹנִים״. [2]כֵּיוָן דַּחֲזַאי כַּמָּה זִימְנֵי דְּעָיֵיל לְבֵית הַכִּסֵּא, וְחָלַץ תְּפִילִּין, וּמַנַּח לְהוּ, וְקָמִצְטַעֵר, [3]אָמְרָה: ״יְהִי רָצוֹן שֶׁיָּכוֹפוּ עֶלְיוֹנִים אֶת הַתַּחְתּוֹנִים״. [4]וְלָא הָווּ שָׁתְקֵי רַבָּנַן מִלְּמִיבָּעֵי רַחֲמֵי. [5]שָׁקְלָה כּוּזָא, שָׁדְיָיא מֵאִיגְּרָא [לְאַרְעָא], [6]אִישְׁתִּיקוּ מֵרַחֲמֵי. וְנָח נַפְשֵׁיהּ דְּרַבִּי. [7]אָמְרוּ לֵיהּ רַבָּנַן לְבַר קַפָּרָא: ״זִיל עַיֵּין״. [8]אֲזַל אַשְׁכַּחֵיהּ דְּנָח נַפְשֵׁיהּ. [9]קְרָעֵיהּ לִלְבוּשֵׁיהּ וְאַהַדְרֵיהּ לִקְרְעֵיהּ לַאֲחוֹרֵיהּ. [10]פָּתַח וְאָמַר: ״אֶרְאֶלִּים וּמְצוּקִים אָחֲזוּ בַּאֲרוֹן הַקֹּדֶשׁ. [11]נִצְּחוּ אֶרְאֶלִּים אֶת הַמְּצוּקִים, וְנִשְׁבָּה אֲרוֹן הַקֹּדֶשׁ״. [12]אָמְרוּ לֵיהּ: ״נָח נַפְשֵׁיהּ״? [13]אֲמַר לְהוּ: ״אַתּוּן קָאָמְרִיתוּ, וַאֲנָא לָא קָאָמִינָא״. [14]בִּשְׁעַת פְּטִירָתוֹ שֶׁל רַבִּי, זָקַף עֶשֶׂר אֶצְבְּעוֹתָיו כְּלַפֵּי מַעְלָה, [15]אָמַר: ״רִבּוֹנוֹ שֶׁל עוֹלָם, גָּלוּי

TRANSLATION AND COMMENTARY

[1]**May it be Your will that the earthly creatures overcome the heavenly creatures,** and that Rabbi Yehudah HaNasi remain among the living." [2]But **when she saw how many times he went to the outhouse, and** first **took off his tefillin, and** then **put them** back on again, **and** how he **suffered** from the intestinal illness that plagued him, [3]**she** altered her prayers and **said: "May it be Your will that the heavenly creatures overcome the earthly creatures,** and that Rabbi Yehudah be relieved of his misery, and laid to his final rest." [4]**But the Rabbis did not silence themselves and stop praying for** God's **mercy,** so that Rabbi Yehudah HaNasi would not be taken from them. [5]So the maidservant **took a pitcher, and cast it** down **from the roof to the ground,** and it smashed to pieces. [6]Alarmed by the sudden noise, the Rabbis **silenced themselves and** momentarily **stopped praying for** God's **mercy, and** in that interim **Rabbi** Yehudah HaNasi **died.** [7]**The Rabbis said to Bar Kappara: "Go** in **and check** on Rabbi Yehudah HaNasi's condition." [8]**He went** in, **and found that he had died.** [9]Bar Kappara immediately **rent his garment** as a sign of mourning, **but he** then **turned** the garment around so that **the rent** was **behind him,** and could not be seen. When he came out and reported back to the Rabbis, [10]**he began** to eulogize Rabbi Yehudah HaNasi **and said:** "Both **the angels and the mortals seized the Holy Ark,** [11]but in the end it was **the angels** who **defeated the mortals, and the Holy Ark was taken captive."** Unwilling to interpret this riddle on their own, [12]the Rabbis **asked** Bar Kappara outright: **"Did** Rabbi Yehudah HaNasi **die?"** Remembering that it had been decided earlier that nobody would announce Rabbi Yehudah HaNasi's death, [13]Bar Kappara **said to them: "You said it, not I."**

בִּשְׁעַת פְּטִירָתוֹ [14]It was further related that **at the time that** Rabbi Yehudah HaNasi **was dying, he pointed his ten fingers upwards** to Heaven, [15]**and said: "Master of the Universe, it is revealed and known to you that**

LITERAL TRANSLATION

[1]May it be [Your] will that the earthly creatures overcome the heavenly creatures." [2]When she saw how many times he went to the outhouse, and took off his tefillin, and put them on, and was in distress, [3]she said: "May it be [Your] will that the heavenly creatures overcome the earthly creatures." [4]But the Rabbis did not silence themselves [and refrain] from praying for mercy. [5]She took a pitcher, [and] cast it from the roof to the ground, [6][and] they silenced themselves, [refraining] from [praying for] mercy. [7]And Rabbi died. The Rabbis said to Bar Kappara: "Go [and] check." [8]He went, [and] found that he died. [9]He rent his garment, and turned the rent behind him. [10]He began (lit., "opened") and said: "The angels and the mortals seized the Holy Ark. [11]The angels defeated the mortals, and the Holy Ark was taken captive." [12]They said to him: "Did he die?" [13]He said to them: "You said it, but I did not say it."
[14]At the time of Rabbi's passing, he pointed his ten fingers upwards, [15][and] said: "Master of the Universe, it is revealed

RASHI

דעל כמה זימנין לבית הכסא – דחולי מעיים הוה ליה. **וחלץ תפילין ומנח להו** – וקא מצטער לחלוץ ולהניח. **פתח ואמר** – הספד. **אראלים ומצוקים** – מלאכים וצדיקים מצוקי ארץ.

NOTES

fought over Rabbi Yehudah HaNasi. On the one hand, Rabbi Yehudah HaNasi's soul would reach new spiritual heights once it was separated from his body, but on the other hand, only when it is linked to his body could it perform God's will on earth. By breaking the earthenware pitcher so that it no longer had any use, the maidservant hinted Rabbi Yehudah HaNasi's broken body and impending death (see Ecclesiastes 12:6).

אֶרְאֶלִּים וּמְצוּקִים **The angels and the mortals.** The term *er'elim* refers to the angels, as the verse states (Isaiah 33:7): "Behold, the *er'elim* shall cry outside, angels of peace shall weep bitterly." And the term *metzukim* refers to the righteous, as the verse states (I Samuel 2:8): "For the pillars (*metzukei*) of the earth are the Lord's, and He has set the world upon them," and as is stated elsewhere that the righteous are the foundation of the world (see *Rashi* and *Rivan*).

TRANSLATION AND COMMENTARY

all my life **I labored with my ten fingers** in the study of Torah and performance of the commandments, **and** all that time **I did not** derive **benefit from** the labor of **even one small finger.** [1]**May it be Your will that there will be peace in my rest."** [2]**A heavenly voice issued forth** immediately, **and said** in the words of the Prophet Isaiah (57:2): [3]**"He shall come in peace; they shall rest in their graves."**

עַל מִשְׁכָּבְךָ [4]The Gemara asks: But surely the heavenly voice **should have said:** "He shall come in peace; he shall rest **in his grave."**

מְסַיַּיע לֵיהּ [5]The Gemara answers: **This** formulation **supports Rabbi Ḥiyya bar Gamda, for Rabbi Ḥiyya bar Gamda said in the name of Rabbi Yose ben Shaul:** [6]**When a righteous man departs from the world, the ministrating angels say before the Holy One, blessed is He:** [7]**"Master of the Universe, the righteous man, so-and-so, has come** to Heaven." [8]God then **says to** the angels: **"Let the righteous men** who have already passed away **come and go to meet** the newcomer. [9]They **say to him: 'He shall come in peace, and then** those other righteous men can again **rest in their graves.'"**

אָמַר רַבִּי אֶלְעָזָר [10]**Rabbi Elazar said: When a righteous man departs from the world, three groups of ministrating angels go out to meet him,** and they greet him with the words of Isaiah (57:2). [11]**One** group **says to him: "Come in peace."** [12]**The second** group **says** to him: **"He that walks in his righteousness."** [13]**And the third** group

וְיָדוּעַ לְפָנֶיךָ שֶׁיָּגַעְתִּי בְּעֶשֶׂר אֶצְבְּעוֹתַי בַּתּוֹרָה, וְלֹא נֶהֱנֵיתִי אֲפִילּוּ בְּאֶצְבַּע קְטַנָּה. [1]יְהִי רָצוֹן מִלְּפָנֶיךָ שֶׁיְּהֵא שָׁלוֹם בִּמְנוּחָתִי". [2]יָצְתָה בַּת קוֹל, וְאָמְרָה: [3]"יָבֹא שָׁלוֹם, יָנוּחוּ עַל מִשְׁכְּבוֹתָם".

[4]"עַל מִשְׁכָּבְךָ" מִיבָּעֵי לֵיהּ!

[5]מְסַיַּיע לֵיהּ לְרַבִּי חִיָּיא בַּר גַּמְדָּא, דְּאָמַר רַבִּי חִיָּיא בַּר גַּמְדָּא אָמַר רַבִּי יוֹסֵי בֶּן שָׁאוּל: [6]בְּשָׁעָה שֶׁהַצַּדִּיק נִפְטָר מִן הָעוֹלָם, אוֹמְרִים מַלְאֲכֵי הַשָּׁרֵת לִפְנֵי הַקָּדוֹשׁ בָּרוּךְ הוּא: [7]"רִבּוֹנוֹ שֶׁל עוֹלָם, צַדִּיק פְּלוֹנִי בָּא". [8]אוֹמֵר לָהֶם: "יָבוֹאוּ צַדִּיקִים וְיֵצְאוּ לִקְרָאתוֹ, [9]וְאוֹמְרִים לוֹ: 'יָבֹא בְשָׁלוֹם, יָנוּחוּ עַל מִשְׁכְּבוֹתָם'".

[10]אָמַר רַבִּי אֶלְעָזָר: בְּשָׁעָה שֶׁהַצַּדִּיק נִפְטָר מִן הָעוֹלָם, שָׁלֹשׁ כִּיתּוֹת שֶׁל מַלְאֲכֵי הַשָּׁרֵת יוֹצְאוֹת לִקְרָאתוֹ. [11]אַחַת אוֹמֶרֶת לוֹ: "בֹּא בְשָׁלוֹם". [12]וְאַחַת אוֹמֶרֶת: "הוֹלֵךְ נְכֹחוֹ". [13]וְאַחַת אוֹמֶרֶת

LITERAL TRANSLATION

and known to you that I labored with my ten fingers in Torah, and I did not benefit with even the small finger. [1]May it be Your will that there will be peace in my rest." [2]A heavenly voice issued forth, and said: [3]"He shall come in peace, they shall rest in their graves." [4]It should have said: "In your grave"! [5]This supports Rabbi Ḥiyya bar Gamda, for Rabbi Ḥiyya bar Gamda said in the name of Rabbi Yose ben Shaul: [6]When a righteous man departs from the world, the ministrating angels say before the Holy One, blessed is He: [7]"Master of the Universe, the righteous man, so-and-so, has come." [8]He says to them: "Let the righteous men come and go out to meet him, [9]and say to him: 'He shall come in peace; [and then] they shall rest in their graves.'" [10]Rabbi Elazar said: When a righteous man departs from the world, three groups of ministrating angels go out to meet him. [11]One says to him: "Come in peace." [12]And one says: "He that walks in his righteousness." [13]And one says

RASHI

ולא נהניתי בעולם הזה – [אפילו] לפי טורח שיגעתי באצבע קטנה שלי. **יבואו צדיקים ויצאו לקראתו ויבא בשלום** – ואחר כך ינוחו צדיקים על משכבותם. **הולך נכחו** – בדרך ישרה.

NOTES

לֹא נֶהֱנֵיתִי אֲפִילּוּ בְּאֶצְבַּע קְטַנָּה I did not benefit with even the small finger. *Rivan* explains that Rabbi Yehudah HaNasi meant that even though he labored with his ten fingers, meaning with all his strength, in the study of Torah, he did not derive benefit from the labor of even one small finger. *Tosafot* understand that Rabbi Yehudah HaNasi meant that he did not enjoy any worldly pleasures whatsoever. Elsewhere, *Tosafot* note that while it is reported that Rabbi Yehudah HaNasi was extremely wealthy and nothing was ever missing from his table, he himself did not derive any pleasure from all his riches.

שֶׁיְּהֵא שָׁלוֹם בִּמְנוּחָתִי That there will be peace in my rest. *Ri'af* explains that the Sages say that sometimes a righteous man will die so that he is spared the calamities that are about to fall on the world, and sometimes he dies to atone for the sins of the generation. Thus Rabbi Yehudah HaNasi asked that there be peace in his rest, meaning that his death should be an atonement and that there would be peace in the world after his passing.

שָׁלֹשׁ כִּיתּוֹת Three groups. *Be'er HaGolah* writes that these three groups of ministering angels and their three statements correspond to the three aspects of man's activity in this world — thought, speech, and action.

הוֹלֵךְ נְכֹחוֹ He that walks in righteousness. *Rashi* understands this verse as referring to the past: Throughout his life the saintly man walked in the straight path, the path

TRANSLATION AND COMMENTARY

says to him: "He shall come in peace, they shall rest in their graves." [1]On the other hand, when an evil man perishes from the world, three groups of angels of destruction go out to meet him, and they greet him with the words of the prophets. [2]One group says to him: "There is no peace, says the Lord, for the wicked (Isaiah 48:22)." [3]The second group says to him: "You shall lie down in sorrow (see Isaiah 50:11)." [4]And the third group says to him: "Go down, and be laid with the uncircumcised (Ezekiel 32:19)."

MISHNAH כָּל זְמַן [5]When a widow **lives in her father's house,** and is being maintained there by her late husband's heirs, **she may collect her ketubah** settlement, **whenever she so desires.** [6]But **when she** spends her widowhood **in her** late **husband's house,** so that she has access to the property of her husband's estate, **she may** only **collect her ketubah** settlement **for up to twenty-five years** from her husband's death. [7]**For** we assume that **in** the course of those **twenty-five years, she** must have **done favors** for others and given them food or spices belonging to her husband's estate, the combined value of which **corresponds to** the value of **her ketubah** settlement, she is regarded as having already received it. [8]**This is the position of Rabbi Meir who said** what he said **in the name of Rabban Shimon ben Gamliel.**

לוֹ: "יָבֹא שָׁלוֹם, יָנוּחוּ עַל מִשְׁכְּבוֹתָם". [1]בְּשָׁעָה שֶׁהָרָשָׁע נֶאֱבָד מִן הָעוֹלָם, שָׁלֹשׁ כִּיתּוֹת שֶׁל מַלְאֲכֵי חַבָּלָה יוֹצְאוֹת לִקְרָאתוֹ. [2]אַחַת אוֹמֶרֶת: "אֵין שָׁלוֹם, אָמַר ה׳ לָרְשָׁעִים". [3]וְאַחַת אוֹמֶרֶת לוֹ: "לְמַעֲצֵבָה יִשְׁכָּב". [4]וְאַחַת אוֹמֶרֶת לוֹ: "רְדָה, וְהָשְׁכְּבָה אֶת עֲרֵלִים".

משנה [5]כָּל זְמַן שֶׁהִיא בְּבֵית אָבִיהָ, גּוֹבָה כְּתוּבָּתָהּ לְעוֹלָם. [6]כָּל זְמַן שֶׁהִיא בְּבֵית בַּעְלָהּ, גּוֹבָה כְּתוּבָּתָהּ עַד עֶשְׂרִים וְחָמֵשׁ שָׁנִים, [7]שֶׁיֵּשׁ בְּעֶשְׂרִים וְחָמֵשׁ שָׁנִים שֶׁתַּעֲשֶׂה טוֹבָה כְּנֶגֶד כְּתוּבָּתָהּ. [8]דִּבְרֵי רַבִּי מֵאִיר שֶׁאָמַר מִשּׁוּם רַבָּן שִׁמְעוֹן בֶּן גַּמְלִיאֵל.

LITERAL TRANSLATION

to him: "He shall come in peace, they shall rest in their graves." [1]When an evil man perishes from the world, three groups of angels of destruction go out to meet him. [2]One says: "There is no peace, says the Lord, for the wicked." [3]And one says to him: "You shall lie down in sorrow." [4]And one says to him: "Go down, and be laid with the uncircumcised."

MISHNAH [5]As long as she is in her father's house, she may collect her ketubah at any time (lit., "forever"). [6]As long as she is in her husband's house, she may collect her ketubah up to twenty-five years, [7]for over twenty-five years she does favors corresponding to her ketubah. [8][These are] the words of Rabbi Meir who said in the name of Rabban Shimon ben Gamliel.

RASHI

משנה כל זמן שהיא בבית אביה — והיורשים זנוה שם. גובה כתובתה — כשתרצה. שתעשה טובה — מנכסי יתומים נותנת לחם ומלח לשכניה.

NOTES

of righteousness. *Rivan* suggests that the verse refers to the present: The righteous man will continue to walk in the straight path, and be rewarded in accordance with his good deeds.

שֶׁתַּעֲשֶׂה טוֹבָה She does favors. Whenever the widow derives benefit from the heirs' property to which she has no right, she is regarded as having received a portion of her ketubah settlement to the value of that benefit. It may be asked: If so, then even when her husband was living, she would forfeit her ketubah settlement after twenty-five years, for surely she does favors for people with her husband's property! *Rabbenu Crescas Vidal* suggests that during her husband's lifetime the husband makes sure that she does not spend any money to which she is not entitled. Or alternatively, during his lifetime the husband waives his right to all that she spends on favors to outsiders.

עֶשְׂרִים וְחָמֵשׁ שָׁנִים Twenty-five years. Some of the Geonim try to explain how the Sages arrived at the figure of twenty-five years. They suggest that each year the woman spends a sela on favors, which is one twenty-fifth of the settlement due to a woman who was a virgin at the time of her marriage (two hundred dinars, or twenty-five selas). But the Tosefta records a different figure, and states that the widow forfeits her settlement after thirty years. It would therefore appear that these figures are simply rough assessments of how long it takes for the widow to consume her ketubah settlement doing favors for others.

HALAKHAH

כָּל זְמַן שֶׁהִיא בְּבֵית אָבִיהָ As long as she is in her father's house. "In a place where it is not customary for a ketubah deed to be written, and the widow was living in her late husband's house, she is entitled to collect her settlement at any time. If she was living in her father's house, she may only collect it for up to twenty-five years. But if she allowed twenty-five years to pass without demanding her settlement, her years of silence are understood as a waiver," following the Sages of our Mishnah. (*Rambam, Sefer Nashim, Hilkhot Ishut* 16:21-23; *Shulḥan Arukh, Even HaEzer* 101:1.)

PEOPLE

מַרְתָּא בַּת בַּיְיתוֹס Marta the daughter of Baitos. Marta the daughter of Baitos was one of the exceedingly wealthy women living in Jerusalem. She might have been a member of the Baitos family that is listed among the families of High Priests in *Pesahim* 57a. After having once been widowed, Marta married Yehoshua ben Gamla, and by way of her wealth and influence brought about his appointment to the High Priesthood. Marta seems to have lived until the very end of the Second Temple period, when, despite her great wealth, she died of starvation (*Gittin* 56a).

TRANSLATION AND COMMENTARY

וַחֲכָמִים אוֹמְרִים [1]**But the Sages say** just the opposite: [2]**When** a widow **lives in her** late **husband's house, she may collect her ketubah** settlement **at any time.** For we say that since the woman was treated well by her husband's heirs, she was too embarrassed to demand her settlement from them. [3]But **when she** spends her widowhood **in her father's house, she may** only **collect her ketubah** settlement **for up to twenty-five years** from her husband's death, for we assume that a woman who allows twenty-five years to pass without demanding her ketubah settlement has waived her right to collect it. [4]If the widow **died,** the woman's **heirs may demand her ketubah** settlement from her late husband's heirs **for up to twenty-five years.**

GEMARA אָמַר לֵיהּ [5]**Abaye asked Rav Yosef:** Rabbi Meir maintains that over twenty-five years the widow does favors for other people with her late husband's property, the accumulated value of which corresponds to her ketubah settlement. [6]Does it stand to reason that **the poorest woman in Israel** who has only a small ketubah settlement forfeits it because of the benefit that she derives from her husband's property **for twenty-five years,** [7]**and** so too a wealthy woman like **Marta the daughter of Baitos** who has a very large ketubah settlement forfeits it because of the benefit that she derives from her late husband's property **over twenty-five years?** Surely it should take the wealthy woman much longer to drive benefit from her husband's property equal in value to her much larger ketubah settlement!

אָמַר לֵיהּ [8]Rav Yosef **said to** Abaye: People say: **According to** the strength of **the camel** — so is the size of **its burden.** A wealthy woman may have a larger ketubah settlement than a poor woman, but she also does more and larger favors for her neighbors than the poor woman.

אִיבַּעְיָא לְהוּ [9]**The following problem arose in discussion** of our Mishnah among the Sages: **According to Rabbi Meir** who maintains that after twenty-five years a widow is regarded as having received her ketubah

[1]וַחֲכָמִים אוֹמְרִים: [2]כָּל זְמַן שֶׁהִיא בְּבֵית בַּעְלָהּ, גּוֹבָה כְּתוּבָּתָהּ לְעוֹלָם, [3]כָּל זְמַן שֶׁהִיא בְּבֵית אָבִיהָ, גּוֹבָה כְּתוּבָּתָהּ עַד עֶשְׂרִים וְחָמֵשׁ שָׁנִים. [4]מֵתָה, יוֹרְשֶׁיהָ מַזְכִּירִין כְּתוּבָּתָהּ עַד עֶשְׂרִים וְחָמֵשׁ שָׁנִים.

גמרא [5]אָמַר לֵיהּ אַבַּיֵי לְרַב יוֹסֵף: [6]עֲנִיָּיה שֶׁבְּיִשְׂרָאֵל — עַד עֶשְׂרִים וְחָמֵשׁ שָׁנִים, [7]וּמַרְתָּא בַּת בַּיְיתוֹס — עַד עֶשְׂרִים וְחָמֵשׁ שָׁנִים? [8]אָמַר לֵיהּ: לְפוּם גַּמְלָא שִׁיחֲנָא. [9]אִיבַּעְיָא לְהוּ: לְרַבִּי מֵאִיר,

LITERAL TRANSLATION

[1]And the Sages say: [2]As long as she is in her husband's house, she collects her ketubah at any time. [3]As long as she is in her father's house, she collects her ketubah up to twenty-five years. [4][If] she died, her heirs mention her ketubah up to twenty-five years.

GEMARA [5]Abaye said to Rav Yosef: [6]The poorest woman in Israel — up to twenty-five years, [7]and Marta the daughter of Baitos — up to twenty-five years?

[8]He said to him: According to the camel the burden.

[9]It was asked of them: According to Rabbi Meir,

RASHI

וחכמים אומרים — לא הוזכרו עשרים וחמש לענין הטובה שמעשה, ולא אפסדוה רבנן כתובה. וכשהוזכרו עשרים וחמש — לענין המחילה הוזכרו; דהואיל ושתקה ולא תבעה כל השנים הללו — מחלתה. הלכך, כל זמן שהיא בבית בעלה — אין שתיקתה מחילה, אלא מפני שמכבדין אותה היא בושה למחות על כתובתה. אבל בבית אביה, משתקה עשרים וחמש שנים — מחילה היא. **מתה יורשיה מזכירין כתובתה כו'** — כלומר, צריכה למחות על כתובתה בתוך עשרים וחמש שנים.

גמרא **ענייה שבישראל** — שכתובתה מועטת, אידה לרבי מאיר בטובה שעושה בעשרים וחמש שנים. **ומרתא בת בייתוס** — שהיתה עשירה, וכתובתה מרובה — תפסיד כתובתה בטובה של עשרים וחמש שנים. **לפום גמלא שיחנא** — המשוי לפי הגמל. אף כאן, לפי עושרה טובתה.

NOTES

כָּל זְמַן שֶׁהִיא בְּבֵית אָבִיהָ As long as she is in her husband's heirs' home. According to the Sages, we are not concerned about how much money the widow spent on favors performed for others, for the heirs would be ready to waive those amounts, and might even want the woman to perform favors for others with their money (*Meiri*).

יוֹרְשֶׁיהָ מַזְכִּירִין כְּתוּבָּתָהּ עַד עֶשְׂרִים וְחָמֵשׁ שָׁנִים Her heirs mention her ketubah settlement up to twenty-five years. Some understand that this means that the widow's heirs can demand her ketubah settlement for up to twenty-five years from her husband's death. Others explain that they can demand their mother's ketubah for up to twenty-five years after her death (see *Melekhet Shlomo* and others).

מַזְכִּירִין כְּתוּבָּתָהּ They mention her ketubah settlement. *Rivan* understands this to mean that the heirs must demand their mother's ketubah settlement within twenty-five years. Others understand the word מַזְכִּירִין according to its literal sense, "mention": The woman's heirs are not required to demand their mother's ketubah within twenty-five years. Rather they must mention their intention to collect to her husband's heirs during that period, in order to show that they have not forgiven the debt (*Rabbi Crescas Vidal, Ran*).

¹מַהוּ שֶׁתְּשַׁלֵּשׁ?
²תֵּיקוּ.
³״וַחֲכָמִים אוֹמְרִים: כָּל זְמַן״.
⁴אֲמַר לֵיהּ אַבַּיֵי לְרַב יוֹסֵף: אֲתַאי קוֹדֶם שְׁקִיעַת הַחַמָּה, ⁵גּוֹבָה כְּתוּבָּתָהּ; ⁶לְאַחַר שְׁקִיעַת הַחַמָּה, לָא גָּבְיָא. ⁷בְּהַהִיא פּוּרְתָּא אַחֵילְתָּא!
⁸אֲמַר לֵיהּ: אִין. כָּל מִדַּת חֲכָמִים כֵּן הִיא. ⁹בְּאַרְבָּעִים סְאָה, טוֹבֵל. ¹⁰בְּאַרְבָּעִים סְאָה חָסֵר קוֹרְטוֹב, אֵינוֹ יָכוֹל לִטְבּוֹל בָּהֶן.
¹¹אֲמַר רַב יְהוּדָה אֲמַר רַב: הֵעִיד רַבִּי יִשְׁמָעֵאל בְּרַבִּי יוֹסֵי לִפְנֵי רַבִּי שֶׁאָמַר מִשּׁוּם אָבִיו: ¹²לֹא שָׁנוּ אֶלָּא שֶׁאֵין שְׁטַר כְּתוּבָּה יוֹצֵא מִתַּחַת יָדֶיהָ.

LITERAL TRANSLATION

¹what about decreasing [the ketubah]? ²Let [the question] stand [unresolved]. ³"And the Sages say: As long as." ⁴Abaye said to Rav Yosef: [If] she came before sunset, ⁵she collects her ketubah; ⁶after sunset, she does not collect. ⁷During that short [time] she waived [her rights]? ⁸He said to him: Yes. All the measures of the Sages are like that. ⁹In forty *se'ahs* he immerses himself. ¹⁰In forty *se'ahs* minus a *kortov*, he may not immerse himself in them. ¹¹Rav Yehudah said in the name of Rav: Rabbi Yishmael the son of Rabbi Yose testified before Rabbi that he said in the name of his father: ¹²They only taught [this twenty-five year restriction] when a ketubah deed does not go out from under her hands.

TRANSLATION AND COMMENTARY

settlement by way of the benefit which she derived from her husband's property over that period, ¹**do we decrease** the size of the widow's ketubah settlement in proportion to the time that had passed since her husband's death? Does she lose one twenty-fifth of her ketubah settlement for each of these years?

תֵּיקוּ ²Not having any apparent solution, the Gemara concludes: Let this **question stand unanswered.**

וַחֲכָמִים אוֹמְרִים ³We learned in our Mishnah: **"The Sages say: When** a widow lives in her late husband's house, she may collect her ketubah settlement at any time. But when she spends her widowhood in her father's house, she may only collect it for up to twenty-five years after her husband's death. ⁴**Abaye asked Rav Yosef:** The Mishnah implies that **if** the widow **came** and demanded her ketubah settlement **before sunset** of the last day of the twenty-fifth year, ⁵**she may** indeed **collect her ketubah** settlement, because she did not waive it. ⁶But if she came and demanded it **after sunset** of that day, **she may not collect** it, because we assume that she did indeed waive it. ⁷Now is it reasonable to assume that **during that short time** — while the sun was setting — the widow **waived** the right to collect her ketubah settlement?

אֲמַר לֵיהּ ⁸Rav Yosef **said to** Abaye: **Yes. All the standards** and measures taught by **the Sages are like that:** If the designated measure is met, the law is one way, but if it is not, the law is another way. ⁹For example, **a person can immerse himself in forty *se'ahs*** of water and be cleansed of ritual impurity. ¹⁰But, **he may not immerse himself in forty *se'ahs* minus a *kortov*** of water and be cleansed of ritual impurity.

אֲמַר רַב יְהוּדָה ¹¹**Rav Yehudah said in the name of Rav: Rabbi Yishmael the son of Rabbi Yose testified before Rabbi** Yehudah HaNasi **that** Rabbi Yishmael **said in the name of his father** Rabbi Yose: The Sages' position that a widow living in her father's house may collect her ketubah settlement only for twenty-five years ¹²**only applies when** the woman **does not have a ketubah deed in her hand,** such as in a community

RASHI

מהו שתשלש – לרבי מאיר, דטעמא משום טובה. **שתשלש** – שנחשוב טובתה לחשבון כתובתה לפי חשבון השנים, להפסיד לכל שנה אחת מעשרים וחמש בכתובתה, אם לא שהתה עשרים וחמש שנים אלא חציין, או שלישית או רביעית. **תשלש** – לשון חלוקה לפי חשבון הוא, כדתנן (מכות ה,א): משלשין בממון ואין משלשין במכות. **כל מדת חכמים כן** – העמידוה יחד ולא תמוט.

NOTES

מַהוּ שֶׁתְּשַׁלֵּשׁ What about adjusting. The Rishonim note: If Rabbi Meir maintains that the widow forfeits her ketubah settlement after twenty-five years, because we assume that in that time she must have done favors for her neighbors with property belonging to her husband's estate, the accumulated value of which corresponds to the value of her ketubah settlement. It stands to reason that we should adjust the size of the widow's ketubah settlement in proportion to the time that passed since her husband's death. According to *Talmidei Rabbenu Yonah,* even Rabbi Meir agrees that the widow's forfeiture of her ketubah settlement is based on her waiver: Since she benefited from the heirs' property for twenty-five years, she is ready to waive her right to a settlement. But before twenty-five years have passed, she might not be ready to waive any of her ketubah settlement. Therefore, the Gemara asks whether or not we adjust the size of her settlement to reflect the time that passed since her husband's death. *Rid* explains that the Gemara thinks that the widow does not forfeit her settlement unless the benefit she derived corresponds to its value. But if the benefit that she derived corresponds to only a fraction of her settlement, since she can surely still collect the rest of it, perhaps she can still collect it all.

TRANSLATION AND COMMENTARY

in which it is not customary for a ketubah deed to be written. [1]**But when** the woman **has a ketubah deed in her hand, she may** indeed **collect her ketubah** settlement **at any time.** [2]**Rabbi Elazar** disagreed and **said: Even if** the woman **has a ketubah deed in her hand,** [3]**she may** still **only collect** her ketubah **for up to twenty-five years.**

מְתִיב רַב שֵׁשֶׁת [4]**Rav Sheshet** raised an **objection** to what Rav Yehudah said in the name of Rav from the following Baraita: **"A creditor may collect** the money that is owed him even if many years have passed since the payment was due, and even **if he did not remind** his debtor that he still expects payment." [5]**How do we visualize the case?** [6]**If** you say that the Baraita is dealing with a creditor who **does not possess a bill** of indebtedness against his debtor, there is a difficulty, for without such a bill, **with what does he collect** if the debtor denies liability? [7]**Rather,** the Baraita must be dealing with a creditor who **holds a bill** of indebtedness against his debtor. [8]**And** the Baraita implies that **it is** only **a creditor** who may collect his debt no matter how much time had elapsed, for **he is not likely to have waived** the money owed him. [9]**But a widow** may not collect her ketubah settlement after a certain amount of time has passed since her husband's death. For even if she holds her ketubah deed, we assume that after so many years she must have **waived** it.

הוּא מוֹתִיב לָהּ [10]Rav Sheshet **raised the objection, and he resolved** the difficulty: [11]The Baraita is **in fact** dealing with a creditor who **does not hold a bill of indebtedness** against his debtor. [12]**And we are dealing here with a debtor** who **admits** that he owes the money. The Baraita teaches that a creditor may always collect the money owed him, for he is not likely to have forgiven the debt. But a widow who does not possess a ketubah deed may not collect her ketubah settlement twenty-five years subsequent to after her husband's death, even if his heirs admit that she had not been paid. For we assume that after so many years, she must have waived it. But a widow who possesses a ketubah deed may indeed collect her ketubah settlement at any time, for we assume that holding the deed, she would not have waived her settlement.

[1]אֲבָל שְׁטַר כְּתוּבָּה יוֹצֵא מִתַּחַת יָדֶיהָ, גּוֹבָה כְּתוּבָּתָהּ לְעוֹלָם. [2]וְרַבִּי אֶלְעָזָר אָמַר: אֲפִילּוּ שְׁטַר כְּתוּבָּה יוֹצֵא מִתַּחַת יָדֶיהָ, [3]אֵינָהּ גּוֹבָה אֶלָּא עַד עֶשְׂרִים וְחָמֵשׁ שָׁנִים.

[4]מְתִיב רַב שֵׁשֶׁת: "בַּעַל חוֹב גּוֹבֶה שֶׁלֹּא בְּהַזְכָּרָה". [5]הֵיכִי דָּמֵי? [6]אִי דְּלָא נָקֵט שְׁטָרָא, בְּמַאי גָּבֵי? [7]אֶלָּא, דְּנָקֵיט שְׁטָרָא. [8]וּבַעַל חוֹב הוּא דְּלָאו בַּר אַחוּלֵי הוּא. [9]הָא אַלְמָנָה אַחֵילְתָּא!

[10]הוּא מוֹתִיב לָהּ, וְהוּא מְפָרֵק לָהּ: [11]לְעוֹלָם, דְּלָא נָקֵיט שְׁטָרָא. [12]וְהָכָא בְּמַאי עָסְקִינַן כְּשֶׁחַיָּיב מוֹדֶה.

LITERAL TRANSLATION

[1]But [when] a ketubah deed goes out from under her hands — she can collect her ketubah at any time. [2]And Rabbi Elazar said: Even if a ketubah deed goes out from under her hands, [3]she can only collect up to twenty-five years.

[4]Rav Sheshet objected: "A creditor collects without a reminder." [5]How do we visualize the case (lit., "what is it like?") [6]If he does not hold a bill [of indebtedness], with what does he collect? [7]Rather, [it is] when he holds a bill. [8]And it is a creditor who is not likely to waive. [9]But a widow — waives!

[10]He asked it, and he resolved it: [11]In fact, [it is] where he does not hold a bill. [12]And here we are dealing with [a case] where the liable one admits [to the debt].

RASHI

אבל שטר כתובה יוצא – בבית דין מתחת ידה. **גובה כתובתה לעולם** – שאילו מחלתה, היתה מוסרת להם שטר הכתובה. **שלא בהזכרה** – אם שתק עשרים וחמש שנים, ולא מיחה על חובו – לא הפסיד בכך. **אלמנה בת אחולי היא** – שנהנית מהן כל השנים הללו, וכתובתה אינה מלוה, ולא חיסרה בה ממון. **לעולם דלא נקיט** – הלכך דווקא בעל חוב, הא אלמנה דלא נקטא שטרא – אחילתה. ודקשיא לך: במאי גביא? – כשחייב מודה.

NOTES

שְׁטַר כְּתוּבָּה יוֹצֵא מִתַּחַת יָדֶיהָ **A ketubah deed goes out from under her hands.** *Rivan* explains that when the widow possesses a ketubah deed, she is not concerned that she will not be able to collect the settlement, and so her twenty-five years of silence on the matter does not testify to a waiver.

HALAKHAH

אֲבָל שְׁטַר כְּתוּבָּה יוֹצֵא מִתַּחַת יָדֶיהָ **But where a ketubah deed goes out from under her hands.** "If a widow has her ketubah deed in her possession, she may take an oath and collect her settlement at any time, even after twenty-five years," following Rabbi Yose. (*Rambam, Sefer Nashim, Hilkhot Ishut* 16:21; *Shulḥan Arukh, Even HaEzer* 101:1.)

בַּעַל חוֹב גּוֹבֶה שֶׁלֹּא בְּהַזְכָּרָה **A creditor collects without a reminder.** "When a creditor presents his debtor with an authenticated promissory note, the debtor is obligated to

[1] וְהָאָמַר רַבִּי אֶלְעָא: שׁוֹנִין: [2] "גְּרוּשָׁה הֲרֵי הִיא כְּבַעַל חוֹב". [3] הֵיכִי דָּמֵי? [4] אִי דְּלָא נְקִיטָא כְּתוּבָּה, בְּמַאי גָּבְיָא? [5] אֶלָּא, לָאו דִּנְקִיטָא כְּתוּבָּה? [6] וּגְרוּשָׁה הִיא דְּלָאו בַּת אַחוּלֵי הִיא. [7] הָא אַלְמָנָה אַחֵילְתָא! [8] הָכָא נַמִי, כְּשֶׁחַיָּיב מוֹדֶה. [9] אֲמַר רַב נַחְמָן בַּר יִצְחָק: [10] תָּנֵי רַב יְהוּדָה בַּר קָזָא בְּמַתְנִיתָא דְּבֵי בַּר קָזָא: [11] "תָּבְעָה כְּתוּבָּתָהּ,

LITERAL TRANSLATION

[1] But surely Rabbi El'a said: They teach: [2] "A divorcee is like a creditor. [3] "How do we visualize the case? [4] If she does not hold a ketubah, with what does she collect? [5] Rather, is it not when she holds a ketubah? [6] And it is a divorcee who is not likely to waive. [7] But a widow — waives.

[8] Here too, where the liable one admits.

[9] Rav Naḥman bar Yitzḥak said: [10] Rav Yehudah bar Kaza taught in the Baraita of the academy of Bar Kaza: [11] "[If] she claimed her ketubah,

TRANSLATION AND COMMENTARY

וְהָאָמַר רַבִּי אֶלְעָא [1] **But surely Rabbi El'a said:** The Sages **taught** in a Baraita: [2] "**A divorcee is like a creditor,** and so she may forever collect her ketubah settlement no matter how much time has passed since her divorce, even if she did not remind her husband that he still owes her the money. For we assume that a divorcee does not waive her ketubah." [3] **How do we visualize the case?** [4] If you say that the Baraita is dealing with a woman who **does not possess a ketubah** deed, there is a difficulty, for without such a deed, **with what does she collect** her ketubah settlement? The document is evidence of his obligation, if the ex-husband says it was paid. [5] **Rather, it must be** that the Baraita is dealing with a woman who **holds her ketubah** deed in her hand. [6] **And** the Baraita implies that **it is** only **a divorcee** who may collect her ketubah settlement, whenever she wishes, for **she is not likely to have waived** the debt. [7] **But a widow** may not collect her ketubah settlement after an extensive period has passed since her husband's death. For even if she possesses her ketubah deed, we assume that after so many years she must have **waived it**, contrary to what Rav Yehudah said in the name of Rav!

הָכָא נַמִי [8] The Gemara replies: **Here too** you can say that the Baraita is dealing with a divorcee who does not possess her ketubah deed, but **the liable one,** her husband, **admits** that she never received her settlement. A divorcee may collect her ketubah settlement at any time, for it is unlikely that she would have waived it. But a widow who does not have her ketubah deed may not collect her settlement after twenty-five years, even if her husband's heirs admit that she did not receive it. After so many years, we assume that she must have waived it. But if the widow has kept her ketubah deed, she too may collect her ketubah settlement at any time, for in such a case we assume that she did not waive it.

אֲמַר [9] **Rav Naḥman bar Yitzḥak said:** [10] **Rav Yehudah bar Kaza taught in a Baraita** that was taught in **the academy of Bar Kaza:** [11] "If a widow **claimed her ketubah** settlement from his heirs before twenty-five years

RASHI

שונין – בעלי ברייתא. **גרושה הרי היא כבעל חוב** – לגבות לעולם שלא בהזכרה, דוודאי לא מחלה. **כשחייב מודה** – שלא נתקבלה כתובתה. **בר קזא** – שם חכם.

NOTES

גְּרוּשָׁה הֲרֵי הִיא כְּבַעַל חוֹב **A divorcee is like a creditor.** *Rivan* says that there are two reasons to say that a divorcee did not mean to waive her ketubah settlement, even if twenty-five years have passed since her divorce. First, a divorcee usually leaves the marriage on bad terms with her husband, so there is no reason to assume that she waived anything to him. Second, since a divorcee does not receive maintenance from her husband's property, there is no reason to assume that she would be ready to waive her ketubah settlement.

HALAKHAH

repay the debt. Even if many years had passed during which the creditor did not demand his money, we do not assume that he waived the debt," following the Baraita. "The same law applies if the creditor does not have a promissory note, but the debtor admits the debt," following Rav Sheshet. Even if we heard that the creditor had given up hope of ever collecting the debt, he may still collect the debt. (*Shulḥan Arukh, Ḥoshen Mishpat* 98:1.)

גְּרוּשָׁה הֲרֵי הִיא כְּבַעַל חוֹב **A divorcee is like a creditor.** "A divorcee may collect her ketubah settlement at any time, for we assume that she would never waive it," following Rabbi El'a (and *Rashi,* who maintains that we say with certainty that a divorcee does not waive her ketubah settlement). (*Shulḥan Arukh, Even HaEzer* 101:4.)

תָּבְעָה כְּתוּבָּתָהּ **If she demanded her ketubah settlement.** "If a widow claimed her ketubah settlement within twenty-years of her husband's passing, we count twenty-five years from when she made the claim. *Rema* adds that even if she only mentioned her ketubah, explaining that her silence on the matter did not mean that she waived anything, she is regarded as having claimed the settlement (*Ran*)." (*Rambam, Sefer Nashim, Hilkhot Ishut* 16:23; *Shulḥan Arukh, Even HaEzer* 101:1.)

TRANSLATION AND COMMENTARY

had passed since her husband's death, [104B] [1] **she is regarded as if she were** once again **at the beginning** of her widowhood. She now has another twenty-five years to collect her ketubah settlement, for by claiming it, she demonstrated that she had no intention of waiving it. [2] **And if the** woman **has a ketubah deed in her possession, she may collect her ketubah** settlement at any time. As long as the woman retains a ketubah deed, we assume that she did not waive her settlement."

שְׁלַח לֵיהּ [3] **Rav Naḥman bar Rav Ḥisda sent to Rav Naḥman bar Ya'akov:** [4] **Teach us, our master,** do Rabbi Meir and the Sages **disagree** in our Mishnah **about** a widow who **has her ketubah deed in her possession,** [5] **or about** one who **does not have her ketubah deed in her possession, and according to whom does the law** follow?

שְׁלַח לֵיהּ [6] Rav Naḥman bar Ya'akov **sent** back **to** Rav Naḥman bar Rava Ḥisda: The Tannaim **disagree** about a widow who **does not have her ketubah deed in her possession.** Rabbi Meir maintains that if she is living in her father's house, she may collect her ketubah settlement at any time, and the Sages disagree and say that she may only collect it for up to twenty-five years from her husband's death. [7] **But** when a widow **has a ketubah deed in her hand,** all agree — both Rabbi Meir and the Sages — that she may **collect her ketubah** settlement **at any time.** [8] **And the law is in accordance with** the position of **the Sages.**

כִּי אֲתָא [9] **When Rav Dimi came** from Eretz Israel to Babylonia, **he reported** the following dispute: [10] **Rabbi Shimon ben Pazzi said in the name of Rabbi Yehoshua ben Levi who said in the name of Bar Kappara:** The Sages' position that a widow living in her father's house may only collect her ketubah for up to twenty-five years, [11] **only applies to** the main portion of her ketubah settlement to which every woman is entitled by law — **a maneh** in the case of a woman who was not a virgin at the time of her marriage, **or two hundred** dinars in the case of a woman who was a virgin at marriage. [12] **But** regarding **the increment** to which her husband had added on his own, even the Sages agree that **she may collect** that at any time. [13] **And Rabbi Abbahu**

[104B] [1] הֲרֵי הִיא כְּבַתְּחִלָּה. [2] וְאִם הָיָה שְׁטַר כְּתוּבָּה יוֹצֵא מִתַּחַת יָדֶיהָ, גּוֹבָה כְּתוּבָּתָהּ לְעוֹלָם.
[3] שְׁלַח לֵיהּ רַב נַחְמָן בַּר רַב חִסְדָּא לְרַב נַחְמָן בַּר יַעֲקֹב: [4] יְלַמְּדֵנוּ רַבֵּינוּ: כְּשֶׁשְּׁטַר כְּתוּבָּה יוֹצֵא מִתַּחַת יָדָהּ מַחֲלוֹקֶת, [5] אוֹ כְּשֶׁאֵין שְׁטַר כְּתוּבָּה יוֹצֵא מִתַּחַת יָדָהּ. וַהֲלָכָה כְּדִבְרֵי מִי?
[6] שְׁלַח לֵיהּ: בְּשֶׁאֵין שְׁטַר כְּתוּבָּה יוֹצֵא מִתַּחַת יָדָהּ מַחֲלוֹקֶת. [7] אֲבָל שְׁטַר כְּתוּבָּה יוֹצֵא מִתַּחַת יָדָהּ, גּוֹבָה כְּתוּבָּתָהּ לְעוֹלָם. [8] וַהֲלָכָה כְּדִבְרֵי חֲכָמִים.
[9] כִּי אֲתָא רַב דִּימִי, אָמַר: [10] רַבִּי שִׁמְעוֹן בֶּן פָּזִי אָמַר רַבִּי יְהוֹשֻׁעַ בֶּן לֵוִי מִשּׁוּם בַּר קַפָּרָא: [11] לֹא שָׁנוּ אֶלָּא מָנֶה מָאתַיִם. [12] אֲבָל תּוֹסֶפֶת יֵשׁ לָהּ. [13] וְרַבִּי אַבָּהוּ

LITERAL TRANSLATION

[104B] [1] she is like at the beginning. [2] And if the ketubah deed went out from under her hand, she collects her ketubah at any time."

[3] Rav Naḥman bar Rav Ḥisda sent to Rav Naḥman bar Ya'akov: [4] Let our master teach us: Is the dispute about when the ketubah deed goes out from under her hand, [5] or about when the ketubah deed does not go out from under her hand, and according to whom is the law?

[6] He sent to him: The dispute is when the ketubah deed does not go out from under her hand. [7] But when the ketubah deed goes out from under her hand, she collects her ketubah at any time. [8] And the law is in accordance with the Sages.

[9] When Rav Dimi came, he said: [10] Rabbi Shimon ben Pazzi said in the name of Rabbi Yehoshua ben Levi who said in the name of Bar Kappara: [11] They only taught [this] about a maneh or two hundred [dinars]. [12] But the increment she has. [13] And Rabbi Abbahu

RASHI

הרי היא כבתחלה — ומונה עשרים וחמש שנים משעת תביעה. **והלכה כדברי מי** — כדברי רבי מאיר, או כדברי חכמים? **לא שנו** — דבעשרים וחמש שנים מחלה. **אלא מנה מאתים** — שהם שם כתובה. **אבל תוספת יש לה** — דמתנה היא, ולאו כתובה.

NOTES

וַהֲלָכָה כְּדִבְרֵי מִי **And according to whom is the law.** The question is raised: Why did Rav Naḥman bar Rav Ḥisda ask this question? There is a general rule that the law follows the majority opinion, and so in this dispute between Rabbi Meir and the Sages, the law should certainly be decided in favor of the view of the Sages! *Ayelet Ahevim* suggests that this question was justified because Rabbi Meir expressed his opinion in the name of Rabban Shimon ben Gamliel whose opinions as recorded in the Mishnah are generally accepted as law (see also *Ramat Shmuel,* who asks why in fact does the law not follow his opinion here).

תּוֹסֶפֶת **The increment.** The Rishonim note that the discussion here is limited to the actual increase, that amount which the husband adds on his own to his wife's ketubah. But the dowry that a woman brings into her marriage is treated as any other debt that a husband owes his wife. It may therefore be collected at any time (*Rosh* and others).

אֲבָל תּוֹסֶפֶת יֵשׁ לָהּ **But the increment she has.** Our commentary follows *Rashi.* But *Rif* had the opposite reading: "Rabbi Shimon ben Pazzi said in the name of

אָמַר רַבִּי יוֹחָנָן: [1]אֲפִילּוּ תּוֹסֶפֶת אֵין לָהּ, [2]דְּאָמַר רַבִּי אַיְיבוּ אָמַר רַבִּי יַנַּאי: תְּנַאי כְתוּבָּה [3]כִּכְתוּבָּה דָּמֵי.

[4]אִתְּמַר נַמִי: [5]אָמַר רַבִּי אַבָּא אָמַר רַב הוּנָא אָמַר רַב: [6]לֹא שָׁנוּ אֶלָּא מָנֶה מָאתַיִם. [7]אֲבָל תּוֹסֶפֶת יֵשׁ לָהּ. [8]אֲמַר לֵיהּ רַבִּי אַבָּא לְרַב הוּנָא: ״אֲמַר רַב הָכִי״? [9]אֲמַר לֵיהּ: ״אִישְׁתִּיקַן קָאָמְרַתְּ, [10]אוֹ אַשְׁקְיַין קָאָמְרַתְּ״? [11]אֲמַר לֵיהּ: ״אִישְׁתִּיקַן קָאָמִינָא״.

[12]חֲמַתֵּיהּ דְּרַב חִיָּיא אֲרִיכָא אִינְתַּתְ אֲחוּהּ הֲוַאי, [13]וְאַלְמָנָה

LITERAL TRANSLATION

said in the name of Rabbi Yoḥanan: [1]She does not have even the increment, [2]for Rabbi Aivo said in the name of Rabbi Yannai: A condition [added to] the ketubah [3]is like the ketubah.

[4]It was also stated: [5]Rabbi Abba said in the name of Rav Huna who said in the name of Rav: [6]They only taught [this] regarding the maneh or two hundred [dinars]. [7]But the increment she has. [8]Rabbi Abba said to Rav Huna: "Did Rav say this?" [9]He said to him: "Did you say [this] to silence me, [10]or to give me to drink?" [11]He said to him: "I said [this] to silence you."

[12]The mother-in-law of Rabbi Ḥiyya the Tall was his brother's wife, [13]and she was [living as] a widow

TRANSLATION AND COMMENTARY

said in the name of Rabbi Yoḥanan: [1]**Even the increment** to her ketubah **may not be collected** after twenty-five years have passed since her husband's death. [2]**For Rabbi Aivo said in the name of Rabbi Yannai: A condition added to the ketubah** — for example, the additional sum added by the husband, or any other financial obligation imposed on him and specified in the ketubah deed — [3]**is** treated **like** the main portion of **the ketubah:** If she loses her right to collect the main portion, she also loses the increment.

אִתְּמַר נַמִי [4]**It was also stated** that other Amoraim disagree about the same issue: [5]**Rabbi Abba said in the name of Rav Huna who said in the name of Rav:** The Sages' position that a widow living in her father's house may only collect her ketubah for up to twenty-five years [6]**only applies to** the main portion of her ketubah, **the maneh or two hundred** dinars to which every woman is entitled by Rabbinic enactment. [7]**But** regarding **the increment** to the woman's ketubah which her husband had added on his own, even the Sages agree that **she may collect** it at any time. [8]**Rabbi Abba asked Rav Huna: "Did Rav** really **say this?"** [9]Rav Huna **asked** Rabbi Abba: "What did you mean by your question? **Did you** ask me because you disagree with that position, and you wish **to silence me,** [10]**or** because you agree with that position and were so overjoyed with the support of Rav that you wished **to give me** wine **to drink** to mark the occasion? [11]Rabbi Abba **said to** Rav Huna: **"I said** what I said because I disagree and I wished **to silence you."**

חֲמַתֵּיהּ דְּרַב חִיָּיא [12]It was related that **Rabbi Ḥiyya the Tall's mother-in-law** was also **his brother's wife.** (That is to say, Rabbi Ḥiyya married his brother's wife's daughter from a previous marriage.) When the brother died without children, his estate was inherited by Rabbi Ḥiyya, [13]**and** his **widow** went back to live

RASHI

תנאי כתובה – תוספת. **אישתיקן קאמרת או אשקיין קאמרת** – האי דמתמהת ואמרת "אמר רב הכי?" – משום דלא סבירא לך הוא ולאשתיקן קאמרת, או משום דחביבה עלך, ולאשקיין קאמרת? דאי אמרה רב – משקית לי חמרא, דשפיר אמר. **אינתת אחוה הואי** – ומת בלא בנים, וירשו רב חייא אחיו.

NOTES

Rabbi Yehoshua ben Levi who said in the name of Bar Kappara: They only taught [this] regarding the maneh or two hundred. But the increment she does not have. And Rabbi Abbahu said in the name of Rabbi Yoḥanan: Even the increment she has." *Rif* understands that this discussion refers to a woman who may collect her ketubah settlement at any time. According to Rabbi Shimon ben Pazzi, this law applies to the main portion of her ketubah settlement at any time, but not the increment. And Rabbi Abbahu disagrees and says that she may even collect the increment at any time. *Rivan* has the standard reading, but at one point he explains that reading in accordance with the position of *Rif.* (See also *Meiri,* who cites the various readings and explanations.)

אִישְׁתִּיקַן **To silence me.** *Rav Hai Gaon* (cited by *Arukh*), who had a slightly different reading of this text, understands that the question as to whether Rav actually said that the widow can collect the increment was actually proposed to Rav himself. And the Gemara asks, if when Rav was asked the question, he was silent, perhaps he never said such a thing? Or was he drinking at the time, so that he could not answer, and we do not know what his position was on the matter?

אִינְתַּתְ אֲחוּהּ הֲוַאי **She was his brother's wife.** *Rivan* explains that this relationship can be constructed in two ways: Either Rabbi Ḥiyya the Tall was married to his

HALAKHAH

אֲפִילּוּ תּוֹסֶפֶת אֵין לָהּ **She does not have even the increment.** "If a widow forfeits her ketubah settlement by failing to claim it, she forfeits not only the main portion of her ketubah settlement, but the increment as well," following Rabbi Yoḥanan. Neither *Rambam* nor *Shulḥan Arukh* state this law explicitly, but the commentators to those

TRANSLATION AND COMMENTARY

in her father's house. [1]Using his brother's property, Rabbi Ḥiyya **maintained** the widow **in her father's house for twenty-five years.** [2]When **at the end** of that period, Rabbi Ḥiyya stopped maintaining the woman, **she said to him: "Give my maintenance."** [3]Rabbi Ḥiyya **said to her: "You are no** longer **entitled to maintenance."** [4]So the woman said to him: **"Give me** then my **ketubah** settlement." [5]Rabbi Ḥiyya **said to her: "You are entitled neither to maintenance nor to** your **ketubah** settlement, for a widow living in her father's house who did not claim her ketubah settlement for twenty-five years is assumed to have waived it and is assumed to have forfeited her right to maintenance as well." [6]The widow **sued** Rabbi Ḥiyya for her ketubah settlement **before Rabbah bar Shela.** [7]Rabbah bar Shela **said to** Rabbi Ḥiyya: **"Tell me** precisely **the facts of the case."** [8]Rabbi Ḥiyya **said to him: "I maintained** my brother's widow **for twenty-five years** while she was living **in her father's house.** [9]I swear **by the life of Master,** that I personally **brought** the woman **her maintenance on my** very own **shoulders."** [10]After hearing this, Rabbah bar Shela **said to** Rabbi Ḥiyya: **"What is the reason that the Sages said** in our Mishnah: [11]**'When** a widow **lives in her** late **husband's house, she may collect her ketubah** settlement at any time, even after twenty-five years? [12]**Because we say that it was** only **on account of** the woman's **embarrassment that she did not demand her ketubah** settlement all those years. [13]**Here too** then we can say that it was only **on account of** her **embarrassment** that your brother's wife **did not demand** her ketubah settlement from you all these years. Since you treated her so well, she was too embarrassed to demand it from you. But she never meant to waive it. [14]So you must **go** now and **give it to her."** [15]Rabbi Ḥiyya **did not heed** Rabbah bar Shela's ruling, [16]so Rabbah bar Shela then **wrote** the woman a writ of seizure **on** Rabbi Ḥiyya's **property,**

בְּבֵית אָבִיהָ הֲוַאי. [1]וְזָנָהּ עֶשְׂרִים וְחָמֵשׁ שְׁנִין בְּבֵי נָשָׁא. [2]לְסוֹף, אָמְרָה לֵיהּ: ״הַב לִי מְזוֹנֵי״. [3]אֲמַר לָהּ: ״לֵית לָךְ מְזוֹנֵי״. [4]״הַב לִי כְּתוּבָּה״. אֲמַר לָהּ: [5]״לָא מְזוֹנֵי אִית לָךְ וְלָא כְּתוּבָּה אִית לָךְ״. [6]תְּבַעְתֵּיהּ לְדִינָא קַמֵּיהּ דְּרַבָּה בַּר שֵׁילָא. [7]אֲמַר לֵיהּ: ״אֵימָא לִי אִיזִי, גּוּפָא דְּעוּבְדָא הֵיכִי הֲוָה״. [8]אֲמַר לֵיהּ: ״זָנֵיתָהּ עֶשְׂרִים וְחָמֵשׁ שָׁנִים בְּבֵי נָשָׁא. [9]בְּחַיֵּי דְּמָר, דִּבְכַתְפַּאי אַמְטַאי לָהּ״. [10]אֲמַר לֵיהּ: ״טַעְמָא מַאי אֲמוּר רַבָּנַן: [11]׳כָּל זְמַן שֶׁהִיא בְּבֵית בַּעְלָהּ גּוֹבָה כְּתוּבָּתָהּ לְעוֹלָם׳? [12]דְּאָמְרִינַן מִשּׁוּם כִּיסוּפָא הוּא דְּלָא תָּבְעָה. [13]הָכָא נַמִי, מִשּׁוּם כִּיסוּפָא הוּא דְּלָא תָּבְעָה. [14]זִיל הַב לָהּ״. [15]לָא אַשְׁגַּח. [16]כָּתַב

LITERAL TRANSLATION

in her father's house. [1]And he maintained her for twenty-five years in her father's house. [2]Afterwards, she said to him: "Give me my maintenance." [3]He said to her: "You no [longer] have maintenance." [4]"Give me [my] ketubah." [5]He said to her: "You have neither maintenance nor a ketubah." [6]She summoned him [to come] to judgment before Rabbah bar Shela. [7]He said to him: "Tell me, then, how was the actual case." [8]He said to him: "I maintained her for twenty-five years in her father's house. [9]By the life of Master, on my shoulders I brought her [maintenance]." [10]He said to him: "What is the reason that the Sages said: [11]'As long as she is in her husband's house she collects her ketubah at any time? [12]Because we say [that it was] on account of embarrassment that she did not claim [her ketubah]. [13]Here too, on account of embarrassment she did not claim [it]. [14]Go give [it to] her." [15]He did not heed. [16]He wrote

RASHI

לא כתובה ולא מזוני — דאלמנה בבית אביה אינה גובה אלא עד עשרים וחמש שנים, כרבנן. **בכתפאי אמטאי לה** — מזונותיה מיום ליום. **הא נמי משום כיסופא** — מחמת הכבוד הזה שעשית לה.

NOTES

brother's wife's daughter from a previous marriage, and his brother had no children of his own. Or else Rabbi Ḥiyya's wife was his brother's only daughter, and he inherited his brother's estate through her.

מִשּׁוּם כִּיסוּפָא On account of embarrassment. *Rabbenu Ḥananel* writes (and so too the Jerusalem Talmud) that the widow's right to collect her ketubah settlement at any time does not actually depend upon where she was living, but on whether she was being maintained by her late husband's heirs. Even if the woman was living in her father's house, if she was being maintained by the heirs, we assume that she was too embarrassed to demand her ketubah settlement, and so she may collect it at any time. This also follows from the story regarding Rabbi Ḥiyya's

HALAKHAH

codes infer this ruling from other rulings that are stated explicitly. (See *Rambam, Sefer Nashim, Hilkhot Ishut* 16:22; *Shulḥan Arukh, Even HaEzer* 101:3.)

דִּבְכַתְפַּאי אַמְטַאי לָהּ I brought her maintenance on my shoulders. "Even if the widow is being maintained in her father's house, if her late husband's heirs honor her and personally deliver the maintenance to her, she may collect her ketubah settlement even after twenty-five years, for her silence is attributed to embarrassment, rather than a waiver on her part," following Rabbah bar Shela. (*Rambam, Sefer Nashim, Hilkhot Ishut* 16:24; *Shulḥan Arukh, Even HaEzer* 101:2.)

TRANSLATION AND COMMENTARY

giving her the right to seek and seize property belonging to Rabbi Ḥiyya in order to recover payment of her ketubah settlement. [1]Rabbi Ḥiyya then **came before Rava, and said to him: "Master, see how** Rabbah bar Shela **judged me."** [2]After hearing the details of the case, Rava **said to him:** "Rabbah bar Shelah **judged you well."** [3]The woman then **said to** Rava: **"If so,** then **let** Rabbi Ḥiyya **go and return to me the produce** of his property that I was entitled to seize **from** the time that the writ entitled me to enjoy that produce **until now."** We learned elsewhere (*Bava Metzia* 35b) that a creditor is entitled to the usufruct of property specified in a writ of seizure. Thus, argued the widow, she should be entitled to the usufruct of the property which she may seize from the time that the public announcements were completed. [4]Rava **said to her: "Show me your writ of seizure."** [5] **He saw that** the following clause **was not written in the writ**: **"And we, the court, know that the property** described in this writ **belonged** originally **to the deceased,** the widow's late husband, and that it passed into his brother's possession upon his death." [6]Rava then **said to** the woman: **"The writ of seizure was not written properly.** It authorizes you to seize any property belonging to Rabbi Ḥiyya, but only the property which he inherited from your late husband can be taken for your ketubah." [7]The widow **said to** Rava: **"Leave the writ of seizure aside.** Let **me** at least **take** the produce **from the day that the days of announcement were completed and until now**. After I received the writ, I located property that had in fact belonged to my late husband, and I showed my husband's brother or its present owner the writ authorizing me to seize the property, and the court sent assessors to value the land that I had wished to confiscate, and the property was publicly offered for sale to ensure that no one else was willing to pay more for it than the court's evaluation, a procedure that takes thirty days. Even if I am not entitled to the produce from the time that I had received the writ, I should be entitled to the produce from the time

LITERAL TRANSLATION

for her a writ of seizure on his property. [1]He came before Rava, [and] said to him: "Master, see how he judged me." [2]He said to him: "He judged you well." [3]She said to him: "If so, let him go [and] return to me the produce [of the field] from that day until now." [4]He said to her: "Show me your writ of seizure." [5]He saw that there was not written in it: "And it was known to us that this property belonged to the deceased." [6]He said to her: "The writ of seizure is not well written." [7]She said to him: "Let the writ of seizure go. I will take [produce] from the day that the days of announcement were completed

לָהּ אַדְרַכְתָּא אַנִּיכְסֵיהּ. [1]אֲתָא לְקַמֵּיהּ דְּרָבָא, אֲמַר לֵיהּ: ״חֲזִי מָר הֵיכִי דָּנַן״! [2]אֲמַר לֵיהּ: ״שַׁפִּיר דָּנָךְ״. [3]אָמְרָה לֵיהּ: ״אִי הָכִי, לֵיזִיל לִהֲדַר לִי פֵּירֵי דְּמִן הַהוּא יוֹמָא עַד הָאִידָּנָא״! [4]אֲמַר לָהּ: ״אַחֲוִי לִי אַדְרַכְתֵּיךְ. [5]חַזְיֵיהּ דְּלָא הֲוָה כָּתוּב בָּהּ: ״וְאִישְׁתְּמוֹדַעְנָא דִּנְכָסִים אֵלּוּ דְּמִיתְנָא אִינּוּן״. [6]אֲמַר לָהּ: ״אַדְרַכְתָּא לָאו שַׁפִּיר כְּתִיבָא״. [7]אֲמַר לֵיהּ: ״תֵּיזִיל אַדְרַכְתָּא. אֵישְׁקוֹל מִיּוֹמָא דִּשְׁלִימֵי יוֹמָא אַכְרַזְתָּא

RASHI

אדרכתא — פסק דין לגבות נכסיו בכל אשר תמצא. אמרה ליה — לרבא. ליהדר לי פירי — דארעא, דשיעור כתובתאי, דהא מיומא דאיכתיבא לי אדרכתא עלייהו, שמאותו היום הם ברשותי. דהכי אמר רבה בפרק ״המפקיד״ (בבא מציעא לה,ב) גבי שומת בית דין: לוקח מאימתי אכיל פירי? אמר רבה: מכי מטי אדרכתא לידיה, אביי אמר: משנחתמה, רבא אמר: מכי שלמו יומי אכרזתא. אישתמודענא — הכרנו שהנכסים הללו שכתבנו אדרכתא זו עליהם — של מת היו, שמשועבד כתובתה של זו עליהם. לאו שפיר כתיבא — שנכתבה על כל שדות של זה, ושדות שלו אינן משועבדות לכתובתיך, אלא אותן שירש מבעליך. תיזיל אדרכתא — דלא שפיר כתיבא. אשקול — פירי מיום שמצאתי שדה משדות המת, והראתי אדרכתא שבידי לבית דין, ושמאוה, והכריזו עליה שלשים יום כמשפט. דאפילו לרבא דמרע כח הלוקח טפי בפרק ״המפקיד״ (שם לה,ב) מודה דמכי שלמו יומי אכרזתא — אכיל לוקח פירי.

CONCEPTS

אַדְרַכְתָּא A writ of seizure. After the court finds in favor of the creditor, it issues a writ of seizure, called an *adrakhta*, which authorizes the creditor to seize the debtor's property in satisfaction of his debt. The word *adrakhta* is understood to mean "pursue," for it allows the creditor to pursue the debtor's property and exact payment from it. After the creditor locates property belonging to the debtor, the court appraises its value, and then publicly announces its sale, making it possible to find a buyer who might purchase it for more than its assessed value. After the days of announcement are finished, the property is either sold or given to the creditor as payment for his debt. In *Bava Metzia* 35b, the Amoraim disagree about whether the creditor is entitled to the usufruct of the property from the time that the writ was issued (the position of Abaye), or from the time that the creditor gets the writ (the position of Rabbah), or is he only entitled to the usufruct from the time that the public announcements regarding the sale were completed (the position of Rava). (See *Tosafot* regarding the various readings in our passage.)

NOTES

mother-in-law. The widow's right to collect her ketubah settlement at any time depends on whether or not she was treated well by her husband's heirs.

HALAKHAH

דְּלָא הֲוָה כָּתוּב בָּהּ: וְאִישְׁתְּמוֹדַעְנָא It was not written in it: "And it was known." "When a writ of seizure is issued against heirs, whether they are minors or adults, it must state: 'And we the court know that this property for which we are issuing this writ belonged originally to the deceased.' If such a clause was not inserted, the writ is not valid, and the creditor may not enjoy the usufruct of the property belonging to the deceased, even after the days of public announcement are completed." This ruling is derived from following the incident reported in our Gemara. (*Rambam, Sefer Mishpatim, Hilkhot Malveh* 12:9; *Shulḥan Arukh, Ḥoshen Mishpat* 109:2.)

אֵישְׁקוֹל מִיּוֹמָא דִּשְׁלִימֵי יוֹמָא אַכְרַזְתָּא I will take from the day that the days of announcement were completed. "A creditor on behalf of whom a writ of seizure was issued may enjoy the usufruct of his debtor's property from the time that the days of public announcement are completed." (*Rambam, Sefer Mishpatim, Hilkhot Malveh* 22:12; *Shulḥan Arukh, Ḥoshen Mishpat* 98:9.)

LITERAL TRANSLATION

and until now." [1]He said to her: "This applies (lit., "these words") where a mistake was not written in the writ of seizure. [2]But where a mistake was written in the writ of seizure — we have no [regard] for it." [3]She said to him: "But surely it is Master who said: [4][A missing] guarantee is a scribal error." [5]Rava said to her: "Regarding this, we do not say [it is] a scribal error, for regarding this, [6]even Rabbah bar Shela erred. [7]At first he maintained: These and those are his. [8]What [difference] is it to me [if] from these or from those? [9]But it is not so. [10]Sometimes she may go and improves them, [11]and those of her husband become ruined. [12]And he says to her: 'Take yours, and give me mine.' [13]And they will come and utter (lit., "bring out") slander against the court."

עַד הַשְׁתָּא״. [1]אֲמַר לָהּ: ״הָנֵי מִילֵּי הֵיכָא דְּלָא כְּתִיב טָעוּתָא בְּאַדְרַכְתָּא. [2]אֲבָל הֵיכָא דִּכְתִיב טָעוּתָא בְּאַדְרַכְתָּא — לֵית לָן בָּהּ״. [3]אָמְרָה לֵיהּ: וְהָא מָר הוּא דְּאָמַר: [4]אַחֲרָיוּת טָעוּת סוֹפֵר הוּא! [5]אֲמַר לָהּ רָבָא: ״בְּהָא לֵיכָּא לְמֵימַר טָעוּת סוֹפֵר הוּא, דִּבְהָא, [6]אֲפִילּוּ רַבָּה בַּר שֵׁילָא טָעֵי. [7]מֵעִיקָּרָא הוּא סְבוּר: הָנֵי וְהָנֵי דִּידֵיהּ. [8]מַה לִּי מֵהָנֵי מַה לִּי מֵהָנֵי? [9]וְלָא הִיא. [10]זִימְנִין דְּאָזְלָה וּמַשְׁבְּחָה לְהוּ, [11]וּדְבַעְלָהּ מִכְסְפֵי. [12]וַאֲמַר לָהּ: ׳שְׁקֵיל דִּידָךְ, וְהַב לִי דִּידִי׳. [13]וְאָתֵי לְאַפּוּקֵי לַעַז עַל בֵּי דִּינָא״.

הדרן עלך הנושא

RASHI

אבל היכא — דאדרכתא בטעות כתיבא — לא זכית בה עד דמטיא ארעא לידך, שהרי מכח אדרכתא שמאוה בית דין והכריזו. **והא מר הוא דאמר** — בפרק ״שניס אוחזין״ (בבא מציעא טו,ב). **אחריות טעות סופר הוא** — שטר שאין בו אחריות גובה מנכסים משועבדים, שלא הלוה זה מעות אלא באחריות שיעבוד נכסיו, והסופר טעה. הכא נמי, בית דין צוו לסופר לכתוב אדרכתא הוגנת, והוא טעה דלא כתב ״אישתמודענא״, והכל יודעים שלא נכתבה אלא על נכסי המת. **בהא רבה בר שילא** — שצוה לכתוב ליך אדרכתא, טעה וסבור שתגבה מנכסים שלו. **דאזלה ומשבחה להו** — לשדה ששמו לה בית דין. **ודבעלה מכספי** — שלא ישביחם היורש, שהוא בטוח שיחזור ויקח את שלו מידה, ויאמר לה: טלי שלי המשועבד ליך. **ואתי לאפוקי לעז על בית דין** — שלא עיינו בתקנתא של זו.

הדרן עלך הנושא

TRANSLATION AND COMMENTARY

that the public announcements regarding the sale of the property were completed." [1]Rava **said to** the widow: **"That only applies** if **there are no mistakes in the writ of seizure. [2]But where there is a mistake in the writ of seizure,** the announcement **has no** legal implications and you are only entitled to the produce from the time that the property actually entered your possession." [3]The widow **said to** Rava: **"But surely it is Master** himself **who said:** [4]The omission of the clause **guaranteeing a** repayment of a loan or the sale of property **is** considered **a scribal error.** It is taken for granted that in the case of a loan the debtor will pledge his land as security for repayment, and in the case of a sale of property the seller pledges his other land as security in case the sold property is seized by a creditor. Thus, even if the clause mentioning this guarantee is omitted from the relevant document, the guarantee is still in force. Thus, the writ of seizure should be regarded as valid, and I should be entitled to the produce from the time that the public announcements of sale were completed." [5]**Rava said to** the widow: **"In this** case **we do not say** that the omission should be attributed to **a** mere **scribal error, for regarding this** matter, [6]**even Rabbah bar Shela erred.** When he instructed the scribe to draw up the writ of seizure, he thought that the widow could collect her ketubah settlement from any property found in her husband's brother's possession. The Gemara now explains Rabbah bar Shela's mistake: [7]**At first** Rabbah bar Shela **thought** that since the property that had always been owned by Rabbi Ḥiyya, **and the property** that he had inherited from his brother all now **belong to** Rabbi Ḥiyya, [8]**what difference** should it make if the widow collects **from this** property **or from that** property? [9]**But this is not so,** [10]for it could happen that the widow **may improve** the property that had been assessed for her by the court, but which had not been part of her late husband's estate, [11]**and the** property that had belonged **to her husband will go to waste.** The husband's heir will not maintain it, because he knows that it is mortgaged to the widow's ketubah settlement. [12]One day **he will say to** her: **"Take** what is **yours, and give me** back what is **mine."** He will receive the property that his father's widow improved, and she will be forced to take the property that he allowed to deteriorate. [13]Thus people **will come to slander the court,** saying that it did not adequately protect the widow's interests. Consequently, the writ of seizure must specify that it authorizes the widow to seize property that had belonged to her late husband and which was subject to her ketubah. Since Rabbah bar Shela had erred about this matter, the writ that had been drawn up for the widow is not valid.

NOTES

אָמְרָה לֵיהּ: וְהָא מָר She said to him: But surely it is master. Some amended the text so that it reads: They [= Rava's disciples] said to him: "But surely it is master," for it does not seem reasonable that the widow was so conversant with the intricacies of the law (*Rabbenu Yehonatan* and others).

Conclusion to Chapter Twelve

If a man has promised to support his wife's daughter, this promise has validity similar to any deed of donation, and it is not connected to the marriage contract between the man and his wife, the girl's mother. Hence the husband must keep this promise in any event, even if his marriage to the girl's mother is dissolved, and it takes priority over the conditions of the ketubah.

Regarding a widow's dwelling place, it was agreed that she continues to live in her late husband's house, and there she continues to enjoy the same conditions she had enjoyed during her husband's lifetime, as if her husband were abroad. The widow's right to live in her late husband's house refers specifically to the very house where they lived together, and if he did not have a house, or the house was destroyed, although his heirs must see that his widow is housed, they are not required to place her in their home. If a widow prefers to return to her father's house, her husband's heirs who continue to support her may deduct what they lose because they cannot feed her together with themselves. However, if there were good reasons for the widow to live in her father's house, she loses nothing.

A widow who lives in her father's house may collect her ketubah settlement at any time, but if she continues to live in her late husband's house, and she has not demanded her ketubah settlement for twenty-five years, we assume that she has waived it.

In this chapter we also find stories about the death and testament of Rabbi Yehudah HaNasi.

Introduction to Chapter Thirteen

שְׁנֵי דַיָּינֵי

This chapter fills in several laws concerning ketubah obligations, but since since it mentions controversies among the Sages during Second Temple times, it also contains several discussions that are not about the main subject of this tractate.

One problem concerned a man who went abroad and left his wife without support. If his wife appears before a court and demands that she be given support from her husband's property, how is the court to ascertain that her husband did not in fact leave her money for support, so that she would be taking his property illicitly. Another question arose regarding a person who voluntarily supported a wife in this situation. To what degree does her husband, upon his return, have a legal obligation to recompense that person?

Another problem connected to ketubot relates to the couple's dwelling place. In what instances can one of the spouses force the other to change his place of residence?

Another problem relates to the currency used to pay the ketubah settlement. If the ketubah did not specify in what currency the payment was to be made, it must be ascertained whether payment is made in the currency of the place where the ketubah was written or in the place where it is paid.

Only two of the other differences of opinion mentioned in this chapter are related to the main subject of the tractate. One concerns a man who left only a small estate after his death, and it is insufficient to pay the ketubah settlement, to support his daughters from his property, and also to support his sons. Who has priority over whom? The other problem concerns cases in which a groom may put off the marriage if his father-in-law does not give him the dowry promised him.

The other differences of opinion presented in this chapter revolve upon a single axis: incomplete confessions. Is it permissible to draw conclusions from indirect evidence, which can be interpreted so that it proves nothing? For example: a defendant who admits to part of a claim, but in a matter that is dissimilar from the claim, but still related to it; a man who lays claim to something that is certainly his, but he cannot lay the claim against a specific person; or someone who has done a deed or testified in a manner that appears to infringe upon his claim in that matter.

LITERAL TRANSLATION

MISHNAH [1]There were two judges decreeing fines in Jerusalem — [2]Admon and Ḥanan ben Avishalom. [3]Ḥanan said two things. [4]Admon said seven.

[5][If] someone went abroad, and his wife demands maintenance, [6]Ḥanan says: [105A] [7]She must take an oath at the end, [8]but she does not take an oath at the beginning.

[9]The sons of the High Priests disagreed with him, [10]and said: She must take an oath at the beginning and at the end.

[11]Rabbi Dosa ben Horkinas said as they said. [12]Rabbi Yoḥanan ben

שְׁנֵי

[1]דַּיָּינֵי גְזֵירוֹת הָיוּ בִּירוּשָׁלַיִם — [2]אַדְמוֹן וְחָנָן בֶּן אֲבִישָׁלוֹם. [3]חָנָן אוֹמֵר שְׁנֵי דְבָרִים. [4]אַדְמוֹן אוֹמֵר שִׁבְעָה.

[5]מִי שֶׁהָלַךְ לִמְדִינַת הַיָּם, וְאִשְׁתּוֹ תּוֹבַעַת מְזוֹנוֹת, [6]חָנָן אוֹמֵר: [105A] [7]תִּשָּׁבַע בַּסּוֹף, [8]וְלֹא תִּשָּׁבַע בַּתְּחִלָּה.

[9]נֶחְלְקוּ עָלָיו בְּנֵי כֹּהֲנִים גְּדוֹלִים, [10]וְאָמְרוּ: תִּשָּׁבַע בַּתְּחִלָּה וּבַסּוֹף.

[11]אָמַר רַבִּי דּוֹסָא בֶּן הָרְכִּינָס כְּדִבְרֵיהֶם. [12]אָמַר רַבָּן יוֹחָנָן בֶּן

RASHI

משנה שני דייני גזירות — מפרש בגמרא. חנן אומר שני דברים — שלא היו חכמים מודים לו. תשבע בסוף — כשישמעו בו שמת, ותבא לגבות כתובתה — תשבע שלא עכבה בידה משל בעלה כלום. ולא תשבע בתחלה — בשעת גיבוי מזונות.

TRANSLATION AND COMMENTARY

MISHNAH שְׁנֵי דַּיָּינֵי גְזֵירוֹת [1]Among the various courts which sat in Jerusalem during the Second Temple period were special courts which established fines that were imposed in cases of robbery. Our Mishnah reports that **there were two judges** who sat on such a court that **established fines in Jerusalem,** [2]one named **Admon and** the other named **Ḥanan ben Avishalom.** [3]**Ḥanan said two things** that were disputed by the sons of the High Priests, [4]and **Admon said seven things** that were disputed by other Sages, as will be explained in the course of the chapter.

מִי שֶׁהָלַךְ [5]The Mishnah now discusses the first of Ḥanan ben Avishalom's disputed rulings: **If someone went abroad,** leaving his wife behind, **and his wife** claims that her husband left her with insufficient means and **demands** that the court award her **maintenance** from his property, Ḥanan and the sons of the High Priests disagree about whether the woman must take an oath to confirm her claim. [6]**Ḥanan says:** [105A] [7]The woman **must take an oath at the end,** following her husband's death, to collect her ketubah settlement. At that time she must swear that her husband did not leave her money from which to collect the ketubah . [8]**But she is not obligated to take** such **an oath at the beginning** when she comes to court claiming maintenance from her husband's property in his absence.

נֶחְלְקוּ עָלָיו [9]**The sons of the High Priests disagreed with** Ḥanan ben Avishalom, [10]**and said:** The woman **must take an oath** both **at the beginning** when she comes to collect her maintenance, **and at the end** when she comes to collect her ketubah settlement.

אָמַר [11]**Rabbi Dosa ben Horkinas agreed with** the sons of the High Priests. [12]**Rabban Yoḥanan ben Zakkai said:**

BACKGROUND

בְּנֵי כֹּהֲנִים גְּדוֹלִים **The sons of the High Priests.** Towards the end of the Second Temple period, the High Priest's office was not passed from father to son; instead, various members of the priestly families were appointed to this position (sometimes, after bribing the authorities). By Herod's time, though, the High Priests were generally members of a small group of families, who shared the Temple functions among themselves (see *Pesaḥim* 57a). Thus, there was apparently a certain group of "sons of High Priests" which also dealt with Halakhic matters possibly in the framework of a priestly court.

NOTES

דַּיָּינֵי גְזֵירוֹת **Judges decreeing fines.** According to an alternative reading, the Mishnah reads: שְׁנֵי דַיָּינֵי גְזֵילוֹת, "two judges of [cases of] robbery" (and so too the Mishnah in the Jerusalem Talmud). However, the Gemara below raises an objection against the Mishnah from a Baraita with that same reading. Thus if one were to accept this alternative reading of the Mishnah, the reading of the Baraita must be amended to read like the standard reading of our Mishnah.

וְחָנָן בֶּן אֲבִישָׁלוֹם **And Ḥanan ben Avishalom.** The Mishnah mentions the name of Ḥanan's father, for as we see from a Baraita cited in the Gemara, there was another judge named Ḥanan, Ḥanan the Egyptian, and the Mishnah wishes to distinguish clearly between them (*Shittah Mekubbetzet*).

מִי שֶׁהָלַךְ לִמְדִינַת הַיָּם **If someone went abroad.** *Ramban* and others understand that the same law applies to a widow who claims maintenance. According to Ḥanan she can collect her maintenance from her husband's estate without first taking an oath, and she only has to take an oath when she wishes to collect her ketubah settlement. But according to *Rambam,* all agree that a widow cannot collect maintenance from her husband's heirs without first taking an oath that she had not already received anything for her maintenance. We are concerned that her husband may have given her money for her maintenance after his death, so that she will not have to humble herself by requesting support from his heirs.

תִּשָּׁבַע בַּתְּחִלָּה וּבַסּוֹף **She must take an oath at the beginning and at the end.** According to *Rashi* and most other Rishonim, the sons of the High Priest maintain that the woman must take an oath at the beginning, when she comes to collect her maintenance, and then another oath at the end, after it is established that her husband has died and she wishes to collect her ketubah settlement. *Rambam,* in his *Commentary to the Mishnah,* explains that the woman must take an oath at the beginning, when she comes to collect her maintenance, and then another oath at the end, when her husband returns and claims that he had left his wife with money for support.

כְּדִבְרֵיהֶם **As they said.** *Shittah Mekubbetzet* argues that a

TRANSLATION AND COMMENTARY

Ḥanan said well: [1]The woman **is only obligated to take an oath at the end** when she comes to collect her ketubah settlement, but not at the beginning when she comes to collect her maintenance.

GEMARA וּרְמִינְהִי [2]**A contradiction may be raised** between our Mishnah and the following related Baraita: [3]**"There were three judges** who sat on a court that dealt **with cases of robbery in Jerusalem** one named **Admon ben Gadai,** [4]a second named **Ḥanan the Egyptian, and** a third named **Ḥanan ben Avishalom."** [5]**There is a difficulty** regarding the number of judges who sat on the court, for the Baraita speaks of **three** judges, whereas the Mishnah spoke of only **two;** [6]and **there is** also **a difficulty** regarding the function of their court, for the Mishnah referred to them as sitting on a court that established **fines,** whereas the Baraita refers to them as sitting in cases of **robbery!**

בִּשְׁלָמָא [7]**Granted that** the Baraita which speaks of **three** judges and the Mishnah spoke of **two** judges **does not pose** any real **difficulty,** [8]for it can be argued that the Tanna of our Mishnah **mentioned** only those judges whom he considered to be most **well-regarded,** [9]and those whom he did **not** consider as **well-regarded, he did not mention.** [10]**But there is a** real **difficulty** regarding the designation which these judges were given, for the Mishnah referred to them as judges who established **fines,** whereas the Baraita refers to them as judges in cases of **robbery!**

אָמַר [11]**Rav Naḥman bar Yitzḥak said:** In fact, one can explain that both the Mishnah and the Baraita refer to judges **who established fines** that were imposed **in cases of robbery.** [12]**As it was taught** in another Baraita: **"If** someone's animal entered another person's property, and caused damage by **breaking off the top of a** young **sapling,** [13]**Rabbi Yose says:** The judges **who established fines** for cases of robbery said:

זַכַּאי: יָפֶה אָמַר חָנָן: [1]לֹא תִּשָּׁבַע אֶלָּא בַּסּוֹף.

גמרא [2]וּרְמִינְהִי: [3]״שְׁלֹשָׁה דַּיָּינֵי גְזֵילוֹת הָיוּ בִּירוּשָׁלַיִם: אַדְמוֹן בֶּן גַּדַּאי, [4]וְחָנָן הַמִּצְרִי, וְחָנָן בֶּן אֲבִישָׁלוֹם״. [5]קַשְׁיָא תְּלָת אַתְּרֵין, [6]קַשְׁיָא גְּזֵירוֹת אַגְּזֵילוֹת!

[7]בִּשְׁלָמָא תְּלָת אַתְּרֵין לָא קַשְׁיָא — [8]דַּחֲשִׁיב לֵיהּ, קָתָנֵי, [9]דְּלָא חֲשִׁיב לֵיהּ, לָא קָתָנֵי. [10]אֶלָּא גְּזֵירוֹת אַגְּזֵילוֹת קַשְׁיָא! [11]אָמַר רַב נַחְמָן בַּר יִצְחָק: שֶׁהָיוּ גּוֹזְרִין גְּזֵירוֹת עַל גְּזֵילוֹת. [12]כִּדְתַנְיָא: ״קִיטְמָהּ נְטִיעָה, [13]רַבִּי יוֹסֵי אוֹמֵר: גּוֹזְרֵי גְזֵירוֹת

LITERAL TRANSLATION

Zakkai said: Ḥanan said well: [1]She must only take an oath at the end.

GEMARA [2]A contradiction was raised (lit., "cast them together"): [3]"There were three judges in cases of robbery in Jerusalem: Admon ben Gadai, [4]and Ḥanan the Egyptian, and Ḥanan ben Avishalom." [5]There is a difficulty [from] three to two, [6][and] there is a difficulty [from] fines to robbery!

[7]Granted that there is no difficulty [from] three to two — [8]he who was important to him, he taught, [9]he who was not important to him, he did not teach. [10]But there is a difficulty [from] fines to robbery!

[11]Rav Naḥman bar Yitzḥak said: [Judges] who decreed fines for robbery. [12]As it was taught: "[If the animal] broke off the top of a sapling, [13]Rabbi Yose says: Those who decree fines

RASHI

גמרא אדמון בן גדאי. גוזרין גזירות — קנסות.

NOTES

precise reading of the Mishnah teaches that whereas Rabban Yoḥanan ben Zakkai took a stand in the disagreement between Ḥanan and the sons of the High Priest in favor of Ḥanan, Rabbi Dosa did not state his opinion to favor one of the two positions (as he may not even have been familiar with the statement of Ḥanan). Rather he voiced his opinion independently, an opinion which was identical to that of the sons of the High Priests.

דַּחֲשִׁיב לֵיהּ **He who was well-regarded by him.** *Rivan* explains that the Mishnah mentioned only the most well-regarded judges, whereas the Baraita included judges who were less well-regarded. *Tosafot* points out a difficulty with this explanation: The Baraita mentions Ḥanan the Egyptian before Ḥanan ben Avishalom, implying that the former, who was mentioned only in the Baraita, was more well-regarded than the latter, who was mentioned also in the Mishnah. They suggest that Ḥanan ben Avishalom was indeed more important than Ḥanan the Egyptian, but Ḥanan the Egyptian was mentioned first because he came from a more distinguished family. *Rabbenu Tam* understands the Gemara differently: The Mishnah listed only those judges whose opinions were disputed by other Sages, but it did not count judges like Ḥanan the Egyptian, whose views are not recorded in our chapter.

גּוֹזְרִין גְּזֵירוֹת **Those who decree fines.** *Rashi* explains that these judges established fines for robbery. *Ritva* notes that

HALAKHAH

גּוֹזְרִין גְּזֵירוֹת **Those who decree fines.** "Those who examined the sacred scrolls in Jerusalem and the judges who sat in judgment over the robbers in Jerusalem took their salaries from the Temple treasury funds. They would

TRANSLATION AND COMMENTARY

[1] **For a one-year-old sapling,** the animal's owner must pay the injured party **two silver me'ahs,** [2] and **for a two-year-old sapling,** he must pay him **four silver me'ahs."**

וּרְמִינְהִי [3] The Gemara now **raises a contradiction** between the Baraita cited above and another Baraita, in which it was taught: [4] **"There were three judges** for **cases of robbery in Jerusalem,** [5] one named **Admon,** a second named **Ḥanan, and** a third named **Naḥum."** This second Baraita deviates from the earlier Baraita which listed Ḥanan the Egyptian, and not Naḥum, as the third judge who sat on this court!

אֲמַר רַב פַּפָּא [6] **Rav Pappa said:** This is also not difficult. **Who mentioned Naḥum** among the judges who established fines that were imposed in cases of robbery? [7] **It was Rabbi Natan, for it was taught** in another Baraita: [8] **"Rabbi Natan says: Naḥum the Median was also among those** judges who **established fines** for robbery **in Jerusalem.** [9] **But the Sages did not agree with him."**

וְתוּ לֵיכָּא [10] The Gemara asks: Why split hairs over the names of individual judges? **Were there no more** judges in Jerusalem? [11] **But surely Rabbi Pineḥas said in the name of Rabbi Oshaya: There were three hundred and ninety-four** different **courts** of twenty-three judges **in Jerusalem,** [12] **and a corresponding number of synagogues** for prayer, **and a corresponding number of academies** for advanced Talmud study, **and a corresponding number of schools** for young children."

שֶׁבִּירוּשָׁלַיִם אוֹמְרִים: [1] נְטִיעָה בַּת שְׁנָתָהּ — שְׁתֵּי כֶסֶף, [2] בַּת שְׁתֵּי שָׁנִים — אַרְבַּע כֶּסֶף".

[3] וּרְמִינְהִי: [4] "שְׁלֹשָׁה דַּיָּינֵי גְזֵירוֹת הָיוּ בִּירוּשָׁלַיִם: [5] אַדְמוֹן, וְחָנָן, וְנַחוּם"!

[6] אֲמַר רַב פַּפָּא: מַאן תָּנָא נַחוּם? [7] רַבִּי נָתָן הִיא, דְּתַנְיָא: [8] "רַבִּי נָתָן אוֹמֵר: אַף נַחוּם הַמָּדִי מִגּוֹזְרֵי גְזֵירוֹת שֶׁבִּירוּשָׁלַיִם הָיָה. [9] וְלֹא הוֹדוּ לוֹ חֲכָמִים.

[10] וְתוּ לֵיכָּא? [11] וְהָאָמַר רַבִּי פִּנְחָס אָמַר רַבִּי אוֹשַׁעְיָא: שְׁלֹשׁ מֵאוֹת וְתִשְׁעִים וְאַרְבָּעָה בָּתֵּי דִינִין הָיוּ בִּירוּשָׁלַיִם, [12] כְּנֶגְדָּן בָּתֵּי כְנֵסִיּוֹת, וּכְנֶגְדָּן בָּתֵּי מִדְרָשׁוֹת, וּכְנֶגְדָּן בָּתֵּי סוֹפְרִים!

LITERAL TRANSLATION

in Jerusalem say: [1] [For] a one-year-old sapling — two silver [me'ahs], [2] [for] a two-year-old [sapling] — four silver [me'ahs]."

[3] But [another] contradiction may be raised: [4] "There were three judges in cases of robbery in Jerusalem: [5] Admon, and Ḥanan, and Naḥum!"

[6] Rav Pappa said: Who taught Naḥum? [7] It is Rabbi Natan, for it was taught: [8] "Rabbi Natan said: Naḥum the Median was also [one] of those who decreed fines in Jerusalem. [9] But the Sages did not agree with him."

[10] Are there no more? [11] But surely Rabbi Pineḥas said in the name of Rabbi Oshaya: There were three hundred and ninety-four courts in Jerusalem, [12] and a corresponding [number of] synagogues, and a corresponding [number of] academies, and a corresponding [number of] primary schools.

RASHI

קיטמה נטיעה גרסינן — בבבא קמא גבי בהמה שנכנסה לרשות הניזק והזיקה, קטמה נטיעת אילן כמה שמין אותה? שתי כסף — שתי מעות. בתי דינין — של עשרים ושלשה. בתי כנסיות — להתפלל. בתי מדרשות — למשנה ולתלמוד. בתי סופרים — ללמוד תינוקות.

NOTES

the term "fines" used by *Rashi* cannot be precise, for the compensation that a robber must pay his victim is an ordinary monetary obligation, and not a fine. Rather, these judges established fixed monetary penalties for specific types of damage, to avoid the necessity of assessing the damage in each individual case. *Talmidei HaRashba* (cited by *Shittah Mekubbetzet*) suggest that these judges imposed special fines upon robbers, whenever they thought that such penalties would deter them from repeating their crimes. The Jerusalem Talmud explains that these judges sat in judgment only over cases of robbery. *Rabbenu Yehonatan* notes that robbery was not a common crime, and a small number of judges could easily handle all the cases.

שְׁלֹשׁ מֵאוֹת וְתִשְׁעִים וְאַרְבָּעָה Three hundred and nintey-four. *Maharsha* cites *Rashi* to Isaiah 1:21, who writes that there were four hundred and eighty-one courts in Jerusalem, corresponding to the numerical value of the word מלאתי, "full," in the verse: "It was full of judgment."

HALAKHAH

receive ninety maneh per annum, and if that sum did not suffice for them, even if they did not want to receive more, their salaries would be raised in accordance with their own needs and the needs of their households," following Rav Yehudah and the Gemara's conclusion.

In later generations, judges were remunerated from a special communal fund that was established for that purpose, and which would be collected either at the beginning or at the end of the year. *Rema* (following *Tur*) writes that it is preferable to collect the money for this fund at the beginning of each year, so that money be readily available, and it not be necessary for the judges to ask people for loans and owe them a favor. (*Rambam, Sefer Zemanim, Hilkhot Shekalim.*4:7; *Shulḥan Arukh, Ḥoshen Mishpat* 9:3.)

[1]דַּיָּינִין — טוּבָא הָווּ. [2]וְכִי קָאָמְרִינַן, [3]אַגּוֹזְרֵי גְזֵירוֹת קָאָמְרִינַן.
[4]אָמַר רַב יְהוּדָה אָמַר רַב אַסִי: [5]גּוֹזְרֵי גְזֵירוֹת שֶׁבִּירוּשָׁלַיִם, הָיוּ נוֹטְלִין שְׂכָרָן תִּשְׁעִים וְתֵשַׁע מָנֶה מִתְּרוּמַת הַלִּשְׁכָּה. [6]לֹא רָצוּ, מוֹסִיפִין לָהֶם.
[7]לֹא רָצוּ? [8]אַטּוּ בִּרְשִׁיעֵי עָסְקִינַן?
[9]אֶלָּא, לֹא סָפְקוּ, [10]אַף עַל פִּי שֶׁלֹּא רָצוּ, מוֹסִיפִין עֲלֵיהֶן.
[11]קַרְנָא הֲוָה שָׁקֵיל אִיסְתֵּירָא מִזַּכַּאי [12]וְאִיסְתֵּירָא מֵחַיָּיב, [13]וְדָאֵין לְהוּ דִּינָא.
[14]וְהֵיכִי עָבֵיד הָכִי? [15]וְהָכְתִיב: ״וְשֹׁחַד לֹא תִקָּח״.

LITERAL TRANSLATION

[1]Judges — there were many. [2]But when we spoke, [3]we spoke about those who decreed fines.
[4]Rav Yehudah said in the name of Rav Assi: [5]Those who decreed fines in Jerusalem would take as their remuneration ninety-nine manehs from the [Temple fund called] *terumat halishkah* (lit., "contribution to the [Temple treasury] chamber"). [6][If] they did not agree, they added to it.
[7][If] they did not agree? [8]Are we dealing with wicked people?
[9]Rather, [if] it did not suffice, [10]even if they did not agree [to take more], they added to it.
[11]Karna would take an istira (half a dinar) from the innocent party [12]and an istira from the guilty party, [13]and judge them.
[14]How could he do this? [15]But surely it is written: "And you shall take no bribe"!

TRANSLATION AND COMMENTARY

דַּיָּינִין [1]Yes! **There were** indeed **many judges.** [2]**But when we spoke** here of a limited number of judges, [3]**we were speaking about** the members of a special court that **established fines** that were imposed for robbery.

אָמַר רַב יְהוּדָה [4]**Rav Yehudah said in the name of Rav Assi:** [5]The judges **who** sat on the court that **established fines** for robbery **in Jerusalem would take ninety-nine manehs from the** Temple fund called ***terumat halishkah*** ("the contribution to the [Temple treasury] chamber") **as their** annual **salary.** [6]**If they did not agree** to this amount, their salary **would be raised.**

לֹא רָצוּ [7]The Gemara questions this ruling: Can it be that **if** the judges **did not agree** to the salary offered them, their salary would be raised? [8]**Are we dealing** here **with wicked people** who demand exorbitant salaries?

אֶלָּא [9]**Rather,** Rav Assi meant as follows: **If** ninety-nine manehs a year **did not suffice** to meet their needs, [10]then **even if they did not agree,** their salary **would be raised,** so that they could devote themselves entirely to their communal responsibilities.

קַרְנָא הֲוָה שָׁקֵיל [11]It was related that when a case would be brought before the renowned jurist **Karna** for adjudication, he **would take an istira** (half a dinar) **from the party** who might be judged as **innocent** [12]**and an istira from the party** who might be judged as **guilty,** [13]**and** only then would he **judge them.**

וְהֵיכִי עָבֵיד הָכִי [14]The Gemara asks: **How could** Karna **do this?** [15]**But surely the verse states** (Exodus 23:8): **"And you shall take no bribe,"** which teaches that a judge may not accept any money from the litigants who appear before him!

RASHI

נוטלין שכרן – ומתפרנסין הימנו, לפי שלא היו עסוקין במלאכתן. ברשיעי עסקינן – שנוטלין שכר לדון יותר מכדי חייהן? לא ספקו – למזונות. אף על פי שלא רצו – ליטול. איסתירא – סלע.

NOTES

מִתְּרוּמַת הַלִּשְׁכָּה **From the *terumat halishkah*.** The literal meaning of the term *terumat halishkah* is "the contribution of [money for] the [Temple treasury] chamber." Each year, every adult Jewish male was obligated to donate a half-shekel to the Temple. These half-shekels were brought to Jerusalem and stored in a specific chamber in the Temple complex. The money collected was divided into two parts: Three large containers of nine *se'ahs* each were set aside as the *terumat halishkah,* and whatever was left over was called the *sheyarei halishkah,* "the surplus of the Temple treasury chamber." Three times a year — fifteen days before Passover, fifteen days before Shavuot, and on the 29th of Elul — a priest would enter the chamber with three smaller containers and take out three *se'ahs* from each of the larger containers holding the *terumat halishkah.* This money was used mainly for the purchase of the communal offerings and other needs of the Temple. According to our Gemara, the judges who sat on the court that established fines for robbery were remunerated from funds taken from the *terumat halishkah.* According to a reading in the Jerusalem Talmud, these judges were remunerated from the *sheyarei haliskhah,* funds that were used also for communal expenses that were not necessarily connected to the Temple service.

HALAKHAH

וְשֹׁחַד לֹא תִקָּח **And you shall take no bribe.** "A judge is forbidden to accept a fee for his services, even if it was given to him so that he would convict the guilty and acquit the innocent. A judge who accepts a bribe violates a negative prohibition, and is liable for the curse, 'Cursed be he who takes a bribe' (Deuteronomy 27:25). He is obligated to return the money to the party who gave it to him, should he claim it back from him." (*Rambam, Sefer Shofetim, Hilkhot Sanhedrin* 23:1.)

TRANSLATION AND COMMENTARY

וְכִי תֵּימָא [1]The Gemara suggests a rationale for Karna's practice, but immediately rejects it: **You might** perhaps **say that the verse** forbidding a judge to take money from the litigants only **applies** if he **did not take** money **from both** of them. [2]If he takes from only one of the parties, **he may come to pervert justice,** and rule unjustly in favor of the party who gave him the money. [3]**But** in the case of **Karna, since he would take** money **from both** litigants, [4]there was **no** concern that he **would pervert justice.** [5]**But** this is difficult, for **is it** really **permitted** for a judge to accept money, even **when** there is **no** concern that **he will come to pervert justice?** [6]**But surely it was taught** in a Baraita: "The verse states (Exodus 23:8): **'And you shall take no bribe'** — [7]**what does it teach** us? [8]**If** you say it **teaches that** the judge **may not** take a bribe to **acquit the guilty** party, [9]**or to convict the innocent** party, [10]this is difficult, for **surely it was already stated** (Deuteronomy 16:20): **'You shall not pervert judgment'!** [11]**Rather,** you must say that the verse teaches that a judge may never take money from a litigant appearing before him, **even** when there is no concern that he will allow the money to influence his decision, and he is confident that he will still **acquit the innocent, and convict the guilty,** [12]for **the Torah said: 'And you shall take no bribe.'"**

הָנֵי מִילֵּי [13]The Gemara proposes another rationale for Karna's practice: **This law** forbidding a judge to take money from litigants **only applies** if he **takes the money as a bribe.** [14]**But Karna took money as a fee** for his services.

וּבְתוֹרַת אַגְרָא [15]The Gemara asks: **But is it** really **permitted** for a judge to accept **a fee** for his services? [16]**But surely we have learned** otherwise in a Mishnah (*Bekhorot* 29a): **"If someone takes a fee to judge, his judgment is invalid."**

[1]וְכִי תֵּימָא הָנֵי מִילֵּי הֵיכָא דְּלָא שָׁקֵיל מִתַּרְוַיְיהוּ, [2]דִּלְמָא אָתֵי לְאַצְלוּיֵי דִּינָא. [3]קַרְנָא כֵּיוָן דְּשָׁקֵיל מִתַּרְוַיְיהוּ, [4]לָא אָתֵי לְאַצְלוּיֵי דִּינָא. [5]וְכִי לָא אָתֵי לְאַצְלוּיֵי דִּינָא, מִי שָׁרֵי? [6]וְהָתַנְיָא: "'וְשֹׁחַד לֹא תִקָּח' [7]מַה תַּלְמוּד לוֹמַר? [8]אִם לְלַמֵּד שֶׁלֹּא לְזַכּוֹת אֶת הַחַיָּיב, [9]וְשֶׁלֹּא לְחַיֵּיב אֶת הַזַּכַּאי — [10]הֲרֵי כְּבָר נֶאֱמַר: 'לֹא תַטֶּה מִשְׁפָּט'! [11]אֶלָּא, אֲפִילּוּ לְזַכּוֹת אֶת הַזַּכַּאי, וּלְחַיֵּיב אֶת הַחַיָּיב, [12]אָמְרָה תּוֹרָה: 'וְשֹׁחַד לֹא תִקָּח'".

[13]הָנֵי מִילֵּי הֵיכָא דְּשָׁקֵיל בְּתוֹרַת שׁוֹחַד. [14]קַרְנָא בְּתוֹרַת אַגְרָא הֲוָה שָׁקֵיל.

[15]וּבְתוֹרַת אַגְרָא מִי שָׁרֵי? [16]וְהָתְנַן: "הַנּוֹטֵל שָׂכָר לָדוּן, דִּינָיו בְּטֵלִין"!

LITERAL TRANSLATION

[1]And if you say [that] these words [apply] where he did not take from both of them, [2]lest he come to pervert the judgment. [3][But] since Karna would take from both of them, [4][he] would not come to pervert the judgment. [5]But when he does not come to pervert the judgment, is it permitted? [6]But surely it was taught: "'And you shall take no bribe' — [7]what does the verse teach us? [8]If to teach that he must not acquit the guilty, [9]and that he must not convict the innocent — [10]surely it was already stated: 'You shall not pervert judgment'! [11]Rather, even to acquit the innocent, or to convict the guilty, [12]the Torah said: 'And you shall take no bribe.'"

[13]This [verse] applies where he took [the money] as a bribe. [14][But] Karna took [the money] as a fee.

[15]But is it permitted as a fee? [16]But surely we have learned: "[If] someone takes a fee to judge, his judgments are void"!

RASHI

בתורת שוחדא — שלא תחייבני אם זכאי אני. **בתורת אגרא** — שכר טורח. **הנוטל שכר לדון** — משנה היא במסכת בכורות (כט,א).

SAGES

קַרְנָא **Karna.** A first-generation Babylonian Amora, sometimes called Rav Karna. Karna was a colleague of Shmuel, and both greeted Rav when he came to Babylonia.

Elsewhere (*Sanhedrin* 17a) the Gemara states that the expression דַּיָּינֵי הַגּוֹלָה, "the judges of the Diaspora," refers to Karna, who served as a Rabbinical judge in Neharde'a. Karna edited a collection of Baraitot called נְזִיקִין דְּבֵי קַרְנָא, "the torts of Karna's school." As the Gemara states here, he earned his livelihood as a wine-taster.

NOTES

דְּשָׁקֵיל מִתַּרְוַיְיהוּ **He would take from both of them.** Many Aḥaronim ask: If a judge is forbidden to accept a bribe because it will make him partial to the party from whom he received the money, then why is he not permitted to accept a bribe from both parties? *Ayelet Ahevim* suggests that once a judge receives a bribe from a litigant, then even if he rules against him, he will not impose the punishment that he deserves. *Ḥever ben Ḥayyim* proposes that a judge is instructed to treat the litigants appearing before him as wicked people. He must suspect that they are lying and investigate the matter until the truth emerges. But once a judge receives a bribe from a litigant, he will be unable to consider him in that light. *Meiri* dealt with this issue and writes that if a judge accepts money from both parties, he will be partial to both of them. He will aim for a decision that compromises between them, rather than judge them according to the letter of the law.

הַנּוֹטֵל שָׂכָר לָדוּן **If someone takes a fee to judge.** Judges

HALAKHAH

הַנּוֹטֵל שָׂכָר לָדוּן **If someone takes a fee to judge.** "If a judge takes a fee for his services, all of his decisions are invalid

[1]הָנֵי מִילֵּי אֲגַר דִּינָא. [2]קַרְנָא אֲגַר בְּטֵילָא הֲוָה שָׁקֵיל. [3]וַאֲגַר בְּטֵילָא מִי שָׁרֵי? [4]וְהָתַנְיָא: ״מְכוֹעָר הַדַּיָּין שֶׁנּוֹטֵל שָׂכָר לָדוּן, אֶלָּא שֶׁדִּינוֹ דִּין״. [5]הֵיכִי דָּמֵי? [6]אִילֵימָא אֲגַר דִּינָא, דִּינוֹ דִּין? [7]וְהָתַנְיָא: ״הַנּוֹטֵל שָׂכָר לָדוּן, דִּינָיו בְּטֵילִין״! [8]אֶלָּא, אֲגַר בְּטֵילָא. [9]וְקָתָנֵי: ״מְכוֹעָר הַדַּיָּין״! [10]הָנֵי מִילֵּי בְּטֵילָא דְּלָא מוֹכְחָא. [11]קַרְנָא בְּטֵילָא דְּמוֹכְחָא הֲוָה שָׁקֵיל, [12]דַּהֲוָה תָּהֵי בְּאַמְבָּרָא דְּחַמְרָא, [13]וְיָהֲבֵי לֵיהּ זוּזָא. [14]כִּי הָא דְּרַב הוּנָא, כִּי הֲוָה אָתֵי דִּינָא לְקַמֵּיהּ, [15]אֲמַר לְהוּ: ״הֲבוּ לִי גַּבְרָא דְּדָלֵי לִי בַּחֲרִיקַאי, [16]וְאֵידוּן לְכוּ דִּינָא״.

TRANSLATION AND COMMENTARY

הָנֵי מִילֵּי [1]The Gemara seeks another way to justify Karna's practice: Perhaps **this** only **applies** if the judge takes the money as **a fee for his judgment.** [2]But **Karna would take** the money as **compensation for his** being **idle** from pursuing his usual trade.

וַאֲגַר בְּטֵילָא [3]The Gemara argues that even that is problematic: **But is** a judge really **permitted** to accept **compensation for his idleness?** [4]**But surely it was taught** in a Baraita: **"It is unbecoming for a judge to take a fee to judge, but his judgment is** nevertheless **valid."** [5]The Gemara asks: **How do we visualize the case** dealt with by the Baraita? [6]**If you say** that the Baraita is dealing with a judge who takes **a fee for his judgment, is his judgment** really **valid?** [7]**But surely it was taught** in the Mishnah cited above: **"If someone takes a fee to judge** a case, **his judgment is invalid"!** [8]**Rather,** the Baraita must be dealing with a judge who accepts **compensation for his idleness.** [9]**And it teaches:** "It is **unbecoming** for a **judge** to take a fee"! How then could Karna have legitimately behaved in that manner?

הָנֵי מִילֵּי [10]The Gemara answers: **This applies** only **to compensation for idleness that is not clearly evident,** when the judge cannot prove that his sitting in judgment causes him a loss. [11]But **Karna would take compensation for idleness** whose resultant loss **was clearly evident,** [12]**for** when he was not sitting on the judge's bench, **he would examine stores of wine** to see which barrels could remain in storage, and which were about to turn sour, [13]**and he would be given a zuz** for each barrel that he examined. Thus, when he served as a judge, he was clearly forgoing income. [14]Karna's situation was **similar to that of Rav Huna,** who **when a case would be brought before him** for adjudication, [15]**would say to** the litigants: "I have to irrigate my field. **Bring me somebody to draw water in my place,** [16]**and I will** be glad to **judge you."**

LITERAL TRANSLATION

[1]This applies to a fee for judgment. [2]Karna would take compensation for [his] idleness.

[3]But is compensation for idleness permitted? [4]But surely it was taught: "Unbecoming is the judge who takes a fee to judge, but his judgment is a [valid] judgment." [5]How do we visualize the case (lit., "what is it like")? [6]If you say a fee for [his] judgment, is his judgment a [valid] judgment? [7]But surely it was taught: "[If] someone takes a fee to judge, his judgments are void"! [8]Rather, compensation for idleness. [9]And it teaches: "Unbecoming is the judge"!

[10]This applies [to compensation for] idleness that is not clearly evident. [11]Karna would take [compensation for] idleness that was clearly evident, [12]for he would examine stores of wine, [13]and they would give him a zuz. [14]Like that of Rav Huna, when a judgment came before him, [15]he would say to them: "Bring me a man who will draw [water] in my place, [16]and I will judge you."

RASHI

אגר דינא – לא אומר לכם הדין כי אם בשכר כך וכך. אגר בטילא – שהיה בטל ממלאכתו. דהוה תהי באמברי דחמרא – מריח באוצרות יין, אי זה ראוי להתקיים. והקרוב להתקלקל – ימכרוהו מיד, ושכר זה היה מצוי לו בכל יום. כי הא – דבטילא דמוכח שרי. הבו לי גברא דדלי – מיא, משקה שדותי. בחריקאי = במקומי. חריקאי – אומר אני שהוא לשון פגום, כמו קרניס חרוקות ד״שחיטת חולין״ (נט,ב) כלומר: שאני מסתלק ונפגם מקומי.

LANGUAGE

אַמְבָּרָא Store. From the Middle Persian *anbar* (*ambar* in related languages), meaning "granary, storehouse."

NOTES

may not accept fees for their services because, just as the Torah was given by God to the people of Israel free of charge, so too it must be taught free of charge by the scholars of every generation.

HALAKHAH

(except those cases regarding which he did not take a fee). But the judge is permitted to take money as reimbursement for the loss which he suffers by sitting in judgment, provided that it is clear that he forgoes income while serving as a judge, and that he takes the reimbursement in equal shares from both parties. But he may not take reimbursement for a loss which is not clearly evident, for example, if he does not have a profession from which he must be idle while serving as a judge, it is not sufficient to claim that business might have come his way while he was serving as a judge." (*Rambam, Sefer Shofetim, Hilkhot Sanhedrin* 23:1; *Shulḥan Arukh, Ḥoshen Mishpat* 9:5.)

TRANSLATION AND COMMENTARY

אָמַר רַבִּי אַבָּהוּ [1]Bribery can certainly not be condoned **Rabbi Abbahu said: Come and see how blind are the eyes of** judges **who accept bribes.** [2]**A person who feels pain in his eyes** is ready to **give** all the **money** in the world **to a doctor** in the hope of a cure, [3]**when** in fact the matter is **in doubt whether he will be cured or he will not be cured.** [4]Yet when corrupt judges **take** meager bribes to **the value of a perutah,** the Scripture warns them that **they** thereby **blind their eyes,** [5]**as the verse states** (Exodus 23:8): **"For the bribe blinds the clear-sighted."**

תָּנוּ רַבָּנַן [6]**Our Rabbis taught** in a Baraita: "The verse states (Deuteronomy 16:20): **'For a bribe blinds the eyes of the clear-sighted'** — [7]**and all the more so** does a bribe blind the eyes **of the stupid.** [8]The same verse continues: **'And perverts the words of the righteous'** — **and all the more so** does a bribe pervert the words **of the wicked.'"** [9]The Gemara asks: **Are the stupid and the wicked fit to** sit in **judgment?** Thus the inferences from "clear-sighted" to "stupid" and from "righteous" to "wicked" are problematical.

אֶלָּא [10]**Rather,** the Baraita means to **say as follows: "For a bribe blinds the eyes of the clear-sighted"** — [11]**even if a** judge began as **a great** [12]**Sage, if he takes a bribe,** [13]**he will not depart from the world without blindness of the mind,** i.e., he will end up as a fool. [14]**"And it perverts the words of the righteous"** — [105B] [15]**even if** a judge is **an absolutely righteous man,** once **he takes a bribe,** [16]**he will not depart from the world without confusion of the mind.**

כִּי אֲתָא [17]**When Rav Dimi came** from Eretz Israel to Babylonia, **he said: Rav Naḥman bar Kohen expounded:** [18]**What is the meaning of the verse that states** (Proverbs 29:4): **"The king by justice establishes the land; but he who exacts gifts overthrows it"?** [19]**If a judge is similar to a** wise and wealthy **king who does not need anything,** [20]and is therefore independent, **he will establish** justice throughout **the land.** [21]**But if** the judge **is like a priest who must pass among the granaries** to collect the priestly gifts,

[1]אָמַר רַבִּי אַבָּהוּ: בֹּא וּרְאֵה כַּמָּה סְמוּיוֹת עֵינֵיהֶן שֶׁל מְקַבְּלֵי שׁוֹחַד. [2]אָדָם חָשׁ בְּעֵינָיו נוֹתֵן מָמוֹן לְרוֹפֵא, [3]סָפֵק מִתְרַפֵּא, סָפֵק אֵינוֹ מִתְרַפֵּא. [4]וְהֵן נוֹטְלִין שָׁוֶה פְּרוּטָה וּמְסַמִּין עֵינֵיהֶן, [5]שֶׁנֶּאֱמַר: "כִּי הַשֹּׁחַד יְעַוֵּר פִּקְחִים".

[6]תָּנוּ רַבָּנַן: "'כִּי הַשֹּׁחַד יְעַוֵּר עֵינֵי חֲכָמִים' — [7]קַל וָחוֹמֶר לַטִּפְּשִׁין. [8]'וִיסַלֵּף דִּבְרֵי צַדִּיקִם' — קַל וָחוֹמֶר לָרְשָׁעִים". [9]מִידֵי טִפְּשִׁים וּרְשָׁעִים בְּנֵי דִּינָא נִינְהוּ?

[10]אֶלָּא, הָכִי קָאָמַר: "כִּי הַשֹּׁחַד יְעַוֵּר עֵינֵי חֲכָמִים" — [11]אֲפִילּוּ חָכָם גָּדוֹל וְלוֹקֵחַ שׁוֹחַד — [12]אֵינוֹ נִפְטָר מִן הָעוֹלָם בְּלֹא סַמְיוּת הַלֵּב. [13]"וִיסַלֵּף דִּבְרֵי צַדִּיקִם" — [105B] [14]אֲפִילּוּ צַדִּיק גָּמוּר וְלוֹקֵחַ שׁוֹחַד — [15]אֵינוֹ נִפְטָר מִן הָעוֹלָם בְּלֹא טֵירוּף דַּעַת.

[16]כִּי אֲתָא רַב דִּימִי, אֲמַר: דָּרַשׁ רַב נַחְמָן בַּר כֹּהֵן: [17]מַאי דִּכְתִיב: "מֶלֶךְ בְּמִשְׁפָּט יַעֲמִיד אָרֶץ וְאִישׁ תְּרוּמוֹת יֶהֶרְסֶנָּה"? [18]אִם דּוֹמֶה דַּיָּין לְמֶלֶךְ, שֶׁאֵינוֹ צָרִיךְ לִכְלוּם, [19]יַעֲמִיד אָרֶץ. [20]וְאִם דּוֹמֶה לְכֹהֵן שֶׁמְּחַזֵּר עַל

LITERAL TRANSLATION

[1]Rabbi Abbahu said: Come and see how blind are the eyes of those who accept bribes. [2]A person who feels pain in his eyes gives [much] money to a doctor [and] perhaps he will be cured, [3][but] perhaps he will not be cured. [4]But they take the value of a perutah [as a bribe], and blind their eyes, [5]as it is stated: "For the bribe blinds the clear-sighted."

[6]Our Rabbis taught: "'For a bribe blinds the eyes of the clear-sighted" — [7]and all the more so of the stupid. [8]'And perverts the words of the righteous' — and all the more so of the wicked." [9]Are the stupid and the wicked fit for judgment?

[10]Rather, he said as follows: "For a bribe blinds the eyes of the clear-sighted" — [11]even if he is a great Sage and he takes a bribe — [12]he will not depart from the world without blindness of the heart. [13]"And it perverts the words of the righteous" — [105B] [14]even if he is an absolutely righteous man and he takes a bribe — [15]he will not depart from the world without confusion of the mind.

[16]When Rav Dimi came, he said: Rav Naḥman bar Kohen expounded: [17]What is [it] that is written: "The king by justice establishes the land; but he who receives gifts overthrows it"? [18]If a judge is like a king, who does not need anything, [19]he will establish the land. [20]But if he is like a priest who passes among

RASHI

אינו נפטר מן העולם — והכי קאמר: קל וחומר שיסמא את עיניו כשיהא טפש בסופו וישב לדון. שאינו צריך כלום — שהוא עשיר, ואין צריך להחניף.

NOTES

אִם דּוֹמֶה דַּיָּין לְמֶלֶךְ **If a judge is like a king.** *Rivan* cites two explanations: If a judge is like a king in that he is wealthy

TRANSLATION AND COMMENTARY

[1]**he will destroy** the judicial process, for he is dependent upon others and will not have the strength to resist the pressures of those upon whom he is dependent.

אָמַר [2]**Rabbah bar Rav Shela said:** A **judge who borrows things** from other people [3]**is disqualified from serving as a judge.** [4]But **we only say this** with respect to a judge **who does not have anything to lend.** [5]**But if he** himself **has to lend** to others, he is qualified to judge, for **we are not concerned** that his decisions will be influenced by his borrowing.

אִינִי [6]The Gemara asks: But **is it** really **so** that someone who only borrows, but does not lend, is disqualified from serving as a judge? [7]**But surely Rava** was a judge, and he **borrowed things from the house of Bar Maryon,** [8]**even though they did not borrow** anything **from him!**

הָתָם [9]The Gemara answers: Rava was himself a wealthy man, and he borrowed from them because **he wanted to show them honor.** Thus, there was no reason for Rava to feel indebted to the house of Bar Maryon, and so there was no concern that his decisions would be influenced by his borrowing from them.

אָמַר רָבָא [10]**Rava said: What is the reason** that taking **a bribe** is prohibited, even if the judge intends to ignore it? It is because bribes make impartiality impossible. [11]**When** a judge **receives a bribe from** someone, [12]**he develops an intimate relationship with that person, and** regards him **as himself,** [13]**and one is unable to see guilt in oneself.** Moreover, the Hebrew term for bribe alludes to this explanation:

הַגְּרָנוֹת, [1]יֶהֶרְסֶנָּה.

[2]אֲמַר רַבָּה בַּר רַב שֵׁילָא: הַאי דַּיָּינָא דְּשָׁאֵיל שְׁאֵילָתָא [3]פָּסוּל לְמֵידַן דִּינָא. [4]וְלָא אֲמָרַן אֶלָּא דְּלֵית לֵיהּ לְאוֹשׁוּלֵי. [5]אֲבָל אִית לֵיהּ לְאוֹשׁוּלֵי — לֵית לָן בָּהּ.

[6]אִינִי? [7]וְהָא רָבָא שָׁאֵיל שְׁאֵילָתָא מִדְּבֵי בַּר מָרְיוֹן, [8]אַף עַל גַּב דְּלָא שָׁיְילֵי מִינֵּיהּ!

[9]הָתָם לְאַחְשׁוּבִינְהוּ הוּא דְּבָעֵי.

[10]אֲמַר רָבָא: מַאי טַעְמָא דְּשׁוּחֲדָא? [11]כֵּיוָן דְּקַבֵּיל לֵיהּ שׁוּחֲדָא מִינֵּיהּ, [12]אִיקַּרְבָא לֵיהּ דַּעְתֵּיהּ לְגַבֵּיהּ וְהָוֵי כְּגוּפֵיהּ, [13]וְאֵין אָדָם רוֹאֶה חוֹבָה לְעַצְמוֹ.

LITERAL TRANSLATION

the granaries, [1]he will destroy it.

[2]Rabbah bar Rav Shela said: That judge who borrows things [3]is disqualified from judging. [4]And we only say [this] where he does not have [anything] to lend. [5]But if he has [something] to lend — we are not concerned.

[6]Is it so? [7]But surely Rava borrowed something from the house of Bar Maryon, [8]even though they would not borrow from him!

[9]There he wanted to give them esteem.

[10]Rava said: What is the reason of [the prohibition of] bribery? [11]If one receives a bribe from somebody, [12]one becomes close to him, and one becomes like the same person, [13]and a person does not see guilt in himself.

RASHI

דשאיל שאילתא — דרגיל לישאל מבני עירו בהמות וכלים. **מאי טעמא דשוחדא** — למה אסור ליטלו לזכות את הזכאי? **אין אדם רואה חובה לעצמו** — אין דעתו מתקרב לצד החובה לחייב את עצמו, ואפילו מתכוין לדין אמת.

NOTES

and therefore not dependent upon the good will of others, he will establish justice in the land. Alternatively, the judge will establish justice in the land if his wealth of knowledge is similar to the material wealth of a king and he has sufficiently mastered the law so that he is not dependent on scholarly consultations with others. *Tosafot* cites *Rabbenu Tam* who argues that both explanations are correct. *Rambam,* in his introduction to the Mishnah, writes that a judge must be similar to a king, who feels that he is dependent upon no one and has no necessity to seek wealth or honor.

דְּשָׁאֵיל שְׁאֵילָתָא Who borrows things. *Rivan* writes that a judge who regularly is in need of borrowing from other people is disqualified from sitting in judgment, for he must maintain good relations with others so that they continue to lend things to him. Alternatively, a judge who regularly borrows from a certain person is disqualified from sitting in judgment over that person (see also *Meiri*). *Ḥever ben Ḥayyim* notes a judge who borrowed money is surely disqualified from judging his creditor, for the verse states (*Proverbs* 22:7): "The borrower is servant to the lender."

מַאי טַעְמָא דְּשׁוּחֲדָא What is the reason for the prohibition of bribery. Our commentary follows *Rashi,* who explains that the Gemara is trying to explain why a judge may not take any money for his services, even to convict the guilty and acquit the innocent. *Iyyun Ya'akov* writes that the Gemara is not searching for the rationale underlying the Biblical commandment, but rather it is trying to account for

HALAKHAH

דַּיָּינָא דְּשָׁאֵיל שְׁאֵילָתָא A judge who borrows things. "A judge who borrowed something is disqualified from sitting in judgment over the lender. This only applies if the judge does not have anything to lend to others. But if the judge has things to lend, he is fit to serve as a judge, for the party who lent him can borrow back from him as well," following Rabbah bar Rav Shela. *Rema* (in the name of *Maharik*) writes that this regulation only applies if the judge

TRANSLATION AND COMMENTARY

[1]**What is** the derivation of the word שֹׁחַד, **"bribe"?** שֶׁהוּא חַד — **that he,** the judge, **is one** with the person who gave him the bribe.

אָמַר רַב פַּפָּא [2]**Rav Pappa said:** A judge **should not judge the case of someone whom he likes,** [3]**nor** the case of **someone whom he hates.** [4]He should not judge the case of someone **whom he likes,** [5]for **he is not able to find fault with him,** [6]and he should not judge the case of someone **whom he hates,** [7]for **he is not able to see merit in him.**

אָמַר אַבַּיֵי [8]**Abaye said:** If a **Rabbinic scholar is** well-**liked by** his **townspeople,** [9]**it is not because he is more outstanding** than others, [10]**but because he does not rebuke them** sufficiently **about religious matters.** He can be said to be bribing them by his indulgent attitude.

אָמַר רָבָא [11]**Rava said: At first** before I became a judge **I used to** think that my townsmen, **the people of Meḥoza, all like me.** [12]**When I became a judge,** I began to **think** that it stands to reason that **some of** the people will now **hate me,** because I found them guilty, [13]**and some of the** people will now **like me,** because I ruled in their favor. [14]**Now that I see that** the same person **whom I find guilty today, I might acquit tomorrow,** [15]**I say:** My popularity should not depend on a particular ruling. **If** there is reason **to like** me, then **all of** the people **will like me;** [16]and **if** there is reason **to hate** me, then **all of them will hate me.**

[1]מַאי "שׁוֹחַד"? שֶׁהוּא חַד. [2]אֲמַר רַב פַּפָּא: לָא לֵידוּן אִינִישׁ דִּינָא לְמַאן דְּרָחֵים לֵיהּ, [3]וְלָא לְמַאן דְּסָנֵי לֵיהּ. [4]דְּרָחֵים לֵיהּ — [5]לָא חָזֵי לֵיהּ חוֹבָה. [6]דְּסָנֵי לֵיהּ — [7]לָא חָזֵי לֵיהּ זְכוּתָא.

[8]אֲמַר אַבַּיֵי: הַאי צוּרְבָא מֵרַבָּנַן דִּמְרַחֲמִין לֵיהּ בְּנֵי מָתָא, [9]לָאו מִשּׁוּם דִּמְעַלֵּי טְפֵי, [10]אֶלָּא מִשּׁוּם דְּלָא מוֹכַח לְהוּ בְּמִילֵּי דִּשְׁמַיָּא.

[11]אֲמַר רָבָא: מֵרֵישׁ הֲוָה אָמִינָא: הָנֵי בְּנֵי מְחוֹזָא כּוּלְּהוּ רַחֲמוּ לִי. [12]כֵּיוָן דַּהֲוַאי דַּיָּינָא, אָמִינָא: מִינַּיְיהוּ סָנוּ לִי, [13]וּמִינַּיְיהוּ רַחֲמוּ לִי. [14]כֵּיוָן דַּחֲזַאי דְּמַאן דְּמִיחַיַּיב לֵיהּ הָאִידָּנָא קָא זָכֵי לְמָחָר, [15]אָמִינָא: אִם מִרְחַם, כּוּלְּהוּ רַחֲמוּ לִי; [16]אִי מִסְנוּ — כּוּלְּהוּ סָנוּ לִי.

LITERAL TRANSLATION

[1]What is [the word] "bribe"? That he is one.

[2]Rav Pappa said: A person should not judge the case of someone whom he likes, [3]nor someone whom he hates. [4]He whom he likes — [5]he sees no guilt in him. [6]He whom he hates — [7]he sees no merit in him.

[8]Abaye said: A Rabbinic scholar whom the townspeople like — [9]it is not because he is more outstanding, [10]but because he does not rebuke them about heavenly matters.

[11]Rava said: At first I used to say: Those people of Meḥoza all like me. [12]Since I became a judge, I said: Some of them [will] hate me, [13]and some of them [will] like me. [14]Since I saw that he whom I find guilty today would be acquitted tomorrow, [15]I said: If [there is reason] to like, all of them [will] like me; [16]if to hate, all of them [will] hate me.

RASHI

שהוא חד — הנותן והמקבל נעשים לב אחד. בני מחוזא — עירו של רבא. מינייהו — מקצתם אוהבים אותי, אותם שזכיתי. אם מרחם — אם אוהבים — נעשו כולם אוהביי.

NOTES

the restrictions added by the Sages who forbade not only an outright bribe but anything that remotely resembles one. Therefore, the Gemara had to explain that a bribe is not forbidden because of the benefit received by the judge, but rather because of the intimacy which it fosters between the judge and the litigant, which will influence the judge's decision.

שֶׁהוּא חַד **That he is one.** *Ayelet Ahevim* proposes a novel interpretation: God is with a judge when he sits in judgment and helps him arrive at a just decision, as the verse states (Psalms 82:1): "He judges among judges." When a judge accepts a bribe, God departs from him, and the judge is left all by himself.

לְמַאן דְּרָחֵים לֵיהּ **Someone whom he likes.** *Hafla'ah* writes that Rav Pappa's statement may be understood as meaning that not only is a judge disqualified from sitting in judgment

HALAKHAH

borrows from a person on a regular basis, but if he once happened to borrow from him, and there is no evidence that he lent it to him because of his case, the judge is fit to sit in judgment over him. If the judge borrowed only in order to show someone honor, he is fit to judge him, as was related about Rava (*Shakh* in the name of *Tur*). (*Rambam, Sefer Shofetim, Hilkhot Sanhedrin* 23:4; *Shulḥan Arukh, Ḥoshen Mishpat* 9:1.)

לָא לֵידוּן אִינִישׁ **A person should not judge.** "A judge may not sit in judgment over someone with whom he has a personal relationship — whether he likes or dislikes him. Rather, a judge must have equal regard for both of the parties to the dispute. Optimally, the judge does not know either party. *Rema* writes that if a judge sat in judgment over someone whom he likes or dislikes, his judgment is nevertheless valid (*Hagahot Oshri*). But according to some authorities (*Tur*), if the judge adjudicated the case of someone whom he hated — someone with whom he had

TRANSLATION AND COMMENTARY

תָּנוּ רַבָּנַן [1] **Our Rabbis taught** the following Baraita: "The verse states (Exodus 23:8): **'And you shall take no bribe.'** [2] **It is not necessary to say** that the verse prohibits only **a monetary bribe,** [3] **for even a favor** 'a bribe of action' **is forbidden.** How do we know this? [4] **For the verse does not state: 'You shall take no money,'** which would imply that only a monetary bribe is forbidden."

הֵיכִי דָּמֵי [5] **How** precisely **do we visualize the case of a** forbidden **favor?** [6] It is **like** what happened **when Shmuel was crossing a bridge,** [7] **and a man gave him his hand** to help him over. [8] Shmuel **said to him: "What business** brings you here?" [9] **He answered: "I have a case** which I wish to bring before you **for judgment."** [10] Shmuel **said to him:** "Then I **am disqualified to judge you,** for you did me a favor by helping me across the bridge."

אַמֵימָר [11] A similar story is told about **Amemar** who **was** once **sitting and judging a case.** [12] **A feather fell on his head, and a man came and removed it.** [13] Amemar **said to him: "What business** brings you here?" [14] **He answered: "I have a case** which I wish to bring before you **for judgment."** [15] Amemar **said to him:** "Since you did me a favor, **I am disqualified to judge you."**

מָר עוּקְבָא [16] It was related that someone **cast spit** on the ground **in front of Mar Ukva, and a man came and covered it.** [17] Mar Ukva **said to him: "What business** brings you here?" [18] **He answered: "I have a**

[1] תָּנוּ רַבָּנַן: "'וְשֹׁחַד לֹא תִקָּח' — [2] אֵינוֹ צָרִיךְ לוֹמַר שׁוֹחַד מָמוֹן, [3] אֶלָּא אֲפִילּוּ שׁוֹחַד דְּבָרִים נַמִּי אָסוּר, [4] מִדְּלָא כְּתִיב: 'בֶּצַע לֹא תִקָּח'". [5] הֵיכִי דָּמֵי שׁוֹחַד דְּבָרִים? [6] כִּי הָא דִּשְׁמוּאֵל הֲוָה עָבַר בְּמַבָּרָא, [7] אֲתָא הַהוּא גַּבְרָא יָהֵיב לֵיהּ יְדֵיהּ. [8] אֲמַר לֵיהּ: "מַאי עֲבִידְתָּיךְ"? [9] אֲמַר לֵיהּ: "דִּינָא אִית לִי". [10] אֲמַר לֵיהּ: "פְּסִילְנָא לָךְ לְדִינָא".

[11] אַמֵימָר הֲוָה יָתֵיב וְקָא דָאֵין דִּינָא. [12] פָּרַח גַּדְפָּא אַרֵישֵׁיהּ, אֲתָא הַהוּא גַּבְרָא שְׁקַלֵיהּ. [13] אֲמַר לֵיהּ: "מַאי עֲבִידְתָּיךְ"? [14] אֲמַר לֵיהּ: "דִּינָא אִית לִי". [15] אֲמַר לֵיהּ: "פְּסִילְנָא לָךְ לְדִינָא".

[16] מָר עוּקְבָא הֲוָה שְׁדִי רוּקָא קַמֵּיהּ, אֲתָא הַהוּא גַּבְרָא כַּסְיֵיהּ. [17] אֲמַר לֵיהּ: "מַאי עֲבִידְתָּיךְ"? [18] אֲמַר לֵיהּ: "דִּינָא

LITERAL TRANSLATION

[1] Our Rabbis taught: "'And you shall take no bribe.' [2] It is not necessary to say a monetary bribe, [3] for even a favor (lit., 'bribe of action') is also forbidden, [4] for it is not written: 'You shall take no money.'"

[5] How do we visualize the case of a [forbidden] favor? [6] Like [what happened] when Shmuel was crossing a bridge, [7] [and] a certain man gave him his hand. [8] He said to him: "What is your business?" [9] He said to him: "I have a [case for] judgment." [10] He said to him: "I am disqualified to judge you."

[11] Amemar was sitting and judging a case. [12] A feather fell on his head, [and] a certain man came and removed it. [13] He said to him: "What is your business?" [14] He said to him: "I have a [case for] judgment." [15] He said to him: "I am disqualified to judge you."

[16] Spit was cast before Mar Ukva, [and] a certain man came [and] covered it. [17] He said to him: "What is your business?" [18] He said to him: "I have a [case for]

RASHI

במברא = גשר. **יהיב ליה ידא** — לסומכו.

NOTES

over someone whom he likes or dislikes, but he is also disqualified from judging a person who likes or dislikes him. For as the verse states (Proverbs 27:19): "As in water [the reflection of] face answers to face, so the heart of a man [answers] to man." A judge cannot avoid being influenced by feelings toward him. This explains the connection between Rav Pappa's statement and the remarks of Abaye and Rava which follow.

פְּסִילְנָא לָךְ לְדִינָא **I am disqualified to judge you.** *Ritva* writes in the name of *Ramah* that a judge is not disqualified by law from sitting in judgment over a person who did him a favor or showed him a courtesy like those reported in

HALAKHAH

not spoken for three days because of the ill-feelings between them — or the case of someone whom he loved, his judgment is not valid. Some say that a judge is permitted to judge the case of someone with whom he has a personal relationship, provided that he does not actually hate him or love him, and it is an act of exceptional piety to refrain from sitting in judgment over such a person. Thus, it is permitted in cases of arbitration for each party to choose a judge whom he likes. And so too it is permitted for a judge to sit in judgment of his disciple (*Maharik*)." (*Rambam, Sefer Shofetim, Hilkhot Sanhedrin* 23:6; *Shulḥan Arukh, Ḥoshen Mishpat* 7:7.)

שׁוֹחַד דְּבָרִים **A favor.** "A judge must take extraordinary care not to take any sort of bribe — not only a monetary bribe, but a favor as well. A 'bribe of action' includes any favor or courtesy shown to the judge by a person who brings a case before him for adjudication," as in the incidents recorded in the Gemara. (*Rambam, Sefer Shofetim, Hilkhot Sanhedrin* 23:3; *Shulḥan Arukh, Ḥoshen Mishpat* 9:1.)

TRANSLATION AND COMMENTARY

case that I wish to bring before you **for judgment."** [1]Mar Ukva **said to him:** "You did me a favor, and so **I am disqualified to judge you."**

רַבִּי יִשְׁמָעֵאל בְּרַבִּי יוֹסֵי [2]It was further related that **Rabbi Yishmael the son of Rabbi Yose** had a **tenant farmer** who **was accustomed to bring** him **a basket** full **of fruit every Friday,** fruit which grew in Rabbi Yishmael's own orchard. [3]**Once** the tenant **brought** the fruit **to** Rabbi Yishmael **on Thursday.** [4]Rabbi Yishmael **said to him: "What is different today** that you brought me my fruit earlier than usual?" [5]The tenant **said to him: "I have a case** that I wanted to bring before you **for judgment,** [6]**so I said** to myself: 'Since I have to be in court on Thursday, the day that the court convenes, **I might as well bring** the fruit **to Master.'"** [7]Rabbi Yishmael **did not accept the fruit from him.** [8]**He said to him: "I am disqualified to judge you."** [9]**He established a pair of Rabbis** as a court, **and they judged** the tenant farmer. [10]**While he was coming and going,** Rabbi Yishmael **said** to himself: [11]**"If** my tenant farmer **wants, he can argue like this, and if he wants, he can argue like that,"** constantly thinking of arguments that the tenant farmer could have presented in his favor. Seeing how partial he had become to his tenant's cause, [12]Rabbi Yishmael **said: "May the souls of those** judges **who take bribes depart.** [13]**If I, who did not take** anything from my tenant farmer — [14]**and had I taken, I would have taken** only **my own** fruit — [15]**if I am like that** and am so easily swayed by anything that remotely resembles a bribe, then **those who accept bribes — all the more so** do they obstruct justice."

רַבִּי יִשְׁמָעֵאל בַּר אֱלִישָׁע [16]**A man** once **brought Rabbi Yishmael bar Elisha** who was a priest **the first shearing** of his sheep, in keeping with the obligation to give a priest the first portion of fleece shorn from a flock (see Deuteronomy 18:4). Not recognizing the person who gave him the fleece, [17]Rabbi Yishmael **asked him: "Where are you from?"** [18]**He told him:** "I come **from such-and-such place."** Seeing that the man had traveled

אִית לִי״. [1]אֲמַר לֵיהּ: ״פְּסִילְנָא לָךְ לְדִינָא״.

[2]רַבִּי יִשְׁמָעֵאל בְּרַבִּי יוֹסֵי הֲוָה רְגִיל אֲרִיסֵיהּ דַּהֲוָה מַיְיתֵי לֵיהּ כָּל מַעֲלֵי שַׁבְּתָא כַּנְתָּא דְּפֵירֵי. [3]יוֹמָא חַד אַיְיתֵי לֵיהּ בְּחַמְשָׁא בְּשַׁבְּתָא. [4]אֲמַר לֵיהּ: ״מַאי שְׁנָא הָאִידָּנָא״? [5]אֲמַר לֵיהּ: ״דִּינָא אִית לִי, [6]וְאָמִינָא: ׳אַגַּב אוֹרְחִי אַיְיתֵי לֵיהּ לְמָר׳״. [7]לָא קַבֵּיל מִינֵּיהּ. [8]אֲמַר לֵיהּ: ״פְּסִילְנָא לָךְ לְדִינָא״. [9]אוֹתֵיב זוּזָא דְּרַבָּנַן, וְקָדָיְינִין לֵיהּ. [10]בַּהֲדֵי דְּקָאָזֵיל וְאָתֵי, אֲמַר: [11]״אִי בָּעֵי, טָעֵין הָכִי, וְאִי בָּעֵי, טָעֵין הָכִי״. [12]אָמַר: ״תִּיפַּח נַפְשָׁם שֶׁל מְקַבְּלֵי שׁוֹחַד. [13]וּמָה אֲנִי, שֶׁלֹּא נָטַלְתִּי, [14]וְאִם נָטַלְתִּי, שֶׁלִּי נָטַלְתִּי, [15]כָּךְ, מְקַבְּלֵי שׁוֹחַד עַל אַחַת כַּמָּה וְכַמָּה״.

[16]רַבִּי יִשְׁמָעֵאל בַּר אֱלִישָׁע אַיְיתֵי לֵיהּ הַהוּא גַּבְרָא רֵאשִׁית הַגֵּז. [17]אֲמַר לֵיהּ: ״מֵהֵיכָא אַתְּ״? [18]אֲמַר לֵיהּ: ״מִדּוּךְ פְּלָן״.

LITERAL TRANSLATION

judgment." [1]He said to him: "I am disqualified to judge you."

[2]The tenant farmer of Rabbi Yishmael the son of Rabbi Yose used to bring him a basket of fruit every Friday. [3]One day he brought [it] to him on Thursday. [4]He said to him: "What is different today?" [5]He said to him: "I have a [case for] judgment, [6]and I said: 'On my way I will bring it to Master.'" [7]He did not accept it from him. [8]He said to him: "I am disqualified to judge you." [9]He set up a pair of Rabbis, and they judged him. [10]While [Rabbi Yishmael] was going and coming, he said: [11]"If he wants, he can argue like this, and if he wants, he can argue like that." [12]He said: "May the souls of those who take bribes depart. [13]If I, who did not take, [14]and [even] had I taken, I would have taken [only] what is mine, [15][if I] am like that, those who accept bribes all the more so."

[16]A certain man brought Rabbi Yishmael bar Elisha the first shearing. [17]He said to him: "Where are you from?" [18]He said to him: "From such-and-such place."

LANGUAGE

כַּנְתָּא Basket. Some derive this word from the Greek κανήτιον, *kanetion,* "small reed basket." (The Greek, in turn, might be related to the Hebrew, קנה.)

RASHI

כנתא דפירי — סל פירות מפרדס של רבי ישמעאל. **זוזא** — זוג. **בהדי דאזיל ואתי** — בכל אשר הולך ובא היה לבו לזכותו של אותו אריס, ובאין לו פתחי זכיות, ואומר בלבו: הלואי ויטעון כך וכך ויזכה בדין. **ראשית הגז** — בכל שנה שגוזז אותן חייב ליתן לכהן אחד מששים.

NOTES

our Gemara. But rather the cases described here were only acts of piety that go beyond the letter of the law.

Meiri notes that for a judge to accept a favor is only forbidden when it is accompanied by some act, as in the cases cited in our Gemara, but words alone do not constitute a bribe (see also *Sma*). Moreover, a judge who was shown a favor is only disqualified from serving as a single judge, but not when he sits on a court with two other judges.

אוֹתֵיב זוּזָא דְּרַבָּנַן He set up a pair of Rabbis. The question was raised: Why did Rabbi Yishmael set up a court of two judges, when we learned elsewhere that a court should

LANGUAGE

גִּילְדָנֵי דְּבֵי גִּילֵי Small marsh fish. Some derive this from the Greek Χεκιδών, *chelidon,* which means "flying fish" (inter alia). However, the word גִּילְדָנֵי apparently refers to several different types of fish, both large fish and small fish. These fish are therefore described here as גִּילְדָנֵי דְּבֵי גִּילֵי — to indicate that they were small (*Berakhot* 44b).

TRANSLATION AND COMMENTARY

a considerable distance to bring him the fleece, [1]Rabbi Yishmael asked: **"And** along all that way **from there to here, was there no priest to whom you could have given** the fleece? Why did you travel all that distance just to give the fleece to me?" [2]The visitor **said to him: "I have a case** which I wanted to bring before you **for judgment, so I said** to myself: [3]**'Since the master** is a priest, **I might** as well **bring him** the fleece.'" [4]Rabbi Yishmael **said to him: "I am disqualified to judge you," [5]and he refused to accept** the fleece **from him.** [6]**He established a pair of Rabbis** as a court, **and they judged** the man. [7]**While he was coming and going,** Rabbi Yishmael **said** to himself: [8]**"If he wants, he an argue like this, and if he wants, he can argue like that,"** all the time thinking of arguments that the man could have presented in his favor. Seeing how partial he had become, [9]Rabbi Yishmael **said: "May the souls of those** judges **who take bribes depart.** [10]**If I, who did not take** what had been offered me — [11]**and had I taken** anything, **I would have taken** only **what is mine** — [12]if I **am like that,** and am so easily influenced by anything that resembles a bribe, then **those who accept bribes — all the more so** do they obstruct justice."

רַב עָנָן [13]**A man brought Rav Anan a basket of small fish.** [14]Rav Anan **said to him: "What business** brings you here?" [15]The man **said to him: "I have a case** which I wish to bring before you **for judgment."** [16]Rav Anan **refused to accept** the fish **from him, and said to him:** [17]"Since you brought me the basket of fish, **I am disqualified to judge you."** [18]The man **said to** Rav Anan: **"I do not want master's judgment, [19]but may master** still **accept** my gift, **so that master not deprive me bringing** him **first fruits."** What did the man mean when he spoke of first fruits? [20]**It was taught** in a Baraita: "The verse states (II Kings 4:42): **'And there came a man from Ba'al-shalisha, and he brought the man of God bread of the first fruits, twenty loaves of barley, and full ears of corn in his sack.'** [21]**Was Elisha**

[1]״וּמֵהָתָם לְהָכָא לָא הֲוָה כֹּהֵן לְמֵיתְבָא לֵיהּ״? [2]אֲמַר לֵיהּ: ״דִּינָא אִית לִי, וְאָמִינָא: [3]׳אַגַּב אוֹרְחַאי אַיְיתֵי לֵיהּ לְמָר׳״. [4]אֲמַר לֵיהּ: ״פְּסִילְנָא לָךְ לְדִינָא״, [5]לָא קַבֵּיל מִינֵּיהּ. [6]אוֹתֵיב לֵיהּ זוּגָא דְּרַבָּנַן, וְקָדָיְינִי לֵיהּ. [7]בַּהֲדֵי דְּקָאָזֵיל וְאָתֵי, אֲמַר: [8]״אִי בָּעֵי טָעֵין הָכִי, וְאִי בָּעֵי, טָעֵין הָכִי״. [9]אֲמַר: ״תִּיפַּח נַפְשָׁם שֶׁל מְקַבְּלֵי שׁוֹחַד. [10]וּמָה אֲנִי, שֶׁלֹּא נָטַלְתִּי, [11]וְאִם נָטַלְתִּי, שֶׁלִּי נָטַלְתִּי, [12]כָּךְ, מְקַבְּלֵי שׁוֹחַד עַל אַחַת כַּמָּה וְכַמָּה״.

[13]רַב עָנָן אַיְיתֵי לֵיהּ הַהוּא גַּבְרָא כַּנְתָּא דְּגִילְדָנֵי דְּבֵי גִּילֵי. [14]אֲמַר לֵיהּ: ״מַאי עֲבִידְתֵּיךְ״? [15]אֲמַר לֵיהּ: ״דִּינָא אִית לִי״. [16]לָא קַבֵּיל מִינֵּיהּ, אֲמַר לֵיהּ: [17]״פְּסִילְנָא לָךְ לְדִינָא״. [18]אֲמַר לֵיהּ: ״דִּינָא דְּמָר לָא בָּעֵינָא, [19]קַבּוּלֵי לְקַבֵּיל מָר, דְּלָא לִמְנְעַן מָר מֵאַקְרוּבֵי בִּכּוּרִים״. [20]דְּתַנְיָא: ״׳וְאִישׁ בָּא מִבַּעַל שָׁלִישָׁה וַיָּבֵא לְאִישׁ הָאֱלֹהִים לֶחֶם בִּכּוּרִים עֶשְׂרִים לֶחֶם שְׂעוֹרִים וְכַרְמֶל בְּצִקְלֹנוֹ׳. [21]וְכִי

LITERAL TRANSLATION

[1][He said to him:] "And from there to here was there no priest to give it to?" [2]He said to him: "I have a [case for] judgment, and I said: [3]'On my way I will bring it to master.'" [4]He said to him: "I am disqualified to judge you," [5][and] he did not accept it from him. [6]He set up a pair of Rabbis, and they judged him. [7]While he was going and coming, he said: [8]"If he wants, he can argue like this, and if he wants, he can argue like that." [9]He said: "May the souls of those who take bribes depart. [10]If I, who did not take, [11]and [even] had I taken, I would have taken [only] what is mine, [12][if I] am like that, those who accept bribes all the more so." [13]A certain man brought Rav Anan a basket of small fish. [14]He said to him: "What is your business?" [15]He said to him: "I have a [case for] judgment." [16]He did not accept [it] from him, [and] he said to him: [17]"I am disqualified to judge you." [18]He said to him: "I do not want master's judgment, [19][but] may master accept [it], so that master not deprive me of bringing first fruits." [20]As it was taught: "'And there came a man from Ba'al-shalisha, and he brought the man of God bread of the first fruits, twenty loaves of barley, and full ears of corn in his sack.' [21]But

RASHI

גילדני דבי גילי — דגים קטנים.

NOTES

consist of three judges, and that a court of two is considered arrogant? *Meiri* suggests that perhaps he added a third judge afterward. Or perhaps the two were expert judges who were authorized to judge the case singly.

Maharsha proposes that Rabbi Yishmael himself was the third judge, for he was only disqualified from serving alone (see previous Note.)

TRANSLATION AND COMMENTARY

a priest **who** is permitted to **eat first fruits,** one of the priestly gifts? [1] **Rather,** the verse comes **to teach you** that **whoever brings a gift to a Torah scholar is regarded as if he brought first fruits** to the Temple." [2] Rav Anan **said to** the man: "At first **I did not want to accept** your gift, [3] but **now that you have explained the reason,** I am ready to **accept it.** [4] Rav Anan then **sent** the man **to Rav Naḥman, and sent him** a message saying: [5] **"Let master judge this man, for I, Anan, am disqualified to judge him."** [6] Rav Naḥman **thought: "Since** Anan **sent me such** a message, this man **must be his relative."** [7] It so happened that **a case involving orphans was pending before him** at the very same time, and so Rav Naḥman had to choose which case to hear first. [8] **He said** to himself: [106A] [9] "I am bound by **one positive commandment** to consider the case of the orphans first **and** by another **positive commandment** to consider the case sent to me by Rav Anan first, for there is an obligation to show honor to Torah scholars and their family. I will judge the case sent to me by Rav Anan first, [10] for **the positive commandment of honoring the Torah** and its scholars **takes precedence** over my other obligation." [11] And so Rav Naḥman **removed the case involving the orphans** from the top of his docket, **and adjudicated the case** of the litigant sent to him by Rav Anan whom he mistakenly assumed was his relative. [12] **When** that man's **opponent saw the honor that**

LITERAL TRANSLATION

could Elisha eat first fruits? [1] Rather, to teach you: Whoever brings a gift to a Torah scholar [is regarded] as if he brought first fruits. [2] He said to him: "I did not want to accept [it]. [3] [But] now that you have explained [your] reason, I will accept it." [4] He sent him to Rav Naḥman, [and] sent him: [5] "Let master judge this man, for I, Anan, am disqualified to judge him." [6] [Rav Naḥman] thought: "Since [Anan] sent me [a message], he must be his relative." [7] A case regarding orphans was standing before him, [8] [and] he said: [106A] [9] "This is a positive commandment, and this is a positive commandment. [10] The positive commandment of honoring the Torah takes precedence." [11] He pushed off the case of the orphans, and took up his case. [12] When the opponent saw the honor that [Rav Naḥman]

אֱלִישָׁע אוֹכֵל בִּכּוּרִים הֲוָה? [1] אֶלָּא, לוֹמַר לְךָ: כָּל הַמֵּבִיא דּוֹרוֹן לְתַלְמִיד חָכָם כְּאִילּוּ מַקְרִיב בִּכּוּרִים. [2] אֲמַר לֵיהּ: ״קַבּוּלֵי לָא בָּעֵינַן דְּאִיקַּבֵּיל. [3] הָשְׁתָּא דְּאָמְרַתְּ לִי טַעְמָא, מְקַבֵּילְנָא״. [4] שְׁדַרֵיהּ לְקַמֵּיהּ דְּרַב נַחְמָן, שְׁלַח לֵיהּ: [5] ״נִידַיְינֵיהּ מָר לְהַאי גַּבְרָא, דַּאֲנָא, עָנָן, פְּסִילְנָא לֵיהּ לְדִינָא״. [6] אֲמַר: ״מִדְּשָׁלַח לִי הָכִי, שְׁמַע מִינָּהּ קְרִיבֵיהּ הוּא״. [7] הֲוָה קָאֵים דִּינָא דְּיָתְמֵי קַמֵּיהּ, [8] אֲמַר [106A] [9] ״הַאי עֲשֵׂה וְהַאי עֲשֵׂה. [10] עֲשֵׂה דִּכְבוֹד תּוֹרָה עֲדִיף. [11] סַלְּקֵיהּ לְדִינָא דְּיָתְמֵי, וְאַחְתֵּיהּ לְדִינֵיהּ״. [12] כֵּיוָן דַּחֲזָא בַּעַל דִּינֵיהּ יְקָרָא דְּקָא

RASHI

וכי אלישע אוכל ביכורים היה — והלא לא כהן היה, שהרי מצינו בדברי הימים שנתייחס אביו על שבט גד, דכתיב "ויעני ושפט בבשן" ומצינו במסכת פסחים ב"אלו דברים" (סח,א) דשפט דהאי קרא הוא אביו של אלישע. **שמע מינה קריביה הוא** — להכי פסול ליה לדינא. **שמע מינה קריביה הוא** — להכי פסול ליה לדינא. **האי עשה והאי עשה** — מצות הדיינים עשה "ושפטתם צדק". **עשה דכבוד תורה** — דיניה דהאי גברא דהוא עשה, דאיכא כבוד תורה דרב ענן בהדיה — עדיף.

NOTES

כָּל הַמֵּבִיא דּוֹרוֹן לְתַלְמִיד חָכָם Whoever brings a gift to a Torah scholar. Just as the first fruits of the new harvest which a Jew must give to the priests serve as an expression of his gratitude to God for the gift of Eretz Israel to the Jewish people, so too the gifts which a person brings to a Torah scholar serve as an expression of his gratitude for the gift of the Torah and its teachers (*Iyyun Ya'akov*).

הַאי עֲשֵׂה וְהַאי עֲשֵׂה This is a positive commandment, and this is a positive commandment. *Rashi* writes that regarding the case of the orphans Rav Naḥman was required to fulfill the positive commandment given to all judges (Deuteronomy 1:16): "And judge righteously between every man and his brother." Some ask: But how does this verse indicate that he must take their case first? He could fulfill this command whenever he hears the case.

It could, however, be suggested that righteous judgment requires a judge to deal with a case as rapidly as possible. The case now before him thus has priority and cannot be postponed *Ritva* explains that Rav Naḥman was bound to consider the case of the orphans first because of the positive commandment (Deuteronomy 1:17): "But hear the small as well as the great." Some suggest that Rav Naḥman was bound by the general obligation to fulfill a commandment as soon as it presents itself, and not to pass over one commandment in order to fulfill another. According to *Rambam,* there is a special obligation to give precedence to the case of orphans.

עֲשֵׂה דִּכְבוֹד תּוֹרָה The positive commandment of honoring the Torah. Some Rishonim understand from our Gemara that the obligation of honoring Torah scholars includes an

HALAKHAH

עֲשֵׂה דִּכְבוֹד תּוֹרָה עֲדִיף The positive commandment of honoring the Torah takes precedence. "A judge must give precedence to the case that was brought before him first. But a case involving a Torah scholar is given precedence,

עָבֵיד לֵיהּ, [1] אִיסְתַּתַּם טַעֲנָתֵיהּ. [2] רַב עָנָן, הֲוָה רָגִיל אֵלִיָּהוּ דְּאָתֵי גַּבֵּיהּ, דַּהֲוָה מַתְנֵי לֵיהּ סֵדֶר דְּאֵלִיָּהוּ. [3] כֵּיוָן דַּעֲבַד הָכִי אִיסְתַּלַּק. [4] יְתֵיב בְּתַעֲנִיתָא וּבְעָא רַחֲמֵי וַאֲתָא. [5] כִּי אֲתָא הֲוָה מַבְעֵית לֵיהּ בָּעוּתֵי, [6] וַעֲבַד תֵּיבוּתָא וִיתֵיב קַמֵּיהּ, עַד דְּאַפֵּיק לֵיהּ סִידְרֵיהּ. [7] וְהַיְינוּ דְּאָמְרִי: סֵדֶר דְּאֵלִיָּהוּ רַבָּה, סֵדֶר אֵלִיָּהוּ זוּטָא.

LITERAL TRANSLATION

granted him, [1] he was unable to plead (lit., "his plea was stopped up"). [2] Elijah was accustomed to come to Rav Anan, [and] teach him *Seder Eliyahu* (The Order of Elijah). [3] When he did this, he left. [4] He sat in a fast, and prayed for mercy, and [Elijah] came. [5] When he came, he frightened him, and he constructed a box, [6] and sat before him, until he taught him his Order. [7] And this is what they say: *Seder Eliyahu Rabbah, Seder Eliyahu Zuta.*

TRANSLATION AND COMMENTARY

Rav Naḥman **was showing him,** [1] **he** was intimidated and **unable to plead** his arguments effectively. As a result he lost the case. By referring the case to Rav Naḥman, Rav Anan, unwittingly and indirectly, caused an injustice to be carried out. Until then, [2] the prophet **Elijah was accustomed to appear before Rav Anan, and teach him** what was later committed to writing in the work known as ***Seder Eliyahu.*** [3] But **when this** injustice **happened** as a result of Rav Anan's misleading message to Rav Naḥman, Elijah **ceased appearing** before him. [4] Rav Anan then **fasted and prayed for mercy, and** Elijah once again **appeared** before him. [5] But now **when** Elijah **appeared**, his appearance **frightened** Rav Anan, **and** so he **constructed** for himself **a box,** [6] in which **he would sit, until** Elijah finished **teaching him the work,** *Seder Eliyahu.* [7] **And this** is why people **refer** to the work as ***Seder Eliyahu Rabbah*** (the "major" *Seder Eliyahu*), which was composed when Anan faced Elijah directly, and ***Seder Eliyahu Zuta*** (the "minor" *Seder Eliyahu*), which was composed when Anan was sitting in his box.

RASHI

סדר אליהו רבה – שלמד חוץ לתיבה, **סדר אליהו זוטא** – שלמד בתוך התיבה.

BACKGROUND

סֵדֶר אֵלִיָּהוּ *Seder Eliyahu.* A Midrashic work by this name is extant, although it is not clear whether this work is the same as the *Seder Eliyahu* mentioned in the Gemara. The present-day *Seder Eliyahu* (which is also called תַּנָּא דְּבֵי אֵלִיָּהוּ, *Tanna deVei Eliyahu*), is divided into two parts, like the one mentioned in the Gemara. *Seder Eliyahu Rabbah,* the larger part, has thirty-one chapters (in some versions, twenty-nine chapters), while *Seder Eliyahu Zuta* has fifteen (other versions have different numbers of chapters). *Seder Eliyahu* is written in Hebrew. Many biblical verses are explained in this work, which also recounts historical events from various periods in Jewish history and tells stories about the Prophet Elijah (related in the first person), which sometimes begin: "Father Elijah said."

Many passages from our *Seder Eliyahu* are quoted in the Talmud, where they are attributed to *Tanna deVei Eliyahu."*

NOTES

obligation of honoring their family members as well. *Pnei Yehoshua* notes however that while we find an obligation to honor the wife of a Torah scholar, for a man's wife is considered as an extension of himself, we do not find a more inclusive obligation of honoring other members of a Torah scholar's family. Rather, Rav Naḥman understood that Rav Anan was asking him to honor his relative, and that acceding to that request was actually a manifestation of honor to Rav Anan himself.

Ritva cites the position of *Ra'ah* that Rav Naḥman had not yet begun to consider the case of the orphans, for had he started to hear that case, he would surely not have been permitted to interrupt the hearing in order to consider the case of a Torah scholar's relative.

אִיסְתַּתַּם טַעֲנָתֵיהּ He was unable to plead. In fact, a Torah scholar himself is indeed given precedence over other cases, and we are not concerned that the honor displayed to him will intimidate his opponent. Here, however, the opponent was intimidated because he knew that the man whom Rav Naḥman had mistakenly taken as Rav Anan's relative was neither a Torah scholar nor the relative of a Torah scholar, and so he thought that Rav Naḥman was biased in his favor (*Ritva*).

הֲוָה מַבְעֵית לֵיהּ בָּעוּתֵי He frightened him. *Maharsha* writes that Rav Anan committed two errors. First, he ate the fish which he should have refused, as did Rabbi Yishmael the son of Rabbi Yose and Rabbi Yishmael bar Elisha. Second, he caused Rav Naḥman to think that the man that he had sent to him was his relative, which led to the intimidation of his opponent. He atoned for his first offense by fasting, but he was unable to atone for his second offense. Just as the opponent was intimidated, so too Rav Anan was punished in that he was henceforth frightened i.e., intimidated by Elijah's appearance, and therefore he was unable to learn from him as before.

Arukh writes that Elijah had at first appeared before Rav Anan in a human form, and so Rav Anan was able to face him. But after Rav Anan committed his mistake, Elijah appeared before him as an angel, and so Rav Anan was unable to look at him directly.

סֵדֶר אֵלִיָּהוּ זוּטָא *Seder Eliyahu Zuta.* *Rivan* writes that Rav Anan was unable to learn for extended periods while he

HALAKHAH

even if it was brought before the judge after another case. *Rema* writes that when a Torah scholar comes to court, his case is given precedence, even if the judges already started to hear another case, so that the Torah scholar would not have to sit idle. But when the relative of a Torah scholar comes to court, if the judges already began to hear another case, they do not stop. Only if they have not yet begun to hear the other case is the relative's case given precedence as a show of honor to the Torah scholar (*Bet Yosef* in the name of *Ritva*). If various cases were brought before a court for adjudication, a case involving orphans is given precedence over a case involving a widow, a case involving a widow is given precedence over a case involving a Torah scholar, a case involving a Torah scholar is given precedence over a case involving an ordinary person, and a case involving a woman is given precedence over a case involving a man. Objections were raised against this ruling from our Gemara, which implies that a case involving a relative of a Torah scholar is given precedence over a case involving orphans (see *Leḥem Mishneh* and *Baḥ*). *Be'er HaGolah* argues that this ruling is in fact based on our passage, for the story concludes that the relative's opponent was intimidated when the Torah scholar's relative was accorded that honor." (*Rambam, Sefer Shofetim, Hilkhot Sanhedrin* 21:6; *Shulḥan Arukh, Yoreh De'ah* 15:1-2.)

TRANSLATION AND COMMENTARY

בִּשְׁנֵי דְּרַב יוֹסֵף [1]**During the years of Rav Yosef, God displayed** His **anger** and brought famine to the world. [2]**The Rabbis said to Rav Yosef: "Let master pray for mercy** on our behalf!" [3]Rav Yosef **said to them: "Now,** the Prophet **Elisha, who when his Rabbinic disciples left his** academy at the conclusion of the lesson, [4]**twenty-two hundred disciples remained** behind and ate at Elisha's table. [5]If Elisha himself who fed all these disciples **did not pray for mercy when** God displayed His **anger** and brought famine, [6]**can I pray for mercy** at this time?"

וּמִמַּאי [7]The Gemara asks: **From where do we know that** twenty-two hundred of Elisha's disciples **remained** behind to be maintained at Elisha's table? [8]**For the verses state** (II Kings 4:42-43): "And there came a man from Ba'al-shalisha, and he brought the man of God bread of the first fruits, twenty loaves of barley, and full ears of corn in his sack. And he said: Give to the people that they may eat. [9]**And his attendant said: What! Should I set this before one hundred men?** He said again: Give the people that they may eat; for thus says the Lord, They shall eat, and shall leave over." Now, the man from Ba'al-shelisha brought twenty-two loaves one of the first fruits of barley, twenty other loaves of barley, and one of the full ears of corn. [10]**What** did the attendant mean when he asked: "Should I set this — the twenty-two loaves — **before one hundred men**"? [11]**If** he asked about setting **all** twenty-two loaves **before one hundred men,** there is a difficulty, [12]for **in years of drought** twenty-loaves for one hundred men **is a lot!** [13]**Rather,** we must understand that the attendant asked about setting a **single** loaf **before one hundred men.** Thus, it follows that there were twenty-two hundred disciples who ate at Elisha's table.

כִּי הָווּ [14]It was related that **when the Rabbis left Rav's academy** at the conclusion of the lesson, **twelve hundred Rabbis remained** behind to eat with Rav himself. [15]And when **the Rabbis left Rav Huna's academy** at the conclusion of their studies, **eight hundred Rabbis remained** behind and were maintained at Rav Huna's table.

[1]בִּשְׁנֵי דְּרַב יוֹסֵף, הֲוָה רִיתְחָא. [2]אָמְרִי לֵיהּ רַבָּנַן לְרַב יוֹסֵף: "לִיבְעֵי מָר רַחֲמֵי"! [3]אֲמַר לְהוּ: "הָשְׁתָּא, — וּמָה אֱלִישָׁע, דְּכִי הָווּ רַבָּנַן מִיפַּטְרִי מִקַּמֵּיהּ, [4]הָווּ פָּיְישֵׁי תְּרֵי אַלְפָּן וּמָאתָן רַבָּנַן — [5]בְּעִידָּן רִיתְחָא לָא הֲוָה בָּעֵי רַחֲמֵי — [6]אֲנָא אִיבְעֵי רַחֲמֵי"? [7]וּמִמַּאי דְּפָיְישֵׁי הָכִי? [8]דִּכְתִיב: [9]"וַיֹּאמֶר מְשָׁרְתוֹ מָה אֶתֵּן זֶה לִפְנֵי מֵאָה אִישׁ"? [10]מַאי לִפְנֵי מֵאָה אִישׁ? [11]אִילֵּימָא דְּכוּלְּהוּ לִפְנֵי מֵאָה אִישׁ — [12]בִּשְׁנֵי בַּצּוֹרֶת טוּבָא הָווּ! [13]אֶלָּא, דְּכָל חַד וְחַד קַמֵּי מֵאָה אִישׁ. [14]כִּי הָווּ מִיפַּטְרִי רַבָּנַן מִבֵּי רַב, הָווּ פָּיְישֵׁי אַלְפָּא וּמָאתָן רַבָּנַן. [15]מִבֵּי רַב הוּנָא — הָווּ פָּיְישֵׁי תְּמָנֵי מֵאָה רַבָּנַן.

LITERAL TRANSLATION

[1]During the years of Rav Yosef, there was [God's] anger. [2]The Rabbis said to Rav Yosef: "Let master pray for mercy!" [3]He said to them: "Now, if — Elisha, who when the Rabbis would take leave from him, [4]two thousand and two hundred Rabbis would remain — [5]did not pray for mercy in a time of anger — [6]I should pray for mercy?"

[7]And from where [do we know] so [many] they remained? [8]For it is written: [9]"And his attendant said: What! Should I set this before one hundred men?" [10]What is [meant by] "before one hundred men"? [11]If we say: All of [those loaves] before one hundred men — [12]in years of drought [that] is a lot! [13]Rather, each one before one hundred men.

[14]When the Rabbis would leave the house [of study] of Rav, a thousand and two hundred Rabbis would remain. [15]From the house of Rav Huna, eight hundred Rabbis would remain.

RASHI

הוה ריתחא — כעס של מקום, ובא רעב לעולם. דכי מיפטרי — תלמידיו ממנו, לעמוד מבית המדרש. הוו פיישי גביה — אוכלי שלחנו, תרי אלפים ומאתים. דכתיב "עשרים לחם ולחם בכורים" — הא עשרים וחד, וכרמל — הרי עשרים ותרתין. וכל אחד לפני מאה איש — הרי תרי אלפין ומאתים.

NOTES

sat inside the box which he had constructed to serve as a barrier between himself and the prophet Elijah. *Seder Eliyahu Zuta* is, therefore, much shorter than *Seder Eliyahu Rabbah.*

בְּעִידָּן רִיתְחָא **In a time of anger.** *Maharsha* notes: We find in tractate *Ta'anit* and elsewhere that many Talmudic Rabbis offered special prayers in times of famine. Surely they did not all support more disciples than did the prophet Elisha! He explains that in all those cases the famine was severe that it endangered the people with starvation and death. Thus the Rabbis interceded with their prayers on behalf of the community. Here, however, Rav Yosef was asked to offer prayers to end a famine that threatened only to raise food prices. He, therefore, declined arguing that he was no better than the Prophet Elisha. *Eshel Avraham* suggests that it is not fitting for a Torah scholar to intercede with his prayers in order to avert a heavenly decree hanging over his community, if the members of that community do not first examine their acts to discover why they are being threatened with calamity, and then repent.

מַאי לִפְנֵי מֵאָה וכו' **What is meant by "before one hundred men etc."** *Maharsha* understands that the Gemara's answer

TRANSLATION AND COMMENTARY

רַב הוּנָא [1]It was further related that **Rav Huna would expound** his discourse **with** the help of **thirteen Amoraim.** It was the Amora's function to listen closely to the master's discourse and transmit it to the assembled gathering, who due to their vast multitudes would otherwise not have been able to hear Rav Huna's actual words. The following story is further evidence of the great number of Rav Huna's disciples: [2]**When the Rabbis would stand up in Rav Huna's academy** in Sura after he completed his lesson, **and** they would **shake out their cloaks,** [3]there was so much **dust** that it **would rise** up **and block out the daylight.** [4]When the sky grew dark **in Eretz Israel,** the people there **would say:** [5]The Rabbis must have just **stood up in the academy of Rav Huna the Babylonian.**

כִּי מִיפַּטְרִי [6]**When the Rabbis left the academy of Rabbah and Rav Yosef** at the end of the lesson, only **four hundred Rabbis remained** behind. [7]**And they called themselves orphans,** with respect to the students of Rav Huna, eight hundred of whom were supported. [8]And **when the Rabbis took leave from Abaye's academy (and some say from Rav Pappa's academy, and** still **others say from Rav Ashi's academy)** [9]only **two hundred Rabbis would remain** behind, **and they called themselves orphans of orphans**, with respect to the students of Rabbah and Rav Yosef, four hundred of whom were supported.

אָמַר [10]It was stated earlier (105a) that the judges who imposed fines in cases of robbery were remunerated from the *terumat halishkah.* The Gemara now discusses the other uses to which those funds were put. **Rabbi Yitzḥak bar Redifa said in the name of Rabbi Ammi:** [11]**The inspectors of animal blemishes in**

[1]רַב הוּנָא הֲוָה דָּרֵישׁ בִּתְלֵיסַר אֲמוֹרָאֵי. [2]כִּי הָווּ קָיְימִי רַבָּנַן מִמְּתִיבְתָּא דְּרַב הוּנָא וְנַפְצִי גְּלִימַיְיהוּ, [3]הֲוָה סָלֵיק אַבָקָא וְכָסֵי לֵיהּ לְיוֹמָא. [4]וְאָמְרִי בְּמַעַרְבָא: [5]קָמוּ לֵיהּ מִמְּתִיבְתָּא דְּרַב הוּנָא בַּבְלָאָה.

[6]כִּי מִיפַּטְרִי רַבָּנַן מִבֵּי רַבָּה וְרַב יוֹסֵף — הָווּ פָּיְישֵׁי אַרְבַּע מֵאָה רַבָּנַן, [7]וְקָרוּ לְנַפְשַׁיְיהוּ יַתְמֵי. [8]כִּי הָווּ מִיפַּטְרִי רַבָּנַן מִבֵּי אַבַּיֵי, וְאָמְרִי לָהּ מִבֵּי רַב פַּפָּא, וְאָמְרִי לָהּ מִבֵּי רַב אַשִׁי, [9]הָווּ פָּיְישִׁי מָאתָן רַבָּנַן וְקָרוּ נַפְשַׁיְיהוּ יַתְמֵי דְּיַתְמֵי.

[10]אָמַר רַבִּי יִצְחָק בַּר רְדִיפָא אָמַר רַבִּי אַמִּי: [11]מְבַקְּרֵי מוּמִין

LITERAL TRANSLATION

[1]Rav Huna would expound with thirteen Amoraim. [2]When the Rabbis would stand up in the academy of Rav Huna and shake out their cloaks, [3]the dust would rise and block the daylight. [4]And they said in Eretz Israel (lit., "the West"): [5]They [must have already] stood up in the academy of Rav Huna the Babylonian.

[6]When the Rabbis would leave the house of Rabbah and Rav Yosef, four hundred Rabbis would remain, [7]and they called themselves orphans. [8]When the Rabbis would leave the house of Abaye, and some say from the house of Rav Pappa, and some say from the house of Rav Ashi, [9]two hundred Rabbis would remain, and they called themselves orphans of orphans.

[10]Rabbi Yitzḥak bar Redifa said in the name of Rabbi Ammi: [11]The inspectors of [animal] blemishes

RASHI

בתליסר אמוראי — השומעין מפיו ומשמיעין לרבים, זה מכאן וזה מכאן, ומלפניס ומלאחור. ומתחלקין למקומות הרבה, שהיה העם רב. **ובסי ליה ליומא** — מאפיל את החמה, והיה ניכר בארץ ישראל.

NOTES

is based on the use of the singular term זֶה, "this," in the expression "should I set *this* before one hundred men," rather than the plural term אֵלּוּ, "these." This teaches that the attendant was asking about setting each loaf before one hundred men.

הֲוָה סָלֵיק אַבָקָא The dust would rise. This story about the dust which would rise and cover the daylight was understood in various ways: Not only was the Torah that was studied in Rav Huna's academy significant, but even the dust rising from the Rabbis' cloaks, a metaphor for the character traits of those scholars, was so impressive, that it covered the daylight, stripping the power of those who worshipped the sun and other idols (*Maharsha*). Others suggest that the dust symbolizes the Torah teachings of the Rabbis studying in Rav Huna's academy which spread in all directions until they even reached Eretz Israel (*Derash Moshe*).

Pnei Yehoshua understands that the Gemara does not mean to say that the dust rising in Babylonia was visible in Eretz Israel. Rather it means that the dust that filled the air when Rav Huna's disciples shook out their cloaks gave rise to a popular saying. Whenever the skies grew dark in Eretz Israel as a result of a dust storm, people would say that the skies are now like the skies in Babylonia when Rav Huna's disciples rose from their studies.

מְבַקְּרֵי מוּמִין The inspectors of animal blemishes. *Tosafot* explains that the inspectors would examine the animals that were brought to the Temple for sacrifice to ensure that they

HALAKHAH

מְבַקְּרֵי מוּמִין The inspectors of animal blemishes. "Those who inspected animals for blemishes in Jerusalem, and the Torah scholars who taught the priests the laws of ritual slaughter and 'taking a fistful of the meal-offerings,' and

TRANSLATION AND COMMENTARY

Jerusalem would take their salaries from the *terumat halishkah*. Because certain types of blemishes or defects render an animal unfit to be sacrificed, inspectors were required in Jerusalem to determine whether a sacrifice was fit or not. These experts were paid from the *terumat halishkah*.

אָמַר רַב יְהוּדָה [1]**Rav Yehudah said in the name of Shmuel: The Torah scholars who taught the priests the laws of ritual slaughter** needed to carry out the sacrificial service **would take their salaries from the *terumat halishkah*.**

אָמַר רַב גִּידֵּל [2]**Rav Gidel said in the name of Rav: The Torah scholars who taught the priests the laws regarding taking a fistful of the meal-offerings would take their salaries from the** *terumat halishkah*. Most meal-offerings require that a handful of the offering together with its oil and frankincense be removed and burned on the altar (see Leviticus 2:2). The priest would scoop out a portion of the offering with the three middle fingers of his right hand, using his thumb and little finger to remove the surplus (see *Menaḥot* 11a). This was an act that required training.

אָמַר [3]**Rabbah bar Bar Ḥanah said in the name of Rabbi Yoḥanan: Those in Jerusalem who examined the** sacred Torah **scrolls for mistakes** and made the necessary corrections **would take their salaries from the *terumat halishkah*.**

שֶׁבִּירוּשָׁלַיִם, הָיוּ נוֹטְלִין שְׂכָרָן מִתְּרוּמַת הַלִּשְׁכָּה.
[1]אָמַר רַב יְהוּדָה אָמַר שְׁמוּאֵל: תַּלְמִידֵי חֲכָמִים הַמְלַמְּדִין הִלְכוֹת שְׁחִיטָה לַכֹּהֲנִים, הָיוּ נוֹטְלִין שְׂכָרָן מִתְּרוּמַת הַלִּשְׁכָּה.
[2]אָמַר רַב גִּידֵּל אָמַר רַב: תַּלְמִידֵי חֲכָמִים הַמְלַמְּדִים הִלְכוֹת קְמִיצָה לַכֹּהֲנִים, נוֹטְלִין שְׂכָרָן מִתְּרוּמַת הַלִּשְׁכָּה.
[3]אָמַר רַבָּה בַּר בַּר חָנָה אָמַר רַבִּי יוֹחָנָן: מַגִּיהֵי סְפָרִים שֶׁבִּירוּשָׁלַיִם, הָיוּ נוֹטְלִין שְׂכָרָן מִתְּרוּמַת הַלִּשְׁכָּה.

LITERAL TRANSLATION

in Jerusalem would take their salaries from the [Temple fund called] *terumat halishkah* (lit., "contribution of the [Temple treasury] chamber").

[1]Rav Yehudah said in the name of Shmuel: The Torah scholars who taught the priests the laws of ritual slaughter would take their salaries from the *terumat halishkah*.

[2]Rav Gidel said in the name of Rav: The Torah scholars who taught the priests the laws regarding taking a fistful of the meal-offerings would take their salaries from the *terumat halishkah*.

[3]Rabbah bar Bar Ḥanah said in the name of Rabbi Yoḥanan: Those in Jerusalem who examined [Torah] scrolls for mistakes would take their salaries from the *terumat halishkah*.

RASHI

מגיהי ספרים – של כל אדם ואדם, שאסור להשהות ספר שאינו מוגה, משום "אל תשכן באהליך עַוְלָה". וראו בית דין שהיו מתעצלין בדבר, והפקירו תרומת הלשכה לכך.

NOTES

were not afflicted with blemishes that rendered them unfit to be sacrificed. However, those who examined first-born animals in order to determine whether they were free from blemishes and therefore could be offered on the altar in the Temple, or whether they were disqualified from being sacrificed and could therefore be slaughtered and eaten like any other nonsacred kosher animal were forbidden to receive payment. *Meiri* understands that all the inspectors of animal blemishes would take their salaries from the *terumat halishkah,* both those who examined the animals that were brought to the Temple for sacrifice, as well as those who examined first-born animals.

תַּלְמִידֵי חֲכָמִים **Torah scholars.** *Tosafot* (105a, s.v., גוזרי) and others discuss the circumstances under which Torah scholars and judges may take salaries. As a rule, a Torah scholar may not charge for the Torah that he teaches, nor may a judge charge for the ruling that he issues. However, a Torah scholar or a judge may be reimbursed for the income that he could otherwise have earned while he was offering instruction or rendering a legal decision. Moreover, a Torah scholar who devotes all his time to community service is entitled to take a salary and support himself and his family from communal funds. *Rabbenu Crescas Vidal* notes that this is the legal basis for the salaries paid to communal Rabbis and yeshiva heads. (See also *Rambam's Hilkhot Talmud Torah* and comments of *Kesef Mishneh.*)

הִלְכוֹת קְמִיצָה **The laws regarding taking a fistful of the meal-offerings.** *Rivan* notes that the procedure of scooping out a handful of the meal-offering, known as *kemitzah,* was one of the most difficult tasks in the Temple, for an exact handful had be scooped out, no more and no less. *Tosafot* note that special instruction was also offered regarding *melikah,* the pinching of the necks of the turtledoves and pigeons offered as sacrifices in the Temple, for that too was an especially difficult task to perform. These courses had to be repeated each week, for the shift of priests serving in the Temple changed weekly. The experts who offered this training were paid from the *terumat halishkah*.

מַגִּיהֵי סְפָרִים **Those who examined the scrolls for mistakes.** *Rashi* and *Rivan* understand that the Gemara is

HALAKHAH

the women who raised their children in ritual purity so that they could participate in the ceremony involving the Red Heifer would all be remunerated from the *terumat halishkah* contributions to the treasury," following Rav and the anonymous Tanna of the Baraita. (*Rambam, Sefer Zemanim, Hilkhot Shekalim* 4:4.)

מַגִּיהֵי סְפָרִים **Those who examined the scrolls for mistakes.** "Those who examined and corrected the Torah scrolls in

TRANSLATION AND COMMENTARY

אָמַר רַב נַחְמָן [1]**Rav Naḥman said in the name of Rav: The women who wove the curtains** for the Temple **would take their salaries from the** ***terumat halishkah.*** [2]**And I** myself **say** that they were not remunerated from the *terumat halishkah,* the fund based on the half-shekel levy that was imposed upon everyone, but rather **from the funds that** people voluntarily **consecrated for the Temple maintenance.** Why so? [3]**Because the curtains were used** in the Temple **instead of the building of walls,** and it was appropriate to pay for them with funds dedicated to the physical upkeep of the Temple, and not from the funds that were to be used for the Temple service.

מֵיתִיבֵי [4]**An objection was raised** against Rav Naḥman from a Baraita in which it was taught: **"The women who wove the curtains** for the Temple, **and** the members of **the house of Garmu** who were in charge of **the production of the shewbread,** [5]**and** the members of **the house of Avtinas** who were in charge of **the production of incense, would all take their salaries from the** ***terumat halishkah."*** Thus, the Baraita supports Rav and is against Rav Naḥman!

הָתָם בְּדְבָבֵי [6]The Gemara answers: The Baraita **there** is dealing with the curtains **of the** Temple **gates** that were hung for the sake of privacy and beauty. Those curtains were not considered part of the actual physical structure of the Temple, and so they were not acquired with funds donated for Temple maintenance, but rather from the *terumat halishkah.* Rav Naḥman, on the other hand, refers to the curtains that were hung in the Temple in place of walls. These separated the Sanctuary from the Holy of Holies in the Second Temple and replaced the cubit-thick wall that had stood there in the First Temple. Those curtains were indeed considered part of the actual physical structure of the Temple, and so they were acquired with funds donated for Temple maintenance. [7]That there were different types of curtains in the Second Temple is learned from what **Rabbi Zera said in the name of Rav:** [8]**There were thirteen curtains in the Second Temple:**

[1]אָמַר רַב נַחְמָן אָמַר רַב: נָשִׁים הָאוֹרְגוֹת בַּפָּרֹכוֹת, נוֹטְלוֹת שְׂכָרָן מִתְּרוּמַת הַלִּשְׁכָּה. [2]וַאֲנִי אוֹמֵר: מִקָּדְשֵׁי בֶּדֶק הַבַּיִת, [3]הוֹאִיל וּפָרֹכוֹת תַּחַת בִּנְיָן עֲשׂוּיוֹת.

[4]מֵיתִיבֵי: ״נָשִׁים הָאוֹרְגוֹת בַּפָּרֹכוֹת, [5]וּבֵית גַּרְמוּ עַל מַעֲשֵׂה לֶחֶם הַפָּנִים, וּבֵית אַבְטִינָס עַל מַעֲשֵׂה הַקְּטֹרֶת, כּוּלָּן הָיוּ נוֹטְלוֹת שְׂכָרָן מִתְּרוּמַת הַלִּשְׁכָּה״!

[6]הָתָם בִּדְבָבֵי, [7]דְּאָמַר רַבִּי זֵירָא אָמַר רַב: [8]שְׁלֹשָׁה עָשָׂר פָּרֹכוֹת

LITERAL TRANSLATION

[1]Rav Naḥman said in the name of Rav: The women who wove curtains [for the Temple] would take their salaries from the *terumat halishkah.* [2]And I say: From funds consecrated for Temple maintenance, [3]for the curtains were used instead of building [walls].

[4]They raised an objection: "The women who wove curtains, and the house of Garmu for the production of the shewbread, [5]and the house of Avtinas for the production of incense, would all take their salaries from the *terumat halishkah*!"

[6]There [it refers] to those of the gates, [7]for Rabbi Zera said in the name of Rav: [8]There were thirteen curtains

RASHI

בית אבטינס ובית גרמו — במסכת יומא (לח,א). בדבבי — בפרכות שכנגד הפתחים, דלצניעותא עבידי, ואינן תחת בנין. אבל כל צורך בנין, כגון פרכות המבדילות בין היכל לקדשי הקדשים, שהיו במקדש שני במקום אמה טרקסין שעשה שלמה בבנין ראשון. ואנשי הגולה עשו את ההיכל גבוה מאד, ולא יכול בנין בעובי אמה להתקיים בגובה כזה. ולהרחיבו לא יכלו — לפי שמקצרים את ההיכל או את קדשי הקדשים. ועשו שתי פרכות וביניהם אמה, כדאמרינן במסכת יומא (נא,ב). ואותן פרכות נעשו מקדשי בדק הבית.

LANGUAGE

אַבְטִינָס **Avtinas.** This is clearly a Greek word although its precise etymology remains obscure. Some interpret this as εὐ-θύινος, *euthuinos,* "good for incense." Thus, Avtinas' name reflects his occupation, preparing incense. Others take this as εὔθυνος, *euthunos,* "righteous judge, public examiner." According to this explanation, "Avtinas" might be equivalent to the Hebrew שפטיה.

BACKGROUND

בֵּית גַּרְמוּ וּבֵית אַבְטִינָס **The house of Avtinas and the house of Garmu.** Elsewhere (*Yoma* 38a) the Gemara states that these two groups refused to disclose how they prepared the incense and baked the shewbread and the twin loaves of bread (שְׁתֵּי הַלֶּחֶם, "two loaves") offered on Shavuot, keeping these matters a family secret.

NOTES

referring to those who examined Torah scrolls belonging to private individuals. Even though a person is forbidden to keep an uncorrected Torah scroll in his possession, the Rabbis saw that people had become lax about the matter, and so they decided to allow the scroll examiners to be paid from the *terumat halishkah. Talmid HaRashba* (cited by *Shittah Mekubbetzet*) writes that the Gemara refers to those who examined the Torah scrolls belonging to the priests from which they would study the laws governing the Temple service. According to the reading of the Jerusalem Talmud in tractate *Shekalim,* and according to *Ra'avad,* this regulation refers to those who examined *sifrei Ezra,* "the scrolls of Ezra" (or *sifrei ha'azarah,* "the scrolls of the Temple courtyard"), the scrolls belonging to the Temple itself, so that the *terumat halishkah* were indeed spent for their stated purpose, the actual needs of the Temple.

HALAKHAH

Jerusalem were remunerated from the *terumat halishkah,"* following Rabbi Yoḥanan. (*Rambam, Sefer Zemanim, Hilkhot Shekalim* 4:7.)

נָשִׁים הָאוֹרְגוֹת בַּפָּרֹכוֹת **The women who wove curtains.** "The curtains that hung in the Sanctuary were paid for from the funds consecrated for the maintenance of the Temple," following Rav Naḥman. But the curtains which covered the Temple gates were paid for from the *terumat halishkah.* (*Rambam, Sefer Zemanim, Hilkhot Shekalim* 4:2.)

הָיוּ בְּמִקְדָּשׁ שֵׁנִי: [1]שִׁבְעָה כְּנֶגֶד שִׁבְעָה שְׁעָרִים, אֶחָד לְפִתְחוֹ שֶׁל הֵיכָל, וְאֶחָד לְפִתְחוֹ שֶׁל אוּלָם, [2]שְׁתַּיִם בַּדְּבִיר, [3]שְׁתַּיִם כְּנֶגְדָּן בַּעֲלִיָּה.

[4]תָּנוּ רַבָּנַן: נָשִׁים הַמְגַדְּלוֹת בְּנֵיהֶן לְפָרָה, הָיוּ נוֹטְלוֹת שְׂכָרָן מִתְּרוּמַת הַלִּשְׁכָּה. [5]אַבָּא שָׁאוּל אוֹמֵר: נָשִׁים יְקָרוֹת שֶׁבִּירוּשָׁלַיִם הָיוּ זָנוֹת אוֹתָן וּמְפַרְנְסוֹת אוֹתָן.

[6]בְּעָא מִינֵּיהּ רַב הוּנָא מֵרַב [106B] [7]כְּלֵי שָׁרֵת, מַהוּ שֶׁיֵּעָשׂוּ מִקָּדְשֵׁי בֶּדֶק הַבַּיִת? [8]צוֹרֶךְ מִזְבֵּחַ נִינְהוּ, [9]וּמִקָּדְשֵׁי בֶּדֶק הַבַּיִת אָתוּ? [10]אוֹ צוֹרֶךְ קָרְבָּן נִינְהוּ,

LITERAL TRANSLATION

in the Second Temple: Seven corresponding to the seven gates, [1]one for the entrance to the Sanctuary, one for the entrance to the vestibule, [2]two for the Holy of Holies, [3][and] two corresponding to them in the upper story.

[4]Our Rabbis taught: "The women who raised their children for the [Red] Heifer would take their salaries from the *terumat halishkah*. [5]Abba Shaul says: The wealthy women in Jerusalem would maintain them and support them."

[6]Rav Huna asked Rav: [106B] [7]Sacred vessels, may they be made (lit., "what about making them") from funds consecrated for the Temple maintenance? [8]Are they [considered to be] necessary for the altar, [9]and [so] they come from funds consecrated for Temple maintenance? [10]Or are they [considered to be] necessary for the sacrifice,

TRANSLATION AND COMMENTARY

Seven corresponding to the seven gates that opened into the Temple courtyard, [1]**one** covering **the entrance to the Sanctuary, one** hung across **the entrance to the vestibule,** [2]**two** curtains that divided **the Holy of Holies** from the Sanctuary, [3]**and two corresponding** curtains **in the upper story** of the Temple, that divided the portion over the Holy of Holies from the portion over the Sanctuary.

תָּנוּ רַבָּנַן [4]**Our Rabbis taught** a Baraita that states: **"The women who raised their children** in special places that were not susceptible to ritual impurity, so that those children would remain ritually pure and be able to participate in the ceremony of **the** Red **Heifer would take their salaries from the *terumat halishkah*.** Children who had never contracted ritual impurity would take part in the burning of the red heifer and the drawing of the water which was later mixed with the heifer's ashes. The women who raised children with the special precautions to prevent them from becoming ritually impure were remunerated from the *terumat halishkah*. [5]**Abba Shaul says:** Rather **the wealthy women of Jerusalem would maintain and support them,** providing them with food and clothing as needed."

בְּעָא מִינֵּיהּ [6]**Rav Huna asked Rav:** [106B] [7]Regarding the **sacred vessels** and utensils that were used in the Temple service, **may they be made from the funds** that were **consecrated for Temple maintenance?** The Gemara now elucidates the root of this question. [8]**Are** the sacred vessels regarded as serving the **needs of the altar** on which the sacrifices are placed? [9]In that case, the sacred utensils **should be purchased with funds consecrated for the maintenance of the Temple,** for they should be considered as part of the physical structure of the Temple, just like the altar. [10]**Or are** the sacred vessels regarded as serving the **needs of the sacrifices,** for without them, sacrifices could not be offered on the

RASHI

שבעה שערים — לעזרה. **שתים בדביר** — תחת אמה טרקסין. **ושתים כנגדן בעליה** — להבדיל בין עליית היכל לעליית קדשי הקדשים, וגם הן במקום אמה טרקסין. **המגדלות בניהן לפרה** — בחצרות הבנויות בסלעים בירושלים, ותחתיהם חלל מפני קבר התהום, כדתנן במסכת פרה (פרק ג משנה ב), ומייתינן לה בפרק "הישן תחת המטה" (סוכה כא,א). ובאין נשים עוברות ויולדות שם, ומגדלות שם בניהם לצורכי פרה אדומה, לעסוק בשריפתה ומילוי מימיה ולהזות כל שבעה על כהן השורפה, כדאמרינן במסכת יומא (ד,א) ומעלה זו עשו לה, להתעסק בה תינוקות שלא נטמאו מימיהם, מפני שזלזלו בה לעשותה בטבול יום, כדתנן: מטמאין היו הכהן השורף את הפרה, ומטבילין אותו, להוציא מלבן של צדוקין שהיו אומרין: במעורבי שמש היתה נעשית. **נשים יקרות** — עשירות. **מפרנסות** — בלבוש וכסות. **כלי שרת** — שמשרתין בהן במזבח החיצון, שהוא בנין של אבנים.

BACKGROUND

שִׁבְעָה שְׁעָרִים Seven gates. How many gates the Temple had seems to be the subject of a Tannaitic dispute (see the lengthy discussion in *Tosafot* s.v. שבעה). Some claim that it had five, while others speak of seven, eight, or even ten different gates. However, it is possible that all the Tannaim agreed about how many gates the Temple courtyard had, and they only disagreed about which of these gates were used regularly (and therefore deserved to be counted), and which were not.

NOTES

כְּלֵי שָׁרֵת, מַהוּ שֶׁיֵּעָשׂוּ Sacred vessels, may they be made. *Hafla'ah* asks: Why does the Gemara not derive the law applying to the sacred vessels for the Temple service from what the Torah tells us about the money donated for the Tabernacle, for there it is obvious that the same funds were used both for the construction of the Tabernacle and fashioning the sacred vessels? He answers that we are unable to derive this matter from the Tabernacle, for at that time the *terumat halishkah* funds did not yet exist. Therefore, the sacred vessels had to be fashioned from the money donated for the Tabernacle. But once various funds were collected for the Temple, after the *terumat halishkah* funds had already been established, it is legitimate to ask whether the sacred vessels are fashioned from funds of *terumat halishkah* or those consecrated for Temple maintenance.

[1]וּמִתְּרוּמַת הַלִּשְׁכָּה הָיוּ עוֹשִׂין אוֹתָן?
[2]אֲמַר לֵיהּ: אֵין נַעֲשִׂין אֶלָּא מִתְּרוּמַת הַלִּשְׁכָּה.
[3]אֵיתִיבֵיהּ: [4]״וּכְכַלּוֹתָם הֵבִיאוּ לִפְנֵי הַמֶּלֶךְ וִיהוֹיָדָע (הַכֹּהֵן) אֶת שְׁאָר הַכֶּסֶף וַיַּעֲשֵׂהוּ כֵלִים לְבֵית ה׳ כְּלֵי שָׁרֵת וגו׳״.
[5]אֲמַר לֵיהּ: דְּאַקְרְיָיךְ כְּתוּבֵי לָא אַקְרְיָיךְ נְבִיאֵי: [6]״אַךְ לֹא יֵעָשֶׂה בֵּית ה׳ סִפּוֹת וגו׳ כִּי לְעֹשֵׂי הַמְּלָאכָה יִתְּנֻהוּ״.
[7]אִי הָכִי, קָשׁוּ קְרָאֵי אַהֲדָדֵי!
[8]לָא קַשְׁיָא. [9]כָּאן שֶׁגָּבוּ, וְהוֹתִירוּ. [10]כָּאן שֶׁגָּבוּ, וְלֹא הוֹתִירוּ.
[11]וְכִי גָּבוּ, וְהוֹתִירוּ, מַאי הָוֵי?

LITERAL TRANSLATION

[1]and [so] they would make them from *terumat halishkah* [funds]?

[2][Rav] said to him: They are made only from *terumat halishkah* [funds].

[3][Rav Huna] raised an objection: [4]"And when they had finished it, they brought the rest of the money before the king and Yehoiadah (the priest), and of it were made vessels for the house of the Lord, etc."

[5]He said to him: He who taught you the Hagiographa did not teach you the Prophets: [6]"But there were not made for the house of the Lord bowls....for they gave that to the workmen."

[7]If so, the verses contradict one another!

[8]There is no difficulty. [9]Here, they collected [for the Temple], and there was left over. [10]Here, they collected, and there was nothing left over.

[11]And if they collected, and there was left over, what of it?

TRANSLATION AND COMMENTARY

altar? [1]In that case they **should be purchased from *terumat halishkah* funds,** just like the communal sacrifices.

אֲמַר לֵיהּ [2]Rav **said to** Rav Huna: The sacred utensils **must be purchased from *terumat halishkah* funds,** and not from the funds that were consecrated for the maintenance of the Temple.

אֵיתִיבֵיהּ [3]Rav Huna **raised an objection** against Rav from the following verse (II Chronicles 24:14): [4]**"And when they had finished it** (the Temple repairs), **they brought the rest of the money before the king** (Yehoash) **and Yehoiadah** (the priest), **and of it were made vessels for the house of the Lord,** vessels for service, and for offering, and spoons, and vessels of gold and silver." This verse supports Rav Huna's contention that the sacred vessels were made with money that had been donated for Temple maintenance.

אֲמַר לֵיהּ [5]Rav **said to** Rav Huna: **Whoever taught you the Hagiographa did not teach you the Prophets,** for the parallel verse in the Prophets states (II Kings 12:14-15): [6]**"But there were not made for the house of the Lord bowls** of silver, snuffers, basins, trumpets, or any vessels of gold, or vessels of silver, from the money that was brought into the house of the Lord; **for they gave that to the workmen,** and they repaired with it the house of the Lord." This verse states explicitly that the sacred vessels were not made from the Temple maintenance funds!

אִי הָכִי [7]**If so,** there is a difficulty, for **the verses contradict each other!**

לָא קַשְׁיָא [8]The Gemara answers: **There is** really **no difficulty,** since from the description given in Chronicles and Kings we are dealing with two different collections for Temple repair. [9]**Here** in the book of Chronicles we are dealing with a case **where** money **was collected** by Yehoiadah for repairing the Temple, **and** some of it **was left over.** Those surplus funds could be used for the sacred vessels. [10]And **here** in the book of Kings the verse is dealing with a case **where** money **was collected** for Temple repairs, **and nothing was left over** to be used for the sacred vessels.

וְכִי גָּבוּ [11]The Gemara asks: **What** difference does it make **if** money **was collected** for repairing the Temple, **and** some **was left over?** Being left over does not mark that money as being consecrated for the sacred vessels!

RASHI

וככלותם – לחזק את בדק הבית בימי יהואש. ופסוק זה בדברי הימים. שגבו – לצורך בדק הבית. והותירו, שאין צריכין לכולו – עושין מן המותר כלי שרת. מאי הוי – הא לא לקודשת קרבן גבו.

NOTES

מִתְּרוּמַת הַלִּשְׁכָּה **From *terumat halishkah* funds.** *Tosafot* and other Rishonim note that the Gemara does not mean that the sacred vessels were purchased from that year's *terumat halishkah* funds, for those funds were reserved for the purchase offerings actually sacrificed on the altar. Rather, the Gemara means that the sacred vessels were purchased with what remained from last year's *terumat halishkah* after the first of Nisan, when it was no longer used for the communal sacrifices, as stated explicitly in the Baraita cited below.

שֶׁגָּבוּ, וְהוֹתִירוּ **When they collected, and there was left over.** *Maharsha* (unlike *Rashi* and our commentary) explains that the Gemara is talking here about the half-shekels which were collected each year from each and every Jew. If money is left over from those funds, the sacred vessels may be bought from them. Otherwise, they

TRANSLATION AND COMMENTARY

אָמַר רַבִּי אַבָּהוּ [1]Rabbi Abbahu said: When issuing the order to take up the collection, the **court's intention was to stipulate** that **if** the money **is needed** for repairs, [2]**it is to be used** for that purpose, and not for anything else. [3]But **if** some remains and is **not** needed for repairing the Temple, **it may be used for sacred vessels.**

תָּנָא [4]**A Sage of the house of Rabbi Yishmael taught** a Baraita: **"The sacred vessels come from the** ***terumat halishkah,*** [5]**as the verse states** (II Chronicles 24:14): 'They brought **the rest of the money** before the king and Yehoiadah, and of it were made vessels for the house of the Lord.' [6]**Which money** always **has a surplus — say that** the verse **is** referring to **the** ***terumat halishkah,*** for after they were set aside from the half-shekels that were collected from every adult Jewish male, for the communal offerings, there was money left over, known as the surplus treasury fund (*sheyarei halishkah*), which was used to defray other expenses.

וְאֵימָא [7]If that is the case, the Gemara asks: The Baraita should have **said** that **the surplus** treasury fund **itself** was to be used for the sacred vessels, and not the *terumat halishkah,* for the verse states that the vessels were made from "the rest of the money"!

כְּדַאֲמַר רָבָא [8]The Gemara answers: That verse in II Chronicles should be explained in the same way that **Rava explained** an entirely different matter: From where do we know that the daily morning sacrifice was the first sacrifice offered each morning, and that no other offering could be brought before it? For the verse states (Leviticus 6:5): [9]"And the priest shall burn wood on it (the altar) every morning, and he shall lay **the burnt-offering** in order upon it." The superfluous letter *he* in the word הָעוֹלָה ("the burnt-offering") teaches that the verse is referring to **the** specific **burnt-offering** that is mentioned first in the Torah passage describing the various sacrifices (Numbers 28), the daily morning sacrifice. [10]**So too** here, the superfluous letter *he* in the word הַכֶּסֶף, "*the* **money,"** teaches that the verse is referring to **the money** that is set aside **first, the** *terumat halishkah,* the half-shekel donations of all Jewish males, which always leaves a surplus.

[1]אָמַר רַבִּי אַבָּהוּ: לֵב בֵּית דִּין מַתְנֶה עֲלֵיהֶן: [2]אִם הוּצְרְכוּ, הוּצְרְכוּ, [3]וְאִם לָאו, יְהוּ לִכְלֵי שָׁרֵת.

[4]תָּנָא דְּבֵי רַבִּי יִשְׁמָעֵאל: ״כְּלֵי שָׁרֵת בָּאִין מִתְּרוּמַת הַלִּשְׁכָּה, [5]שֶׁנֶּאֱמַר: ״אֶת שְׁאָר הַכֶּסֶף״, אֵיזֶהוּ כֶּסֶף שֶׁיֵּשׁ לוֹ שִׁירַיִים? [6]הֱוֵי אוֹמֵר: זֶה תְּרוּמַת הַלִּשְׁכָּה.

[7]וְאֵימָא שִׁירַיִים גּוּפַיְיהוּ!

[8]כְּדַאֲמַר רָבָא: [9]״הָעוֹלָה״ עוֹלָה רִאשׁוֹנָה. [10]הָכִי נַמִי, ״הַכֶּסֶף״ כֶּסֶף רִאשׁוֹן.

LITERAL TRANSLATION

[1]Rabbi Abbahu said: It was the intention of the court to stipulate about them: [2]If [all the moneys] are needed, they are needed, [3]and if not, they will be for the sacred vessels.

[4][A Sage] of the house of Rabbi Yishmael taught: "The sacred vessels come from the *terumat halishkah,* [5]as it is stated: 'The rest of the money.' [6]Which money has a surplus — say that it is the *terumat halishkah.*"

[7]But say [from] the surplus itself!

[8]As Rava said: [9]"The burnt-offering" means the first burnt-offering. [10]So too, "the money" [means] the first money.

RASHI

כסף שיש לו שיריים — כסף הקופות שהוא נתרם מן הלשכה, ושיריים נשארים בלשכה. זה תרומת הלשכה — כסף שבקופות. ואימא שיריים גופייהו — משיריים הנותרים בלשכה כלי שרת באין, ולא מן התרומה עצמה. העולה עולה ראשונה — מנין שלא יהא דבר קודם על המערכה לתמיד של שחר — תלמוד לומר ״וערך עליה העולה״. והוינן בה: מאי תלמודא? ואמר רבא: ״העולה״ משמע העולה האמורה ראשון בסדרי קרבנות, והיא עולת הבקר. שנאמר ״ואמרת להם זה האשה כו׳״ וה״א יתירא קא דריש. והכא נמי ״את שאר הכסף״ — בכסף שיש לו שאר.

NOTES

are purchased from money donated for repairing the Temple. *Maharshal* argues that the Gemara cannot be referring to money consecrated for the repair of the Temple, for that money is donated and the term "collected" would be inappropriate.

אֵיזֶהוּ כֶּסֶף שֶׁיֵּשׁ לוֹ שִׁירַיִים Which money has a surplus. According to its plain sense, this verse refers to the contributions made for the repair of the Temple, and not with *terumat halishkah.* However, Rabbi Yishmael apparently understands the verse as follows: They brought before the king and Yehoiadah what remained of the money that was contributed for the repair of the Temple, and also what remained of other funds, including the *terumat halishkah.*

וְאֵימָא שִׁירַיִים גּוּפַיְיהוּ Say the surplus itself. Most Rishonim understand the Gemara's question as did *Rashi*: Why not say that the sacred vessels were to be purchased with money taken from the surplus treasury funds, rather than from *terumat halishkah* themselves? *Ra'ah* understands that the Gemara is asking: Why not say that the verse is referring to the surplus of money that was contributed for Temple repair. It answers that the verse is talking about a fund regarding which there is "first money" and "second money," which must be the half-shekel obligation, for it is divided between *terumat halishkah* and the surplus treasury fund (*sheyarei halishkah*).

TRANSLATION AND COMMENTARY

מֵיתִיבֵי [1] **An objection was raised** against what was stated here from a Baraita in which it was taught: **"The incense and all the communal sacrifices come from the *terumat halishkah*.** [2] **The golden altar, the frankincense, and the sacred vessels** all **come from the surplus of the libations.** The Temple treasurers paid suppliers to provide the Temple with wine, oil, and flour throughout the year. If the suppliers agreed to provide flour worth a particular fixed sum each week, and the price fell, the suppliers would have to provide the Temple with more commodities for the same amount of money. These extra goods were called 'the surplus of the libations.' Furthermore, the suppliers would provide the flour using heaping measures, whereas the sacrifices were brought using level measures. The difference between the two measures of flour was also included in the surplus of the libations. These surpluses would be sold and used for the golden altar, the frankincense, and the sacred vessels. [3] **The altar for the burnt-offering, the chambers, and the courtyards** all **come from the funds consecrated for the Temple maintenance,** for they are all part of the physical structure of the Temple. [4] **Whatever** is built **outside the wall of the Temple courtyard** (the women's courtyard, the surrounding walls, and the towers) **comes from the surplus treasury fund.** [5] **This is what we have learned** in the Mishnah (*Shekalim* 4:2): **The wall of the city** of Jerusalem, **and its towers, and all the needs of the community,** such as the digging of water cisterns, street repairs, and security measures, all **come from the surplus treasury fund."** Thus, we see that the sacred vessels come from the surplus of the libations and not from the *terumat halishkah*!

[1] מֵיתִיבֵי: ״הַקְּטוֹרֶת וְכָל קׇרְבְּנוֹת צִבּוּר בָּאִין מִתְּרוּמַת הַלִּשְׁכָּה. [2] מִזְבַּח הַזָּהָב, וּלְבוֹנָה, וּכְלֵי שָׁרֵת בָּאִין מִמּוֹתַר נְסָכִים. [3] מִזְבַּח הָעוֹלָה, הַלְּשָׁכוֹת, וְהָעֲזָרוֹת בָּאִין מִקׇּדְשֵׁי בֶּדֶק הַבַּיִת. [4] חוּץ לְחוֹמַת הָעֲזָרָה בָּאִין מִשְּׁיָרֵי הַלְּשָׁכוֹת. [5] זוֹ הִיא שֶׁשָּׁנִינוּ: חוֹמַת הָעִיר וּמִגְדְּלוֹתֶיהָ וְכָל צׇרְכֵי הָעִיר בָּאִין מִשְּׁיָרֵי הַלִּשְׁכָּה!

LITERAL TRANSLATION

[1] They raised an objection: "The incense and all the communal sacrifices come from the *terumat halishkah*. [2] The golden altar, and the frankincense, and the sacred vessels come from the surplus of the libations. [3] The altar for the burnt-offering, the chambers, and the courtyards come from the funds consecrated for Temple maintenance. [4] [What is] outside the wall of the Temple courtyard comes from the surplus [treasury] funds. [5] This is what we have learned: The city wall and its towers and all the communal needs come from the surplus treasury funds."

RASHI

מזבח הזהב – כלי הוא ולא בנין. שאינו מחובר לאדמה, ויכולין לטלטלו, לפיכך נידון ככלי. **ולבונה** – של לחם הפנים. **מותר נסכים** – פליגי בה במסכת מנחות בפרק ״שתי מדות״ (צ,א): רבי חייא בן רבי יוסף אמר: בירוצי מדות, שהמספקין סלתות, שקבלו מעות הקדש לספק סלתות כל ימות השנה, מודדין להקדש במדה מבורצת – טפופה ולא מחוקה, והמקריבן מוחק המדה, והם מותר נסכים, ומוכרים אותן. ורבי יוחנן אמר: כאותה ששנינו: המקבל עליו לספק [כל ימות השנה להקדש] סלתות מארבע סאין בסלע ועמדו משלש, שנתייקרו – מספק מארבע. והמקבל לספק משלש והוזלו ועמדו מארבע – מספק ארבע. וזו היא ששנינו: מותר נסכים לקיץ המזבח. **מזבח העולה** – שהוא בנין, בא מקדשי בדק הבית. **חוץ לחומת העזרה** – כגון עזרת נשים, והחיל, וחומת העיר ומגדלותיה – באים משיריים הנותרים בלשכה כשתרמוה בקופות.

NOTES

מִזְבַּח הַזָּהָב, וּלְבוֹנָה **The golden altar, and the frankincense.** *Rivan* asks: Why should the frankincense come from the surplus of the libations? Surely the frankincense was placed on the table together with the shewbread, and as such it should be regarded as a sacrifice and be brought from the *terumat halishkah* funds! Indeed, the *Vilna Gaon* removes the word "frankincense" from the passage. *Talmid HaRashba* (cited by *Shittah Mekubbetzet*) argues that since the frankincense was only offered once a week, and since it was not offered on the altar, it is not treated like other sacrifices.

HALAKHAH

הַקְּטוֹרֶת וְכָל קׇרְבְּנוֹת צִבּוּר **The incense and all the communal sacrifices.** "The daily sacrifices, the additional sacrifices, and all the other communal offerings and their libations, the incense, and the fee paid to those who produce it, all come from the *terumat halishkah*," following the Mishnah cited here. (*Rambam, Sefer Zemanim, Hilkhot Shekalim* 4:1.)

כְּלֵי שָׁרֵת **The sacred vessels.** "The menorah and the sacred vessels were supposed to be purchased with the surplus of the libations," following Rabbi Akiva. (*Rambam, Sefer Zemanim, Hilkhot Shekalim* 4:2.)

מִזְבַּח הָעוֹלָה **The altar for the burnt-offering.** "The altar for the burnt-offering, the Sanctuary, and the Temple courtyards were built from the surplus Temple treasury funds (following the Jerusalem Talmud; see *Kesef Mishneh*, who asks why *Rambam* rules in accordance with the Jerusalem Talmud, and against the Babylonian Talmud). And so too whatever was built outside the wall of the

[1]תַּנָּאֵי הִיא, דִּתְנַן: [2]״מוֹתַר תְּרוּמָה מֶה הָיוּ עוֹשִׂין בָּהּ? [3]רִיקּוּעֵי זָהָב צִיפּוּי לְבֵית קָדְשֵׁי הַקֳּדָשִׁים. [4]רַבִּי יִשְׁמָעֵאל אוֹמֵר: מוֹתַר פֵּירוֹת לְקֵיץ הַמִּזְבֵּחַ, [5]מוֹתַר תְּרוּמָה לִכְלֵי שָׁרֵת. [6]רַבִּי עֲקִיבָא אוֹמֵר: מוֹתַר תְּרוּמָה לְקֵיץ הַמִּזְבֵּחַ, [7]מוֹתַר נְסָכִים לִכְלֵי שָׁרֵת. [8]רַבִּי חֲנִינָא סְגַן הַכֹּהֲנִים אוֹמֵר: מוֹתַר נְסָכִים לְקֵיץ הַמִּזְבֵּחַ, [9]מוֹתַר תְּרוּמָה לִכְלֵי שָׁרֵת. [10]וְזֶה וָזֶה לֹא הָיוּ מוֹדִים בְּפֵירוֹת״.

TRANSLATION AND COMMENTARY

תַּנָּאֵי הִיא [1]The Gemara explains: This matter **is** the subject **of a Tannaitic dispute, for we have learned** elsewhere in the Mishnah (*Shekalim* 4:4): [2]**"What was done with the** yearly **remainder of the** *terumat halishkah* after the first of Nisan? On that date, the communal sacrifices started to be brought from the shekels that had just been collected. [3]That money was used to purchase the **gold plates that covered the walls,** floor, and ceiling **of the Holy of Holies.** [4]**Rabbi Yishmael says: The surplus of the 'fruits'** (the meaning of which is explained below) was used **for supplying the altar** with sacrifices **when it was idle.** When there were no other sacrifices being offered on the altar, voluntary burnt-offerings would be financed from this Temple fund, so that the altar would not remain idle. [5]**The remainder of the** previous year's *terumat halishkah* was used **for the** purchase of **sacred vessels.** [6]**Rabbi Akiva says: The remainder of** the previous year's *terumat halishkah* was used **for supplying the altar** with voluntary burnt-offerings **when it was idle.** [7]**The surplus of the libations** was used **for** the purchase of **the sacred vessels.** [8]**Rabbi Ḥanina the deputy of the Priests says: The surplus of the libations** was used **for supplying the altar** with voluntary burnt-offerings **when it was idle.** [9]**The remainder of** the previous year's *terumat halishkah* was used **for the** purchase of **sacred vessels.** [10]**And neither this one** — Rabbi Akiva — **nor that one** — Rabbi Ḥanina — **agrees** with Rabbi Yishmael **about** the surplus of fruit, for according to them, there was no such fund in the Temple." Thus, we see that the Tannaim disagree about the fund from which the sacred vessels were purchased. Therefore, Rav, who said that sacred vessels are purchased from the *terumat halishkah* funds, followed the opinion of the Baraita of the house of Rabbi Yishmael and Rabbi Ḥanina of the Mishnah in *Shekalim*. While the above anonymous Baraita, "The incense and all the communal sacrifices," follows the opinion of Rabbi Akiva of that Mishnah. One, therefore, cannot use that anonymous Baraita to dispute Rav.

LITERAL TRANSLATION

[1]It is [a dispute among] the Tannaim, for we have learned: [2]"What did they do with the [yearly] remainder of the *terumat [halishkah]*? [3]Beaten gold [plates] for covering the walls of the Holy of Holies. [4]Rabbi Yishmael says: The surplus of the 'fruits' [was used] for supplying the altar [with sacrifices] when it was idle. [5]The [yearly] remainder of the *terumat* [*halishkah* was used] for sacred vessels. [6]Rabbi Akiva says: The [yearly] remainder of the *terumat* [*halishkah* was used] for supplying the altar [with sacrifices] when it was idle. [7]The surplus of the libations [was used] for the sacred vessels. [8]Rabbi Ḥanina the deputy of the Priests says: The surplus of the libations [was used] for supplying the altar when it is idle. [9]The [yearly] remainder of the *terumat* [*halishkah* was used] for the sacred vessels. [10]And this one and that one did not agree about the 'fruits.'"

RASHI

תנאי היא – דאיכא למאן דאמר כלי שרת מתרומת הלשכה באין. **מותר תרומה** – הנשאר בקופות בראש חדש ניסן. שמכאן ואילך אין לוקחין קרבנות צבור אלא מתרומה חדשה, כדאמרינן בראש השנה (ז,א): קרבנות צבור הבאין באחד בניסן – מצוה להביא מן החדש. **ציפוי לבית קדשי הקדשים** – מחפין בהם הרצפה והכתלים. **מותר ריות פירות** – ולקמן מפרש מאי ניהו. **לקיץ המזבח** – כשהוא בטל מנדרים ונדבות לוקחין עולות ומקריבין; בשר למזבח ועורות לכהנים. **וזה וזה** – רבי עקיבא ורבי חנינא. **לא היו מודין** – שיהא שום מותר בפירות.

LANGUAGE

קֵיץ הַמִּזְבֵּחַ **The dry season of the altar.** A Baraita (see *Shevuot* 12a) takes the word קֵיץ as "dates"; thus, just as dates were often eaten after the main meal was finished as a dessert, so too קֵיץ הַמִּזְבֵּחַ were additional burnt-offerings, brought after the regular sacrifices had been offered, so the altar would not be left idle. Hence, it was not known in advance how many קֵיץ הַמִּזְבֵּחַ sacrifices would be offered, since there was no need for such offerings if enough people brought sacrifices to the Temple on their own.

HALAKHAH

Temple courtyard, such as the city walls and its towers, and all the needs of the community were funded by the surplus treasury funds." (*Rambam, Sefer Zemanim, Hilkhot Shekalim* 4:8.)

מוֹתַר תְּרוּמָה **What remained of the *terumat halishkah*.** "Whatever remained of the *terumat halishkah* (after the first of Nisan) and the surplus treasury funds was used for the purchase of male sacrificial animals that were offered as burnt-offerings whenever the altar was otherwise idle," following Rabbi Akiva. (*Rambam, Sefer Zemanim, Hilkhot Shekalim* 4:9.)

מוֹתַר נְסָכִים **The surplus of the libations.** "The surplus of the libations was used for the purchase of sacred vessels for the Temple. If there was no such surplus, the sacred vessels were purchased from the *terumat halishkah*," following Rabbi Akiva, and assuming that Rabbi Akiva agrees with Rabbi Yishmael when nothing remains of the libations; *Kesef Mishneh*. (*Rambam, Sefer Zemanim, Hilkhot Shekalim* 4:2.)

[1] ״פֵּירוֹת״ מַאי הִיא? [2] דְּתַנְיָא: ״מוֹתַר תְּרוּמָה מָה הָיוּ עוֹשִׂין בָּהּ? [3] לוֹקְחִין פֵּירוֹת בְּזוֹל, וּמוֹכְרִין אוֹתָם בְּיוֹקֶר, [4] וְהַשָּׂכָר מְקַיְּצִין בּוֹ אֶת הַמִּזְבֵּחַ. [5] וְזוֹ הִיא שֶׁשָּׁנִינוּ: ״מוֹתַר פֵּירוֹת לְקֵיץ הַמִּזְבֵּחַ״.

[6] מַאי ״זֶה וְזֶה לֹא הָיוּ מוֹדִין בְּפֵירוֹת״? [7] דִּתְנַן: ״מוֹתַר שְׁיָרֵי לִשְׁכָּה מָה הָיוּ עוֹשִׂין בָּהֶן? [8] לוֹקְחִין בָּהֶן יֵינוֹת, שְׁמָנִים, וּסְלָתוֹת, וְהַשָּׂכָר לַהֶקְדֵּשׁ. [9] דִּבְרֵי רַבִּי יִשְׁמָעֵאל. [10] רַבִּי עֲקִיבָא אוֹמֵר: אֵין מִשְׂתַּכְּרִין בְּשֶׁל הֶקְדֵּשׁ [11] אַף לֹא בְּשֶׁל עֲנִיִּים״. [12] בְּשֶׁל הֶקְדֵּשׁ, מַאי טַעְמָא לָא? [13] אֵין עֲנִיּוּת בְּמְקוֹם עֲשִׁירוּת.

LITERAL TRANSLATION

[1] What are "fruits?" [2] As it was taught: "What would they do with the [yearly] remainder of the *terumat* [*halishkah*]? [3] They would buy fruit [when] cheap, and sell it dear, [4] and the profit would [be used to] supply the altar when it was idle." [5] And this is what we have learned: "The surplus of the 'fruits' [was used] for supplying the altar when it was idle."

[6] What is [meant by]: "This one and that one did not agree about the 'fruits'"? [7] As we have learned: "What would they do with the [yearly] remainder of the surplus [treasury] funds? [8] They would buy wine, oil, and flour, and the profit becomes Temple property. [9] [These are] the words of Rabbi Yishmael. [10] Rabbi Akiva says: They do not make profits from sacred property [11] nor from [collections] for the poor." [12] With sacred property, what is the reason not? [13] There is no poverty in a place of riches.

TRANSLATION AND COMMENTARY

פֵּירוֹת [1] The Gemara now clarifies what had been mentioned above regarding the profit on the fruit: **What is** the Mishnah referring to when it speaks of **"fruits"? As it was taught** in a Baraita: [2] **"What was done with the remainder of** the previous year's *terumat halishkah* after the first of Nisan, when it was no longer used for the communal sacrifices? [3] The Temple treasurers **would** use the money to **buy fruit at a low price, and** then they would **sell** the fruit **at a higher price,** [4] **and with the profit they would supply the altar** with voluntary burnt-offerings **when** the altar **was idle."** [5] **And this is what we have learned** in the Mishnah: **"The surplus of 'the fruits'** was used **for supplying the altar** with voluntary burnt-offerings **when it was idle."**

מַאי [6] The Gemara asks: **What** did the Mishnah mean when it stated: **"Neither this one** — Rabbi Akiva — **nor that one** — Rabbi Ḥanina — **agrees** with Rabbi Yishmael **about** the surplus of (profits on) the **fruits?"** The Gemara answers: Rabbi Akiva and Rabbi Ḥanina both follow Rabbi Akiva's opinion stated elsewhere, [7] **as we have learned** in the Mishnah (*Shekalim* 4:3): **"What was done with the** yearly **remainder of the surplus treasury funds?** [8] The Temple treasurers **would buy wine, oil, and flour** with the money, and sell them to people who needed wine for a libation, or oil and flour for a meal-offering, **and** any **profit** that would be made becomes **Temple property.** [9] **This is the position of Rabbi Yishmael.** [10] **Rabbi Akiva** disagrees and **says:** The Temple treasurers **may not make profits from sacred property** or money belonging to the Temple. [11] **And** similarly, the treasurers of a charity fund may **not** make profits from **money** collected **for the poor."** Since Rabbi Akiva and Rabbi Ḥanina maintain that the Temple treasurers may not do business with money belonging to the Temple treasury, they deny the existence of a fund made up of profits from such business. Therefore the voluntary burnt-offerings which were brought when the altar was otherwise idle had to be purchased from some other fund.

בְּשֶׁל הֶקְדֵּשׁ [12] The Gemara now asks: For **what reason** does Rabbi Akiva say that the Temple treasurers may **not** do business **with sacred** money or property **belonging to the Temple?** [13] The Gemara explains: **There is no poverty where there is wealth.** The affairs of the Temple must be conducted in an atmosphere of opulence, and so the Temple treasurers may not act like paupers and involve themselves in business dealings for trifling profits.

RASHI

והשכר מקיצין בהן – והקרן לכלי שרת, כדקאמר רבי ישמעאל. **מאי זה וזה לא היו מודים** – מאי פירושא ד״לא היו מודים״ – כדתנן, דפליג רבי עקיבא אדרבי ישמעאל, ולא הודה לו שיהו משתכרין בשל הקדש.

HALAKHAH

אֵין מִשְׂתַּכְּרִין בְּשֶׁל הֶקְדֵּשׁ There is no poverty in a place of riches. "Since *Rambam* does not cite Rabbi Yishmael's position about what is done with what money left over from the surplus of the treasury funds, it would appear that he rules in accordance with Rabbi Akiva, and also he ruled so explicitly in his *Commentary to the Mishneh*." (*Rambam, Sefer Zemanim, Hilkhot Shekalim* 4:4.)

אַף לֹא בְּשֶׁל עֲנִיִּים Also not with that of the poor. "Business may not be conducted with charity funds which are supposed to be distributed to the poor, lest a poor person come and there be nothing to give him," following our Gemara. But regarding an endowment fund, where the principle is not to be distributed, but only the income, the principle may indeed be entirely invested in a business. (*Bet Yosef,* in the name of *Sefer Terumot* and *Hagahot Maimoniyot; Shulḥan Arukh, Yoreh De'ah* 259:1, *Rema.*

TRANSLATION AND COMMENTARY

בְּשֶׁל עֲנִיִּים [1]The Gemara asks: And for **what reason** does Rabbi Akiva say that the treasurers of a charity fund may **not** do business **with** money **belonging to the poor?** [2]The Gemara answers: They may not invest the money in a business, because **a pauper might come** and ask for money, [3]**and there will be nothing to give him.**

מִי שֶׁהָלַךְ [4]We have learned in the Mishnah: **"If someone went abroad,** and his wife demands that the court award her maintenance from his property, the Tannaim disagree about the law." [5]**It was stated** that the Amoraim disagree about the following matter: **Rav said:** [107A] [6]If a husband leaves home and his wife claims that he did not leave her with means of support, the court **awards maintenance to the woman** from her husband's property. [7]**And Shmuel said:** The court **does not award a married woman maintenance** from her husband's property. [8]**Shmuel said: Abba** (i.e., Rav) **agrees with me** that during **the first three months** after he left, the court does not award his wife maintenance from his property, [9]**for** we assume that **a man does not leave his house empty.** Surely he must have left her with sufficient means to support herself for a short time.

בְּשֶׁשָּׁמְעוּ בּוֹ [10]The Gemara limits the issue in dispute: **Where people have heard that** the husband **died** while he was away from home, [11]**everyone** — both Rav and Shmuel — **agree** that the court awards his wife maintenance from his property. [12]The Amoraim only **disagree about** how to rule when **they did not hear that** the husband **died** while he was away: [13]**Rav said** that in such a case, the court **awards** his wife maintenance from her husband's property, **for** the husband **is obligated to** provide his wife with maintenance, and while he is absent her maintenance is collected from his property. [14]**And Shmuel said:** In such a case, the court **does not award** the wife maintenance from her husband's property.

[1]בְּשֶׁל עֲנִיִּים, מַאי טַעְמָא לָא? [2]דִּלְמָא מִתְרַמֵּי לְהוּ עַנְיָא, [3]וְלֵיכָּא לְמֵיתְבָא לֵיהּ. [4]"מִי שֶׁהָלַךְ לִמְדִינַת הַיָּם". [5]אִיתְּמַר: רַב אָמַר: [107A] [6]פּוֹסְקִין מְזוֹנוֹת לְאֵשֶׁת אִישׁ. [7]וּשְׁמוּאֵל אָמַר: אֵין פּוֹסְקִין מְזוֹנוֹת לְאֵשֶׁת אִישׁ. [8]אָמַר שְׁמוּאֵל: מוֹדֶה לִי אַבָּא בִּשְׁלֹשָׁה חֳדָשִׁים הָרִאשׁוֹנִים, [9]לְפִי שֶׁאֵין אָדָם מַנִּיחַ בֵּיתוֹ רֵיקָן.

[10]בְּשֶׁשָּׁמְעוּ בּוֹ שֶׁמֵּת, [11]כּוּלֵּי עָלְמָא לָא פְּלִיגִי; [12]כִּי פְּלִיגִי בְּשֶׁלֹּא שָׁמְעוּ בּוֹ שֶׁמֵּת. [13]רַב אָמַר: פּוֹסְקִין, דְּהָא מְשׁוּעְבָּד לָהּ. [14]וּשְׁמוּאֵל אָמַר: אֵין פּוֹסְקִין.

LITERAL TRANSLATION

[1]With that of the poor, what is the reason not? [2]Perhaps a pauper will happen [to come], [3]and there will be nothing to give him.

[4]"If someone went abroad." [5]It was stated: Rav said: [107A] [6]They award maintenance to a married woman. [7]And Shmuel said: They do not award maintenance to a married woman. [8]Shmuel said: Abba agrees with me about the first three months, [9]for a man does not leave his house empty.

[10]When they heard that he died, [11]everyone agrees (lit., "the whole world does not disagree"); [12]when they disagree is about when they did not hear that he died. [13]Rav said: They award, for he is obligated to her. [14]And Shmuel said: They do not award.

RASHI

פוסקין מזונות — בית דין יורדין לנכסי מי שהלך למדינת הים, ופוסקין מזונות לאשתו. **בששמעו בו שמת כולי עלמא לא פליגי** — דפוסקין, דלמאי ניחוש להו? אי לגרוי — הרי סופה לגבות כתובתה, ותשבע שלא עיכבה משלהם כלום. ואי לשמא אמר לה "לאי מעשה ידיך במזונותיך" וקבלה עליה — משמת אינה משועבדת לו מעשה ידיה. ואם תאמר: והרי היא משועבדת ליתומים, ואף הם יאמרו לה כן? אף הוא לא היה יכול לומר לה אלא אם כן היא מתרצה.

NOTES

אַבָּא Abba. *Rivan* (and so too *Rashi* in various places) understands that Shmuel referred to Rav as Abba (literally, "father"), because he recognized Rav as being his father in wisdom, or else he used that name as a term of endearment. But according to a tradition reported by the Geonim, Rav's real name was Abba. His disciples and others referred to him as "Rav" without any further specification, but his colleague Shmuel referred to him by his given name (see *Arukh*, s.v., אביי.)

בְּשֶׁשָּׁמְעוּ בּוֹ שֶׁמֵּת Where people heard that he died. *Ritva* notes that the Gemara is not dealing with two witnesses who came and testified to the husband's death, for then his wife is surely awarded maintenance like any other widow. Rather the Gemara is dealing with two witnesses who testified in court that they had heard from two other people who had been abroad that the husband had died.

HALAKHAH

פּוֹסְקִין מְזוֹנוֹת לְאֵשֶׁת אִישׁ They assign maintenance to a married woman. "If a man went abroad, and his wife claimed her maintenance from his property, the court does not award her maintenance during the first three months following the husband's departure, for we assume that he left her with the means to support herself during that period. But after three months, the court awards her maintenance from her husband's property," following Rav. (*Rambam, Sefer Nashim, Hilkhot Ishut* 12:16; *Shulḥan Arukh, Even HaEzer* 70:5.)

LITERAL TRANSLATION

[1]What is the reason?

[2]Rav Zevid said: Say that he gave her bundles [of money].

[3]Rav Pappa said: [4]We are concerned that he may have said to her: [5]"Spend your handiwork on your maintenance."

[6]What is [the difference] between them?

[7]There is [a difference] between them [regarding] an adult, and [her handiwork] does not suffice. [8]Or alternatively (lit., "if also"), a minor [wife], and [her handiwork] suffices.

[1]מַאי טַעֲמָא?

[2]רַב זְבִיד אֲמַר: אֵימָא צְרָרֵי אַתְפְּסָהּ.

[3]רַב פַּפָּא אֲמַר: [4]חָיְישִׁינַן שֶׁמָּא אָמַר לָהּ: [5]"צְאִי מַעֲשֵׂה יָדַיִךְ בִּמְזוֹנוֹתַיִךְ".

[6]מַאי בֵּינַיְיהוּ?

[7]אִיכָּא בֵּינַיְיהוּ גְּדוֹלָה, וְלָא סָפְקָה. [8]אִי נַמִי, קְטַנָּה, וְסַפְקָה.

TRANSLATION AND COMMENTARY

מַאי טַעֲמָא [1]The Gemara asks: For **what reason** does Shmuel say that a wife is not maintained from her absent husband's property?

רַב זְבִיד אֲמַר [2]**Rav Zevid said:** The court does not award a wife maintenance from her husband's property, because we **say that** before he left the husband may **have given** her **bundles of money** for her maintenance. She is certainly not entitled to collect her maintenance allowance twice.

רַב פַּפָּא אֲמַר [3]**Rav Pappa said:** The court does not award a wife maintenance from her husband's property, [4]because **we are concerned that perhaps** the husband **had said to** her: [5]"Go and **use your handiwork for your maintenance,"** and she agreed to the arrangement. As we learned earlier in the tractate (47b), a wife is entitled to be maintained by her husband, in return for which she must give him her handiwork and other earnings. But if a man allowed his wife to keep her handiwork and other earnings and use them for her support, and she agreed, he is no longer liable for maintenance. Not knowing the nature of their financial arrangement, the court may not forcibly award her maintenance from his property.

מַאי בֵּינַיְיהוּ [6]The Gemara asks: **What is** the practical difference **between** these two explanations, that of Rav Zevid and that of Rav Pappa?

אִיכָּא בֵּינַיְיהוּ [7]The Gemara answers: **There is** a practical difference **between** the two where the woman is **an adult** who might have been entrusted by her husband with money for her maintenance, **and** her earnings **do not suffice** her needs, either because food prices are high, or she lacks a marketable skill. According to Rav Zevid, she cannot collect maintenance from her husband's property, for there is reason to think that he left her money for that purpose before he left. According to Rav Pappa, she can collect her maintenance from her husband's property, for there is no reason to think that she had agreed to maintain herself from her earnings. [8]**Alternatively,** there is a practical difference between the two if the wife is **a minor** whose husband would not have left her with money for her maintenance, **but** whose earnings **suffice** for her maintenance. According to Rav Zevid, she can collect her maintenance from her husband's property, whereas according to Rav Pappa, she cannot do so, for she might have agreed to support herself from her earnings.

RASHI

צררי — צרורות כספים נתן בידה למזונות. חיישינן שמא אמר לה צאי מעשה ידיך במזונותיך — וקבלה עליה. איכא בינייהו גדולה — הראויה להתפיסה מעות, ולא ספקה מזונות במעשה ידיה, שהן שני בצורת או שאינה בעלת מלאכה. לצררי — איכא למיחש, ל"צאי מעשה ידיך במזונותיך" — ליכא למיחש, דכיון דלא ספקה — לא קבלה עליה. אי נמי קטנה — ובעלת מלאכה, והשנים כתקנן. וספקה — לרב זביד פוסקין, דלא עביד איניש

NOTES

Even though a woman may remarry on the basis of such rumors, monetary matters as a rule cannot be decided by them. Our Gemara teaches that if the court received such a hearsay report that the husband had died while abroad, it may award his wife maintenance from his property.

אֵימָא צְרָרֵי אַתְפְּסָהּ **Say that he gave her bundles.** *Ritva* writes that we are only concerned that the husband might have left his wife with maintenance money, or that he might have arranged with her that she would maintain herself from her own earnings, if he planned to be away for a long time. But if he had intended to be gone for only a short time, and then he decided to stay away longer, such concerns do not apply. The court then awards his wife maintenance from his property even during the first three months of his absence.

Ritva adds that if there is concern that the husband may have left his wife with maintenance money, she may not collect maintenance from his property even if she takes an

HALAKHAH

גְּדוֹלָה, וְלָא סָפְקָה **An adult, and it does not suffice.** "When the court awards a woman maintenance from her husband's property, it is not required to consider the woman's own earnings. However, when the husband returns, he is entitled to take her earnings (for it would appear from the Gemara that according to Rav she is assigned maintenance

TRANSLATION AND COMMENTARY

תְּנַן [1]The Gemara raises an objection against Shmuel from our Mishnah, in which **we have learned: "If someone went abroad,** leaving his wife behind, **and his wife** claims that her husband left her with insufficient means of support and **demands** that the court award her **maintenance** from his property, Ḥanan and the sons of the High Priests disagree about the law. [2]**Ḥanan says:** The woman **must take an oath at the end,** after it is established that her husband has died, and she comes to collect her ketubah settlement. At that time, she must take an oath that she has no money or other property of her husband's in her possession from which she could collect her ketubah settlement. [3]**But she is not obligated to take an oath at the beginning** when she comes to court and demands maintenance from her husband's property in his absence. [4]**The sons of the High Priests disagreed with** Ḥanan ben Avishalom, **and said:** [5]She **must take an oath** both **at the beginning,** to collect her maintenance, **and at the end,** to collect her ketubah settlement." [6]Now, Ḥanan and the sons of the High Priest **only differ about** whether or not she must take **an oath** to confirm that her husband had left her with no money. [7]**But** they both agree that the court must **assign maintenance for her** from her husband's property, against Shmuel!

תַּרְגְּמָה שְׁמוּאֵל [8]The Gemara answers: **Shmuel can explain** the Mishnah in accordance with his position: It is dealing a ruling made after **people heard that** the husband **had died.** In such a case Shmuel agrees with Rav that the court awards the widow maintenance from her husband's property.

תָּא שְׁמַע [9]The Gemara raises another objection against Shmuel from a Baraita: **Come and hear: "If someone went abroad,** leaving his wife behind, **and his wife** claims that her husband left her without the means to support herself, and she **demands** that the court award her **maintenance** from his property, [10]**the sons of the High Priests say:** She **must** first **take an oath** that her husband had not left her any money. [11]**Ḥanan** disagrees and **says: She need not take an oath** in order to collect her maintenance.

[1]תְּנַן: ״מִי שֶׁהָלַךְ לִמְדִינַת הַיָּם, וְאִשְׁתּוֹ תּוֹבַעַת מְזוֹנוֹת, [2]חָנָן אָמַר: תִּשָּׁבַע בַּסּוֹף, [3]וְלֹא תִּשָּׁבַע בַּתְּחִלָּה. [4]נֶחְלְקוּ עָלָיו בְּנֵי כֹּהֲנִים גְּדוֹלִים, וְאָמְרוּ: [5]תִּשָּׁבַע בַּתְּחִלָּה וּבַסּוֹף״. [6]עַד כָּאן לָא פְּלִיגִי אֶלָּא לְעִנְיַן שְׁבוּעָה. [7]אֲבָל מְזוֹנֵי יָהֲבִינַן לָהּ!

[8]תַּרְגְּמָהּ שְׁמוּאֵל: בְּשֶׁשָּׁמְעוּ בּוֹ שֶׁמֵּת.

[9]תָּא שְׁמַע: ״מִי שֶׁהָלַךְ לִמְדִינַת הַיָּם וְאִשְׁתּוֹ תּוֹבַעַת מְזוֹנוֹת, [10]בְּנֵי כֹּהֲנִים גְּדוֹלִים אוֹמְרִים: תִּשָּׁבַע. [11]חָנָן אוֹמֵר: לֹא תִּשָּׁבַע.

LITERAL TRANSLATION

[1]We have learned: "[If] someone went abroad, and his wife demands maintenance, [2]Ḥanan says: She must take an oath at the end [regarding her ketubah], [3]but she does not take an oath at the beginning [regarding the maintenance]. [4]The sons of the High Priests disagreed with him, and said: [5]She must take an oath at the beginning and at the end." [6]Up to here they do not differ except regarding an oath. [7]But maintenance they give [it to] her.

[8]Shmuel explained it: Where they heard that he had died.

[9]Come [and] hear: "[If] someone went abroad, and his wife demands maintenance, [10]the sons of the High Priests say: She must take an oath. [11]Ḥanan says: She need not take an oath.

RASHI

דמתפים נררי לקטנה. לרב פפא אין פוסקין, דאיכא למימר: ״לאי מעשה ידיך למזונותיך״ אמר לה.

NOTES

oath that she had not received any money. We assume that it is nearly certain that a man will provide for his wife if he goes on an extended trip. This case differs from that of a widow who is believed to collect her ketubah settlement with an oath that she received nothing from her husband to cover payment of her ketubah settlement. The difference between these cases derives from the fact that it is more likely that the husband had left his wife with money for her maintenance while he was abroad than that he had left her with money that she was to use after his death.

HALAKHAH

even if her earnings could support her; *Maggid Mishneh*). But according to *Rosh,* the court only awards the woman maintenance if she cannot support herself (so too is the position of *Rema, Even HaEzer* 70:10; *Helkat Meḥokek*)." (*Rambam, Sefer Nashim, Hilkhot Ishut* 12:16; *Shulḥan Arukh, Even HaEzer* 70:5.)

תִּשָּׁבַע בַּסּוֹף **She must take an oath at the end.** "If a woman's husband went abroad, and she did not go to court to claim maintenance, but rather she sold her husband's property on her own, the sale is valid. The sale does not require a public announcement. Nor is the wife required to take an oath until the husband returns and claims that he had left her with money for her maintenance, or until he dies and she comes to collect her ketubah settlement. At that time she must take an oath that she only sold enough of her husband's property to supply her maintenance," following Ḥanan. (*Rambam, Sefer Nashim, Hilkhot Ishut* 12:16; *Shulḥan Arukh, Even HaEzer* 70:5.)

TRANSLATION AND COMMENTARY

[1]**But if** the husband later **returned and said:** 'Before I left, I **gave** my wife money that was to be used for **her maintenance** while I was away,' [2]**he is believed,** and she must return to him whatever property had been awarded to her by the court." According to this Baraita, Ḥanan and the sons of the High Priest both agree that the court awards her maintenance from her husband's property, against Shmuel!

הָכָא נַמִי [3]The Gemara answers: **Here too,** Shmuel can say that the Baraita is dealing with a ruling issued after **people heard that** the husband **had died,** for in such a case he agrees with Rav that the court awards the widow maintenance from her husband's property.

וְהָא [4]The Gemara asks: **But surely** the Tanna of the Baraita **said: "If** the husband later **returned and said** that he had left enough money with his wife, he is believed." The Baraita must be dealing with a husband who is still alive!

אִם בָּא [5]The Gemara answers: Indeed, this is so, but the rumor had spread before he returned, and on the basis of that rumor the court awarded his wife maintenance from his property. The Baraita teaches that if the husband **returned** home **following** such **a rumor,** and claimed that he had left his wife with sufficient means to support herself, he is believed.

תָּא שְׁמַע [6]The Gemara raises yet another objection against Shmuel: **Come and hear** what was taught in the following Baraita: **"If someone went abroad, and his wife** claims that he left her without the means to support herself in his absence, and she **demands maintenance** from his property, the court awards her maintenance. [7]If her husband later **returns** home **and says:** Before I left, I said to my wife: **'Spend your handiwork on your maintenance,' he is believed.** [8]**If the court** proceeded to **award** the woman maintenance before the husband returned home, [9]**what they awarded** to her **they awarded,** and nothing need be returned." Thus, we see that the court awards a woman maintenance from her absentee husband's property, against Shmuel!

[1]וְאִם בָּא וְאָמַר: ׳פָּסַקְתִּי לָהּ מְזוֹנוֹת׳, [2]נֶאֱמָן״!
[3]הָכָא נַמִי בְּשֶׁשָּׁמְעוּ בּוֹ שֶׁמֵּת.
[4]וְהָא ״אִם בָּא וְאָמַר״ קָאָמַר!
[5]אִם בָּא לְאַחַר שְׁמוּעָה.
[6]תָּא שְׁמַע: ״מִי שֶׁהָלַךְ לִמְדִינַת הַיָּם וְאִשְׁתּוֹ תּוֹבַעַת מְזוֹנוֹת, [7]וְאִם בָּא וְאָמַר: ׳צְאִי מַעֲשֵׂה יָדַיִךְ בִּמְזוֹנוֹתַיִךְ׳, רַשַּׁאי. [8]קָדְמוּ בֵּית דִּין וּפָסְקוּ, [9]מַה שֶּׁפָּסְקוּ פָּסְקוּ״.

LITERAL TRANSLATION

[1]And if he came and said: 'I gave her maintenance,' [2]he is believed."

[3]Here too, where they heard that he had died.

[4]But surely he said: "If he came and said"!

[5]If he came after the rumor.

[6]Come [and] hear: "[If] someone went abroad, and his wife demands maintenance, [7]and if he came and said: 'Spend your handiwork on your maintenance,' he is permitted. [8][If] the court proceeded and awarded [her maintenance], [9]what they awarded they awarded."

RASHI

ואם בא ואמר פסקתי לה מזונות – אתפסתיה זוזי. **נאמן** – ובשבועה ומחזרת מה שנתנו לה בית דין. **לאחר שמועה** – לאחר ששמעו בו שמת, כו'.

NOTES

וְאִם בָּא וְאָמַר: פָּסַקְתִּי לָהּ מְזוֹנוֹת And if he came and said: I gave her maintenance. Our commentary follows *Rashi,* who explains that if the husband returned home and said that before he left he had given his wife money for her maintenance, he is believed. After he takes an oath confirming his claim, his wife is obligated to return to him whatever the court had given her of his property. *Tosafot* explains that since the husband is believed, if his wife had borrowed money from others for her maintenance, she cannot collect that sum from her husband unless she first takes an oath denying his claim. *Ramban* explains that if the husband returned home before the court awarded his wife maintenance from his property, he is believed, so that she cannot collect what she had borrowed from others, even with an oath. *Ramban* notes that the husband is only believed regarding the past, but he cannot come and say that he had already provided his wife maintenance money for the next ten years. Were he believed with respect to such a claim, a widow could never collect her maintenance from her husband's property.

HALAKHAH

וְאִם בָּא וְאָמַר: פָּסַקְתִּי לָהּ מְזוֹנוֹת And if he came and said: I gave her maintenance. "If a woman did not demand maintenance in court while her husband was away, nor did she sell any of his property, but rather she borrowed money for her maintenance, when her husband returns, he must take a *hesset* oath, affirming that he had left her means for support. After this he is exempt from all obligation, and she is liable for her debt." (*Rambam, Sefer Nashim, Hilkhot Ishut* 12:21; *Shulḥan Arukh, Even HaEzer* 70:10.)

אִם בָּא וְאָמַר: צְאִי מַעֲשֵׂה יָדַיִךְ And if he came and said: Spend your handiwork. "If, before leaving home the husband told his wife that she should spend her earnings on her maintenance, and she did not protest, she cannot later claim her maintenance from him or his property. But a husband cannot force this arrangement upon his wife against her will (*Maggid Mishneh*)." (*Rambam, Sefer Nashim, Hilkhot Ishut* 12:20; *Shulḥan Arukh, Even HaEzer* 70:9.)

קָדְמוּ בֵּית דִּין וּפָסְקוּ If the court proceeded to assign her maintenance. "If the court awarded a woman maintenance, and the court or the woman sold some of her

[1]הָכָא נַמִי בְּשֶׁשָּׁמְעוּ בּוֹ שֶׁמֵּת. [2]תָּא שְׁמַע: ״מִי שֶׁהָלַךְ לִמְדִינַת הַיָּם, וְאִשְׁתּוֹ תּוֹבַעַת מְזוֹנוֹת, [3]בֵּית דִּין יוֹרְדִים לִנְכָסָיו, וְזָנִין וּמְפַרְנְסִין לְאִשְׁתּוֹ, [4]אֲבָל לֹא בָּנָיו וּבְנוֹתָיו, וְלֹא דָּבָר אַחֵר״. [5]אֲמַר רַב שֵׁשֶׁת: בְּמַשְׁרֶה אֶת אִשְׁתּוֹ עַל יְדֵי שָׁלִישׁ. [6]אִי הָכִי, בָּנָיו וּבְנוֹתָיו נַמִי! [7]כְּשֶׁהִשְׁרָה לָזוֹ וְלֹא הִשְׁרָה לָזוֹ. [8]מַאי פָּסְקָא?

LITERAL TRANSLATION

[1]Here too, where they heard that he had died.

[2]Come [and] hear: "[If] someone went abroad, and his wife demands maintenance, [3]the court confiscates (lit., "goes down into") his property, and maintains and supports his wife, [4]but not his sons and daughters, and not something else."

[5]Rav Sheshet said: Where he provided for his wife through a trustee.

[6]If so, his sons and his daughters too!

[7]Where he provided for this one [through the trustee], but he did not provide for those (lit., "that one") [through the trustee].

[8]Why the [arbitrary] decision?

RASHI

ולא דבר אחר – מפרש לקמיה. במשרה אשתו על ידי שליש – העמיד אפוטרופוס לזונה ועכשיו מסך האפוטרופוס את ידו, דהשתא ודאי לגררי ליכא למיחש, ולא לשמא אמר לה ״צאי מעשה ידיך למזונותיך״. אי הכי – דהשרה אותה על ידי שליש – אפילו בניו ובנותיו נמי, דהא גלי דעתיה דניחא ליה שיהו נזונין משלו.

TRANSLATION AND COMMENTARY

הָכָא נַמִי [1]The Gemara answers: **Here too,** Shmuel can say that the Baraita is dealing with a ruling issued after **people heard that** the husband **died.** For in such a case he agrees with Rav that the court awards the widow maintenance from her husband's property.

תָּא שְׁמַע [2]The Gemara continues with another objection raised against Shmuel: **Come and hear** what was taught in the following Baraita: **"If someone went abroad, and his wife** comes to court and **demands maintenance** from her husband's property, [3]**the court confiscates** the husband's **property, and maintains and supports his wife,** [4]**but** does **not** support **his sons and daughters, and** the court does **not** give her money for **something else."**

אֲמַר רַב שֵׁשֶׁת [5]**Rav Sheshet said:** The Baraita is dealing with a husband who **had appointed a trustee to provide his wife** with maintenance in his absence, and now the trustee does not want to continue to act for the husband. In such a case, even Shmuel agrees that the court awards the woman maintenance from her husband's property, for her husband clearly had not left her money for her maintenance, nor did his wife agree to maintain herself with her own earnings.

אִי הָכִי [6]The Gemara asks: **If** it is **so** that the Baraita is dealing with a husband who had appointed a trustee to maintain his family, then **his sons and daughters** should **also** be awarded maintenance from his property, as he clearly desired them to receive support!

כְּשֶׁהִשְׁרָה לָזוֹ [7]The Gemara answers: No, the Baraita ruling refers to a husband who **had appointed the trustee to provide** his wife with maintenance, **but he did not appoint that trustee to maintain** his sons and daughters.

מַאי פָּסְקָא [8]The Gemara asks: **What is the basis for this arbitrary decision** that assumes that a husband would want to support his wife but not his children?

NOTES

אִי הָכִי, בָּנָיו וּבְנוֹתָיו נַמִי **If so, his sons and daughters too.** According to Rav, the Baraita is not dealing with a husband who had appointed a trustee to maintain his family in his absence. Thus we understand the distinction that is made here between the man's wife and his children. The wife is awarded maintenance from her husband's property, because he is obligated to maintain her, but the children are not awarded maintenance, for their father is not obligated to maintain them, even though it is meritorious for him to do so. But according to Shmuel, who understands that the Baraita is dealing with a husband who had appointed a trustee, why distinguish between the man's wife and his children? (See *Tosafot* and *Ritva*.)

HALAKHAH

husband's landed property to pay for it, and the husband returned and claimed that he had left his wife with money, she must take a Mishnaic oath that she had not received anything from him, following Ḥanan. But if she sold movable goods belonging to her husband, she is only required to take a *hesset* oath (*Vilna Gaon*)." (*Rambam, Sefer Nashim, Hilkhot Ishut* 12:21-22; *Shulḥan Arukh, Even HaEzer* 70:10.)

בֵּית דִּין יוֹרְדִים לִנְכָסָיו **The court confiscates his property.** "If the court awarded a woman maintenance, and her husband has property, the court may confiscate the property and sell it for her maintenance," following the Baraita. (*Rambam, Sefer Nashim, Hilkhot Ishut* 12:16; *Shulḥan Arukh, Even HaEzer* 70:5.)

וְלֹא דָּבָר אַחֵר **And not something else.** "If a man went abroad, and his wife demands her maintenance, the court awards her money for maintenance, clothing, and a suitable residence. But she is not awarded money for ornaments or

TRANSLATION AND COMMENTARY

אֶלָּא [1]**Rather, Rav Pappa said:** The Baraita is dealing with a **woman who heard from a single witness that** her husband **had died.** [2]Regarding **a woman** in this situation, **who if she wished to** remarry **on the basis of** the testimony of **that single witness, would be permitted to** remarry. This is due to a special leniency instituted to prevent her from becoming an *agunah* — [3]**we** then **also give her maintenance** on the basis of that testimony, even according to Shmuel. [4]But regarding the man's **sons and daughters, if they wished to take possession of his property on the basis of** the testimony of **that single witness,** [5]they **would be unable to take possession,** for they may only succeed to their father's estate if there are two witnesses who testify to his death. [6]Therefore **we also do not give them maintenance** from his property on the basis of that testimony.

מַאי ״דָּבָר אַחֵר״ [7]The Gemara asks: We learned in the above Baraita that if one went abroad, and his wife demands her maintenance, the court confiscates the husband's property, and maintains and supports the woman, but it does not award her money for "something else." **What** does the Baraita **mean by "something else"?**

רַב חִסְדָּא [8]**Rav Ḥisda said:** The court does not award the woman **ornaments** or perfumes as part of her living expenses from the husband's property.

רַב יוֹסֵף [9]**Rav Yosef said:** The court does not award her or other poor people **charity** from the husband's property.

מַאן דְּאָמַר [10]The Gemara notes: Rav Ḥisda **who said** that the court does not award the woman **ornaments** or perfumes from her husband's property, **all the more so** must he agree with Rav Yosef that [107B] the court does not award her or other poor people **charity** from his property, for the court may not award charity from a person's property without his consent. [11]But Rav Yosef **who said** that the court does not award poor people **charity** from the husband's property disagrees with Rav Ḥisda and says that the court [12]**gives** a woman **ornaments** and perfumes from her husband's property, [13]**for** we assume that **it is not pleasing to** a husband **that** his wife **suffer the disgrace** of being without her ornaments and perfumes.

תָּא שְׁמַע [14]The Gemara raises another objection against Shmuel: **Come and hear** what was taught in a Baraita: "A woman whose husband died without children and is waiting for her husband's brother to take her as his **levirate wife** or to release her from the levirate tie by performing the *ḥalitzah* ceremony

[1]אֶלָּא אֲמַר רַב פַּפָּא: כְּשֶׁשָּׁמְעָה בּוֹ שֶׁמֵּת בְּעֵד אֶחָד. [2]הִיא, דְּאִי בָּעֵית אִינְסוּבֵי בְּעֵד אֶחָד מָצֵי מִינְסְבָא, [3]מְזוֹנֵי נַמִּי יָהֲבִינַן לָהּ. [4]בָּנָיו וּבְנוֹתָיו, דְּאִי בָּעוּ לְמֵיחַת לִנְכָסָיו בְּעֵד אֶחָד [5]לָא מָצוּ נָחְתֵי, [6]מְזוֹנֵי נַמִּי לָא יָהֲבִינַן לְהוּ.

[7]מַאי ״דָּבָר אַחֵר״?

[8]רַב חִסְדָּא אָמַר: תַּכְשִׁיט.

[9]רַב יוֹסֵף אָמַר: צְדָקָה.

[10]מַאן דְּאָמַר תַּכְשִׁיט, כָּל שֶׁכֵּן [107B] צְדָקָה. [11]מַאן דְּאָמַר צְדָקָה, [12]אֲבָל תַּכְשִׁיט יָהֲבִינַן לָהּ, [13]דְּלָא נִיחָא לֵיהּ דְּתִיתְנַוָּול.

[14]תָּא שְׁמַע: ״הַיְּבָמָה שְׁלֹשָׁה

LITERAL TRANSLATION

[1]Rather, Rav Pappa said: Where she heard that he died from one witness. [2]She, who if she wishes to marry on the basis of one witness, may marry, [3]we also give her maintenance. [4]His sons and his daughters, who if they wish to confiscate (lit "go down to") his property on the basis of one witness [5]are unable to seize it, [6]we also do not give them maintenance.

[7]What is [meant by] "anything else"?

[8]Rav Ḥisda said: An ornament.

[9]Rav Yosef said: Charity.

[10]He who said [she does not get] an ornament, all the more so [107B] charity. [11]He who said charity, [12]but an ornament, we give her, [13]for it is not pleasing to him that she be disgraced.

[14]Come [and] hear: "A levirate wife [during] the first three

RASHI

צדקה – אין בית דין פוסקין צדקה לעניים מנכסיו, בזמן ששאר בני העיר פוסקין עליהן צדקה. תכשיט – בשמים, להתקשט בהן אשתו.

NOTES

לָא מָצוּ נָחְתֵי **They are unable to take over.** In order to save a woman from the fate of an *agunah,* who may not remarry, the Rabbis instituted a leniency and accepted the testimony of a single witness as evidence of her husband's death. They imposed certain stringencies upon the woman in the case that the single witness's testimony proves to have been false, so that she will take great care and verify the matter before she remarries on the basis of that testimony. Even though the testimony is accepted not only to allow the woman to remarry, but also to allow her to collect her ketubah settlement, it is not regarded as valid testimony for other civil matters. Thus the man's heirs may not take possession of his estate unless there are two witnesses who can testify to his death.

שְׁלֹשָׁה חֳדָשִׁים רִאשׁוֹנִים **The first three months.** During the first three months of her widowhood, a woman whose

HALAKHAH

perfumes," following the Baraita and Rav Ḥisda (according to tradition, Rav Ḥisda was Rav Yosef's teacher, and regarding those generations of Amoraim, the law is in accordance with the earlier authority; *Vilna Gaon*). (*Rambam, Sefer Nashim, Hilkhot Ishut* 13:7; *Shulḥan Arukh, Even HaEzer* 70:5.)

הַיְּבָמָה **A levirate wife.** "If a man died childless, his wife is maintained for three months from her husband's property,

TRANSLATION AND COMMENTARY

is maintained for the first three months following her husband's death **from her husband's property,** for a widow must wait at least three months before she remarries, and she is entitled to maintenance from her late husband's property until she remarries. [1]**From then** the widow **is not maintained from her husband's property.** She does not remarry because she is bound to the levir by the levirate tie, [2]but she is also **not** maintained **from the levir's property,** because he has not married her yet. [3]**If** the levir **was brought before a court,** and the widow demanded that he either take her as his levirate wife, or perform *ḥalitzah,* **and** the levir **ran away,** [4]the woman **is maintained from the levir's property."** One may infer that if the court awards a widow maintenance from the levir's property in his absence, then surely it should award her maintenance from her husband's property if he left her without the means to support herself. This conclusion contradicts Shmuel!

אָמַר לָךְ שְׁמוּאֵל [5]The Gemara answers: **Shmuel can say to you** that he agrees that a widow may collect maintenance from the levir's property, [6]for **what should we be concerned about regarding** a woman who is waiting for her brother-in-law to take her in levirate marriage? [7]**If** you suggest that before running away, the levir might have given her **bundles of money** for her maintenance, [8]I can reply that the levir **was not** yet all that close to **her,** so he would not have given her money. [9]**If** you suggest that she might have agreed to maintain herself from **her handiwork,** [10]I can reply that **she is not obligated** to hand over her handiwork **to** the levir, so she surely would not have agreed to such an arrangement. But in the case of a married woman whose husband left home, we have reason to suppose that he might have left her with money for her maintenance, or she might have agreed to spend her handiwork on her maintenance.

תָּא שְׁמַע [11]The Gemara continues to attack Shmuel's position: **Come and hear** what was taught in the following Baraita: **"If a woman went abroad together with her husband, and** later **she returned** home alone

חֳדָשִׁים הָרִאשׁוֹנִים נִיזּוֹנֶת מִשֶּׁל בַּעְלָהּ. [1]מִיכָּן וְאֵילָךְ אֵינָהּ נִיזּוֹנֶת לֹא מִשֶּׁל בַּעְלָהּ, [2]וְלֹא מִשֶּׁל יָבָם. [3]עָמַד בַּדִּין וּבָרַח, [4]נִיזּוֹנֶת מִשֶּׁל יָבָם"! [5]אָמַר לָךְ שְׁמוּאֵל: [6]לְמַאי נֵיחוּשׁ לָהּ לְהַאי? [7]אִי מִשּׁוּם צְרָרֵי, [8]לָא מִיקַּרְבָא דַּעְתֵּיהּ לְגַבָּהּ. [9]אִי מִשּׁוּם מַעֲשֵׂה יָדֶיהָ, [10]לָא מִשְׁתַּעְבְּדָא לֵיהּ. [11]תָּא שְׁמַע: "הָאִשָּׁה שֶׁהָלְכָה הִיא וּבַעְלָהּ לִמְדִינַת הַיָּם,

LITERAL TRANSLATION

months is maintained from [the property of] her husband. [1]From then on she is not maintained from [the property of] her husband, [2]nor from [the property of] the levir. [3][If] he stood in court and [then] ran away, [4]she is maintained from [the property of] the levir."

[5]Shmuel can say to you: [6]About what should we be concerned regarding this [woman]? [7]If because of bundles [of money], [8]he (lit., "his intention") is not close to her. [9]If because of her handiwork, [10]she is not obligated to him.

[11]Come [and] hear: "[If] a woman went abroad, she and her husband,

RASHI

שלשה חדשים הראשונים — שאינה יכולה לא להנשא ולא להתייבם — ניזונת משל בעלה. **עמד בדין** — ואמרה לו "כנוס או חלוץ".

NOTES

husband died without children can neither enter into levirate marriage nor undergo *ḥalitzah,* for she might be pregnant with her late husband's child. Since she is temporarily forbidden to marry on account of her late husband, she is considered as being still bound to him. Therefore she is entitled to maintenance from his property. After three months, unlike an ordinary widow, she is no longer entitled to maintenance from her late husband's property. Because she is bound to her brother-in-law on account of the levirate tie, she may not marry anyone else. However, she is also not entitled to maintenance from the levir, because they are not married yet, and the levirate tie is even weaker than betrothal (see *Rivan*).

לְמַאי נֵיחוּשׁ About what should we be concerned. The Gemara apparently entertained the possibility that even in the case of the widow who was waiting to be taken in levirate marriage, the levir might have given the woman bundles of money for her maintenance, for he had already

HALAKHAH

and during that period the levir is entitled to her handiwork. From then on the widow is not maintained either from her husband's property, or from the levir's property. If the levir was brought before a court, and the widow demanded that he either marry her, or perform *ḥalitzah,* and he agreed to marry her, but then took ill or was even forced to flee, the levir is liable for her maintenance," following the Baraita. (*Rambam, Sefer Nashim, Hilkhot Ishut* 18:15; *Shulḥan Arukh, Even HaEzer* 160:1.)

הָאִשָּׁה שֶׁהָלְכָה הִיא וּבַעְלָהּ לִמְדִינַת הַיָּם If a woman went abroad, she and her husband. "If a woman went abroad together with her husband, and she returned alone and said that her husband had died, she is believed and may collect either her maintenance or her ketubah settlement. But if she returned and said that she had been divorced, she is not believed and may only collect her maintenance up to the value of her ketubah." (*Rambam, Sefer Nashim, Hilkhot Ishut* 18:24; *Shulḥan Arukh, Even HaEzer* 93:17.)

TRANSLATION AND COMMENTARY

and said: [1]**'My husband died** while we were away,' [2]**If she wishes, she may receive maintenance** from her husband's property, [3]**and if she wishes, she may collect her ketubah** settlement, for a woman is believed when she claims that her husband died. This is the normal situation of a widow who may collect her ketubah settlement or receive maintenance from her husband's estate until she remarries. If the woman returned home alone and said: [4]**'My husband divorced me,'** but she is unable to present the bill of divorce, [5]**she continues to be supported** from her husband's property **up to the value of her ketubah** settlement. Without a bill of divorce or witnesses, she is not believed to say that she was divorced. However she may collect maintenance up to the value of her ketubah settlement. For if she was in fact divorced, she is entitled to it, and if she was not divorced, her husband is obligated to maintain her." Now, this is inconsistent with Shmuel's ruling, the court does not award a married woman maintenance from her husband's property in his absence!

הָכָא נַמִי [6]The Gemara answers: **Here too,** Shmuel can say that the Baraita is dealing with a case **where they heard that** the husband had **died,** and here he agrees with Rav that the court awards the widow maintenance from her late husband's property.

וּמַאי שְׁנָא [7]The Gemara asks: If we heard that the husband died, **what is the difference** here **that** the woman **is only entitled to maintenance up to the value of her ketubah** settlement? We do not accept her claim of being divorced.

דְּאִיהִי [8]The Gemara answers: Here it is the woman **herself who caused herself a loss.** Although, without a bill of divorce, the court does not believe she is divorced, it does believe that she was widowed and awards her maintenance. However, by claiming she was divorced, the woman damaged her claim for maintenance, because divorcees are not entitled to maintenance.

תָּא שְׁמַע [9]Shmuel's position has withstood all attacks, but the Gemara raises one last objection against it: **Come and hear** what was taught in the following Baraita: A minor orphan girl who was given in marriage by her mother or brothers under a Rabbinic arrangement may subsequently annul her marriage before reaching her legal majority. [10]**"In what case did** the Rabbis **say that** such a girl **may not collect**

וּבָאת וְאָמְרָה: [1]'מֵת בַּעְלִי' — [2]רָצְתָה, נִיזּוֹנֶת, [3]רָצְתָה, גּוֹבָה כְּתוּבָּתָהּ. [4]'גֵּירְשַׁנִי בַּעְלִי' — [5]מִתְפַּרְנֶסֶת וְהוֹלֶכֶת עַד כְּדֵי כְּתוּבָּתָהּ"!

[6]הָכָא נַמִי, כְּשֶׁשָּׁמְעוּ בּוֹ שֶׁמֵּת. [7]וּמַאי שְׁנָא עַד כְּדֵי כְּתוּבָּתָהּ? [8]דְּאִיהִי הִיא דְּאַפְסִידָה אַנַּפְשָׁהּ. [9]תָּא שְׁמַע: [10]"כֵּיצַד אָמְרוּ

LITERAL TRANSLATION

and she came and said: [1]'My husband died' — [2][if] she wishes, she is maintained, [3][and if] she wishes, she collects her ketubah. [4]'My husband divorced me' — [5]she continues to be supported up to the value of her ketubah."

[6]Here too, where they heard that he had died.

[7]And what is the difference [here that she gets only] up to the value of her ketubah?

[8]Because it was she who caused herself the loss.

[9]Come [and] hear: [10]"In what circumstances did [the Sages] say

RASHI

רצתה ניזונת כו' — שהאשה נאמנת לומר "מת בעלי" ותינשא. וכשם שנאמנת לינשא — כך נאמנת ליטול כתובתה, כדאמרינן במסכת יבמות: מספר כתובתה נלמד "לכשתנשאי לאחר תטלי מה שכתוב ליכי". **מתפרנסת והולכת כו'** — כתובתה לא גביא — שמא לא גירשה, ובגירושין לא האמינוה. אבל מזוני יהבינן לה. ובפרעון כתובה, ממה נפשך; אם גירשה — הרי נטלתן בכתובתה, ואם לאו — הרי הוא חייב במזונותיה. **איהי היא דאפסדה אנפשה** — שאמרה "גרשני", וגרושה אין לה מזונות. וכי תימא: כיון דשמעה שמת תגבה כתובתה יחד — אין הכי נמי. והאי דקאמר מתפרנסת והולכת — אם אינה רוצה ליטול כתובתה, דסבורה שמא לא מת, ונוח לה ליטול בשם מזונות. שאם יבא בעלה — תהא כל כתובתה קיימת. ומתפרנסת עד כדי כתובתה, ותו לא יהבינן לה.

NOTES

been brought before a court and ordered either to take her as his levirate wife or perform *ḥalitzah*. *Ritva* argues that we see from here that while Rav Pappa adds his own explanation, he does accept Rav Zevid's explanation as to why the court does not award a woman maintenance from her absentee husband's property.

מִתְפַּרְנֶסֶת וְהוֹלֶכֶת עַד כְּדֵי כְּתוּבָּתָהּ She continues to be supported up to the value of her ketubah. The Jerusalem Talmud maintains that until a divorcee receives full payment of her ketubah settlement, her former husband is obligated to provide her with maintenance. *Rif* claims that the Babylonian Talmud does not accept this position, for the Baraita cited in our Gemara implies that once a divorcee receives maintenance to the value of her ketubah, she has no further claim against her former husband — neither for maintenance, nor for her ketubah. *Rosh* argues that our Gemara does not contradict what is stated in the Jerusalem Talmud. He understands that the Rabbis enacted that a man is obligated to maintain his divorced wife until she has received full payment of her ketubah settlement, in order to encourage him to pay her at once, rather than in installments. But if a woman returned from abroad and claimed that she had been divorced, she cannot collect her ketubah settlement in one payment, for she cannot prove

TRANSLATION AND COMMENTARY

maintenance? [1]You cannot say that she was a minor living with her husband, [2]for her husband is then liable for her maintenance. [3]Rather, say that her husband went abroad, and she borrowed money to maintain herself. [4]Then she arose and declared her refusal to continue living with her husband. In such a case he is not obligated to repay the loan taken by the girl for her maintenance." [5]Now, it may be inferred from this Baraita that the reason he is free from paying the maintenance is that she declared her refusal. [6]But if she did not declare her refusal, she would indeed be given back the maintenance money that she borrowed in her husband's absence. This Baraita thus contradicts Shmuel!

אָמַר לָךְ שְׁמוּאֵל [7]The Gemara answers: However, Shmuel can say to you that here he agrees that the girl may collect her maintenance from her husband's property, [8]for with what should we be concerned? [9]If you say that he might have given her bundles of money for her maintenance, [10]people do not give bundles of money to a minor. [11]And if you say she agreed to maintain herself from her handiwork, [12]a minor's handiwork does not suffice for her maintenance. Surely she would not have agreed to such an arrangement. But regarding a married woman whose husband left home, the court does not award her maintenance from his property, either because he might have left her with money for maintenance or because they might have agreed that she would maintain herself from her handiwork.

מַאי הֲוָה עֲלַהּ [13]Having repeatedly failed to dismiss the position of Shmuel, the Gemara asks: What conclusion was reached on this matter? What is the final Halakhic ruling regarding this issue? [14]The Gemara answers: When Rav Dimi came from Eretz Israel to Babylonia, he said: [15]An incident involving a woman whose husband left home without leaving her the means to support herself once came before Rabbi Yehudah HaNasi in Bet She'arim, [16]and he awarded the woman maintenance from her husband's property. [17]A similar incident came before Rabbi Yishmael in Sepphoris, [18]and he did not award the woman maintenance from her husband's property.

תָּהֵי בָּהּ [19]Rabbi Yoḥanan expressed his wonder about this ruling: [20]What did Rabbi Yishmael see that he did not award the woman maintenance from her husband's property? [21]Surely the sons of the High Priests

מְמָאֶנֶת אֵין לָהּ מְזוֹנוֹת? [1]אִי אַתָּה יָכוֹל לוֹמַר בְּיוֹשֶׁבֶת תַּחַת בַּעְלָהּ, [2]שֶׁהֲרֵי בַּעְלָהּ חַיָּיב בִּמְזוֹנוֹת. [3]אֶלָּא, כְּגוֹן שֶׁהָלַךְ בַּעְלָהּ לִמְדִינַת הַיָּם, לָוְתָה וְאָכְלָה, [4]עָמְדָה וּמֵיאֲנָה. [5]טַעְמָא דְּמֵיאֲנָה". [6]הָא לָא מֵיאֲנָה יָהֲבִינַן לָהּ!

[7]אָמַר לָךְ שְׁמוּאֵל: [8]הָכָא לְמַאי נֵיחוּשׁ לָהּ? [9]אִי מִשּׁוּם צְרָרֵי, [10]צְרָרֵי לִקְטַנָּה לָא מַתְפִּיס. [11]וְאִי מִשּׁוּם מַעֲשֵׂה יָדֶיהָ, [12]קְטַנָּה לָא סַפְקָה.

[13]מַאי הֲוָה עֲלַהּ? [14]כִּי אֲתָא רַב דִּימִי אֲמַר: [15]מַעֲשֶׂה בָּא לִפְנֵי רַבִּי בְּבֵית שְׁעָרִים, [16]וּפָסַק לָהּ מְזוֹנוֹת. [17]לִפְנֵי רַבִּי יִשְׁמָעֵאל בְּצִפּוֹרִי, [18]וְלֹא פָּסַק לָהּ מְזוֹנוֹת. [19]תָּהֵי בָּהּ רַבִּי יוֹחָנָן: [20]וְכִי מָה רָאָה רַבִּי יִשְׁמָעֵאל שֶׁלֹּא פָּסַק לָהּ מְזוֹנוֹת? [21]הָא לָא נֶחְלְקוּ

LITERAL TRANSLATION

that a girl who refuses [marriage] gets no maintenance? [1]You cannot say when she is living with her husband, [2]for her husband is [then] liable for her maintenance. [3]Rather, when her husband went abroad, she borrowed and ate, [4][and then] arose and refused [the marriage]." [5]The reason is that she refused [the marriage]. [6]But if she did not refuse, we give [it to] her!

[7]Shmuel can say to you: [8]Here about what should we be concerned? [9]If because of bundles [of money], [10]he does not give bundles [of money] to a minor. [11]If because of her handiwork, [12][the handiwork of] a minor does not suffice.

[13]What was the final decision here (lit., "what was there about it")? [14]When Rav Dimi came, he said: [15]An incident came before Rabbi in Bet She'arim, [16]and he awarded her maintenance. [17]Before Rabbi Yishmael in Sepphoris, [18]and he did not award her maintenance.

[19]Rabbi Yoḥanan wondered about it: [20]What did Rabbi Yishmael see that he did not award her maintenance? [21]Surely the

NOTES

that she is divorced. However, she may collect her maintenance up to the value of her ketubah, for if she is divorced, she is entitled to it, and if she is not divorced, she is entitled to maintenance.

HALAKHAH

מְמָאֶנֶת אֵין לָהּ מְזוֹנוֹת **A girl who refuses marriage does not have maintenance.** "If a girl under the age of twelve was orphaned from her father and then married off by her mother or brothers, the husband is liable for her maintenance and her ransom as long as she lives with him. But if he went abroad, and she borrowed money for her maintenance or her ransom, and then she declared her refusal to remain married, he is not required to repay her loan," following the Baraita. (*Rambam, Sefer Nashim, Hilkhot Ishut* 24:5; *Shulḥan Arukh, Even HaEzer* 116:5.)

בְּנֵי כֹּהֲנִים גְּדוֹלִים וְחָנָן אֶלָּא לְעִנְיַן שְׁבוּעָה, [1]אֲבָל מְזוֹנֵי יָהֲבִינַן לַהּ!
[2]אֲמַר לֵיהּ רַב שֶׁמֶן בַּר אַבָּא: כְּבָר תַּרְגְּמָהּ רַבֵּינוּ שְׁמוּאֵל בְּבָבֶל: [3]כְּשֶׁשָּׁמְעוּ בּוֹ שֶׁמֵּת.
[4]אֲמַר לֵיהּ: פָּתְרִיתוּ בָּהּ כּוּלֵּי הַאי?
[5]כִּי אֲתָא רָבִין אֲמַר: [6]מַעֲשֶׂה בָּא לִפְנֵי רַבִּי בְּבֵית שְׁעָרִים, [7]וְלֹא פָּסַק לָהּ מְזוֹנוֹת. [8]לִפְנֵי רַבִּי יִשְׁמָעֵאל בְּצִיפּוֹרִי, וּפָסַק לָהּ מְזוֹנוֹת.
[9]אֲמַר רַבִּי יוֹחָנָן: מָה רָאָה רַבִּי שֶׁלֹּא פָּסַק לָהּ? [10]דְּהָא לֹא נֶחְלְקוּ חָנָן וּבְנֵי כֹּהֲנִים גְּדוֹלִים אֶלָּא לְעִנְיַן שְׁבוּעָה, [11]אֲבָל מְזוֹנוֹת יָהֲבִינַן לַהּ!
[12]אֲמַר לֵיהּ רַב שֶׁמֶן בַּר אַבָּא: כְּבָר תַּרְגְּמָהּ שְׁמוּאֵל בְּבָבֶל: [13]כְּשֶׁשָּׁמְעוּ בּוֹ שֶׁמֵּת.
[14]אֲמַר לֵיהּ: פָּתְרִיתוּ בָּהּ כּוּלֵּי הַאי?

LITERAL TRANSLATION

sons of the High Priests and Ḥanan only disagreed about an oath, [1]but maintenance we give [it to] her!

[2]Rav Shemen bar Abba said to him: Rabbenu Shmuel already explained it in Babylonia: [3]Where they heard that he had died.

[4][Rabbi Yoḥanan] said to him: Did you explain all this?

[5]When Ravin came, he said: [6]An incident came before Rabbi in Bet She'arim [7]and he did not award her maintenance. [8]Before Rabbi Yishmael in Sepphoris, and he awarded her maintenance.

[9]Rabbi Yoḥanan said: What did Rabbi see that he did not award her? [10]Surely Ḥanan and the sons of the High Priests only disagreed about an oath, [11]but maintenance we give [it to] her!

[12]Rav Shemen bar Abba said to him: Shmuel already explained it in Babylonia: [13]Where they heard that he had died.

[14]He said to him: Did you explain all this?

TRANSLATION AND COMMENTARY

and Ḥanan only disagreed in the Mishnah **about** whether or not she must take **an oath** to confirm her claim that her husband had left her without the means to support herself. [1]**But** they both agree that the court **gives her** maintenance from her husband's property, contrary to Rabbi Yishmael's ruling!

אֲמַר לֵיהּ [2]**Rav Shemen bar Abba said to** Rabbi Yoḥanan: **Rabbenu Shmuel already explained** the matter **in Babylonia:** [3]The Mishnah is dealing with a case **when they heard that** the husband **died.** In such a case all agree that the court awards the woman maintenance from her husband's property.

אֲמַר לֵיהּ [4]Impressed with Rav Shemen's answer, Rabbi Yoḥanan **said to him: Did you** already **resolve all** the difficulties relating to this matter? I was not aware that you had already studied the issue in such great depth.

כִּי אֲתָא [5]**When Ravin came** from Eretz Israel to Babylonia, **he reported** a different version of these rulings: [6]**An incident** involving a woman whose husband left home without leaving her the means to support herself once **came before Rabbi** Yehudah HaNasi **in Bet She'arim,** [7]**and he did not award** the woman **maintenance** from her husband's property. [8]A similar incident came **before Rabbi Yishmael in Sepphoris, and he awarded** the woman **maintenance** from her husband's property.

אֲמַר רַבִּי יוֹחָנָן [9]**Rabbi Yoḥanan said: What did Rabbi** Yehudah HaNasi **see that he did not award** the woman maintenance? [10]**Surely Ḥanan and the sons of the High Priests only disagreed** in the Mishnah **about** whether or not a woman must take **an oath** to confirm her claim that her husband had left her without the means to support herself. [11]**But** they both agree that the court **gives her** maintenance from the husband's property, contrary to Rabbi Yehudah HaNasi's ruling!

אֲמַר לֵיהּ [12]**Rav Shemen bar Abba said to** Rabbi Yoḥanan: **Shmuel already explained** the matter **in Babylonia** that the Mishnah is dealing with a case [13]**where they heard that** the husband **died,** for in such a case all agree that the court awards the woman maintenance from her husband's property.

אֲמַר לֵיהּ [14]Rabbi Yoḥanan **said to him: Did you** already **resolve all** the difficulties relating to this matter? I did not know that you had already studied the issue in such great depth.

NOTES

פָּתְרִיתוּ בָּהּ כּוּלֵּי הַאי **Did you resolve all this.** *Rivan* offers two explanations of this expression. According to his first explanation, Rabbi Yoḥanan expressed his astonishment: Have your already resolved all the difficulties relating to this matter? According to his second explanation, Rabbi Yoḥanan raised an objection: If you have already studied the issue in such great depth, you should have resolved the difficulty in a different manner! It would appear from the Jerusalem Talmud that Rabbi Yoḥanan and Resh Lakish disagreed about the same issue that is disputed here between Rav and Shmuel, and that Rabbi Yoḥanan follows the position of Rav.

TRANSLATION AND COMMENTARY

וְהִלְכְתָא [1]The Gemara concludes the discussion with the following ruling: **The law is in accordance with** the position of **Rav** that **a married woman** whose husband left home without leaving her with the means to support herself **is awarded maintenance** from her husband's property, even though Shmuel's position was never actually refuted.

וְהִלְכְתָא [2]Having cited this ruling, the Gemara now records two additional rulings: **The law is in accordance with** the position of **Rav Huna who said** what he said **in the name of Rav.** [3]**For Rav Huna said in the name of Rav: A woman can say to her husband:** [4]**"I will not** exercise my right to **be maintained** by you, **and I will not work** for you." When the Rabbis enacted the rights and duties of husband and wife, the wife's right to maintenance was the primary enactment, instituted for her benefit. In return for the husband's duty to maintain his wife, the Rabbis enacted that he should be entitled to her handiwork, in order to avoid the animosity that might arise between husband and wife if he were required to support her but not entitled to the proceeds from her handiwork. Since the wife's right to maintenance is primary, she is entitled to forfeit that right and keep the proceeds of her handiwork.

וְהִלְכְתָא [5]On a totally different matter, the Gemara reports: **The law is in accordance with Rav Zevid with regard to glazed** utensils. [6]**For Rav Zevid said:** Regarding **glazed** earthenware **utensils,** certain varieties absorb food that is cooked in them, so that they become permanently forbidden for use if non-kosher foods are cooked in them. Other types do not absorb the food that is cooked in them, so that after a thorough washing they are permitted for further use, even if they were used with non-kosher foods. [7]**White and black** glazed earthenware utensils **are permitted,** even if they were used to cook non-kosher food, for they do not absorb the food that is cooked in them, [8]and **green** glazed earthenware utensils **are forbidden,** if they were used

[1]וְהִלְכְתָא כְּוָתֵיהּ דְּרַב, וּפוֹסְקִין מְזוֹנוֹת לְאֵשֶׁת אִישׁ.

[2]וְהִלְכְתָא כְּוָתֵיהּ דְּרַב הוּנָא אָמַר רַב. [3]דְּאָמַר רַב הוּנָא אָמַר רַב: יְכוֹלָה אִשָּׁה שֶׁתֹּאמַר לְבַעְלָהּ: [4]״אֵינִי נִיזּוֹנֶת, וְאֵינִי עוֹשָׂה״.

[5]וְהִלְכְתָא כְּוָתֵיהּ דְּרַב זְבִיד בְּקוּנְיָא, [6]דְּאָמַר רַב זְבִיד: הָנֵי מָאנֵי דְּקוּנְיָא — [7]חִיוָּרֵי וְאוּכָּמֵי שָׁרוּ, [8]יְרוּקֵי אֲסִירֵי.

LITERAL TRANSLATION

[1]And the law is in accordance with Rav, and they award maintenance to a married woman.

[2]And the law is in accordance with Rav Huna who said in the name of Rav. [3]For Rav Huna said in the name of Rav: A woman can say to her husband: [4]"I will not be maintained, and I will not work."

[5]And the law is in accordance with Rav Zevid about glazing, [6]for Rav Zevid said: Glazed utensils — [7]white and black are permitted, [8]green are forbidden.

RASHI

מאני דקוניא — כלי חרס שמחפין עליהם עופרת, שקורין *פלומבלי״ר בלע״ז. ירוקי אסורי — לענין חמץ בפסח, וגיעולי עובדי כוכבים, ויין נסך. חיורי שרו — לפי שהעופרת מחליק את החרס, ואינו מניחו לבלוע. אבל הירוקים — מעורב צריף שקורין **אלו״ס בתוך העופרת, והוא עז, ומחלחל את החרס ובולע והכי אמרינן במסכת עבודה זרה (לג,ב): דמצרפי ובלעי.

NOTES

וְהִלְכְתָא כְּוָתֵיהּ דְּרַב זְבִיד **And the law is in accordance with Rav Zevid.** This ruling is recorded here, even though it deals with a matter that is totally unrelated to the subject matter of our Gemara, because the three rulings that are recorded here were all issued at the same time and in the same place (*Ritva*). Others explain that since our Gemara dealt above with Rav Zevid's explanation of Shmuel's position that the court does not award a woman maintenance in her husband's absence, it now brings a ruling that the law is in accordance with Rav Zevid's position on an entirely different matter.

מָאנֵי דְּקוּנְיָא **Glazed utensils.** *Rashi* understands that we are dealing here with earthenware utensils that are plated with lead. *Tosafot* follows *Rabbenu Ḥananel* and *Arukh* who understand that we are dealing with earthenware utensils that are glazed. Following the Gemara in *Pesaḥim* and *Avodah Zarah*, *Rif* and *Tosafot* note that Rav Zevid's allowance regarding white and black utensils is limited to

HALAKHAH

פּוֹסְקִין מְזוֹנוֹת לְאֵשֶׁת אִישׁ **They assign maintenance to a married woman.** "If a man went abroad, the court awards his wife maintenance from his property," following Rav. *Rambam* writes that the Geonim disagreed about whether a woman whose husband went abroad is awarded maintenance even if she does not have a ketubah deed. *Rambam* rules that she is awarded maintenance even without producing her ketubah deed, for she is entitled to maintenance by Torah law. (*Rambam, Sefer Nashim, Hilkhot Ishut* 12:18; *Shulḥan Arukh, Even HaEzer* 70:5.)

אֵינִי נִיזּוֹנֶת, וְאֵינִי עוֹשָׂה **I will not be maintained, and I will not work.** "The Rabbis enacted that a husband is entitled to his wife's handiwork in return for the maintenance that he must provide her. Therefore, if a woman says that she wishes to surrender her right to maintenance and keep her handiwork for herself," we allow that, following Rav Huna. (*Rambam, Sefer Nashim, Hilkhot Ishut* 12:4; *Shulḥan Arukh, Even HaEzer* 69:4.)

מָאנֵי דְּקוּנְיָא **Glazed utensils.** "Lead-plated or glazed earthenware utensils that are green because they contain

LANGUAGE

קוּנְיָא **Glazed utensils.** From the Greek κονια, *konia*, meaning "dust, plaster."

REALIA

מָאנֵי דְּקוּנְיָא **Glazed utensils.** The Gemara apparently refers to pottery which was coated with various chemicals, particularly mineral salts before being fired in the kiln. What type of glazing resulted and how water-resistant it was depended, in large measure, on the temperature of the kiln and the glazing agent.

Even today, pottery is frequently glazed by adding lead and other mineral salts (cf. also *Rashi*). Other chemicals are often added to color the glaze, and such chemicals are likely to affect the final product. Thus, certain types of glaze are water-resistant, while others are porous, and pottery glazed with these substances will absorb liquid kept there.

LANGUAGE (RASHI)

פלומבלי״ר* From the Old French *plomer,* meaning "to plate with lead."

אלו״ם** From the Old French *alum,* meaning "alum."

LANGUAGE (RASHI)

קריבצי"ש* (read: קיריויני"ש). From the Old French *crevaces*, meaning "crevices."

[1]וְלָא אֲמָרַן אֶלָּא דְּלֵית בְּהוּ קַרְטוּפְנֵי, [2]אֲבָל אִית בְּהוּ קַרְטוּפְנֵי, אֲסִירֵי.

משנה [3]מִי שֶׁהָלַךְ לִמְדִינַת הַיָּם, וְעָמַד אֶחָד וּפִירְנֵס אֶת אִשְׁתּוֹ, [4]חָנָן אוֹמֵר: אִיבֵּד אֶת מְעוֹתָיו. [5]נֶחְלְקוּ עָלָיו בְּנֵי כֹּהֲנִים גְּדוֹלִים, וְאָמְרוּ: [6]יִשָּׁבַע כַּמָּה הוֹצִיא, וְיִטּוֹל.

[7]אָמַר רַבִּי דּוֹסָא בֶּן הָרְכִּינַס כְּדִבְרֵיהֶם. [8]אָמַר רַבִּי יוֹחָנָן בֶּן זַכַּאי: יָפֶה אָמַר חָנָן. [9]הִנִּיחַ מְעוֹתָיו עַל קֶרֶן הַצְּבִי.

TRANSLATION AND COMMENTARY

to cook non-kosher food, for they absorb the food that is cooked in them. [1]**And we only say** that the white and black utensils are permitted **if they have no cracks** in the glaze, [2]**but if they have cracks** in the glaze, **they** too are forbidden if they have been used for non-kosher foods, for it is absorbed into the utensils through the cracks.

MISHNAH מִי שֶׁהָלַךְ [3]**If someone went abroad,** leaving his wife without the means to support herself, **and someone else stood and supported the wife** without her husband having asked him to do so, how should the court rule if her husband returns and the lender demands reimbursement? [4]**Hanan says:** The one who supported the absentee husband's wife has **lost his money.** [5]**The sons of the High Priests disagreed with** Hanan, **and said:** [6]The one who maintained the woman **may swear how much he spent** on her support, **and recover** it from her husband.

אָמַר [7]**Rabbi Dosa ben Horkinas agreed with** the sons of the High Priests. [8]**Rabbi Yohanan ben Zakkai said: Hanan said well** in this case, for the one who maintained the woman without having been asked to do so is regarded as if [9]**he had put his money on the horn of a deer,** meaning that he has absolutely no claim to the money.

LITERAL TRANSLATION

[1]And we only say this when they have no cracks, [2]but if they have cracks, they are forbidden.

MISHNAH [3][If] someone went abroad, and someone [else] stood and supported his wife, [4]Hanan says: He lost his money. [5]The sons of the High Priests disagreed with him, and said: [6]He may swear how much he spent, and take [it back].

[7]Rabbi Dosa ben Horkinas said as they said. [8]Rabbi Yohanan ben Zakkai said: Hanan said well. [9]He put his money on a deer's horn.

RASHI

קרטופנא — ביקועי *קיריויני"ש בלעז. **משנה** חנן אומר איבד את מעותיו — שלא אמרתי לך: הלוני ואני אפרע. אבל אם הלוה את האשה מעות למזונותיה על מנת שתשלם לו, הוא תובעה, והיא תובעת הבעל, וישלם, כדאמר לעיל בממאנת ולוותה ואכלה ועמדה ומיאנה: טעמא — דמיאנה, הא לא מיאנה — משלם.

NOTES

utensils that had been used for cold foods, such as non-kosher wines. But if those utensils were used for hot foods, even Rav Zevid agrees that they are permanently forbidden, for once an earthenware utensil absorbs forbidden food matter, there is no way to restore it to use.

וְעָמַד אֶחָד וּפִירְנֵס And someone else stood and supported. *Rashi* and most other Rishonim maintain that the Mishnah's ruling is limited to the case when the other person did not provide the maintenance as a loan. But if he loaned the woman money, he may demand it back from her. She in turn may demand it from her husband, and the husband is required to pay. But some Geonim disagree and say that the Mishnah's ruling applies in all cases, and that the husband is never required to pay the other person for maintaining his wife. *Rashba* and *Ra'ah* disagree about how to rule if the other person provided the maintenance without specifying the nature of the arrangement. According to *Rashba,* unless he specified that he was relying on the woman's husband to pay him back, he is regarded as having extended her a loan. *Ra'ah* maintains that he is only regarded as having extended the woman a loan, if he stated so explicitly. Otherwise, it is assumed that he was relying on her husband to pay him back.

Nimmukei Yosef explains that even though a person is generally entitled to compensation if he benefited another person in some way, someone who supports a woman in her husband's absence without having been asked to do so is not entitled to compensation from her husband, for the

HALAKHAH

alum are permanently forbidden for use once they have been used for non-kosher foods. White or black utensils, if they are smooth and have no cracks are treated like metal utensils. If they have cracks, they are treated like earthenware utensils," following Rav Zevid. (*Rambam, Sefer Kedushah, Hilkhot Ma'akhalot Asurot* 11:19; *Shulhan Arukh, Yoreh De'ah* 135:6.)

עָמַד אֶחָד וּפִירְנֵס אֶת אִשְׁתּוֹ Somebody arose and supported his wife. "If a man went abroad, and someone else supported his wife from his own property without being asked to do so by her husband, the husband is not obligated to pay him back for his expenses. He never asked the other person to maintain his wife in his absence, and she did not accept the maintenance as a loan. *Rema* (following *Hagahot Mordekhai*) writes that if someone owed the husband money, and he supported his wife while he was away, the amount which he spent on her maintenance is deducted from his debt. Some authorities note that if someone supported the woman from her husband's property, he is not required to pay the husband back (*Bet Shmuel, Helkat Mehokek,* and others)." (*Rambam, Sefer Nashim, Hilkhot Ishut* 12:19; *Shulhan Arukh, Even HaEzer* 70:8.)

גמרא

[1]תְּנַן הָתָם: [2]"הַמּוּדָּר הֲנָאָה מֵחֲבֵירוֹ [108A] [3]שׁוֹקֵל לוֹ אֶת שִׁקְלוֹ, [4]וּפוֹרֵעַ אֶת חוֹבוֹ, [5]וּמַחֲזִיר לוֹ אֲבֵידָתוֹ. [6]וּבְמָקוֹם שֶׁנּוֹטְלִין שָׂכָר, [7]תִּפּוֹל הֲנָאָה לַהֶקְדֵּשׁ".

LITERAL TRANSLATION

GEMARA [1]We have learned elsewhere: [2]"[If] one is forbidden by a vow from benefiting from another person, [108A] [3]he may pay his [half-]shekel for him, [4]or repay his debt, [5]or return to him his lost object. [6]And in a place where they take a fee, [7]the benefit goes to (lit., 'falls to') the Temple treasury."

TRANSLATION AND COMMENTARY

GEMARA תְּנַן הָתָם [1]**We have learned elsewhere** in the Mishnah: [2]**"One who is forbidden by a vow from benefiting from another person** — whether he forbade himself with a vow from deriving any benefit from that other person, or that other person forbade him with a vow from deriving any benefit from him — [108A] [3]that other person **may pay the half-shekel on his behalf.** Each year every Jew is obligated to contribute half a shekel to the Temple treasury for the communal sacrifices, and even if one has sworn not to benefit from somebody else, one may pay the half-shekel for that person. Similarly, if one owes money, [4]the person from whom one has sworn not to derive any benefit may **repay that debt.** [5]Similarly, if one has lost property, that other person may **return the lost object to him.** [6]**In** some **places,** people who restore lost objects to their rightful owners generally **take a fee** for their services. In such a place, if the person who returned the lost object to the one who was forbidden to derive any benefit from him refuses to accept a fee, the rightful owner would derive an actual benefit from him, namely, the fee which he is ready to waive, since he has sworn to derive no benefit from that person, [7]**the benefit,** the waived fee, **must be given to the Temple treasury."**

RASHI

שוקל לו את שקלו — שוקל בשבילו שקל שהוא חייב לכל שנה לקרבנות לבור. **ופורע לו את חובו** — אם חייב ממון לנושה — מותר לזה שיפרענו בשבילו. **ומחזיר לו אבידתו** — אם ראה חמורו תועה — מותר להשיבו. **במקום שנוטלין שכר** — על טורח השבתה. **תפול** — הניית השכר להקדש, שהרי שניהן מודרין בהנאה זה מזה.

NOTES

husband can argue that had the other person not provided his wife with maintenance, she would have reduced her expenses and maintained herself from her own earnings. Thus the husband did not actually benefit from what the other person did.

וּמַחֲזִיר לוֹ אֲבֵידָתוֹ **He may return to him his lost object.** *Rid* explains that even though the owner benefits when his lost object is returned to him, the party who vowed that the other individual receive no benefit from him or his property can argue that he had no intention of causing him any benefit, but only to perform the commandment of restoring a lost object.

וּבְמָקוֹם שֶׁנּוֹטְלִין שָׂכָר **And in a place where they take a fee.** By law no one is entitled to a fee for restoring a lost object to its rightful owner, for all are bound by both a positive and a negative commandment to do so. But in some communities it was customary for the owner to give the finder a reward. There are also situations where the finder has to make great efforts and take time off from his own work in order to care for the lost object and/or return it to its owner. In such a case, the owner of the lost object is obligated to compensate the finder for his expenses and his lost income.

תִּפּוֹל הֲנָאָה לַהֶקְדֵּשׁ **The benefit goes to the Temple treasury.** The Rishonim ask: If the owner of the lost object is forbidden to derive benefit from the finder, why must the finder's fee be given to the Temple treasury? Let it be given to the finder himself! He has not sworn not to derive benefit from the owner. *Rashi* understands that both parties are forbidden to derive benefit from one another. Therefore the finder is forbidden to take a fee from the owner of the lost object. *Ritva* objects that even in such a case the finder

HALAKHAH

שׁוֹקֵל לוֹ אֶת שִׁקְלוֹ **He may pay his half-shekel.** "If someone was forbidden by a vow from deriving benefit from another person, that other person may pay on his behalf the half-shekel obligation that he owes the Temple treasury." (*Rambam, Sefer Hafla'ah, Hilkhot Nedarim* 6:4.)

וּפוֹרֵעַ אֶת חוֹבוֹ **And repay his debt.** "If someone was forbidden by a vow from deriving benefit from another person, that other person may repay his debt on his behalf. Even if the debtor had given his creditor a pledge, and the other person from whom he was forbidden to derive benefit repaid his debt and recovered the pledge, that other person must return the pledge to the debtor. This ruling follows Ḥanan and the Jerusalem Talmud, which understands that Ḥanan's position applies to all debts, and not only the husband's obligation to maintain his wife (see *Tosafot, s.v.,* הא)." (*Rambam, Sefer Hafla'ah, Hilkhot Nedarim* 6:4; *Shulḥan Arukh, Yoreh De'ah* 221:1.)

וּמַחֲזִיר לוֹ אֲבֵידָתוֹ **And return to him his lost object.** "If someone was forbidden to derive benefit from another person, and he lost certain property, that other person may return it to him if he finds it. In a place where it is customary for a person who restores lost property to its rightful owner to take a fee for his services, the following distinctions apply: If the finder was forbidden to derive benefit from the owner, the finder must return the lost object to its rightful owner free of charge. If the owner was forbidden to derive benefit from the finder, the finder may not return the lost object to the rightful owner without

[1]בִּשְׁלָמָא שׁוֹקֵל לוֹ אֶת שִׁקְלוֹ — [2]מִצְוָה קָעָבֵיד, [3]דִּתְנַן: [4]"תּוֹרְמִין עַל הָאָבוּד, [5]וְעַל הַגָּבוּי, [6]וְעַל הֶעָתִיד לִגָּבוֹת". [7]וּמַחֲזִיר לוֹ אֲבֵידָתוֹ

LITERAL TRANSLATION

[1]Granted that he may pay his [half-]shekel on his behalf — [2]he performs a commandment, [3]for we have learned: [4]"They set aside for what was lost, [5]and for what was collected, [6]and for what was yet to be collected." [7]And [granted] that he may return to him his lost object

TRANSLATION AND COMMENTARY

בִּשְׁלָמָא [1]The Gemara probes the meaning of this Mishnah: **Granted that** a person **may pay the half-shekel** levy **on behalf** of another person who is forbidden to derive any benefit from him, [2]for all that **he** does is **fulfill the commandment** of contributing a half-shekel to the Temple treasury. The other person derives no benefit from him, since every individual has a share in the communal sacrifices. [3]**For we have learned:** "When the Temple treasurers set aside the *terumat halishkah*, the fund for supporting communal sacrifices, from the shekalim that were collected from every adult male, [4]**they set it aside** not only on behalf of the shekalim that were actually deposited in the Temple treasury, but even **on behalf of** shekalim **that were lost,** [5]**and on behalf of** shekalim **that were collected** by the agent and had not yet reached the Temple, [6]**and on behalf of** shekalim **that were yet to be collected."** The half-shekel contribution was intended to assure the participation of the entire nation in the communal sacrifices brought as part of the Temple service. Thus when the Temple treasurers set aside *terumat halishkah,* they did so even on behalf of the people whose shekalim were stolen or lost before reaching the Temple treasury. They did so for people whose shekalim had been collected and were on the way to Jerusalem. Moreover, they even set it aside on behalf of people who have not yet contributed their shekalim, and will not do so in the future. Therefore the person for whom the half-shekel was paid received no benefit from this act because the Temple treasurers had already given him a share in the communal sacrifices. [7]**And granted** also **that** a person **may return a lost object to** someone who is forbidden to derive any benefit from him, for all that

RASHI

מצוה קא עביד — כלומר: מצוה בעלמא קא עביד, ואינו מהנהו לזה. שאם לא שקל עליו — לא הפסיד כלום, שיש לו חלק בקרבנות. דתנן תורמין — את הלשכה בשלש קופות. על האבוד — אף על מי ששלח שקלו ואבד. ועל הגבוי — שעדיין לא הגיע כאן. ועל העתיד לגבות — ואפילו לא נגבה לאחר מכאן — יש לו חלק בתרומה ובקרבנות, אלא שחיסר מצוה. נמצא שכר המצוה על הנותן.

NOTES

should be entitled to his fee, for it is not regarded as a benefit that the finder derives from the owner, but rather as a payment for the services which he rendered. Therefore, argues *Ritva* (see also *Nimmukei Yosef*), it must be the finder who wishes to waive the fee to which he is entitled. In such a case, the owner of the lost object may not keep the money, but rather he must hand it over to the Temple treasury.

עַל הָאָבוּד, וְעַל הַגָּבוּי **For what was lost, and for what was collected.** Our commentary follows *Rashi,* who explains that shekalim "that were lost" refers to shekalim that were lost on the way to the Temple treasury, shekalim "that were collected" refers to shekalim that were collected and are now on their way to Jerusalem, and shekalim "that were yet to be collected" refers to shekalim that were not yet collected and might never be collected. *Ritva* objects that according to this explanation, there is no order to the Mishnah, for if *terumat halishkah* is set aside for shekalim that were lost, surely it is set aside for shekalim that are on their way to Jerusalem. Nor can it be argued that the Mishnah follows the stylistic principle of arranging cases in an anticlimactic order ("this and it is unnecessary to say this"), because that principle cannot account for the position of the third case regarding the shekalim that might never be collected at all, for that case is certainly the most novel one. Rather, argues *Ritva* (see also *Tosafot*), shekalim "that were lost" refers to shekalim that already reached the Temple treasury and then were lost; shekalim "that were collected" refers to shekalim that reached the hands of the Temple treasurer but were lost before they were brought into the Temple treasury; and shekalim "that were yet to be collected" refers to shekalim that were lost while on the way to Jerusalem. Thus the Mishnah proceeds from the simplest case to the more novel one. *Kesef Mishneh* understands that *Rambam* (see Halakhah) did not read "for what was lost", and had only: "They set aside for what was collected, and for what was yet to be collected." *Ritva* suggests that shekalim "that were yet to be collected" refers to shekalim that will arrive in the Temple treasury after Sukkot when the *terumat halishkah* that was to be used for

HALAKHAH

accepting a fee. If the two were forbidden to derive any benefit from one another, the finder may not accept a fee, nor may he return the lost object without charging a fee. A fee must be taken and then donated to the Temple treasury." (*Rambam, Sefer Hafla'ah, Hilkhot Nedarim* 7:1; *Shulhan Arukh, Yoreh De'ah* 221:3.)

תּוֹרְמִין עַל הָאָבוּד **They set aside for what was lost.** "When the Temple treasurers set aside the *terumat halishkah,* they have in mind to set it aside on behalf of what was collected and is found in the Temple treasury, and on behalf of what was collected but had not yet reached the Temple treasury, and on behalf of what was still to be collected (see *Kesef Mishneh*)." (*Rambam, Sefer Zemanim, Hilkhot Shekalim* 2:9.)

TRANSLATION AND COMMENTARY

he does **also fulfills the commandment** of restoring lost property to its rightful owner. The recipient derives no actual benefit from him, because the property was his even before it was returned. [1]**But** why is a person permitted to **repay the debt** of someone who is forbidden to derive any benefit from him? [2]**Surely, he causes him to profit,** because he no longer has to repay the debt.

אָמַר רַב אוֹשַׁעְיָא [3]**Rav Oshaya said:** According to **whose** viewpoint **was** the Mishnah in *Nedarim* stated? [4]**It follows** the viewpoint of **Ḥanan, who said** in our Mishnah: "If someone went abroad, leaving his wife without the means of support, and somebody arose and supported her, without her husband's request, and when the husband returned, he demanded reimbursement, Ḥanan says: [5]The person who supported the absentee husband's wife **lost his money.**" And this same law applies to any other debt. If someone other than the debtor repaid the debt, he cannot demand reimbursement. Thus, a person is permitted to repay the debt of someone who is forbidden to derive any benefit from him. Since the person who repaid the debt cannot demand the reimbursement, he does not benefit him when he waives reimbursement. Even though the debtor is no longer obligated to pay his debt, since he received nothing from the person who repaid his debt, that person is not regarded as having benefited him. He merely spared him a potential loss.

— נַמִי מִצְוָה קָעָבֵיד. [1]אֶלָּא פּוֹרֵעַ לוֹ אֶת חוֹבוֹ — [2]הָא קָמִשְׁתָּרְשִׁי לֵיהּ!

[3]אֲמַר רַב אוֹשַׁעְיָא: הָא מַנִּי? [4]חָנָן הִיא, דַּאֲמַר: [5]אִיבֵּד אֶת מְעוֹתָיו.

LITERAL TRANSLATION

— he also performs a commandment. [1]But repaying his debt — [2]surely he benefited!

[3]Rav Oshaya said: [According to] whom is this? [4]It is Ḥanan, who said: [5]He lost his money.

RASHI

משתרשי ליה = מרויחו. חנן היא דאמר: איבד מעותיו — זה שפרנס את אשת חבירו, ונתכוון לשם הלואה, שישלם לו בעלה — איבד מעותיו. ואין יכול לומר לו: את חובך פרעתי, שלם לי. והוא הדין נמי לכל חוב שעליו ועמד חברו ופרעו, וזה לא אמר לו "הלויני" — אינו חייב לו כלום. וכיון דאילו פריעה לשם הלואה לאו הלואה היא, כי פריעה נמי לשם מחילה — לאו מידי יהיב ליה.

NOTES

the communal sacrifices had already been set aside for the last time that year. These shekalim will be treated like the surplus treasury funds (*sheyarei halishkah*) and used for other purposes. But the people who sent those shekalim have a part in the communal sacrifices.

נַמִי מִצְוָה קָעָבֵיד **He also performs a commandment.** *Ritva* notes that even though a person is permitted to restore lost property to a person who is forbidden to derive any benefit from him, he may not give him charity, even though the giving of charity is also a commandment. He is permitted to return the lost object, for that object already belongs to the person who is forbidden to derive benefit from him. Charity, however, is a more direct benefit because the recipient is getting money that he otherwise would not have.

הָא מַנִּי? חָנָן הִיא **According to whom is this? It is Ḥanan.** *Rid* notes that once the Gemara offers this answer, it is no longer necessary to say as we said above that a person may pay the half-shekel levy on behalf of another person who is forbidden to derive benefit from him, because even without contribution every individual still has a share in the communal sacrifices. For according to Ḥanan it can be argued that since he paid the half-shekel levy on behalf of the other person without having been asked to do so, he cannot later demand reimbursement. Since he cannot demand reimbursement, he is not considered as benefiting him when he decides not to ask for it.

חָנָן הִיא **It is Ḥanan.** The Rishonim (see *Tosafot* and others) discuss at length why according to Ḥanan if a person vows that another individual may derive no benefit from him, he may nevertheless repay his debts. Surely he causes him to benefit, since the debtor no longer owes the money. Following the Gemara in *Nedarim* 33a, they explain that a person is permitted to repay the debt of another person who is forbidden to derive benefit from him, because he is not considered directly as benefiting him, but only as "chasing a lion away from him," that is to say he is sparing him a loss. *Rosh* and *Tosafot* add that this indirect type of benefit is permitted only because the man repaying the debt may not claim the money back from the debtor. Thus his act had no direct legal bearing on the man forbidden to benefit from him, but only the incidental consequence of his not having to repay the debt. *Ritva* formulates the explanation in a slightly different manner: A person is permitted to repay the debt of another person who is forbidden to derive benefit from him, because the benefit derived is not clear and obvious to all. The debtor does not receive any tangible benefit.

The Jerusalem Talmud cites another opinion according to which the Mishnah in *Nedarim* follows not only Ḥanan, but the sons of the High Priests as well. In our Mishnah, the sons of the High Priests who maintain that a person who supports a woman in her husband's absence without having been asked to do so can later recover from the husband what he spent on the woman's maintenance. According to the opinion cited in the Jerusalem Talmud, the sons of the High Priests agree that a person who repays another person's debt without his consent cannot later collect the money from the debtor. The woman's maintenance can be recovered from the husband, because we assume that he did not want his wife to starve in his absence, so he would be ready to compensate anybody who maintains her. But as for someone who repaid someone else's debt, the debtor can argue that he would

LITERAL TRANSLATION

[1]And Rava said: You can even say the Rabbis. [2]What we are dealing with here? [3]Where he borrowed on condition that he not repay.

[4]Granted [that] Rava did not say like Rav Oshaya, [5]for he establishes it like the Rabbis. [6]But what is the reason that Rav Oshaya did not say like Rava?

[7]Rav Oshaya can say to you: [8]Granted that he does not have [direct] benefit, [108B] but does he not have embarrassment [if does not repay]. [9]There he also has benefit — [10]with that enjoyment that he is [no longer] embarrassed by him.

[1]וְרָבָא אֲמַר: אֲפִילּוּ תֵּימָא רַבָּנַן. [2]הָכָא בְּמַאי עָסְקִינַן? [3]שֶׁלָּוָה עַל מְנָת שֶׁלֹּא לִפְרוֹעַ.

[4]בִּשְׁלָמָא רָבָא לָא אֲמַר כְּרַב אוֹשַׁעְיָא, [5]דְּמוֹקֵים לָהּ כְּרַבָּנַן. [6]אֶלָּא רַב אוֹשַׁעְיָא מַאי טַעֲמָא לָא אֲמַר כְּרָבָא?

[7]אָמַר לָךְ רַב אוֹשַׁעְיָא: [8]נְהִי דַּהֲנָאָה לֵית לֵיהּ [108B] כִּיסּוּפָא מִי לֵית לֵיהּ. [9]הָתָם נַמִי אִית לֵיהּ הֲנָאָה — [10]בְּהַהִיא הֲנָאָה דְּמִיכְסִיף מִינֵּיהּ.

TRANSLATION AND COMMENTARY

וְרָבָא אֲמַר [1]The Gemara cites an alternative answer: **Rava said: You can even say** that the Mishnah in *Nedarim* follows the viewpoint of **the Rabbis** of our Mishnah, (the sons of the High Priests), who disagreed with Ḥanan. They said that the person who, on his own, maintained the absentee husband's wife may swear how much he spent on her support, and recover it from the husband. The same law applies to any other debt. If someone other than the debtor repaid it, he may indeed demand the money back from the debtor. Thus, ordinarily, a person from whom a debtor has sworn not to derive benefit may not repay the debt for him, because he is entitled to demand reimbursement. Thus when he waives reimbursement, he benefits the debtor. [2]But **what we are dealing with here** in the Mishnah in *Nedarim* [3]**is someone** who **borrowed** money **on condition that he not** be required to **repay** the loan at any specific time. In such a case, a person from whom the debtor has sworn to derive no benefit may repay the loan on his behalf. The creditor could not have demanded the money from the debtor, and so the debtor did not derive any benefit when the other person repaid it for him.

בִּשְׁלָמָא [4]The Gemara continues: **Granted that Rava did not explain** the Mishnah in *Nedarim* **as** did **Rav Oshaya,** [5]**for he** wanted to **explain** it **in accordance with** the position of **the Rabbis** of our Mishnah, and not just in accordance with the position of Ḥanan. [6]**But what is the reason that Rav Oshaya did not explain** the Mishnah **as** did **Rava?**

אָמַר לָךְ [7]The Gemara answers: **Rav Oshaya can say to you:** [8]Even **if** the debtor **does not enjoy** any present **benefit** when the other person repays his debt, for he had stipulated with his creditor that he would not be required to repay his loan at any specific time, [108B] **does** the debtor **not suffer** constant **embarrassment** because he is in debt? [9]**There too** the debtor **enjoys a benefit** when somebody else repays his loan — [10]**that benefit** being **that he** will no longer suffer the **embarrassment** of being in debt. Thus, the Mishnah in *Nedarim* cannot follow the position of the Sages of our Mishnah, but must follow the position of Ḥanan.

RASHI

אפילו תימא רבנן — דאמרי: חייב, אף על פי שלא אמר לו הלויני. וגבי שאר חוב נמי — חייב לשלם, וכי מחיל — אסור במודר הנאה. והכא דקתני פורע לו את חובו — בשלוה זה תחלה הלואה מן המלוה על מנת שלא לפרוע עד שירצה, לא יוכל הנושה ללחצו, הלכך לאו מידי יהיב ליה. כיסופא מי לית ליה — דקא מיכסיף מן המלוה תמיד. הלכך, אי רבנן היא, דאמרי דלענין חוב לוה על מנת לפרוע ופרע חברו בשבילו — חייב לשלם, וגבי מודר הנאה מחילה היא, ואסיר. כי לוה על מנת שלא לפרוע — נמי הנאה היא, ומחילה מחיל גביה, ואסיר. אלא חנן היא, ובין בחוב העומד לפרוע, בין בעומד שלא לפרוע — לית ליה גביה מידי, ולאו מחילה היא, ואף על גב דסלקיה מפרעון ומכיסופא.

NOTES

have persuaded his creditor to waive the debt. And this would apply even if the creditor held a pledge, and even if the creditor was pressing the debtor to repay the money that he owed him.

The Rishonim, however, disagree whether one who paid off his friend's debt can, in fact, demand repayment. According to many (*Rashi, Rif, Rambam,* and others), at least according to Ḥanan, there is no difference between a person who maintained somebody else's wife in his absence and a person who repaid another person's debt. Neither may recover the money that he laid out. Others (*Rabbenu Tam,* and others) maintain that Ḥanan's ruling is limited to the case of a person who maintained somebody else's wife in his absence. But a person who repaid another person's debt can indeed recover the money from the debtor, unless it was a debt taken on condition that he not necessarily have to repay (following *Rava*).

עַל מְנָת שֶׁלֹּא לִפְרוֹעַ **On condition that he not repay.** This is not to suggest that the loan was extended on condition that the borrower would not be obligated to repay the loan. That would not be a loan, but rather a present. Rather, Rava is talking about someone who borrowed money on condition that he not be required to repay the loan at any specific time (*Rashi*), or else he borrowed money on condition that if he fails to repay the loan on time, the lender would not take him to court (*Rivan*).

כִּיסּוּפָא מִי לֵית לֵיהּ **Does he not have embarrassment.** *Rashi* understands that according to Rav Oshaya, the Mishnah

TRANSLATION AND COMMENTARY

MISHNAH אַדְמוֹן אוֹמֵר [1]As was stated already in the first Mishnah of the chapter, **Admon said seven** things that were disputed by the sons of the High Priests: [2]**If someone died and left sons and daughters,** and the sons now claim inheritance to which they are entitled by Torah law, and the daughters come and demand maintenance from their father's estate to which they are entitled by Rabbinic enactment (see *Ketubot* 49a), [3]**when the** inherited **property is extensive,** i.e., when the property of the estate will suffice to maintain both the sons and the daughters until the daughters reach the age of majority, [4]**the sons inherit** the entire estate **and the daughters receive** their **maintenance** from it until they reach majority or are betrothed. [5]**But when the property is limited,** i.e., when the estate will not suffice to maintain both the sons and the daughters until the daughters reach majority, [6]**the daughters receive** from the estate their **maintenance.** Whatever is left is given to the sons for their maintenance, [7]**and** when the estate assets run out, **the sons** must **go begging,** if they are unable to earn enough to cover their living expenses.

אַדְמוֹן אוֹמֵר [8]**Admon said:** Just **because I am male, should I lose** out? If a father's estate will not suffice to maintain both the sons and the daughters until the daughters reach majority, both the sons and the

משנה [1]אַדְמוֹן אוֹמֵר שִׁבְעָה: [2]מִי שֶׁמֵּת וְהִנִּיחַ בָּנִים וּבָנוֹת, [3]בִּזְמַן שֶׁהַנְּכָסִים מְרוּבִּין — [4]הַבָּנִים יוֹרְשִׁים וְהַבָּנוֹת נִזּוֹנוֹת, [5]וּבִנְכָסִים מוּעָטִים — [6]הַבָּנוֹת יִזּוֹנוּ [7]וְהַבָּנִים יְחַזְּרוּ עַל הַפְּתָחִים.

[8]אַדְמוֹן אוֹמֵר: בִּשְׁבִיל שֶׁאֲנִי

LITERAL TRANSLATION

MISHNAH [1]Admon says seven: [2][If] someone died and left sons and daughters, [3]when the property is extensive (lit., "large") — [4]the sons inherit and the daughters are maintained. [5]But [when] the property is limited (lit., "small"), [6]the daughters are maintained, [7]and the sons go begging (lit., "go around the doors").

[8]Admon says: Because I am

RASHI

משנה נכסים מועטין – מפרש בבבא בתרא: שאין בהן פרנסת שנים עשר חדש לזכרים ולנקבות. הבנות יזונו והבנים ישאלו על הפתחים – תקנת חכמים היא.

NOTES

in *Nedarim* cannot agree with the position of the sons of the High Priests of our Mishnah. Even if the borrower stipulated with his creditor that he would not be required to repay his loan at any particular time, the borrower nevertheless suffers embarrassment because he is in debt. When the other person repays the loan on his behalf, he removes his embarrassment, and thus causes him to derive benefit from him. (The last line of the Gemara, "There also, etc.," seems to be superfluous, and *Rabbi B. Ronsburg* notes in his emendations that those words apparently are not found in the texts used by the Rishonim.) *Ritva* understands the Gemara differently: A person who borrows money with the stipulation that he is not required to repay it at any particular time is embarrassed because he is in debt. Therefore he is considered to be under even greater obligation to his lender than one who borrows money that must be repaid on a particular date. Thus, if repaying somebody else's loan is regarded as a benefit, then all the more so is repaying a loan that does not have to be repaid on any particular date, not because he removed the other person's embarrassment, but because he removed the sense of obligation that that embarrassment generated.

וּבִנְכָסִים מוּעָטִים **But when the property is limited.** *Rashi* explains that a limited estate is one that will not suffice to maintain the sons and the daughters for twelve months. Others point out that the definition of "limited property" is the subject of an Amoraic dispute in *Bava Batra* 139b, and that *Rashi* here explains our Mishnah in accordance with Rav. However, the law is in accordance with the view of Shmuel, who says that property is considered limited if it will not suffice to maintain both the sons and the daughters until the daughters reach the age of majority. (This matter is the subject of dispute in the Jerusalem Talmud as well.) *Rashi* often adopts the simplest explanation of the Mishnah, even if that explanation does not follow the view that is accepted as law.

אַדְמוֹן אוֹמֵר **Admon says.** According to *Rabbenu Tam, Rosh,* and others, Admon does not actually disagree with the first Tanna of the Mishnah; he merely expresses astonishment about the judgment. Similarly, when Rabban Gamliel says that he agrees with Admon's position, it does not mean that he rules that way. Rather it only means that he agrees that the position of the first Tanna of the Mishnah is indeed astonishing.

בִּשְׁבִיל שֶׁאֲנִי זָכָר **Because I am male.** Why did the Gemara ask a question about the meaning of Admon's remark? It

HALAKHAH

בִּזְמַן שֶׁהַנְּכָסִים מְרוּבִּין **When the property is great.** "If someone died, leaving sons and daughters, the sons inherit the entire estate, and they are obligated to maintain the daughters until they reach majority or until they are betrothed. This applies in a case where the father left an estate which will suffice to maintain both the sons and the daughters until the daughters reach the age of majority (where the property is 'great'). But if the estate will not suffice to maintain both the sons and the daughters until the daughters reach majority, a portion is set aside for the daughters' maintenance, and the rest goes to the sons, and when the estate assets run out, the sons must go begging," following the anonymous Tanna of the Mishnah against Admon. This only applies in a case where the father left landed property. But in a case where he left movable goods, since the daughters are only maintained from such goods by Geonic enactment, the daughters do not push the sons aside, but rather the sons and the daughters receive their maintenance from the movable goods in equal measure. (*Rambam, Sefer Nashim, Hilkhot Ishut* 19:17-18; *Shulḥan Arukh, Even HaEzer* 112:11-12).

TRANSLATION AND COMMENTARY

daughters should receive maintenance from the father's estate, and when nothing is left, they must all go begging.

אָמַר רַבָּן גַּמְלִיאֵל [1]**Rabban Gamliel said: I agree with the position of Admon.**

GEMARA מַאי קָאָמַר [2]The Gemara asks: **What did** Admon add when **he said:** Just because I am male, should I lose out?

אָמַר אַבַּיֵי [3]**Abaye said:** Admon meant to **say as follows:** [4]**Because I am male and fit to engage in Torah** study, is it proper that [5]**I should lose** out in advancing my knowledge and have to go begging, while my father's daughters receive maintenance from his estate?

אֲמַר לֵיהּ [6]**Rava said to** Abaye: Does a son's right to his father's estate depend on his engaging in Torah study? If so, if a man had two sons, one of whom engages in Torah study, and the other one does not, the son **who engages in Torah study inherits** from his father, [7]**and** the son **who does not engage in Torah** study **does not inherit** from **him.** But surely, this is not the law!

אֶלָּא [8]**Rather, Rava said:** Admon meant to **say as follows:** [9]Just **because I am male and fit to inherit** from my father **when the property** of his estate **is extensive,** [10]**should I lose** out **when the property** of his estate **is limited?**

MISHNAH הַטּוֹעֵן אֶת חֲבֵירוֹ [11]If a person admits to part of a claim brought against him in court, he must pay the amount that he admitted owing and take a Torah oath that he does not owe his creditor the remainder of the claim. However, this only applies if the defendant admits owing property of the same kind that the plaintiff had demanded of him, for example, where the plaintiff claims that he is owed a hundred bushels of wheat, and the defendant admits owing him only fifty bushels of wheat. But if the plaintiff claims that he is owed a hundred bushels of wheat, and the defendant admits owing fifty bushels of barley, the defendant is regarded as having denied the plaintiff's entire claim. He pays the fifty bushels of barley, but is not liable for an oath by Torah law on the wheat. Now, **if someone claimed pitchers of oil from another person, and** the other person **admitted** that he owed him empty **containers,** the Tannaim disagree about

זָכָר הִפְסַדְתִּי?

[1]אָמַר רַבָּן גַּמְלִיאֵל: רוֹאֶה אֲנִי אֶת דִּבְרֵי אַדְמוֹן.

גמרא [2]מַאי קָאָמַר? [3]אָמַר אַבַּיֵי: הָכִי קָאָמַר: [4]בִּשְׁבִיל שֶׁאֲנִי זָכָר וְרָאוּי לַעֲסוֹק בַּתּוֹרָה, [5]הִפְסַדְתִּי? [6]אֲמַר לֵיהּ רָבָא: מַאן דְּעָסֵיק בַּתּוֹרָה הוּא דְּיָרֵית, [7]מַאן דְּלָא עָסֵיק בַּתּוֹרָה לָא יָרֵית? [8]אֶלָּא, אֲמַר רָבָא: הָכִי קָאָמַר: [9]בִּשְׁבִיל שֶׁאֲנִי זָכָר וְרָאוּי לִירַשׁ בִּנְכָסִים מְרוּבִּין, [10]הִפְסַדְתִּי בִּנְכָסִים מוּעָטִין?

משנה [11]הַטּוֹעֵן אֶת חֲבֵירוֹ כַּדֵּי שֶׁמֶן וְהוֹדָה בְּקַנְקַנִּים.

LITERAL TRANSLATION

male, should I lose?

[1]Rabban Gamliel said: I see the words of Admon.

GEMARA [2]What is [Admon] saying?

[3]Abaye said: This is what he says: [4]Because I am male and fit to engage in Torah [study], [5]I should lose?

[6]Rava said to him: He who engages in Torah [study] inherits, [7]and he who does not engage in Torah [study] does not inherit?

[8]Rather, Rava said: Thus he said: [9]Because I am male and fit to inherit when the property is extensive, [10]I should lose when the property is limited?

MISHNAH [11][If] someone claimed pitchers of oil from his fellow, and he admitted to [empty] containers,

RASHI

הפסדתי — בתמיה.

גמרא מאי קאמר — ״אם בשביל שאני זכר הפסדתי״, משמע: אם בשביל שאני זכר וכחי יפה הפסדתי, ומהו יפוי כחו?

משנה והודה לו בקנקנים — רקים, בלא שמן.

NOTES

seems to be quite clear: Just because he is a male and inherits his father's estate by Torah law, and his sisters are female and entitled to maintenance by Rabbinic enactment, should he therefore lose out when the estate is limited? *Shittah Mekubbetzet* suggests that the Gemara is troubled by the formulation of Admon's remark, "Because I am male" (rather than "Because a son is male"), which implies that Admon personally has some advantage over other males.

הִפְסַדְתִּי **I should lose.** Our commentary follows *Rashbam* (in *Bava Batra* 139b) and others, who say that Admon does not mean to say that the sons should exclude the daughters completely, so that they receive nothing. Rather, the sons should not lose out entirely. Thus both the sons and the daughters should receive maintenance from their father's estate until there is nothing left, and then they should all go begging.

Some suggest, in response to Admon's question, that his complaint, why should the sons go begging, incorporates its own answer. Since it is not appropriate for young girls to beg for their keep, the humiliation that they would suffer would be far greater than that of their brothers.

הַטּוֹעֵן אֶת חֲבֵירוֹ כַּדֵּי שֶׁמֶן וְהוֹדָה בְּקַנְקַנִּים **If he claimed pitchers of oil from his fellow, and he admitted to empty containers.** The question has been raised: Why did the Tanna of the Mishnah describe a claim of "pitchers [כַּדִּים] of oil," and an admission of "containers [קַנְקַנִּים]"? Some suggest that the term "pitcher" is ambiguous, for it can refer

LITERAL TRANSLATION

[1] Admon says: Since he admitted to part of the claim, he must take an oath. [2] And the Sages say: [Here] there is no partial admission of [any of the] aspects (lit., "the kind") of the claim.

[3] Rabban Gamliel said: I see the words of Admon.

GEMARA [4] Infer from this that according to the Sages, [5] [if] he claimed from him wheat and barley, and he admitted barley, he is exempt. [6] Say that this is a refutation of [what] Rav Naḥman said in the name of Shmuel. [7] For Rav Naḥman said in the name of Shmuel: [If] he claimed from him wheat and barley, and he admitted to him one of them, he is liable [to take an oath].

[8] Rav Yehudah said in the name of Rav: [9] [The Mishnah teaches] where he claimed from him a measure.

[1] אַדְמוֹן אוֹמֵר: הוֹאִיל וְהוֹדָה בְּמִקְצָת הַטַּעֲנָה, יִשָּׁבַע. [2] וַחֲכָמִים אוֹמְרִים: אֵין הוֹדָאַת מִקְצָת מִמִּין הַטַּעֲנָה. [3] אָמַר רַבָּן גַּמְלִיאֵל: רוֹאֶה אֲנִי אֶת דִּבְרֵי אַדְמוֹן.

גמרא [4] שְׁמַע מִינָּהּ לְרַבָּנַן, [5] טְעָנוֹ חִטִּין וּשְׂעוֹרִין וְהוֹדָה בִּשְׂעוֹרִין, פָּטוּר. [6] לֵימָא תֶּהֱוֵי תְּיוּבְתָּא דְּרַב נַחְמָן אָמַר שְׁמוּאֵל. [7] דְּאָמַר רַב נַחְמָן אָמַר שְׁמוּאֵל: טְעָנוֹ חִטִּין וּשְׂעוֹרִים וְהוֹדָה לוֹ בְּאֶחָד מֵהֶן, חַיָּיב! [8] אָמַר רַב יְהוּדָה אָמַר רַב: [9] בְּטוֹעֲנוֹ מִדָּה.

RASHI

גמרא בטוענו מדה — לא תבע ממנו קנקנים, אלא: שמן הפקדתי אצלך. ומאי "כדי שמן" דקתני מתניתין — מדה; אלא עשרה כדי שמן, דהוי ליה טענו חטים והודה לו בשעורים.

TRANSLATION AND COMMENTARY

the law: [1] **Admon says: Since** the defendant **admitted to part of the claim** which the plaintiff brought against him, the pitchers, **he must take an oath** by Torah law that he does not owe him the oil, too. [2] **The Sages** disagree and **say: There was no partial admission** by the defendant **of any** of the **aspects of that claim.** The plaintiff claimed both containers and oil. And the defendant admitted that he owed all the pitchers but denied any of the oil. Therefore, he is not liable for an oath by Torah law.

אָמַר רַבָּן גַּמְלִיאֵל [3] **Rabban Gamliel said: I agree with the position of Admon.**

GEMARA שְׁמַע מִינָּהּ [4] The Gemara tries to draw an inference regarding an Amoraic dispute: **Infer from** our Mishnah that **according to the Sages** who disagree with Admon, [5] **if** the plaintiff **claimed** that the defendant owed him both **wheat and barley, and** the defendant denied owing him the wheat but **admitted** owing him the **barley,** the defendant **is exempt** from taking an oath by Torah law. For this case is parallel to our Mishnah where the plaintiff claimed that the defendant owed him pitchers of oil, and the defendant admitted owing him the pitchers and denied owing him oil. [6] Thus, we should **say that this** Mishnah **is a refutation of what Rav Naḥman said in the name of Shmuel.** [7] **For Rav Naḥman said in the name of Shmuel: If** the plaintiff **claimed** that the defendant owed him both **wheat and barley, and** the defendant denied owing him the wheat but **admitted** owing him the **barley,** the defendant **is required to take** an oath by Torah law, for he is regarded as having admitted to part of the claim brought against him.

אָמַר רַב יְהוּדָה [8] **Rav Yehudah said in the name of Rav:** Our Mishnah does not refute Shmuel, for the Mishnah is not dealing with a plaintiff who claimed that the defendant owed him both pitchers and oil. [9] Rather **he claimed from him a** certain volume **measure** of oil, — so-and-so many pitchers of oil, and the defendant denied owing him any oil but admitted that he owed him those many empty containers. Thus, the case in the Mishnah is analogous to a claim that the defendant owed wheat, and the defendant admitted that he owed barley. As noted, in such a case we rule that there was no partial admission on the part of the defendant of the kind of property that was claimed from him, and so the defendant is not required to take an oath by Torah law.

NOTES

either to the measure of liquid held by that utensil or it can refer to the utensil itself, but the term "container" always refers to the utensil itself (see *Shittah Mekubbetzet, Melekhet Shelomo*).

לֵימָא תֶּהֱוֵי תְּיוּבְתָּא דְּרַב נַחְמָן **Say that this is a refutation of what Rav Naḥman said.** *Tosafot* and others ask: How can the Gemara raise an objection against Rav Naḥman from the position of the Sages? It is clear from the Gemara in *Shevuot* (40b) that the ruling of Shmuel quoted by Rav Naḥman follows the viewpoint of Admon! *Ritva* answers that the Gemara here understood that Rav Naḥman stated his opinion according to everybody, and therefore it raised a question from the opinion of the Sages who appear to disagree.

טְעָנוֹ חִטִּין וּשְׂעוֹרִים **If he claimed from him wheat and barley.** The Rishonim note that the discussion of this topic

HALAKHAH

טְעָנוֹ חִטִּין וּשְׂעוֹרִים וְהוֹדָה לוֹ בְּאֶחָד מֵהֶן **If he claimed from him wheat and barley, and he admitted to him one of them.** "If the plaintiff claimed that the defendant owed him two different kinds of property, and the defendant admitted

[1]אִי הָכִי, מַאי טַעֲמָא דְּאַדְמוֹן? [2]אֶלָּא, אֲמַר רָבָא: דְּכוּלֵּי עָלְמָא, [3]הֵיכָא דַּאֲמַר לֵיהּ: ״מְלֹא עֲשָׂרָה כַּדֵּי שֶׁמֶן יֵשׁ לִי בְּבוֹרְךָ״ — [4]שֶׁמֶן קָטָעֵין לֵיהּ, [5]קַנְקַנִּים לָא קָטָעֵין לֵיהּ. [6]״עֲשָׂרָה כַּדֵּי שֶׁמֶן מְלֵאִים יֵשׁ לִי אֶצְלְךָ״ — [7]שֶׁמֶן וְקַנְקַנִּים קָטָעֵין לֵיהּ. [8]כִּי פְּלִיגִי — [9]הֵיכָא דַּאֲמַר לֵיהּ: ״עֲשָׂרָה כַּדֵּי שֶׁמֶן יֵשׁ לִי אֶצְלְךָ״. [10]אַדְמוֹן אוֹמֵר: יֵשׁ בַּלָּשׁוֹן הַזֶּה לְשׁוֹן קַנְקַנִּים. [11]וְרַבָּנַן סָבְרֵי: אֵין בַּלָּשׁוֹן הַזֶּה לְשׁוֹן קַנְקַנִּים.

LITERAL TRANSLATION

[1]If so, what is the reasoning of Admon? [2]Rather, Rava said: According to everyone, [3]when he said to him: "I have ten pitchers of oil in your pit" — [4]oil he claimed from him, [5]containers he did not claim from him. [6]"I have ten full pitchers of oil with you" — [7]the oil and the containers he claimed from him. [8]When do they disagree — [9]where he said to him: "I have ten pitchers of oil with you." [10]Admon says: This [choice of] expression includes the containers. [11]And the Sages maintain: The [choise of] expression does not include the containers.

TRANSLATION AND COMMENTARY

אִי הָכִי [1]The Gemara asks: **If so,** then **what is the reasoning of Admon?** Since there was no partial admission of the claim, how can Admon require him to swear?

אֶלָּא [2]The Gemara answers: **Rather, Rava said: According to everyone** — both Admon and the Sages — [3]if the plaintiff **said to** the defendant: **"I have ten pitchers of oil in your pit,"** and the defendant admitted owing him empty containers, the defendant is not required to take an oath by Torah law, [4]for the plaintiff **claimed** a certain measure of **oil from** the defendant, [5]but **he did not claim** any **containers from him,** and so there was no partial admission on the part of the defendant of what was claimed from him. And they also all agree that if the plaintiff said to the defendant: [6]**"I have ten full pitchers of oil with you,"** and the defendant admitted owing him empty containers, the defendant is required to take an oath by Torah law, [7]for the plaintiff **claimed** both **oil and containers from** the defendant. Therefore the defendant is regarded as having admitted to part of the claim that was brought against him. [8]**In which case do** Admon and the Sages **disagree?** [9]They only disagree about when the plaintiff **said to** the defendant: **"I have ten pitchers of oil with you,"** and the defendant admitted owing the plaintiff empty containers. [10]**Admon says** that the plaintiff's choice of **expression includes** a claim for both the oil and **the containers,** and so the defendant is regarded as having admitted to part of the claim. [11]**And the Sages** who disagree with Admon **maintain** that the plaintiff's choice of **expression does not include** a claim for **containers,** but only for oil, and so there was no partial admission on the part of the defendant.

RASHI

בבורך — בור שלפני הבד. **קנקנים לא טעין ליה** — וכי הודה לו בקנקנים — לאו הודאה היא. **כדים מלאים** — כדים ושמן משמע. **עשרה כדי שמן** — ולא אמר "מלאים". **יש בלשון הזה לשון קנקנים** — כיון דלא אמר ליה "מלא עשרה" — אין זה טוענו מדה, אלא עשרה כדים מלאים, והוה ליה טענו חטים ושעורים.

NOTES

found in our Gemara cannot be reconciled with the parallel discussion in tractate *Shevuot* (see *Ritva,* and others). The Jerusalem Talmud also deals with this issue, in particular with the question of whether or not Rabbi Yoḥanan agrees with the position of Shmuel (and Resh Lakish in the Jerusalem Talmud) that if the plaintiff demanded wheat and barley, and the defendant admitted owing one of them, the defendant is liable for an oath.

יֵשׁ לִי בְּבוֹרְךָ I have in your pit. The Aḥaronim note that there is a variant reading in this passage, בְּיָדְךָ, "in your hand," rather than בְּבוֹרְךָ, "in your pit." *Rambam* and others understand that the formulation, "I have ten pitchers of oil with you," by itself — even without reference to the pit — implies that the plaintiff is demanding a certain measure of oil, and not utensils.

יֵשׁ בַּלָּשׁוֹן הַזֶּה This choice of expression includes. The Jerusalem Talmud asks the obvious question: Why not ask the plaintiff what he meant when he demanded pitchers of oil? Did he mean only to claim oil, or did he also claim the utensils in which the oil was stored? It answers that

HALAKHAH

to one, but denied the other — e.g., the plaintiff claimed that the defendant owed him wheat and barley, and the defendant admitted owing him the one, but denied owing him the other — the defendant is regarded as having partially admitted to the claim brought against him, and so he is liable for an oath for that part of the claim that he denied," following Shmuel. (*Rambam, Sefer Mishpatim, Hilkhot To'en VeNit'an* 3:11; *Shulḥan Arukh, Ḥoshen Mishpat* 88:12.)

עֲשָׂרָה כַּדֵּי שֶׁמֶן Ten pitchers of oil. "If the plaintiff claimed that the defendant owed him ten pitchers of oil, and the defendant admitted owing him ten empty pitchers, he is exempt from an oath, for the plaintiff claimed oil, and the defendant admitted to containers. But if the plaintiff claimed that the defendant owed him ten pitchers of oil, and the defendant admitted owing him ten empty pitchers, he is liable for an oath," following Admon. (*Rambam, Sefer Mishpatim, Hilkhot To'en VeNit'an* 3:13; *Shulḥan Arukh, Ḥoshen Mishpat* 88:18.)

[1]אֶלָּא טַעְמָא דְּאֵין בַּלָּשׁוֹן הַזֶּה לְשׁוֹן קַנְקַנִּים, [2]הָא יֵשׁ בַּלָּשׁוֹן הַזֶּה לְשׁוֹן קַנְקַנִּים, חַיָּיב. [3]לֵימָא תֶּיהֱוֵי תְּיוּבְתָּא דְּרַבִּי חִיָּיא בַּר אַבָּא. [4]דְּאָמַר רַבִּי חִיָּיא בַּר אַבָּא: טְעָנוֹ חִטִּין וּשְׂעוֹרִים, וְהוֹדָה לוֹ בְּאֶחָד מֵהֶם, פָּטוּר!

[5]אָמַר רַב שִׁימִי בַּר אַשִׁי: [6]נַעֲשָׂה כְּמִי שֶׁטְּעָנוֹ רִימּוֹן בִּקְלִיפָּתוֹ.

[7]מַתְקִיף לָהּ רָבִינָא: רִימּוֹן בְּלֹא קְלִיפָּתוֹ לָא מִינְטַר. [8]שֶׁמֶן מִינְטַר בְּלֹא קַנְקַנִּים!

[9]אֶלָּא, הָכָא בְּמַאי עָסְקִינַן? [10]דַּאֲמַר לֵיהּ: ״עֲשָׂרָה כַּדֵּי שֶׁמֶן יֵשׁ לִי אֶצְלְךָ״, [11]וַאֲמַר לֵיהּ אִידָךְ: ״שֶׁמֶן לֹא הָיוּ דְּבָרִים מֵעוֹלָם; [12]קַנְקַנִּים נַמִי — חֲמִשָּׁה אִית לָךְ, [13]וַחֲמִשָּׁה לֵית לָךְ״. [14]אַדְמוֹן אוֹמֵר: יֵשׁ בַּלָּשׁוֹן

LITERAL TRANSLATION

[1]But the reason the Sages argue is because this expression does not include containers, [2]if this expression would include the containers, he would be liable [to swear]. [3]Say that this is a refutation of Rabbi Ḥiyya bar Abba. [4]For Rabbi Ḥiyya bar Abba said: [If] he claimed from him wheat and barley, and he admitted to him one of them, he is freed of liability [to take an oath].

[5]Rav Shimi bar Ashi said: [6][In the Mishnah] it is as if he claimed from him a pomegranate in its rind.

[7]Ravina objected to this: A pomegranate without its rind does not keep. [8]Oil without containers keeps!

[9]Rather, with what we are dealing here? [10]When he said to him: "I have ten pitchers of oil with you," [11]and the other one said to him: "Oil — there was never such a thing; [12]the containers too — five you have [with me], [13]and five you do not have [with me]." [14]Admon says: This [choice of] expression

TRANSLATION AND COMMENTARY

אֶלָּא [1]The Gemara asks: The Sages disagree with Admon about the case where the plaintiff said that the defendant owes him ten pitchers of oil, because they maintain that the plaintiff's **expression does not include containers.** [2]**But** it follows from this that **if** the plaintiff's **formulation included** a claim for both the oil and **the containers,** and the defendant admitted owing the plaintiff either one or the other, even the Sages would agree that the defendant **is required** to take an oath by Torah law, for he is regarded as having admitted to part of the claim. [3]Thus, we should **say that this** Mishnah **is a refutation of Rabbi Ḥiyya bar Abba.** [4]**For Rabbi Ḥiyya bar Abba said: If** the plaintiff **claimed** that the defendant owed him both **wheat and barley, and** the defendant **admitted** owing him **one of them,** either the wheat or the barley, the defendant **is free** of an oath, for he is not regarded as having admitted to part of the claim brought against him!

אָמַר [5]**Rav Shimi bar Ashi said:** Rabbi Ḥiyya bar Abba can argue that the Mishnah does not refute his position, for a claim of wheat and barley is different from a claim of pitchers of oil. The claim of wheat and the claim of barley are separate claims, so the admission of one is not regarded as a partial admission. But if a plaintiff claimed pitchers of oil, [6]**it is** regarded **as if he claimed from him a pomegranate in its rind.** The claim of oil cannot be separated from that of the pitchers.

מַתְקִיף לָהּ [7]**Ravina objected to this** answer: Rav Shimi bar Ashi's comparison is not valid, for **a pomegranate does not keep without its rind,** and so a claim of a pomegranate in its rind is regarded as a single claim. [8]But **oil keeps** in a pit **without containers,** and so a claim of pitchers of oil should be treated just like a claim of wheat and barley! If an admission regarding the containers obligates the defendant to take an oath regarding the oil, the Mishnah stands as a contradiction to Rabbi Ḥiyya bar Abba!

אֶלָּא [9]The Gemara suggests another answer: **Rather,** Rabbi Ḥiyya bar Abba can say that **here** in the Mishnah **we are dealing with** a plaintiff [10]who **said to** the defendant: **"I have ten pitchersful of oil with you,"** [11]**and** the defendant **said to** the plaintiff: "As for your claim that I owe you **oil — there was never such a thing.** I never borrowed any oil from you. [12]As for **the containers — five** pitchers **I do** indeed **owe you,** [13]**but** the other **five I do not owe you."** [14]**Admon says** that the plaintiff's choice of **expression includes** a claim for

RASHI

אלא טעמא כו׳ — לשון קושיא הוא, לאותובי למאן דאמר פטור. דדוקיא דמתניתין כרב נחמן, מדקתני: הטוען את חבירו כדי שמן, ולא קתני: כדים מלאים שמן — שמעינן מינה דמשום דאין בלשון הזה לשון קנקנים פטרי רבנן, הא אם תבעו שניהם — חייב. **נעשה כמי שתבעו רימון בקליפתו** — לא דמו כדים ושמן לחטים ושעורים, דכולי חדא מילתא הוא, וממין הטענה הוא. **שמן** — בלא קנקנים, מנטר בבור. **אלא הכא במאי עסקינן כו׳** — אלא לא תימא כמו שטענו רימון, אלא רבי חייא מוקי למתניתין — כגון שהודה במקצת קנקנים ומקצתם כפר, דבקנקנים גופייהו איכא כפירה והודאה. ואי יש בלשון התביעה לשון קנקנים — מיחייב עלייהו שבועה. ושבועה דשמן דקא מחייב אדמון — משום גלגול היא, דקסבר: יש בלשון התביעה לשון קנקנים.

NOTES

the plaintiff presented his claim and then was struck dumb, and there was no way for us to clarify what he had meant by his claim.

הַזֶּה לְשׁוֹן קַנְקַנִּים, [1]וּמִגּוֹ דְּקָמִשְׁתַּבַּע אַקַּנְקַנִּים, [2]מִשְׁתַּבַּע נַמִּי אַשֶּׁמֶן עַל יְדֵי גִּלְגּוּל. [3]וְרַבָּנַן סָבְרִי: אֵין בַּלָּשׁוֹן הַזֶּה לְשׁוֹן קַנְקַנִּים. [4]מַה שֶּׁטְּעָנוֹ לֹא הוֹדָה לוֹ, [5]וּמַה שֶּׁהוֹדָה לוֹ לֹא טְעָנוֹ.

מִשְׁנָה [6]הַפּוֹסֵק מָעוֹת לַחֲתָנוֹ, [7]וּפָשַׁט לוֹ אֶת הָרֶגֶל [109A] [8]תֵּשֵׁב עַד שֶׁתַּלְבִּין רֹאשָׁהּ.

LITERAL TRANSLATION

includes the containers, [1]and since he swears about the containers, [2]he swears also about the oil by extension. [3]And the Rabbis maintain: This [choice of] expression does not include the containers. [4]What he claimed from him, he did not admit to him, [5]and what he admitted to him, he did not claim from him.

MISHNAH [6][If] someone undertakes to give money to his son-in-law, [7]and he claimed poverty (lit., "stretched out [his] foot before him"), [109A] [8]she sits [unmarried] until her head turns white.

TRANSLATION AND COMMENTARY

both the oil and **the containers,** [1]**and since** the defendant is obligated to **take an oath about the containers,** for he admitted to part of the claim that was brought against him, [2]**he** is also obligated to **take an oath about the oil by extension.** When a defendant is obliged to take an oath to free himself of a liability, the plaintiff can require him to include a denial of other claims, which ordinarily would not require a defendant to take an oath. Here the defendant should not be liable for an oath regarding the oil, for, as Rabbi Ḥiyya bar Abba said, if the plaintiff claimed that the defendant owed him both wheat and barley, and the defendant admitted owing him only one of them, the defendant is not required to take an oath. Similarly the defendant's admission regarding the containers should not obligate him to take an oath regarding the oil. But since the defendant is liable for an oath regarding the five pitchers which he denied owing the plaintiff, the plaintiff can require him to include in his oath a denial of his claim regarding the oil as well. [3]**And the Sages** who disagree with Admon **maintain** that the plaintiff's choice of **expression does not include** a claim for **the containers,** but only for oil. Therefore the defendant is not required to take any oath. [4]**That which** the plaintiff **claimed from him,** the oil, the defendant **did not admit** owing, [5]**and that which** the defendant **admitted** owing, the five pitchers, the plaintiff **did not claim from him.**

MISHNAH הַפּוֹסֵק מָעוֹת [6]**If someone undertook** at the time of his daughter's betrothal **to give** a certain amount of **money to his** future **son-in-law** as his daughter's dowry, [7]**and** then after betrothal and before the marriage **he stretched out the leg to** his son-in-law, i.e., told him that he became impoverished and did not have the money to meet his obligation, [109A] the groom cannot be compelled to marry the woman in the absence of the dowry, nor can he be forced to grant her a divorce. [8]Therefore, she **can** end up **sitting** unmarried in her father's house **until her head turns white.**

RASHI

משנה ופשט לו את הרגל — לשון בזיון הוא, ואמר נואש, שאינו חש לדבריו: טול טיט שעל גבי רגלי. ואני שמעתי: תלה אותי על עץ, ואין לי מה ליתן.

NOTES

וּפָשַׁט לוֹ אֶת הָרֶגֶל And he extended him the foot. The Rishonim offer various explanations of this expression, which in modern Hebrew has come to mean "to go bankrupt." *Rashi* cites two explanations, and *Rivan* three: According to one explanation, this is an expression of contempt: A person extending his shoe before his claimant and telling him to take the mud that is on his shoe for he is not going to give him anything else. According to a second explanation, one person extends his foot to the other, telling him that even were he to hang him from a tree by his foot, he can give him nothing, as he has no money. According to a third explanation, one person tells the other that he is offering him his foot as payment. He has nothing else to offer him to clear the debt. Others understand that this expression simply means that the person fled (*Rambam, Ra'avad, Rav Natan Av HaYeshivah,* and *Ritva*). *Meiri* suggests that it means that he died.

תֵּשֵׁב עַד שֶׁתַּלְבִּין רֹאשָׁהּ She sits until her hair turns white. *Tosafot* and others ask: Why should the woman be forced to sit in her father's house until she grows old? Why not compel the father to pay his daughter's dowry as he had promised? *Ritva* notes that this question does not arise according to those who explain the Mishnah to be referring to a father who has no money, or is dead or gone. But the question is relevant according to those who explain that the father has money, but refuses to hand it over to his son-in-law.

Why then do we not force the father to keep his promise? Moreover, we learned in the previous chapter (*Ketubot* 102b) that the obligations undertaken by the father of the bride prior to his daughter's betrothal are valid and binding, even if no act of acquisition was performed. If so, the bridegroom has a lien on the father's property and is able to obtain what is his through the courts! *Rashbam* answers that the obligations undertaken by the father of the bride are only binding if the betrothal took place immediately after those obligations were undertaken. But here the betrothal only took place later, so the father has no legal responsibility to fulfill his promise. Others suggests that the obligations were undertaken after the betrothal, in which

[1]אַדְמוֹן אוֹמֵר: יְכוֹלָה הִיא שֶׁתֹּאמַר: [2]״אִילּוּ אֲנִי פָּסַקְתִּי לְעַצְמִי, [3]אֵשֵׁב עַד שֶׁתַּלְבִּין רֹאשִׁי. [4]עַכְשָׁיו שֶׁאַבָּא פָּסַק, מָה אֲנִי יְכוֹלָה לַעֲשׂוֹת? אוֹ כְּנוֹס אוֹ פְּטוֹר״.

[5]אָמַר רַבָּן גַּמְלִיאֵל: רוֹאֶה אֲנִי אֶת דִּבְרֵי אַדְמוֹן.

גמרא [6]מַתְנִיתִין דְּלָא כִּי הַאי תַּנָּא, [7]דְּתַנְיָא: ״אָמַר רַבִּי יוֹסֵי בְּרַבִּי יְהוּדָה: [8]לֹא נֶחְלְקוּ אַדְמוֹן וַחֲכָמִים עַל הַפּוֹסֵק מָעוֹת לַחֲתָנוֹ, [9]וּפָשַׁט לוֹ אֶת הָרֶגֶל, [10]שֶׁיְּכוֹלָה הִיא שֶׁתֹּאמַר: ׳אַבָּא פָּסַק עָלַי מָה אֲנִי יְכוֹלָה לַעֲשׂוֹת׳? [11]עַל מָה נֶחְלְקוּ? [12]עַל שֶׁפָּסְקָה הִיא עַל עַצְמָהּ, [13]שֶׁחֲכָמִים אוֹמְרִים: תֵּשֵׁב עַד

LITERAL TRANSLATION

[1]Admon says: She can say: [2]"Had I undertaken for myself [to give you money], [3]I would sit [unmarried] until my head turns white. [4]Now that Father undertook [to give you money], what can I do? Either marry [me] or free [me]." [5]Rabban Gamliel said: I see the words of Admon.

GEMARA [6]Our Mishnah is not in accordance with this Tanna, [7]for it was taught: "Rabbi Yose the son of Rabbi Yehudah said: [8]Admon and the Sages did not disagree about one who undertook to give money to his son-in-law, [9]and he claimed poverty (lit., 'he stretched out [his] foot before him'), [10]for she can say: 'Father undertook for me; what can I do?' [11]About what did they disagree? [12]About one who undertook to give money for herself, [13]for the Sages say: She sits until

TRANSLATION AND COMMENTARY

אַדְמוֹן אוֹמֵר [1]**Admon** disagrees and **says:** The daughter **can say** to her bridegroom: [2]**"Had I** myself **undertaken** to give you money **on my behalf,** and then failed to meet my obligation, it would be right that [3]**I would** have to **sit unmarried** in my father's house **until my head turns white.** [4]But **since** it was **Father** who **undertook** to give you money as my dowry, and it was he who was unable to meet his obligation, **what can I do?** You must **either marry me, or free me** with a divorce."

אָמַר רַבָּן גַּמְלִיאֵל [5]**Rabban Gamliel said: I agree with the position of Admon.**

GEMARA מַתְנִיתִין [6]**Our Mishnah does not follow the Tanna,** [7]whose position **was taught** in the following Baraita: **"Rabbi Yose the son of Rabbi Yehudah said:** [8]**Admon and the Sages did not disagree about** a man **who** at the time of his daughter's betrothal **undertook to give** a certain amount of **money to his** future **son-in-law** as his daughter's dowry, [9]**and** then as the wedding date approached **he claimed poverty** and told the groom that he would be unable to meet his obligation. [10]In such a case, all agree that the daughter **can say: 'Father undertook** to give you money **as my** dowry, and he broke his promise, but **what can I do?'** The bridegroom must either marry his betrothed bride or grant her a divorce. [11]**About which** case then **did they disagree?** [12]They disagreed **about** a woman **who undertook to give** a certain amount of **money** to her future husband **as her** dowry. [13]**The Sages say:** The bridegroom cannot be compelled to marry his bride, nor to grant her a divorce, for it was she who did not keep her promise. Therefore, **she** can end up **sitting**

NOTES

case the obligations not being binding without an act of acquisition. Some Rishonim cite the Jerusalem Talmud, which maintains that the obligations undertaken by the father of the bride at the time of his daughter's betrothal are only binding if this is her first marriage, but here the daughter had been married previously. *Ritva* concludes that the simplest solution is to say that the father is absent or has no money. The Aḥaronim discuss whether a father who has no money because of circumstances beyond his control and is therefore unable to provide his daughter with her dowry, should be regarded as if he had fulfilled his part of the agreement.

שֶׁפָּסְקָה הִיא עַל עַצְמָהּ **About one who undertook to give money for herself.** According to the Jerusalem Talmud, the Mishnah refers to a father who obligated himself to his future son-in-law in the presence of his daughter. Only in

HALAKHAH

יְכוֹלָה הִיא שֶׁתֹּאמַר **She can say.** "If someone undertook at the time of his daughter's betrothal to give his son-in-law a certain sum of money, and then went abroad (*Rambam*), or was otherwise unable to meet his obligation (*Rashi*), the daughter can argue that she had not undertaken any obligation toward her bridegroom, and so he must now either marry her or grant her a divorce," following Admon. *Rema* adds that this only applies in a case where the daughter does not have the means to meet her father's obligation, but if she has the means to meet his obligation, she must do so, and she cannot demand that her bridegroom either marry her or grant her a divorce (following *Hagahot Alfasi* and others). And furthermore, this only applies before the couple marries. But after the marriage, the husband can certainly not divorce his wife on the grounds that he had not received what had been promised him (*Hagahot Mordekhai*). (*Rambam, Sefer Nashim, Hilkhot Ishut* 23:16; *Shulḥan Arukh, Even HaEzer* 52:1.)

פָּסְקָה הִיא עַל עַצְמָהּ **About one who undertook to give money for herself.** "If the woman herself undertook to give her husband a certain amount of money, but she was later unable to meet that obligation, she must sit in her father's

TRANSLATION AND COMMENTARY

unmarried in her father's house **until her head turns white.** [1] **And Admon** disagrees and **says:** [2] The woman **can say** to her bridegroom: 'When I promised you the money, **I thought that Father would give it to you on my behalf.** [3] **Now that Father does not** wish to **give you** money **on my behalf, what can I do?** [4] **Therefore, you must either marry me, or free me** with a divorce.' [5] **Rabban Gamliel said: I agree with the position of Admon.** The woman has no money of her own. So it is reasonable to assume that she relied on her father to provide her dowry."

תָּנָא [6] **A Tanna taught: "In what case does the ruling apply?** [7] If the woman who undertook to give a dowry to her future husband was **an adult** when she undertook the obligation, she may have to wait in her father's house until she can assemble the dowry. [8] **But** if she undertook the obligation as a **minor,** her obligation is not binding and **we resolve the matter through coercion."**

כּוֹפִין לְמַאן [9] The Gemara asks: **Whom do we coerce? If you say** that the Baraita means that we coerce **the father** to provide his daughter with a dowry, there is a difficulty. [10] For then, the cases **should have been reversed!** If we compel the father to provide the dowry, that should be for an adult daughter, for her obligation was binding. But for a minor daughter, we should not compel the father to provide her with a dowry, because the daughter's obligation has no validity! Why then does the Baraita teach that coercion is applied to the case of a minor daughter and not to that of an adult daughter?

LITERAL TRANSLATION

her head turns white. [1] [And] Admon says: She can say: [2] 'I thought that Father would give [it] for me. [3] And now that Father does not give [it] for me, what can I do? [4] Either marry [me] or free [me].' [5] Rabban Gamliel said: I see the words of Admon." [6] [A Tanna] taught: "In what [case] are these things said? [7] In [the case of] an adult. [8] But in [the case of] a minor, we coerce." [9] We coerce whom? If you say the father, [10] [the cases] should have been reversed!

שֶׁתַּלְבִּין רֹאשָׁה. ¹אַדְמוֹן אוֹמֵר:
יְכוֹלָה הִיא שֶׁתּאמַר: ²'כִּסְבוּרָה
אֲנִי שֶׁאַבָּא נוֹתֵן עָלַי. ³וְעַכְשָׁיו
שֶׁאֵין אַבָּא נוֹתֵן עָלַי, מָה אֲנִי
יְכוֹלָה לַעֲשׂוֹת. ⁴אוֹ כְּנוֹס אוֹ
פְּטוֹר'. ⁵אָמַר רַבָּן גַּמְלִיאֵל:
רוֹאֶה אֲנִי אֶת דִּבְרֵי אַדְמוֹן".
תָּנָא: ⁶"בַּמֶּה דְּבָרִים אֲמוּרִים?
⁷בִּגְדוֹלָה. ⁸אֲבָל בִּקְטַנָּה, כּוֹפִין".
⁹כּוֹפִין לְמַאן? אִילֵימָא לָאָב,
¹⁰אִיפְּכָא מִיבָּעֵי לֵיהּ!

RASHI

במה דברים אמורים — אַבָּרַיְיתָא קָאֵי.
איפכא מיבעי ליה — אִם בָּאת לִכוֹף
אֶת הָאָב — אִיפְּכָא מִסְתַּבְּרָא טְפֵי, לְפִי
שֶׁהַגְּדוֹלָה תְּנָאָה תְּנָאֵי.

NOTES

such a case do the Sages maintain that she must sit in her father's house until she grows old, for the bridegroom can argue that she too was involved in the agreement. But if the daughter was not present, all agree that she can demand that her bridegroom either marry her, or grant her a divorce.

In a similar vein, *Rosh* and others understand that in the Baraita, which says that Admon and the Sages are in disagreement where it was the woman who undertook to provide her own dowry, her undertaking was carried out in her father's presence. Admon maintains that in such a case, we interpret the father's silence as tacit agreement. Thus the daughter can argue that she can do nothing if her father refuses to honor his commitment. Her bridegroom must either marry her or grant her a divorce. But if the woman undertook the obligation in her father's absence, even Admon agrees that she must sit in her father's house until she grows old.

תָּנָא: בַּמֶּה דְּבָרִים אֲמוּרִים? **A Tanna taught: In what case are these things said?** Our commentary follows *Rashi* and others, who understand that this Baraita qualifies the previous one: The ruling that the daughter who undertook to give a dowry to her future husband must wait in her father's house until she can meet that obligation only applies if the woman was an adult when she undertook the obligation. Others maintain that this Baraita qualifies the Mishnah. The introductory term תָּנָא supports this position, for it is a term that is used to introduce a Tosefta that explains a Mishnah, but not a Baraita that explains another Baraita.

אֲבָל בִּקְטַנָּה, כּוֹפִין **But with a minor, we coerce.** Following the position that this Baraita qualifies the Mishnah (see previous Note), *Meiri* explains that although it was her father and not she who had obligated himself to provide her the dowry, the Sages still say that the woman must sit in her father's house until she grows old, if she was an

HALAKHAH

house until she finds the money, or until she dies, and her husband cannot be compelled to divorce her," following the Sages of the Baraita. (*Rambam, Sefer Nashim, Hilkhot Ishut 23:16; Shulḥan Arukh, Even HaEzer 52:1.*)

בַּמֶּה דְּבָרִים אֲמוּרִים? בִּגְדוֹלָה **In what case are these things said? With an adult.** "This ruling that the daughter must sit in her father's house until she finds the money to meet

the obligation that she undertook toward her husband only applies in the case where she undertook that obligation when she was already an adult. But if she undertook that obligation while she was still only a minor, the husband can be compelled to divorce her if he is unwilling to marry her without receiving her dowry." (*Rambam, Sefer Nashim, Hilkhot Ishut 23:16-17; Shulḥan Arukh, Even HaEzer 52:1.*)

TRANSLATION AND COMMENTARY

אֶלָּא [1]Rather, Rava said: The Baraita means to say that if the daughter was a minor when she undertook the obligation, [2]it is the husband who is coerced to either marry her or give her a bill of divorce.

אָמַר [3]Rabbi Yitzḥak ben Elazar said in the name of Ḥizkiyah: "Wherever Rabban Gamliel said: [4]'I agree with the position of Admon,' the law is indeed in accordance with Admon."

אֲמַר לֵיהּ [5]Rava said to Rav Naḥman: [6]Does this ruling apply even where Rabban Gamliel said in a Baraita that agreed with the position of Admon?

אֲמַר לֵיהּ [7]Rav Naḥman said to Rava: "Did we say that wherever Rabban Gamliel said in a Mishnah that he agreed with the position of Admon, the law is in accordance with that position?" [8]"We said that wherever this statement of Rabban Gamliel appears," the law is in accordance with Admon!

אָמַר רַבִּי זֵירָא [9]Rabbi Zera said in the name of Rabbah bar Yirmeyah: [10]Regarding the two things that Ḥanan said, the law is like the Tanna who agrees with him, Rabban Yoḥanan ben Zakkai. [11]But regarding the seven things that Admon said, [12]the law is not like the Tanna who agrees with him, Rabban Gamliel.

מַאי קָאָמַר [13]The Gemara asks: What did Rabbi Zera mean when he said this? [14]If you say that he meant as follows: Regarding the two things that Ḥanan said, [15]the law is like him and like that the Tanna who agrees with him, [16]but regarding the seven things

[1]אֶלָּא, אָמַר רָבָא: [2]כּוֹפִין לַבַּעַל לִיתֵּן גֵּט.

[3]אָמַר רַבִּי יִצְחָק בֶּן אֶלְעָזָר מִשְּׁמֵיהּ דְּחִזְקִיָּה: [4]"כָּל מָקוֹם שֶׁאָמַר רַבָּן גַּמְלִיאֵל 'רוֹאֶה אֲנִי אֶת דִּבְרֵי אַדְמוֹן' — הֲלָכָה כְּמוֹתוֹ".

[5]אֲמַר לֵיהּ רָבָא לְרַב נַחְמָן: [6]אֲפִילּוּ בְּבָרַיְיתָא?

[7]אֲמַר לֵיהּ: מִי קָאָמְרִינַן: "בְּמִשְׁנָה"? [8]"בְּכָל מָקוֹם שֶׁאָמַר רַבָּן גַּמְלִיאֵל" קָאָמְרִינַן.

[9]אָמַר רַבִּי זֵירָא אָמַר רַבָּה בַּר יִרְמְיָה: [10]שְׁנֵי דְבָרִים שֶׁאָמַר חָנָן — הֲלָכָה כַּיּוֹצֵא בּוֹ. [11]שִׁבְעָה דְבָרִים שֶׁאָמַר אַדְמוֹן — [12]אֵין הֲלָכָה כַּיּוֹצֵא בּוֹ.

[13]מַאי קָאָמַר? [14]אִילֵימָא הָכִי קָאָמַר: שְׁנֵי דְבָרִים שֶׁאָמַר חָנָן, [15]הֲלָכָה כְּמוֹתוֹ וְכַיּוֹצֵא בּוֹ. [16]וְשִׁבְעָה דְּבָרִים שֶׁאָמַר אַדְמוֹן,

LITERAL TRANSLATION

[1]Rather, Rava said: [2]We coerce the husband to give a bill of divorce.

[3]Rabbi Yitzḥak ben Elazar said in the name of Ḥizkiyah: [4]"Wherever Rabban Gamliel said: 'I see the words of Admon,' the law is in accordance with him."

[5]Rava said to Rav Naḥman: [6]Even in a Baraita?

[7]He said to him: Did we say: "In the Mishnah"? [8]We said: "Wherever Rabban Gamliel said."

[9]Rabbi Zera said in the name of Rabbah bar Yirmeyah: [10]The two things that Ḥanan said — the law is like he who agrees (lit., "goes out") with him. [11]The seven things that Admon said — [12]the law is not like he who agrees with him.

[13]What did [Rabbi Zera] say? [14]If you say that he said as follows: The two things that Ḥanan said, [15]the law is like him and like he who agrees with him. [16]And the seven things that Admon said,

RASHI

אפילו בברייתא – כשפסקה היא לעצמה. הכי גרסינן: אמר רבי אמר רבי זירא אמר רבה בר ירמיה שני דברים שאמר חנן הלכה כיוצא בו שבעה דברים שאמר אדמון אין הלכה כיוצא בו. מאי קאמר כו׳. כיוצא בו דחנן – רבן יוחנן בן זכאי, כיוצא בו דאדמון – רבן גמליאל. אין הלכה כיוצא בו – שלא ראה את דבריו אלא בשלשה, שהיה לו לראות את דבריו בכולם.

NOTES

adult when her father undertook the obligation. As an adult, she must have understood that her father was trying to deceive her future husband, and that he never intended to provide her with a dowry. But if the daughter was a minor at the time, she certainly does not share any of the guilt. The bridegroom in this case can be compelled either to marry her, or grant her a divorce.

אֲפִילּוּ בְּבָרַיְיתָא Even in a Baraita. *Rashi* understands that when Rava asked whether or not the law is in accordance with Admon, even when Rabban Gamliel's agreement is stated in a Baraita, he was referring to the Baraita in our Gemara dealing with a woman who obligated herself to provide her future husband with a dowry. *Rif,* however, does not rule in accordance with Admon's position in that Baraita. *Ramban* explains that Rava was not asking about this particular Baraita, but about Baraitot in general. *Ramban* adds that the Gemara cannot be referring to our Baraita, for if the law is in accordance with Admon of our Mishnah, it cannot be in accordance with Admon in this Baraita.

הֲלָכָה כַּיּוֹצֵא בּוֹ The law is like he who agrees with him. *Rashi, Rivan,* and others understand that the expression כַּיּוֹצֵא בּוֹ is used here in an unusual sense, "like he who goes out with it," meaning the Tanna who agrees with him. *Rabbenu Ḥananel, Rif,* and others understand the expression in its usual sense, "in cases that go out with it," in similar cases. *Rashi's* explanation is supported by the unusual expression used at the end of the passage: אֵין הֲלָכָה כְּמוֹתוֹ אֶלָּא כַּיּוֹצֵא בּוֹ, which according to *Rashi* means: The law is not like Admon, but rather like the Tanna who [sometimes] agrees with him, [but here disagrees with him]. (See *Maharshal,* who emends that text according to the other explanation, so that it reads וְכַיּוֹצְאוֹ בּוֹ.)

אֵין הֲלָכָה כְּמוֹתוֹ [1] וְלֹא כַּיּוֹצֵא בּוֹ — [2] וְהָאָמַר רַבִּי יִצְחָק בֶּן אֶלְעָזָר מִשְּׁמֵיהּ דְּחִזְקִיָּה: [3] כָּל מָקוֹם שֶׁאָמַר רַבָּן גַּמְלִיאֵל: "רוֹאֶה אֲנִי אֶת דִּבְרֵי אַדְמוֹן", [4] הֲלָכָה כְּמוֹתוֹ!

[5] אֶלָּא הָכִי קָאָמַר: שְׁנֵי דְבָרִים שֶׁאָמַר חָנָן, [6] הֲלָכָה כְּמוֹתוֹ וְכַיּוֹצֵא בּוֹ. [7] שִׁבְעָה דְּבָרִים שֶׁאָמַר אַדְמוֹן, אֵין הֲלָכָה כַּיּוֹצֵא בּוֹ. [8] הָא כְּמוֹתוֹ הֲלָכָה בְּכוּלְּהוּ.

[9] וְהָאָמַר רַבִּי יִצְחָק בֶּן אֶלְעָזָר מִשְּׁמֵיהּ דְּחִזְקִיָּה: [10] כָּל מָקוֹם שֶׁאָמַר רַבָּן גַּמְלִיאֵל: "רוֹאֶה אֲנִי אֶת דִּבְרֵי אַדְמוֹן", [11] הֲלָכָה כְּמוֹתוֹ. [12] אָמַר, אִין; [13] לֹא אָמַר, לָא.

[14] אֶלָּא הָכִי קָאָמַר: [15] שְׁנֵי דְבָרִים שֶׁאָמַר חָנָן, [16] הֲלָכָה כְּמוֹתוֹ וְכַיּוֹצֵא בּוֹ. [17] שִׁבְעָה דְּבָרִים שֶׁאָמַר אַדְמוֹן, יֵשׁ מֵהֶן שֶׁהֲלָכָה כְּמוֹתוֹ וְכַיּוֹצֵא בּוֹ, [18] וְיֵשׁ מֵהֶן שֶׁאֵין הֲלָכָה כְּמוֹתוֹ אֶלָּא כַּיּוֹצֵא בּוֹ. [19] בְּכָל מָקוֹם שֶׁאָמַר רַבָּן גַּמְלִיאֵל: "רוֹאֶה אֲנִי אֶת דִּבְרֵי אַדְמוֹן", [20] הֲלָכָה כְּמוֹתוֹ; [21] אִינָךְ, לָא.

מַשְׁנָה [22] הָעוֹרֵר עַל הַשָּׂדֶה,

LITERAL TRANSLATION

the law is not like him, [1]and not like he who agrees with him — [2]but surely Rabbi Yitzḥak ben Elazar said in the name of Ḥizkiyah: [3]Wherever Rabban Gamliel said: "I see the words of Admon," [4]the law is like [Admon]!

[5]Rather, he said as follows: The two things that Ḥanan said, [6]the law is like him and like he who agrees with him. [7]The seven things that Admon said, the law is not like he who agrees with him. [8]But is the law like him in all of these cases.

[9]But surely Rabbi Yitzḥak ben Elazar said in the name of Ḥizkiyah: [10]Wherever Rabban Gamliel said: "I see the words of Admon," [11]the law is like [Admon]. [12][Where] he said, yes; [13][where] he did not say, no!

[14]Rather, he said as follows: [15]The two things that Ḥanan said, [16]the law is like him and like he who agrees with him. [17]The seven things that Admon said, there are those that the law is like him and like he who agrees with him, [18]and there are those that the law is not like him, but rather like he who [sometimes] agrees with him. [19]Wherever Rabban Gamliel said: "I see the words of Admon," [20]the law is like [Admon]; [21]the others, not.

MISHNAH [22][If] someone contested a field,

TRANSLATION AND COMMENTARY

that Admon said, the law is not like him, [1]**and not like** the Tanna **who agrees with him,** there is a difficulty. [2]For **surely Rabbi Yitzḥak ben Elazar said in the name of Ḥizkiyah:** [3]**Wherever Rabban Gamliel said: "I agree with the position of Admon,"** [4]**the law is** indeed **in accordance with** Admon! How could Rabbi Zera contradict that ruling of Ḥizkiyah, who was of the first generation of Amoraim and is considered to have the Halakhic status of a Tanna.

אֶלָּא הָכִי קָאָמַר [5]**Rather,** Rabbi Zera meant to **say as follows:** Regarding **the two things that Ḥanan said,** [6]**the law is like him and like** the Tanna **who agrees with him.** [7]Regarding **the seven things that Admon said, the law is not like** the Tanna **who agrees with him,** for Rabban Gamliel agrees with Admon only regarding his first three rulings, but he disagrees with him about his next four rulings, [8]**and the law is** in fact **like** Admon **regarding all** seven **cases.**

וְהָאָמַר [9]**But surely Rabbi Yitzḥak ben Elazar said in the name of Ḥizkiyah:** [10]**Wherever Rabban Gamliel said: "I agree with the position of Admon,"** [11]**the law is** indeed **in accordance with** Admon. [12]Now, this implies that **where** Rabban Gamliel **said** that he agrees with Admon, the law is **indeed** in accordance with Admon, [13]but **where** Rabban Gamliel **did not say** that he agrees with Admon, the law is **not** in accordance with Admon, which contradicts Rabbi Zera!

אֶלָּא הָכִי קָאָמַר [14]**Rather,** Rabbi Zera meant to **say as follows:** [15]Regarding **the two things that Ḥanan said,** [16]**the law is like him and like** the Tanna **who agrees with him.** [17]But regarding **the seven things that Admon said, there are among them things** regarding which **the law is like him and like** the Tanna **who agrees with him,** [18]**and there are among them things** regarding which **the law is not like him, but rather like** the Tanna **who** sometimes **agrees with him.** How so? [19]**Wherever Rabban Gamliel said: "I agree with the position of Admon,"** [20]**the law is** in fact **like Admon.** [21]But regarding **the other** rulings of Admon with which Rabban Gamliel did not agree, the law is **not** like Admon.

MISHNAH הָעוֹרֵר עַל הַשָּׂדֶה [22]**If someone contested** another person's title **to a field and** the plaintiff had

RASHI

משנה העורר על השדה כו׳ — ראובן מערער על שדה שביד שמעון, ואומר: לוי שמכרה לך גזלה ממני.

HALAKHAH

הָעוֹרֵר עַל הַשָּׂדֶה **If someone contested about a field.** "If Reuven sold a field to Shimon, and Levi was one of the witnesses who signed the bill of sale, and later Levi came and contested the sale, arguing that Reuven had stolen the

וְהוּא חָתוּם עָלֶיהָ בְּעֵד, [1]אַדְמוֹן אוֹמֵר: הַשֵּׁנִי נוֹחַ לִי, [2]וְהָרִאשׁוֹן קָשֶׁה הֵימֶנּוּ. [3]וַחֲכָמִים אוֹמְרִים: אִיבֵּד אֶת זְכוּתוֹ.

[4]עֲשָׂאָהּ סִימָן לְאַחֵר, [5]אִיבֵּד אֶת זְכוּתוֹ.

גמרא [6]אָמַר אַבַּיֵי: לֹא שָׁנוּ אֶלָּא עֵד, [7]אֲבָל דַּיָּין —

LITERAL TRANSLATION

and he is signed on [the deed] as a witness, [1]Admon says: [He may say:] The second [occupant] is easier for me [to oppose], [2]and the first is more difficult than he. [3]And the Sages say: He lost his right [to the field].

[4][If] he made it a [boundary] mark for someone else, [5]he lost his right.

GEMARA [6]Abaye said: They only taught [this] regarding a witness, [7]but a judge —

TRANSLATION AND COMMENTARY

signed the deed of sale for the property **as a witness,** the Tannaim disagree about the law. [1]**Admon says:** Even though the plaintiff's signature upon the bill of sale would seem to be an acknowledgment that the sale was valid, he can still claim that the field belongs to him and not to the one who sold it. He can argue as follows: I signed the bill of sale because **I preferred** that the property be in the hands of **the second occupant,** [2]because **the first occupant,** the seller, **is** a much **more difficult** person to deal with in court **than he.** I had no hopes of recovering the property from the one who stole it and sold it, but I thought that I would be able to recover it from the buyer. Thus, if the plaintiff can establish with witnesses that he had once been the rightful owner of the property, he is regarded as having presumptive possession of it, and the first occupant must prove his ownership. [3]**The Sages** disagree and **say:** the plaintiff **lost his right** to the property. His signature on the bill of sale is regarded as an admission that the property was not his.

עֲשָׂאָהּ סִימָן לְאַחֵר [4]If the plaintiff **designated** the adjacent contested property **as a boundary mark** in a bill of sale that he drew up when selling property **to someone else,** and in that bill of sale he recognized the seller as the owner of that property, all agree — both Admon and the Sages — [5]that the plaintiff **lost his right** to the property.

GEMARA אָמַר אַבַּיֵי [6]**Abaye said:** The disagreement between Admon and the Sages recorded in our Mishnah **only applies** if the plaintiff had attached his signature as **a witness** to the bill of sale transferring the property. [7]**But** if he served as **a judge** whose signature authenticated the signatures of the witnesses on the bill of

RASHI

והוא חתום – על שטר המכירה שכתב לוי לשמעון, כשמכרה לו. **אדמון אומר** – יכול הוא שיאמר: מה שלא ערערתי בשעה שלקחת מלוי, וחתמתי בתוך השטר עד – לפי שלוי אדם חזק, וקשה להוציאה מידו, ונוח לי שתהא בידך, שאוציאנה ממך בדין. **איבד את זכותו** – דהואיל וחתם – הודה שאין לו עסק בה. **עשאה** – המוחזק בה סימן לאחר, שלא מכר לראובן זה העורר עליה, אלא לאיש אחר היה מוכר שדה מצד זו, ומצר לו ארבעת מצרי השדה, וכתב לו במצרים: מצר פלוני שדה שלי, ועשה שדה זו סימן מצר ללוקח, ובשמו של מוכר. וזה חתם על אותו שטר, ולא ערער. **איבד את זכותו** – אפילו לאדמון. דאין לומר כאן: השני נוח לי.

גמרא אבל דיין – שהובא שטר המכירה בבית דין לקיימו, כמשפט קיום שטרות, שהעדים באין ומעידין על כתב ידם, והדיינין כותבין: שטרא דנן נפקא לקדמנא ואסהידו סהדי אחתימות ידייהו, ואישרנוהי וקיימנוהי.

NOTES

וְהוּא חָתוּם עָלֶיהָ בְּעֵד **And he signed it as a witness.** *Ritva* notes that the Sages' position that the plaintiff lost his right to the property only applies if he actually signed the bill of sale transferring the property, or performed some other clear act that can be interpreted as an admission that the property was not his. But if he was merely present at the time of the sale and remained silent, or even if he encouraged the other person to purchase the property, he did not forfeit his right to it.

עֲשָׂאָהּ סִימָן לְאַחֵר **If he made it a boundary mark for someone else.** *Rashi* understands that this phrase refers to the situation where the occupier of the disputed land sold

HALAKHAH

field from him, we do not listen to Levi nor consider the evidence that he adduces in support of his claim, for he lost all his rights to the field when he signed the bill of sale which transferred the property to Shimon, following the Sages. This only applies in a case where he signed the bill of sale together with another witness, but if he alone signed the bill, he did not forfeit his rights, for he knew that the signature of a single witness has no legal validity (following *Ritva*). So too if he added his signature as an honorary gesture after two witnesses had already signed the bill, he did not forfeit his rights (following *Rivash*). If Levi rented the property from Reuven, he is treated in the same manner as if he had signed a bill of sale transferring the property to a third person." (*Rambam, Sefer Mishpatim, Hilkhot To'en VeNit'an* 16:1; *Shulhan Arukh, Hoshen Mishpat* 147:1.)

עֲשָׂאָהּ סִימָן לְאַחֵר **If he made it a sign for someone else.** "If Levi the contester had signed a bill of sale relating to the adjacent property which identifies that other property as bordering on the property belonging to Reuven, he forfeited all rights to the property which he now claims was stolen from him by Reuven (following the Jerusalem Talmud). And all the more so if he himself drew up a bill of sale identifying the adjacent property as bordering on property belonging to Reuven (*Maggid Mishneh*)," following the Mishnah. (*Rambam, Sefer Mishpatim, Hilkhot To'en VeNit'an* 16:1; *Shulhan Arukh, Hoshen Mishpat* 147:4.)

לֹא שָׁנוּ אֶלָּא עֵד **They only taught this about a witness.**

TRANSLATION AND COMMENTARY

sale, all agree that he **did not lose his right** to the property which he now claims is his. Such validation of a bill of indebtedness is required before it may be used to collect the debt or prove ownership of a field. Even if the plaintiff was a member of the court that authenticated the signatures of the witnesses attached to the bill of sale, he can still contest the purchaser's title to that property, for a judge is not required to read a document before he authenticates the signatures on it. [1]**For Rabbi Ḥiyya taught** the following Baraita: **"Witnesses may not sign a bill unless they** first **read it,** for when they sign the bill they are regarded as testifying to the subject matter of the document. [109B] [2]**But judges may sign** the validation certificate that they append to a document, **even if they did not read** the document itself, for they only authenticate the signatures of the witnesses, and not the veracity of the subject matter of the document."

עֲשָׂאָהּ סִימָן [3]We learned in the next clause of the Mishnah: **"If** Reuven **designated** the contested property **as a boundary mark** in a bill of sale that he drew up **for** the sale of land to **a third party,** mentioning Shimon as the owner of that property, all agree that Reuven lost his right to the land." [4]**Abaye said:** This regulation **only applies** when Reuven designated the contested property as a landmark in a bill of sale which he drew up **for someone else.** That is to say, he sold the adjacent property, and described it in the bill of sale as

לֹא אִיבֵּד אֶת זְכוּתוֹ. [1]דְּתָנֵי רַבִּי חִיָּיא: ״אֵין הָעֵדִים חוֹתְמִין עַל הַשְּׁטָר אֶלָּא אִם כֵּן קְרָאוּהוּ, [109B] [2]אֲבָל הַדַּיָּינִין חוֹתְמִים אַף עַל פִּי שֶׁלֹּא קְרָאוּהוּ״. [3]״עֲשָׂאָהּ סִימָן לְאַחֵר״. [4]אָמַר אַבַּיֵי: לֹא שָׁנוּ אֶלָּא לְאַחֵר,

LITERAL TRANSLATION

he did not lose his right. [1]For Rabbi Ḥiyya taught: "Witnesses may not sign a bill unless they read it, [109B] [2]But the judges may sign even if they did not read it."

[3]"[If] he made it a [boundary] mark for someone else." [4]Abaye said: They only taught [this] for [a sale to] someone else,

RASHI

לא איבד זכותו — שלא ידע מה כתוב בו, שיערער עליו. **דתני רבי חייא אין העדים חותמין על השטר אלא אם כן קראוהו** — שהרי על דברי השטר הם באים להעיד. **אבל הדיינים חותמין** — בקיום, אף על פי שלא קראוהו, שהרי אינן מעידין אלא שטר זה בא לפנינו והעדים הכירו שהיא חתימתן. **לא שנו אלא לאחר** — דוקא נקט מתניתין סימן לאחר. אבל עשאה המוחזק בה סימן לעצמו של ראובן זה העורר עליה, שהיה שמעון מוכר שדה שבצדה לראובן זה העורר עליו, וכשמכר לו סימני המצרים כתב על שדה זו ״מיצר פלוני שלי״, ולא מיחה ראובן.

NOTES

an adjacent field which was his to a third party. When he drew up the deed of sale for that second field he wrote that the property being sold bordered on property now being disputed. And the plaintiff was signed on that deed. In such a case, all agree that the plaintiff lost his right to the property by acknowledging the seller's ownership. *Ramban, Rosh,* and others argue that while this ruling is indeed correct, the case being discussed by the Mishnah is where the plaintiff sold his own adjacent property to a third person, and in the bill of sale he wrote that it bordered on property belonging to the party whose title to the property he later contested.

אִיבֵּד אֶת זְכוּתוֹ He lost his right. The Rishonim write (and so *Rambam* rules) that the plaintiff lost all his rights to the property, so that even if he produces witnesses that the property had belonged to his father, or witnesses that the property had been stolen from him, we do not rely on those witnesses, but rather on his implied admission that the property does not belong to him.

אֲבָל הַדַּיָּינִין But the judges. *Ritva* notes that before the judges sign the endorsement validation certificate they append to a document, they must indeed examine it. However, this is done in order to ascertain that the witnesses are not related to the principals, but they are not required to read it closely in order to familiarize themselves with its contents.

לֹא שָׁנוּ אֶלָּא לְאַחֵר They only taught this for someone else. The Jerusalem Talmud maintains that the plaintiff loses his right to the contested property not only if he himself designated it as a border mark in a bill of sale which he drew up for someone else, but also if he signed a bill of sale which somebody else drew up, designating the contested property as a border.

HALAKHAH

"It is only a witness who had attached his signature to a bill of sale who cannot come later and contest the sale arguing that the seller had stolen the property from him. But a judge who had authenticated the signatures of the witnesses on the bill of sale can later contest the sale and claim that the property had been stolen from him, for he can argue that he had not actually read the document." (*Rambam, Sefer Mishpatim, Hilkhot To'en VeNit'an* 16:2; *Shulḥan Arukh, Ḥoshen Mishpat* 147:4.)

אֵין הָעֵדִים חוֹתְמִין Witnesses may not sign. "Witnesses may only sign a document after having carefully read it." (*Rambam, Sefer Mishpatim, Hilkhot To'en VeNit'an* 16:2; *Shulḥan Arukh, Ḥoshen Mishpat* 45:2,5; see also *Ḥoshen Mishpat* 68:2.)

אֲבָל הַדַּיָּינִין חוֹתְמִים But the judges may sign. "Judges are permitted to sign the validation certificate which they append to a document, even if they did not read the document itself." (*Rambam, Sefer Mishpatim, Hilkhot To'en VeNit'an* 16:2; *Sefer Shofetim, Hilkhot Edut* 6:8; *Shulḥan Arukh, Ḥoshen Mishpat* 46:2; 147:4.)

TRANSLATION AND COMMENTARY

bordering on the property belonging to Shimon. [1]**But** if Reuven designated the contested property as a boundary mark in a bill of sale which he drew up **for himself,** i.e., if he purchased the adjacent property from Shimon, [2]all agree that **he did not lose his right** to the contested property, [3]for Reuven **can say: "Had I not done this for** Shimon, **he would not have sold me** the other property. [4]**What possible argument do you** have preventing me from claiming the contested property? [5]Do you say that **should I have made a** prior **declaration** before two witnesses that the bill of sale which I was drawing up for the other property was formulated under duress? I could not make such a declaration, [6]for as they say: **Your friend has a friend, and your friend's friend has a friend.** Word would quickly have spread that I was contesting Shimon's title to the adjacent property, and he would not have sold me the property that I desired to buy from him."

ההוא [7]A man once **designated** certain property **as a boundary mark** in a bill of sale that he drew up **for someone else,** identifying that property as belonging to another person. [8]Later **he contested** that person's title to the property, claiming that he himself was the rightful owner, **and** then **he died** before the matter was resolved. Before he died **he had appointed a guardian** to take charge of the property that would be inherited by his minor children. [9]**The guardian came before Abaye** and presented a claim for the contested property, [10]but Abaye rejected the claim and **said to him:** "Surely we learned in the Mishnah: 'If Reuven **designated** the contested property **as a boundary mark** in a bill of sale that he drew up **for someone else,** and in that bill of sale he recognized Shimon as its owner, [11]all agree that Reuven **lost his right** to the property, and can no longer challenge Shimon's title.'" [12]The guardian **said** to Abaye: **"Were the father of the orphans** still **alive,** surely **he would have been able to claim** as follows: 'When I described the property that I sold as bordering on your property, I did not mean that the whole field is yours. [13]Rather, I only meant to **designate as yours** the area occupied by **a single furrow** at its edge! Since the deceased could have put forward such an argument, I who stand in his place

[1]אֲבָל לְעַצְמוֹ, [2]לֹא אִיבֵּד אֶת זְכוּתוֹ, [3]דַּאֲמַר: "אִי דְּלָא עֲבַדִי לֵיהּ, הָכִי לָא הֲוָה מְזַבֵּין לָהּ נִיהֲלִי. [4]מַאי אִית לָךְ לְמֵימַר? [5]אִיבָּעֵי לִי לְמִימְסַר מוֹדָעָא? [6]חַבְרָךְ חַבְרָא אִית לֵיהּ, וְחַבְרָא דְּחַבְרָךְ חַבְרָא אִית לֵיהּ".

[7]הַהוּא דַּעֲשָׂאָהּ סִימָן לְאַחֵר, [8]עִרְעֵר וּשְׁכִיב, וְאוֹקִים אַפּוֹטְרוֹפָּא. [9]אֲתָא אַפּוֹטְרוֹפּוֹס לְקַמֵּיהּ דְּאַבַּיֵי, [10]אֲמַר לֵיהּ: "עֲשָׂאָהּ סִימָן לְאַחֵר, [11]אִיבֵּד אֶת זְכוּתוֹ". [12]אֲמַר: "אִי הֲוָה אֲבוּהוֹן דְּיָתְמֵי קַיָּים, הֲוָה טָעֵין וַאֲמַר: [13]'תֶּלֶם אֶחָד עָשִׂיתִי

LITERAL TRANSLATION

[1]but for [a sale to] himself, [2]he did not lose his right, [3]for he can say: "Had I not done this for him, he would not have sold it to me. [4]But what do you have to say? [5]I should have made a declaration? [6]Your friend has a friend, and your friend's friend has a friend."

[7][There was] a certain person who made it a [boundary] mark for someone else, [8]he contested and died, and appointed a guardian. [9]The guardian came before Abaye, [10][who] said to him: "[If] he made it a sign for someone else, [11]he lost his right." [12]He said: "Were the father of the orphans alive, he could have claimed and said: [13]'I made [only] one furrow of it

RASHI

אי לאו דעבדי הכי – אם לא שתקתי. **למימסר מודעא** – לומר לעדים בסתר: הוו יודעין שעל שדה זו שאצל זו שאני לוקח אני מערער, ומה ששתקתי למה שכתבה במצריה בשמו – שאם אני מוחה לא ימכור לי זאת. **חברך חברא אית ליה** – ויודיעוהו, ושוב לא ימכור לי. **תלם אחד** – מענית המחרישה על פני כל השדה שמכר הודיתי לו, בין שדה זו שאני עורר ובין אותה שמכר.

NOTES

אֲבָל לְעַצְמוֹ לֹא אִיבֵּד אֶת זְכוּתוֹ But for himself, he did not lose his right. Our commentary follows *Rashi,* who explains that the party in possession of the contested property sold an adjacent property to the plaintiff and designated the contested property as a border mark. The reading in the standard editions, "He would not have sold it to me," supports this explanation. But *Rabbenu Ḥananel, Tosafot,* and most of the Rishonim understand that the party in possession of the contested property bought the adjacent property from the plaintiff, and designated the contested property as a landmark. According to this interpretation, the Gemara must read: "He would not have bought it from me."

HALAKHAH

אֲבָל לְעַצְמוֹ But for himself. "This ruling is not brought by *Rambam* nor by *Shulhan Arukh. Bet Yosef* suggests that perhaps it follows from the ruling regarding someone who designated the contested property as a landmark in a bill of sale which he drew up for someone else. If Reuven designated the contested property as a landmark in a bill of sale which he drew up for himself, he did not forfeit his rights to the property." (*Rambam, Sefer Mishpatim, Hilkhot To'en VeNit'an* 16:1, *Maggid Mishneh*; *Tur, Ḥoshen Mishpat* 147, *Bet Yosef;* and see *Shulḥan Arukh, Ḥoshen Mishpat* 147:2.)

תֶּלֶם אֶחָד עָשִׂיתִי לְךָ I did for you one furrow. "If the

LANGUAGE

רִיכְבָּא דְּדִיקְלֵי **A nursery of palm trees.** *Rashi* (cf. also *Arukh*) explains this as "a row of palm trees planted very close to one another." Others, however, explain רִיכְבָּא דְּדִיקְלֵי as "the stump of a palm tree."

TRANSLATION AND COMMENTARY

should also be able to do so.'" [1]Abaye **said to** the guardian: **"You said well,** [2]**for Rabbi Yoḥanan said: If** a person who had designated property as a boundary mark in a bill of sale that he drew up for someone else later **claimed:** 'When I described the property as bordering on property that belongs to you, [3]I only meant to **designate as yours** the area occupied by **a single furrow** at its edge.' The plaintiff **is believed.** If the plaintiff can establish with witnesses that he had once been the rightful owner of the property, the other person must prove that he owes it." [4]Abaye added: "But **now,** you must **go** and **give** that other person the area of **a single furrow** along the edge of the property, for you have admitted that section belongs to him." [5]**A row of palm trees stood** on the furrow along the edge, and the guardian was not willing to waive them. [6]So **he said to** Abaye: **"Were the father of the orphans** still **alive,** surely **he would be able to claim** as follows: 'When I identified the adjacent property as belonging to that other person, it did indeed belong to him, for I had sold it to him. [7]But later **I bought it back from him.'** Since the deceased could have put forward such an argument, I who stand in his place should also be able to do so." [8]Abaye **said to** the guardian: **"You said well,** [9]**for Rabbi Yoḥanan said: If** a person who had designated property as a boundary mark in a bill of sale which he drew up for someone else, and later **claimed:** 'I had indeed sold the property to him, but later **I bought it back from him,'** the plaintiff **is believed.** If the plaintiff can establish with witnesses that he had once been the rightful owner of the property, the other person must prove that he owns it."

לְךָ׳״. [1]אֲמַר לֵיהּ: ״שַׁפִּיר קָאָמְרַתְּ, [2]דְּאָמַר רַבִּי יוֹחָנָן: אִם טָעַן וְאָמַר: [3]׳תֶּלֶם אֶחָד עָשִׂיתִי לְךָ׳, נֶאֱמָן. [4]זִיל, הַב לֵיהּ מִיהַת תֶּלֶם אֶחָד״. [5]הֲוָה עֲלָהּ רִיכְבָּא דְּדִיקְלֵי. [6]אֲמַר לֵיהּ: ״אִי הֲוָה אֲבוּהוֹן דְּיָתְמֵי קַיָּים, הֲוָה טָעֵין וְאָמַר: [7]׳חָזַרְתִּי וְלָקַחְתִּי מִמֶּנּוּ׳״. [8]אֲמַר לֵיהּ: ״שַׁפִּיר קָאָמְרַתְּ, [9]דְּאָמַר רַבִּי יוֹחָנָן: ׳אִם טָעַן וְאָמַר חָזַרְתִּי וּלְקַחְתִּיו מִמֶּנּוּ׳, נֶאֱמָן״.

LITERAL TRANSLATION

yours.'" [1]He said to him: "You said well, [2]for Rabbi Yoḥanan said: If he claimed and said: [3]'I made [only] one furrow of it yours,' he is believed. [4]Go, give him in any case one furrow." [5]There was a row of palms on [that furrow]. [6]He said to him: "Were the father of the orphans alive, he could have claimed and said: [7]'I bought [the field] back from him.'" [8]He said to him: "You said well, [9]for Rabbi Yoḥanan said: If he claimed and said: 'I bought it back from him,' he is believed."

RASHI

ועל אותו תלם כתב: מצר פלוני שלי, וחתמתי על השטר ולא מחיתי. הב ליה מיהת תלם אחד — לאחר שהביא אפוטרופוס של יתומים ראיה שהיתה של אביהם וגזלה הימנו, ולא היה למחזיק זכות בה אלא לפי שעשאה אביהן סימן בשמו של מחזיק, אמר ליה אביי לאפוטרופוס: זיל הב ליה למחזיק מיהת תלם אחד. הוה — על אותו תלם. ריכבא דדקלא — שורת דקלים מורכבין זה על גב זה. חזרתי ולקחתיו הימנו — לאחר שעשיתיו סימן בשמו. נאמן — דהפה שאסר הוא הפה שהתיר. דמאחר שיש עדים שהיתה שלו ונגזלה הימנו — אין לזה זכות באותו תלם אלא על פיו של זה, שעשאה סימן לאחר, והרי חזר ואמר: לקחתיו.

NOTES

שַׁפִּיר קָאָמְרַתְּ **You said well.** The Rishonim note: If the arguments presented by the guardian were indeed valid, Abaye should have put them forward himself. There is a rule that a court must present all possible arguments that are advantageous to the orphans. Various solutions are suggested: *Tosafot* suggest that Abaye had forgotten the ruling of Rabbi Yoḥanan, and did not remember that the orphans could enter such pleas (see also *Rid*). Others propose that when a guardian is looking out for the orphans' interests, the court need not present arguments on their behalf. Rather it waits for the guardian to enter all of his pleas, for surely he is more familiar with the circumstances (see *Ritva, Rabbenu Crescas* in the name of *Rashba*). *Rosh* answers that Abaye did not put those arguments forward because he wanted to test the guardian and see whether he would fulfill his responsibility. *Rid* argues that the court only presents common pleas that on behalf of orphans, but unusual pleas, such as those mentioned in our passage, are not presented by the court.

HALAKHAH

contester claims that when he designated property as a landmark, describing it as belonging to someone else, he only meant to designate as that other person's property the area occupied by a single furrow along the edge, his claim is accepted, and he did not forfeit his rights to the rest of the property." (*Rambam, Sefer Mishpatim, Hilkhot To'en VeNit'an* 16:2; *Shulḥan Arukh, Ḥoshen Mishpat* 147:3.)

חָזַרְתִּי וְלָקַחְתִּי **I bought it back from him.** "If the contester claims that even the single furrow which he had designated as a landmark, describing it as belonging to another person, he had already bought back from him, his claim is accepted, and he did not forfeit his rights to the property." (*Shulḥan Arukh, Ḥoshen Mishpat* 147:3 in *Rema.*)

[1]אָמַר אַבַּיֵי: הַאי מַאן דְּמוֹקֵים אַפּוֹטְרוֹפָּא, [2]נוֹקִים כִּי הַאי דְּיָדַע לְאַפּוּכֵי בִּזְכוּתָא דְּיָתְמֵי.

מִשְׁנָה [3]מִי שֶׁהָלַךְ לִמְדִינַת הַיָּם, וְאָבְדָה דֶּרֶךְ שָׂדֵהוּ, [4]אַדְמוֹן אוֹמֵר: יֵלֵךְ לוֹ בַּקְּצָרָה. [5]וַחֲכָמִים אוֹמְרִים: יִקְנֶה לוֹ דֶּרֶךְ בְּמֵאָה מָנֶה, אוֹ יִפְרַח בָּאֲוִיר.

גְּמָרָא [6]מַאי טַעֲמָא דְּרַבָּנַן? [7]שַׁפִּיר קָאָמַר אַדְמוֹן!

LITERAL TRANSLATION

[1]Abaye said: Someone who appoints a guardian should appoint [someone] like him, [2]who knows how to uncover favorable arguments for the orphans.

MISHNAH [3][If] someone went abroad, and the path to his field was lost, [4]Admon says: He may go by the shortest path. [5]But the Sages say: He must buy himself a path for a hundred manehs, or fly in the air.

GEMARA [6]What is the reason of the Sages? [7]Admon said well!

TRANSLATION AND COMMENTARY

אָמַר אַבַּיֵי [1]The Gemara concludes this discussion with the following advice: **Abaye said: If someone appoints a guardian** over property that will be inherited by his minor children, [2]he **should appoint someone like** this guardian **who knows how to uncover favorable arguments for the orphans.**

MISHNAH מִי שֶׁהָלַךְ [3]Someone owned a field that was surrounded by property belonging to other people, and he owned a path leading to his field through the neighboring property. **If he went abroad, and** while there **the path to his field was lost,** plowed over by the owner of the property through which it passed, so that it could no longer be located, [4]**Admon says: He may go** to his field **via the shortest path,** meaning that he may seize property that forms the shortest path to his field. [5]**The Sages** disagree and **say: He must buy himself a path** from his neighbor, even if that neighbor charges him **a hundred maneh** for it, **or** else he must **fly in the air** to get to his field, for his neighbors may object to his crossing their property in order to reach his field.

GEMARA מַאי טַעֲמָא דְּרַבָּנַן [6]The Gemara at first assumes that the field discussed in the Mishnah was surrounded on all four sides by property belonging to a single individual. So it asks: **What is the reasoning of the Rabbis** who disagree with Admon? [7]Surely **Admon said well.** Since he once owned a path through the neighbor's land, he can take another.

RASHI

משנה ואבדה דרך שדהו – שהחזיקו בה בעלי השדות שבמצריו. ילך לו בקצרה – על כרחם יטול לו דרך לשדהו. אבל דרך קצרה יברור לו, שלא ירבה ליטול.

גמרא שפיר קאמר אדמון – דהא סלקא דעתך כשארבעת השדות שסביבותיו של אדם אחד הן, דממה נפשך אורחיה גביה הוא.

NOTES

אָבְדָה דֶּרֶךְ שָׂדֵהוּ **The path to his field was lost.** According to some commentators, the owner of the inner field has full title to the path that cuts across his neighbor's property. Others understand that he only has the right of passage through his neighbor's property. However, even according to the Sages who may require him to purchase a path from his neighbors, this means that he must purchase the right of way, but not the path itself (see *Eshel Avraham*).

יֵלֵךְ לוֹ בַּקְּצָרָה **He goes on the shortest path.** This does not mean that the owner of the lost path may choose a path that is shortest for him. Rather it means that he must choose the path that cuts across the least of his neighbor's property and causes him the least damage (*Rivan, Talmidei Rabbenu Yonah*).

יִקְנֶה לוֹ דֶּרֶךְ **He must buy himself a path.** The Jerusalem Talmud asks: Did not Joshua enact that a person may cross another person's property in order to get to where he must go? Why then must the owner of the lost path buy a path from his neighbor? It answers that Joshua enacted that when a person is lost, he may cross another person's property until he regains his bearings. Otherwise he may not cross property without the owner's consent. Alternatively, one may say that Joshua enacted that a person may cross his neighbor's property by himself, but he may not lead his animals across that property without his neighbor's consent. Thus, the owner of the lost path must buy a path from his neighbor if he wishes to go to his field on a regular basis or if he wishes to take his animals there.

שַׁפִּיר קָאָמַר אַדְמוֹן **Admon said well.** *Tosafot* and others note that all agree that if one person bought all the

HALAKHAH

הַאי מַאן דְּמוֹקֵים אַפּוֹטְרוֹפָּא **Someone who appoints a guardian.** "When the court appoints a guardian to be in charge of orphans' property, it must select a person who is trustworthy, strong, and capable of defending the rights of the orphans. He should understand business matters so that he can preserve their capital and even generate profits." (*Rambam, Sefer Mishpatim, Hilkhot Nahalot* 10:6; *Shulḥan Arukh, Ḥoshen Mishpat* 290:2.)

אָבְדָה דֶּרֶךְ שָׂדֵהוּ **The path to his field was lost.** "If someone went abroad, and while he was away the path leading to his field by way of his neighbor's property was lost, and the properties surrounding his field belonged to four different people (or they belonged to a single person, but he had purchased them from four different people), each of his neighbors can push him off with the argument that perhaps his path had cut across the property belonging to one of the other neighbors. In such a case, the owner of the lost path has no other recourse but to purchase a new path from one of his neighbors. But if the surrounding properties had always belonged to a single person, the

[1]אָמַר רַב יְהוּדָה אָמַר רַב: כְּגוֹן שֶׁהִקִּיפוּהָ אַרְבָּעָה בְּנֵי אָדָם מֵאַרְבַּע רוּחוֹתֶיהָ.

[2]אִי הָכִי, מַאי טַעְמָא דְּאַדְמוֹן?

[3]אֲמַר רָבָא: בְּאַרְבָּעָה דְּאָתוּ מִכֹּחַ אַרְבָּעָה, [4]וְאַרְבָּעָה דְּאָתוּ מִכֹּחַ חַד, [5]כּוּלֵּי עָלְמָא לָא פְּלִיגִי דְּמָצֵי מַדְחֵי לֵיהּ. [6]כִּי פְּלִיגִי בְּחַד דְּאָתֵי מִכֹּחַ אַרְבָּעָה. [7]אַדְמוֹן סָבַר: "מִכָּל מָקוֹם, דַּרְכָּא אִית לִי גַּבָּךְ". [8]וְרַבָּנַן סָבְרִי: [9]"אִי שָׁתְקַתְּ, שָׁתְקַתְּ. [10]וְאִי לָא, מַהֲדַרְנָא שְׁטָרָא לְמָרַיְיהוּ, [11]וְלָא מָצֵית לְאִשְׁתַּעוּיֵי דִּינָא בַּהֲדַיְיהוּ".

[12]הַהוּא דַּאֲמַר לְהוּ: "דִּיקְלָא לִבְרָת". [13]אֲזוּל יָתְמֵי פְּלוּג

LITERAL TRANSLATION

[1]Rav Yehudah said in the name of Rav: When [the fields of] four people surrounded it from four directions.

[2]If so, what is Admon's reason?

[3]Rava said: Where the four derived (lit., "came from") four, [4]or the [other] four derived [ownership] rights from one, [5]everyone agrees (lit., "does not disagree") that they can push him off. [6]Where they disagree is when one derived [ownership] rights from four. [7]Admon maintains: "In any case, I have a path with you." [8]And the Rabbis maintain: [9]"If you remain silent, you are silent. [10]But if not, I will return the deed to their owners, [11]and you will not be able to bring a case against them."

[12][There was] a certain [dying] person who said to them: "A date palm to [my] daughter." [13]The orphans went [and] divided

TRANSLATION AND COMMENTARY

אָמַר רַב יְהוּדָה [1]**Rav Yehudah said in the name of Rav:** The property belonged to **four** different **people,** which **surrounded** the field **on four sides.** The owner of each field can claim that the path was on his neighbor's field. Since the owner of the lost path cannot prove his claim against any one of his neighbors, he must buy himself a path, even at an exorbitant price.

אִי הָכִי [2]The Gemara asks: **If so, what is the reasoning of Admon** who says that he may seize the shortest path to his field?

אֲמַר רָבָא [3]**Rava said: When the four** present neighbors **derived their ownership rights from four** previous owners, [4]**or the four** present neighbors **derived their rights from a single** previous owner. [5]**Everyone agrees** — both Admon and the Rabbis — **that** each of the neighbors **can push off** the owner of the lost access path. [6]**They** only **disagree** about the case **where one** current neighbor **derived his rights from four** previous neighbors. [7]**Admon maintains** that the owner of the lost access path may seize the shortest path to his field, arguing: **"In any case, I own a path** that cuts **across your** property." [8]**And the Rabbis** disagree and **maintain** that the owner of the lost access path must buy a path from his neighbor, for the neighbor can say to him: [9]**"If you are silent, you are silent,** and perhaps I will agree to sell you an access path at a reduced price. [10]**But if not** — if you insist on receiving an access path free of charge — **I will return the deed** of sale **to the** previous **owner** of that land, [11]**and you will not be able to conduct a case against** any one of **them,** since I and any of the previous owners push you off!"

הַהוּא [12]**A man said to those** who stood around him as he lay on his deathbed: "I wish to give **a date palm to my daughter."** By Rabbinic decree, a gift given by a person on his deathbed is valid even if no act of acquisition was performed, and so the daughter had the right to receive a date palm from her father's estate. [13]After the man died, his male **heirs divided** their father's **property, and did not give** their sister **a date palm**

RASHI

ארבעה בני אדם — דכל חד וחד מדחי ליה: דרכך לאו גבאי הוא. **וארבעה דאתו מכח חד** — שלקחוה מאיש אחד, אחר שהלך זה. **אי שתקת שתקת** — ואוזיל גבך כשתקנה הדרך ממני. **ההוא דאמר** — בשעת מיתתו.

NOTES

property surrounding the field belonging to the person whose access path was lost from a single owner, he may not threaten to sell it to four different people, to frustrate the claim of the owner of the lost path. Since the first owner was unable to evade this man's clear claim against his property by selling it, so the man who succeeded him may not do so.

מַהֲדַרְנָא שְׁטָרָא לְמָרַיְיהוּ I will return the deeds to their former owners. The Rishonim ask: Why cannot the person whose access path was lost say to his neighbor: Go return the deeds of sale to the four previous owners? Why should we reject his claim on the basis of a threat that the surrounding neighbor clearly does not want to carry out? *Rosh* explains that since the neighbor has the possibility of

HALAKHAH

owner of the lost path may seize from his neighbor property that forms the shortest path to his field. If the owner of the lost path seized property from his neighbor claiming that it was his, the neighbor cannot remove him from the property without clear proof that the path did not belong to him, for he put forward his claim with certainty (*Maggid Mishneh*)." (*Rambam, Sefer Mishpatim, Hilkhot To'en VeNit'an* 15:11; *Shulḥan Arukh, Ḥoshen Mishpat* 148:1-2.)

הַהוּא דַּאֲמַר לְהוּ: דִּיקְלָא לִבְרַת There was a certain person who said to them: A date palm for my daughter. "If a dying person left instructions that a certain property be given to a certain person, but after he died, his heirs

TRANSLATION AND COMMENTARY

to which she was entitled. [1]When the matter was brought before **Rav Yosef** for a ruling, he first **thought to say:** [2]**This** case **is** similar to the case of **our Mishnah.** Just as each landowner can argue that the path went through his neighbor's field, each of the heirs can push her away by arguing that the date palm belonging to the sister stood on the portion taken by his brother.

אָמַר לֵיהּ אַבַּיֵי [3]Hearing Rav Yosef's argument, **Abaye said to him: Are** the two cases **similar?** [4]**There** in our Mishnah **each of** the neighbors **can** rightly **push off** the owner of the lost access path, as it went through only one of their fields. [5]But **here** the responsibility to give her **a date palm fell on** all **of them.** When their father instructed that his daughter be given a date palm, all of his property was in his possession, and so the obligation to give the daughter her date palm falls equally upon all of the heirs who succeed to that property. Hence, each of the heirs now owes his sister his proportionate share of a date palm. [6]The Gemara asks: **What is their remedy?** How can the sister be given a date palm without one of the brothers suffering a loss? [7]The Gemara explains: The brothers **should give** the sister **a date palm, and then divide once more** all **the** remaining **property,** giving each brother a reevaluated portion of the father's estate.

הַהוּא [8]**A man once said to those** who stood around him as he lay on his deathbed: "I wish to give **a date palm to my daughter."** [9]After **he died,** it turned out that **he left** as part of his estate **half-titles to two of his date palms.** He and a partner had jointly owned two date palms, so that half of each tree fell into his estate. The heirs desired to give the daughter those two halves of a date palm rather than a whole date palm, because of the greater difficulty of caring for two partly-owned trees. [10]When the matter was brought before **Rav Ashi** for a ruling, he **sat and pondered the** following **difficulty:** [11]**Do people call two half-titles to a date palm a date palm, or not?**

לְנִכְסֵי, לָא יָהֲבוּ לָהּ דִּיקְלָא. [1]סָבַר רַב יוֹסֵף לְמֵימַר: [2]הַיְינוּ מַתְנִיתִין.
[3]אֲמַר לֵיהּ אַבַּיֵי: מִי דָּמֵי? [4]הָתָם, כָּל חַד וְחַד מָצֵי מַדְחֵי לֵיהּ. [5]הָכָא, דִּיקְלָא גַּבַּיְיהוּ הוּא. [6]מַאי תַּקַּנְתַּיְיהוּ? [7]לֵיתְבוּ לָהּ דִּיקְלָא, וְלִיהַדְרוּ וְלִיפְלְגוּ מֵרֵישָׁא.
[8]הַהוּא דַּאֲמַר לְהוּ: "דִּיקְלָא לִבְרָת". [9]שְׁכֵיב וְשָׁבֵיק תְּרֵי פַּלְגֵי דְּדִיקְלָא. [10]יְתֵיב רַב אַשִׁי וְקָא קַשְׁיָא לֵיהּ: [11]מִי קָרוּ אֱינָשֵׁי לִתְרֵי פַּלְגֵי דִיקְלֵי דִּיקְלָא, אוֹ לָא?

LITERAL TRANSLATION

the property, [but] did not give her a date palm.
[1]Rav Yosef thought to say: [2]This is our Mishnah.
[3]Abaye said to him: Are they similar? [4]There, each of them can push him off. [5]Here, the date palm was with [all of] them. [6]What is their remedy? [7]They should give her a date palm, and then divide [the estate] again (lit., "from the beginning").
[8][There was] a certain [dying] person who said to them: "A date-palm to my daughter." [9]He died, and he left half-[titles] to halves of a date palm. [10]Rav Ashi sat and had a difficulty: [11]Do people call two halves of a date palm a date palm, or not?

RASHI

היינו מתניתין – דאזלא גבי כל חד וחד, ומצי מדחי לה כרבנן. כל חד וחד מצי מדחי ליה – של מזרח אומר לו: בצפון דרך שלך, ואין לך אצלי כלום. וכן כל אחד ואחד. הכא דקלא גבייהו הוא – שהרי כל הנכסים היו יחד בשעת צוואה, ועל כולם הטיל הדקל, ולא פירש איזהו. ושבק תרי פלגי דדקלא – שהיה לו בשותפות. ושאר דקלים הרבה היו לו. והיתומים היו נותנין לה אותן שני חצאין, שיש טורח בהן יותר.

NOTES

returning the deeds to the previous owners, he is regarded as if he had already done so. *Rid* and *Ritva* say that the argument that the neighbor will return the deeds to their former owners is the theoretical basis for his refusal to accede to the plaintiff's demand. The neighbor's real claim is that, since the four previous owners would have pushed off the owner of the lost access path, he can also push him off, for he purchased all of their rights regarding the property.

תְּרֵי פַּלְגֵי דְּדִיקְלָא **Half-titles to two date palms.** Our commentary follows *Rashi,* who understands that the deceased had also left other date palms, but the heirs

HALAKHAH

divided up his estate without giving anything to that other person, their distribution of the estate has no validity, and so they must give that other person the property that had been promised him, after which they must redivide the estate among themselves, following Abaye. *Rema* (following *Tur* in the name of *Rosh*) writes that if one of the heirs was willing to give that other person the property that had been promised him, and accept monetary compensation from the other heirs, he may do so." (*Rambam, Sefer Mishpatim, Hilkhot Naḥalot* 10:2; *Shulḥan Arukh, Ḥoshen Mishpat* 288:2.)

תְּרֵי פַּלְגֵי דְּדִיקְלָא **Two halves of a date palm.** "If a dying person left instructions that a certain person be given a date palm, and it turned out that he left as part of his estate two halves of a date palm, that other person takes the two halves of a date palm, for two halves of a

TRANSLATION AND COMMENTARY

אֲמַר לֵיהּ [1]**Rav Mordekhai said to Rav Ashi: Avimi from Hagronya said in the name of Rava as follows:** [2]**People** do indeed **call the two half-titles of a date palm a date palm,** and they may give her the two half-owned trees.

[110A] **MISHNAH** הַמּוֹצִיא שְׁטַר [3]**If someone produces a** past-due **promissory note against another person,** and demands that the debt be repaid, [4]**and that** other **person** claims that he has repaid the debt but lost the receipt, and the debtor **produces a bill** of sale proving **that** the creditor **had sold him a field** after the promissory note had already become due, the Tannaim disagree about the law. [5]**Admon says:** We accept the debtor's claim that he repaid the debt, for **he can say** to the creditor: **"If** indeed I still **owed you** the money that I had once borrowed from you, [6]**you should have collected what was yours when you sold me the field.** You should not have sold me the field and accepted my money as payment for the property, but rather you should have collected the money as repayment of the debt. The fact that you sold me the field proves then that my debt must already have been repaid."

וַחֲכָמִים אוֹמְרִים [7]**The Sages** disagree with Admon and **say:** The creditor **was clever when he sold** the debtor **the land,** for he was concerned that the debtor might default on the loan. [8]To make certain he had assets to seize, he sold him the land, and now **he can take it** back **as a pledge,** and collect his debt from it.

[1]אֲמַר לֵיהּ רַב מָרְדְּכַי לְרַב אַשִׁי: הָכִי אֲמַר אֲבִימִי מֵהַגְרוֹנְיָא מִשְּׁמֵיהּ דְּרָבָא: [2]קָרוּ אֱינָשֵׁי לִתְרֵי פַּלְגֵי דִיקְלֵי דִּיקְלָא.

[110A] **משנה** [3]הַמּוֹצִיא שְׁטַר חוֹב עַל חֲבֵרוֹ, [4]וְהַלָּה הוֹצִיא שֶׁמָּכַר לוֹ אֶת הַשָּׂדֶה, [5]אַדְמוֹן אוֹמֵר: יָכוֹל הוּא שֶׁיֹּאמַר: ״אִילּוּ הָיִיתִי חַיָּיב לְךָ, [6]הָיָה לְךָ לְהִפָּרַע אֶת שֶׁלְּךָ כְּשֶׁמָּכַרְתָּ לִי אֶת הַשָּׂדֶה״. [7]וַחֲכָמִים אוֹמְרִים: זֶה הָיָה פִּקֵּחַ שֶׁמָּכַר לוֹ אֶת הַקַּרְקַע, [8]מִפְּנֵי שֶׁהוּא יָכוֹל לְמַשְׁכְּנוֹ.

LITERAL TRANSLATION

[1]Rav Mordekhai said to Rav Ashi: Thus said Avimi from Hagronya in the name of Rava: [2]People call the two half-[titles] to two date palms a date palm.

[110A] **MISHNAH** [3][If] someone produces a bill of indebtedness against another person, [4]and that [person] produces [a deed] that he sold him a field, [5]Admon says: He can say: "If I owed you, [6]you should have collected what was yours when you sold me the field."

[7]And the Sages say: He was clever when he sold him the land, [8]for he can take it as a pledge.

RASHI

קרו אינשי כו׳ — ועל כרחה ידה על התחתונה, שהנכסים בחזקת היתומים, וזו אינה באה עליהם אלא מכח הלוואה. **משנה** והלה הוציא שמכר לו שדה — הלוה הוציא עליו שטר מכירה מאוחרת לשטר ההלואה, ואומר: שטרך מזוייף או פרוע, שאם הייתי חייב לך — לא היית מוכר לי את השדה, שהיה לך לגבות את חובך. זה היה פקח שמכר לו את השדה — לפי שהיה זה מבריח מטלטליו ולא היה לו מהיכן ימשכננו על חובו, ועכשיו יטול את הקרקע.

NOTES

preferred to give the daughter the two half-titles to a date palm, to avoid the extra work of caring for two half-owned trees. *Ritva* (following *Ra'ah*) argues that in such a case the brothers would surely have to give the daughter a full date-palm, for "a date palm" is surely understood to mean "one complete date palm," if indeed the father had one in his possession. Rather, the deceased did not leave any complete date palms, but only two separate halves of date palms. The heirs wished to deprive the daughter of any portion of their father's estate, arguing that "a date palm" does not mean two separate halves of date palms.

שֶׁמָּכַר לוֹ אֶת הַשָּׂדֶה **That he sold him a field.** The Jerusalem Talmud records an Amoraic dispute about whether Admon and the Sages only disagree when the debtor who purchased property from his creditor that was equal in value to his debt, but if the property was worth less the Sages admit to Admon, or do they disagree even where he purchased property that was worth less than his debt.

The Jerusalem Talmud also asks: We understand the position of the Sages if the debtor had no other property. But if the debtor had other property, how can his creditor argue that he only sold him the property so that he would

HALAKHAH

date-palm can be referred to as one date palm, following Avimi from Hagronya. *Rema* writes that even if the deceased also left a whole date palm, the heirs can argue that he had meant that the other person receive the two halves of a date palm (*Tur* following *Rosh;* see also *Sma* who understands that *Bet Yosef* disagrees with this)." (*Rambam, Sefer Kinyan, Hilkhot Zekhiyah* 11:22; *Shulḥan Arukh, Ḥoshen Mishpat* 253:22.)

הַמּוֹצִיא שְׁטַר חוֹב **If someone produces a promissory note.** "If someone produces a promissory note against another person, and that other person produces a bill of sale attesting to the fact that the creditor had sold him a field after his debt had become due — in a place where first the buyer gives the seller the purchase money, and only then does the seller write him a deed of sale, the promissory note is invalid, for the creditor should have accepted the purchase money as repayment of the debt owed him. In such a case the debtor is believed to say that he had repaid his debt, and that he had been given a receipt, but it was subsequently lost. Some authorities (*Rosh)* maintain that the

גמרא [1]מַאי טַעֲמָא דְּרַבָּנַן? [2]שַׁפִּיר קָאָמַר אַדְמוֹן! [3]בְּאַתְרָא דְּיָהֲבִי זוּזֵי, [4]וַהֲדַר כָּתְבֵי שְׁטָרָא, כּוּלֵּי עָלְמָא לָא פְּלִיגִי [5]דְּמָצֵי אָמַר לֵיהּ: [6]״הָיָה לְךָ לִפְרוֹעַ אֶת שֶׁלְּךָ כְּשֶׁמָּכַרְתָּ לִי אֶת הַשָּׂדֶה״. [7]כִּי פְּלִיגִי בְּאַתְרָא דְּכָתְבֵי שְׁטָרָא, וַהֲדַר יָהֲבִי זוּזֵי. [8]אַדְמוֹן סָבַר: אִיבָּעֵי לֵיהּ לְמִימְסַר מוֹדָעָא. [9]וְרַבָּנַן סָבְרִי: [10]חַבְרָךְ חַבְרָא אִית לֵיהּ, וְחַבְרָא דְּחַבְרָךְ חַבְרָא אִית לֵיהּ.

TRANSLATION AND COMMENTARY

GEMARA מַאי טַעֲמָא [1]The Gemara asks: **What is the reasoning of the Rabbis** who disagree with Admon? [2]Surely **Admon said well** that the bill of sale in the debtor's possession proves that his debt was repaid! Why should the creditor have taken the money for the field, given him the field, and then take it back as a pledge?

בְּאַתְרָא דְּיָהֲבִי זוּזֵי [3]The Gemara answers: **In a place where** it is common practice for the buyer to **give** the seller **the** purchase **money,** [4]**and** only **then** does he **write** the buyer **a deed** of sale, **everyone agrees** — both Admon and the Rabbis — **that** we accept the debtor's claim that he had already repaid the debt, [5]for **he can say to the** creditor: "If indeed I still owed you the money that I had once borrowed from you, [6]**you should have collected what was yours** out of the money I gave you **when you sold me the field.**" [7]**They** only **disagree** about **a place where** it is the common practice for the seller **to write** the buyer **a deed** of sale, **and** only **then** does the buyer **give** him **the** purchase **money.** [8]**Admon maintains** that if the debt was still outstanding, the creditor **should have made a declaration** before two witnesses that he was only selling the property to the debtor so that he would be able to take it back as a pledge for his debt. [9]**And the Sages maintain** that the creditor can argue that he had good reason not to make such a notification, for as they say: [10]**Your friend has a friend, and your friend's friend has a friend.** Had he made such a declaration before witnesses, word would quickly have spread to the debtor, who would have canceled the sale. Admon assumes that the debtor is honest, so he protects him from a creditor who may try to collect a debt twice. The Sages assume that the creditor is honest, and they try to protect him from a debtor who may try to refuse to pay his debt.

LITERAL TRANSLATION

GEMARA [1]What is the reason of the Rabbis? [2]Admon said well!

[3]In a place where they give money, [4]and then they write the deed [of sale], everyone agrees (lit., "does not disagree") [5]that he can say to him: [6]"You should have collected what was yours when you sold me the field." [7]They disagree in a place where they write the deed, and then they give money. [8]Admon maintains: He should have made a declaration. [9]And the Sages maintain: [10]Your friend has a friend, and your friend's friend has a friend.

RASHI

גמרא באתרא שהלוקח יהיב זוזי והדר כתבי שטר מכירה כולי עלמא לא פליגי — שהיה למוכר לעכב בחובו המעות שקיבל, ולא יכתוב לו השטר. וכיון שכתבו — הוכיח שאין לו עליו חוב. למימסר מודעא — ואיני מוכר לו אלא שאוכל למשכנו. חברא אית ליה — ויודיעהו, ולא יקח עוד השדה.

NOTES

be able to take it back from him as a pledge and collect his debt from it? It answers by constructing cases where the creditor has reason to collect his debt from the particular property that he had sold to his debtor. *Rivan* suggests that the creditor can argue that he did not wish to rely on the debtor's other property, for it might be mortgaged to somebody else or there might be prior creditors.

אִיבָּעֵי לֵיהּ לְמִימְסַר מוֹדָעָא **He should have made a declaration.** The Rishonim ask: The positions taken by Admon and the Sages in our Mishnah seem to contradict their own positions in an earlier Mishnah (109a) dealing with a person who came to contest another person's title to a field, after having signed a bill of sale affirming that other person's sale of the field to a third party. For in our Mishnah, the Sages maintain that the creditor can argue that he had sold property to the debtor so that he could collect it back from him as a pledge for his debt, and Admon argues that the creditor should have made a declaration to that effect before two witnesses. In the earlier Mishnah, Admon maintains that the plaintiff can argue that he had signed the bill of sale because he preferred to have the property in the hands of the third party. The Sages argue that the plaintiff lost his right to the property, for he should have declared his intentions before two witnesses. *Meiri* explains that in the earlier Mishnah, Admon maintains that the plaintiff did not have to make a declaration, for had he done so, the buyer might not have purchased the property, and he might have suffered a loss.

HALAKHAH

debtor is also believed if he says that the promissory note had been forged. Others (*Ran*) disagree. But in a place where first the seller writes the buyer a deed of sale, and only then does the buyer give the seller the purchase money, the promissory note is valid, for the creditor can argue that he had sold the property to the debtor, so that he would be able to take it back from him as a pledge for the money that was owed him." (*Rambam, Sefer Mishpatim, Hilkhot Malveh VeLoveh* 24:11; *Shulḥan Arukh, Ḥoshen Mishpat* 85:1.)

TRANSLATION AND COMMENTARY

MISHNAH שְׁנַיִם שֶׁהוֹצִיאוּ [1]**If two people produced promissory notes against each other,** and one was dated later than the other, and the party holding the later note claimed that his own debt he had already repaid, the Tannaim disagree about the law. [2]**Admon says:** We accept the claim put forward by the party holding the later bill, for he can say to the other party: **"If indeed I** still **owed you** the money of that first loan, [3]**why did you borrow** money **from me,** rather than take the money I gave you as repayment of the loan."

וַחֲכָמִים אוֹמְרִים [4]**The Sages** disagree with Admon and **say:** We do not accept this argument, but rather **this** party **collects the debt** recorded in his promissory note, [5]**and that** party **collects the debt** recorded in the other promissory note.

GEMARA אִתְּמַר [6]**It was stated** that the Amoraim disagree about the following matter: **If two people produced promissory notes against each other,** [7]**Rav Naḥman said: This** party **collects** the debt recorded in his promissory note, **and that** party **collects** the debt recorded in the other one. [8]**Rav Sheshet** disagreed and **said:** If the debts are for an equal amount **why change bags** of equal weight from one side of the animal to the other? [9]**Rather,** let them cancel each other out, so that **this** party **keeps his** property, **and this** party **keeps** his property.

LANGUAGE

מַטְרָתָא **Bags.** Some derive this word from the Greek μετρητής, *metretes,* meaning "measuring utensils." Thus, Rav Sheshet claimed that two people carrying measuring vessels of equal size gain nothing by changing them off. The Geonim (see also the *Arukh*), however, suggest that מַטְרָתָא means "a saddle with two bags of equal size." Thus, Rav Sheshet meant that one gains nothing by reversing the respective positions of the saddle-bags.

משנה [1]שְׁנַיִם שֶׁהוֹצִיאוּ שְׁטַר חוֹב זֶה עַל זֶה, [2]אַדְמוֹן אוֹמֵר: ״אִילּוּ הָיִיתִי חַיָּיב לְךָ, [3]כֵּיצַד אַתָּה לֹוֶה מִמֶּנִּי״? [4]וַחֲכָמִים אוֹמְרִים: זֶה גּוֹבֶה שְׁטַר חוֹבוֹ, [5]וְזֶה גּוֹבֶה שְׁטַר חוֹבוֹ.

גמרא [6]אִתְּמַר: שְׁנַיִם שֶׁהוֹצִיאוּ שְׁטַר חוֹב זֶה עַל זֶה, [7]רַב נַחְמָן אָמַר: זֶה גּוֹבֶה וְזֶה גּוֹבֶה. [8]רַב שֵׁשֶׁת אָמַר: ״הַפּוּכֵי מַטְרָתָא״ לָמָּה לִי? [9]אֶלָּא זֶה עוֹמֵד בְּשֶׁלּוֹ וְזֶה עוֹמֵד בְּשֶׁלּוֹ.

LITERAL TRANSLATION

MISHNAH [1][If] two people produced bills of indebtedness against one another, [2]Admon says: "If I owed you, [3]how did you borrow from me?" [4]And the Sages say: This one collects his debt, [5]and this one collects his debt.

GEMARA [6]It was stated: [If] two people produced bills of indebtedness against one another, [7]Rav Naḥman said: This one collects and this one collects. [8]Rav Sheshet said: Why "change bags"? [9]Rather, this one stands with his, and this one stands with his.

RASHI

משנה שנים שהוציאו שטר חוב זה על זה — ראובן על שמעון ושמעון על ראובן, שטר שהוציא ראובן מוקדם ושל שמעון מאוחר. אדמון אומר — יכול שמעון לומר לראובן. אילו חייב הייתי לך — כדברי שטרך, כילד אתה לוה ממני אחרי כן? היה לך לתבוע את חובך ממני. זה גובה וזה גובה — אפילו החוב שוה, אין אומרים: יעכב זה מלוה של חברו בשביל מלוה שהלוהו, אלא בית דין יורדין לנכסי כל אחד, ומגבין לשכנגדו את חובו.

גמרא הפוכי מטרתא למה לי — הנושא שני מרצופין של עור ומשאן שוה, מה יתרון לו להפוך של ימין לשמאל ושל שמאל לימין?

NOTES

But in our Mishnah, the creditor was holding a promissory note, and so there was no reason to think that he would have suffered a loss had he made a declaration. Moreover, he should indeed have made a declaration, so that people would not think that he had sold his property because his fortunes had declined, and he needed the money. The Sages maintain that in the earlier Mishnah, since it was the plaintiff himself who signed the bill of sale affirming the other person's sale of the field to a third party, surely he should have made a declaration regarding his intentions. If he did not, he lost his rights to the property. But in our Mishnah, there was no admission on the creditor's part that the debt had been repaid, so there was no reason for him to make a declaration and unnecessarily jeopardize his chances of recovering his money (see also *Tosafot* and *Rashba*).

רַב שֵׁשֶׁת אָמַר **Rav Sheshet said.** The dispute between Rav Naḥman and Rav Sheshet is also cited in the Jerusalem Talmud. There it is explained that Rav Sheshet's position is based on the regulation governing two oxen that gored one another, each causing damage to the other. In such a case, we do not say that each party pays the other the damage which was caused by his animal. Rather the party whose animal caused the greater amount of damage pays the other the excess. Rav Naḥman's position is understood as being based on the opinion of the Sages of our Mishnah, that "this one collects his debt, and this one collects his debt." The Jerusalem Talmud argues that this does not disprove Rav Sheshet's position, for the Sages of the Mishnah only disagree with Admon, who says that only one of the parties collects his debt. Even they agree that the two debts cancel each other out, and it is only the difference between the larger debt and the smaller debt that actually passes from one party to the other.

HALAKHAH

שְׁנַיִם שֶׁהוֹצִיאוּ שְׁטַר חוֹב **If two people produced promissory notes against each other.** "If two people produced notes against each other, the party holding the later note cannot say to the one holding the earlier note that if it were true that he had still owed him money, why did he borrow money from him rather than collect the money that was owed him. But rather each party collects the debt recorded in the promissory note in his hands," following the Sages of the Mishnah. (*Rambam, Sefer Mishpatim, Hilkhot Malveh VeLoveh* 24:10; *Shulḥan Arukh, Ḥoshen Mishpat* 85:3.)

[1]דְּכוּלֵּי עָלְמָא, [2]עִידִּית וְעִידִּית, [3]בֵּינוֹנִית וּבֵינוֹנִית, [4]זִיבּוּרִית וְזִיבּוּרִית — [5]וַדַּאי "הַפּוּכֵי מַטְרָתָא" הוּא. [6]כִּי פְּלִיגִי דְּאִית לֵיהּ לְחַד בֵּינוֹנִית וּלְחַד זִיבּוּרִית. [7]רַב נַחְמָן סָבַר: זֶה גּוֹבֶה וְזֶה גּוֹבֶה. [8]קָסָבַר: בְּשֶׁלּוֹ הֵן שָׁמִין. [9]אָתֵי בַּעַל זִיבּוּרִית וְגָבֵי לֵיהּ לְבֵינוֹנִית, [10]דַּהֲוָה גַּבֵּיהּ עִידִּית, [11]וַאֲתָא הַהוּא [12]וְשָׁקֵיל זִיבּוּרִית. [13]וְרַב שֵׁשֶׁת אָמַר: הַפּוּכֵי מַטְרָתָא לָמָּה לִי? [14]קָסָבַר: בְּשֶׁל כָּל אָדָם הֵן שָׁמִין.

LITERAL TRANSLATION

[1]According to everyone, [2]land of the best quality and land of the best quality, [3]land of intermediate quality and land of intermediate quality, [4]land of the poorest quality and land of the poorest quality — [5]it is surely "changing bags." [6]They disagree when one has land of intermediate quality and one has land of the poorest quality. [7]Rav Naḥman maintains: This one collects and this one collects. [8]He maintains: They assess according to his. [9]The owner of the land of the poorest quality comes and collects land of intermediate quality, [10]which is for him land of the best quality, [11]and the other one comes [12]and collects land of the poorest quality. [13]And Rav Sheshet said: Why change bags? [14]He maintains: They assess according to everybody.

TRANSLATION AND COMMENTARY

דְּכוּלֵּי עָלְמָא [1]The Gemara now clarifies the issue that is in dispute. The quality of land is divided into three legal categories: Excellent, intermediate, and poor. If the law requires a person to make a payment of money, and he is unable to do so, his land may be confiscated as payment. The type of land that may be impounded depends upon the type of obligation. In the case of a debt, if the debtor has land of different qualities, his creditor is entitled to collect his debt from the land of intermediate quality. Now, **according to everyone** — both Rav Naḥman and Rav Sheshet — [2]if the one party had only **land of the best quality and** the other party also had only **land of the best quality**, [3]or if the one party had only **land of intermediate quality and** the other party also had only **land of intermediate quality**, [4]or if the one party had only **land of the poorest quality and** the other party also had only **land of the poorest quality**, the court will not confiscate property from each of the parties and hand it over to the other, [5]for **surely** that would be tantamount to **changing bags** of equal weight from one side of the animal to the other. [6]**They** only **disagree when one** party **had land of intermediate quality and the other** party **had land of the poorest quality.** [7]**Rav Naḥman says** that **this** party **collects** his debt **and that** party **collects** his debt. [8]**He maintains** that **we assess** each **debtor's own** property, and determine the quality of each parcel of land in relation to all of his holdings. [9]Therefore, **the owner of the land of the poorest quality** in relation to all the land in that region **may come and collect** his debt from **the land of intermediate quality** belonging to his debtor. [10]**For him** it is **land of the best quality,** since the rest of his property is land of the poorest quality. [11]**Therefore** the **other** party cannot **come and** seize it back from him as payment of the debt. [12]Rather he must **collect** his debt from the **land of the poorest quality** in his debtor's possession. Hence, the party who started with land of the poorest quality now has land of intermediate quality, and the party who started with land of intermediate quality now has land of the poorest quality. [13]**Rav Sheshet** disagrees and **says: Why change bags** of equal weight from one side of the animal to the other? [14]**He maintains** that **we** determine which portion of each debtor's land is land of the best quality and which portion is land of intermediate quality by **assessing** the property belonging to **all people** in the region. Thus, a creditor is entitled to collect land belonging to his debtor if it is considered land of intermediate quality in that region, even if it is the best land the debtor owns. Therefore, there is no reason to allow

RASHI

בשלו הן שמין – מה שאמרו חכמים: בעל חוב בבינונית – בקרקעות הלוה שמין. שאם יש ללוה שדה שהיא בינונית לכל אדם, ואצלו היא עידית שאשר שדותיו גרועות הימנה – אין בעל חוב גובה הימנה. ורב ששת סבר בשל כל אדם הן שמין – וסוף סוף, כי הדר אתי האי למיגבי – בינונית שהיתה שלו שקיל.

NOTES

עִידִּית וְעִידִּית **Land of the best quality and land of the best quality.** Not only do Rav Naḥman and Rav Sheshet agree when each debtor has equivalent quality land, but even if one creditor had money to pay his debt, and the

HALAKHAH

עִידִּית וְעִידִּית **Land of the best quality and land of the best quality.** "If two people produced promissory notes against each other for the same amount, and they each had land of the best quality, or they each had land of intermediate quality, or they each had land of the poorest quality, or one had land of the best quality or land of intermediate quality, and the other had land of the poorest quality, or one had land of intermediate quality and land

TRANSLATION AND COMMENTARY

the two parties to collect their debts one from the other. [1]For **in the end,** the debtor who delivered intermediate quality land to cover his debt, will **come** and **take** back **his own land of intermediate quality.** Both parties will then end up with exactly as they started.

וּלְרַב נַחְמָן [2]The Gemara questions this explanation: Now we have explained the disagreement between **Rav Naḥman** and Rav Sheshet where one creditor has land of poor quality and the other land of intermediate quality. But **why,** according to **Rav Naḥman, do we say that the owner of the land of the poorest quality came first,** so that he collects the land of intermediate quality belonging to his debtor, who then collects his debt from the land of the poorest to cover what is owed to him, so that the two end up with different holdings? [3]Why not say that **the owner of the land of intermediate quality came first and collects** from his debtor **land of the poorest quality,** for the debtor has no other property from which the debt can be collected. The creditor's own land of intermediate quality is now considered land of the best quality, relative to the rest of his land, so that when the second debtor collects his debt, [4]he must **collect** back **from him** the same land of the poorest quality which had earlier been seized from him. Thus, according to Rav Naḥman, both parties would end up as they started, and the argument still remains: Why change bags of equal weight from one side of the animal to the other?

לָא צְרִיכָא [5]This analysis leads to the conclusion that the dispute between Rav Naḥman and Rav Sheshet **only applies if** the owner of the land of the poorest quality **presented his claim first.**

סוֹף סוֹף [6]The Gemara objects: What difference does it make who presented his claim first? **In the end, when** they **collect** their debts, **they come together.**

אֶלָּא [7]The Gemara answers: **Rather,** the dispute between Rav Naḥman and Rav Sheshet **only applies when one** party **has land of the best quality as well as land of intermediate quality,** [8]**and** the other party **has** only **land of the poorest quality.** [9]**This master** — Rav Naḥman — says that each collects the debt that is owed him, because he **maintains** that **we assess** the quality of **the debtor's** property **according** to the property he possesses. Therefore, no matter which party collects his debt first, the owner of the land of the poorest quality gains. For if he collects first, he collects land of intermediate quality. Then, when the other party

[1]סוֹף סוֹף, כִּי אָתֵי הַהוּא, בֵּינוֹנִית דְּנַפְשֵׁיהּ קָשָׁקֵיל.
[2]וּלְרַב נַחְמָן, מַאי חָזֵית דְּאָתֵי בַּעַל זִיבּוּרִית בְּרֵישָׁא? [3]לֵיתֵי בַּעַל בֵּינוֹנִית בְּרֵישָׁא וְלִיגְבֵּי זִיבּוּרִית, [4]וְלִיהֲדַר וְלִיגְבֵּי נִיהֲלֵיהּ!
[5]לָא צְרִיכָא דְּקָדֵים תְּבָעֵיהּ.
[6]סוֹף סוֹף, כִּי אָתוּ לְמִגְבֵּי, בַּהֲדֵי הֲדָדֵי קָאָתוּ!
[7]אֶלָּא, לָא צְרִיכָא, דְּאִית לֵיהּ לְחַד עִידִּית וּבֵינוֹנִית, [8]וְאִית לֵיהּ לְחַד זִיבּוּרִית. [9]מָר סָבַר: בְּשֶׁלּוֹ

LITERAL TRANSLATION

[1]In the end, when he comes, he takes [back] his own land of intermediate quality.

[2]And according to Rav Naḥman, what [reason] do you see that the owner of the land of the poorest quality comes first? [3]Let the owner of the land of intermediate quality come first and collect land of the poorest quality, [4]and then [the other] would collect it from him!

[5]It was only necessary where he claimed from him first.

[6][But] in the end, when they come to collect, they come together!

[7]Rather, it was only necessary when one has land of the best quality and land of intermediate quality, [8]and one has land of the poorest quality. [9]One master maintains:

RASHI

ולרב נחמן — נהי נמי דבשלו הן שמין, מאי חזית כו׳. **סוף סוף כי אתו למיגבי בהדי הדדי אתו** — שהרי שניהן הוציאו שטרותיהן בבית דין. **מר סבר בשלו הן שמין** — ולאו הפוכי מטרתא הוא. דממה נפשך איכא רווחא לבעל זיבורית, דאי חבריה

NOTES

other had only land there would be also a canceling out of the debts. That is because once the party who did not have money receives the money from the other party, he can recover his land, for any land that is confiscated for payment of a debt can forever be redeemed by the original owner (*Rosh*).

HALAKHAH

of the poorest quality, and the other had land of the poorest quality, each party keeps the property that is in his possession," following Rav Sheshet. (*Rambam, Sefer Mishpatim, Hilkhot Malveh VeLoveh* 24:10; *Shulḥan Arukh, Ḥoshen Mishpat* 85:3.)

דְּאִית לֵיהּ לְחַד עִידִּית וּבֵינוֹנִית Where one has land of the best quality and land of intermediate quality. "If one party had land of the best quality and land of intermediate quality, and the other party had only land of the poorest quality, this one collects from land of intermediate quality, and the other one collects from land of the poorest quality," following Rav Naḥman against Rav Sheshet. (*Rambam, Sefer Mishpatim, Hilkhot Malveh VeLoveh* 24:10; *Shulḥan Arukh, Ḥoshen Mishpat* 85:3.)

בְּשֶׁלּוֹ הֵן שָׁמִין They assess according to his. "If the debtor now has land of intermediate quality and land of the

TRANSLATION AND COMMENTARY

collects his debt, he can only collect land of the poorest quality. In relation to all his debtor's property, the land of intermediate quality that he had collected is regarded as land of the best quality, from which the creditor cannot collect. Conversely, if the owner of the land of the best and intermediate quality collects first, he collects land of the poorest quality. Then when the other party collects his debt from him, he collects the land of intermediate quality which he is entitled to. [1] **And the** other **master** — Rav Sheshet — says that each party keeps the property that is his, because he **maintains** that **we assess** property in relation to that belonging to all people in the region. Therefore, if the owner of the property of the poorest quality collected his debt first, he would collect property of intermediate quality, and then when the other party collected his debt from him, he would take back the land of intermediate quality.

תְּנַן [2]The Gemara raises an objection against Rav Sheshet: **We have learned** in our Mishnah: **"The Sages** disagree with Admon and **say:** If two people produced promissory notes against each other, [3]**this one collects** his debt, **and that one collects** his debt," against Rav Sheshet who maintains that the two debts cancel each other out!

תִּרְגְּמָהּ רַב נַחְמָן [4]**Rav Naḥman** himself **explained** the Mishnah **according to Rav Sheshet,** for the Mishnah is dealing with a case **in which the one** party **borrowed** money **for ten years,** [5]**and the other** party borrowed money **for** only **five** years. In such a case even Rav Sheshet agrees that we cannot invoke the argument why change bags of equal weight from one side of the animal to the other.

הֵיכִי דָּמֵי [6]The Gemara wishes to clarify the matter: **How precisely do you visualize the case?** [7]**If you say** that **the first** party borrowed money **for** a period of **ten years,** [8]**and** then at the end of the first year **the second** party borrowed money back **for** a period of **five** years, there is a difficulty, [9]for **could Admon say about this** that the first party can say to the second: [10]**"If** indeed I still **owed you** the money that I had borrowed from you, **why did you borrow** money **from me,** rather than collect what I owed you?" [11]**Surely, the time** for repayment by the first party **had not yet arrived,** and the second party could not have collected his debt, but rather he had to borrow the money from the first party!

הֵן שָׁמִין. [1]וּמָר סָבַר: בְּשֶׁל כָּל אָדָם הֵן שָׁמִין.

[2]תְּנַן: "וַחֲכָמִים אוֹמְרִים: [3]זֶה גּוֹבֶה וְזֶה גּוֹבֶה".

[4]תַּרְגְּמָהּ רַב נַחְמָן אַלִּיבָּא דְּרַב שֵׁשֶׁת: כְּגוֹן שֶׁלָּוָה זֶה לְעֶשֶׂר, [5]וְזֶה לְחָמֵשׁ.

[6]הֵיכִי דָּמֵי? [7]אִילֵימָא רִאשׁוֹן לְעֶשֶׂר, [8]וְשֵׁנִי לְחָמֵשׁ — [9]בְּהָא לֵימָא אַדְמוֹן: [10]"אִילּוּ הָיִיתִי חַיָּיב לְךָ, כֵּיצַד אַתָּה לֹוֶה מִמֶּנִּי"? [11]הָא לָא מְטָא זִמְנֵיהּ!

LITERAL TRANSLATION

They assess according to [the debtor]. [1]And the other master maintains: They assess according to everybody.

[2]We have learned: "And the Sages say: [3]This one collects and this one collects."

[4]Rav Naḥman explained it according to Rav Sheshet: As when this one borrowed for ten [years], [5]and this one for five.

[6]How do we visualize the case (lit., "what is it like")? [7]If you say: The first one for ten [years], [8]and the second for five — [9]could Admon say about this: [10]"If I owed you, how did you borrow from me?" [11]Surely his time [to repay] did not [yet] arrive!

RASHI

קדיש ברישא וגבי — איכא גביה עידית ובינונית וזיבורית, ומגבי להאיך בינונית. ואי איהו קדים וגבי בינונית — הויא גביה עידית, ומגבי לחבריה זיבורית. ומר סבר בשל עולם הן שמין — וכיון דבהדדי אתו למיגבי, יהבי בית דין בינונית לבעל זיבורית ברישא, והדר גבי לה מיניה — הלכך הפוכי מטרתא הוא. תנן זה גובה וזה גובה — נהי נמי דאית להו לרבנן ששניהם השטרות כשרים יעמוד זה בשלו וזה בשלו, אלמא שמע מינה: בשלו הן שמין, ולאו הפוכי הוא. כגון שלוה זה לעשר — שלא יוכל הנושה לתובעו עד עשר שנים, דאיכא רווחא דהמתנה. אילימא ראשון לעשר — ושני בא אצלו לסוף שנה, ולוה לחמש. בהא לימא אדמון כו׳ הא לא מטא זמניה — ונוח היה לו לזה שהלוהו ויתבענו לסוף חמש, ועדיין יהא חובו מעוכב בידו עד השלמת עשר, משיהא פורע לו בחובו.

HALAKHAH

poorest quality, but at the time of the loan he also had land of the best quality, he must pay his debt with land of intermediate quality. But if he never had land of the best quality, he may pay his debt with land of the poorest quality, for in determining from which land to collect a debt, we assess the debtor's own property, following Rav Naḥman." (*Rambam, Sefer Mishpatim, Hilkhot Malveh VeLoveh* 19:4; *Shulḥan Arukh, Ḥoshen Mishpat* 102:4.)

זֶה לְעֶשֶׂר, וְזֶה לְחָמֵשׁ **This one for ten years, and this one for five.** "If two people produced promissory notes against each other, and the later promissory note was dated prior to the due date of the earlier promissory note, each party collects the debt recorded in the note that is in his hands. But if the later promissory note was dated only after the earlier promissory note had become due, the party holding the later note can argue that if the earlier note were really valid, his debtor should have collected the note rather than borrow from him. According to *Shakh* (following the majority of Rishonim), in all cases each party collects the debt recorded in the note that he is holding." (*Shulḥan Arukh, Ḥoshen Mishpat* 85:3.)

LITERAL TRANSLATION

[1]Rather, the first one for five [years], [2]and the second for ten [years]. [3]How do we visualize the case? [4]If his time [to repay] had arrived, [5]what is the reason of the Sages? [6]And if his time had not [yet] arrived — [7]surely his time had not arrived, [8]and what is the reason of Admon?

[9]It was only necessary where he came on the day that completed the five [years]. [10]One Sage maintains: A person is likely to borrow for a day. [11]And the other Sage maintains: A person is not likely to borrow for a day.

[12]Rami bar Ḥama says: Here we are dealing with orphans, [13]for orphans collect, [14]but [others] do not collect from them.

[1]אֶלָּא, רִאשׁוֹן לְחָמֵשׁ, [2]וְשֵׁנִי לְעֶשֶׂר. [3]הֵיכִי דָּמֵי? [4]אִי דִּמְטָא זִמְנֵיהּ, [5]מַאי טַעֲמָא דְּרַבָּנַן? [6]וְאִי דְּלָא מְטָא זִמְנֵיהּ — [7]הָא לָא מְטָא זִמְנֵיהּ, [8]וּמַאי טַעֲמָא דְּאַדְמוֹן?

[9]לָא צְרִיכָא, דַּאֲתָא בְּהַהוּא יוֹמָא דְּמִשְׁלַם חָמֵשׁ. [10]מָר סָבַר: עָבִיד אִינִישׁ דְּיָזֵיף לְיוֹמֵיהּ. [11]וּמָר סָבַר: לָא עָבִיד אִינִישׁ דְּיָזֵיף לְיוֹמֵיהּ.

[12]רָמִי בַּר חָמָא אָמַר: הָכָא בְּיַתְמֵי עָסְקִינַן, [13]דְּיַתְמֵי מִיגְבָּא גָּבֵי, [14]אַגְבּוּיֵי לָא מַגְבִּינַן מִינַּיְיהוּ.

TRANSLATION AND COMMENTARY

אֶלָּא [1]**Rather, the first** party must have borrowed money **for five years,** [2]**and** later **the second** party borrowed money back **for ten years.** But this too requires clarification: [3]**How** precisely **do you visualize the case?** There appears to be a flaw in both positions. [4]**If the time** when the first party was obligated to repay his debt **had** already **arrived** when the second party borrowed the money from him, [5]**what is the reasoning of the Sages** who disagree with Admon? If the first party had really not yet repaid his debt, why would the second party have borrowed the money from him, rather than taking it as repayment for the money that he was owed? [6]**And if the time** when the debt was due **had not** yet **arrived** when the second party borrowed the money back from him, [7]**surely the time** when the first party was obligated to repay his debt **had not** yet **arrived** either? Therefore the second party could not yet have collected the money that was owed him! [8]**What** then **is the reasoning of Admon** who says that the second loan proves that the first loan must have been repaid?

לָא צְרִיכָא [9]The Gemara answers: The dispute between Admon and the Sages **only applies when** the second party **came** and borrowed money from the first party **on the very day that completed the five-year** period for which the first party had received his loan from the second party. [10]**One Sage,** the Rabbis, **maintains** that **a person is** indeed **likely to borrow** money even if he only needs it **for a** single **day.** Therefore each of the parties may collect the debt recorded in the promissory note in his possession. [11]**And this Sage,** Admon, **maintains** that **a person is not likely to borrow** money if he only needs it **for a day.**

רָמִי בַּר חָמָא [12]The Gemara now cites an alternative explanation: **Rami bar Ḥama says: Here** in the Mishnah **we are dealing with orphans** who seek to collect money that was owed to their father. [13]**The orphans** may indeed **collect** their father's debt from his debtor's property, [14]**but** if the deceased did not leave his heirs any land, the other party **may not collect** his debt **from them,** for the movable goods which an heir inherits are not charged to the debts of the deceased. In this case, Rav Sheshet's argument why change bags of equal weight from one side of the animal to the other, does not apply.

RASHI

אי דמטא זמניה — אם שלמו חמשת השנים כשבא המלוה ללוות מן הלוה. **מאי טעמא דרבנן** — דמכשרי שטרו של מלוה ראשון? הרי הגיע זמנו והיה לו לתובעו ולא ללוות, ד"עבד לוה לאיש מלוה". **לא צריכא דאתא** — לגביה ולוה הימנו ביומא דמשלם חמש. **ביתמי עסקינן** — שמת אחד מהן והיתומים באים ותובעים, ואין להם קרקע שיהא שכנגדם גובה שטרו מהן, דלא משעבדי מטלטלי דיתמי לבעל חוב. **הכי גרסינן:** ולוקמה דאית להו ליתמי זיבורית ואית ליה לדידיה עידית ובינונית דאי נמי בשל כל אדם הן שמין אין נפרעים כו'.

NOTES

אִי דִּמְטָא זִמְנֵיהּ **If his time arrived.** *Ramban* asks: Why not say that we are dealing here with a place where it is the common practice to first draw up the promissory note, and then hand over the loan money? In that case, the second party could not have kept the money received from the first party in payment of the debt, for he had already given him a promissory note obligating himself to return the money to him. This is why the Sages allow both to collect. He answers that if so, our Mishnah would have been unnecessary, for the law regarding that case could have been derived from the previous Mishnah (see also *Meiri*).

HALAKHAH

בְּהַהוּא יוֹמָא דְּמִשְׁלַם חָמֵשׁ **On that day that completed the five years.** "If two people produced promissory notes against each other, each party collects the debt recorded in the note that he is holding, even if the later loan had been extended a day before the earlier loan became due." (*Shulḥan Arukh, Ḥoshen Mishpat* 85:3.)

TRANSLATION AND COMMENTARY

וְהָא זֶה [1]The Gemara notes: **But surely** the Mishnah **states:** "The Sages say: If two people produced promissory notes against one another, [2]**this one collects** his debt, **and that one collects** his debt," while according to Rami bar Ḥama's explanation, only the orphans collect their debt!

זֶה גּוֹבֶה [3]The Gemara responds: The Mishnah means to say as follows: **This** party, the orphans, **collect** their debt, **and the other** party **is fit to collect,** [4]**but** the orphans **do not have** any property from which to collect.

זֶה גּוֹבֶה [5]**Rava said: There are two arguments against this explanation.** [6]**First,** the Mishnah **states: "This one collects** his debt, **and that one collects** his debt." The plain sense of these words is that both parties actually collect their debts. [7]**And furthermore, let** the other party **give the orphans land** in payment of the debt that he owed to their father, [8]**and then let him collect** that land back **from them** as payment for the debt that their father owed him, [9]as **Rav Naḥman** said. **For Rav Naḥman said in the name of Rabbah bar Avuha:** [10]**If orphans collected land** as payment **for a debt which had been owed to their father,** their father's own **creditor** may **then collect** that land **from them.**

קַשְׁיָא [11]**This is** indeed **difficult** according to Rami bar Ḥama's explanation.

וְלוֹקְמַהּ דְּאִית לְהוּ [12]**But let us establish** the Mishnah according to Rami bar Ḥama as dealing with **orphans** who **have land of the poorest quality,** [13]**and** the other party who **has land of the best quality and land of intermediate quality.** [14]**For** in such a case **the orphans** may **go and collect** the debt that had been owed their father from **land of intermediate quality,** [15]**and** the orphans themselves may **give land of the poorest quality** in payment for their father's debt. [16]**Even if we** determine which portion of the debtor's land is of the best quality and which is of intermediate quality by **assessing** the property belonging to **everyone** (so that both parties should be entitled to land of intermediate quality), the law is that if a debtor died, [17]his creditor may **only collect** his debt **from his heirs' property from land of the poorest quality.** It is a meritorious deed for heirs to pay the debts of the deceased, and if they inherit land, which is mortgaged to the creditor, they may be compelled to do so. However, those debts may be recovered only from the poorest quality land. Thus, even according to Rami bar Ḥama's explanation of the Mishnah, one of the parties died, and his heirs seek to collect money that had been owed their father, the Mishnah can be understood according to its plain sense that both parties collect their debts. Even Rav Sheshet would agree that the parties collect land of different qualities, so the debts do not cancel each other out.

[1]״וְהָא זֶה גּוֹבֶה וְזֶה גּוֹבֶה״ [2]קָתָנֵי!
[3]זֶה גּוֹבֶה, וְזֶה רָאוּי לִגְבּוֹת, [4]וְאֵין לוֹ.
[5]אָמַר רָבָא, שְׁתֵּי תְּשׁוּבוֹת בַּדָּבָר: [6]חֲדָא, ״דְּזֶה גּוֹבֶה וְזֶה גּוֹבֶה״ קָתָנֵי. [7]וְעוֹד, לַגְבֵּינְהוּ אַרְעָא לְיָתְמֵי, [8]וְלִיהֲדַר וְלִיגְבִּינְהוּ מִינַּיְיהוּ, [9]כִּדְרַב נַחְמָן. דְּאָמַר רַב נַחְמָן אָמַר רַבָּה בַּר אֲבוּהּ: [10]יְתוֹמִים שֶׁגָּבוּ קַרְקַע בְּחוֹבַת אֲבִיהֶן, בַּעַל חוֹב חוֹזֵר וְגוֹבֶה אוֹתָן מֵהֶן.
[11]קַשְׁיָא!
[12]וְלוֹקְמַהּ דְּאִית לְהוּ לְיָתְמֵי זִיבּוּרִית, [13]וְאִית לֵיהּ לְדִידֵיהּ עִידִית וּבֵינוֹנִית, [14]דְּאָזְלֵי יָתְמֵי גָּבוּ בֵּינוֹנִית, [15]וּמַגְבּוּ לֵיהּ זִיבּוּרִית, [16]דְּאִי נַמִּי בְּשֶׁל כָּל אָדָם הֵן שָׁמִין, [17]הָא אֵין נִפְרָעִין מִנִּכְסֵי יְתוֹמִים אֶלָּא מִזִּיבּוּרִית!

LITERAL TRANSLATION

[1]But surely, it states: [2]"This one collects and this one collects"!

[3]This one collects, and this one is fit to collect, [4]but he does not get.

[5]Rava said: [There are] two arguments against (lit., "answer to") this matter. [6]First, it states: "This one collects and this one collects." [7]And furthermore, let him give land to the orphans [for his debt], [8]and then let him collect from them, [9]like Rav Naḥman. For Rav Naḥman said in the name of Rabbah bar Avuha: [10][If] orphans collected land for their father's debt, a creditor then collects it from them.

[11]It is difficult!

[12]But let us establish it if the orphans have land of the poorest quality, [13]and he has land of the best quality and land of intermediate quality, [14]for the orphans go [and] collect land of intermediate quality, [15]and give him land of the poorest quality, [16]for even if they assess according to all people, [17]surely one only collects from the property of orphans' land of the poorest quality!

NOTES

וְלוֹקְמַהּ **But let us establish it.** Some understand that the Gemara is asking why not establish the Mishnah according to Rami bar Ḥama as dealing with orphans who have land of the poorest quality, and the other party has land of the best and of intermediate quality. In such a case, Rava's questions would fall away. Others understand that this is a question posed to Rami bar Ḥama himself: Why did he not explain the Mishnah in this manner (see *Rivan, Ritva*)? Some

הָנֵי מִילֵּי הֵיכָא דְּלָא תָּפַס.[1] אֲבָל הֵיכָא דְּתָפַס, תָּפַס.[2]

מִשְׁנָה שָׁלֹשׁ אֲרָצוֹת[3] לְנִשּׂוּאִין: יְהוּדָה, וְעֵבֶר הַיַּרְדֵּן, וְהַגָּלִיל. אֵין מוֹצִיאִין מֵעִיר[4] לְעִיר, וּמִכְּרַךְ לִכְרַךְ.[5] אֲבָל[6] בְּאוֹתָהּ הָאָרֶץ מוֹצִיאִין מֵעִיר

LITERAL TRANSLATION

[1] These words [apply] where he did not seize. [2] But where he seized, he seized.

MISHNAH [3] There are three regions regarding marriage: Judea, Transjordan, and Galilee. [4] They do not take out from [one] town to [another] town, [5] or from [one] city to [another] city [in different regions]. [6] But in the same region they take out from town

TRANSLATION AND COMMENTARY

הָנֵי מִילֵּי [1] However, the Gemara rejects this suggestion. True, there is a rule that payment of creditors from the estate of a deceased party is done with the poorest quality land. However, **this rule only applies** if the **creditor had not seized** land of intermediate quality belonging to the debtor before he died. [2] **But where he had** previously **seized** such land, **the seizure is valid.** In our case, the land of intermediate quality that the debtor has to give the orphans for his own debt was his during the father's lifetime, and therefore it can be considered to have been "seized" by him to secure the debt that the father owed him. Therefore, after having given this land of intermediate quality to the orphans in payment of his debt, the father's debtor would be allowed to claim this same land back, as it had already been in his possession. Thus Rami bar Ḥama's explanation that our Mishnah deals with orphans cannot accord with Rav Sheshet, for here too the two parties could not collect their debts from one another as no net change of property would occur.

MISHNAH שָׁלֹשׁ אֲרָצוֹת לְנִשּׂוּאִין [3] Eretz Israel is considered as **three** separate **regions regarding marriage: Judea, Transjordan, and Galilee.** If a man marries a woman in one of those regions (and he himself came from that region), he cannot compel her to go and live with him in one of the other two regions. [4] The husband **cannot compel** his wife **to move** from one region to another, even **from** a **town** in the one region **to** a **town** in the other region, [5] **or from** a **city** in the one region **to** a **city** in the other region. [6] **But within the same region,** the husband **can compel** his wife **to move** with him **from the town** in which they had been

RASHI

משנה שלש ארצות לנשואין — שלש ארצות הן בארץ ישראל חלוקות לענין נשואי אשה, שאם נשא אשה באחת מהן אינו יכול לכופה לילך אחריו מארץ אל ארץ. אין מוציאין — מזו לזו לא מעיר לעיר ולא מכרך לכרך. כרך גדול מעיר, והוא מקום שווקים, ומכל סביביו באים שם לסחורה, וכל דבר מצוי בו.

NOTES

ask: Why not say that the Mishnah is referring to orphans who are still minors? In such a case, all agree that nothing may be collected from them until they reach majority. *Ritva* answers that this would be essentially the same as the case of the debtors, one of whom borrowed for five years, and the other borrowed for ten. *Rabbenu Crescas Vidal* answers that even in such a case we would say that if the creditor seized intermediate quality property from the orphans, his seizure is valid.

יְהוּדָה, וְעֵבֶר הַיַּרְדֵּן, וְהַגָּלִיל **Judea, Transjordan, and Galilee.** *Tosafot Yom Tov* asks: Why does the Mishnah separate between Judea and Galilee inserting Transjordan between them? *Rashash* answers that Judea and Galilee were separated by a region inhabited by the Samaritans, so that Judea was more closely connected to Transjordan than to Galilee.

אֵין מוֹצִיאִין **They do not take out.** Our commentary follows *Rashi* and most of the Rishonim, who maintain that the Mishnah is dealing here with the question of whether a man can compel his wife to leave her family and birthplace. *Rabbenu Tam* understands that it is obvious that a woman cannot be compelled to move to another region. First, travel is more difficult for a woman than for a man, and so it would be almost impossible for her to visit her family from a different region. Moreover, the verse states (Genesis 2:24): "That is why a man leaves his father and his mother, and cleaves to his wife." Rather, the Mishnah is asking whether a woman can compel her husband to leave his home and move to her country.

HALAKHAH

שָׁלֹשׁ אֲרָצוֹת לְנִשּׂוּאִין **There are three countries regarding marriage.** "The world is divided into different countries regarding marriage and the possibility of one spouse compelling the other to move. Eretz Israel is divided into three countries for this purpose: Judea, Transjordan, and Galilee. *Rivash* explains that countries are defined for this purpose as territories with their own political or linguistic identity." (*Rambam, Sefer Nashim, Hilkhot Ishut* 13:16; *Shulḥan Arukh, Even HaEzer* 75:1.)

אֵין מוֹצִיאִין **They do not take out.** "If a man married a woman from another country, he can compel her to return with him to his own country, for we assume that he married her on that condition, even if he did not stipulate so explicitly. But if he married a woman from his own country, he cannot compel her to move with him to another country. He can, however, compel her to move with him from one city to another or from one village to another within the same country. *Rema* writes that a woman can also compel her husband to move with her from one city to the next within the same country. According to some authorities (*Terumat HaDeshen*), a man who is unable to support himself in one place can compel his wife to move with him to a place where he can support himself. Other authorities (*Bet Yosef* and others) disagree." (*Rambam, Sefer Nashim, Hilkhot Ishut* 13:17; *Shulḥan Arukh, Even HaEzer* 75:1.)

TRANSLATION AND COMMENTARY

living to another town, [1]or from the city in which they had been residing to another city. [110B] [2]But even within the same region, the husband cannot compel his wife to move from a town to a city, nor from the city to a town, for there are certain advantages to living in a town and other advantages to living in a city, and the woman cannot be obliged to give up those advantages against her will. [3]The husband can compel his wife to move with him from an unpleasant dwelling to a more pleasant dwelling, [4]but he cannot compel her to move with him from a more pleasant dwelling to an unpleasant dwelling. [5]Rabban Shimon ben Gamliel disagrees and says: The husband cannot even compel his wife to move with him from an unpleasant dwelling to a more pleasant dwelling, [6]for a pleasant dwelling tries the body of someone who is not used to pleasant surroundings. Any change can be detrimental to a person's physical health.

GEMARA בִּשְׁלָמָא [7]The Gemara asks: **Granted** that a husband cannot compel his wife to move with him **from the city to a town,** even if the two are in the same region, [8]**for in a** big **city** a woman **can find all the things** that she might want, **whereas in a** smaller **town** she can**not find all the things** that she needs. [9]**But what is the reason** that a husband cannot compel his wife to move with him **from the town to a** larger city?

לְעִיר, [1]וּמִכְּרַךְ לִכְרַךְ [110B] [2]אֲבָל לֹא מֵעִיר לִכְרַךְ וְלֹא מִכְּרַךְ לְעִיר. [3]מוֹצִיאִין מִנָּוֶה הָרָעָה לַנָּוֶה הַיָּפָה, [4]אֲבָל לֹא מִנָּוֶה הַיָּפָה לַנָּוֶה הָרָעָה. [5]רַבָּן שִׁמְעוֹן בֶּן גַּמְלִיאֵל אוֹמֵר: אַף לֹא מִנָּוֶה רָעָה לְנָוֶה יָפָה, [6]מִפְּנֵי שֶׁהַנָּוֶה הַיָּפָה בּוֹדֵק.

גמרא [7]בִּשְׁלָמָא מִכְּרַךְ לְעִיר — [8]דְּבִכְרַךְ שְׁכִיחִי כָּל מִילֵּי, בָּעִיר לָא שְׁכִיחִי כָּל מִילֵּי. [9]אֶלָּא מֵעִיר לִכְרַךְ, מַאי טַעֲמָא?

LITERAL TRANSLATION

to town, [1]and from city to city, [110B] [2]but not from town to city, nor from city to town. [3]They take out [their wives] from an unpleasant dwelling to a pleasant dwelling, [4]but not from a pleasant dwelling to an unpleasant dwelling. [5]Rabban Shimon ben Gamliel says: Not even from an unpleasant dwelling to a pleasant dwelling, [6]for a pleasant dwelling tries (lit., "tests") [the body].

GEMARA [7]Granted from a city to a town — [8]for in a city all things are found, [and] in a town not all things are found. [9]But from a town to a city, what is the reason?

RASHI

אבל לא מעיר לכרך – בגמרא מפרש טעמא. **שהנוה היפה בודק** – את הגוף, למי שבא מנוה רע, ומתוך כך חלאים באים עליו.

NOTES

נָוֶה Dwelling. *Talmidei Rabbenu Yonah* understand that the term נָוֶה refers to a tiny settlement with very sparse population. Thus, the types of settlements in descending order of size are as follows: city, כְּרַךְ — the largest type of settlement usually having a wall; town, עִיר — smaller than a city, but still having a relatively large population; village, כְּפָר — smaller than a town; and dwelling-place, נָוֶה — the smallest of all. But judging from the context, the term נָוֶה might have a more general meaning — any dwelling-place. Some understand that "a pleasant dwelling" refers to a place where prices are low, and merchandise is readily available. But it can refer to any place that is more desirable than others, whether for its climate, its population, or any other reason.

שֶׁהַנָּוֶה הַיָּפָה בּוֹדֵק For a pleasant dwelling is trying on the body. Our commentary follows *Rashi* and others who explain that even if a person moves to more pleasant surroundings, the change itself is taxing on the body and might lead to illness. *Rivan* explains that the pleasant surroundings can reveal illnesses that might not have been noticeable before. *Rambam (Hilkhot Ishut* 13:18) explains that a man cannot compel his wife to move with him, not even from an unpleasant dwelling-place to a more pleasant one. In a more pleasant place, people are more concerned about their personal appearance, and the woman will have to examine herself more carefully so that she not be unattractive. *Maggid Mishneh* and *Ran* note that according to this explanation, that which the Gemara states below: "A change of routine is the beginning of bowel diseases," is not an explanation of the Mishnah's statement that "a pleasant dwelling is trying on the body," but only an example of a situation in which a change can lead to undesirable results.

The Jerusalem Talmud adduces Scriptural support for this statement (Genesis 19:19): "I cannot escape to the mountain, lest some evil take me, and I die." Even though Lot was fleeing to a place which was better and more secure, he was concerned that evil would overtake him there.

HALAKHAH

אַף לֹא מִנָּוֶה רָעָה Not even from an unpleasant dwelling. "If a husband wishes to move his wife from region to region or from city to city within the same country, he cannot compel her to move from a more pleasant dwelling to a less pleasant dwelling, nor even from a less pleasant dwelling to a more pleasant dwelling, following Rabban Shimon ben Gamliel," whose positions in the Mishnah are accepted as the law. (*Rambam, Sefer Nashim, Hilkhot Ishut,* 13:18; *Shulḥan Arukh, Even HaEzer* 75:2.)

LITERAL TRANSLATION

[1] [This] supports Rabbi Yose bar Ḥanina. [2] For Rabbi Yose bar Ḥanina said: From where [do we derive] that city-dwelling is difficult? [3] For it is stated: "And the people blessed all the men, who willingly offered to dwell in Jerusalem."

[4] "Rabban Shimon ben Gamliel says, etc." [5] What is [meant by] "trying"?

[6] In accordance [with the opinion of] Shmuel, for Shmuel said: A change of routine is the beginning of bowel disease.

[7] It is written in the book of Ben Sira: "All the days of the poor are evil." [8] But surely there is Shabbat and the Festivals! [9] In accordance [with] Shmuel, for Shmuel said: A change of routine is the beginning of bowel disease.

[10] Ben Sira [continued and] said: "Even the nights, among the lowest of roofs is his roof, [11] and on the height of the hills is his vineyard; [12] the rain of the roofs to his roof, [13] and the earth of his vineyard to the vineyards."

MISHNAH [14] All can be compelled to go up to Eretz Israel, but no one (lit., "not all") can be compelled to leave.

[1] מְסַיֵּיע לֵיהּ לְרַבִּי יוֹסֵי בַּר חֲנִינָא. [2] דְּאָמַר רַבִּי יוֹסֵי בַּר חֲנִינָא: מִנַּיִן שֶׁיְּשִׁיבַת כְּרַכִּים קָשָׁה? [3] שֶׁנֶּאֱמַר: "וַיְבָרְכוּ הָעָם לְכֹל הָאֲנָשִׁים הַמִּתְנַדְּבִים לָשֶׁבֶת בִּירוּשָׁלָיִם".

[4] "רַבָּן שִׁמְעוֹן בֶּן גַּמְלִיאֵל אוֹמֵר כו׳". [5] מַאי "בּוֹדֵק"?

[6] כִּדְשְׁמוּאֵל, דְּאָמַר שְׁמוּאֵל: שִׁינּוּי וֶסֶת תְּחִלַּת חוֹלִי מֵעַיִם.

[7] כָּתוּב בְּסֵפֶר בֶּן סִירָא: "כָּל יְמֵי עָנִי רָעִים". [8] וְהָאִיכָּא שַׁבָּתוֹת וְיָמִים טוֹבִים! [9] כִּדְשְׁמוּאֵל, דְּאָמַר שְׁמוּאֵל: שִׁינּוּי וֶסֶת תְּחִלַּת חוֹלִי מֵעַיִם.

[10] בֶּן סִירָא אוֹמֵר: "אַף לֵילוֹת; [11] בְּשֵׁפֶל גַּגִּים גַּגּוֹ וּבִמְרוֹם הָרִים כַּרְמוֹ; [12] מִמְּטַר גַּגִּים לְגַגּוֹ, [13] וּמֵעֲפַר כַּרְמוֹ לִכְרָמִים".

מִשְׁנָה [14] הַכֹּל מַעֲלִין לְאֶרֶץ יִשְׂרָאֵל, וְאֵין הַכֹּל מוֹצִיאִין.

TRANSLATION AND COMMENTARY

מְסַיֵּיע לֵיהּ [1] The Gemara answers: **This** ruling of the Mishnah **supports Rabbi Yose bar Ḥanina.** [2] **For Rabbi Yose bar Ḥanina said: From where do we derive that city-dwelling is hard** on a person? [3] **For the verse states** (Nehemiah 11:2): **"And the people blessed all the men, who willingly offered to dwell in Jerusalem."**

רַבָּן [4] We learned in our Mishnah: **"Rabban Shimon ben Gamliel says:** The husband cannot even compel his wife to move with him from an unpleasant dwelling to a more pleasant dwelling. [5] The Gemara asks: **What does the Mishnah mean** when it says that a pleasant dwelling **tries** the body of someone who is not used to pleasant surroundings?

כִּדְשְׁמוּאֵל [6] The Gemara answers: **This accords with the** objection of **Shmuel, for Shmuel said: Any change of routine is the beginning of bowel disease.**

כָּתוּב [7] The Gemara notes: A similar idea **is found in the book of Ben Sira** (see Proverbs 15:15): **"All the days of the poor are evil."** It may be asked: How can it be said that *all* the days of the poor are evil? [8] **Surely there is Shabbat and the Festivals,** upon which even the poor eat well! [9] It is **like** what **Shmuel said: A change of routine is the beginning of bowel disease.**

בֶּן סִירָא [10] Having cited this verse, the Gemara continues with the continuation of this verse from the book of Ben Sira: **Ben Sira said: "Even the nights** of the poor are evil, **among the lowest of roofs is his roof** for his house is situated in the lowest part of town, [11] **and on the height of the hills is his vineyard** for he cannot afford to purchase property in a more suitable location; [12] **the rain** that falls on all **the** other **roofs** spills out **onto his roof** for his house is lower than all others, [13] **and the earth of his vineyard** is carried away by the rain **to** other people's **vineyards** situated on lower ground."

MISHNAH הַכֹּל מַעֲלִין [14] **Anybody can compel** the members of his family **to settle** with him **in Eretz Israel,**

RASHI

גמרא ישיבת כרכין קשה – שהכל מתיישבין שם, ודוחקין ומקרבים הבתים זו לזו ואין שם אויר, אבל בעיר יש גנות ופרדסים סמוכים לבתים, ואוירן יפה. **שנוי וסת** – אפילו לטובה. **במרום הרים כרמו** – שאין בידו ממון לקנות במקום טוב, וקונה בראש ההר, וכל זבלים שהוא מוליך לו נופל וזב לכרמים שתחתיו.

משנה הכל מעלין – את כל בני ביתו אדם כופה לעלות ולישב עמו בירושלים.

LANGUAGE

וֶסֶת **Routine.** Here this word means "habit, routine" (and, by extension, "diet"); usually, though, וֶסֶת means "menstrual period." This word is derived from the Greek ἔθος, *ethos,* meaning "habit, routine."

BACKGROUND

בֶּן סִירָא **Ben Sira.** One of the apocryphal books, which was appended to the Bible in the Septuagint. The Talmudic Sages frequently cite this work, prefacing quotations from it with the term דִּכְתִיב, "as it is written," as if it were a Biblical book.

Since this was not a holy book, it was preserved in a number of versions, also evidenced by the differences between the various ancient translations and manuscripts of this work, and it is possible that the Talmudic Sages were referring to a completely different work, "the Alphabet of Ben Sira," which was one of the reasons why the Sages treated the book with a certain degree of suspicion.

The citation adduced here is not found in either the ancient versions or the Hebrew manuscripts of Ben Sira (although it does appear as a marginal addition in one manuscript). Part of this quote is taken from Proverbs 15:15, "All the days of the poor are evil," while the additional material is attributed to Ben Sira.

שִׁינּוּי וֶסֶת **Change of diet.** Eating food to which one is not accustomed, or overindulging in food after restricting one's food intake, can adversely affect the digestive system, causing discomfort and occasionally even pain, if not actual illness.

NOTES

יְשִׁיבַת כְּרַכִּים קָשָׁה **City-dwelling is hard.** *Rivan* and *Rid* explain that population is denser in a big city, so that each person has less space and less air. *Rabbenu Ḥananel* suggests that urban living is hard on a person, because prices are generally higher in the city. *Talmidei Rabbenu Yonah* add that the larger population of the city leads to an increase in the demand for goods, and this raises prices. Moreover, in a city there is greater social pressure to live a more luxurious style, which adds significantly to the cost of urban living.

HALAKHAH

הַכֹּל מַעֲלִין לְאֶרֶץ יִשְׂרָאֵל **All can compel to go up to Eretz Israel.** "A man can compel his wife to move with him to Eretz Israel, even from a pleasant dwelling to an unpleasant dwelling, and even from a place the majority of whose

TRANSLATION AND COMMENTARY

but no one can compel the members of his family **to leave** Eretz Israel. [1] **Anybody** living in Eretz Israel **can compel** the members of his family **to settle** with him **in** the city of **Jerusalem, but no one can compel** the members of his family **to leave** Jerusalem and live elsewhere. [2] This law applies to **both men and women.**

נָשָׂא אִשָּׁה [3] **If someone married a woman in Eretz Israel, and** later **divorced her in Eretz Israel,** and the woman's ketubah deed did not specify the currency in which her ketubah settlement would be paid, [4] the husband **pays** out his wife's ketubah settlement with **money of Eretz Israel.**

נָשָׂא אִשָּׁה [5] **If someone married a woman in Eretz Israel, and** later **divorced her in Cappadocia** (a country in Asia minor), where the coins are slightly larger and therefore more valuable than the coins with the same nominal value in Eretz Israel, and the woman's ketubah deed did not specify the currency in which her ketubah settlement would be paid, [6] the husband may **pay** out his wife's ketubah settlement with **money of Eretz Israel.**

נָשָׂא אִשָּׁה [7] **If someone married a woman in Cappadocia, and** later **divorced her in Eretz Israel,** where the coins are slightly smaller and therefore less valuable than the coins with the same nominal value in Cappadocia, and the woman's ketubah deed did not specify the currency in which her ketubah settlement would be paid, [8] the husband may **pay** out his wife's ketubah settlement with **money of Eretz Israel.**

רַבָּן שִׁמְעוֹן בֶּן גַּמְלִיאֵל [9] **Rabban Shimon ben Gamliel says:** Since the man married the woman in Cappadocia, **he** must **pay** out his wife's ketubah with **money of Cappadocia.**

נָשָׂא אִשָּׁה [10] **If someone married a woman in Cappadocia, and** later **divorced her in Cappadocia,** [11] all agree that the husband must **pay** out his wife's ketubah settlement with **money of Cappadocia.**

GEMARA הַכֹּל מַעֲלִין [12] We learned in our Mishnah: **"Anybody can be compelled** by the head of the family (or his wife) to settle in Eretz Israel with him." [13] The Gemara asks: **What** does the word "anybody" come **to include?**

[1] הַכֹּל מַעֲלִין לִירוּשָׁלַיִם, וְאֵין הַכֹּל מוֹצִיאִין. [2] אֶחָד הָאֲנָשִׁים וְאֶחָד הַנָּשִׁים.

[3] נָשָׂא אִשָּׁה בְּאֶרֶץ יִשְׂרָאֵל, וְגֵרְשָׁהּ בְּאֶרֶץ יִשְׂרָאֵל, [4] נוֹתֵן לָהּ מִמְּעוֹת אֶרֶץ יִשְׂרָאֵל.

[5] נָשָׂא אִשָּׁה בְּאֶרֶץ יִשְׂרָאֵל, וְגֵרְשָׁהּ בְּקַפּוֹטְקִיָּא, [6] נוֹתֵן לָהּ מִמְּעוֹת אֶרֶץ יִשְׂרָאֵל.

[7] נָשָׂא אִשָּׁה בְּקַפּוֹטְקִיָּא, וְגֵרְשָׁהּ בְּאֶרֶץ יִשְׂרָאֵל, [8] נוֹתֵן לָהּ מִמְּעוֹת אֶרֶץ יִשְׂרָאֵל.

[9] רַבָּן שִׁמְעוֹן בֶּן גַּמְלִיאֵל אוֹמֵר: נוֹתֵן לָהּ מִמְּעוֹת קַפּוֹטְקִיָּא.

[10] נָשָׂא אִשָּׁה בְּקַפּוֹטְקִיָּא וְגֵרְשָׁהּ בְּקַפּוֹטְקִיָּא, [11] נוֹתֵן לָהּ מִמְּעוֹת קַפּוֹטְקִיָּא.

גמרא [12] ״הַכֹּל מַעֲלִין״. [13] לְאֵתוּיֵי מַאי?

LITERAL TRANSLATION

[1] All can be compelled to go up to Jerusalem, no one can be compelled to leave. [2] [This includes] men and women alike.

[3] [If] someone married a woman in Eretz Israel, and divorced her in Eretz Israel, [4] he gives her money of Eretz Israel.

[5] [If] someone married a woman in Eretz Israel, and divorced her in Cappadocia, [6] he gives her money of Eretz Israel [for her ketubah settlement].

[7] [If] someone married a woman in Cappadocia, and divorced her in Eretz Israel, [8] he gives her money of Eretz Israel.

[9] Rabban Shimon ben Gamliel says: He gives her money of Cappadocia.

[10] [If] someone married a woman in Cappadocia, and divorced her in Cappadocia, [11] he gives her money of Cappadocia.

GEMARA [12] "All can be compelled." [13] To include what?

BACKGROUND

קַפּוֹטְקִיָּא **Kapotkya.** Kapotkya refers to the district of Cappadocia in Asia Minor, which bordered on the Euphrates. Cappadocia was originally an independent state; in Talmudic times, it became a Roman province. As stated here, Cappadocian coins were worth more than the corresponding currency from Eretz Israel, because they contained a higher percentage of precious metal.

RASHI

אחד האנשים ואחד הנשים – אף האשה כופה את בעלה לעלות ולדור שם, ואם לאו – יוציא ויתן כתובה, כדקתני בברייתא בגמרא בהדיא. **מעות קפוטקיא** – גדולות ושוקלות יותר משל ארץ ישראל.

HALAKHAH

inhabitants are Jews to a place the majority of whose inhabitants are gentiles. He cannot compel his wife to leave Eretz Israel with him, even to go from an unpleasant dwelling to a pleasant dwelling, or from a place the majority of whose inhabitants are gentiles to a place the majority of whose inhabitants are Jews," following the Mishnah and the Gemara. (*Rambam, Sefer Nashim, Hilkhot Ishut,* 13:19; *Shulḥan Arukh, Even HaEzer* 75:3.)

הַכֹּל מַעֲלִין לִירוּשָׁלַיִם **All can compel to go up to Jerusalem.** "The same laws that apply with respect to moving to or from Eretz Israel apply with respect to moving within Eretz Israel to or from Jerusalem, for anybody living in Eretz Israel can compel the members of his family to settle in Jerusalem, but nobody can compel the members of his family to leave Jerusalem and live elsewhere in Eretz Israel." (*Rambam, Sefer Nashim, Hilkhot Ishut,* 13:20; *Shulḥan Arukh, Even HaEzer* 75:4.)

TRANSLATION AND COMMENTARY

לְאַתּוּיֵי עֲבָדִים [1]The Gemara explains: The word "anybody" **includes** Hebrew **slaves,** meaning that a master can compel his Hebrew slave to emigrate to Eretz Israel with him.

וּלְמַאן [2]The Gemara asks: **And according to the one** below **who taught explicitly** in the Mishnah that this regulation applies even to Hebrew **slaves,** for there is a reading of the Mishnah which states: "This law includes men, women and slaves alike" [3]**what** does the term "anybody" come **to include?**

לְאַתּוּיֵי [4]The Gemara answers: The word "anybody" comes **to include** that a man or a woman may even compel his or her spouse to leave **a pleasant dwelling** outside Eretz Israel and go and live in **an unpleasant dwelling** in Eretz Israel.

וְאֵין [5]Our Mishnah continues: **"But no one can be compelled** by the head of the family (or his wife) **to leave** Eretz Israel and live outside Eretz Israel." [6]**What** does this clause come **to include?**

לְאַתּוּיֵי [7]The Gemara answers: **It adds** that if **a** Canaanite **slave ran away from** his master who lived **outside Eretz Israel** and he fled **to Eretz Israel,** the master cannot compel him to leave and return home with him, [8]**for we say to** the master: **"Sell him here, and go** home without him," [9]**because** he is fulfilling the commandment of **dwelling in Eretz Israel,** and increasing the number of its inhabitants.

הַכֹּל מַעֲלִין [10]The next clause of our Mishnah reads: **"Anybody** living in Eretz Israel **can be compelled** by the head of the family (or his wife) **to settle** with him **in** the city of **Jerusalem."** [11]**What** does the term "anybody" come **to include?**

לְאַתּוּיֵי [12]The Gemara answers: It **adds** that a man or a woman may even compel his or her spouse to leave **a pleasant dwelling** somewhere in Eretz Israel and settle with him **in an unpleasant dwelling** in the city of Jerusalem.

וְאֵין הַכֹּל [13]Our Mishnah continues: **"But no one can be compelled** by the head of the household (or his wife) **to leave** the city of Jerusalem and live elsewhere." [14]**What does** this clause **come to include?**

[1]לְאַתּוּיֵי עֲבָדִים.
[2]וּלְמַאן דְּתָנֵי עֲבָדִים בְּהֶדְיָא,
[3]לְאַתּוּיֵי מַאי?
[4]לְאַתּוּיֵי מִנָּוֶה הַיָּפָה לְנָוֶה הָרָעָה.
[5]״וְאֵין הַכֹּל מוֹצִיאִין״. [6]לְאַתּוּיֵי מַאי?
[7]לְאַתּוּיֵי עֶבֶד שֶׁבָּרַח מִחוּצָה לָאָרֶץ לָאָרֶץ, [8]דְּאָמְרִינַן לֵיהּ: ״זַבְנֵיהּ הָכָא וְזִיל״, [9]מִשּׁוּם יְשִׁיבַת אֶרֶץ יִשְׂרָאֵל.
[10]״הַכֹּל מַעֲלִין לִירוּשָׁלַיִם״.
[11]לְאַתּוּיֵי מַאי?
[12]לְאַתּוּיֵי מִנָּוֶה הַיָּפָה לְנָוֶה הָרָעָה.
[13]״וְאֵין הַכֹּל מוֹצִיאִין״.
[14]לְאַתּוּיֵי מַאי?

LITERAL TRANSLATION

[1]To include [Hebrew] slaves.
[2]And according to the one who taught slaves explicitly, [3]to include what?
[4]To include from a pleasant dwelling to an unpleasant dwelling.
[5]"But no one can be compelled to leave." [6]To include what?
[7]To include a Canaanite slave who ran way from outside Eretz [Israel] to Eretz [Israel], [8]for we say to his [master]: "Sell him here and go [back]," [9]on account of [the command of] dwelling in Eretz Israel.
[10]"All can be compelled to go up to Jerusalem." [11]To include what?
[12]To include from a pleasant dwelling to an unpleasant dwelling.
[13]"But no one can be compelled to leave." [14]To include what?

RASHI

גמרא לאתויי עבדים – היה לו עבד עברי ילך העבד אחריו על כרחו.

NOTES

לְאַתּוּיֵי עֲבָדִים **To include slaves.** Our commentary follows *Rashi* and others who understand that when the Gemara says that the Mishnah's teaching, that anybody can compel the members of his family to go with him to Eretz Israel, includes slaves, it is referring to Hebrew slaves, and means that a master can compel his Jewish slave to emigrate to Eretz Israel with him. *Ra'avad* understands that the Gemara is referring to Canaanite slaves (as the unspecified term "slaves" generally means in the Talmud). Since, like a woman, a Canaanite slave is obligated to fulfill the Torah's commandments, just as a woman can compel her husband to either move to Eretz Israel or grant her a divorce, so too a Canaanite slave can compel his master to either move to Eretz Israel or emancipate him.

זַבְנֵיהּ הָכָא **Sell him here.** *Rabbenu Tam* (see *Tosafot* and *Tosafot Rosh*) notes that the term "sell" is not precise, for it follows from the Gemara in *Gittin* 45a, that the master may not sell a slave to another Jew, but rather he must "sell" him to the slave himself. He must emancipate him and receive from the slave a promissory note for his value.

HALAKHAH

לְאַתּוּיֵי עֲבָדִים **To include slaves.** "If a non-Jewish slave wishes to move to Eretz Israel, we compel his master to move there with him, or to sell him to someone who is moving there. If a master wishes to leave Eretz Israel, he cannot force his slave to move with him against his will. These laws apply at all times, even when Eretz Israel is under foreign rule." (*Rambam, Sefer Kinyan, Hilkhot Avadim,* 8:9; *Shulḥan Arukh, Yoreh De'ah* 267:85.)

TRANSLATION AND COMMENTARY

לְאַתּוּיֵי [1]The Gemara explains: It **adds** that a man or a woman may not **even** compel his or her spouse to leave **an unpleasant dwelling** in the city of Jerusalem and go with him **to a pleasant dwelling** somewhere else. This could have been inferred from the previous clause in the Mishnah — for if one spouse can compel the other to move from a pleasant dwelling outside Jerusalem to an unpleasant dwelling in Jerusalem, then certainly one spouse cannot compel the other to move from an unpleasant dwelling in Jerusalem to a pleasant dwelling outside Jerusalem. [2]Nevertheless **since an earlier clause** of the Mishnah **taught: "No one can be compelled to leave** Eretz Israel to live outside Israel," [3]this **later clause also taught: "No one can be compelled to leave** the city of Jerusalem and live somewhere else in Eretz Israel."

תָּנוּ רַבָּנַן [4]**Our Rabbis taught** a Baraita which stated: **"If the** husband **says** that he wishes **to settle** in Eretz Israel or in Jerusalem, [5]**and she says** that she does **not** wish **to settle** there, **she can be compelled to settle** in Eretz Israel or in Jerusalem with her husband. [6]**And if** she does **not** accede to his wishes, **she can be divorced without** receiving payment of **her ketubah** settlement. [7]**If** the wife **says** that she wishes **to settle** in Eretz Israel or in Jerusalem, **and he says** that he does **not** wish **to settle** there, [8]**he can be compelled to settle** in Eretz Israel or in Jerusalem with his wife. [9]**And if** he does **not** accede to her wishes, **he must grant her a divorce with payment of her ketubah** settlement. [10]**If** the wife **says** that she wishes **to leave** Eretz Israel or Jerusalem, **and he says** that he does **not** wish **to leave,** [11]**she can be compelled to stay** in Eretz Israel or Jerusalem. [12]**And if** she does **not** accede to his wishes, **she can be divorced without** receiving payment of **her ketubah** settlement. [13]**If** the husband **says** that he wishes **to leave** Eretz Israel or Jerusalem, **and she says** that she does **not** wish **to leave,** [14]**he can be compelled to stay in** Eretz Israel or Jerusalem. [15]**And if** he does **not** accede to her wishes, **he must grant her a divorce with payment of her ketubah** settlement."

נָשָׂא אִשָּׁה [16]Our Mishnah continues: **"If someone married a woman** in Eretz Israel, and later divorced her in Cappadocia, he may pay his wife's ketubah settlement with the poorer money of Eretz Israel. If someone married a woman in Cappadocia, and later divorced her in Eretz Israel, he may pay his wife's ketubah settlement with money of Eretz Israel." [17]**This itself is difficult,** for there is an internal contradiction between

[1]לְאַתּוּיֵי אֲפִילּוּ מִנָּוֶה הָרָעָה לַנָּוֶה הַיָּפָה. [2]וְאַיְּידֵי דְּתָנָא רֵישָׁא: "אֵין מוֹצִיאִין", [3]תָּנָא סֵיפָא נַמִי: "אֵין מוֹצִיאִין".
[4]תָּנוּ רַבָּנַן: "הוּא אוֹמֵר לַעֲלוֹת, [5]וְהִיא אוֹמֶרֶת שֶׁלֹּא לַעֲלוֹת, כּוֹפִין אוֹתָהּ לַעֲלוֹת. [6]וְאִם לָאו, תֵּצֵא בְּלֹא כְּתוּבָּה. [7]הִיא אוֹמֶרֶת לַעֲלוֹת, וְהוּא אוֹמֵר שֶׁלֹּא לַעֲלוֹת. [8]כּוֹפִין אוֹתוֹ לַעֲלוֹת. [9]וְאִם לָאו, יוֹצִיא וְיִתֵּן כְּתוּבָּה. [10]הִיא אוֹמֶרֶת לָצֵאת, וְהוּא אוֹמֵר שֶׁלֹּא לָצֵאת, [11]כּוֹפִין אוֹתָהּ שֶׁלֹּא לָצֵאת. [12]וְאִם לָאו, תֵּצֵא בְּלֹא כְּתוּבָּה. [13]הוּא אוֹמֵר לָצֵאת, וְהִיא אוֹמֶרֶת שֶׁלֹּא לָצֵאת, [14]כּוֹפִין אוֹתוֹ שֶׁלֹּא לָצֵאת. [15]וְאִם לָאו, יוֹצִיא וְיִתֵּן כְּתוּבָּה".
[16]"נָשָׂא אִשָּׁה כּוּ'". [17]הָא גּוּפָא

LITERAL TRANSLATION

[1]To include even from an unpleasant dwelling to a pleasant dwelling. [2]And since the first clause taught: "No [one] may compel to leave," [3]the last clause also taught: "No [one] may compel to leave."

[4]Our Rabbis taught: "[If] he says to go up, [5]and she says not to go up, we compel her to go up. [6]And if not, she goes out without a ketubah. [7][If] she says to go up, and he says not to go up, [8]we compel him to go up. [9]And if not, he must divorce [her] and pay her ketubah. [10][If] she says to leave, and he says not to leave, [11]we compel her to stay (lit., "not to leave"). [12]And if not, she goes out without a ketubah. [13][If] he says to leave, and she says to stay, [14]we compel him to stay. [15]And if not, he must divorce [her] and pay her ketubah."

[16]"[If] someone married a woman, etc." [17]This itself is

RASHI

ואיידי דתנא כו׳ – דאילו משום מנוה הרע לנוה היפה לא איצטריך, כיון דאשמעינן דמעלין מנוה היפה לנוה הרע – כל שכן דאין מוציאין, אפילו מן הרע ליפה. **לעלות** – מחוצה לארץ לארץ, וכן משאר גבולין לירושלים. **לצאת** – או מארץ לחוצה לארץ.

HALAKHAH

הוּא אוֹמֵר לַעֲלוֹת **He says to go up.** "If the husband says that he wishes to settle in Eretz Israel, and the wife says that she does not wish to settle there, he can divorce her without payment of her ketubah. And similarly, if the wife wishes to settle in Eretz Israel, and the husband does not wish to do so, he can be compelled to grant her a divorce with payment of her ketubah. Some authorities maintain that we can only compel a spouse to move to Eretz Israel when it is not dangerous to do so (*Rashbatz*). The authorities disagree about whether or not there is a commandment today to settle in Eretz Israel. Since the matter has not been decided, a spouse cannot be compelled to move there against his or her will. (*Pithei Teshuvah* cites a number of responsa that conclude that even today there is a commandment to settle in Eretz Israel.)" (*Rambam, Sefer Nashim, Hilkhot Ishut,* 13:20; *Shulhan Arukh, Even HaEzer* 75:4-5.)

TRANSLATION AND COMMENTARY

these two rulings. [1]The Mishnah first **states: "If someone married a woman in Eretz Israel, and** later **divorced her in Cappadocia,** [2]**he** may **pay** his wife's ketubah settlement with money of Eretz Israel." [3]Now, **this implies that** in determining the currency in which a ketubah settlement must be paid, **we follow** the place where **the** ketubah **obligation** had been established, and since the ketubah was established at the time of marriage, he must pay his wife's settlement in the currency of the place where they were married. [4]But let us now **consider the next clause** of the Mishnah which states: **"If someone married a woman in Cappadocia, and** later **divorced her in Eretz Israel,** [5]the husband may **pay** out his wife's ketubah settlement with **money of Eretz Israel."** [6]Now, **this implies that** in determining the currency in which a ketubah settlement must be paid, **we follow** the place of **collection** where the divorce was granted!

קַשְׁיָא. [1]קָתָנֵי: ״נָשָׂא אִשָּׁה בְּאֶרֶץ יִשְׂרָאֵל, וְגֵרְשָׁהּ בְּקַפּוֹטְקִיָּא, [2]נוֹתֵן לָהּ מִמְּעוֹת אֶרֶץ יִשְׂרָאֵל״. [3]אַלְמָא בָּתַר שִׁיעְבּוּדָא אָזְלִינַן. [4]אֵימָא סֵיפָא: ״נָשָׂא אִשָּׁה בְּקַפּוֹטְקִיָּא, וְגֵרְשָׁהּ בְּאֶרֶץ יִשְׂרָאֵל, [5]נוֹתֵן לָהּ מִמְּעוֹת אֶרֶץ יִשְׂרָאֵל״. [6]אַלְמָא בָּתַר גּוּבַיְינָא אָזְלִינַן! [7]אֲמַר רַבָּה: מִקּוּלֵּי כְּתוּבָּה שָׁנוּ כָּאן. קָסָבַר: [8]כְּתוּבָּה דְּרַבָּנַן. [9]״רַבָּן שִׁמְעוֹן בֶּן גַּמְלִיאֵל אוֹמֵר: נוֹתֵן לָהּ מִמְּעוֹת קַפּוֹטְקִיָּא״. [10]קָסָבַר: כְּתוּבָּה דְּאוֹרַיְיתָא.

LITERAL TRANSLATION

difficult! [1]It states: "[If] someone married a woman in Eretz Israel, and divorced her in Cappadocia, [2]he gives her money of Eretz Israel." [3]This implies that we follow the [place of] obligation. [4]Consider the last clause: "[If] someone married a woman in Cappadocia, and divorced her in Eretz Israel, [5]he gives her money of Eretz Israel." [6]This implies that we follow the [place of] collection!

[7]Rabbah said: They taught here [one] of the leniencies of a ketubah. [8]He maintains: A ketubah is by Rabbinic decree.

[9]"Rabban Shimon ben Gamliel says: He gives her [the high-quality] money of Cappadocia." [10]He maintains: A ketubah is by Torah law.

RASHI

מקולי כתובה שנו כאן — כאן הקלו בכתובה, וזו אחת מקולי כתובה. **קסבר כתובה דאורייתא** — הילכך בתר שיעבוד אזלינן כדין כל שטרי חוב.

אֲמַר רַבָּה [7]**Rabbah said:** Our Mishnah **taught one of the leniencies** which apply **regarding a ketubah:** Whether the marriage or the divorce took place in Eretz Israel, the husband may pay his wife's ketubah settlement with money of Eretz Israel, [8]for the Tanna of our Mishnah **maintains** that the ketubah obligation **is** only **by Rabbinic decree,** and the Rabbis wanted to make it easier for the man to pay the settlement.

רַבָּן שִׁמְעוֹן בֶּן גַּמְלִיאֵל [9]Our Mishnah continues: **"Rabban Shimon ben Gamliel says:** If the man married his wife in Cappadocia, **he must pay her** ketubah settlement **with money of Cappadocia."** [10]The Gemara explains: Rabban Shimon ben Gamliel **maintains** that the **ketubah** obligation **is by Torah law,** and therefore the currency in which a ketubah settlement must be paid follows the place where the ketubah obligation had been established, as is the case with other promissory notes.

NOTES

קָסָבַר כְּתוּבָּה דְּאוֹרַיְיתָא A ketubah is by Torah law. The Rishonim ask: If Rabban Shimon ben Gamliel maintains that the ketubah is a Biblical ordinance, then it must be paid according to the Tyrian silver standard (the standard used for all Biblical obligations) In that case, it should make no difference whether the ketubah settlement is paid in Cappadocian money or money from Eretz Israel, for either way the amount of the money paid will be adjusted to the same standard? Some answer that even if the value of the money is the same, Cappadocian money is preferred because it circulates more easily. Others suggest that indeed it makes no difference regarding the main portion of the woman's ketubah settlement, but there is a difference regarding payment of the increment, which the husband may add of his own (see *Ritva*). *Ramban* and others argue that even according to Rabban Shimon ben

HALAKHAH

נָשָׂא אִשָּׁה בְּאֶרֶץ יִשְׂרָאֵל If someone married a woman in Eretz Israel. "If a man married a woman in one place, and divorced her somewhere else (and she was living there with him at the time of the divorce, but if he sent her the bill of divorce to the place where they had married, the law is different; *Bet Yosef* in the name of *Rashba*), and he had not specified the currency in which the ketubah settlement would be paid out, the law is as follows: If the money in the place where they had married is better than the money in the place where he granted her the divorce, he pays out the ketubah settlement with money from the place of the divorce. And if the money in the place where he granted her the divorce is better than the money in the place where they had married, he pays out the ketubah settlement with money from the place where they had married, for the law is in accordance with the Sages that the ketubah obligation is by Rabbinic decree, and so we are lenient about it. But in any event, the husband may not pay his wife less than what the Rabbis established as the minimal ketubah settlement (*Maggid Mishneh*). If the husband specified the currency in which he would pay out his wife's ketubah settlement, he must pay out the ketubah settlement in that currency." (*Rambam, Sefer Nashim, Hilkhot Ishut,* 16:6; *Shulḥan Arukh, Even HaEzer* 100:5.)

TRANSLATION AND COMMENTARY

תָּנוּ רַבָּנַן [1] **Our Rabbis taught** a related Baraita: **"If someone produces a promissory note against another person, and** the note **mentions Babylonia** as the place where the loan was made, the debtor **pays** his creditor **with Babylonian money.** [2] If the note **mentions Eretz Israel,** the debtor **pays** his creditor **with money from Eretz Israel.** [3] If the note **was written without specifying** any place, **and he produced it in Babylonia,** the debtor **pays** his creditor **with Babylonian money.** [4] **If he produced it in Eretz Israel,** [5] the debtor **pays** his creditor **with money from Eretz Israel.** [6] If the note **mentions** a certain sum of **silver, without specifying** the denomination — [7] **the borrower pays** the creditor **whatever he wishes,** even if he does so with silver coins of the smallest denomination. [8] **This is not the case regarding a** woman's **ketubah** settlement (as will be explained below)."

אַהַיָּיא [9] The Gemara asks: **To which** portion of the Baraita does this last line apply, in distinguishing between the law applying to a ketubah and the law applying to other promissory notes?

אָמַר רַב מְשָׁרְשִׁיָּא [10] **Rav Mesharshiya said:** The last line of the Baraita relates to the law recorded **in the first clause** of the Baraita that if someone produces a promissory note that mentions Babylonia as the place of the loan, the debtor pays his creditor with Babylonian money, even if the promissory note was presented to him in Eretz Israel, With respect to promissory notes, we follow the place where the obligation was first established. But this is not the law regarding a woman's ketubah, for a ketubah written in Babylonia and paid in Eretz Israel is paid with money from Eretz Israel. [11] This comes **to the exclusion of** the opinion of **Rabban Shimon ben Gamliel, who said** that the obligation to pay **the ketubah** settlement **is by Torah law,** and therefore the currency in which a ketubah settlement must be paid follows the place where the ketubah obligation had been established, as is the case with ordinary promissory notes.

כָּתוּב בּוֹ [12] It was taught in the Baraita: **"If the note mentions** a certain sum of **silver without specifying**

[1] תָּנוּ רַבָּנַן: "הַמּוֹצִיא שְׁטַר חוֹב עַל חֲבֵירוֹ, כָּתוּב בּוֹ בָּבֶל, מַגְבֵּהוּ מִמְּעוֹת בָּבֶל. [2] כָּתוּב בּוֹ אֶרֶץ יִשְׂרָאֵל, מַגְבֵּהוּ מִמְּעוֹת אֶרֶץ יִשְׂרָאֵל. [3] כָּתוּב בּוֹ סְתָם, הוֹצִיאוֹ בְּבָבֶל, [4] מַגְבֵּהוּ מִמְּעוֹת בָּבֶל. [5] הוֹצִיאוֹ בְּאֶרֶץ יִשְׂרָאֵל, מַגְבֵּהוּ מִמְּעוֹת אֶרֶץ יִשְׂרָאֵל. [6] כָּתוּב בּוֹ כֶּסֶף סְתָם, [7] מַה שֶּׁיִּרְצֶה לֹוֶה מַגְבֵּהוּ, [8] מַה שֶּׁאֵין כֵּן בִּכְתוּבָּה". [9] אַהַיָּיא? [10] אָמַר רַב מְשָׁרְשִׁיָּא: אַרֵישָׁא, לְאַפּוּקֵי מִדְּרַבָּן שִׁמְעוֹן בֶּן גַּמְלִיאֵל, [11] דְּאָמַר: כְּתוּבָּה דְּאוֹרַיְיתָא. [12] "כָּתוּב בּוֹ כֶּסֶף סְתָם, מַה

LITERAL TRANSLATION

[1] Our Rabbis taught: "If someone produces a promissory note against another person, [and] it was written in it Babylonia, he gives him Babylonian money. [2] [If] it was written in it Eretz Israel, he gives him money of Eretz Israel. [3] [If] it is written without specification, [and] he produced it in Babylonia, [4] he gives him Babylonian money. [5] [If] he produced it in Eretz Israel, he gives him money of Eretz Israel. [6] [If] there is written in it silver without specification, [7] whatever the borrower wishes he gives him, [8] which is not the case regarding a ketubah."

[9] To which [clause] does this refer?

[10] Rav Mesharshiya said: To the first clause, [11] to the exclusion of Rabban Shimon ben Gamliel, who said: A ketubah is by Torah law.

[12] "[If] there is written in it silver without specification, whatever

RASHI

כתוב בו כסף סתם — מאה כסף, ולא פירש אם סלעין אם דינרין אם פונדיונין.

NOTES

Gamliel who maintains that the ketubah is a Biblical ordinance, it was only the Rabbis who set the amount of the ketubah settlement at two hundred dinars. Unless the ketubah states specifically that it is to be paid according to the standard of provincial silver (one-eighth of the Tyrian standard), it amounts to two hundred silver coins according to the local standard, Thus, there can be a significant difference between paying the ketubah settlement in Cappadocian money or in money from Eretz Israel. And since Rabban Shimon ben Gamliel maintains that the ketubah is a Biblical ordinance, the currency in which it must be paid out follows the place where the ketubah obligation had been established, as is the case with other promissory notes.

HALAKHAH

הַמּוֹצִיא שְׁטַר חוֹב If someone produces a promissory note. "If someone produces a promissory note against another person, and the note mentions Babylonia, the debtor pays his creditor with Babylonian money. And if the note mentions Eretz Israel, he pays him with money from Eretz Israel. If the note does not mention any place, the debtor must pay his creditor with money of the country in which the promissory note was produced. If the note mentions a certain sum without specifying the denomination, the debtor may pay the creditor whatever he wishes," following the Baraita. (*Rambam, Sefer Mishpatim, Hilkhot Malveh Ve-Loveh,* 17:9; *Shulḥan Arukh, Ḥoshen Mishpat* 42:14.)

REALIA

נַסְכָא **Silver money.** In ancient times, coins were usually the value of the precious metal they contained. Therefore, small silver coins were generally not usable. A perutah contained less than half a gram of silver, and a coin of this size was normally rather small. While small silver coins were used in Greece for a certain period of time, such coins were later displaced by copper coins.

TRANSLATION AND COMMENTARY

the denomination, **the borrower pays** the creditor **whatever he wishes,** even if he does so with silver coins of the smallest denomination." The Gemara asks: If the notes mention silver without specifying any denomination, [1]**say** that borrower may pay the lender with **an** unminted **bar of silver!**

אָמַר רַבִּי אֶלְעָזָר [2]**Rabbi Elazar said:** The Baraita is dealing with a case **where the note mentioned** "silver **coins"** — to the exclusion of an unminted bar of silver — but it does not specify the denomination.

וְאֵימָא: [3]The Gemara asks: But **say** then that the borrower can pay the lender with **perutot,** the smallest denomination of coin in circulation!

אָמַר רַב פַּפָּא [4]The Gemara answers: **Rav Pappa said:** Coin manufacturers **do not make perutot of silver,** but only of copper. And since the promissory note speaks of silver coins, it can indeed be paid with silver coins of the smallest denomination, but it cannot be paid with perutot or any other copper coins.

תָּנוּ רַבָּנַן [5]The Gemara enters now into a discussion regarding the issue underlying our Mishnah, the obligation of living in Eretz Israel. **Our Rabbis taught** the following Baraita: **"A person should always live in Eretz Israel, even in a town the majority** of whose inhabitants **are non-Jews.** [6]**And he should not live outside of Eretz Israel, even in a town the majority** of whose inhabitants **are Jews.** [7]**For anyone who lives in Eretz Israel is considered like someone who has a God,** [8]**and anyone who lives outside of Eretz Israel is considered like someone who does not have a God,** [9]**as the verse states** (Leviticus 25:38): **'To give you the land of Canaan**

שֶׁיִּרְצֶה לֵיהּ מַגְבֵּהוּ״. [1]וְאֵימָא: נַסְכָא!

[2]אָמַר רַבִּי אֶלְעָזָר: דִּכְתִיב בֵּיהּ מַטְבֵּעַ.

[3]וְאֵימָא: פְּרִיטֵי!

[4]אָמַר רַב פַּפָּא: פְּרִיטֵי דְּכַסְפָּא לָא עָבְדִי אֱינָשֵׁי.

[5]תָּנוּ רַבָּנַן: ״לְעוֹלָם יָדוּר אָדָם בְּאֶרֶץ יִשְׂרָאֵל, אֲפִילּוּ בְּעִיר שֶׁרוּבָּהּ גּוֹיִם. [6]וְאַל יָדוּר בְּחוּצָה לָאָרֶץ, וַאֲפִילּוּ בְּעִיר שֶׁרוּבָּהּ יִשְׂרָאֵל. [7]שֶׁכָּל הַדָּר בְּאֶרֶץ יִשְׂרָאֵל, דּוֹמֶה כְּמִי שֶׁיֵּשׁ לוֹ אֱלוֹהַּ, [8]וְכָל הַדָּר בְּחוּצָה לָאָרֶץ, דּוֹמֶה כְּמִי שֶׁאֵין לוֹ אֱלוֹהַּ, [9]שֶׁנֶּאֱמַר: ׳לָתֵת לָכֶם אֶת אֶרֶץ כְּנַעַן לִהְיוֹת לָכֶם

LITERAL TRANSLATION

the borrower wishes he gives him." [1]Say: A bar [of silver]!

[2]Rabbi Elazar said: Where it is written in it [silver] coin?

[3]Say perutot!

[4]Rav Pappa said: People do not make perutot of silver.

[5]Our Rabbis taught: "A person should always live in Eretz Israel, even in a town that is mostly non-Jewish. [6]And he should not live outside of Eretz Israel, even in a town that is mostly Jewish. [7]For anyone who lives in Eretz Israel is considered like he who has a God, [8]and anyone who lives outside of Eretz Israel is considered like he who does not have a God, [9]as it is stated: 'To give you the land of Canaan to be for you

RASHI

מה שירצה לוה מגבהו — ואפילו איסרין. **ואימא נסכא** — חתיכות כסף היה, לכך לא פירש? **ואימא פריטי** — ותאמר שיתן לו נחשת, או כסף שוה מאה פרוטות?

NOTES

דּוֹמֶה כְּמִי שֶׁיֵּשׁ לוֹ **Is considered as if.** *Maharsha* notes that the Gemara does not query the Baraita's statement that "anyone who lives in Eretz Israel is considered like someone who has a God," for Scripture describes God as "God of the land [= Eretz Israel]," and so He is the God of all those who reside therein. But the Gemara asks about the second half of the Baraita's statement that anyone who lives outside of Eretz Israel is considered like he who does not have a God: How can this be? Surely God is also described as "God of the earth," and the Jews are His people wherever they might be found? The Gemara answers that the Baraita means that anyone living outside of Eretz Israel is considered as an idol-worshipper. The Aḥaronim deal with this issue at length. The *Zohar* states in several places that the countries outside of Eretz Israel are under the sovereignty of heavenly officers, whereas Eretz Israel is under the direct control of God Himself (see *Ri'af,* and others).

כָּל הַדָּר בְּחוּצָה לָאָרֶץ **Anyone who lives outside of Eretz Israel.** *Rivan* (and so too it would appear from *Rambam*) understands that this refers to someone who leaves Eretz Israel to live outside of Eretz Israel. *Meiri* explains that the countries outside of Eretz Israel are the fixed seats of idolatrous practices, and it is impossible for a Jew living outside of Eretz Israel not to be influenced by them in some degree.

HALAKHAH

וְאֵימָא: נַסְכָא **Say: A bar of silver.** "If the promissory note reads: 'So-and-so borrowed silver from so-and-so,' the debtor may repay the debt with the smallest bar of silver. If it reads: 'So-and-so borrowed silver coins from so-and-so,' the debtor may repay the debt with silver coins of the smallest denomination that circulate in that area, even perutot." (*Rambam, Sefer Mishpatim, Hilkhot Malveh VeLoveh* 17:9; *Shulḥan Arukh, Ḥoshen Mishpat* 42:13.)

לְעוֹלָם יָדוּר אָדָם בְּאֶרֶץ יִשְׂרָאֵל **A person should always live in Eretz Israel.** "A person should always live in Eretz Israel, even in a town the majority of whose residents are Gentiles, rather than live outside of Eretz Israel, even in a town the majority of whose residents are Jews, for whoever leaves Eretz Israel is regarded as if he were worshipping idols." (*Rambam, Sefer Shofetim, Hilkhot Melakhim* 5:12.)

TRANSLATION AND COMMENTARY

to be for you a God.' It may be asked: [1]Can this mean that **someone who does not live in Eretz Israel does not have a God?!** [2]**Rather,** the verse comes **to teach you** that **anyone who lives outside of Eretz Israel is considered as an idol-worshipper.** [3]**And similarly regarding** King **David** the verse **says** (I Samuel 26:19): **'For they have driven me out this day from being joined to the inheritance of the Lord, saying: Go, serve other gods.'** It may be asked: [4]**Did someone** actually **say to David: Go, serve other gods?** [5]**Rather,** the verse comes **to teach you: Anyone who lives outside of Eretz Israel is considered as an idol-worshipper."**

רַבִּי זֵירָא [6]It was related that **Rabbi Zera would** try to **avoid Rav Yehudah, because** Rav Zera **wanted to settle in Eretz Israel,** and he knew that Rav Yehudah was opposed to such a move. [7]**For Rav Yehudah said: Whoever emigrates from Babylonia to Eretz Israel violates a positive commandment,** [8]**for the verse states** (Jeremiah 27:22): [111A] [9]**"They shall be carried to Babylonia, and there shall they be until the day that I take heed of them, says the Lord."** Rav Yehudah inferred from this verse that those who were exiled to Babylonia are bound by a positive commandment to remain there.

וְרַבִּי זֵירָא [10]The Gemara asks: **And** how did **Rabbi Zera,** who wished to settle in Eretz Israel, understand this verse?

הַהוּא [11]In his view, **that verse was written about the sacred vessels** that were removed from the Temple and taken to Babylonia, as the previous verse states explicitly (Jeremiah 27:21): "For thus says the Lord of hosts, the God of Israel, concerning the vessels that remain in the house of the Lord, and in the house of the king of Judea and of Jerusalem."

וְרַב יְהוּדָה [12]The Gemara asks: **And** what does **Rav Yehudah** say to refute this interpretation of Rabbi Zera?

כְּתִיב קְרָא [13]The Gemara answers: There is yet **another verse** supporting Rav Yehudah, which **states** (Song of Songs 2:7): [14]**"I adjure you, O daughters of Jerusalem, by the gazelles, and by the hinds of the field,** that you stir not up, nor awake my love, till it please." Rav Yehudah learned from this verse that there is a prohibition against taking active steps to hasten the time of redemption, including settling in Eretz Israel.

וְרַבִּי זֵירָא [15]The Gemara asks: **And** how does **Rabbi Zera** understand this verse?

הַהוּא [16]The Gemara explains: **That verse teaches that** all of **Israel should not return** to Eretz Israel **as one,**

לֵאלֹהִים׳. [1]וְכָל שֶׁאֵינוֹ דָּר בָּאָרֶץ אֵין לוֹ אֱלוֹהַּ?! [2]אֶלָּא לוֹמַר לְךָ: כָּל הַדָּר בְּחוּצָה לָאָרֶץ כְּאִילּוּ עוֹבֵד עֲבוֹדָה זָרָה. [3]וְכֵן בְּדָוִד, הוּא אוֹמֵר: ׳כִּי גֵרְשׁוּנִי הַיּוֹם מֵהִסְתַּפֵּחַ בְּנַחֲלַת ה׳ לֵאמֹר לֵךְ עֲבוֹד אֱלֹהִים אֲחֵרִים׳. [4]וְכִי מִי אָמַר לוֹ לְדָוִד: לֵךְ, עֲבוֹד אֱלֹהִים אֲחֵרִים? [5]אֶלָּא, לוֹמַר לְךָ: כָּל הַדָּר בְּחוּצָה לָאָרֶץ כְּאִילּוּ עוֹבֵד עֲבוֹדָה זָרָה״.

[6]רַבִּי זֵירָא הֲוָה קָמִשְׁתַּמֵּיט מִינֵּיהּ דְּרַב יְהוּדָה, דִּבְעָא לְמִיסַּק לְאֶרֶץ יִשְׂרָאֵל. [7]דְּאָמַר רַב יְהוּדָה: כָּל הָעוֹלֶה מִבָּבֶל לְאֶרֶץ יִשְׂרָאֵל עוֹבֵר בַּעֲשֵׂה, [8]שֶׁנֶּאֱמַר: [111A] [9]״בָּבֶלָה יוּבָאוּ וְשָׁמָּה יִהְיוּ עַד יוֹם פָּקְדִי אוֹתָם נְאֻם ה׳״.

[10]וְרַבִּי זֵירָא?

[11]הַהוּא בִּכְלֵי שָׁרֵת כְּתִיב.

[12]וְרַב יְהוּדָה?

[13]כְּתִיב קְרָא אַחֲרִינָא: [14]״הִשְׁבַּעְתִּי אֶתְכֶם, בְּנוֹת יְרוּשָׁלַיִם, בִּצְבָאוֹת אוֹ בְּאַיְלוֹת הַשָּׂדֶה וגו׳״.

[15]וְרַבִּי זֵירָא?

[16]הַהוּא שֶׁלֹּא יַעֲלוּ יִשְׂרָאֵל

LITERAL TRANSLATION

a God.' [1]And someone who does not live in Eretz Israel has no God?! [2]Rather, to teach you: Anyone who lives outside of Eretz Israel is like an idol-worshipper. [3]And similarly regarding David, it says: 'For they have driven me out this day from being joined to the inheritance of the Lord, saying: Go, serve other gods.' [4]Did someone say to David: Go, serve other gods? [5]Rather, to teach you: Anyone who lives outside of Eretz Israel is like an is idol-worshipper."

[6]Rabbi Zera would slip away from Rav Yehudah, because he wanted to go up to Eretz Israel. [7]For Rav Yehudah said: Whoever goes up from Babylonia to Eretz Israel violates a positive commandment, [8]as it is stated: [111A] [9]"They shall be carried to Babylonia, and there shall they be until the day that I take heed of them, says the Lord."

[10]And Rabbi Zera?

[11]That [verse] was written about the sacred vessels.

[12]And Rav Yehudah?

[13][In] another verse it is written: [14]"I adjure you, O daughters of Jerusalem, by the gazelles, and by the hinds of the field, etc."

[15]And Rabbi Zera?

[16]That [verse teaches] that Israel should not go up

RASHI

וכי מי אמר לו לדוד כן — אלא מפני שהיה צריך לברוח ולצאת מארץ ישראל אל מלך מואב ואל אכיש. **דבעי רבי זירא למיסק** — ורב יהודה מוחה בידו, להכי הוה משתמיט מיניה. **בכלי שרת כתיב** — קרא דלעיל מיניה כתיב ״כי כה אמר ה׳ אל העמודים ועל הים ועל המכונות וגו׳״. **שלא יעלו בחומה**

NOTES

שֶׁלֹּא יַעֲלוּ בַּחוֹמָה **That they should not go up as one.** Our commentary follows *Rashi* who understands this expression

בַּחוֹמָה.
[1] וְרַב יְהוּדָה?
[2] ״הִשְׁבַּעְתִּי״ אַחֲרִינָא כְּתִיב.
[3] וְרַבִּי זֵירָא?
[4] הַהוּא מִיבָּעֵי לֵיהּ לְכִדְרַבִּי יוֹסֵי בְּרַבִּי חֲנִינָא, דְּאָמַר: [5] שָׁלֹשׁ שְׁבוּעוֹת הַלָּלוּ לָמָּה? [6] אַחַת, שֶׁלֹּא יַעֲלוּ יִשְׂרָאֵל בַּחוֹמָה. [7] וְאַחַת, שֶׁהִשְׁבִּיעַ הַקָּדוֹשׁ בָּרוּךְ הוּא אֶת יִשְׂרָאֵל שֶׁלֹּא יִמְרְדוּ בְּאוּמּוֹת הָעוֹלָם. [8] וְאַחַת, שֶׁהִשְׁבִּיעַ הַקָּדוֹשׁ בָּרוּךְ הוּא אֶת הַגּוֹיִם שֶׁלֹּא יִשְׁתַּעְבְּדוּ בָּהֶן בְּיִשְׂרָאֵל יוֹתֵר מִדַּאי.
[9] וְרַב יְהוּדָה?
[10] ״אִם תָּעִירוּ וְאִם תְּעוֹרְרוּ״ כְּתִיב.
[11] וְרַבִּי זֵירָא?
[12] מִיבָּעֵי לֵיהּ לְכִדְרַבִּי לֵוִי, דְּאָמַר: [13] שֵׁשׁ שְׁבוּעוֹת הַלָּלוּ לָמָּה? [14] תְּלָתָא — הָנֵי דַּאֲמָרַן. [15] אִינָךְ — שֶׁלֹּא יְגַלּוּ אֶת הַקֵּץ, וְשֶׁלֹּא יְרַחֲקוּ אֶת הַקֵּץ,

LITERAL TRANSLATION

as one (lit., "as a wall").
[1] And Rav Yehudah?
[2] Another "I adjure you" is written.
[3] And Rabbi Zera?
[4] That [verse] is needed for that of Rabbi Yose the son of Rabbi Ḥanina, who said: [5] Why those three oaths? [6] One, that Israel not go up as one. [7] And one, that the Holy One, blessed be He, administered an oath to Israel that they not rebel against the nations of the world. [8] And one, that the Holy One, blessed be He, administered an oath to the nations of the world that they not subjugate Israel too much.
[9] And Rav Yehudah?
[10] It is written: "That you stir not up, nor awake."
[11] And Rabbi Zera?
[12] It is needed for that of Rabbi Levi, who said: [13] Why those six oaths? [14] Three — those which we said. [15] The others — that they not reveal the end [of the exile], and that they not push off the end,

TRANSLATION AND COMMENTARY

at the same time, and with a great show of force. But individuals may return.

וְרַב יְהוּדָה [1] The Gemara asks: **And** how does **Rav Yehudah** counter this argument?

הִשְׁבַּעְתִּי [2] The Gemara answers: There is a **second**, identical **verse** which **states** (Song of Songs 3:5): **"I adjure you,** O daughters of Jerusalem, by the gazelles, and by the hinds of the field, that you stir not up, nor awake my love, till it please," from which Rav Yehudah can derive his prohibition to settle in Eretz Israel.

וְרַבִּי זֵירָא [3] The Gemara asks: **And** how does **Rabbi Zera** account for this duplication?

הַהוּא מִיבָּעֵי לֵיהּ [4] The Gemara explains: **That** second **verse is needed for what Rabbi Yose the son of Rabbi Ḥanina said:** [5] **Why** were **three oaths** necessary — Song of Songs 2:7, 3:5, and 8:4? [6] **One,** to adjure **Israel** that it **not return** to Eretz Israel **as one,** but rather as individuals. [7] **And the second, that the Holy One, blessed be He, administered an oath to Israel that they not rebel against the nations of the world** under whose subjugation they will be placed. [8] **And the third, that the Holy One, blessed be He, administered an oath to the nations of the world that they not subjugate Israel too much.**

וְרַב יְהוּדָה [9] The Gemara asks: **And** from where does **Rav Yehudah** derive his general prohibition to settle in Eretz Israel? Does he not need the verse in Song of Songs (3:5) for the oath not to rebel against the nations of the world?

אִם תָּעִירוּ [10] The Gemara answers: Rav Yehudah can derive it from the end of **the verse** (*ibid.* 2:7) **"That you stir not up, nor awake."** This duplication adds another oath forbidding Jews to return to Israel even as single individuals.

וְרַבִּי זֵירָא [11] The Gemara asks: **And** what does **Rabbi Zera** say about this?

מִיבָּעֵי לֵיהּ [12] The Gemara answers: The apparent duplication in all three of the above verses **is needed for what Rabbi Levi said:** [13] Why were **six oaths** necessary? The three oaths cited above are all worded doubly, "That you stir not up, nor awake," giving us six oaths. [14] **Three** oaths are those **that were given** above. [15] **The other** three oaths were as follows: **That** the prophets among them were adjured **not** to **reveal** when **the end**

RASHI

— יחד, ביד חזקה. אם תעירו ואם תעוררו — שתי שבועות בכל אחת. שלא יגלו את הקץ — נביאים שביניהם. ושלא ירחקו את הקץ — בעונם. לישנא אחרינא: "שלא ידחקו" גרסינן — לשון דוחק, שלא ירבו בתחנונים על כך יותר מדאי.

NOTES

to mean that Israel should not return to Eretz Israel as one, and with a great show of force. (According to some readings, and also *Rabbi Ya'akov Emden,* the text reads: כַּחוֹמָה, "as a wall," meaning at once.) *Maharsha* suggests that it also means that they may not return to Israel and rebuild its walls without the permission of the non-Jewish authorities, for that would be regarded as a rebellion against the nations of the world.

שֶׁלֹּא יְרַחֲקוּ אֶת הַקֵּץ **That they not push off the end.** *Rashi* explains that this means that Israel should not push off the end with their sins. Alternatively, *Rashi* has a second reading: שֶׁלֹּא יִדְחֲקוּ, "that they not press for it," meaning

[1] וְשֶׁלֹּא יְגַלּוּ הַסּוֹד לַגּוֹיִם.
[2] ״בִּצְבָאוֹת אוֹ בְּאַיְלוֹת הַשָּׂדֶה״.
[3] אָמַר רַבִּי אֶלְעָזָר, אָמַר לָהֶם הַקָּדוֹשׁ בָּרוּךְ הוּא לְיִשְׂרָאֵל: [4] אִם אַתֶּם מְקַיְּימִין אֶת הַשְּׁבוּעָה, מוּטָב. [5] וְאִם לָאו, אֲנִי מַתִּיר אֶת בְּשַׂרְכֶם כִּצְבָאוֹת וּכְאַיְלוֹת הַשָּׂדֶה.
[6] אָמַר רַבִּי אֶלְעָזָר: כָּל הַדָּר בְּאֶרֶץ יִשְׂרָאֵל שָׁרוּי בְּלֹא עָוֹן, שֶׁנֶּאֱמַר: [7] ״וּבַל יֹאמַר, שָׁכֵן, חָלִיתִי; הָעָם הַיּוֹשֵׁב בָּהּ נְשֻׂא עָוֹן״.
[8] אֲמַר לֵיהּ רָבָא לְרַב אַשִׁי: אֲנַן בְּסוֹבְלֵי חֳלָאִים מַתְנִינַן לָהּ.
[9] אָמַר רַב עָנָן: כָּל הַקָּבוּר בְּאֶרֶץ יִשְׂרָאֵל, כְּאִילּוּ קָבוּר

LITERAL TRANSLATION

[1] and that they not reveal the secret to Gentiles. [2] "By the gazelles, and by the hinds of the field." [3] Rabbi Elazar said: The Holy One, blessed be He, said to Israel: [4] If you keep the oath, good. [5] But if not, I will [declare] your flesh free [for slaughter] like the gazelles and the hinds of the field.

[6] Rabbi Elazar said: Whoever dwells in Eretz Israel lives without sin, as it is stated: [7] "And the inhabitant shall not say, I am sick; the people that dwell therein shall be forgiven their iniquity."

[8] Rava said to Rav Ashi: We teach this [verse] regarding those who suffer from disease.

[9] Rav Anan said: Whoever is buried in Eretz Israel [is considered] as if he were buried

RASHI

ושלא יגלו את הסוד – אמרי לה סוד העבור, ואמרי לה סוד טעמי התורה. **מתיר את בשרכם** – לשון הפקר. **ובל יאמר שכן חליתי** – כלומר: אל יתרעם לומר: צר לי, כי כולם נשואי עון.

TRANSLATION AND COMMENTARY

of the exile would take place, **and that they not push off the end** by sinning (see Note), [1] **and that they not reveal to the Gentiles the secrets** known only to Israel.

בִּצְבָאוֹת [2] The verse states (Song of Songs 2:7): "I adjure you, O daughters of Jerusalem, **by the gazelles, and by the hinds of the field,** that you stir not up, nor awake my love, till it please." [3] **Rabbi Elazar said: The Holy One, blessed be He, said to Israel:** [4] **If you keep the oath,** all will be well. [5] **But if** you do **not** keep the oath, **I will declare your flesh** to be **free** for slaughter **like** that of **the gazelles and the hinds of the field.**

אָמַר רַבִּי אֶלְעָזָר [6] **Rabbi Elazar said: Whoever dwells in Eretz Israel lives without sin, as the verse states** (Isaiah 33:24): [7] **"And the inhabitant shall not say, I am sick; the people that dwell therein** — in Eretz Israel — **shall be forgiven their iniquity."**

אֲמַר לֵיהּ [8] **Rava said to Rav Ashi: We teach** that **this** promise was given to **those who suffer from diseases,** as the verse itself states: "And the inhabitant shall not say, I am sick." It is those that suffer with sickness who shall be forgiven their iniquity, and not those who merely dwell in Eretz Israel.

אָמַר רַב עָנָן [9] **Rav Anan said: Whoever is buried in Eretz Israel is considered as if he were buried under**

NOTES

that they should not devote themselves to excessive supplications regarding the matter. Others suggest that this means that they should not speak too much about it, for according to Rabbi Zera in tractate *Sanhedrin,* excessive talking about the end of days pushes it off even further. *Maharsha* proposes that this means that Israel should not put the end far off in their minds, saying that the end will not come for a very long time, but rather they should hope that the end will arrive at any moment.

שֶׁלֹּא יְגַלּוּ הַסּוֹד לַגּוֹיִם That they not reveal the secret to Gentiles. According to *Rabbenu Ḥananel, Rashi's* first explanation, and *Tosafot,* this means that Israel should not reveal to the Gentiles the secrets regarding the intercalation of the year. According to *Rashi's* second explanation, it means that Israel should not reveal the secret reasons of the Torah to non-Jews. *Eshel Avraham* suggests that the Gemara means that Israel should not reveal to the Gentiles the existence of these secret oaths.

שָׁרוּי בְּלֹא עָוֹן Lives without sin. It has been asked: Surely, many people living in Eretz Israel have sinned, as we find throughout the books of the Prophets! Some suggest that in Eretz Israel sins are quickly atoned for and pardoned. Alternatively, the merit of observing the commandment of living in Eretz Israel helps a person to avoid sin. It has also been proposed that a precise reading of the text indicates that he who dwells in Eretz Israel lives without *avon,* "unintentional sin," for the merit of living in Eretz Israel helps him avoid such transgressions. But regarding transgressions committed intentionally there is no difference between a person living inside Eretz Israel and a person living outside of it (*Iyyun Ya'akov*).

וּבַל יֹאמַר, שָׁכֵן, חָלִיתִי And the inhabitant shall not say, I am sick. *Ri'af* notes that the proof that the verse is referring to the inhabitants of Eretz Israel is found in one of the earlier verses (Isaiah 33:20): "Look upon Zion, the city of our solemnities."

כְּאִילּוּ קָבוּר תַּחַת הַמִּזְבֵּחַ As if he were buried under the altar. *Maharsha* writes that this means that whoever is

HALAKHAH

כָּל הַדָּר בְּאֶרֶץ יִשְׂרָאֵל Whoever dwells in Eretz Israel. "The Sages have said about anyone who lives in Eretz Israel that his sins are pardoned," following Rabbi Elazar. (*Rambam, Sefer Shofetim, Hilkhot Melakhim* 5:11.)

כָּל הַקָּבוּר בְּאֶרֶץ יִשְׂרָאֵל Whoever is buried in Eretz Israel. "Whoever is buried in Eretz Israel has achieved atonement for his sins, and the place in which he is buried is regarded as altar of atonement," following Rav Anan. (*Rambam, Sefer Shofetim, Hilkhot Melakhim* 5:11.)

BACKGROUND

שֶׁלֹּא יְגַלּוּ הַסּוֹד So they will not reveal the secret. *Rashi* explains that this refers to revealing the secrets of the Torah, or the secrets of intercalation.

However, the Gemara might be referring to other types of secrets. Thus, an inscription discovered in Ein Gedi curses those who "reveal the secret of the city" (see below).

This might have been a security-related secret (such as a list of hidden roads) or a professional secret. Other sources indicate that Jews who revealed their professional secrets eventually lost their jobs, whereas those who kept such information secret did not.

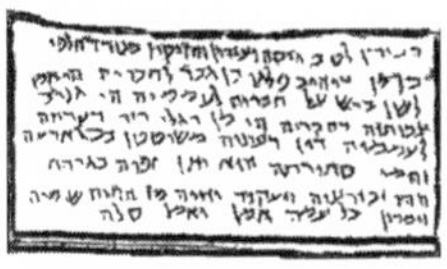

A Mosaic Inscription From Ein-Gedi (sixth-century C.E.)

"May Yose and 'Iron and Hezekiah the sons of Hilfi be remembered for good.

"[Regarding] anyone who causes strife between one person and another, or who denounces someone to the Gentiles, or who steals someone else's property or reveals the secret of the city to the Gentiles — May He whose eyes roam throughout the earth and behold hidden things set His countenance against that man and his seed, and uproot him from beneath the heavens. And let all the people say: Amen and Amen, Selah."

תַּחַת הַמִּזְבֵּחַ. [1]כְּתִיב הָכָא: "מִזְבַּח אֲדָמָה תַּעֲשֶׂה לִּי", [2]וּכְתִיב הָתָם: "וְכִפֶּר אַדְמָתוֹ עַמּוֹ".

[3]עוּלָּא הֲוָה רְגִיל דַּהֲוָה סָלֵיק לְאֶרֶץ יִשְׂרָאֵל. [4]נָח נַפְשֵׁיהּ בְּחוּץ לָאָרֶץ. [5]אֲתוֹ אָמְרוּ לֵיהּ לְרַבִּי אֶלְעָזָר. [6]אָמַר: "אַנְתְּ עוּלָּא, [7]'עַל אֲדָמָה טְמֵאָה תָּמוּת'"! [8]אָמְרוּ לוֹ: "אֲרוֹנוֹ בָּא". [9]אָמַר לָהֶם: "אֵינוֹ דּוֹמֶה קוֹלַטְתּוֹ מְחַיִּים לְקוֹלַטְתּוֹ לְאַחַר מִיתָה".

[10]הָהוּא גַּבְרָא דִּנְפַלָה לֵיהּ יְבָמָה בֵּי חוֹזָאָה. [11]אֲתָא לְקַמֵּיהּ דְּרַבִּי חֲנִינָא, אֲמַר לֵיהּ: [12]"מַהוּ לְמֵיחַת וּלְיַבְּמַהּ"? [13]אֲמַר לוֹ: "אָחִיו נָשָׂא כּוּתִית וּמֵת. [14]בָּרוּךְ הַמָּקוֹם שֶׁהֲרָגוֹ. וְהוּא יֵרֵד אַחֲרָיו"?

LITERAL TRANSLATION

under the altar. [1]It is written here: "An altar of earth you shall make for me," [2]and it is written there: "And His land (lit., 'earth') will atone for His people."

[3]Ulla would regularly go up to Eretz Israel. [4]He died (lit., "his soul rested") outside Eretz Israel. [5]They came [and] told Rabbi Elazar. [6]He said: "For you, Ulla, [the verse said] [7]'you shall die in an unclean land.'" [8]They said to him: "His bier came." [9]He said to them: "Someone who was received during [his] lifetime cannot be compared to someone who was received after death."

[10][There was] a certain man before whom fell a woman [requiring] levirate marriage in Bei Hoza'ah. [11]He came before Rabbi Ḥanina, [and] said to him: [12]"What about going down and taking her in levirate marriage?" [13]He said to him: "Your (lit., 'his') brother married a Cuthean woman and died. [14]Blessed is God who killed him. And you (lit., 'he') she should go down after him?"

TRANSLATION AND COMMENTARY

the altar of the Temple. How do we know this? [1]**In one place the verse states** (Exodus 20:21): **"An altar of earth** [אֲדָמָה] **you shall make for me,"** [2]**and in another place the verse states** (Deuteronomy 32:43): "For He will avenge the blood of his servants, and will render vengeance against His adversaries; **and His land** [אַדְמָתוֹ] **will atone for His people."** The verses teach that burial in Eretz Israel, His land [אַדְמָתוֹ], is considered like burial under the earthen altar [which is also אֲדָמָה].

עוּלָּא הֲוָה רְגִיל [3]It was related that **Ulla would regularly go up** and visit **Eretz Israel,** [4]but **he died outside Eretz Israel.** [5]People **came and told Rabbi Elazar** of Ulla's passing. [6]Rabbi Elazar then **said:** "Woe to **you, Ulla,** through whom the following verse was fulfilled (Amos 7:17): [7]**'You shall die in an unclean land.'"** [8]The people **said to Rabbi Elazar:** "Ulla may have died abroad, but **his bier** already **came,** so that he can be buried in Eretz Israel." [9]Rabbi Elazar **said to them: "Someone who was received** in Eretz Israel **during his lifetime** and then died there **cannot be compared to someone who was received** there only **after** his **death."**

הָהוּא גַּבְרָא [10]It was related that **there was a certain man** living in Eretz Israel whose brother died in Babylonia, and his widow **fell before him for levirate marriage in** the far-off district of **Bei Hoza'ah.** [11]The surviving brother **came before Rabbi Ḥanina, and said to him:** [12]**"What** is the law **regarding leaving** Eretz Israel in order to **take** my brother's widow **in levirate marriage?"** [13]Rabbi Ḥanina **said to him: "Your brother married a Cuthean woman** — that is, he left Eretz Israel in order to marry a certain woman — **and died.** [14]**Blessed is God who killed him.** He deserved that punishment for leaving Eretz Israel. **And** now you ask whether you, his surviving brother, **should leave** in order to take his sister-in-law as his levirate wife?"

RASHI

אתה על אדמה טמאה תמות – מקרא הוא בנבואת עמוס. **ארונו בא** – לקוברו בארץ ישראל.

SAGES

עוּלָּא Ulla. A third-generation scholar from Eretz Israel, Ulla was one of the most important *neḥotei* (scholars who traveled from Babylonia to Eretz Israel and vice-versa, transmitting the traditions of each country to the other). Ulla seems to have commuted frequently between Babylonia and Eretz Israel, traveling from place to place to teach Torah. He was a student of Rabbi Yoḥanan. Ulla's full name was apparently Ulla bar Yishmael.

The Babylonian scholars esteemed Ulla very highly. Rav Ḥisda would refer to him as רַבּוֹתֵינוּ הַבָּאִים מֵאֶרֶץ יִשְׂרָאֵל "our teachers who come from Eretz Israel." Rav Yehudah sent his son to Ulla to see how he conducted himself.

Ulla's teachings are also cited in the Jerusalem Talmud, where he is usually identified by his full name, Ulla bar Yishmael [or Ulla Naḥota]), and many of the scholars of the following generation were his students.

Nothing is known about his personal life, although the Amora Rabbah bar Ulla might have been his son.

Ulla died in Babylonia during one of his journeys to that country, but he was buried in Eretz Israel.

NOTES

buried in Eretz Israel is considered as if he were buried under the altar in a place of purity. The Sages say that Adam was created from dust taken from the place where the altar would later stand. Therefore, a person being buried under the altar symbolizes that the person is being returned to his original place and in his original condition — without sin.

אַנְתְּ עוּלָּא You, Ulla. What is told here regarding Ulla fits in well with what was stated above, that Ulla went up regularly to visit Eretz Israel, for he was one of the Sages, who would travel between Eretz Israel and Babylonia in order to bring the Torah of Eretz Israel to Babylonia. Thus, it was particularly ironic that Ulla who would regularly visit and spend time in Eretz Israel should die in a land of the Gentiles.

אֵינוֹ דּוֹמֶה קוֹלַטְתּוֹ מְחַיִּים Someone who was received during his lifetime. The Jerusalem Talmud cites Rabbi Meir (who also died abroad) as offering the following saying:

HALAKHAH

אֵינוֹ דּוֹמֶה קוֹלַטְתּוֹ מְחַיִּים Someone who was received during his lifetime cannot be compared. "There is no comparison between someone who arrived in Eretz Israel during his lifetime and someone who was brought there only after his death," following Rabbi Elazar. But the greatest of Sages would still bury their dead in Eretz Israel, following in the ways of our forefathers, Jacob and Joseph. (*Rambam, Sefer Shofetim, Hilkhot Melakhim* 5:11.)

TRANSLATION AND COMMENTARY

אָמַר רַב יְהוּדָה [1]**Rav Yehudah said in the name of Shmuel: Just as it is forbidden to leave Eretz Israel to live in Babylonia,** [2]**so** too **it is forbidden to leave Babylonia for other countries,** for Babylonia is the seat of academies in which Torah study flourishes. [3]**Rabbah and Rav Yosef both said:** It is **even** forbidden to move from the Torah center of **Pumbedita to** its suburb of **Bei Kuvei.**

הַהוּא דְּנָפַק [4]It was related there was **someone who left** the city of **Pumbedita to** live in **Bei Kuvei, and Rav Yosef put him under a ban** for the move. [5]It was further related that **there was someone who left** the Babylonian city of **Pumbedita to** live outside Babylonia in **Astonya,** and shortly after his move **he died.** [6]**Abaye said: If that Torah scholar had wanted,** he would have stayed in Pumbedita and **he would** still **be alive.**

רַבָּה וְרַב יוֹסֵף [7]**Rabbah and Rav Yosef both said: The worthy people in Babylonia** will be **received in Eretz Israel,** [8]whereas **the worthy people in** all **other countries** will be **received in Babylonia.**

לְמַאי [9]The Gemara asks: **To what** does this acceptance refer? [10]**If you say** that Rabbah and Rav Yosef refer to acceptance of family **lineage** regarding marriage, that the worthy people of Babylonia will be well received when they come to seek out a suitable marriage partner in Eretz Israel, and that the worthy people of all other countries will be well received when they seek their partner in Babylonia, there is a difficulty. [11]For **surely the master said** elsewhere: **All** other **lands** (except Babylonia) **are** regarded as **dough with respect to Eretz Israel.** The communities outside Eretz Israel are suspected of having had alien elements mixed into them, which no family can prove to be absent in their lineage. Therefore they would not be well received by the Babylonians who had purer lineage. [12]**And Eretz Israel is** regarded as **dough with respect to Babylonia.** The Jews in Babylonia regarded their own lineage as purer than that of the Jewish community in Eretz Israel, and would not seek partners in Eretz Israel.

[1]אָמַר רַב יְהוּדָה אָמַר שְׁמוּאֵל: כְּשֵׁם שֶׁאָסוּר לָצֵאת מֵאֶרֶץ יִשְׂרָאֵל לְבָבֶל, [2]כָּךְ אָסוּר לָצֵאת מִבָּבֶל לִשְׁאָר אֲרָצוֹת. [3]רַבָּה וְרַב יוֹסֵף דְּאָמְרִי תַּרְוַיְיהוּ: אֲפִילּוּ מִפּוּמְבְּדִיתָא לְבֵי כּוּבֵי.
[4]הַהוּא דְּנָפַק מִפּוּמְבְּדִיתָא לְבֵי כּוּבֵי, שַׁמְתֵּיהּ רַב יוֹסֵף. [5]הַהוּא דְּנָפַק מִפּוּמְבְּדִיתָא לְאַסְתּוֹנְיָא, שְׁכֵיב. [6]אֲמַר אַבַּיֵי: אִי בָּעֵי הַאי צוּרְבָא מֵרַבָּנַן, הֲוָה חַיֵּי.
[7]רַבָּה וְרַב יוֹסֵף דְּאָמְרִי תַּרְוַיְיהוּ: כְּשֵׁרִין שֶׁבְּבָבֶל אֶרֶץ יִשְׂרָאֵל קוֹלַטְתָּן. [8]כְּשֵׁרִין שֶׁבִּשְׁאָר אֲרָצוֹת בָּבֶל קוֹלַטְתָּן. [9]לְמַאי? [10]אִילֵימָא לְיוֹחֲסִין — [11]וְהָאָמַר מָר: כָּל הָאֲרָצוֹת עִיסָּה לְאֶרֶץ יִשְׂרָאֵל, [12]וְאֶרֶץ יִשְׂרָאֵל עִיסָּה לְבָבֶל!

LITERAL TRANSLATION

[1]Rav Yehudah said in the name of Shmuel: Just as it is forbidden to leave Eretz Israel for Babylonia, [2]so it is forbidden to leave Babylonia for other countries. [3]Rabbah and Rav Yosef both said: Even from Pumbedita to Bei Kuvai.

[4][There was] someone who left Pumbedita for Bei Kuvei, [and] Rav Yosef put him under a ban. [5][There was] someone who left Pumbedita for Astonya, [and] he died. [6]Abaye said: If that Torah scholar had wanted, he would be alive.

[7]Rabbah and Rav Yosef both said: The worthy ones in Babylonia are received in Eretz Israel. [8]The worthy ones in other countries are received in Babylonia.

[9]For what? [10]If you say: For [assumedly pure] lineage — [11]but surely the master said: All lands are dough for Eretz Israel, [12]and Eretz Israel is dough for Babylonia!

RASHI

כך אסור לצאת מבבל — לפי שיש שם ישיבות המרבילות תורה תמיד. **דנפק מפומבדיתא לבי כובי** — לגור שם. **ארץ ישראל קולטתן** — כדמפרש. **אילימא ליוחסין** — שנושאין נשים מארץ ישראל, והא בבל מיוחס טפי! דאמר מר בפרק "עשרה יוחסין" (קדושין עא,א). **כל הארצות** — הרי הן אצל בבל. **בעיסה** — המעורבת, שאין ניכר בה מה בתוכה. כך כל המשפחות ספק.

BACKGROUND

בֵּי כּוּבֵי **Bei Kuvei.** A village near Pumbedita, located six parasangs (about twenty-four kilometers) from that city.

אַסְתּוֹנְיָא **Astonya.** Some take this as a common noun, derived from the Persian *astan*, "district"; thus, Astonya denotes the city where the local government was located. Alternatively, this might be a proper noun. The context suggests that this was the city of Peruz (Shevor), which was located near Pumbedita. Some identify this city as Westania, where many of the Talmudic Sages lived.

NOTES

"You cannot compare someone who returns his soul to his mother's bosom to someone who returns his soul to the bosom of a strange woman."

כָּךְ אָסוּר לָצֵאת מִבָּבֶל **So it is forbidden to leave Babylonia.** Our commentary follows *Rashi,* who explains that one is forbidden to leave Babylonia for other countries, because Babylonia is a seat of Torah with flourishing Torah academies (see also *Meiri,* who discusses the matter at length). (*Rabbi Ya'akov Emden* and others note that Babylonia should not enjoy any special status today, for the

HALAKHAH

כָּךְ אָסוּר לָצֵאת מִבָּבֶל **So it is forbidden to leave Babylonia.** "Just as one is forbidden to leave Eretz Israel, so too one is forbidden to leave Babylonia for other countries, as the verse states: 'They shall be carried to Babylonia, and there they shall be.' *Kesef Mishneh* writes that it would appear from *Rambam* that one is forbidden to leave Babylonia even for Eretz Israel." (*Rambam, Sefer Shofetim, Hilkhot Melakhim* 5:12.)

BACKGROUND

הוּצַל דְּבִנְיָמִין Hutzal of Benjamin. This city, which was very old, was located near Neharde'a, near the Euphrates river. Elsewhere the Gemara states that Hutzal existed as a walled city during Joshua's time, and there was a Jewish settlement there in King Yehoakhin's time. This city was called "Hutzal of Binyamin" because its first residents were exiles from the tribe of Binyamin. Elsehwere the Gemara states that the Divine Presence rested upon the synagogue in Hutzal. This city was a major center of Torah study for a long time, and many Tannaim of the last generation lived there. During the Amoraic period, too, it apparently had a yeshivah, and many of the Talmudic Sages studied there.

TRANSLATION AND COMMENTARY

אֶלָּא [1]The Gemara explains: **Rather,** Rabbah and Rav Yosef are dealing with **the matter of burial,** claiming that the worthy people in Babylonia are buried in Eretz Israel, and the worthy people of all other countries are buried in Babylonia.

אָמַר רַב יְהוּדָה [2]**Rav Yehudah said: Whoever lives in Babylonia is considered as if he were living in Eretz Israel,** [3]**as the verse states** (Zechariah 2:11): **"Escape, O Zion, that dwells with the daughter of Babylonia."** Although the previous verse describes Jewry as being "spread abroad as the four winds of heaven," there is a special comparison here between the daughters of Zion dwelling with the daughters of Babylonia.

אָמַר אַבַּיֵי [4]**Abaye said:** We **have** it on the authority of tradition that the Jewish community of **Babylonia will not experience the sufferings** which are to precede the advent **of the Messiah.** [5]Abaye **explained** this tradition **as referring to** the Babylonian city of **Hutzal,** the home of an ancient Jewish community of the tribe **of Benjamin,** [6]**and** which people **call "the corner of salvation,"** because it will be spared the birth pangs of the Messianic age.

אָמַר רַבִּי אֶלְעָזָר [7]**Rabbi Elazar said: The dead outside Eretz Israel will not be resurrected** in the time of the resurrection, [8]**as the verse states** (Ezekiel 26:20): **"And I shall set up my glory** [צְבִי] **in the land of the living."** Rabbi Elazar interprets the word צְבִי as "desire," and the phrase צְבִי בְּאֶרֶץ as "land of desire." Thus, the verse should be understood as follows: [9]**The dead of the land of my desire** — Eretz Israel — **will be resurrected,** so that they are once again among the living, [10]whereas **the dead of the lands, which are not of my desire, shall not be resurrected.**

מָתִיב [11]**Rabbi Abba bar Memel raised an objection:** Surely, the verse states (Isaiah 26:19): **"Your dead men shall live,** even **my dead body shall arise."** [12]**Is it not that "Your dead men shall live" refers to the dead in Eretz Israel,** [13]**and that "my dead body shall arise" refers to the dead outside Eretz Israel?** Even the dead outside Eretz Israel will be resurrected! [14]**What** then **is the meaning of** the verse: **"And I shall set up my glory** [צְבִי] **in the land of the living"?** The word צְבִי should be understood there according to its alternative meaning as "deer," [15]and the verse may be understood as **referring to Nebuchadnezzar,** king of Babylonia, **for God said:** [16]**I will bring upon** the people of Israel **a king who is as swift as a deer.**

[1]אֶלָּא, לְעִנְיַן קְבוּרָה.

[2]אָמַר רַב יְהוּדָה: כָּל הַדָּר בְּבָבֶל כְּאִילּוּ דָּר בְּאֶרֶץ יִשְׂרָאֵל, [3]שֶׁנֶּאֱמַר: "הוֹי, צִיּוֹן, הִמָּלְטִי יוֹשֶׁבֶת בַּת בָּבֶל".

[4]אָמַר אַבַּיֵי: נְקִטִינַן: בָּבֶל לָא חָזְיָא חֶבְלֵי דְּמָשִׁיחַ. [5]תַּרְגְּמָהּ: אַהוּצַל דְּבִנְיָמִין, [6]וְקָרוּ לֵיהּ "קַרְנָא דְּשֵׁיזַבְתָּא".

[7]אָמַר רַבִּי אֶלְעָזָר: מֵתִים שֶׁבְּחוּץ לָאָרֶץ אֵינָם חַיִּים, [8]שֶׁנֶּאֱמַר: "וְנָתַתִּי צְבִי בְּאֶרֶץ חַיִּים" [9]— אֶרֶץ שֶׁצִּבְיוֹנִי בָּהּ מֵתֶיהָ חַיִּים, [10]שֶׁאֵין צִבְיוֹנִי בָּהּ אֵין מֵתֶיהָ חַיִּים.

[11]מָתִיב רַבִּי אַבָּא בַּר מֶמֶל: "יִחְיוּ מֵתֶיךָ, נְבֵלָתִי יְקוּמוּן". [12]מַאי לָאו "יִחְיוּ מֵתֶיךָ" מֵתִים שֶׁבְּאֶרֶץ יִשְׂרָאֵל, [13]"נְבֵלָתִי יְקוּמוּן" מֵתִים שֶׁבְּחוּץ לָאָרֶץ? [14]וּמַאי "וְנָתַתִּי צְבִי בְּאֶרֶץ חַיִּים"? [15]אַנְּבוּכַדְנֶצַּר הוּא דִּכְתִיב, דְּאָמַר רַחֲמָנָא: [16]מַיְיתֵינָא עֲלַיְיהוּ מַלְכָּא דְּקַלִּיל כִּי טַבְיָא!

LITERAL TRANSLATION

[1]Rather, for the matter of burial.

[2]Rav Yehudah said: Whoever lives in Babylonia [is considered] as if he were living in Eretz Israel, [3]as it is stated: "Escape, O Zion, that dwells with the daughter of Babylonia."

[4]Abaye said: We maintain: Babylonia will not see the sufferings of the [period preceding the] Messiah. [5]He explained it [as referring] to Hutzal of Benjamin, [6]and they called it "the corner of salvation."

[7]Rabbi Elazar said: The dead outside Eretz Israel will not be resurrected, [8]as it is stated: "And I shall set my glory (lit., 'beauty') in the land of the living" — [9]the dead [in] the land of my desire will be resurrected; [10][in the land] that is not of my desire the dead will not be resurrected.

[11]Rabbi Abba bar Memel raised an objection: "Your dead men shall live, [even] my dead body shall arise." [12]Is it not [that] "Your dead men shall live" [refers to] the dead in Eretz Israel, [13][and that] "my dead body shall arise" [refers to] the dead outside Eretz Israel? [14][Then] what is [the meaning of] "And I shall set my glory in the land of the living"? [15]That is written regarding Nebuchadnezzar, for the Merciful said: [16]I will bring upon them a king who is as swift as a deer.

RASHI

אלא לענין קבורה — של בבל מוליכין ארונותיהם ליקבר בארץ ישראל, ושל שאר ארצות הרחוקים מארץ ישראל וקרובים לבבל — קוברים בבבל, שיש שם זכות תורה. **וקרו ליה** — לימות המשיח.

NOTES

Torah academies set up there in Talmudic times.) But it would appear from *Rambam* that this prohibition is based on the special Scriptural command (Jeremiah 27:22): "They shall be carried to Babylonia, and there they shall be."

[1]אֲמַר לֵיהּ: רַבִּי, מִקְרָא אַחֵר אֲנִי דּוֹרֵשׁ: [2]״נוֹתֵן נְשָׁמָה לָעָם עָלֶיהָ, וְרוּחַ לַהוֹלְכִים בָּהּ״. [3]וְאֶלָּא הָכְתִיב: ״נְבֵלָתִי יְקוּמוּן״! [4]הַהוּא בִּנְפָלִים הוּא דִּכְתִיב. [5]וְרַבִּי אַבָּא בַּר מֶמֶל, הַאי ״נוֹתֵן נְשָׁמָה לָעָם עָלֶיהָ״ מַאי עָבֵיד לֵיהּ?

[6]מִיבָּעֵי לֵיהּ לְכִדְרַבִּי אַבָּהוּ, [7]דְּאָמַר רַבִּי אַבָּהוּ: אֲפִילּוּ שִׁפְחָה כְּנַעֲנִית שֶׁבְּאֶרֶץ יִשְׂרָאֵל מוּבְטָח לָהּ שֶׁהִיא בַּת הָעוֹלָם הַבָּא. [8]כְּתִיב הָכָא: ״לָעָם עָלֶיהָ״, [9]וּכְתִיב הָתָם: ״שְׁבוּ לָכֶם פֹּה עִם הַחֲמוֹר״ — עַם הַדּוֹמֶה לַחֲמוֹר. [10]״וְרוּחַ לַהוֹלְכִים בָּהּ״. [11]אָמַר רַבִּי יִרְמְיָה בַּר אַבָּא אָמַר רַבִּי יוֹחָנָן: [12]כָּל הַמְהַלֵּךְ אַרְבַּע אַמּוֹת בְּאֶרֶץ יִשְׂרָאֵל מוּבְטָח לוֹ שֶׁהוּא בֶּן הָעוֹלָם הַבָּא״.

[13]וּלְרַבִּי אֶלְעָזָר, צַדִּיקִים שֶׁבְּחוּץ לָאָרֶץ אֵינָם חַיִּים? [14]אָמַר רַבִּי אֶילְעָא: עַל יְדֵי גִלְגּוּל.

LITERAL TRANSLATION

[1]He said to him: My master, I expound another verse: [2]"He that gives breath to the people upon it, and spirit to them that walk therein." [3]But surely it is written: "My dead body shall arise"! [4]That is written about still-born babies. [5]And Rabbi Abba bar Memel, what does he do with, "He that gives breath to the people upon it"? [6]That is needed for that of Rabbi Abbahu, [7]for Rabbi Abbahu said: Even a Canaanite maidservant in Eretz Israel is promised that she is fit for the world to come. [8]It is written here: "To the people upon it," [9]and it is written there: "Stay here with the ass" — a people that is similar to an ass. [10]"And spirit to them that walk therein." [11]Rabbi Yirmeyah bar Abba said in the name of Rabbi Yoḥanan: [12]Whoever walks four cubits in Eretz Israel is promised that he is fit for the world to come."

[13]And according to Rabbi Elazar, the righteous outside Eretz Israel will not be resurrected? [14]Rabbi El'a said: Through rolling [to Eretz Israel].

TRANSLATION AND COMMENTARY

אֲמַר לֵיהּ [1]Rabbi Elazar **said to** Rabbi Abba bar Memel: **My master,** I based what I said upon the **exposition of another verse** (Isaiah 42:5): [2]**"He that gives breath to the people upon it, and spirit to them that walk therein,"** which implies that only the "people upon it," that is, the dead of Eretz Israel, will be resurrected, and not the dead of other countries.

וְאֶלָּא הָכְתִיב [3]The Gemara asks: **But surely the verse** cited above **states: "My dead body shall arise,"** which as was suggested above, comes to add that even the dead outside Eretz Israel will be resurrected!

הַהוּא בִּנְפָלִים [4]The Gemara answers: **That verse refers to still-born babies,** who will be resurrected in the time of the resurrection.

וְרַבִּי אַבָּא בַּר מֶמֶל [5]The Gemara asks: **What does Rabbi Abba bar Memel do with** the verse: **"He that gives breath to the people upon it,"** which implies that only the dead of Eretz Israel will be resurrected?

מִיבָּעֵי לֵיהּ [6]Rabbi Abba bar Memel can say that **that** verse **is needed for that of Rabbi Abbahu.** [7]**For Rabbi Abbahu said: Even a Canaanite maidservant in Eretz Israel is promised that she will have a place in the world to come.** [8]**Here the verse states:** "He that gives breath **to the people** [עָם] **upon it,"** [9]**and elsewhere the verse states** (Genesis 22:5): **"Stay here with the ass** [עִם הַחֲמוֹר]," which the Rabbis understand as עַם הַדּוֹמֶה — **a people that is similar to an ass,** the Canaanites. Since the Canaanites are referred to as a "people," the words of the prophet also refer to them, and they too are promised a place in the world to come.

וְרוּחַ [10]The verse in Isaiah continues: **"And gives spirit to them that** *walk* **therein."** [11]**Rabbi Yirmeyah bar Abba said in the name of Rabbi Yoḥanan:** [12]It may be inferred from here that **whoever walks four cubits in Eretz Israel is promised that he has a place in the world to come."**

וּלְרַבִּי אֶלְעָזָר [13]The Gemara answers: **According to Rabbi Elazar,** is it really true that **the righteous** buried **outside Eretz Israel will not be resurrected** in the time of the resurrection?

אָמַר רַבִּי אֶילְעָא [14]**Rabbi El'a said:** Their bones will first **roll** underground until they reach Eretz Israel, and only then will they be resurrected.

RASHI

לעם עליה — על ארץ ישראל. **ההוא בנפלים כתיב** — ולעולם בארץ ישראל. **אינן חיים** — בתמיה. **על ידי גלגול** — מתגלגלים העצמות עד ארץ ישראל, וחיין שם.

NOTES

אֲפִילּוּ שִׁפְחָה כְּנַעֲנִית Even a Canaanite maidservant. *Maharsha* notes that a Canaanite maidservant is on the lowest level of those connected to the Jewish people, for even a Canaanite manservant is on a higher level, since he is circumcised.

HALAKHAH

הַמְהַלֵּךְ אַרְבַּע אַמּוֹת Whoever walks four cubits. "Even if a person only walked four cubits in Eretz Israel, he is promised

[1]מַתְקִיף לָהּ רַבִּי אַבָּא סַלָּא רָבָא: [2]גִּלְגּוּל לַצַּדִּיקִים צַעַר הוּא!

[3]אָמַר אַבַּיֵי: מְחִילוֹת נַעֲשׂוֹת לָהֶם בַּקַּרְקַע.

[4]"וּנְשָׂאתַנִי מִמִּצְרַיִם, וּקְבַרְתַּנִי בִּקְבֻרָתָם". [5]אָמַר קַרְנָא: דְּבָרִים בְּגוֹ. [6]יוֹדֵעַ הָיָה יַעֲקֹב אָבִינוּ שֶׁצַּדִּיק גָּמוּר הָיָה. [7]וְאִם מֵתִים שֶׁבְּחוּצָה לָאָרֶץ חַיִּים, [8]לָמָּה הִטְרִיחַ אֶת בָּנָיו? [9]שֶׁמָּא לֹא יִזְכֶּה לִמְחִילוֹת. [10]כַּיּוֹצֵא בַּדָּבָר אַתָּה אוֹמֵר: [11]"וַיַּשְׁבַּע יוֹסֵף אֶת בְּנֵי יִשְׂרָאֵל וגו׳". [12]אָמַר רַבִּי חֲנִינָא: דְּבָרִים בְּגוֹ. [13]יוֹדֵעַ הָיָה יוֹסֵף בְּעַצְמוֹ שֶׁצַּדִּיק גָּמוּר הָיָה. [14]וְאִם מֵתִים שֶׁבְּחוּצָה לָאָרֶץ חַיִּים, [15]לָמָּה הִטְרִיחַ אֶת אֶחָיו אַרְבַּע מֵאוֹת פַּרְסָה? [16]שֶׁמָּא לֹא יִזְכֶּה לִמְחִילוֹת.

[17]שָׁלְחוּ לֵיהּ אֲחוּהִי לְרַבָּה: "יוֹדֵעַ הָיָה יַעֲקֹב שֶׁצַּדִּיק גָּמוּר

LITERAL TRANSLATION

[1]Rabbi Abba Sala Rava strongly objected: [2]For the righteous, rolling is suffering!

[3]Abaye said: Underground passages will be made for them.

[4]"And you shall carry me out of Egypt, and bury me in their burying place." [5]Karna said: [There is] something [hidden] in this. [6]Jacob our forefather knew that he was an absolutely righteous man. [7]And if the dead outside Eretz Israel will be resurrected, [8]why did he trouble his sons? [9]Perhaps he would not merit underground passages. [10]Similarly you may say: [11]"And Joseph took an oath of the children of Israel, etc." [12]Rabbi Ḥanina said: [There is] something [hidden] in this. [13]Joseph knew himself that he was an absolutely righteous man. [14]And if the dead outside Eretz Israel will be resurrected, [15]why did he trouble his brothers [to carry him] four hundred Persian miles? [16]Perhaps he would not merit underground passages.

[17]His brothers sent to Rabbah: "Jacob knew that he was an absolutely righteous man,

TRANSLATION AND COMMENTARY

מַתְקִיף לָהּ [1]**Rabbi Abba Sala the Great strongly objected:** [2]**For the righteous, rolling** underground **is** certainly a form of **suffering,** which they do not deserve!

אָמַר אַבַּיֵי [3]**Abaye said: Underground passages will be prepared** for the righteous, at the end of which they will emerge in Eretz Israel and rejoin the living.

וּנְשָׂאתַנִי מִמִּצְרַיִם [4]The verse states that Jacob instructed his sons as follows (Genesis 47:30): **"And you shall carry me out of Egypt, and bury me in their burying place."** [5]**Karna said:** A secret **matter is hidden** here: [6]**Jacob our forefather knew** very well **that he was an absolutely righteous man,** and therefore assured of a place in the world to come. [7]**If** then it is true that **the dead** buried **outside Eretz Israel and will be resurrected,** [8]**why did he trouble his sons** and ask that he be carried out of Egypt and buried in Eretz Israel? [9]Jacob was afraid that **perhaps he would not merit** to make his journey to Eretz Israel through the **underground passages** and did not want to suffer the underground rolling of his bones to Eretz Israel. [10]**Similarly you may explain the verse** in which Joseph instructs his brothers as follows (Genesis 50:25): [11]**"And Joseph took an oath of the children of Israel,** saying, God will surely visit you, and you shall carry up my bones from here." [12]**Rabbi Ḥanina said:** A secret **matter is hidden** here. [13]**Joseph knew himself to be an absolutely righteous man.** [14]**If** then it is true that even **the dead buried outside Eretz Israel will be resurrected,** [15]**why did he trouble his brothers** and ask them to carry him **four hundred parasangs** (1536 km., 960 ml.) through the wilderness? [16]Joseph was afraid that **perhaps he would not merit** to make his journey through the **underground passages** that were prepared for the righteous, and he did not want to suffer the underground rolling of his bones.

שָׁלְחוּ לֵיהּ [17]It was related that **Rabbah's brothers sent him** a letter from Eretz Israel to Babylonia trying to persuade him to settle there. The letter included the discussion cited above about **"Jacob,** who though **he knew that he was an absolutely righteous man,"** did not want to be buried outside Eretz Israel. The letter also

RASHI

מחילות נעשה להם בקרקע — ועומדים על רגליהם והולכים במחילות עד ארץ ישראל, ושם מגלגלין ויוצאים. **דברים בגו** — יש כאן דברים מסותרים בדבר זה, וצריך לתת להם לב. **שצדיק גמור היה** — ולא היה צריך לזכות ארץ ישראל. **שלחו ליה אחוהי לרבה** — רבה בר נחמני בפומבדיתא היה, והיה לו אחים בארץ ישראל, ושלחו אגרת זו כדי שיעלה אצלם.

NOTES

דְּבָרִים בְּגוֹ **There is something [secret] in this.** Regarding Jacob it might have been said that he wished to be buried alongside his forefathers. But Joseph was not buried alongside his forefathers, but rather in Shechem, and so there must be a secret matter hidden here (*Pnei Yehoshua*).

HALAKHAH

a place in the world to come," following Rabbi Yoḥanan. (*Rambam, Sefer Shofetim, Hilkhot Melakhim* 5:11.)

הָיָה, וכו׳״. [1]אִילְפָא מוֹסִיף בָּהּ דְּבָרִים: מַעֲשֶׂה בְּאֶחָד שֶׁהָיָה מִצְטָעֵר עַל אִשָּׁה אַחַת וּבִיקֵּשׁ לֵירֵד. [2]כֵּיוָן שֶׁשָּׁמַע כָּזֹאת, גִּלְגֵּל בְּעַצְמוֹ עַד יוֹם מוֹתוֹ. [3]אַף עַל פִּי שֶׁחָכָם גָּדוֹל אַתָּה, אֵינוֹ דּוֹמֶה לוֹמֵד מֵעַצְמוֹ לְלוֹמֵד מֵרַבּוֹ. [4]וְאִם תֹּאמַר: אֵין לְךָ רַב! [5]יֵשׁ לְךָ רַב, וּמַנּוּ? רַבִּי יוֹחָנָן. [6]וְאִם אֵין אַתָּה עוֹלֶה, הִזָּהֵר בִּשְׁלֹשָׁה דְּבָרִים: [7]אַל תַּרְבֶּה בִּישִׁיבָה, שֶׁיְּשִׁיבָה קָשָׁה לְתַחְתּוֹנִיּוֹת. [8]וְאַל תַּרְבֶּה בַּעֲמִידָה, שֶׁעֲמִידָה קָשָׁה לַלֵּב. [9]וְאַל תַּרְבֶּה בַּהֲלִיכָה, שֶׁהֲלִיכָה קָשָׁה לָעֵינַיִם, [10]אֶלָּא שְׁלִישׁ בִּישִׁיבָה, שְׁלִישׁ בַּעֲמִידָה, שְׁלִישׁ בְּהִילּוּךְ. [11]כָּל יְשִׁיבָה שֶׁאֵין עִמָּהּ סְמִיכָה — עֲמִידָה נוֹחָה הֵימֶנָּה.

[12]עֲמִידָה סָלְקָא דַּעְתָּךְ? [13]וְהָאָמַרְתְּ: עֲמִידָה קָשָׁה לַלֵּב? [14]אֶלָּא: יְשִׁיבָה [111B] שֶׁאֵין בָּהּ סְמִיכָה — [15]עֲמִידָה שֶׁיֵּשׁ בָּהּ סְמִיכָה נוֹחָה הֵימֶנָּה.

[16]וְכֵן אָמְרוּ: [17]יִצְחָק, וְשִׁמְעוֹן, וְאוֹשַׁעְיָא אָמְרוּ דָּבָר אֶחָד: [18]הֲלָכָה כְּרַבִּי יְהוּדָה בַּפְּרָדוֹת.

LITERAL TRANSLATION

etc." [1]Ilfa added things: It once happened that someone desired (lit., "was distressed over") a certain woman and he wanted to leave [Eretz Israel]. [2]When he heard this, he suffered (lit., "rolled") with himself until the day of his death. [3]Even though you are a great Sage, someone who studies on his own cannot be compared to someone who learns from his master. [4]And if you say: You do not have a master! [5]You have a master, and who is he? Rabbi Yoḥanan. [6]And if you do not go up [to Eretz Israel], beware of three things: [7]Do not sit excessively, for sitting is hard on hemorrhoids. [8]And do not stand excessively, for standing is hard on the heart. [9]And do not walk excessively, for walking is hard on the eyes. [10]Rather, one-third sitting, one-third standing, one-third walking. [11]Any sitting that does not have support — standing is more comfortable than it.

[12]Can standing enter your mind? [13]But surely you said: Standing is hard on the heart? [14]Rather, [any] sitting [111B] that does not have support — [15]standing that has support is more comfortable than it.

[16]And they also said: [17]Yitzḥak, and Shimon, and Oshaya said the same thing: [18]The law is in accordance with Rabbi Yehudah regarding mules.

TRANSLATION AND COMMENTARY

included other teachings to try to influence Rabbah to settle in Eretz Israel, [1]such as what **Ilfa added: It once happened that someone desired a certain woman** living outside Eretz Israel **and he wanted to leave** Eretz Israel in order to marry her. [2]**When he heard** how important it was to live in Eretz Israel, he decided to remain, and **he suffered with himself until the day he died.** The brothers also added the following: [3]**Even though you are a great Sage, someone who studies on his own cannot be compared to someone who learns from his master** (as head of the Pumbedita Yeshivah, Rabbah had no greater Sage from whom to learn), and so it would be better for you to come to Eretz Israel. [4]**And if you say** that **you do not have a master** in Eretz Israel from whom to learn, [5]**you** do indeed **have** such **a master, that is, Rabbi Yoḥanan.** [6]**And if** you decide in the end **not to settle** in Eretz Israel, **beware of three things:** [7]**Do not sit excessively, for** extensive **sitting** causes **hemorrhoids.** [8]**And do not stand excessively, for standing is hard on the heart.** [9]**And do not walk excessively, for walking is hard on the eyes.** [10]**Rather,** divide your time into three, and spend **one-third sitting, one-third standing,** and **one-third walking.** They added one further piece of advice: [11]**Any sitting that does not have support — standing is easier than it.**

עֲמִידָה [12]The Gemara asks: **Can you imagine** that they meant that **standing** is easier on the body than sitting without support? [13]**But surely they said** that **standing is hard on the heart!**

אֶלָּא [14]**Rather,** they meant to say as follows: In comparison to **sitting** [111B] on something **that does not give** a person adequate **support,** such as a bench or stool, [15]**standing** next to something **that gives support,** such as next to a wall or a pillar, **is more comfortable** and easier on the body.

וְכֵן אָמְרוּ [16]Rabbah's brothers **also said** to him in their letter: [17]**Yitzḥak, Shimon, and Oshaya** all **said the same thing** [18]that **the law is in accordance with** the position of **Rabbi Yehudah regarding mules.**

RASHI

אילפא מוסיף בה דברים — עוד שלחו לו כן. מעשה באחד שהיה מצטער על אשה אחת — שנתן בה עיניו, והיא בחוץ לארץ. ואף על פי שחכם אתה — יפה לך לעלות כאן ללמוד מפי רב, שאין דומה הלומד מעצמו כו׳. ואם תאמר אין לך רב — כאן שיוכל ללמדך. שאין בה סמיכה — כמו במטות או בקתדראות יש סמיכה, בספסלין וכסאות — אין סמיכה.

HALAKHAH

הֲלָכָה כְּרַבִּי יְהוּדָה בַּפְּרָדוֹת **The law is in accordance with Rabbi Yehudah regarding mules.** "A hybrid animal (that is regarded as *kilayim*) may be mated with a similar hybrid animal, provided that the mothers of the two animals are

[1]דְּתַנְיָא: ״רַבִּי יְהוּדָה אוֹמֵר: פִּרְדָּה שֶׁתָּבְעָה, [2]אֵין מַרְבִּיעִין עָלֶיהָ לֹא סוּס וְלֹא חֲמוֹר, אֶלָּא מִינָהּ״.
[3]אָמַר רַב נַחְמָן בַּר יִצְחָק: יִצְחָק — זֶה רַבִּי יִצְחָק נַפָּחָא. [4]שִׁמְעוֹן — זֶה רַבִּי שִׁמְעוֹן בֶּן פָּזִי; [5]וְאָמְרִי לָהּ: רֵישׁ לָקִישׁ. [6]אוֹשַׁעְיָא — זֶה רַבִּי אוֹשַׁעְיָא בְּרַבִּי.
[7]אָמַר רַבִּי אֶלְעָזָר: עַמֵּי הָאֲרָצוֹת אֵינָן חַיִּים, [8]שֶׁנֶּאֱמַר: ״מֵתִים בַּל יִחְיוּ וגו׳״.
[9]תַּנְיָא נַמִי הָכִי: ״׳מֵתִים בַּל יִחְיוּ׳. [10]יָכוֹל לַכֹּל? [11]תַּלְמוּד לוֹמַר: ׳רְפָאִים בַּל יָקֻמוּ׳. [12]בִּמְרַפֶּה עַצְמוֹ מִדִּבְרֵי תוֹרָה הַכָּתוּב מְדַבֵּר״.

LITERAL TRANSLATION

[1]For it was taught: "Rabbi Yehudah says: A female mule that was in heat — [2]we may not mate it with a horse, nor with a donkey, but rather with its own kind."

[3]Rav Naḥman bar Yitzḥak said: Yitzḥak — this is Rabbi Yitzḥak Nappaha. [4]Shimon — this is Rabbi Shimon ben Pazzi; [5]and some say: Resh Lakish. [6]Oshaya — this is Rabbi Oshaya the son of Rabbi.

[7]Rabbi Elazar said: Uneducated people will not be resurrected, [8]as it is stated: "They are dead, they shall not live etc."

[9]It was also taught thus: "'They are dead; they shall not live.' [10]I might have thought all. [11]Therefore it states: '[They are] weak; they shall not rise.' [12]Scripture speaks about those who are lax about the matters of the Torah."

TRANSLATION AND COMMENTARY

[1]**For it was taught** in a Baraita: **"Rabbi Yehudah says: If a female mule** (the offspring of a horse and a donkey) **is in heat, [2]it may not be mated with a horse, nor with a donkey, but only with** an animal of **its own kind,** a male mule." The Torah prohibits crossbreeding different species of animals (Leviticus 19:19). The Rabbis maintain that an animal's species regarding this prohibition is determined by its dam, and not its sire. Thus, a female mule whose mother is a mare is regarded as a horse, and so it may be mated with a stallion; and a female hinny, whose mother is a jenny, is regarded as a donkey, and so it may be mated with a jackass. Rabbi Yehudah disagrees and says that an animal's species is determined by its father as well. Thus, a female mule may not be mated with a stallion, for it is part donkey, nor may it be mated with a jackass, for it is part horse. Thus it may only be mated with another mule. The three Rabbis mentioned above all ruled in accordance with the position of Rabbi Yehudah.

אָמַר [3]**Rav Naḥman bar Yitzḥak** identified the authorities mentioned in the letter to Rabbah and **said: Yitzḥak — this is Rabbi Yitzḥak Nappaha.** [4]**Shimon — this is Rabbi Shimon ben Pazzi,** [5]**and some say** that this is **Resh Lakish.** [6]**Oshaya — this is Rabbi Oshaya the son of Rabbi.**

אָמַר רַבִּי אֶלְעָזָר [7]**Rabbi Elazar said: Uneducated people will not be resurrected** at the end of the days, [8]**as the verse states** (Isaiah 26:14): **"They are dead, they shall not live;** they are weak, they shall not rise."

תַּנְיָא נַמִי הָכִי [9]**The same** idea **was also taught** in the following Baraita: "The verse states: **'They are dead, they shall not live.'** If I had only this part of the verse, [10]**I might have thought** that **none** of the dead will be revived. [11]**Therefore** the verse **continues: 'They are weak, they shall not rise.'** [12]**Scripture speaks here about those who are** uneducated and therefore **lax about the matters of the Torah.** They will not rise from their graves, but others will indeed be resurrected."

RASHI

אין מרביעין עליה לא סוס ולא חמור — מספקא ליה אי חוששין לזרע האב אי לא. הלכך אפילו היא בת חמורה נקבה — אין מרביעין עליה חמור, שמא חוששין לזרע האב ונמצא מרביע כלאים. ורבנן פליגי עליה, ואמרי: אין חוששין לזרע האב, ואם בת סוסיא היא מרביעין עליה סוס, ואם בת חמורה היא — מרביעין עליה חמור, הכי איתא בפרק ״אותו ואת בנו״. רפאים בל יקומו — [ב]מרפה עצמו מדברי תורה.

NOTES

עַמֵּי הָאֲרָצוֹת אֵינָן חַיִּים **Uneducated people will not be resurrected.** The commentators note that Rabbi Elazar did not mean that the uneducated will have no part in the resurrection, for all the dead will rise from their graves on the day of the final judgment. Rather, Rabbi Elazar meant that the uneducated will not remain among the living after the day of judgment, for they will be judged in accordance with their deeds and perish. *Meiri* writes that while all but

HALAKHAH

of the same species. For example, a male mule whose mother is a donkey may be mated with a female mule whose mother is also a donkey. But if the mothers are of two different species, the two offspring may not be mated together. If someone went ahead and mated two such animals, he is liable for lashes. So too, if he mated the hybrid offspring with a pure-bred animal of its mother's species, he is liable for lashes," following Rabbi Yehudah. (*Rambam, Sefer Zeraim, Hilkhot Kilayim* 9:6; *Shulḥan Arukh, Yoreh De'ah* 297:6,9.)

TRANSLATION AND COMMENTARY

אֲמַר לֵיהּ [1]**Rabbi Yoḥanan said to** Rabbi Elazar: **It is not pleasing to the Master** of the uneducated people — God — **that you speak about them like that.** [2]For **that** verse **refers to one who is lax about idolatry.** Such a person will not be revived in the time of resurrection, but the uneducated masses will be resurrected.

אֲמַר לֵיהּ [3]Rabbi Elazar **said to** Rabbi Yoḥanan: I also based my teaching that the uneducated will not be resurrected on the **exposition of a different verse,** [4]**for the verse states** (Isaiah 26:19): "Your dead men shall live, even my dead body shall arise. Awake and sing, you that dwell in dust. **For Your dew is a dew of lights, and the earth shall cast out the dead"** — [5]**Whoever uses the light of the Torah** ("the dew of lights"), **the light of the Torah will** later **revive him.** [6]**And whoever does not use the light of the Torah,** the uneducated, **the light of the Torah will not revive him.**

כֵּיוָן דְּחַזְיֵיהּ [7]It was further related that **when** Rabbi Elazar **saw that** Rabbi Yoḥanan **was** greatly **distressed** about the fate of the uneducated, [8]**he said to him: "My master, I found them a remedy in the Torah** that will allow them to be resurrected, despite their ignorance, for the verse states (Deuteronomy 4:4): [9]**'But you that did cleave unto the Lord your God are alive every one of you this day.'** Now, it may be asked: [10]**Is it** at all **possible to cleave unto the Divine Presence?** [11]**But surely** another **verse states** (Deuteronomy 4:24): **'For the Lord your God is a consuming fire'!** [12]**Rather,** the verse means as follows: **Whoever marries his daughter to a Torah scholar, or conducts business on behalf of Torah scholars,** joining their assets to his own and earning them a profit, [13]**or benefits Torah scholars with his property** in some other way — [14]**Scripture regards him as if**

[1]אֲמַר לֵיהּ רַבִּי יוֹחָנָן: לָא נִיחָא לְמָרַיְיהוּ דְּאָמְרַתְּ לְהוּ הָכִי. [2]הַהוּא בִּמְרַפֶּה עַצְמוֹ לַעֲבוֹדָה זָרָה הוּא דִּכְתִיב!

[3]אֲמַר לֵיהּ: מִקְרָא אַחֵר אֲנִי דּוֹרֵשׁ, [4]דִּכְתִיב: "כִּי טַל אוֹרֹת טַלֶּךָ וָאָרֶץ רְפָאִים תַּפִּיל" — [5]כָּל הַמִּשְׁתַּמֵּשׁ בְּאוֹר תּוֹרָה, אוֹר תּוֹרָה מְחַיֵּיהוּ. [6]וְכָל שֶׁאֵין מִשְׁתַּמֵּשׁ בְּאוֹר תּוֹרָה — אֵין אוֹר תּוֹרָה מְחַיֵּיהוּ.

[7]כֵּיוָן דְּחַזְיֵיהּ דְּקָמִצְטָעֵר, [8]אֲמַר לֵיהּ: "רַבִּי, מָצָאתִי לָהֶן תַּקָּנָה מִן הַתּוֹרָה: [9]'וְאַתֶּם הַדְּבֵקִים בַּה' אֱלֹהֵיכֶם חַיִּים כּוּלְּכֶם הַיּוֹם'. [10]וְכִי אֶפְשָׁר לְדַבּוּקֵי בַּשְּׁכִינָה? [11]וְהָכְתִיב: 'כִּי ה' אֱלֹהֶיךָ אֵשׁ אוֹכְלָה'! [12]אֶלָּא, כָּל הַמַּשִּׂיא בִּתּוֹ לְתַלְמִיד חָכָם, וְהָעוֹשֶׂה פְּרַקְמַטְיָא לְתַלְמִידֵי חֲכָמִים, [13]וְהַמְהַנֶּה תַּלְמִידֵי חֲכָמִים מִנְּכָסָיו — [14]מַעֲלֶה עָלָיו

LITERAL TRANSLATION

[1]Rabbi Yoḥanan said to him: It is not pleasing to their Master that you speak about them like that. [2]That is written about one who is lax about idolatry.

[3]He said to him: I [have also] expounded a different verse, [4]for it is written: "For Your dew is a dew of lights, and the earth shall cast out the dead" — [5]whoever uses the light of the Torah, the light of the Torah revives him. [6]And whoever does not use the light of the Torah, the light of the Torah does not revive him.

[7]When he saw that he was distressed, [8]he said to him: "My master, I found them a remedy from the Torah: [9]'But you that did cleave unto the Lord your God are alive every one of you this day.' [10]Is it possible to cleave to the Divine Presence? [11]But surely it is written: 'For the Lord your God is a consuming fire'! [12]Rather, whoever marries his daughter to a Torah scholar, or conducts business on behalf of Torah scholars, [13]or benefits Torah scholars with his property — [14]Scripture regards him

RASHI

וארץ רפאים תפיל — ואלרץ לרפאים תפיל. מצאתי להם תקנה — יהנו לתלמידי חכמים מנכסיהם. העושה פרקמטיא — מתעסק בממון תלמידי חכמים כדי להגיע לידם שכר, והם פנויין לעסוק בתורה על ידי אלו, וכתיב "חיים כולכם היום" — על ידי דיבוקן של תלמידי חכמים יזכו לחיות.

LANGUAGE

פְּרַקְמַטְיָא **Business.** From the Greek πραγματεία, *pragmateia,* meaning "business, trade."

NOTES

the wicked will enjoy eternal life, the uneducated will not enjoy the same quality of life after the resurrection as will the righteous scholars.

וְאַתֶּם הַדְּבֵקִים **But you that did cleave.** *Midrash Yelamdenu* offers the following analogy: Just as the cover of a Torah scroll may be rescued from a fire (in violation of the Sabbath law) together with the Torah scroll itself, so too those who cleave to Torah scholars will have a share in their reward (*Iyyun Ya'akov*).

כָּל הַמַּשִּׂיא בִּתּוֹ **Whoever marries his daughter.** *Maharsha* notes that the Gemara proposes three ways of cleaving unto a Torah scholar: Cleaving unto him physically by

HALAKHAH

כָּל הַמַּשִּׂיא בִּתּוֹ **Whoever marries off his daughter.** "It is a mitzvah to cleave unto Torah Sages and their disciples in order to learn from their ways, as the verse states: 'And that you may cleave unto him.' Therefore, a person must

הַכָּתוּב כְּאִילּוּ מְדַבֵּק בַּשְּׁכִינָה. [1]כַּיּוֹצֵא בַּדָּבָר אַתָּה אוֹמֵר: [2]״לְאַהֲבָה אֶת ה׳ אֱלֹהֶיךָ... וּלְדָבְקָה בוֹ״. [3]וְכִי אֶפְשָׁר לְאָדָם לִידָּבֵק בַּשְּׁכִינָה? [4]אֶלָּא, כָּל הַמַּשִּׂיא בִּתּוֹ לְתַלְמִיד חָכָם, וְהָעוֹשֶׂה פְּרַקְמַטְיָא לְתַלְמִידֵי חֲכָמִים, וְהַמְהַנֶּה תַּלְמִידֵי חֲכָמִים מִנְּכָסָיו, [5]מַעֲלֶה עָלָיו הַכָּתוּב כְּאִילּוּ מְדַבֵּק בַּשְּׁכִינָה״.

[6]אָמַר רַבִּי חִיָּיא בַּר יוֹסֵף: עֲתִידִין צַדִּיקִים שֶׁמְּבַצְבְּצִין וְעוֹלִין בִּירוּשָׁלַיִם, [7]שֶׁנֶּאֱמַר: ״וְיָצִיצוּ מֵעִיר כְּעֵשֶׂב הָאָרֶץ״, [8]וְאֵין ״עִיר״ אֶלָּא יְרוּשָׁלַיִם, [9]שֶׁנֶּאֱמַר: ״וְגַנּוֹתִי אֶל הָעִיר הַזֹּאת״.

[10]וְאָמַר רַבִּי חִיָּיא בַּר יוֹסֵף: עֲתִידִים צַדִּיקִים שֶׁיַּעַמְדוּ בְּמַלְבּוּשֵׁיהֶן. [11]קַל וָחוֹמֶר מֵחִטָּה: [12]מַה חִטָּה שֶׁנִּקְבְּרָה עֲרוּמָה יוֹצְאָה בְּכַמָּה לְבוּשִׁין, [13]צַדִּיקִים שֶׁנִּקְבְּרוּ בִּלְבוּשֵׁיהֶן, [14]עַל אַחַת כַּמָּה וְכַמָּה!

[15]וְאָמַר רַבִּי חִיָּיא בַּר יוֹסֵף: עֲתִידָה אֶרֶץ יִשְׂרָאֵל שֶׁתּוֹצִיא גְּלוּסְקָאוֹת וּכְלֵי מֵילַת,

LITERAL TRANSLATION

as if he were cleaving to the Divine Presence. [1]Similarly, it states: [2]'That you may love the Lord your God...and that you may cleave to Him.' [3]But is it possible for a person to cleave to the Divine Presence? [4]Rather, whoever marries his daughter to a Torah scholar, or conducts business on behalf of Torah scholars, or benefits Torah scholars with his property [5]is regarded by Scripture as if he were cleaving to the Divine Presence."

[6]Rabbi Ḥiyya bar Yosef said: In the future the righteous will break through [the ground] and rise in Jerusalem, [7]as it is stated: "And may they break through in the city like the grass of the earth." [8]And "city" only [means] Jerusalem, [9]as it is stated: "For I will defend this city."

[10]And Rabbi Ḥiyya bar Yosef said: In the future, the righteous will rise in their clothing. [11][Derive this] by way of an *a fortiori* inference from wheat: [12]If wheat that is buried naked issues forth with several [protective] structures (lit., "garments"), [13]righteous men who are buried in their clothing, [14]all the more so!

[15]And Rabbi Ḥiyya bar Yosef said: In the future, Eretz Israel will issue forth fine breads and fine wool garments,

TRANSLATION AND COMMENTARY

he were cleaving to the Divine Presence. [1]**Similarly, the verse states** (Deuteronomy 30:20): [2]**'That you may love the Lord your God...and that you may cleave to Him.'** [3]It may be asked: **Is it** at all **possible for a person to cleave to the Divine Presence?** [4]**Rather, whoever marries his daughter to a Torah scholar, or conducts business on behalf of a Torah scholar, or benefits Torah scholars with his property** in some other way — [5]**Scripture regards him as if he were cleaving to the Divine Presence."**

אָמַר [6]**Rabbi Ḥiyya bar Yosef said: In the future** at the time of the resurrection, **the righteous will break through** the ground **and rise** up **in Jerusalem,** [7]**as** a verse referring to the days of the Messiah **states** (Psalms 72:16): **"And may they break through in the city like the grass of the earth."** [8]**And** the word **"city" refers** here **to Jerusalem,** [9]**as the verse states** (II Kings 19:34): **"For I will defend this city."**

וְאָמַר [10]**And Rabbi Ḥiyya bar Yosef** also **said: In the future** at the time of the resurrection, **the righteous will rise** up from the ground **in their clothing.** [11]We may derive this **by way of an *a fortiori* inference from wheat:** [12]**If a wheat** seed **that is buried naked, issues forth** covered **with several** layers of straw and chaff, [13]then **righteous men who are buried in their shrouds,** [14]**all the more so** will they emerge in the time of resurrection fully attired!

וְאָמַר [15]**And** furthermore **Rabbi Ḥiyya bar Yosef said: In the future, Eretz Israel will issue forth** loaves of **fine**

LANGUAGE

גְּלוּסְקָאוֹת Loaves of fine bread. This word is apparently derived from the Greek κόλλιξ, *kollix,* meaning "loaf of bread."

מֵילַת Wool. This word is apparently of Greek origin, although its precise etymology is unclear. Some derive it from μαλλός, *mallos,* meaning "wool shearings," while others explain it as μηλωτή, *melote,* meaning "sheepskin." Still others associate this term with Μίλητος, Miletos, a Greek city where fine woolen clothing was made. Elsewhere the Talmud indicates that מֵילַת is wool of the highest quality, which was taken from lambs and sheep specially designated for this purpose.

RASHI

גלוסקאות וכלי מילת — דרוש ״פסת בר״ לשון פיסת היד

NOTES

marrying one's daughter to him; cleaving unto him financially by allowing him to benefit from one's property; and cleaving unto him emotionally by doing whatever is in one's power to allow him to derive some form of benefit.

וְאֵין עִיר אֶלָּא יְרוּשָׁלַיִם And "city" only means Jerusalem. We find elsewhere that Jerusalem is referred to as "the city" without further specification, e.g. (Ezekiel 40:1): "In the fourteenth year after the city [=Jerusalem] was smitten." In Rabbinic literature, Jerusalem is commonly referred to as "the city."

שֶׁיַּעַמְדוּ בְּמַלְבּוּשֵׁיהֶן Will rise in their clothing. A disagreement regarding this matter is recorded in the Jerusalem Talmud as to whether the righteous will rise from their graves in the clothing in which they had been buried, their shrouds, or in other clothing (see *Tosafot*).

שֶׁתּוֹצִיא גְּלוּסְקָאוֹת Will issue forth breads. *Hafla'ah* writes

HALAKHAH

make efforts to marry the daughter of a Torah scholar, and to marry off his daughter to a Torah scholar, and to eat and drink with Torah Sages, and to do business with them, and to join with them in every possible way." (*Rambam, Sefer HaMada, Hilkhot De'ot* 6:2; *Shulḥan Arukh, Even HaEzer* 2:6.)

TRANSLATION AND COMMENTARY

bread and silk garments, [1]**as the verse states** (Psalms 72:16): **"May there be abundance of corn** [פִּסַּת בַּר] **in the land."** Rabbi Ḥiyya bar Yosef understands the word פסים in the sense of כתנת פסים, "fine wool garment," and the word בַּר he understands in the sense of bread, so that the verse teaches that in the future the land will bring forth food and clothing in their finished form.

תָּנוּ רַבָּנַן [2]**Our Rabbis taught** a Baraita which stated: "The verse states (Psalms 72:16): [3]**'May there be abundance of corn in the land on the tops of the mountains.'** [4]The Rabbis **said: In the future, wheat** (פִּסַּת בַּר) **will grow tall like palms, and rise up** even **to the top of mountains.** [5]**And lest you say** that if the wheat grows that tall, **it will be toilsome** and laborious **to harvest.** [6]**Therefore the verse** itself **states: 'May its fruit rustle like the Lebanon.'** [7]**The Holy One, blessed be He, will bring a wind from His treasure house,** [8]**and cause** the wind **to blow upon** the wheat, **and cause its best flour to fall** to the ground, [9]**and a person will** then **go out to the field, and bring** in **a handful** of the flour, [10]**which will suffice for his** own **maintenance and the maintenance of his** entire **household."**

עִם חֵלֶב [11]The verse states (Deuteronomy 32:14): **"With the fat of kidneys of wheat."** [12]The Rabbis **said: In the future,** a kernel of **wheat will be** as big **as the two kidneys of a large ox.** [13]**And do not be surprised** that wheat can grow to that size, **for** it once happened that **a fox made a nest** in which to bear its young **in a** large **turnip** by hollowing out its center, [14]**and** people came and **weighed** the turnip, **and found** that even after its center had been hollowed out, the turnip still weighed **sixty pounds of the pounds of Sepphoris** (approximately the same as a modern pound).

תַּנְיָא [15]And similarly, **it was taught** in a Baraita: **"Rav Yosef said:** [16]**It once happened in Shihin that someone was left three branches of mustard by his father,** [17]**and one of** the branches **broke off** from its stalk, **and** they

1 שֶׁנֶּאֱמַר: "יְהִי פִסַּת בַּר בָּאָרֶץ".
2 תָּנוּ רַבָּנַן: 3 "'יְהִי פִסַּת בַּר בָּאָרֶץ בְּרֹאשׁ הָרִים'. 4 אָמְרוּ: עֲתִידָה, חִטָּה שֶׁתִּתַמֵּר כַּדֶּקֶל וְעוֹלָה בְּרֹאשׁ הָרִים; 5 וְשֶׁמָּא תֹּאמַר: יֵשׁ צַעַר לְקוֹצְרָהּ? 6 תַּלְמוּד לוֹמַר: 'יִרְעַשׁ כַּלְּבָנוֹן פִּרְיוֹ'. 7 הַקָּדוֹשׁ בָּרוּךְ הוּא מֵבִיא רוּחַ מִבֵּית גְּנָזָיו, 8 וּמְנַשְּׁבָה עָלֶיהָ וּמַשְׁרָה אֶת סָלְתָּהּ, 9 וְאָדָם יוֹצֵא לַשָּׂדֶה וּמֵבִיא מְלֹא פִּיסַּת יָדוֹ, 10 וּמִמֶּנָּה פַּרְנָסָתוֹ וּפַרְנָסַת אַנְשֵׁי בֵּיתוֹ".
11 "עִם חֵלֶב כִּלְיוֹת חִטָּה". 12 אָמְרוּ: עֲתִידָה חִטָּה שֶׁתְּהֵא כִּשְׁתֵּי כִּלְיוֹת שֶׁל שׁוֹר הַגָּדוֹל. 13 וְאַל תִּתְמַהּ, שֶׁהֲרֵי שׁוּעָל קִינֵּן בְּלֶפֶת, 14 וּשְׁקָלוּהוּ, וּמָצְאוּ בּוֹ שִׁשִּׁים לִיטְרִין בְּלִיטְרָא שֶׁל צִפּוֹרִי.
15 תַּנְיָא: "אָמַר רַב יוֹסֵף: 16 מַעֲשֶׂה בְּשִׁיחִין בְּאֶחָד שֶׁהִנִּיחַ לוֹ אָבִיו שְׁלֹשָׁה בַּדֵּי חַרְדָּל, 17 וְנִפְשַׁח אֶחָד

LITERAL TRANSLATION

[1]as it is stated: "May there be abundance of corn in the land."

[2]Our Rabbis taught: [3]"'May there be abundance of corn in the land on the tops of the mountains.' [4]They said: In the future, wheat will grow tall like palms, and rise to the top of mountains. [5]And lest you say: There is toil in harvesting it? [6]Therefore the verse states: 'May its fruit rustle like the Lebanon.' [7]The Holy One, blessed be He, brings a wind from His treasure house, [8]and causes it to blow upon it, and causes its best flour to fall, [9]and a person goes out to the field, and brings a handful, [10]and [has] from it his maintenance and the maintenance of his household."

[11]"With the fat of kidneys of wheat." [12]They said: In the future, wheat will be like the two kidneys of a large ox. [13]And do not be surprised, for a fox made a nest in a turnip, [14]and they weighed it, and found in it sixty pounds of the pounds of Sepphoris.

[15]It was taught: "Rav Yosef said: [16]It once happened in Shihin that someone whose father left him three branches of mustard, [17]and one of them broke off,

RASHI

שהיא רחבה, וחטה רחבה לא משכחת אלא פת אפויה. וכלי מילת דרוש "פסת" לשון כתונת פסים. שתתמר – לשון תומר = דקל. קינן בלפת – ניקב בו עד שעשה לידתו בתוכו. ואף על פי כן – שקלו את המותר ששים ליטרין. נפשח – נגדל אחד מהן מן הקלח.

NOTES

that according to God's original plan for the world, the earth was to have brought forth food and clothing in their finished form, but the earth was cursed as a result of Adam's sin. At the end of days when man actualizes his full potential, the earth too will actualize its full potential and bring forth food and clothing in their final form.

Rambam (in his introduction to his Commentary to the Mishnah) writes that the descriptions found here are allusions to the great abundance that will fill the world in the end of days, allowing people to devote all their time and attention to the study of Torah.

BACKGROUND

לֶפֶת **Turnips.**

The turnip (*Brassica rapa*) is a common garden vegetable, whose bulbs were normally eaten cooked. Large turnip bulbs were often cut into pieces before being sold. Turnip bulbs are usually not that big, although they can sometimes grow very large. Thus, cases have been documented of turnips seventy centimeters long, weighing more than twelve kilograms, and a fox could easily make its nest in a bulb this size.

חַרְדָּל **Mustard.**

Mustard is produced from the seeds of several different plants, such as white mustard (*Sinapis alba*), black mustard (*Brassica nigra*), and other, related plants. These plants belong to the Cruciferae family, and grow wild in Israel. Black mustard has spreading branches and bundles of large flowers, which grow close to one another. It is the largest member of the Cruciferae family in Israel. It grows from half a meter to two meters high, sometimes even reaching a height of five meters.

LANGUAGE

פִּטּוּס Cask. From the Greek πίθος, *pithos,* meaning "a large earthenware cask."

BACKGROUND

פִּטּוּס Cask.

Casks were the largest earthenware containers manufactured in ancient times. Some casks have been found which are taller than people.

גֶּפֶן Grapevines. Grapevines can live for a long time, and they sometimes grow very large. A grapevine's trunk may reach up to a meter and a half in circumference, and the main trunk can sometimes be more than forty meters long. Accordingly, large numbers of grape clusters grow on such huge vines.

TRANSLATION AND COMMENTARY

found nine ***kavs*** (12.7 l., 13.5 qt.) **of mustard** seeds **in it,** [1]**and** the branch was so big that **with its** the **woody parts they covered a potter's hut.** [2]And so too **Rabbi Shimon ben Tahlifa said: Father left us a cabbage stalk,** [3]**and** it was so tall that **we would** have to **ascend and descend on a ladder** in order to reach its upper portion."

וְדַם עֵנָב [4]The verse states (Deuteronomy 32:14): "'**And you drank wine of the pure blood of the grape.'** [5]**The Rabbis said: The world to come is not like this world.** [6]**In this world, it is toilsome** and laborious **to pick** grapes **and tread** upon them. [7]**In the world to come,** a person **will bring** home **a single grape on a wagon or a ship,** [8]**and put it down in the corner of his house, and take his supply** of wine **from it,** [9]**as if it were a** very **large cask** filled with wine, **and the woody parts** of the grape **he will kindle under his pot.** [10]**No grape will yield less than thirty** ***se'ah*****-kegs** (1 *se'ah* = 8.5 l., 9qt.) **of wine,** [11]**as the verse states: 'And you drank wine** (חָמֶר) **of the pure blood of the grape.'** [12]**Do not read** the word according to the traditional Masoretic vocalization as **'*hamer,*'** 'wine' — [13]**but rather** read the word as if it were vocalized **'*homer,*'** 'thirty *se'ahs.*' "

כִּי אֲתָא [14]**When Rav Dimi came** from Eretz Israel to Babylonia, **he said:** [15]**What is the meaning of the verse, which states** (Genesis 49:11-12): "Binding his foal to the vine, and the ass's colt to the choice vine; he washes his garments in wine, and his clothes in the blood of grapes. His eyes are red with wine, and his teeth white with milk." [16]**"Binding his foal to the vine"** — in the future, [17]there will be **no grapevine in Eretz Israel that does not require a whole city for the harvest,** Rav Dimi interpreting the word for foal, *iro,* in the sense of *iro,* "his city." [18]**"And his ass's colt to the choice vine"** — in the future, [19]**there will no tree** that had before been **fruitless that will not yield a load of** fruit that will have to be carried by **two asses.** Rav Dimi relates the word שֹׂרֵקָה (translated here as "choice vine") to the word סרק ("fruitless tree"), and he understands the phrase בְּנִי אֲתֹנוֹ (translated here as "his ass's colt") as hinting at two asses, as if the word were vocalized as the plural *benei.* [20]**And lest you say** that the vines might indeed produce a great number of grapes, but those grapes **might not yield** very much **wine,** [21]**therefore the verse states: "He washes his**

מֵהֶן, וְנִמְצְאוּ בּוֹ תִּשְׁעָה קַבִּין חַרְדָּל, [1]וְעֵצָיו סִיכְּכוּ בּוֹ סוּכַּת יוֹצְרִין. [2]אָמַר רַבִּי שִׁמְעוֹן בֶּן תַּחֲלִיפָא: קֶלַח שֶׁל כְּרוּב הִנִּיחַ לָנוּ אַבָּא, [3]וְהָיִינוּ עוֹלִים וְיוֹרְדִים בּוֹ בְּסוּלָּם".

[4]"וְדַם עֵנָב תִּשְׁתֶּה חָמֶר". [5]אָמְרוּ: לֹא כָּעוֹלָם הַזֶּה הָעוֹלָם הַבָּא. [6]הָעוֹלָם הַזֶּה יֵשׁ בּוֹ צַעַר לִבְצוֹר וְלִדְרוֹךְ. [7]הָעוֹלָם הַבָּא מֵבִיא עֲנָוָה אַחַת בְּקָרוֹן אוֹ בִּסְפִינָה, [8]וּמַנִּיחָהּ בְּזָוִית בֵּיתוֹ, וּמְסַפֵּק הֵימֶנָּה כְּפִטּוּס גָּדוֹל, [9]וְעֵצָיו מַסִּיקִין תַּחַת הַתַּבְשִׁיל. [10]וְאֵין לְךָ כָּל עֲנָבָה וַעֲנָבָה שֶׁאֵין בָּהּ שְׁלֹשִׁים גַּרְבֵּי יַיִן, [11]שֶׁנֶּאֱמַר: 'וְדַם עֵנָב תִּשְׁתֶּה חָמֶר'. [12]אַל תִּקְרֵי 'חָמֶר', [13]אֶלָּא 'חוֹמֶר'".

[14]כִּי אֲתָא רַב דִּימִי אֲמַר: [15]מַאי דִּכְתִיב: [16]"אֹסְרִי לַגֶּפֶן עִירֹה" — [17]אֵין לְךָ כָּל גֶּפֶן וְגֶפֶן שֶׁבְּאֶרֶץ יִשְׂרָאֵל שֶׁאֵין צָרִיךְ עִיר אַחַת לִבְצוֹר. [18]"וְלַשֹּׂרֵקָה בְּנִי אֲתֹנוֹ" — [19]אֵין לְךָ כָּל אִילָן סְרָק שֶׁבְּאֶרֶץ יִשְׂרָאֵל שֶׁאֵינוֹ מוֹצִיא מַשּׂוֹי שְׁתֵּי אֲתוֹנוֹת. [20]וְשֶׁמָּא תֹּאמַר: אֵין בּוֹ יַיִן? [21]תַּלְמוּד לוֹמַר:

LITERAL TRANSLATION

and nine *kavs* of mustard were found in it, [1]and with its woody parts they covered a potter's hut. [2]Rabbi Shimon ben Tahlifa said: Father left us a cabbage stalk, [3]and we would ascend and descend it on a ladder."

[4]"'And you drank wine of the pure blood of the grape.' [5]They said: The world to come is not like this world. [6][In] this world, there is toil in picking and treading [grapes]. [7][In] the world to come, one brings in one grape on a wagon or a ship, [8]and puts it down in the corner of the house, and takes his supply from it, as if it were a large cask, [9]and its woody parts [are used] as kindling under the cooking pot. [10]And there is not a single grape that does not yield thirty kegs of wine, [11]as it is stated: 'And you drank wine of the pure blood of the grape.' [12]Do not read '*hamer,*' ['wine'], [13]but rather '*homer,*' ['thirty *se'ahs*']."

[14]When Rav Dimi came, he said: [15]What is [the meaning of] that which is written: [16]"Binding his foal [עירה] to the vine" — [17]there is not a single grapevine in Eretz Israel that does not require a [whole] city [עיר] for the harvest. [18]"And his ass's colt to the choice vine" — [19]there is not a single fruitless tree that will not produce a load [of fruit] for two asses. [20]And lest you say: It has no wine? [21]Therefore the verse states:

RASHI

והיינו עולים בסולם — ללקט עליו העליונים. **ודם ענב תשתה** — מתוך הענבה תשתהו. ולא תצטרך לדורכו. **חומר** — כור, והוא שלשים סאין. **גרבי** — סאה. **אין לך כל אילן סרק** — שלא יעשה פרי. **אין בו יין** — אין בו ליחלוח בפרי.

TRANSLATION AND COMMENTARY

garments in wine." [1]**And lest you say** that those grapes might indeed yield wine in great quantities, but the wine **might not be** choice **red,** [2]**therefore the verse states** elsewhere (Deuteronomy 32:14): **"And you drank wine of the pure blood of the grape."** [3]**And lest you say** that the wine might indeed be red, but it will be of poor quality, so that **it will not intoxicate** those who drink it, [4]**therefore the Torah states: "And his clothes** [״סותה״] **in the blood of the grapes."** Rav Dimi interprets the word סותה (translated here as "his clothes") as stemming from the word הֲסָתָה, "incitement," so that the word alludes to the inciting and fomenting qualities of the wine. [5]**And lest you say** that while the wine might be strong and intoxicating, **it will have no taste,** [6]**therefore the Torah states: "His eyes are red** [חַכְלִילִי] **with wine"** — [7]**every palate that tastes it will say:** "More **for me,** more **for me."** Rav Dimi interprets the word חַכְלִילִי (translated here as "red") as if it were three words חֵיךְ לִי לִי, "the palate [says]: For me, for me." [8]**And lest you say** that while the wine **might** indeed **be good for young lads, it will not be good for old people,** [9]**therefore the Torah states: "And his teeth white with milk."** [10]**Do not read** the words according to the traditional Masoretic vocalization as *l'ven shinayim,* "whitened teeth," [11]**but rather** read the words as if they were vocalized *l'ven shanim,* "for a man of years."

פְּשָׁטֵיהּ דִּקְרָא [12]The Gemara asks: **What is the plain sense of the verse** (Genesis 49:12): "His eyes are red with wine, and his teeth white with milk"? [13]**When Rav Dimi came** from Eretz Israel to Babylonia, **he said: The congregation of Israel said before the Holy One, blessed be He:** [14]**"Master of the Universe, show us with Your eyes a hint** of Your feelings of affection toward us, [15]**for that is sweeter than wine, and show us** Your love **with Your teeth** — smile at us — **for that is sweeter than milk."**

[16]The Gemara notes: **This** exposition of the verse **supports** the statement **of Rabbi Yoḥanan,** [17]**for Rabbi Yoḥanan said: Someone who whitens his teeth to another person** and smiles at him **is better** for him **than**

"כִּבֵּס בַּיַּיִן לְבֻשׁוֹ". [1]וְשֶׁמָּא תֹּאמַר, אֵינוֹ אָדוֹם? [2]תַּלְמוּד לוֹמַר: "וְדַם עֵנָב תִּשְׁתֶּה חָמֶר". [3]וְשֶׁמָּא תֹּאמַר: אֵינוֹ מְרַוֶּה? [4]תַּלְמוּד לוֹמַר: "סוּתֹה". [5]וְשֶׁמָּא תֹּאמַר: אֵין בּוֹ טַעַם? [6]תַּלְמוּד לוֹמַר: "חַכְלִילִי עֵינַיִם מִיָּיִן" — [7]כָּל חֵיךְ שֶׁטּוֹעֲמוֹ אוֹמֵר: לִי, לִי. [8]וְשֶׁמָּא תֹּאמַר: לִנְעָרִים יָפֶה, וְלִזְקֵנִים אֵינוֹ יָפֶה? [9]תַּלְמוּד לוֹמַר: "וּלְבֶן שִׁנַּיִם מֵחָלָב". [10]אַל תִּיקְרֵי "לְבֶן שִׁנַּיִם" [11]אֶלָּא "לְבֶן שָׁנִים".
[12]פְּשָׁטֵיהּ דִּקְרָא, בְּמַאי כְּתִיב? [13]כִּי אֲתָא רַב דִּימִי אֲמַר, אָמְרָה כְּנֶסֶת יִשְׂרָאֵל לִפְנֵי הַקָּדוֹשׁ בָּרוּךְ הוּא: [14]"רִבּוֹנוֹ שֶׁל עוֹלָם, רְמוֹז בְּעֵינֶיךָ דִּבְסִים מֵחַמְרָא, [15]וְאַחְוֵי לִי שִׁינֶּיךָ דִּבְסִים מֵחַלְבָּא".
[16]מְסַיַּיע לֵיהּ לְרַבִּי יוֹחָנָן, [17]דְּאָמַר רַבִּי יוֹחָנָן: טוֹב הַמַּלְבִּין שִׁינַּיִם לַחֲבֵירוֹ יוֹתֵר

LITERAL TRANSLATION

"He washes his garments in wine." [1]And lest you say: It is not red? [2]Therefore the verse states: "And you drank wine of the pure blood of the grape." [3]And lest you say: It does not intoxicate? [4]Therefore the Torah states: "And his clothes [in the blood of the grapes]." [5]And lest you say: It has no taste? [6]Therefore the Torah states: "His eyes are red with wine," [7]every palate that tastes it says: For me, for me. [8]And lest you say: It is good for young lads, but it is not good for old people? [9]Therefore the Torah states: "And his teeth white with milk." [10]Do not read *l'ven shinayim* (lit., "white of the teeth") [11]but rather *l'ven shanim* (lit., "to a son of years").

[12][According to] the plain sense of the verse, to what does it refer? [13]When Rav Dimi came, he said: The congregation of Israel said before the Holy One, blessed be He: [14]"Master of the Universe, hint to us with Your eyes, for that is sweeter than wine, [15]and show us with Your teeth, for that is sweeter than milk."

[16]This supports that of Rabbi Yoḥanan, [17]for Rabbi Yoḥanan said: Someone who whitens his teeth (smiles) before another person is better than someone

RASHI

סותה — לשון הסתה, שהיין מסית את השכור. **רמוז לי בעיניך** — ותתרגם לשון שחוק ומחוך: חוך לי בעינים שלך, וטוב לי מיין כשתראני פנים צהובות ושוחקות. **ואחוי לי שיניך** — אף זו לשון שחוק, שהשוחק שיניו נגלין.

NOTES

פְּשָׁטֵיהּ דִּקְרָא **The plain sense of the verse.** *Maharsha* notes that while the interpretation which the Gemara offers here is not really the plain sense of the verse, it is closer to the plain sense of the verse than the previous interpretation. See also Onkelos who generally offers a literal translation of the Torah's text, but with respect to this verse deviates from his usual practice, for here the plain sense of the verse is clearly not the same as its literal meaning.

LITERAL TRANSLATION

who gives him milk to drink. [1]As it is stated: "And his teeth white with milk." [2]Do not read *l'ven shinayim* (lit., "white of teeth") [3]but rather *libbun shinayim* ("whitening of teeth")."

[4]Rav Ḥiyya bar Adda was the teacher of Resh Lakish's children. [5]He tarried three days and did not come. [6]When he came, [Resh Lakish] said to him: "Why did you tarry?" [7]He said to him: "Father left me one grapevine, [8]and I picked from it on the first day three hundred clusters, [9][each] cluster [yielding] a keg. [10]On the second day I picked three hundred clusters, [11]two clusters [yielding] a keg. [12]On the third day I picked from it three hundred clusters, [13]three clusters [yielding] a keg. [14]And I renounced ownership of more than half of it." [15]He said to him: "Had you not tarried, [16]it would have produced more."

[17]Rami bar Yeḥezkel happened to be in Bene Berak. [18]He saw certain goats grazing under fig trees, [19]and honey dripped from the figs, [20]and milk dripped from them, and they got mixed together. [21]He said: "This is the meaning of 'flowing with milk and honey.'"

[22]Rabbi Ya'akov ben Dostai said: "From Lod to Ono is three miles. [23]Once I left early in the morning,

מְמַשְׁקֵהוּ חָלָב. [1]שֶׁנֶּאֱמַר: "וּלְבֶן שִׁנַּיִם מֵחָלָב". [2]אַל תִּקְרֵי "לְבֶן שִׁנַּיִם" [3]אֶלָּא "לִבּוּן שִׁנַּיִם".

[4]רַב חִיָּיא בַּר אַדָּא מַקְרֵי דַּרְדְּקֵי דְּרֵישׁ לָקִישׁ הֲוָה. [5]אִיפַּגַּר תְּלָתָא יוֹמֵי וְלָא אֲתָא. [6]כִּי אֲתָא, אֲמַר לֵיהּ: "אַמַּאי אִיפַּגְרַתְּ"? [7]אֲמַר לֵיהּ: "דָּלִית אַחַת הִנִּיחַ לִי אַבָּא, [8]וּבָצַרְתִּי מִמֶּנָּה יוֹם רִאשׁוֹן שְׁלֹשׁ מֵאוֹת אֶשְׁכּוֹלוֹת, [9]אֶשְׁכּוֹל לְגָרָב. [10]יוֹם שֵׁנִי בָּצַרְתִּי שְׁלֹשׁ מֵאוֹת אֶשְׁכּוֹלוֹת, [11]שְׁתֵּי אֶשְׁכּוֹלוֹת לְגָרָב. [12]יוֹם שְׁלִישִׁי בָּצַרְתִּי מִמֶּנָּה שְׁלֹשׁ מֵאוֹת אֶשְׁכּוֹלוֹת, [13]שָׁלֹשׁ אֶשְׁכּוֹלוֹת לְגָרָב. [14]וְהִפְקַרְתִּי יוֹתֵר מֶחֶצְיָהּ". [15]אֲמַר לֵיהּ: "אִי לָאו דְּאִיפַּגְרַתְּ, [16]הֲוָה עָבְדָא טְפֵי".

[17]רָמִי בַּר יְחֶזְקֵאל אִיקְּלַע לִבְנֵי בְרַק. [18]חֲזָנְהוּ לְהָנְהוּ עִיזֵּי דְּקָאָכְלָן תּוּתֵי תְּאֵינֵי, [19]וְקָנָטֵיף דּוּבְשָׁא מִתְּאֵינֵי, [20]וַחֲלָבָא טָיֵיף מִנַּיְיהוּ, וּמִיעָרַב בַּהֲדֵי הֲדָדֵי. [21]אֲמַר: "הַיְינוּ 'זָבַת חָלָב וּדְבַשׁ'".

[22]אָמַר רַבִּי יַעֲקֹב בֶּן דּוֹסְתַּאי: "מִלּוּד לְאוֹנוֹ שְׁלֹשָׁה מִילִין. [23]פַּעַם אַחַת קִדַּמְתִּי בַּנֶּשֶׁף,

TRANSLATION AND COMMENTARY

someone who gives him milk to drink, [1]**as the verse states: "And his teeth white with milk."** [2]**Do not read** the words according to the traditional Masoretic vocalization as ***l'ven shinayim,*** [3]**but rather** read it as if it were vocalized ***libbun shinayim,*** "whitening of the teeth." Whitening one's teeth to a person is better than (the letter *mem* in the word *me-ḥalav* is used here as a particle indicating comparison) offering him milk to drink.

רַב חִיָּיא בַּר אַדָּא [4]The Gemara offers another anecdote to demonstrate the abundance found in Eretz Israel. **Rav Ḥiyya bar Adda was the teacher of Resh Lakish's children.** [5]**He tarried three days and did not come** to teach his young pupils. [6]**When he** finally **came,** Resh Lakish **said to him: "Why did you tarry?"** [7]Rav Ḥiyya bar Adda **said to him:** "When **Father** died, he **left me one grapevine.** I could not come these past three days, because I was busy harvesting the grapes. [8]**On the first day** that I did not come, **I picked from** the vine **three hundred clusters** of grapes, [9]each **cluster** yielding **a** *se'ah*-**keg** of wine. [10]**On the second day I picked three hundred clusters** of grapes, [11]every **two clusters** of grapes yielding **a keg** of wine. [12]**On the third day I picked from** the vine **three hundred clusters** of grapes, [13]every **three clusters** yielding **a keg** of wine. [14]I had so much wine that **I renounced ownership of more than half of it,** allowing anybody who wanted it to take it for himself." [15]Resh Lakish **said to him: "Had you not tarried,** and thus left my children idle, [16]your grapevine **would have produced** even **more** wine. Its yield diminished from day to day, showing that you were being punished for not coming and fulfilling your obligation to teach my children Torah."

רָמִי בַּר יְחֶזְקֵאל [17]It was related that **Rami bar Yeḥezkel arrived in Bene Berak.** [18]**He saw** a flock of **goats grazing under** a grove of **fig trees.** [19]**Honey dripped** to the ground **from the figs,** [20]**and milk dripped** to the ground **from** the animals. [21]Seeing this sight, Rami bar Yeḥezkel **commented:** "Surely **this is the meaning** of the verse that describes Eretz Israel as a 'land **flowing with milk and honey.**'"

אָמַר רַבִּי יַעֲקֹב בֶּן דּוֹסְתַּאי [22]**Rabbi Ya'akov ben Dostai said: "From Lod to Ono is** a distance of **three miles** (2.88 km., 1.8 mi.). [23]**Once I left early in the morning, and walked** along the road **up to my ankles in the fig**

RASHI

איפגר – לשון בטול. דלית – כרם המודלה על גבי כלונסות, *טריליי"ה בלעז. הוה עבדא טפי – שהרי ראית שבכל יום היין מתמעט מן האשכולות, וזהו עונש הבטול. קדמתי בנשף – קודם עמוד השחר.

LANGUAGE (RASHI)

טריליא"ה* From the Old French *treille,* meaning "trained vine."

וְהָלַכְתִּי עַד קַרְסוּלַּי בִּדְבַשׁ שֶׁל תְּאֵינִים״.
[1]אֲמַר רֵישׁ לָקִישׁ: ״לְדִידִי חֲזִי לִי זָבַת חָלָב וּדְבַשׁ שֶׁל צִפּוֹרִי, [2]וְהָוֵי שִׁיתְסַר מִילִין אַשִּׁיתְסַר מִילִין״.
[3]אֲמַר רַבָּה בַּר בַּר חָנָה: [4]״לְדִידִי חֲזִי לִי זָבַת חָלָב וּדְבַשׁ שֶׁל כָּל אֶרֶץ יִשְׂרָאֵל, [112A] [5]וְהָוְיָא כְּמִבֵּי מִיכְסִי עַד אַקְרָא דְּתוּלְבַּנְקִי, [6]עֶשְׂרִים וְתַרְתֵּין פַּרְסֵי אוּרְכָּא וּפוּתְיָא שִׁיתָּא פַּרְסֵי.
[7]רַבִּי חֶלְבּוֹ וְרַבִּי עֲוִירָא וְרַבִּי יוֹסֵי בַּר חֲנִינָא אִיקְלְעוּ לְהַהוּא אַתְרָא. [8]אַיְיתוּ קַמַּיְיהוּ אַפַּרְסְקָא דַּהֲוָה כְּאִילְפַּס כְּפַר הִינוֹ. [9]וְאִילְפַּס כְּפַר הִינוֹ כַּמָּה הָוֵי? [10]חָמֵשׁ סְאִין. [11]אָכְלוּ שְׁלִישׁ, וְהִפְקִירוּ שְׁלִישׁ, וְנָתְנוּ לִפְנֵי בְּהֶמְתָּן שְׁלִישׁ. [12]לְשָׁנָה, אִיקְלַע רַבִּי אֶלְעָזָר לְהָתָם וְאַיְיתוּ לְקַמֵּיהּ. [13]נַקְטוֹ בִּידֵיהּ, [14]וַאֲמַר: ״אֶרֶץ פְּרִי לִמְלֵחָה מֵרָעַת יוֹשְׁבֵי בָהּ״.
[15]רַבִּי יְהוֹשֻׁעַ בֶּן לֵוִי אִיקְלַע לְגַבְלָא. [16]חֲזַנְהוּ לְהָנְהוּ קְטוּפֵי דַּהֲווּ קַיְימֵי כִּי עִיגְלֵי. [17]אֲמַר: ״עֲגָלִים בֵּין הַגְּפָנִים״? [18]אָמְרוּ לֵיהּ: ״קְטוּפֵי נִינְהוּ״. [19]אֲמַר: ״אֶרֶץ, אֶרֶץ, הַכְנִיסִי פֵּירוֹתַיִךְ! [20]לְמִי אַתְּ מוֹצִיאָה פֵּירוֹתַיִךְ — [21]לַגּוֹיִים הַלָּלוּ שֶׁעָמְדוּ

LITERAL TRANSLATION

and walked up to my ankles in the honey of figs." [1]Resh Lakish said: "I myself saw [the area of] flowing milk and honey of Sepphoris, [2]and it was sixteen miles by sixteen miles."

[3]Rabbah bar Bar Ḥanah said: [4]"I myself saw [the area of] flowing milk and honey of all of Eretz Israel, [112A] [5]and it is like from Bei Mikhsi to the fortress of Tulbanki, [6]twenty-two *parasangs* long and six *parasangs* wide.

[7]Rabbi Ḥelbo, and Rabbi Avira, and Rabbi Yose bar Ḥanina happened to be in a certain place. [8]They brought before them a peach that was as a stew-pot of Kefar Hino. [9]And how was a stew-pot of Kefar Hino? [10]Five *se'ahs*. [11]They ate a third, renounced ownership of a third, and placed a third before their animals. [12]A year later, Rabbi Elazar happened to be there and they brought [a peach] before him. [13]He held it in his hand, [14]and said: "A fruitful land into barrenness, because of the wickedness of those who dwell therein."

[15]Rabbi Yehoshua ben Levi happened to be in Gavla. [16]He saw certain [grape] clusters that stood like calves. [17]He said: "[Are there] calves among the grapevines?" [18]They said to him: "They are clusters." [19]He said: "O land, O land, take in your fruit! [20]For whom do you bring forth your fruit — [21]for those nations that stood

RASHI

והוה כמבי מיכסי עד אקרא דתולבנקי – כשתצרף כל המקומות ישתער לכך. נקטו בידיה – מלאן קטנות, נאחזות בידו אחת. קטפי = אשכולות, כדמתרגמינן (ויקרא כה) ״לא תבצור״ – לא תקטוף.

TRANSLATION AND COMMENTARY

honey that dripped from the fig trees which lined the way."

אֲמַר רֵישׁ לָקִישׁ [1]**Resh Lakish said: "I myself saw the area** described as the land **flowing with milk and honey** in the vicinity **of Sepphoris,** [2]**and it was sixteen miles** long **by sixteen miles** (15.36 km. x 15.36 km., 9.6 mi. x 9.6 mi.) wide."

אֲמַר [3]**Rabbah bar Bar Ḥanah said:** [4]**"I myself saw the area** described as the land **flowing with milk and honey of all of Eretz Israel,** [112A] [5]**and it is as** big as the area **between** the city **of Bei Mikhsi and the fortress of Tulbanki,** [6]an area that is **twenty-two** ***parasangs*** **long and six** ***parasangs*** **wide** (84.49 km. x 23.04 km. 52.8 mi. x 14.4 mi).

רַבִּי חֶלְבּוֹ [7]**Rabbi Ḥelbo, Rabbi Avira, and Rabbi Yose bar Ḥanina happened to come to a certain place,** [8]where **a peach that was as big as a stew-pot of Kefar Hino was brought before them.** [9]**And how big was a stew-pot of Kefar Hino?** [10]**Five** ***se'ahs*** (43 liters). [11]The peach was so large that the Rabbis **ate a third** of it, **renounced ownership of a third,** allowing anybody who wanted to come and eat it, **and placed** the remaining **third before their animals** for them to eat. [12]**A year later, Rabbi Elazar happened to come** to that same place, **and** he too **was** offered a peach. [13]But the fruit of this year's crop was much smaller, so Rabbi Elazar could **hold** the peach **in his hand.** Commenting on the small size of this year's fruit, Rabbi Elazar cited a verse (Psalms 107:34), [14]**and said: "A fruitful land into barrenness, because of the wickedness of those who dwell therein."**

רַבִּי יְהוֹשֻׁעַ בֶּן לֵוִי [15]It was related that **Rabbi Yehoshua ben Levi happened** once **to come to** the town of **Gavla,** [16]where **he saw clusters** of grapes in the vineyard **that** were so large that they looked to him **like calves standing** among the grapevines. [17]He **asked** the townspeople: **"Are those** really **calves** standing **among the grapevines?"** [18]They **said to him: "They are** nothing but **clusters** of grapes." [19]**He said** to them: **"O land, O land, take in your fruit!** [20]**For whom do you bring forth your fruit?** [21]**For those nations that stood** up

NOTES

לַגּוֹיִים הַלָּלוּ **For those nations.** *Maharsha* writes that Rabbi Yehoshua ben Levi meant to say that even if the peoples

LANGUAGE

אַפַּרְסְקָא **Peach.** This word is apparently derived from the Greek Περσικόν, *persikon,* meaning "Persian (fruit)," the Greek name for peaches.

אִילְפַּס **Stew pot.** From the Greek λοπάς, *lopas,* a type of pot used primarily for cooking.

REALIA

אִילְפַּס **A stew pot.**

A closed stew pot and its cover, from the end of the Talmudic period in Eretz Israel.

The Talmudic sources describe the stew pot as an earthenware container with a broad bottom, a wide mouth and straight sides. The stew pot's sides were usually thinner than those of regular pots (קְדֵירָה). Moreover, unlike other pots, stew pots usually came with covers, which had sharp and sometimes perforated tops. Like other pots, stew pots were apparently used for cooking all types of food, particularly food which could be cooked quickly, or which only needed to be warmed up, after being cooked in a regular pot.

BACKGROUND

קְטוּפֵי הַגֶּפֶן **Grape clusters.** Grape clusters usually grow from thirty to forty centimeters long, although they may sometimes grow considerably longer. Irregular clusters (עוֹלְלוֹת) occasionally grow more than a meter long, and there have even been cases of normal clusters about a meter in length. Such a cluster can be seen from far away, and it can be mistaken for an animal in the vineyard.

עָלֵינוּ בְּחַטָּאתֵינוּ״? [1]לְשָׁנָה, אִיקְלַע רַבִּי חִיָּיא לְהָתָם. [2]חָזַנְהוּ דְּהָווּ קַיְימֵי כְּעִיזֵּי. [3]אֲמַר: ״עִזִּים בֵּין הַגְּפָנִים״? [4]אָמְרוּ לֵיהּ: ״זִיל, לָא תַּעֲבֵיד לָן כִּי חַבְרָךְ״.

[5]תָּנוּ רַבָּנַן: ״בְּבִרְכוֹתֶיהָ שֶׁל אֶרֶץ יִשְׂרָאֵל, בֵּית סְאָה עוֹשָׂה חֲמֶשֶׁת רִיבּוֹא כּוֹרִין. [6]בִּישִׁיבָתָהּ שֶׁל צוֹעַן, בֵּית סְאָה עוֹשָׂה שִׁבְעִים כּוֹרִין״. [7]דְּתַנְיָא: ״אָמַר רַבִּי מֵאִיר: [8]אֲנִי רָאִיתִי בְּבִקְעַת בֵּית שְׁאָן בֵּית סְאָה עוֹשָׂה שִׁבְעִים כּוֹרִין. [9]וְאֵין לְךָ מְעוּלָּה בְּכָל אֲרָצוֹת יוֹתֵר מֵאֶרֶץ מִצְרַיִם, [10]שֶׁנֶּאֱמַר: ׳כְּגַן ה׳ כְּאֶרֶץ מִצְרַיִם׳. [11]וְאֵין לְךָ מְעוּלָּה בְּכָל אֶרֶץ מִצְרַיִם יוֹתֵר מִצּוֹעַן, דְּהָווּ מְרַבּוּ בָּהּ מְלָכִים, [12]דִּכְתִיב: ׳כִּי הָיוּ בְצֹעַן שָׂרָיו׳. [13]וְאֵין לְךָ טְרָשִׁים בְּכָל אֶרֶץ יִשְׂרָאֵל יוֹתֵר מֵחֶבְרוֹן, דְּהָווּ קָבְרִי בָּהּ שִׁיכְבֵי. [14]וַאֲפִילּוּ

LITERAL TRANSLATION

against us on account of our sins?" [1]A year later, Rabbi Ḥiyya happened to be there. [2]He saw that they stood like goats. [3]He said: "[Are there] goats among the grapevines?" [4]They said to him: "Go, do not do to us as [did] your colleague!"

[5]Our Rabbis taught: "When Eretz Israel is blessed, a *bet se'ah* produces fifty thousand *kors.* [6]When Tzo'an is settled, a *bet se'ah* produces seventy *kors.*" [7]As it was taught: "Rabbi Meir says: [8]I saw in the valley of Bet She'an a *bet se'ah* producing seventy *kors.* [9]And there is nothing better among all the lands than the land of Egypt, [10]as it is stated: 'Like the garden of the Lord, like the land of Egypt.' [11]And there is nothing better in all the land of Egypt than Tzo'an, where they would raise kings, [12]as it is written: 'For his princes were at Tzo'an.' [13]And there is no stonier land in all of Eretz Israel than Hebron, where they would bury the dead. [14]And even so,

TRANSLATION AND COMMENTARY

against us on account of our sins? Surely it would be better if the land did not produce such large fruit, for it will be taken away by our enemies!" [1]**A year later, Rabbi Ḥiyya happened to come** to that same place. [2]He **saw** clusters of grapes that were not as large as the previous year's crop, but still so large that they looked **like goats standing** among the grapevines. [3]**He asked: "Are those** really **goats** standing **among the grapevines?"** [4]The townspeople **said to him: "Go** from here, and **do not do to us** what **your colleague** did! A year ago he pronounced a curse upon our grapes, and the fruit of this year's crop has already diminished in size!"

תָּנוּ רַבָּנַן [5]**Our Rabbis taught** a Baraita which stated: **"When Eretz Israel is blessed,** an area of **a *bet se'ah*** (576 sq.m. or 142 acre) **produces fifty thousand *kors*** (12,400 cu.m. or 350,000 bushels) of produce. [6]This stands in contrast to the Egyptian city of **Tzo'an,** where, even **when** it **was** well **settled,** an area of **a *bet se'ah* produced** only **seventy *kors*** (17.4 cu.m. or 490 bushels) of produce." [7]**As it was taught** in another Baraita: **"Rabbi Meir says:** [8]**I saw in the Bet She'an valley** — an area that was considered in Second Temple times to be outside of Eretz Israel — that an area of **a *bet se'ah* produces seventy *kors*** of produce. [9]**And** if such a yield is obtained in the Bet She'an valley, then surely such a yield is obtained in Egypt, for **there in no more fertile** land **among all the lands** of the world **than the land of Egypt,** [10]**as the verse states** (Genesis 13:10): **'Like the garden of the Lord, like the land of Egypt.'** [11]**And there is no more fertile** land **in all the land of Egypt than** the area surrounding the city of **Tzo'an, where the** future **kings would be raised,** [12]**as the verse states** (Isaiah 30:4): **'For his princes were at Tzo'an'** — the kings of Israel relied on the alliances with the kings of Egypt, and so their princes and officers were always found in Tzo'an at the court of the Egyptian kings. [13]**And there is no stonier land in all of Eretz Israel than** that which is found in the **Hebron** area, and which would be used for the **burial of the dead,** because of its poor quality for agriculture. [14]**And even so,** agricultural

RASHI

לשנה — לסוף שנה. **בברכותיה** — כשהשנה מבורכת. **בישיבתה של צוען** — כלומר, כדמפרש ואזיל, ומצוען אתה למד לארץ ישראל, כדמפרש ואזיל. **אני ראיתי בבקעת בית שאן** — שהיא משאר ארצות. **בית סאה עושה שבעים כורים** — וכיון דבשאר ארצות יש שבעים כורים, כל שכן בארץ מצרים. שאין לך מעולה בכל הארצות כמצרים, שהרי נמשלה לגן ה׳, ואין במצרים מדינה מעולה כצוען. **דמרבו בה מלכי** — מצרים, שנאמר "כי היו בצוען שריו". על מלכי ישראל הכתוב מדבר לגנאי, שמרדו בהקדוש ברוך הוא וסמכו על מלכי מצרים, ותמיד היו שריהם ושלוחיהם מצויין בצוען, שלוחים למלך מצרים, מביאין תשורה.

NOTES

who take over Eretz Israel are not wicked, it is not right that they enjoy the special blessings bestowed upon the Land. The Land was not given to them as their inheritance, and it is only on account of the sins of the Jewish people that they are there.

בְּבִקְעַת בֵּית שְׁאָן **In the valley of Bet She'an.** *Rashi* writes that Bet She'an is outside of the boundaries of Eretz Israel. *Maharsha* notes that Rabbi Meir follows his own opinion stated elsewhere that Bet She'an is outside the area that was settled by those who returned to Eretz Israel from the

TRANSLATION AND COMMENTARY

yields in **Hebron were seven times as successful as** those in **Tzo'an,** [1]**as the verse states** (Numbers 13:22): **'And Hebron was built** (נִבְנְתָה) **seven years before Tzo'an in Egypt.'** [2]**What is the meaning of** the word ***nivnetah*** (translated literally as 'built')? [3]**If you say** that the word *nivnetah* should be understood **literally** to mean 'built,' there is a difficulty, [4]**for is it possible that a person** — Ham — **built a house for his younger son** — Canaan — **before he built a house for his older son** — Mitzrayim? [5]**For the verse states** (Genesis 10:6): **'And the sons of Ham: Kush, and Mitzrayim [=Egypt], and Put, and Canaan'?** Since Mitzrayim was older than Canaan, surely then their father would have built Tzo'an in Egypt before he built Hebron in Canaan! [6]**Rather,** the verse must mean that the agricultural yields obtained in the city of Hebron **were seven times more successful than** those **in Tzo'an,** so that if a *bet se'ah* in Tzo'an yielded seventy *kors,* a similar area in Hebron yielded four hundred and ninety *kors."* [7]The Gemara adds: **This only applies to the stony land** found around Hebron, **but** in other areas of Eretz Israel where **the land is not** as **stony,** the yield obtained was **five hundred** *kors.* [8]And furthermore, **this only applies** in years **when** Eretz Israel **was not blessed,** [9]**but** in years **when it was blessed,** the yield obtained was a hundred times larger, [10]**as the verse states** (Genesis 26:12): **"Then Isaac sowed in that land,** and received in the same year a hundredfold," meaning a hundred times the size of the usual crop. Using this calculation, we arrive at the figure mentioned in the previously-cited Baraita, that when Eretz Israel is blessed, a *bet se'ah* of land produces fifty thousand *kors* of produce (a hundred times five hundred *kors*).

תַּנְיָא [11]**It was taught** in a Baraita: **"Rabbi Yose said:** [12]A ***se'ah*** of wheat **in Judea would produce five *se'ahs*** of flour after the various stages of grinding and sifting: [13]**A *se'ah* of flour, a *se'ah* of fine flour, a *se'ah* of bran-flour, a *se'ah* of coarse bran-flour, and a *se'ah* of poor-quality flour."**

הָכִי חֶבְרוֹן מְבוּנָּה עַל אַחַת מִשִּׁבְעָה בְּצוֹעַן, [1]דִּכְתִיב: 'וְחֶבְרוֹן שֶׁבַע שָׁנִים נִבְנְתָה לִפְנֵי צֹעַן מִצְרָיִם'. [2]מַאי "נִבְנְתָה"? [3]אִילֵימָא נִבְנְתָה מַמָּשׁ, [4]אֶפְשָׁר אָדָם בּוֹנֶה בַּיִת לִבְנוֹ קָטָן קוֹדֶם שֶׁיִּבְנֶה לִבְנוֹ גָּדוֹל, [5]שֶׁנֶּאֱמַר: 'וּבְנֵי חָם כּוּשׁ וּמִצְרַיִם וּפוּט וּכְנָעַן'? [6]אֶלָּא, שֶׁמְּבוּנָּה עַל אַחַת מִשִּׁבְעָה בְּצוֹעַן'. [7]וְהָנֵי מִילֵּי בַּטְּרָשִׁים, אֲבָל שֶׁלֹּא בַּטְּרָשִׁים, חֲמֵשׁ מֵאָה. [8]וְהָנֵי מִילֵּי שֶׁלֹּא בְּבִרְכוֹתֶיהָ, [9]אֲבָל בְּבִרְכוֹתֶיהָ, [10]כְּתִיב: 'וַיִּזְרַע יִצְחָק בָּאָרֶץ הַהִיא וגו'".

[11]תַּנְיָא: "אָמַר רַבִּי יוֹסֵי: [12]סְאָה בִּיהוּדָה הָיְתָה עוֹשָׂה חָמֵשׁ סְאִין: [13]סְאָה קֶמַח, סְאָה סֹלֶת, סְאָה סוּבִּין, סְאָה מוּרְסִין, וּסְאָה קִיבּוּרַיָּא".

LITERAL TRANSLATION

[agriculture in] Hebron was seven times as successful as [in] Tzo'an, [1]as it is written: 'And Hebron was built [נִבְנְתָה] seven years before Tzo'an in Egypt.' [2]What is [the meaning of] *nivnetah?* [3]If you say *nivnetah,* literally ["built"], [4]is it possible that a person builds a house for his younger son before he builds [a house] for his older son, [5]for it is stated: 'And the sons of Ham: Kush, and Mitzrayim [=Egypt], and Put, and Canaan? [6]Rather, that its [agriculture] was seven times as successful as [in] Tzo'an." [7]And these words [refer] to stony lands, but not stony lands, five hundred. [8]And these words [apply] when it is not blessed, [9]but when it is blessed, [10]it is written: "Then Isaac sowed in that land, etc." [11]It was taught: "Rabbi Yose said: [12]A *se'ah* in Judea would produce five *se'ahs:* [13]A *se'ah* of flour, a *se'ah* of fine flour, a *se'ah* of bran-flour, a *se'ah* of coarse bran-flour, and a *se'ah* of poor-quality flour."

RASHI

מבונה — בנויה בכל טוב. "מבונה" — לשון פרי, כדכתיב (בראשית ל): "ואבנה גם אנכי ממנה". לבנו הקטן — לכנען. לבנו גדול — למצרים. על אחת משבעה — הרי שבע פעמים שבעים כורים, הרי ארבע מאות ותשעים. ובמקום שאינו טרשים כחברון — יש להוסיף עד חמש מאות. ובברכותיה כתיב "מאה שערים", על אחת שבשאר שנים נתברך למאה. מאה פעמים חמש מאות — הרי חמשת ריבוא. סאה קמח — הוא אבק דק היוצא מן הנפה. והחטין טוחנין ברחיים של גריסין ואין טוחנין דקין, והנפה מוציאה הקמח וקולטת פסולת, ומחזיר מה שבנפה לריחים. סובין — שהמכתשת מוציאה, כשלותתין חטין לסולת כותשין אותן במכתשת. מורסין — הן סובין היוצאין באחרונה. קיבוריא — קמח שאינו יפה, שעושים ממנו פת קבור, וקורין *שאנדי"ר.

BACKGROUND

סְאָה קֶמַח A *se'ah* of flour. In ancient times, all parts of the wheat (including the husk) were ground together, after which the different types of flour were separated from one another by sifting the meal. The highest quality flour, which is called סֹלֶת, "fine flour," constitutes a relatively large percentage of the inside of the wheat grains. Next in quality is קֶמַח, "ordinary flour," the thinnest part of the meal. Cibar flour is the lowest quality flour, which apparently had some of the wheat sprouts mixed with it. The bran and coarse bran apparently came from the ground wheat husks. Most commentaries hold that bran (סוּבִּין) was finer than coarse bran (מוּרְסִין).

LANGUAGE

קִיבּוּרַיָּא Coarse meal, bread. From the Latin *cibarius (panis),* or from the Greek κιβαρός, *kibaros,* a loanword from the Latin, meaning "plain bread, black bread."

LANGUAGE (RASHI)

שאנדי"ר* From the Old French *seondier,* meaning "second-rate."

NOTES

Babylonian exile, and thus it was not endowed with the sanctity of Eretz Israel during the Second Temple period. Even though Bet She'an is within the boundaries of Eretz Israel that was conquered by Joshua, Rabbi Meir apparently feels that the special blessings bestowed upon Eretz Israel are only conferred upon those places that make up the primary areas of settlement of the Jewish people in their land.

שֶׁבַע שָׁנִים Seven years. The word *shanim* ("years") is understood here in the sense of the word *shonim* ("times") (*Maharsha*).

TRANSLATION AND COMMENTARY

אָמַר לֵיהּ [1]It was related that **a certain heretic said to Rabbi Ḥanina: "Well do you praise your land,** [2]for my **father left me** but **one** ***bet se'ah*** of land in Eretz Israel, **from which** I have **oil, wine, grain,** and **legumes,** and **on which my flocks graze."**

אָמַר לֵיהּ [3]It was further related that **a certain Emorite said to a** Jewish **resident of Eretz Israel,** shortly after he entered the country: [4]**"That date palm which stands on the bank of the Jordan** River, **how many** dates **did you pick from it?"** [5]The Jew **said to him:** "I harvested **sixty** ***kors*** of dates from that tree." [6]The Emorite **said to him: "You have barely entered** Eretz Israel, **and you have** already begun to **destroy it,** for when the country was still in our hands, [7]**we would pick** from that date palm **a hundred and twenty** ***kors*** of dates." [8]The Jew **said to** the Emorite: **"When I said** that I picked sixty *kors* of dates from the tree, **I was referring to** only **one side of the date palm,** for I have not yet had a chance to harvest the other side."

אָמַר רַב חִסְדָּא [9]**Rav Ḥisda said: What is** the meaning of the verse in which **it is written** (Jeremiah 3:19): **"I shall give you a pleasant land, an inheritance of choice** [נַחֲלַת צְבִי]"? The word צְבִי, usually understood here to mean "choice," also bears the meaning of "deer." [10]**Why,** it may be asked, **is Eretz Israel compared to a deer?** [11]**Just as a deer's hide** once it is removed from the animal **cannot** again **cover** the animal's **flesh,** for it shrinks after it is taken off the animal's body, [12]**so too Eretz Israel** once its fruit is harvested **cannot** again **store** all **the fruit** which grew there, for the yields are so large. [13]**Another explanation** of the use of the word צְבִי: **Just as a deer is the swiftest-**running **of all animals,** [14]**so too Eretz Israel is the swiftest of all lands to ripen its fruit.** [15]And **lest you say** that the comparison between Eretz Israel and a deer extends even further, so that **just as a deer is swift** in running, **but its meat is not fatty,** [16]**so too Eretz Israel is swift to ripen its fruit, but its fruit are not fat.** [17]**Therefore the Torah states** (Exodus 3:8 and various other places): "A land **flowing with milk and**

[1]אָמַר לֵיהּ הַהוּא מִינָא לְרַבִּי חֲנִינָא: ״יָאֶה מַשְׁבְּחִיתוּ בָּהּ בְּאַרְעֲכוֹן. [2]בֵּית סְאָה אַחַת הִנִּיחַ לִי אַבָּא, מִמֶּנָּה מִשְׁחָה, מִמֶּנָּה חֲמַר, מִמֶּנָּה עִיבּוּר, מִמֶּנָּה קִיטְנִיּוֹת, מִמֶּנָּה רוֹעוֹת מִקְנָתִי״.

[3]אָמַר לֵיהּ הַהוּא בַּר אֱמוֹרָאָה לְבַר אַרְעָא דְּיִשְׂרָאֵל: [4]״הַאי [תָּאלְתָּא], דְּקַיְימָא אַגּוּדָא דְּיַרְדְּנָא, כַּמָּה גָּדְרִיתוּ מִינָּהּ״? [5]אָמַר לֵיהּ: ״שִׁיתִּין כּוֹרֵי״. [6]אָמַר לֵיהּ: ״אַכַּתִּי לָא עַיְילִיתוּ בָּהּ אַחֲרִיבְתּוּהָ. [7]אֲנַן מְאָה וְעֶשְׂרִים כּוֹרֵי הֲוָה גָּזְרִינַן מִינָּהּ״. [8]אָמַר לֵיהּ: ״אֲנָא נַמִי מֵחַד גִּיסָא קָאָמִינָא לָךְ״.

[9]אָמַר רַב חִסְדָּא: מַאי דִּכְתִיב: ״וְאֶתֶּן לָךְ אֶרֶץ חֶמְדָּה נַחֲלַת צְבִי״? [10]לָמָּה אֶרֶץ יִשְׂרָאֵל נִמְשְׁלָה לִצְבִי? [11]לוֹמַר לָךְ: מָה צְבִי זֶה אֵין עוֹרוֹ מַחֲזִיק בְּשָׂרוֹ, [12]אַף אֶרֶץ יִשְׂרָאֵל אֵינָהּ מַחֲזֶקֶת פֵּירוֹתֶיהָ. [13]דָּבָר אַחֵר: מָה צְבִי זֶה קַל מִכָּל הַחַיּוֹת, [14]אַף אֶרֶץ יִשְׂרָאֵל קַלָּה מִכָּל הָאֲרָצוֹת לְבַשֵּׁל אֶת פֵּירוֹתֶיהָ. [15]אִי מָה צְבִי זֶה קַל וְאֵין בְּשָׂרוֹ שָׁמֵן, [16]אַף אֶרֶץ יִשְׂרָאֵל קַלָּה לְבַשֵּׁל וְאֵין פֵּירוֹתֶיהָ שְׁמֵנִים? [17]תַּלְמוּד לוֹמַר: ״זָבַת חָלָב

LITERAL TRANSLATION

[1]A certain heretic said to Rabbi Ḥanina: "Well do you praise your land. [2]Father left me one *bet se'ah*, from which [I have] oil, from which [I have] wine, from which [I have] grain, from which [I have] legumes, [and] on which my flocks to graze."

[3]A certain Emorite said to a resident of Eretz Israel: [4]"That date palm, which stands on the bank of the Jordan, how much do you pick from it?" [5]He said to him: "Sixty *kors*." [6]He said to him: "You have not yet entered [Eretz Israel, and] you have destroyed it. [7]We would cut from it a hundred and twenty *kors*." [8]He said to him: "I too, what I said was about one side [of the date palm]."

[9]Rav Ḥisda said: What is [it] that is written: "I shall give you a pleasant land, an inheritance of choice"? [10]Why is Eretz Israel compared to a deer? [11]To say to you: Just as a deer — its hide does not contain its flesh, [12]so too Eretz Israel does not contain its fruit. [13]Another thing: Just as a deer is the swiftest of all animals, [14]so too Eretz Israel is the swiftest of all lands to ripen its fruit. [15]If [you say] just as this deer is swift but its meat is not fat, [16]so too Eretz Israel is swift to ripen [its fruit] but its fruits are not fat — [17]therefore the Torah states: "Flowing with milk

RASHI

יאה משבחיתו בה בארעכון — יפה אתם משבחין אותה. **בית סאה הניח לי אבא** — בארץ ישראל. **אמר ליה ההוא בר אמוראה** — אחד מבני האמורי אמר ליהודי, תחלת ביאתו לארץ. הך תאלתא דקיימא אגודא דירדנא — דקל פלוני העומד על שפת הירדן. **כמה גדריתו מינה** — כמה תמרים אתם גודרים הימנו? לקיטת תמרים קרויה גדירה בלשון [משנה, וגוזרה בלשון] ארמי. **אין עורו מחזיק את בשרו** — שהעור כווץ וגומד לאחר הפשטו. **אינה מחזקת פירותיה** — עושה פירותיה מרובין, עד אין מקום להכניסן.

וּדְבַשׁ״, [1]שְׁמֵנִים מֵחָלָב וּמְתוּקִים מִדְּבַשׁ.
[2]רַבִּי אֶלְעָזָר כִּי הֲוָה סָלֵיק לְאֶרֶץ יִשְׂרָאֵל, [3]אֲמַר: ״פָּלְטִי לִי מֵחֲדָא״. [4]כִּי סְמָכוּהוּ, אֲמַר: [5]״פָּלְטִי לִי מִתַּרְתֵּי״. [6]כִּי אוֹתְבוּהוּ בְּסוֹד הָעִיבּוּר, [7]אֲמַר: ״פָּלְטִי לִי מִתְּלָת, [8]שֶׁנֶּאֱמַר: ׳וְהָיְתָה יָדִי אֶל הַנְּבִיאִים הַחֹזִים שָׁוְא וגו׳׳, [9]׳בְּסוֹד עַמִּי לֹא יִהְיוּ׳ — זֶה סוֹד עִיבּוּר. [10]׳וּבִכְתָב בֵּית יִשְׂרָאֵל לֹא יִכָּתֵבוּ׳ — זֶה סְמִיכָה. [11]׳וְאֶל אַדְמַת יִשְׂרָאֵל לֹא יָבֹאוּ׳ — כְּמַשְׁמָעוֹ״.
[12]רַבִּי זֵירָא כִּי הֲוָה סָלֵיק לְאֶרֶץ יִשְׂרָאֵל, לָא אַשְׁכַּח מַבְּרָא לְמִעֲבַר. [13]נְקַט בְּמִצְרָא וְקָעָבַר. [14]אֲמַר לֵיהּ הַהוּא מִינָא: ״עַמָּא פְּזִיזָא, דְּקָדְמִיתוּ פּוּמַיְיכוּ לְאוּדְנַיְיכוּ, [15]אַכַּתִּי בִּפְזִיזוּתַיְיכוּ קַיְימִיתוּ״! [16]אֲמַר לֵיהּ: ״דּוּכְתָּא דְּמֹשֶׁה וְאַהֲרֹן לָא זָכוּ לָהּ, [17]אֲנָא מִי יֵימָר דְּזָכֵינָא לָהּ״!

LITERAL TRANSLATION

and honey" — [1]fatter than milk and sweeter than honey.

[2]When Rabbi Elazar went up to Eretz Israel, [3]he said: "I have been saved from one [curse]." [4]When they ordained him, he said: [5]"I have been saved from two." [6]When they place him on the council for intercalation, [7]he said: "I have been saved from three [curses], [8]as it is stated: 'And My hand shall be against the prophets that see vanity, etc.' [9]'They shall not be in the counsel of my people' — this is the council for intercalation. [10]'Neither shall they be written in the writing of the house of Israel' — this is ordination. [11]'Neither shall they enter into Eretz Israel' — [in] its literal sense."

[12]When Rabbi Zera was going up to Eretz Israel, he did not find a ferry with which to cross. [13]He held a [strung] rope and crossed. [14]A certain heretic said to him: "An overhasty people, that put your mouths before your ears, [15]you still persist in your haste!" [16]He said to him: "A place that Moses and Aaron did not merit, [17]who says that I will merit it?"

TRANSLATION AND COMMENTARY

honey" — [1]a land whose fruits are **fatter than milk and sweeter than honey.**

רַבִּי אֶלְעָזָר [2]It was related that **when Rabbi Elazar emigrated** from Babylonia **to Eretz Israel,** [3]**he said: "I have been saved from one** Biblical curse." [4]**When** Rabbi Elazar **was** later **conferred with** Rabbinic **ordination, he said:** [5]**"I have** now **been saved from a second** Biblical curse." [6]And **when he was** later **placed on the council** of the Sanhedrin which was responsible **for intercalating** the year, [7]**he said: "I have** now **been saved from a third** Biblical curse, [8]**as the verse states** (Ezekiel 13:9): **'And My hand shall be against the prophets that see vanity** and that divine lies; they shall not be in the counsel of my people, neither shall they be written in the writing of the house of Israel, neither shall they enter into the Land of Israel, and you shall know that I am the Lord God.' [9]**'They shall not be in the counsel of my people' — this** refers to **the council** of the Sanhedrin that was responsible **for intercalation** of the year. [10]**'Neither shall they be written in the writing of the house of Israel' — this** refers to Rabbinic **ordination.** [11]**'Neither shall they enter into the Land of Israel'** — this should be understood **literally."** Rabbi Elazar rejoiced that none of these curses were fulfilled in him.

רַבִּי זֵירָא [12]It was further related that **when Rabbi Zera emigrated** from Babylonia **to Eretz Israel, he did not find a boat to cross** the Jordan River. [13]**He** therefore **held** on to **a rope** that was stretched across the river like a bridge, **and** thus he **crossed.** [14]When **a certain heretic** saw what Rabbi Zera was doing, he **said to him:** "From the outset you were **an overhasty people, for you put your mouths ahead of your ears,** and promised to obey God even before you heard what He expected of you (see Exodus 24:7). [15]And **you still persist in your haste.** You should have waited for a boat, rather than endanger yourself by crossing the river with a rope." [16]Rabbi Zera **said to him:** "Eretz Israel is a **place into which** even **Moses and Aaron did not merit** to enter. [17]**Who said** then **that I would merit** to go into the land? I was in a hurry to cross the river as quickly as possible, lest I tarry and later be prevented from entering into the Land."

RASHI

פלטי לי מחדא — נצלתי מאחת מהן, מן הקללות האמורות במקרא. **נקט במצרא** — יש מקום שאין גשר, ומשליכין עץ על רוחב הנהר משפה לשפה, ואינו רחב לילך עליו, כי אם אוחז בידיו בחבל המתוח למעלה הימנו, קשור שני ראשיו בשתי יתידות אחת מכאן ואחת מכאן בשני עברי הנהר. **עמא פזיזא** = עם בהול. **דקדמיתו פומייכו לאודנייכו** — מתחלתכם הייתם בהולים, שהקדמתם ״נעשה״ ל״נשמע״, ועודכם בבהלתכם כבתחלה, למהר לעשות דבר בלא עתו.

NOTES

שְׁמֵנִים מֵחָלָב Fatter than milk. Since the verse, "a land flowing with milk and honey," was stated about the fruit of Eretz Israel, and milk does not grow from the land, Rav Ḥisda explained the verse as referring to the fruit of Eretz Israel, which is fatter than milk (*Maharsha*).

סוֹד הָעִיבּוּר The council for intercalation. This expression refers to the special council of Sages that met to decide upon the intercalation of the year. This council had seven

LANGUAGE

מִיגַּנְדַּר Roll. This verb means "roll" in the Talmud. A similar word is found in Aramaic and Syriac. This word also means "adorn, embellish," a meaning which is also attested in modern Hebrew (cf. also *gandor* in spoken Arabic, which means "adorning one's self, pleading").

קַטֵיגוֹרְיָא Prosecution. From the Greek κατηγορία, *kategoria*, meaning "prosecution, accusing."

TRANSLATION AND COMMENTARY

רַבִּי אַבָּא מְנַשֵּׁק [1]The Gemara continues with several anecdotes which illustrate the love and affection that the Amoraim felt for Eretz Israel: **Rabbi Abba would kiss the stones of Akko,** when he entered the Land from the north. [2]**Rabbi Ḥanina would remove the obstacles** from the roads, so that passers-by not injure themselves and speak ill of Eretz Israel. [3]**Rabbi Ammi and Rabbi Assi** [112B] **would move** on hot days **from the sun to the shade,** [4]**and** on cold days **from the shade to the sun,** as the changes in temperature would dictate, so that they would always be comfortable, and not voice any complaints about the discomforts of living in Eretz Israel. [5]**Rabbi Ḥiyya bar Gamda would roll in the dust** of Eretz Israel, [6]**as the verse states** (Psalms 102:15): **"For Your servants hold her stones dear, and cherish her very dust."**

אָמַר רַבִּי זֵירָא [7]Returning to the discussion concerning the Messianic period and the end of days, the Gemara continues: **Rabbi Zera said in the name of Rabbi Yirmeyah bar Abba:** [8]In **the generation during which** the Messiah **the son of David will come,** [9]**there will be** many **accusations** raised **against Torah**

[1]רַבִּי אַבָּא מְנַשֵּׁק כֵּיפֵי דְעַכּוֹ. [2]רַבִּי חֲנִינָא מְתַקֵּן מַתְקָלֵיהּ. [3]רַבִּי אַמִי וְרַבִּי אַסִי [112B] קָיְימֵי מִשִּׁמְשָׁא לְטוּלָּא, [4]וּמִטּוּלָּא לְשִׁמְשָׁא. [5]רַבִּי חִיָּיא בַּר גַּמְדָא מִיגַּנְדַּר בְּעַפְרָהּ, [6]שֶׁנֶּאֱמַר: "כִּי רָצוּ עֲבָדֶיךָ אֶת אֲבָנֶיהָ וְאֶת עֲפָרָהּ יְחֹנֵנוּ". [7]אָמַר רַבִּי זֵירָא אָמַר רַבִּי יִרְמְיָה בַּר אַבָּא: [8]דּוֹר שֶׁבֶּן דָּוִד בָּא, [9]קַטֵיגוֹרְיָא בְּתַלְמִידֵי חֲכָמִים.

LITERAL TRANSLATION

[1]Rabbi Abba kissed the stones of Akko. [2]Rabbi Ḥanina removed obstacles. [3]Rabbi Ammi and Rabbi Assi [112B] moved [on hot days] from the sun to the shade, [4]and [on cold days] from the shade to the sun. [5]Rabbi Ḥiyya bar Gamda rolled in its dust, [6]as it is stated: "For Your servants hold her stones dear, and cherish her very dust."

[7]Rabbi Zera said in the name of Rabbi Yirmeyah bar Abba: [8]The generation during which the son of David will come — [9]there will be accusations [raised] against Torah scholars.

RASHI

כיפי = אלמוגים. לישנא אחרינא: **כיפי דעכו** — סלעים. **מתקן מתקליה** — משוה ומתקן מכשולי העיר. מחמת חיבת הארץ, שהיתה חביבה עליו, ומחזר שלא יצא שם רע על הדרכים. **קיימי משמשא לטולא** — כשהשמש הגיע למקום שהן יושבין וגורסין, וחמה מקדרת עליהן — עומדין משם לישב בצל. ובימי הצנה עומדין מן הצל ויושבין בחמה, כדי שלא יוכלו להתרעם על ישיבת ארץ ישראל. **כי רצו עבדיך את אבניה ואת עפרה יחוננו. קטיגוריא** — הרבה מסטינים ומלמדים חובה יעמדו עליהם.

NOTES

members, and its meetings were not open to the public as were academy sessions, but only to the Sages who were specifically invited to participate, as is explained at length in tractate *Sanhedrin*.

מְנַשֵּׁק כֵּיפֵי Kissed the stones. According to *Rashi's* first explanation, the word *keifei* means corals. According to this, Rabbi Abba would show his affection even for the corals that were found in the bay of Acko. *Rambam* and *Tosafot* (following the Gemara at the beginning of tractate *Gittin*) understand that Akko was situated along the northern border of the territory endowed with the sanctity of Eretz Israel during the Second Temple period and afterward, and it was the stones that marked the border of Eretz Israel that Rabbi Abba would kiss.

מְתַקֵּן מַתְקָלֵיהּ Removed the obstacles. *Tosafot* had the reading: מְתַקֵּל מַתְקָלֵיהּ, "he weighed the stones." Following the Midrash, *Tosafot* explain that Rabbi Ḥanina would weigh the stones as he approached Eretz Israel. As long as they were light, he knew that he had not entered the land, but once they were heavy, he knew that they were the stones of Eretz Israel. According to *Midrash Tanḥuma* (ed. Buber), when Rabbi Ḥanina came across stones that were harder, he knew that he had reached Eretz Israel. See also *Arukh*, who adds that Rabbi Ḥanina's test to see whether or not he had already entered into Eretz Israel was based on the verse (Deuteronomy 8:9): "A land whose stones are iron."

מִיגַּנְדַּר בְּעַפְרָהּ Rolled in its dust. It has been suggested that by rolling in the dust of Eretz Israel, Rabbi Ḥiyya bar Gamda would intimate that he did not desire Eretz Israel for its blessings, but rather because of his love for the Land, for even its rocks and dirt were important to him.

דּוֹר שֶׁבֶּן דָּוִד בָּא The generation during which the son of David will come. *Tosafot* explains that after the Gemara told of the blessings at the end of days, it now tells of the troubles that will accompany the advent of the Messiah. *Pnei Yehoshua* adds that these troubles might be mentioned to teach that there is also a positive aspect to these troubles, for they cleanse and purify the people of Israel of their impurities.

קַטֵיגוֹרְיָא בְּתַלְמִידֵי חֲכָמִים There will be accusations raised against Torah scholars. *Ri Migash* explains in one of his responsa that the Torah scholars will be hated by the nations of the world. Thus, they will raise accusations against them, just as a prosecutor levels accusations against the defendant in a court of law. Some of the Geonim had the reading: קַרְטִיגְיָא, which they explained to mean "smelting." It has also been suggested that in the period of the advent of the Messiah hatred will reign even among the Torah scholars themselves (as is implied by the particle *bet* which means "among") (*Etz Yosef*).

HALAKHAH

רַבִּי אַבָּא מְנַשֵּׁק Rabbi Abba kissed. "The greatest Sages used to kiss the ground along the borders of Eretz Israel, and kiss its rocks, and roll in its dust," as is reported in our Gemara. (*Rambam, Sefer Shofetim, Hilkhot Melakhim* 5:10.)

TRANSLATION AND COMMENTARY

scholars. [1]Rabbi Zera continues: **When I said this before Shmuel, he added:** At that time, Torah scholars will undergo **one** stage of **refinement** by trial and persecution **after another,** vastly reducing their numbers, but increasing their quality, [2]**as the verse states** (Isaiah 6:13): **"And if one-tenth remain in it, then that shall again be eaten up."**

תָּנֵי רַב יוֹסֵף [3]**Rav Yosef taught** a Baraita which stated: "In the days of the advent of the Messiah, [4]Israel will be attacked by **plunderers,** and then by the **plunderers of** those **plunderers."**

אָמַר [5]**Rav Ḥiyya bar Ashi said in the name of Rav:** [6]**In the future** at the end of days, **all the fruitless trees in Eretz Israel will bear fruit,** [7]**as the verse states** (Joel 2:22): **"For the tree bears its fruit, the fig tree and the vine do yield their strength."**

[1]כִּי אָמְרִיתָהּ קַמֵּיהּ דִּשְׁמוּאֵל, אָמַר: צֵירוּף אַחַר צֵירוּף, [2]שֶׁנֶּאֱמַר: "וְעוֹד בָּהּ עֲשִׂירִיָּה וְשָׁבָה וְהָיְתָה לְבָעֵר". [3]תָּנֵי רַב יוֹסֵף: [4]"בָּזוֹזֵי וּבָזוֹזֵי דְבָזוֹזֵי". [5]אָמַר רַב חִיָּיא בַּר אַשִׁי אָמַר רַב: [6]עֲתִידִין כָּל אִילָנֵי סְרָק שֶׁבְּאֶרֶץ יִשְׂרָאֵל שֶׁיִּטְעֲנוּ פֵּירוֹת, [7]שֶׁנֶּאֱמַר: "כִּי עֵץ נָשָׂא פִרְיוֹ תְּאֵנָה וָגֶפֶן נָתְנוּ חֵילָם".

הדרן עלך שני דייני גזירות
וסליקא לה מסכת כתובות

LITERAL TRANSLATION

[1]When I said this before Shmuel, he said: Refinement [by trial] after refinement, [2]as it is stated: "And if one-tenth remain in it, then that shall again be eaten up." [3]Rav Yosef taught: [4]"Plunderers, and plunderers of plunderers."

[5]Rav Ḥiyya bar Ashi said in the name of Rav: [6]In the future, all the fruitless trees in Eretz Israel will bear fruit, [7]as it is stated: "For the tree bears its fruit, the fig tree and the vine do yield their strength."

RASHI

צירוף אחר צירוף – גזירות על גזירות. ועוד בה עשיריה – כשתשעה החלקים יהיו אבודין, ולא נותר כי אם העשירית – אף היא תשוב והיתה לבער. בזוזי ובזוזי דבזוזי – שוללים אחר שוללים. כי עץ נשא פריו – מדכתיב "תאנה וגפן נתנו חילם" – הרי עץ פרי אמור, מה תלמוד לומר "כי עץ נשא פריו" – אף אילני סרק ישאו פרי.

הדרן עלך שני דייני גזירות

NOTES

בָּזוֹזֵי וּבָזוֹזֵי דְבָזוֹזֵי **Plunderers, and plunderers of plunderers.** *Arukh* explains that those who plunder Israel will themselves be plundered by others, and those other plunderers will then come and plunder Israel again.

עֲתִידִין כָּל אִילָנֵי סְרָק **In the future, all the fruitless trees.** *Tosafot* note that this statement does not really belong here, but rather it should have been brought earlier in the context of the discussion concerning the future fertility of Eretz Israel. It was cited here only in order to conclude the chapter and the tractate on a positive note. *Pnei Yehoshua* adds that this statement is nevertheless related to the preceding discussion, for the verse which was cited above (Isaiah 6:13) concludes: "But like a terebinth and like an oak, whose stock remains when they cast their leaves, so [shall remain] the stock of the holy seed." The terebinth and the oak are fruitless trees, but in the future they too will bear fruit. According to the Midrash and *Ramban*'s commentary to the Torah (Genesis 1:11), at the beginning of creation, all trees bore fruit. It was only following Adam's sin and the earth's being cursed, that certain trees lost their ability to do so. In the future, when all of the world's sins will be pardoned, and the world will reach a state of perfection, so too the earth's curse will be pardoned and all the trees growing from it will reach a state of perfection and bear fruit.

Conclusion to Chapter Thirteen

Regarding a man who has gone abroad, it was concluded that the court allocates support to his wife in any event, and it does not make her take an oath, except if she comes to collect her ketubah settlement. Although in this matter the court is absolutely required to support the wife from her husband's property, if another person supported her of his own free will, he cannot obligate her husband to pay him back, unless he specifically advanced the money to the wife as a loan.

Regarding a couple's dwelling place, it was agreed that neither spouse may force the other to move to another country, and, within the same country, neither may force the other to move to another town or city, whether it be larger or smaller, worse or better. However, there is an exception to this rule, which is immigration to the Land of Israel (even if this entails a decline in living standards), and the same principle applies between any place in the Land of Israel and Jerusalem.

Since the Sages disagreed about certain matters related to the ketubah, it was agreed that whenever it was not stated specifically in what currency the ketubah settlement was to be paid, the husband may pay either according to the place where the ketubah was written or according to the place where payment is made, as is convenient to him.

If a man left only a small estate, his daughters are to be supported. They collect according to the conditions of the ketubah, and the sons are not supported. Regarding a groom who was promised a dowry and did not receive it, in any event this is not his wife's fault, and she can demand that he marry her or give her a bill of divorce.

In the differences of opinion regarding confessions and claims, it was agreed that when a man confesses to his fellow in a manner that can be understood as admitting part of a claim, he is regarded as having made a partial confession, and he is required to take an oath. It was also concluded that a person who has lost the path to his field can receive a path only if he has a clear claim against a specific person. Otherwise the defendants refute him one by one until he compromises with them. If a person challenges ownership of a field and has signed as a witness on a deed that implies that the field does not belong to him, he has lost his rights. But if someone has lent money and then returns and borrows from the same person, or he has sold his field to the borrower, this is no proof that he has admitted to him that there was never any loan.

In the course of discussion it also emerged that it was forbidden for a judge to receive anything from any of the litigants before him, not only a bribe, but also wages. A judge may only receive a proven compensation for his lost time, or he may receive a salary from the community, if he works only for the public good.

By way of stories, this chapter also sings the praises of the Land of Israel in the present, and, the more so, in the future.

List of Sources

Aḥaronim, lit., "the last," meaning Rabbinic authorities from the time of the publication of Rabbi Yosef Caro's code of Halakhah, *Shulḥan Arukh* (1555).

Arba'ah Turim, code of Halakhah by Rabbi Ya'akov ben Asher, b. Germany, active in Spain (c. 1270-1343).

Arukh, Talmudic dictionary, by Rabbi Natan of Rome, 11th century.

Avnei Nezer, novellae on the Talmud by Rabbi Avraham Bornstein of Sokhochev, Poland (1839-1908).

Ayelet Ahavim, novellae on *Ketubot* by Rabbi Aryeh Leib Zuenz, Poland, 19th century.

Ba'al HaMa'or, Rabbi Zeraḥyah ben Yitzḥak HaLevi, Spain, 12th century. Author of *HaMa'or,* Halakhic commentary on *Hilkhot HaRif.*

Ba'er Hetev, commentary on *Shulḥan Arukh, Ḥoshen Mishpat,* by Rabbi Zeḥaryah Mendel of Belz, Poland (18th century).

Baḥ (Bayit Ḥadash), commentary on *Arba'ah Turim,* by Rabbi Yoel Sirkes, Poland (1561-1640).

Bereshit Rabbah, Midrash on the Book of Genesis.

Bertinoro, Ovadyah, 15th century Italian commentator on the Mishnah.

Bet Aharon, novellae on the Talmud, by Rabbi Aharon Walkin, Lithuania (1865-1942).

Bet Shmuel, commentary on *Shulḥan Arukh, Even HaEzer,* by Rabbi Shmuel ben Uri Shraga, Poland, second half of the 17th century.

Bet Ya'akov, novellae on *Ketubot,* Rabbi Ya'akov Lorberboim of Lissa, Poland (1760-1832).

Bet Yosef, Halakhic commentary on *Arba'ah Turim* by Rabbi Yosef Caro (1488-1575), which is the basis of his authoritative Halakhic code, *Shulḥan Arukh.*

Birkat Avraham, novellae on the Talmud, by Rabbi Avraham Erlinger, Israel (20th century).

Bnei Ahuvah, novellae on *Mishnah Torah,* by Rabbi Yehonatan Eibeschuetz, Poland, Moravia, and Prague (c. 1690-1764).

Derash Moshe, novellae on *Ein Ya'akov,* by Rabbi Moshe ben Yitzhak, Moravia, 16th century.

Derishah and *Perishah,* commentaries on *Tur* by Rabbi Yehoshua Falk Katz, Poland (c. 1555-1614).

Eliyah Rabbah, commentary on *Shulḥan Arukh, Orah Ḥayyim,* by Rabbi Eliyahu Shapira, Prague (1660-1712).

Eshel Avraham, by Rabbi Avraham Ya'akov Neimark, novellae on the Talmud, Israel (20th century).

Even HaEzer, section of *Shulḥan Arukh* dealing with marriage, divorce, and related topics.

Geonim, heads of the academies of Sura and Pumbedita in Babylonia from the late 6th century to the mid-11th century.

Giddulei Shmuel, by Rabbi Shmuel Gedalya Neiman, novellae on the Talmud, Israel (20th century).

Gra, by Rabbi Eliyahu ben Shlomo Zalman (1720-1797), the Gaon of Vilna. Novellae on the Talmud and *Shulḥan Arukh.*

Hafla'ah, novellae on *Ketubot,* by Rabbi Pinḥas HaLevi Horowitz, Poland and Germany (1731-1805).

Hagahot Asheri (Oshri), glosses on the *Rosh* by Rabbi Yisrael of Krems, 14th century.

Hagahot Mordekhai, glosses on the *Mordekhai,* by Rabbi Shmuel ben Aharon of Schlettstadt, Germany, late 14th century.

Halakhot Gedolot, a code of Halakhic decisions written in the Geonic period. This work has been ascribed to Sherira Gaon, Rav Hai Gaon, Rav Yehudah Gaon and Rabbi Shimon Kayyara.

Ḥatam Sofer, responsa literature and novellae on the Talmud by Rabbi Moshe Sofer (Schreiber), Pressburg, Hungary and Germany (1763-1839).

Ḥaver ben Ḥayyim, novellae on the Talmud by Rabbi Ḥizkiyah Ḥayyim Ploit, Lithuania, 19th century.

Ḥelkat Meḥokek, commentary on *Shulḥan Arukh, Even HaEzer,* by Rabbi Moshe Lima, Lithuania (1605-1658).

Hokhmat Manoaḥ, commentary on the Talmud by Rabbi Manoaḥ ben Shemaryah, Poland, 16th century.

Ḥoshen Mishpat, section of *Shulḥan Arukh* dealing with civil and criminal law.

Ir Binyamin, novellae on *Ein Ya'akov,* by Rabbi Binyamin Ze'ev Darshan, Germany, 17th century.

Ittur, Halakhic work by Rabbi Yitzḥak Abba Mari, Provence (1122-1193).

Iyyun Ya'akov, commentary on *Ein Ya'akov*, by Rabbi Ya'akov bar Yosef Riesher, Prague, Poland, and France (d. 1733).

Kesef Mishneh, commentary on *Mishneh Torah,* by Rabbi Yosef Caro, author of *Shulḥan Arukh.*

Korban HaEdah, commentary on the Jerusalem Talmud by Rabbi David ben Naftali Frankel, Germany (1707-1762).

Kovetz Shiurim, novellae on the Talmud by Rabbi Elḥanan Wasserman, Lithuania (1875-1941).

Leḥem Mishneh, commentary on the Mishneh Torah by Rabbi Avraham di Boton, Salonica (1560-1609).

Magen Avraham, commentary on *Shulḥan Arukh, Oraḥ Ḥayyim,* by Rabbi Avraham HaLevi Gombiner, Poland (d. 1683).

Maggid Mishneh, commentary on *Mishneh Torah,* by Rabbi Vidal de Tolosa, Spain, 14th century.

Maharal, Rabbi Yehudah Loew ben Betzalel of Prague (1525-1609). Novellae on the Talmud.

Maharam of Rotenburg, Rabbi Meir of Rotenburg, Tosafist and Halakhic authority, Germany (c. 1215-1293.)

Maharam Schiff, novellae on the Talmud by Rabbi Meir ben Ya'akov HaKohen Schiff (1605-1641), Frankfurt, Germany.

Maharsha, Rabbi Shmuel Eliezer ben Yehudah HaLevi Edels, Poland (1555-1631). Novellae on the Talmud.

Maharshal, Rabbi Shlomo ben Yeḥiel Luria, Poland (1510-1573). Novellae on the Talmud.

Meiri, commentary on the Talmud (called *Bet HaBeḥirah*), by Rabbi Menaḥem ben Shlomo, Provence (1249-1316).

Mekhilta, Halakhic Midrash on the Book of Exodus.

Melekhet Shlomo, commentary on the Mishnah by Rabbi Shlomo Adeni, Yemen and Eretz Israel (1567-1626).

Melo HaRo'im, commentary on the Talmud by Rabbi Ya'akov Tzvi Yolles, Poland (c. 1778-1825).

Mishnah Berurah, commentary on *Shulḥan Arukh, Oraḥ Ḥayyim,* by Rabbi Yisrael Meir HaKohen, Poland (1837-1933).

Mishneh LeMelekh, commentary on *Mishneh Torah*, by Rabbi Yehudah ben Shmuel Rosanes, Turkey (1657-1727).

Mitzpeh Eitan, glosses on the Talmud by Rabbi Avraham Maskileison, Byelorussia (1788-1848).

Mordekhai, compendium of Halakhic decisions by Rabbi Mordekhai ben Hillel HaKohen, Germany (1240?-1298).

Nimmukei Yosef, commentary on *Hilkhot HaRif,* by Rabbi Yosef Ḥaviva, Spain, early 15th century.

Or Sameaḥ, novellae on *Mishnah Torah,* by Rabbi Meir Simḥah HaKohen of Dvinsk, Latvia (1843-1926).

Oraḥ Ḥayyim, section of *Shulḥan Arukh* dealing with daily religious observances, prayers, and the laws of the Sabbath and Festivals.

Perishah, see *Derishah.*

Pitḥei Teshuvah, compilation of responsa literature on the *Shulḥan Arukh* by Rabbi Avraham Tzvi Eisenstadt, Russia (1812-1868).

Pnei Moshe, commentary on the Jerusalem Talmud by Rabbi Moshe ben Shimon Margoliyot, Lithuania (c. 1710-1781).

Pnei Yehoshua, novellae on the Talmud by Rabbi Ya'akov Yehoshua Falk, Poland and Germany (1680-1756).

Porat Yosef, by Rabbi Yosef ben Rabbi Tzvi Hirsch, novellae on tractate *Ketubot* (19th century).

Ra'ah, see *Rabbi Aharon HaLevi.*

Ra'avad, Rabbi Avraham ben David, commentator and Halakhic authority. Wrote comments on *Mishneh Torah*. Provence (c. 1125-1198?).

Rabbenu Gershom, commentator and Halakhic authority, France (960-1040).

Rabbenu Ḥananel (ben Ḥushiel), commentator on the Talmud, North Africa (990-1055).

Rabbenu Shimshon (ben Avraham of Sens), Tosafist, France and Eretz Israel (c. 1150-1230).

Rabbenu Tam, commentator on the Talmud, Tosafist, France (1100-1171).

Rabbenu Yeḥiel, French Tosafist (d. 1268).

Rabbenu Yehonatan, Yehonatan ben David HaKohen of Lunel, Provence, Talmudic scholar (c. 1135-after 1210).

Rabbenu Yeruḥem, Rabbi Yeruḥem ben Meshullam, Halakhist, Spain, 14th century. Author of *Toledot Adam VeḤavah.*

Rabbenu Yonah, see *Talmidei Rabbenu Yonah.*

Rabbi Aharon HaLevi, Spain 13th century. Novellae on the Talmud.

Rabbi Akiva Eger, Talmudist and Halakhic authority, Posen, Germany (1761-1837).

Rabbi Avraham ben Isaac of Narbonne, French Talmudist (c. 1110-1179).

Rabbi Benyamin Musafiya, Italy and Amsterdam (c.1606-1675). Author of *Musaf Arukh.*

Rabbi Cresdas Vidal, Spanish Talmudist and commentator, 14th century.

Rabbi Elḥanan Wasserman, Talmudic scholar and Halakhic authority, Lithuania (1875-1941).

Rabbi Moshe the son of Rabbi Yosef of Narbonne, French Talmudist of the twelfth century, France and Eretz Israel.

Rabbi Shlomo of Montpellier, French Talmudist of the thirteenth century.

Rabbi Shmuel HaNagid, Spain (993-1055 or 1056). Novellae on the Talmud found in *Shittah Mekubbetzet.*

Rabbi Ya'akov Emden, Talmudist and Halakhic authority, Germany (1697-1776).

Rabbi Yosef of Jerusalem, French Tosafist of the twelfth and thirteenth centuries, France and Eretz Israel.

Rabbi Zeraḥyah ben Yitzḥak HaLevi, Spain, 12th century. Author of *HaMa'or*, Halakhic commentary on *Hilkhot HaRif.*

Radbaz, Rabbi David ben Shlomo Avi Zimra, Spain, Egypt, Eretz Israel, and North Africa (1479-1574). Commentary on *Mishneh Torah.*

Rambam, Rabbi Moshe ben Maimon, Rabbi and philosopher, known also as Maimonides. Author of *Mishneh Torah,* Spain and Egypt (1135-1204).

Ramban, Rabbi Moshe ben Naḥman, commentator on Bible and Talmud, known also as Naḥmanides, Spain and Eretz Israel (1194-1270).

Ran, Rabbi Nissim ben Reuven Gerondi, Spanish Talmudist (1310?-1375?).

Rash, Rabbi Shimshon ben Avraham, Tosafist, commentator on the Mishnah, Sens (late 12th- early 13th century).

Rashash, Rabbi Shmuel ben Yosef Shtrashun, Lithuanian Talmud scholar (1794-1872).

Rashba, Rabbi Shlomo ben Avraham Adret, Spanish Rabbi famous for his commentaries on the Talmud and his responsa (c. 1235-c. 1314).

Rashbam, Rabbi Shmuel ben Meir, commentator on the Talmud, France (1085-1158).

Rashbatz, Rabbi Shimon ben Tzemaḥ Duran, known for his book of responsa, *Tashbatz,* Spain and Algeria (1361-1444).

Rashi, Rabbi Shlomo ben Yitzḥak, the paramount commentator on the Bible and the Talmud, France (1040-1105).

Rav Aḥa (Aḥai) Gaon, author of *She'iltot.* Pumbedita, Babylonia and Eretz Israel, 8th century. See *She'iltot.*

Rav Hai Gaon, Babylonian Rabbi, head of Pumbedita Yeshivah, 10th-11th century.

Rav Natan Av HaYeshivah, Eretz Israel, 12th century. Commentary on the Mishnah.

Rav Natronai Gaon, of the Sura Yeshivah, 9th century.

Rav Sherira Gaon, of the Pumbedita Yeshivah, 10th century.

Rav Tzemaḥ Gaon, Tzemaḥ ben Ḥayyim, Gaon of Sura from 889 to 895.

Rema, Rabbi Moshe ben Yisrael Isserles, Halakhic authority, Poland (1525-1572).

Remah, novellae on the Talmud by Rabbi Meir ben Todros HaLevi Abulafiya, Spain (c. 1170-1244). See *Yad Ramah.*

Ri, Rabbi Yitzḥak ben Shmuel of Dampierre, Tosafist, France (died c. 1185).

Ri HaLavan, French Tosafist (12th century).

Ri Korkos, Rabbi Yosef Korkos, Spain, 15th-16th century. Responsa literature.

Ri Migash, Rabbi Yosef Ibn Migash, commentator on the Talmud, Spain (1077-1141).

Rid, see *Tosefot Rid.*

Rif, Rabbi Yitzḥak Alfasi, Halakhist, author of *Hilkhot HaRif,* North Africa (1013-1103).

Rishonim, lit., "the first," meaning Rabbinic authorities active between the end of the Geonic period (mid-11th century) and the publication of *Shulḥan Arukh* (1555).

Ritva, novellae and commentary on the Talmud by Rabbi Yom Tov ben Avraham Ishbili, Spain (c. 1250-1330).

Rivan, Rabbi Yehudah ben Natan, French Tosafist, 11th-12th centuries.

Rivash, Rabbi Yitzḥak ben Sheshet, Spain and North Africa (1326-1408). Novellae on the Talmud mentioned in *Shittah Mekubbetzet.*

Rosh, Rabbi Asher ben Yeḥiel, also known as Asheri, commentator and Halakhist, German and Spain (c. 1250-1327).

Sefer HaYashar, novellae on the Talmud by Rabbenu Tam. France (c. 1100-1171).

Sefer Mikkaḥ U'Mimkar, by Rav Hai Gaon. Treatise on the laws of commerce.

Sefer HaTerumot, Halakhic work by Rabbi Shmuel ben Yitzḥak Sardi, Spain (1185-1255).

Sha'ar HaTziyyun, see *Mishnah Berurah.*

Shakh (Siftei Kohen), commentary on the *Shulḥan Arukh* by Rabbi Shabbetai ben Meir HaKohen, Lithuania (1621-1662).

She'iltot, by Aḥa (Aḥai) of the Pumbedita Yeshivah, 8th century. One of the first books of Halakhah arranged by subjects.

Shittah Mekubbetzet, a collection of commentaries on the Talmud by Rabbi Betzalel ben Avraham Ashkenazi of Safed (c. 1520-1591).

Shulḥan Arukh, code of Halakhah by Rabbi Yosef Caro, b. Spain, active in Eretz Israel (1488-1575).

Sifrei, Halakhic Midrash on the Books of Numbers and Deuteronomy.

Sukkat David, by Rabbi David Kviat, novellae on tractate *Ketubot,* America (20th century).

Talmidei Rabbenu Yonah, commentary on *Hilkhot HaRif* by the school of Rabbi Yonah of Gerondi, Spain (1190-1263).

Taz, abbreviation for *Turei Zahav.* See *Turei Zahav.*

Terumot HaDeshen, responsa literature and Halakhic decisions by Rabbi Yisrael Isserlin, Germany (15th century).

Tiferet Yisrael, commentary on the Mishnah by Rabbi Yisrael Lipshitz, Germany (1782-1860).

Tosafot, collection of commentaries and novellae on the Talmud, expanding on Rashi's commentary, by the French-German Tosafists (12th and 13th centuries).

Tosafot Yeshanim, one of the editions of the *Tosafot* on the Talmud, 14th century.

Tosefot Rosh, an edition based on *Tosefot Sens* by the *Rosh,* Rabbi Asher ben Yeḥiel, Germany and Spain (c. 1250-1327).

Tosefot Rid, commentary on the Talmud by Rabbi Yeshayahu ben Mali de Trani, Italian Halakhist (c. 1200-before 1260).

Tosefot Sens, the first important collection of *Tosafot,* by Rabbi Shimshon of Sens (late 12th-early 13th century).

Tosefot Yom Tov, commentary on the Mishnah by Rabbi Yom Tov Lipman HaLevi Heller, Prague and Poland (1579-1654).

Tur, abbreviation of *Arba'ah Turim,* Halakhic code by Rabbi Ya'akov ben Asher, b. Germany, active in Spain (c. 1270-1343).

Turei Zahav, commentary on *Shulḥan Arukh* by Rabbi David been Shmuel HaLevi, Poland (c. 1486-1667).

Yoreh De'ah, section of *Shulḥan Arukh* dealing mainly with dietary laws, interest, ritual purity, and mourning.

Zuto Shel Yam, by Rabbi Moshe Leiter, glosses on the Aggadah in the Talmud (20th century).

About the Type

This book was set in Leawood, a contemporary typeface designed by Leslie Usherwood. His staff completed the design upon Usherwood's death in 1984. It is a friendly, inviting face that goes particularly well with sans serif type.